MANAGEMENT OF INDIAN FINANCIAL INSTITUTIONS

MANAGEMENT OF INDIAN FINANCIAL INSTITUTIONS

Prof. R.M. Srivastava
Former Head and Dean,
Faculty of Management Studies,
Banaras Hindu University.
Director, Northern Coal Fields Ltd.

and

Dr. Divya Nigam
Asstt. Professor,
Lala Lajpat Rai College of Commerce,
Mumbai

ISO 9001:2015 CERTIFIED

First Edition	:	**1984**
Second Revised Edition	:	**1991**
Third Revised Edition	:	**1996**
Fourth Edition	:	**1997**
Fifth Edition	:	**1998**
Sixth Edition	:	**1999**
Seventh Edition	:	**2000**
Eighth Edition	:	**2008**
Ninth Revised Editiion	:	**2013**
Edition	:	**2014, 2017**
Edition	:	**2019**
Edition	:	**2021**

Published by : Mrs. Meena Pandey for **Himalaya Publishing House Pvt. Ltd.,**
"Ramdoot", Dr. Bhalerao Marg, Girgaon, **Mumbai - 400 004.**
Phone: 022-23860170/23863863, Fax: 022-23877178
E-mail: himpub@bharatmail.co.in; **Website:** www.himpub.com

Branch Offices :

New Delhi : Pooja Apartments, 4-B, Murari Lal Street, Ansari Road, Darya Ganj, New Delhi - 110 002. Phone: 011-23270392, 23278631; Fax: 011-23256286

Nagpur : Kundanlal Chandak Industrial Estate, Ghat Road, Nagpur - 440 018. Phone: 0712-2738731, 3296733; Telefax: 0712-2721216

Bengaluru : Plot No. 91-33, 2nd Main Road Seshadripuram, Behind Nataraja Theatre, Bengaluru - 560020. Phone: 08041138821, Mobile: 09379847017, 09379847005

Hyderabad : No. 3-4-184, Lingampally, Besides Raghavendra Swamy Matham, Kachiguda, Hyderabad - 500 027. Phone: 040-27560041, 27550139

Chennai : New No. 48/2, Old No. 28/2, Ground Floor, Sarangapani Street, T. Nagar, Chennai - 600 017. Mobile: 09380460419

Pune : First Floor, Laksha Apartment, No. 527, Mehunpura, Shaniwarpeth (Near Prabhat Theatre), Pune - 411 030. Phone: 020-24496323, 24496333; Mobile: 09370579333

Lucknow : House No. 731, Shekhupura Colony, Near B.D. Convent School, Aliganj, Lucknow - 226 022. Phone: 0522-4012353; Mobile: 09307501549

Ahmedabad : 114, SHAIL, 1st Floor, Opp. Madhu Sudan House, C.G. Road, Navrang Pura, Ahmedabad - 380 009. Phone: 079-26560126; Mobile: 09377088847

Ernakulam : 39/176 (New No. 60/251), 1st Floor, Karikkamuri Road, Ernakulam, Kochi - 682011. Phone: 0484-2378012, 2378016; Mobile: 09387122121

Cuttack : New LIC Colony, Behind Kamala Mandap, Badambadi, Cuttack - 753 012, Odisha. Mobile: 9338746007

Kolkata : 108/4, Beliaghata Main Road, Near ID Hospital, Opp. SBI Bank, Kolkata - 700 010, Phone: 033-32449649; Mobile: 07439040301

DTP by : Sudhakar Shetty

Printed at : Geetanjali Press Pvt. Ltd., Nagpur. On behalf of HPH.

Dedicated

*To Our Most Beloved & Revered Mother &
Grand Mother Smt. Phool Kumari
who has been perennial source of
exuberance, inspiration and effervescent spirit*

R.M. Srivastava

Divya Nigam

PREFACE TO THE NINTH REVISED EDITION

The prime objective of the present comprehensively revised edition is to capture the latest developments in financial system in India and around the world including the U.S. sub-prime crisis and Euro Sovereign debt crisis with their cascading effects on economies of developed and developing nations, and remarkable dynamism and vibrance displayed by players of financial markets in their strategic thinking and action and in terms of adopting with unswerving speed new concepts, skills, paradigms, new architecture, innovative roles and financial mechanics and world class practices, and convey them candidly to the learners in structured and stimulating manner.

The immanent features of the present edition, structured around decision making are:

- The present edition has been exhaustively revised and streamlined by updating the data, incorporating the latest developments, rewriting some chapters and adding new chapters so as to add value to the text in the changed milieu.
- As many as 10 chapters (I, II, IV, V, VI, XIII, XVII, XXVI, XXVII and XXVIII) have been rewritten and 14 chapters updated to render the materials more meaningful to the learners.
- To improve further the quality and coverage of the text as many as 9 chapters have been added.

  Thus, two new chapters on 'Global Financial Turmoil — Threat to Financial Stability' and 'Micro Finance Institutions' have been incorporated to equip the learners with the contemporary developments in financial system around the globe.
- A new section comprising 7 chapters on 'Management of Financial Services' has been added so as to enrich the learners with the ongoing operations of the players in financial services sector.
- Conceptual questions at the chapter end would enable the learners to test their understanding of the text.
- Key terms crucial to understanding of various dimensions of financial institutions have been highlighted throughout the book.

As such, the present edition, the authors indubitably believe, will be highly appreciated by the students of commerce and management, those pursuing specialised professional programmes in the sphere of finance and practising managers.

R. M. Srivastava

Divya Nigam

CONTENTS

Introduction

Section One

Section I: Learning Objectives

- The present section attempts to provide background material in terms of economic growth and financial institutions, global financial crisis, types of financial institutions and recent trends in Indian financial market.

Section Outline

- Economic Growth and Financial Institutions.
- Global Financial Turmoil — Threat to Financial Stability.
- Types of Financial Institutions.
- Recent Developments in Indian Financial System

Chapter 1

Economic Growth and Financial Institutions

Learning Objectives:

The present chapter attempts to provide:

- An insight into economic growth and capital formation
- An understanding of the process of capital formation and problems involved therein.
- An incisive view of nature, significance and components of financial system.
- A critical view of roles played by financial institutions.
- A synoptic view of financial stability and its Indian perspective.

Chapter Outline:

- Capital formation as an Engine of Economic growth
- Ingredients of capital formation
- Problems of capital formation in under-developed countries
- Financial system — Nature and significance
- Role of financial institutions
- Financial stability
- Conclusions

A. CAPITAL FORMATION AS AN ENGINE OF ECONOMIC GROWTH

Economic growth implies a long-term rise in per capita national output. Such an increase in output in developed countries has been associated with radical changes in production techniques and organisations, in the institutional set-up and in the socio-cultural and psychological environment and attitudes of the people. While the process, pattern and rate of growth have differed between countries over periods of time, and initiating impulses and sustaining forces have similarly varied, there have been certain marked similarities in regard to certain features of economic growth. Thus, during the growth process, there has invariably been a shift of population from agricultural and other primary-producing sectors to the industrial sector and an increase in capital-labour ratio and a more than proportionate increase in labour output ratio. Of these, the first two have generally attracted greater attention of the underdeveloped countries; and economic growth has been thought to be associated with industrialisation, to the neglect of agriculture and primary production, and with a high rate of capital formation (again to the neglect of the human factor in development).

Industrialisation is necessary for the rapid economic growth of underdeveloped regions because of the need for providing gainful employment to millions of unemployed and under-employed persons, for a higher rate of productivity in industry than in agriculture, owing to the advantage of the large-scale of operation and the slower operation of the law of variable proportions; for higher income elasticity of demand for industrial products, and because of technical advances in agricultural and primary production, which is itself dependent upon industrialisation. Moreover, industrialisation imparts the necessary dynamism to the economy for changing the socio-psychological environment of its traditional, economic and social structure. However, a necessary condition of industrialisation is the generation of an agricultural surplus and the increasingly absorptive capacity of the market. Accordingly, though industrialisation is necessary, it is influenced by the rate of agricultural progress.

In any case, whatever be the pattern of growth, the basic conditions determining the rate of growth are three, *viz.*, Effort, Capital and Knowledge. In the post-Second World War period, there has been an upsurge in the desire for economic growth following rapid political and other developments, and increasing impatience in the countries of Asia, Africa and South America with their existing economic conditions. The keen desire for development has tended to minimise the significance of the factors associated with *effort*. As regards *knowledge*, it has been suggested that there already exists a vast amount of knowledge in developed countries; all that they have, therefore, to do is to borrow, adapt and apply it; and no particular emphasis is required on the growth of knowledge (which is a slow and expensive process) insofar as these countries are concerned. This reasoning has led to emphasis being laid on increasing capital formation as the most crucial factor in the economic growth of the underdeveloped countries. Thus, an increase in the rate of capital formation, though not sufficient, is a necessary condition of economic growth.

But it may be recognised that the factors associated with effort, enterprise, social and psychological environment and institutions, absorptive capacity, technical know-how, and adaptation of technology which is much more than mere imitation or importation of knowledge and technology in the form in which it has been applied in developed countries and organisational and management aspects are no less important. The rate of capital formation in underdeveloped countries has, therefore, to be greatly stepped up if the already existing wide disparities in the levels of economic prosperity in them and in the developed countries are not to increase further.

B. INGREDIENTS OF CAPITAL FORMATION

Capital formation signifies the diversion of the productive capacity of the economy to the making of capital goods which increase future productive capacity. In its broad sense, the term is used to include human as well as material capital.[1] Investment in human skills, education and health have contributed to an increase in productive capacity no less than have the investments in material capital — plant and machinery, tools and equipment, transport facilities, power generation, etc. However, in a restricted sense, capital formation refers to an increase in the stocks of material capital only.

In a money economy, current money income represents the remuneration of productive services as they are committed to the production of goods and services of current consumption and of capital goods which would be used in future for further production. The recipients of income spend major part of it on goods of current consumption and save the rest which represents a claim on the society for goods and services in the future. These claims are lent out to investors who thereby (or through created claims) commit resources to the production of capital goods, or to other goods, in exchange of which they may acquire capital goods from outside and thus add to the productive capacity of the economy. Thus, three ingredients of capital formation are:

(*i*) Saving;
(*ii*) Investment;
(*iii*) Finance.

◆ Saving

Savings constitute the first ingredient of capital formation. The term *saving* refers to the activity by which claims to resources, which might be put to current consumption, are set aside and so become available for other purposes. It represents the excess of income over current consumption. The total volume of savings in an economy, therefore, depends mainly upon the size of its material income and its average propensity to consume, which, in its turn, is determined by the level and distribution of the incomes, tastes and habits of the people, their expectations about the future, etc. As the size of the national income increases, the volume and ratio of savings may generally be expected to rise, unless the marginal propensity to consume is either equal to, or higher than the average propensity. This is very likely to be the case in countries where the standards of living are very low, and where the development policy places a heavy emphasis on the social objectives of raising the living standards of the poorer sections of the community, or where the spending habits of the people are strongly influenced by the "demonstration effect."

Total savings are composed of public savings and private savings. Public savings constitute the savings of the government through normal budgetary channels and the retained earnings of public enterprises. The volume of such savings depends largely upon the functions assumed by the state, the general state of the economy, the tax structure, the fiscal policy of the government, its pricing and investment policies. Private savings include household savings and business savings. They occupy, by far, the most important position in democratic countries. The size of household savings depends on the capacity and ability and willingness of the people to save, which are influenced by a multitude of social, psychological and political factors, in addition to the economic factors, the most important of which are the level and distribution of income and the general fiscal, monetary and economic policies of the state.

Business savings in the form of retained savings and depreciations and other provisions, claim relatively large proportions of the total savings in developed countries. Such savings are identified generally with corporate savings because the savings of other forms of business enterprises are not only relatively small but are not easily distinguishable from household savings. Corporate savings depend chiefly on the profitability of the enterprises and their policies of the distribution of dividends, provision for depreciation, etc., and the retention of current earnings for financing expansion programmes. These, in their turn, are largely influenced by the general state of the economy (and of industry in particular), the fiscal policies of the state and expectations about the future.

Investment

Another important ingredient of capital formation is investment which represents the end activity that adds to the volume of productive capital. The level of investment in an economy depends upon the decisions of entrepreneurs to invest. These are governed by the expectations of these entrepreneurs about their future earnings and the prevailing rate of interest at which claims for resources may be obtained. Expected future earnings, in turn, are a function of the state of the industry and the economy, their potential for development and their future expectations about it, the existing stock of capital, technological innovation, government policies, etc. The existence of a sizeable class of entrepreneurs, able and willing to seize the opportunity for new investments is, however, an essential condition.

Finance

Savings and investment activities in an economy are connected by finance and financial mechanism through which savings (claims to resources) of myriads of savings are pooled together and then are put into the hands of those able and willing to invest. The financial mechanism (also known as financial system) comprises a wide range of financial markets, institutions and instruments which cater, on the one hand, to the safety, liquidity and profitability notions of the savers and on the other, to the varied types of financial requirements of the investors.

Financial system does not directly add to the volume of real capital formation, though it is a necessary link between savers and investors in a free enterprise economy.[2] By providing facilities and services for profitable use of savings and by ensuring their safety and liquidity, it encourages or rather facilitates savings. Likewise, by assuring the entrepreneurs of supply of funds at a reasonable price and thus, reducing their botherations and burden of pooling financial resources, financial system indirectly aids in the process of investment as well.

C. PROBLEMS OF CAPITAL FORMATION IN UNDERDEVELOPED COUNTRIES

Capital formation in underdeveloped countries is inhibited by factors working at each of the three stages in the process, *i.e.*, saving, investment and finance. Of these, the factors inhibiting saving and investment are the crucial ones. Moreover, a circular relationship exists between such factors. As Nurkse has stated, in the vicious circle of poverty that afflicts the poor countries, perhaps the most important circular relationships are those "that afflict the accumulation of capital."[3]

The volume of saving in underdeveloped countries is low because of the low level of income which, in turn, is due to the low productivity of agriculture. The income of the vast majority of the people is hardly adequate for a bare subsistence level of living. No saving, therefore, is possible in their case. Alongside this, the uneven distribution of income may also be held responsible for the low level of savings because a large proportion of the total savings accrues in the hands of non-profit earning classes comprising, in the main, of the landed aristocracy and feudal classes. The savings of these people generally flow into conspicuous consumption — the purchase of jewellery, building of churches, ornate temples, tombs, monuments and prestige house construction, etc., and are misdirected and dissipated in unproductive channels. Another important aspect of the problem is that the marginal propensity to consume is very high. Even when incomes are increasing, the proportion that is saved does not register any marked increase. This is explained by the low levels of living and the strong demonstration effect.

The investment activity in underdeveloped countries is hampered by the small size of the domestic market, lack of entrepreneurial ability and rigidity, and market imperfections. Not only is the supply of capital limited by the low volume of saving but, owing to poverty, the final demand is small and the inducement to invest is limited. Moreover, the size of the entrepreneurial class is small because of socio-cultural, demographic and other factors. Entrepreneurs are generally reluctant to enter into long-range commitments. Entrepreneurship is unfortunately lacking in underdeveloped countries. Further, owing to ignorance, backwardness, lack of mobility and other imperfections of the market, the investment activity is retarded in these countries.

The financial mechanism in most of the economically backward countries is underdeveloped. Not only are there not enough institutions to take care of the different requirements of businesses, but their operations are generally limited to direct lending, and participation in equity capital does not form an important part of their activity. It may, however, be admitted that these limitations of the financial mechanism are essentially due to the low volume of savings and investment in these countries. Such institutions may, therefore, be expected to grow as development takes place.

D. FINANCIAL SYSTEM

◆ Nature and Significance

An organised and well functioning financial system is indispensible for an economy to grow rapidly and achieve sustainable competitive edge over others, for the fact that it facilitates channelisation of funds from those who have surplus income to those who need it for productive investment. Such a movement of funds is imperative for efficient utilisation of resources in the vital interests of the society. Financial system of a country comprises complex and interdependent set of financial instruments, financial markets and financial institutions as also policies, strategies, procedures and practices pursued by these segments.

Primary function of financial system is to link surplus spending units (SSUs) to deficit spending units (DSUs). SSUs represent those having surplus of income over expenditure for a given period of time.[4] Households, business enterprises, national and foreign governments and foreign organizations represent the SSUs. DSUs, on the other hand, represent those whose receipts fall short of their expenditures. DSUs are businesses, local and state governments and at times foreigners.

Another key function of financial system is to provide for efficacious mechanism for payment of personal, business and government transactions through wide range of financial instruments and intermediaries.

Financial system also provides ways and means to manage financial risks through risk-pooling and risk sharing. These mechanisms are built in hedging, diversification and insurance. Hedging is a technique to move from a risky asset to riskless asset, while diversification seeks to pool and subdivide risks. In insurance, the insured retains the economic benefits of ownership while laying off the probable loss.

A sound financial system furnishes useful information that facilitates coordination of decision-making operations. Information about existing interest rates and securities enable individuals in making financial decisions and aid the managers of enterprises in choosing suitable investment projects and funding thereof.

A well-functioning financial system, by facilitating efficient allocation of resources from savers to investors, promotes economic growth. One of the most influential theories which recognized the role of financial development in economic growth through improvements in productivity was propounded by Joseph Schumpeter.[5] For a long time, however, this view did not get due attention. The importance of financial system in the economic growth process gained prominence again in the early 1970s, when it was recognized that financial system has a two-pronged effect, *viz,* enhancing the efficiency of investments and augmenting savings and hence, the scale of investments.

In recent years, theories of endogenous growth have led to a better understanding of the criticality of efficient financial systems in development. The consensus now is that there is a positive two-way casual relationship between economic growth and financial development.[6] Financial intermediation enhances economic growth by channeling savings into productive areas of investment, while allowing individuals to reduce the risks associated with their liquidity needs. According to Levine,[7] financial services affect economic growth through five main channels, *viz,* saving mobilisation, resource allocation, risk management, management monitoring and trade facilitation. Each of the five main channels contributes to both capital accumulation and the process of technological innovation.

The role of financial system in growth has also been validated by empirical work by Gelb,[8] Greene and Villanueva,[9] Gertler and Rose,[10] De Gregurio and Guidotti,[11] Levine and Zerves.[12] Most of these studies are based on cross-country analysis, which find that a measure of financial development, such as credit or market capitalisation, has a positive and significant effect on growth. There is evidence that financially developed economies seem to allocate their resources more efficiently.[13] King and Levine,[14] using data for 80 countries for 1960-1989, found a significantly positive relationship between several measures of financial development, including total credit extended to the private sector by banks and economic growth. Demirguekunt and Maksimovic[15] using 40 countries found that in more financially developed economies, large proportion of firms grew above the maximum rate of growth achievable by similar firms when they lacked access to external finance.

◈ Components of Financial System

Financial system of a country comprises three interdependent constituents, viz. financial instruments, financial markets and financial institutions.

◈ Financial Instruments

Financial instruments represent legal claims to some future benefit where value does not bear relation to the form, physical or otherwise in which these claims are recorded. Financial instruments provide useful devices through which savings of the lenders-savers are attracted by the borrowers-spenders for investment purposes. The exchange of funds between SSUs and DSUs is evidenced by pieces of paper representing a financial asset to the holder and a financial liability to the issuer.

In order to cater to the diverse needs of both the suppliers of funds and those who need them, an array of financial instruments, having varying maturity denominations, claims to income and assets and controlling power and traded in financial markets. These may be classified into two broad categories, viz, short-term and long-term financial instruments.

Among short-term financial instruments, commercial bills, treasury bills, negotiable certificate of deposit, commercial paper are the important ones which companies and government units issue to obtain short-term funds.

Commercial bills represent an important short-term financial instrument that emanates out of commercial transactions. When a buyer is unable to make the payment immediately, the seller draws a bill upon him payable after a certain period. The buyer accepts the bill and returns the same to the seller who either retains till the due date or gets it discounted from some bank to get cash.

Treasury Bills are the most popular device employed by the government to procure funds from the market. These bills represent direct obligations of the government and are almost risk free. They have maturities spanning from three months to one year. Financial institutions, companies and individuals buy treasury bills to satisfy their liquidity and safety needs.

Negotiable Certificate of Deposit (CD) is a special type of time deposit of a commercial bank. It has maturities of one to twelve months and is issued in denominations ranging from $1,00,000 to $1 million. CDs are sold only by the largest and most credible banks and have a very low default risk.

A **commercial** paper represents unsecured promissory notes with a fixed maturity, usually, between 7 days and three months, issued in a bearer form and on a discount basis. Companies and financial intermediaries float commercial paper. It is important to note that default risk of commercial paper is quite low because only well-established firms can sell it. It is marketed through a handful of dealers or it may be issued directly to the issuing firm.

Long-term financial instruments are used by companies and governments to raise funds for longer period of time. Households are the major suppliers of funds for these instruments. Given their long maturity, these instruments experience wide price fluctuations in the secondary markets than do money market instruments.

Among various long-term financial instruments, equity shares and bonds are the most popular. Equity shares are certificates representing partial ownership in the companies that issue them. Equity shares are considered cornerstone of finances of a company without which a company cannot be founded. The holders of equity shares are residual owners who have unrestricted claims on income and assets and possess all the voting power in the company. It is noteworthy that equity shares bring in permanent capital to the company, which is not under contractual obligation to refund during its life time. Further, equity shareholders are residual owners whose claims on income arise only after creditors and preferred shareholders' claims are met. They are the last claimants to assets of the company. Another redeeming feature of equity shareholders is that controlling power rests with them. Every equity shareholder has the right to vote on every resolution placed before the company and his voting right on a poll is in proportion to his share of the paid-up capital of the company.

Bonds are long-term debt obligations issued by companies and government agencies to support their operations. Bonds usually provide a return to investors in the form of interest income (coupon payments) every six months or annually. Since bonds represent debt, they specify the amount and timing of interest and principal payments to investors who purchase. At maturity, investors holding the bonds are paid the principal. Bonds can be sold in the secondary market if the investor do not want to hold them until maturity. Long-term debt securities tend to have a higher expected return than short-term debt securities. It is important to note that bond-holders have priority of claim to income and assets over equity shareholders. However, they do not have controlling power.

Thus, equity shares differ from bonds in as much as while equity shareholders are owners of the company, bondholders are creditors. Further, equity shares do not involve any fixed obligation on the part of the company to refund the capital nor pay dividend to its holders. Bonds, on the contrary, involve fixed obligations of interest and principal payments and thus bring in their wake an element of risk.

Besides, short-term and long-term financial instruments, derivative securities are also traded in financial markets. **Derivative securities** represent financial contracts whose values are derived from the values of underlying assets (such as debt securities or equity shares). The primitive and simplest form of derivatives is forward contract. It goes on to take complex forms like swaps, futures, options and their different variations.

There are certain unique features of derivative securities. In the first instance, value of a financial derivative is derived from some other asset. Secondly, derivatives are used as vehicle for transferring risk from risk averse investors to risk-bearing investors. Thirdly, financial derivatives provide commitments to prices for the future dates or give protection against adverse movements of prices or exchange rates and thereby reduce the magnitude of financial risk. Finally, derivative securities are highly levered.

◆ Financial Markets

Financial markets are exclusively concerned with dealing in financial instruments with a view to garnering funds from those who have surplus funds to channelise them to those who need them for profitable deployment. This economic function of a financial market is shown schematically in Figure 1.1.

In Figure 1.1, those who have saved and are lending funds, the lender-savers, are at the left and those who have to borrow funds to finance their spending, the borrower-spenders, are at the right. The principal lender-savers are households, business firms and the domestic government as well as foreigners. The most important borrowers-spenders are businesses and

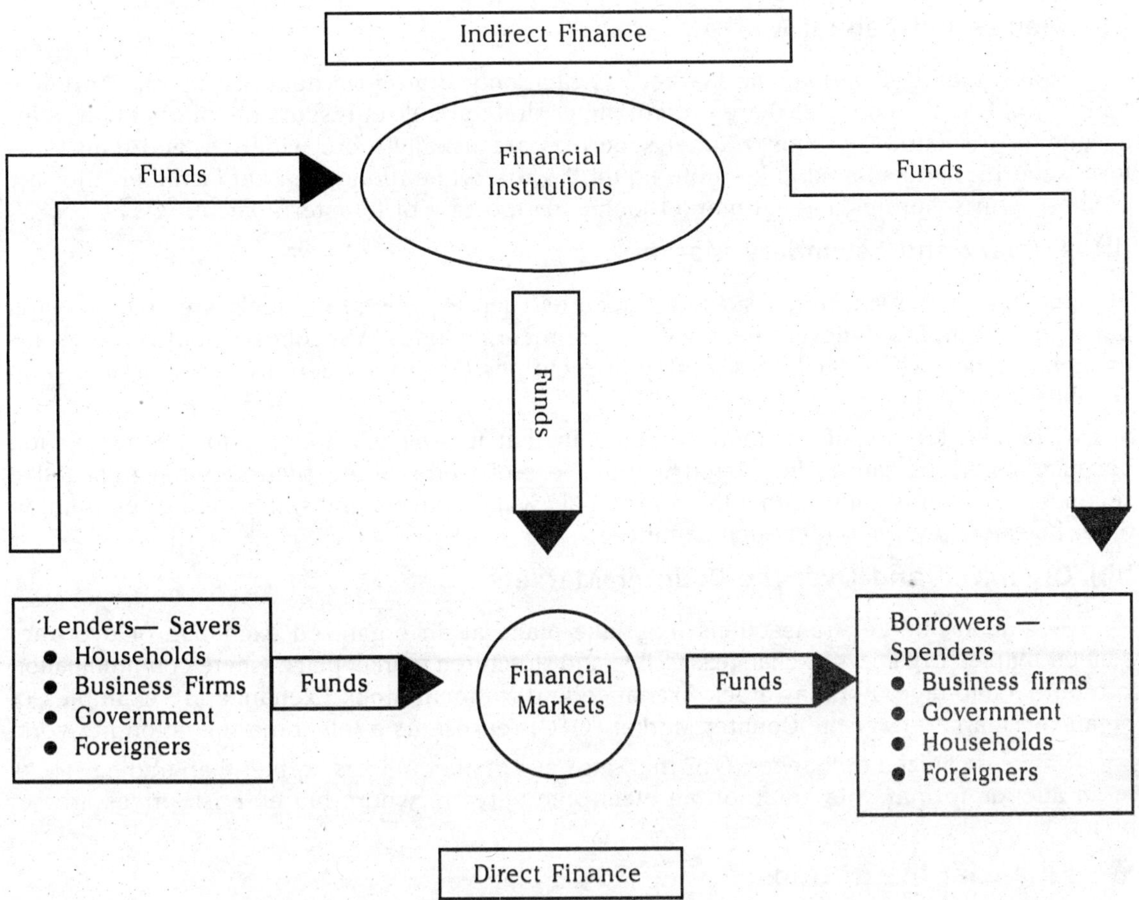

Fig. 1.1: Flow of Funds through Financial System

the government, but households and foreigners also borrow money to fund their requirements. The arrows in the figure show that funds flow from lender-savers to borrower-spenders via two routes — direct and indirect.

In the direct route (route at the bottom of Figure 1.1) also designated as direct finance, borrowers borrow money directly from lenders in financial markets by their financial assets (also called financial instruments), which represent claims on the borrower's future income or assets. However, for direct finance to take place, the borrowers must be willing to issue an instrument with a denomination, maturity and other characteristics that suit the desires and preferences of the savers. So long as their needs are not satisfied simultaneously, there will hardly be any transfer of funds. Financial institutions intervene in the process of transfer of funds. They buy the instrument with one set of characteristics (i.e., terms to maturity, denomination, etc.) from the borrower-spenders and transfer them into indirect instruments with a different set of features which they sell to the lender-savers. This process of transformation is called 'intermediation' which constitutes an indirect route to financing. Thus, indirect finance has been evolved to overcome problems involved in direct finance. The top half of Figure 1.1 exhibits the flow of money through indirect route.

Thus, financial markets play crucial role in economic development of a country by allowing funds to move from those having built up saving but lack productive investment opportunities to people who have such opportunities. This facilitates an efficacious allocation of funds which contribute to higher production and efficiency for the overall economy.

There are many different types of financial markets and each market can be distinguished by the maturity structure and trading structure of its securities.

(i) Money and Capital Markets

Money market is a financial market in which only short-term debt instruments (original maturity of less than one year) are traded, the capital market represents the market that deals in long-term securities. Money market securities are usually more widely traded than long-term securities and so tend to be more liquid.[16] Thus, while money market facilitates the sale of short-term securities, capital market facilitates the sale of long-term securities.

(ii) Primary and Secondary Markets

In primary market, new issues of a security such as a bond or stock, are sold to initial buyers by a company or government agency for procuring funds. A secondary market represents financial market which facilitates trading of securities that have been previously issued (and are thus second hand).

A radiant feature of secondary market in that it provides liquidity to the transaction because securities can be liquidated without loss of value. Some securities have an active secondary market, signifying that there are many willing buyers and sellers at a given point in time. Investors always prefer such securities.

(iii) Organized and Over-the-Counter Markets

Secondary market transactions may take place at an organized exchange or over-the-counter market. Organized exchange is visible and structured market place where communication is often face-to-face. Bombay Stock Exchange and National Stock Exchange are examples of organised market. Over-the-Counter Market (OTC) represents a telecommunication network.

Unlike organized exchanges, OTC markets have market makers. Rather than trading stocks in an auction format, they trade on an electronic network where bid and ask prices are set by market makers.

◈ Financial Institutions

Financial institutions, also known as financial intermediaries, represent third segment of financial system of a country. They perform the major function of mobilising funds from those who have surplus funds and directing them in the hands of those who need them. Besides, they also render various kinds of financial services.

A peep into the history of economic thought vividly brings out the various roles which financial institutions have been playing in course of their operations. Broadly speaking, these roles can be categorised as:

(*i*) Role as a financial intermediary
(*ii*) Role as a catalytic agent
(*iii*) Role as a creator of money
(*iv*) Role as a provider of financial services.

E. ROLE OF FINANCIAL INSTITUTIONS AS A FINANCIAL INTERMEDIARY

Financial institutions playing the role of a financial intermediary provide the means and mechanism of transferring command over resources from those who have an excess of income over expenditure to those who can make use of the same with a view to adding to the volume of productive capital. On the one hand, they create claims in the form of their shares, debentures, deposits, etc., against themselves, which they induce the savers to accept in exchange for their savings (claims on society for goods and services in the future). On the other hand, they acquire claims against the investors investing in their shares and debentures and by granting direct loans to them. It is here that the role of financial institutions' originate. They provide a convenient and effective link between savings and investment. They pool the savings of myriads of people with peculiar characteristics and notions about safety, liquidity and profitability by means of a wide range of financial instruments, offering various degrees of the mix of liquidity, return and safety of the savings.

In an underdeveloped country, the role of these institutions as mobilisers of savings becomes more pronounced in view of the fact that there are a large number of savers, each with small amounts of savings. These savers are generally reluctant to invest their surplus income because of their lack of adequate knowledge about complicated investment affairs. Moreover, their resources are small, and they can, at best, hold securities of one or two or a few industrial units; the fate of their savings and the prospects of earnings therefrom are therefore, tied to the fate of such unit or units. Thus, they are exposed to greater risk which constrain them to abstain from investing their savings.

Financial institutions take care of both these problems. Investment in an outlet of a financial institution minimises the risk involved in it. The investment policies of these institutions centre on the diversification of investments in terms of securities, units, industries and geographical regions. Thus, the total investment portfolio of the institution will probably have a lower risk element than if the thousands of individuals invested their limited funds in one or a few business firms. Since these individuals have a claim on the financial institutions, they participate in the benefits of diversification. Furthermore, these institutions employ expert investment analysts, and professional knowledge and expertise goes into the selection and supervision of their investment portfolio.

Diversification and expert investment knowledge ensure steady and regular earnings for the companies and a share in the general prosperity. Accordingly, investors in the outlets of financial institutions are assured of the triple benefits of low risk, steady return and capital appreciation. By taking upon themselves the problems which confront the small savers in investing their savings and dealing with them effectively, financial institutions not only help to garner savings but promote thrift among the masses, which is conducive to the creation of savings. By adding the ingredients of industrialisation, such as capital, entrepreneurship and management, these institutions are a direct instrument for increasing income and thereby increasing savings.

Financial institutions channel the funds mobilised by them to those who require more funds than they have, such as business firms. One of the major problems facing a business firm is how to approach thousands of small savers with a view to raising the desired amount of funds, which means diversion from main business activity. On the other hand, those willing to save, say ₹ 25 a month, need a convenient outlet for their savings. Financial institutions provide just such an outlet. These institutions, while themselves raising resources from a large number of small savers, make funds available to industrial concerns in relatively bigger lots, and thus reduce their burden and the botheration involved in raising resources directly from individual savers. In this way, financial institutions act as conduits through which scattered savings are first aggregated and then disaggregated among many business firms. This is why financial institutions are regarded as "gap fillers."

Besides representing the dichotomy between the savings and investment activities, financial institutions help in the allocation of funds among different industries and different sectors of the economy in consonance with the priorities laid down in a plan. They channel savings into those industries which build a strong base for the rapid industrialisation of the country and which carry forward the phase of industrial development. By providing financial help on softer terms to entrepreneurs setting up enterprises in backward areas, they help in correcting regional imbalances in the country. Further, when the programmes of rapid industrialisation get bogged down due to the inadequacy of finance through the existing sources, the government can approach these institutions, which render valuable assistance in the form of loans, investment in securities and underwriting thereof.

◆ Role as a Catalytic Agent

Financial institutions play the role of a catalytic agent to bring about economic and social change in a country through dynamism and innovativeness in their operations. Well functioning banks and other financial intermediaries such as venture capital funds also spur technological innovation by identifying and funding intrepreneurs who are perceived to have the best chances of developing new products successfully and for implementing innovative production processes. Further, financial institutions facilitate the development of physical and social infrastructure, which is essential prerequisite for rapid economic advancement by extending financial support to infrastructural projects. Funding infrastructural sector provides exciting investment opportunities to entrepreneurs.

Besides, financial institutions can catalyse the social change which, in fact, is imperative for all-round economic growth of a developing country. Through introduction of special assistance schemes for weaker and helpless sections and relatively isolated segments of society like tribals, financial institutions play crucial role in banishing poverty and improving standard of living of the people.

Through their widely spread network, financial institutions make their presence felt in far flung areas of the country, promote the habit of thrift among the people living in those regions and help them with credit in gainful activity and join the mainstreams of development.

◆ Role as a Creator of Money

Financial institutions, apart from playing the role of intermediary and catalytic agent, create money and thus act as catalyst in the process of money supplier. Through acceptance of public deposits and lending money against it for funding transactions they create further deposits. This role has assumed greater importance in the present age of consumerism with increased desire for goods and services by all segments of society.

◆ Role as a Provider of Financial Services

Besides rendering services associated with mobilizing and allocating savings activities, financial institutions act as entrepreneur to prompten the pace of growth of underdeveloped countries. As an entrepreneur, a financial institution endowed with skills and resources undertakes the task of assessing growth potentialities of various regions of the country, identifying specific project ideas, evaluating these ideas so as to determine their feasibility in financial and non-financial terms. Based on the survey, financial institutions discern need-based, resource-based and foot-loose or merchant type of industrial projects. In order to ensure that these projects are implemented properly, they take the responsibility of identifying individuals with entrepreneurial traits and motivate them to an entrepreneurial career by providing training facilities and dispensing financial, technical and managerial support so that the latter sets up industries.

Financial institutions provide services on the basis of non-fund activities also. This is called 'fee-based' activity. It includes management of pre-issue and post-issue activities relating to the capital issues, making arrangements for the placement of capital and debt instruments, providing credit syndication services and assisting in the process of getting all Government and other clearances.

Financial institutions also help industrial development of a country by advising corporate enterprises on when to exit a business and how to better manage their portfolio. As a friend, philosopher and guide, financial institutions counsel corporate borrowers regarding selling off assets not needed for the organizational success, building optimal investment portfolio, effective portfolio monitoring, identifying potential non-performance early and expeditious remedies and foreclosure to minimize.

F. FINANCIAL STABILITY

◆ A Backdrop

Financial stability is *sine quo non* for smooth and efficient functioning of financial system and achieving sustained economic growth. This is why financial stability has always been of concern to monetary authorities. However, in recent years it has received greater attention due to globalization, advances in information technology and communications networking and deregulation of the financial sector in emerging market economies which meant that weaknesses in the financial system could engender serious and far more disruptive consequences than was previously the case and could increasingly engender contagion effects extending well beyond national boundaries. Several episodes of financial fragility that have occurred in the latter half of the 1990s across the globe, such as the Mexican crisis of 1994-95, the East Asian crisis of 1997-98 and the more recent crisis in Argentina and Turkey and first global level crisis of 2008 followed by a deep, structural and multifaceted crisis, which entailed enormous costs for the financial system of several countries, have further underlined the need for a safe and sound financial sector.

Traditionally, it is believed that monetary stability leads to financial stability. While there are complementaries between these two objectives in the long run, the relationship can be very different in the short-run. In this regard, a stable macroeconomic environment can often downplay the risks posed to the financial system. Accordingly, episodes of financial instability often follow periods of protracted macro economic booms.

◈ Conceptual underpinning

Despite widespread usage of the term, there is no widespread agreement on a useful working definition of the term. Some define financial stability in terms of what it is not — the absence of financial instability. Others take a more macro-prudential view and specify financial stability in terms of limitation of risks of significant real output losses in the presence of episodes of system wide financial distress. Absence of widely accepted concept is because the analysis of financial stability is still in its infant stage of development and practice, as compared with, for example, the analysis of monetary and/or macroeconomic stability.

In view of absence of a framework, a set of models, or even a concept of equilibrium it is difficult to define financial stability precisely. However, it would be useful to factor in key principles for understanding the term financial stability.

The first principle is that financial stability is a broad concept, encompassing the different aspects of finance — infrastructure, institutions, and markets. Both private and public persons participate in markets and in vital components of the financial infrastructure (including the legal system and official frameworks for financial regulation, supervision and surveillance). Accordingly, the term "financial system" can be seen as encompassing both the monetary system with its official understandings, agreements, conventions, and institutions as well as the processes, institutions and conventions of private financial activities. Given the tight inter linkages between all of these components of the financial systems, expectations of disturbances in any of the individual components can undermine the overall stability, requiring a systematic perspective. At any given time, stability or instability could be the result of either private institutions and actions or official institutions and actions, or both simultaneously and/or iteratively.

A second principle is that financial stability not only implies that financial system adequately fulfills its role in allocating resources and risks, mobilizing savings and facilitating wealth accumulation, development and growth; it also signifies that the systems of payment throughout the economy function smoothly. This requires that fiat (or central bank) money and its close-substitute, derivative money can adequately fulfill its role as the universally accepted means of payment and unit of account and, when appropriate, as a short-term store of value. Thus, financial stability and monetary stability overlap to a large extent.

A third principle is that the concept of financial stability relates not only to the absence of actual financial crisis but also to the ability of the financial system to limit, contain and deal with the emergence of imbalances before they pose a threat to itself or economic processes. In a well-functioning and stable financial system, this occurs in part through self-corrective, market-disciplining mechanisms that create resilience and prevent problems from festering and growing into system-wide risks. Thus, financial stability entails both preventive and remedial dimensions.

A fourth important principle is that financial stability should be coughed in terms of the potential consequences for the real economy. Disturbances in financial markets or at individual financial institutions need not constitute financial instability if they do not impair overall economic functioning. Illustratively, a closer of a small financial institution, or for that matter, movement in asset prices within certain limits or even minor corrections in financial market need not necessarily hamper stability. On the contrary, fluctuations in asset and other prices in financial markets may actually be good for overall financial stability as adjustment mechanisms. What is important from macroeconomic standpoint are issues related to contagion and systematic risk, which can lead to economy-wide upheavals and would, therefore, need to be monitored on an ongoing basis.[17]

Further, financial stability should be thought of as occurring along a continuum. The continuum for financial stability can be thought of as multidimensional and occurring across a multitude of observable and measurable variables. As a continuum, financial stability can be seen practically as somewhat broader and less precise than the ability to return to a single and sustainable position or time path after a shock or perturbation.

Taking the above principles into consideration, financial stability can be broadly defined in terms of the financial system's ability to facilitate both an efficient allocation of economic resources and enhance economic process, manage risks and absorb shocks. Moreover, financial stability is considered a continuum changeable over time and consistent with multiple combinations of the constituent elements of finance. Basically, it refers to the smooth and efficient functioning of the financial markets and institutions but it does not mean absence or avoidance of crisis but presence of conditions conducive to efficient functioning without disruption. The relevant legal, institutional and policy frameworks are wide ranging and policy instruments at the disposal of authorities very varied. In a way, the financial stability objective is shared with a set of public policy bodies and professional bodies but the primary responsibility for overall financial sector efficiency, and stability generally rest with the central bank. The plausible reasons for such a responsibility are the major elements contributing to financial stability, *viz.*, the oversight of the financial infrastructure, in particular payments systems, regulation and supervision of financial institutions, crisis management and provision of liquidity and macro financial stability monitoring not only the behaviour of all important players in the financial sector but also non- financial sector balance sheets as well as that of the government.[18]

◈ Significance of Financial Stability

Financial stability contributes significantly to a country in achieving robust economic growth on an enduring basis. This is sought to be done through efficient allocation of resources, absorbing shocks, and preventing these from having a disruptive effect on the real economy or on other financial systems. The importance of financial stability is perhaps most viable in situations of financial instability. For example, banks may be reluctant to finance profitable projects, asset prices may deviate excessively from their underlying intrinsic values, as has happened in sub-prime crisis of the USA in 2008, or payments may not be settled in time. In extreme cases, financial instability may even lead to bank runs, hyper inflation, or a stock market crash. Financial instability harms the financial condition of non- financial units such as households, enterprises and governments to the extent that the flow of finance to them becomes restricted. It can also disrupt the operations of particular financial institutions and markets so that they are less able to continue financing the rest of the economy.

Financial stability signifies that the financial system is robust to disturbances in the economy so that it is able to mediate financing, carry out payments and redistribute risk in a satisfactory manner.

Financial stability in the 21st century has moved to centre-stage nationally as well as in discussions relating to the future of the global monetary and financial. Basic factors that have brought this about are the rapid pace of technological innovation across the globe, increasing diversity of financial instruments and the emergence of a large number of financial conglomerates, cutting across not only various financial sectors, but also across countries. The role of financial intermediaries is also getting redefined with their ability to effectively compete by appropriate transformation of risk. Further, the source of financial disturbances has become more unpredictable mainly due to integration of financial markets across national boundaries, thereby exacerbating the possibility of contagion. The progressive dismantling of capital controls since the 1990s has led to substantial cross-border capital flows and volatile exchange rates. Sharp movements in exchange rates have had an adverse impact, particularly in emerging market economies posing a potential source of instability.

Globalization has also brought in its wake episodes of financial instability which indicated that rapid movements of capital could be detrimental to economies with weak institutional frameworks. Moreover, the institutional backdrop has become more complex over the past twenty five years as the hedge fund industry, which is relatively opaque in operations, has significantly grown in size. Such a large industry carries the risk of 'herd behaviour' and with high concentration of assets, this has already posed a threat to financial stability. Another factor contributing to increased financial vulnerability in several countries is existence of deficiencies in key economic and social infrastructure. These include (*a*) inappropriate and ineffective prudential regulation and supervision; (*b*) inefficacy of bank intervention and resolution; (*c*) policy-induced distortions such as administered interest rates and weak government finances; (*d*) inadequate accounting practices, property rights and corporate governance; and (*e*) lack of institutional framework and adequate provisions, especially in the legal system.

Precisely speaking, the importance of financial stability emanates from four major trends in financial systems noticed in recent years. These are: (*i*) an imbalance of growth between the financial sector and the real economy; (*ii*) a change in mode of operations due to financial deepening; (*iii*) emergence of a globally integrated financial system; and (*iv*) an evolution of sophisticated financial instruments and attendant risks.

◈ Financial Stability: An Indian Perspective

As in other countries, in India too financial stability has emerged as a key consideration in the conduct of monetary policy since the 1990s, consequent upon the structural reforms initiated in the early 1990s, the gradual opening up of the Indian economy and the transformation of the financial system from a planned and administered regime to a market-oriented financial system. Financial stability in India, according to former RBI Governor, means ensuring uninterrupted settlements of financial transactions (both internal and external), maintenance of a level of confidence in the financial system amongst all the participants and stakeholders and absence of excess volatility that unduly and adversely affects real economic activity.[19]

The overall approach of the RBI to maintain financial stability is three-pronged: maintenance of overall macroeconomic balance, improvement in the macro-prudential functioning of institutes and markets and strengthening micro-prudential institutional soundness through regulation and supervision. Monetary stability is an important precondition for financial stability and therefore, the most significant contribution that monetary policy can make to financial stability is through maintaining low and stable inflation. Since the second half of the 1990s, inflation has been brought down to an average of 5 per cent per annum compared to an average of around of 8-9 per cent per annum in the preceding two and a half decades. The reduction in inflation since the early 1990s has also enabled inflation expectations to stabilize. Low and stable inflation expectations increase confidence in the domestic financial system and thereby contribute in an important way to the stability of the domestic financial system.

The RBI took a number of measures to widen, deepen and integrate various segments of the financial markets in order to strengthen price discovery mechanism, lower the transaction costs and enhance the liquidity in the markets. Further, the RBI ensured orderly conditions in the financial markets so as to maintain financial stability. Operating procedures and instruments of monetary policy have evolved over time to meet the objectives of financial stability. For instance, with persistent capital flows, a new facility in the form of **Market Stabilisation Scheme (MSS)** was put in place effective April 2004. The MSS has provided the RBI greater flexibility in its market operations. Similarly, India's exchange rate policy of focusing on managing volatility with no fixed rate target, while allowing the underlying demand and supply conditions to determine the exchange rate movements over a period in an orderly way has stood the test of time. Prudent external sector management with a cautious approach to capital account liberalization has been an important component of macroeconomic policies to ensure financial stability. Overall, the RBI's approach is to minimize volatility in the financial markets and minimize knee-jerk reactions, while focusing on price stability and the underlying inflation. The objective has been to ensure that there are no avoidable uncertainties in policy, while mitigating undue pressures on the functioning of markets without undermining market efficiency.

In its strive to strengthen and institutionalize the mechanism for maintaining financial stability, monitor macro-prudential supervision of the economy functioning of large financial conglomerates, and inter-regulatory coordination issues, the Government of India announced during 2010 Budget about setting up the Financial Stability and Development Council (FSDC). FSDC seeks to institutionalize financial stability. The RBI already has a financial stability unit whose primary task is to identify and analyse potential risks. While FSDC, with its full-time secretariat, improves upon the present arrangement wherein the RBI has in place multidisciplinary teams from diverse departments — banking supervision and regulation, financial markets and so on? More importantly, how will it 'administer' financial stability? This is one of the key functions of the central bank. Macro-prudential supervision is a specialized complex and sensitive task as it deals with risks to do financial system as a whole. This role is being executed by the RBI with insights gathered from its economic analysis, market operations performed in pursuit of monetary policy as well as supervision and regulation of banks and non-bank. It is, therefore, imperative to ensure that the RBI and FSDC do not function at cross-purposes, particularly as monetary policy decisions and macro-prudential policy can diverse, indicating the nuanced nature of decision-making. The RBI has already raised eyebrows on the formation of the FSDC as a super regulator and it should rather confine itself to financial literacy and inclusion. In its communication to the Ministry of Finance in August 2010, the RBI has made a strong case for being designated the "systematic regulator", a role it has already been performing. It is of the opinion that the central bank being the monetary policy authority and the lender of the last resort in the county, is in an ideal position to perform that role. It is of the view that the responsibility for financial stability and macro-prudential regulation of the financial sector should "vest explicitly" with the RB1.[20]

The Finance Ministry has, of late, removed the misgivings of the RBI by ruling out a role of super regulator to FSDC.[21]

G. CONCLUSIONS

Three factors determining the rate of growth of a country are effort, capital and knowledge. Among these, increasing capital formation has been recognized as the most crucial factor in fostering economic growth of the underdeveloped countries. Capital formation involves three distinct but interdependent activities, *viz.*, saving, finance and investment. Low capital formation has been the most potent cause for backwardness of a country. Process of capital formation in underdeveloped countries is inhibited by factors working at each of the above three stages in the process.

An economy to grow rapidly and achieve sustainable competitive edge over others must have organized and well-functioning financial system. Primary function of financial system is to link SSUs to DSUs. It also provides efficacious mechanism for payment of transactions through wide range of financial instruments and intermediaries.

Financial system of a country is composed of financial instruments, financial markets and financial institutions. Financial instruments represent claims to some future benefit whose value does not bear relation to the form in which claims are recorded. Financial instruments may be short-term and long-term. Short-term instruments comprise commercial bills, treasury bills, commercial paper, certificate of deposits, etc. Long-term financial instruments include shares and bonds.

Another component of financial system is financial market which is concerned with dealing in financial instruments in order to mobilizing funds from those who have surplus funds to channelize them to those who need them. Financial market may be money and capital markets, primary and secondary markets, organized and over the counter markets.

Financial institutions representing third segment of financial system play the role of a financial intermediary, a catalytical agent, a creator of money and as a provider of financial services.

Financial stability is essential for smooth and efficient functioning of financial system and achieving sustained and rapid growth. Financial stability refers to the financial system's ability to facilitate an efficient allocation of economic resources and enhance economic process, manage risks and absorb shocks. However, it does not mean absence or avoidance of crisis but presence of conditions conducive to efficacious functioning without disruption.

The overall approach which the RBI pursues to maintain financial stability is three-pronged: maintenance of overall macro-economic balance, improvement in the macro-prudential functioning of the institutions and markets and strengthening micro-prudential institutional soundness through regulation and supervision.

KEY TERMS

- Bonds
- Capital Market
- Capital Formation
- Certificate of Deposits
- Commercial Bills
- Commercial Paper
- Deficit Spending Units
- Direct Financing
- Economic Growth
- Finance
- Financial Assets
- Financial Institutions
- Financial Instruments
- Financial Stability
- Financial System
- Indirect Financing
- Money Market
- Organized Market
- Over-the-Counter Market
- Primary Market
- Secondary Market
- Shares
- Surplus Spending Units
- Treasury Bills

DISCUSSION QUESTIONS

1. Discuss the role of capital formation in economic growth of a country.
2. What is capital formation? How is it created?
3. Why is level of capital formation low in an underdeveloped country?
4. Discuss nature and significance of financial system.
5. What are ingredients of financial system? Discuss each of them in brief.
6. What are the financial instruments? Distinguish between short-term and long-term financial instruments.
7. What role do financial markets play in economic development of a country?
8. Distinguish between money and capital markets.
9. What is primary market? How does it differ from secondary market?
10. Discuss various roles that financial institutions play in fostering growth of a country.
11. "Financial Institutions do more than simply transfer money and securities between entrepreneurs and savers". Elucidate.
12. What is financial stability? Discuss the approach the Reserve Bank has pursued to maintain financial stability in the country.

REFERENCES

1. Ragnar Nurkse, Problem of Capital Formation in underdeveloped countries, Basil Blackwell, Oxford Press, 1955, p. 2.
2. G.M. Meir and R.E. Baldwin, Economic Development — Theory, History and Policy, John Wiley & Sons Inc, New York, 1957, p. 338.
3. Ragnar Nurkse, *op. cit.*, p. 4.
4. R.N. Goldsmith, The Flow of Capital Funds in the Post War Economy, New York, Columbia, 1965, p. 28.
5. Joseph Schumpeter, The Theory of Economic Development, Harvard University Press, Cambridge 1911.
6. Green Wood J. and B. Jovanovic, Financial Development, Growth and Distribution of Income, The Journal of Political Economy, 98 (5 Part 1) 1990.
7. R. Lavine, Financial Development and Economic Growth: Views and Agenda, Journal of Economic Literature, 1997.
8. Gelp, "Financial Policies, Growth and Efficiency; World Bank PPR Working Paper, 202, 1989.
9. J. Greene and D. Vilanueva, "Private Investment in Developing Countries", IMF Staff Papers Papers 18, March 1991.
10. M. Gertler and A. Rose, "Finance Growth and Efficiency", Policy Research Working Paper Series, 814, The World Bank, 1991.
11. J. De Gregoria and P. Guidotti, "Financial Development and Economic Growth", World Development, 23 (3), March, 1995, pp. 433-48.
12. R. Levine and S. Zervos, "Stock Markets, Banks and Economic Growth", American Economic Review, 88(3) 1998, p. 537-58.
13. W. Carlin and C. Mayor, "Finance, Investment and Growth", Journal of Financial Economics 69(1), 2003, pp. 199-226.
14. R. King and R. Levine, "Financial Intermediation and Economic Development in Financial Intermediation in the construction of Europe" Eds, Colin Mayer and Xavier Vives, London; Centre For Economic Policy Research, 1999, pp. 156-89.
15. A. Demirgue-Kunt and V. Maksimovic, "Funding Growth in Bank-Based and Market-Based Financial Systems; Evidence from Firm-Level Data", Journal of Financial Economics 65(3), September, 2002 pp. 337-363.
16. Frederic S. Mishkin and Stanley G. Eakins, Financial Markets and Institutions, Pearson Education, Delhi, 2007, p. 22.
17. Rakesh Mohan, Central Banks and Risk Management: "Pursuing Financial Stability, RBI Bulletin, December, 2006, p. 1505.
18. Y.V. Reddy, Financial Sector Reform and Financial Stability, RBI Bulletin, April, 2006.
19. *Ibid.*
20. Business Standard, August 3, 2010.
21. Business Standard, April 1, 2011.

❊ ❊ ❊

Global Financial Turmoil — Threat to Financial Stability

Chapter 2

Learning Objectives

The present Chapter attempts to:

- Provide vivid view of origin, causes and impact of global financial turmoil of 2008.
- Present, in brief, international response to the crisis.
- Describe genesis, causes and impact of global financial crisis of 2011.
- Evaluate measures taken to solve the problem.
- Offer suggestions to avoid threats to international financial stability.

Chapter Outline:

A. PRELUDE

Two successive financial crises of gargantuan proportions during a short period of three years having a domino effect on the global financial system, panicking the entire world, pushing the economies of the developed countries into recession and slowing down the pace of emerging economies have, of late, again raised concern on financial globalisation. Critiques of globalisation have reemphasised that globalisation does not bring any additional gains that what can already come from free trade. Countries, they argue, that have benefitted most from free-market globalisation are not those that have embraced it wholeheartedly but those that have adopted parts of it selectively. Open market, it is contended, succeeds only when embedded within social, legal and political institutions that provide them legitimacy by ensuing that the benefits of capitalism are widely shared.[1]

In contrast, advocates of financial globalisation opine that policies promoting sound macro economy, financial sector development, institutional quality and trade openness appear to help developing countries derive the benefits of financial integration.[2]

In recent times following the occurrence of financial disaster at global level, doubts are being expressed about the efficacy of national monetary, fiscal and trade policies in guarding the economy against the risks of financial instability arising out of rapid transmission of shocks from the US and Europe in the wake of integration of financial system of countries. Although the impact of globalisation on national economic policy effectiveness is ultimately an empirical issue, it would not be correct to say that domestic economic policies become redundant with increased openness. In fact, under globalisation national policies need to be more carefully calibrated and fine-tuned to maximise the benefits of globalisation while minimising its costs.

A perspicacious analysis of the circumstances leading to outburst of global level financial meltdown in 2008 and 2011 as also their impact on economic and financing system of developed and emerging economies, and measures taken at national and global level to counteract threat to financial stability will serve as guideposts to both national and international monetary and fiscal authorities in formulating monetary, fiscal and financial rules in such a way as to prevent recurrence of such crisis in future and to provide adequate safeguards to national authorities to minimise their impact on economic and financial systems of the respective countries. And hence the following discussions.

B. GLOBAL FINANCIAL TURMOIL — 2008

◆ Origin and Escalation

Unprecedented global financial crisis witnessed since mid 2008 following sustained period of growth with only moderate fluctuations coupled with low inflation posed perilous threat to financial stability across advanced as well as emerging market economies (EMEs) including India. The crisis emanated from sub-prime mortgage lending lending to non-credit worthy clients) in the U.S. which triggered burgeoning financial loss to the U.S. banking system ($1.4 trillion) owing to heavy defaults.

The sub-prime crisis in the U.S. was seeded and fertilized by the U.S. government's liberal policy of housing finance to generate cheap money through the dot com bubble in the late 1990s and had gone on a high growth mode. But as the third millennium opened, the dot com hopes collapsed and recession set in. The terror attack on the U.S. in the September 2001 coincided with the recession. To overcome the problem, the idea of predatory sub-prime lending formed part of economic modeling in the U.S. The US Federal Reserve devised to almost no interest policy, encouraging the investors to seek returns through riskier investments and lenders to take even greater risks. With the sudden risk of cheap money chasing houses, the value of houses shot up. The owners of houses used the increase in value as additional equity and borrowed to shop. The unworthy borrowers were exhorted to borrow and spend for a national cause. About $5.26 trillion money went through shopping malls in the U.S., China and elsewhere, driving the global economy in the bargain.

However, the dotcom crisis overcome by sub-prime lending sector hit the sub-prime mortgage market when the housing bubble prices nosedived in 2006, reducing the value of the security for loans and unworthy borrowers not paying their instalments, leading to large foreclosures and consequent write-offs.

What made the crisis worse was that the sub-prime loans were sold to wall street firms, who, in turn, bundled thousands of mortgage loans from lenders into mortgage-backed securities, sliced and diced into different structures, called 'Collateralized Debt Obligations' (CDOs) and sold to investment banks and insurance companies such as Merril Lynch, Lehman Brothers and American International Group (AIG). The CDOs were so complicated that even the regulators and financial experts failed to assess the risks inherent in them with rising defaults on home loans, CDO price stated plummeting, denting investment banker's portfolio and destroying their capital. Since mid 2007 most mortgage banks having given NINJA (No Income, No Job or Asset Loans) began facing problems in their balance sheets. With intensification of crisis, banks grew increasingly suspicious about each other's solvency and ability to honour commitment, resulting in shrinkage of inter-bank market and thus hurting the flow of funds to the 'real' economy .

The crisis that emerged in the U.S. soon escalated into widespread financial stress, and spilled over to financial markets of developed countries quickly and subsequently spread to emerging and developing economies through various channels — financial, trade and confidence — despite their relatively sound macro-economic fundamentals and policy frameworks.

The depth and breadth of the crisis was unprecedented. The initial estimate of actual and potential global write downs held by banks and other financial institutions, which started at about U.S. $50 billion in mid-2007, increased to around U.S. $ 4.0 trillion by end-2008. In April 2010 it was scaled down to $2.3 trillion.

◆ Causes of the Financial Turmoil

The global level financial disaster was the outcome of myriad of forces which were interwined. While the immediate cause of the crisis could be attributed to the problems persisting in the sub-prime mortgage sector of the U.S., the subsequent disruption of financial markets is the long-run consequence of the easy global money and credit conditions existing particularly from the beginning of the decade. The persistence of global imbalances since the beginning of the current decade also contributed to the chaos.[3] The U.S. Fed's very low interest rates, that were maintained for a very long time, did contribute to a housing and asset price bubble.[4] Equally important cause was the lack of recognition of asset prices in policy formulation.[5] According to some, the Basel Accord was also a cause of the crisis; banks' efforts to circumvent the capital adequacy requirements of the Basel Accord caused the financial disruption.[6]

Another potent cause of the crisis was widespread use of highly complex structured debt instruments and the inadequacy of banking supervision in coping with financial innovations.

Failure of governance on the part of central banks has also been blamed for the crisis. They focused excessively on CPI inflation at the expense of financial vulnerability.[7] The global level crisis reflected a collapse of the market as well as the state, since governance in both private and public sectors failed.[8]

Many players can be blamed for the origin and escalation of the crisis, *viz,* Mortgage lenders doling out NINJA loans, miserable failure of credit rating agencies in assessing the potential impact of adverse events for structured credit products, Wall Street firms who structured mind-numbingly complex and opaque products and sold them to investment institutions and failure of regulatory authorities to take effective action to check identified vulnerabilities in the financial sector and to address deterioration in the risk management standards and inadequate regulatory arrangements.

◈ Impact of the Financial Turmoil

In view of increasingly integrated global trading and financial systems, there had been rapid transmission of shocks from the U.S. and Europe to the rest of the world. The impact of the crisis was felt on financial system, external sector and real sector in almost all the economies of the world in varying degrees.

Although the crisis began spreading financial markets and countries from August 2007, the collapse of large U.S. investment bank, Lehman Brothers in September 2008 aggravated panic in the financial markets, distorting the financial intermediation process, causing severe shortages of market liquidity in security and commercial paper markets and repricing of risk. Financial markets of EMEs also came under severe strain with increased volatility.

Inter-bank/money market experienced serious disruptions and banks in developed countries increased their demand for liquid funds and became reluctant to lend to one another. This tightened funding conditions in interbank credit markets leading to decline in credit growth in these countries.

Stock markets all over the world felt the heat of the global crisis in terms of high volatility and sharp decline in prices. The impact of the crisis was more pronounced on the EME stock markets. Corporate bond market in EMEs also suffered severely from the second half of 2008.

Foreign exchange markets experienced a substantial increase in volatility due to significant dislocations in their financial markets. As a result, there was steady depreciation of the U.S. dollar against the euro after June 2007. Sterling depreciated by almost 15 per cent. Russian rouble also depreciated by steadily during July 2007 to April 2008. However, the Japanese yen exhibited an appreciating trend. Development in foreign exchange markets of EMEs broadly reflected developments in their equity market. Capital outflows during 2008 and early part of 2009 significantly weakened currencies in India, Korea, New Zealand and Vietnam.

The crisis brought to the fore major weaknesses inherent in the U.S. financial system and regulatory framework that failed to recognize the systematic risks posed by the 'shadow banking system' and the build-up of housing and credit bubbles. Over time, the shadow banking institutions became almost as important as commercial banks in providing credit to the U.S. economy without the same regulatory controls. These institutions became more vulnerable because they borrowed short-term money to purchase long-term illiquid and risky assets. Further, these entities as well as certain regulated banks did not have a financial cushion sufficient to absorb large loan defaults. All these forces together made the U.S. financial system increasingly fragile and vulnerable to risk.

The pressure built up in the U.S. financial system spread rapidly to Europe. Apart from the U.K., the crisis transmitted rapidly to the euro area which had deep financial linkages with the U.S. Many euro banks and financial institutions had large exposure to U.S. assets and were leveraged. As a result, with the onset of the crisis, they started getting affected. Access to funds became more difficult and expensive. Financial health of the banks in the U.S. and Europe plummeted sharply.

U.S. investment banks suffered more than commercial banks. The top 5 U.S. investment banks, *viz.*, Lehman Brothers, Bear Sterus, Merril Lynch, Goldman Sachs and Morgan Stanley, incurred over U.S.$ 4.1 trillion in debt for fiscal year 2007, constituting 30 per cent of the U.S. nominal GDP. Securities underwritten by them during 2008 declined as primary market issuance slowed. As a result, Lehman Brothers was liquidated, Bear Stearns and Merril Lynch were sold at low prices and Goldman Sachs and Mortgan Stanley turned into commercial banks. These institutions received government support.

The two U.S. government sponsored enterprises, owned or guaranteed, *viz,* Fanvie Mac and Fredric Mac were placed in conservatorship by the U.S. government in September 2008. These seven entities together had US $ 9 trillion in debt or guarantee obligations, reflecting on enormous concentration of risk, yet were not subject to the same regulation as depository banks.

Insurance companies also suffered badly. The main effect of the turmoil was on their financial performance. The U.S. insurance company, AIG, suffered heavily during second and third quarters of 2008 resulting in its rating downgrades in September, 2008. AIG was unable to raise enough capital to meet demands for collateral quickly enough, which the Federal Reserve of New York to offer AIG a two-year loan of upto US$ 85 billion to give the ailing insurer the opportunity to sell some of its assets in an orderly way. The near-collapse of AIG was directly linked to the underwriting of credit risk.

Banks in Asia remained relatively resilient and had limited exposures to U.S. sub-prime mortgages. They held comfortable domestic currency liquidity cushions during the crisis.

Impact of the crisis was felt across the world. The year 2009 witnessed sharpest decline of 12.2 percent in world trade in more than 70 years.[8] Among developed countries, Germany and Japan were the worst affected by their declining exports of manufactures. Australia and Canada were also affected by a fall in commodity prices.

Following the slowdown in advanced countries, developing economies in Asia felt a strong contraction, current account surplus turned into deficit.

As for global capital flows, capital flows to developing countries declined from around U.S. $ 1.2$ trillion in 2007 to U.S. $780 billion in 2008. This was due to sharp decline in portfolio equity and debt flows. FDI inflows in Europe and Central Asia declined significantly. In contrast, Net FDI flows to EMEs such as China and India, witnessed spike during 2008, despite deepening of the crisis, reflecting the long-term view of FDI investors on growth potentials of these economies.

The global crisis badly impacted the real sector of the developed countries, as reflected in decline asset prices, fall in consumer and business sentiment and contraction in expenditure on housing construction.

Thus, while advanced countries experienced slowdown rapidly, EMEs appeared relatively insulated from the financial disaster in the initial phases. However, the latter was also affected subsequently after the failure of Lehman Brothers in September, 2008. The GDP growth of the EMEs, as per the IMF estimate, declined to 2.4 per cent in 2009 from 6.1 per cent in 2008.

◈ International Response to the Financial Turmoil

So as to minimize the impact of the disaster, national authorities across the globe responded quickly through monetary and fiscal policy interventions and financial regulation and supervision. The international response was unparalleled in terms of scale, magnitude and exceptional coordination.

Adoption of soft interest rate policy of central banks of almost all the developed countries was one of the important moves. Initially, monetary policy response in terms of interest rate cuts began at the individual level which became more coordinated afterwards. Thus, on October 8, 2008, six major central banks undertook the first-ever round of coordinated action in policy rate cuts. Other central banks also followed this policy swiftly. By the end of May 2009, the Federal Reserve, the Bank of Japan, the Bank of England, the Bank of Canada and the Swiss National Bank had brought policy rates close to zero.

Besides softening interest rates, central banks in many developed countries undertook other measures to ease liquidity position in the market. These measures included (*i*) easing the terms and availability of existing central bank facilities like standing lending windows, (*ii*) enhancing the access to the central bank lending, (*iii*) easing conditions for lending highly liquid securities against less liquid market securities, (*iv*) easing stipulations on the provision of reserves, and (*v*) liberalizing credit conditions in the non-banking sector to improve liquidity and reduce risk in non-banking operations.

In EMEs, central banks adopted the policy of softening interest rates, cutting reserve requirement ratios and introducing reserve averaging and hiking exemption thresholds. They also eased the terms of existing foreign exchange facilities.

Fiscal policy measures were also undertaken to provide direct financial support and/or deposit insurance/guarantee to troubled financial institutions in order to make them solvent and stabilize the financial system. Thus, financial support programmes initiated in the U.S., U.K., Switzerland and other European countries involved a combination of direct support by way of sale of distressed and illiquid assets and equity injection and extending guarantees on bank deposits, inter-bank loans and bonds. The U.S., European and other developed countries provided extensive assurances to bank depositors and creditors that the government would not allow important institutions to fail. This was intended to enhance the level of confidence in the financial system.

The government support to financial institutions ranged from 0.7 per cent of GDP in Italy to a high of 20.0 percent in the U.K., with the majority of the developed countries providing far more than 5.0 per cent of GDP as on June, 2009. In case of EMEs, it ranged from nil in a number of them to 3.5 per cent of GDP in Hungary.

Besides the above monetary and fiscal policy interventions, various initiatives were taken jointly at the international level to improve regulation of financial system and governance standards. An outline of major initiatives is given below.

(*i*) Financial Stability Board (FSB) called upon countries for significantly stronger capital standards and the G-20 committed to developing rules to improve both the quantity and quality of bank capital.

(*ii*) The Group of Central Bank Governors and Heads of Supervision broadly agreed in their meeting in July 2010 to the definition of capital adequacy, counterparty credit risk, leverage ratio and the global liquidity standard.

(*iii*) The Communique of the G-20 meeting of Finance Ministers and Central Bank Governors held in September 2010 reaffirmed commitment on fully implementing the new capital and liquidity framework within the agreed time frame; the phased implementation would start from January 1, 2013.

(*iv*) Basel Committee on Banking Supervision (BCBs) and Financial Stability Board (FSB) are currently engaged in developing a well integrated approach to systematically important financial institutions (SIFIs) which would include combinations of capital surcharges, contingent capital and bail-debt. The FSB is also mulling on measures to enhance the effectiveness of SIFI supervision.

(*v*) In order to strengthen the effectiveness of supervisory practices for international bank group, the BCBs evolved a set of good practice principles on supervisory colleges in October, 2010. These principles pertain to objectives and structure of supervising colleges, appropriate sharing of information by the college members with respect to principal risks and risk management practices of the banking group, integrity and confidentiality of information exchange, promoting collaborative work between members, interacting with institutions, complementing the crisis management structures and tailoring the supervision of large internationally active financial conglomerates to their systematic importance.

(*vi*) Following the initiatives of the G-20 countries, nearly all FSB members adopted the International Accounting Standards Board (IASB) standards. The FSB has made considerable progress in achieving converged accounting standards in the areas of impairment of financial assets, de-recognition of repurchase of agreements as off-balance sheet exposures, valuation under uncertainty in fair value measurement guidance and netting of financial instruments.

(*vii*) So as to reduce the conflict of interest at the credit rating agencies (CRAs) and encourage due diligence on the part of investors, the G-20 member countries agreed to a regulatory oversight regime for CRAs consistent with IOSCO's CRA code of conduct. CRAs have been prohibited from structuring advice, replacing issuer-pay model by investor-pay model, introduction of pay-for performance and wait-to-rate models and reducing reliance on ratings for meeting prudential requirements.

(*viii*) For introducing a credible and transparent deposit insurance system for maintaining public confidence in the banking system, International Association of Deposit Insurers (IADI) and BCBs jointly developed the core principles for effective deposit insurance systems in June 2009. It consisted of a voluntary framework based on best international practices for bringing about changes in existing system or setting up a new deposit insurance system. These principles focus on operational independence, transparency and accountability for deposit insurer and call for having effective relationships with other safety-net participants while delineating the approach to be followed in respect of cross-border issues, membership and coverage, funding, public awareness, legal issues, failure resolution, reimbursing depositors and recoveries.

C. GLOBAL FINANCIAL TURMOIL - 2011

◈ Genesis

Despite massive stimulus packages totaling over $2.3 trillion in the past three years, coupled with a negative real rate of interest, U.S. economy continues to be in horrible shape, economy recovery is fragile, unemployment is stuck at more than 9 percent, real per capita output has not budged in six years, the national savings rate is zero and domestic investment is miserable 4 per cent of national income. The U.S. fiscal deficit has touched 10 per cent of GDP and its tax system is collecting the least revenue per dollar of output since World War II. U.S. Federal debt held by the public shot up from 36 per cent of GDP in 2007 to 62 per cent of GDP in 2010. Expansionary fiscal policies played a critical role in averting a deeper U.S. recession. But the policy has also resulted in rise in federable debt. There are several reasons for this sluggishness, the most important being the overhang of household debt that is a legacy of the housing bubble. But one significant factor in the U.S. continuing economic weakness is the fact that government in America has slashed spending in the face of a depressed economy.

Downgrading of the U.S. Sovereign credit rating by Standard and Poor's (S&P) in September 2011 for the first time since 1917 is a sordid reflection on the effectiveness, stability and predictability of American policy making and political institutions in managing economic and financial systems of the country. Unlike the crisis of 2008, the 2011 crisis is not a financial crisis; this is a crisis of confidence, which has had its deleterious effect on global economy.

After a major slump in economic growth in 2009, the global economy witnessed optimism in the year 2010 due to 'two speed' recovery in advanced and emerging economies. The beginning of 2011 witnessed the optimum giving way to greater concerns on account of a projected slowdown in the U.S. economy, with challenges arising from the global financial system as well as the emerging fiscal and economic growth scenario across countries. The risks to global financial stability, according to the Global Financial Stability Report in September, 2011, increased during the past three years, signaling a partial reversal in the progress made during this period.

The current crisis owing to lackluster performance of the U.S. economy was aggravated by escalating sovereign risks in the Euro zone emanating from possible sovereign debt defaults in Greece, Ireland and Portugal and the weakening sovereign balance sheets in Italy and Spain. And Europe is fast emerging as the epicentre of the unfolding global economic turmoil.

The situation in Europe is worse than the U.S. in the euro zone. The financial and banking crisis has been followed by much more dangerous sovereign debt crisis, with several governments on the brink of defaults, what began as a problem affecting the small peripheral economies of Greece, Ireland and Portugal has subsequently buffeted Spain and Italy, with even France facing investors anxieties.

The Euro crisis, which has now assumed menacing proportions, has been caused mainly by fiscal irresponsibility and lack of political coordination among euro leaders. Euro zone countries have had an incentive to run reckless policies financed by the easy availability of bank loans within the European Union (EU). There was a widely shared perception that if they were in trouble, they would be bailed out by deep-pocketed neighbours like Germany and France. At the heart of this system clearly was a great deal of 'moral hazards'. Thanks to the key rules regarding money creation within the Euro zone, all the big European banks acquired substantial portfolios of short-term sovereign debt as sovereigns kept borrowing. The perception was that the European Central Bank (ECB) or the EU would never let a sovereign fail. There was excessive leverage at all levels — Sovereign, Corporate and Household. For example, uncontrolled government spending, high fiscal deficit funded through sovereign borrowings year after year and European banks owe € 5.4 trillion or 45 per cent of EU's GDP within the next 24 months. They sold $ 413 billion worth of bonds in 2011, equivalent to two-thirds of the $ 654 billion due to be returned to investors in 2011 as the debt matures. The resulting gap of $ 241 billion was the first time European lenders have collectively been unable to replace their maturing debt with new bonds for the past 5 years. Bond issues of European banks could hardly raise 15 per cent of the amount. Credibility of different sovereigns was so low that declining GDP in Greece, Italy and other Euro zone countries resulted in a situation where the sovereign borrowings were over 150 per cent of the national GDP. At such an unsustainable level of borrowings, debt servicing became a great concern. Investors are not only shunning government bonds but also shying clear of the region's banks themselves large holders of sovereign debt, engendering a credit crunch that has now proved to be very dangerous for the Europe's economy.

◈ Impact

The current level of global economic and financial crisis seems to be more serious than the previous one and has greater cascading effects on economies of the world. This is for the fact that the earlier crisis emanated from sub-prime mortgage lending; people were caught unaware. So the response was a little knee-jerking. Once the problem flared up, countries across the world joined together, employing all the arrows in the armoury of monetary and fiscal tools to combat the crisis. The present crisis, what has been brewing in Europe, has been known to everyone for almost two years. Everyone knew it was a sovereign debt issue but there was no political willingness to reach an agreement on a specific bailout plan to stave off the crisis. In fact, inaction and stubborn attitude of richer nations of EU allowed the crisis to worsen with contagion to affect other economies of the world. Furthermore, euro crisis is more serious and more threatening than the crash of 2008 because collapse of the euro will have catastrophic consequences, not only for Europe, but also for the global financial system due to inter-connectedness.

In view of the above, impact of 2011 crisis particularly on the USA and Europe has been disastrous. As noted above, the White House's fiscal policy initiatives since 2008 have failed to push growth and employment. The U.S. economy has been limping along with a growth rate of less than 2 per cent during 2011-12, with similarly dim prospects in 2012-13. The situation is worse in Europe. Gross domestic product (GDP) is likely to contract 4.7 per cent in 2012-13 in Greece and 3.3 per cent in Portugal. Eurozone unemployment has risen to its highest level of 10.4 per cent since euro single currency was introduced in June 1998. Unemployment at Greece is 21.7 per cent and 15 per cent in Spain and 24 per cent in Portugal. Germany's unemployment rate fell to 6.7 per cent in January, 2012. In 2010, only 5 per cent of Europe's debt was considered highly risky. By late 2011, this had grown to 46 per cent. And it had spread to Ireland, Portugal, Spain, Italy and Belgium — some of them with public debt ranging from 110 per cent of GDP to 166 per cent. Even the better placed economies are reported to have a debt in the 80-90 per cent of GDP range. The credit crunch in the Eurozone banks on the periphery remains severe. Unable to achieve the nine per cent capital target by raising private capital, banks are selling their assets and contracting credit, thus making the Eurozone recession more severe. Spain's borrowing costs reached around 7% in July, 2012. The highest ever since the birth of the euro.

The U.S. and Euro economic problems impacted the global economy. After recovering strongly in the first half of 2010, the global economy encountered heightened downside risks. The global recovery lost some momentum in the second half of the year in the advanced countries, especially in the US and Japan. Growth in the world industrial production also exhibited signs of declaration after attaining peaks in March, 2010.

Stock markets around the world were showing signs of distress. German and French stock markets shed a third of their value since their peaks in 2010 while U.K. and U.S. shares lost a fifth. Continuing uncertainty in the eurozone crisis and global risk aversion has had deleterious effect on economic health of India as is reflected in slowdown in GDP growth rate from 9% during 2009-10 to 6.5% during 2011-12, increase in current account deficit to over 4% as on December end 2011 as against 3.3% during 2010-11, continued withdrawals of FIIs from stock markets since February, 2012, FDI outflows to the tune of $10.7 billion in 2011 and consequent depreciation of value of rupee since February, 2012, touching its life time low of ₹ 56.38 to a dollar on May 25, 2012 and decline in BSE sensex from 21,207 in September, 2010 to 15,847 on May 23, 2012.

Corporate India is also experiencing pinch of confidence deficit. While the slow down is a common factor in both 2008 and 2011, what makes it worse this time is that confidence has taken several hard knocks; there is complete frustration, unlike in 2008. According to a survey conducted by the FICCI, companies doing business in Europe are feeling the punch of the crisis in the Eurozone. About three-fourth of Indian companies doing business in Europe suffered a loss of 20 per cent or more.

Against the depressing scenario comes a new United Nations report that says "the world is on the brink of one more recession." Indeed "World Economic Situation and Prospects 2012', predicts 2012 will be a "make or break" years for the global economy.

◈ European Response to Euro Zone Crisis

Sensing gravity of the euro zone crisis with the contagion moving to the euro-areas, core and other economies around the world, European leaders, after prolonged deliberations, took the following key measures to contain the problem.

(*i*) Italian Parliament passed a euro 30-billion austerity package to help stem a debt crisis threatening to overwhelm the euro zone. The package, dubbed a "Save Italy" aimed to raise more than euro 10 billion ($13.4 billion) from a new property tax, a new tax on luxury items, increase in value added tax, crackdown on tax evasion and measures to increase the pension age.

(*ii*) EU decided to create a euro 500-billion European Stability Mechanism as early as July 2012. It will be permanent, and perhaps would be able to borrow directly, as needed, from the ECB.

(*iii*) In a complementary, confidence-seeking short-term gesture, EU also agreed to ask their respective central banks to give the IMF euro 200 billion to buttress the euro 440-billion European Financial Stability Facility.

(*iv*) EU agreed to more centralized oversight and control of the fiscal budgets of individual countries and possible sanctions for countries that break public debt undertakings.

(*v*) EU members agreed on a new treaty (called a fiscal compact) that would oblige them never to have a cyclically adjusted budget deficit of more than 0.5 per cent of GDP.

(*vi*) Euro zone finance ministers sealed a 130-billion euro ($ 172 billion) bailout for Greece on February 21, 2012 to avert a chaotic default in March, 2012 after persuading private bondholders to take greater losses and Athens to commit to deep cuts.

Despite the above initiatives, the eurozone has been sinking deeper in the last 12 months of 2012. The debt to GDP ratio remains the same or has even increased in many countries; unemployment has soared; and prospects for a recovery have receded even further. Europe now faces a Grand Canyon — like divide between countries trapped in impoverishment and despair and a small group of countries regrouping around Germany who are holding up — so far. European Central Bank Governor's bold decision "to do whatever it takes to save the euro" and to unveil — despite German's opposition — an unlimited bond-buying programme, if subject to strict conditionalities, has kept the markets quiet and allowed pressured countries to issue sovereign debt at affordable rates.

While some welcome structural reforms have taken place across Europe, the one bit of institutional progress to be noted is the agreement on a single supervisory mechanism as a step towards a European banking union. However, as with almost every eurozone agreement, this has to be taken with a grain of salt. First, Berlin has ensured that the supervisory mechanism will only cover the 200 biggest banks. Germany does not want outsiders to poke their nose into its regional banks, which are the envy of Chinese banks in terms of cronyism and political interference in lending decisions. Second, a lot of very important elements remain to be negotiated and, of course, the level is in the details. Third, the whole mechanism — along with a joint deposit guarantee scheme and a joint resolution fund to wind down failed banks — will not come into force before spring 2014.

Even if CDS payments are not triggered in the near term, concerns about fundamentals and fiscal path of Greece and other distressed nations might deviate from prescribed deficit targets on the back of weak growth and growing public discontent over "austerity paradox" that austerity slows growth further and actually worsens a government's budget balances instead of improving them. Hence unless the struggling nations get a growth impulse that will boost revenues and help in reducing the debt-to-GDP ratio, the crisis is likely to continue to fester. This argument is gaining prominence among European leaders.

However, a lower deficit must lead overtime to a lower debt ratio even if this ratio worsens in the short run. After all, most models used to assess the economic impact of fiscal policy imply that a cut in expenditure, for example lowers demand in the short run, but that the economy recovers after a while to its previous level. So, in the long run, fiscal policy has no lasting impact on output. This implies that whatever short-run negative impact lower demand may have on the debt ratio should be offset later (in the medium to long run) by the rebound in demand that brings the economy back to its previous output level. This conclusion was already reached and reflected in the U.S. Congressional Budget. Hence, this should be all the more true for euro-zone countries like Italy or Spain.[12]

Thus, in the long run, austerity measures at all levels need to be the order of the day. These countries need to spend less and save more even to service the lower debt level after the write offs and bailout. Everyone needs to learn to live within their means.

D. SUGGESTIONS TO OVERCOME THREATS TO GLOBAL FINANCIAL STABILITY

Although economies are showing some signs of recovery from the worst crisis consequent upon various monetary and fiscal interventions across the world, the recovery has been fragile and uneven. Outburst of Euro crisis posing threat to global economies provides enough clue to the inadequacies of the existing policy measures. So as to minimise future threats to financial stability emanating out of irresponsible monetary and fiscal policy measures of a country, it would be pertinent to take the following measures:

(*i*) Financial regulations of different countries need to be proactive so as to avoid falling behind financial innovations and emerging new business models. This demands continuous sharpening of regulatory and supervisory skills and instruments. The financial regulators should be equipped with super skills to assess utility of structured products and derivatives in credit markets which have implications for financial stability. In this regard, a thorough examination of the relative superiority of different modes of trading and settlement practices would be necessary in order to address the weaknesses inherent in the "originate-to-distribute" models.

(*ii*) In view of growing inter-connectedness among financial markets of countries and financial institutions becoming more global in nature, international financial policy makers and supervisors are increasingly required to take a cooperative and coordinated approach to deal effectively with episodes of financial stress. Areas that need a better coordination mechanism at the global level include coordination of resolution tools for financial entities, consistency and coordination in depositor and investor's protection and clear legal obligations and powers to share information between house and host countries.

It is gratifying to note that BCBs and FSB have, of late, developed an integrated approach to address issues like combinations of capital surcharges, contingent capital and bail-debt, supervision of important financial institutions. Furthermore, as noted earlier, FSB has released a set of principles for cross-border cooperation on crisis management. The BCBs, as discussed earlier, brought out in October, 2010 a set of sound principles for strengthening effectiveness of supervisory practices for international bank growth.

(*iii*) So as to ensure financial stability, role of the central bank of a country has to be broadened. A central bank can discharge its lending of last resort-function more effectively if its mandate extends beyond merely monitoring financial institutions to taking preventive actions. This would be possible if the central bank also has responsibility for bank supervision.

E. MOVE TOWARDS GREATER GLOBAL CONVERGENCE IN THE BANKING REGULATION

The recent financial crisis has redefined the broad contours of regulation of the banking sector globally. The need for convergence in banking regulation stems from the fact that while banking has become global, banking regulation is national. Therefore, addressing the issue of regulatory arbitrage is at the centre-stage of policy concern. The international standard-setting bodies have been attempting to achieve convergence by issuing broad principles that should shape national regulatory frameworks.

In the post-crisis period, the Financial Stability Board (FSB) has emerged as the most important international body to address the vulnerabilities in the global financial system and to guide the development and implementation of strong regulatory, supervisory and other policies in the interest of financial stability. Besides, implementation of Basel III capital requirements, the FSB is addressing the issue of systematically important financial institutions (SIFIs), which involves determination of SIFIs and their loss absorbency, resolution tools and regimes for them; and supervisory intensity and effectiveness of such SIFIs with the aim of reducing both the probability and the impact of a SIFI.

The broader endeavour of global convergence in the banking regulation will, however, have to account for country-specific circumstances to enable customised adoption of guidance of international standard setting bodies as already recognized in many cases by the Basel Committee on Banking supervision (BCBS). To the extent that the systematically important jurisdictions harmonise and converge to agreed international best practices, there are positive externalities from India's standpoint. In particular, the BCBs guidance on conduct of the countercyclical capital buffer for India may require some changes, as the recommended metric of credit-to-GDP ratio could potentially impact the structural drivers underlying credit growth in India. Thus, there may be a need for some adjustments to capital buffer guidance. The issue is being examined by an internal group in the RBI.

F. MOVE TOWARDS REFORM IN FINANCIAL SECTOR REGULATIONS IN INDIA

With a view to strengthening the mechanism for maintaining financial stability, financial sector development and inter-regulatory coordination, the Government of India, in consultation with the financial sector regulators, set up Financial Sector Legislative Reforms Commission (FSLRC) in December 2010 under the Chairmanship of Justice B.N. Srikrishna. The FSLRC, which submitted its report on 22nd March, 2013, has proposed an Indian Financial Bill to enable creation of a unified financial regulator while limiting the role of the Reserve Bank of India (RBI) to monetary management.[13]

As per the proposed regulatory architecture, the Unified Financial Agency (UFA) and not a unified financial regulator, the Commission has asserted, will comprise four existing agencies which will be merged into one. These are the Securities and Exchange Board of India (SEBI), the Forward Markets Commission (FMC), the Insurance Regulatory and Development Authority (IRDA) and the Pension Fund Regulatory and Development Authority (PFRDA).

Envisioning a full transition into a set of small and implementable measures, the FSLRC observed the existing RBI will continue to exist, though with modified functions.

Apart from the RBI along with the UFA, the Commission has suggested Financial Sector Appellate Tribunal (FSAT), Resolution Corporation, Financial Redressal Agency, Public Debt Management Agency and FSDC (Financial Stability and Development Council). The existing Securities Appellate Tribunal (SAT), it said, will be subsumed into FSAT and the existing Deposit Insurance and Credit Guarantee Corporation of India (DICGC) will be subsumed into the Resolution Corporation.

While the existing FSDC will continue to exist though with modified functions and a statutory framework, the Commission has recommended two new creations — a Financial Redressal Agency (FRA) and a new Debt Management Office.

The Commission also recommended that the finance ministry should frame the rules governing capital controls on inbound flows into the country, in consultation with the RBI, while the RBI should make regulations about outbound capital flows in consultation with the Central Government.[13]

The Commission has also proposed a single investment vehicle for investment in India, a sound legal process while making rules for capital account transactions and granting approvals; a framework for imposition of controls in emergency situations, review or restrictions on capital account transactions on national security considerations and a principle that once controls are imposed at the entry level, there must be equal treatment for Indian investors and foreign investors.

The focus of the recommendations of the Commission is on a unified financial sector regulator as response to the recent financial crisis. Virtually, all diagnoses of the crisis identified lack of regulatory coordination as one of the contributory factors. This is why, the US set up the financial stability oversight council in 2010, creating a formal structure of regulatory coordination mandated by the Dodd Frank Act. But the moves were not all unidirectional. The UK, which had moved on regulatory integration, establishing the Financial Services Authority in 1997, saw disadvantages in moving perhaps too far in the other direction. And hence, the UK through the revised framework brought banking supervision back to the Bank of England, in the form of a subsidiary entity, the Prudential Regulation Authority, while restricting the remaining regulatory tasks within the Financial Conduct Authority, which has an explicit mandate for consumer protection with respect to all financial products and services.

The FSLRC recommendations on unification broadly follow along the lines of the revised UK framework. Thus, bank supervision remains part of the RBI's mandate, based on the premise that the lender of the last resort to the banking system must always have full visibility of the risks and potential threats to the system. The integration of financial and commodity market regulators on the one hand and insurance and pension sector regulators on the other is based on the "Consumer first" principle, allowing all financial services to be subject to common standards of transparency and the conduct of providers. This framework potentially allows for uniform treatment of innovation, wherever it may originate.

Some experts express doubts about the effectiveness of the unified regulatory agency. According to C.S. Rao, Former Chairman, IRDA, "this proposal might not help at a time when some countries, that had adopted a super regulator model, are turning back to the original regulatory structure of individual regulators. He added that, in small nations like Singpore, it could be feasible, where this model would help avoid overlaps In a large country like India, you need expertise in each field. This proposal would lead to a situation where people at the lateral level would have very little background of the segment (For example, Insurance or Stock markets) that they are working for. In some situations, a stock market expert could be working on insurance issue or vice-versa."[14]

Lack of clarity could also be an issue, said some ex-regulators. According to J. Hari Narayan, former IRDA Chairman, "the proposed model would lead to further confusion in the system. The proposal lacks clarity. It has been adopted from the English model, which has its own faults. Dilution of regulations seem to be the purpose behind the proposal."[15]

G. CONCLUSIONS

Unprecedented financial crisis that emanated from sub-prime mortgage lending in mid-2007 and transformed itself into a global disaster can be attributed to a myriad of factors ranging from excessive leverages and risk appetite fuelled by an extended period of unusually low interest rates and large global imbalances, unbridled financial innovation and weaknesses in the regulatory and supervisory arrangements.

The financial crisis, which adversely affected all segments of financial markets in both advanced countries and emerging market economies, evoked unparalleled policy response both domestically and internationally in terms of their scale, magnitude and coordination across various jurisdictions. For advanced countries, the policy priority was on strengthening financial regulation and supervision. In the EMEs, dealing with the collapse of trade and the outflow of capital occupied the policy attrition.

Despite massive stimulus packages during the past three years, U.S. and other economies could not recover; their rate of recovery was slow mainly because of contagion effect of Euro zone crisis which has been brewing in Europe for the last two years. Euro zone crisis emanating from sovereign debt defaults in Greece spread to other euro countries.

The Euro crisis has been caused mainly by fiscal irresponsibility and lack of political willingness to solve the problem. Because of the euro crisis situation in euro zone countries became worse and was on the brink of collapse. The whole global economy has experienced heightened downside risks. Stock markets around the world are showing signs of distress.

Sensing the gravity of the crisis, European leaders have, of late, taken several measures, such as austerity package, creation of European stability mechanism, centralised oversight and control of the fiscal budgets of individual countries, agreement on a new treaty called a fiscal compact and sealing of a 130-billion bailout for Greece. These measures have evoked positive response in terms of improvement to the euro fortunes. But in the long run it is important for every country to live within its means so as to avoid such crisis.

In the wake of increasing inter-connectedness of financial markets of countries around the world, it would be in the interest of every nation to take certain measures so as to minimise future threats to financial stability arising out of monetary and fiscal irresponsibilities of a nation. In the first instance, financial regulation of every country has to be proactive. Regulatory authorities need to be adequately equipped to assess implications of various derivative products on financial stability. Further, international financial authorities are required to take a cooperative and coordinated approach to deal effectively with episodes of financial stress. Furthermore, role of central bank of a country should be broadened to include not only monitoring functions but also supervisory function.

Of late, Indian financial system is seriously seized with developing unified regulatory agency so as to have financial stability, financial sector development and inter-regulatory coordination. FSLRC's recommendations are in this direction.

KEY TERMS

- Basal Committee on Banking and Supervision (BCBS)
- Collateralised debt obligations
- Collection Account Clauses
- Committee on Payment and Settlement System
- European Stability Mechanism
- Financial Stability Board (FSB)
- Fiscal compact
- FSLRC
- International Organization for Securities Commission (IOSCO)
- Lender of Last resort
- NINJA
- Securitization Market
- Securitised Products
- Shadow banking
- Sub-prime Lending

DISCUSSION QUESTIONS

1. What is sub-prime lending? How did it create global crisis?
2. Outline the various forces that led to the outburst of global financial meltdown of 2008.
3. How did global financial crisis impact various countries of the world?
4. What measures were taken by policy authorities both at domestic and international level to minimize the impact of the crisis?
5. What is euro crisis? How did it arise?
6. In what way has euro crisis affected various euro countries?
7. "Euro crisis is more dangerous than the sub-prime crisis". Comment.
8. "Euro crisis is more political than economic". Do you agree with the statement?
9. What steps have, of late, been taken by European authorities to solve the problem?
10. What suggestions would you offer to avoid threat to financial stability due to monetary and fiscal irresponsibilities of a nation?
11. Discuss in brief, recommendations of FSLRC.

REFERENCES

1. Dani Rodrick, The Globalisation Paradox, www Norton & Company, 2011.
2. A. Ayhan Kose, Eswar Prasad, Kenneth Rogoff and Shangsin was, "Financial Globalisation and Economic Policies", IZA Discussion Paper No. 4037, 2009.
3. Bank for International Settlements, 79th Annual Report, 2009.
4. J.B. Taylor, "The Financial Crisis and the Policy Responses: An Empirical Analysis of what went wrong", NBER working Paper Series, No. 14631, 2009.
5. W. White, opening Remarks at the Seventh BIS Annual Conference on 'Whither Monetary Policy? Monetary Policy Challenges in the Decade Ahead", BIS Papers No. 45, June 26-27, 2009.
6. V. Acharya and Mathew Richardson, "Causes of the Financial Crisis", New York University, April 2009.
7. IMF, World Economic Outlook: Crisis and Recovery, April 2009.
8. World Trade Organizations, "The Trade Situation in 2008-09".
9. RBI Report on Trend and Progress of Banking in India, 2010-11.
10. Daniel Gros, Director of the Centre for European Policy Studies, Business Standard, January 17, 2012.
11. *Ibid.*

12. Daniel Gros; Answering Attacks on Austerity, Business Standard, February 21, 2012.
13. HINDU, March 29, 2013.
14. Business Standard, March 25, 2013.
15. *Ibid.*

Chapter 3

Types of Financial Institutions

Learning Objectives:

The present chapter attempts to provide:

- An overview of money market and capital market institutions.
- An understanding of nature and functions of money market institutions.
- An overview of nature and functions of capital market institutions.
- An understanding of universal and virtual banking, vulture funds and mutual banking.

Chapter Outline:

A. EPILOGUE

There are numerous ways (and forms) in which savings of different types of savers may be mobilised and transferred to real investors. Each of these ways represents a specialised activity requiring expert knowledge and information and is carried out by specialist institutions, though, in all the cases, the general nature of their functions is virtually the same, *viz.*, "to spread information, to provide brokerage, to limit obligation, to create liquidity and to transform the relatively risky liabilities, which are the only kind that the business (and real investors) usually can afford to accept into the relatively safe assets, which are the only kind that savers can usually afford to hold.[1]

Broadly speaking, financial institutions may be categorised into two groups, *viz.*, Money Market Institutions and Capital Market Institutions.

B. MONEY MARKET AND CAPITAL MARKET INSTITUTIONS

Money market institutions refer to those financial institutions which cater to the notions of savers of high liquidity and safety alongwith profitability and which provide working capital to trade and industries mainly in the form of loans and advances. Money market is concerned with the supply of and the demand for investible funds. Essentially, it is a reservoir of short-term funds. Money market provides a mechanism by which short-term funds are lent out and borrowed; it is through this market that a large part of the financial transactions of a country are cleared. It is a place where a bid is made for short-term investible funds at the disposal of financial and other institutions by borrowers comprising institutions, individuals and the Government itself.

Thus, money market covers monetary and financial assets which are close substitutes for money. The money market is generally expected to perform the following three broad functions:[2]

(*i*) To provide an equilibrating mechanism to even out demand for and supply of short-term funds.

(*ii*) To provide a focal point for central bank intervention for influencing liquidity and general level of interest rates in the economy.

(*iii*) To provide reasonable access to providers and users of short-term funds to fulfil their borrowing and investment requirements at an efficient market clearing price.

Capital market is the place where the medium-term and long-term financial needs of business and other undertakings are met by financial institutions which supply medium and long-term resources to borrowers. These institutions may further be classified into *investing institutions* and *development banks* on the basis of the nature of their activities and the financial mechanism adopted by them. Investing institutions comprise those financial institutions which garner the savings of the people by offering their own shares and stocks, and which provide long-term funds, especially in the form of direct investment in securities and underwriting capital issues of business enterprises. These institutions include investment banks, merchant banks, investment companies and the mutual funds and insurance companies. Development banks include those financial institutions which provide the sinews of development, *i.e.*, capital, enterprise and know-how, to business enterprises so as to foster industrial growth.

However, metamorphic environmental developments in and outside the country following the policy of liberalisation and globalisation with the walls cocooning the economy being torn down and revolution in the computer and telecommunications technology have led to geographical and functional integration of international financial markets in recent years. Further, deregulation and intensification of competition among banks and also from non-banking financial intermediaries in advanced countries as well as in developing countries have almost blurred the boundaries between money and capital markets culminating in the emergence of more diversified multipurpose financial institutions and financial innovations of unprecedented dimensions.

C. KINDS OF MONEY MARKET INSTITUTIONS

◆ Central Bank

Nature: The Central Bank is the apex monetary institution in the money market which acts as the monetary authority of the country, and serves as the government bank as well as the bankers' bank. It undertakes the major financial operations of the government; by its conduct of these operations and by other means, it influences the behaviour of financial institutions to ensure that they support the economic policy of the government. The Central Bank differs from other financial institutions. First, it differs in that it is controlled by the people who are more or less closely connected with other organs of government. Second, it does not exist to earn profit, which is the principal aim of a commercial bank. Third, the Central Bank must have a special relation with the commercial banks whereby it may influence the operations of these institutions in the implementation of the government's economic policy. In brief, the Central Bank is an organ of the government which, by reason of its operations, influences the working of financial institutions of the country.

Evolution of central banking is essentially a twentieth century phenomenon in as much as there are at present about 160 central banks in the world where there were only about a dozen banks at the turn of the Twentieth Century.[3] The need for having a central bank in a country arose with increased complexity of banking business and the consequent vicissitudes experienced by banks and their depositors. Further, it was strongly felt to have a central bank which could issue currency, act as a banker and lender to the government, regulate and serve as a lender of last-resort. In recent years, central bank is also expected to focus on price stability along with financial stability.

The following paragraphs are devoted to provide insights into the tasks assigned to central bank in a country.

The main function of a central bank is to regulate the monetary mechanism comprising of the currency, banking and credit systems. For this purpose, the bank is given wide power. Another important function of the central bank is to conduct the banking and financial operations of the government. Besides, it discharges certain other functions. These functions are performed with the service motive and not for making profits. The functions of the central bank and the obligations resting upon it are of a very special character, calling for skill, experience and judgement of a kind different from those required from a commercial bank.

The functions of a central bank may be described broadly under four main headings:

- ***Issue of Currency Notes*:** One of the principal functions of a central bank is the issue of legal tender currency. In our country, the Reserve Bank of India has been given the sole monopoly for the issue of currency other than one-rupee coins and notes and subsidiary coins. For this purpose, the Bank maintains a separate department, known as the Issue Department. Notes are issued on the basis of a minimum currency reserve system.
- ***Government Banker:*** The central bank acts as the agent and adviser of the state. As the government's banker, it conducts the government departments, boards and enterprises; it makes temporary advances to the government in anticipation of the collection of taxes or raising of loans from the public. The central bank is also called upon to discharge certain other functions; for example, that of the government's financial agent; and it generally acts as the financial advisor to the government.

In addition, the bank is often entrusted with the management of the public debt and the issue of new loans and treasury bills on behalf of the government.

Finally, the central bank is the principal advisor of the government on various financial and economic matters. It assists the government in the formulation of its economic and financial policies. The advice of the bank is also sought on matters of international finance.

At times, central banks finance governments through monetisation as and when the need arose for expansionary fiscal policy which has been often in developing countries. War Warning through monetisation has also been the worm for developed countries.

- ***Bankers' Bank:*** In view of the fact that it is the sole authority of note-issue and the government's banker, the central bank stands in a privileged position in the money market. As the bankers' bank, it holds a certain portion of deposits of the commercial banks of the country. By varying the cash reserve ratio, the central bank effectively controls the credit creation capacity of scheduled banks, and thereby exercises credit control with a view to bringing about monetary stability in the country. To a certain extent, it is also possible for the central bank to influence the credit policy of scheduled banks by means of an open market operations policy.

As bankers' banker, the most important duty of the central bank is to extend financial facilities to commercial banks when there is a banking crisis. It extends financial accommodation through rediscounting of first rated bills of exchange, government securities and such other eligible papers.

Being the holder of the balances of commercial bank, the central bank serves as a bank of central clearance. The Bank of England was the first central bank to act as a bank of central clearance. The plan adopted was to offset inter-bank indebtedness by effecting transfers in the accounts kept by the various banks with the Bank of England. Since then, many central banks have adopted the function of central clearance. The main advantage of central clearance is that it minimises the necessity of the bank to hold large cash reserves.

- ***Foreign Exchange:*** The central bank of the country is also entrusted with the responsibility of maintaining the external stability of the currency. It enjoys monopoly power to control and regulate foreign exchange.

It is obvious from these functions of the central bank that it plays a pivotal role in a country's money market.

◈ Commercial Banks: Nature and functions

Commercial banks constitute another important segment of the money market. These banks are concerned with accepting deposits of money from the public at large, repayable on demand or otherwise, and withdrawable by cheque, draft, order or otherwise, and employing the deposits so pooled in the form of loans and investment to meet the financial needs of business and other classes of society.

Like other financial intermediaries, commercial banks act as mobilisers of public savings for their productive utilisation. However, the mechanism they provide for performing this function is fundamentally different from that of other institutions. A commercial bank is the only institution which accepts funds from the public in the form of demand deposits, i.e., deposit accounts which are subject to withdrawal by the owner on demand and subject to transfer to a third party by means of a cheque. A clear line of demarcation, therefore, exists in the functions of a commercial bank and all other financial institutions. Deposits with other financial institutions do not circulate as money, while those in the commercial banks do. In the field of lending also, commercial banks have specialised in providing funds to the business community with a view to satisfying their working capital needs. The provision of short-term loan by means of cash credit, discounting bills, hundis, promissory notes and other debt instruments distinguishes commercial banks from other financial intermediaries. In the process of the acceptance of deposits and provision of loans, commercial banks create money. This too is a characteristic feature of their function which sets them apart from other financial institutions.

The foregoing description of the nature of commercial banks indicates that these institutions act as repositories of public deposits and lenders of money. Besides, they manufacture money. We shall now dwell upon each of these functions.

- ***Repository Function of Commercial Banks:*** As repository of savings, commercial banks provide to their customers a range of deposits tailored to the individual and institutional depositors' needs.

Commercial banks offer two types of deposits, viz., chequable deposits and non-transaction deposits. *Chequable* deposits are bank accounts that allow the owner of the account to write cheques to their parties. Such deposits include all accounts on which cheques can be drawn: non-interest bearing chequing accounts (demand deposits), interest-bearing negotiable order or withdrawal accounts and money market deposit accounts. Chequable deposits and money market deposit accounts are payable on demand. A chequable deposit is an asset for the depositor because it is part of his/her wealth. Conversely, chequable deposits are a liability because the depositor can withdraw funds from an account that the bank is obligated to pay. Chequable deposits are usually the lowest-cost source of bank funds because depositors are willing to forego some interest in order to have access to a liquid asset that can be used to make purchases.

In *Non-transaction deposits* owners can write cheques on non-transaction parties. The interest rates are usually higher than those on chequable deposits. Such deposits are primary source of bank funds. There are two basic types of non-transaction deposits: savings account and time deposits (also called certificates of deposits or CDs). In savings account, to which funds can be added or from which funds can be withdrawn at any time, transactions and interest payments are recorded in a passbook held by owner of the account.

Time deposits have a fixed maturity length, ranging from several months to over five years and have penalties for early withdrawal. Small-denomination time deposits are less liquid for the depositor than passbook savings, earn interest rates, and are a more costly source of funds for the banks. Large-denomination time deposits (CDs) are typically bought by companies or other banks.

- ***Deployment Function of Commercial Banks:*** The second major function of commercial banks is that of the employment of funds in different sectors of the economy. Commercial banks utilise their funds by way of granting loans and advances, investing them in industrial securities and by underwriting industrial issues.

A major portion of the funds is employed by commercial banks in loans. Loans are provided in a variety of ways, according to their form, security, maturity, method of repayment, origin and purpose.

By form, bank loans can be categorised into four groups. Loans and advances, overdrafts, cash credit and bills discounting. In *loans*, a bank makes an advance in a lumpsum, which is repaid in one single instalment. Once the loan is sanctioned, the borrower is required to draw out the amount and pay interest on the whole amount sanctioned. An overdraft is an arrangement whereby the customer is allowed to overdraw his account. It is usually granted against collateral securities. Interest is charged on the exact amount overdrawn, subject to the payment of a minimum amount by way of interest. In the *cash credit* arrangement, the customer is allowed to borrow up to a certain limit against either a bond of credit by one or more sureties or against certain securities. The credit may be secured or unsecured, depending upon the credit standing of the party and the relationship between the bank and the borrower. Unlike the loan arrangement, the borrower in a cash credit arrangement is not bound to avail himself of the whole advance sanctioned to him. Within the limits of the sanction, he can draw any amount according to his convenience. Furthermore, he is not obliged to draw the amount in a lumpsum. Technically, a cash credit advance is repayable on demand without any specific date of repayment. But, in actual practice, it continues for a long period. The customer has to pay the interest only on the amount actually utilised by him and not on the limit granted. Another characteristic feature of the cash credit form of the bank loans is that the securities furnished by the borrower can be raised or reduced according to the amount withdrawn, and he is at liberty also to replace one kind of security for another till the value thereof is adequate from the bank's point of view. Cash credit is very popular in India, and accounts for about 20 per cent of the total bank finance.

Loans are also given by way of *discounting of bills of exchange.* When a credit transaction takes place, the seller draws a bill of exchange upon the buyer, requesting him to pay the amount mentioned therein after the lapse of the period of the credit. These bills are then discounted with commercial banks which collect the payment from the acceptor of the bill on the maturity date. Banks discount only usance bills maturing within 90 days. For this service, the bank charges the customer. This charge is known as a *discount.* It includes interest for the unexpired period of the bill for which the bank is required to retain it and compensation for the expense and trouble in realising it. The banker may sometimes purchase bill instead of discounting them. However, this is generally done in the case of documentary bills and that, too, from approved customers. Documentary bills are supported by title to goods, such as bills of lading or lorry and railway receipts.

By security, bank loans may be *secured or unsecured.* A secured loan is made on the security of a specific collateral, *viz.*, stock-in-trade, accounts receivables, plant, equipment and premises, corporate stocks and bonds, gold, silver, etc. The basic requirement of such assets is their marketability. Banks generally prefer to provide secured loans because security provides added protection against the risk of non-payment of loans. In the event the borrower defaults in repaying the loan at maturity; the security pledged can be liquidated to clear the dues. Bankers insist on security of loans, particularly from those borrowers whose financial conditions are not beyond reproach.

An *unsecured loan,* also called a clean loan, is granted against the promissory note of the borrower. In some instances, this loan is supported by guarantees of partners, directors, banks or other persons who undertake to discharge the liability in the event the borrower refuses or he is unable to repay. But a distinguishing feature of unsecured loans is that no tangible security is offered to the bank. Such types of loans are given to businessmen and others with a continuing credit reputation in society and strong financial strength. These loans are made only after a careful investigation into the creditworthiness of the borrower.

By *maturity*, bank loans may be grouped into short, intermediate and long-term loans. Short-term loans may be made for a period of 30, 60 or 90 days, for a year or on demand basis. *Demand* loans have no definite maturity date, but they are callable at any time by the lenders, and are payable at any time at the option of the borrower.

Term loans are granted normally for a period of 1-5 years. However, in practice, it has frequently been noted that a loan made for a period of ten years has been regarded as an *intermediate loan.*

Long-term loans are provided for a period of more than five years. Such loans are provided for financing the expansion of projects, the rehabilitation and modernisation of old plants and for financing permanent working capital requirements. Real estate loans for the purchase of houses and financing of industrial and commercial buildings are the most important type of long-term loans. Such loans involve financial planning and budgeting, which are not necessary in the case of short-term lending.

Commercial banks of the USA and the industrial banks of Japan provide long-term loans to industrial enterprises. In India, these banks until recently have confined their operation to short-term lending business. However, during post-reform period, the banking system in the country has shown a remarkable resilience and vitality. It has tended to adapt itself to the sweeping changes in the economy, with the result that there has been an interesting diversification of banking functions. A redeeming feature of this has been the diversification of banking business in medium and long-term financing, and non-funding activities.

Commercial bank loans may be classified according to the method of repayment as lumpsum loans and instalment loans. In lumpsum loans, usually referred to as *straight loans,* the borrower is required to repay the entire principal amount at one final maturity date. The interest on the loan may be payable at various intervals, usually every six months.

In the *instalment loans*, the borrower is required to repay the loan periodically along with the interest. Payments may be either monthly, quarterly, semi-annually, or annually. The instalment based on the principle of amortization by which principal and interest payments are amortized over the life of the contract. The repayment schedule in this case is tailored to the income flows of the borrowers.

By *type of borrowers*, bank loans to customers are distinguished from loans to outsiders made in the open market. The term *customers' loans* implies loans to regular depositors of the bank and are characterised by personal relations between the bank and its depositors. In the customers' loan market, the banker is under pressure to grant the reasonable requests of his customers or loans because the continued success of the bank depends on its ability to retain the patronage of its customers. Extension and renewals of the customers' loans are common. Loans to outsiders are impersonal, the lender who purchases the open market paper does not anticipate the establishment of a continuous debtor-creditor relationship with the borrower who offers the paper for sale by turning it over to a middleman, who in turn finds a buyer for it. When an open market loan matures, it must be paid.

Bank loans may be further classified according to the *purpose* for which they are sought by the borrowers. They may take the form of commercial and industrial loans, real estate loans, loans to other banks, loans to other financial institutions, loans to brokers and dealers in securities, loans to farmers and loans to individuals. This classification is made on the basis of the information which the bank collects on the uses of the funds requested. But the information supplied by the borrower may not always be true. Funds sought for a particular purpose may be co-mingled with other funds and used for different purposes. More often than not, the proceeds of a loan sought for business or agricultural purposes have been utilised for the acquisition of consumer goods. It is also possible that borrowers may change their minds regarding the use of funds after they have been secured.

- ***Commercial Banks Manufacture Money:*** Banks are not only purveyors of money but its creators as well. A considerably large portion of money in an advanced economy is the money which commercial banks create out of their lending and investing operations. Banks are profit seeking enterprises and, therefore, they utilise the deposits which they get from the people by loaning them and investing them in securities. Banks know that all the depositors will not turn up at the same time to run down their deposits. Whatever demands are made are more than offset by new deposits. Banks can, therefore, manage to satisfy the depositors' claims by carrying a portion of the total deposits, and employing the balance to earn profits. Thus, loans and investments are created by deposits. But the reverse is also true, when banks lend or invest.

When a bank grants a loan to a customer, it does not pay him in cash but simply credits the amount of the borrower with the amount of the loan. The borrower may draw out some of the loan in cash, but generally he spends it by cheque, in which case the amount withdrawn from the borrower's account may come back to the same bank when the payee of the cheques deposit them. In case the payee has an account with some other bank, the deposits of that other bank increase.

Thus, a large portion of the loans granted by the banker is taken back in the shape of deposits, and the liabilities of the bank become liabilities not to that customer but to the payees of the cheques. The deposits which come back to the bank are also lent out, which further increases the deposits of the bank. Through this process of credit creation, a bank manufactures money several times the original amount of the deposit, which is termed as *cash or primary deposit*. For example, if a bank has an initial cash deposit of ₹ 100 and out of its experience, it decides to hold 10 per cent of the primary deposit in cash, it can create deposits to the tune of ₹ 1,000. The deposits which the banks create are referred to as *derivative deposits*. The mechanism of credit creation may better be understood with the help of the following example.

Let us assume the Bank A has deposits of ₹ 5,000. Let us also assume that the bank carries a reserve of 10 per cent. The bank will, therefore, utilise the balance of ₹ 4,500 in a profitable manner. Suppose the bank lends this surplus money to Mr. X. Mr. X utilises the amount to make payments to his creditors. The balance sheet of Bank A will then stand as below:

Liabilities	₹	*Assets*	₹
Deposit	5,000	Cash	500
		Loan to X	4,500
Total	5,000		5,000

Let us further assume that the creditor of Mr. X deposits the amount of ₹ 4,500 in his bank, *e.g.*, Bank B. It is also possible that the creditor may deposit the amount with Bank A itself. The balance sheet of Bank B will then be:

Liabilities	₹	*Assets*	₹
Deposit	4,500	Cash	4,500

After holding a cash reserve of ₹ 450, *i.e.*, 10 per cent, the bank lends the balance of ₹ 4,050. Suppose the bank lends this sum to Y. Its balance sheet will then show the following state of affairs:

Liabilities	₹	*Assets*	₹
Deposit	4,500	Cash	450
		Loan	4,050
Total	4,500	Total	4,500

If Y uses this loan to make payments to his creditor who deposits the money with Bank C, the balance sheet of Bank C will be:

Liabilities	₹	*Assets*	₹
Deposit	4,050	Cash	4,050

Bank C after carrying a reserve of ₹ 405, *i.e.*, 10% of the deposit, lends the balance, ₹ 3,645 to Z who uses the amount to pay his creditors. When the creditors deposit the sum with their bank, the deposit liabilities will increase further. The process of a deposit becoming a loan and the latter being converted into a new deposit will continue so long as the initial cash deposit of ₹ 5,000 is completely used. By that time, original bank deposit will have increased ten times. This is how the multiple creation of money takes place.

Making a loan is not the only way in which deposits can be created. When a bank lends, it issues cheques on itself in favour of the sellers of the securities. The sellers deposit the cheques which they receive in payment of the securities in one of the banks. The purchase of securities by any banker will increase the deposit of his own bank or some other bank by the amount of investment in securities.

It should, however, be remembered that credit creation capacity of banks is conditioned by the amount of cash reserve which they have to carry to honour the customer's claims. The larger the proportion of cash reserves, the less would be the expansion of derivative deposits because, in that case, only a smaller balance is left for investment elsewhere. Banks have to hold two types of reserves — a legal reserve and a working reserve. Every bank is required to carry the legal minimum reserve. In addition, they have to carry working reserves.

The nature of working conditions also sets a limit to the ability of the banks to manufacture money. During the period of a boom, there is expansion in business activity, and businessmen need a large amount of loans to finance their increased requirements. The provision of a larger amount of loans results in the creation of more deposits. Contrary to this, in times of depression, there is a contraction of credit.

The availability of good securities restricts the ability of banks to create money. A bank may agree to loan money only when the securities offered are found acceptable. If approved securities are not available, the banks cannot create deposits without inviting difficulties or disaster. Moreover, the credit creation capacity of a bank is limited by the availability of honest and sound borrowers.

The monetary policy of a country influences, both directly and indirectly, the extent of credit creation capacity of commercial banks.

Thus, commercial banks' credit money are subject to certain restrictions, which represent the safety measures for the continued existence of a bank.

Banks have historically developed comparative advantage vis-a-vis other types of intermediates over different functions such as liquidity and payment services, credit supply and information provision). Banks are called special financial institutions as they not only accept and deploy large amounts of uncollateralised public funds in a fiduciary capacity, but also leverage such funds through credit creation. Banks, thus, have a fiduciary responsibility. The deployment of funds mobilized through deposits involves banks in financing economic activity and providing the life time for the payment system. The banking system is something that is central to nation's economy, and that applies whether the banks are local or foreign.

It is interesting to note that owners of the banks have only a minor state and the considerable leveraging capacity of banks (more than ten to one) puts them in control of very large amount of public funds inspite of their being very small. In a sense, therefore, the owners act as trustees and as such must be fit and proper for the deployment of funds enrusted to them. The sustained success and growth depend on the public confidence in individual bank and the banking system.

Concentrated shareholding banks controlling huge public funds does these issues related to the risk of concentration of ownership because of the moral hazard problem and linkages of owners with business. Hence, diversification of ownership is desirable as also ensuring fit and proper status of such owners and directors. However, with diversified ownership, there is, perhaps, even greater concern over corporate governance and professional management in order to safegaurd depositors' interests and ensure systemic stability. It would, therefore, be in fitness of thing for regulatory and supervisory authorities to develop mechanism to ensure that banks have adequate capital to cushion risks that are inevitable in their operation, follow prudent and transparent accounting practices and are managed in accordance with the best practices for risk management.

In view of the above, banks are not only departmental store of finance but also represent special type of financial intermediaries that need a differentiated treatment by regulating authorities.

- ***Miscellaneous Functions:*** Commercial banks render a variety of services to their customers. For this purpose, they perform a number of functions which may be categorised in two broad groups, *viz*., agency functions and general utility functions.

A bank acts as the agent of its customers in various ways. It undertakes, on behalf of its customers, the payment of subscriptions, insurance premiums, rents, income-tax, etc., and the collection of cheques, bills, salaries, dividends, interest, etc. It purchases and sells, on behalf of its customers, shares, debentures and bonds on the stock exchanges. Banks also arrange to transfer money from one place to another by means of cheques or bank drafts or by mail transfer. They also act as representatives of or correspondents for their customers. They act as trustees, executors, administrators and attorneys. As trustees, they take care of the funds of the customers. As executors, they carry out the desires of the deceased customer in terms of the will left by him. They sign transfer forms and documents as attorneys on behalf of their customers.

Commercial banks perform a number of other functions which are of a general utility nature. These include the safe keeping of valuables and documents, the issue of credit instruments to promote an easy transfer of funds from one part of the country to another, the collection of credit information regarding customers, acting as referees for their customers.

In their frenetic effort to attract new customers and retain the existing ones commercial banks have of late, offered myriad of services to the account holders, *viz*, multi-city/payable at par (PAP), cheque facility, anywhere banking facility, credit card, mobile bank and Real Time Gross Settlement (RTGS). Foreign banks are expanding products on offer, their complexity such as derivatives, leverage financing. Door step banking facilities are being offered by some of these banks to cater to convenience the life style of its customers. Private sector banks are extending services including wealth maximization and equity trading apart from credit cards.

◈ Indigenous Financial Agencies: Nature and Functions

Indigenous financial agencies occupy an important position in the Indian money market. They comprise moneylenders and indigenous bankers. The Central Banking Enquiry Committee defined an indigenous banker as "any individual or private firm receiving deposits and dealing in hundis or lending money" and moneylenders as "those whose primary business is not banking but moneylending." In spite of these definitions, it is difficult to draw a definite line between moneylenders and indigenous bankers. In many states, while there were moneylenders who received deposits, there were indigenous bankers who did not accept deposits but were still regarded as indigenous bankers. The Banking Commission observed that "while the former lends his own funds, the latter acts as a financial intermediary by accepting deposits, or avails himself of bank credit; in other words, the indigenous banking system is regarded as a true financial intermediary in the sense that its ability to purvey funds is largely dependent on the outside sources it is able to mobilise. Another distinguishing feature is that the transactions of the moneylender are conducted in cash while those of the indigenous banker are based on the dealings in short-term credit instruments for financing the production and distribution of goods and services."[4]

The indigenous bankers may be defined as those individuals and firms which accept deposits or rely on bank credit for the conduct of their business and are close to, or on the periphery of, the organised money market and are professional dealers in short-term credit instruments (*hundis*) for financing the production and distribution of goods and services. The total number of indigenous bankers has been estimated in the neighbourhood of 2,000 to 2,500.[5]

By and large, indigenous bankers are urban-based and have not penetrated into rural areas. While some have been prominent in areas where the growth of commercial banking has been slow (for example, in Assam), a much larger number have prospered even in areas where commercial banks have developed considerably. For instance, the Multani bankers have concentrated their activities in the metropolitan areas of Mumbai and Chennai, while the Gujarat Shroffs have been active in the industrial and trading centres of Gujarat and Maharashtra.

The normal business of indigenous bankers is to finance inland trade, including the movement of agricultural commodities, such as cotton, oil seeds, and sugar; they do not generally finance the agriculturists directly. Their main clients are non-agriculturists.

Usually, indigenous bankers lend money on written promissory notes or on receipts signed by the borrowers, acknowledging the loan and stating the agreed rate of interest. They also lend money against bonds written out on stamped legal forms, which state all the conditions of the loan in detail. The drawing and discounting of *hundis* is another method of lending money. Indigenous bankers lend money on the mortgage of houses, land or other immovable property.

One of the most important characteristics of the operations of indigenous bankers is that they give prompt, flexible, informal and personal service. Although the rates of interest are high in relation to those charged by banks, the loan is otherwise tailored to suit the individual borrower's needs. Also, funds are often provided on a risk basis, and risk financing is often what the small man needs. In view of these reasons, the services of these bankers have been much sought after. Their flexible lending policy stemming out of their close personal knowledge of their clients has given them an edge over their industrial counterparts with their more formal methods of working.

Moneylenders may be broadly classified into professional moneylenders and non-professional moneylenders. Professional moneylenders may again be divided into resident and itinerant. The Mahajans or Soukars come under the category of resident moneylenders, while the Pathans from the North West Frontier come under the category of itinerant moneylenders. The non-professional moneylenders are those people who have not taken to moneylending as their business but who occasionally utilise the surplus funds at their disposal in the business of moneylending. Under this category may be included landowners, large agriculturists, merchants and traders, pensioners, priests, etc.

The methods of business of these moneylenders are not uniform. They vary from place to place, and from money lender to money lender. Generally, loans are given on personal security, and even without any written agreement. However, when the amount is large or the transaction represents the renewal of an old loan, promissory notes are taken. It is not unusual for these moneylenders to give loans even to borrowers from the neighbouring villages with whom they may not have any personal acquaintance. In such cases, they charge a very high rate of interest to cover the risk. Often, moneylenders are very reasonable as regards the period for which the loans are granted. The period for short-term loans are so fixed that they become due soon after the harvest. Sometimes, moneylenders, make advances to cultivators against the security of crops. Usually, no interest is charged on such loans because, as per the terms of lending, the cultivator is bound to sell his crops to them at a price which is generally lower than the market price by 5 to 15 per cent.

◈ Discount Houses: Nature and Functions

Discount houses are specialised firms which transact the bulk of the total discount business in the London money market. There are 12 discount houses in the London money market. Each of the discount houses is a public company owned and operated independently of other financial institutions.

These agencies are concerned with the discounting of trade bills. After having discounted the bills, they arrange them according to their maturity and sell them to commercial banks after one month. Thus, the discount houses also provide an active market in commercial bills. When a bill, bought on the London market, is sold by a discount house, it is endorsed, that is, the discount house adds its name to the bill and thus assumes responsibility for its payment at maturity in the event of default.

A further function of the discount houses consists in dealing in short-dated government bonds.

The organisation of the discount houses is extremely simple, and the number of their employees is quite small, although they turn over huge sums of money every day. The capital of these institutions is relatively small. Their profits are made mainly by borrowing money more cheaply than they lend it, and, to some extent, from commissions and from dealer profits on selling the assets in which they invest.

The discount houses borrow "at call' from banks and other financial institutions. In this way, they provide a means whereby the banks are able to reduce to a minimum the amount of money they must keep unemployed to meet the calls upon them by their customers for cash, and at the same time earn interest on the surplus funds which they may have at any given time. In this way, the discount market provides a very flexible instrument whereby the bankers are able to adjust their cash position at will by lending to, or withdrawing funds from discount houses according to their day-to-day requirements.

The money borrowed by discount houses is mainly invested in British Government Treasury Bills, Commercial Bills and British Government Securities with a life of upto 5 years. They also hold bills and bonds issued by local authorities and public corporation and sterling dollar certificates of deposit.

Should any of these discount houses become short of money, e.g., by calling in of loans by the banks, they may have recourse to the Bank of England as the lender of the last resort. In such circumstances, the practice of the Bank of England is to lend them against the security of eligible bills of exchange, Treasury Bills or short-dated government securities. It is open to the discount with the Bank of England eligible bills of exchange or Treasury Bills, but this facility is very seldom used in practice.

◈ Accepting Houses: Nature and Function

Another important constituent of the London Money Market is Accepting Houses. Accepting houses maintain accounts both with the Bank of England and commercial banks. They borrow short period loans from banks with a view to lending them out to the money market.

Acceptance credit is the basic business of these houses which has been described as fundamentally a three-month operation. These houses finance exports from, and imports to, Britain and to other markets by means of bills of exchange. A bill of exchange is drawn on an acceptance house either by the seller or by the buyer of goods. After it has been accepted by the house against documents, the drawer can then receive immediate cash by discounting the bills with a discount house.

The other activities traditionally financed by the Accepting Houses include normal banking facilities for customers, including the foreign banks which regulate open credits with them. They also advise on the shipping and insurance problems arising out of the financing of trade.

The activities of Acceptance Houses have, in recent years, extended beyond their traditional short-term acceptance credit business to the arranging of medium and even long-term finance for major projects. They play a leading part in forming consortia of leading deposit banks and sometimes other institutions, which provide the bulk of the credit required.

◈ Money Market Mutual Funds (MMMFs)

Money market mutual funds, sometimes called money market funds, are relatively new financial institutions having portfolio of money market (short-term) instruments constructed and managed by investment companies. The portfolio is divided into shares that are sold to individual investors. All MMMFs are open-end investment funds that invest only in money market securities. Most funds do not charge investors any fee for purchasing or redeeming shares.

A key feature of MMMFs is that shareholders can write cheques against the value of their shareholdings. However, there may be restrictions on the number of cheques written per month or on the minimum amount of the cheque.

MMMFs have a low level of credit risk. There may be some concern that an economic downturn could cause frequent defaults on commercial paper or other short-term instrument. But MMMFs can quickly shift away from securities issued by any particular enterprises that may fail in the near future.

◈ Shadow Banking Institutions

Shadow banking institutions represent non-bank financial institutions which do not accept deposits like a commercial bank but play an increasingly critical role in lending businesses the money necessary to operate.

The term "shadow banking system" is attributed to Paul McCulley who coined it at the Jackson Hole Conference in 2007, where he defined it as "the whole alphabet soup of levered up non-bank investment conduits, vehicles, and structures."[6] Many "shadow bank" like institutions and vehicles emerged in American and European markets, between the years 2000 and 2008, and played an important role in providing credit across the global financial system.

Operationally, shadow institutions, like investment banks borrow from investors in short-term, liquid markets, meaning that they would have to frequently repay and borrow again from these investors. At the same time, they use the funds to lend to corporations or to invest in longer-term, less liquid assets. When the housing market began to deteriorate and the ability to obtain funds from investors through investments such as mortgage-backed securities declined, these investment banks were unable to fund themselves.

Technically, these institutions are subject to market risk credit risk and especially liquidity risk, since their liabilities are more long-term and illiquid. This creates a potential problem in that they are not depository institutions and do not have direct or indirect access to their central bank's lender-of-last-resort support. Therefore, during periods of market liquidity, they could go bankrupt if unable to refinance their short-term liabilities. They were also highly leveraged.

In early, 2007, lending through the shadow banking system slightly exceeded lending via the traditional banking system based on outstanding balances which contributed to the freezing of credit markets in the USA.[7]

◆ Finance Companies

Finance companies, mostly popular in the US financial sector, are concerned with providing short and intermediate term credit to consumers and small businesses. Although other finance institutions provide this service, only finance companies specialize in it.

The three major types of finance companies are: Sales finance institutions, personal credit institutions and business credit institutions. *Sales finance institutions* specialise in making loans to customers of a specific retailer or manufacturer. *Personal credit institutions* specialize in making instalment and other loans to consumers. These institutions make loans to customers with low income or a bad credit history, whom depository institutions find too risky to lend to. They compensate for the additional risk by charging higher interest rates than depository institutions. *Business Credit Institutions* provide financing to companies, especially through equipment leasing and factoring, in which the finance company purchases accounts receivable from corporate customers at a discount from face value and the finance company assumes the responsibility for collecting the accounts receivable.

Finance companies provide three types of loans: real estate, consumer and business. Business and consumer loans account for major part of the loan portfolio of finance companies.

Finance companies raise funds by selling commercial paper and by issuing stocks and bonds. Besides, they borrow from commercial banks. These loans can provide a continual source of funds, although some finance companies use bank loans mainly to fund seasonal savings in their business.

However, finance companies cannot accept deposits. Rather, to finance assets, they rely heavily on short-term commercial paper, with many having programmes, in which they sell commercial paper directly to mutual funds and other institutional investors on a continuous day-by-day basis.

D. KINDS OF CAPITAL MARKET INSTITUTIONS

◆ Investment Banks: Nature and functions

In American economy, the investment banking institution is one of the major financial intermediaries charged with the responsibility of garnering the savings of myriads of thrifty people and directing these funds into the business enterprises seeking capital for the acquisition of plant and equipment and for holding inventories. The following are some of the cardinal features of this kind of institution which make it distinct from other financial intermediaries:

- Investment banks are mainly concerned with the long-term financing of business enterprises and the marketing of stocks and bonds. In this, they differ from commercial banks.
- Investment bankers carry out their financing function by acting as *security middlemen*. They are merchandisers whose stock-in-trade is stocks and bonds. They buy securities from issuing companies and sell them at wholesale prices to security dealers and at retail prices to individual and traditional institutional investors.

- Besides acting as security middlemen, investment bankers render expert advice on the type and form of securities that will appeal to investors.
- An investment bank may exercise something less than its full function as a merchant. Instead of making an outright purchase of security, it may act as an "insurer" of a successful sale when a company is offering new issues to its existing stockholders through rights. It may contract with the issuing company to distribute an issue on the "best effort basis." It may act as an agent in the direct placement of the issue of securities with one or a limited number of investing institutions. The last two are technically brokerage functions, but are closely associated with investment banking because they are linked with the original distribution of securities.

The functions of investment bankers, as presently performed by them in the USA, may be categorised into two broad groups:

(*i*) Function concerning the formation of new capital for a new and established businesses and for state and local government bodies; and

(*ii*) Functions that are subordinate to capital formation and are associated with outstanding securities and securities markets.

◈ Functions Concerning the Formation of New Capital

The primary function of an investment banker is to participate in the formation of new capital for new and established business enterprises and for state and local government bodies. This comprises activities relating to the origination, underwriting, purchase and sale of securities. Besides, investment bankers render such services as are useful and helpful to the company seeking the new capital.

- ***Origination:*** Investment bankers assist the issuing company in working out the details of the financing, including the preparation of the Securities and Exchange Commission registration statement and prospectus in case of a public issue, arrangement with lawyers, accountants and engineering firms and companies, and compliance with legal requirements.
- ***Underwriting:*** In order to ensure the successful sale of a new issue and relieve the company of the uncertainties associated with it, investment bankers perform the underwriting function. In underwriting, investment bankers enter into an agreement with the issuer to take up all such securities as are not bought by the public. The most common situation, in which a stand-by agreement is used occurs when the corporation issues to present common stockholders rights to subscribe to an additional issue of common stock, at a certain price within a limited period of time.

The underwriting of issues may be done on the basis of negotiation or on competitive bidding. Under the negotiated purchase plan, the issuer and investment banker engage in negotiations to determine the essential features of the issue. Together, they discuss and negotiate a price for the security and timing of the issue. Depending upon its size, two or more investment bankers join to underwrite it.

Under competitive bidding the issuing company invites bids on the price from investment bankers which will be paid to the company. Usually, two or more bankers join together for the purpose of bidding on a security issue. The security issue is offered for sale to the highest bidder.

- ***Purchase of Securities:*** The nerve centre of the investment banking business lies in the purchase of securities. Investment bankers purchase the securities outright and make payment therefor, and arrange to distribute them to investors. Where the size of the issue is large, and a single investment banker finds it difficult to buy the entire issue, they invite other bankers to form a purchase syndicate.

Before agreeing either to pay or underwrite, the investment banker analyses the business of the company from every angle. If, on investigation, he is satisfied that he can sell the securities successfully, the question of fixing the price is decided. The price is determined by the process of bargaining.

- ***Selling the Securities:*** Another major function of the investment banker is to dispose off securities to investors. He sells securities in three ways:
  (*i*) By sales representatives;
  (*ii*) By correspondence; and
  (*iii*) By advertising.

Generally speaking, all the three methods are used in one selling transaction; but the investment banking firm invariably relies on its sales representatives for the sale of securities. Investment bankers usually do not face problems in the distribution of securities because investors have complete faith in them.

In addition to simply disposing off securities, the selling function may involve at least two other related responsibilities. First, when the issuing company is selling securities for the first time, the investment banker frequently creates an after-market for the securities. In making market, the underwriters maintain a position in the stock market and stands ready to buy and sell them at the "ask and bid prices" he quotes. These questions are based upon supply and demand conditions. With a secondary market, the stock has greater liquidity for investors; this appeal enhances the success of the original offering. Second, to minimize the potential of a large block of share falling into the hands of a few investors, companies often provide for a wide geographical distribution when they issue new stock.

For large issues, investment bankers form a selling syndicate analogous to the purchase syndicate, comprising a large number of firms.

◈ Functions Subordinate to Capital Formation

The functions which are subordinate to capital formation include such activities as secondary distribution of large blocks of outstanding securities, acting as broker or dealer, offering security, advice and portfolio management, security substitution and allied services.

- ***Secondary Distribution of Large Blocks of Outstanding Securities:*** Modern investment bankers play an important part in distributing the outstanding securities of corporate enterprises so as to affect the transfer of a part or all of the ownership of the companies. Frequently, owners of large block of securities like to liquidate their holdings in cash. This they can do with the help of investment bankers. Sometimes, owners of a closely held company desire to have a public market for their remaining holdings upon their death or to establish the availability of a market for further disposition so as to meet their liabilities and other obligations.

When a company is contemplating the acquisition of another company or when it wants to merge with another company, the services of investment bankers are very often utilized for the purpose of negotiating the terms of acquisition or merger. Besides, if new financing is required by the company after the merger, investment bankers may be called in to effect a public distribution of the securities issued to raise the required cash.

- ***Acting as Broker or Dealer in Security Market:*** Being a member of the stock exchange as a broker or an agent, the investment banker deals in securities and helps the holders to liquidate their holdings. The company and individual customer contacts established by large investment banking houses afford considerable opportunity for brokerage business.
- ***Advisory and Technical Services:*** Investment bankers render investment advice to individual companies for the management of their security portfolio. In view of their constant contacts with securities and their markets, their expert investment analysis and trained staff, these institutions perform their functions effectively and efficiently.
- ***Security Substitution:*** The investment banker performs the function of security substitution in making available, as a substitute for outstanding securities, a different security

which caters to the needs of the investors in better ways. The securities of an investment trust is a clear-cut example of security substitution on a large-scale.

- ***Allied Services:*** Investment bankers render a number of services connected with securities, such as acting as paying agents or transfer agents for corporation's securities, acting as exchange or subscription agents, holding securities for the clients in safekeeping, undertaking periodic review of securities markets, and supplying information to their clients. Investment bankers provide many other services involved in the securities business.

◈ Mutual Funds: Nature and Functions

A mutual fund is an institutional device through which the investors pool their funds to invest in a diversified portfolio of securities, thus spreading and reducing risk. It is an investment vehicle through which small and large investors pool their funds under the direction of the investment manager. These funds are invested in a wide variety of securities in such a way as to minimise risk while ensuring steady return.

Thus, shareholders pool their money to create the mutual fund which, in turn, contracts with an investment management firm to manage the assets.

As a matter of fact, mutual fund is akin to making an investment trust which is concerned with garnering savings of the individuals and institutions and channelisation of these savings essentially in corporate securities in such a manner as to ensure to its investors a triple benefit of steady return and capital appreciation along with low risk. There are basically two types of investment trusts, *viz.*, open-end and closed-end. Open-end investment trust continuously offers new shares for sale and always stands ready to buy securities at any time. Thus, the capitalisation of the trusts is constantly changing as investors buy and sell their shares directly with the funds. Closed-end trust has a fixed number of shares that can be owned by the investing public. It is just like any other incorporated association with a fixed amount of capital. The investors cannot buy or redeem directly with the investment trust.

Mutual fund or investment trust is not an investment company as such. An investment company is constituted under the Companies Act and it has the same type of capital structure as an industrial or commercial company. In contrast, mutual fund is a trust at law. Further, mutual fund is obliged to buy back units whenever an investor desires to sell them, an investment company can not buy back its shares from its shareholders. Further, mutual funds cannot raise long-term debt from the market while an investment company can do so. In the case of mutual fund, there always exists direct relation between the value of the unit and the value of the fund (underlying assets.) This is not necessarily so in the case of an investment company. Finally, while mutual fund may offer both open-end and closed-end schemes for mobilisation of savings, investment companies are usually closed-end companies with fixed capitalisation.

Mutual fund refers only to open-end investment trust whose distinctive feature is regular sale and purchase of securities. Further, mutual funds must redeem their shares at the funds' current net asset value at the time the shareholders request redemption. In sum, mutual fund is a form of collective investment brought in by a large group of investors. Each fund is divided into equal portions or units. Anyone investing in the funds is allocated units in proportion to the size of one's investment. The price of these units is governed principally by value of the underlying investments held by the funds.

◈ Types of Mutual Funds

So as to cater to varying needs and preferences of large number of savers, many types of funds are offered to them. Choice of a saver of a fund would depend on what he desires his money earn for him and how much risk he is willing to assume. Thus, we have a variety of mutual funds, important among them are discussed below:

◈ Stock Funds

These funds invest primarily in common stocks. There is a broad range of common stock funds — from those that invest almost exclusively in high quality "blue chip" companies to those that invest solely in the new, unestablished companies.

There may be several sub-divisions of stock funds. Thus, Growth and Income Funds place relatively equal weight on capital growth and dividend income and accordingly invest in equity and preference stocks. Growth Funds invest their funds in common stocks primarily for capital growth purpose. They meet the investor's need for appreciation, high risk-bearing capacity and ability to defer liquidity. As such, the investments by growth oriented funds are predominantly made in equities. Income Funds aim at ensuring to their investors high current income; growth in the value of the portfolio is of small importance. Such funds employ their funds in high yielding common stock. There are two basic groups within the income funds; those that stress constant income at relatively low-risk and those that attempt to achieve the maximum income possible even with the use of leverage. Naturally, the higher anticipated return of any investment, the higher the potential risk of the investment.

◈ Bond Funds

Bond funds solely employ their funds in bonds so as to ensure regular and fixed income to their investors. In the USA, it is common to have two types of bond funds, one emphasising high-yielding but risky bonds and the other low-yielding but high grade bonds.

◈ Balanced Funds

Balanced funds combine bond and/or preferred stocks with the ownership of common stock, usually some pre-determined percentage relationship. Several balanced funds keep one-half of the portfolio in common stocks and one-half in bonds and preferred stocks. Balanced portfolios are more conservative than common stock funds, and they generally do not have significant price movement either up or down. The main purpose of balance funds is to achieve an adequate return in the form of interest and dividends from the fixed portion of the portfolio, while at the same time gaining a modest growth in the common-stock portion.

◈ Specialised Funds

There are a number of funds that directly invest in a specialized group of securities. Funds may specialise in securities of firms in certain industries or producers of specific products, or of specific income-producing securities. Investors interested in a particular group of securities might want to invest in a specialised mutual fund.

◈ Leverage Funds

Leverage mutual funds are common-stock funds whose main objective is to maximise capital appreciation. The special techniques these funds use make them speculative and risky. Leverage funds use borrowed funds to their utmost in order to increase the size of the value of the portfolio. Hopefully, the gain received will exceed the cost of the borrowed funds, and the balance of the gain will benefit the shareholders.

Some leverage funds use the short sales, which permits the management of the fund to take advantage of declining market in order to realize gains in the portfolio. The proper use of short sales reduces the loss of the portfolio in a declining market, but it also decreases the gain in a rising market if a proportionally large short position is maintained.

Some leverage funds use options, specially call options to give the purchaser the right to buy a security at a pre-determined price for a stipulated length of time, regardless of the fluctuation of the market price of the security on which the option is written. Because of the exceptionally high risk, call options are not used as often as borrowed funds and short sales are.

◈ Taxation Funds

Mutual funds designed to provide tax exemption benefits to the investors, whether in the domestic or foreign capital markets are called taxation funds. Tax saving Magnum of SBI Capital Markets Limited is an example of the domestic type and UTI's US & CO. Million India fund based in the US is an example of the latter type. Offshore mutual funds avail the tax exempt status in tax havens.

◈ Off-Shore Mutual Funds

Off-shore mutual funds refers to cross border flow of funds. Thus, they attract foreign capital for investment purpose in the country of the issuing company. Further, they open its domestic capital markets to the international investors and global portfolio investment. e.g., IITI's India fund (1986) and SBI's India Magnum (1989).

The chief objective of overseas mutual funds is to take advantage of pockets of international growth; by investing in foreign securities, the fund manager can augment his overall returns.

◈ Significance of Mutual Funds

Mutual funds are financial intermediaries concerned with mobilising savings of those who have surplus income and channelisation of these savings in those avenues where there is demand of funds. These institutions employ their resources in such a manner as to afford for their investors the combined benefits of low risk, steady return, high liquidity and capital appreciation through diversification and expert management.

Savers of moderate means in the underdeveloped regions are generally reluctant to invest in corporate securities because of their lack of adequate knowledge about complicated investment affairs. Moreover, their resources being small, they can at best hold securities of one or two or just a few industrial concerns only and as such, the fate of their savings and prospects of earnings therefrom are tied to the fate of such unit or units. Investment in securities of mutual funds takes care of both these problems, for such investment, in effect, represents a part of the funds' entire portfolio diversified in terms of securities, units, industries and geographic regions. The institutions employ expert investment analysts and thus professional knowledge and expertise go into the selection and supervision of their investment portfolio. Diversification and expert investment knowledge ensure steady and regular earnings to the funds and a share in the general prosperity. Accordingly, investors in the shares of mutual funds are assured of low risk, steady return, liquidity and capital appreciation. By taking upon themselves the problems which confront the small savers in investing their savings and dealing with them affectively, mutual funds help mobilise savings of the people and promote thrift.

Savings pooled by mutual funds are invested largely in industrial securities. They usually finance long-term business requirements largely by way of direct subscription to share capital of industrial enterprises. Mutual funds, while themselves raising resources from a large number of small savers, make funds available to industrial concerns in relatively bigger lots and thus reduce their burden and botheration involved in raising finance directly from individual savers.

Thus, by playing the role of financial intermediation mutual funds provide a convenient and effective link between saving and investment. Well managed mutual funds would be mutually beneficial arrangement. While, on the one hand, they help the investing community by offering a share of corporate growth; on the other, they have a salutary impact on the stock markets. By blending caution with aggression and analysis with intuition, the funds can successfully convert market opportunities into lucrative returns for the investors.

Role of the mutual fund is not limited to domestic sphere only. In addition to attracting domestic savings, these funds can offer their units abroad and attract foreign capital just as UTI, SBI, Canara Bank and some private sector mutual funds have recently done by offering Indian Fund and India Growth Fund schemes. Similarly, they may serve as useful institutions for securing profitable investment avenues abroad or domestic savings. Investment in foreign industrial securities requires fairly detailed knowledge of the state of the foreign economy in general and industries in particular as also of fiscal and monetary policies, state of the money and capital markets and of the financial position of industrial enterprises and their future prospects. As a result, despite attractive investment prospects abroad for surplus domestic savings, individual investors would find it an extremely difficult task to make foreign investments on their own. Mutual funds have, as in the case of domestic investment, stepped in to solve these problems for the savers.

◈ Insurance Companies

Insurance companies represent such financial institutions as are concerned with pooling savings of the people and investing them in productive outlets. They pool savings through premiums by providing life cover protection against fortuitous events. They are, in fact, contractual savings agencies which receive without fail a steady inflow of regular funds in the form of premiums or regular contributions to pension funds. The savings so pooled are essentially invested in government and semi-government securities, corporate securities and in socio-economic productive schemes. As custodians of the policyholders' savings, the responsibility of the insurance companies to the public is very heavy.

Broadly speaking, there are two categories of insurance companies, *viz.*, Life Insurance Companies and General Insurance Companies. Life Insurance Companies provide life insurance protection to the masses at a reasonable cost. They garner savings of policyholders by promising them and/or their beneficiaries a large sum either in later life or upon death and deploy their resources in long-term productive channels.

The major part of insurance business is life insurance, the operations of which depend on the laws of mortality. Life Insurance Companies play a vital role in pooling of the personal savings of millions of individuals. They are relatively better placed in doing so because they are the only institutions which besides creating huge savings, provide protection to the family against any misfortune. The contractual nature of life insurance helps these institutions in the mobilisation of savings because it binds the individual to stick to his decision and pays his premiums regardless of the fluctuations in his income. It is because of these reasons that life insurance companies have emerged as one of the prominent reservoir of long-term savings in different countries of the world.

General insurance companies are those financial intermediaries which pool savings by covering risks arising from fortuitous occurrences such as personal accident, fire, illness, damage to property, loss to crops, livestock, poultry, horticulture, etc.

The general insurance policies of the GIC are not similar to those of the LIC. They do not represent financial claims like the life insurance policies. The thrust of general insurance business is on pooling of risks arising from uncertain occurrences. Unlike life insurance policies, general insurance policies are for shorter period of time and policies have to be renewed every year on the same terms or on any other terms. Further, in the case of LIC, the claim is fixed, whereas in the case of GIC the claim is variable and it is ascertainable only after the occurrence of the event. Still another distinguishing operating feature of the GIC is that it holds assets in relatively liquid form, so as to take care of unpredictable claims of short-term in nature.

◈ Development Banks

Concept of Development Banking: The concept of development banking is relatively a new concept which was used for the first time in the post-Second World War period to refer to the institutional financial machinery built for fostering industrial growth in the country. In the post-Second World War period several newly liberated underdeveloped countries in Asia, Africa and Latin America became restless and wanted to solve their chronic problems of squalor and poverty. In their anxiety to hasten the pace of industrialisation, they established special financial institutions to supply the basic ingredients of development — capital, knowledge and entrepreneurship — for the rapid industrial growth of the country. Development banks are not only financial agencies which are engaged in providing medium and long-term assistance to business undertakings in the form of loans, underwriting and investment, but which act as catalytic agents in promoting balanced and viable development by assuming the promotional role of discovering project ideas, undertaking feasibility studies, providing technical, financial and managerial assistance for the implementation of projects and, on some occasions, for the establishment and management of industrial units. Providing financial assistance and rendering promotional services are the minimal functions of development banks, besides a number of other activities, such as the development of infrastructure and social utilities, which are also included among the functions of development banks.

A development bank is thus a hybrid institution which combines in itself the functions of a finance corporation and a development corporation. A finance corporation is an institution which is concerned primarily with long-term loan capital, while a development corporation is concerned primarily with equity capital and with fostering and managing specific companies as well as providing financial support.[8]

The development banks, which have been established in underdeveloped countries, are so diverse in their form, structure, objectives and methods of operation that there is no universal model which suits every developing country. Every country has tended to design a model which might best suit its peculiar social, political and economic conditions. But in spite of their wide diversity, there is a close similarity among them so far as the scope of their basic purpose and functions are concerned. They have all been established to supply the sinews of economic development so as to accelerate the pace of economic progress. A development bank is intended to provide the necessary capital, enterprise, managerial and technical know-how where these are clearly inadequate or non-available, and to assist in building up the financial and socio-economic infrastructure which will promote quick economic development. The emphasis on its various activities has shifted from one country to another, depending on its peculiar needs and circumstances. In some countries, for example, the focus has been on finance; in some others on promotion; in yet others on technical know-how; and elsewhere on economic planning itself.[9]

Although the development bank is a post-Second World War institutional device, it cannot be regarded as an untried innovation because prototype of these banks had already been in existence even before World War I. The origin of such prototype may be traced as far back as 1822, when the "Societe General de Belgique" was established in Belgium to finance commercial and industrial ventures. However, its activity did not arouse much interest. Contrary to this, the French Credit Mobiliser, established in 1852, caught the imagination of industrial financiers throughout the world. The principal object of this institution was to function as a financing institution which would mobilise resources through the issue of bonds and promissory notes to encourage investment in the securities of new undertakings. It became a model for similar investment banks in Germany, Austria, Belgium, the Netherlands, Italy, Switzerland and Spain. Throughout the 19th century, the Credit Mobiliser had an appeal for all those countries which were anxious to develop a suitable machinery for financing a rapid rate of industrial progress. Even a country like Japan founded the Industrial Bank of Japan in 1902 on the model of Credit Mobiliser for the purpose of financing her industrial development. Although the Japanese bank provided financial support to industrial development, it cannot be regarded as a development bank in the sense in which the word is used in underdeveloped countries. The Japanese Industrial Bank was not a specialist institution designed to provide finance and enterprise for industrial development, but a hybrid institution which combined in itself the functions of an issue house, a commercial bank and a mortgage institution. The Bank was authorised, by virtue of the power granted under its charter, to float and underwrite government and municipal bonds, to subscribe to and underwrite the shares and debentures of companies, to grant loans against the security of real estate and factory buildings and against the mortgage of ships and to engage in commercial banking business such as the discounting of bills and the receipt of deposits. In respect of industrial financing, the Bank was required to seek the approval of the Ministry of Finance. Unlike the development banks set-up in different underdeveloped countries to provide long-term loans for more than five years, the Bank in Japan was empowered to provide loans for not more than a period of five years. However, in the case of mortgage loans, the Bank could grant loans for 15 years; but these loans were given only to the shipping industry. In subsequent years, when the shipping industry was caught in a slump, the Industrial Bank offered mortgage loans to all the industries and thus became a long-term financier. Besides, it played a very significant role as an issue house and underwriter. After the financial panic of 1927, the Bank decided to lend support to small-scale industries. Both the Credit Mobiliser and the Industrial Bank of Japan were pioneering financial institutions which attracted the attention of different countries of the world. Since the emergence of these two institutions, development of financial and promotional devices was observed.

The first phase of institutional development was witnessed on the European continent in the period following the First World War. Every country in Europe saw the creation of specialised financial institutions to provide industrial finance for the reconstruction, modernisation and development of war-shattered industries. These institutions were exclusively mortgage banks, which were authorised to grant long-term loans to industrial undertakings on the first mortgages of the industrial real property, factories, buildings, machinery and plant. Among the most important mortgage banks were the Industrial Mortgage Bank of Finland Ltd., the National Hungarian Mortgage Institute Limited, the Provincial Mortgage Bank of Saxony and the National Economic Bank of Poland. These banks played an important role in the construction and development of the war-shattered economies of Europe by providing long-term loans to various categories of industries. Unfortunately, they were soon dragged into the throes of great depression.

The post-depression period witnessed the second phase of industrial development. During this period, the need for catering to the requirements of small-scale industries was recognised. Accordingly, specialised financial institutions were formed in several countries. Unlike the industrial mortgage banks of the nineteen-twenties, which were purely lending institutions, financial institutions created during the post-depression period showed a keen interest in carrying out the functions of capital underwriting and direct subscription, along with lending activities. The Industrial Credit Company of Ireland was an instance of such intermixture of functions, and it offered extended coverage as well. Another instance is furnished by the Netherlands in the share capital of industrial enterprises in addition to being authorised to grant term loans.

In the last phase of the industrial development observed in the years after World War II, a new institutional device was evolved. Contrary to the pure lending business of mortgage banks in the period following World War I, and the growing interest amongst some of the post-depression industrial credit companies in assuming the combined responsibility of underwriting and lending, financial institutions which emerged in the period after World War II showed a remarkable preference for underwriting and direct investment activity, besides mortgage lending business. Since 1944, several interesting developments took place in the machinery for financing post-war industry in Great Britain and other advanced countries. The Industrial Development Bank of Canada (1944), the Finance Corporation of Industry Ltd. (FCI), the Industrial and Commercial Finance Department of the Commonwealth Bank of Australia (1946) are important examples of institutions engaged in financing the establishment of industries in developed countries. Although the Canadian institution used the words ‘Development Bank’ for the first time, it hardly performed any promotional functions which characterise most of the development banks in underdeveloped countries today. It confined itself to financing activity only. In contrast with this, the Industrial Finance Department of the Commonwealth Bank of Australia was established to assist in the development of industrial undertakings in addition to providing institutional finance, although it was not expressly nomenclatured as a development bank. These institutions were closely similar, not only in their basic functions and their underlying objectives, but also in their methods of financing industrial enterprises. They offered not only term loans against the security of the fixed assets of industrial undertakings but also participated in the risk capital of companies.

None of the above institutions could be regarded as true development banks in the sense in which the term is understood in developing countries. They were not set-up to supply the sinews of development as the development bank does. As a matter of fact, they represented special institutional machineries designed to broaden the existing source of finance for the development of small and medium size industries during the period of transition from a war-time to a peace-time economy.

The above discussion leads us to the unmistakable conclusion that the financial institutions which emerged in developed countries bear the characteristics of term financial institutions and may be designated as finance corporations. In sharp contrast, institutional machinery has been devised in underdeveloped countries to undertake, besides lending funds, promotional activities to help develop new industrial undertakings in the country with a view to fostering accelerated economic growth in the country. They, therefore, resemble the concept of a development bank which is closely related to the upsurge on the part of an undeveloped country to accomplish a quick rate of all-round economic development and its search for an appropriate instrument through which such development can be promoted and financed.

- ***Functions of Development Banks:*** The principal objective of a development bank is to help alleviate endemic problems of poverty and unemployment and for that purpose, it acts as a catalyst for quickening industrial development in the country. In an underdeveloped county, where not only there is scarcity of capital but also dearth of entrepreneurial talent, the development bank does not restrict its activity to the conventional function of providing term capital to entrepreneurs, but goes far beyond it to assume a promotional role by undertaking potential industrial surveys and identifying growth projects, preparing feasibility reports, and providing technical, managerial and other assistance to interested entrepreneurs right from the stage of project formulation to the commissioning and operation of the project. In order to widen the entrepreneurial base, the development bank organises training programmes for potential entrepreneurs.

While performing these functions, development banks have to keep in view the socio-economic objectives of the country. In developing countries today, particularly in India, there is considerable emphasis on the redistribution of income and productive assets, on social justice, self-reliance, prevention of concentration of economic power, regional balanced growth, and on the promotion of a class of new technician entrepreneurs. Economic growth with an almost simultaneous and just distribution of its benefits is the primary objective. In an economy, where the resources are scarce, this requires not only the investment of all available investible resources but their qualitative composition and geographical distribution. Development banks have to act within this framework.

Development banks need to adapt their lending and investment strategy and activities to the national objectives. Their lending has to be far more purposeful. It is quite a complex task to work towards the simultaneous achievement of what may sometimes turn out to be conflicting objectives. Growth and equity, after a certain point, may not move in the same direction. A project to be established in a less developed region may be more expensive than in some other region. The incentives offered to the entrepreneurs for development of less developed region may lead to a further concentration of productive assets in the hands of the top few. These are complex issues which a development bank must face. It has to decide about the various trade-offs between the likely benefits and the costs involved, and must evolve a delicate blend of objectives.

The social objectives of the country need to be translated into action. Development banks have to define their objectives within the territory of their statute in such a manner as to serve these social objectives. Translated into a blue-print for action, the criteria for the allocation of assistance, they define priorities of assistance by the development banks. Today, the priority areas in the country are:

(*i*) Projects coming up in the backward regions;

(*ii*) Projects coming up in the small-scale sector;

(*iii*) Projects promoted by new and technician entrepreneurs;

(*iv*) Projects producing goods of mass consumption; and

(*v*) Projects in the nature of export promoting and import substituting industrial units.

(*vi*) Infrastructural projects

In addition to these long-term priorities, development banks have to work out short-term priorities by adapting their lending strategies to the changing circumstances so as not to create inflationary conditions, or not to create idle capacity in certain sectors where the demand is slack or where critical raw materials or utilities are not easily available, or not to create a situation of shortages or gluts of certain commodities at some future dates.

Development banks can help in optimising resources. Finance is the main instrument of the working of these banks. But the mere creation of finance without a corresponding creation of goods and services within a reasonable time would be inflationary.

A development bank cannot be merely a lending agency. It has to take into account certain factors so that it may command all the resources and exploit their strength for the maximum benefit of the nation. The manner in which finance is disbursed to projects very much determines the claims of assisted units of such resources as power, fuel and transport. By following an appropriate location policy while assisting projects, it can help determine the geographical dispersal of industries and facilitate a reduction in regional imbalances by the creation of incomes and employment in the relatively backward areas of the country. And depending on the kind of entrepreneurs it assists, it can also determine the emerging pattern of the ownership of the means of production.

But even with its best efforts, a development bank may find that viable projects in the socially desirable sectors are not forthcoming. As stated earlier, entrepreneurship is a very scarce factor in the country. And whatever new entrepreneurs may be located, they generally prefer to be at a safer place where economies of conglomeration are available, i.e., they prefer to operate in developed regions. Development banks are not supposed to wait for the socially most desired projects to come. Waiting has its own social cost, nor can they afford to fritter away their assistance to basically doubtful or socially less desirable projects. There is no guarantee that there will be an autonomous increase in the supply of locally desirable and beneficial projects. While the willingness to lend is there, there are no right kinds of projects or entrepreneurs. The supply of right projects or entrepreneurs has to be induced. This they can do by rendering promotional services to them.

The minimal functions of development banks are the provision of financial assistance and the performance of promotional activities. But the development banks which have emerged in the post-war years are authorised to provide financial facilities in various forms, such as granting loans to industrial enterprises, subscribing to the shares and debentures of companies, guaranteeing the loans raised by them from other sources, guaranteeing deferred payments for the import of plant and equipment, and underwriting the issue of industrial stocks, shares, bonds and debentures. As part of their promotional activity, development banks conduct techno-economic surveys with a view to identifying growth potentialities in different parts of the country and discovering project ideas, commissioning project reports and preparing feasibility studies in order to elicit entrepreneurial interest in project ideas. They also provide technical and managerial assistance to those willing to implement the projects.

Between these minimal functions of a development bank, there is a wide range of possible activities which it may undertake. For instance, it may assume responsibility for developing infrastructure and social utilities, for organising consultancy services to benefit entrepreneurs and training programmes for new entrepreneurs with a view to widening the entrepreneurial base.

- ***Types of Development Banks:*** The urge for economic development has triggered the emergence of variety of development bank. The variations in development banks are found across the globe in respect of the sectors of their operations, ownership, the type of assistance they render, their geographical coverage, the size of the units assisted and the size of the assistance. A brief account of different varieties of development banks is presented below:
- ***Sectors of Operations:*** On the basis of the sectors of their operations, development banks may be broadly categorised into two groups: *general development banks* and *specialised development banks*. General development banks are established to assist

projects of all the sectors, including agriculture, power, transport and manufacturing. They make no distinction between public sector and private sector projects. Specialised development banks, however, confine their operations to only one sector. Thus, there are separate development banks for assisting industrial projects and agricultural projects. Further, a number of development banks have been set-up only to promote and assist enterprises in the private sector. Development banks which assist only the public sector projects have also come into existence. Mixed development banks, which are authorised to help both the public sector and the private sector projects, have gained popularity in recent years. The scope of the operations of several development banks, which were initially set up to assist private sector projects, have of late, been broadened to cover the government projects as well. The scope of a development bank's business should not be unduly restricted. As it gains experience in one line of activity, it may extend its operations to other fields which will help in improving its profitability. The experience of both the Canadian and British institutions, which extended their business into the spheres of trade and services, bears testimony to this fact.

- ***Ownership:*** From the viewpoint of ownership, development banks may be classified into banks that are owned by the government, by the central bank or by the private sector or they may be owned jointly by the government, the central bank and private interests. A majority of the development banks belong to the first and second categories. It is obvious that few such institutions would be established by private entrepreneurs because they are diffident of entering in the field of experimental and risky ventures like those of development banks. Besides, the profit prospects of these institutions are bleak because they are supposed to finance and nurse enterprises, irrespective of profit consideration and in the interest of the community at large. But even if private capital is available, a privately owned development bank would need some sort of government support in the form of a guarantee of principal and/or interest on the bank's capital and bond issues, of interest-free loans or some kind of subsidy.

Privately owned banks have definite advantages over public sector banks in that they are free from the political pressures and interference by politicians which public banks are subject to. They have the opportunity to take investment decisions on purely economic considerations. The government development banks also have certain advantages over their counterparts in the private sector. Unlike private banks, public sector banks need not worry every time about declaring a dividend. They can extend their area of operations to assist large, medium and small industries, can venture into new and pioneering fields, and can undertake growth potential surveys if the situation warrants. Privately-owned bank cannot engage in these activities in view of their limited financial resources.

In sum, there is nothing sacrosanct about private development bank. Private sector banks are not necessarily efficient any more than public banks and are necessarily susceptible to political pressures and bureaucratic influence. Much would depend upon the degree of autonomy given to a bank in its day-to-day working and upon the persons at the helm of its affairs.

- ***Types of Financial Assistance:*** On the basis of forms of financial assistance, development banks fall into three categories:
  - (*i*) Development banks confined to lending activity;
  - (*ii*) Development banks confined to loans and guarantees and underwriting activity; and
  - (*iii*) Development bank providing assistance in all forms, including managerial and technical services.

There is a general tendency in favour of the mixed type of development banks which are authorised to provide both loan and risk capital to industrial concerns. Recently, some of the development banks have assumed a promotional role and render managerial and technical services to needy entrepreneurs.

◈ Geographical Coverage

Development banks may be international, national or provincial, depending on the geographical areas of their operations. An *international bank* is one which is authorised by its charter to satisfy the financial and promotional needs of business enterprises of the different countries of the world. The International Bank for Reconstruction and Development, which was established in 1946 to assist in the reconstruction and development of the territories of members, epitomises the best and most essential features of an international development bank. International banks do not confine their activities within a nation but extend them beyond the frontiers of their own countries, and provide assistance for expansion and development of individual industrial enterprises in them.

E. UNIVERSAL BANKING

◈ Concept

The term Universal bank in general refers to a financial institution offering commercial as well as investment banking services. Thus, universal banking not only includes services related to savings and loans but also investments. In practice, the term Universal banks comprise those institutions which offer a wide range of financial services, beyond commercial banking and investment banking and various other activities including insurance. As such, Universal bank is a financial super market supplying multifarious products under one roof. It is one stop-shopping for a customer who is willing to deal in several financial products. However, Universal banking does not mean that every institution conducts every kind of business with every type of customer. In fact, universal banking is an option, a pronounced business emphasis in terms of products, customer groups and regional activity which can be observed in most cases.

Generally, the concept of universal bank is based on two financial models. One is German type in which the big German banks carry comprehensive banking activities including banking operations as well as other services and insurance. The other model of universal banking is British-American type in which specialised banks in accordance with change of financial environment, pursue diversification in securities and investment.

◈ Forms of Universal Banking

Universal banking existing in different countries of the world has taken various forms, *viz.*, in-house fully integrated universal banking, universal banking subsidiary structure and holding company structure, depending on varying regulatory regions, and with varying degree of specialisation or universalisation of financial services by the participants concerned.

◈ In-House Fully Integrated Universal Banking

This is the purest form of universal banking in which a single institution offers a complete range of banking and other products to satisfy the need of the customers. In this type of universal banking, various activities like commercial banking, investment banking, insurance, leasing, etc., are undertaken by the different departments of the organisation.

◈ Universal Banking Subsidiary Structure

In this form of universal banking, there exists a net work of principal institution and subsidiaries. While principal institution undertakes both banking and investment activities, for other activities subsidiaries have to be set up. This type of structure exists in Germany. Under the German banking statutes all activities could be carried out within the structure of the parent bank except insurance, mortgage banking and mutual funds, which require legally separate subsidiaries. In the U.K., broad range of financial activities are allowed to be conducted through separate subsidiaries of the bank.

◈ Holding Company Structure

In this structure, one financial holding company owns both banking and non-banking subsidiaries which are legally separate and individually capitalised in so far as financial services other than banking are allowed by law. This model exists in the U.S.

◈ Utility of Universal Banking

Universal banking concept is becoming popular all over the world in view of several in-built advantages in the system. One such advantage, as put forth by the advocates, is greater economic efficiency in the form of lower cost, higher output and better products. This is for the fact that a financial institution having freedom to choose the size and product mix of its operations configurates its activities in such a way as to optimalise the use of its resources. An universal bank derives the advantage of economies of scale because costs involved in offering products at a time by one institution are always lower than those incurred on various activities individually by different units. A large size and range of operations provide greater scope for better utilisation of resources. It is also advocated that universal banking helps in avoiding the wasteful duplication of marketing, research and development and information gathering efforts. Further, large scale operations enable the institution to make use of modern information technologies which will go a long way in improving its effectiveness and competitiveness.

In highly competitive scenario with finicky customers ruling the market and fast changing demands, the advocates contend that it may be difficult for a specialised institution to change its operations to suit the needs without incurring substantial risks of future. On the contrary, universal banking equipped to undertake varieties of business can easily cope with the situations by shifting the resources within the organisation without substantial costs.

Finally, it has been argued that universal banking helps the organisation to develop and maintain customer relations on an ongoing basis by offering need based financial products through a single window. Customers prefer to do business with an universal bank because he gets services at one place and is saved from the botheration of running after specialised institutions for his varied demands.

However, it is argued that customers' interests are not well protected by universal banks because combining commercial and investment banking gives rise to conflict of interest. The universal banks may not objectively advise their clients on optimal means of financing. Conflicts of interests, according to Saunders (1985), arise from the following:

(*a*) Conflict between the investment banker's promotional role and the commercial banker's obligation to provide disinterested advice;

(*b*) Using the bank's securities department or affiliate to issue securities to repay unprofitable loans;

(*c*) Placing unsold securities in the bank's trust accounts;

(*d*) Marketing bank loans to support the price of a security which is underwritten by the bank or its securities affiliate;

(*e*) Making imprudent loans to issuers that the bank or its securities affiliate underwrites;

(*f*) Direct lending by a bank to its securities affiliate; and

(*g*) Informational advantages regarding competitors.

Another criticism of universal banking is that failure of a large financial institution will have serious ramifications for the entire economic system of the country. It is also argued that universal banks are particularly vulnerable because of assumption of business of underwriting and distributing securities.

Another argument given against universal banking is that such institution by virtue of its size of operation would become monolithic undesirable leading to adverse economic consequences.

Further, universal banks, argued by critics, tend to be bureaucratic and inflexible in course of their operations and as such may work primarily with large established customers at the expense of smaller and newly set up organisations.

It may, however, be observed that the empirical evidence available on economies of scale and flexibility is not categorical.[10]

Further, universal banks in Germany were not found exerting excessive influence to the detriment of interest of the economy.[11]

◆ Universal Banking — A Global View

In view of globalization and economic liberalization, financial deregulation and digitalization all over the world leading to increased competitiveness in every sector of the economy including financial sector, financial institutions in their bid to retain their existing market share, ensure growth in future, arrest deteriorating performance, and to capitalize on emerging opportunities have, of late, been emphasizing on attracting new customers and retaining the existing ones by offering wide array of customized products and services at economical rate and in convenient manner under one roof and hence euphoria of universal banking system across the globe since the beginning of the 20th century. Although the universal banking system had been in existence in the USA in the beginning of the 20th century but due to serious conflict of interests of commercial and investment banking the USA passed the Banking Act, 1933 prohibiting banks from combining investment and commercial banking activities. The legal provisions of the Banking Act, 1933 (Glass-Steagall Act) established a distinct separation between commercial banking and investment banking, and made it almost impossible for the same organization to combine these activities.

Banks in the USA began adopting the system in the late 1990s, led by financial giant citigroup. US banks are permitted to deal in government securities and stock-brokerage activities. But corporate securities underwriting and dealing activities must be conducted through specially authorized affiliates, which must limit such activities to 10 per cent of gross revenues. U.S. banks are, however, not allowed to do insurance business. The resistance to softening the separation of banking activities, as enshrined in the Glass-Steagall Act, continues to exist.

Universal banking is a long tradition in Europe. The principal financial institutions in these countries typically are universal banks offering the entire range of banking services. Continental European banks are engaged in deposit taking, real estate and other forms of lending, foreign exchange, trading as well as underwriting. Universal banking in Germany, France and Switzerland has helped in maintenance of the safety of financial system and protection of the Central bank against the excessive demands as the lender of last resort. This is for the fact that in these countries universal banking evolved gradually over a long period of time, giving time for appropriate institutions, practices, experience and conventions to be developed and a body of formal as well as non-formal guidelines for regulatory purposes to be established.

A mélange of environmental forces and unique historical events enabled banks in different European countries to establish themselves in particular segments of the corporate financial market.

In countries like Germany, Australia, Austria, Denmark, Finland, France, Hong Kong, Poland and Sweden, banks can undertake in-house commercial banking and investment banking business. But Brazil, Canada, Japan, Korea, Mexico, Netherland, New Zealand, Norway, Thailand and U.K. have adopted conglomerate route and set up subsidiaries to take up diversified banking activities. Banks in these countries, except Japan and Korea, can also engage in insurance business through their subsidiaries.

In the Anglo-Saxon countries and in Japan, commercial and investment banking tend to be separated. In recent years, though most of these countries have lowered the barriers between commercial and investment banking, they have refrained from adopting the Continental European System of Universal banking.

While deposit-taking and loan-making remain the primary business functions of Chinese banks, ambitious commercial lenders are now encroaching upon the non-banking financial business territories of trust companies and equity funds. It is expected that Universal banking, in the next few years, will become the new hallmark of Chinese financial market. As the China

Banking Regulatory Commission prepares to issue, in the near future, regulations allowing the country's commercial lenders to command trust and investment companies, the China Securities Regulatory commission is calling for regulation to allow banks to access the fund-management business. Once China's commercial banks receive decision-makers' approval to establish trust companies as their subsidiaries, the era of universal banking will begin in the country.[12]

Swiss banking system is based on the concept of universal banking wherein all banks can provide all banking services such as credit/lending business, asset management and investment financial analysis. However, several bank groups are now fully or partially specialized. For instance, UBs AG is the world's leader in wealth management and also Switzerland for individual and corporate client. It is also an important global player in investment banking and the securities business. Another leading bank of Switzerland, the Credit Suisse Group, is a globally active financial services provider. Besides offering comprehensive financial advise to private clients, it offers solutions through the Winterthur insurance company to pension and insurance questions and as a financial intermediary it also serves global companies and institutions as well as public corporations.[13]

◈ Emergence of Universal Banking System in India

Universal banking system in India is of recent origin especially after adoption of new economic policy of liberalization, privatization and globalization in 1991 and the consequent financial reforms. Until the economic reforms, commercial banks following British banking system remained confined to accepting public deposits and making short-term loans to meet working capital requirements of industry, trade and agriculture. These banks (which have been government-owned) were hitherto operating in protected economy which provided comforts to them in areas of liquidity management. While in an administered interest regime, discretion of management was limited and consequently, the risk parameters in these spheres were hazy and not quantifiable. Further, with tremendous growth of banks during the post-nationalization period came inefficiency and loss of control over widely spread branches resulting in rise in costs, poor quality of assets, and decline in profitability, operational irregularities, and monitoring arrears in reconciliation were order of the day. The competitive efficiency of banks was at a low ebb. Customer service became the least available commodity, and the customers were most dissatisfied with the services of the banks. The financial strengths and operational efficiency of the Indian banks were not measuring up to international standards. The global and domestic developments called for corrections primarily with a view to strengthening the banking system, improving operating performance, and bringing it on par with international financial system.

Like commercial banks, Indian financial institutions comprising Development Financial Institutions (DFIs) and refinancing institution, which came into existence to meet specific sectoral needs and to provide long-term resources at concessional terms confined themselves to the role of channeling agency. Thus, the DFIs hitherto have been only for long-term both on the assets and liabilities sides while commercial banks catered to 'short-term' business. There was a marked demarcation, though not a 'Chinese wall' between these two. Closing the gap to improve the performance of both the categories of financial institutions and provide satisfactory customer services came to receive greater attention of policy makers and Reserve Bank of India. The concept of universal banking was considered an effective mechanism to fill this gap. Persistently rising NPAs, declining profitability and dearth of avenues for the financial institutions in the wake of falling market sentiments in the recent past have accelerated the process. For a few of the financial institutions, survival itself was in danger.

Under the circumstances, the basic issue plaguing the Government, Reserve Bank of India, management of banks and DFIs was how to rationalize and harmonize the relative roles of these institutions in future. This, in itself, required perspicacious probe into: *(i)* How to solve the problems faced by DFIs in raising long-term resources at reasonable cost in lieu of concessional resources that were available until recently? *(ii)* Can improved access to short-term resources through the traditional banking route help the DFIs? *(iii)* Do the problems faced by the DFIs now or in the immediate future require their conversion into universal bank? *(iv)* In case of conversion of DFIs into universal banks, how can they fulfill prudential requirements as also entry conditions applicable to the banks? *(v)* What would be the transition path and period? *(vi)* What would be appropriate regulatory regime for universal banking? *(vii)* What would be the mix of services which DFIs and commercial banks, when converted into universal banks, would be providing to customers? *(viii)* How far are the DFIs and commercial banks capable enough to undertake universal banking on a competitive basis?

In its frenetic bid to evolve an effective, resilient, vibrant and customer friendly financial system and for that purpose to explore the possibility of establishing universal banks by converting the existing DFIs and commercial banks, Reserve Bank of India constituted on December 8, 1997 a Working Group under the Chairmanship of Shri S.H. Khan to look into the above issues. Earlier, Narsimham Committee looked into these issues. The important highlights of these committees are brought out below:

◈ Narasimham Committee Recommendations on Universal Banking

The Narsimham Committee while taking note of the strong phenomena of consolidation and convergence which the financial system is now experiencing globally and even in those countries where there are legal or regulatory impediments to provide on combination of commercial, investment and other banking service, relaxation of restriction is being contemplated at present and there has been blurring of the boundaries among suppliers of various financial products and services, and in India too, banks and DFIs are moving closer to each other in the scope of their activities, and banks are already providing a range of financial services such as investments, merchant banking, leasing and hire purchase and project finance and DFIs are undertaking bank like activities, such as short-term non-project lending and retail deposit taking, recommended that DFIs should, over a period of time, convert themselves into banks. The Committee further suggested that there should be only two forms of intermediaries, *viz*., banking companies and non-banking finance companies.

The Committee also observed that mergers between banks and DFIs need to be based on synergies and location and business specific complementarities of the converged institutions must be made on commercial footing.

◈ Khan Working Group (KWG) Recommendations on Universal Banking

The Khan Working Group (KWG) was constituted to review the role, structure and operations of Development Financial Institutions (DFIs) and commercial banks in emerging operating environment and suggest changes to examine whether DFIs could be given increased access to short-term funds and the regulatory framework needed for the purpose and to suggest measures for strengthening of organisation, human resources, risk management practices and other related issues in DFIs and commercial banks in the wake of Capital Account Convertibility.

The KWG Committee noted that over the years a wide variety of financial institutions have come into existence and they perform the developmental role in their respective areas, in addition to catering to the financial needs of different sectors. However, there are some significant differences among them. While most of them extend direct finance, IDBI extends direct as well as indirect finance. It also extends finance by discounting and rediscounting of bills/promissory notes and refinances term loans given by SFCs and commercial banks. IDBI also exercises supervisory role over SFCs. IDBI, NABARD and NHB are mainly refinancing institutions. Even in case of three major financial institutions in the industrial sector, *i.e.*, IDBI, ICICI and IFCI, there is a difference in the ownership pattern and the organisation structure of these institutions. The operating environment for DFIs, especially with regard to long-term operation funds and government guaranteed bonds have undergone remarkable changes. Similarly, the Committee noted that there have been changes in the regulatory environment for DFIs-IDBI, IFCI and ICICI, etc., inasmuch as these institutions have been brought under the regulatory framework of the RBI.

The KWG also noted that while deregulation and securitization have effaced traditional distinctions between commercial and investment banks in other countries, commercial banks in India have developed subsidiaries engaged in regular security issues and trading. Competition in banking field has enhanced following the entry of private sector banks as also of foreign banks. Banking environment in the country has, of late, led to reduction in statutory preemptions and greater freedom to banks to decide on most of their operations.

The KWG also noted that diversification of business by banks into investment banking and beyond has been occurring during the last decade of the 20th century and subsidiaries have been set up to undertake various activities, such as investment banking, factoring, primary dealership, broker's business, mutual funds, credit card business, housing finance, securities exchange, securities trading and custodial services, merchant banking, leasing, hire purchase, development of Software and computer related activities and trusteeship.

Keeping in view the above, the KWG made the following recommendations:

(*i*) The approach to universal banking should be guided by international experience and domestic requirements.

(*ii*) In terms of institutional structure of the capital market, there should be only two categories of financial institutions, *viz*., Banks and Non-banking financial intermediaries (NBFCs).

(*iii*) In the long run DFIs will have to be converted into universal banks or NBFCs, depending upon the choice of each DFI. The universal banks will be allowed to give various type of services to their customers and at the same time could raise funds directly from the public. However as NBFCs, they would be asked to address the needs of a particular segment of the market.

(*iv*) In view of the fact that in the present institutional infrastructure DFIs continue to have a special niche carved out for them until the long-term debt market improved in terms of liquidity and depth; small and medium-sized firms continue to depend on DFIs for long-term financing; DFIs have project appraisal capabilities which other intermediaries are yet to develop and the financial sector along with all financial markets have to render adequate competitive services among all financial intermediaries; DFIs should be allowed to continue to play the existing role in the medium term.

(*v*) The DFIs should have the freedom to remain DFIs, specializing in their own activities. However, if a DFI chooses to become a bank, venturing into commercial banking activities, that option should also be available. In that case, the 'Converted' DFI, should be prepared to fully conform to all prudential, regulatory and supervisory norms which are applicable to banks.

(*vi*) The question of transformation of DFI into a bank should ideally be considered after a period, say of five years from now, in view of the factors stated above. When a DFI chooses to transform itself into a bank, the transitionary arrangements on a time-bound basis, could be worked out, after a detailed examination by the RBI, on a case by case basis. This case by case approach is essential because each DFI would be in a unique position in terms of its capacity to transform into a bank, necessitating a transition path which needs to be worked out.

There is, however, no particular advantage in stipulating a time limit, even after 5 years, on DFIs to exercise an option to become a bank in as much as it would always continue as a NBFC, subject to all the regulatory requirements of NBFCs. Thus, depending on the evolving situation, a DFI could choose to provide specialized services as an NBFC or continue to adopt the conglomerate route with a banking subsidiary or transform itself into a bank.

(*vii*) If a DFI chooses to provide banking services by itself through a wholly owned subsidiary route, permission to set up a fully owned subsidiary could also be considered by the RBI. However, whenever there is a bank, as a subsidiary of a DFI in a conglomerate with a DFI, adoption of a consolidated approach for regulation and supervision of such institutions is essential in view of the special status of banks in the financial sector.

(*viii*) If a DFI does not acquire a banking licence within a stipulated period, it would be categorized as a NBFC.

(*ix*) Management and shareholders of banks and DFIs should be permitted to explore and enter into gainful mergers. These mergers should be possible not only between banks but also between banks and DFIs. These mergers need to be based on synergies so as to make a case where the whole is greater than the sum of its parts and have a force multiplier effect.

(*x*) Due to the overlap of regulations, the KWG has suggested that super regulations be established to supervise and coordinate the activities of the multiple regulations in order to ensure uniformity in regulatory treatment.

◈ Present status of Universal Banking in India

Following the recommendations of the Narsimham Committee as also the KWG, Commercial banks were permitted to undertake new activities like consumer credit, credit cards, merchant banking, leasing, mutual funds, etc. A number of banks set up subsidiaries for merchant banking, leasing and mutual funds. The banks have also commenced factoring and securitization. Recently, the banks have been permitted to enter into long-term project financing and to engage in insurance business. Thus, public sector banks assumed the character of universal banks during the post reform period. SBI and its subsidiary SBI life has strategic allowance for selling their products. SBI has got its own mutual funds. Nationalized banks like Punjab National Bank, Allahabad Bank, Union Bank of India, Oriental Bank of Commerce and Bank of Baroda, have, of late, engaged into merchant banking and investment banking business.

Among the new private sector banks, ICICI bank, Kotak Mahindra Bank, HDFC Bank Ltd., and Development Credit Bank Ltd., are reported to be very aggressive in marching towards universal banking. These banks have forged strategic alliances with several foreign insurance companies for selling the insurance products both in life and general branches.

Realizing the benefits of Universal banking way back in 1996, the ICICI decided to transform itself from a term lending institution into a virtual universal bank to provide corporate and retail financial services through its various divisions and group companies. These include term lending activities, life and general insurance personal, finance, mortgages, investment banking international banking and private equity. During the last decade, the ICICI plunged into consumer banking, making an early call on the acceptance of technology-based services by Indian consumer. Retail credit has been the primary growth driver over the last few years. The Corporation foresees continuing growth momentum driven by under penetration and rising household incomes. Thus, ICICI Bank has become a global player in universal banking activities with robust presence in Indian and foreign markets.

HDFC Bank Ltd., is another private sector universal bank, having extended its business to insurance and investment services. This Bank is also a global player in financial market as an universal bank.

The Government facilitated DFIs to diversify their activities through legislative amendments. ICICI and IDBI were enabled to convert themselves into universal banks through merger route. A move is on to merge IFCI with a new entity so as to create a mega bank.

F. VIRTUAL BANKING

In view of fast technological development and highly competitive landscape with exclusive focus on customers, virtual banking is emerging as powerful method of rendering services to customers who are increasingly moving away from the confines of traditional branch banking and care, seeking the convenience of remote electronic banking services.

Broadly speaking, virtual banking denotes the provision of banking and related services through extensive use of information technology without direct recourse to the bank by the customer.[14] The salient features of virtual banking are the overwhelming reliance on information technology and absence of physical bank branches to deliver services to the customers. The origin of virtual banking in the developed countries can be traced back to the seventies with the installation of Automated Teller Machines (ATMs). Subsequently, driven by the competitive environment as well as various technological and customer pressures, other types of virtual banking services have grown in prominence all over the world.

Services rendered by a virtual bank comprise Automated Teller Machines (ATMs), shared ATM network, Electronic Funds Transfer at Point of Sale (EFTPOS), Smart Cards, Stored-value Cards, phone-banking and more recently, internet and intranet banking.

Virtual banking in different parts of the globe has passed through three distinct phases — inception phase, growth phase and maturity phase.

In the inception phase, technological application is in its infancy and a substantial amount of investment is required so as to make the application widely available commercially. In the growth phase, technology behind the application is widely available and customers are provided its services. In the maturity phase, application of technology is in wider use and institutions not offering such applications are outsmarted by their rivals making use of the technology in their operations.

Virtual banking is gaining popularity all over the world because of its manifold advantages. In the first instance, cost of handling a transaction via the virtual resource is less than that incurred via branch. Secondly, virtual banking responds to customers' needs much more speedily than branch banking. Thirdly, the outcome of the above two is reflected in relatively higher profits and access to a larger number of potential customers' for the bank without the concomitant costs of physically opening branches. Virtual banking is more cost effective than branch banking because of lower cost of operating branch network alongwith the reduced staff costs. Another advantage of virtual banking lies in improved quality and an enlarged range of services being made available to large number of customers to their satisfaction.

However, cost involved in acquiring and installing technological appliances is substantially high. It would, therefore, be advisable for the bank to examine viability and feasibility of the technology and its associated applications. In fact, it is utility of the technology for the customers and not its inherent sophistication that needs to be assessed before going ahead with such technological interventions.

Virtual banking has made start in the Indian banking system in recent few years. ATMs have been installed by almost all the major banks in major metropolitan cities. Electronic Funds Transfer (EFT) mechanism has also been initiated by major commercial banks. The Shared Payment Network System (SPNS) has been installed by banks in Mumbai. The operationalisation of the Very Small Aperture Terminal (VSAT) is expected to provide a significant thrust to the development of Indian Financial Network (INFINET) which will further facilitate connectivity within the financial sector.

Despite the rudimentary stage of internet banking in India, in order to promote safety and soundness for e-banking activities as a precautionary measure, the RBI constituted working group on internet Banking and recommended technology, security, legal and operational standards keeping in view international best practices.

The Committee classified the internet banking products into 3 types based on the levels of access granted, *viz.*, Information only systems, Electronic Information Transfer System and fully Electronic Transaction System. Its recommendations covered the risks associated with internet banking, the technology and security standards for internet banking, legal issues relating to this new type of activity and the regulatory and supervisory concerns of the central bank. Based on its recommendations the RBI issued guidelines to banks for implementation in phased manner.[15]

G. VENTURE CAPITAL

An emerging institutional source of long-term business financing playing a crucial role in recent years in corporate development is venture capital.

Venture capital, as defined by ICRA Information Services, signifies financing provided by venture capitalists who invest alongside innovative entrepreneurs in relatively new, high-growth companies.

These could have a reasonable, though not assured, potential to develop into highly profitable ventures, exhibiting high risk (of failure) and high return (in terms of large appreciation in capital invested) characteristics.

Venture capitalists supply risk capital in the form of equity capital for the formation and setting up of firms particularly to those specializing in new ideas or new technologies. They also provide input of skills needed to set the firm up, design its marketing strategy organize and manage. Thus, venture capital financing is usually early and expansion stage financing and venture capitalists are equity partners who work in the same spirit of an entrepreneur. They help start ups to develop into significant economic contributors by actively participating in it. They work in development of new products and services, provide, networking, management and marketing support. In short, venture capitalists have a long-term orientation.

The unique blend of risk financing and handholding of entrepreneurs by venture capitalists creates an environment suitable for knowledge and technology-based enterprises. The experience of US, Taiwan and Israel show that venture capital markets and technological innovation go hand in hand. In the U.S.A, venture firms have played a unique role in the formation and commercialization of entirely new industries: personal computers, cellular, communications, micro computer software, biotechnology and over night delivery. Industries such as consumer products, retailing, construction, transportation, industrial, financial services and forestry have also flourished. Thanks to venture capitalists.

Venture capitalists could be generalists investing in various industry sectors, different stages of venture life cycle or geographical areas. Or, they could be specialists focusing only on a particular industry sector or geographical area. Venture capitalists sometimes specialize in providing equity funding for firms in different stages, *viz.*, early-stage need financing or start up financing, development stage financing to support initial production, expansion-stage or second stage financing to provide working capital or for expansion of capacity, bridge or mezzanine financing to fund companies that expect to go public or raise term debt in the near future. Venture capital industry in its present form started in the USA in 1946, the year of formation in Bostons of the American Research and Development Corporation. The legislation used spur venture capital was small business investment companies with tax advantage and government loan money. By 1962 there were 585 such companies with 205 million in capital between them. However, these companies ran into problems due to lack of understanding of venture capital principles on the part of the management and their inexperience. In appropriate, government legislation also contributed to the failures.

Learning from the experience of the 60's, new venture capital companies were formed. These were the years when venture capitalists became more involved in development financing both for their portfolios and for new investments. In 1988 there were 587 active venture capital firms in the USA, of which 200 formed the core of the industry. There were $24.1% billion funds under the management. The buoyancy in American venture capital activity was due to abundant technological opportunities for creation and commercialization of new goods and services, freedom of foreign investment in the USA, large potential gains associated with equity, management participation in technology ventures and tax relief.

In the UK, venture capital activity flourished in the years since 1980. In 1987 Britain had 140 such companies with total investments of £ 800 million. The major factors contributing to the phenomenal growth of venture capital in the UK were strengthening of the enterprise culture i.e., public acceptability of being in business of taking risks for one self, of starting a business, of trying to make a profit and development of the securities market.

In some countries, venture capital firms came into existence with the support of international finance corporation (IFC) since 1978. For example, IFC played crucial role in setting up SOFINNOYA in Spain, VIBES I Philippines, Brasilpai in Brazil, IPS in Kenya, KDIC in Korea and SEAVI in South East Africa.

In recent years, few venture capital firms came up in Korea, Taiwan and Malaysia on the initiative of some private sector institutions. In Korea, for instance, number of venture capital firms have been established with the help of Korea Technology Advancement Corporation (KTAC).

H. VULTURE FUNDS

Vulture funds, as an institutional agency, are coming into existence in different countries of the world to help companies in overcoming their financial crisis. These funds are financial funds that look for pickings among dying or dead companies. They represent funds that buy securities in distressed investments such as high yield bonds in or near default, or equities that are in or near bankruptcy. Even highly leveraged firms may be targeted if there is a chance that the owners will not be able to make all required debt payments. These funds are like circling vultures patiently waiting to pick over the remains of a rapidly weakening company. The goal of vulture funds is high returns at bargain prices. Some people look down upon hedge funds that operate like vulture funds, which have preyed on the cheap debt of struggling companies and forced these companies to pay it back, plus interest.[16]

Vulture funds have the financial wherewithall and the risk capacity to purchase deeply discounted debt of troubled companies in the expectation of increasing its value. The fundamental principle underlying the operation of a vulture fund is picking up assets at dirt cheap valuation and then disposing them off at a tidy profit.

These are companies which are typically viable businesses, but burdened by huge debts. They are badly structured but shareholders' value can be created once they are restructured. Vulture funds provide best opportunities to such companies.

Another area where vulture funds can be significantly useful to organizations is of consolidation, where in existing promoters may be willing to sell their equity rather than face the embarrassment of receiving bank notices threatening the takeover of the company's assets.

Still another area of opportunity for vulture funds lies in picking up of assets like real estate and machinery of defaulting companies and then starting new ventures around these assets. This would require the fund to have special skill sets.

Vulture funds are specialized in buying distressed debt. In the U.S.A. and Japan vulture funds are doing good business. These funds have played a big role in South East Asia following the region's economic melt-down.

There are two types of vulture funds; one seeks to acquire a controlling interest in the company through ownership of either equity or debt when the equity has no value or voting power. The second type of vulture funds acquires the debt with the expectation that its value is higher than the purchase price or that its value can be enhanced by a skilled owner. The US capital market has both the types of funds. But European countries have none.[17]

A vulture fund, as the name indicates, buys over the asset of such companies and sells them for a profit or also funds take over of the another entity. The business functions on the principles of picking up assets of dirt cheap valuations and the disposing them off at tidy profits.

The enactment of the Securitization Act in 2002 has offered tremendous opportunities to vulture funds in India. Not only they get the opportunity of buying over the assets of sick companies and selling them for huge profits but an opportunity of restructuring sick companies whose businesses are typically viable but burdened by huge debts and badly managed and where shareholders' value can be created once they are restructured. Another opportunity for vulture funds is in the area of consolidation, wherein existing promoters may be willing to sell their equity rather than notices threatening the takeover of the company's assets. The fourth area of opportunity lies in picking up assets like real estate and machinery of defaulting companies and then starting new ventures around these assets, this would require the fund to have specific skill sets.

To encash the above opportunities, vulture funds have, of late emerged in Indian financial markets.

A host of foreign commercial banks such as Deutsche Bank, Bank of America, and Barclay Bank are exploring business opportunity in acquiring non-performing assets in India. Sun F and C which has been highly successful in post liberalization Russian market, is also planning to set up a vulture fund.

Foreign commercial banks are looking at investing in stressed assets in India. They are interested more in buying single exposures rather than acquiring a portfolio of bank loans. A lot of funds in Germany are also considering investing in bad loans in India. Foreign banks are also keen on setting up assets reconstruction companies in India, which is seen having a $ 25-30 million market of bad loans.[18]

ICICI ventures has also decided to embrace this market while others like New Bridge and CDC also seem to be interested in this opportunity. The burgeoning size of non-performing assets of the Indian financial sector (estimated to be ₹ 1,00,000 crore) is a big lure for vulture funds.

I. MUTUAL BANKING

In recent years, mutual banking is emerging across the globe as a powerful financial instrument to offer customers mutual funds products through banks.

Under the new concept of mutual banking, formal tie up is made between banks and mutual funds (MFs) to make use of each others' services to tap savings of the retail investors through innovative product and service offering. Banker having mass base can act as effective distribution channel of MFs' products and significantly generate their fee-based income. The synergetic advantages in mutual banking device are beneficial to both banks and MFs because of the mass appeal of mutual banking products. Customers get opportunity to avail of non-banking financial products with multiple return matrix from their banking services providers without the hassle of shopping in the market. They can get counseling support from the bank and the MF personnel.

However, success of mutual banking depends essentially on choice of customer oriented products offering attractive return with minimum risk over a period of time, selection of competent marketing staff with the right kind of aptitude and attitude and their training as also increasing awareness among potential investors by educating them about the mutual banking and its nuances in proper perspective.

J. MICRO FINANCE INSTITUTIONS[45]

Micro Finance Institutions (MFIs) have now come to be recognized across the globe as the basic institutional agency to help the poor and neglected sectors, especially women to improve their economic and social status. MFIs represent that segment of financial system which are exclusively concerned with rendering financial and non-financial services to the most poor and unprivileged swatches of the society who are otherwise unreached by mainstream financial institutions.

MFIs' are unique financial institutions because of their organizational and operating features distinct from other financial institutions, as can be noted below:

- The mission of the MFIs is to outreach credit and other services for the most poor and hapless sections of the society. MFIs are concerned with providing small amount of finance to the most neglected for productive purpose so as to improve their economic conditions of local communities and alleviate poverty.
- Thrust of the MFIs operations is on women's development and emancipation, by empowering them by providing financial and non-financial services which include training and capacity building.

- Basic philosophy of the MFIs is that poor people, with access to savings, credit insurance and other financial services, are more resilient and can cope with the everyday crisis they face more successfully. Access to credit allows poor people to take advantage of economic opportunities.
- Financial support by the MFIs is rendered at reasonable and affordable price.
- The MFIs provide financial services at the door step of the poor.
- They render financial support without collateral security and against group guarantee.
- Operations of MFIs are basically based on no-profit or loss basis.
- The MFIs use two basic methods in delivering financial services to their clients, viz. Group method and Individual method.

Group method primarily involves a group of individuals, which becomes the basic unit of operations of the MFIs. Since MFIs provide collateral free loans, group method helps in creating social collateral (peer pressure) that can effectively substitute physical collateral. Thus, a group becomes a basic unit with which MFIs deal.

The advantage of group method is that groups are trained to own joint responsibility for loans that are taken by individuals in the group. Groups ensure repayments from all individuals in that group and in case of a default. groups function as the forum where the credit discipline and other related issues are discussed. Groups also help credit appraisal and provide opinion on the creditworthiness of each individual in the group. They also help in controlling cost. In view of these advantages, group method is widely used in micro-finance across the world.

- The MFIs across the globe have emerged in various forms such as, non-profit mutual benefit for profit, cooperative societies and banks charitable trusts, company mutual benefit, non-banking financial intermediary (NBFC).

Although credit unions and lending cooperatives have been around hundreds of years, the pioneering of modern microfinance is often credited to Dr. Mohammad Yunus, who began experimenting with lending to poor women in the village Jobra, Bangladesh during his tenure as a Professor of economics at Chittagong University in the 1970s. He would go on to set up Grameen Bank in 1983. Since then, innovation in microfinance has continued and providers of financial services to the poor continue to evolve. Today, the World Bank estimates that about 160 million people in developing countries are served by micro finance.[19]

A peep into the history of MFIs reveals that between the 1950s and 1970s, governments and donors focused on providing subsidized agricultural credit to small and marginal farmers, in hopes of raising productivity and incomes. During the 1980s, micro-enterprise credit concentrated on providing loans to poor women to invest in tiny businesses, enabling them to accumulate assets and raise household income and welfare. These experiments resulted in the emergence of non-governmental organizations (NGOs) that provided financial services to the poor. In the 1990s, many of these institutions transformed themselves themselves into formal financial institutions in order to access and on lend client savings, thus enhancing their outreach.

As regards ownership, MFIs can be government-owned, like the rural credit co-operatives to China; member-owned, like the credit-unions in West Africa, socially minded shareholders, like many transformed NGOs in Latin America, and profit-maximizing shareholders, like the microfinance banks in Eastern Europe.

K. CONCLUSIONS

Wide spectrum of financial institutions both in money and capital markets with Central bank as the apex body have come into existence across the globe to cater to varied needs of savers and investors. Among money market institutions, commercial banks, indigenous agencies, discount houses, finance companies, money market mutual fund and acceptance houses are important players. Among capital market institutions, investment banks, merchant banks, mutual funds, insurance companies, development banks universal banks, virtual banks, venture capitalists, vulture funds, and mutual banking are notable agencies engaged principally in providing term financing to investors and entrepreneurs. Of late, MFIs have emerged as population agency to help the downtrodden, especially women to improve their economic and social status.

Recent macro level economic and technological developments and growing liberalization and globalization across the globe as also deregulation and intensification of competition among banks and from non-banking financial intermediaries have almost blurred the boundaries between money and capital markets culminating in the emergence of more diversified multi-purpose financial institutions.

KEY-TERMS

- Accepting houses
- Balanced Funds
- Bond Funds
- Capital market
- Central Bank
- Chequable deposits
- Commercial Bank
- Development banking
- Discount houses
- Finance companies
- Indigenous financial agencies
- Insurance companies
- Investment Banks
- Leverage Funds
- Microfinance Institutions
- Money market
- Money market Mutual Fund,
- Mutual Banking
- Mutual funds
- Non-transaction deposits
- Off-shore mutual funds
- Specialised funds
- Stock funds
- Taxation funds
- Universal Banking
- Venture capital
- Vulture funds

DISCUSSION QUESTIONS

1. Define money market. How is it different from capital market?
2. Who are the major players in the money market? Discuss in brief, their nature and functions.
3. How is Central bank of a country distinct from other financial institutions?
4. 'Central Bank of a country, acts as lender of the last resort.' Comment.
5. Discuss the nature and functions of commercial banks.
6. How does a Commercial bank manufacture money?
7. Bring out redeeming features of finance companies.
8. What is the function of discount houses? How are they different from accepting houses?
9. What are the major functions of investment banks?
10. Define mutual funds. Discuss the main features of various kinds of mutual funds.
11. What is money market mutual fund? Discuss its major function.
12. What is development banking? How is it different from commercial banking?
13. Why is universal banking gaining more prominence in recent years?
14. What is venture capital? In what respect is it different from vulture funds?
15. Discuss, in brief, nature and functions of mutual banking.
16. How are micro finance institutions distinct from other financial institutions? Why are they becoming more popular across the world?

REFERENCES

1. Abramortiz Mosses, *Capital Formation and Economic Growth*, University Press, Princeton, 1955, p. 4.
2. Y. V. Reddy, *Development of Money Market in India*, RBI Bulletin, March, 1999, p. 388.
3. Report of the Central Banking Enquiry Vol.I, Part I Government of India, 1931, p. 73.
4. Banking Commission Report, Government of India, 1977, pp. 440-441.
5. *Ibid.*
6. Mc Culley Paul, "Teton Reflections: Global Central Bank Focus," Jackson Hole Conference, August/September, 2007.
7. Timothy Geithner, "Reducing Systematic Risk in a Dynamic Financial System," Remarks at Economic Club of New York, June, 2008.
8. William Diamond, *Development Banks*, The John Hopkins Press, Baltimore, Maryland, p. 2.
9. RBI discussion paper on Harmonizing the Role and Operations of Development Financial Institutions and Banks, January, 1991, p. 2.
10. *Op. cit.*, p. 11.
11. www.Bank net India.com/banking/ unfeature.htm
12. www.Chinadaily.com. Cn/English/doc/2004-08/16/content 365914 htm
13. www.Swiss banking. Org/en/home/fsa-alegemein.htm
14. RBI Report on Trends and Progress of Banking in India, RBI 1998-99, pp. 25-26.
15. RBI Report on Trends and Progress of Banking in India, 2000-01, pp. 70-71.
16. Vulture Fund, Investopedia.com
17. In Price of Vultures, Global Investor Magazine.com, July-August, 2001.
18. Foreign Banks, Eyeing Stressed Loan Assets, Business Standards, March 09, 2005.
19. www.Kiva.org/about/microfinance.

Chapter 4

Recent Developments in Indian Financial System — An Overview

Learning Objectives:

The present Chapter aims at providing a vivid and critical view of recent developments in Indian financial system

Chapter Outline:

- Prelude.
- Financial markets — Heading towards greater stability, liquidity and transparency.
- Innovation, diversification and restructuring of term-financing institutions.
- Changing profile of Indian banking industry.
- Conclusions.

A. PRELUDE

The post reform period since early 1990s has witnessed significant transformation in Indian financial system in terms of increased breadth and depth of financial markets, enhanced resilience, dynamism and sophistication of financial institutions and evolution of innovative financial products. While wide range of regulatory and institutional reforms has led to opening of avenues of business for financial institutions, they have intensified competition both in domestic and international fields. Financial institutions in their strive to survive and thrive in competitive landscape have changed their strategy and adopted new paradigms and business models. Cross-border flows and entry of new products have had significant impact on the financial sector forcing Indian financial institutions to dovetail their product mix to cope with rapidly changing environment and remain competitive in the globalised scenario.

As a result, structure and operations of financial system in India are becoming increasingly complex and correspondingly exposed to greater risks. So as to ensure that financial system and its various segments grow along sound lines, a robust prudential regulatory framework has been put in place. Financial regulation and supervision have been progressively aligned with international best practices with appropriate adaptation. The corporate governance framework in financial institutions is being strengthened.[1]

B. FINANCIAL MARKETS — HEADING TOWARDS GREATER STABILITY, LIQUIDITY AND TRANSPARENCY

The policy of financial liberalization, privatization and globalization pursued by the Government since 1991 and frenetic efforts of the Government, the RBI and other agencies to execute the various policy guidelines have substantially improved every segment of financial market of the country both quantitatively and qualitatively, as may be noted below:

◈ Money Market

In recent years, the RBI took several measures to deepen the money market of the country and improve its liquidity. The first such measure was liberalization of the RBI policy relating to entry into the **call/notice money market** in order to widen and provide more liquidity. Thus, entities that could evidence of surplus funds were permitted to route their lendings through Primary dealers (PDs). Further, the RBI took steps to develop the call/notice money market into pure interbank market in a phased manner. Lending in call money market by non-bank participants was caped to 85 per cent of their average lending in 2000-01 which was subsequently reduced to 75 per cent. Since August 6, 2005 non-bank participants, except PDs were completely phased out. Prudential limits have been placed on borrowings and lendings of banks and PDs in the market.

So as to activate the **term money market** the RBI dismantled the administered interest rate system in this market and widened the participation by allowing select financial institutions in 1993 to borrow from the term money market for a period of 3-6 months. Further, no limits were stipulated for transactions in the term money market.

In order to widen the participation of commercial paper (CP), the RBI undertook a host of initiatives such as permitting corporates, PDs and secondary dealers (SDs) to issue CP, directing banks, financial institutions, PDs and SDs to make fresh investments and held CP in only dematerialized form with effect from June 30, 2001 and reducing the minimum maturity period of CP from 15 days to 7 days in October, 2004.

In tandem with the phasing out of non-banks from the call money market, the RBI endeavoured to render other avenues for their short-term investments attractive. The minimum maturity of certificates of deposits was reduced to 7 days to bring them at par with other short-term instruments.

With a view to paving the way for the emergence of a risk free rate which could become a benchmark for pricing the other money market instruments, the RBI abolished ad hoc Treasury Bills (T-Bills) and introduced regular auctions of T-Bills. A uniform price auctions for 91-days was also introduced. With effect from December 11, 2002, the auction format of 91-days of T-Bills was changed to multiple price auctions from uniform price auction to encourage more responsible bidding from the market participants.[2] The RBI has allowed interest rate futures (IRFs) trading on 91-day Treasury Bills. This helped develop the market, the final settlement price of the contract was based on the weighted average price or yield obtained in the weekly auction of the 91-day T-Bills on the date of expiry the contract.[3]

So as to provide an additional short-term avenue to investors and to bring money market instruments within the reach of individuals, the RBI introduced **MMMFs**. These institutions were sponsored by financial institutions and banks. The RBI took several measures to make them more flexible and attractive. Thus, the ceiling for raising resources and stipulations regarding the minimum size of MMMFs were done away with and the prescription on limits for investment was withdrawn except in respect of CP. In October, 1997, MMMFs were allowed to invest in reputed corporate bonds and debentures with a residual maturity of upto one year, within the ceiling existing for CP.

The recent thrust of the RBI policy regarding development of the money market has been the positioning of Liquidity Adjustment Facility (LAF) as an instrument for modulating liquidity and signaling the monetary stance and for creating conditions for orderly market activity. The first stage of LAF introduced with effect from June 5, 2000 was followed by refinement made in May, 2001.

In order to improve liquidity conditions in the money market, the RBI opened in November, 2010 a second LAF window and additional liquidity support under LAF upto 1 per cent of net demand time liabilities (NDTL). Both the measures were made available till December 16, 2010.

In line with the objective of widening and deepening of the money market and imparting liquidity to the market, the RBI introduced market repo and Collateralized Borrowing and Lending obligations (CBLo). These instruments have provided avenues for non-banks to manage their short-term liquidity mismatches and facilitated the transformation of the call money market into a pure inter-bank market. The RBI has been using its repo instrument effectively for absorbing excess liquidity and for infusing funds to ease the liquidity. Since March 2010, the RBI raised its repo rate, at which it lends money to banks, thirteen times taking the rate to 8.0 per cent in its relentless efforts to squeeze liquidity and tame inflation.

In its endeavour to improve liquidity position of banks, the RBI enhanced the borrowing limit for banks under the marginal standing facility to 2 per cent of net demand and time liabilities in April, 2012 from 1 per cent earlier.

CBLo was operationalised as a money market instrument through the Clearing Corporation of India Ltd. (CCIL) in January 2003.

The RBI established the Discount and Finance House of India (DFHI) in 1988 as a money market institution in association with public sector banks and financial institutions to facilitate the smoothening of short-term liquidity imbalance by developing active primary and secondary money markets. DFHI discounts not only commercial bills but also treasury bills and other money market instruments. The thrust of the DFHI since inception has been on call money, T-Bills and commercial bills. In February, 1996, the DFHI was accredited as a PD. Since then it continues to participate in primary and secondary markets for government securities.

In August 2009, the RBI introduced new short-term bills, *viz.*, Cash Management Bills, to help the government tide over temporary cash flow mismatches. This instrument has maturity of less than 91 days and is issued at a discount. The tenure, amount and date of the bills would depend on the cash requirement of the government. These bills are tradeable and used for repo transactions.

Consequent upon the various initiatives of the RBI since the early 1990s, the Indian money market has undergone transformation in terms of instruments, participants and technological infrastructure, leading to emergence of deep, liquid and vibrant money market. Along with the shifts in the operating procedures of monetary policy, the liquidity management operations of the RBI have also been fine tuned to enhance the effectiveness of monetary policy signalling.

Money market and its various segments have been developed in line with shifts in policy emphasis. Thus, there was surge in total value of business transacted in the money market by over four times from ₹ 22,709 crore in 1997-98 to ₹ 90,275 crore in February, 2010. An important factor contributing to expansion of the money market was repo market (outside the LAF) which tended to shot up from ₹ 6,895 crore in 1999-00 to ₹ 19,820 crore in February, 2010.

Likewise, CBLo spurted spectacularly from ₹ 30 crore in 2002-03 to ₹ 63,645 crore in February, 2010 indicating emergence of CBLo as the predominant segment in the money market.

As regards, the call money market, the average daily turnover in call market from ₹ 22,709 crore in 1997-98 rose to ₹ 35,144 crore in 2001-02, reflecting increase in pressure on call money market, mainly due to stock market boom and rise in demand for loans for industrial and commercial purposes. However, there was sharp decline in daily turnover in the market in 2002-03 when it tumbled to ₹ 29,421 crore and further to ₹ 8,990 crore in 2005-06, showing amply slow down in stock market business and contraction in bank deposits. During the subsequent three years — 2006-07 – 2008-09 there was surge in daily turnover of the call money market mainly because of economic and business boom and bullish state of the stock market on the one hand and tightening of liquidity conditions, on the other.

A noteworthy development noted was the substantial migration of money market activity from the uncollateralized call money segment to the collateralized market repo and CBLo. This migration has been largely the result of the considered policy of phasing out non-banking participants from the call money market.

In respect of Treasury bill segment of the Indian money market, the RBI's recent moves to increase the notified amount in each auction of the T-Bills from ₹ 100 crore to ₹ 1,000 crore have rendered the T-bills market vibrant and provided an additional avenue of investment to the non-bank entities. The 91-day T-bills have been most prominent in terms of gross turnover, although both the 91-day and 364-day T-bills have been the main stay of T-bills market in India. The total outstanding amount in treasury bills stood at ₹ 1,21,541 crore as on July 1, 2011 up from ₹ 72,329 crore a year ago. The government had auctioned ₹ 1,17,000 crore of treasury bills and ₹ 38,000 crore of cash management bills during April-June, 2011. The amount borrowed through treasury bills was ₹ 87,000 crore and that, through cash management bills was ₹ 12,000 crore.

Besides the quantitative growth, there has also been tremendous qualitative improvement in Indian money market, as reflected in participation of a large number of institutional participants in trading of call money market, treasury bill market, bill market, CP and CDs market. The RBI's relentless efforts have minimized default risk and achieved a balanced development of various segments. Growth of collateralized segment has improved options for liquidity management while reducing risk. Developments in institutional infrastructure have also helped in improving transparency, facilitating price discovery process and providing avenues for a better liquidity and risk management. Operationalisation of a screen-based negotiated quote-driven for dealings in the call/notice and term money markets (NDs-Call) with effect from September 18, 2006 developed by the CCIL has helped in improving the case of transactions while also bringing about greater transparency and efficient price discovery.[4]

The RBI's efforts to set prudential limits on borrowing and lending in the call money market has encouraged migration towards the collateralized segments and developed derivative instruments for hedging market risks to minimize risks arising out of interest rate fluctuations.

Administered interest rate system following the introduction of auction system of sale of T-bills and withdrawal of ceiling on the interest rates on inter-bank call market, and inter-bank short-term deposits paved way to a market-based interest rate. Further, there has been decline in volatility in call rates over the years, especially after the introduction of the LAF.

Policy initiatives by the RBI in terms of widening of market-based instruments and shortening of maturities of various instruments have not only helped in promoting market integration but also enabled better liquidity management and transmission of policy signals by the RBI.[5]

Indian money market has thus become reasonably deep, vibrant and liquid, as reflected in bid-ask spread in the overnight rates. With the development of market repo and CBLo, the call money market has emerged as a pure inter-bank market from August, 2005. There has also been significant migration of money market activity from the uncollateralized call market segment to the collateralized market repo and CBLo markets.

The RBI's initiatives have also facilitated integration of different segments of money market and so also other financial markets, as reflected in the close co-movement of turnovers and rates of return of different segments and instruments. Empirical studies conducted in Indian context have provided reasonably robust evidence of integration between the money market segments, *i.e.*, call money, reverse repo, CPs and CDs. The 91-day T-bills was observed to have the potential of emerging as a reference rate.[6]

The global financial meltdown, however, adversely affected the Indian money market and its various segments. The failure of Lehman Brothers and a few other global financial institutions in mid-September 2008 led to the freezing of money market activities in major financial centres including India. With the increasing uncertainty in global markets, the volatility in the call market also increased significantly during mid-September 2008. But the measures initiated by the RBI thereafter augmented liquidity, and the weighted average call money rate declined. Furthermore, volumes in the money market have also grown from January 2007, suggesting that inter-bank money market has been functioning normally, liquidity conditions improving leading to reduction in policy rates.

Thus, persistent efforts of the RBI have certainly increased size of activity in different segments of the money market, broadened participation, evolved innovative instruments and technologies, enhanced transparency and improved signaling mechanism in monetary policy, resulting in the emergence of liquid and vibrant money market in the country.

However, Indian money market needs to be developed further and its various segments need greater coordination for ensuring greater financial stability. As such, initiatives to further deepen the various segments of the money market will have to be pursued in future.

There is also strong need to improve ALM practices by banks and other market participants which would enable banks to evolve suitable prudential limits on their call money exposures from their internal control system.

Furthermore, there is also a need to expand the eligible set of underlying collateral securities for repo transactions.

It is also necessary to strengthen the CP market so as to exploit its potential fully.

◆ Capital Market

Capital market in India has recorded landmark developments during the post liberalization period, as listed below:

(*i*) Institutionalization and sophistication of capital market in terms of setting up of Securities Exchange Board of India (SEBI) in 1992 and Constitution of National Stock Exchange (NSE) in 1992, establishment of Over the Counter Exchange of India (OTCEI), Institutionalization of the stock exchanges by opening the gates of the stock market to FIIs and constitution of a depository to facilitate scripless trading. All this provided impetus to new issue market in India.

(*ii*) Strengthening equity market by way of complete switch over to rolling, an extension of derivatives trading in equity to index options, stock options and stock futures. The onset of a full range of equity derivative is a remarkable development in Indian stock market.

(*iii*) Expansion and sophistication of secondary market due to opening of the market to FIIs and their increasing participation in stock trading, growing participation of mutual funds in securities of stock exchange, remarkable shift in portfolio allocations towards debt instruments and constitution of Credit Rating Information Services of India Ltd. (CRISIL).

(*iv*) Demutualization of stock exchanges involving separation of trading rights from ownership and management control and conversion of non-profit organization into a for-profit organization mark another milestone in the Indian capital market.

(*v*) Growing financial depth of capital market both in breadth and coverage of formal finance, broadening the access of funds to wider strata of population across the country.

(*vi*) Permitting Qualified Foreign Investors (QFIs) in 2011 to invest upto $10 billion, or ₹ 45,000 crore, in India's stock markets through mutual funds under the supervision of the SEBI so as to boost the capital market. It was subsequently raised to $ 20 million. In addition, SEBI allowed overseas investors on July 18, 2012 to invest in corporate banks and debt schemes of mutual funds without any lock-in period.

(*vii*) Initiation of several measures by the SEBI to strengthen mutual funds industry and increase competitiveness in stock market by permitting MCX to offer equity and equity derivative contracts in July 2012.

Various segments of Indian capital market, *viz.*, new issue market, secondary market, government securities and corporate debt market recorded significant improvement both quantitatively and qualitatively due to incredible policy interventions of the Government and its agencies during post reform period.

(I) New Issue Market

Until the post reform period new issue market in India was not as much developed in terms of quantity and quality of activities as also financial depth and sophistication as in the U.S., UK and European countries. However, in recent years, it has grown spectacularly in tandem with scorching pace of economic and industrial growth of the country and emerged as robust and resilient constituent of the financial market to cope with the competitive challenges across the country. Dynamism in the new issue market in India, as reflected in the volume of new issue activity, use of innovative instruments to garner funds, methods of distribution of securities, pricing of issues and broadening of market base over a period of time is because of the following inexorable policy intervention, rapid industrialization of the country, path-breaking technological developments, entry of financial institutions and foreign investors willing to take direct investment risks and strong support by Indian stock market.

In its endeavour to bolster new issue activity in India, the Government of India and the SEBI undertook the following reformatory measures during post liberalization period:

- Pursuance of the policy of deregulation and delicensing;
- Repeal of capital issue (Control) Act, and abolition of capital issues in 1992;
- Introduction of market-based pricing system;
- Constitution of the SEBI to promote the development of the securities market and protect the interests of investors in securities.
- Permission to Indian companies to raise resources abroad through the issue of Global Deposit Receipts (GDRs) and Foreign Currency Convertible Bonds (FCCBs);
- Disinvestment by the Government of India in public sector undertakings;
- Opening up of the market for portfolio investments by FIIs and encouraging foreign private participation in financial services including stock broking;
- Permitting public sector financial institutions and commercial banks to raise equity share capital from the market;
- Permitting introduction of innovative financial instruments such as warrants, cumulative convertible preference shares, non-voting shares, sweet equity shares and a host of hybrid bonds and debentures;

- Making it mandatory on the part of promoters to disclose the details of shares held by them in listed entities promoted by them;
- Simplifying regulatory framework for issuance and listing of non-convertible debt securities by an issuer company, public sector undertaking or statutory corporation;
- Enhancing the application limit for retail investors from ₹ 1 lakh to ₹ 2 lakh in October, 2010 for investment in public issue;
- Reducing the time between issue closures and listing to 12 days for all offers from May 1, 2011 so as to make the public issue process more efficient;
- Permitting the retail investors having being allotted shares at a discount in initial public offerings (IPOs) to apply at the discounted price rather than the cut-off price from June 15, 2011;
- Raising the investment limit of FIIs to $25 billion in corporate bonds issued by companies in the infrastructure sector with residual maturity of over 5 years;
- Permitting FIIs to invest in domestic mutual funds upto $10 billion from August, 2011; the ceiling was subsequently raised to $ 20 billion. In order to give fillip to sagging new issue market and to shore up the inflow of foreign funds, and thereby stem the steady depreciation of the rupee against the dollar, the Government on May 29, 2012 threw open the securities markets to direct investment by all residents of the Gulf and EU nations. Thus, the government allowed QFIs from six member countries of the Gulf Cooperation Council (GCC), viz, Saudi Arabia, Bahrain, the United Arab Emirates, Oman, Qatar and Kuwait, and 27 countries of EC to invest in Indian capital market. Alongside, it also opened the doors to individual overseas investors to bring up to $1 billion in the country's debt and corporate bond market. Thus, a $1-billion window over and above the current $20-billion has been created for QFI investment in corporate bonds and mutual fund debt schemes.
- Making it mandatory through an amendment to the Securities Contract (Regulations) Act, in June 2010 for private sector listed companies to ensure 25 per cent public holding to ensure over the next 3 to 5 years with a view to increasing depth and liquidity in the market, attracting good quality, long-term investors to the stock;
- IPOs of companies with paid-up capital of upto ₹ 25 crore will not require the SEBI's permission to raise capital from September, 2011.

  On August 16, 2012, the SEBI took the following steps to strengthen new issue market and improve the reach of initial public offerings (IPOs):

  (*a*) Every retail applicant will get allotment, irrespective of application size.

  (*b*) Minimum application size for all investors increased to ₹ 10,000-15,000 from ₹ 5,000-7,000.

  (*c*) Implemented a framework to increase the reach and use of the Application Supported by Blocked Amount (ASBA).

  (*d*) Brokers will be given more incentives to encourage the use of ASBA by retail investors.

  (*e*) Broker network of stock exchanges at more than 1,000 locations for e-IPOs so as to widen the distribution network of IPOs.

Most of the new measures, though appearing to be just tinkering of existing rules are really part of a larger process of bringing the Indian primary markets and its regulation up-to-date. This will certainly improve investors' confidence.

The above initiatives have brought about cataclysmic changes in the landscape of the new issue market and its related activities, heralding the emergence of matured and resilient market in the country, as evidenced from the following discussions.

There has been spectacular increase in amount of new capital issues during the last decade, rising from ₹ 7,613 crore through 65 issues in 1999-2000 to about ₹ 84,000 crore through 115 issues in 2007-08. What is interesting to note is that the private sector companies were the predominant players in the new issues market, accounting for over 76 per cent of the resources mobilized by way of public issues in 2007-08. This can be explained partly by various positive efforts of the Government and the SEBI and partly by the strong macro-economic fundamentals and higher growth rate trajectory embarked upon by the Indian economy, buoyancy in the secondary market, encouraging both issuers and investors to enter the primary market, country-wide enthusiasm among entrepreneurs to enlarge and modernize manufacturing capacities to meet domestic as well as foreign demand and higher rate of return on equity investments in the face of decline in interest rates on deposits.

However, the new issue market subdued considerably during 2008-09 when the number of IPOs in the private sector plummeted to 45 and resources mobilized declined sharply to ₹ 14,671 crore. This slump was driven by heightened volatility and uncertainty in the financial markets and slowdown in growth and incumbent demand for investment and dampened sentiment due to depressed secondary markets.

The new issue market activities, however, revived since June 2009 and picked up sharply during the last quarter of 2009-10 when funds mobilized through 36 issues amounted to about ₹ 16,000 crore.[7] During the period 2009-10, as many as 65 issues were floated to raise ₹ 25,153 crore from the market.

New issue market activities gained momentum since June 2009. As a result, as many as 71 issues were floated to garner ₹ 32,607 crore during 2009-10. Upswing in the new issue activity continued during 2010-11 also when 77 companies floated new issues in the market to raise ₹ 37,620 crore.

Resource mobilisation in the primary market was significantly lower (65.8 per cent) during 2011-12 over the previous year. Dampened secondary market conditions, and the poor performance of IPOs after their listing affected investor and promoter sentiment. Firms almost abstained from mobilising resources through public issues during October-January, 2012 when investor's risk appetite was low. However, during February-June, 2012, the primary market witnessed a few issuances. Overall, primary market sentiment remained subdued during the year. 51 issues were floated during 2011-12 to mobilise ₹ 128.6 crore.

Another significant development noted in new issue market in recent years is predominance of premium equity issued. Thus in 2004-05 and 2005-06, 99 per cent of capital issues were premium issues as compared to 74 per cent in 2000-01. This is indicative of increased confidence of investors. But it needs to be noted that institutional investors like FIIs and mutual funds and to some extent, banks and financial institutions have been the major contributors for investment in premium issues with over subscription. Betting high on the Indian market, FIIs have purchased stocks and bonds worth ₹ 10 lakh crore in financial year ending March 2011.[8]

Another landmark development of the new issue market during the post reform period is growing participation of retail investors in the equity market. Individuals, several of them from middle-class households, have entered the market through mutual funds and through portfolio management schemes. It has been estimated that retail investors have pumped in about ₹ 17,500-18,000 crore into the equities during 2006. Several factors, such as rising exposure levels, changing life-styles and attitudes and decline of fixed deposits as a viable investment option, contributed to this trend.

However, retail investors' enthusiasm for equity offering disappeared during 2008-09 because of their cautious approach and volatility in markets in the wake of global financial crisis. According to data compiled by Bombay Stock Exchange Research Bureau, the share of retail investors in the market capitalization of actively traded stocks on Bombay Stock Exchange (BSE) has slumped to a five-year low. At the end of March 2011, retail investors accounted for 15.86 per cent market capitalization of 3214 actively-traded stocks on BSE, which is much lower than the 19 per cent they held in 2,486 actively traded companies at the end March 2006. Interestingly, the decline has coincided with the expanding 711 (prior) during the past two years on back of record inflows in 2009 and 2010.[9]

However, participation of retail investors in new equity market is low. Reasons for the poor retail participation in the market are low return and high volatility.

As a result, the pattern of ownership has changed. The share of the public and other category was 14 per cent in December 2012 from 22 per cent in March 2001, that of domestic mutual funds halved to 3.5 per cent during the period. The stake held by promoters went up to 51 per cent from 49.9 per cent during this period and of foreign institutional investors (FIIs) from 14.7 per cent to 22.7 per cent.[11]

In view of uncertainties in new issue market and low investor's appetite for equity shares, many private sector companies including Jindal Power, Reliance Infratel, Sterlite Energy and Lodha Developers have decided not to raise funds through equity issues.[12]

Thus, the new issue market in the country witnessed phenomenal changes during the post liberalization and compares well with other emerging economies in terms of sophisticated market design of equity market, participation of FIIs, mobilization of funds through Euro issues.

However, the growth of equity markets still remains low and largely skewed in comparison to the USA, Malaysia and South Korea, indicating immense latent potential. Further, the new issue market of the country continues to be shallow. Despite inflation, only 2 per cent of Indian household savings are invested in the market as against 20 per cent in developed economies and about 51 per cent in the USA.

A myriad of factors such as lack of transparency, overpricing of issues and high transaction costs have stonewalled the full-fledged growth of the new issue market of the country. Due to recent global financial crises the new issue market suffered grievously with investors confidence at its lowest ebb.

To rev up the market and sustain its growth, it would be most desirable to restore investors' confidence. For this, the SEBI should make listing requirements more stringent, install an efficient institutional arrangement, and direct the companies to adhere strictly codes of corporate governance.

There is a strong need to kick-start the new issue market, not just through regulation and policy initiatives but through a proactive role by market participants and intermediaries.

In its attempt to attract more retail investors in equities, the Government recently introduced the Rajiv Gandhi Equity Savings Scheme (RGESS). The scheme announced in the budget of 2012, would provide a 50 per cent tax deduction on investments upto ₹ 50,000 to retail investors whose annual taxable income is below ₹ 10 lakhs.

The most striking development that took place in new issue market during 2011-12 was mobilisation of resources by Indian corporates through issue of preference shares. After the regulatory change in January 2012 whereby the SEBI lifted restrictions on insurance companies and mutual funds subscribing to preferential issues of companies, fund mobilisation through preferential issues has risen sharply in 2011-2012 by over ₹ 23,000 crore being raised by over 100 Indian companies as compared to the entire calendar year 2011.

(II) Secondary Market

Post liberalization period witnessed perceptible and palpable improvement in Indian secondary market (stock market) in terms of proliferation of size of the operations, enhanced liquidity, transparency, efficiency and stability because of myriad of initiatives taken by the Government and the SEBI; important ones are listed below:

- Empowering the SEBI in January 1992 for regulating the transactions of stock exchanges in such a way as to protect investors' interests and ensuring the orderly development of the secondary market.
- Incorporating the National Stock Exchange (NSE) in 1992 for bringing about improvement in trading systems and providing nationwide stock trading facilities in an efficient, transparent and fair manner.
- Establishing OTCEI in 1992 for increasing sophistication of Indian stock market.
- Opening of Indian stock markets in 1992 to FIIs.

- Setting up of National Securities Depository Ltd. (NSDL) in 1995 and Central Depository Services (India) Ltd. in 1999 which heralded the beginning of paperless trading in the exchanges.
- Corporatization and demutualisation of stock exchanges by which ownership, management and trading membership have been segregated from each other.
- Lifting of 30-year old ban on forward trading in securities in 1999.
- Introducing trading in derivatives such as Index futures, stock index options, futures and options is individual in 2000 to provide hedging options to the investors and to provide price discovery mechanism in the market.
- Setting up of the investor protection fund (IPF) by the stock exchanges.
- Requiring the listed companies to publish unaudited financial results on a six monthly basis as also to incorporate in the listing agreement segment reporting related party disclosures, consolidated financial results and financial statements.
- Setting up of credit rating agencies to add value to the market by assigning ratings to debt instruments and by continuous monitoring and dissemination of the ratings.
- Permitting short selling and securities lending and borrowing schemes to all classes of investors with effect from April 21, 2008 so as to provide adequate liquidity to market participants and facilitate price discovery.
- SEBI permitting two leading stock exchanges — the National Stock Exchange (NSE) and the Bombay Stock Exchange (BSE) to have a separate trading platform, for SMEs and issuing guidelines therefor. Companies having a post issue paid-up capital of upto ₹ 10 crore will be covered under the SME platform, while companies with a post-issue paid-up capital between ₹ 10 crore and ₹ 25 crore will be listed on the SME platform.
- SEBI allowing stock exchanges to appoint market makers in the derivatives segment so as to increase liquidity in a transparent manner.
- SEBI allowing in principle physical settlement in equity derivatives.
- SEBI allowing stock exchanges in April 2012 for listing of their shares on other stock exchanges, subject to certain riders, after three years from the date of approval.
- SEBI allowing in April 2012, 51 per cent stake of bourses to be held with the public, diversified ownership in stock exchanges with curbs on single-investor participation.
- SEBI laying down provisions in April 2012 to form an independent governance committee in each stock exchange that will have a significant role in the regulatory functions of the exchange, such as listing, trading and surveillance, independent directors to form the majority of the committee and one of them to head it.
- Permitting MCX Stock Exchange in July 2012 to deal in equities and same kinds of futures.

Consequent upon multi-pronged policy initiatives during the post-liberalization period secondary market in India witnessed remarkable progress in terms of increase in size of operations, improvement in liquidity, transparency and stability as also institutionalization and sophistication of the market.

As regards expansion of the secondary market, it may be observed that the number of stock exchanges surged from 8 in 1970 to 25 at present, with a number of companies listed in various stock exchanges having shot up from less than 10 lakhs in 1970 to over 1.5 crore at present. Market capitalization of stock markets in India to GDP recorded phenomenal spurt from 17.8 per cent in 1991 to over 154.6 per cent in 2007. A host of factors such as improvement in fundamentals of economy, technological advancement and increase in institutional efficiency contributed to this upsurge. With global crisis, the market capitalization of stock exchanges in India suffered drastically in 2008. However, the market bounced back in 2010 when stock market capitalization surged to 101.9 per cent due to reduction in policy rates and positive results of corporate and banks.

Market capitalization of the BSE increased tremendously from ₹ 5,72,198 crore in 2002--03 to ₹ 61,64,157 crore in 2009-10. Similarly, NSE's market capitalization soared during the corresponding period, more than 11 times rise during the period.

There has been significant improvement in liquidity of stock market transactions during the post liberalization period, as evidenced from increase in turnover ratio (total value of shares traded on the country's stock exchanges divided by the stock market capitalization) from 20.3 per cent in 1991-91 to over 100 per cent in 2009-10.[13]

Derivatives as a means of reducing exposure to investment risks and protecting interests of the investors are becoming popular in India since 2000 when the SEBI allowed BSE and NSE to commence trading in financial derivatives. Thus, the turnover of derivative segment during the period 2002-03 to 2007-08 shot up by about ten-fold in the BSE and thirty-fold in the NSE. Activity in financial derivatives, which was adversely affected by the financial crisis, saw significant improvement in 2009-10 led by adequate liquidity in the system and return of stability in the domestic markets.

In this connection, it may be noted that in the BSE, turnover of cash segment still claims predominant portion of the transaction where as the reverse is true in the case of the NSE where derivative segment represents about four-fifths of the total. The NSE features among the top derivative exchanges of the world in terms of the numbers of contracts traded. If one takes into account commodity futures, MCX occupies in top slot in some commodities.

In view of the recommendations of the derivatives market review committee set up by the SEBI, Indian stock market will witness a bouquet of offering in the futures and options space and introduction of derivatives based on foreign indices, *viz.*, S&P 500 and Dow Jones Industrial Average in the ensuing years. Indian investors will thus get an opportunity to bet on the US market, and that too, in their local currency.

Institutionalization of the stock market in terms of active participation of mutual funds, FIIs, Public Provident Funds, UTI, LIC and other financial institutions including banks in stock market activities, is another landmark development during the post-liberalization period. Major industrial investors in the stock market have been FIIs and mutual funds. FIIs have started deploying funds in equity particularly from 2003-04 when the Indian stock market showed buoyancy and economic conditions improved. Between April 2007 and January, 2008, FIIs invested ₹ 66,898 crore in the Indian equity market. However, they made net sales of ₹ 14,324 crore between January 2008 and March, 2008. In contrast, mutual funds have been heavily investing in debt. In 2007-08, it deployed about four-fifths of their funds in debt, indicating clearly that their risk appetite is less than FIIs.

A remarkable change in the pattern of institutional investments was noticeable during 2008-09. As a part of the global deleveraging process and general increase in risk aversion towards emerging markets, the FIIs withdrew large amount of their investments from the Indian market so much so that their large net purchases in 2007-08 turned into large net sales in 2008--09. Investments of mutual funds in equities also declined during the period, whereas their investments in debt increased, reflecting the lesser risk involvement in government debt. FIIs returned with net purchases and retail investors and mutual funds also made a swift reversal with a buying spree from March 2009 following the decline in the volatility in the stock markets and recovery of asset prices from their previous lows across countries. Betting high on the Indian market, FIIs have invested ₹ 10 lakh crore in stocks and bonds during 2010-11.[14] According to market experts, it was strong FII inflows that provided the much needed warmth to Indian capital market at times when the global economy continued to reel under the pressure of financial crisis.

In fact, FIIs accounted for nearly 8 per cent of capital investments in India in financial year 2011 — up from a 1.1 per cent iin finanial year 2005.

After slow down during January-November 2011 when foreign investors were net sellers to the tune of $500 million, FIIs invested over $ 621 billion during January-December, 2012.[15]

It is interesting to note that FIIs poured more money into Indian equities in the financial year ending March 2013 than they have in any year since they were permitted to invest in these 21 years ago. They were net buyers by ₹ 1.4 lakh crore during 2012-13, according to data from the SEBI. This is higher than both 2010 and 2011, both of which saw net inflows of ₹ 1.1 lakh crore.

It is interesting to observe that Indian markets have generally been in a bull market in the past decade, except a few instances such as the end of April and early May, 2011 when the Nifty rallied from a low of 5364, crossed the 200 DMA and scaled a high of 5908 in a span of 15 days, up 10 per cent. Similar trends were also seen in April 2001 and November 2002 when the index was trading below the 200-DMA and the markets rallied almost 12 per cent in 14-22 days. During the 2008 bear market, the rallies were vicious; the index jumped 18.5 per cent in a short time frame of 8-9 days. Most of these rallies were followed by sharp corrections, and the markets giving up almost all the gains. However, according to technical analysts, the Indian markets are looking weak as the short-term 500-Day Moving Average is below the 200-Day Moving Average.[16]

Another trend lurking in recent years is domination of the Indian stock market by foreign money. It is not Indian money that drives or sustains the BSE and the NSE. Indian stock market is more identified with the Indian geography than with Indian savings or Indian money. When foreign money rushes in, the sensex goes up and the vice-versa. The correlation between FII inflows and the movement of the sensex is crystal clear. The $51 billion that flowed in propelled the 3o-share index from sub-4,000 level in 2003 to over 20,000 by early 2008. The outflows of 2008 resulted in the sensex sinking to 8,500-level.

FII inflows of ₹ 1 lakh crore in 2010-11 pushed the BSE benchmark sensex to the level of 21,207 in September 2010.

The sensex plunged sharply to 15190 and Nifty fell to 4613.10 on December 20, 2011 on heavy selling of shares by FIIs due to slowing growth and weakening rupee amid declining global markets. On February 15, 2012, heavy FII buying pushed sensex to 18,202 and Nifty to 5,531.95. However, the sensex declined sharply to 15,847 on May 23, 2012 due to continued eurozone crisis, global risk aversion, rupee depreciation, flight of FIIs, decrease in FDI and above all due to weak fundamentals of the economy. The positive sentiments riding on the optimism surrounding the delay in implementation of the controversial tax avoidance rules and hopes of policy rate cuts pushed the sensex above 20,000 mark on January 15, 2013.

It is also important to note that the movements of Indian stock markets in recent years have been highly synchronized with advanced and emerging market economies. The regional stock markets in Asia including India, Hong Kong and Singapore and global markets such as the US, UK and Japan shared a single & long-run co-integrating relationship in terms of stock price indices. The Indian market held the key to this integration process.[17]

In recent years, the Indian stock market has seen multi-faceted growth in terms of products traded in the market. i.e., equities and bonds issued by the government and companies, futures on benchmark indices as well as stocks, options on benchmark indices as well as stocks, currency derivatives, Exchange Traded Funds and futures on interest rate products such as 91-day Treasury Bills, 10-year Zero Coupon Bond and 6 per cent 10-year Bond, etc.

Of late, Indian stock exchanges have embarked on consolidation and expansion in order to increase their volume of business, expand their reach, and improve services to the investors and thus gain market share. There is a race among Indian exchanges for global alliance, as all the top branches are banking on over-the-counter derivatives market to be moved to the exchange platform in the next five years. Thus, the MCX-SX--D inked a tie up with global index provider FTSE while the NSE went ahead and tied up with the London Stock Exchange (LSE). Later, the LSE became the largest shareholder of FTSE. London-based FTSE is an independent company, managing over 1,20,000 equity, bond and alternative asset class indices. In the USA, the NSE has partnered with the Chicago Mercantile Exchange (CME), a rival of NYSE Euronext group.

In Asia, NSE has a tie-up with the Singapore Stock Exchange (SGX), which competes with the Singapore Mercantile Exchange (SMX).

NSE's tie-up with CME group helps it increase its reach as the latter has ties with Brazil's Bolsa de Mercadories & Futuros, Bovesper, Bursa Malaysia, Dubai Mercantile Exchange, KRX Exchange of Korea, Paril Bourse SBF SP, Montreal Exchange, Spains MEFF and SGX. Members of all these exchanges get several trading privileges in terms of direct access and cross-margining.

Of late, Indian stock exchanges have embarked on consolidation and expansion in order to increase their volume of business, expand their reach, and improve services to the investors and thus win market share. Thus, the NSE has a license to list Dow Jones Industrial Average and S&P 500 through its alliance with the Chicago Mercantile Exchange (CME). The NSE has also forged deal with the London Stock Exchange for working out a joint business strategy. This will lead NSE's equity benchmark index, S&P CNX Nifty to become a globally traded contract. Also, NSE will be able to offer a basket of top traded global indices once the FTSE 100 index is listed on its floor in India.

The BSE has tied up with the Deutsche Boarse Group, a strategic investor in it, to explore cross-listing of indices and other products. This will enable the BSE to have a greater reach in Europe. The BSE has also roped in the US-based International Securities Exchange to develop and launch derivative products.

So as to improve its volume of business the BSE has forged an alliance with three regional stock exchanges, *viz.* Madhya Pradesh Stock Exchange (MPSE), the Vadodara Stock Exchange (VSE) and Jaipur Stock Exchange (JSE). BSE already has a tie-up with the Calcutta Stock Exchange (CSE), in which it has a 5 per cent stake. The NSE has already joined hands with the Madras Stock Exchange and signed MoUs with MPSE, VSE and JSE. It is also in talks with the Ahmedabad Stock Exchange (ASE) and CSE for an alliance.

To protect their turf from future competition, the two are wooing brokers by reducing charges and introducing new products.

It is noteworthy that competitive environment in stock market has tended to become fierce following the establishment of MCX-SX. MCX-SX has embarked on an aggressive membership drive, offering favourable terms for fees, deposits and networth criteria, including discounts for professionals and members from non-urban areas. The NSE has countered by creating a new Alpha membership fees and allowed existing members to convert to Alpha. Though the NSE's deposit and networth criteria are higher than in the MCX-SX structure, transaction costs will reduce to near zero for some NSE members. The BSE, which has the lowest deposit structure, will likely respond similarly, since it cannot afford to be left behind. And then there is the Delhi Stock Exchange, which is setting up a state-of-the art trading platform in collaboration with the London stock Exchange.

Competition between the exchanges could lead to an expansion of high frequency trading in particular. Members with co-located terminals directly linked to exchanges stand to gain.

It is most exciting to note that two arch rivals for over 15 years, the BSE and the NSE have, of late, decided to form alliance so as to expand the volume of business and meet competitive challenge from MCX-SX. As per the terms of the alliance, BSE's online trading platform (Bolt) will be made available on NSE's in-house software Neat-on-Web (Now). Traders using this platform will get access to more than 70,000 stocks listed on BSE. BSE will get access to NSE's over 2,00,000 trading terminals in 1,400 towns across India. Effectively, this strategic move signifies integration of trading terminals and widening the reach.[18]

Thus, the secondary market in India has emerged more efficient and liquid during the post liberalization period and has grown in volume of business and product offerings. However, it still remains much smaller than many advanced countries, such as the US, UK, Australia and Japan. Further, the role of corporate sector is limited, given the size of the economy. Actually, the entire corporate sector listed on the bourses and unlisted, accounts for just 14 per cent of GDP.[19] Further, 90 per cent of the business of exchanges is from the four metros. The top 100 companies account for 95 per cent of trading and less than 5 per cent of Indians invest in stocks.[20] As a result, the capital raised from the securities market has remained quite small, despite some surge in issues in recent years.

Retail investors have been net sellers in equities during the past four years, as uncertain market prospects prompted them to stay from stocks or sell these at higher levels.

According to a recent study by broking firm CLSA, retail investors sold about ₹ 15,400 crore in equities in the past four years through all the three routes — direct, mutual funds and insurance products.

The aversion to stocks has resulted in the ratio of equity holding as a percentage of total financial assets of the country's households to dip to 7 per cent in September, 2012 from 10 per cent about 4 years earlier.[21]

In view of growing demand of funds from the corporate sector, it would be useful to ensure that the stock market is well positioned. There is also a need to develop strong institutional investors, which would serve many purposes. As the market evolution is an ongoing process, the Indian equity market would have to continuously strive to keep up to the international standards.

(III) Foreign Exchange Market

Prior to the pre-liberalization period, the Indian foreign exchange market was highly regulated with restrictions on transactions, participants and use of instruments. However, post liberalization period has witnessed a wide range of regulatory and institutional reforms resulting in substantial development of the rupee exchange market as it is observed today. Market participants have become sophisticated and acquired reasonable expertise in using various instruments and managing risks. As a part of reforms process, several derivative instruments have been introduced resulting in significant growth of the Indian foreign exchange market. The daily average turnover has seen an almost ten-fold rise during the 10-year period from 1997-98 to 2007-08 from US$ 5 billion to US$ 48 billion. This resulted in rise in the share of India in global foreign exchange market turnover from 0.3 per cent in April 2004 to 0.9 per cent in April 2007.

With the increasing global integration, efficiency in the foreign exchange market has improved as evident from the low bid-ask spreads. It was noted that the spread is almost flat and very low. The normal spot market quote has a spread of 0.25 paise to 1 paise while swap quotes are available at a 1 to 2 paise spread. Thus, the foreign exchange market in India has evolved overtime as a deep, liquid and efficient market as against what existed prior to pre-reform period.

In recent years, external sector developments in India have been marked by robust capital flows, which resulted in tendency appreciation of exchange rate of the Indian rupee up to 2007-08. The exchange rate policy is primarily guided by the need to reduce excess volatility, prevent the emergence of speculative activities, help maintain an adequate level of reserves, and develop an orderly foreign exchange rate market. This has served well in maintaining orderly market conditions.

However, outburst of global financial crisis in general and failure of the Lehman Brothers' in particular in mid-September 2008 led to reversal and/or modulation of capital flows, particularly FII flows, ECBs and trade credit with concomitant pressures on the foreign exchange market across the globe including India. The rupee depreciated sharply, breaching the level of ₹ 50 per US dollar on October 27, 2008. To control the situation the RBI scaled up its intervention operations during the month of October, 2008.

With the return of some stability in international financial markets and relatively better growth performance of the Indian economy, there has been a revival in FII investment since the beginning of 2009-10. As compared with depreciation of 21.5 per cent during 2008-09, the rupee appreciated by around 13 per cent in 2009-10.

Though, there has been some recovery in the forex turnover during 2009-10, it has not yet picked up to the pre-crisis levels. The volatility in exchange rate, measured in terms of the difference between high and low remained elevated since July 2008 but subsided somewhat from the beginning of 2009-10 after the introduction of the forex swap facility by the RBI from November 7, 2008.

Volatility has always been an essential feature of foreign exchange markets, it is only after the onset of the global financial crisis in 2007 that it has increased exponentially. Over a two month period, the rupee has been on a roller coaster ride, gaining nearly 7 per cent in September, 2012 and losing 4 per cent in October, 2012. Consequently, banks and corporate entities have to reckon with a far higher degree of exchange risk than ever before.[22]

The RBI has been taking steps to minimise volatility. The supply of dollars to the domestic market has been encouraged by relaxing relevant rules on inward remittances while, as a general strategy that is the right thing to do, some of the specific steps are controversial. The greater leeway given to companies, for instance, to fund their long-gestation projects in India through short-period external commercial borrowings smacks of myopia. It will result in a balooning of near-term external debt and that will not be good news for the balance of payments. Even more to the point, the RBI has found that many corporates run a serious exchange rate risk by not hedging their foreign exchange positions on the repayment of these loans.

The reasons vary from unfamiliarity with hedging techniques — in which case banks need to strengthen their customer education programmes — to a dangerous tendency to speculate in foreign exchange rate movements. The RBI has tried to counter such practices by tightening the rules and directing banks to monitor uncovered foreign exchange exposures move closely.

C. FINANCIAL INSTITUTIONS

C1. Innovation, Diversification and Restructuring of Term-financing institutions

Accelerating liberalization and deregulation coupled with radical reforms in financial sector, rapid technological developments and fierce competition in the wake of sharp increase in the pace of innovation and structural changes in the international financial markets brought about tremendous changes in corporate policies and strategies and so also business mix of Indian financial institutions, thereby blurring the distinction between money and capital market institutions and changing their fundamental character from mere lending institutions to full-fledged financial institutions and catalytic agents of growth.

With a view to overcoming challenges of the emerging competitive environment, Indian financial institutions re-oriented their strategies to bring about innovation in their products and diversify their activities — both fund-based and non-fund based. Until recently, these institutions confining themselves to dispensing loans to traditional industrial sectors located in a few advanced regions of the country. Except UTI, no financial institution endeavoured to mobilize savings of the community. In fact, they performed the role of a channeliser rather a financial intermediary. However, financial institutions, sensing the ferocity of competition ushered in by change in the Government policy, transcended their traditional role to assume the role of a full fledged financial institution to render various financial services to the needy entrepreneurs in addition to project finance.

Thus, Industrial Financial Corporation of India (IFCI), Industrial Credit and Investment Corporation of India (ICICI) and Industrial Development Bank of India made direct access to new issue market, since the traditional sources of Government guaranteed and other low cost funds were on the wane to raise funds. The IDBI Act was amended in 1995 to enable them to undertake fund raising functions. The IFCI was reconstituted as a company under the Companies Act to impart higher degree of operational flexibility.

As a financier, term financial corporations recently decided to bring about innovation of new products, diversify into new business and improve the quality of products and services so as to attain internationally accepted standards as linkages are developed with overseas market participants and these face competitive challenges more effectively. Although project finance has had been the sheet anchor of their business, the financial corporations embraced financial services in recent few years. They diversified both fund-based and non-fund based activities, and took up project counseling, loan syndication and debenture trusteeship assignments. Besides, financial corporations introduced variegated schemes of leasing equipment, equipment procurement, equipment credit, supplier's credit, buyer's credit, finance to hire purchase, financial leasing and hire purchase concerns, supply non-revolving line of credit to machinery and equipment and computer manufacturing concerns for sale of their products, modernization of sugar, textile and jute industries, financing of corporate hospitals and multi-disciplinary health centres and providing assistance for technological upgradation. Venture capital schemes were also introduced by financial institutions to inculcate entrepreneurship among the qualified technocrats. The IDBI also provided on a large scale bridge loans against public rights issues in view of the increasing number of companies accessing the capital market for financing their projects.

Following the metamorphic changes in economic policy of the Government in 1991 financial institutions launched a new scheme for working capital finance. As a matter of fact, these institutions are now focusing more on short-term lendings because of their high exposure to infrastructural projects causing asset-liability mismatch. They are trying to reduce their average credit maturity by emphasizing on short-term lending not exceeding a period of three years.

Indian financial institutions have also started rendering merchant banking services to provide professional advice and services to entrepreneurs in formulating and implementing projects and helping them in raising capital from the market and availing of financial assistance from various financial intermediaries.

Introduction of the concept of consortium financing and lead institution in project financing, standardization of common forms and legal documents and installation of inter-institutional mechanism by all-India financial institutions are some of the steps which were taken so as to ensure quick and convenient supply of assistance to industrial enterprises. The formalized system of consortium financing is now being replaced by an informal system of loan syndication. The mandatory convertibility clause on institutional loan has been abolished.

Entry of term financing institutions like IDBI, ICICI, UTI and SIDBI and HDFC in banking business is another striking development which took place in recent years. As a matter of fact, these institutions set up banks as their subsidiaries to undertake normal banking operations in the long run. Further, these financial institutions have also embraced short-term financing activity and started providing working capital to the corporates.

Another historic move taken by the Government recently was opening of the insurance sector to both domestic and foreign institutions. Thus, the enactment of the Insurance Regulatory and Development Authority (IRDA) Act, 1999 allowed banks and private players to do insurance business subject to the fulfillment of certain terms and conditions. Thus, the IDBI, ICICI, HDFC, SBI and other banks entered into insurance business.

In another respect too, capital markets witnessed phenomenal growth. The spread of the equity culture amongst savers led to mushroom growth of non-bank financed companies (NBFCs). These non-banks encroached upon the turf exclusively reserved for the commercial banks in the past. A greater overlap in product coverage has occurred between commercial banks and non-banks as both are performing the intermediation function.

Mutual funds have emerged as popular institutions to garner savings of the people since 1987 when leading public sector banks and insurance companies set up their own funds. Thus, till 1992, eight new mutual funds were sponsored by the SBI, CanBank, PNB, Indian Bank, Bank of Baroda, Life Insurance Corporation (LIC) and General Insurance Corporate of India (GIC). The industry gained buoyancy from 1993 onwards when it was opened for private sector to infuse greater competitions in the capital market. As a result, a number of mutual funds were opened by big corporate houses, development financial institutions, *viz.*, IDBI, ICICI and HDFC and foreign asset management companies (such as, by Morgan Stanley and DSP Merrill Lynch). Of historic significance is the development in February 2003 (following the repeal of the UTI Act, 1963). When UTI was bifurcated into two separate entities, called specified undertaking of UTI and UTI Mutual Fund Ltd. Over the past four decades, the industry has, however, grown manifold in terms of players, schemes and unit holders. It has also witnessed several innovations and upgradation of skills of the agency forces, rationalizations of product distribution arrangements continuous R&D for improved product handling and phased shifts from scheme-oriented investor services to single window personalized client oriented services.

While the last decade of 20th century witnessed innovation, sophistication and diversification in operations of development financial institutions (DFIs), restructuring and reorganization of these institutions has been the phenomenon since the beginning of 21st century. In their relentless endeavour to improve productivity, profitability, make their operations cost effective and enhance their competitiveness in fiercely competitive environment, DFIs, at the instance of the Government of India, pursued restructuring strategy. Several policy initiatives have been taken to facilitate the process of transition of DFIs opting for conversion into banks through a series of measures aimed at financial restructuring so as to embrace the character of an universal bank and provide wide variety of financial services to customers under one roof. Both ICICI and IDBI decided to reposition themselves to become one of the largest universal banks in the country to meet global challenges and opted for merger route. ICICI merged with its erstwhile subsidiary ICICI Bank with effect from October, 2002 and IDBI with IDBI Bank with effect from October 2004. The RBI issued a notification in September, 2004 to incorporate IDBI as a scheduled bank under the RBI Act. Top non-banking finance companies (NBFCs) are being directed by RBI to convert themselves into banks provided they fulfill the very stiff criteria. Thus, the activities of these DFIs, like investment banking, advisory services, merchant banking services are extended by the new entities making them universal banks.

Close on the heels of the merger of IDBI with IDBI Bank, a move is on to merge IFCI with the new entity so as to create a mega bank with a development finance role. As per the plans, the Stressed Assets Stabilization Fund (SASF) would form the vehicle for the revival of sick assets of IFCI that have a substantial commonality amongst the institutions like IDBI, IFCI and IIBI.

Likewise, during the last few years, the Government took several measures to contain the fallout of the events in the UTI which adversely affected investors' perception and to improve working of the Trust. Accordingly, on August 31, 2002, the Unit Trust of India Act, 1963 was repealed through an ordinance on October 30, 2002. The ordinance also sought to restructure the UTI by splitting it into two parts, *viz.*, UTI-I comprising US-64 and assured return schemes to be placed under a Government appointed Administrator, and UTI-II, later named as UTI Mutual Fund (UTIMF) consisting of the NAV-based schemes, professionally managed and brought under the regulatory purview of SEBI. At present, all the schemes of UTI-I are being managed by specified undertaking of UTI run by the Administrator. The Government also signed a Memorandum of Undertaking with the four sponsors of UTIMF, *viz.*, State Bank of India, Punjab National Bank, Bank of Baroda and LIC, which marked the transition of UTI from a hybrid institution to a mutual fund.

The Government is also contemplating to merge Infrastructure Development Finance Corporation (IDFCI) with SBI so as to enable the former to meet the burgeoning infrastructural needs of the economy more effectively.

C.2 Changing Profile of Indian Banking Industry

The profile of Indian banking industry has undergone tectonic transformation during the post liberalization period. Various policy initiatives of the Government and the RBI changed the basic character of Indian banking from class banking to mass banking, from one engaged in short-term lending and offering pure deposit type products to universal banking, offering a bouquet of customized products through multiple channels to wide spectrum of customers.

Dynamism in banking system has been witnessed in every domain of banking business including creation and intensification of competitive environment, ownership of banks, corporate governance, diversification of business, adoption of the financial inclusion in bank financing, focus on customer service, financial literacy, strengthening of institutional machinery and restructuring of banks.

The post-reform period has also witnessed unprecedented growth of banking industry not only in terms of number of banking branches and consequent increase in banking penetration but also in quantum leap on resource mobilization and change in structure of deposits, as reflected in growing predominance of time deposits in total bank deposits.

There has also been remarkable progress regarding deployment of funds by banks. There has been wondrous surge in bank credit, resulting in rise in its proportion to the GDP. Pattern of credit distribution has also undergone change.

Following the Government and the RBI policy of financial inclusion and increased access to formal financial system by the unprivileged and deprived sections of the society, the commercial banks in India have adopted multi-pronged strategy to channel their resources. They are trying to reach the poor people in unbanked areas through self-help groups and business-correspondents.

Post reform period has also witnessed tremendous improvement in financial health of banking industry, particularly in terms of improvement in productivity, operating earnings, profitability, capital adequacy and quality of assets. However, there still remains scope for banks to expand their asset base in relation to their input usage by adopting innovations in product technology and to control operating cost. There is also a strong need to improve further the efficiency and productivity of banks through reduction of intermediation cost, operating cost, improvement in labour productivity and enhancing non-interest sources of income.

D. CONCLUSIONS

Indian financial system has undergone tremendous transformation during the post liberalization period in terms of increased breadth and depth of financial markets, enhanced resilience, dynamism and sophistication of financial institutions and evolution of innovative financial products. Financial institutions in their endeavour to survive and thrive in competitive environment have changed their strategy and pursued new paradigm and business models.

Incredible interventions of the RBI have helped widening and deepening the money market in India particularly with reference to magnitude of business in different segments of the market, broadened participation, new instruments and technologies, increased transparency and improved signaling mechanism of monetary policy. This led to the emergence of liquid and vibrant money market in the country. However, there is still a need to develop the market further and increase integration of various segments of the money market in order to ensure greater financial stability.

Post liberalization period has witnessed significant development in capital market in India, as reflected in institutionalization and sophistication of the market, strengthening of equity market, expansion of secondary market, and demutualization of stock exchanges.

Consequent upon various initiatives of the Government and its agencies, new issue market in India has witnessed phenomenal changes, both quantitatively and qualitatively, increasing depth and sophistication of the operations of the market as also resilience of the market to cope with the new economic challenges. It compares with other emerging economies. However, the growth of debt and equity market remains low and largely skewed in comparison to the U.S., Malaysia and South Korea. A host of factors such as inadequate information disclosures, overpricing of issues, high transaction costs, etc. have stonewalled the full-fledged growth of the new issue market of the country.

Indian secondary market has also witnessed perceptible dynamism and vibrance in terms of proliferation of trading, improvement in trading and settlement infrastructure, risk management systems and levels of transparency leading to improved liquidity and reduced cost. Increased institutionalization of the market, demutualization of stock exchanges and short-selling were other remarkable developments during post-reform period.

There has been substantial development of the foreign exchange market in India during the post-reform period. Market participants have become sophisticated and acquired expertise in using various instruments and managing risks. With increasing global integration, efficiency in the foreign exchange market has improved as is evident from the low bid-ask spreads. However, outbreak of global financial crisis affected FII inflows, ECBs and trade credit, exerting pressure on the foreign exchange market of the country and concomitant increase in volatility in exchange rate.

Post-liberalization period has witnessed remarkable change in strategies and business models of financial institutions, changing their basic character from mere lending institutions to full-fledged financial institutions and catalytic agents of growth.

The whole profile of Indian banking industry has also undergone cataclysmic change during the post liberalization period because of the various policy initiatives of the Government and the RBI since 1991. The commercial banks assumed the character of universal banks offering bouquet of banking and non-banking products to wide sections of the society. There has been unprecedented expansion of banking industry during the post-reform period, especially in terms of number of branches, increase in banking penetration, mobilization of resources, and pattern of credit deployment. Financial health of the Indian banks — both public and private sectors — has significantly improved.

KEY TERMS

- Bolt
- Call Money Market
- Class Banking
- Collateralised borrowings and lendings
- Commercial Paper
- Demutualization
- Derivatives
- Financial Inclusion
- Liquidity adjustment Facility
- Mass Banking
- MMMFS
- OTCEI
- Primary Dealers
- Securities lending and borrowing
- Short Selling
- Treasury Bills
- Universal Banks

DISCUSSION QUESTIONS

1. In what respects has money market in India developed during the post liberalization period? What measures did the RBI take to strengthen the money market in the country?
2. What policy initiatives were taken by the RBI to replace administered interest rate by market-based interest rate?
3. "Recent policy initiatives of the RBI have deepened and broadened various segments of Indian money market." Comment.
4. "Despite significant improvement in the operations of Indian money market, there is still a need to further develop the money market." In the light of this statement, list out the steps that should be taken to improve dynamism of the market.
5. Bring out the recent developments in Indian capital market.
6. Discuss, in brief, various measures taken by the Government to develop new issue market in India.
7. How far have the various policy initiatives of the Government impacted the post-liberalization period?
8. What reformatory measures were undertaken during the post-liberalization period to develop stock market in the country?
9. How has Indian stock market improved its efficiency, liquidity and risk management systems in recent years?

10. In what respects has foreign exchange market in India improved during the post-reform period?
11. Trace out the recent developments in financial institutions in India.
12. "Various reformatory measures initiated by the Government and the RBI during the past decades have changed the basic character of Indian banking industry." Comment.

REFERENCES

1. RBI Annual Report, 2000-01, p. 82.
2. RBI Annual Report, 2002-03, p. 188.
3. Business Standard, March 8, 2011.
4. RBI Annual Report, 2006-07, pp. 147-148.
5. RBI Report on Currency and Finance, 2008-09, p. 202.
6. RBI Annual Report, 2000-01, p. 82.
7. RBI Report on Currency and Finance, 2008-09, p. 211.
8. RBI Annual Report, 2009-10.
9. Business Standard, June 9, 2011.
10. RBI Annual Report, 2004-05.
11. Business Standard, April 5, 2013.
12. Business Standard, July 26, 2011.
13. RBI Annual Report, 2009-10.
14. Business Standard, April 4, 2011.
15. Business Standard, December 13, 2012.
16. Business Standard, July 12, 2011.
17. Business Standard, September 2011.
18. RBI Report on Currency and Finance, 2008-09, pp. 213-14.
19. Business Line, November 6, 2007.
20. Business Today, May 31, 2009.
21. Business Standard, December 13, 2012.
22. Hindu, November 9, 2012.

Management of Commercial Banks in India

Section Two

Section II: Learning Objectives

The present section aims at:

- Providing a succinct view of Reserve Bank of India.
- Providing deep insights into the pattern of Development of Commercial Banks in India and Retail Banking Business.
- Familiarising with the Fundamentals of Corporate Governance in Commercial Banks.
- Evolving Strategy to meet Challenges to Indian Commercial Banks.
- Focusing on Commerical Banks Restructuring.
- Dilating upon Human Resource Management in Commercial Banks.
- Analysing Managerial Aspects of Capital and Deposits.
- Shedding lurid light on Relationship Banking.
- Acquainting with Managerial Dimensions of Bank Credit
- Providing an understanding of Asset-Liability Approach in Commercial Banks.
- Assessing Efficiency of Commercial Banks in India

Section Two

Section Outline

- Reserve Bank of India — Karnel of Indian Banking System
- Commercial Banking in India.
- Financial Deepening and Inclusion.
- Retail Banking in India.
- Corporate Governance in Commercial Banks.
- Strategy to meet Competitive Challenges to Commercial Banks in India.
- Commercial Bank Restructuring.
- Strategic Human Resource Management in Commercial Banks.
- Management of Capital Funds in Commercial Banks.
- Management of Deposits by Banks.
- Relationship Banking.
- Management of Loans in Commercial Banks.
- New Norms of Working Capital Financing by Banks.
- Asset-Liability Management in Commercial Banks.
- Management of NPAs in Commercial Banks.
- Management of Income in Commercial Banks.
- Operational Efficiency of Commercial Banks in India.
- Performance Budgeting in a Commercial Bank.
- Zero-Base Budgeting in a Commercial Bank.

Reserve Bank of India (RBI) — Karnel of Indian Banking System

Learning Objectives:

The present chapter aims at:

- Familiarizing with the objectives and tasks of the RBI
- Throwing light on structure of the RBI
- Providing deep insights iinto the RBI's monetary policy

Chapter Outline:

- Epilogue.
- Global evolution of central banking.
- Historical antecedents of central banking in India.
- Objectives and tasks of the RBI.
- Structure of the RBI.
- Monetary policy of the RBI.
- Conclusions.

A. EPILOGUE

The most important player in financial markets throughout the world is Central bank — the exclusive authority in charge of monetary policy. The Central bank's actions affect interest rates, the amount of credit, and the money supply, all of which have direct impacts not only on financial markets but also on aggregate output and inflation. It is, therefore, pertinent to understand how Central banks have evolved around the world as also in India, role that they play in financial markets and the overall economy, how monetary policy is conducted and what challenges they are facing in performing their operations.

B. GLOBAL EVOLUTION OF CENTRAL BANKING

Evolution of central banking is essentially a twentieth century phenomenon as there were only about a dozen central banks in the world at the turn of twentieth century. In contrast, at present, there are nearly 160 central banks. This is reflection of the pressing need for effective central banking authority to cope with growing business and banking complexities. The many vicissitudes experienced by banks and their depositors inevitably led to cries for their regulation. Growing member of states during the twentieth century was also responsible for proliferation of central banks as a latter is essentially a nation state phenomenon. During the twentieth century the need was strongly felt to constitute central monetary authority to issue currency; to be a banker and lender to the government; to regulate and supervise banks and financial entities, and to serve as a lender of last resort.

C. HISTORICAL ANTECDENTS OF CENTRAL BANKING IN INDIA

Evolution of central banking in India can be traced to the 18th century when the Governor of Bengal in British India recommended the establishment of a General Bank in Bengal and Bihar. Accordingly, the Bank was established in 1773. However, it was wound up subsequently. It was in the early 20th century that, consequent to the recommendations of the Champerlain Commission (1914), proposing the amalgamation of the three Presidency Banks, the Imperial Bank of India was constituted in 1921 to carry out the functions of central banking in addition to commercial banking. In 1926, Hilton Young Commission (the Royal Commission on Indian currency and Finance) recommended for the establishment of a Central bank to be designated as the Reserve Bank of India so as to augment banking facilities across the country. Accordingly, a Bill to establish RBI was introduced in Parliament and passed in 1934 and the RBI Act came into force on January 1, 1935. The RBI was inaugurated on April 1, 1935 as a shareholders' institution and the Act provided for the appointment by the Central Government of the Governor and two Deputy Governors. The RBI was nationalised on January 1, 1949 in terms of the Reserve Bank of India (Transfer to Public Ownership) Act, 1948.[1]

D. OBJECTIVES AND TASKS OF THE RBI

The objectives of the RBI, as laid down in the Preamble, are to regulate the issue of bank notes and keep reserves with a view to securing monetary stability in India and generally to operate the currency and credit system of the country to its advantage.

So as to achieve the above objectives, the RBI has been assigned the responsibility of maintaining the external value of the rupee, acting as bankers' bank, Government bank, playing developmental role and ensuring better customer services.

◈ Maintaining Exchange Stability

The RBI as a central bank is endowed with the major responsibility of maintaining the external value of the rupee. Until 1975, the rupee was linked with pound sterling. In late 1975, the rupee was delinked from pound sterling and the value was determined with reference to a basket of currencies until 1991. Thereafter, the exchange rate regime shifted from a basket-linked managed float to a market-based system in March 1993, after a short experiment with a dual exchange rate regime between March 1992 and February 1993.

The RBI seeks to maintain the stability of the exchange value of the rupee through its domestic policies and the regulation of the foreign exchange market. As a regulator of the foreign exchange market, the RBI is seized with the task of administering the foreign exchange control, choosing the exchange rate system and fixing or managing the exchange rate between the rupee and other currencies, managing exchange reserves and negotiating with the monetary authorities of different countries of the world and with international financial institutions such as the IMF, World Bank and Asian Development Bank.

◈ Banker's Bank

As a banker's bank the RBI acts as a source of reserves to the banking system and serves as a lender of the last resort. The RBI has also been assigned the responsibility of ensuring that the banks are established and run on sound lines with focus on protecting the depositors' interests.

Following the large scale bank failures mainly due to ad hoc enactments such as the Banking Companies (Inspection) Ordinance, 1946 and the Banking Companies (Restriction on Branches) Act, 1946, the need for a statutory bank regulator became more pressing. Consequently, a special legislation called the Banking Companies Act was passed in March 1949, which was renamed as the Banking Regulation Act in March, 1966.

As banker's bank, the RBI controls the volume of reserves of commercial banks and thereby determines the deposits/credit creating ability of the banks.

As bankers' bank, the RBI regularly monitors and supervises operations of the commercial banks. At present, the RBI uses CAMELS (Capital adequacy, Asset quality, Management, earnings, liquidity and systems and control) method to assign ratings to Indian banks. CAMELS, which goes from A+ to D is assigned to a bank while finalising annual financial inspection (AFI) report.

The RBI has found the CAMELS method of rating inadequate as it represents only bank's past year performance and does not capture the risks that could cause a bank to fail. As such, the RBI decided in September, 2012 to replace CAMELS by INROADS (Indian Risk-oriented and Dynamic Rating System) from the next round of annual financial inspection in 2013.

◈ Government Banker

The RBI also performs the function of an agent and advisor of the Government. As the government banker, it administers the government departments, boards and organizations; it makes temporary advances to the government when needed. On behalf of the government the RBI manages public debt, issue of new loans and treasury bills. It also negotiates, on behalf of the government, with foreign countries on matters pertaining to currencies and acts as advisor to the government on international finance. It also helps the government in the formulation of its economic, trade and financial policies.

With the onset of economic planning, the RBI's role as the government banker tended to be diversified. With the emancipation from centuries old colonial rule, the RBI has decided to play active role in the nation building process. This it strived through large public investment facilitated by accommodative monetary and enabling debt management policies. The role of the RBI in bridging the resource gap of the Government in plan financing by monetizing government debt and maintaining interest rates at artificially low levels for government securities to reduce the cost of government borrowing has been considerably significant.

However, it was noted with concern that a fiscal-monetary-inflation nexus led to monetization of fiscal deficit filled inflation. The RBI, therefore, decided to restrict the monetary impact of budgetary imbalances by raising the required reserve ratios to be maintained by banks. Since the growth of pre-empted resources was not sufficient to cater to the government's requirements, it has to perforce borrow funds from outside the captive market through postal savings and provident funds by offering substantial fiscal incentives and at administered low rates of interest. This pushed the money into the throes of financial repression.

So as to check the unbridled automatic monetization of fiscal deficits, the First Supplemental Agreement between the RBI and the Government of India was entered into on September 9, 1994 to set out a system of limits for creation of ad hoc Treasury Bills during the three-year period ending March, 1997. In pursuance of the Second Supplemental Agreement between the RBI and the Government of India on March 6, 1997, the ad hoc Treasury Bills were completely phased out by converting the outstanding amount into special undated securities and were replaced by a system of 'Way and Means Advances'. The participation by the RBI in primary auctions of the Government has also been discontinued with effect from April, 2006 under the provision of Fiscal Responsibility and Budget Management Act, 2003 (FRBM).[2] Similar other measures, that have been initiated since 1991, are deregulation of interest rates and lowering of statutory ratios.

As Government banker, the RBI is endowed with the role of regulating and supervising financial system and institutions so as to prevent systematic risk, avoid financial crisis, protect depositors' interest and reduce asymmetry of information between depositors and financial institutions. Earlier, the RBI's role in this regard was limited because of predominant Government ownership of banks with more than 90 percent of banking assets owned by the Government by the 1990s.

However, after the change in banking policy in 1991 focusing on competitiveness, deregulation of interest rate and elimination of credit allocation, the RBI's regulatory and supervisory role increased. In the wake of introduction of competition through entry of new private sector banks and expansion of foreign banks along with the philosophy of equal regulatory treatment of private and public sector banks, there was a strong need for adoption of modern regulation and supervision. This was further reinforced for the sake of promoting safety and soundness of the banking system and protection of depositors.

The thrust of the RBI, while playing the role of a regulator and supervisor, has been to ensure that banks are financially robust, well managed and that they do not pose a threat to the interest of their depositors. The RBI shifted its emphasis from the traditional Capital Assets, Management, Earnings, Liquidity and Interest rate sensitivity approach to a more risk-based approach in sync with Basel II's three-pillar concept of minimum capital requirements, supervisory review and market discipline.

In consonance with changed economic milieu the RBI has changed its role of financial regulation and supervision, laying less emphasis on 'micro' regulation but more focus on 'prudential' supervision and risk assessment and containment. As the Commercial banks are scheduled to start implementing Basel II with effect from March end, 2007 (now extended to March end 2008), the RBI will continue to lay focus on supervisory capacity building measures to identify the gaps and to assess as well as to quantify the extent of additional capital which banks have to maintain to cope with operational and market risks.

In view of the importance of consolidation, competition and risk management to the future of banking, the RBI will continue to lay accent on corporate governance, ownership pattern of private banks, expansion of foreign banks and financial inclusion.

Another role which the RBI has begun playing more effectively after liberalization of the economy in 1991 was in the sphere of the development of financial markets, especially the money, government securities and forex markets in view of their critical role in the transmission mechanism of monetary policy. The money market is the focal point for intervention by the RBI to equilibrate short-term liquidity flows on account of its linkages with the foreign exchange market. Likewise, the government securities market has become significant for the entire debt market since it serves as a benchmark to price other debt market instruments.

The RBI has pursued a gradual and well-calibrated policy to facilitate the development of markets through institutional and financial structure by improving market microstructure.

There has been close coordination between the Central Government and the RBI, as also between different regulatory bodies, which helped in orderly and smooth development of the financial markets in India. The new economic and financial policies leading to inorganic growth in size, depth and activity have paved way for flexible use of indirect instruments by the RBI to achieve its objectives. The RBI has been continuously seized with revisiting and refining its operating procedures and instruments as also various aspects of financial institutions, markets and financial infrastructure in line with global best practices.

◈ Development Function

Unlike Central banks in developed countries, the RBI has assumed the role of fostering growth of the economy since its inception. The thrust of the RBI's developmental role has been to raise the savings ratio to enhance investment necessary for growth. In this endeavour, the RBI has played crucial role in establishing a myriad of specialized financial institutions in the agricultural, industrial and infrastructural sectors and in widening the facilities for term-finance and for facilitating the institutionalization of savings. It was because of incredible efforts made by the RBI, institutions like the Industrial Finance Corporation, State Finance Corporations, Industrial Credit and Investment Corporation of India, Infrastructure Development Finance Corporation, Unit Trust of India, National Bank for Agricultural and Rural Development, National Housing Bank, Discount and Finance of India, and Clearing Corporation of India were set up with its varying degrees of involvement.

More recently, the Board for Regulation and Supervision of Payment and Settlement System was constituted in 2005 and the Banking Codes and Standards Board of India in 2006 to develop a comprehensive code of conduct for fair treatment of banks customers.

The RBI has been continuously involved in setting up or supporting these institutions with varying degrees of involvement, including equity contributions and extension of lines of credit.

Although the RBI has been actively involved in setting up financial institutions and evolving financial systems, its general practice has been to hive them off as they come of age, or if a perception arose of potential conflict of interest. There can be little doubt that the establishment of these institutions has helped financial development in the country greatly, even though some of them have been less than successful in their operations.[3]

Another developmental role of the RBI, which is common to most central banks, is the development of efficient payment and settlement system which is essential for successful conduct of modern financial system. Until the constitution of the RBI, clearing associations were formed in the presidency towns and the final settlement between member banks was effected by means of cheques drawn on the Presidency Banks and establishment of the Imperial Bank in 1921, settlement was done through cheques on that bank. After the establishment of the RBI in 1935, the Clearing houses in the Presidency Towns were taken over by the RBI, and continued for more than five decades.

Taking cognizance of the significance of payment and settlement systems, the RBI took upon itself the responsibility of setting up a safe, efficient and robust payment and settlement system for the country for more than a decade now.

Very recently, the RBI introduced "Real Time Gross Settlement (RTGS)" system which has been operationalized since March 2004. This was done with a view to further improving payment and settlement system. It is believed that this system once fully operationalized would take care of all kinds of inter-bank transactions.

Sensing positive response to cataclysmic reforms in the financial sector and the consequent changes in banking practices, the RBI has, of late, decided to delegate the actual management of retail payment and settlement systems to the Commercial banks. Thus, the Commercial banks have now taken over the task of setting up new MICR based cheque processing centres. In view of satisfactory result of this approach the RBI is thinking to get the normal processing functions arranged and operated by professional organizations which could be set up through participation of Commercial banks. This would also be applicable to the Clearing Houses which will perform the clearing activities. However, the settlement function will continue to rest with the RBI.

It is along this line that the Clearing Corporation of India Ltd., has been entrusted with the task of affecting the clearing processes related to money, government securities and foreign exchange market. But the RBI will continue to have regulatory supervision over such operations. The RTGS, which provides for funds transfers across participants in electronic mode with reduced risk, will continue to be operated by the RBI.

◈ Customer Centric Function

One of the crucial functions of the RBI has been the protection of the interests of the bank depositors. In fact, the RBI's mandate for depositor's protection is enshrined in a statute dating as far back as 1949 when concepts like customer service, customer experience, customer relationship and customer centricity did not find an entry into the lexicon of the linking world.

As the regulator of the banking sector, the RBI has been seized, from its inception, with the task of reviewing, examining and evaluating customer service in the banks. It has been rejigging the progress periodically and has been continually spurring the Indian banks to become more customer friendly and customer centric in its conduct and business practices.[4]

Sensing a general feeling that the customer does not get satisfactory service even after demanding it and there has been a disenchanment of the depositors, the RBI has had abiding concern for high quality customer service and played enduring in enabling customer empowerment and re-enfranchisement of the customer. Although on set of competitive environment during the post-reform period was expected to provide high-quality customer service to meet the long-standing aspirations of the bank customers, the RBI felt that the forces of competition alone could not ensure at a justifiable price, determined in a transparent manner. Accordingly, the RBI took initiatives to put in place the requisite institutional mechanisms in order to improve quality of customer service in the banking sector. Highlights of important steps taken recently by the RBI to improve customers services are discussed below:

(i) Banking Ombudsman Scheme

With a view to providing an expeditious and inexpensive forum to bank customers for resolution of their grievances regarding banking services, the RBI introduced the Banking Ombudsman scheme way back in 1995. The scheme was revised in 2002 and then in 2006 to cover several new areas of customer complaints. Under the revised scheme, the complainants can file their complaints in any form, including online and can also appeal to the RBI against the awards and other decisions of the Banking Ombudsman.

(ii) Customer Service set up in the Banks

Following the recommendations of Tarapore Committee appointed by the RBI in December 2003 on Procedure and Performance Audit of Public Services (CPPAPS – Tarapore Committee) to suggest improvement in the quality of customer service rendered by banks, the RBI directed the banks to put in place an institutional machinery comprising of (a) a Customer Service Committee of the Board including, as invitees, experts and representatives of customers, to enable the bank to formulate policies and assess the compliance thereof internally, (b) Standing Committee of Executives on customer service to periodically review the policies and procedures and working of the bank's own grievance redressal machinery; and (c) a nodal department official for customer service at the Head office and each controlling office, whom customers with grievances could approach in the first instance and with whom the Banking Ombudsman (BO) and the RBI could laise.

(iii) Customer Service Department in the RBI

So as to provide focused attention to the customer service dimension of the banking sector, the RBI set up a new department, called Customer Service Department, on July 1, 2006 to carry out a variety of activities relating customer service and grievance redressal in the RBI and the banking sector including matters pertaining to the Banking Ombudsman Scheme and the Banking Codes and Standards Board of India.

(iv) Banking Codes and Standards Board of India (BCSBI)

In view of the existence of the institutional gap in measuring the performance of the banks against codes and standards based on established global best practices, the RBI set up the Banking Codes and Standards Board of India (BCSBI). The BCSBI, an autonomous and independent body, provides for voluntary registration of banks with the Board as its members and committing to provide customer services as per the agreed standards and codes. The Board monitors and assesses the compliance with codes and standards which the banks have agreed to. In July 2006, the Board released a code of Bank's Commitment to customers to provide a framework for a minimum standard of banking services. By setting the minimum standards of reliability, transparency and accountability in the provision of customer service, the code outlines how each bank is expected to deal with the customer's day-to-day requirements, and accordingly, what each customer could reasonably expect from his/her bank. So far, as many as 70 out of 74 Scheduled banks are registered with the Board.

(v) Fair Practices Codes for Lenders

The RBI has also been concerned to ensure fair deal to the borrowing community from the bankers. Accordingly, it formulated a Fair Practices Code for Lenders which was communicated to the banks in 2003 to safeguard the rightful interest of the borrowers and guard against undue hassles by the lenders. The code was revised in March, 2007 to include the requirement that the banks should provide to the borrowers' comprehensive details regarding the loans as also the reasons for rejection of the loan applications of the prospective borrowers.

(vi) Transparency and Reasonableness of Bank Charges

In order to ensure fair practices in banking services, the RBI has made it obligatory for the banks to display and update on an ongoing basis, in their offices/branches as also on the home page of their websites, the details of various service charges and fees, in a format approved by the RBI, to provide for better comparability.

The RBI constituted a Working Group to formulate a scheme for ensuring reasonableness of bank charges and to incorporate the same in the Fair Practices Code; the compliance with which would be monitored by the BSCBI. The Group, which submitted its report in August 2006, has recommended broad principles for determining reasonableness of the bank charges for the identified basic banking services. The recommendations of the Group were accepted and conveyed to the banks for implementation in February, 2007.

(vii) Customer Service and Financial Inclusion

So as to ensure that banking facilities are available to the masses, especially the under privileged, pensioners, self employed and those employed in the unorganized sector, the RBI has decided to implement policies to encourage the banks which provide extensive services while disincentivising those which were not responsive to the banking needs of the community. The RBI also monitors the nature, scope and cost of services rendered by the banks with a view to ascertaining if there was denial, implicit or explicit, of the basic banking services to the common person. Accordingly, the banks were directed to review their existing practices to align them with the objective of financial inclusion.

Further, the RBI advised the banks in November 2005 to make available a basic banking 'no-frills' account either with 'nil' or very low minimum balances as well as charges that would marginal accounts accessible to vast sections of population. This was aimed at achieving the objective of greater financial inclusion. The banks were also advised to give wide publicity to the facility of such a 'no-frills' account indicating the facilities and charges in a transparent manner.

On July 1, 2010, the RBI issued Master Circular on customer service incorporating various issues, such as customer service, operations of deposit accounts, levy of service charges, service at counters, disclosure of information, operation of accounts by old and incapacitated persons, facilities to visually impaired persons, guardianship in deposit accounts, remittances, drop box facility, collection of instruments, dishonour of cheques, dealing with complaints, etc.

E. STRUCTURE OF THE RBI

The organization of the RBI can be divided into three parts, viz., Central Board of Directors, Local Boards and the offices of the RBI.

(i) The Central Board of Directors

The RBI operates under the overall supervision and control of the Central Board of Directors. The Central Board of Directors is composed of 20 members comprising one Governor, four deputy Governors and fifteen directors.

The Governor is the highest authority of the RBI. He is appointed by the Government of India for term of five years He can be reappointed for another term.

Four Deputy Governors are nominated by the Central Government for a term of five years.

Fifteen directors of the Central Board are appointed by the Central Government. Out of these, four directors, one each from four local boards are nominated by the Central Government.

Ten directors nominated by the Central Government are among the experts of commerce, industries, finance, economics and cooperation. The finance secretary of the Government of India is also nominated as Government officer in the Board for a period of 4 years. In December 2011, the RBI Act 1934 was amended to have two government representatives on the board. This was intended to improve coordination between the government and the central bank.

The Governor acts as the Chief Executive Officer and Chairman of the Central Board. In his absence, a deputy governor nominated by the Governor acts as the Chairman of the Board. The Deputy Governor and Government's Officer nominee are not entitled to vote at the meetings of the Board. The Governor and four deputy governors are full time officers of the RBI.

(ii) Local Boards

Besides the Central Board, there are local boards for four regional areas of the country with the headquarters at Mumbai, Kolkata, Chennai and New Delhi. Local boards consist of five members each, appointed by the Central Government for a term of four years to represent territorial and economic interests and the interest of co-operatives and indigenous banks. The function of local boards is to advise the Central Board on general and specific issues, referred to them and, to perform duties which the Central Board delegates. The final control of the RBI vests in the Central Board.

(iii) Offices of the RBI

The Head Office of the RBI is situated in Mumbai and the offices of local boards are situated in Delhi, Kolkata and Chennai. In order to maintain smooth working of banking system the RBI has opened local offices or branches in Ahmedabad, Bangalore, Bhopal, Bhubaneshwar, Chandigarh, Guwahati, Hyderabad, Jaipur, Kanpur, Nagpur, Patna, Jammu, Thiruvananthpuram, Kochi, Lucknow and Byculla (Mumbai). The RBI can open its offices with permission of the Government of India. In places where it has no offices, the RBI is represented by the State Bank of India and its associate banks as its agents.

The internal organizational set up of the RBI has been modified and expanded from time to time in order to cope with the increasing volume and range of the Bank's activities. The underlying principle of internal organization is functional specialisation with adequate coordination. In order to perform its various functions, the RBI has organised a large number of departments.

◆ Financial Supervision

The RBI performs this function under the guidance of Board for Financial Supervision (BFS). The Board was constituted in November, 1994 as a Committee of Central Board of Directors of the RBI. The Board is constituted by co-opting four directors from the Central Board as members for a term of 2 years and is chaired by the Governor. The deputy governors of the RBI are ex-officio members. One deputy governor, usually the deputy governor in charge of banking regulation and supervision, is nominated as the Vice-Chairman is nominated as the Vice-Chairman of Board BFS meetings.

The BFS is normally required to meet once every month. It considers inspection reports and other supervisory issues placed before it by the supervisory departments. The BFS oversees thc functioning of Department of Banking Supervision (DBS), Department of Non-Banking Supervision (DNBS) and Financial Institutions Division (FID) and gives directions on the regulatory and supervisory issues.

Organisation structure of the RBI is graphically shown in Figure 5.1.

Fig. 5.1

Organization Structure of the RBI

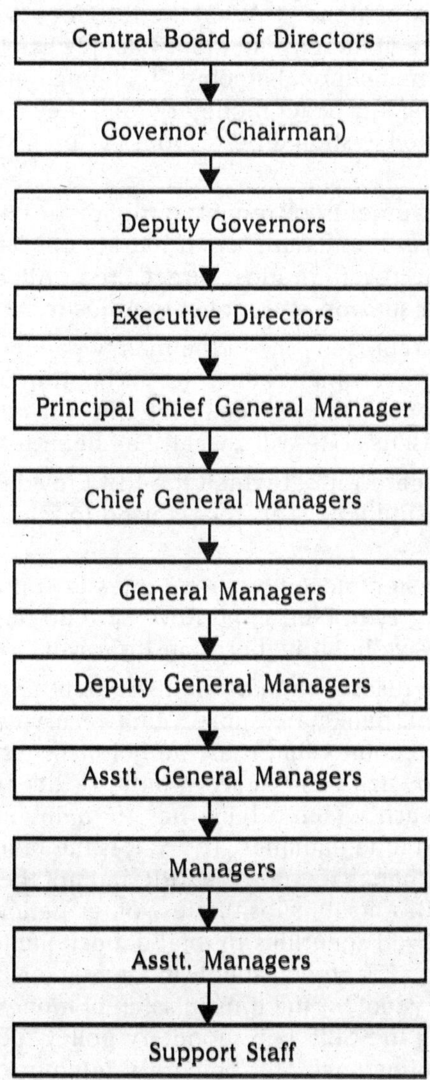

F. MONETARY POLICY OF THE RBI

◈ Monetary Policy Instruments of the RBI

One of the major responsibilities of the RBI is to formulate monetary policy and execute it in such a way as to promote full employment, economic growth, price stability and a sustainable pattern of international trade. Thrust of monetary policy is controlled expansion of bank credit and money supply with special attention to seasonal requirements for credit. The RBI is essentially concerned with managing supply of money in the light of price variations without affecting the output. The containment of inflationary pressures without jeopardising the growth potential has been the primal focus of the RBI's monetary policy.

It is important to note that the RBI believes in discretionary monetary policy and has refrained from prescribing any rigid monetary rule or rate of growth of money supply as a target in the course of monetary management. The approach to the question of the right quantum of monetary expansion is essentially an exercise in discretion rather than an application of mechanistic formula.[5] "Money supply does matter ... however, money supply is only an indicator of the demand pressures on the economy.... The pursuit of a sound monetary policy, therefore, is not as simple or mechanical a matter as might be implied by the deceptive simplicity of the Quantity Theory of Money."[6] What the RBI does is to state some kind of rough working rule such as ... "the rate of increase in money supply has to be somewhat higher than the projected rate of growth of real national income."[7] Although the monetary authorities have at times not refrained from fixing any exact monetary rule, they also seem to regard any such rule as harmful, for monetary policy should be responsive to changing economic scenario — both national and foreign.

The RBI uses various instruments of monetary policy to control supply of money and ensure price stability. These instruments are: open market operations, bank rate, Repo Rate and Reverse Repo rate, variable reserve ratios, Direct Credit Allocation and Credit rationing, selective credit controls, moral suasion and Liquidity Adjustment Facility.

Open market operations represent one of the main weapons of monetary control which involves purchase and sale of government securities in open market. There is no restriction on the quantity or maturity of government securities the RBI can buy or sell or hold. This instrument, as the following discussions will reveal, has been least used by the RBI.

The **Bank rate** is the standard rate at which the RBI provides financial accommodation to banks and other financial institutions. This tool is used to regulate the cost of financing of banks and other institutions.

In recent years, the RBI has employed two repo rates to control money supply vis., Repo rate, at which the RBI lends money to banks and Reverse repo rate at which the RBI borrows from banks. Repo rate has always been higher than the reverse repo rate.

The RBI also uses variable reserve ratio as an instrument to control the money supply in the economy. In this instrument, banks are subject to a reserve requirement ratio, which is proportionate to their deposit accounts that must be held as reserves. A bank is required to carry two kinds of reserve ratio, viz., Cash Reserve Ratio (CRR) and Statutory Liquidity Ratio (SLR). The CRR refers to the cash which a bank has to maintain with the RBI as a certain percentage of their demand and time liabilities. The SLR is the ratio of cash in hand (exclusive of cash balances maintained by banks to meet the CRR, but not the excess reserves), balances in current account with the SBI and its subsidiaries, other nationalised banks and the RBI; gold and unencumbered, approved securities to total deposit liabilities of banks. By changing the CRR and SLR the RBI tries to affect credit supply in the market. The Reserve Bank considers the CRR as more effective policy tool for the transmission of monetary policy than other policy rates. The Bank rules out using the SLR as a monetary policy tool, as it thinks any increase in this measure is retrogressive because of it being a safety pool of money and not a policy instrument.

Direct credit allocation and credit rationing is another credit control technique which the RBI employs to control credit supply. In this technique, the Bank seeks to allocate credit among different sectors, borrowers and users. A variant of this technique, which has been very much used, is to prescribe average and incremental credit-deposit ratio.

Selective Credit Controls (SCCs) are the most actively used technique in India. SCCs seek to change the composition of credit; they are used to reduce the supply of credit in certain directions and to encourage it in desired directions. The RBI uses SCCs normally in three forms: (*i*) fixation of margin requirements, (*ii*) fixation of separate minimum lending rates on credit covered by SCCs, and (*iii*) fixation of ceiling on ex-ante flows of credit.

Moral suasion is another most actively and consistently employed technique of monetary policy. It takes the form of writing letters and holding discussions between the RBI and the banks about trends in the economy in general and in money, credit and finance in particular, and about the measures which ought to be taken from time to time in the light of national objectives.

Introduction of Liquidity Adjustment Facility (LAF) by the RBI in June 2000 followed by refinement in May 2001 is an innovative instrument for modulating liquidity and signalling the monetary stance and for creating conditions for orderly market activity.

◈ The Monetary Policy Process of the RBI

In order to make monetary policy decisions central bank management assesses the current economic situation, using statistics on recent economic growth, inflation and the unemployment rate. It also reviews global economic conditions and their relationship with conditions of the house country. Then, the members of the management board discuss their main concerns about the domestic economy. They also consult the experts and stakeholders across the country before taking final monetary policy stance for a certain period.

The formulation of monetary policy in the RBI reflects an extensive consultative process where the views and suggestions of various stakeholders are solicited and analysed. While the pre-policy consultations with industry associations, bankers and economists contribute to the information set used for policy making, the surveys conducted by the RBI targeted at the common man, corporates and professional forecasters also provide important lead information. After the policy, as part of the communication process, questions from the press and analysts are answered, which help in receiving post-policy feedback. The Institutional framework for consultation on important technical aspects of policy making is a critical part of the monetary policy process in India.

The Technical Advisory Committee (TAC) on Monetary Policy reviews macroeconomic and monetary developments and advises the RBI Board on the stance of monetary policy and monetary measures. The TAC's role is advisory in nature and the responsibility, accountability and time path of decision-making remains entirely with the RBI. Between the usual quarterly cycles formalised for policy announcements, monetary measures can be announced at any point of time depending upon the evolving macroeconomic conditions.

In its attempt to render the policy making process move consultative, the RBI introduced with effect from October 2005, pre-policy consultation meetings with the IBA, market participants (FIMMDA, FEDAI and PDAI), representatives of trade and industry (CII, FICCI, ASSCHAM and FIEU), Credit Rating Agencies (CRISIL and ICRA) and other institutions (UCBs, MFIs, SMEs, NBFCs, rural cooperatives and RRBs). These meetings focus on macro-economic developments, liquidity position, interest rate environment and monetary and credit developments alongwith forward-looking suggestions. In addition, meetings are also held with economists, media persons, analysts and journalists on a half-yearly basis in April and October to know their views on the global/domestic macroeconomic situation and solicit their advice on monetary policy measures.

Institutional arrangements have been put in place internally to guide the policy formulation process. The inter-departmental Financial Markets Committee (FMC) holds a daily meeting to review developments in the money, foreign exchange and government securities markets as well as assess liquidity conditions to guide appropriate market interventions.

The Internal Monetary Policy Strategy Group meets regularly to review monetary and credit conditions and takes a medium-term view on the stance of the monetary policy. The inter-departmental technical group has been constituted to prepare reviews/forecasts of inflation and GDP growth for policy purposes. Besides, the inter-departmental corporate sector performance group submits quarterly reports on the performance and outlook for the private corporate sector.

The RBI also takes note of suggestions and feedback received through letters, e-mails or any other means of communication from stakeholders and individuals.

Given the complex nature of many challenges following the global crisis, the RBI had to scale up its usual consultative process. It organised the first International Research Conference to solicit the best possible suggestions at the international level on some such challenges that the RBI would have to deal with in future.

◈ Recent Trends in Conduct of the RBI's Monetary Policy

The monetary policy of the RBI has always been eclectic having accent on control of money supply, curb on the increase in money supply corresponding to inward remittances of foreign exchange and control on the requirement of credit for financing the purchase of foodgrains. However, in recent years there has been some change in this policy to the extent the role of money supply in the economy is stressed a little more now than before. According to the RBI Governor, "While the need to monitor the monetary aggregates has all along been recognized, in the recent period there has been a sharper focus on movements in the monetary aggregates.... our monetary policy deals essentially with the volume and cost of money."[8] Monetary policy, according to C. Rangarajan, concerns itself both with the regulation of money supply and interest rates.[9]

Following the policy of economic liberalisation and globalisation leading to increased integration of the Indian economy with global economies and emergence of market orientation, the role of the RBI has moved away from exercising control and discretion towards becoming an active player in the market through practising timely and effective intervention to modulate conditions and signal a policy stance.

A key feature of Indian monetary policy formulation during the post reform period has been to look at not only domestic factors but also at developments in the global economic situation, the international inflationary situation, interest rate scenario, exchange rate movements and capital flows. The RBI has been according due weightage to considerations relating to minimizing output and employment in addition to price stability.

Thus, the overall stance of monetary policy in India in recent years has been:

(*i*) To ensure a monetary and interest rate environment that supports export and investment demand in the economy so as to enable continuation of the growth momentum while re-inforcing price stability with a view to anchoring inflation expectations.

(*ii*) To maintain the emphasis on macroeconomic and in particular, financial stability.

(*iii*) To consider promptly all possible measures as appropriate to the evolving global and domestic situation.

Before the intensification of the global financial meltdown from September 2008, the monetary policy measures in the country were guided by an overriding intention to contain spiralling inflationary expectations that were largely driven by international commodity prices. Monetary policy was striving to dampen demand-side pressures through monetary tightening.[10] Accordingly, the RBI decided in March, 2007 to limit the daily reverse absorptions to a maximum of ₹ 3,000 crore to facilitate the maintenance of appropriate liquidity in the system and active liquidity management through the market stabilisation scheme (MSS). However, this ceiling was withdrawn subsequently from August, 2007. During 2006-07, the cash reserve ratio (CRR) of commercial banks was increased by 100 basis points in four stages to 6.00 per cent from 5.00 per cent of NDTL of the banks. During 2007-08, the CRR was further increased by 150 basis points in four stages to 7.50 per cent. During 2008-09, the CRR was further increased by

150 basis points and repo rate by 125 basis points to 9.00 for both. The Government of India, in consultation with the RBI raised the ceiling under the MSS from ₹ 1,10,000 crore for the year 2007-08 to ₹ 2,50,000 crore from November 7, 2007 in order to give greater manoeuvrability to the RBI in the conduct of monetary policy.

The intensity of global financial crisis since September 2008 reinforced the importance of placing special emphasis on preserving financial stability and stimulating growth. The monetary policy challenge, accordingly was to strike an optimal balance between preserving financial stability, maintaining price stability, anchoring inflation expectations and sustaining the growth momentum, with the use of both conventional (CRR, reverse repo and SLR and open market operations) and unconventional (opening refinancing facilities to SIDBI and Exim Bank and prudent norms in regard to provisioning and risk weights) tools.

In the wake of uncertain global environment and continued pressure of global recession and significant slowdown in the domestic economic activity with deceleration in growth seen in all constituent sectors of the economy and the consequent liquidity constraint, the RBI pursued accommodative monetary policy during the first half of 2009-10 and accordingly took a series of pre-emptive measures comprising repo rate, reverse repo rate, CRR, SLR as well as specific refinancing windows for accommodating the distressed sectors of the economy. Thus, the CRR was decreased from 9 per cent in August, 2008 to 5 per cent in January 2009; Repo rate from 9 per cent in July 2008 to 4.75 per cent in August, 2009 and Reverse repo rate from 6 per cent in April 2008 to 3.25 per cent in April 2009.[11] The underlying consideration was to maintain a monetary and interest rate regime supportive of price stability and financial stability.[12]

The RBI exited from monetary expansion and adopted aggressive monetary policy strategy in order to moderate inflation by reining in demand pressures and inflationary expectations while maintaining financial conditions conducive to sustaining growth.

The dominant factor that shaped the strong monetary policy of the RBI in 2010-11 and onwards has been high inflation. The anti-inflationary policy stance of the RBI is based on its assessment of national and global scenario, contours of which are given below:

(*i*) Persistently high inflation rate due to domestic structural demand — supply imbalances, worsening inflationary expectations,

(*ii*) Uncertainties in the areas of global commodity prices, global macro economic environment and capital flows,

(*iii*) Existence of the large fiscal deficit causing increase in demand pressure, and

(*iv*) Corporates having increasingly regained their pricing power in many sectors and thus raising the possibility of accentuation of demand pressures.

Accordingly, the RBI raised policy rates thirteen times since March, 2010. Thus, the repo rate was raised from 5.00 per cent in March, 2010 to 8.50 per cent in October, 2011; the reverse repo rate from 3.50 per cent to 7.50 per cent during the period. On April 17, 2012, the RBI reduced the repo rate by 50 basis points to 8.00 per cent and reverse repo rate to 7.00 per cent. The CRR, however, was raised once from 5.75 per cent in March 2010 to 6.00 per cent in April, 2010 while policy repo rates remain unchanged in view of stubbonly inflationary pressures, CRR was reduced successively to 4.25 per cent on October 30, 2012 in order to ease liquidity position of the banks.

The 2011 May policy statement of the RBI is very significant in as much as it has reset the parameters of the monetary policy with a new overnight call money rate, an innovation called marginal standing facility and a new fixed relationship between the repo and reverse repo rates, with the former defined as the single policy rate to which all other rates have to adjust in a predictable manner. The move towards a single rate regime will help reduce volatility in money markets and improve transmission of policy signals.

Thus, the monetary policy actions of the RBI were intended to moderate inflation by reining the demand pressures and inflationary expectations while maintaining financial conditions conducive to sustaining growth. The RBI's strong policy signal in the form of hike in repo and reverse repo rates continuously since March, 2010 amply suggests the central bank's commitment to fairness and equity, as soaring inflation hurts the people more.

Despite pursuance of the tightening monetary policy, while rate of growth of GDP slackened, inflation rate hike has not significantly relented mainly because of the failure of the Government to improve the quality of expenditure.[13]

However, since the beginning of the year 2012, the RBI has changed the monetary policy stance to provide greater liquidity cushion to banks and space for growth. Thus, in January, 2012 the RBI reduced the CRR by 50 basis points from 6.0 per cent to 5.50 per cent, injecting a liquidity of ₹ 31,500 crore into the banking system. It was followed by further reduction of CRR by 75 basis points from 5.5 per cent to 4.75 per cent with effect from March 10, 2012 to pump in around ₹ 48,000 crore into the banking system and to ensure smooth flow of credit to productive sectors of the economy. It was further brought down to 4.25 per cent, freeing up ₹ 17,500 crore of additional funds. On January 29, 2013, CRR was further reduced to 4.00 per cent to improve liquidity position by releasing an additional ₹ 18,000 crore into the system.

For the first time in three years, the RBI reduced in April 2012 repo rate by 50 basis points to 8.0 per cent from 8.50 per cent to boost economic growth. However, the RBI Governor warned there was limited scope for further cuts, at least in the near term. According to the monetary policy statement, 2012, "It must be emphasized that the deviation of growth from its trend is modest. At the same time, upside risks to inflation persist. These considerations inherently limit the space for further reduction in policy rates, the policy stance would change based on how growth inflation dynamics panned out."[14] On January 29, 2013, the RBI further cut the repo rate by 25 basis points to 7.75 per cent and 7.50 per cent on March 19, 2013 to prop up growth.

Thus, the monetary policy actions of the RBI were intended to moderate inflation by reining in demand pressures and inflationary expectations while maintaining financial conditions conducive to sustaining growth. The RBI's strong policy signal in the form of hike in repo and reverse rates continuously since March, 2010 amply suggests the Central bank's commitment to fairness and equity, as soaring inflation hurts the people more.

Nevertheless anti-inflationary hike in policy rates during 2 years has slackened price of growth, the RBI is found according preference to fight inflation at the altar of growth. Despite pursuance of aggressive monetary policy, inflation rate hike has not significantly relented because of the Government's failure to control the large fiscal deficit.

However, since the beginning of 2012, monetary policy stance of the RBI seems to have changed to provide greater liquidity cushion to the financial systems over to ease growth rate.

G. FUTURE CHALLENGES

Since the Government embarked on the strategy of globalization, liberalization and privatization, ushering metamorphic changes in financial systems, the RBI has transformed itself continuously both functionally and structurally to cope with the changing needs of the economy and Government policies. The RBI continues to pursue the developmental role, making ceaseless efforts to develop financial markets, build institutions and encourage use of modern technology in the financial system.

However, the RBI is going to face new challenges in the ensuing years owing mainly to the enactment of the Fiscal Responsibility and Budget Management Bill, encouraging the greater participation of private and foreign banks, increasing globalization and continued liberalization of capital account. Further, rapid growth of the economy demanding higher savings and investment rate and so also enhanced need for financial intermediation, will demand banking institutions to improve further their existing services like banking, e-commerce, mutual funds, insurance and money market operations and integrate these services in a efficient manner. All these call for convergence of activities and supervision of financial conglomerates, introduction of new technology, improvement in credit risk appraisal, encouragement of financial innovation, improvement in internal controls and establishment of suitable legal framework. The RBI is, therefore, expected to play the role of facilitator, enabling the banks to compete and innovate without foregoing safety and soundness of the banking system.

Another future challenge of the RBI would be to further develop the financial markets so as to enhance the efficacy of the transmission mechanism, along with the corporate debt market.

The RBI is also expected to continue to shoulder the responsibility of bringing about greater price stability and financial stability keeping in view expected increase in credit expansions and global integration.

The last but not the least challenge, which the RBI is expected to face, relates to social security and investment of pension and insurance funds.

The RBI with its dexterous skills, competencies and experiences, it is expected, can successfully meet the above challenges and address the emerging national issues with greater confidence.

H. CONCLUSIONS

As a karnel of Indian financial system, the RBI acts as the monetary authority of the country, serves as the government bank and acts as the bankers' bank with focus on price stability along with financial stability. Unlike Central banks of developed countries, the RBI also acts as the principle institution in bringing about development and growth in the economy.

As the banking regulator, the RBI has taken wide-ranging proactive measures with a view to securing better customer service for the bank customers.

Over the years, the RBI has transformed itself functionally and structurally to cope with the challenges arising out of the Government's new economic and banking policy.

The RBI performs its functions under the overall supervision of Central Board of Directors comprising one Governor, four Deputy Governors and fifteen directors. Besides, there are local boards and offices of the RBI to assist the central board.

The RBI's major responsibility is to formulate monetary policy and execute it in order to promote economic growth, price stability and financial stability and a sustainable pattern of international trade. Main policy instruments, which the RBI employs to achieve these objectives, are open market operations, bank rate, repo rate, reverse repo rate, CRR, direct credit allocation and credit rationing and selective credit control techniques.

The RBI's approach to formulating monetary policy is consultative where the views and suggestions of wide sections of the country are solicited and analysed. It also undertakes comprehensive survey of the current and future economic, industrial and financial environment of the country and offshore countries.

The monetary policy of the RBI has always been eclectic with focus on control of money supply and credit so as to ensure price stability and financial stability.

In the wake of global financial crisis, the RBI laid special emphasis in its policy stance on preserving financial stability and stimulating growth and used both conventional tools to strike an optimal balance between preserving financial stability, maintaining price stability, anchoring inflation expectations and sustaining the growth momentum. The bank adopted accommodative monetary policy during the first half of 2009-10. However, this policy remained short lived as it was replaced by aggressive policy since March, 2010 to contain inflation. The policy rates, viz. repo rate, and reverse repo rate were continuously raised to moderate inflation by reining in demand pressure and inflationary expectations while maintaining financial conditions conducive to sustaining growth.

Although the RBI is performing its role effectively, it is expected to help the financial institutions to integrate their service and encourage financial so as to promote deepening of the market. The RBI will also have to take the responsibility of enhancing efficiency of transmission mechanism.

KEY TERMS

- Accommodative Monetary Policy
- Aggressive Monetary Policy
- Bankers' Bank
- Banking Ombudsman Scheme
- Board for Financial Supervision
- CAMELS
- Central Board of Directors
- Cash Reserve Ratio
- Government Bank
- INROADS
- Lender of Last Resort
- Liquidity Adjustment Facility
- Local Boards
- Monetary Tightening
- Moral Suasion
- Open Market Operations
- Repo Rate
- Reverse Repo Rate
- Selective Credit Controls

DISCUSSION QUESTIONS

1. Why is he Reserve Bank of India considered apex bank of India?
2. What role does the Reserve Bank play as Government banker?
3. What measures have the Reserve Bank taken in recent years to improve services to banks' customers?
4. How is the RBI managed? What role does Central Board of Directors play in managing the operations of the RBI?
5. Discuss, in brief, various monetary policy instruments which the RBI uses in controlling supply of money and credit and ensuring price stability.
6. Outline the procedure which the RBI adopts while formulating monetary policy of the country.
7. "The overall approach of the RBI to formulating monetary policy is consultative." Comment.
8. "Monetary policy of the RBI has been eclectic." Comment.
9. How has the Government policy of liberalisation and globalisation influenced monetary policy strategy of the RBI?
10. Assess the monetary policy of the RBI during post-global financial crisis.
11. "Despite aggressive monetary policy pursued by the RBI in recent years, it has not been able to check soaring prices." Comment.

REFERENCES

1. Mevvyu King, *"The Institutions of Monetary Policy"*, American Economic Review, 2004, Vol. 94.
2. History of *Reserve Bank of India*, RBI Bulletin, May 2005
3. Rakesh Mohan, *Evolution of Central Banking in India*, RBI Bulletin, June 2006.
4. V. Leeladhar, Customer Centricity and the Reserve Bank, RBI Monthly Bulletin, November, 2007.
5. RBI Bulletin, April 1966, p. 340.
6. RBI Bulletin, February 1979, p. 94.
7. RBI, Functions and Working, Bombay, 1970, p. 34.

8. R.N. Malhotra, "India's Monetary Policy and the Role of Banking System in Economic Development," RBI Bulletiin, March, 1990, p. 200.
9. C. Rangarajan, "Issues in Monetary Management", Indian Economic Association, Presidential Address, 1988, pp. 14-22.
10. RBI report on Currency and Finance, 2008-09.
11. RBI Report on Trend and Progress of Banking in India, 2009-10.
12. RBI Annual Report, 2009-10.
13. Business Standard, July 27, 2011.
14. Business Standard, April 18, 2012.

Chapter 6

Commercial Banking In India —A Snap Shot

Learning Objectives:

The present chapter attempts to:

- Provide insight into Evolution and Growth of Commercial Banking in India.
- Focus on Geographical Expansion of Indian Commercial Banks.
- Sensitise to Deposit Structure of Indian Commercial Banks.
- Dilate on Credit Pattern of Indian Commercial Banks.
- Acquaint with Priority Sector Financing by Indian Commercial Banks.
- Familiarize with technological developments in Commercial Banks in India

Chapter Outline:

A. AN INTRODUCTION

It is well appreciated that the gains in the real sector of an economy are spurred and sustained by the strength of the financial sector which is at its back. Within the financial sector, it is the strength and structure of the banking sector and how its strengths and weaknesses make or break an economy has been very amply demonstrated by the recent experiences in the South East Asian and global crises. It is now widely recognized that in South East Asian economies, one of the important reasons of the crisis was the weak structure of the banking system and its resultant inability to cope up with the changes that were taking place in the real sector. Likewise, latest global financial crises were the outcome mainly of weak regulatory and supervisory arrangements. Indian economy has largely remained protected against these crises and has shown considerable resilience purely on account of strong fundamentals and sound regulatory financial system.

The present banking system in India was evolved basically to meet the financial needs of trade and industry. The constituents of the present banking system in India have been of varying origin and sizes. At the apex is the Reserve Bank of India, the Central Bank of the country. The Reserve Bank of India is followed by the State Bank of India which was created in July 1955 by nationalising the Imperial Bank of India; the State Bank of India's subsidiaries; 20 major nationalised scheduled banks; other joint stock banks that were formed in India in the later half of the 19th century; co-operative banks which had their first existence in 1904 in the garb of co-operative credit societies; *nidhis* and *chit funds*, which have been in existence since the last quarter of the 18th century. Besides, there are indigenous banks and bankers who are centuries old. Regional Rural Banks (RRBs) were also formed in 1975 to particularly assist rural folk. Thus, the banking sector in India comprises the public sector commercial banks, private sector banks, co-operative banks and regional rural banks.

Commercial banking system, existing in India, can be split into scheduled and non-scheduled banks.

◈ Scheduled Banks

A scheduled bank is one which is registered in the second schedule of the Reserve Bank of India. The following conditions must be fulfilled by a bank for inclusion in the schedule:

(*i*) The banker concerned must be in business of banking in India;

(*ii*) It is either a company defined in Section 3 of the Indian Companies Act, 1956, or corporation or a company incorporated by or under any law in force in any place outside India or an institution notified by the Central Government in this behalf;

(*iii*) It must have paid-up capital and reserves of an aggregate real or exchangeable value of not less than rupees five lakhs;

(*iv*) It must satisfy the Reserve Bank of India that its affairs are not conducted in a manner detrimental to the interests of its depositors.

The minimum capital requirement for setting up banks in the private sector was prescribed at ₹ 100 crore. Upon review of the position of the capital funds of old private sector banks in 1998-99 it was indicated that old private sector banks having net worth of less then ₹ 50 crore were to attain the level of ₹ 50 crore by March end, 2001. Subsequently, the RBI directed that capital requirement of old private sector banks should be on par with that of new private sector banks at ₹ 200 crore with commitment to increase it to ₹ 300 crore with in three years. It also directed that all banks would have a net worth of at least ₹ 300 crore.

Scheduled banks come under the purview of the various credit control measures of the Reserve Bank of India. They are required to maintain a certain minimum balance in their accounts with the RBI, and do certain things prescribed by law. The scheduled banks are entitled to borrowings and rediscounting facilities from the RBI. These banks are similar to the member banks of the U.S.A.

Scheduled Banks may be classified into two groups: *Indian Scheduled Banks and Foreign Scheduled Banks*. The Indian Scheduled Banks are those which have their registered offices in India and are registered in the second schedule of the RBI. As against this, foreign scheduled banks comprise those commercial banks which are registered in the said schedule but have their registered offices outside India. These banks have played a prominent role in India's foreign trade; in fact, they had complete sway in this sphere until the Second World War. Since then, a number of leading Indian scheduled banks entered the field of foreign trade and have in the course of time achieved an important position in this field.

Indian scheduled banks may be distinguished in two broad sectors:

(*a*) Public sector commercial banking comprising the State Bank of Indian and its subsidiaries and the twenty nationalised banks;

(*b*) Private sector commercial banking comprising all the other Indian scheduled banks that do not fall in the above group.

◈ Non-Scheduled Banks

Banks, which are not included in the Second Schedule of the RBI, are known as non-scheduled banks. They may be classified into four groups:

(*a*) Banks with paid-up capital and reserves in excess of ₹ 5 lakhs;

(*b*) Banks with paid-up capital and reserves ranging between ₹ 50,000 and one lakh of rupees;

(*c*) Banks with paid-up capital and reserves ranging between one lakh rupees and five lakhs;

(*d*) Banks with paid-up capital and reserves below ₹ 50,000.

Non-scheduled banks are not entitled to all those facilities that the scheduled banks avail of from the Reserve Bank of India. Since the enactment of the Banking Regulation Act in 1949, non-scheduled banks have also come under the ambit of the RBI control. It has become obligatory on the part of these banks to carry a portion of their deposits with the RBI or in vault with the bank itself, and prepare their annual accounts and balance sheets in accordance with the requirements stipulated in Section 29 of the Banking Companies Act.

B. EVOLUTION AND GROWTH OF BANKING SYSTEM IN INDIA

So as to understand present make-up of banking sector in India and have an idea of how it will shape up in facing the new millennium challenges, it will be in fitness of things to look at its development in a somewhat longer historical perspective.

The past five decades and particularly the last three decades witnessed cataclysmic change in the sphere of commercial banking all over the world. Indian banking system has also followed the same trend. As a matter of fact, the changes here have been far more pronounced than anywhere else.

In over six decades since independence, banking system in India has passed through five distinct phases, *viz.*,

Evolutionary phase	(prior to 1948)
Foundation phase	(1948-1967)
Expansion phase	(1968-1984)
Consolidation phase	(1985-1990)
Reformatory phase	(1991 and onwards)

◈ Evolution Phase (Prior to 1950)

Enactment of the RBI Act 1935 gave birth to scheduled banks in India, and some of these banks had already been established around 1881. The prominent among the scheduled banks is the Allahabad Bank, which was set up in 1865 with European management. The first bank which was established with Indian ownership and management was the Oudh Commercial Bank formed in 1881, followed by the Ayodhya Bank in 1884, the Punjab National Bank in 1894 and Nedungadi Bank in 1899. Thus, there were five Banks in existence in the 19th century. During the period 1901-1914, twelve more banks were established, prominent among which were the Bank of Baroda (1906), the Canara Bank (1906), the Indian Bank (1907), the Bank of India (1908) and the Central Bank of India (1911).

Thus, the five big banks of today had come into being prior to the commencement of the First World War. In 1913, and also in 1929, the Indian Banks faced serious crises. Several banks succumbed to these crises. Public confidence in banks received a jolt. There was a heavy rush on banks. An important point to be noted here is that no commercial bank was established during the First World War, while as many as twenty scheduled banks came into existence after independence - two in the public sector and one in the private sector. The United Bank of India was formed in 1950 by the merger of four existing commercial banks. Certain non-scheduled banks were included in the second schedule of the Reserve Bank. In view of these facts, the number of scheduled banks rose to 81. Out of 81 Indian scheduled banks, as many as 23 were either liquidated or merged into or amalgamated with other scheduled banks in 1968, leaving 58 Indian schedule banks. The age-wise distribution of these 58 Indian scheduled Banks is given in Table 6.1.

TABLE 6.1: Age-wise Distribution of Indian Scheduled Banks

	Established during	*No. of Banks*
1.	19th Century	2
2.	Pre-First World War	14
3.	Inter-War Period	21
4.	Second World War	3
5.	Post-Second World War	18
	Total	58

It may be emphasized at this stage that banking system in India came to be recognized in the beginning of 20th century as powerful instrument to influence the pace and pattern of economic development of the country. In 1921 need was felt to have a State Bank endowed with all support and resources of the Government with a view to helping industries and banking facilities to grow in all parts of the country. It is towards the accomplishment of this objective that the three Presidency Banks were amalgamated to form the Imperial Bank of India. The role of the Imperial Bank was envisaged as "to extend banking facilities, and to render the money resources of India more accessible to the trade and industry of this country, thereby promoting financial system which is an indisputable condition of the social and economic advancement of India."

Until 1935 when RBI came into existence to play the role of Central Bank of the country and regulatory authority for the banks, Imperial Bank of India played the role of a quasi-central bank. It functioned as a commercial bank but at times the Government used it for regulating the money supply by influencing its policies. It was by making it the sole repository of all its funds and by changing the volume of its deposits with the Bank as and when desired by it, the Government tried to influence the base of deposits and hence credit creation by Imperial Bank and by rest of the banking system. Thus, Imperial Bank was not given fully the role of a commercial bank, otherwise the line of its growth and influence over the Indian economy would have been substantially different and the growth pattern of the Indian industry and so also of small scale industries and agriculture would also have been different.

The newly constituted Imperial Bank acted true to its name and lived more by the risk-averse culture which pervaded the then Government's most favoured Presidency Bank — the Bank of Bengal. In contrast to the two favoured Presidency Banks — Bank of Bengal and Bank of Bombay which had not developed any such culture — Bank of Madras had already pioneered the financing of small-scale industries, which head way was largely lost on its amalgamation with other two Presidency Banks.

Thus, the role of commercial banks in India remained confined to providing vehicle for the community's savings and attending to the credit needs of only certain selected and limited segments of the economy. Banks' operations were influenced primarily by commercial principle and not by developmental factor. Regulation was still only being introduced and unhealthy practices in the banks were then more rules than exceptions. Failure of banks was common as governance in privately owned joint stock banks left much to be desired.

◈ Foundation Phase (1948-1967)

The banking scenario prevalent in the country during the period 1948-1968 presented a strong focus on class banking with accent on security rather than on purpose. The emphasis of the banking system during this period was on laying the foundation for a sound banking system in the country. Consequently, this phase witnessed the development of the necessary legislative framework for facilitating reorganisation and consolidation of the banking system in the country. Banking Regulation Act was passed in 1949 to conduct and control operations of the commercial banks in India. Another major step taken during this period was the transformation of Imperial Bank of India into State Bank of India and a redefinition of its role in the Indian economy, strengthening of the co-operative credit structure and setting up of institutional framework for providing long-term finance to agriculture and industry. Banking sector, which during the pre-independence India was catering to the needs of the government, rich individuals and traders, opened its door wider and set out for the first time to bring the entire productive sector of the economy — large as well as small, in its fold.

During this period the number of commercial banks declined remarkably (Table 6.2). There were 566 banks as on December, 1951; of this, the number of scheduled banks was 92 and the remaining 474 were non-scheduled banks. This number went down considerably to the level of 281 at the close of 1968. The sharp decline in the number of banks was due to heavy fall in the number of non-scheduled banks which touched an all time low level of 210.

It may be interesting to observe that upto the Second Plan period, non-scheduled banks were dominant in number but following a sharp decline in their number, they were outnumbered by scheduled banks. The major factor underlying the perceptible change was the consolidation and strengthening of the banking structure and the organisational drive started by the RBI after the enactment of the Banking Regulation Act 1949 with a view to improving the quality of banking services and widening the geographical and functional spread of their activity. The process of liquidation and consolidation, which began in 1960, continued in subsequent years. As many as 115 banks were either liquidated or amalgamated with other banks.

TABLE 6.2: Number of Commercial Banks During 1951-1968

Particulars	*December 1951*	*December 1956*	*December 1968*
(*a*) Scheduled Banks	92	89	71
(*b*) Non-scheduled Banks	474	334	210
Total	566	423	281

Before 1968, only RBI and Associate Banks of SBI were mainly controlled by the Government. Some associates were fully owned subsidiaries of SBI and in the rest, there was a very small shareholding by individuals and the rest by RBI.

◈ Expansion Phase (1968-1984)

This phase witnessed socialisation of banking in 1968. Commercial banks were viewed as agents of change and social control on banks. However, inadequacy of social control soon became apparent because all banks except the SBI and its seven associate banks were in the private sector and could not be influenced to serve social interests. Therefore, banks were nationalised (14 in 1969 and 6 in 1980) in order to control the heights of the economy in conformity with national policy and objectives. This period saw the birth and growth of what is now termed as 'directed lending' by banks. It also saw commercial banking spreading to far and wide areas in the country with great pace during which a number of poverty alleviation and employment generating schemes were sought to be implemented through commercial banks. Thus, this period was characterised by the death of private banking and the dominance of social banking over commercial banking. It was hardly realised that banks were organisations with social responsibilities but not social organisations. This period also witnessed the birth of Regional Rural Banks (RRBs) in 1975 and NABARD in 1982 which had priority sector as their focus of activity.

Although number of commercial banks declined from 281 in 1968 to 268 in 1984, number of scheduled banks shot up from 71 to 264 during the corresponding period, number of non-scheduled banks having registered perceptible decline from 210 to 4 during the period under reference. The rise in the number of scheduled banks was, as stated above, due to the emergence of RRBs.[1]

The fifteen years following the banks' nationalisation in 1969 were dominated by the banks' expansion at a pathbreaking pace. As many as 50,000 bank branches were set up; three-fourths of these branches were opened in rural and semi-urban areas. Thus, during this period a distinct transformation of far reaching significance occurred in the Indian banking system as it assumed a broad mass-base and emerged as an important instrument of socio-economic changes. With the completion of this process, the basic objective of banks was accomplished and the banking industry achieved unparalleled growth in terms of reach, business parameters and employment. There is some recent evidence that the branch expansion programme since nationalization of banks succeeded in encouraging commercial banks in opening branches in backward rural locations and reaching the rural poor. Further, it offered opportunities for households to save. Thus, social banking programmes employed by the Government served to redistribute resources to the rural poor, impacting positively on poverty and non-agricultural output.[2] In fact, so rapid was the growth in these areas that the banking industry hardly had any time to consider other issues such as support systems required for efficient operations, control mechanisms and profitability. Thus, with growth came inefficiency and loss of control over widely spread offices. Moreover, retail lending to more risk-prone areas at concessional interest rates had raised costs, affected the quality of assets of banks and put their profitability under strain. The competitive efficiency of the banks was at a low ebb. Customer service became least available commodity. Performance of a bank/banker began to be measured merely in terms of growth of deposits, advances and other such targets and quality became a casualty.

◈ Consolidation Phase (1985-1990)

A realisation of the above weaknesses thrust the banking sector into the phase of consolidation. This phase began in 1985 when a series of policy initiatives were taken with the objective of consolidating the gains of branch expansion undertaken by the banks, and of relaxing albeit marginally, the very tight regulation under which the system was operating. Although number of schedule banks increased from 264 in 1984 to 276 in 1990, branch expansion of the banks slowed down. Hardly 7,000 branches were set up during this period. For the first time, serious attention was paid to improving housekeeping, customer services, credit management, staff productivity and profitability of the banks and concrete steps were taken during this period to rationalise the rates of bank deposits and lending. Measures were initiated to reduce the structural constraints which were then inhibiting the development of money market.

However, this phase was just an extension of the earlier phase and commercial banks were yet to see the worst in the form of Agricultural and Rural Debt Relief Scheme 1990. By this time about 90% of commercial banks were in the public sector and closely regulated in all its facets. Prices of assets and liability were fixed by the RBI; prices of services were fixed uniformly by the Indian Banking Association (IBA); composition of assets was also somewhat fixed in as much as 63.5% of bank funds were mopped up by CRR and SLR and the remainder was to be directed towards priority sector lending and small loaning; salary structure was negotiated by the IBA and validated by the Government. Thus, there was no autonomy in vital decisions. Commercial approach in operations and drive towards efficiency were almost non-existent. The result was that during this period, the banks ended up consolidating their losses rather than the gains. However, they tried to keep up their morale by continuing to post profits through antiquated accounting methods.

◈ Reformatory Phase (1991 and onwards)

The pre-reform period witnessed following major regulatory constraints on the banking sector which not only distorted the efficiency of the interest rate mechanism but also adversely affected the viability and profitability of banks.

- Large pre-emptions — both in terms of the statutory holding of Government securities and cash reserve ratio and
- Complex structure of administrated interest rates.

The financial strengths and operational efficiency of Indian banks working in a highly protected and regulated environment were not measuring up to international standards. The global and domestic developments called for corrections primarily with a view to strengthening the financial system and bringing it on par with institutions abroad. The need for reform was further reinforced when the country faced grave economic crisis in 1991. For the first time in its history, India faced the problem of defaulting on its international commitments. The access to external commercial credit markets was completely denied; international credit ratings had been downgraded and the international financial community's confidence in India's ability to manage its economy had been severally eroded. The economy suffered from serious inflationary pressures, emerging scarcities of essential commodities and breakdown of fiscal discipline.

The Government took swift action to restore international confidence in the economy and redress the imbalances. Various macro economic structural reformatory measures were undertaken in the field of foreign trade, tax system, industrial policy and financial and other sectors. The objective was to improve the underlying strength of the economy, attempt to ensure against future crises and further the fundamental developmental objectives of growth with equity and self reliance.

Banking sector in India, as noted above, had gone metamorphosis during the last two decades. While banking sector contributed to a great extent in creating a vital infrastructure for national building, generating employment opportunities and expanding business, it suffered during the course of its expansion from many deficiencies in regard to their efficiency and quality of their operations. It had hardly any time to consider other issues such as support systems required for efficient operations, control mechanism and profitability. Thus, growth of banking industry accompanied inefficiency, and loss of control over widely spread offices. There were other extraneous factors which contributed to inefficiencies. These factors were:

- Over-regulation leading to weakening of the management function;
- Directed lending leading to hobbling of the innovative skills of the banker;
- Social control came to be synonymous with political control with loan write off completely eroding the basic character of banking business;
- Trade Unions muscle power increased with massive branch expansion leading to day-to-day interference in individual credit decision making and internal management and poor work culture;
- Customer service became the greatest casuality.

- Too much expansion at too fast a pace had left certain management areas weak, adversely affecting quality of bank assets and its profitability.

Hence, from 1991 a process of financial sector reforms was set in 6 months. Narasimham Committee was constituted as a part of a broader programme of structured economy reforms.

RECOMMENDATIONS OF NARASIMHAM COMMITTEE - I

◈ Salient Features of the First Phase of the Committee Report

The persistent deterioration in the financial health and the looming danger to the banking system called for quick but comprehensive remedial measures, failing which there was perilous threat to erosion of the real value of and return on the saving entrusted to them leading to loss of public confidence. Accordingly, the Government of India constituted in August, 1991 a high power committee under the Chairmanship of Shri M. Narasimham, then Dy. Governor, R.B.I., to examine all aspects relating to the structure, organisation, functions, and problems of the financial system and recommend measures to improve efficiency and effectiveness of Indian financial system. The Committee submitted its report in November, 1991. The salient features of the Committee's recommendations were:[3]

◈ Phased Reduction of Statutory Pre-emptions

The Committee recommended that SLR should be reduced to 25% and CRR to 10% over a time period so that the funds of banks are deployed by them in more remunerative loan assets.

◈ Interest Rate on CRR Balances

The Committee had recommended payment of interest on eligible balances (i.e., cash balances above the basic minimum of 3%) related to bank's average cost of deposits.

◈ Phasing out of Directed Credit Programme

The Committee recommended that priority sector should be redefined to comprise the small and marginal farmers, the tiny sector of industry, small business and transport operators, village and cottage industries, rural artisans and other weaker sections. The target for this redefined sector should be fixed at 10% of aggregate credit, subject to taking a review after three years.

◈ Interest Rate Deregulation

The Committee felt that the existing interest structure on loans and deposits is very complex and hence suggested that there should be some market orientation.

At the same time, the Committee believed that a reasonable degree of macro economic balance through a reduction in the fiscal deposit was necessary for successful deregulation of interest rates. Premature moves to market determined interest rates could pose the danger of excessive bank lending at high nominal rates to borrowers of dubious creditworthiness, eventually creating actual problems for both the banks as well as the borrowers. Accordingly, the Committee recommended that for the present, interests rates on bank deposits might continue to be regulated, the ceiling on such rates being raised as the SLR was reduced progressively.

◈ Capital Adequacy Ratio (CAR)

The Committee had recommended that BIS norms on capital adequacy should be achieved over a period of three years by March, 1996. The Committee suggested that the banks and financial institutions should achieve a minimum 4% capital adequacy ratio in relation to risk weightage assets by March, 1993. The BIS standards of 8% should be achieved by March, 1996.

Income Recognition

Before arriving at the CAR for each bank, the Committee felt the evaluation of assets of the banks should be done on the basis of their realisable values. Accordingly, it proposed that the banks and financial institutions adopt uniform accounting practices particularly in regard to income recognition and provisioning against doubtful debts. The Committee also emphasised on the need for adopting sound practices in regard to valuation of investments on the lines suggested by the Ghosh Committee on final accounts.

As regards income recognition, the Committee recommended that no income should be recognized in the accounts in respect of non-performing assets. An asset would be considered non-performing if interest on such assets remains past due for a period exceeding 180 days at the balance sheet date. The Committee further recommended that banks and financial institutions be given a period of three years to move towards the norms in a phased manner.

Asset Classification

The Committee suggested that the assets should be classified, using the health code classification which is in vogue in banks and financial institutions, into four categories, *viz.*, standard, sub-standard, doubtful and Loss Assets. In regard to sub-standard assets, a general provision should be created equal to 10% of the total outstanding under this category. In respect of doubtful debts, provision should be made to the extent of 100% of the security shortfall. As regards secured portion of some doubtful debts, further provision should be made, ranging from 20% to 50%, depending on the period for which such assets remain in the doubtful category. Loss assets should either be fully written off or provision be made to the extent of 100 per cent. The Committee was of the view that a period of 4 years should be given to the banks and financial institutions to conform to these provisioning requirements in phased manner. But in respect of doubtful debts 100% of the security shortfall was to be fully provided for in the shortest possible time.

Transparency

The Committee recommended that the format of bank balance sheet and profit and loss account should be modified in such a manner that the bank's balance sheets disclose more information.

Tax Treatment of Provisions

The Committee suggested that the criteria recommended for non-performing assets and provisioning requirements be given due recognition by the tax authorities. Accordingly, it recommended that instead of deductions under 36 (i) (vii) being restricted to 5% of the total income and 2% of the aggregate average advances by rural branches, it should be restricted to 0.5% of the aggregate average advances by rural branches.

Loan Recovery

The Committee recommended that government should take steps to ensure recovery of bank dues by creating some special recovery tribunals and provide for quick recovery process.

Tackling Doubtful Debts

The Committee recommended that Asset Reconstruction Fund (ARF) should be created to take over bad debt of the banks on discount, and bank balance sheet should be made clean as a one time exercise. The ARF should be provided with special powers for recovery. The capital of the ARF should be subscribed by the public sector banks and financial institutions.

Restructuring the Banks

The Committee recommended that the banks be restructured by creating 3-4 large banks which would become international in character, 8-10 national banks with network of branches throughout the country engaged in universal banking, local banks in specific regions and rural banks for rural areas.

It was further suggested by the Committee that this revised system should be market driven and based on profitability considerations and brought about through a process of mergers and acquisitions.

◆ Entry of Private Banks

The Committee proposed that the Government should indicate that there would be no further nationalisation of banks. This will remove the existing disincentive for the more dynamic private banks to grow. It also recommended that there should not be any difference in treatment between the public sector and private sector banks. The Committee proposed that there should be no bar to new banks in the private sector being set up provided they conform to the start-up capital and other requirements as may be prescribed by the RBI and the maintenance of prudential norms with regard to accounting, provisioning and other aspects of operations.

◆ Branch Licensing

The Committee recommended that branch licensing be abolished and the matter of operating branches or closing of branches (other than rural branches for the present) be left to the commercial judgement of the individual banks.

◆ Foreign Banks

The Committee recommended that foreign banks be allowed to open offices in India either as branches or where the RBI considers it appropriate, as subsidiaries. However, they should be subjected to the same requirements as applicable to domestic banks.

◆ Supervision of Banks

The Committee felt that the Indian banking system at present was over-regulated and over administered. It recommended that supervision should be based on evolving prudential norms and regulations which should be adhered to rather than excessive control over administrative and other aspects of bank organisation and functioning. The Committee emphasised on internal audit and internal inspection system of banks. The inspection by the supervisory authorities should be based essentially on the internal audit and inspection reports. Their main concern should be to ensure that audit and inspection machinery is adequate and conforms to well laid down norms.

◆ Control of Banking System

The Committee was of the firm opinion that the duality of control over the banking system between the RBI and the Banking Division of the Ministry of Finance should end and that the RBI should be the primary agency for the regulation of the banking system. The supervisory function over the banks and other financial institutions, the Committee suggested, should be hived off to a separate authority to operate as a quasi-autonomous body under the aegis of the RBI.

◆ Action on the Recommendations of Narasimham Committee-I

The recommendations of Narasimham Committee were implemented by the Government, as outlined below:

The CRR of schedule Commercial banks which was 15 per cent of net demand and time liabilities between July 1, 1990 and October 8, 1992 was brought down in phases to 5.0 per cent effective October 2, 2004. CRR on January 29, 2013 was 4.00.

The statutory liquidity ratio (SLR) has been progressively brought down from the peak rate of 38.5 per cent to the statutory minimum of 25.0 per cent in October 1997. The SLR has now been reduced to 23.0 per cent.

(a) ***Interest Rate on CRR Balances:*** As per the recommendation, interest on eligible cash balances is paid at 4%.

(b) ***Phasing out of Directed Credit Programme:*** The Government did not accept the recommendation of the Committee to reduce the level of priority sector lending from 40% to 10%. However, the priority sector definition was enlarged to include certain categories of advances which were hitherto not part of the priority sector.

(c) ***Interest Rate Deregulation:*** Banks are given freedom to have their own reference rate known as Prime Lending Rate instead of floor and ceiling rates and fix individual borrower's interest rate within a band over PLR.

(d) ***Capital Adequacy Norms:*** RBI implemented the Committee's recommendations on capital adequacy norms and as on 31st March 1997 only two banks (UCO and Indian Bank) were not able to achieve the norm of 8%.

(e) ***Assets Classification:*** The banks with effect from 1.4.92 had implemented the guidelines of the RBI and classified their loan assets based on record of recovery and also started recognizing income based on this. During the period 31st March 1993 to 31st March 1997 many banks reported huge losses due to the implementation of these directives.

(f) ***Transparency:*** In deference to the recommendation of the Narasimham Committee the format of bank balance sheet and profit and loss accounts was modified by the RBI and Government w.e.f. March 1992 and the banks started preparing their financial statements as per the modified format. During 1996 and 1997 more significant additions such as break-up of capital adequacy ratio, provisions made for the year, NPA percentage, etc., were introduced. In 1998 banks were further directed to disclose critical ratios relating to productivity and profitability.

(g) ***Tax Treatment Provisions:*** The limit of admissible deductions was enhanced to 5% of the income and 10% of average aggregate advances of rural branches.

(h) ***Loan Recovery:*** As recommended by the Committee, the Government passed an Act during August 1993 providing for creation of recovery tribunals for loan accounts with outstanding balance of ₹ 10 lakh or more. It also established 8 such tribunals and an Appellate Tribunal in Mumbai which upto March 1998 covered 20 states and 4 union territories.

(i) ***Tackling Doubtful Debts:*** No steps have so far been taken in regard to creation of Asset Reconstruction fund, as recommended by the Committee.

(j) ***Restructuring of the Banks:*** No progress in this respect was made except that on 4.9.93 a loss making bank, *viz.*, New Bank of India was merged with Punjab National Bank.

◆ Private Banks

The Banking Regulation (Amendment) Act 1994 was passed to permit private sector to enter into banking field. Accordingly, the RBI gave license to 9 private banks to start their operations towards the end of April 1994.

RBI allowed entry of foreign banks subject to reciprocity and other prudential considerations. Since 1992 till March 1998, 19 new foreign banks with total of 47 branches were allowed. These banks were asked to achieve minimum target of 3% (with SSI minimum 10% and export minimum 12%) of net bank credit of priority sector lending by March, 1994.

The revised guidelines for licensing of new banks in the private sector were issued which stipulated a minimum initial paid-up capital of the new bank of ₹ 200 crore to be raised to ₹ 300 crore with in three years from the commencement of business with minimum 40 per cent as promoter's contribution subject to a lock-in period of 5 years and dilution of any excess stake after one year. The rest could be raised through public issue or private placement with NRI participation in the primary equity limited to 40 per cent and within this limit a restriction of 20 per cent for any foreign banking company or finance company as a technical collaborator or a co-promoter. However, while new banks should not be promoted by an industrial house, individual companies can invest up to 10 per cent of the bank's equity.

◈ Recommendations of Narasimham Committee-II

◈ Salient Features

Narasimham Committee was again constituted in 1997 to suggest measures to strengthen the banking sector of the country. The Committee submitted its report in April 1998. Main recommendations of the Committee were:

(*a*) There should be a merger of strong public sector banks in view of its multiplier effect on industry. Strong banks should not be merged with the weak as it will have negative impact on the asset quality of the stronger bank because of the contaminated portfolio of the weak banks. The committee was of the opinion that mergers would be meaningful and useful only when they were not a mere arithmetical merger of balance sheets and staff. Mergers would have to yield benefits in terms of staff and branch network.

(*b*) Public sector banks should be given greater autonomy with respect to recruitment and personnel in general management of staff and also in determining their organisation structure.

(*c*) Underlying the need for dealing with the issue of weak banks separately, the committee recommended that for potentially viable weak banks corrective measures such as recapitalisation be undertaken. But those where early or complete correction was not possible, alternative approaches including closure should be carefully examined.

(*d*) Banks would have to move away from excessive concentration on asset management and adopt a more general approach of asset-liability management with a view to modifying their liability in consonance with the desired asset structure.

(*e*) Banks should understand the growing interdependence of various market segments and develop the necessary expertise for forecasting the relevant variable taking into account this interdependence.

(*f*) There should be greater specialisation by banks in different niches of the market such as retail agriculture, export, SSI and corporate sector.

(*g*) Banks should place greater reliance on non-fund business such as advisory and consultancy services, guarantees and custody service.

(*h*) Banks should have thrust on greater financial intermediation with large companies, accessing securities debt domestically and from financial markets abroad.

(*i*) Banks should concentrate on management of credit risk and better management of non-performing advances.

(*j*) So as to improve financial health of the banks and the banking system as a whole, the Committee recommended that capital adequacy ratio be raised to 9% by March end, 2000 and 10% by 2002.

In order to strengthen the banking system the Committee felt that capital adequacy requirements should take into account market risks in addition to credit risk. The entire portfolio of government securities, the Committee recommended, should be marked to market in the next three years. There should be a 5% weight for market risk for government and approved securities.

(*k*) The Committee suggested that an asset should be classified as doubtful if it is in the substandard category for 18 months in the first instance and eventually for 12 months and lost if it had been so identified but not written off.

(*l*) It was recommended by the Committee that the Government guaranteed advances which have turned sticky should be classified as NPAs. Income recognition, asset classification and provisioning norms should apply to Government guaranteed advances in the same manner as for any other advances.

(*m*) The Committee recommended that a general provision of 1% on standard assets should be introduced. Banks and financial institutions should avoid the practice of evergreening (by making fresh advances to their troubled constituents only with a view to settling interest dues and avoiding classification of the loans in question as NPAs).

(*n*) The Committee recommended that Government should guarantee issue of bonds for tier II capital by banks. These instruments would be eligible for SLR investment.

(*o*) Realising the necessity of priority sector advances the Committee recommended that this should be continued. Branch managers of banks should be fully responsible for the identification of beneficiaries, interest subsidy element in credit should be eliminated and interest rates on loans under ₹ 2 lakhs should be deregulated for scheduled commercial banks.

(*p*) The Committee suggested that functions of boards and management need to be reviewed so that the boards remain responsible for enhancing shareholder's value through formulation of corporate strategy. It also made a strong pitch for professionalisation and depoliticisation of bank boards, especially in respect of non-official directors.

◆ Action on the Recommendations of Narasimham Committee-II

In conformity with the Committee's recommendations, the RBI announced a package of measures in October, 1998. These relate to increasing the minimum capital adequacy ratio in the banking system from 8% to 9% by March 31, 2000 and 10% by march 2002 recognising the market risks and prescribing a risk weight of 2.5% in Government/approved securities by March 31, 2000; providing 100% risk weight for foreign exchange and gold open position limits from the year ended March 31, 1999; moving towards tighter asset classification, income recognition and provisioning norms. As per the RBI directive, an asset will be classified as doubtful if it has remained in substandard category for 18 months instead of 24 months by March 31, 2001.

The Government guaranteed advances, which have turned sticky, have to be classified as NPAs as per the existing prudential norms with effect from 1st April, 2000.

The RBI has reiterated that banks should adhere to the prudential norms on asset classification, provisioning, etc., and avoid the practice of evergreening.

Further, banks have been advised to put in place a formal asset-liability management system with effect from 1st April, 1999.

In line with the Committee's recommendations, the RBI directed the banks to ensure a loan review mechanism for larger advances soon after the sanction and continuously monitor the weaknesses developing in the accounts for initiating corrective measures in time.

Further, acting upon the recommendations of the Narasimham Committee the Government reduced its ownership from 67 per cent to 51 per cent in 1994 and decided to further reduce its minimum equity holding to 33 per cent in 19 public sector banks. However, this decision will not apply to the SBI and the RBI will continue to hold a majority stake in the SBI.

The RBI modified norms for classification of assets as standard and sub-standard. According to the changed norms, an asset, including a leased asset, becomes non-performing when it ceases to generate income for the bank. Banks have to classify a loan as non-performing if interest and or instalment of principal remain due for more than 90 days. An asset is classified as substandard if it remains non-performing for 12 months. An asset becomes doubtful if it remains sub-standard for 12 months. A loss asset is one whose loss has been identified by internal auditors or RBI but the amount has not been written off wholly.

RBI mandates 100 per cent provisioning for loss assets. For doubtful assets, 20 per cent provisioning is required for three years. After more than three years, the loss has to be fully provided for.

C. RECENT REFORMING MEASURES OF THE RBI

In its strive to serve the customers and improve banking penetration in the country, the RBI has, of late, taken the following initiatives:

- In January, 1993 the RBI permitted the Self-help Groups (SHGs) to open savings bank account with banks.
- The RBI directed in January, 2006 for engagement of Business Correspondents (BCs) by banks for providing banking and financial services in addition to the traditional brick and mortar model. Under this BC Model, banks have been permitted to use the services of various entities like Non-Governmental organisations/Self-help Groups (NGOs/ SHGs), Micro Finance Institutions (MFIs) and other civil society organizations (CSOs) registered under Section 25 of the Companies Act, 1956, retired Government employees and ex-servicemen to act as BCs.[4] Banks were further allowed to appoint as BCs: individual owners of kirana/medical/fair price shops/individual PCO operators, agents of small savings schemes of GOI/insurance companies, individuals who own petrol pumps retired teachers, authorised functionaries of well-run self-help groups which are linked to banks and any other individuals including those operating common service centre as BCs.[5]
- In November 2009, the RBI advised banks to draw up a road map to provide banking services through a banking outlet in every village having a population of over 2000 by March 2012.
- In January, 2010 the RBI directed the banks to draw up specific Board approved Financial Inclusive Plans (FIP) with a view to rolling them out over the next three years. Banks were advised to devise FIPs matching with their business strategy and to make the FIPs an integral part of their corporate plans.[6]
- From July 1, 2010, banks were directed to switch over to the base rate mechanism for pricing loans, marking the end of the benchmark prime lending rate (BPLR) regime.[7]

Base rate is the minimum rate at which banks can lend (barring specified exemptions, such as to export and agricultural sectors). According to the RBI guidelines, it is calculated, factoring in a bank's cost of deposits, operating costs, the cost of statutory drafts on bank funds imposed by the RBI (CRR and SLR) and the profit margin. The RBI has stipulated that banks cannot change below the base rate for most loans.

The new model will lead to a single rate, while earlier banks had separate BPLRs for retail and corporate loans, now all borrowers will consider only the base rate. Also, the transmission of policy guidelines, such as lowering of rates, is expected to be much faster in the new regime.

The new model will ensure greater transparency; it need not mean lower lending rates for borrowers. In fact, banks' blue-chip corporate borrowers could see some increase in their cost of borrowing because the banks now can not lend to corporate borrowers at "sub-PLR rates" which they were doing earlier. Further, the base rate would prevent to a degree what regulators term "predation" — the phenomenon of large banks dropping loan rates way below costs to grab market share. There have been recent instances of predation in retail credit markets breeding the risk of credit bubbles building upon on the back of these exceptionally cheap loans.[8]

Besides freeing lending rates, the RBI deregulated deposit interest rates in April 1992 by replacing the maturity-wise prescriptions by a single ceiling rate of 13 per cent for all deposits above 46 days. The ceiling was brought down to 12 per cent in April 1995. Banks were allowed to fix the interest rates on deposits with maturity of over 2 years in October 1995 which was further relaxed to maturity of over one year in July 1996. The ceiling rate for deposits of 30 days upto 1 year was linked to the bank rate less 200 basis points in April 1997. In October 1997, the deposit rates were fully deregulated by removing the linkage to the Bank Rate. Accordingly, the RBI gave the freedom to commercial banks to fix their own interest rates on domestic term deposits of varying maturities with the prior approval of their respective Board of Directors/Asset Liability Management Committee (ALCo). In April, 1998 the RBI lifted the restrictions on banks that they must offer the same rate on deposits of the same maturity in respect of deposits of ₹ 15 lakh and above with the bank board's laying down policy in this regard. Thus, banks have had complete freedom in fixing their domestic rates, except interest rate on savings deposits.

In line with the deregulation of domestic deposit rates, banks were given complete freedom in September 1997 to decide interest rates on Non-residential External (NRE) term deposits across all maturities. Likewise, with regard to foreign currency Non-Resident Bank (FCNR-B) scheme banks were permitted to determine the interest rates (fixed or floating with an interest reset period of 6 months) subject to a prescribed ceiling effective from April 16, 1997. In response to changing conditions in the financial markets, interest rates on NRE term deposits were linked to the international rates by way of a ceiling of 250 basis points over and above the US dollar, LIBOR/Swap rates of corresponding maturities from July 17, 2003. The ceiling rates were progressively reduced during subsequent period and brought closer to LIBOR from April 24, 2007.

As a precursor to complete deregulation of the deposit rates, the RBI in its annual monetary policy 2011 raised saving bank deposit interest rate (SBDR) to 4 per cent on May 3, 2011 from 3.5 per cent to align it to closer to short-term market rates. On October 25, 2011 the RBI decided to regulate savings deposit rates — the last bastion of administered rates — with immediate effort. Accordingly, the RBI allowed banks to decide on their own, the interest on savings deposits. However, banks were directed to pay a uniform rate on savings deposits up to ₹ 1,00,000 irrespective of the amount in the account. Further, there should not be any discrimination from customer to customer on interest rates for a similar amount of deposit.

In our country, where a significant portion of household savings (particularly in semi-urban and rural areas) is still held in the form of cash, deregulation of interest rate on savings bank deposit resulting in competition among banks for rise in interest rates, will bring into the banking system a part of this household savings. A market-based savings interest rate will accelerate greater financial inclusion of the unbanked, and also augment a higher savings propensity, thereby creating a multiplier effect.

Savings rate deregulation is expected to provide greater scope for product innovation and service excellence and a better opportunity for banks to cross-sell. The rates would essentially be driven by relationship value, future potential and efficient transaction costs. Market forces will also ensure that banks make additional efforts to educate their customers on banking services and product features. Unfortunately Indian bankers have not been so creative and proactive in this respect mainly due to their "lazy banking" attitude.[9]

There are fears of unhealthy competition amongst banks, which may lead to a fall in profitability. However, these are untenable in view of the positive experience of deregulation in term deposit rates and other interest rates including interest rates on loans over the past decade. Though there may be some immediate impact on the cost of deposits, resulting in a compression of net interest margins, in the long-run the spin-offs of healthy operations and higher mobilisation of savings will surely benefit those banks that are service-oriented and provide tangible value to their small savings depositors. This is what happened in insurance, telecom and pharmaceuticals once they were aligned to free market principles. India is likely to emulate Hong Kong's phased deregulation of savings rate, which was followed by the launch of several new products, revised fee charges and minimum balance requirements and the introduction of a tiered structure of interest rates.

Thus, savings rate deregulation will create a win-win situation for both the retail depositor and the banking system.

◆ A Critique

The Reserve Bank of India (RBI) issued on February 23, 2013 final guidelines for setting up of new banks in the private sector including corporate houses and non-banking finance companies (NBFCs) through a wholly-owned Non-Operative Financial Holding company (NOFHC). Public sector companies are also to apply. The RBI will allow applicants for new licenses until July 1, 2013.

Main highlights of these guidelines are:

- Promoters/promoter groups should have a past record of sound credentials, integrity and should be financially sound and have a successful track record of running their business for at least 10 years.
- Promoter groups business model and business culture should not be aligned with the banking model and their business should not potentially put the bank and the banking system at risk on account of group activities such as those which are speculative in nature or subject to high asset price volatility.
- The initial minimum paid-up voting equity capital for a bank would be ₹ 500 crore. The NOFHC would initially hold a minimum of 40 per cent of the paid-up voting equity capital of the bank which would be locked for five years and which would be brought down to 15 per cent within 12 years.
- The bank shall get its shares listed on the stock exchanges within three years of the commencement of business.
- The aggregate foreign shareholding at the new bank would not exceed 49 per cent for the first five years after which it would be as per the extant policy.
- At least 50 per cent of the directors of the NOFHC would be independent directors.
- The NOFHC and the bank would not have any exposure to the promoter group.
- The bank shall not invest in the equity/debt capital instruments of any financial entities held by the NOFHC.
- The new bank should open at least 25 per cent of its branches in un-banked rural centres (population upto 9,999 as per the latest to census).

The RBI's norms on new bank licenses may not have discriminated against any particular category, but its stringent conditions would not likely keep non-serious players out of the fray. Given that financial inclusion should be the core of their strategy, aspirants for new bank licenses will have to be prepared for a long haul before they hit the profitability highway.

It is, thus, evident that every conceivable entity — financial institutions, public sector organisations and of course, corporate groups — is eligible to apply. In the public discussions during the last one year, some experts, including nobal laureate Joseph Stiglitz have come out against granting licences to unequivocally favoured the idea. Obviously, an enormous amount of corporate lobbying has taken place. But the RBI's norms on new bank licences are stringent. Foremost among them is that to get license, an entity has to be 'fit and proper', has a 10-year successful track record, be financially sound and has "sound credentials and integrity".

It makes sense for an NBFC to become a bank and for the financial arm of a corporate biggie to become a bank. But given all the restrictions there will be to prevent a bank from extending help or accommodation to anything linked to its promoting group, the question really is: what is there in a bank license for a large business group? It can access any amount of institutional finance at home or abroad, and a new bank will take a long time to make real money. A bank will allow a business house to dispense favours to lesser business mortals; beyond that, the most powerful business houses may be using their clout to own a bank simply because they find it prestigious to own a trophy bank.

Given the regulatory costs (SLR, CRR and priority sector requirements) of converting an NBFC into a bank, it is doubtful if many promoters who are already running successfully NBFCs will think twice before applying for a banking license.

The formidable challenge, which prospective banking entrants are likely to face, pertains to human resource. Many new banks may find it is too difficult to get sufficient skilled manpower willing to work in branches located in those unbanked locations. According to experts, new banks would be able to get talent to those areas only if they are able to pay a higher salary.

However, one of the constraints for paying attractive salary is that these branches may not become profitable immediately.

E. PRESENT STRUCTURE OF COMMERCIAL BANKING IN INDIA

The present structure of commercial banking, as it exists today in India, is graphically shown through Chart 6.1.

Chart 6.1: Scheduled Commercial Banking Structure in India as on March 31, 2012

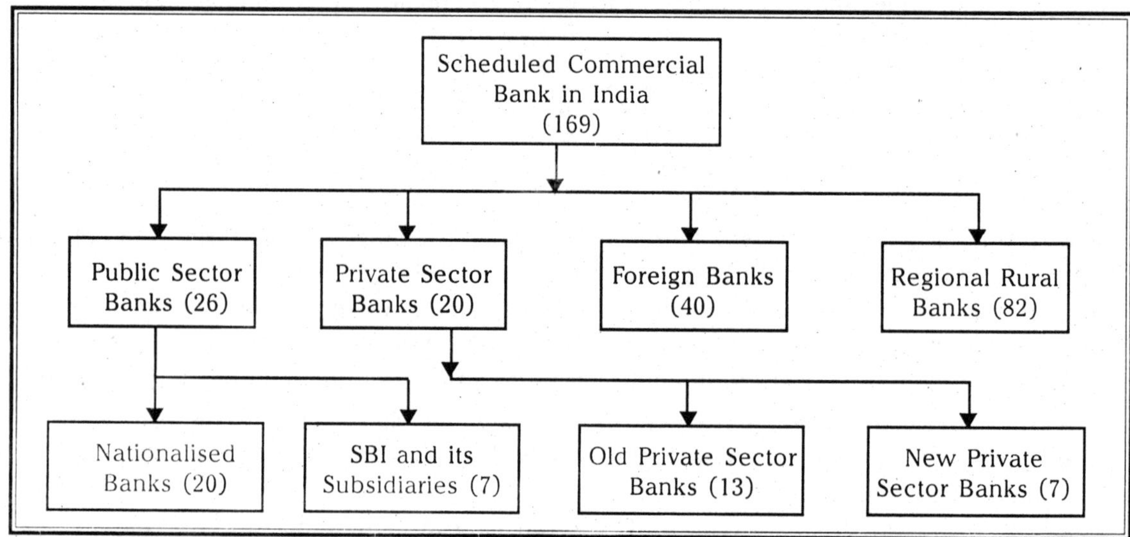

It may be noted from Chart 6.1 that number of scheduled commercial banks in India as on March 31, 2012 stood at 169, much lower than what existed on the eve of economic liberalisation (1991) being 272. The decline in the number of commercial banks was essentially due to merger of banks and liquidation of weak institutions.

Scheduled commercial banks (SCBs) operating in India comprise 26 public sector banks (PSBs), 20 private sector banks — 13 old private sector and 7 new private sector banks, 40 foreign banks operating in India and 82 regional rural banks (RRBs)

Number of RRBs, which stood at 196 as on March 31, 2005 tended to decline sharply to 82 as on March end 2012 due to amalgamation of a large number of unviable RRBs in recent years.

F. GEOGRAPHICAL EXPANSION OF INDIAN COMMERCIAL BANKS

There has been unprecedented expansion of banking operations in India particularly during the post nationalization period, as is vividly brought out in Table 6.3. Thus, its may be noted that on the eve of nationalization of banks number of commercial banks was 89 with total branches of 8,262. During the post nationalization period there has been massive expansion of number of banks and their branches from 89 in 1969 to 276 in 1986 and from 8,262 to 53,287 during the corresponding period. This resulted in steep decline in the average population per bank branch from 64,000 to 19,000 during the corresponding points of time.

TABLE 6.3: Number of Scheduled Commercial Banks Branches

	At the end of March								
	1969	1986	1991	1995	2000	2005	2010	2011	2012
1. No. of Bank Branches	8,262	53,287	60,570	64,234	67,868	68,339	71,998	72,300	83,229
2. Population per branch (----)	64	16	14	15	15	16	14	14	14

This expansionary trend was the outcome of the Government policy to penetrate unbanked areas of the country.

Number of bank branches rose to an all time high level of 83,229 as at March end, 2012. This resulted in steep decline in size of population served by a branch from 64,000 as on March end, 1969 to as low as 14,000 as on March end, 2012.

Bank-groupwise expansion of branches (Table 6.4) reveals that nationalized banks with their 43,187 branches as on March end 2010 represented about three-fifths of the total branches followed by SBI and its associates with 18,114 branches. Private sector banks had only 10,387 branches. Thus, geographical penetration by public sector banks has been remarkable showing the Government concern to service the customers across the country.

G. SPATIAL DISTRIBUTION OF COMMERCIAL BANK BRANCHES

Since nationalisation of banks the Government and the RBI made it a policy to expand banking business in all unbanked areas including rural and semi-urban areas. Accordingly, the RBI issued a directive in December 1969 according to which a bank having 60 per cent or more of its offices in rural and semi-urban areas at the end of 1969 would be eligible for opening one office each in an urban and a metropolitan port town for every two offices in rural/semi-urban areas; in other cases, the ratio was one office for every three offices in rural/semi-urban areas.

In January, 1977 significant changes were made in the branch licensing policy so as to provide more weightage to rural areas. According to the new policy, a bank willing to open one office each in a metropolitan and a banked centre was required to open four branches in the unbanked rural centres.

TABLE 6.4: Bank Groupwise Number of Scheduled Commercial Banks branches as on:

Bank Group	As on June 30, 1979	As on March end 2010	As on March end 2012
1. SBI and its Associates	13,265	18,114	19,787
2. Nationalised Banks	32,421	43,187	50,527
3. Private Sector Banks	4,983	10,387	13,408
4. Foreign Banks in India	186	310	317
Total	50,855	71,998	84,039

Source: Statistical Tables relating to Banks, RBI.

In view of the several problems which banks had to face in regard to manpower, control mechanism, training, overall efficiency, etc. created by the above policy, a new directive was issued in which the district was made the focus of attention. A minimum of 4,500 new branches were to be set-up during 1978-81 in the rural/semi-urban areas of different districts — a district having more population for bank office than the national average of 20,000. This policy was carried forward in the subsequent years with a modification in March 1985 for one bank branch on an average for a population of 17,000.

The main criterion for branch expansion was to open branches in the areas having no banking facilities irrespective of their commercial viability. As a result, branch expansion programme created a number of operating problems such as increased development expenditure, inadequacy of trained staff, loosening head office control which in turn, adversely affected productivity and efficiency and so also profitability of the banks. All these forced the RBI to change the norms of branch expansion and the population coverage criterion was dropped for giving licences for opening new branches. According to the RBI directive, future growth of bank offices would depend on well established need business — potential and financial viability of the proposed offices. There would be no need for envisaging any branch expansion programme as such for any period with targets like population coverage per bank office, as the objective of having a bank office for population not exceeding 17,000 had been achieved. As such, the RBI decided to allow branch expansion in rural areas only if the existing rural branch shows an increase in business. Additional branches might also be permitted if it was found that service area allocated to the branch was too large to handle efficiently.

Branch licensing policy was liberalised in October 1992 to empower banks to shift their existing branches within the same locality, open specialised branches for industrial finance/ SSIs/NRIs/Treasury, open extension counters and convert the existing rural branches into satellite offices if the existing branches are found non-viable after complying with certain minimal guidelines.

The RBI further liberalised branch expansion policy in 1993-94, and private sector banks were permitted to open branches without seeking its prior approval provided they satisfied the RBI's capital adequacy requirements. In its directive to PSBs issued in August, 1995, the Government of India asked them to consider opening of specialised branches at key small-scale industry and agricultural centres including conversion of existing branches into specialised branches.

In its strive to encourage banks to penetrate in unbanked areas, the RBI permitted banks in October 2009 to open branches in rural and semi-urban centres termed Tier-3 to Tier-6 centres. The number of branches opened by a bank in such areas will remain criterion for the RBI in allowing the bank to open branches in Tier-1 and Tier-2 cities, in addition to the bank's performance in financial inclusion.[10]

With financial inclusion being a key agenda of both the RBI and the Government, the RBI through its policy directive issued in July 2011 linked new branch licensing to the number of rural branches that banks open. The RBI advised banks should allocate at least 25 per cent of the total number of branches proposed to the opened during a year in unbanked rural (Tier-5 and Tier-6) centres.

TABLE 6.5: Spatial Distribution of Commercial Bank Branches (Per cent)

Centers	At the end of March					
	1971	1981	1991	2001	2011	2012
Rural	35.6	48.6	58.4	49.1	37.4	36.0
Semi-urban	33.6	21.8	18.8	22.1	25.2	25.5
Urban	16.1	15.2	13.3	15.6	19.8	20.3
Metropolitan	14.7	14.4	09.5	13.2	17.6	18.2
Total	100.0	100.0	100.0	100.0	100.0	100.0

Source: Basic Statistical Returns of Scheduled Commercial Banks in India.

Consequent upon liberalisation of the RBI's branch expansion policy, massive penetration of banks in rural and semi-urban regions of the country has taken place during the post nationalisation period. Thus, it may be noted from Table 6.5 that more than half of the branches were represented by rural and semi-urban regions as on March end 2012. Period-wise analysis of the spatial distribution of commercial bank branches reveals that until 1991 more than 70 per cent bank branches were in rural/semi-urban areas and urban and metropolitan branches represented hardly less than 30 per cent. However, there was a steep decline in the relative proportion of rural and semi-urban branches in total bank branches (from 77.2% in 1991 to 61.5% in 2012). This was mainly due to change in the RBI's branch expansion policy which laid greater emphasis on the criteria of business potential and financial viability of the newly set up branch. It is most interesting to note that not only banks have scaled down their presence, albeit marginally, but also at the same time enhanced their presence in urban and metropolitan areas in as much as new and old banks were found competing vigorously with one another to lure each other's customers. Obviously, either the RBI gave up on the cardinal principle of banking reputation held by it or is guilty of being a mute witness to the banking industry flouting its licensing norms.

H. STATE-WISE DISTRIBUTION OF BANK BRANCHES

Another redeeming feature of geographical expansion of banking services in India during the post nationalization period has been greater focus on relatively under developed states. Thus, on the eve of nationalization, relatively developed states such as Karnataka, Tamil Nadu, Punjab, Maharashtra, Haryana, Gujarat and West Bengal with total number of branches of 4,708 had claimed about 57 per cent of the total branches. But owing to establishment of increasingly large number of bank branches in less developed states since 1969 and onward, the proportionate share of advanced states declined to 45 per cent as on March 31, 2012. On the contrary, the share of banks branches in states like Andhra Pradesh, Rajasthan, Bihar, M.P. U.P and other undeveloped states surged to 55 per cent from 43 per cent as on June 30, 1969, clearly showing greater flow of banking facilities in underdeveloped states (Table 6.7).

TABLE 6.7 State/Union Territory-wise Distribution of Banks' Branches

Name of State/ Union Territory	Number of Branches of Banks as on		
	June end 1969	March end 2010	March end 2012
Northern Region	**762**	**13,495**	**16,780**
Haryana	173	2,361	3,034
Himachal Pradesh	15	1,000	1,164
Punjab	116	3,460	4,385
Rajasthan	164	4,090	4,944
Chandigarh	20	270	369
Delhi	274	2,314	2,884
North-Eastern Region	**90**	**2,113**	**2,451**
Arunachal Pradesh	68	80	96
Assam	07	1,434	1,641
Manipur	02	81	95
Meghalaya	3	208	240
Nagaland	10	88	108
Tripura	—	222	271
Eastern Region	**781**	**13,962**	**17,385**
Bihar	273	4,029	4,666
Jharkhand	—	1,804	2,186
Sikkim	—	74	91
West Bengal	508	5,200	6,119
Andaman & Nicobar Islands	—	37	—
Orissa	—	2,818	3,323
Central Region	**1,090**	**16,795**	**20,006**
Madhya Pradesh	343	4,133	4,823
Uttar Pradesh	747	10,191	12,121
Chattisgarh	—	1,295	1,459
Uttarakhand	—	1,176	1,603
Western Region	**1,958**	**12,964**	**15,784**
Goa	85	418	523
Gujarat	752	4,572	5,552
Maharahstra	1,118	7,928	9,635
Dadra & Nagar Haveli	0	19	34
Daman & Diu	3	27	740
Southern Region	**2,996**	**23,586**	**28,164**
Andhra Pradesh	567	6,949	8,422
Karnataka	756	6,050	7,201
Kerala	601	4,227	5,022
Tamil Nadu	1,060	6,214	7,336
Lakshadweep	—	11	12
Pondicherry	12	135	171

Regarding the penetration of banking services, a peep into the average population per bank branch — a better indicator of the penetration of banking services — shows that the penetration of banking services has been on a consistent increase in India in the recent years (Table 6.8). However, the rate of increase in the penetration of banking services in rural areas was much lower than in urban areas.

TABLE 6.8: Population per bank branch

(Number of Population in '000)

	2007	2008	2009	2010	2012
Population per bank branch in rural areas	17.8	17.0	16.6	16.1	16.0
Population per bank branch in urban areas	12.7	11.7	11.0	10.4	10.5
Total population per bank branch	16.0	15.1	14.5	14.0	13.9

Source: RBI's Report on Trend and Progress of Banking in India, 2009-10.

At the regional level, there was a striking differential in the degree of penetration of banking services. On the one hand, were northern, southern and western regions, where the population per bank branch was in the range of 10,000 to 13,900 at end-March 2012 (Table 6.9). On the other hand, in the central, eastern and north-eastern regions, the population per bank branch was fairly higher in the range of 18,000 to 19,000. It may, however, be emphasised that population per bank branch was on a decline across all regions in the recent years signifying growing penetration of banking services across all regions. This can be attributed to, as noted above, liberalisation of the branch authorisation policy in December, 2009 giving freedom to domestic scheduled commercial banks to open branches at Tier 3 to 6 centres (with population of upto 49,999 as per the population census of 2001) without having the need to take permission from the RBI in each case subject to reporting.

TABLE 6.9: Population per bank branch by Region

(Number of persons in '000)

Regions	2007	2008	2009	2010
Central Region	20.0	19.0	18.5	17.2
Eastern Region	20.0	19.0	18.7	17.4
North Eastern Region	22.0	21.0	20.0	19.1
Northern Region	11.5	11.5	10.5	10.0
Southern Region	11.5	10.4	10.0	9.5
Western Region	15.0	13.8	13.0	12.5

Source: Statistical Tables relating to Banks in India, 2009-10, RBI.

I. OWNERSHIP OF BANKS

The owners or shareholders of banks have only a minor stake, and the considerable leveraging capacity of banks (more than ten to one) puts them in control of very large volume of public funds inspite of their own stake being small. As such, the owners act as trustees and therefore, must be fit and proper for the deployment of funds entrusted to them.

In India, lion's share of banking business (90%) was accounted for by the Public sector during the pre-reform period. As part of the reforms programme, initially there was infusion of capital by the Government in Public Sector Banks (PSBs), which was followed by expanding the capital base with equity participation by the private investors. This led to decline in the share of the PSBs in the aggregate assets of the banking sector from 90 per cent in 1991 to around 70 per cent at present.

There has been further increase in private shareholding of PSBs in recent years. Though government shareholding in PSBs had remained above 51 per cent during 2011-12, majority of the PSBs (11 out of 21) were very close to the floor (Table 6.10).

TABLE 6.10: Public Sector Banks classified by percentage of private shareholding as at end-March 2012

Class of shareholding	Total Private shareholding	Private resident shareholding	Private non-resident shareholding
Upto 10 per cent	—	—	17
More than 10 per cent and upto 20 per cent	2	5	9
More than 20 per cent and upto 30 per cent	4	8	—
More than 30 per cent and upto 40 per cent	6	8	—
More than 40 per cent and upto 49 per cent	14	5	—

Source: RBI's Report on Trend and Progress of Banking in India, 2009-10.

As at end-March 2012, 10 out of 26 PSBs had private shareholding ranging from 20 per cent to 40 per cent. In addition, foreign shareholding in the PSBs was only upto 17.4 per cent. In contrast, foreign shareholding in private sector banks was upto 70.7 per cent which was within the stipulated limit of 74 per cent.

TABLE 6.11: Public and Private Sector Banks classified by percentage of foreign shareholding during 2009-10

Class of Shareholding	Public Sector Banks	New Private Sector Banks	Old Private Sector Banks
Nil	1	—	2
Upto 10 per cent	9	—	3
More than 10 per cent and upto 20 per cent	11	—	1
More than 20 per cent and upto 30 per cent	—	1	4
More than 30 per cent and upto 40 per cent	—	1	3
More than 40 per cent and upto 50 per cent	—	2	1
More than 50 per cent and upto 60 per cent	—	1	—
More than 60 per cent and upto 70 per cent	—	2	1

Source: RBI's Report on Trend and Progress of Banking in India, 2009-10.

So as to ensure that the control of private sector banks is well diversified to minimise the risk of misuse or imprudent use of levered funds, the RBI has a stipulated that shareholding or control in any bank in excess of 10 per cent of the paid-up capital by any single entity or group of related entities requires its prior approval. Banks (including foreign banks having branch presence in India)/financial institutions are not allowed to exceed equity holding of 5 per cent of the equity capital of the investee bank. Large industrial houses are allowed to acquire shares not exceeding 10 per cent of the paid-up capital of the bank subject to the

RBI's prior approval. The RBI could permit a higher level of shareholding on a case by case basis for restructuring of problem/weak banks or in the interest of consolidation in the banking sector.

As regards aggregate foreign investment in private banks from all services (FDI, FII, NRI), the guidelines stipulate that it cannot exceed 74 per cent of the paid-up capital of a bank. If FDI (other than by foreign banks or foreign bank groups) in private banks exceeds 5 per cent, the entity acquiring such stake would have to meet the 'fit and proper' criteria. The aggregate limit for all FII investments is restricted to 24 per cent which can be raised to 49 per cent with the approval of the board/shareholders. The current aggregate limit for all NRI investments in 24 per cent with the individual NRI investments is 24 per cent with the individual NRI investments is 24 per cent with the individual NRI limit being 5 per cent, subject to the approval of the board/shareholders.

In many private sector banks such as IndusInd Bank, Development Credit Bank, Kotak Mahindra Bank and Yes Bank, promoter shareholding has been found to be high. Taking cognizance of the high promoter shareholding of some private banks, the RBI, in its attempt to provide level playing field for all the players, has now decided to put a cap at 15 per cent of the paid-up capital on the promoter's shareholding in the bank.

Diversification of ownership has led to greater market accountability and improved efficiency. Since the initiation of reforms, infusion of funds by the Government into the PSBs for the purpose of recapitalization amounted, on a cumulative basis, to less than one per cent of India's GDP, a figure much lower than that for many other countries. Even after accounting for the reduction in the Government's shareholding on account of losses set off, the current market value of the share capital of the Government in PSBs has increased manifold and as such what was perceived to be a bail-out of PSBs by the Government seems to be turning out to be a profitable investment for the Government.

J. COMMERCIAL BANKS' DEPOSITS AND THEIR PATTERN

Being repositories of deposits, commercial banks garner savings of the people by offering myriad of innovative products. In India, Commercial banks have in recent years played significant role in mopping up burgeoning resources from individuals and others for fostering growth of the country. Table 6.12 exhibiting the amount of scheduled banks deposits at different points of time, shows that there has been notable acceleration in amount of the banks deposits from ₹ 4,661 crore as on June end, 1969 to ₹ 64,53,700 crore as on March end 2012. Per capita deposits surged from ₹ 3,910 crore in 2010 to ₹ 5,110 crore in 2012. Reasons for this remarkable growth are tremendous branch expansion and increased penetration in unbanked areas across the country, rise in interest rates and introduction of innovative and attractive saving schemes.

TABLE 6.12: Scheduled Commercial Banks' Deposits

As on	Amount in crore of ₹
June end, 1969	4,661
March end, 1991	2,00,569
March end, 2001	10,55,386
March end, 2005	18,37,557
March end, 2006	21,64,477
March end, 2007	26,08,309
March end, 2008	33,20,061
March end, 2009	40,63,203
March end, 2010	47,52,456
March end, 2011	56,16,432
March end, 2012	64,53,700

The pattern of bank deposits registered far-reaching changes particularly during the post nationalisation period, as evidenced from Table 6.13. Demand deposits accounted for major portion of total bank deposits before nationalisation of banks. However, post nationalisation period witnessed volte-face in the structure of bank deposits.

TABLE 6.13: Composition of Bank Deposits as on ....

(Percentages)

	June 1951	June 1966	June 1969	March 1991	July 2000	March 2006	March 2007	March 2008	March 2009	March 2010	March 2011	March 2012
Demand Deposits	63.0	50.3	45.0	17.0	14.0	17.0	13.0	16.9	11.5	10.2	10.4	9.8
Time Deposits	37.0	49.7	55.0	83.0	86.0	83.0	87.0	83.1	88.5	89.8	89.6	90.2
	100.0	100.0	100.0	100.0	100.0	100.0	100.0	100.0	100.0	100.0	100.0	100.0

Thus, it may be noted from Table 6.13 that time deposits tended to increase consistently and significantly from 37% as on June end, 1951 to over 90 per cent as on March end, 2012 with the result demand deposits reached an all time low level of 10 per cent during the year. This marked change in the composition of bank deposits may be explained by the following factors:

(*a*) Banks undertook an extensive publicity campaign to attract fixed deposits.

(*b*) Banks started penetrating into less commercially sophisticated areas where current accounts are not so common.

(*c*) The sharper rise in rates of interest on fixed deposit has attracted people to put their savings in fixed deposits.

(*d*) Introduction of numerous short-term deposit schemes tailored for people with varied notions has infused saving habits among the people and encouraged them to put their savings in term deposits of commercial banks.

It is interesting to note from the table that there was a surge in relative share of demand deposits in 2001 and also 2008. This can be attributed to public preference to park their savings in banks to derive benefits of safety along with reasonable income. Besides, money from mutual fund redemptions may have also found its way into banks.[11]

Analysis of deposits according to ownership of the banks reveals that a decade ago PSBs garnered major portion of public deposits in the country to the extent of over 82 per cent and the remaining less than one-fifth was mobilized by private sector and foreign banks operating in India. However, during the last five years, growth rate of deposits in the case of the PSBs was lower in comparison to newly set up private sector banks and foreign banks with the result that the share of the public sector banks in total deposit nose-dived from 82.4 per cent in 2001 to 52.9 per cent in 2005, while that of new private sector banks surged from 5.9 per cent to 11.0 per cent during the corresponding period. In case of foreign banks, the per centage share of their deposits buoyed up sharply from 4.8 per cent to 31.8 per cent.

TABLE 6.14: Deposits according to Ownership of Banks

(Rs. in crore)

	As On 31st March, 2001		As on 31st March, 2005	
	₹	%	₹	%
Public Sector Banks	8,59,462	82.4	14,20,750	52.9
Old Private Sector Banks	70,965	6.9	1,05,564	3.8
New Private Sector Banks	62,888	5.9	3,14,630	11.5
Foreign Banks in India	49,974	4.8	86,505	31.8
Total	10,43,289	100.00	27,27,449	100.0

This is reflection of competitive challenge which public sector banks, having hitherto enjoyed monopoly position, are facing from the newly emerging banks who are able to attract more new customers by dint of their superior services and better product-mix.

K. SPATIAL DISTRIBUTION OF DEPOSITS OF SCHEDULED COMMERCIAL BANKS

There has been chequered development in respect of spatial distribution of deposits of SCBs during the post-nationalisation period. Thus, it may be noted from Table 6.15 that the shares of rural, semi-urban and urban deposits in total bank deposits declined from their peaks in the 1980s and the early 1990s. This was because of increased competition from post offices. In contrast, the proportionate share of metropolitan deposits in total deposits of banks increased from the early 1990s, partly reflecting the growing significance of new private sector banks, which are operating largely in urban and metropolitan areas.

TABLE 6.15: Spatial Distribution of Deposits of Scheduled Commercial Banks

(Per cent)

End of March	*Rural*	*Semi-urban*	*Urban*	*Metropolitan*
1980	12.6	23.1	25.1	39.3
1990	15.3	21.2	24.7	38.9
2001	14.7	19.6	22.9	42.8
2007	9.7	13.8	20.5	56.0
2010	9.2	13.5	20.7	56.6

Source: Basic Statistical Returns of Scheduled Commercial Banks in India, RBI.

L. COMMERCIAL BANKS CREDIT AND ITS PATTERN OF DEPLOYMENT

Commercial banks being socio-economic institutions deploy buck of their resources by way of lending to different sections of the society not only to satisfy their credit needs but also to maximise their return as loaning is considered the most profitable source.

TABLE 6.16: Total Credit provided by Scheduled Commercial Banks

As on	*Amount in crore of ₹*
June end 1969	3,599
March end 1991	1,21,865
March end 2001	5,17,560
March end 2005	11,00,428
March end 2006	15,07,077
March end 2007	18,48,166
March end 2008	24,76,936
March end 2009	30,00,906
March end 2010	34,97,054
March end 2011	42,98,704
March end 2012	43,71,400

Source: RBI report on Trend and Progress of Banking in India.

Table 6.16 exhibits amount of loans granted by the scheduled commercial banks.in India during different points of time. It may be glanced from the table that there was quantum jump in amount of credit facilities provided by the banks since nationalisation of banks, rising from

₹ 3,599 crore as on June end 1969 to as high as ₹ 43,71,400 crore as on March end 2012. As a result, per capita bank credit soared from ₹ 69 to ₹ 3,991 during the corresponding period. This momentous growth in bank credit is because of massive branch expansion and new credit policy of the RBI directing banks to focus on rendering financial support to priority sectors and the recent strategy of the banks to provide retail loans including housing loans.

A peep into Table 6.16 reveals that bank credit during the period 2005-2008 recorded robust growth from ₹ 11,00,000 crore as on March end, 2005, bank loans shot up remarkably to ₹ 34,77,000 crore as on March end 2008. This can be explained by resounding economic growth, moderation in inflation, decline in real interest rates and rising income of household. Enormous investments in sectors such as infrastructure, retail, agriculture, SMEs and capacity expansion by companies, financial deepening from low base structural shifts in supply elasticities and improvement in efficiency of credit markets also contributed to this phenomenal rise. However, there was a decline in the growth of bank credit during the last three years. This was primarily due to global financial meltdown and tightening policy of the RBI in terms of rise in CRR, repo rate and reverse repo rate which led to revere liquidity crunch forcing banks to scale down retail loans, especially to housing sector.

It is interesting to note that despite the widespread concerns with regard to slowdown in credit off-take in the context of monetary policy, on a year-to-year basis, the loan and advances of the banking sector recorded higher growth in 2010-11 as compared with the previous year. While the economic recovery, from the recent financial turmoil increased the demand for credit; from the supply side, higher growth in deposits as well as growth in capital facilitated higher credit growth.

However, during the period 2011-2012, credit growth slowed, partly reflecting the slower economic activity and the portfolio adjustment to the non-performing assets. Thus, bank advances during this period grew 10.7 per cent compared to 16 per cent in the corresponding period last year. Further, the decline in credit growth for public sector banks was the sharpest (15%) reflecting risk aversion. This led to portfolio switch to safer investments of government securities. Credit growth of private sector banks saw a decline from 28.2% to 18.5% in the same period. Foreign banks, however, bucked the trend with a moderate increase of 20.6 per cent in advances at the end of December 2011, as compared with 19.8 per cent growth in the year-up period.

While credit flow from banks declined, the share of credit flow from non-bank sources increased to 53.9 per cent in the first nine months of 2011-12, compared with 43 per cent in the corresponding period last year.

It may further be interesting to observe that the pattern of distribution of bank credit has undergone a sea-change. A close perusal of Table 6.17 brings out the following facts:

(*i*) The industry sector had bagged the bulk of assistance in the form of loans and advances before the nationalisation.

(*ii*) Until the Second Plan period, commerce and trade remained the largest recipients of bank loans. However, the industry sector emerged as a prominent recipient during the Second Plan. From the Third Plan period onwards, the industry sector alone claimed about two-thirds of the total bank loans. The increasing tempo of industrial development, particularly after the beginning of the Second Plan, the rise in working capital requirements as well as the Reserve bank's efforts to discourage speculative hoarding of goods by the trade with the help of bank finance are believed to have shifted bank advances by giving preference to industries.

(*iii*) Until recently, commercial banks had been lackadaisical in giving loans to the agricultural sector because of the relatively greater credit risks inherent in them.

(*iv*) Following nationalization of banks there has been a marked shift in the sectoral deployment of credit. Thus, the share of industries sector declined from 67.5 per cent in 1968 to as low as 48.2 per cent in 1991. Likewise, trade sector suffered fall in its share of bank credit from 19.3 per cent to 14.7 per cent during the corresponding period. In sharper contrast to this, proportionate share of credit to farming sector buoyed up from 0.4 per cent in 1968 to 14.8 per cent in 1991.

TABLE 6.17: Sectoral Distribution of Bank Credit (Percentages) as on March 31

	1951	1956	1961	1966	1968	1974	1980	1985	1988	1991	1999	2000	2001	2002	2003	2004	2005	2006	2007	2008	2009	2010-2011	2011-2012
Industries	33.5	36.2	50.2	62.1	67.5	62.7	53.3	40.3	38.7	48.2	36.5	37.3	34.7	32.1	36.6	32.4	37.6	30.4	38.8	39.4	40.5	44.2	45.7
Trade	40.4	41.1	31.3	21.3	19.3	17.4	8.0	23.4	28.3	14.7	4.4	4.2	3.3	3.8	3.8	3.3	3.4	4.1	6.2	5.5	5.5	NA	NA
Agriculture & allied activities	2.1	2.0	3.1	2.4	0.4	7.2	10.4	17.6	18.1	14.8	11.7	11.1	12.0	11.3	10.7	11.8	12.6	12.3	12.8	12.8	13.0	12.5	12.1
Others	24.0	20.7	15.4	14.2	12.8	12.7	28.3	17.7	14.9	22.3	47.4	47.4	50.0	52.8	48.9	52.5	46.4	53.2	52.2	42.3	41.0	43.3	42.2
Total	100.0	100.0	100.0	100.0	100.0	100.0	100.0	100.0	100.0	100.0	100.0	100.0	100.0	100.0	100.0	100.0	100.0	100.0	100.0	100.0	100.0	100.0	100.0

The above sea change in the pattern of bank credit distribution was the outcome of new credit policy of the Government and the RBI according high priority to farming sector, entrepreneurs and small business and stipulating targets for lending to priority sectors.

(*v*) Changes in sectoral distribution of bank credit witnessed during post-nationalization period continued during the post-reform period. Bank credit to agriculture, which suffered fall until 2003, tended the surge from 10.7 per cent in 2003 to 13 per cent in 2009. This is further going to spurt because of the Government policy to double the flow of credit to agriculture during the eleventh plan.

As a matter of fact, credit to agriculture has been the major thrust area in recent years. Several initiatives have been taken as a follow-up to the announcement made by the Government in June 2004 to double the flow of credits to agriculture over the next three years.[12] In terms of financial inclusion, policy efforts were directed towards increasing the coverage of farmers by commercial banks by extending finance at the rate of 100 farmers/branch and financing of 50 lakh new farmers in a year. Further, the banks were asked in April 2007, to dispense with the requirement of 'no dues' certificates for loans upto ₹ 50,000 to small farmers and obtain self-declaration from the borrower. In August 2008, banks were advised that where landless labourers, sharecroppers and oral lesses faced problems in getting the necessary certificates from the local administration/panchayat raj institutions regarding cultivation of crops, they could submit affidavits regarding their occupational status.

(*vi*) The next thrust area of the policy is credit to the small and medium enterprises (SME) sector and several banks have initiated measures to encourage their credit flows to this sector. Until a few years ago, banks hardly looked at SMEs as they were not perceived to be an attractive business proposition because its was felt that they lacked a viable business model. But during the last few years, SMEs have slowly metamorphosed themselves into a performing sector across all industries, be its agri-products, food processing, industrial goods NIT services or any other areas of services. In view of their tremendous export and employment potentialities, banks are sensing a good business opportunity in this sector, as has been happening across Asia and elsewhere in the world.

So as to ensure smooth and greater flow of banks' credit to SMEs the RBI took several measures during 2004-05. First, the composite loan limit through a single window for SSI entrepreneurs was enhanced from ₹ 50 lakh to ₹ 1 crore. Second, in order to encourage securitization of loans to the SSI sector, investments made by banks in securitized assets representing direct lending to the SSI sector were permitted to be treated as their direct lending to the SSI sector under the priority sector, provided the pooled assets represent loans to the SSI sector. Third, interest rates on the deposits placed by foreign banks with SIDBI in lieu of shortfall in their priority sector lending obligations were restructured and the tenor of deposits increased from one year to three years from financial year 2005-06. Fourth, investment limit in plant and machinery for seven items belonging to sports goods, which figure in the list of items reserved for manufacturer in the SSI sector, was enhanced from ₹ 1 crore to ₹ 5 crore.

On August 19, 2005 the RBI advised banks to take the following measures to augment flow of credit to SMEs.[17]

- Enhancement of composite loan limit through a single window for SSI entrepreneurs from ₹ 50 lakh to ₹ one crore;
- Raising investment limit in plant and machinery for 7 items belonging to sports goods from ₹ 1 crore to ₹ 5 crores.
- Financing to SSI units (upto ₹ 10 crore) to be included in the priority sector;
- Banks to fix self-target for financing to SME sector to achieve higher disbursement over the preceeding year;

- Banks to adopt cluster-based approach as a thrust;
- Banks to set up specialized branches in identified clusters/centres with preponderance of medium enterprises to enable the SME entrepreneurs to have an easy access to the bank credit.
- The Board of Directors to formulate comprehensive and more liberal policies in respect of loans to the SSI sector, based on the guidelines on lending to this sector.

Consequent upon the above initiatives, there has been modest increase in the share of SSI sector to total credit to industry from 16.9 per cent in 2007 to 17.9 per cent in 2008.

Expressing concern over the slow growth of lending to small and micro enterprises, the RBI of late, urged banks to step up credit to this sector to 55 per cent of the total SME financing by 2012 and 60 per cent by 2013. The RBI has set up Standing Advisory Committee under the chairmanship of one of its Dy. Governor's to review credit flow to SMEs regularly.

(vii) As regards financing to industry sector, commercial banks deployed more than two-thirds of their funds in industry sector until 1974 where after there has been steep decline in its share to reach an all time low level of 30.4 per cent in 2006. This is attributed to change in lending policies of the banks in tune with the Government policy according high priority to rural and service sectors, on the one hand and greater reliance of large corporates on internal as well as alternative sources of external financing. There was significant improvement in relative share of bank credit to industry sector during the subsequent years when its share soared to over 40 per cent. This was primarily due to banks' greater concern for financing expanding demand of industry sector.

(viii) There has been tremendous expansion of bank credit to 'others' which claimed bulk of the credit (53.2%) facilities of the banks. This is mainly because of credits to housing sector which recorded gargantuan increase to the tune of ₹ 1,86,429 crore as on March end, 2006.

M. SPATIAL DISTRIBUTION OF BANK CREDIT

Spatial distribution of bank credit (Table 6.18) presents disconcerting picture. It may be seen from the table that the share of credit is lower than that of deposits in all regions except metropolitan, implying that resources get intermediated into metropolitan areas. This in itself may not necessarily be undesirable or unexpected if resources are being intermediated to their best uses. However, they do provide some indication for concern because it typifies financial exclusion practices of Indian banks. Retail credit has grown during the last 8 years by nearly 50 per cent mostly at urban centres. As incomes increase, there is growing demand for retail credit in rural areas which is perhaps being met by informal sector. Anecdotal evidence suggests that money lenders in rural areas force more competition from other informal money lenders rather than from Indian banks.

TABLE 6.18: Spatial Distribution of Bank Credit (Per cent)

Regions	*1969*	*1996*	*2005*	*2010*
Rural	3.3	11.4	9.5	11.5
Semi-urban	13.1	13.1	11.3	11.0
Urban	21.8	17.7	16.4	17.8
Metropolitan	61.8	57.8	62.7	59.7
Total	100.0	100.0	100.0	100.0

According to the RBI study, the spatial distribution of bank credit showed high level of concentration of credit at the top 100 centres. At the March-end 2010, the top 100 centres accounted for 78.0 per cent of the total bank credit in India, which was marginally lower than

TABLE 6.19: Industry-wise Deployment of Gross Bank Credit

Industry	Outstanding as on last reporting Friday of March											
	1992	2002	2003	2004	2005	2006	2007	2008	2009	2010	2011	2012
Industry (Small, Medium and Large) *of which*	**65240**	**229523**	**295562**	**313065**	**423136**	**550444**	**697339**	**858344**	**1054390**	**1311452**	**1620848**	**1967454**
1. Coal	246	1409	1334	1165	2139	4146	7704	—	—	—	—	—
2. Mining and quarrying including Coal	—	1593	1769	1635	4146	7704	7582	12277	14241	18084	22857	32495
3. Iron and steel	3692	20042	28065	26295	35742	50991	63744	82696	99159	127464	163189	192749
4. Other Metal and Metal Products	2312	6496	8556	8168	11273	14905	19993	24899	29604	35465	46705	62881
5. All Engineering	14842	24199	26272	26348	28934	34878	43762	15843	65807	73820	93367	113567
of which: electronics	2092	5941	7831	8421	9114	11004	13511	54439	18912	22100	24986	319192
6. Electricity	1298	9343	11173	14090	—	—	—	—	—	—	—	—
7. Cotton textiles	4278	11744	15762	17166	22782	29781	38049	47746	51307	61288	74143	81044
8. Jute Textiles	330	737	860	1051	910	1053	967	1080	1469	1380	1572	1392
9. Other Textiles	3970	13455	15075	15941	19446	24577	35812	42288	43521	47096	58214	66053
10. Sugar	899	5028	5726	6363	6928	8776	11551	16080	17309	19255	25080	31163
11. Tea	658	986	1052	1222	1627	1851	2340	2483	2731	1995	2368	2317
12. Food Processing	1241	7285	8577	9872	24025	30946	40011	49397	53779	65677	84931	102411
13. Vegetable oils (including vanaspati)	898	2729	2919	3219	3591	5077	6114	7243	6763	10380	13371	14352
14. Tobacco and tobacco products	550	861	756	891	1943	4002	4774	—	—	—	—	13510
15. Paper and paper products	1501	3741	5049	5990	6863	9148	11588	13469	15983	19074	21143	25171
16. Rubber and rubber products	1077	2246	2662	2593	3966	7250	9250	11213	13587	15617	21923	25751

17. Chemicals, Dyes, paints, etc.	8280	25988	31805	30629	39021	48638	55900	8779	75555	85713	94527	112503
of which												
(*i*) Fertilisers	1357	5463	6923	6249	8165	10569	9837	62562	14265	13847	10538	15194
(*ii*) Petro-chemicals	814	6663	7735	7221	7177	6965	8318	9186	8782	10046	12374	18441
(*iii*) Drugs and Pharmaceuticals	1127	6393	7892	8667	12335	16273	18653	23502	29755	35980	41572	47204
18. Cement	986	4224	6431	5689	8005	7799	9410	12544	19220	24722	28557	37185
19. Leather and leather products	1086	2352	2940	3167	3264	4486	4774	5742	6146	6232	7116	7449
20. Gems and jewellery	1300	6456	7533	9178	14156	20559	23850	25101	28537	31751	39427	50366
21. Construction	1344	4000	4891	5978	8321	13303	19997	27945	38505	44219	50135	56703
22. Petroleum	19	11320	14743	12266	15261	25150	35886	42067	68147	78579	57567	70055
23. Automobiles including trucks	—	4454	5629	5302	12045	18628	20855	29323	34642	38780	44491	51610
24. Computer software	—	1665	2611	3029	2760	3637	5156	—	—	—	—	—
25. Infrastructure	—	14809	26297	37224	78999	112853	143375	34476	269972	379888	526612	619086
of which												
(*i*) Power	—	7373	15042	19655	38235	60157	73158	205336	124447	187841	269196	328860
(*ii*) Telecommunications	—	3972	5779	8408	15705	18455	19446	95075	50326	59362	100425	93594
(*iii*) Roads and Ports	—	3464	5476	9161	14500	19695	24984	38282	47060	73569	92569	114383
26. Ships acquired from abroad *under new scheme*	68											
27. Other industries	14365	41861	57075	60458	84506	80975	97977	90698	102028	124822	150704	221883

that end-March 2009 (78.5%). The top 100 centres, however, accounted for only 69.4 per cent of the deposits at end-March 2010 and 69.2 per cent at March-end 2009.[18]

At the regional level too, bank credit was concentrated in the western, southern and northern regions of the country. The amount of credit per capita in western region was about 11 times the corresponding amount in the north-eastern region and about six to eight times the amount in the central and eastern regions at end-March 2010.[18]

It is interesting to note that Indian banks are lending more than what they get as deposits — this is what was the RBI's Governer's concern during the third quarterly review of the monetary policy for the year 2010-11. The Governor said "The incremental credit-deposit (C/D) ratio of the banking sector was 1.2 per cent as at the end of December 2010, up from 58 per cent in the corresponding period of the previous year."[19]

Ideally, banks cannot lend, for example, more than ₹ 70 for every ₹ 100 they mobilised as deposits, because they need to set aside ₹ 30 in the form of cash reserve ratio (CRR) and statutory liquidity ratio (SLR). But RBI says, for every additional ₹ 100 deposits, banks are lending ₹ 102, even after meeting CRR and SLR obligations.

Banks have managed this by borrowing from the call money market and the liquidity adjustment facility of the RBI. If this trend continues, it can give rise to widening the asset-liability gap, which is not a healthy trend. This is why the RBI asked banks to manage their resources portfolio to sustain credit deployment.

N. INDUSTRY-WISE DEPLOYMENT OF BANK CREDIT

Table 6.19 contains information pertaining to industry-wise distribution of gross bank credit. It is revealing to note from the table that the banks in India have diffused their funds among large number of industries so as to maximise returns alongwith reduced risks. However, plan priority industries such as engineering chemicals, food processing and infrastructure received greater attention of the banks.

O. CREDIT-DEPOSIT RATIO OF SCHEDULED BANKS

Credit-deposit ratio (C-D ratio) is an important index for analysing the role of banks in promoting productive sectors and contributing to economic growth of the country. In a bank-based financial system, the C-D ratio assumes greater significance as an aggressive measure for gauging the effectiveness of delivery system. Higher C-D ratio signifies greater credit orientation of banks.

It may be noted from Table 6.20 that C-D ratio has ballooned significantly from 60.0 as on June end 1969 to 78.0 as on March-end 2012. This is indicative of greater deployment of deposits for financing productive sectors.

TABLE 6.20: C-D Ratio of Scheduled Commercial Banks

	At the end of				
	June 1969	*March 1991*	*March 2001*	*March 2011*	*March 2012*
Credit-Deposit Ratio	60.0	60.0	58.7	77.0	78.1

At a time when the Government and the RBI are emphasizing inclusion and increase in credit delivery to those without access to formal sources of finance, private sector banks are found to have low C-D ratios in rural areas as compared to their public sector counterparts. According to RBI data, the C-D ratio in private sector banks was 42 per cent at the end of March, 2011 in rural areas while it was 60 per cent in public sector banks. Accordingly, the RBI directed banks in November, 2011 to have a C-D ratio of at least 50 per cent in rural areas.

The banking system in India is significantly different across the country owing to the desperate economic, geographic and social structures and economic activity is reflected in banking operations. Despite the RBI advisory for the last three decades, variations in C-D ratio persist across the country. Thus, it may be noted from Table 6.21 that western and southern regions have had much higher C-D ratio as compared to other regions, suggesting greater deployment of garnered resources by the banks for productive purpose. In north-eastern region, about one-third of the deposits was utilised for lending purpose.

State/territory-wise analysis of C-D ratio brings to the forth the sharper disparities in C-D ratio, showing variation from 134 per cent in Chandigarh to mere 8 per cent in Lakshadweep. Among the states, Tamil Nadu and Andhra Pradesh top the list with C-D ratio above 100 per cent. Not far behind there is Rajasthan with C-D ratio of 96 per cent. Karnataka, Haryana, Maharashtra and Gujarat are among the advanced states with a moderately high C-D ratio in the range of 75-80 per cent. On the contrary, Goa and Bihar have the lowest credit off-take with less than 30 per cent C-D ratio. The north-eastern states of Tripura, Meghalaya and Arunachal Pradesh have a very low credit inflow while Uttarakhand and Jharkhand are the other two states with C-D ratio of less than 40. In many as 16 states, the C-D ratio is less than 50 per cent.

Though the rise in the aggregate C-D ratio over the last decade has been encouraging existence of widespread disparities in credit off-take across the states goes against the mission of inclusive growth and hence causing great concern to the RBI. To address this problem, the RBI is working through the state-level Bankers' committees for capacity-building initiatives, with financial literacy cum credit counselling centres and rural self-employment training institutes in each district.

TABLE 6.21: Region-wise C-D Ratio of Scheduled Commercial Banks in India

Region	As on March end				
	2008	2009	2010	2011	2012
Northern	67.7	68.9	74.6	82.5	90.1
North-eastern	40.7	36.0	34.4	33.8	33.8
Eastern	51.5	56.2	50.3	51.4	50.0
Central	46.1	44.3	46.7	46.7	47.3
Western	88.6	85.6	77.8	79.5	74.1
Southern	89.1	87.9	92.2	94.5	94.8

A granular look at Table 6.22 reveals that in sync with higher growth rates, the shares of service sector credit and personal loans increased in the total outstanding non-food credit from 34.3 per cent at March end 2009 to 44 per cent at end-March 2012. In contrast, the share of agricultural sector, which offers employment to large sections of population, declined from 15.9 per cent to 10.5 per cent during the same period. The share of industrial credit recorded modest rise. However, there was increase in the share of credit to industry sector during 2012 as compared to 2011 owing to improvement in industrial condition of the country. Out of the total industrial credit, the share of infrastructure increased from 29 per cent in 2009-10 to 33 per cent in 2010-11. There was phenomenal growth in credit to telecommunications sector

TABLE 6.22: Sectoral deployment of Gross Bank Credit as on March end

(Percentages)

Sector	2009	2010	2011	2012
1. Agricultural & Allied activities	15.9	13.7	12.6	10.5
2. Industry	49.8	43.1	44.1	45.5
3. Personal loans	10.3	19.2	18.2	17.5
4. Services	24.0	24.0	24.4	26.5
Total	100.0	100.0	100.0	100.0

P. PRIORITY SECTOR FINANCING BY COMMERCIAL BANKS IN INDIA

◈ Priority Sector Lending Policies — A Synoptic View

One of the major objectives of the nationalisation of banks, as noted earlier, was to direct larger volumes of credit flows of the banking sector into the priority sector comprising agriculture, small-scale industries, small traders, artisans, self-employed persons and similar other weak sections of society which had hitherto been ignored by the banks. To accomplish this objective, the banks were asked to adopt a new credit policy. The cardinal features of this policy are:

(*a*) The banks would pursue the production nexus approach instead of the asset nexus approach while dispensing assistance to the priority sectors. For example, the viability of the project would be judged on the basis of whether the incremental income that would be generated by undertaking an activity with the help of bank finance would be sufficient to ensure the repayment of the loan. The bank would not insist on security and personal guarantee for loan purposes. Priority sectors would receive lending facilities on relaxed terms and conditions. The normal security requirements of banks are dispensed with in their case.

(*b*) Under the new policy, a commercial bank would entertain viable proposals even for composite finance. Besides providing funds for short-term capital requirements, it would provide term lending facilities to farmers to cover their credit needs for the purchase of inputs, pesticides, the development of land, the installation of tubewells with diesel/electric pumpsets, minor irrigation schemes, etc.

(*c*) Commercial banks would provide concessional lending facilities to the priority sectors, under which the latter will receive loans at a relatively lower interest rate and for a longer period of time.

The banks were also asked by the Reserve Bank to adopt target-oriented programmes of financing the priority sectors. In 1977, the public sector banks in India were advised to enlarge the flow of credit to the priority sectors so as to reach a level of 33 1/3 per cent of their outstanding credit by the end of March 1979. Subsequently, in 1980 this ratio was raised to 40 per cent to be achieved over a period of five years (by March 1985). With a view to ensuring an equitable distribution of bank credit among the priority sectors, they have been directed to lend not less than 16 per cent of the total bank credit facilities to the agricultural sector by 1985 which was subsequently raised to 18 per cent. Further, direct advances to weaker sectors in agriculture should reach a level of at least 10.0 per cent of the total direct lending to agriculture and allied activities by 1985. In the small-scale industries sector, the weaker sections should get 12.5 per cent of the total bank advance by 1985. Banks have also been advised to ensure that by March 1985, 25 per cent of their priority sector would be advances are deployed for those below the poverty line.

Foreign banks operating in India were also advised to progressively increase their advances to the priority sector to reach a level of 15 per cent of their net bank credit (NBC) by end March 1992. In April 1993, this ratio was further raised to 32 per cent, two sub-targets of 10 per cent in respect of SSI and 12 per cent for exports were fixed.

On the basis of the revised guidelines on lending to the priority sector, the priority sector lending target/sub-targets were linked to adjusted net bank credit (ANBC) or credit equivalent amount of off-balance sheet exposures, whichever is higher, with effect from April 30, 2007.

Narasimham Committee had recommended for reduction of the level of priority sector lending from 40% to 10%. However, the Government did not accept the recommendation and both domestic scheduled commercial banks and foreign banks were required to extend a minimum of 40 per cent and 32 per cent, respectively, of their net bank credit to the priority sector. Within this target of 40 per cent, sub-targets of 18 per cent and 10 per cent of net bank credit, respectively, were stipulated for lending to agriculture and weaker sections of the population. In case of foreign banks, out of the target of 32 per cent, the aggregate credit to SSI sector should not be less than 10 per cent of the net bank credit and that to the export sector should not be less than 12 per cent of the net bank credit.

In order to align bank credits to the changing needs of the society, the scope and definition of priority sector were fine-tuned over time by including new items as also by enhancing credit limit of the constituent sub-sectors. As a part of this process, some more measures were initiated in 2004-2005. First, the ceiling on credit limit to farmers against pledge / hypothecation of agricultural produce (including warehouse receipts) was increased from ₹ 5 lakh to ₹ 10 lakh under the priority sector. Second, the limit on advances under the priority sector for dealers in agricultural machinery was increased from ₹ 20 lakh to ₹ 30 lakh and for distribution of inputs for allied activities from ₹ 25 lakh to ₹ 40 lakh. Third, banks were permitted to extend direct finance to the housing sector up to ₹ 15 lakh, irrespective of location as part of their priority sector lending. Fourth, investments by banks in the mortgage backed securities (MBS) have been classified as direct lending to housing within the priority sector lending subject to certain conditions. Fifth, loans advanced to distressed urban poor to prepay their debit to non-institutional lenders against appropriate collateral or group security have been classified as advances to weaker sections within the priority sector. Sixth, investment limit in plant and machinery for seven items belonging to sports good, which figure in the list of items reserved for manufacture in the small scale industries (SSI) sector, was enhanced from ₹ 1 crore to ₹ 5 crore for the purpose of classification under priority sector advances. Seventh, banks were urged to make efforts to increase their disbursements to small and marginal farmers to 40 per cent of their direct advances under special agricultural credit plans (SACP) by March 2007. All Private sector banks were also asked to formulate SACP targets from 2005-06 with an annual growth rate of at least 20-25 per cent of credit disbursements to agriculture. Eighth, investments by banks in securitized assets representing direct lending to the SSI sector have been classified as their direct lending to the SSI sector under priority sector.[20]

Besides, the RBI has directed banks not to insist for any collateral security/third party guarantees for all advances under priority sector upto ₹ 25,000. No service or processing fee is to be recovered by banks in such cases. Banks have also been given a time bound schedule with in which they are required to sanction the advances to borrowers falling under priority sector.

The revised guidelines on lending to the priority sector, effective April 30, 2007 have enlarged the basis of the priority sector lending.

The broad categories of the priority sector for all scheduled commercial banks will be as under.

(i) Agriculture (Direct and Indirect Finance)

Direct finance to agriculture shall include short, medium and long-term loans given for agriculture and allied activities such as dairy, fishery, piggery, poultry, bee keeping.

Indirect finance to agriculture shall include loans give for specified entities in the areas of agriculture and allied activities.

With a view to providing adequate and timely credit to farmers, it was decided during 2011-12 to introduce a separate Short-Term Refinance Facility from NABARD for Central Co-operative Banks (CCBs) with sound financial position and a new line of short-term refinance support for PSBs and RRBs for financing in PACs in such areas where CCBs are weak. The quantum of refinance is fixed at a uniform rate of 45 per cent of the Realistic Lending Programme. The facility is available at an interest rate of 4.5 per cent per annum provided that the rate charged to the ultimate borrower for crop loans upto 0.3 million does not exceed 7 per cent.

(ii) Small Enterprise (Direct and Indirect Finance)

Direct finance to small enterprises shall include all loans given to micro and small enterprises, engaged in both manufacturing (production, processing or preservation of goods) and service activities and whose investment in plant and machinery and equipment does not exceed the specified amounts. The micro and small (service) enterprises will include small road and water transport operators, small business, professional and self-employed persons and certain other service enterprises.

Indirect finance to small enterprises shall include finance to any person providing inputs to or marketing the output of artisans, village and cottage industries, handlooms and to cooperatives of producers in this sector.

(iii) Retail Trade

Retail trade shall include retail traders/private retail traders dealing in essential commodities (fair price shops) and consumer cooperative stores.

(iv) Micro Credit

Micro credit shall include provision of credit and other financial services and products of very small amounts not exceeding ₹ 50,000 per borrower, either directly or indirectly through a SHG/JLG mechanism or to NBFC/MFI for on-lending upto ₹ 50,000 per borrower.

(v) Education Loans

Education loans shall include loans and advances granted to individuals (but not to institutions) upto ₹ 10 lakh for studies in India and ₹ 20 lakh for studies abroad.

(vi) Housing Loans

Housing loans shall include loans upto ₹ 20 lakh to individuals for purchase/construction of one dwelling unit per family and loans given for repairs to the damaged dwelling units of families upto ₹ 1 lakh in rural and semi-urban areas and upto ₹ 2 lakh in urban and metropolitan areas.

In December 2008, the RBI in its attempt to provide support to the housing sector, directed banks to grant loans to housing finance companies (HFCs) for on-lending to individuals for purchase/construction of a dwelling unit per family. Such loans could be classified as housing loans under priority sector, provided the loans granted by HFCs did not exceed ₹ 20 lakh per dwelling unit. The maximum amount of loans granted by banks to HFCs, that would be eligible for classification as housing loans under priority sector, could not exceed 5.0 per cent of the bank's total priority sector lending.[21]

The RBI in its latest directive issued on July 20, 2012 said that banks have to disburse 13.5 per cent of 40 per cent priority sector loan, directly to the agricultural sector. The latest directive excluded infrastructure sector from priority sector category. Indirect lending to housing finance companies and most NBFCs no longer qualify for priority sector lending.

Foreign banks in India having 20 or more branches in the country must extend 40 per cent of their net credit to the priority sector, a norm hitherto applicable only for domestic banks. These banks have been given five years, starting April 2013, to meet the new norms. They have been asked to file an action plan by December, 2012 for achieving the targets over a specific time frame, needing RBI approval.

◆ Trend in Scheduled Commercial Banks' advances to priority sector

Consequent upon various measures taken by the Government and the RBI, there has been substantial growth in the banks' advances to priority sector. Thus, it may be noted from Table 6.23 that the amount of priority sector advances by the banks surged from ₹ 441 crore as on June end 1969 to ₹ 14,97,600 comes as on March end 2012.

An analysis of priority sector advances according to ownership of banks reveals that domestic and foreign banks had more than met their overall priority sector lending targets of 40 and 32 per cent, respectively. (Table 6.24) However, the private sector banks excelled their public sector counterparts in lending to the priority sector.

As regards the target achieved by the PSBs in lending to agriculture sector, it may be observed by Table 6.24 that advances to agriculture sector constituted 16.5 per cent as on March end 2011. Nevertheless, PSBs have increasingly raised allocation of priority sector advances to this sector, they have not been able to achieve the target stipulated for this sector. In contrast, they have more than achieved the target stipulated for the small scale sector.

TABLE 6.23: Scheduled Commercial Banks' Advances to Priority Sector

Year as on	Amount in ₹ crore
June end 1969	441
June end 1991	42,093
March 2001	1,49,116
March 2004	3,11,336
March 2005	4,00,775
March 2006	5,46,773
March 2007	7,03,756
March 2008	8,24,772
March 2009	9,65,773
March 2010	11,40,000
March 2011	12,77,543
March 2012	14,97,600

Source: RBI's Report on Trends and Progress of Banks in India for relevant years.

TABLE 6.24: Lending by Banks according to Priority Sector Segments

(₹ in crore)

	Public Sector Banks						Private Sector Banks					
	2006	2007	2009	2010	2011	2012	2006	2007	2009	2010	2011	2012
Priority Sector advances	4,09,748 (40.3)	5,21,180 (39.6)	7,24,150 (42.7)	8,64,564 (41.6)	10,28,615 (41.3)	11,30,100 (37.2)	1,06,586 (42.8)	1,43,768 (42.7)	1,87,849 (46.2)	2,15,552 (45.9)	2,48,828 (46.6)	2,86,400 (39.4)
of which: Agriculture	1,55,220 (15.3)	2,05,091 (5.6)	2,99,415 (17.6)	3,70,730 (17.1)	4,14,991 (16.5)	4,78,600 (15.8)	36,712 (13.6)	52,056 (12.8)	76,102 (8.7)	89,769 (15.6)	92,136 (15.9)	1,04,200 (14.3)
of which: Micro and Small Enterprises	82,434 (8.1)	1,04,703 (8.0)	1,91,408 (11.3)	2,78,398 (13.2)	3,76,625 (15.1)	68,54,000 (22.6)	10,421 (4.2)	13,063 (3.9)	46,656 (11.5)	64,534 (13.7)	87,857 (16.4)	1,49,400 (20.6)

Source: RBI Report on Trend and Progress of Banking Institute for relevant years.

Almost the same tendency was noticeable in respect of private sector banks.

At the aggregate level, both public and private sector banks were below the sub-target of 18 per cent for agriculture at end-March 2010. At the disaggregated level, more than half of PSBs (15 out of 27) and exactly half of the private sector banks (11 out of 22) could not meet the agricultural sub-target. Within private sector banks, the performance was relatively poor in the case of old private sector banks, while most new private sector banks were able to meet the sub-target under agriculture.

Non-achievement of agriculture lending target by many public and private sector banks has been due to low capital formation in agriçulture resulting in poor credit absorption and write-off of non-performing loans leading to reduction in the outstanding advances in the case of some banks.

◆ Problems faced by Banks in Priority sector Lending

The above discussion reveals that the scheduled banks have made commendable progress in financing poor and neglected sectors of the society. However, two major problems are causing great concern to Indian bankers in respect of bank lending to priority sectors. The first such problem is high volume of overdues and the other is the ever increasing cost of supervision. The recovery position continues to plague the system.

Though in the short run the bankers would have to garner their resources and to undertake recovery camps, this could not continue to be the normal practice for long. As a long-term measure, there must be an inducement for the borrower to go to the banker and pay his dues and if there was a wilful default some action would be operative against them. The second area of concern is the test of supervised credit. Presently, the quality of supervision leaves much to be desired. Just improving the supervision machinery in the traditional manner would not help.

The main domain of the banks is credit system. If the banks are to survive successfully, they have to ensure proper utilisation of credit. They have to ensure the recycling of credit.

Finally, large-scale priority sector lending have imposed overwhelming stresses and strains on banks. In recent years, while earnings per unit of resources of the banks have been declining due to channelization of an increasing proportion of their advances to the priority sectors and other weaker sections, the cost of operations of banks has gone up. As a result, the banking system is operating today on a thin margin which is progressively getting thinner. The bankers cannot afford to ignore their responsibility to function as viable financiers by overlooking their profitability, balance sheet strength, liquidity and quality of assets. Both micro level and macro level efforts have to be made to arrest the deteriorating profitability trend and put the banking on viable keel.

Q. LONG-TERM FINANCING BY COMMERCIAL BANKS

Following the recommendations of the Narasimham Committee, the RBI permitted commercial banks in India to engage in long-term financing business. Accordingly, Indian commercial banks entered into long-term financing activity and provided term loans, leasing and hire purchase loans, invested in shares, bonds/debentures of corporate enterprises, units of mutual funds and shares of financial institutions. Participation of commercial banks in long-term financing has been facilitated by change in composition of banks' deposits with term deposits accounting for preponderant share of total resources mobilised by them.

TABLE 6.25: Non-SLR Investments of Scheduled Commercial Banks

(Per cent)

Instrument	Upto October 2007	Upto October 2008	Upto September 2010	Upto October 2011	Upto September 2012
1. Commercial paper	4.6	14.3	17.7	8.1	10.9
2. Shares	13.9	25.7	15.2	15.0	13.2
3. Bonds/debentures	34.2	47.5	42.7	47.0	61.2
4. Units of Mutual funds and Instruments issued by financial institutions	47.3 —	12.5 —	24.4 —	14.6	14.8
Total	100.0	100.0	100.0	100.0	100.0

Table 6.25 brings out data pertaining to long-term investments (Non-SLR) of Scheduled commercial banks. It may be noted from the table that bulk of the funds was invested in bonds/debentures of public sector undertakings and private companies followed distantly by investment in commercial paper. In recent years, commercial banks' preference for shares, bonds and debentures of organisations has dwindled in favour of commercial paper, mutual funds and financing institutions. This can be attributed to subdued conditions in the capital market.

Nevertheless banks are growingly participating in long-term financing business, funding long-term assets like infrastructure and homes with resources (mostly deposits) are landing them in a serious spot. Investing in infrastructure bonds of 10-15 years and providing home loans for a period of 15-20 years against the 7.4% deposits having a maturity period of more than 5 years is causing burgeoning problem of asset-liability mismatch to the banks.

To avert the impending risk, the commercial banks have resorted to 'Take-out-finance' route. Take-out financing is a method of providing finance for long projects (say 15 years) by sanctioning medium-term loans (five-seven years). It involves an understanding that the loan will be taken out of the books of the financing bank within a pre-fixed period and taken over by another institution, thereby preventing any possible asset-liability mismatch. India infrastructure Finance Company Ltd. is already working on a proposal to take infrastructure loans of commercial banks on its books.

To promote infrastructure investment in July 2010, the RBI permitted take-out financing arrangement through External Commercial Borrowings (ECB), under the approval route and subject to specified conditions, for the purpose of refinancing of rupee currency loans availed of from the domestic banks by the sea port and airport, roads including bridges and power sectors for the development of new projects.

Commercial banks' investment in non-SLR outlets witnessed decline during 2010-2012 primarily due to decline in investment in commercial paper shares and mutual funds. On the contrary, banks' investment in debentures soared significantly. This trend partly reflected increase in risk aversion by banks with a growing preference to park funds in safer instruments, against the backdrop of weak macro-economic outlook.

R. COMMERCIAL BANKING AND INSURANCE BUSINESS

During the last few decades commercial banks across the world embraced insurance business so as to offer package of banking and insurance services to customers under one roof and thereby improve their earnings. The convergence of banking and insurance business is termed as "Bancassurance" in financial jargon. Bancassurance, also known as Allfinaz (Germany) is the arrangement whereby branches of the bank distribute insurance products.

Bancassurance having its humble beginning in 1980s in France, has grown in different countries at different pace and is different terms, depending upon the demography, economic and legislative prescriptions in those countries. It has its deep roots in the European countries particularly in France, Spain, Belgium, Luxemburg and Italy where banks distribute more than 50 per cent of the total life policies. However, in the US, Germany, the U.K. and Canada, growth of bancassurance is limited.

In Asia, bancassurance is a relatively new concept. Among Asian countries, Malaysia and Taiwan with their market share of 25 per cent and 35 per cent, respectively are forerunners in bancassurance. In Indonesia, a bank can sell insurance products of two insurance companies. In Philippines, banks are permitted to own 100 per cent of the insurance company and bank is permitted to lease part of its premises to an insurance company. In Argentina, sale of insurance products to bank customers is done through a separate entity. In Brazil, insurance products are distributed through all channels including banks except agents because of prohibitory regulations. In Japan, an insurance company is authorised to set up banking subsidiaries and life and non-life insurance companies are authorized to sell each other's products. In Singapore and South Korea, banks can act as brokers.

In India, the Government vide its notification issued under Banking Regulation Act allowed Indian banks in August 2000 to do insurance business under the IRDA Act, 1999, provided the bank had minimum networth of ₹ 500 crore and satisfied other criteria in respect of capital adequacy, profitability, NPA level and had track record of existing subsidiaries. Maximum equity holding by a bank will normally be 50 per cent in the joint venture. However, the RBI can, on a highly selective basis, permit a higher contribution by a promoter bank initially, pending divestment of equity within the stipulated period. Banks, which were not eligible as joint venture participants can participate without risk participation basis up to 10 per cent of their networth or ₹ 50 crore, whichever is, lower, in an insurance company for providing infrastructure and service support without taking on any contingent liability.

Insurance companies have also been permitted under IRDA Act to opt for banks as distribution channel to sell their insurance policies.

Following permission of the RBI to engage in insurance business under IRDA Act, several banks including PSBs like SBI, Bank of India and PNB and private sector banks including ICICI and HDFC forged strategic alliance with private insurance companies to undertake insurance business. Interestingly, there has been increasing focus by major banks on joint ventures and ownership models. During the last decade as many a 17 banks in India have tied up with insurers to undertake bancassurance.

Increasing interest of banks in India in bancassurance is triggered by the recognization in financial circle that bancassurance can serve as a potent source of improving profitability and enhancing competitiveness of both banks and insurance companies. Because of their complementary strengths, banks and insurance companies gain synergistic advantages. For banks, bancassurance is a means of product diversification and additional source of fee income. For instance, commercial banks in India can use their networks of over 70,000 branches to cross sell various type of insurance products, meet shareholders' concern of banks' shrinking bottomlines, improve their profit margin and shareholders' value by earning substantial fee income and leverage their brand equity. For insurance companies, bancassurance is a tool for deepening their market penetration without any additional cost, providing greater opportunity of introducing new hybrid products and assuring economies of scale in administrative cost.

The synergistic advantages to both banks and insurance companies ostensibly add value to the customers who stand to gain by way of getting better quality financial products under one roof at reduced price and that too at their doorsteps.

Bancassurance has already shown tangible results. It collected 219 billion rupees of premium, which accounted for 7.31 per cent of total premium of life and non-life sectors in March 2010. By 2012, bancassurance is expected to generate about 40 per cent of new business for private life insurance sector in India, according to a 2010 survey by Towers Watson.[22]

Banks are now realizing that bancassurance can be an effective source to ramp up their income. SBI Life's profits for financial year 2010-11 grew up by 33 per cent to reach ₹ 366 crore which was attributed to its bancassurance foray. HDFC Standard Life gets 50 per cent of its annual revenues from bancassurance.[23]

Private insurers have also come to realize that bancassurance is the most cost effective way to reach customers. They have already increased their market share from 14.25 per cent in 2006 to 31.44 per cent in 2010.

Taking cognizance of the tremendous potentiality of bancassurance in the country, IRDA is reviewing a proposal to allow banks to sell products for more than one insurance company in the life, non-life and health sectors in a bid to accelerate penetration. The regulator's move to open up bancassurance distribution is a positive development for India's insurance industry to enhance penetration and new development.

However, the pace of growth of bancassurance in India is much slower compared to China where its bancassurance sales made up 80 per cent of its 2010 revenues. The reasons for this slower growth may be traced in several challenges which bancassurance are facing. The most common challenges to success are poor management, lack of a sales culture within the bank, no involvement by the branch manager, insufficient product promotions, failure to integrate marketing plans, marginal database expertise, poor sales channel linkages, inadequate incentives, resistance to change, negative attitudes towards insurance and unwieldy marketing strategy. Another serious challenge lies in conflict of interest that arises when banks try to sell insurance policies. In India, insurance is often seen as a savings rather than as a risk management tool and this puts it directly against savings and term deposits. Obviously, the priority for banks then would be to sell their deposit schemes before insurance policies.

Thus, future prospects of bancassurance depends on how effectively banks and insurance companies attend to above problems.

S. COMMERCIAL BANKS IN INDIA AND VALUE CHAIN FINANCING

Financing of value chain activities of firm, *viz*., designing, producing, marketing, delivering and supporting, also known as "Supply Chain Financing" is gaining prominence in banks' loan portfolio and emerging as one of the fastest growing segments in the banking sector in foreign countries as also in India. The business in this area is expected to surge by 50-100% during the year 2007. The reason underlying the growing popularity of this kind of business is banker's conviction that funding of a firm having strong value chain will not only improve the firm's competitiveness and profitability but also enhance value to the bank in terms of improved profit margin and reduced risk.

Although value chain financing (VCF) is akin to working capital financing (WCF), the two differ in as much as while in the former banks perceive each entity on its own merit and go by fairly high standard and rigid "permissible bank financing" kind of norms, in VCF bank's thrust is on value chains clustering around a company, say, a manufacturing company having networked with entities engaged in designing, supplying, marketing, distribution and supporting. Major consideration influencing credit decision in respect of loans to the manufacturing company is the creditworthiness of entities engaged in each of the value chain of the company. This concept of financing is found useful to all parties in the value chain including the manufacturing companies, for the fact that it ensures uninterrupted production and distribution at reduced cost mainly due to availability of required credit facilities to smaller entities.

Modus operandi in the case of VCF is that bank opens a line of credit for a vendor of the manufacturing company on its recommendation. This line of credit is very specific in the sense that vendor supplies to the manufacturer and credit facility is provided against the guarantee of the latter. The recovery of the loan is linked to the vendor supplying to the manufacturing company on schedule. Once the vendor supplies, the manufacturer's payment may be routed through escrow account to give further comfort to the bank. This arrangement will minimize the possibility of vendor diverting funds somewhere else. Where the vendor provides discount to the manufacturer, the bank may even pay the former upfront and collect the same from the latter. As such, the bank can monitor production, distribution, collections as also financial health of the vendor.

VCF adds value to both the vendor and manufacturer. The vendor gets credit support as and when required as the bank is in know of order commitments of the manufacturer. The manufacturing company is also benefitted on two scores, *viz*; better and smooth supply from the vendor and reduction in its working capital requirements due to less inventory holding.

Besides financing supplier on value chain of the manufacturer, banks are also providing financial support to the entities on distribution chain. Usually, banks provide working capital to selected distributors after consulting the manufacturer by allowing the former to lift produce from the latter. There is also provision of an escrow account type of mechanism where the sales of the distributor gets credited to an account with the bank. The manufacturing company has access to this bank account and can get the payment from this account.

This kind of arrangement is beneficial to all parties. The manufacturing company finds no problem in getting payment which it was facing earlier in traditional WCF because it was selling against post dated cheques (PDC) to dealers with no guarantee whether the PDC will bounce or get realized. The financing bank can monitor sales and receipts of the distributor. It also saves lot of charges for collection, processing and security.

This new arrangement of bank financing provides an opportunity to the manufacturers to outsource the applicant's processing part of their accounting departments because banks have complete records of every single shipment to the dealer. They are also in a position to link payment to bills and shipments.

However, success of VCF is contingent upon extensive geographical reach and IT. Geographical reach is essential for collecting or making payments while IT enables the banks to render value added services to various value chain entities. IT, in fact, has significantly helped private sector banks in gaining competitive edge over their public sector counterparts by providing a myriad of innovative banking services.

T. TECHNOLOGY IN COMMERCIAL BANKS IN INDIA

Technology has been playing crucial role in the banking sector across the globe. Information Technology (IT) has emerged as a key business facilitator to banks for improving their own internal processes and for developing new products and offering range of need-based services to customers. As IT's role has become pervasive, it provides a competitive advantage to organizations in attracting/servicing customers. Furthermore, with the large scale increase in the number of transactions handled by banks, IT has become a prime factor in efficient handling of transaction processing. It has also the potential of furthering financial inclusion by making small ticket retail transactions cheaper, easier and faster for the banking sector as well as for the small customers.

The early 1980s were instrumental in the introduction of mechanisation and computerisation in Indian banks. This was the period when banks as well as the RBI went very slow on mechanisation, carefully avoiding the use of computers to avoid resistance from employee's unions. However, this was the critical period acting as the icebreaker, which led to the slow and steady move towards large scale technological adoption.

The process of computerisation, which marked the starting point of all initiatives, is reaching near completion in most of the banks. After migrating to the use of stand-alone systems a decade ago, the old banks (both public and private) started the migration towards core banking systems (CBS), while new private banks had commenced operations with a complete IT based background. CBS has opened up new vistas for banks to offer a variety of facilities to new customers. Facilities such as 'anywhere and anytime' got a fillip due to a centralised information pool with banks. Constituents are now treated as customers of the bank as a whole instead of being attached to a particular branch alone. In addition, newer delivery channels based on technology have also gained ground. Some of these include internet banking, mobilise banking, ATMs and shared ATM networks for availing of banking services on a much broader scale than ever before.

The most fundamental way in which technology has enabled banks to revolutionalise the availability of its services, as noted earlier, has been through computerisation. While new private sector banks have an edge in this regard, PSBs have been investing for upgrading their operations by way of computerisation of the total number of PSB's branches, 97.8 per cent were fully computerised at end-March, 2010 (Table 6.26). All branches of the SBI group were fully computerised. Over ₹ 22,000 crore spent on computerisation by PSBs between September 1999 and March 2010.

TABLE 6.26: Computerisation in Public Sector Banks

(Percentage of Total Bank branches)

Category	2006	2007	2008	2009	2010
Fully computerised branches [(*i*) + (*ii*)]	77.5	85.6	93.7	95.0	97.8
(*i*) Branches under CBS	28.9	44.4	67.0	79.4	90.0
(*ii*) Branches already computerised	48.5	41.2	26.6	15.6	7.9
Partially computerised branches	18.2	13.4	6.3	5.0	2.2

Source: RBI Report as Trend and Progress of Banking in India for relevant years.

A technology development is closely related to computerisation in bank branches in the adoption of the CBS by the banks. In this respect, there was a significant increase in the percentage of branches of the PSBs implementing CBS during the past five years; the percentage increased from 44.4 at end-March 2006 to 90.0 at March-end, 2010. The percentage of branches under CBS was much larger for the SBI group as compared to nationalised banks.

The third major technological development, which has revolutionised the delivery channel in the banking sector, has been the Automated Teller Machines (ATMs). ATMs, particularly off-site ATMs, act as substitutes for bank branches in offering a means of anytime cash withdrawal to customers. Commercial banks in India have made satisfactory progress in this aspect during the last few years. (Table 6.27). It may be noted from the table that total number of ATMs installed by the scheduled commercial banks in India surged from 27,088 as on March end 2007 to 74,508 as at March end 2011, registering over 250 per cent growth during the period. Growth rate of PSBs in installation of ATMs was much higher compared to their private sector counterparts. However, private sector banks had larger share of off-site ATMs in total ATMs installed as at March end, 2011 as compared to the PSBs.

Sustained increase in total number of ATMs is indicative of growing move towards door-step bankiing.

During 2011-12, an additional 21,000 ATMs were deployed by banks. PSBs accounted for more than 60 per cent of the total number of ATMs as at end March 2012, while close to one-third of the total ATMs, were attributable to new private sector banks.

TABLE 6.27 Number of ATMs of Scheduled Commercial Banks in India
(As at March end ...)

	2007			2011			2012		
	On-site ATMs	Off-site ATMs	Total ATMs	On-site ATMs	Off-site ATMs	Total ATMs	On-site ATMs	Off-site ATMs	Total ATMs
1. Public Sector Banks	10,289	6,040	16,329	29,795	19,692	49,487	34,012	24,181	58,193
(i) Nationalised banks	6,634	3,254	9,888	15,691	9,145	24,836	18,277	12,773	31,050
(ii) SBI Group	3,655	2,786	6,441	14,104	10,547	24,651	15,735	11,408	27,143
2. Private Sector Banks	4,259	5,541	9,799	10,648	13,003	23,651	13,249	22,830	36,079
(i) Old private sector banks	1104	503	1,607	2,641	1,485	4,126	3,342	2,429	5,771
(ii) New private sector banks	3154	5,038	8,192	8,007	11,518	19,325	9,907	20,401	30,308
3. Foreign banks	249	711	960	286	1,081	1,367	284	1,130	1,414
Total ATMs of SCBs	14,797	12,292	27,088	40,729	33,776	74,508	47,545	48,141	95,686

It is also interesting to note that there was increase in the penetration of ATMs in recent years as evident from a fall in the population per ATM (Table 6.28) while there was a greater concentration of ATMs in urban areas than in rural area, the number and percentage of ATMs in rural areas was on a steady rise in the recent years (Table 6.29).

TABLE 6.28: Population per ATM

(Number of person in '000)

Year	Population per ATM in rural areas	Population per ATM in urban areas	Total population per ATM
2007	125.6	15.9	43.0
2008	89.3	12.6	33.2
2009	68.1	10.4	26.8
2010	43.5	8.1	19.7

TABLE 6.29: Percentage share of ATMs located at various centres

	Rural centres	Semi-urban centres	Urban centres	Metropolitan centres
2007	4.8	19.9	35.5	39.8
2008	5.4	21.4	34.8	38.4
2009	6.3	22.1	33.9	37.7
2010	8.6	24.1	32.9	34.4

The percentage of ATMs located in rural areas accounted for 28.4 per cent of the total ATMs in the country at end March 2009 which increased to 32.7 per cent at end-March, 2010. A large part of the increase in ATMs in rural areas was due to PSBs. The growing penetration of ATMs in rural areas could also be seen from a continued fall in the population per ATM in rural areas (Table 6.28).

In sync with increase in ATMs, number of debit cards issued by the banks grew tremendously during the last five years, from 74.98 millions in 2006-07 to 279 millions in 2011-12 (Table 6.30). It may further be noted that more than three-fourths of the total debt cards were issued by PSBs at end-March, 2012. In contrast, more than half of the outstandng credit cards as at the end of March, 2012 were issued by new private sector banks.

TABLE 6.30: Debit cards issued by commercial banks

(in millions)

Bank Group	Outstanding Number of Debit Cards					
	2006-07	2007-08	2008-09	2009-10	2010-11	2011-12
1. Public sector banks	44.09	64.33	91.7	129.69	170.34	215.0
2. Private sector banks	27.19	34.1	41.34	47.85	53.58	60.0
3. Foreign banks	3.70	4.02	4.39	4.43	3.92	3.8
All SCBs	74.98	102.44	137.43	181.97	227.87	278.8

TABLE 6.31: Credit cards issued by commercial banks

(in millions)

Bank Group	Outstanding Number of Credit Cards					
	2006-07	2007-08	2008-09	2009-10	2010-11	2011-12
1. Public sector banks	4.14	3.93	3.44	3.26	3.08	3.06
2. Private sector banks	10.68	13.29	12.18	9.5	9.32	9.67
3. Foreign banks	8.31	10.33	9.08	5.57	5.64	4.92
All SCBs	23.12	27.55	24.70	18.33	18.04	17.65

A trend in favour of cashless payments is discernible in recent years with both volume and volume of transactions through major electronic modes of payments registering an increase. (Table 6.32)

There has been significant increase in volume and value of electronic transactions by scheduled commercial banks. (Table 6.32). Among the various electronic modes of payment, the centralised version of Electronic Fund Transfer (EFT) — National EFT (NEFT) has become an important means of retail payments, while the Real Time Gross Settlement (RTGS) has shown substantial growth as a means of settling large value payments. NEFT registered a steep growth in 2011-12 over the previous year.

TABLE 6.32: Volume and value of electronic transactions by Scheduled Commercial banks *(as at end-March 2012)*

Volume in million, Value in ₹ crore

Transactions	Volume		Value		
	2009-10	2010-11	2009-10	2010-11	2011-12
ECS credit	98.1	117.3	1,17,613	1,81,680	1,83,800
ECS Debit	149.3	156.7	69,524	73,646	83,400
NEFT	66.3	132.3	4,09,507	9,39,149	17,90,300
RTGS	33.3	49.3	3,97,53,359	4,84,87,234	5,39,30,700

It may be noted that there has been a steady increase in the ratio of total value of electronic payments to GDP showing growing preference for the electronic mode of payments in recent years.

Having reached computerisation in general and CBS in particular near completion, banks need to leverage on to this technological advancement to look at areas beyond CBS that can help in not just delivering quality and efficient services to customers but also generating and managing information effectively. With regard to the second aspect of information management, a system of receiving data from banks by the Reserve Bank in an automated manner without any manual intervention is under examination.

Going forward, there are a number of issues with regard to development of banking technology that need to be addressed. These relate to further improvement in back office management in the form of streamlining MIS, strengthening centralised processing, Customer relationship management (CRM) and IT Governance. The back office technological advancement would help in diverting banks' resources more towards the front office management thereby increasing customer focus of their services and support greater financial penetration and inclusions.

U. AUTONOMY OF BANKING INDUSTRY IN INDIA

Public sector banks that continue to occupy a pivotal position in the Indian financial sector have been upset over the Government meddling in their operations during the last one year (2011-12). They say that over the past one year, the Government has been issuing as many as 36 directives setting new rules as well as reiterating existing ones. All these, it is claimed, impinge on their freedom to take independent decisions even in areas that are considered very basic.[24]

Earlier in July 2012, the finance ministry asked the banks not to extend short-term, unsecured loans without the board approval. It also directed banks to provide information about the non-performing asset creation from such loans.

The reform of the financial sector was intended to confer autonomy on the PSBs so that they could take commercial decisions independent of the government. The extent of such autonomy has varied from bank to bank but in all cases, it was hoped that the government would respect their autonomous status.

The existing arrangements between banks and the government in tilted towards the latter. However, it would be desirable if the Government sticks to policy making and allow banks the freedom to take decisions in an increasingly competitive environment. The RBI governor, D. Subba Rao and his predecessor, Y.V. Reddy, have come out on the side of the banks, arguing that micro-managing is bad for banks and, in the long run, hurts the interests of the major shareholder, the Government too of course, minority shareholders suffer the most and in these days of shareholder activism the government should not risk antagonising them. Dr. Reddy rightly pointed out that the Government should demonstrate exemplary corporate governance by exercising its ownership rights through its nominees on the boards of banks.

V. CONCLUSIONS

Liberalised economic and financial policy of the Government and the RBI have brought about tectonic change in the overall profile of commercial banks in India. Reformatory measures changed the basic character of Indian banking from class banking to mass banking, from the one engaged in short-term lending and offering pure deposit type products to universal banking offering a wide variety of customised products through multiple channels to wide spectrum of customers. Entry of foreign banks and private sector banks rendered the operating environment highly competitive for the public sector banks. Ownership of the PSBs has also changed remarkably in favour of private shareholding.

Unprecedented growth of banking industry in India, penetrating in rural hinterlands has been noticeable during the post-liberalisation period. Not only has there been quantum leap in deposits mobilised by the banks, structure of bank deposits also underwent remarkable charge, as reflected in preponderance of time deposits in total bank deposits.

Quantity and quality of bank lending have also registered palpable and perceptible change during the post-liberalisation period. There has been magnificent surge in bank credit, resulting in rise in its proportion to the GDP.

Post-liberalisation period has also witnessed diversification of banking business in the country. Not only has it entered into long-term financing but also engaged in insurance business and formed strategic alliance with private insurance companies in order to improve their earnings.

What is most gratifying to note is that banks in India have adopted latest technology to improve their services to customers and offer wide variety of products through multiple channels. However, commercial banks in India, despite significant expansion in geographical operations and remarkable change in spatial distribution of a banking credit facilities, more than 60 per cent of rural areas still remain outside the coverage of the formal banking sector and the poor still continue to depend on informal sources of credit, including the usurious village moneylenders. This has led to the emergence of alternative sources of financing poor rural households including Micro finance Institutions (MFIs). A detailed discussion on this alternative source has been made in chapter 30.

KEY TERMS

- Bancassurance
- Base rate
- Benchmark prime lending rate
- Business correspondents
- Capital adequacy ratio
- Core banking solutions
- Credit-deposit ratio
- Credit reserve ratio
- Directed lending
- Lazy banking attitude
- Predation
- Priority sector financing
- Self-help group
- Statutory liquidity ratio
- Take out financing
- Value chain financing

DISCUSSION QUESTIONS

1. What is scheduled bank? How is it different from non-scheduled banks?
2. Present a brief view of growth of banking industry in India.
3. What pre-empted the Government and the RBI to reform Indian banking system despite nationalisation of banks?
4. Briefly bring out recommendations of Narasimham Committee.

5. What steps have been taken by the Reserve Bank to implement the Narasimham Committee recommendations?
6. How have these steps changed the profile of Indian banking industry?
7. Critically examine the RBI policy regarding bank licensing to private corporate houses.
8. Briefly discus the present structure of commercial banking in India.
9. Give a brief account of geographical and spatial distribution of commercial banks in India.
10. How far has ownership of public sector banks in India changed during post-reform period?
11. In what respects have pattern of deposits and lending of the banks changed during the reform post-reform period?
12. Discuss the role of commercial banks in India in financing priority sectors.
13. What is bancassurance? Why have Indian banks shown greater interest in bancassurance?
14. Outline technological developments in Indian banking industry.

REFERENCES

1. RBI's Report on Trend and Progress of Banking in India, 2000-01, p. 63.
2. RBI's Report on Trend and Progress of Banking in India 2002-03, p. 76.
3. Narasimham Committee Recommendations – Report on Trend and Progress of Banking in India, 1997-98.
4. RBI's Report on Trend and Progress of Banking in India, 2009-10. p. 33.
5. *Ibid.*
6. RBI's Report on Trend and Progress of Banking in India, 2009-10, p. 33.
7. Business Today, August 22, 2010.
8. Business Standard, July 1, 2010.
9. Business Standard, May 11, 2011.
10. Business Standard, October 28, 2009.
11. RBI's Report on Trend and Progress of Banking in India, 2005-06, p. 23.
12. RBI's Report on Trend and Progress of Banking in India, 2004-05, p. 16.
13. RBI's Report on Trend and Progress of Banking in India, 2005-06, p. 23.
14. Business Standard, July 6, 2011.
15. Business Standard, February 8, 2011.
16. RBI's Report on Trend and Progress of Banking in India, 2009-10.
17. *Ibid.*
18. Annual Report, RBI, 2005-06.
19. Annual Report, 2008-09, RBI.
20. RBI's Report on Trend and Progress of Banking in India, 2009-10.
21. RBI's Report on Trend and Progress of Bank in India, 2008-09.
22. Insurance news.net.com
23. *Ibid.*
24. Hindu, August 14, 2012.

Retail Banking

Learning Objectives:

The present chapter attempts to:

- An understanding of concept and redeeming features of retail banking.
- An insight into utility of retail banking.
- A synoptic view of retail banking in foreign countries.
- A vivid account of retail banking in India and its future prospects.

Chapter Outline:

- Introduction.
- Concept of retail banking.
- Distinguishing features of retail banking.
- Utility of retail banking.
- Retail banking in foreign countries.
- Retail banking in India.
- Future of retail banking.
- Government policy for retail banking.
- Conclusions

Chapter 7

A. INTRODUCTION

In view of tectonic changes in socio-economic milieu across the globe leading to enhanced competitiveness, path breaking developments in information technology, acceleration of disintermediation process, the evolving macro-economic environment owing to financial market reforms and myriad of micro-level demand and supply side factors and fast changing personal, familial and social values of the people, commercial banks shifted from traditional banking activities to a broad-based retail banking business. Thus, retail banking has emerged as core segment of the banking business all over the world and gained prominence in recent years to meet the competitive challenges, to improve quality of services and profit margin. As such, it is pertinent to comprehend the concept of retail banking, its distinguishing features, utility, and retail banking developments in India and abroad.

B. CONCEPT OF RETAIL BANKING

Retail banking refers to the dealing of commercial banks with individual customers both on liabilities and assets sides of the balance sheet. It encompasses fixed, current and saving deposit linked products on the liabilities side, mortgages, loans (e.g., personal, housing, auto and educational) and other financial products on the assets side. Generally, the pure retail banking is conceived to be provision of mass banking products and services to individuals for personal consumption as opposed to whole sale banking having thrust on corporate (proprietary, partnership firm, private limited and public limited companies) and institutional (societies, trusts and clubs, etc.) clients. Over the years, the concept of retail banking has been expanded to include in many cases the services provided to small and medium sized businesses. In Europe some banks even include their private banking services to high network individuals in their retail banking portfolio. In sum, retail banking includes various financial services and products forming part of the assets as well as the liabilities segment of the banks.

C. DISTINGUISHING FEATURES OF RETAIL BANKING

- The essence of retail banking lies in individual customers. It is akin to mass banking which lays focus on masses rather than on class. In retail banking, all the banking needs of the individual customers are taken care of in an integrated manner. Though the term retail banking and retail lending are often used synonymously, the two, however, differ. While retail lending is reflection on asset side of the balance sheet, retail banking comprises products of liabilities and asset sides.
- Retail banking business today is multi-products, and multi-customers. It offers multiple products like deposits, credit cards, insurance, investments and securities to multiple customer groups comprising consumer, small business and corporates.
- Unlike plain vanilla class banking products that the banks world over offered until the recent past, leaving no option to customers but to take or leave, commercial banks under retail banking business offer wide variety of customized products at most competitive rates through multiple channels to cater to their needs of wide variety of individual customers.

Wide range of products, that banks are now offering, encompass both the deposits and loans related products packaged with several value additions in different permutations and combinations and attractive brand names and released in the market with wide publicity. Banks continuously and constantly monitor the utility of their existing products and services portfolio in the context of fast changing expectations of customers and make necessary modifications therein wherever necessary.

Retail banking products for different groups of customers like, children, salaried persons, senior citizens, professionals, technocrats, businessmen, retail traders and farmers, etc. include flexi-deposit, saving bank, recurring deposit, short-term deposit and deferred pension linked deposit schemes. Today, pure deposit type products are being replaced by multi-benefit, multi-access genres of banking products.

Retail banking products for depositors in various segments like salaried class, professionals, children, housewives, pensioners, farmers, technologists, etc., include saving bank accounts, flexi-deposit accounts, recurring deposit accounts, short-term deposits and deferred pension linked deposit schemes. Most of the inncvation is taking place in saving bank accounts to make the paltry 3-4 per cent interest a bit attractive. Most of the banks now offer sweep in and sweep out accounts, called 2-in-1 accounts or value added savings bank accounts. This account is a combination of savings bank and term deposit accounts and offers twin benefits of liquidity of a savings bank accounts and higher interest earning of term deposits accounts.

Among the various lending products being offered by banks under retail banking business, important ones are: housing loans, loan for consumer goods, personal loans for marriage, medical treatment and holidaying, etc., education loans, auto loans, old loans, event loans, festival loans, insurance products, loan against rent receivables, loan against pension receivables to senior citizens, debit and credit cards, international cards, loans to medical practitioners to set up their own clinics or for purchase of medical equipments, loan to women entrepreneurs, etc.

To make their products and services more alluring and attractive so as to woo maximum number of customers, the banks are vying with each other with whole lot of frills, goodies, freebies and add-ons.

Besides offering several frills and goodies, banks are also offering various retail banking services to their customers. These service are payment of utility bills, insurance premiums on due dates, payment of monthly/quarterly education fee of children to their respective schools, remittance of funds from one account to another, demoting of shares, bonds, debentures and mutual funds, payment of credit card bills on due dates and finally filing of income tax returns and payment of income tax.

Thus, we are seeing the replacement of broad-brush generic products and services with solutions targeted at specific segments.

In retail banking, retail lending is made at the point of sale. Commercial banks are increasingly entering into tie up arrangements with leading automobile, electronic and consumer goods dealers, builders and real agents, universities and colleges, etc., for promoting and selling their retail banking products to customers at the very point of sale.

- Another striking feature of retail banking is that retail loans are less susceptible to ups and downs in the economy. In contrast, corporate loans are subject to economic oscillations.
- An emerging product of retail banking in India is bancassurance. With assumption of insurance business, most of the banks in India have, of late, entered into tie up arrangement with multinational insurance companies for selling their insurance products in life and non-life segments as corporate agents for a fee. Bancassurance, as noted earlier, is a package of banking and insurance services which are offered under one roof. The customers can avail the banking and insurance services together at one point. The introduction of bancassurance products has broadened the scope of retail banking. It is expected to give fillip to fee-based income of banks in the context of declining interest margins.

In view of the above, retail banking has come to be regarded as "hotter than vindaloo". Considering the fact that vindaloo, the Indian-English innovative curry available in umpteen number of restaurants of London, is indeed very hot and spicy, it seems that retail banking is perceived to be the in-thing in Fodey's world of banking.[1] Today, retail banking is in an exciting developmental phase with new products and services arriving on the market almost every week.

- Another redeeming feature of retail banking industry is that it has multiple delivery channels such as call centres, branches, ATM internets, telebanking. Besides, many new delivery channels are emerging to explore and exploit market opportunities. While customers continue to access retail banks by walking into their local branch and they are also using ATMs to access a relatively simple range of banking services, automated methods of access are on the increase and the internet is undoubtedly the strongest growth story of the European industry, with millions of customers already choosing to bank this way. Crux of retail banking business is technology because automated access gives the considerable benefits of greater speed and accuracy, which can result in all-important reduction in overall costs. Much can be achieved in automated access by working with existing technology and infrastructures, which, therefore, enables banks to optimize return on the investments they have already made.

D. UTILITY OF RETAIL BANKING

In ferociously competitive environment, as it exists today, successful survival and growth of organizations and more so of service organizations like banks depend essentially on cost, quality, speed and risk factors that help immensely not only in attracting new customers but also in customer retention. Retention of customers leading to increase in market share is now receiving greater attention of banking organizations, for the fact that 5 per cent increase in customer retention can increase profitability by 35 per cent in banking business, 50 per cent in insurance and brokerage, and 125 per cent in the consumer credit market.

Retail banking with its immanent features of customers, multi channels of products, and diversity of risk as also economies of scale and system has come to be acknowledged as powerful tool in the hands of commercial banks and other financial institutions to deeply penetrate markets, enhance the market share and thereby improving their competitiveness on sustaining basis. Multi-channel strategies clearly enable banking organizations to extend their reach and increase their contact with multiplatform consumers.

Technology fueled retail banking facilities strengthen balance sheets and income structures of banks. Technology has enabled a significant reduction in cost of external finance to the borrowers, while banks have benefitted from product innovation and lower transaction cost associated with collection, processing and use of information. Further, automated access gives considerable benefits of greater accuracy which can result in an all-important reduction in overall costs. This, in its wake, offers banks better techniques for risk management and pricing of products. Electronically induced retail banking can help banks in diversifying risks in their credit portfolio and containing the menace of NPAs. By finding out more about customer risks, banks can manage their risks more effectively and open the door to more customers and greater profits.

Retail banking allows banks to cross sell other products and services as it is far more easier to sell other products to the same customer rather than search for absolutely new ones. Cross selling is one of the best avenues for relationship banking and retention of customers.

It is noteworthy that banks are not sharing the same pie of retail business; the pie itself is growing exponentially. Retail banking, as a matter of fact, has fuelled a considerable quantum of purchasing power through a slew of retail products.

Retail banking can help banks to attract new customers, retain the existing ones and thus widen their customer base by offering them multiple choices in terms of innovative products, services and channels, which suit their lifestyles and tastes and financial needs as well. Because of advanced technology, it has become possible for banks to deliver services throughout the branch network, providing instant updates to checking accounts and rapid movement of money for stock transfers.

Clearly, new products and services have a key role to play in customer retention. When a banker is increasing the number of products held by each customer, the customers are likely to be less deflected to his competitors. However, it is important to deliver these products and services in the most effective ways.

As a matter of fact, retail banking is transforming commercial banks into one stop financial super markets and thereby honing their competitive position.

In view of the above, retail banking is emerging as the most crucial segment of commercial banks. However, the surge in retail lending has certain limitations. For instance, retail lending may accentuate indebtedness of households, with implications for sustainability of private consumption and saving in the medium to longer horizon. Rapid increase in retail loans may impinge on bank credit for investment activities with implications for economic growth. Several cross section studies suggest that retail lending may pose various risks with implications for banks' asset quality.[2] Even management of large number of clients may become a problem if IT systems are not robust. There may be network management whereby keeping these complex, distributed networks and applications operating properly in support of business objectives becomes essential.

Finally, cost of maintaining large number of small value transactions in branch networks will be relatively high if the customers do not use alternate delivery channels like ATM, internet and phone banking, etc., for carrying out banking transactions.

E. RETAIL BANKING IN FOREIGN COUNTRIES

The British credit markets have been traditionally crystallized by banks' collusive practices for years. Regulatory changes like competition and credit control in 1971 and the increasing pressure imposed by American banks in the domestic market compelled British financial institutions including banks to embark on an unusual ride in search of new areas of profitability and hence the emergence of retail banking business in the U.K. After the mid- 1970s the automated procedures moved from the back- to the front-office, boosting the number as well as the variety of customer services. During the 1970s, electronic transactions were intended as a cheaper alternative to speed up common transactions and save on labour cost. Less than 20 years after the introduction of the revolutionary cash machines, the banking system experienced the mushrooming of a great variety of alternative payment services, all incarnating and reinforcing the common purpose of 'taking banking outside the banks', that is, away from the traditional brick- and mortar premises.

The organization of retail payments in the U.K. has undergone significant changes during the last two and half decades. Not only the volume of such transactions has grown, but also the ways in which these can be carried out have expanded, thanks to the possibilities opened up by the development of information and communication technologies.

The emergence of a unique ATM network is a relatively recent accomplishment in the U.K., made possible by a collective interbank agreement which has instituted LINK Interchange Network Ltd., as the transaction management company incharge for switching and selling shared ATM transactions. This included banks to pursue alternative strategies to capture and/ or to keep customers with new products and services.

Today, the U.K. has a wide spectrum of different types of banking organization, from the traditional, fully integrated bank to the 'virtual' Internet-only banks through the vast and heterogeneous populations of organization that supply financial services and compete with the former either over the whole product range or, more likely, in a niche.

The U.K. market for retail banking services increased by 10.5 per cent between 2002 and 2003 to reach a value of 1,470 billion. Lending makes up the largest proportion (57%) of the U.K. retail banking market.[3] Barclays is the leading player with an 18.2% share of total U.K. retail banking in 2003.

The U.S. banks' thrust on retail banking is on electronic commerce and payments, electronic delivery channels, making electronic remote banking more available for the small business customers but with a different product mix for their specialized needs.

The retail banking services market in the USA expanded by 3% to US$ 1,244.48 million in 2003. In the USA, real estate loans constitute the largest sector in the retail banking services with a growth rate of 17% during the review period from US $ 670.5 billion in 1999 to US $ 787 billion in 2003 to capture approximately 63% of the market.[4] Retail banking services market remains fragmented with many small regional players and the five largest companies accounting for only 35.4% of the total market value in 2003. Citigroups is the largest company in retail banking with 10% market share.

After more than a decade wallowing in debt and seemingly unable to turn themselves around, Japan's banks appear to be looking to new products and client segments to rejuvenate their business models and spread risk throughout the system. Hence, Japanese banks embraced retail banking on a growing scale in recent few years so as to improve their profitability. While lending portfolios at most of the major banks, partly as a result of meeting the FSA target to reduce NPLs by March 2005, Japanese banks are moving down the credit curve, targeting smaller business to improve profitability. Sumitomo Mitsui Banking Corporation (SMBC) introduced its uncollateralised Business Select Loan (BSL) in 2002 with a view to assisting small business with annual sales of upto ₹ 1 bn ($9.25 m). Firms can borrow upto ₹ 50m (average borrowings are ₹ 20,000 – ₹ 30,000). By the end of March 2004, the Bank had lent ₹ 1100 bn.[5] SMBC is heralded as a particularly strong success story because 50% of the 17,000 borrowers taking loans under the BSL scheme are new customers of the bank.

Recent trends in Japanese banks are indicative of emergence of a universal model on long-term basis which comprises a mix of retail and commercial banking, retail and institutional securities sales and investment banking.[6] This kind of structure offers the ability for Japanese banks to smooth their revenue streams and to reduce vulnerability to cyclical markets.

Another major bank of Japan 'Shinsei Bank' after sensing customers dissatisfaction with existing services has offered new and free services to retail customers resulting in significance improvement of its bottomline by $ 50m in the third year of its existence. The Bank has also built a diversified investment banking business including structured trading, speciality finance, corporate advisory, private equity, asset management and financial markets.

Japanese banks have plenty of opportunity to intermediate in the development of the capital markets where there is relatively little retail activity. These banks have a prime opportunity to package investment banking products for retail investors. They are evincing keen interest in making big changes in their business portfolio with a view to attracting new customers and retaining the existing ones.

In Germany, retail banking companies comprise two sectors, viz; loans and deposits. The German market for retail banking services has grown by 3 per cent since 2002 to reach a value of US $ 4.05 trillion in 2003 and US $ 4.77 trillion in 2005. The major players accounted for 22.2 per cent market share in the German retail banking business in 2003, postbank lending with a market share of 9.1 per cent. Deutsche Bank is the leading German banking group and a world leader in financial services based in Frankfurt, Germany. Dresdner Bank is a leading German banking institution and a leader among European banks based in Frankfurt.[7]

F. RETAIL BANKING IN INDIA

Since the beginning of the current decade the developing countries market for retail lending has been zooming ahead.

Retail banking in India is not a new phenomenon. It has always been in existence in different forms. However, in recent few years, it has emerged as an important segment of banks' portfolio.

The year 1995 marked the starting point of Retail Banking Revolution with Foreign Banks and new generations private banks taking the lead. Till 90s, only foreign banks were the main players in retail banking activities. However, there has been paradigm shift in banking business of Indian Commercial banks from wholesale banking to retail banking. The typical products, which Indian retail banking segment is offering, are housing loans, consumption loans for purchase of durables, auto loans, credit cards and education loans. The loans are marketed under attractive brand names to differentiate the products offered by different banks.

Retail banking in India has been the main story and a key profit driver for banks in the recent times with retail portfolio constituting 21.5 per cent of total outstanding advances as on March 2004.[8] The loans are generally for duration of five to seven years with housing loans granted for a longer duration of 15 years. Credit card is another rapidly growing sub-segment of this product group. Another redeeming feature of retail lending in India is that overall impairment of the retail loan portfolio is worked out to 2.5 per cent and compares favourably with the gross NPA ratio for the entire loan portfolio.

TABLE 7.1: Retail Portfolio of Scheduled Commercial Banks in India

(Amt. in ₹ crore)

Item	At end-March						
	2006	2007	2008	2009	2010	2011	2012
1. Housing loans	1,79,060	2,24,481	2,52,932	2,63,235	3,15,862	3,67,364	4,11,800
2. Consumer durables	4,469	7,296	4,802	5,431	3,032	4,555	2,700
3. Credit card receivables	12,434	18,317	27,437	29,941	21,565	18,655	22,300
4. Auto loans	61,369	22,562	87,998	83,915	78,346	1,00,155	1,16,200
5. Other personal loans	1,18,351	1,55,204	1,97,879	2,11,294	2,03,947	2,53,243	30,69,000
Total Retail Loans	3,75,683	4,87,860	5,71,048	5,93,815	6,22,752	7,43,972	8,59,900
Percentage of total retail loans to Total loans	25.5	25.8	24.5	21.3	19.0	18.5	18.4

Source: RBI's Report on Trend and Progress of Banking in India for relevant years.

Table 7.1 shows retail loans and its composition during the period 2006-12. It may be noted from the table that there has been significant acceleration in the amount of retail loans granted by scheduled commercial banks in India from ₹ 3,75,683 as on March end 2006 to ₹ 8,59,900 crore as on March end 2012, recording annual growth rate of 18 per cent during the period. This was lower than the annual growth rate of the retail loans during the period 1992-93 to 2006-07, being 19.5 per cent. As a result, the proportionate share of retail loans in total banks' loans soared from 8.3 per cent at end-March 1993 to 25.8 per cent at end March 2007.

However, relative share of retail loans in total banks' loans tended to decline steadily in recent years, from 25.8 per cent at end March 2007 to 18.4 per cent at end March 2012. This is to be accounted for by decline in credit for consumer durables, credit card receivables, auto loans and other personal loans.

During the last decade commercial banks in India have shown preference for retail lending. There are host of factors that compelled Indian banks to shift focus from class banking to mass and retail banking in the recent past; important amongst these are:

- The Government policy of liberalization, privatization and globalization leading to increased competitiveness, financial dis-intermediation and consequent reduction in interest spreads and drain on their profitability has forced banks to go for retail business because they find that it is the activity where many major banks are making most of their money but also because of the more recurrent nature of its earnings.
- During the last 10 years after 1992 Indian economy has recorded an average growth rate of 6.8 per cent and continues to grow even at higher rate. This has obviously led to economic prosperity and the resultant increase in purchasing power of consumers.
- Fast changing consumer demographics offer tremendous potential for growth in consumption both qualitatively and quantitatively. India with majority of population (70%) below 35 years provides great scope for growth of retail business.
- The adherence to stringent asset classification norms has resulted in growing menace of NPAs in corporate loans, affecting adversely the asset quality, profitability and capital adequacy. The risks involved in corporate loans tend to be very high as banks

have to keep all their eggs in one basket. On the contrary, the retail advances are highly diversified and hence less risky and they are repayable normally in a short period of 3-5 years except housing loans and from fixed source of income like salaries.

- Another temptation for Indian banks to go for retail banking is that retail advances offer higher interest spread of 3 to 4 per cent as compared to corporate loans which give average return of just 0.5 to 1.5 per cent only. This is for the fact that retail borrowers are relatively less sensitive than the corporates. Further, the retail customers, unlike corporates, are too fragmented to bargain effectively.
- Technological forces have played significant role in making retail banking business more convenient, quicker and cheaper. Convenience banking in the form of debit cards, internet and phone banking, anywhere and anytime banking has lured many new customers into the banking field. Thus, technological innovations have contributed to growing popularity of retail banking in India, as elsewhere.
- Technology induced product innovations and competitive pricing strategies have enabled Indian Commercial banks to foster customer relations resulting in retaining the existing clients and attracting new ones.
- So as to arrest declining profit margin because of the decrease in the treasury income of the banks in recent few years, they decided to shift to retail banking. In view of the fact that retail's share in impaired assets is far lower than the overall bank loans and advances, retail loans have put comparatively less provisioning burden on banks apart from diversifying their income streams.
- Increasing amount of consumers in the country with upswing in income levels of middle class having high prosperity to consume and changing mindsets and preferences for improving their quality of life have nudged retail banking business in India.

A break-up of retail loans granted by Indian banks signifies the prominance of housing loans followed distantly by other personal loans. Over the period 2006-2010, housing loans picked up more sharply (17.5%) in comparison to other segments of retail loans. A myriad of factors has contributed to this trend. One important factor was high economic growth in recent years and concomitant increase in job opportunities and rise in income levels, especially of young people that triggered the craze for owning a house by availing of the housing loans. The increase in IT and IT-related activities had a positive impact on demand for housing loan. Further, tax incentives offered to salaried people made housing loans more attractive. Another significant factor for increase in retail loans was rise in personnel consumption. Convenience banking in the form of credit/debit cards, internet and phone banking anywhere and anytime attracted many new customers in the banking field. Lower interest rate, that prevailed during most part of 2009-10, was also responsible for pick up in retail loans during 2009-10.

In their effort to entice potential borrowers for housing loans, many banks — both PSBs like SBI, PNB, Indian Bank, Corporation Bank and Private sector banks like ICICI Bank, HDFC Bank, Axim Bank have launched 'Teaser Loan Scheme' in which loans are fixed in the initial years and became floating later. Interest rates that are a mixture of these two (fixed and floating) are called teaser rates. Under the scheme, ICICI and HDFC offer home loans at a fixed rate for the initial three or five years and at a floating rate thereafter. Fixed interest rate offered in the initial years is comparatively lower, after which rates are reset at higher rates. Teaser products (loans) are legitimate and approved by the RBI. However, the RBI has directed banks to make higher provisioning for such products at 2 per cent which is five times higher than the one applicable to other categories of retail loans.

With a view to according relief to house loan borrowers, the RBI issued directive on October 25, 2011 to banks to waive the prepayment charged on floating rate loans. This has given relief to home loan borrowers who are already stretched and grappling with rising interest rates. In its strive to improve their level of earnings through retail loans, new private sector banks are contemplating forays into the secured retail loan market through distribution tie-ups, instead of launching their own loan products. According to analysts, the low base of core deposits has forced these banks to choose the distribution model. The banks, however, say higher fees incomes are encouraging them to take this route.[9]

IndusInd Bank has signed an agreement in May 2011 with HDFC to sell housing loans through its branches. According to IndusInd Bank Chief Operating Officer, "we do not like the returns that we would get from our own housing loan products. The yields on retail assets are typically in the range of 16-17 per cent, while those for mortgage are at 10-11 per cent. So, we decided not to have our capital blocked in these products."

Yes Bank too, is exploring distribution parts with both housing and auto finance companies. It is already in talks with HDFC and Dewan Housing Finance for distribution partnerships in mortgage products. For auto loans, the private sector bank is weighing similar tie-ups with vehicle finance companies that are owned and managed by automobile manufacturers.

In future, this route of retail loan is going to be popular among the banks so as to avert asset-liability mismatches. Typically, a housing loan of 15-20 years tenure is backed by deposits of a maturity period of at least seven-eight years. so, if one enters the home loan business, one needs to have a strong long-term deposit base. This is why some banks are choosing distribution tie-ups.

Nevertheless, retail banking has been the focus of Indian banks, they have still miles to traverse. It constitutes less than 7 per cent of the GDP in India which is far less than in other Asian countries (35 per cent). It is also notable that retail lending in India is mostly confined to urban and metropolitan regions, leaving very little scope for this segment in rural hinterlands of the country.

G. FUTURE OF RETAIL BANKING

Retail banking segment of banks' business has a very bright future prospects especially in a growing economy like India mainly because of increasing prosperity and the consequent increase in purchasing power of the people, changing demographies with young population having high propensity to consume coupled with more liberal attitudes toward personal debt. Even in developed countries like the US, retail banking is likely to represent nearly half of the US $ 450 billion in financial services revenues in the region. However, key to success of retail banking in India and abroad lies in how affectively commercial banks are capable of meeting the challenges. Retail banking will probably undergo the most change in the next few years of any banking sector. The major challenge is how to deliver in a competitive landscape that is complex and rapidly evolving. From an historic position of strength the traditional banks now must fight how to sell new products. Consumers no longer automatically turn to their primary bank for additional services and most current accounts are loss-making. Besides, the core banking relationship itself is being challenged by product specialists and non-financial services players exploiting the power of retail brands.

A new generation of confident consumers is driving a fundamental change in consumer behaviour. Younger consumers are far more finicky and demanding, switching fastly to a new offer. According to a research study of Asian consumers, nearly 50% customers are dissatisfied with the service they receive from their banks and many would be prepared to switch if offered new opportunities. Banks will have, therefore, to be more watchful, monitoring changing consumer behaviour and accordingly bringing about change in product, price and channel so as to offer superb product and customized service on a continuing basis.

Competition remains strong right across retail financial services; in credit and debit cards, mortgages, loans and insurance. Good margins, deregulation and lower entry costs have attracted new competitors. Players from the US card market have tried to exploit expertise in customers segmentation and operations. Retailers and others have tried to exploit a strong existing brand and CRM capabilities.

Growing ferocity of competitiveness in the sphere of retail banking will result in reduction of geographic barriers. Thus, geographic convenience could make little difference in future.

In that case, the consumer will choose banking services largely on the basis of price consideration. A time may come in the not–too–distant future when the consumer will be able to conduct a large amount of highly automated "Comparison shopping", usually so-called "Intelligent – agent" software programmes to search for and look at products from banks all over the country, not just from those banks that happen to be located near the consumers' home or work place.

In addition, the "electronic comparison" shopping will not necessarily always be for a "complete bundle" of banking services from a single bank, but could be on a product-by-product basis or, as financial products become increasingly standardized as they become automated on a "accommodate-by commodity" basis. Thus, electronic delivery of banking services could erode the brand-name loyalty consumers. Moreover, for retail products like credit cards, mortgages, auto loans and some investment and savings products, there will also be non-bank competitors, specializing in being a very large provider of just one product to gain the lowest unit cost through economies of scale in processing.

Commercial banks are going to face new challenges from their competitors who are now relying on new, sophisticated technology, but are thinking of other ways to compete, cut costs and gain access to the consumer, and at the same time avoiding direct competition in those areas where non bank competitors already have a big advantage. For example, rather than relying on conventional branches, or setting up internet sites, and waiting for the consumer to take the initiative and eventually come to the bank in person, or electronically, the US banks are putting small branches in super market (large grocery-store) chains where many consumers, including the customers of their competitors, are virtually certain to come a few times each week. These scaled-back, but strategically placed, branches might help these banks capture that is not ready for total electronic delivery of financial products or those who might not actively seek information about financial products. In any case, this innovating approach to bank branching is considerably less expensive than conventional, stand-alone branches and is one of the alternative branch configurations many banks in the USA considering.[10]

Another challenge which banks could be facing in near future is new forms of risks such as the potential risk for losing the competitive edge by underestimating the potential for electronics in banking, inadequate planning for electronic security, and the possibility for onerous regulation if banks do not provide reliable electronic banking products.

Finally, retail banking will become more expensive for banks in future. To meet the evolving needs of different segments, to develop new products, and to introduce services like internet banking and remodelled branches will all require a level of investment with which Asian banks are unfamiliar. Historically, banks in Asia have earned good returns partly because they were able to keep investments low and because they did not face stiff competition. That era is over.

To meet the above challenges and ensure retail banking to survive and thrive, customers and customer service should be the kernel of retail banking business. This demands constant innovation in retail banking. In bracing for tomorrow, there is a paradigm shift in bank financing through innovative constant upgradation and revalidation of the banks' internal systems and processes. To use retail as a growth trigger requires product development and differentiation, innovation and business process re-engineering, micro-planning, marketing, prudent pricing customization, technological upgradation, home/electronic/mobile banking, cost reduction and cross-selling.[11]

Thus, while there exists immense opportunities for growth of retail banking in India and abroad, the challenges are equally daunting. To what extent retail banking can exploit growth opportunities would depend upon the core competency of the banks to counterpoise the challenges and make use of opportunities profitably. However, the competitive edge of the banks in the field of retail banking would depend essentially on the kind of technology used and the efficiency of operations.

H. GOVERNMENT POLICY FOR RETAIL BANKING

At a recent bankers' conference, the finance minister hinted at the possibility of bringing in a law to provide sanction for collection, sharing and regulation of credit information. In view of high degree of risks involved in retail lending, there is a strong need to develop suitable risk mitigation techniques in order to sustain the stability of earning from these loans. The regulations have recently introduced some intigating measures in the form of increased risk weightage for arriving at regulating capital. As per the old norms, the banks had to weigh housing loans at 50 per cent and other retail loans at 100 per cent to calculate the total risk weighted assets (RWA) and then provide capital of a per cent of the RWA. With the risk weights for housing loans raised to 75 per cent and other retail loans at 125 per cent, the capital requirements have increased. Even under the standardized approach of the Basel-II norms for capital adequacy, the risk weight for mortgages (including home loans) is 40 per cent and that for other retail loans is 75 per cent. However, such tightening needs to be balanced against the credit needs of this segment and the resultant opportunity for revenue generation.

I. CONCLUSIONS

Retail banking has, of late, emerged as core segment of the banking business all over the world and gained prominence to meet the competitive challenges, improve quality of services and profit margin.

The essence of retail banking lies in individual customers. While retail lending is reflection on asset side of the balance sheet, retail banking comprises products of liabilities and assets sides. Retail banking business today is multi-products and multi-customers. Unlike plain vanilla class banking products that the banks world over offered until the recent past, banks under retail banking scheme offer wide variety of customized products at most competitive rates through multiple channels to cater to the needs of wide variety of individual customers.

Retail banking business is making rapid progress during the last decade not only in developed economies but also in developing economies. In Brazil, Russia, India and China, the loan to individuals has grown more than triple from $ 145 bn in 2001 to an estimated $ 477 bn in 2005. In mature economies like Germany alone, the retail lending totalled about $ 1700 billion in 2005.

Retail banking in India has been the main story and key profit driver for banks in the recent times with retail portfolio constituting 19.0 per cent of total outstanding advances as on march end 2010. There is, however, still much scope for retail banking in the country.

Future of retail banking in India is very bright mainly because of increasing prosperity and the consequent increase in purchasing power of the people, changing demographics with young population having high propensity to consume coupled with more liberal attitudes toward personal debt.

To what extent retail banking can exploit growth opportunities would depend upon the core competency of the banks to counterpoise the challenges and make use of opportunities profitably. However, the competitive process of the banks in the field of retail banking would depend essentially on the kind of technology used and the efficiency of operations.

KEY TERMS

- Accommodate-by commodity
- Bancassurance
- Core-banking relationship
- Electronic comparison shopping
- Hotter than vindaloo
- Mass banking
- Primary bank
- Retail lending
- Teaser loan

DISCUSSION QUESTIONS

1. What is retail banking? What are the unique features of retail banking?
2. Discuss the significance of retail banking in competitive environment.
3. Evaluate recent trends in retail banking in India.
4. Why is retail banking gaining prominence in the loan portfolio of commercial banks in India in recent years?
5. What is the future of retail banking in India?
6. What challenges banking industry across the world are likely to face in future in the field of retail banking? What measures would you suggest for combating these challenges?

REFERENCES

1. Retail Banking – Opportunities and Challenges, key note address by Shyamla Gopinath, Dy. Governor at the IBA – Banking Frontiers International conference on May 28, 2005 in December 2005.
2. www.euromonitor.com/Retail banking services in h-k., October, 2004.
3. www.euromonitor.com/Retail banking services in USA (mmp) October. 2004.
4. www.The banker.com/news/full story php/aid/1847/Japan % 925 banks rebuilt.html.
5. www.euromonitor — /Retail-banking services in Germany, October 2004.
6. Report on Trend and Progress of Banking in India, 2003-04, p. 59.
7. *Ibid.*
8. www.ny.frb.org/new servants speeches/1997 EPQ 71030.html.
9. Business Standard, May 2011.
10. Business Line, August 30, 2007.
11. The Economic, Times, October 28, 2007.

Corporate Governance in Commercial Banks

Chapter 8

Learning Objectives:

The present chapter attempts to provide:

- a historic evolution of the term corporate governance.
- conceptual exposition of corporate governance and its relevance to commercial banks in India.
- an insight into the fundamentals of corporate governance.
- an overview of code of effective corporate governance for commercial banks in India.
- a synoptic view of corporate governance practices in commercial banks in India.

Chapter Outline:

- Emergence of corporate governance.
- Corporate governance and commercial banks.
- Concept of corporate governance.
- Objectives of corporate governance in commercial banks in India.
- Fundamentals of corporate governance.
- Prescribing code of effective corporate governance practices for commercial banks.
- Corporate governance in commercial banks in India.
- RBI and corporate governance in banks in India.
- Government of India and corporate governance in commercial banks.
- Conclusions.

A. EMERGENCE OF CORPORATE GOVERNANCE PHILOSOPHY

The term corporate governance is much in use these days; everybody and anybody having anything to do with the corporate sector talks of good corporate governance. Certainly corporate governance is not just a buzz word or management fad but has become need of the hour for every organisation if it is to survive and grow successfully and achieve competitive edge over its competitors in fast paced and brutally competitive landscape and enhance its legitimacy in a highly awakened society.

Concept of corporate governance gained prominence in the wake of major corporate debauches, corporate failures, collapses and gross financial irregularities in developed countries of the USA, the UK, Canada, France and Australia in the late 1980s and early 1990, causing shareholders, banks and other investors to worry about their investments. Scandals plagued such companies as Adelpine Communications (family misuse of corporate funds), Enron (off balance sheet activities and the use of fictitious corporate entities), Health South (CEO greed and falsified accounts), Tyco International (alleged CEO expropriation of corporate loan and cash for personal use), Worldcom (one of the biggest bankruptcy in US corporate history and falsified accounting records), Imclone systems (CEO's blatant insider trading of company stock), Lehman Brothers (biggest bankruptcy in US financial market due to bad mortgage against housing loans), to name just a few.

Recent failures of top management of Indian organisations, as evidenced by the indifference of ITC Board toward evasion of excise duties and violation of the FERA for years, lapse of the Shaw Wallace Board in detecting financial machinery and mute watch of the Bata Board members to its Chairman frittering away the Company's brand equity among middle class customers, connivance of top management of BPL, Sterlite Industries and Videocon International with big bull Harshad Mehta in rigging the prices of their shares and spate of other corporate scandals, including the latest massive financial fraud committed by Satyam erstwhile Chairman B. Ramlinga Raju, bear sufficient testimony to the Boards being decorative and decorous baubles behaving like anesthetized witnesses, and rubber stamping the decisions already made by the Chief Executive. Recent misgovernance by the State Bank of India is a case in point. (Illustrative case 8.1).

Illustrative Case 8.1

Misgovernance in State Bank of India

With change in Chairmanship of the SBI after five years in 2010, the top management decided to make unprecedented additional provisioning in the last quarter of the year to cover up inadequate provisioning for non-performance assets (NPAs) and pension liability for the preceding three quarters as required by the RBI prudential norms and applicable accounting standards. This caused the Bank's profit to decline 99 per cent to ₹ 20.88 crore in January-March 2011 from ₹ 1,867 crore, devastating the investors' confidence and credibility in financial reporting. This impacted the SBI's share price plummeting to one of its lowest marks.

The RBI's financial prudence norms stipulated that all banks should provide for 70 per cent of their NPAs and had set September 2010 deadline. But while most banks made incremental provisions in each quarter to reach the prescribed level, the SBI opted not to follow them till March, 2010. So the SBI's NPA coverage was just 44.36 per cent compared to Bank of Baroda's 74.46 per cent. ICICI Bank, ranked second in India by assets, reported 59.48 per cent coverage and Punjab National Bank 69.46 per cent.

The SBI, being the leader in the banking industry is expected to have set an example by taking the lead to achieve the required coverage instead of waiting till the last quarter.

Again, according to the RBI's directive in November, 2010, all banks offering term home loans had to provide higher provisioning of 2 per cent instead of 0.2 per cent earlier — which worked out to ₹ 500 crore for the SBI. Though its auditors asked it to make the higher provision for the quarter to December, 2010, the SBI made the provision only in the fourth quarter.

The fact that there are wide fluctuations in the SBI's profitability whenever the leadership changes is a sad reflection on the quality of governance in the Bank, despite the RBI's stringent norms and the entire gamut of corporate governance system in place. The overwhelming power and influence of the chairman in deciding when and how mandatory provisioning should be carried out seems to prove that the pillars of the corporate governance architecture — board of directors, audit committee, the internal control framework, internal and external auditors — abdicate their collective wisdom and fell in line helplessly with the dominant leadership.

The issue deserves to be examined. The judicious application of prudential norms and accounting standards over the years could have averted erratically fluctuating stock prices owing to inappropriate reporting of quarterly financial results.

As a matter of fact, the Board members have been found shying away from discharging their legitimate responsibilities. It was only when the organisation and its chief executive's performance is berated and proscribed in public that the Board members woke up from slumber and came into action to stem the organisation and its chief out of the crisis. This phenomenon has been global, as evidenced by the study of the Business Week of American companies in 1996 showing the existence of the different degrees of quality of corporate governance ranging between 9.9 and 97.8 (out of score of 100) and desperate attempts to rehaul the functioning of corporate boards in the US and UK — best symbolized by the now famous recommendations of the Cadbury Committee and the Greenbury Committee on Corporate governance that the UK-based corporations are adopting and by the lead set by the General Motors.

Thus, emergence of competitive environment with customers — both external and internal — dictating the organisations to perform best in their interests and maximize their value and highly awakened investors demanding greater transparency and adoption of international standards of disclosures have forced organisations to practice good governance for sake of existence and hence the emerging concept of governance. As a matter of fact, organisations are increasingly realising that good governance can be a source of competitive advantage.

In recent few years, the tide of board room activism has been steadily rising and some events of recent years suggest that Boards taking exception to their CEOs are becoming the rule.

B. CORPORATE GOVERNANCE AND COMMERCIAL BANKS

The significance of governance process lies in its contribution both to business prosperity and accountability. Good governance ensures that the shareholders are taken into confidence on matters concerning the company's business activity. Given the important role of banks in financial intermediation in the economy and the need to safeguard depositors' money, corporate governance is of immense value to banking entities.

The issue of corporate governance in banks is not exactly the same as that of manufacturing corporations. In the case of traditional manufacturing enterprises, the issue has been that of safeguarding and maximising the shareholder's value. In the case of banking industry, the risk involved for depositors and the possibility of contagion assumes greater significance than that of consumers of manufactured products. Further, the involvement of Government is discernibly higher in banks due to importance of stability of financial system and the larger interests of the public. This is true for Indian banking industry which is largely Government owned.

In India, the corporate governance in the context of PSBs was non-existent until a few years ago. These banks operating in a subsidized and protected environment until the early 1990s had no autonomy to operate. The entire banking sector was highly regulated, over administered and subject to discretionary controls. There was hardly any competition from other existing institutions. They commanded a lion's share in the banking business. The bank customers did not have much freedom of choice because of standardized products and regimented interest rates. Even the capital requirements of the PSBs were met by the Government through budgetary support.

There was no threat to the operations of the PSBs from external front because of the automatic flow of the business of the public sector occupying the commanding heights of the economy to them. The Government was omnipresent and growth impulses emanated from the Government. Bank depositors were rest content with the safety of their deposits due to availability of deposit insurance cover and ownership of banks.

However, tectonic changes in economic policy of the Government in 1991 and afterwards altogether changed the turf on which the PSBs operated. The operating environment in the banking field has become much more competitive while the rules of the game have been made stricter. In a deregulated environment, the banks need autonomy in their decision making. However, such autonomy needs to be accompanied by greater accountability on part of their board to the stakeholders. The root cause of Indian banks' deteriorating performance and the recent banking crisis in South-East Asia and global financial meltdown can be traced in the collective myopia and anathema of the board members, supervisors and institutional shareholders. Had they been more vigilant, these problems could have been averted.

The Indian commercial banks have, of late, started realizing that their continued strength and stability are matter of general public interest and concern both in regard to its linkages with the real sector and for providing a payment and settlement system. Further, they have come to firm belief that they can develop in healthy manner and fund their operations only so long as they enjoy the confidence of the public. More so, when the central bank is justifiably prescribing better prudential requirements and capital adequacy norms. If some additional capital has to be raised by these institutions, they should be able to convince the capital market and shareholders that it is worth investing their money in. It will, therefore, be in the vital interest of the banks to put in place and assure the market that their system of corporate governance is such that they can be trusted with shareholders' money. They may outsource global capital by way of ADRS, FDI, CDRs and financing by way of debt if highest standards of governance are maintained.

With broadening of the ownership of the PSBs and growing importance of the external constituencies of institutional and individual shareholders, credible and widely accepted governance and responsiveness of the top management are required so as to strengthen the position of the banks in the primary and secondary markets. The government decision to substantially reduce its stake in the banks and allow greater participation of public in their ownership further necessitates qualitative change in governance so that the expectations of external constituencies are met and opportunities arising out of liberalization are exploited fully. In fact, good governance momentum all over the world is coming from powerful institutional investors and money managers who demand greater disclosure, more transparent explanation for major decisions. The existence of private shareholders implies that issues like enhancing shareholders' value, protecting shareholders value and right become extremely important. Such a situation did not exist in most of the public sector banks until a few years back.

Although the RBI has been taking various regulatory measures — both quantitative and qualitative — to safeguard the interests of depositors, there is a need to attach greater importance to qualitative standards such as internal controls and risk management, composition and role of the Board and disclosure standards and hence the growing importance to corporate governance of the commercial banks.

In view of the above, the term corporate governance has almost become a rhetoric in Indian organisations including banks and financial institutions; like all rhetorics it is the most spoken but least meant.

C. CONCEPT OF CORPORATE GOVERNANCE

Concept of corporate governance is subtle and elusive. It has been defined differently by managerial scholars and management practitioners. The Cadbury Committee defined Corporate Governance as the system by which companies are directed and controlled,[1] thus placing the Board of Directors of a company at the centre of the governance system. In Canada, the Toronto Stock Exchange's guidelines define corporate governance as "the process and structure . . . to direct and manage the business and affairs of the corporate with the objective of enhancing shareholders value, which includes ensuring the financial viability of the business."[2] The OECD'S Business Sector Advisory Group Report, however, takes a much more pragmatic view on the subject : "Corporate governance comprehends that structure of relationships and corresponding responsibilities among a core group consisting of shareholders, board members and managers designed to best foster the competitive performance required to achieve the corporate's primary objective."[3] In India, the Kumar Mangalam Birla Report asserts that the "The fundamental objective of corporate governance is the enhancement of the long-term shareholder value while at the same time protecting the interests of other shareholders."[4]

Thus, corporate governance is all about conducting the affairs of an organization in such a way as to ensure fairness to customers, employees, investors, creditors, vendors, the government and society at large.

Corporate governance, in fact, is a philosophy of management by which owners and managers are expected to be perennially responsive to other entities such as minority shareholders, promoters, institutional shareholders, depositors, creditors, customers, employees and institutional lenders. Corporate governance has its in-built interest in overall employee involvement for quality and cost, empowerment and accountability towards the stakeholders. The essence of corporate governance is a framework in which owners and managers are expected to be perennially responsive to the stakeholders. It is all about conducting the company's affairs in such a manner as to ensure fairness to customers, employees, investors, creditors, vendors, government and the society.

Corporate governance provides a set of systems and processes which ensure that a company is managed in the best interest of all the stakeholders. Although the issue of corporate governance focuses on enhancing shareholders' value and protecting interests of employees, creditors and customers and holding management accountable for their performance, it would be a pity if corporate governance acquires a restrictive definition of improving shareholders' lot by way of adequate return. A company is no longer responsible simply for making a profit or producing goods but for simultaneously contributing to the solution of extremely complex ecological, moral, political, racial and social problems.

Corporate governance is, thus, an instrument for benefitting all stakeholders of a corporate entity. It entails driving the corporation's strategy and overseeing the day-to-day business with each process through creation of checks and balances. In its wide sense, corporate governance is almost akin to a trusteeship. It is about creating an out performing organisation which leads to increasing customer satisfaction, shareholders' value and safeguarding interests of other stakeholders.

Corporate governance has as its backbone a set of transparent relationships between an institution's management, its board, shareholders and other shareholders. It should, therefore, take into account a number of aspects, such as enhancement of shareholder's value, protection of rights of shareholders, competition and role of PRO and of directors integrity of accounting practices and disclosure norms and internal control system. As far as the banking industries is concerned, corporate governance relates to the manner in which the business and affairs of individual banks are directed and managed by their Board of Directors and senior management. It also provides the structure through which objectives of the institution are set; the strategy of attaining those objectives is determined and the performance of the institution is monitored.[5]

It is useful to recognize that it is a dynamic concept, in terms of scope, thrust and relevance. For example, the issue is approached very differently today compared to original view of the Cadbury Committee on the subjects. East Asian crisis gave a new dimension to corporate governance in the context of financial stability. In the USA, regulatory regimes, post-corporate scandals are very different from those of the early 90's. The OECD set out its corporate governance principles in 1999 but revived them in 2004. The Basel Committee on banking supervision published guidelines on corporate governance in banks in 1999. As an update, in July 2005, the Basel Committee had issued a Consultative Document on enhancing corporate governance for banking operations on boards of the banks. Thus, corporate governance should be viewed as an ongoing process subject to rapid changes based on experiences, developments and policy setting.[6]

Another important point to be noted is that there is considerable divergence in the understanding and practice of corporate governance, in general, and in respect of banks in particular, but there is also increasing tendency towards convergence. The cultural context may be difficult to capture but the legal, institutional and attitudinal contexts do vary perceptibly across countries - say between Anglo Saxon, Europeans and Japanese situations. At the same time, the trend toward greater convergence is for several reasons. The corporates are getting listed in multiple stock exchanges in different countries and carry out corporate operations in several jurisdictions while the cross-border financial flows seek an assurance of some commonly understood standards of governance, which have a mutually reinforcing tendency. Banks, in particular, have been subject of special interest for governance, especially in view of their fiduciary role. The cross-border operations of banks provide an added impetus for convergence in such standards.[7]

D. OBJECTIVE OF CORPORATE GOVERNANCE IN COMMERCIAL BANKS IN INDIA

The principal objective of corporate governance in commercial banks in India is to help the latter to grow and develop in healthy manner on self sustaining basis in highly competitive environment. This is why there is growing thrust on raising the level of corporate governance in the country from the angle of creating shareholders' value and also being more transparent in the operations. In India and so also in other countries banks and other financial institutions can succeed in deregulated environment only if they manage public savings operations with integrity and responsibility and adopt sound business practices. Irregularities on the part of the financial institutions may lead to mistrust among public. If they have to attract local and foreign capital, they have to demonstrate better standards of governance and place greater emphasis on their financial soundness and viability. Once this is assured, the shareholders' value will not only be retained but enhanced. A sound corporate governance culture enforces better discipline upon corporate management and ensures maximum value to the shareholders, keeping in view the interests of other shareholders, such as customers, employees and above all, the society at large.

E. FUNDAMENTALS OF CORPORATE GOVERNANCE

There are certain well established principles of corporate governance which apply to banks also. However, in view of their unique status, and safety nets provided to them, certain principles of corporate governance require a re-orientation.

- Corporate governance represents a set of systems which include certain structural and organisational aspects, and processes that embrace how things are done within such structures and organisational systems. These systems and processes are built up keeping in view the interests of each of the stakeholders. The company being an artificial and juristic entity cannot function by itself. The persona of a company is manifested through the Board of Directors. In fact, the most important body in the corporate system is its Board of Directors. It is often said that the cause of corporate governance is served depending on how well the Board of Directors of a company is organised and structured. This is why issues like size of the Board, its composition, role of directors, personal competencies and qualification of individual directors, frequency of change of composition, representation of the stakeholders in the Board, etc., constitute cornerstones of corporate governance.

Corporate governance also refers to the management processes which should be so devised as to ensure that the best interests of the stakeholders are met effectively. The Board of Directors with its different committees and the chairman should develop the right kind of processes for organisational effectiveness. These processes could be performance management systems, periodic business reviews, environmental audit, energy audit, security audit, secretarial and legal audit, bench marking customer satisfaction, etc.

- Crux of Corporate governance is separation of ownership from management. It is mistaken to believe that the Board has nothing to do with the management of the company. In fact, the Board is supposed to be involved with strategy and conduct of the management while ensuring that it follows the direction of the Board. The Board should strive for excellence through corporate objectives, *viz.*, maximization of customers' satisfaction and shareholders' value.
- The philosophy underlying corporate governance is that the Board of Directors should not confine itself to statutory functions alone but become an effective pivot ensuring direction and management. The Board should ensure that the bank is run with integrity, complies with all legal requirements and regulatory standards. The essence of good corporate governance is management's freedom to drive their companies forward, but to exercise it within a framework of effective accountability.
- Independence is the cornerstone of accountability and independent boards are essential to a sound governance structure. In most of the Indian banks the CEO and Chairman's position is combined. There has been much debate concerning the wisdom and feasibility of an independent chairman. The Cadbury Committee had stated that there should be a clearly accepted division of responsibilities at the top level of a company which will ensure a balance of power and authority in such a way that no one individual has unfettered powers of decision. Where the Chairman is also the chief executive, it is essential that there should be a strong and independent element on the Board with a recognized senior member. This principle has also been acknowledged by the US corporate Governance. It states that a substantial majority of the board should consist of directors who are independent.

  Shri S.H. Khan, former Chairman IDBI in his discussion paper observed that "to avoid the concentration of power in the hands of a single individual and in recognition of the pivotal role of the Chairman in securing good corporate governance, it is important that the roles of the Chairman and of the CEO be separated and different individuals appointed to the position. The Chairman should ideally be a non-executive director of the institution."
- Corporate governance goes far beyond regulations and laws. It deals with laws, procedures, practices and implicit rules that determine a company's ability to take informed managerial decisions and refers to an economic, legal and institutional environment that allows organisation to grow, diversify, restructure and compete. Mere compliance with regulatory pressures is a minimal requirement of good corporate governance. The road to efficiency lies in minimizing regulatory prescriptions and maximizing voluntary codes to ensure excellence in corporate governance among banks.
- Corporate governance implies self regulation. As suppliers, potential collaborators, investors and customers start rewarding companies with good corporate governance practices, companies realize that governance can be a source of competitive advantage.

This is why code of governance should not be imposed on companies. Every company has to evolve its own code to sub-serve the interests of its stakeholders.

- Transparency has come to be regarded as the golden rule for the orderly behaviour of the financial system. There are several reasons for this development. First, transparency backed by prudent supervision enhances the accountability or the financial system. This, in turn, builds in a check against undue risk-taking and reduces the probability of failures and systematic risk. Secondly, it provides a payment and settlement system to the economy and have important linkages with the rural sector. Shareholders get all the relevant information necessary to judge whether their interests are being taken care of. Transparency and disclosures also serve as an important adjunct to the supervising process as they facilitate market discipline of the banks. They also facilitate translation into allocative efficiency and a clear perception of the risk-returns trade-off embedded in investment proposals.

In addition, the PSBs being owned partly or wholly by the Government of India, the government has a stake in the profitable and functioning of these banks.

In the aftermath of the East-Asian crisis of 1997-98, and global financial crisis of 2008 it was realized that information available in the markets, prior to the crisis, did not reflect the underlying reasons. Hence, considerable attention is being devoted to developing standard transparency codes and substantial progress has been made. The IMF has also developed voluntary standards of transparency and disclosure.

As such, it is imperative for the Board of Directors, Chairman, External auditors and supervisors of the PSBs to strive hard to achieve higher degree of openness, transparency, integrity and accountability in the working of the institution.

F. PRESCRIBING CODE OF EFFECTIVE CORPORATE GOVERNANCE FOR COMMERCIAL BANKS

Code of corporate governance refers to rules prescribed for different functionaries of the organisation to achieve the necessary high standards of corporate behaviour. These rules should set norms on size of Board of Directors, composition of the Board, role and responsibilities of the Directors, Chairman and executive committee of the Board, role and responsibilities of the Audit Committee, conduct of annual general meeting and disclosure standards and transparency.

Although several models of corporate governance such as Cadbury model, Greenbury model, CII model, SEBI model and World Bank model, International Corporate Governance Network and ICICI model have been formulated as reactions to corporate disasters so as to guide the conduct of the affairs of the enterprises in the best interests of the stakeholders, no single model can, however, work necessarily for all the companies. In fact, every organisation has to evolve its own code of corporate governance keeping in view the fundamentals of governance enumerated above, the special conditions under which the PSBs function in India, and the veritable fact that it has to be such as to serve as competing advantage to the bank in highly competitive and unforgiving society.

◈ Size of the Board of Directors

Various studies on optimum size of the Board have been undertaken in the USA and UK. One conclusion emerging from these studies is that a Board should ideally have 12 directors. This, of course, does not take into account the peculiarities which a banking company may have, warranting a variation from this number. The Companies' Act 1956 also talks of a maximum number of 12 directors. In his discussion paper, Shri, Khan, former Chairman, IDBI, observed that the Board of Directors of any institution may ideally consist of 12 to 15 Directors.

In fact, the size of the Board should be such that sufficient non-executive directors exist to perform the assigned function to oversight committees.

The SBI's Board consists of 11 members and Bank of Baroda has 14 directors. Private sector banks such as ICICI Bank and HDFC have 16 and 12 members in their Boards, respectively.

◈ Composition of the Board

In view of the growing competitive pressure, the task of the Board of Directors has become formidable in as much as it has to steer clear the bank through turbulent times, make crucial decisions pertaining to product pricing and develop competing strategies and execute them to meet the challenges posed by the new players.

Composition of the Board should be decided keeping in view the above tasks. Further, while determining the Board composition, the focus should be on balancing independence, expertise, knowledge and business experience of the individual directors as also the diversity of backgrounds likely to make the Board most effective. The Board should also be diverse. Empirical studies suggest that Board diversity has a positive relationship with stockholders' value. Board diversity can help corporate management broaden their perspectives, which might become overly narrow with a homogenous Board. A diverse Board may strengthen the ability of the entire Board to act more independently, since the Board members with non-traditional backgrounds might be considered the ultimate outsiders.

◈ Responsibilities of Board of Directors

The governance of firms rests with the Board of Directors. Accordingly, conceptualizing the future and seeing what others cannot see has to be the hallmark of Board of Directors of an organization. They are expected to conceive the vision and share it with employees, customers, suppliers, collaborators, investors and other enlightened groups of the society to solicit that opinions which will enable him to crystallize it in terms of corporate purpose and mission. Sharing of the vision generates excitement, brings order out of chaos and builds confidence and trust among the employees who will work harder to make it succeed. It also helps the Board in refining and making it operational. While articulating strategic ambition it would be ensured that it is not so broad as to convey little meaning or guidance to people deep in the organization. It needs to be so spelt out as to capture employee's attention and interest. The articulated corporate ambition should be such as to ensure commitment of the people to the purpose the organization has helped to develop.

Based on SWOT analysis the Board has to evolve strategic policy guidelines in respect of nature and scope of business, approach to growth, development of resource, structuring of organization, etc.

The Board of Directors has to play actively the role of change agent, entrepreneur, facilitator and coordinator to enable the organization to cope with competitive challenges through strategy building and restructuring. The Directors are expected to set in consultation with corporate executives corporate objectives in various critical business activities with ultimate focus on excellence and not effectiveness. Objectives of high productivity and total quality and developing human capital should also receive overriding emphasis in evolving corporate objective mix.

The Board of Directors has to take the responsibility of finding position in the market place that best suits the firm's competencies. In the changed environment they should consider strategy in terms of 'fit' and 'stretch' that demand focus on leveraging of resources in addition to the allocation so as to capitalize on the opportunities with the minimum resources.

While making above strategic exercise, the Directors must follow collaborative approach and share the strategic thoughts with their young and enlightened executives and evolve the strategy by consensus. At present, the chief executive considers himself as the chief strategist with full control of setting corporate objectives and determining priorities. This mindset need to be changed in an environment where fast changing knowledge and expertise required to take strategic decisions are usually found on all front-liners. The frontline managers must, therefore, be encouraged to provide foresight and a compelling view of the future.

The Board of Directors has to assume mantle of translating the strategy into action. They must have a game plan that takes care of the overall picture, with each piece of the picture well defined, well thought, and well put. It is the ultimate responsibility of the Board to see that operational plans are tethered to the overall objective and strategy. They have to oversee the operational guidelines formulated by the senior executives to serve as guide posts for the development of functional and tactical strategies.

In their efforts to execute the strategy the Board of Directors have to strive for developing organizational structure which is proactive and responsive to the market place and which reconfigures resources to address emerging opportunities. Creation of self-managed teams with focused objectives and tasks are the demand of the day.

They are, therefore, expected to guide the managers in designing and developing lean, thin and flat structure so as to enhance organizational responsiveness, augment productivity, reduce costs and improve quality. Role and responsibilities of executives in organizational hierarchy need to be clearly defined and the same be communicated to all concerned.

Time has come when the Board members have to involve themselves directly in acquisition, development and maintenance of human resource of the organization. They have to guide human resource managers in tailoring the manpower planning to corporate plans and drawing a long-term hiring programme so as to track down people endowed with knowledge, skills and attitudes best suited to achieving corporate objectives. Retaining talents requires team-based rewards system, which pegs rewards of entire manpower of the business division to the achievement of its goals.

A comprehensive, systematic and continuing training system linked to the corporate strategy needs to be installed by the Board. Prominent on the agenda of the training programmes should be developing an overall global business perspective as well as understanding of business strategy formulation and relationships between cross functional areas and developing competencies for personal growth. This will go a long way in retention of employees and improving their marketability, which may, in fact serve as powerful investment of motivation.

So as to motivate and prod the people to contribute their best to the organization the Board of Directors must assume the responsibility of a change agent to transform perception and mindsets of the senior managers and change the style of their leading the people. They must ensure that their employees are not treated as a cost to be controlled but as an asset to be developed. Instead of chastising the employees, corporate managers should be directed to support, coach and mentor them to contribute their best to the organization. It is the ultimate responsibility of the board to convert the contractual employees of an economic entity into committed members of a purposeful organization.

The Board of Directors must recognize that they can influence their employees by team leadership and not by command leadership. They must move from exercising gross power of authority, which only produces compliance to the subtle power of influence which secures commitment and passes ownership down the line. They have to learn to direct their employees through vision, imagination and ideas and fire their desire to reach the destination. They should build an organizational climate where individuals are free to take any initiative necessary to fulfill quality goals. They have to foster trust, generate a sense of pride and ownership in the organization and provide life satisfaction to them and sustain it through culture, useful traditions, practices and systems.

Above all, employees can be influenced not by virtue of traits and behaviour of the corporate managers alone but also on account of his mastery over a process which is crucial to the organization. In the age where competitive advantages must be polished till they shine, the Board of Directors must champion this specific proprietary expertise, by not only making it the pivotal of the organization's strategy, but also ensuring that it is passed up, down and across the organization.

Further, the Board should ensure that the firm is run with integrity, complies with all legal requirements and regulatory standards and conducts its business in accordance with high ethical standards.

The Board has also to ensure that proper control systems exist and are functioning and that the operations of the firm are conducted with due regard to assurance that necessary provisions are made and all statutory and other directives are complied with.

So as to ensure that the Board members are discharging their duties dexterously and skillfully, they should be sufficiently exposed to various aspects of banking such as banking law, regulatory requirements, current trends in global banking and nuances of Indian and International financial markets. Newly appointed members should undergo a proper process of induction into banks affairs.

◈ The Role and Responsibilities of Chairman

The chairman of a bank is next to the Board in the management hierarchy. As a top executive of the organisation he represents the central authority who has overall control and accountability for effective functioning and performance in terms of a set of norms for co-ordination of the product businesses within the bank and the various functional managers. It is the chairman of the bank who has to ensure that the collective ability of the Board provides both the leadership and the checks and balances which effective governance demands. He has also to ensure that the non-executive directors receive timely and relevant information tailored to their needs and they are properly briefed on the issues arising at meetings so as to make them effective board members.

◈ Chairman and Chief Executive Officer (CEO)

The moot issue relating to corporate governance is whether the chairman should be different from the CEO of the Bank. The Cadbury Committee which went into the financial aspects of corporate governance in the UK had recommended that the Chairman of the board should be a person different from the CEO of the company. It felt that this would ensure the right accountability of the CEO to the Board and that the independence of the Board to a large extent would be whittled down if the Chairman and the CEO are one and the same person. It would be advisable to have as Chairman a person of high stature and eminence who is not in the executive management of the company. This will further ensure greater independence and creditability in Board meetings.

◈ Role and Responsibilities of Non-executive Directors

Among the non-executive directors are independent directors who have a key role in the entire mosaic of corporate governance. According to the Kumar Mangalam Committee, independent directors are those who apart from director's remuneration, do not have any material pecuniary relationship of transactions with the company, its promoters, its management or its subsidiaries, which in the judgement of the Board may affect their independence of judgment. About the role of independent directors, the Committee is of the view that non-executive directors including independent directors help bring an independent judgment to bear on Board's deliberations, especially on issues of strategy, performance, management of conflicts and standards of conducts.

◈ Role and Responsibilities of Nominee Directors

In recent years, financial institutions in India have nominated their executives in the boards of companies assisted by them. In many cases it has been found that these nominees have remained content with safeguarding the interests of the institutions vis-à-vis of the company.

There is a general impression that whenever a conflict arises between the interests of the financial institutions and that of the company, the nominees invariably safeguard only the interests of their institutions. This impression is wholly erroneous. What is good for the company should be good for the financial institutions too. If the nominee directors ensure that things happen in the best interests of the company, rarely will the interests of financial institutions be jeopardised. After all, in the ultimate analysis only if the company did well the investments of the financial institutions will be protected.

The nominee directors should exercise their influence for maintaining high standards of corporate governance. They should encourage regular and systematic contact at senior executive level to exchange views and information on strategy performance, board membership and quality of management. They should also play a significant role in the appointment of non-executive directors of the requisite calibre, dexterity, experience and objectivity.

◈ Personal Competencies and Skills of Individual Directors

To be an effective member on the board of a commercial bank, besides stature and eminence, he/she must be honest, above board, trustworthy and possess appropriate skills and experience. A bank director, apart from having an independent mind, should have a close insight into how banks operate, what are statutory requirements under Banking Companies' Act and what is the banking scenario in and outside the country. Besides, a bank director should be able to think in a top of the line manner. He should be well-versed in the macro economic trends as well as specific trends in the banking business. Personal attributes like ability to listen, being open minded and being articulate will go a long way in making a bank director quite effective.

In order to have competencies and skills in an ever-changing environment, it is important that the directors also undergo exposure programme especially with respect to latest developments in economic and banking fields both at domestic and global levels.

◈ Audit Committee of the Board of Directors (ACBs)

Audit Committee of the Board acts as an important link in the corporate governance of a commercial bank. This body provides direction and function in the bank. As per the guidelines laid down by the Reserve Bank, the ACB should review various aspects of the internal inspection/ audit function including the system, its quality and effectiveness in terms of follow-up. It is also supposed to evaluate the inspection reports of specialised and extra large branches and all branches having unsatisfactory ratings. While reviewing inspection reports focus should be on certain areas such as inter-branch adjustment accounts, unreconcited long entries in inter-bank accounts, arrears in balancing of books at various branches, frauds and all other major house keeping. The ACB may also, if necessary, seek the assistance of the outside consultants for assessing the effectiveness of the total audit function.

The ACB should also pay serious attention to the area of disclosure standards. No doubt, the RBI prescribes disclosure standards to be followed by every bank while preparing financial statements and other reports. There is, however, an ample scope for improving upon them. If disclosure standards of the PSBs are to be in line with globally accepted standards, concepts such as consolidation of accounts and segmental reporting would have to be introduced. This will keep the investors better informed about the division/groupwise performances of the subsidiary on the working of the bank. Adoption of international standards of disclosures and transparency can facilitate the PSBs in accessing global financial markets and getting their shares listed on the international stock markets.

◈ Role and Responsibilities of Secretary of the Board

Secretary of the Board has to play significant role in corporate governance. It is his responsibility that all the agenda items are properly placed before the Board and its various committees. So as to discharge his responsibilities properly only a qualified company secretary with adequate experience and legal background should be appointed.

Unfortunately, there is no system of recruiting a professional person for this purpose. This system has got to be changed and a Chartered Accountant or Company Secretary should be appointed as the secretary of the Bank. A professionally qualified secretary will also acquaint the non-executive director with details of the functioning of the board.

◆ Remuneration of CEO and Directors

Remuneration of CEO and Executive Directors of Board of a bank should be good enough to attract, retain and motivate them of the quality required. However, it should be commensurate with the performance of the bank.

CEO compensation has always been a hotly debated topic in the USA. Of late, the debate has spread to India. A study by XLRI found that in the past eight years, CEO pay in India has risen faster than profits, average employee pay, return on capital employed or even return on equity. The study showed that between 1992-93 and 2000-01, the top management salaries grew by 33.1% while the compounded annual growth rate of sales was 11.52%, of PBDIT was 13.84% and of pay themselves wages was 9.81%.

According to CII, Indian CEOs cannot pay themselves too much. It feels that Indian corporates cannot follow the US model of paying the CEOs excessive amounts. Indian CEOs should have some limit in mind in terms of personal emoluments, structure. It emphasized that companies should bridge the salary gap between the CEO and the second rung of command.

At a conference on CEO pay, Narayan Murthy reiterated that CEO compensation should not be more than 15-18 times the pay of the lowest level of employee in the firm.

What is most important to note that in India it is not possible to find out the actual compensation of CEO even if the firm happens to be publicity listed and faithfully files the CEO salary information in its annual reports, for the fact that the information disclosed represents only the base amount and constituents a mere fraction of the money and perks the CEO compensation under accounting heads.

Under the circumstances, it is imperative that a company must have credible and transparent policy in determining an accounting for remuneration of the directors. The overriding principle in respect of directors' remuneration is that of openness and the shareholders are entitled to a full and clear statement of available to the directors.

It is in this context that the Kumar Mangalam Committee recommended that the board set up a remuneration Committee to determine on their behalf and on behalf of the shareholders with agreed terms of reference, the company's policy on specific remuneration packages for executive directors including pension rights and any compensation payment.

◆ Conduct of the Annual General Meeting

In view of growing broadening of ownership of the commercial banks, conduct of the Annual General Meeting (AGM) has assumed great significance. AGM provides a platform where the individual shareholders can express their views freely on the working of the Bank and the Chairman takes the shareholders into confidence about the state of banking in general and his bank in particular.

However, the existing laws have reduced the conduct of the AGM to a mere ritual and many directors do not think it necessary even to attend the AGM. This sorry state of affairs needs to be changed to render the corporate governance effective. The Board of Directors should treat the AGM with the sanctity it deserves and necessary amendments in the law governing the banks need to be made in order to give substance to the concept of shareholders' democracy.

◆ Disclosure Standards and Transparency

Transparency, as observed earlier, is an important element of corporate governance. This is why the Cadbury Committee emphasized on openness and transparency because it feels that the "life blood of markets is information" and barriers to the flow of relevant information represent imperfections in the market." The Committee further added that the cardinal principle of financial reporting is that the view presented should be true and fair. The Board should aim for the highest level of disclosure consonant with presenting reports which are understandable and with avoiding damaging to their competitive position. They should also aim to ensure the integrity and consistency of their reports and they should meet the spirits as well as the letter of reporting standards."

The Basel Committee on Banking Supervision in its Report on "Enhancing Bank Transparency" (September 1998) recommended that banks in their financial reports must provide timely information which would facilitate market participants' assessment of banks. Accordingly, a bank should furnish details of its working results as well as of its subsidiaries. There should also be information on allocation of capital to different business groups or activities within the banks so that activity-wise/business group-wise return on capital is revealed.

Besides, the bank should also disclose information about directors' experience, qualifications and other positions held by them in order to guard against conflicts of interest.

G. CORPORATE GOVERNANCE IN COMMERCIAL BANKS IN INDIA

Ownership and governance of banks assume special significance in view of the fact that they accept and deploy large amount of uncollateralized public funds, leverage such funds through credit creation as also administer the payment mechanism. Accordingly, legal provisions relating to ownership and governance laid down in the Banking Regulation Act, 1949 have been supplemented by regulating prescriptions issued by the RBI from time to time.

In India, the existing legal framework and significant current practices cover the following aspects: *(i)* Composition of Board of Directors; *(ii)* guidelines on corporate governance; *(iii)* guidelines for acknowledgement of transfer and allotments of shares in private sector banks and foreign investment in the banking sector which is governed by the Press Note of March 5, 2004 issued by the Ministry of Commerce and Industry, Government of India.

The advent of corporate governance norms across the globe and the introduction of the recommendations of the Kumar Mangalam Board Committee on corporate governance set up by SEBI in 2000 on clause 49 of the listing agreement further set in motion new obligations of PSBs in terms of transparency and disclosure norms. The recommendations of Narayan Murthy Committee on corporate governance were made part of clause 49 applicable to PSBs by adding a rider that the clause would be applicable to the extent it does not violate their respective statutes, and guidelines or directives issued by the regulating authorities.

The clause 49 of the listing agreement includes, among others, composition of the Board, Audit Committee, subsidiary companies, disclosures, (EO/CFO certification, report an corporate governance and comprises. Section 9(3) of the acts of 1970/1980 dealing with the composition of the Board of a PSB was introduced in 1994. It already provides for a framework of directors such as two whole time directors designated as Chairman and Managing Director, Executive Director, a nominee of the RBI, a nominee of the union government, a director each from workmen, non-workmen categories, a chartered accountant and six more directors to be nominated by the union government. Section 9(3) (i) of the Acts 1970/1980 based on the non-government holding provides for a certain number of directors to be elected from shareholders other than the union government. This section discusses the areas of expertise and knowledge, which would be required from shareholder directors.

The Basel Committee on Banking Supervision principle have been adopted for Indian banks after adjusting for local rules, regulations and the governance standard requirements. In February 2005, the RBI released a road map for the presence of foreign banks in India and also guidelines on ownership/governance in private sector banks. The recommendations of the Ganguly Committee on corporate governance also serve as a regulatory framework on corporate governance for banks. The Committee highlighted the role and responsibility of independent non-executive directors, qualification and other eligibility criteria (fit and proper criteria) for their appointment, training the directors and keeping them up-to-date with the latest developments.

Besides, the committee set the philosophy of corporate governance at a level much higher than just compliance with legal and regulatory requirements. It expressed the need to maintain business ethics and maximize value for all the stakeholders, besides effective management and control.

The recent experience indicates that the PSB Boards have been strengthened with persons of eminence and high specialization. Boards of Union Bank of India, Bank of Baroda and Bank of India have attracted people who are experts in their respective fields. As the process of accessing capital markets of the PSBs got strengthened, SEBI categorised the Union Government as a promoter, thereby enabling only shareholder directors of listed PSBs to be deemed as independent directors. Under the current region of clause 49, directors appointed/nominated by the Union Government are categorized as promoter directors and shareholder directors of listed PSBs to be deemed as independent directors.

The recent initiatives like managerial autonomy to the PSBs, mandatory and non-mandatory provisions such as code of conduct and training to directors are giving a new sense of direction to decision making and corporate governance in the PSBs. Many brands of PSBs have also realized that the voluntary adoption of good corporate practices is today fast becoming a prerequisite for better valuation of stock prices and enhanced visibility. It also gives room for profitable disinvestment. With increased holding in PSBs by reputed mutual funds such as Calpers and other FIIs, PSBs might be subject to greater pressure for good governance practices such as transparency, disclosure, fair business dealings, equity approach to shareholders, interests and social transformation initiatives.

H. RESERVE BANK OF INDIA AND CORPORATE GOVERNANCE IN BANKS IN INDIA

Taking cognizance of crucial role of Board of Directors, the RBI has directed banks to set up Audit Committees of the Board Chaired by non-executive Chairman and consisting of non-executive directors. The Audit Committee should be responsible for ensuring the efficiency of the entire internal control system and audit functions of the banks besides compliance with the inspection reports of the RBI and internal and concurrent auditors.

RBI's approach to regulation of operations of commercial banks in the recent past has some features that would enhance the need for and usefulness of good corporate governance in financial sector. The transparency aspects have been emphasized by expanding the coverage of information, timeliness of such information and analytical content.[8]

Banks, for example, have been directed to put in place appropriate systems to ensure that investment in privately placed unrated investments were made in accordance with the systems and procedures prescribed under the respective bank's investments policy approved by the Board. They were also advised to introduce suitable format of disclosure requirements in respect of private placement of issues on the lines of the Model Format recommended by the Technical Group on Non-SLR investments with the approval of the Board.

The Boards of banks have been asked to lay down policy and prudential limits on investments in bonds and debentures. It should prescribe stringent appraisal of issues especially by non-borrower customers, provide for an internal system of rating for non-borrower customers, stipulate entry level minimum ratings/quality standards, lay down proper risk management systems.

Towards bringing about a certain minimum level of uniformity with regard to the content and coverage of the Best Practices Code (BPC) in banks, the RBI prescribed broad guidelines to commercial banks as given below:[9]

- BPC should be integrated with the overall risk management strategy of the bank.
- BPC should be a comprehensive and homogeneous document.
- BPC should, at a minimum, cover all the functional areas of the bank.
- BPC should incorporate recommendations of the various committees advised to banks by the RBI.

- BPC should also take into account the instructions of the Central Vigilance Commission (CVC), Government of India, if any, issued from time to time and instructions relating to a consultative Group of Directors of Banks and Financial Institutions (Chairman: Dr. A.S. Ganguly) to review the supervisory role of Boards of banks and financial institutions, to obtain feedback on the functioning of the Boards, *vis-à-vis* compliance, transparency, disclosures, audit Committees, etc. and suggest measures for making the role of Board of Directors more effective. The Group submitted its recommendations in April 2002 after comprehensively reviewing the existing framework as well as the current practices and benchmarked its recommendations with international best practices as enunciated by Basel Committee on Banking Supervisions (1999) as well as of other Committees and advisory bodies, to the extent applicable in Indian context. The major recommendations of the group are:[10]
    (*i*) Appointment of one more whole-time director on the boards of large-sized nationalized banks. The Government, while nominating directors on the Boards of PSBs, should be guided by certain broad "fit and proper" norms for the Directors.
    (*ii*) The appointment/nomination of independent/ non-executive directors to the Board of banks (both public sector and private sector) should be from a pool of professional and talented people to be prepared and maintained by RBI.
    (*iii*) It should be desirable to take an undertaking from every director to the effect that they have gone through the guidelines defining the role and responsibilities of directors and understood what is expected of them and enter into a covenant to discharge their responsibilities to the best of their abilities, individually and collectively.
- It would be desirable to separate the office of the Chairman and Managing Director in respect of large-sized PSBs. This functional separation will bring about more focus on strategy and vision as also the need thrust in the operational functioning of the top management of the bank.
- The whole-time directors should have sufficiently long tenure to enable them to leave a mark of their leadership and business acumen on the bank's performance.
- The information furnished to the Board should be wholesome, complete and adequate to take meaningful decisions. The Board's focus should be more on strategic issues, risk profile, internal control system, overall performance, etc.
- It would be desirable if the exposures of a bank to stockbrokers and market-makers as a group, as also exposures to other sensitive sectors, *viz*; real estate, etc., are reported to the Board regularly. The disclosures of progress made towards establishing progressive risk management system, the risk management policy strategy, exposures to related entities, the asset classification of such lendings/investments etc., should be in conformity with corporate governance standards, etc.
- Finally, the banks could be asked to come up with a strategy and plan implementation of the governance standards recommended and submit progress of implementation for review after twelve months and thereafter half yearly or annually, as deemed appropriate.

In June 2002, the RBI directed banks (excluding foreign banks, RRBs and CABs) to place the Report as well as the list of recommendations before their respective Board of Directors. Based on the decision taken by the Board, these recommendations could be adopted and implemented in the concerned bank.

The RBI, in consultation with the Government of India, laid down a comprehensive policy framework on February 28, 2005. The broad principles underlying the framework ensure that: (*i*) ultimate ownership and control is well diversified; (*ii*) important shareholders are fit and proper; (*iii*) directors and CEO are fit and proper and observe sound corporate governance principles as per the RBI circular of June 25, 2004; (*iv*) private sector banks maintain minimum capital (initially ₹ 200 crore, with a commitment to increase to ₹ 300 crore within three years)/(₹ 300 crore at all times) for optimal operations and for systematic stability; and policy and processes are transparent and fair.[11]

In determining whether the applicant (including all entities connected with the applicant) is fit and proper to hold the position at the lowest threshold of 5 percent and above, the Reserve Bank takes into account all relevant factors, including among other criteria, the applicant's integrity, reputation and track record in financial matters and compliance with tax laws, which are necessary to protect the interests of the depositors and integrity of the financial system.[12]

In November 2007, the RBI issued directives to determine the 'fit and proper' criteria for elected directors on the boards of the nationalised banks. Accordingly, the banks are required to constitute a 'nomination committee' comprising a minimum of three independent directors who would determine the 'fit and proper' status of the existing elected directors/proposed candidates based on broad criteria such as educational qualification, experience, field of expertise, track record and integrity. All the elected directors have to furnish a simple declaration every year as on 31st March, that the information already provided by them has not undergone any change and where there is a change, requisite details are furnished by the directors forthwith.[13]

The RBI has proposed to restrict the fixed component of the annual salary hikes of CEOs and wholetime directors of private banks to 10-15%. This is part of the RBI's comprehensive guidelines based on the compensation policy formulated by the Financial Stability Board (FSB), a global body for standardisation of rules for the financial sector.

The RBI has also proposed that variable pay (bonuses) could be slashed in case of poor financial performance of the bank. It wants that salaries to top bankers to be adjusted for all types of risks.

The RBI has advised the boards of directors of all banks to ensure that the amount of compensation of a particular employee should be reasonable, taking into account all relevant factors.

The RBI also made it clear that guaranteed bonuses should not be part of the compensation as they were not consistent with sound risk management or the pay for perform principles.[14]

The above guidelines would only be applicable to Indian private sector banks.

Of late, the RBI raised the issue of lack of corporate governance in banks. It has already initiated a process and its supervisory department is to check how much time the bank's top management, like chairman and executive directors, spend in their office, and is to review the governance structure.[15]

I. GOVERNMENT OF INDIA AND CORPORATE GOVERNANCE IN COMMERCIAL BANKS

In the wake of a spate of financial irregularities hitting the financial sector in 2010-11, culminating in the arrest of some public sector bank officials including a board member, the Government directed the board members not to intervene in daily operations and instead concentrate more of policies and practices the bank should follow, like exposure caps; whether to continue lending to certain sectors having stress, branch opening policies and the like.[16]

J. CONCLUSIONS

Effective corporate governance is necessary for commercial banks if they have to grow and compete successfully in liberalised environment. Mere compliance with regulatory requirements is not adequate for good governance. In fact, codes of governance have to be evolved keeping in view the existing demands and effectively acted upon by every institution on its own so as to maximise the value of the stakeholders. Good governance can, in effect, prove to be powerful source of competitive advantage.

Foundations of corporate governance are independence, disclosures and transparency, accountability and self regulation. As a matter of fact, good governance goes beyond regulations and laws.

Governance for banks assumes significance for the fact that they accept and deploy large amount of uncollateralised public funds and leverage these funds through credit creation, as also administer the payment mechanism. This is why legal prescriptions relating to ownership and governance laid down in the Banking Regulation Act, 1949 have been supplemented by regulatory prescriptions issued by the RBI from time to time.

In February 2005, the RBI laid down a comprehensive policy framework for governance of commercial banks. In 2007, the RBI directed the nationalised banks to determine the criteria of 'fit and proper' for their elected directors.

Taking cognizance of a spate of financial irregularities in financial institutions in 2010-11, the Government of India directed the top management of banks in November, 2011 to concentrate more on policies and practices the bank should follow.

Lately, in February 2005, the RBI laid down a comprehensive policy framework for governance of commercial banks.

KEY TERMS

- Audit Committee
- Best Practices Code
- Board Diversity
- Fit and Proper
- Independent Directors
- Transparency and Disclosures

DISCUSSION QUESTIONS

1. What is corporate governance? What are the fundamentals of corporate governance?
2. Corporate governance can serve as a powerful source of competitive advantage in banking organisations. Comment.
3. Discuss the relevance of corporate governance for commercial banks.
4. How should a bank prescribe code for different aspects of corporate governance?
5. What should be the role and responsibilities of Board of Directors of a commercial bank for effective governance of the bank?
6. What is Audit Committee? What role should the audit committee play for effective governance of the bank?
7. Discuss recent steps taken by the RBI for strengthening governance of the commercial banks in India.

REFERENCES

1. The Report of the Financial Aspects of Corporate Governance, The Cadbury Committee Report, 1992.
2. Guidelines for Improved Corporate Governance in Canada, TSE, 1994.
3. Corporate Governance: Improving Competitiveness and Access to Capital in Global Markets, Report of the Ira Millstein Committee, 1988, UECD.
4. Report of the Kumar Manglam Birla Committee on Corporate Governance, SEBI, 2000.
5. Report on Trend and Progress of Banking in India, 2001-02, p. 28
6. Y.V. Reddy, Conference on Corporate Governance for Directors of Indian Banks, The Indian Banker, January, 2006.

7. *Ibid*.
8. Y.V. Reddy, Corporate Governance in Financial Sector, RBI Bulletin, August, 1999, p. 1001.
9. Annual Report, RBI 2003-04, p. 232.
10. RBI (2002) Report of the Consultative Graph of Directors of Banks/Financial Institutions.
11. RBI Report on Trend and Progress of Banking in India, 2004-05, p. 26.
12. RBI Report on Trend and Progress of Banking in India, 2003-04, p. 26.
13. RBI Report on Trend and Progress of Banking in India, 2007-08, pp. 57-58.
14. Times Business, Times of India, July 5, 2010.
15. Business Standard, November, 2011.
16. *Ibid*.

Chapter 9

Competitive Strategy to Meet Challenges to Commercial Banks in India

Learning Objectives:

The present chapter attempts to provide:

- an insight into the challenges facing Indian commercial banks.
- an overview of the opportunities available to Indian commercial banks.
- an idea about strengths and weaknesses of Indian commercial banks.
- an understanding of strategic mechanism to cope with the challenges.

Chapter Outline:

- Epilogue.
- Challenges before Indian commercial banks.
- Opportunities for Indian commercial banks.
- Strengths of Indian commercial banks.
- Weaknesses of Indian commercial banks.
- Strategy to cope with the challenges.
- Conclusions.

A. EPILOGUE

Cataclysmic structural reforms in Indian economic system following the Government policy of tectonic economic liberalisation and tumbling of trade barriers coupled with metamorphic liberalised policy in financial sector in sync with Narasimham Committee recommendations leading to replacement of regulated, overadministered banking industry by greater degree of operational autonomy, crumbling of entry barriers to the banking sector resulting into entry of new players (domestic and foreign), blurring of distinction between banks and non-banks, pathbreaking communicational and computational technological advancements in financial sector, deregulation of interest rate system and free pricing of products, introduction of floating exchange rate system, prescription of prudential norms of asset classification, income recognition and capital adequacy, changes in credit delivery mechanism, flexibility in credit assessment process and growing trend of disintermediation triggered competitive environment in the financial sector in the country with market forces deciding the future of banking and other financial institutions. All these led to the emergence of new banks, new financial institutions, new instruments, new windows and new opportunities, along with new challenges. While deregulation has opened up new vistas for banks to augment revenues, it has unleashed greater competition and consequently greater risks.

In fiercely competitive environments, as it exists today in the country and abroad, banks like other organizations, to survive and thrive and to achieve sustainable competitive prowess over their rivals, have not only to be comparatively better and more efficient but also have to be different for all times to come. For this, they have to be resilient and need to evolve a strategy that is forever morphing, forever conforming itself to emerging opportunities and incipient trends. This demands prognostic diagnosis of the problems and challenges along with emerging opportunities and assessment of existing strengths and weakness of the commercial banks operating in India. The following paragraphs are devoted to dilate upon these issues and formulate strategies to cope with the challenges and capitalize on the opportunities so that the banks remain robust, vibrant and resilient.

B. CHALLENGES BEFORE INDIAN COMMERCIAL BANKS

Major challenges, which Indian Commercial Banks are facing today and which are likely to be more poignant in the ensuing years in view of the irreversible process of the reform and resultant verisimilitude of many more players entering the banking sector, are, as outlined below.

◈ Problem of Pressure on Profitability

The greatest challenge, which PSBs are facing in recent years, arises out of pressure on their profitability. With continuous expansion in number of branches and manpower, thrust on social and rural banking, directed priority sector lending, maintenance of higher reserve ratios, waiver of loans under ARDR-type concessions, repayment defaults by large industrial corporates and other borrowers, etc. had their telling impact on the profitability of the banks.

Further, with the introduction of prudential norms, to be effective from March end 1993 a majority of the commercial banks' balance sheets had shown huge losses. In order to improve financial health of these banks the Government provided a dose of hybrid capital and in return these banks were made to sign a memorandum of understanding with the RBI. The crux of the MOU was on toning up productivity, efficiency, cost reduction, higher recovery. Accordingly, the focus of operations of banks shifted from deposit mobilisation to services marketing, *i.e.,* deposits have to be procured, but keeping profits in mind. On the lending front, credit expansion entered new areas where banks hesitated to venture earlier with total thrust on maintenance of quality of lending. Further, accent of banks' operations shifted to non-fund based business with an eye on capital adequacy achievement and other ancillary business which may cross subsidise the cost of certain unremunerative services, the banks have to offer. Further, rising interest rate on term deposits to mobilise public savings has enhanced cost of financing, leading to increased pressure on the banks' profitability.

◈ Problem of Low Productivity

Another ferocious challenge, which Indian commercial banks are confronting, is low productivity. The low productivity has been due to huge surplus manpower, absence of good work culture, antiquated labour laws, inflexible and inefficient labour force, in PSBs, and absence of employees' commitment to the organisation. The individual excellence of staff members is mostly marred by the group dynamics of strong but militant unions on the one hand, and the callous, ineffective, short-sighted management with their opaque impersonal personnel policies, on the other.

The management having feudal mindsets have continued to prefer not to see the problem in its proper perspective due to the fear of strong unions. They have camouflaged the issue by diverting their attention to such apparent face saving devices like redeployment, repositioning, retraining, etc. The stark reality is that the excess baggage of general cadre low productive staff members has to be removed. There are various ways of minimising the size of the staff, such as voluntary retirement scheme or golden shakehand. The problem before the management at present is how to make fuller use of talents available in the bank and improve its productivity.

◈ Problem of Non-Performing Assets (NPA)

A serious threat to the survival and success of Indian banking system is uncomfortably high level of NPAs. Although NPAs of commercial banks in India declined in recent years until 2009-10 when it dropped for 2.3 per cent. However, it soared to 3.2 per cent by 2012-13, crossing the ₹ 2 trillion (₹ 2,00,000 crore) mark. The RBI fears a further deterioration. In its fifth financial stability report, leased on June 28, the RBI says bad loans could rise to 4.6 per cent in a severe risk scenario. According to a report released by Standard and Poor (S&P) on November 10, 2012 NPAs for the banking industry to excess ₹ 5.8 lakh crore by March 31, 2013, accounting for about 10 per cent of bank loans, a huge jump from 5 per cent in March 2011.

Spiralling NPAs are hurting bank's profitability and even the basic inability of the banking system and loan loss provisioning. Due to slow economic growth, banks are yet to see recovery on their assets quality. According to bankers, the NPA cycle will peak due to factors such as drop in the productivity of Indian companies, larger proportion of long-term loans, exposure to sectors which are cyclical in nature and aggressive lending to the agriculture sector.

◈ Problem of Resource crunch

Commercial banks in India, as noted above, are facing stiff competition from newly emerging and considerably alacre competitors having telling effect upon their resource mobilization efforts. Problem of resource crunch is likely to be deepened in near future. There are indications that the household savings comprising financial savings and physical assets are moving away from bank deposits to more sophisticated form of financial assets such as mutual funds, stock and derivatives or life insurance and pension contributions. There is also increased appetite for physical savings mainly in the form of housing and gold.

◈ Problem of Asset-liability mismatch

With more and more bank credit going for infrastructure lending and commercial real estate financing while the liability structure of the banks is getting shorter and shorter, banks are facing serious problem of asset-liability mismatch. The problem is compounded by the fact that both on the assets and liabilities sides there are rigidities in the absence of tradeable asset and liability instruments.

◈ Problem from Customers

In view of unleashing of competitive forces and fast changing life styles and values of customers who are now better informed and more sophisticated and discerning and who have a wide choice to choose from various banking and non-banking intermediaries have become more demanding and their expectations in terms of products, delivery and price are increasing, the PSBs lacking in customers' orientation are finding it difficult to even retain their highly valued customers what to talk of attracting the new clients particularly when the foreign banks as also the new breed of private sector banks have embarked upon aggressive marketing programme aiming at niche markets. In their efforts to woo the customers, these banks by dint of information technology are offering speedier service and new and complex products. The telebanking, anywhere banking, virtual or Internet banking, ATM, Credit Cards and newly introduced interest rate swap, forward rate agreements, etc. are some of the products innovated by the new players. A fierce war is on among the aggressive new private and foreign banks in metropolis to grab 24-square feet pieces of land to set up ATMs. The pace of installation is so high that one day the ATMs will outnumber the brick and mortar branches in these cities. Although the PSBs are trying to computerise their operations, the pace of progress in this direction has been decidedly slow. Further, experience has shown that consumers' interests are at times not accorded full protection and their grievances are not properly attended to. Feed back received reveals recent trends of levying unreasonably high service/user charges and enhancement of user charges without proper and prior intimation.[1] The combined impact of customers' disenchament is already reflected in decline in the market share of PSBs both in deposits and lendings. This is causing serious concern to the management.

The problem for Indian banks is that their central product i.e., money, is not for most people the realization of their dreams but simply a conduit to that dream house, car, holiday etc. Research suggests that organizations, that excel at creating and maintaining loyal customers can command prices that are 4-7% higher than weaker competitions and as a result also generate significantly higher profits.[2] This will also help them in retaining customers.

◈ Competition from New Players

The commercial banks in India, which enjoyed monopoly position until recently, are facing perilous challenges particularly on quality, cost and flexibility fronts from the newly emerging players who by dint of their invigorating ambience and work culture supported by pragmatic leadership, committed, courteous, affable and trained staff and modern ultra gadgets are offering excellent customer services and making inroads in the business centres.

PSBs operating hitherto in highly protected and regimented system heavily tilted towards deposit mobilisation and social banking responsibilities with little scope or incentive for the bankers to be conscious of their profitability and productivity levels and with high preemption of loanable funds and directed credit at concesssional rate, massive branch expansion on non-economic considerations, high non-performing assets high operating costs, lower productivity and profitability and with unhealthy organizational culture and less motivated employees and mundane approach of managing operations are finding it extremely difficult to thwart the systematic and planned efforts of the new players from taking away their business.

The new banks have set the tone and to some extent also the standard for technological improvements and product innovations which the vastly dominating PSBs will have to bring in their own operations if they have to maintain their present position of dominance.

By resorting to latest methods in human resource management as well as information technology, the new entrants in the field have suddenly sensitised even the ordinary user of the banking services in India to the type and quality of services he can expect from his bank. This is the challenge before the older bigger nationalised banks, who till today are saddled with historical baggage of a work ethic which has given greater weightage to creating employment opportunities over unit efficacy and witty hilly supported status-quo over the need for changes.

The market has become highly competitive and largely customer centric. This calls for an ability to reach the client at his door step and meet his requirements of products and services in a customised manner. The race for customers could at times lead to adverse selections. This situation demands aggression laced with caution which, in turn, calls for highly efficient management by the banks of both liabilities and assets.

These banks have to work in a market which will not know any geographical barriers and therefore will have to develop abilities of product innovation and delivery comparable to the best in the world.

◈ Challenge due to Globalization

Globalisation and integration of Indian financial market with the global financial markets and the consequent entry of foreign players in domestic market has infused, in its wake, brutal competitive pressures on the Indian commercial banks. Foreign players endowed with robust capital adequacy, high quality assets, world-wide connectivity, benefits of economies of scale and stupendous risk management skills are posing serious threats to the existing business of the Indian banks. Cross-border flows and entry of new products, particularly derivative instruments, have impacted significantly on the domestic banking sector, forcing banks in India to adjust the product mix, as also to effect rapid changes in their processes and operations in order to remain competitive in the globalized environment. Indian banks are therefore, in greater pressure to gear themselves to offer not only wide menu of services but also provide these in an increasingly efficient manner in terms of cost, time and convenience.

Further more, globalisation of financial markets signifies that a problem in one country can sometimes adversely impact one or more countries instantaneously, even if they are fundamentally strong. There is also a growing realization that the ability of countries to conduct business across national borders and the ability to cope with the possible downside risks would depend, *inter alia*, on the soundness of the financial system. This demands adoption of a strong and transparent, prudential, regulatory, supervisory, technological and institutional framework in the financial sector on par with international practices. All this necessitates a transformation: a transformation in the mindset, a transformation in the business processes and finally a transformation in knowledge management. This process is not a one shot affair; it needs to be appropriately phased in the least disruptive manner.

◈ Competition from Disintermediation

Indian commercial banks are facing competitive onslaught not only from within the system but also from other quarters. The threat of financial disintermediation has already started looming large. In recent years, Indian corporates are reported to have mobilised funds of ₹ 24,000 crore through commercial paper.

This threat is going to be more deeper in future in view of increased role of market forces. With increasing integration of markets and opening of more avenues to meet financial needs of corporates, capital will flow more freely across Indian borders, good creditworthy borrowers would be able to source cheap finance abroad as well as in domestic capital markets. As the ease of access, transaction costs and other mechanisms in these diverse markets will never converge, corporates will find one market better than the other. Commercial banks will be approached by these corporates only for services. This may, therefore, result in contraction of lending business of the banks who would be called upon to cater to the growing demands for financial services.

The situation is going to be further compounded by the fact that almost every major corporate group has its own non-banking finance company.

With growing disintermediation and intense competition among commercial banks for higher quality business, pressure on spreads is increasing. While in the short run this could cause concern to some, in the long run one has to concede that it is in the best interest of the system. It will force the participants to increase their efficiency, reduce the cost of service, delivery and garner higher volumes of business for maintaining their competitiveness.

The increasing pressure on spreads has already forced the banking system in the country to go in for product innovation and their orientation today is far more towards customers and markets than in the past. Even in non-fund based business, pricing will be under pressure because of customer resistance and his increasing ability to drive a good bargain for himself. It is, therefore, not going to be all that easy to increase fee-based earnings.

◈ Problem of Managing Duality of Ownership

Indian banking is in a peculiar problem of managing conflicting interests of the Government of India and the RBI on the one hand and the private shareholders, on the other. Growing demands of finicky customers are compelling banks to offer a broader range of products through diverse distribution channels. The recent measures taken by the Government and the RBI for opening up India's banking sector to international investors will further increase the pressure of competition. At the same time, there is renewed emphasis by the Government on the social sector together with thrust on rural and agricultural lending. Caught between the competitive pressure, both domestic and external, and the politics of development, banks will have to be on their toes, become even more efficient in managing funds and in meeting the needs and demands of customers.[3]

◈ Problem of Managing Customers of Diverse Strata

Another very important challenge, which PSBs are facing, is managing two ends of spectrum of banking services. PSBs, unlike their counterparts in the private sector as also the foreign banks, have two faces: a commercial side and non-commercial side, each having various strata. In a country like India with wide disparities in needs, standards and ways of living of the people in various regions, the bankers are expected to manage these different strata in its total expanse equally well without ignoring any of them or even performing one at the expense of the other.

In a country as vast as India and wide disparities in standards and ways of living in its rural, semi-urban and metropolitan areas, banking services have been designed and delivered in keeping with the different levels of economic property enjoyed by the populace in each of these areas and their relative needs. Banking needs of a vast majority of the countrymen living in rural and semi-urban regions are extremely simple and for them benefits of modern day technology-driven banking will be a far cry for some time to come. In these areas it is availability of services and its cost and simplicity and not the high quality that matter most.

In view of the fact that rural and semi-urban areas accounted for over 31 per cent of the deposits and about 28 per cent of the aggregate loans, Indian bankers cannot afford to ignore this sector of the economy. The challenge before the system, therefore, lies in managing two ends of the spectrums of banking services, with equal facility and in apportioning its resources equitably over the entire spectrum. The new private sector banks and so also the foreign banks, who operate at only one end of the spectrum, *i.e.*, the most lucrative one where corporates and high value individuals inhabit, are not likely to pick up this challenge.

◈ Problem due to Technological Factor

The decade of 90s has witnessed a sea change in the way banking is done in India. Technology has made tremendous impact in banking. Anywhere and any time banking has become a reality. This has thrown new challenges in the banking sector and new issues have started cropping up which is going to face certain problems in the near future. Indian public sector banks, despite their impressive branch networks, have not been able to meet their customers' expectations due to inefficiencies arising out of inadequate investment in technology. This has already resulted in erosion of their market share.

Foreign banks and the new private sector banks have embraced technology right from the inception of their operations and therefore, they have adapted themselves to the changes in the technology easily. However, PSBs and old private sectors could not keep pace with technological development.

The challenge in this regard will, therefore, be for banks to ensure that they derive maximize advantage out of their investments in technology and to avoid wasteful expenditure arising out of uncoordinated and piecemeal adoption of technology, adoption of inappropriate/ inconsistent technology and adoption of obsolete technology.

◈ Problem of Managing Risk

With the increasing degree of deregulation and exposure of banks to various types of risks, efficient risk management systems have become inevitable. In the initial stages of development of the risk management system, banks were managing each risk in isolation. The current business environment demands a more integrated approach to risk management. It is no longer sufficient to manage each risk independently or in functional silos. Enterprises world over are, therefore, now putting in place an integrated frame work for risk management which is proactive, systematic and spans across the entire organization. Banks in India are also moving from the individual silo system to an enterprise wide risk management system. This is placing greater demands on the risk management skills in banks and has brought to the forefront the need for capacity building.

◈ Challenge of Talent

In a highly competitive and globalised environment where knowledge is the sole differentiating factor that separates good institution from an average one, talent has become the world's most sought after by community because it contributes significantly to product innovation and development and deep understanding of market and customer needs, originality of service and creation of global infrastructure.

One of the major factors for low competitiveness of PSBs in India is inflexible and incapable labour force.[4] Organisations including banks in competitive landscape need high degree of talent because it contributes significantly to product innovation and development, deep understanding of market and customer needs, originality of service and creation of global infrastructure. Indian banking industry like other industries is facing problem of talent crunch. CEOs are vying with each other in attracting talents. Competition for talented people is becoming more fiercer than competition for customers.

According to McKinsey report, the quest for workers is creating a talent crunch that some believe might dull India's competitive edge in outsourcing. Currently, only around 25% of technical graduates and 10-15% of general graduates are suitable for employments. This is an irony that while there are 40 million unemployed, corporate India is busy trying to cope with an unprecedented demand for committed people with right technical and leadership skills. This problem is going to assume alarming propositions in near future. Projections show that by 2,010, the IT/ITES sector will need a work force of 2.3 million to maintain its current market share. However, there will be a potential shortfall of nearly 0.5 million qualified employees.[5]

The problem will not only be in the availability of IT or technical talent but also in the availability of good managers who understand the needs of the global economy and execute accordingly. Further, quality of management talent will also be an issue. Indian banks will need managers with skill sets considerably different from those of the past. They will need a new kind of managers who can think strategically and operate effectively in a global market place in order to compete with global rivals.

Banks in India are going through an unusual manpower crunch. In the next ten years, they will have to hire around one million people to keep their branches running and account for retirement and natural attrition. Finding the right candidate for a leadership position will be even tougher.

According to the Khandelwal Committee, which was set up to address the human resource challenges of the PSBs, the leadership gaps in the PSBs are palpable. In the next five years, 80 per cent of general managers, 65 per cent of deputy general managers, 58 per cent of assistant general managers and 44 per cent of chief managers would be retiring.

So many people leaving at the same time has prompted the RBI to call the 10 years from 2010 to 2020 as the 'decade of retirement.'[6]

◈ Challenge of Qualitative Change in Banking Paradigm

Building adequate capability — individual and institutional-to put in place appropriate strategies and plans for raising fresh capital or to augment capital through internal resources, to redefine their business strategies with a view to altering their profile of risk exposure and to enhance their systems and procedures to international standards and also simultaneously fortify their financial position is the greatest challenge plaguing Indian banks during the post reform period. This is for the fact that any improvement in skills and operational systems calls for change in the mind sets and attitudes of the employees and inculcate work culture. Bank employees in India, as noted earlier, are highly cynical and less motivated with decreasing loyalty towards their work life. They are not very much concerned with their productivity and lack cost consciousness. Strong and militant trade unions resisting any organisational change and archaic approach of managing have also been the barriers to bank development. Above all, ethnocentric mindsets and action flippant bank managers have also been responsible for the present plight of the PSBs. In fact, greatest threat to banking system is not from new players but from the Indian banks' habit of endowing their senior managers with tremendous authority and holding them responsible for little. Lack of individual accountability extends to the organisation with the banks not following any scientific management system. The very ability of management system to change could be source of competitive advantage to Indian bankers. This has also become imperative in view of the changing customers' expectations and behaviour.

C. OPPORTUNITIES FOR INDIAN COMMERCIAL BANKS

Government policy of globalization and liberalization and the consequent integration of domestic markets with international financial markets have offered incredible opportunities to Indian commercial banks to expand and penetrate in domestic markets, diversify and internationalize their operations with greater freedom and to access international financial markets for procuring funds cheaply and deploy funds prudently so as to enhance their financial performance and improve their operational earnings. The banks are now enjoying greater autonomy in revisiting their existing credit and investment portfolio, reviewing extant branch network and greater discretion to reduce amplitude of cross subsidization to priority sector. Banks have now been given managerial autonomy to acquire any company, non-bank finance company, housing finance companies or other business to increase their balance sheet size so as to grow into areas/sectors that they have potential. They can also exit non-profitable areas. Banks have also got freedom to pursue new lines of business as part of overall business strategy.[7] Further, they also enjoy freedom in pricing and structuring their products. They have the opportunity to access foreign markets.

Indian Commercial Banks have tremendous opportunities to grow in almost all the sectors of the economy because of robust economic health of the country and ubiquitous development in different sectors, especially in manufacturing, financial services, information technology, construction, transportation and small and medium enterprises (SMEs). Apart from run away consumerism fuelling demand for retail loans, there is now an equally healthy appetite from a resurgent industry, cutting across both large and SMEs. The growth of credit to industry accelerated at 35.5% in 2005, compared to 8.1% in 2004. This trend looks all set to continue as Corporate India is on an expansion spree. Banks have also to cater to the burgeoning needs of processing sector which at present processes only 2 per cent of fruits and vegetables compared to 20 per cent in Malaysia, 60-70 per cent in the UK and USA and 30 per cent in Thailand. India's share in globalized food process market is absymally less than 1 per cent. There is wastage of $ 350 billion worth of fruits and farm products, necessitating greater focus on processing industry. This demands tremendous support from the banking sector.

The nearly 12 million small scale industrial units across India which account for about 49% of India's exports, over 40% of manufactured output and employ about 30 million people, making a substantial contribution to the country's GAP, have long been ignored by banks in India because it was felt that SMEs lacked a viable business model. But during the last four to five years, SMEs have steadily metamorphosed themselves into a performing sector across all industries, be it agri-products, food processing, industrial goods or IT services or any other areas of services. The number of success stories in this sector has gone up sharply. They are thus emerging as an engine of growth in the country. As a result, banks are sensing a good business opportunity in this sector as has been happening across Asia and elsewhere in the world.[8] There is, therefore, likelihood of banks' lending business to the SMEs soaring by 50 per cent in next few years.

The boom in India's consumer spending offers burgeoning opportunities to banks. The boom in consumer spending is going to be driven not just by youngsters entering the workforce but also by 'empty-nesters- parents' who are enjoying renewed spending power after their children have finished their education, married and left the family home and also by the rising levels of women entering the workforce.

Despite massive branch expansion during post nationalization period, banks have yet not fully exploited their existing potentials in rural hinterlands of the country with the result that even today rural folk remain more dependent on non-institutional agencies like local money lender, friends and relatives not only when it comes to taking loans, but also when it comes to repayment of debt and pay as high as 22% interest to these non-institutional agencies. High priority accorded by the Government to rural development and massive allocation of funds for the purpose and growing interest shown by Corporate India and MNCs towards rural areas offer big green pastures for Indian Banks.

With a population of 600 million to consume there exists huge untapped growth opportunity. Banks have to harness rural India's potential as a growth engine by micro-finance initiatives and efficient credit delivery through a wide range of channels. Over 50 million households in rural areas have moved from low income to high income giving rise to equally number of potentially bankable households. In infrastructure sector, there exists tremendous opportunity for banks to meet the existing vast gap between the demand of funds and supply therefor.

D. STRENGTHS OF INDIAN COMMERCIAL BANKS

One of the greatest strengths of Commercial Banks in India is their titanic branch network (over 71,000 branches) giving an easy access to almost entire spectrum of customers. These branches are manned by staff having intimate knowledge of local environment.

Another great strength of Indian commercial banks is diversification in their operations. In fact, banks have moved from the traditional plain vanilla stuff of 10-15 years ago to offer an entire gamut of services including insurance, investment banking, asset management and private equity, foreign exchange, payment of utility bills of customers, offering mobile and internet banking services, etc. Banks, especially new private sector banks, are on a roll when it comes to pleasing their clients.

Banks are also endowed with large manpower resources having relevant banking skills to manage the operations.

Post reform period has witnessed enormous increase in technological strengths of Indian commercial banks, changing the way banking is done. ATMs, credit cards, telebanking fully computerized branches, country wide networks and internet banking, coupled with many innovative banking products have completely changed the face of traditional banking. Anywhere and anytime banking has become a reality. This has rendered banking services faster, error free and competitive. Most of the banks have already started providing fancy products, driven by technology.

Finally, commercial banks in India have gained in financial strengths in recent few years in terms of productivity and profitability, improved financial soundness so much so that they are outshining their counterparts of advanced nations. However, they have still to traverse a long path to sustain the success.

E. WEAKNESSES OF INDIAN COMMERCIAL BANKS

Indian Commercial banks, particularly PSBs have been ailing from the following weaknesses, which have become bottlenecks in achieving competitive edge over their rivals.

- Low operating size
- High operating costs
- Inadequate deposit mobilization efforts
- Financial exclusion
- Complex and non-responsive organizational structure
- Credit to non-productive sectors like commercial estate
- Poor customers' service
- Under utilized capacity particularly in rural areas
- Unsatisfactory work culture
- Feudalistic attitude of the staff
- Ethnocentric and action flippant management
- Absence of organizational focus on employees leading to their demotivation
- Inadequate access to global financial markets

Inadequate risk management skills particularly to cope with market risks as per Basel II norms.

F. STRATEGY TO COPE WITH THE CHALLENGES

- **Envisioning:** Coping with the challenges demands a paradigm shift towards the approach of managing business as also change in the role of bank managers and their mindsets. Thus, it has become imperative for bankers to switch over to strategic management system which involves visualization of corporate vision and mission of the organization, articulation of corporate and business level objectives and determination of suitable course of action against the background of environmental opportunities and threats and organisational strengths and weaknesses. The primacy of the customer and his needs and a realization that a bank exists only because of its customers have to permeate the entire organisation. Banks should move from product-centric mindset to customer-centric philosophy.

In the present market driven environment when many players are vying with each other to grab market share, a banker has to first of all decide how he intends to position its organisation and what it wants to do to excel locally and compete globally. The corporate bank leader has to decide what a future market will look like and then stretch the organisation skills in such a way as to take advantage of the market. Thus, he has to conceive vision of the bank so as to enable the people in and outside the organisation to know the direction in which it will be moving. The vision so visualised needs to be shared with employees, customers, collaborators, and other enlightened people of the society to solicit their opinions. In sum, path of the bank should be chosen by consensus. It must, however, be noted that primacy of the customer has to be focused while conceptualising vision so that its entire efforts are directed towards customers' satisfaction in terms of cost and quality of services. For instance, a public sector bank can define its vision as 'dedicated to provide hassle-free services to people they want any time, any where.' This simple statement of overall purpose and mission will capture attention of the people in and outside the organisation and provide opportunity to them for interpreting, refining and making it operational.

In the changed scenario when a bank is exclusively concerned with improving its competitiveness in domestic as well as global markets on sustainable basis, primary focus of the organisation must be on customers' delight and enchantment. The overall objective of a bank will, therefore, have to achieve excellence in operations rather than efficiency and effectiveness. Excellence orientation emphasises on performing outstanding and superior things with minimum resources in all the critical areas.

Keeping in view the aspirations of the customers — both external and internal and capabilities of the organisation, long-term objectives should be set. Some of the major parameters for determining objectives could be return on assets, return on equity, capital adequacy, expense-income ratio, ratio of NPA to total loans or total assets, productivity per employee, customer satisfaction index, customer prioritization, customer profitability and development of staff skills, staff involvement, etc. Within the framework of objectives, short-term quantifiable targets should be fixed. These objectives and goals should be set in consultation with those concerned with their accomplishments.

◈ Enabling

Once the overall objectives are set, corporate bank management has to evolve strategy for the organisation as a whole. Focus of the strategy has to be on competition. Competitive advantage is at the heart of the bank's performance in competitive markets. In fact, competition determines the suitability of activities of an enterprise which can contribute to its success. Competitive strategy is the search for a favourable competitive position in an industry, the fundamental arena in which competition occurs. It concerns how to create competitive advantage in each of the business in which a company competes. Competitive strategy involves taking offensive or defensive actions to create a defendable position in an industry to cope successfully with the forces of competition and thereby yield a superior return on investment.

Choice of competitive strategy of a bank is the function of attractiveness of banking business and its competitive position. Determining attractiveness of a business calls for understanding of forces of competition, such as entry of new competitors, the threat of substitutes and bargaining power of customers and rivalry among current competitors. A bank in order to assess its competitive position should scan its strengths and weaknesses in relation to its competitors, and the business.

Keeping in view the above factors, PSBs should identify the areas where the organisation should confront competition and where to avoid it. In the changed environment, it would be in fitness of things for PSBs to concentrate on those businesses where they have core competencies and tremendous opportunities so as to ensure that existing customers are not lost and new customers are attracted. Thus, for instance; critical activities of these banks could centre around acceptance of deposits, provision of credit, security investment, foreign business, merchant banking, leasing, corporate consultancy services, etc. Based on its resources, skills and expertise, every bank has to identify its core businesses which must receive overriding focus in deployment of funds.

To become highly competitive, independent business units for each of the core activities empowered to develop its strategy for directing and running the particular business should be set up. Business unit level strategy should specify how the organisation intends to compete in that specific business and what would be its contribution to the organisation. Thus, a bank may have separate business units to manage different customer groups. A broad configuration of customer groups could be large corporates, mid-sized corporates, trading community, small scale industry, agriculture, government and institutions and retail banking, technology and support services, etc. Priority sector can be looked at as a separate customer group.

Competitive strategy of each of these units as a device of carving a niche for itself in the business and coping successfully with the forces of competition, and based on the concept of fit, must emerge out of perspicacious insight into the forces of competition that determine, attractiveness of an activity and dispassionate winnowing of the units' strength's and weaknesses in relation to its competitors. The concept of fit will have to be supplemented by the 'concept of leverage' which implies that an organisation with limited resources should focus on doing more with less, go for undefended niches rather than confront its competitors, investing on core competencies which the management feels, can help to achieve competitive edge on sustainable basis. In its pursuit to achieve excellence in its operations, the management will have to assume the new responsibilities of leveraging the resources of the bank by converging, accumulating, complementing, conserving and recovering.

Since no bank is in a position to compete in all the operations in the entire market, it would be in the fitness of things for it to adopt segmented approach instead of mass marketing approach and concentrate on greater specialization in different niches of the market so that the bank can deliver greater value to its customers' demographics. Accordingly, every bank should identify potential market segments keeping in view the opportunities and extent of competition and select one or more of them on the basis of its core capabilities and develop products which would be superior to its competitors in terms of price, delivery of services and other attractive features.

Thus, PSBs should avoid continuing and/or entering in those areas where their competitors are superior to them in their core competencies. Foreign banks because of limited domestic resources constraint and superior skills in managing foreign business, generally avoid embracing retail banking and instead concentrate on foreign currency loan business of top corporates either through their own offices abroad or their investment banking arms. Similarly, foreign banks as also new private banks could concentrate more on metropolitan and urban areas and look for high networth individuals. On the contrary, bulk of the business and income will continue to come from domestic operations, that too from agriculture, allied services, trade and transport and PSBs having strengths in terms of deep knowledge of the local market, wide branch network and a deep rooted relationship should concentrate on business of retail banking, trade finance and housing and consumer finance in semi-urban and rural areas with focus on customers' delight so as to retain the existing customers and attract the new ones.

Banks need to adopt strategy of inclusiveness to tap vast savings potentials in rural hinterlands. The focus of this strategy has to be on fuller utilization of existing capacity and developing innovative ways to cater to the typical needs of rural sector. There is a need for well thought out strategy for marketing services in the interiors of the country including kind of delivery channels required for meeting the banking and remittance needs of the rural population.

Fuller utilization of existing capacity can itself give huge dividends. Given the existing number of nearly 48000 rural and semi-urban branches, an increase of loans by ₹ 1 crore per branch could simply add profits of about ₹ 480 crore to the banking system.

Currently, each rural branch services only about 1000 loan account. If we assume that a bank branch can serve atleast 300 households, it would imply at the minimum tripling of the business at rural branches. This might require redeployment and some increase in staff, especially field staff and would be more than worth the effort considering the increase in business and profitability that it would result in.

A potential that remains untapped, thus far, is infrastructure sector. Infrastructural requirements in India during the next five years have been estimated by the approach paper for the eleventh 5-year plan at ₹ 14.5 lakh crores (45,320 billion) against the generation of ₹ 10,000 to ₹ 15,000/- crores a year by financial institutions, leaving a whopping gap to be met by foreign resources. In view of economic sanctions and rating downgrade and global financial crisis, availability of low cost foreign currency funds for infrastructural projects looks like a pipe dream. The management has to be proactive and recognize the burgeoning potentiality of this sector in years to come partly because of growth in supply and maintenance chain for a population that is growing in purchasing power and partly due to the growth in labour industries operating through technical and professional skills like computers and software, information technology, travel and tourism, etc. Software industry is one burning example where the irony is that despite their laudable performance, bankers have been loath to it.

Based on market intelligence of different regions and customers' profile, existing branches can be regrouped into specialised branches with distinct systems and procedures to support farmers, rural artisans, SSI, other target groups particularly with respect to opening of new accounts, issue of various deposit instruments, handling of remittances and collections, transacting loan recoveries, etc. These branches will have to reinvent products with attributes suited to the local clients. Thus, a branch located in a predominantly trading centre should concentrate on efficient collection services of bills and related trade credit products. Likewise, a branch situated in residential area has to offer need based consumer banking services. So as to focus sharply on identification, positioning and competitive advantage of personal banking products among the target group, a bank can think of branding its products such as unfixed deposit, equity advance, any time money, smart money, etc.

SBI is firming up plans to expand its rural business and set up a separate entity for the same within the next three years. The plan is to have a vertical split if the Bank's structural organisation into rural and metro-urban. The rural network would also offer products such as personal and home loans while the metro-urban branches would offer agri-products along with other products. With big corporates such as Reliance, Bharati, ITC and others getting into agri and allied businesses these in scope for such products even in urban areas.[9]

Last decade witnessed PSBs diversifying in fee-based activities like merchant banking, leasing, corporate counselling etc. in their bid to arrest deteriorating profitability performance. However, most of them have not been able to make perceptible dent primarily because of dearth of requisite skills and expertise. At a time when merchant banking business has become competitive with domestic and foreign entities coming in, PSBs have to reassess their capabilities and decide a specific activity in which it can outplace its rivals. Where a critical mass cannot be ensured and corporate customers who otherwise bank with the organisation need to be given this facility, collaboration arrangements may be thought of.

The specialised bank branches especially those in trading centres should be declared as profit centres. With ushering in of freedom of fixing interest rates and introduction of concept of prime lending rate and now base rate resulting in discretions for differential product and pricing between branches and customers based on volume and value, the bank management should evolve a dual and flexible pricing policy. While building and nurturing relationships with good customers will benefit the bank in the long run, rigorous costing will have to be done for appropriately pricing individual transactions for disloyal customers. In this process, unremunerative services may even have to be discouraged if these cannot be priced appropriately.

Two most crucial factors on which hinges competitiveness of a bank are cost and quality of services. As the scope for manoeuverability on the revenue side is limited, vigorous effort is needed on cost control. This will require economising on non-interest costs comprising of transaction costs and establishment expenses on an ongoing basis because interest costs of deposits are more or less determined by overall macro-economic conditions and customer-preferences. Imbibing culture of cost consciousness in the organisation is inevitable.

To compete with global banks in terms of cost, quality and speed of services, Indian banks will have to gain in size and operate efficiency. At present, India has no big banks with assets of over ₹ 1,00,000 crore other than SBI and ICICI Bank. Even small economies in Asia like Thailand and Taiwan have more big banks than India. As such bank's management should explore the possibility for forging mergers and alliances with other domestic banks.[10] This will enable the merging banks to achieve excellence in their operations and become global players by fuller utilization of skills and resources, melding complementary skills, cost savings through rationalization of operations, deep market penetration, diversification of risk, and by way of strengthening their financial, technological, operational and organizational efficiencies.

So as to enchant customers through innovative products and newer forms of services, extensive use of technology is essential. Although PSBs have, of late, started using computers and information technology, extent of its application is low. Vigorous drive is required to ensure telebanking facilities, electronic fund transfer and networking of ATM facilities. Simultaneously, efforts should be made to go into networking of branches, treasury management and a live wire MIS system including data base development and analysis of customer profile and its changes.

According to brand research, the main influencer for customers to choose a brand is the reputation of an organization.[11] Accordingly, companies in the financial services sector will have to develop a high level of brand affinity with the customer and help him or her connect to the brand at a personnel level. Customers always prefer to deal with a brand that instills trust, is ethical and honest and above all stands for superior quality at a fair price which is readily discernible. They like brand which delivers what they need in a timely and unbureaucratic fashion. They also tend to connect to a brand emotionally – their dreams, desires and aspirations are meant to be addressed by the brand they choose.

In its endeavour to improve productivity and profitability greater focus is required on asset-liability management. With progressive reduction in statutory pre-emptions of bank funds, there is tremendous scope for effective management of asset portfolio. Proper credit assessment and risk management mechanisms will have to be evolved so that genuine needs of creditworthy customers are met. This will go a longway in minimizing NPAs. The internal arrangements will have to be supported externally by a proper legal framework to facilitate prompt action against a defaulting borrower. The financial system itself needs to be so geared that a defaulter at one place is recognised as a defaulter by the system.

While making above strategic exercises, top management must follow collaborative approach and share the strategic thoughts with their young and enlightened executives. At present, chief executives consider themselves as the chief strategists with full control of setting corporate objectives and determining priorities. This mindset needs to be changed. Front line managers, who are very close to the customers and competitors, know better than their senior about what is going on and it is they who can define the appropriate product market matrices. The managers at the middle and lowest range must be encouraged to provide foresight and a compelling view of the future.

Another crucial issue concerning management of assets is treasury management. Unfortunately, this is a weak link in the chain of most banking operations. With credit off-take coming down significantly and increasing liquidity of banks, and two successful years of drop in YTM, management should plan for active trading for switching portfolio between gilts, shares and other instruments. Further, integrating domestic and foreign treasury operations with the best of the facilities should be set up without any further delay. It is an area which no bank aspiring for a prominent position can ignore. Adequate control mechanism and reporting coupled with bolt trading limits will have to be introduced to develop the skills of trading.

◈ Enacting

It is important to emphasize that while deciding about strategic course of action to achieve organisational objectives, thoughtful consideration has to be given to feasibility of its implementation. It is here the corporate bank managers have to play a crucial role. The chief executive must have a game plan that takes care of the overall picture, with each piece of the picture well defined, well thought and well-put. He has to help develop operational plans tethered to the strategy. This can be done by a coalition team consisting of senior executives at the corporate level and unit heads.

So as to remain different and competitive for all the time to come, banks should develop their social architecture that generates intellectual capital as the quintessential driver of change. Developing the individual human capacity is an integral element of building capacity and in fact, capacity building initiatives are now increasingly becoming an index of institutional quality.

Taking the bank to the heights of excellence will require a blend of new technologies, better processes of credit and risk appraised treasury management, product diversification responsive structure, internal control and outstanding human resources.

The most crucial factor affecting strategy implementation and determining future of a bank is to attract, retain and motivate talents. This enjoins upon the central and human resource managers, the responsibility of tailoring the manpower planning to corporate plans and drawing a long-term hiring programme so as to track down people endowed with knowledge, skills and attitudes best suited to achieve the bank's objectives. Retaining talents requires team-based reward system which pegs reward of entire manpower of the entire business unit to the achievement of its goals.

A comprehensive, systematic and continuing training system linked to the bank strategy needs to be installed. Prominent on the agenda of the training programmes will have to be developed on overall national and global perspective as well as understanding of strategy making and relationships between cross functional areas and cross sections of the society and finally as developing competencies for personal growth. This will go a long way in retention of employees and improving their marketability which may, in fact, serve as powerful instrument of motivation.

It is also imperative to motivate and prod the people to contribute their best to the organisation. This demands paradigm change in perceptions and mindsets of the managers and change in style of their leading the people. They must treat their employees not as a cost to be controlled but an asset to be developed. They must support and coach their people to meet the challenges of customers' demand and support them to exercise their delegated authority fully. They have to act as catalytic agent and convert the contractual employees of an economic entity into committed members of a purposeful organisation.

Corporate bank managers will have to build an organisational climate where there is least resistance to any change in the organisation. They have to foster trust, generate a sense of pride and ownership in the organisation and provide life satisfaction to them and sustain it through culture, useful traditions, practices and systems. Concept of empowerment will have to be adopted in proper perspective so as to facilitate decision making to move closer to the customers. Barring corporate lending and major decisions, the front-line managers should be empowered to decide about other retail services.

Employees can be influenced not by virtue of traits and behaviour of the corporate managers alone, but also on account of his mastery over a process which is crucial to the organisation. In an age where competitive advantages must be polished till they shine, chief executive and senior managers must champion this specific proprietary expertise, not only making it the pivotal of the organisational strategy but also ensuring that it is passed up/ down and across the organisation.

In view of dynamic character of environment, the management will have to revisit competitive strategies and other mechanisms on a periodical basis so as to assess their utility in the changed environment and wherever necessary, evolve new strategies and mechanisms. For effective review and evaluation of the plans, a comprehensive mechanism at the corporate as well as at the unit level needs to be developed and clear standards and policies which serve as evaluation criteria are developed and communicated to all concerned.

Above all, banks can face the emerging challenges more deftly and confidently, provided the top management exhibit impeccable commitment to change and involve all employees while deciding about any strategic change.

G. CONCLUSIONS

Pursuance of Government policy of liberalization, privatization and globalization has infused competitiveness in every sector of Indian economy, offering tremendous opportunities to banking and other organizations to expand and diversify their operators and improve their operational efficiency. However, Indian banks are facing enormous problems and challenges in squeezing the opportunities.

Coping with the challenges and capitalizing on the environmental opportunities to the fullest extent demands the bank management to switch over to strategic management system which involves visualization of corporate vision and mission of the bank, articulation of objectives and choosing suitable course of action against the background of SWOT analysis. Effective execution of strategy is contingent upon adoption of new technology, better processes of credit and risk appraisal, treasury management, product diversification, responsive structure, internal control and availability of talented man power.

KEY TERMS

- Business unit-level strategy
- Competitive advantage
- Concept of Fit
- Concept of leverage
- Core competence
- Excellence perspective
- Enabling
- Enacting
- Envisioning
- Strategic Management System
- Strategy of inclusiveness.

DISCUSSION QUESTIONS

1. Discuss the major challenges Indian commercial banks are facing.
2. What are the opportunities available to commercial banks in India to expand their business and improving their earnings?
3. What are the greatest strengths of commercial banks in India that can help them to exploit the environment opportunities?
4. "Despite existence tremendous business opportunities and availability of strengths, commercial banks in India have not been able to take full mileage." Do you agree with the statement? If yes, explain the major causes.
5. What strategies should a bank in India pursue to exploit the opportunities to grow?
6. What efforts should be made to execute the strategic plans of the bank?

REFERENCES

1. V. Leeladhar, *Indian Banking — The Challenges Ahead,* Reserve Bank of Indian Bulletin, December, 2005, p. 1132.
2. The Indian Banker, May, 2006, p. 7.
3. V. Leeladhar, *Emerging Challenges Before The Indian Bank — The Road Ahead,* RBI Bulletin, June, 2005, pp. 5 & 6.
4. Asian Banking Outlook, 2006, *Economic Times*, June 19, 2006.
5. Times of India, January, 29, 2006.
6. Business Standard, December 5, 2012.
7. The Business Live, February, 23, 2005.
8. Economic Times, May 16, 2006.
9. Business Line, September 7, 2007.
10. V. Leeladhar, *Emerging Challenges Before the Indian Banks*, pp. 588-589.
11. The Indian Banker, May 2006, pp. 6-7.

***

Chapter 10

Commercial Banking Restructuring

Learning Objectives:

The present chapter attempts to provide:

- An understanding of the concept of corporate restructuring and its various forms.
- An awareness of the designing of corporate restructuring programme.
- An overview of International experiences of bank restructuring .
- A panoramic view of bank's restructuring in India.
- A synoptic view of Government and RBI policies towards restructuring of banks.

Chapter Outline:

- Backdrop.
- Concept of corporate restructuring.
- Forms of corporate restructuring.
- Designing corporate restructuring programme.
- Bank restructuring: International experiences.
- Restructuring of commercial banks in India.
- Role of regulatory authority.
- RBI policy guidelines on mergers and amalgamations of banks.
- Conclusions.

A. BACKDROP

In a brutally competitive and highly uncertain environment, as it exists today, organizations to survive and thrive on sustained basis have not only to be bigger and more profitable than their competitors but also have to be resilient and continuously anticipate the environmental changes, containing opportunities and threats, and reinvent business models and redefine core businesses based on their core competencies faster than the change in circumstances. They have to evolve a strategy that is forever morphying, forever conforming itself to emerging opportunities and incipient trends and build an organization that is constantly making its future rather than defending its past. This is why during the last three decades majority of the companies world-over engaged themselves in restructuring their product-market strategies to concentrate in core business processes so as to ensure their survival and successful growth.

Indian economy witnessed during the last decade or so frenetic activity in corporate field, especially in the sphere of corporate restructuring. The impact of sweeping changes in economic and industrial policies, deregulation of markets, globalization of markets, economic interdependencies, free flow of capital and knowledge, interaction among different financial systems of different countries, and proliferation and convergence of technologies, fast changing demographies of the workforce, changes in personal, social, familial values of people and rapidly moving customers; their penchants and predilections forced corporates to restructure their current product portfolio, and to change organizational culture so as to evolve a cohesive business entity, common set of values and to cut costs and to improve operational efficiencies so as to make themselves globally competitive in terms of cost, quality, speed and services.

The restructuring activity in India reached new heights in the mid-1990s with the re-engineering wave, propelled in many cases by the adoption of computer-based enterprise resource planning systems. The fanfare with which corporate restructuring was introduced in India created an impression that it is panacea for all problems of the firm. Corporate entities both in public and private sectors started rushing into bouts of retructuring sometimes even without assessing the validity of objectives set before them. This led to failure of many restructuring exercises. It would, therefore, be pertinent to explain concept and dimensions of corporate restructuring, and how corporate restructuring programme is designed.

B. CONCEPT OF CORPORATE RESTRUCTURING

Corporate restructuring is about revisiting existing management practices of an enterprise and altering them so as to attain greater adaptability and viability with reference to the current and emerging environmental developments. It involves overhauling strategies, structures and management processes in order to improve competitiveness and/or profitability.

Corporate restructuring, it must be noted, is a proactive and planned decision making exercise to redefine the basic line of business and discover a common thread for the firm's survival and successful growth. It involves altering what it owes, refocuses itself to specific tasks performance. This is sought to be done after making a detailed analysis of itself at a point of time. At times, restructuring may radically alter a firm's product portfolio, capital structure, asset mix and organization structure and culture so as to enhance value of the firm and attain competitive edge on sustainable basis. Thus, the kernel of corporate restructuring exercise is SWOT analysis.

Another salient feature of corporate restructuring is that it is an all permeating process involving an analytical appraisal of the existing strategic policies and practices and wherever necessary redesigning the strategies, the structure of the organization, upgradation of its technology, modernization of its plant and equipment, revamping financial structure, remodeling its human relations ethos, revamping its marketing philosophy and repositioning the firm within the corporate world. It also involves selection of the performance indices in context of which the current and future effectiveness of the firm should be recorded.

In view of its pervasive nature, restructuring at any one level is inter-related with changes at other levels and therefore, it is essential for the management to assess organization-wide implications of any change which is going to be affected. The entire process is based on wholistic approach.

Further, restructuring exercise is a continuing process which has to be done continuously so as to cope with ever changing environmental developments, exploit emerging opportunities and combat impending threats.

Restructuring process may take many forms including strategic alliances, mergers and acquisitions, financial restructuring, company downsizing, product or process restructuring and work reorganization.

Post liberalization period has witnessed restructuring spree in India, prominent being ICICI, IDBI, HLL, Aditya Birla Group, Ranbaxy, Sun Pharma, Lupin Agro, SRF Finance, Jaiprakash Industries, Tata Group, Indian Oil Corporation, Sony Entertainment Television (SET) India, ONGC, Steel Authority of India Ltd., Indian Tobacco Ltd., Coal India Ltd., Blue Star, ICI India, etc.

C. FORMS OF CORPORATE RESTRUCTURING

Corporate restructuring, as stated above, is all pervasive encompassing every business and management policies and practices- strategic, functional and operational. Thus, it covers strategy restructuring and financial restructuring.

◆ Strategy Restructuring

Strategy restructuring is about reviewing the firm's existing vision, mission, objectives and strategies and evaluating their effectiveness in the changed scenario. Thus, this kind of corporate restructuring involves reviewing and modifying fundamental line of the firm's business, revisiting and adjusting current business portfolio, rethinking ways and means to synergize organizational efforts and reviewing and modifying existing priorities for allocation of resources. The underlying idea is to define what the firm should be doing in future.

Strategy restructuring is also concerned with assessing adequacy of existing competitive strategies against the background of environmental changes and bringing alteration therein whenever necessary.

Nokia went for strategy restructuring to enhance its competitive position when it decided to shed its tyres, television and other businesses and focus exclusively on cellular telephony having tremendous global opportunities.

◆ Organizational Restructuring

Corporate strategy restructuring to improve competitiveness of a firm demands transformation of existing structure and organizational culture. Thus, existing structure of a firm needs to be winnowed with reference to types of activities being performed, assignment of these activities amongst various divisions and department, assignment of tasks and responsibilities to subordinates and delegation of authority, organizational hierarchies, co-ordination of activities of various divisions and departments as also pattern of communication among those in the structure, the development of informal as well as formal relationships and resulting motivation.

All these aspects need to be examined with a view to determining their adequacy to cope with change in corporate strategy. The structure of an organization affects cost of operations, the speed with which it does things, the way it meets its customers' needs and the way people behave. The contemporary tendency in structure is to make organization as simple, flat, flexible and transparent as possible so that it is most responsive to the organizational needs.

So as to ensure effective implementation of corporate and business level strategies, it is germane to ensure that the existing culture and operating ethos in the organization are convivial and conducive to enamour and enthrall employees to contribute their best to the organization. There must be complete congruence between strategy and culture. A mismatch poses real obstacles. Just as an organization changes and grows through its life cycle, likewise culture has also to be changed to cope with environmental changes.

Where the occurrence of environmental changes is small or incremental, they need to be synchronized with the existing culture. However, in case of breakthrough changes, as noticed across the globe during the last few decades, it will be kosher for the firm to change their culture otherwise the firm may be in trouble soon.

◈ Manpower Restructuring

In competitive environment people have come to be acknowledged as powerful source of competitive advantage because it is they who make the organizational processes and structure capable enough to achieve the desired results. As such, people should be managed properly. Knowledgeable people cannot be managed by theory X or Y. They cannot be managed as subordinates. They have to be managed in marketing way and need to be supported and mentored so that they give their best to the organization. The top management will have to own responsibility of converting their contractual employees of an economic entity into committed members of the firm. Human resource manager has to establish internal structures and processes for enhancing capability of the people to respond to changes.

◈ Market Restructuring

Market Restructuring is about reviewing existing marketing strategy of the firm and assessing its effectiveness in attracting and retaining customers, creating value for customers and improving its market share. In heightened competitive landscape, customers have come to be accepted as lodestar of a firm and as such, focus has be made on customer relationship management so as to create, maintain and enhance strong bondage with customer's loyalty. The management has to evaluate existing marketing efforts in capturing new customers, cultivating a deeper share of wallet from existing customers and converting them into the firm's ambassadors and wherever necessary bring about modification in current marketing strategies.

◈ Financial Restructuring

Financial Restructuring is the process of reorganizing the company by affecting major changes in ownership pattern, asset mix, operations which are outside the ordinary course of business. Financial restructuring of a bank, which may take the form of mergers, takeovers, divestitures, leveraged recapitalization, spin-offs, carve-outs, and reorganization of capital, is mainly aimed at restoring its solvency.

◈ Operational Restructuring

Operational restructuring attempts to provide the ideal conditions within a bank to ensure that the profitability increases and is sustained over a period. The key elements here are the quality of internal governance and the structure of a bank's operations. The operational restructuring tools may include changes in ownership and management and a drastic re-engineering of its operations to cover, among other things, its business strategy, product mix, and pricing, loan recovery procedures, branch network, staff costs and increased resort to automation and other new technology.

D. DESIGNING CORPORATE RESTRUCTURING PROGRAMME

Corporate restructuring, as stated above, is necessary to keep the vitality of a firm intact. Management should consider corporate restructuring as a normal part of business. It should, therefore, be on agenda of the firm's annual strategic planning sessions. It is always better to make many small adjustments to the firm's direction than an about face after several years of lax oversight. The management should never think about corporate restructuring until the firm faces bankruptcy. Any corporate restructuring programme involves the following steps:

◈ Understanding the Firm's Strategic Architecture and Organizational Characteristics

Corporate restructuring programme in a firm aspiring to remain competitively superior to its rivals for all the time to come must begin with revisiting the existing vision, mission, objectives and strategies, process, structure, management, organizational culture and human and financial resources so as to determine their adequacy to cope with environmental developments.

◈ Assessing Imperativeness of Change

Before embarking on any move to cope with the change requirement, the management must find out what triggers the change. There may be slew of forces that necessitate departure from the present state of affairs. Obviously, the most powerful force that triggers reaction is the change in the environment that exists outside the organization. Even forces within the organization may also necessitate the change. Deep insights into these forces and their implications may signal the need for restructuring.

◈ Determining what should be Changed

Having got in-depth understanding of the existing architecture of the firm and its basic characteristics, the management has to decide if there is a need to alter the current vision of the organization in the changed scenario. For instance, almost all the corporate enterprises in India were forced to change their direction and scope of business with a view to coping with the fast changing environmental demands and ensuring survival and growth in the competitive milieu. In sync with organizational vision and mission, radical changes in the overall and functional strategies have to be affected and to execute these strategies, change in process, structure, people, etc., is necessary.

To add value, a firm needs to examine the extent to which existing processes add value to the product/service. The management should identify the processes having the greatest impact on the company's product/service and customer's choice and the process that do not add value or are in deep trouble need to be remedied. Each process may also be examined to determine whether it is conducive to working as an integrated process.

Adequacy of present organizational structure in terms of departmentalization of activities, role and responsibilities of various functionaries, line and staff relationships, degree of decentralization, skills and competencies of the organizational people, co-ordination of activities, pattern of communication, etc., to cope with the change in strategy should also be examined.

Any change in strategy, process and structure is not possible without full co-operation and support of the people. To restructure the organization, people's beliefs and attitudes need to be changed. This is not so easy a task particularly in strong cultures.

◈ Understanding Organizational Reactions and Analyzing them

People usually react definitely to change depending on their perceptions, circumstances and understanding of the process. Generally, three types of reactions to any restructure programme are observed: *viz.*, alliance, compliance and definance. Those opposing change obviously need rapt attention. Even those who support the change need to be managed properly. The management must try to find why people are opposing change or not supporting change overtly.

◈ Approach to Restructuring Programme

There are two broad approaches to affect restructuring programme, viz, Tactical and Strategic. Tactical approach includes education and communication, participation and involvement, facilitative support, emotional support, manipulation and co-option, incentives and coercion.

Strategic approach to any restructuring programme comprises organizational development (OD). OD is a planned process of change in an organization's culture through the utilization of behavioural science technology, research and theory. This approach is a problem solving approach of dealing with the threats and opportunities in the external environment and focuses on changing certain aspects of people and these changes are based on an overview of structure, technology and all other organizational ingredients. It lays emphasis on participative and collaborative management and emphasis on changing the organization's culture.

The techniques used by OD approach include structural intervention, task-technology intervention and people oriented intervention.

E. BANK RESTRUCTURING: INTERNATIONAL EXPERIENCES

Different countries have opted different strategies, depending on the structure of their banking system. The banking system in many emerging economies is fragmented in terms of the number and size of institutions, ownership, profitability and competitiveness of banks, use of modern technology and other related structural features. Very often, three or four large Commercial banks coexist with a large number of smaller urban and rural banks or under the influence of the public sector bank. In general, few banks, even larger ones, are listed on the stock exchange. Profitability varies widely with some banks earning high returns but operating very inefficiently, and other banks competing fiercely for a narrow segment of the market. Likewise, while some banks in the emerging economies are at the cutting edge of technology and financial innovation, many are still struggling with the basic operations such as credit risk assessment and liquidity management. Finally, recent banking crises have weakened banking systems in a number of countries, and banks in some countries remain on the brink of insolvency.

It is in this context bank mergers have been considered as a possible avenue for improving the structure and efficiency of the banking industry. In the United States, over nine thousands of banks and thrifts were merged or closed to handle the severe banking crisis experienced during the 1980s and the early 1990s. The US banking system was highly segmented geographically and functionally, thereby increasing the risk profile of the banks.[1] Enhanced deposit insurance alongwith financial deregulation and growth in real estate construction fuelled by the incentives encouraged new entrants to the industry and led to higher risk-taking. Combined with poor management, imprudent lending practices and fraud led to an unprecedented crisis in the US banking system. In dealing with troubled banks, the Federal Deposit Insurance Corporation (FDIC) in case of merger with healthier banks entered into "income maintenance agreements", where it stood guarantee for a minimum return on the earning assets that were acquired. The FDIC strategy in respect of failing banks was mostly by way of arranging for "Purchase and Assumption" (P&A), under which the acquirer purchased some or all assets and assumed some or all liabilities of the failed banks. In the case of "clean bank" under scheme of P&As, only the good assets were taken over. When this became difficult to arrange for "small bank" P&A were introduced in which a smaller package of assets including some non-performing loans were taken over by the acquirer.

In a more concentrated banking system, large insolvent banks could be split, the viable parts sold and the rest liquidated. Breaking up of monolithic banking systems was adopted in several emerging market economies of Easter Europe in Nicaragua, Peru and Tanzania; large problem banks were downsized by placing restrictions on asset growth. In Argentina, Estonia, Latvia and Venezuela, several bigger banks were either closed or merged. Simultaneously, some of the countries permitted entry of new banks including foreign banks.

Market driven consolidation is a relatively new phenomenon and has been mainly observed in Central European economies. In Hungary, for instance, some 40 institutions are presently competing in the retail and corporate markets. At the same time, Belgium's KBC and ABN Amro observe their Hungarian operations to exploit market synergies. After the large number of bankruptcies of private banks, in Poland and Czech Republic the number of commercial banks declined significantly, with no dominant bank in the corporate sector.

Sweden is an off-quoted example of successful management of banking crisis by adopting a comprehensive strategy. Its banking problems came to light in late 1990 mainly due to over exposure to the real estate sector. The government opted for a comprehensive approach, the main features of which were as follows:

A separate restructuring authority, known as the "Bank Support Authority" was set up. The government took several steps to raise confidence in the country's financial system. It guaranteed that the banks and all other credit institutions would meet their commitments as and when they arose. Further, transparency and disclosure of information ensured increased confidence at home and abroad. Government support to the needy banks was in the form of capital infusion (86%) and loan guarantees apart from share subscription or share purchases (10 per cent) and interest subsidies (2 per cent).

Bank restructuring in Poland was also successful mainly because of its comprehensive approach. The approach followed was to make a proper assessment of the extent to which a bank was in trouble and then to emphasize organizational restructuring. Privatization was one of the approaches followed for restructuring the banks. The banks to be restructured were first transformed into joint stock companies with the government being the shareholder. To manage these banks in their new form, long-term technical assistance contacts with reputable foreign banks were entered into.

The problems faced by banks in the early 1990s exemplify the special problems in dealing with government-owned banks. Due to non-transparent accounting practices, inadequate provisioning in loan losses and lack of supervision, the banking sector in the Philippines was inherently weak. The banking crisis deepened by the end of 1985, when the Philippines National Bank (PNB) and the Development Bank of the Philippines (DBP) were declared insolvent. These banks accounted for nearly half of the banking system's assets. Their non-performance loans formed about 70 per cent of their combined portfolios and about 21 per cent of the banking system's assets. The rehabilitation programmes adopted for these banks were comprehensive and included downsizing transfer of non-performing assets to the Asset Privatization Trust, recapitalization, writing of government deposits, introduction of new management, closing of branches and cost reduction programmes. As a result, the banks became much smaller; the total assets of PNB were reduced by 54 per cent. By 1987, both banks returned to profitability and improved their capital asset ratios. In 1969, PNB was privatized upto 30 per cent and further to 57 per cent by 1996.

In Asian countries, government led consolidation has gained prominence, motivated by the need to strengthen capital adequacy and the financial viability of many smaller banks affected by the 1997-98 crisis. Malasia Danamodel, a special purpose institution established with the twin objectives of recapitalising the banks and facilitating consolidation and rationalization of the banking system, is a case in point.

Thailand's financial sector had been facing problems since the early 1980s due to weak managerial practices and inadequate supervision. The remedial measure then taken included strengthening of the legal, regulatory and supervision arrangements, government takeovers, changes in management, mergers and closures and financial support at market-related rates. The basic weaknesses, however, persisted and in 1997, deeper structural weaknesses in the economy brought these weaknesses to the fore again.

Immediate regulatory action involved suspension of operation of 58 finance companies, which were required to submit rehabilitation plans. The Financial Sector Restructuring Authority (FSRA) and the Asset Management Corporation (AMC) were created to aid the restructuring process. The FSRA assumed the responsibility of either rehabilitating or liquidating the troubled units.

It is pertinent to note that the Thai financial restructuring programme has been that an entirely new institutional framework was created and the legal and regulatory framework was simultaneously amended to meet requirements of the situation. It was, thus, a fairly comprehensive programme.

The Korean financial crisis that broke out in December, 1997 had its origins in the corporate and financial sectors and a poorly implemented capital account liberalization. The more immediate causes were a determining terms of trade, bankruptcy of important conglomerates and a change in international market sentiment. The failure of some bigger conglomerates in 1997 and the East Asian crisis brought the situations to a head towards the end of 1997. In November, 1997 the government announced a blanket guarantee for deposits maintained with banks and other financial institutions, resulting in restoring public confidence. In December, 1997 a comprehensive reform package was drawn to include exit of unviable financial institutions, restructuring of others and the strengthening of banking regulation and supervision.

In China extensive bank restructuring is being carried out since 1997. Four of the largest state-owned banks, *viz.*, Industrial and Commercial Bank of China, Construction Banks of China, Agricultural Bank of China and Bank of China are undergoing restructuring programme aimed at improving their efficiency and increasing profits which had stagnated due to huge non-performing assets estimated to be at about 20 per cent of total outstanding loans. The poor performance is attributed to decades of government-directed lending and poor management. Each of these banks reportedly has between 800 and 1000 branches and together employ more than 1.5 million employees. The operations are fully guaranteed by the Central government which owns them.

The series of measures taken by the government to improve management, capital and asset quality include increasing banks' independence from local governments, setting up asset management companies, conversion of debt into equity, mergers, closures and liquidation, and direct capital injections from the Central governments. It has been decided to close or merge between 10 and 30 per cent of branches of these banks. A new board of supervisions for the banks has been constituted to oversee the work of the top management of the four banks.

In Latin America, bank mergers arose as a response to inefficient banking structures. In Argentina, bank consolidation has been driven largely by the domestic and external financial liberalization launched in the early 1990s, and the progressive tightening of prudential regulations. Bank consolidation in Mexico, on the other hand, took place in response to the lack of capital after the 1995 banking crisis.

In Malaysia, the government-driven merger programme for domestic banks was initiated in 1999 and concluded in 2002. It resulted in the creation of more than 50 domestic institutions. In 2006, another acquisition brought down the total number of banking groups to nine.

F. RESTRUCTURING OF COMMERCIAL BANKS IN INDIA

Restructuring of Commercial banks in India is not a new phenomenon, nevertheless the intent of the restructuring and the pace of such restructuring have differed from time to time. Thus, Imperial Bank of India was formed in 1921 after amalgamation of the three presidency banks for extending banking facilities and for rendering the money resources of India more accessible to the trade and industry of 'this' country, thereby promoting financial system for social and economic advancement of the country. Thus, in 1961 alone thirty banks were merged compulsorily with other banks. As a consequence of improved atmosphere, bank failure decreased while the number of mergers, amalgamations and transfers increased from 4 in 1950 to 79 in 1964. (Table 10.1).

From 566 reporting Commercial banks at the end of 1951, the number came down remarkably to 292 at the end of 1961, to 100 at the end of 1966 and to 85 by the end of 1969. In 1961 alone above 30 banks were merged compulsorily with other banks. This improved the banking environment. The idea underlying this merger was to strengthen the banking system. Small, weak and insufficient non-scheduled banks, which could hardly become viable, were merged with other scheduled banks so as to check the frequent failure of banks and to save them from facing crisis and maintaining confidence.

The banking scenario prevalent in the country before nationalization depicted strong stress on class banking depriving banking facilities to masses. Hence, 14 banks were nationalized in 1969 and 6 in 1980 and ownership of these banks passed in the hands of the Government. This led to taking geographical expanse of the subcontinent and was thus a critical trigger for financial outreach of institutions and empowerment of the common man. During the period 1969-1989, 14 unsuccessful commercial banks were merged with successful banks including State Bank of India, Chartered Bank, Union Bank, Canara Bank, Punjab National Bank, Allahabad Bank, Bank of Baroda, Indian Overseas Bank, Bank of India and Indian Bank. Here again, these mergers took place at the behest by the RBI so as to protect the interests of the depositors.

TABLE 10.1: Bank Mergers, Amalgamations and Transfers of Assets and Liabilities

Year	Voluntary Amalgamations under Sec. 44-A	Compulsory Mergers under Sector 45	Other Mergers	Transfer of Assets & Liabilities	Total
1950	4	–	–	–	4
1951	2	–	1	–	3
1952	–	–	4	–	4
1953	–	–	1	2	3
1954	–	–	–	1	1
1955	–	–	–	3	3
1956	–	–	–	–	–
1957	2	–	2	–	4
1958	4	–	2	1	7
1959	4	–	–	4	8
1960	2	–	–	5	7
1961	1	30	2	3	36
1962	3	1	2	5	11
1963	2	1	4	15	22
1964	7	9	1	62	79
Total	31	41	19	101	192

Even as the banking system's branch network was growing at a fast pace, by the beginning of 1990s financial strength and operational efficiency of the Indian banks and financial institutions, which were operating in a highly protected and domestic environment — called for corrections primarily with a view to strengthening the financial system and to bring it on par with institutions abroad. Hence, another inflexion point in Indian banking was the financial sector reforms initiative that was launched in the early 1990s. These reforms heralded a dramatic shift in the way banks functioned and operated in India. The changed environment due to liberalization, privatization and globalization policies and the internal compulsions arising from greater competition and the need to improve their market share/profitability gave rise to the quest for greater efficiency and the need to reposition themselves given the realities of the environment and their internal strengths and weaknesses so as to meet competitive challenges. Hence, the Government of India, in its attempt to strengthen banking system and make it globally competitive, constituted Narasimham Committee to recommend measures to improve efficiency and competitiveness of the Indian financial system. The Committee in its Report II had stressed the need to reduce the number of public sector banks and to create a few large banks with large-scale operations and international presence. Mergers between banks, the Committee further emphasized, should be based on synergies and locational and business specific complementaries of the concerned institutions and must obviously make sound commercial sense and such mergers should emanate from the management of banks with the Government as the common shareholder playing a supportive role. Thus, the Committee strongly advocated for the mergers among strong banks so as to derive the inbuilt benefits of megers, *viz.*, cost benefits, revenue benefits, reduced risk and other benefits. The Committee's recommendations were reinforced subsequently when Finance Minister while addressing the IBA's Annual General Meeting in Mumbai in August, 2004 observed "consolidation alone will give banks the muscle, size and scale to act like world-class banks. We have to think global and act local and seek new markets, new classes of borrowers". While replying to a question on the consolidation of Government owned banks in the Lok Sabha on 4th December, 2004 he remarked "larger size entails better management of risk. Small and weak banks pose systematic risks with their low capital adequacy ratio and high non-performing assets." Again, speaking at a banking seminar, the Finance Minister observed "International trends suggest that consolidation has reduced the chances of credit risk. Tata Motors looks and behaves like a global company, Ranbaxy looks and behaves like a global drug company. If Infosys, Wipro and TCS look and behave like global companies, Indian banks need to do the same".

The finance ministry wants the country's nationalized banks to develop better brand equity, and become stronger and smarter. The ministry believes that the merger of existing nationalized banks that will create a stronger identify can help win the confidence of depositors more than any of the mushrooming private banks. Speaking at the centenary event of Bank of India, the Finance Minister observed that seven large public sector banks in the country, *viz.*, SBI, Punjab National Bank, Canara Bank, Bank of India and Central Bank should look at consolidation among themselves or with smaller PSU banks or with private sector banks. Close on heels of the finance ministry pitching for consolidation in the banking sector, the RBI too feels that mergers and amalgamations are imminent.

Thus, in view of positive attitude of the Government and the RBI, mergers of commercial banks during the post reform period were expected to be affected for improving competitiveness of the merged banks. However, merger of New Bank of India with Punjab National Bank of India in 1993-94, Kashinath Seth Bank with State Bank of India in 1995-96, Bari Daob Bank Ltd. with the Oriental Bank of Commerce in 1997, Bareilley Co-operative Bank Ltd. with Bank of Baroda in 1998-99, Benaras State Bank Ltd. with Bank of Baroda in 2002, Nedungadi Bank with Punjab National Bank in 2003, Global Trust Bank with the Oriental Bank of Commerce in 2004 which took place on the explicit advise of the RBI with a view to giving relief to the ailing banks and maintaining public interest and depositors' confidence, do not corroborate this. Even recent mergers of ICICI Corporation with ICICI Bank and IDBI Bank were primarily mooted to save the financial institutions suffering from huge financial losses.

Hence, it can be indubitably observed that merger and amalgamation in Indian Banking until recently has been to provide the safeguard and hedging to weak banks against their failure and that too at the initiative of RBI, rather than to pave the way to initiate the banks to come forward on their own accord for merger purely on economic considerations.

Recent trends and changed attitude of the top management of banks after realizing the sordid truth that consolidation will make the institutions strong and robust and make them highly competitive in terms of productivity, cost effectiveness, better services and efficient risk management provide enough clue to the forging of future mergers on initiative of the management and that too on economic consideration.

Thus, the merger of Bank of Punjab into Centurian Bank-the two relatively small private sector banks- in June 2005 to constitute Centurian Bank of Punjab is the first one since the Government and the RBI started goading the country's banking system and the only consideration of the merger was synergistic. The merged entity will be well capitalized, have a strong management team and will be able to achieve considerable revenue and cost benefits. The synergies arising out of the merger are remarkable, especially on two counts-geographical spread and the product portfolio. While Bank of Punjab is strong in North India and the Centurian Bank in southern and western parts of the country. Further, Bank of Punjab has been strong in the rural areas and has a recent agricultural portfolio. It also works out to be a good match for Centurian, having a limited revenue stream consisting of retail, two-wheeler and personal loans. Thus, the merger will give both banks a wider revenue stream. The merger provides the combined entity the impetus to grow and carve out a niche for itself. The merger of the two banks is indeed a trail blazer for the banking industry in India. Another merger between two private sector banks that followed the above one in October 2005 was acquisition of Lord Krishna bank (LKB) by Kerala-based Federal Bank. The acquisition will boost Federal Bank's presence in the South as it would get a ready customer base there. It will also acquire 111 branches of LKB spread across 11 states. LKB has been forced to explore possibilities of a merger as it needs more capital to adhere to RBI ownership guidelines. The merged entity will have assets over ₹ 19,300 crore, which will be about 15% more than Federal Bank's current assets size.

Accordingly, in September, 2006, the Boards of Centurian Bank of Punjab and LKB decided to merge. Three PSBs, *viz.*, Oriental Bank of Commerce, Indian Bank and Co-operation Bank forged a strategic alliance on September 15, 2006 to help the banks leverage their combined balance sheet strength and share the benefits of economics of scale. The alliance enables the banks to share business – e-payment system, sharing of IT infrastructure, training ATMs, treasury resources, loan syndication, capital market and international forays. In this collaborative arrangement each bank is a separate legal entity.[4] This, thus, heralds a consolidation phase in Indian banking.

General Bank of Kurundwad Ltd., (GBK) was merged with the Federal Bank Ltd., with effect from September 2, 2006 because of deteriorating financial health of the former. Likewise, United Western Bank (UWB) was amalgamated with IDBI on October 3, 2006.

ICICI Bank Ltd., and Sangli Bank Ltd., were amalgamated with effect from April 19, 2007. The Government of India sanctioned the Scheme of Transfer of Undertaking of Bharat Overseas of Bank which was made effect from the close of business on March 31, 2007.

A list showing mergers and amalgamations since 1985 onwards is given in Table 10.2.

Moves are on foot for merger of public sector banks.[5] Already there is talk of a possible merger of the Bank of India and the Union Bank of India. If it goes through, it will create the second largest bank in India after the State Bank of India. There is going to be merger of Bank of Baroda and Dena Bank, Indian Bank and Overseas Bank. Oriental Bank of Commerce, Allahabad Bank, ICICI Bank and Vijaya Bank are also looking for partners. Corporation Bank has already got an enabling clause to this effect, passed recently in the shareholders' meetings.[6] In near future, there is a strong possibility of merger of Bharat Overseas Bank with Indian Overseas Bank and United Bank with Corporation Bank.[7] The Chairman of the SBI group hinted that sooner or later the associate banks of SBI would have to merge into a single entity.[8] Already there exists a virtual merger with integration in information technology, treasury operations, accounting practices, systems and procedures and market information sharing. A strong synergy had already developed among SBI and associate banks in cross-selling products of insurance, mutual funds and credit cards.

The long due merger of State Bank of Maharashtra — a subsidiary of the SBI — with the latter took place in 2008. This merger would help eliminate duplication of branches in the same geographical region and consequent cost savings.

In May 2010, Bank of Rajasthan was merged with ICICI Bank in the wake of regulatory pressure mounting on the promoter of the former. The merger of Bank of Rajasthan with the ICICI Bank, according to the Managing Director and CEO of the ICICI Bank, "will offer a strategic fit as it adds to our network in north and western India. It saves us about three years time to market. In the normal course, it takes about a year to set up 500 branches and then three years for the branches to come upto the kind of deposit levels."[9]

TABLE 10.2: Recent Banks Mergers/Amalgamations in India – 1985 onwards

Banks	Merged/Amalgamated with	Year
Lakshmi Commercial Bank Ltd.	Canara Bank	1985
Bank of Cochin Ltd.	State Bank of India	1985
The Miraj State Bank Ltd.	Union Bank of India	1985
The Hindustan Commercial Bank Ltd.	Punjab National Bank	1986
Traders' Bank Ltd.	Bank of Baroda	1988
United Industrial Bank Ltd.	Allahabad Bank	1989-1990
Bank of Tamilnadu	Indian Overseas Bank	1989-1990
The Bank of Thanjavur	Indian Bank	1989-1990
Parur Central Bank Ltd.	Bank of India	1989-1990
Purbanchel	Central Bank of India	1990-1991
New Bank of India	Punjab National Bank	1993-1994
Bank of Karnataka Ltd.	Bank of India	1993-1994
Kashinath Seth Bank	State Bank of India	1995-1996
Bari Daob Bank Ltd.	The Oriental Bank of Commerce	1997
Punjab Corporative Bank Ltd.	The Oriental Bank of Commerce	1997
Bareilly Corporation Bank	Bank of Baroda	1998-1999
Times Bank	HDFC Bank	2000
Bank of Madura	ICICI	2001
Benares State Bank Ltd.	Bank of Baroda	2002
Nedungandi Bank	Punjab National Bank	2003
South Gujarat Local Area Bank	Bank of Baroda	2004
Global Trust Bank	The Oriental Bank of Commerce	2004
Bank of Punjab	Centurian Bank	2005
Lord Krishna Bank	Federal Bank	2005
Centurian Bank of Punjab	Lord Krishna Bank	2006
United Western Bank Ltd.	IDBI	2006
Ganesh Bank of Kurundwad Ltd.,	Federal Bank Ltd.,	2006
Sangli Bank Ltd.,	ICICI Bank Ltd.,	2007
Bharat Overseas Bank Ltd.,	Indian Overseas Bank	2007
State Bank of Maharashtra	State Bank of India	2008
Bank of Rajasthan	ICICI Bank	2010

It emanates from the above discussions that different sections of the society have now conviction that it is bank restructuring through consolidation that can make banks globally competitive in terms of productivity, profitability, quality of services, risk management and reduced operational cost. However, it would be mistaken to conclude without dispassionately assessing the potentiality of consolidation move from different angles, that consolidation strategy is a panacea to all the present sufferings of Indian banks.

G. CONSOLIDATION AS A SOURCE OF GLOBAL COMPETITIVENESS OF INDIAN COMMERCIAL BANKS

Strategic consolidation with its humungous potentiality of enabling the merging banks to achieve excellence in their operations and become global players by fuller utilization of skills and resources, melding complementary skills, cost savings through rationalization of operations, deep market penetration, diversification of risks, and by way of strengthening their financial, technological, operational and organizational efficiencies has recently been acknowledged as potent source of raving up the growth of the merged entity and bolstering up its global competitive position. In fact, consolidation is regarded as logical response to the globalization of markets, increasing ferocity of competition, the need for turbulent innovation and the growing complexity of technology.

The afforested benefits of consolidation are certainly ascribed to size factor. Size, analysts feel, matters a lot. It not only gives a bank enough strength to take risk but also improves efficiency which is crucial to compete against global players. Larger banks generally command more respect in domestic and international markets, enjoy better and can cut their transaction cost. Large banks are also able to build up financial strengths, capture larger portion of the growing retail business and secure better regional presence. There are cost savings to larger banks that can only be achieved through rationalization of staff and offices. It is further contented that larger banks are capable of providing a fuller range of products and services and have greater ability to impenetrate global markets and raise the desired funds to meet increasing capital adequacy requirements stemming both from natural credit growth and the demands of Basel II. Further, the international exposure of banks compels them to adhere to global best practices.

Technology is the fundamental force driving the merger wave but the benefits of the technology revolution accrue optimally to relatively bigger banks. Technology enables the banks to share customer and product information, thereby, increasing the share of the customer wallet, lowering the cost of servicing a customer and enhancing profitability of even smaller branches. Economies of scale and the ability to absorb the latest technology would enable the consolidated entity to offer world class services to customers at an affordable price.

Through consolidation, the merged banks can spread or reduce risk, even almost eliminate in unfavourable conditions. By choosing the right partners operational risks can be diversified product-wise and geographically.

Further, small sized banks with weaker assets would find it difficult to survive in the long run as they need to meet additional capital requirements. The exit route for such banks will be to get absorbed by banks with strong asset quality. Another added utility of consolidation lies in the maximum utilization of available resource. The consolidation will take care of sharpening the knowledge and skills of the specialized categories of staff members including IT and other professionals on the one hand and utilization of all available resources like locational advantages of the premises, ATMs, IT assets of the banks, on the other.

In view of the above benefits of scale of operations, consolidation has become imperative in Indian banking industry. As a matter of fact, India has no big banks with assets of over ₹ 100,000 crore other than SBI and ICICI Bank. Even small economies in Asia like Thailand and Taiwan have more big banks than India. The list of the world's top 1,000 banks has only 20 Indian banks, of which only 6 are in the top 500. India's only entry in the top 25 Asian Banks (excluding Japan) is SBI at no. 10.[10] SBI, India's largest bank having an asset size of $ 127 billion, is ranked 83rd among the world's banks according to asset size. Although the SBI is catering to a population size which is three times larger than that serviced by Bank of America (BOA), in terms of the assets, the latter ($ 93.75 billion) is more than three times bigger than BOA (trillion dollar assets). There are four banks in China which are among top banks in the world. It must, however, be noted that size alone does not guarantee better performance, nevertheless a minimum size is expected if banks have to attain global aspirations and greater banking synergy. To become globally competitive, Indian banks have not only to be bigger in size but also be robust, strong, efficient and resilient in performance on sustained basis. For that purpose, the merger processes, that are likely to embark in future as a part of the restructuring exercise, should aim at helping the merged entity to become strong and develop ability to withstand the market shocks and meet challenges from both domestic and global players.

The management of the merging banks would have to take certain strategic factors into consideration for gaining maximum mileage of the consolidation and minimizing risks involved therein.

H. STRATEGIC CONSIDERATIONS IN CONSOLIDATION DECISIONS

Strategic issues that need to be addressed perspicaciously by merging banks before arriving at final decision and in post merger scenario comprise economic, technological, human, organizational and cultural ones.

◈ Economic Consideration

Before reaching any final decision, management of merging banks must accord overriding consideration to market-related forces such as increased market share, revenue growth, lower costs, improved return on assets, geographical and distribution synergies and optimal utilization of skills and capabilities. The consolidation process should promote the safety and stability of the financial system. It should result in improving operational efficiency which promotes competition and optimizes resource allocation.

The emerging market dynamics like falling interest rate regime making the spreads thinner, increasing focus on retail banking, enhanced quest for rural credit, felt need for augmenting more profits, especially from operations, reduction of NPAs, need for more capital to augment the technology needs, etc., are the major drivers for mergers and acquisitions for the banking sector. The merger process should also ensure that merged entity will be adequately capitalized to meet the technological requirements as also Basel II capital adequacy norms. In the light of the above, partners should be chosen.

Once the banks are merged, the management must focus on improving long-term profitability of the merged bank. This calls for diversification of lendings across several customer segments, improving quality of lending, streamlining of credit monitoring system, increasing the share of non-fund income by increasing product offerings wherever necessary by better use of technology reducing operating expenses by upgrading banking technology, improving the management and of market risks and finally, reducing the impact of operational risks by putting in place appropriate frameworks to measure risk, mitigating them or insuring them.

◈ Technological Consideration

Another critical consideration influencing merger and acquisition decisions is technology. Most of the banks in their bid to derive competitive business advantage have implemented technology in bits and pieces, some banks have already made inroads into Core Banking Solutions (CBS) by investing huge capital but others are in the initial stages or its process. Hence, in the post-merger scenario, integration of technology initiatives in a cost effective manner especially in the wake of varied business strategies is quite challenging. Another related issue is the reorientation of their technical skills which is relatively cost-intensive. A cautious and practice-oriented approach in enhancing the basic competencies of the merged bank like meaningful integration of technology with cost-effectiveness and quality and improving the skills of the workforce, etc. are expected to yield desired result.

◈ Human Consideration

As the consolidation process is a change initiative, the human related issues are quite crucial which need careful handling so as to avoid the employee's hostility towards the merger move. The management should, therefore, evolve an objective system to communicate the "why" and "what" of the merger move to all the functionaries of both banks so as to dispel their apprehensions on scores of job security, career progress, cultural fit, utilization of the skills, and any other uncertainty. The top management has to play a pivotal role in making the people aware of the new vision and mission and solemn objectives of the post-merged bank so that they know where to focus and what to achieve to enhance the productivity and customer satisfaction. Besides, for clearing of uncertainty, such a communication system should also build a strong platform for trust and goodwill that is essential to bridge the cultural gap between the two banks.

While consolidation decision is driven by financial considerations, its success vitally depends on the motivation of retained staff to contribute to the achievement of merged entity. Merger and acquisition value extraction is impossible without the enthusiastic co-operation of employees.

The merging banks must have adequate skills to complete the integration process successfully. As the skills, knowledge, capabilities and values of the people in different banks are in variance with each other due to factors like age profile, academic background, business strategies, training and development systems, opportunities for growth etc., talent assimilation in the post-merger period is daunting. Providing training and development and reskilling of the people in the post-merger scenario is another vital aspect which requires to be addressed strategically. It is also necessary to undertake re-engineering exercise in order to bridge the skill gap.

Aligning business strategies of the merged bank with people systems in the post-merger period goes a long way in achieving the desired results. This calls for revitalizing the human resource policies, encompassing recruitment, training and development, performance, promotion, placement/transfer, succession planning, etc., by keeping in view the existing policies prevailing in both the banks and also the present and future needs of the post-merger bank.

◈ Organizational Consideration

There is also a dire need to bring about suitable changes in the organizational structures, including staffing patterns, reporting relationships, job roles, systems and procedures, work processes, etc. For this, a thorough analysis of the existing systems prevalent in both the banks should be done and a set of viable and practice-oriented norms acceptable to all should be evolved and implemented.

In the wake of information technology explosion and a host of initiatives on inter-connectivity and networking of operational and administrative functions of the banks, the span of control, which is at present narrow, needs to be made more wider, thereby causing increased redundancy of the tall and multi-layered organizational structures thus heralding flat, lean an meaningful structures which foster continuous and speedy communication processes, paving way for qualitative and faster decisions.

Banks should, therefore, speed up the process of organizational restructuring through elimination of unwarranted intermediary administrative/hierarchical tiers, redefining reporting relationships and by properly empowering employees at various levels. It would be germane to organize self-empowered team comprising of talented persons. The team must have full time job. It would also be pertinent to define and communicate required roles and associated responsibilities of employees of the banks.

◈ Cultural Consideration

So as to ensure that merger of the banks achieves its objectives effectively, cultural issues need to be carefully addressed. One of the prime factors responsible for failure of most mergers and acquisitions has been cultural incompatibility between the two firms. Holding different perceptions, values and beliefs towards critical issues has boomeranged many alliances and mergers.

As such, assessment of the potential compatibility of cultures of the two banks such as leadership styles, decision making pattern, team system of working, reward and punishment systems, organizational capabilities and customer career is necessary before taking merger decision. These attributes are the guiding factors for the people working with, thereby they have imbibed certain cultures, perceptions, beliefs, values, etc.

In view of better experiences gained in the earlier exercise of bank mergers, the merging banks need to be carefully chosen, not only from the point of economic and technological viabilities but also from the angle of reduced response time in getting the cross-cultural integration for the mutual long-term benefit of employees and banks.

Constant monitoring by the top management of the merged bank of external and internal developments and frequent interactions among themselves will not only provide searing insights into the incipient problems which need to be thoroughly looked into but also throw lurid light on the adequacy of the current vision, objectives and strategies of the merged bank in the changed environment.

I. ROLE OF REGULATORY AUTHORITY

There is no doubt that consolidation is imperative to improve their performance, make the organization strong and sound and to attain global aspirations. However, the consolidation has to be addressed not merely to create large behemoths but to reap maximum benefits from the synergies in terms of regional balance, network of branches, HR cultures, asset commonality and ensuring that legal issues are not overlooked. The merger process should, therefore, be facilitated by Government and supervisory authorities through appropriate fiscal and monetary policies supported by a sound regulatory and supervisory framework since bank mergers have the potential to raise anti-trust concerns and can lead to monopoly of banking activities which could be concentrated in a few very large banks and may have serious repercussions to the financial system and the economy. It is, therefore, important for the Government to lay down prudential norms and supervisory guidance. The regulators have to consider the anti-trust aspects of merger process. In this connection, the US Federal Reserve Bank, while considering cases of mergers, keeps the following into consolidation:

- Ensure a safe and sound banking system.
- Preserve benefits of competition for consumers of financial services.
- Meet convenience and need of local communities.
- Allow the firm to evolve with the needs of the market.

The Government of India has clearly indicated that it will support the merger initiatives of the banks so as to develop strong and robust entities capable enough to meet global challenges.[11]

◈ Government of India Policy Regarding Mergers and Acquisitions of Banks

The Government of India has adopted positive attitude towards mergers of banks and clearly indicated that it will support the merger initiatives of the banks because it firmly believes that consolidation will make Indian banks strong and robust capable enough to meet global challenges. While replying to a question on the Consideration of Government owned banks in Lok Sabha on 4th December, 2004 the finance minister remarked "Larger size entails better management of risk." Speaking at the inauguration of the SIDBI's new development centre for small and medium enterprises, the finance minister observed "size and scale matter in public sector banks." Hence, irrational fears need to be dispelled. Consolidation, governance and competition will be the key drivers of growth in the banking sector.

The Government has clearly indicated that it is not an extended activity of the government to bail out sick public sector banks. They should learn from mistakes in the past and follow sound commercial business proportions in order to compete in the sector.[12]

◈ RBI Policy Guidelines on Mergers and Amalgamation of Banks

In pursuance of the recommendations of the Joint Parliamentary Committee (2002), the Reserve Bank had constituted a Working Group to evolve guidelines for voluntary mergers involving banking companies. Subsequently, guidelines for merger/amalgamation of private sector banks were issued on Many 11, 2005.[13] Basic principles underlying the guidelines would also be applicable as appropriate to private sector banks. Highlights of the guidelines are:

- The draft scheme of amalgamation be approved individually by two-thirds of the total strength of the total members of Board of Directors of each of the two banking companies.

- The members of the Board of Directors who approve the draft scheme of amalgamation are required to be signatories of the Deed of covenants as recommended by the, Ganguly Working Group on Corporate Governance.
- The draft scheme of amalgamation be approved by shareholders of each banking company by a resolution passed by a majority in number representing two-thirds in value of shareholders, present in person or by proxy at a meeting called for the purpose.
- The swap ratio be determined by independent valuers having required competence and experience, the Board should indicate whether such swap ratios are fair and proper.
- The value to be paid by the respective banking company to the dissenting shareholders in respect of shares held by them to be determined by the RBI.
- The shareholding pattern and composition of the Board of the amalgamating banking company after the amalgamation are to be in conformity with the RBI guidelines.
- Where an NBFC is proposed to be amalgamated into a banking company in terms of Sections 391 to 394 of the Companies Act, 1956, the banking company is required to obtain the approval of the RBI before the scheme of amalgamation is submitted to the High Court for approval.

J. CONCLUSIONS

In highly competitive environment, organizations to survive and thrive on sustained basis continuously engage themselves in restructuring their product-market strategies in sync with environmental developments. This is why there has been restructuring spree in corporate world during the last two decades. This restructuring has taken various forms.

As in corporate organization, commercial banks the world over have also undertaken restructuring programme of various kinds including mergers, acquisitions, transfers, etc. In fact, consolidation has come to be recognized as powerful source of improving competitiveness of banks because it enables the merging banks to achieve excellence in their operations through fuller utilization of skills and resources, melding complementary skills, cost savings through rationalization of operations, deep market penetration, diversification of risk and by way of strengthening their financial, technological, operational and organizational efficiencies.

Until recently, unsuccessful commercial banks in India had to be merged with successful banks at the behest by the RBI so as to protect the interests of the depositors. However, in recent few years, mergers between banks are taking place mainly to avail synergistic benefits and strengthen the competitive position of banks. This is for the fact that the management has realized the sordid truth that consolidation will make the institutions strong and robust and make them highly competitive in terms of productivity, cost effectiveness, better services and efficient risk management. The Government has also adopted policy of encouraging banks to voluntarily merge with others for gaining the muscle, size and scale and thus becoming global.

KEY TERMS

- Consolidation
- Core Banking Solution
- Financial Restructuring
- Manpower Restructuring
- Mergers
- Operational Restructuring
- Organisational Development
- Orgnisational Restructuring
- Strategy Restructuring

DISCUSSION QUESTIONS

1. What is corporate restructuring? Discuss various forms of corporate restructuring.
2. Why should a bank restructure its strategy?
3. How can consolidation serve as a powerful source of competitive advantage to a bank?
4. What has triggered restructuring of commercial banks in India?
5. In what respects does mergers of banks in recent years differ from the past?
6. What important factors should a bank take into account while acquiring other bank?
7. Discuss the role of regulatory authority in a merger decision.
8. Discuss, in brief, RBI policy towards merger of banks.

REFERENCES

1. http://economictimes.indiatimes.com/guide/verma3a.htm.
2. The HINDU, September 11, 2005.
3. Economic Times, June 20, 2005.
4. http://in.rediff.com/money/2004/nov/30merger.htm.
5. Business Line, October, 2006.
6. Times of India, January 31, 2005.
7. Business Line, October 6, 2005.
8. THE HINDU, May 29, 2005.
9. Business Standard, May 24, 2010
10. The Banker, London, July 2004.
11. P. Chidambaram, *Indian Banking: Realizing Global Aspiration*, IBA Bulletin, January 2005.
12. Business Standard, April 9/10, 2005.

Chapter II

Strategic Human Resource Management in Commercial Banks

Learning Objectives:

The present chapter attempts to provide:

- Familiarity with the relevance of human resource management to commercial banks.
- Shedding lurid light on new paradigms and perspectives of HRM in commercial banks in India.
- Providing a vivid view of how human resource strategy should be formulated for a commercial bank.

Chapter Outline:

A. INTRODUCTION

Human resource strategic management is concerned with the people dimension in management. Since enterprise is a system of people who interact, it has to depend on the people. Organisational success and survival, therefore, largely depend on how well the people in the organisation perform, *i.e.*, on how well human resources are managed.[1] How does an organization identify the types of people it needs and then convince them to join? What does it take to train them, to evaluate their performance, and to encourage them to stay with the organisation and contribute to its objectives? All these tasks fall within the realm of human resource strategic management.

The overall objective of human resource strategic management is to strike best match between people and organisation so as to contribute to the successful survival and growth of the organisation and help the people in achieving satisfaction of their economic and other needs. So as to accomplish this objective, human resource manager has to perform four strategic functions, *viz.*, acquisition, development, motivation and maintenance. Effective performance of these functions is inevitable in order to cope with bewildering complexity and paraxysm of business activity, technological advancement, increasing ferocity of competition, problem of low productivity and high cost and cataclysmic changes leading to change in profile of workers, their style of functioning, attitude towards management, towards work and themselves. This is possible only if fruitful alliance between corporate strategy and human resource management uniting the organisation's direction with that of its employees is made.[2]

B. RELEVANCE OF HUMAN RESOURCE MANAGEMENT TO COMMERCIAL BANKS

Significance of management and development of human resources is felt in all types of organisations like manufacturing, trading, services, etc. It gets added importance in service oriented organisations like banks which are considered wheels of social change for improvement of general standards of prosperity of the society along with public accountability. In a fast moving competitive environment unleashed by Government policy of liberalisation and globalisation, commercial banks will have to focus on customers for their successful functioning and survival. While charting out their future course of action, banks' management will have to remember that to get competitive edge over their rivals on sustaining basis five things are essential — increased productivity, improved quality, innovation in the market, a deep understanding of customer needs and delivery of world class service, and only one factor that could provide all these capabilities is 'knowledge' and human beings are the drivers of the knowledge juggernaut. As such, primary focus of strategic management approach of commercial banks will have to be on effective and efficacious utilisation of human resources. A strong sustained programme on HRD in proper perspective along with internal marketing can bring about the desired attitudinal change in the employees.

Post nationalisation period witnessed cataclysmic change in operations of Indian banking system. Apart from the quantitative dimensions of operations, the range and variety of functions handled by the banking system have been startling. The massive financial resources and unparalleled intensive branch network have often induced the authorities to impose ever increasing responsibilities on the banking system. The resilience of the banking system to adapt to the new responsibilities has further increased additional expectations. The commercial banks felt the exigency of setting up separate department of human resource management development to cope with the increased responsibilities in the mid-70s. However, HRM department geared itself to the needs of expansion through mass recruitment, mass promotions and mass training. Certain unhealthy developments such as increasing overtime, restrictive practices, excessive recruitment and union-activity during working hours, occurred during this period.

The decade of the 80s witnessed a phase of consolidation with greater thrust on internal house-keeping and lesser focus on branch expansion. The Government intervened to improve the state of human resource management in the banking industry. Thus, certain drastic steps such as stoppage of overtimes, introduction of job rotation scheme for the bank staff, freezing new financial benefits over and above industry level awards, compulsory rural and semi-urban postings and an embargo on recruitment, were taken. These measures led the bankers to look towards the government for any initiative in the area of HRM.

While response of the trade unions to the above interventions was lukewarm, employees at the grass root level reacted negatively leading to increased indiscipline, development of no work culture and non co-operation which, in turn, adversely affected productivity and profitability of the banks. Customer orientation among the bank employees has been sadly lacking. Unfortunately, the bank's management hardly did anything to bring about change in work culture, attitude and perception of employees and develop the desired competencies among them.

Consequent upon the wrenching changes affected in the financial sector in 1991, banking industry became highly competitive offering tremendous opportunities of business expansion and diversification nationally as well as globally along with threats from the emergence of new players in the industry. As a result, focus on customers increased. Bankers began to realise that a consistently high quality of customer service would be the key factor for any bank to survive in the competitive market. High quality customers' service requires invigorating work culture and highly motivated employees with customer focused attitude and mind frame and right kind of skills.

C. NEED FOR NEW PARADIGMS AND PERSPECTIVES IN HRM IN COMMERCIAL BANKS IN INDIA

Although commercial banks in India have been carrying out human resource functions, their efforts lacked strategic focus and customer orientation, using archaic techniques and limited skills to manage human resources. It is most intriguing to note that most of the banks' management do not understand what HRD is and what it should be and what its implications and significance are to their organisations. So far, HRD has been identified with training, that too it is unfocused HRD and treated as cost and not an investment. However, recent environmental compulsions, outlined below, necessitated new perspectives and new paradigms in HRM interventions to cope with changing environmental demands.

- In a deregulated and liberalised scenario, a bank can compete successfully in terms of innovation, quality of service, and proper perception of customer needs. All these can be provided by human resources which constitute both the source and conduit of knowledge. It is the knowledge about the customers' needs and bank competencies to meet these needs will help the bank to achieve competitive edge over its rivals. Effective HRD interventions can significantly help the bank to procure right kind of people and harness the intellectual capital within the organisation.
- HRD function is also receiving serious attention of the top management of banks because of increasing demand and growing sophistication of customers. Retention of customers has become the primary agenda before every bank because it has been proved that developing new customers is relatively a costly affair. In order to ensure customer loyalty, quality of interfacing with customers has to be improved remarkably because the scope of product, price and technology differentiation is very limited. It is the ability of the bank people to deliver prompt and courteous service that can improve the service. HRD practices can play useful role here by developing and motivating the employees.
- The new economic environment driven by market forces necessitates qualitative change in the range of service available from the banks and much greater emphasis on the speed of transactions. Simultaneously, technological support for management information systems and processing of information relevant for credit appraisal have to become an integral part of managerial and organisational reforms. Increased use

of information technology demands change in existing policies and practices of manpower planning, training and compensation, etc.

- In their efforts to survive and grow in the liberalised environment, commercial banks embarked on plans of launching new product, product diversification and automation of business. For this, new kinds of skills are required. Bank functionaries will need competencies to operate in ill defined and ever changing environment, deal with non-routine and abstract work process, to work in groups and to operate within expanding geographical and time horizons. This calls for restructuring existing training systems so as to gear it to new business strategies and goals. Skill upgradation will have to be accorded high priority in the training agenda of banks.
- In the competitive environment, banks will have to adopt marketing approach to attract and retain customers. They have to engage in strategic marketing exercises on continuing basis such as analysing opportunities, setting objectives, developing marketing strategies and formulating plans. Banks will have to be innovative and design the work organisations to respond to customer needs. All this requires not only a different kind of skill but change in attitude and a new mind frame at all levels of the bank and hence the need for new paradigms and perspectives in HRM function of Indian commercial banks.

The most pertinent issue, that cries out for change, is the rigidity of the human resource policy that is sapping the competitive vigour of the institutions. As a matter of fact, banking organizations, especially public sector, have been pursuing blinkered approach to managing human resources. From recruitment methods to wage settlements and the appointment of bank chiefs and senior executives, the entire edifice built after 1969 has become not simply outdated but also a cause for moral-crushing income inequalities. Government inaction on this count is matched by bank employees union's obstinate refusal to allow any winds of change to blow in.

At the recent Bancon Conference in Mumbai, Chiefs of PSBs discussed ways to increase productivity, introduce high-tech measure to increase efficiency and a bank-based wage system that would permit individual entities to fix wages to replace the existing industry-based settlement for every grade across banks. However, the idea has spooked the unions which were quick to shoot down the idea of wage fixation by individual banks. A performance-based, bank-based wage fixation process would reward employees on merit. Partly responsible for the sluggish services and inability of PSBs to attract talent at various levels has been the recruitment and compensation process cast in stone over the last four decades.

Trade Unions must realize that their present power to collectively bargain for the status quo flows from the lack of competition among PSBs. But core banking and Basel II norms that are infusing technology will increasingly make their position untenable; banks will simply not recruit certain categories of worker. Before that happens, the unions must leverage their present clout to introduce skill upgrades for appropriate employees and VRS for the rest. Resistance to technology is no longer possible. Employees would be better off joining hands with banks for a merit-based recruitment and wage policy. They would have a lot to gain and a lot more to defend.

If human resources have to be a powerful source of competitive advantage, Indian human resource managers have to act as lynchpin of the organization to reenergize business and enhance competitiveness through continuous value addition and minimization of slippage. They have not only to perform existing function of staffing, training and career development, compensation; performance appraisal and maintenance with new perspectives, new paradigms and innovative approaches and new skills but also to assume the role of strategic partners and participate actively in the front-end of strategic thinking and action, resource leveraging, change initiatives as also to act as an agent among various specialized agencies within and outside the organization.

D. HUMAN RESOURCE MANAGEMENT IN INDIAN BANKS AND RBI

According to the RBI, the central government's increasing interference in day-to-day operations in credit sanctioning, loan pricing and human resource issue is due to the fact that public sector banks lack management capacities. They do not have need-based recruitment planning nor proper performance management system. Commenting on the present decade as "retirement decade" for public sector banks, as lakhs of employees are set to retire by 2020, K.C. Chakraboarty Dr. Governor, RBI emphasized that the banks must formulate strategy to transform the HR processes and implement some new-age concepts.[3]

Emphasizing on acquiring the right people, Chakraborty questioned Banks' enthusiasm to recruit from major management institutions. He expressed his doubt if the people recruited from top management institutions understand the financial inclusion drive and have empathy towards poorest of the poor.[4]

It is important to note that while banks often talk about the challenge of finding people keen to work in rural areas, it is hardly reflected in the way they recruit people. Under the circumstances, it is advisable for banks to recruit people from smaller cities.

Public sector banks do not have proper mechanism of performance management which may lead to disastrous result. According to Chakraborty, "We are all having to deal with the problem of people who are 'promotable' but not 'postable' and people who are 'postable' but not getting promoted. This is because we have failed to discriminate performers and non-performers.[5]

As such, senior management of banks and the board need to spend more time on performance management. They should actively engage in formulating suitable human resource strategy for the bank along the line outlined below.

E. FORMULATING HUMAN RESOURCE STRATEGY FOR COMMERCIAL BANKS IN INDIA

While formulating human resource strategy for the bank, management need to pursue an integrated and multi-pronged approach to manage people. Human resource manager has to play more pragmatic, positive and broader role with electrifying effect.

In the changed environment, coalition of corporate vision with the individuals' aspirations is vitally imperative and it is the human resource manager who has to play crucial role in this respect by communicating the corporate vision to the people in the organisation. He has to strategise human resource function so that its various components are harmonised firmly with corporate strategy towards improving productivity, quality and customer satisfaction.

The above approach should be followed while formulating strategy in the area of acquisition, development, motivation and maintenance of human resources in the bank.

◈ Strategic Approach to Managing Human Resources

HR managers in banks have to perform the strategic human resource function so that its various components are harmonized firmly with corporate strategy towards improving productivity, quality and customer satisfaction.

HR managers playing an integral part of corporate management will have to coalesce human resource objectives and strategies with strategic intent and content of the organization. It is ineluctable for the HR managers to play the role of a coordinator and to concentrate corporate vision and objectives with individual's aspirations.

In conceptualization of the organization's future and determining how it intends to position itself and what it aspires to do to excel locally and compete globally, the top management must call upon the expertise and experience of the HR manager. The involvement of HR managers, who are supposed to be in close and constant touch with customers - external and internal — and are aware of their aspirations and needs and imbued with a perspicacious grasp of all contemporary trends, will help the organization in evolving need based vision by consensus.

In performance driven economy the most daunting task of Indian corporate managers is to contrive strategy on the basis of the concept of fit between opportunities and competencies and create markets that do not exist. They have to stretch beyond the resources available to them and creatively use them so as to develop on sustainable basis, new and innovative products of world class standards to cater to the extant as well as prospective market requirements at competitive price. All this is possible only if the organization has developed core competencies. Core competencies, according to Prahalad and Hamel, is the collective learning in an organization, especially how to coordinate diverse production skills and integrate multiple streams of technologies. It does not form part of physical asset of an organization; instead it is about leveraging the limited resources of a firm by stretching the imagination and aspirations of the people, both by creatively reshaping the way the organization competes. HR managers can play crucial role in creating and honing core competencies of firm through hiring and nurturing the talents, fostering innovation and creativity and inebriating entrepreneurship and encouraging employees to unabashedly embrace their dictum and unashamedly challenge the status-quo.

A strategic plan, howsoever sapient and sound it may be, will be of little value to the bank if it has not been implemented properly. In a melee of continued ups and downs, crests and toughs, key to success of an organization is how fast it can execute and how well it can adapt. While affectuating strategic decisions, top management has to create organizational arrangements that allow the bank to pursue its strategy most effectively through committing the people and the resources to the strategic choice. Efficacious implementation of corporate and business strategies calls for formulation of functional strategies, designing organizational structure and processes, developing plans and evolving management information and control systems. Effectiveness of strategy implementation demands determining clearly to what extent the organization will have to change so as to translate the strategy under consideration and manage the change process. HR manager has to play the role of a facilitator in meaningful implementation of various strategic decisions by carrying out HR activities and proactively handling people related business issues in sync with corporate objectives and strategies. The quality and content of HR services need to be improved to reenergize the business.

◆ Acquisition of Human Resources

HR managers will have to assume the responsibility of tailoring manpower planning to corporate objectives and strategies and drawing a long-term hiring programme so as to track down people endowed with knowledge, skills and behavior best suited to achieving corporate objectives. The recruitment process has to focus on acquisition of right people who could act as missionaries at management level and mercenaries at activity level.

Banks in India are currently facing an unusual manpower crunch mainly due to the outcome of slowdown in recruitment in the 1990s as of lack of retirement planning. A large number of people joined the banking sector in 1972-73 following the nationalisation of banks. The next wave of recruitment came to 1983-84, and then there was a lull in activity. For two decades additional manpower in banking sector was not commensurate with the growth. Thus, the entire decade of the 1990s saw virtually no recruitment. To add to trouble, in 2000, after computers were introduced at branches, a voluntary retirement scheme was launched to shed excess staff. Later, in the second half of 2000-10 when the country returned to the high growth path, recruitment failed to keep pace with business growth.

It is evident from the above that manpower planning in Indian banks is at present based on ad hoc assessment and horse trading due to the fact that work-norms and loads are non-existent or, at best, less definite. There are large differences across banks in the ratio of staff to various indicators of business activity. Excess staff is particularly pronounced in the administrative offices of banks such as Head Office, Zonal/Regional offices and in metropolitan branches. Rural and semi-urban branches remain understaffed. Consequent upon computerization, expansion of new business activities and diversification, manpower planning has to be tailored to corporate purpose and objectives and long-term hiring programme has to be drawn so as to track down people with knowledge, skills and behaviour best suited to achieving corporate objectives. The recruitment process has to focus on identifying people with incisive and creative bent of mind.

It will, therefore, be necessary to build up-to-date data on manpower in terms of competency gaps, talents, etc., work-out plan of acquisition of personnel with specialized skills, working out new job attributes for clerks and officers, chalking out plans for redeployment of staff from surplus to deficit pockets and relocation of staff as a result of computerization.

For fresh recruitment, banks should think of approaching universities particularly those offering course in bank management and conducting campus interviews to attract young specialists in bank management. Alternatively, they can pickup summer trainees from these institutions who can be put to work on real life projects and job offers can be made to those suiting the needs of the bank.

Recruitment of employees, particularly in the supervisory cadre of banks should lay thrust not only on functional expertise but also on attitudes and approaches that match the bank's objectives and cultures. As such, attributes like interests, disposition, attainments, general intelligence, special aptitudes and physical make-up need to be thoroughly glanced. For this purpose, banks may make use of psychographic testing techniques developed by renowned management institutes to prepare psychological profiles of the ideal candidates.

Further, written tests should be conducted to assess the candidates' result orientation, analytical ability, initiative and drive, communication skills and innovativeness. These tests should furnish as much information as possible to the employers to enable them to decide about suitability of a candidate for the job. Tests should be supported by multi-session comprehensive interview to explore various facets of an applicant under different circumstances and under varying degrees of pressure.

Most banks in India rely on management schools to supply fresh recruits but the RBI has questioned the rationale of hiring management graduates for financial inclusion as it believes such students will not be in tune with the problems of banking in far-flung areas.

◈ Development of Human Resources

In a service industry like banking, development of manpower resources assumes greater significance. Development is defined as a planned programme designed to improve performance and to bring about measurable changes in knowledge, skills, attitude and social behaviour of bank employees. It includes both training to enhance skill in performing a specific job, and education to increase general knowledge and understanding of total environment.

In view of banking organisations facing skill shortages and fierce competition from new players for existing experienced staff and new entrants of good calibre, and finding it extremely difficult to buy the required skills in the market place, it has become imperative for the PSBs to accord high priority to training of their employees so as to update their knowledge and competence and develop special skills of self directed leadership, self- motivated team work and self generated creativity.

At present, Indian banks offer training programmes mainly through their own staff training colleges and that of the RBI. These institutions seek to impart functional training by way of lectures, audio visuals, self directed learning, programmed instruction, etc. Though there is no dearth for faculty support on these aspects, trainees are of the opinion that theoretical exposure given to them by the bank's training institution is inadequate. There is, therefore, strong need to supplement the existing exercises by involving reputed management academics.

It will, therefore, be in the interest of a bank to link closely its training system to the corporate strategy. Training programme should so designed and developed as to make it performance oriented. It should address a broader market and the development of creative and innovative thinking in the organisation. Prominent on the agenda of today's and tomorrow's training programmes of the banks should be on developing an overall global business perspective as well as understanding of business strategy formulation and relationships between cross and functional strategies and multiskilling in cross functional areas. This will go a long way in retention of the employees and improving their marketability.

Behavioural training is also necessary to develop the soft skills of employees such as inter-personal communication, team work, innovations and leadership. Such type of training may take the form of games, role playing, simulation, case studies etc. Unfortunately, behavioural training has yet to find its place in staff training colleges of most of the PSBs.

With a view to ensuring that the newly recruited persons are contributing their best to the accomplishment of corporate objectives, HR manager of banks must devise and implement Tailor-made induction module, and holding up role models for them to emulate and the gradual process of indoctrination to familiarize the new recruits with corporate objectives, philosophy policics and procedures and develop attitudes suited to the culture of the organization. Almost all the senior managers should participate in these programmes to share the bank's vision, philosophy and culture.

Retraining should also form part of the training strategy of a bank. This involves unlearning old concepts and acquiring new skills. Retraining is necessary to the existing employees having no experience of working in competitive high tech areas.

◈ Motivating Human Resources

Acquisition of right kind of persons and their training and development do not necessarily ensure enhanced productivity and improved effectiveness of the bank. What is further required is to activate the potential of the employees. In fact, an employee's job performance is the function of his ability and willingness or desire to use his ability in achieving personal or organisational goals. This willingness or desire to act and to behave is what may be called motivation.

Sadly speaking, employees in Indian commercial banks are not motivated adequately. No systematic efforts have been made so far to induce employees to exert energy and effort at an acceptable rate. Banks' management have yet to realise that highly motivated employees are essential element in the success of the institutions.

The Khandelwal Committee in its report submitted in 2010 had suggested some drastic steps, such as performance linked pay on the lines of the private sector to attract talent to the PSBs and motivate them.

It would, therefore, be in fitness of things for the management to inspire the employees. Some of the strategies that have proved their utility in motivating the organisational people are given as under:

Managerial Communication

The most important strategy for bank managers is simply to communicate well with the organisational people. This satisfies such basic human needs as recognition, a sense of belonging and security.[6]

Theory X and Theory Y

Another motivating strategy involves a manager's assumptions about the nature of people. According to Douglas McGregor, Theory X involves negative assumptions which managers often use as the basis for dealing with their people. Theory Y represents positive assumptions which managers strive to use.[7]

The basic rationale for using theory Y rather than theory X in most situations is that managerial activities which reflect theory Y assumptions generally are more successful in satisfying human needs of most organisational members than are managerial activities that reflect theory X assumptions. As such, the bank's managers are advised to employ theory Y for motivating their employees.

However, Abraham H. Maslow in his book on European Management (new edition 1998) observed that different people have to be managed differently. He emphasized on the necessity of developing strategic relationships between employer and employees. Employees used to be managed in marketing way so that their aspirations, needs and values are accorded due consideration. To stay a step ahead of the aspirations of their people, companies have to do more than provide a stimulating work environment. While conventional training programmes may continue, organizations will need to look to keep talented employees enthused by continuously upgrading their knowledge and skills — set by way of cross — divisional transfers working with vendors, collaborating with competitors in the knowledge area and building emotional relations.

◈ Job Design

Two recent job design strategies, *viz.*, Job enrichment and Flexi Time are catching attention of enterprises. Job enrichment is the process of incorporating motivators into a job situation. The job content can be enriched in terms of providing higher responsibility, opportunity for achievement, opportunity for recognition, advancement and learning opportunities.

Thrust of Flexi-time strategy is on permitting employees to choose their own working hours within certain limitations. The choices of starting and finishing times can be as flexible as the organisation allows. To ensure that flexibility does not become counter productive within the organisation, many flexi-time programmes include a core period during which all employees must be on the job.

Flexi-time strategy has been found resulting in greater job satisfaction and increased productivity. It can also result in higher motivation levels of employees.[8] It may also help the management in attracting qualified people for the organisation.[9]

◈ Behaviour Modification

This strategy focuses on encouraging appropriate behaviour as a result of the consequences of that behaviour. According to the Law of Effect,[10] behaviour that is rewarded tends to be repeated and behaviour that is punished tends to be eliminated.

Behaviour modification strategy emphasises on ensuring that appropriate consequences occur as a result of that behaviour.[11] Positive reinforcement is a desirable consequence of a behaviour, and negative reinforcement is the elimination of an undesirable consequence of a behaviour. If an employee's arriving on time is positively reinforced, or rewarded, the probability increases that the employee will arrive on time more often. In addition, if the employee experiences some undesirable outcome on arriving late for work, such as a verbal reprimand, the employee is negatively reinforced when this outcome is eliminated by on-time arrival. Punishment is the presentation of an undesirable behaviour consequence or the removal of a desirable behavioural consequence that decreases the likelihood of the behaviour continuing.

In order to make behaviour modification programmes successful, it is necessary to give different levels of rewards to different employees depending on the quality of their performance, telling employees that they are doing wrong, punishing employees privately so as to avoid any embarrassment to them, and always give rewards and punishments when earned to emphasize that management is serious about behaviour modification efforts.[12]

Another strategic approach to motivating employees is to adopt the system of involving employees in decision making. Improvement, participation and ownership enlist employees commitment to the organisation.

◈ Maintenance of Human Resources

Commercial banks must give serious attention to the maintenance aspect of human resource management. It is primarily concerned with creation and maintenance of such working climate in the organisation as is necessary to attract the best people, retain them and inspire them to give their best.

The existing system of graded salary structure, fixed annual increments and automatic adjustments to inflation devoid of any rewards and recognition to really meritorious employees is now forcing many talented employees to look for greener pastures elsewhere. Entry of private and foreign banks in the banking field has opened a new vista of opportunities for high performers. PSBs have already started experiencing problem of retaining their highly experienced and specialised staff including senior managers.

In the changed environment, banks have to evolve new compensation system under which employee's reward will be linked to the corporate objectives by pegging it to the employee's contribution towards achieving them. Time has come to design a comprehensive reward system that splits employees' compensation between company standards, individual merit and team performance. Thus, the individual rewards should be linked not only to individual performance but also the divisional performance and overall corporate performance. A differential ratio may be adopted for each such factor, which varied for different ranks. For example, at the top level, individual performance may be given a weightage of 10-20 per cent, department performance again the same, whereas the weightage given to overall corporate performance may vary between 60-70 per cent. On the other hand, for an employee at the junior-most level, his own performance may get a weightage of 70-80 per cent and the performance of his department and overall corporate performance may be given a lesser weightage between 10-15 per cent in determining his pay packet and increments.

Banks will also have to provide for fast track promotions to talented and good performers. They should maintain a clear differentiation between the average performers and the stars. The difference between an average performer's bonus and others may be as much as 100 per cent. The laggards can even go without a bonus.

Narasimham Committee has rightly observed that "it would be necessary to reward specially skilled and talented persons of known merit with accelerated promotional opportunities if banks are to retain bright numbers of their staff and not lose them to competitors in financial services industry."

Further, banks should institutionalise non-monetary rewards. By honouring their employees' achievements, singling out outstanding performers and offering benefits to the families, the management can create a positive work culture in the bank and build loyalty.

F. CONCLUSIONS

Survival and sustained success of service organizations like banks depend essentially on how effectively their people are managed. This has gained prominence in the Indian banking system in recent years, especially after the embracement of new economic policy leading to increased competitiveness and the consequent focus on customer.

As such, a bank is expected to formulate suitable human resource strategy and follow integrated and multi-pronged approach to manage their people. It has to focus on acquisition of suitable human resources, train and develop them, and motivate them so that they contribute their best to the organization. Banks should also give serious attention to the maintenance aspect so as to attract the talented people and retain them.

In drawing up human resource plan and implementing it, human resource manager has to play crucial role. He has to play the role of a facilitator and carry out HR activities and proactively handle people related business issues in tandem with corporate objectives and strategies. The quality and content of HR services need to be improved to re-energise the banking business.

The RBI expressed its unhappiness on existing human resource management practices of public sector banks in India.

KEY TERMS

- Behavioural Modification
- Behavioural Training
- Flexi Time
- Job Enrichment
- Strategic approach to human resource management
- Theory X and Theory Y

DISCUSSION QUESTIONS

1. "In competitive environment, survival and success of a commercial bank depends on how it manages its human resources." Comment.
2. What prompted commercial banks in India to adopt new paradigms and perspectives of human resource management?
3. What is strategic approach to managing human resources in a bank?
4. How should a banker formulate its human resource strategy to cope with competitive business challenges?
5. How can a banker motivate its functionaries?
6. Describe the RBI's opinion about HR practices of public sector banks in India.

REFERENCES

1. Cynthin A. Lenguick, Hall and Mark L. Lenguick, Lenguick Hall, *Strategic Human Resource Management, A Review of the Literature and a Proposed Typology*, Academy of Management Review 3, No. 3, 1988, pp. 454-70.
2. Peggy Stuart, *HR and Operations Work Together at Texas Instruments*, Personnel Journal, 71, No. 4, April 1992, p. 64.
3. Business Standard, RBI for overhaul of banks, HR Practices, June 6, 2012.
4. *Ibid.*
5. *Ibid.*
6. Edwin Timbers, *Strengthening Motivation Through Communication*, Advanced Management Journal 31, April 1966, pp. 64-69.
7. Douglas McGregor, *The Human Side of Enterprise*, McGraw-Hill, New York, 1960.
8. Lee A. Graf, *An Analysis of the Effect of Flexible Working Hours on the Management Functions of the First-Line Supervisor.* (Ph.D. Thesis, Mississippi State University).
9. Jill Kanin — Lovers, "Meeting the Challenge of Workforce 2000", *Journal of Compensation and Benefits*, January/February, 1990, pp. 233-36.
10. E.L. Thorndike, "The Original Nature of Man," *Education Psychology* 1, 1903.
11. Fred Luthans and Robert Kreither, *Organisational Behaviour Modifications and Beyond*, Glenview, III, Scott, Foresman, 1985.
12. New Tool, Reinforcement For Good Work, *Psychology Today*, April 1972, pp. 68-69.

Management of Capital Funds in Commercial Banks

Chapter 12

Learning Objectives:

The present chapter attempts to:

- Provide an understanding of concept, functions and genesis of capital funds adequacy.
- Provide a detailed view of standards for measuring capital adequacy in a commercial bank.
- Provide an outline of Basel Committee framework on capital adequacy.
- Provide a vivid account of the capital adequacy norms in Indian commercial banks and the existing capital adequacy position.

Chapter Outline:

- Epilogue.
- Functions of capital funds in commercial banks.
- Genesis of adequacy of capital fund in a commercial bank.
- Concept of adequate capital fund.
- Standards for measuring capital adequacy in a commercial bank.
- Basel Committee and capital adequacy.
- Capital adequacy norms in Indian commercial banks.
- Present position of capital adequacy in Indian commercial banks.
- Conclusions.

A. EPILOGUE

The capital fund constitutes one of the sources of funds for a commercial bank. It represents owned resources, and includes the share capital subscribed by its shareholders as well as reserve built up by the bank by ploughing back a part of its business earnings. Survival and success of a bank depend on its strength which, in turn, infuses public confidence in it. Failure of individual banks, particularly large ones, might erode public confidence in the banking system. This is why regulators all over the world strive to minimise the magnitude and scope of bank failures by clamping minimum capital requirement for banks.

Management of capital funds entails risk-return trade off. Increasing level of capital fund reduces the risk of bank failure by acting as cushion against the losses but at the same time it reduces expected returns on equity, a measure that the investors focus on increasingly as the basis for valuing a bank's share.

As such, it is pertinent for the management to determine optimal size of the capital so as to maximise value of the bank without enhancing its liquidity.

B. FUNCTIONS OF CAPITAL FUNDS IN COMMERCIAL BANKS

Bank capital performs a number of functions which are discussed below:

◈ Bank Capital Acts as Loss Absorber

Like other businesses, a commercial bank needs capital to commence its operations, and to continue its existence as a running business. Commercial and industrial companies require capital initially to finance their operations and secondly to provide a bail-out for creditors or to cover possible losses. From the standpoint of a bank, the reverse is generally true. The primary role of bank capital is to act as a buffer. It provides a cushion to absorb possible losses so that depositors may be fully protected at all times. Although the capital fund is regarded as the absorber of losses arising from the realisation of assets and from other contingencies, yet this function can be fulfilled only in the extreme case of the liquidation of the bank. The true nature of the protection function of the capital fund is that it is the ultimate of final protection from the risk of insolvency. In the short run, a major portion of the bank's losses may be offset by its current earnings, not by its capabilities. Even in the long run, the capital fund may not fulfil the protective role because, if a bank had poor earnings, loses internal control and a large quantity of risk assets — symptoms of bank liquidation — the bank management (and perhaps the Central Bank also) would step in the long before the capital funds were severely impaired.

Thus, it would not be meaningful to look on the function of capital as a "cushion of excess assets with which to absorb losses and still remain solvent."[1] In fact, the real function of the capital fund is to inspire, enjoy and maintain the public confidence which enables the banks to continue in business and prosper. By instilling confidence in depositors, the capital fund helps the management to avert the costly situation of liquidation. It reassures both the depositors and the shareholders that banks are in a position to withstand whatever strains may be placed upon them.

In a recent decision, it was held that the primary function of the bank capital fund is to absorb the losses resulting from events that managerial foresight cannot be reasonably expected to anticipate. It should provide a margin of safety that preferably would allow a bank to continue operations without loss of momentum and, at the least, would buy time for it in which it may re-establish its operational momentum. Normal risks — risks that can be anticipated — should be covered by gross earnings and not by the capital fund.

◈ Bank Capital Supplies Working Tools of Banks

The secondary function of the capital funds is to provide the wherewithal for the acquisition of such fixed assets as buildings, equipment, furniture, etc. The provision of permanent assets is a continuous function of the bank capital fund, mainly because depositors cannot be expected to supply the funds for such assets, say a new branch building. Under conditions of expansion, therefore, the capital base must, of necessity, be strengthened in line with the expansion in the operations of the bank.

◈ Bank Capital Acts as Source of Loan Funds

Another important function of bank capital is the assurance that the bank will be able to fulfil the credit needs of the community and assume the risks inherent in its safety. In other words, there are certain types of investments for which borrowed funds may not be helpful; reliance is placed only on capital funds.

Bank capital represents the public and private ownership of commercial banks, which distinguishes these institutions from the mutual savings associations, co-operative banks, co-operative credit and thrift societies and the post office savings banks, etc., which compete with commercial banks for savings.

C. GENESIS OF ADEQUACY OF CAPITAL FUND IN A COMMERCIAL BANK

The need for adequate capital funds arises because of the following reasons:

- In a country like India, where other factors of public confidence, *viz.*, deposit insurance, banking inspection, sound management policies and the social status of bank management, have not been fully appreciated by the public, an adequate capital fund is indeed needed to bring about solidarity, scope, operation and the ultimate strength of the bank.
- A bank must have an adequate capital fund to cover the normal hazards inherent in its operations. It may have to incur unforeseen operational losses from time-to-time; some of its advances may turn out to be bad or doubtful, or there may be an unanticipated crash in the value of its assets, particularly its security investment. To provide for these contingencies, the bank must have an adequate capital fund. A strong equity base offers a measure of operational freedom to the bank. Since during phases of their expansion and diversification, banks need a greater operational freedom and are also susceptible to unforeseen risks, strengthening of the capital base under such conditions is the *sine qua non* for the maintenance of their strength. The adequacy of the capital fund assumes further importance in the context of a restrictive monetary policy. An increase in the bank rate brings about losses in the value of government securities and bonds. Consequently, banks might face a shrinkage in the value of their assets. Banks with sufficient capital funds might find it easy to absorb this shock.
- There is a strong element of public and social responsibility, for a commercial bank must provide for the nation's credit requirements, and meet the credit risk. Adequate capital funds enable banks to discharge this responsibility. In a country wedded to rapid economic development, there is likely to be a great pressure on the banking sector to finance growing industry and trade. Banks have to make intensive efforts to garner the savings of the community through branch expansion and by increasing the range and efficiency of their services. Their ability to discharge successfully this increasing responsibility depends upon the success with which they are able, on the one hand, to finance the physical and working tools needed for branch expansion and, on the other, to sustain and increase the confidence of their depositors and protect their interests. Moreover, banks have to depend upon their own funds (capital

funds) to finance the working tools and other physical assets. Public confidence is the outcome of an adequate capital fund.

- In a country like ours, adequate capital is necessary to secure the permission of the Reserve Bank of India to open a new branch. According to Section 23 of the Banking Companies Act, 1949, the Reserve Bank of India must be satisfied, among other things, that the capital fund of the bank is adequate. It may withhold all the facilities from the bank which has an insufficient capital.

D. CONCEPT OF ADEQUATE CAPITAL FUND

To define the adequacy of bank capital funds is not an easy job. As a matter of fact, the capital fund of a banking system may not be judged as adequate or inadequate on any *priori* ground.[2] "The more capital, the better" is not the answer to the question. It is question of "how much capital" and for "what purposes." The depositors may favour the maximum amount of capital fund so that the bank may be able to absorb all the losses and the risks which may occur; they would in that case be fully protected. On the other hand, the stockholders may like the bank to operate with the minimum capital, since an excessive amount of capital fund prevents them from earning any reasonable return on the investment. Thus, there is a conflict in the interest of shareholders and depositors. However, this conflict is not as sharp as it appears. The reason is not far to seek. Profitability has also an element of depositors' interest because they expect the shareholders to assume all the risks, and profits serve as a reward to the owners for risk bearing. Likewise, it is in the interest of the shareholders to combine profitability with safety because, in the long run, their shareholdings will remain profitable only if the business continues to exist and prosper, which itself is possible if the banker enjoys public confidence.

As already observed, public confidence is essentially a function of the safety of deposits in the bank. The adequacy of capital funds should, therefore, be determined by effecting a compromise between related but partly antagonistic considerations. This compromise should be brought about in the light of the character of the assets, the liabilities, other than corporate liabilities, and the management. It is also important to consider the history and future prospects of the bank, its customers and the community it serves. The determination of adequate capital is, therefore, a complex problem. It is imprecise and requires a considerable exercise of judgement. However, the necessary exercise of sound judgement can be aided by an objective examination of the factors that should be taken into account; and, over a period of years, various approaches to the problem have been developed and used for this purpose. Before examining these approaches, it would be in the fitness of things to give an account of the legal provisions governing an adequate capital fund.

E. STANDARDs FOR MEASURING CAPITAL ADEQUACY IN A COMMERCIAL BANK

A number of criteria have been devised to determine capital adequacy. Important among these are the ratio of paid-up capital to reserves, the capital-deposit ratio, the risk-asset ratio, and the adjusted risk-asset ratio.

◆ Ratio of Paid-up Capital to Reserve

The size of the reserve of banks in relation to their paid-up capital is an important index of their financial position and strength. It is also a pointer to the management policy regarding the retention of earnings. Since the banks carry on their business mainly with the depositors' funds, an increase in the paid-up capital may not keep pace with that in the reserve. The reserve is expected to follow a rising trend because it is created out of current earnings; the management policy with respect to dividend would, of course, decide the quantum of profits to be retained every year. This measure is simple; but it cannot determine capital adequacy. The very purpose of measuring capital adequacy is to judge whether bank capital is sufficient to absorb the losses. The ratio of reserve to paid-up capital fails to serve this purpose. It does not shed any light on the magnitude of losses to be protected.

◈ Capital-Deposit Ratio

The capital-deposit ratio was very frequently used in the past in the USA and the UK to measure capital adequacy. The banking authorities in India have also considered the adequacy of capital in relation to deposit liabilities. A high capital-deposit ratio is indicative of the fact that the depositors will incur low risks. It has been recognised by some authorities that, with every decline in the ratio of capital to deposits, the risks of depositors tend to increase sharply.

In the 1920s, a rule-of-thumb was developed in the USA, that a bank should have a capital fund which is equal to 10 per cent of its deposit liabilities. It was felt that banks operating on this relationship of capital funds to deposits would be sufficiently profitable to attract the necessary capital by the sale of capital stock. Second, a ratio of lower than 10 per cent would result in a bank operating on too narrow a margin of safety. This ratio came to be widely used and was frequently mentioned as a satisfactory measure for judging capital adequacy.

Though this ratio had the virtue of simplicity, it did not measure the quality and amount of assets in which deposits were invested. According to R.J. Robinson, there can be no scientific basis for this particular ratio; simply a good, round decimal, easy to calculate at a glance. Deposits in themselves contain no risk until they are used to make loans and investments; and the extent of the risk varies with the character of the assets into which deposits are converted.

In the above measures, size of capital is determined independently of the risk profile of individual banks. The regulators stipulated minimum capital to assets ratio but did not pay much attention on quality, riskiness of banks' asset portfolio. Such stipulation enabled two banks of the same asset size to operate with the same amount of capital, irrespective of their risk profiles. The capital requirements imposed no constraint on risk taking, other than limiting growth, when banks felt under pressure to increase earnings in the wake of declining net interest margin due to increased competition and development of substitute products to banks loans and growing distintermediation process with borrowers accessing the securities market for raising funds.

In view of the above, other methods based on relationship between capital and assets of banks were evolved to measure the capital adequacy.

◈ Capital-Assets Ratio

This was conceived as the ratio of capital funds to total assets less cash and investments in government securities. A ratio of 1 : 5 or a risk-asset ratio of 20 per cent was originally considered to be sufficient. A study made by the Illinois Bankers' Association found that the required amount of capital depends upon:

(*i*) The amount of assets subject to risk; and

(*ii*) The extent of risk.

The amount of capital bears no relationship to the amount of deposits, and there is no uniform risk in relation to deposits. The study suggested that each bank review its experience with various kinds of assets during the depression years; and, on the basis of that experience, establish the percentages of capital required for each class of assets.

The above method is ideal for an individual bank. But this has been found to be too complex for practical use by most of the banks, for it calls for an in-depth and time consuming analysis of each assets. Moreover, it fails to provide any norm that may apply to all the banks because each bank's evaluation of its risks would probably differ from that of another.

◈ Adjusted Bank-Assets Ratio

This is an improved version of the risk-assets approach. It came to be widely used by the supervisory authorities in the U.S.A. as one of the tests of capital adequacy. It related capital funds to risk assets, but excluded from the total assets such items, as cash, investments in government securities carrying a maturity period of five years, and loans guaranteed by the government or government agencies. A ratio of 1:6 or $16^2/_3$ per cent was considered as a standard. A slightly higher proportion of risk assets was tolerated if all the other factors were found to be favourable. Undoubtedly, this approach is superior to the other methods of measuring capital adequacy. However, it is not free from certain pitfalls. To ascertain whether a particular asset is risk-free or not is a difficult job. The assets considered to be "riskless" may not be always free from risk. Government securities, for example, do possess a money risk, although the credit risk may be non-existent. Even among risk assets, the extent of risks is not uniform because all the assets may not carry the same amount of credit risk.

The Federal Reserve Bank of New York attempted to indicate the dollar amount of minimum capital funds required by an individual bank on the basis of its own assets distribution. The amount of capital funds thus arrived at is the minimum for a bank, for which all the other factors are favourable. For the purpose of this analysis bank assets were classified in six broad groupings:

(*i*) Primary and secondary reserves;
(*ii*) Minimum risk assets;
(*iii*) Portfolio assets;
(*iv*) Sub-standard and specially mentioned assets;
(*v*) Workout assets;
(*vi*) Fixed assets.

To each of these six categories, a specific capital requirement was assigned, which was large enough not only to absorb probable losses in each category of assets, but to provide enough capital to maintain the authorities' confidence and keep the bank open. Against the capital requirements thus computed, the book capital funds were taken, less estimated losses and half of assets classified as doubtful, plus unused or excess valuation reserves. The capital funds of 25 per cent in excess of the minimum were considered a desirable standard.

The board of governors of the Federal Reserve System developed a similar approach to capital adequacy, which combined the capital adequacy test with the liquidity test, requiring more capital for banks which were less liquid. Bank assets were categorised in eight groups; each group was assigned capital funds ranging from ½ per cent on money market paper to 100 per cent on a fixed asset. The liquidity requirements were put at 47 per cent for demand deposits and 33 per cent for time deposits. Any deficiency is called for additional capital funds to allow for possible loss on the liquidation of the portfolios assets in fully satisfying the computed liquidity requirements.

◈ Primary Capital-to-Risk Ratio

A new ratio has been proposed jointly by The United States and the United Kingdom in February 1987 to evaluate the adequacy of commercial bank capital.

This ratio attempted to measure the capital adequacy by relating the bank's adjusted primary capital to its weighted risk assets. Primary capital here refers to that part of capital fund which should be freely available to absorb current losses while permitting an organisation to function as a going concern. Primary capital would thus consist of two classes of capital funds base — primary capital and limited primary capital. The latter would be limited to a specified percentage of base primary capital.

The base primary capital funds would comprise equity share capital, general reserves for unidentified losses, and minority interests in the equity accounts of consolidated subsidiaries. Other capital instruments would be qualified as limited primary capital to the extent the total does not exceed 50 per cent of tangible base primary capital, *i.e.*, base primary capital reduced by intangible assets. Limited primary capital funds would include perpetual preferred stock, limited life referred stock with an original maturity of at least 25 years, and certain debt that is subordinated to deposits. To qualify, subordinated debt must be unsecured, repayable only with equity similar debt, and convertible to equity if other capital is depleted. It must also permute deferral of interest payments during periods of financial distress.

To determine the weighted risk assets, each of the bank's assets would be assigned to one of five risk categories and weighted according to the relative risk of that category. The determination of asset groupings and the assignment of weights primarily would reflect credit risks considerations, with some sensitivity to liquidity and interest rate risk. The categories would distinguish among broad classes of obligors and to a lesser extent, among maturities and types of collaterization.

A credit equivalent approach would be used in weighing the risk of off-balance sheet activities. Under this approach, the face amount of an off-balance sheet exposure would be multiplied by a credit conversion factor, and the resulting credit equivalent amount would be assigned to the appropriate risk category as if it were a balance sheet item. Assets collateralized by cash or U.S. Government securities would be accorded a lower risk weight, but the approach would not explicitly recognize other forms of collateral or guarantees in weighing asset risk.

F. BASEL COMMITTEE AND CAPITAL ADEQUACY

Consequent upon economic liberalisation and fast changing technology, competitiveness in financial markets increased ferociously, both nationally as well as globally resulting into blurring of dividing lines among financial intermediaries. The major financial intermediaries have become growingly global in geographical coverage and universal in their financial operations, encompassing a wide range of activities including banking, securities markets activities and insurance activities. The increased competition and difficult financial conditions in the early 1980s put downward pressure on profit margins and capital adequacy ratios. The growing concern of commercial banks regarding international competitiveness and capital adequacy ratios led to the formulation of the Basel Accord of 1988.

The Committee on Banking Regulations and Supervisory Practices had in July 1988, released the agreed framework on International Convergence of capital measures and capital standards. The Committee adopted risk assets approach which assigns weights to both on and off balance sheet exposure of a bank according to their perceived risk as a method of measuring capital adequacy. Salient features of the capital accord were:[3]

- Minimum Capital requirement for banks was linked by formula to credit risk as determined by the composition of their assets. The greater the credit risk, the higher the regulatory capital required.
- The minimum capital to risk weighted assets ratio (CRAR) was set at 8 per cent.
- It defined capital in two tiers: Tier 1 and Tier 2. Tier 1 capital (core capital) representing the most permanent, should be at least 4% of the risk weighted assets. The Tier 2 capital, which is less permanent in nature, would be limited to 100% of Tier I capital.
- The regulatory capital requirements were standardized between countries to 'level playing field' so that the banks in one country may not have competitive advantages over banks in other countries due to divergent capital adequacy measures across the countries.
- A four-step process was to be followed by big banks for computing the CRAR.
  (*i*) Classify on-balance sheet assets into one of four risk categories.

(*ii*) Convert off-balance sheet exposures into credit equivalent amounts using the prescribed multipliers and then classify the converted amounts into appropriate risk categories.

(*iii*) Multiply the amount of assets in each risk category by the appropriate risk weight to arrive at risk weighted assets.

(*iv*) Divide the total capital or Tier 1 capital by the risk weighted assets to arrive at CRAR and core CRAR, respectively.

Thus, the Basel I Framework was designed to establish minimum levels of capital for internationally active banks. However, its simplicity encouraged over 100 countries across the world to not only adopt the Basel I Framework but also apply in across the entire Banking segment without restricting it to the internationally active banks. The voluntary adoption of Basel I Framework by several countries has made it, defacto, a globally accepted standard, though not all countries are fully compliant with all the aspects.

◈ The New Basel Norms on Capital Adequacy (BASEL COMMITTEE NORMS II)

Although the Basel norms helped to arrest the erosion of bank's capital ratios, apprehensions were expressed regarding the applicability of capital adequacy ratios in the changed environment of operations. The rule of "one-size-fits-all" approach of Basel I recognized only credit risk without considering market, operational and liquidity risks and was confined to a broad-band categorization of credit exposures without distinguishing between differing risk profiles and risk management standards across risk weights, and so on.

As such, it was not found adequate to hedge against failure. Further, it was noted that most of the banks did not hold actual capital much above the Basel minimum norm. All these led to the amendment in the accord of the Basel Committee on Banking Supervision in 1996.

In view of significant changes in the business of banking, risk management practices, supervising approaches and financial markets, the Basel Committee on Banking Supervision (BCBS) brought out their consultative paper on new Capital Adequacy Framework in June 1999 and a second revision in January, 2001 after an informed public debit with a view to turning the capital adequacy framework to fast paced changes in the institutional structure and to address the dissatisfaction with the 'one-size-fits-all' tenet of the capital adequacy ratio requirements. The new rules were expected to take effect by 2005.

The Accord[4] rests on the three pillars of (*i*) minimum capital requirements; (*ii*) Supervisory Review Process; and (*iii*) market discipline. While the current definition of capital and the minimum requirement of per cent of capital to risk weighted assets has been retained, the revised accord was extended on a consolidated basis to holding companies of banking groups and would refine the measurement of risk. While retaining the measurement of market risk, the Accord emphasizes the measurements of operational risk and credit risk (either by the standardized or the internal rating-based (IRB) approaches). In case of the standardized approach, although the risk measurement would be the same, there would be four categories for claims on corporates — 20 per cent, 50 per cent, 100 per cent and 150 per cent - of risk weightage as against the present single uniform risk weight of 100 per cent.

The second pillar would seek to ensure that each bank has sound internal process in place to assess the adequacy of financial modelling techniques to the prescription of capital adequacy.

The new framework focuses on the importance of bank management in developing an internal capital assessment process and setting targets for capital which are commensurate with the bank's particular risk profile and control environment. Supervisors would be responsible for evaluating how well the banks are assessing the capital adequacy needs relative to their risks. The internal processes would then be subjected to supervisory review and intervention, when appropriate. Supervisors are expected to evaluate how well banks are assessing their capital needs relative to their risks and to intervene where appropriate.

The four basic and complimentary principles on which the pillar 2 rests are: (*a*) A bank should have a process for assessing its overall capital adequacy in relation to its risk profile as well as a strategy for maintaining its capital levels. (*b*) Supervisors should review and evaluate a bank's internal capital adequacy assessment and strategy as well as its compliance with regulatory capital ratios (*c*) Supervisors expect banks to operate above the minimum regulatory capital ratios and should have the ability to require banks to hold capital in excess of the minimum; and supervisors should seek to intervene at an early stage to prevent capital from dipping below prudential levels.

Implementation of pillar 2 requires that a comprehensive assessment of risks be carried out by both the banks (internally) and the supervisors (externally). Banks and Supervisors need to focus on key risks which are not directly addressed under pillar I. Some of the key issues are: (*i*) interest rate risk in banking book; (*ii*) residual risk; (*iii*) credit concentration risk.

The third pillar aims as bolstering market discipline through enhanced disclosure by banks. This is essential to ensure that market participants can better understand bank risk profile and the adequacy of their capital position. The new framework sets out disclosure requirements in several areas, including the way in which banks calculate their capital adequacy and their risk assessment methods.

The new accord is expected to foster a healthy market-based banking system. The advanced risk management techniques could pose a challenge to the emerging economies, especially given the lack of adequate supervisory skills and the need to shift scarce supervisory resources away from direct supervision towards implementation of these specified proposals.[5]

The Basel Committee on Banking Supervision (BCBS) released the Third Consultative paper on the new Basel Capital Accord (Basel II) in July, 2003. The following significant modifications were made in the new accord.[6]

- Fully secured lending will now receive a 35 per cent risk weighting instead of the earlier 40 per cent.
- A minimum Loss Given Defaults (LGDs) value of 10 per cent is proposed for retail exposures secured by mortgages.
- As an alternative to standard or own estimate haircuts for repo style transactions the method of value at risk (VaR) has been continued.
- Advanced and Foundation Internal Rating based (IRB) approaches are presently available for high volatility commercial real estate lending.
- A revolving retail exposures risk weight curve has been recalibrated in the light of the operating results.
- An alternative standard operational risk approach has been developed.

The New Basel Capital Accord popularly known as Basel II, came to be operationalized some time around end 2006. The Accord represented the convergence of research and practice in supervision it attempts to apply state-of-the art.

Basel II provides options for banks and banking systems to determine the capital requirements for credit and operational risks and enables banks / supervisors to select appropriate approaches for their operations and financial markets. At the same time, the new capital framework will help to ensure that capital supervision continues to serve as a corner stone to safety and soundness in the banking system. Both results will help to make banks resilient, less sensitive to the ups and downs of the business cycle, and better able to serve as a source of credit and growth for businesses and consumers.

The implementation of the risk policy principle is fraught with difficulties. Reviewing and monitoring of collateral in terms of appropriate valuation, maintenance of margins and shortfalls and examining limits to different business are also called for.

While Basel–II better aligns regulatory capital with actual risk, it transcends regulatory compliance to provide banks an opportunity to achieve distinctive competitive advantage by adroit risk management. The Basel - II recommendations which are more risk-sensitive, would impact capital requirements, profitability, risk management, borrowers, rating agencies, technology and asset quality in different ways.

Implementation of Basel - II guidelines calls for vastly improved IT architecture for business decisions and to cope appropriately with the Pillar 3 disclosure requirements. Most banks will have to streamline risk management system, evolve prudent asset liability mix, to have adequate capital provision, transparency and disclosure norms.

The Executive Board of the IMF feels that premature adoption of Basel II in countries with limited capacity could inappropriately divert resources from the more urgent priorities, ultimately weakening rather than strengthening supervision. They are of the firm opinion that countries should give priority first to strengthening their financial systems comprising institutions, markets and infrastructure and focus on achieving greater level of compliance with the Basel core principles.[7]

In the wake of financial crisis, the Basel Committee on Banking Supervision (BCBs) initiated several post-crisis reform measures mainly building on the Basel II capital adequacy framework. The framework was bolstered significantly in July 2009 through a series of enhancements to each of the three pillars; notably to address the under capitalisation of trading book exposure of banks. Subsequently, in December 2010, the BCBs released revised set of rules for capital and liquidity regulations, *viz.*, 'Basel III: A Global regulatory framework for more resilient banks and banking systems' and 'Basel III: International Framework for liquidity risk measurement, standards and monitoring' which inter alia aim at promoting a more resilient banking sector and strengthening liquidity regulations. Collectively, the revised Basel II capital framework and the new global standards are commonly referred to as "Basel III".[8]

Though Basel III can be viewed as a modification to Basel II framework, it differs significantly from Basel II in terms of its comprehensiveness. More particularly, apart from revising the definition of regulatory capital, it is much wider in risk coverage and encompass measures to address the systemic risks. Implementation of Basel III has thrown up significant challenges to both banks and the banking supervisors alike.

G. CAPITAL ADEQUACY NORMS IN INDIAN COMMERCIAL BANKS

In India, the Basel I Framework on capital adequacy norms was implemented with effect from 1992-93 which was, however, spread over three years - banks with branches abroad were required to comply fully by end March, 1994 while the other banks were required to comply by end March, 1996. The RBI introduced in April, 1992 a risk weighted assets ratio system for banks (including foreign banks) in India as a capital adequacy norms. The salient feature of this measure were:

- The balance sheet assets, non-funded items and other off balance sheet exposures were assigned weight according to the prescribed risk.
- Capital was defined in two tiers — Tier 1 and Tier 2. Tier 1 capital (core capital) meant paid-up capital, statutory reserves, other disclosed free reserves, capital reserves representing surplus arising out of sale proceeds of assets. Equity investment in subsidiaries, intangible assets and losses in the current period and those brought forward from previous periods, would be deducted from Tier 1 capital.

Tier 2 of the capital would consist of:

(*a*) Undisclosed reserves and cumulative perpetual preference shares;

(*b*) Revaluation of reserves;

(*c*) General Provisions and loss reserves;

(*d*) Hybrid debt capital instruments;

(*e*) Subordinated debt.

For Tier 2 capital the revaluation of fixed assets done by banks for capital adequacy purpose was to be discounted by nearly 55% as against 25% earlier.

RBI devised uniform discounting norms for calculating all scheduled commercial banks' capital adequacy ratio on account of subordinated debt instruments by 100% of the remaining maturity period of less than one year, discount rate would be 80% when the remaining maturity period for less than two years but more than one year, 60% for less than 3 years, 40% for less than 4 years and 20% between 4 years to less than 5 years.

- For these banks having branches abroad, the risk weighted assets ratio of 8% was to be achieved as early as possible and in any case by 31st March, 1995. Other banks were to achieve a capital adequacy norms of 4% by 31st March, 1993 (Tier 1 capital should not be less than 50% of total capital) and the 8% norm in full by 31st March, 1996.
- Foreign banks were to achieve the norm of 8% by 31st March, 1993.
- Risk adopted assets would mean weighted aggregate of funded and non-funded items. The aggregate would be taken into account for reckoning the minimum capital ratio.
- The weights allotted to each of the items of assets and off-balance sheet items were:

◈ Funded Risk Assets of Percentage Weight

(*i*) Cash, balances with RBI, balances with other banks, money at call and short-notice and investments in Government and other trustee securities = 0.

(*ii*) Claims (funded or non-funded) on commercial banks, such as certificates of deposits, etc. = 20.

(*iii*) Other investments = 100.

(*iv*) Investments in subordinated debt instruments or bonds issued by Banks or Financial Institutions for Tier 2, Capital = 20.

(*v*) Loans guaranteed by Government of India, banks, loans to staff members = 0.

(*vi*) Loans guaranteed by State Governments = 100.

(*vii*) Others = 100.

(*viii*) Advances guaranteed by DICGC or ECGC = 50.

(*ix*) Rediscounting of discounted bills accepted by banks or loans due from banks or bills negotiated under LCs of other banks = 20.

(*x*) Premises = 100.

(*xi*) Other Assets = 100.

◈ Off-Balance Sheet (Non-funded) Items

The credit risk exposure attached to off-balance sheet items has to be first calculated by multiplying the face amount of each of the off balance sheet items by the credit conversion factor as given below. This would then have to be again multiplied by the weights attributable to the relevant counter-party as specified above.

◈ Instrument/Credit and Conversion Factor

1. Conversion factor for LC is 20%, for guarantee 50% and financial guarantees and acceptances and endorsements 100%.
2. Direct credit substitutes or financial guarantees, e.g., general guarantees of indebtedness and acceptances = 100.
3. Certain transactions-related contingent items, e.g., performance bonds, bid bonds, warranties and standby letters of credit related to particular transactions = 50%.
4. Short-term self liquidating trade-related contingencies such as documentary credits collateralized by the underlying shipments = 20%.

5. Sale and repurchase agreement and assets sales with recourse, where the credit risk remains with bank = 100%.
6. Forward asset purchase, forward deposits and partly paid shares and securities, which represent commitment with certain draw down = 100%.
7. Note issuance/revolving underwriting facilities = 50%.
8. Other commitments, *e.g.*, formal standby facilities and credit lines, with an original maturity of over one year = 50%.
9. Similar commitments with an original maturity upto one year or which can be unconditionally cancelled at any time = 0%.
10. Foreign exchange contracts original maturity of 14 days or less = 20%.

In this connection, it may be noted that cash margin or deposit shall be deducted before applying the conversion factor. After applying the conversion factor, the adjusted off balance sheet value shall again be multiplied by the weight attributable to the relevant counterparts as specified in domestic operations.

In 1996, the RBI laid down strict prudential norms for weak public sector banks that failed to attain the 8% capital adequacy target before March 31, 1996 deadline. Over half a dozen nationalised banks missed the target. The RBI imposed three major conditions as a measure of prudence:

(*a*) A complete curb on capital expenditure.
(*b*) Strict control over further growth in risk-weighted assets.
(*c*) A complete bank on fresh recruitment of personnel at all levels.

In a circular notified in April 1998, RBI indicated that investments in bonds and debentures where payment of interest and principal was guaranteed by Central or State Government and investments in Indira Vikas Patra, Kisan Vikas Patra would carry zero risk weight while calculating capital adequacy. Other investments would carry 100% risk.

So as to strengthen the capital base of the banking system in order to cope with any additional risk factor, the monetary and credit policy of October 1998 directed banks to achieve a minimum capital adequacy ratio of 9 per cent by March 31, 2000.

◈ Implementation of Basel II Norms in India

India responded to the 1996 amendment to the Basel I framework, which required banks to maintain capital for market risk exposures, by initially prescribing various surrogate capital charges for these risks between 2002-2003. These were replaced with the capital charges as required under the Basel I framework in June 2004, which became effective from March 2005. India has gone a step further than the Basel I requirement and the banks have been required to maintain capital charge for market risks on their 'Available for sales' portfolio also with effect from March, 2006. Thus, the RBI pursued a policy of gradualism in harmonizing its regulations with the global standards.[9]

The RBI directed its policy of conforming to the best international standards and in the process, the emphasis on gradual harmonization with the international best practices, all commercial banks to start implementing Basel II from March 31, 2007 — though a marginal stretching beyond this date should not be ruled out in view of the latest indications on the state of preparedness.

The RBI undertook the following steps for implementation of Basel II norms:[10]

- The RBI announced in its annual policy statement in May, 2004 that banks in India should examine in depth the options available under Basel II and draw a road-map by end - December, 2004 for migration to Basel II and review the progress made at quarterly intervals.

- The RBI organized a two-day seminar in July, 2004 mainly to sensitize the CEOs of banks to the opportunities and challenges emerging from the Basel II norms.
- Soon thereafter all banks were advised in August, 2004 to undertake a self-assessment of the various risk management systems in place, with specific references to the three major risks covered under the Basel II and initiate remedial measures to update the systems to match up to the minimum standards prescribed under the new framework.
- Banks were also advised to formulate and operationalize the Capital Adequacy Assessment Process (CAAP) as required under Pillar II of the new framework.
- The RBI issued a Guidance Note on operational risk management in November, 2005, which serves as a benchmark for banks to establish a specific operational risk management framework.
- The RBI tried to ensure that the banks have suitable risk management framework oriented towards their requirements dictated by the size and complexity of business, risk philosophy, market perceptions and the expected level of capital.
- Risk Based Supervision (RBS) in 23 banks was introduced on a pilot basis.
- As per normal practice, and with a view to ensuring migration to Basel II in a non-disruptive manner, a consultative and participative approach was adopted for both designing and implementing Basel II. A steering committee comprising senior officials from 14 banks (Public, private and foreign) was constituted wherein representation from the Indian Banks' Association (IBA) and the RBI was ensured.

The Steering Committee had formed sub-groups to address specific issues. On the basis of recommendations of the steering committee, draft guidelines to the banks implementation of the New capital Framework have been issued.

- The RBI set up a group for implementation of Pillar II. The group consists of three sub-groups on the internal capital adequacy assessment process, supervisory review and evaluation process and supervisory review process for securitization. Pillar II is meant not only for ensuring adequate capital to support all the risks in a bank but also to encourage banks to adopt better risk management.

With a view to ensuring smooth transition to the revised framework and providing an opportunity to streamline their systems and strategies, the RBI issued the following guidelines:[11]

- Banks in India shall adopt the Standardized Approach for credit risk, and the Basic Indicator Approach for operational risk for computing their capital requirements under the revised framework. Banks shall continue to apply the Standardized Duration Approach for computing their capital requirements for market risk.
- Foreign banks operating in India and Indian banks having operational presence outside India should adopt the revised framework with effect from March 31, 2008. All other commercial banks are encouraged to migrate to the revised framework in alignment with them, but in any case not later than March 31, 2009.
- Banks are required to maintain capital to risk weighted assets ratio (CRAR) of 9 per cent on an ongoing basis. However, taking into account the relevant risk factor and internal capital adequacy assessments of each bank, the RBI may prescribe a higher level of minimum capital ratio to ensure that the capital held by a bank is commensurate with its overall risk profile.
- Banks are required to maintain, at both solo and consolidated level, a minimum Tier I ratio of atleast 6 per cent. Banks below this level must achieve this ratio on or before March 31, 2010.
- The minimum capital maintained by banks on implementation of Basel II norms shall be subject to a prudential floor computed with reference to the requirement as per Basel I framework for credit and market risks. The floor has been fixed at 100 per cent, 90 per cent and 80 per cent for the position as at end March for the first three years of implementation of the revised framework.

- With a view to ensuring smooth transition to the revised framework and providing opportunity to banks to streamline their systems and strategies, banks were advised to have a parallel run for the revised framework.
- Banks may use the credit ratings awarded by the following four credit rating agencies for assigning risk weights for credit risk for capital adequacy purposes, *viz.*, Credit Analysis and Research Ltd., CRISIL Ltd., Fitch India and ICRA Ltd., Banks are allowed to use the credit ratings of following three international rating agencies: Filch, Moody's and Standard and Poor's.
- Claims on domestic sovereigns (Central and State Government) will attract a zero risk weight while those guaranteed by State Governments will attract 20 per cent risk weight.
- Risk weights for claims on banks will be linked to the capital adequacy position of the counter party bank. Scheduled and other banks will receive a differential treatment.
- Claims on corporates will be risk weighted as per the ratings awarded by the chosen rating agencies. Unrated claims on corporates will attract a risk weight of 100 per cent. Claims above ₹ 50 crore sanctioned/renewed on or after April, 2008 will attract a higher risk weight of 150 per cent; this threshold will be lowered to ₹ 10 crore with effect from April, 2009.
- Claims in respect of a few specified categories such as venture capital funds, commercial real estate, consumer credit including personal loans and credit card receivables, capital market exposures, and claims on non-deposit taking systematically important NBFCs will attract risk weights of 125 per cent of 150 per cent.
- Capital requirements for operational risk under the Basic Indicator Approach will be the average of a fixed percentage of positive annual gross income of the previous three completed financial years.
- A set of disclosure requirements has been prescribed to encourage market discipline.
- Banks are required to obtain prior approval of the RBI to migrate to the advanced approaches such as the Internal Rating Based Approach or the Advanced Measurement Approach for operational risk for computing capital requirements.

In January 2006, the RBI allowed Indian banks to augment their capital funds by issue of the following additional instruments so as to enable them to meet additional capital requirements owing to adoption of Basel II framework and expansion of bank credit.

Additional instruments which banks can issue include innovative perpetual debt instruments (IPDI) (eligible for inclusion as Tier I capital), debt capital instruments (eligible for inclusion as upper Tier II capital), perpetual non-cumulative preference shares (eligible for inclusion as Tier I capital) and redeemable cumulative preference shares (eligible for inclusion as Tier-II capital) subject to laws in force from time to time.

The broad features of the above instruments are contained in Table 12.1.

In the light of the feedback from banks, the RBI reviewed the existing guidelines and issued the following amendments, inter alia, on March 31, 2008.[12]

- Innovative Perpetual Debt Instruments (IPDI) in excess of 15 per cent of Tier I capital were allowed to be included a Tier 2 capital.
- A bank's aggregate investment in all types of instruments, eligible for capital status investee banks/FIs/NBFCs/Primary dealers should not exceed 10 per cent of the investing bank's capital funds (Tier I plus Tier 2, after adjustments). Any investment in excess of this limit should be deducted at 50 per cent from Tier I and 50 per cent from Tier 2 capital.
- The direct loan/credit/overdraft exposure, if any, of banks to the state governments and the investment in State Government Securities would attract zero risk weight, while state government guaranteed claims would attract 20 per cent risk weight.

TABLE 12.1: Broad Features of Innovative Instruments

Feature	Innovative Perpetual Debt Instruments	Debt Capital Instruments
Limits	Shall not exceed 15 per cent of total Tier I capital	Shall not exceed 100 per cent of Tier I capital along with other components of Tier II capital.
Maturity	Perpetual	Minimum 15 years.
Put option	Not available	
Call option	Available after ten years with the approval of the Reserve Bank.	
Step up option	Available only once during the life of the instrument, in conjunction with the call option, after lapse of ten years from the date of issue. The step-up shall not be more than 100 basis points.	
Loss absorption	Interest due will not be payable and will be non cumulative if CRAR is/will be less than minimum prescribed.	Interest due and principle on redemption will be deferred, but would be cumulative for interest, if CRAR is/will be less than the minimum prescribed.
	Banks may be allowed to pay with the prior approval of the Reserve Bank when the payment of interest will result in net loss/increase net loss provided CRAR remains above the regulatory norm.	
Seniority of claim	Superior to the claims of investors in equity shares; and Subordinate to the claims of all other creditors.	Superior to the claims of investors in equity shares and in instruments eligible for inclusion in Tier I capital; and Subordinate to the claims of all other creditors.
Discount for the purpose of capital adequacy	Not subjected to progressive discount.	Progressive discount at 20 per cent per year in the last five years before maturity.
FII/NRI Investment	Investment in these instruments by FIIs and NRIs shall be within an overall limit of 49% and 24% of the issue, respectively, subjected to the investment by each FII not exceeding 10% of the issue and investment by each NRI not exceeding 5% of the issue. Investment by FIIs shall be outside the limit for investment in corporate debt instruments i.e., US $ 1.5 billion.	Investment by FIIs in Upper Tier II instrument raised in Indian Rupees shall be outside the limit for investment in corporate debt instruments i.e, US $ 1.5 billion. However, investment by FIIs in these instruments will be subject to a separate ceiling of US $ 500 million. NRIs shall be eligible to invest in these instruments as per existing policy.
Issue of these instruments in foreign currency.	Not more than 49% of the eligible amount can be issued in foreign currency.	The total amount of Upper Tier II instruments issued in foreign currency shall not exceed 25% of the unimpaired Tier I capital. This limit will be distinct from other limits in foreign currency borrowings by authorized dealers.
CRR/SLR requirements	Will not attract CRR/SLR requirements.	Will attract CRR/SLR requirements.

- Consumer credit, including personal loans and credit and receivables but excluding education loans would attract a higher risk weight of 125 per cent or more, if warranted by the external rating or of the counterparty.
- In case of loans collateralised by a bank's own deposits, even if the tenure of deposits was less than 3 months or deposits had maturity mismtach, vis-a-vis the tenure of the loan, the provisions regarding derecognition would not be attracted provided an explicit consent was obtained from the depositor (*i.e.*, borrower) for adjusting the maturity proceeds of such deposits against the outstanding loan or for renewal of such deposits till the full repayment of the underlying loan.
- In view of excess volatility in the stock markets across the world, equity was removed from the list of eligible financial collaterals.

Earlier in October 2007, the RBI enhanced banks' capital raising options for meeting the capital adequacy requirements by issuing guidelines regarding the issue of preference shares as part of regulatory capital.

In February 2010, the RBI revised the existing guidelines for implementation of the Basel II framework in India in line with the changes made by the Basel Committee on Banking supervision to the Basel II framework in July, 2009. The changes in Pillar I (minimum capital requirement) of the framework relating to standardized approaches are mainly aimed at increasing capital requirements for securitisation exposures, both in the banking book and trading book. The revised guidelines on pillar 2 (Supervisory Review Process) are intended to assist the banks in better identifying and capturing firm-wise risks in their internal assessments of capital adequacy and managing them appropriately. The Pillar 3 (Market Discipline) revisions include more granular disclosure requirements for credit risk mitigations and securitised exposures. Detailed guidelines on the standardised approach (TSA) for calculation of capital charge for operational risk and internal models approach (IMA) for measuring the capital charge for market risk were issued in March and April, 2010, respectively.[13]

It is true that adoption of the advanced approaches might help the banks to maintain lower capital. However, it will require superior technology and information systems which aid the banks in better data collection, support high quality data and provide scope for detailed technical analysis needed for the advanced approaches. Availability of appropriate skills and capacity to retain/attract such skills at all points in time and a well established effective and independent control mechanism for supplementing the risk management are prerequisites for effective adoption of advanced approaches.

◆ Roap map set for Basel III Implementation

The Basel on Banking Supervision (BCBS) issued a comprehensive reform package, "Basel III: a global regulatory framework for more resilient banks and banking systems" in December 2010. The objective of the reform package is to improve the banking sector's ability to absorb shocks arising from financial and economic stress, thus reducing the risk of spillover from the financial sector to the real economy. Consequently, the RBI issued final guidelines on Basel III implementation in Indian banks on May 2, 2012 after due consideration of the comments/ suggestions received from various stakeholders in the draft guidelines issued on December 30, 2011.

The key features of the guidelines are as follows:[14]

(i) Minimum capital requirements: Total capital must be at least 9 per cent of risk-weighted assets (RWAs). Tier 1 capital must be at least 7 per cent of RWAs; and Common Equity Tier I (CET I) capital must be at least 5.5 per cent of RWAs.

(ii) Capital Conservation Buffer (CCB): The CCB in the form of common equity of 2.5 per cent of RWAs is required to be maintained; and total capital with CCB will be 11.5 per cent of RWAs.

(iii) Leverage ratio: A non-risk based Tier I leverage ratio has been prescribed. There will be a parallel run for the leverage ratio from January 1, 2013 to January 1, 2017 during which banks should strive to maintain a minimum Tier I leverage ratio of 4.5 per cent. The leverage ratio requirement will be finalised taking into account the final proposal of the Basel Committee.

The implementation period of Basel III capital requirements will begin from January 1, 2013 and will be fully implemented by March 31, 2018, before the timeline (January 1, 2019) indicated in Basel III rules. In India, implementation of Basel III has been advanced by nine months to ensure that full implementation is co-terminus with the financial closure of banks, as indicated in Table 12.2.[15]

TABLE 12.2: Phase-wise Timeline for Basel III Implementation

Minimum Capital Ratios	Jan. 1, 2013	Mar. 31, 2014	Mar. 31, 2015	Mar. 31, 2016	Mar. 31, 2017	Mar. 31, 2018
Minimum Common Equity Tier (CET I)	4.5	5.0	5.5	5.5	5.5	5.5
Capital Conservation Buffer (CCB)	—	—	0.625	1.25	1.875	2.5
Minimum CET I + CCB	4.5	5.0	6.125	6.75	7.375	8.0
Minimum Tier I Capital	6.0	6.5	7.0	7.0	7.0	7.0
Minimum Total Capital	9.0	9.0	9.0	9.0	9.0	9.0
Minimum Total Capital + CCB	9.0	9.0	9.,625	10.25	10.75	11.5
Phase-in of all deductions from CET I (in %)	20.0	40.0	60.0	80.0	100.0	100.0

It is noteworthy that the RBI has always prescribed minimum capital adequacy ratio 1 per cent higher at 9 per cent compared to 8 per cent stipulated by the Basel Committee under Basel I/Basel II capital adequacy framework. The higher prescription has served Indian banking system well over the years. The higher capital adequacy norms will ensure that individual banks are stronger and internationally competitive. The higher prescription also enhances the resilience of the Indian banking system. It is important to consider that banks are exposed to certain risks, which cannot be properly explained and quantified. As such, such risks can be taken case of to a larger extent by the additional capital cushion.

H. PRESENT POSITION OF CAPITAL ADEQUACY IN INDIAN COMMERCIAL BANKS

From the perspective of regulatory and supervisory process, the capital to risk weighted assets ratio (CRAR) constitutes the most important indicator of assessing soundness and solvency of banks.

The overall capital position of commercial banks in India has witnessed a marked improvement during the post reform period (Table 12.3). Thus, as at end-March 2006, 82 out of 84 commercial banks operating in India maintained CRAR at or above 9 per cent. The corresponding figure for 1995-96 was 54 out of 92 banks. Regarding capital position in different categories of commercial banks, it may be noted from Table 12.2 that in 1995-96 scheduled commercial banks had CRAR of 9.6 per cent. As against this, CRAR in case of nationalized banks was 9.5 per cent and that of SBI group 9.9 per cent. CRAR of old Private sector banks had CRAR of 28.7 per cent. In case of foreign banks CRAR was 14.6 per cent. Thus, all the categories of banks in India had CRAR higher than the stipulated rate.

During the period 1995-96 - 2008-09, there has been substantial improvement in CRAR of all categories of banks except foreign banks operating in India. Thus, it is to be seen from the table that the overall CRAR of SCBs at 12.3 per cent was much higher than what it had in 1995-96. The ratio continued to be significantly above the stipulated minimum even after satisfying the new requirements pertaining to the capital charge for market risk. Despite sharp increase in the credit portfolio coupled with the higher risk weight made applicable for housing and consumer loans resulting in a significant rise in the risk weighted assets, banks' capital base kept pace with the sharp rise in risk-weighted assets. This, to an extent, was achieved by increased access to the domestic and international capital markets. To maintain the CRAR, banks have relied mainly on retained earnings, although some banks have tended to supplement their retained earnings with capital issues.

TABLE 12.3: Distribution of Commercial Banks According to CRAR

(Number of Banks)

Year	Between 0-9 Per cent	Between 9-10 Per cent	Above 10 Per cent	Total
1995-96	17	33	42	92
2000-01	5	11	84	100
2004-05	2	8	78	88
2005-06	3	3	79	85
2006-07	2	4	78	84
2007-08	—	2	77	79
2008-09	—	1	78	79

Source: Reports on Trend and Progress of Banks, Reserve Bank of India for relevant years.

At the individual bank level, barring two banks in the old private sector group accounting for a negligible 0.3 per cent of the total assets of the SCBs, the CRAR of all other banks was above the minimum capital requirements of nine per cent.

At the end-March, 2006, scheduled commercial banks were well placed in respect of capital requirements, despite a modest decline in the aggregated capital ratios during the year. The decline in CRAR during 2005-06 could be attributed to the higher rate of increase in total risk weighted assets, *vis-à-vis* the expansion in capital during the year. Higher growth in risk weighted assets, in turn, reflected (*i*) higher growth in the advances portfolio of banks as compared with investment in Government securities (*ii*) increase in risk weights for personal loans, real estate and capital market exposure and (*iii*) application of capital charge of market risk for investments held under the AFS category from March, 2006. Although the overall CRAR declined, the core capital (*i.e.*, Tier I) ratio of the banks increased from 8.4 per cent at end-March, 2005 to 9.3 per cent at end March, 2006 reflecting increased access by banks to primary capital market as also transfer of IFR from Tier II to Tier I capital. The increase in Tier I ratio would provide more headroom to banks in raising capital funds through Tier II, especially in the context of implementation of Basel norms from March 2007. The core capital ratio declined to 8.3 per cent at end-March, 2007. Only one old private sector bank, *viz.*, Sangli Bank, could not comply with the prescribed minimum CRAR at end-March, 2007. This bank was subsequently amalgamated with ICICI Bank.

During 2008-09, the CRAR of major bank groups remained static or improved except for a marginal deterioration observed in case of PSBs. The decline in CRAR of PSBs was mainly contributed by the SBI Group. In fact, the CRAR of PSB group was below the industry average, while that of it was above in the case of other bank groups.

It is important to note that the Indian banking system withstood the pressures of the global financial crisis and a factor that facilitated the normal functioning of the banking system even in the face of one of the largest global financial crisis was its robust capital adequacy.

As all commercial banks in India excluding RRBs became Basel Complaint as on March 31, 2009, it would be pertinent to look at the capital adequacy position both under Basel I and Basel II frameworks.

It may be noted from Table 12.5 that CRAR of Indian banks as end March, 2012 stood at 12.94 per cent and in 14.24 per cent respectively under Basel I and Basel II framework, far above the stipulated minimum ratio by the RBI. This signifies that Indian banks successfully managed to meet the increased capital requirements under the changed framework.

(per cent)

Basel II	
2011	2012
13.1	13.23
13.5	13.03
12.3	13.70
16.5	16.21
14.6	14.12
16.9	16.66
17.2	16.74
14.2	14.24

rime measure of the (measured by Tier I re CRAR ratio of the and II frameworks, s under the Basel II ystem (Table 12.5). In in Tier II CRAR ratio.

nmercial Banks

(Amt. in crore)

Basel II		
10	20	12
7,381	6,70,389	7,78
95,100	4,74,581	5,6
72,281	1,95,808	2,1
,01,396	47,24,933	54,60
14.5	14.2	4.2
10.1	10.0	3.9
4.4		

ging on an average, above nder both frameworks, the bout 4-6 percentage points foreign and private banks ainst this, there was decline ks maintained their position. capital adequacy position of wngraded financial strength of deteriorating quality of assets ion is likely to be more serious ability and more stringent Basel

		12.4					12.5	11.7	12.1	14.1	14.3
	.8	13.4	11.5	12.3	11.3	10.2	12.1	12.6	12.0	14.4	15.1
10.3	10.8	11.9	12.6	12.9	15.2	15.0	14.0	13.0	12.4	13.1	15.1

Source: Reports on Trend and Progress of Banking in India for relevant years.

TABLE 12.5: Capital to Risk Weighted Assets Ratio
(As at end-March)

Bank group	Basel I				Ba	
	2009	2010	2011	2012	2009	201
Public Sector banks	12.3	12.1	11.8	11.88	13.5	13.3
Nationalised banks	12.1	12.1	12.2	11.84	13.2	13.2
SBI group	12.7	12.1	11.0	11.97	14.0	13.5
Private sector banks	15.0	16.7	15.1	14.47	15.2	17.4
Old Private sector banks	14.3	13.8	13.3	12.47	14.8	14.
New private sector banks	15.1	17.3	15.5	14.90	15.3	18.
Foreign banks	15.0	18.1	17.7	17.31	14.3	17.
Scheduled Commercial banks	13.2	13.6	13.0	12.94	14.0	14.

Source: RBI Report on Trend and Progress of Banking in India for relevant years.

Core CRAR reflecting the paid-up and reserves generally forms the financial strength of any bank. In the case of Indian banks, core capital capital) made up about 70 per cent of the total at end March, 2010. C SCBs at end-March 2012 stood at 9.4 and 10.4 per cent under Basel respectively, against much above the RBI's stipulation of 6 per cent framework, underlying the core capital strength of the Indian banking s 2011-12, CRAR declined over the previous year mainly owing to decline

TABLE 12.6: Component-wise capital Adequacy of Scheduled Co
(As at end-March)

	Basel I					
	2009	2010	2011	2012	2009	20
A. Capital funds: (i+ii)	4,88,563	5,72,582	6,74,662	7,81,000	4,87,876	5,6
(*i*) Tier I Capital	3,31,422	3,97,665	4,76,615	5,68,500	3,33,810	3,
(*ii*) Tier II capital	1,57,141	1,79,916	1,98,047	2,12,400	1,54,016	1,
B. Risk-weighted Assets	37,04,372	42,16,565	51,81,583	6,03,750	34,88,303	39
C. CRAR (A as % of B) of which:	13.2	13.6	13.0	12.9	14.0	
Tier I	9.0	9.4	9.2	9.4	9.6	
Tier II	4.2	4.1	3.8	3.5	4.4	

Source: Based on off-site returns submitted by banks to the RBI.

At the bank group-level, each bank group reported a CRAR ra 12 per cent both under Basel I and II frameworks (Table 12.6). U level of CRAR was relatively high for foreign banks, which was a above the levels reported by PSBs. Between 2009 and 2010, bot reported an increase in CRAR (under both Basel I and II). As ag in the capital adequacy ratio for the SBI, while nationalised ban

During the fiscal year 2010-11, financial health including PSBs including SBI has deteriorated so much so that Moody do the Bank. Downgrading of the SBI due to weak Tier-I capital an is a reflection of weakening banking system in India. The situa in the ensuring years due to increasing NPAs, decreasing profi norms.

On January 10, the Government decided to infuse ₹ 12,517 crore in 10 PSBs during 2012-13 to enhance their lending capabilities and also help them in meeting the stricter adequacy norms under Basel III.

To comply with the capital adequacy norms in the previous years also, the government had infused about ₹ 20,117 crore in PSBs during 2010-11 and injected another ₹ 12,000 crore in 2011-12.

Accordingly, to keep pace with the capital requirements in the coming year, the Government decided in principle to provide need-based additional capital infusion in banks from 2013-14 to 2018-19 to ensure compliance with Basel-III global banking norms aimed at minimising financial risks.[16]

I. CONCLUSIONS

Survival and success of a bank depends, *inter alia*, on adequacy of capital as it provides cushion against normal hazards inherent in its operations. Besides, there is a strong element of social responsibility. Adequate capital funds enable a bank to discharge its responsibility. Banks with adequate capital also command public confidence. This is why, Basel Committee on Banking Regulations and Supervisory Practices had in July 1st, 1997 released the agreed framework on international convergence of capital measures and capital standards. The Committee adopted risk assets approach for measuring capital adequacy and set CRAR at 8 per cent.

In view of significant changes in the business of banking, risk management practices, supervisory approaches and financial markets, the Basel Committee brought out new capital adequacy framework in June 1999 which was subsequently revised in January, 2001. The new framework is based on three pillars of minimum capital requirements, supervisory review process and market discipline.

In India the Basel I framework on capital adequacy norms was implemented with effect from 1992-93. The RBI introduced in April, 1992 a risk weighted assets ratio systems for banks in India as a capital adequacy norm. The RBI directed the banks to achieve a minimum capital adequacy ratio of 9 per cent by March 31, 2000.

Pursuant to the RBI policy of conforming to the best international standards and in the process, the emphasis on gradual harmonization with the international best practices, all banks have been directed to start implementing Basel II framework from March 31, 2007. The RBI undertook several measures for ensuring smooth and hassle free implementation of Basel II norms.

As regards capital adequacy position of commercial banks in India, it is gratifying to note that most of the banks have already complied with the stipulated requirements and are in comfortable position. Despite sharp increase in the credit portfolio coupled with the higher risk weight made applicable for housing and consumer loans, banks' capital base kept pace with the sharp rise in risk-weighted assets. This, to an extent, was achieved by access to capital markets.

KEY TERMS

- Adequate Capital Fund
- Basel accord
- Basel Committee on Banking Supervision
- Basic Indicator Approach
- Capital-Asset ratio
- Capital cause and variation buffer
- Capital deposit ratio
- Core Capital
- CRAR
- Financial Health
- Innovative Perpetual debt instruments
- Perpetual non-cumulative preference shares
- Risk-based supervision
- Standardised approach.

DISCUSSION QUESTIONS

1. What do you understand by capital adequacy? Discuss its significance for a commercial bank.
2. What are the major functions of capital funds in a commercial bank?
3. Discuss how capital adequacy of a commercial bank be measured.
4. Discuss Basel Committee norms of capital adequacy for commercial banks.
5. Bring out capital adequacy norms in Indian Commercial banks.
6. Discuss the RBI policy regarding implementation of Basel Committee norms.
7. Comment on the capital adequacy of Indian Commercial banks.
8. What are the challenges public sector banks are going to face and why?

REFERENCES

1. Gay lord A. Freeman, "The Problem of Adequate Bank Capital", quoted by Howard D. Crose in his book on Management Policies for Commercial Banks, p. 158.
2. S.K. Muranjan, Modern Banking in India, p. 123.
3. Report on Trend and Progress of Banking in India, RBI, 1999-2000, pp. 22-23.
4. Basel Committee on Banking Supervision (2001), the New Basel Capital Accord, Bank for International Settlements, Switzerland.
5. L. Mayer, 'The New Basel Capital Proposal', BIS Review, 2001, No. 40.
6. Bank for International Settlement, Third Consultative Paper, Basel, 2003.
7. Dr. Y.V. Reddy, Challenges and Implications of Basel II for Asia, RBI Bulletin, June 2006, pp. 637-38.
8. RBI annual Report, 2010-11. p. 104.
9. *Op. cit.*, Dr. Y.V. Reddy, p. 638.
10. Shyamala Gopinath, Approach to Basel II, RBI Bulletin, June 2006, p. 708.
11. RBI, Annual Report 2006-07.
12. RBI Report on Trend and Progress of Banking in India, 2007-08.
13. RBI Annual Report, 2009-10.
14. RBI Report on Trend and Progress of Banking in India, 2011-12.
15. *Ibid*.
16. HINDU, January 1, 2013.

Management of Deposits

Chapter 13

Learning Objectives:

The present chapter attempts to:

- Discuss the role of banks as mobiliser of deposits.
- Discuss the forces that bear upon deposit mobilization by banks.
- Analyse the trends in deposit mobilization by commercial banks in India.
- Outline the challenges before commercial banks in India.
- Discuss marketing approach to overcome challenges.
- Provide mechanism of formulating marketing strategy for a commercial banks and implementing it.

Chapter Outline:

- Commercial banks as mobiliser of deposits.
- Forces influencing deposit mobilisation by banks.
- Deposit mobilization by commercial banks in India — A trend analysis.
- Challenges before commercial banks in India.
- Strategic marketing approach to overcome the challenges.
- Formulating marketing strategy for a commercial bank.
- Implementing marketing Strategy.
- Conclusions.

A. COMMERCIAL BANKS AS MOBILISER OF DEPOSITS

A well designed and developed banking system promotes growth through effective mobilization of savings and their efficacious allocation to the most productive uses. The historical experience shows that virtually in all the economies, including the market intermediated ones, banks have played a crucial role in resource mobilization and supporting the growth process, and that the development of banks and other intermediaries has itself facilitated the development of financial markets.

The genesis of bank's role in the resource mobilization lies in enterprises relying critically on external sources of finance, especially in their formative stages. In particular, banks have played critical role in coordinating investment efforts in many economies such as Belgium, Germany, Italy and Japan in engineering 'take-offs' during their crucial phases of development. During the 'take-off stages' of these economies powerful banks initially relied on capital contributions from a small number of promoters and thereafter, as their business expanded, they resorted to deposits as a major source of funds. With development of financial markets, borrowings also became an important source of funds for the banks.

In India too, banks have played a significant role in supporting the growth process by mobilising savings, particularly after nationalisation of banks. They have been instrumental in governing deposits from the household sector, the major surplus sector of the economy, which, in turn has helped raise the financial savings of the household sector and hence the overall rise in saving rate.[1]

B. FORCES INFLUENCING DEPOSIT MOBILISATION BY BANKS

A host of forces bears upon the banks' deposit mobilisation efforts. These forces include external forces — environmental forces within which a bank has to operate and internal forces which are related to the internal affairs of the bank.

◆ External Forces

(i) State of National Economy: The magnitude of the deposits of a bank fluctuates with changes in the economic conditions of a country. In times of prosperity, the level of deposits tends to rise. With an improvement in the economic and business conditions of the country and with an expansion in employment opportunities, the per capita income of the people increases. This is likely to result in an increased inflow of primary deposits to the banks. The level of derivative deposits will shoot up sharply. Increased demands are made for loans from the business community, which needs additional funds to meet its expanding needs. Consumers are more disposed to buy durable consumer goods and houses in times of booms, All these result in the creation of more deposits. Moreover, commercial banks liberalise their lending policies and soften their lending terms during periods of prosperity because of improved business conditions. Several marginal firms, which were earlier deprived of lending facilities, may get bank loans because, in good times, banks are inclined to take a somewhat optimistic view of the creditworthiness of marginal borrowers, and are more disposed to make borderline loans. The provision of larger amounts of loans results in the creation of more deposits.

In the declining phase of economic activity, when business demands for loans decline and consumers cut back on the purchase of durables, the banks become more reluctant to lend because they take a dimmer view of the credit standing of marginal borrowers, for it is often the marginal borrowers rather than high class ones who continue to need and apply for loans. The process of credit contraction tends to be exaggerated by the banks themselves during lean times.

(ii) Characteristics of Local Economy: Although the local economy cannot remain immune to changes in general economic conditions, certain peculiar features of the local economy may have their distinct influence on the level of bank deposits and their structure. A bank operating in an agrarian economy will experience an increased demand for loans by farmers during a particular season. Its deposit creation activity gains momentum during that season. Moreover, there is an increased flow of the farmers' deposits to banks immediately after the harvest. The level of deposits, particularly those in the current account, tends to be relatively more stable. In an agricultural economy, where a number of crops are grown, the level of deposits of a bank will not fluctuation as sharply as it will in the case of a bank operating in an economy with a single cash crop. The magnitude of deposit in a bank in an industrial economy records relatively more fluctuations in view of the regular demand for bank loans. Within industry communities, the level of deposits in a bank fluctuates differently, depending on the industrial structure in the locality. The amount of deposits in a commercial bank fluctuates violently if it is situated in a community dependent upon a single industry or a few industries. Not only will the deposits of the business be affected but this trend may also influence the deposits of employees working in the Industry. If the business of the industry is adversely affected by forces originating outside the community, and if the demand for industrial products declines the local bank will experience a decline in the level of deposits not only because of the decrease in business deposits but also because of a fall in the deposits of workers who are affected in some way or the other if the enterprise faces rough whether. The magnitude of fluctuations may not be so sharp in case of those banks which are operating in a community with diversified groups of industries.

A change in the demand for a product may also bring about fluctuations in the level of deposits. The deposits in the local bank will gain in size if the demand for the products of the industry by the community in which it is operating increases. Conversely, a decline In demand of products and so also their prices will result in a decline in bank deposits.

(iii) Role of Government in the Community: The central, and State Government as well as local governments too, substantially influence the magnitude of deposits which an individual bank will hold. A modern government not only plays a regulative role but goes far beyond it to assume promotive responsibilities in order to provide social and economic overheads which are a necessary adjunct of accelerated economic growth. Moreover, the government participates more directly in industrial activities and sets up certain key and strategic industries not only to initiate and carry forward the process of industrial growth but to prevent the emergence of big monopolistic organisations and the concentration of economic power in a few hands. In those communities in which the government has set up a number of industrial enterprises producing the goods that are in demand by other communities, the bank will be in a position to procure and create more deposits. The provision of economic overheads, including transport facilities, is likely to affect the deposits in a bank. With improved transportation facilities, people can move easily and in no time from one place to the other. They will, therefore, no longer tie their deposits to a local small bank, and may, instead, withdraw their deposits from the local bank and keep them in a big bank with diversified services to its customers.

(iv) Relative Changes in Population: The relative changes in population owing to the movements of the people from one place to another influence the level of deposits in local banks. People migrate to other places because of better job opportunities. Migration may also take place when a natural calamity befalls on a particular region and it becomes very difficult for the inhabitants to earn their livelihood. As a result, the a bank in the locality to which people have migrated will gain deposits at the expense of the bank operating in a community from which people shifted.

(v) Economic Policy of Government: Economic and fiscal policies of the central government influence deposit mobilisation efforts of commercial banks. Liberalised policy of the government, opening the economy to both public and private agencies to participate in the developmental programmes and offering level playing fields to all the participants infuses competitiveness in the economy. A myriad of financial institutions emerge in both public and private sectors, vying with each other to attract surpluses of the households and business enterprises through innovative productive offerings. In such an environment, it is banks' strategies and management of product offerings by them that will decide its volume of deposits.

Fiscal policy of the government also affects the magnitude of deposits of banks. Taxation policy of Government of India, for example, offering the tax benefits with maturity of five years and above has certainly helped the scheduled banks to attract large amount of deposits, especially from the household sector. Recent directive of the finance ministry issued on November, 2011 directing the PSBs to increase the share of current and savings accounts deposits to 40 per cent of the total deposits by 2015 will certainly affect composition of deposits of the banks.

In July 2012, the Government of India directed commercial banks to cap on corporate bulk deposits at 10 per cent of total deposits for 2011-12. From the next financial year, the cap would be increased to 15 per cent, but it would comprise certificates of deposits too.

(v) Policy of Central Bank: Monetary policy of the Central bank is another key variable that affects the volume of bank's deposits. Interest rate policy and bank expansion policy of the central bank are the two major vehicles through which banks' volume of deposits are affected. Central bank pursuing policy of deregulation of interest rates both on deposits and loans provides immense opportunities to banks to design and develop attractive schemes tailored to diverse segments of the customers which can enable them to tap unutilised surpluses of the people. Likewise, the central banking policy to permit banks to penetrate in unbanked regions of the country, as has been the policy of the Reserve Bank of India, can enable banks to reach the interiors of the country and attract the savings of the inhabitants.

(vii) Households' decisions: Household savings form a potential pool of resources for intermediation by banks. As such, the evolving dynamics in determinants of household savings have a critical bearing on banks in their management of resource mobilisation. While the banks' accessibility of resources is expected to grow in consonance with the increasing level of household savings, the actual recourse of the same would depend upon the households' decisions on their portfolio composition of savings. The level and composition of household savings in turn, are dependent upon macro economic conditions, financial market development and regulation, alternative income sources, demographics and preferences of the household sector.[2]

◈ Internal Factors

(i) Physical Features of Banks: The physical features of a bank go a long way in attracting potential customers. It has generally been found that people derive pleasure in dealing with a bank with attractive buildings, modernistic teller stations, comfortable benches and easy chairs and a decor in keeping with draped windows and beautiful walls. In order to please customers, bankers now emphasise the importance of better lighting, lighter woods and brighter interiors.

(ii) Personnel of Bank: Personal, courteous and prompt and good quality service makes a profound appeal to the public. The bank staffed with personnel who exude warmth and friendliness is in a better position to attract deposits than one that lacks these attributes. This is why the personnel department of a bank now, lays greater emphasis on public relations. Bank executives and employees are encouraged to participate in various training programmes and conferences. The officers and employees of many banks actively participate in various civic affairs and project works. This they do to impress upon the people that the banks take interest in their welfare. The people of the community expect the banks in their locality to take the initiative in setting up industries and lend a helping hand in mitigating their problems. This has now engaged the attention of the Indian bankers. Some of the commercial banks in India have now set up a new department, known as the Public Relations Department. This department is concerned with all such activities as will help the bank to expand its business. It organises advertising and promotional programmes and conducts area surveys to compile a list of prospects who might be cultivated and solicited to become customers of the bank.

(iii) Services Rendered by Bank: Customers generally prefer to have dealings with the bank offering better and more diversified services and facilities. A bank which renders such services as drive- in teller windows, bank-by-mail, a convenient safe-deposit box scheme, after-hour depository services and devising numerous saving schemes to suit the liquidity and other considerations of savers is placed in a relatively better position to garner the surpluses of the people. Farmers may be attracted to a bank because the latter is staffed by a highly qualified and trained farm executive who is capable of giving advice to farmers having production, marketing or financial problems. Banks with a reputation for caring for their customers appeal to the public more than those who are loath to lend to steady customers in periods of economic strain.

(iv) Fundamental Policies and Financial Position of a Bank: If the level of deposits in a bank is conditioned, in the main, by public confidence in the bank, which itself is a function of sound management policies, the competence of the management, a well-disciplined and stable organisation, and a strong capital position. Presence of outstanding men on the Board, capable officers and employees, and sound investments and loan portfolios help the bank to maintain public confidence.

(v) Size of the Bank: Increase in the size of a bank is likely to affect deposit rates of regional or large nationwide organisations compete in different ways than small, local institutions even when the different organisations have similar local market shares. Furthermore, multi-market banks complete differently than the banks that operate primarily in the local market.

With growth in the size of banks, they have access to more non-deposit liabilities. Typically, this reduces their desire to compete intensively for deposits. Large banks operating in multiple markets become less sensitive to local market conditions. Further, presence of multi-market mega banks instills more aggressive competition among them leading to higher deposit rates.[3]

C. DEPOSIT MOBILIZATION BY COMMERCIAL BANKS IN INDIA — A TREND ANALYSIS

Against the background discussed above, let us analyse the trends in mobilization of deposits by the banks in India during dynamically changing economic conditions existing especially after nationalization of the banks in 1969 and discern the forces that affected the banks' efforts in this field.

As noted earlier, deposits have constituted the preponderant source for the commercial banks in India, accounting for over 90 per cent of the total. These deposits were garnered primarily from households (70 per cent). However, in recent years the share of the private corporate sector and other tended to increase.[4]

For vivid discussions of dynamics of bank deposit growth, the post nationalization period can be divided into four phases, *viz.*, Phase I (1969-1984); Phase II (1984-1995); Phase III (1995-2005); and Phase IV (2005 and onwards).

◈ Phase I (1969-1984)

In a first phase, the aggregate deposits growth of SCBs increased sharply averaging 19.2 per cent during 1969-84 as compared to 9.5 per cent during the pre-nationalization phase (1951-1969). This phenomenal growth can be attributed to remarkable surge in net financial savings of the household sector by 49.2 per cent in a single year 1970-71 and large expansion of banks particularly in rural and semi-urban areas following nationalization of banks in 1969 and 1980.

As a result, the share of rural deposits in total deposits shot up from 3.1 per cent in 1969 to 14.4 per cent by 1984, which was primarily responsible for raising the overall deposit growth during the period.

TABLE 13.1: Growth in Bank Deposits
(Annual Average)

(Per cent)

Period of Averages	Demand and saving	Term	Aggregate
1951-52 to 1968-69	7.1	13.1	9.5
1969-70 to 1983-84	13.3	22.7	19.2
1984-85 to 1994-95	19.5	18.2	18.4
1995-96 to 2004-05	12.6	16.4	15.7
2005-06 to 2007-08	22.5	21.3	21.4
2008-09	12.2	24.4	22.4
2009-10	27.3	13.1	17.0

Source: Handbook of Statistics on the Indian Economy, Reserve Bank of India.

In contrast, the share of metropolitan deposits in total deposits plunged sharply from 45 per cent to around 39 per cent over the same period.

It is interesting to note from Table 13.2 that the proportionate share of bank deposits in gross financial savings of the household sector increased remarkably from 35.7 per cent in 1970-71 to 42.5 per cent in 1983-84, reflecting the impact of bank branch expansion (Table 13.2).

TABLE 13.2: Financial Assets of the Household Sector
(Average Pattern of Distribution)

(Per cent)

Particulars	1970-71 to 1983-84	1984-85 to 1994-95	1995-96 to 2004-05	2005-06 to 2006-07	2010-11
Currency	13.4	15.3	9.3	8.7	13.4
Bank Deposits	44.6	36.5	36.9	50.9	44.5
Non-banking deposits	3.6	5.2	4.6	0.6	2.8
Life Insurance Fund	8.6	8.2	12.9	14.5	24.2
Provident and Pension Fund	19.0	17.5	17.7	9.9	9.1
Claims on Government	5.7	10.4	15.2	9.9	6.5
Shares and Debentures (including units of Mutual Funds)	2.6	11.3	3.8	5.6	–0.4
Trade debt (Net)	2.6	–0.5	–0.5	00	–0.1
Changes in Financial Assets	100.0	100.0	100.0	100.0	100.0

Source: Handbook of Statistics on the Indian Economy, 2006-07, RBI.

A compositional analysis of bank deposits reveals that the proportionate share of term deposits, which was 55.7 per cent at end-March 1980, declined to around 51 per cent in 1981-82 reflecting a switch towards the new 12 percent 6-year National Savings Certificates (NSC), which was introduced during the year. There was also a sharp increase in the issue of shares and debentures, particularly convertible debenture, by the corporate sector.

◆ Phase II (1984-1995)

This phase witnessed marginal deceleration in the aggregate deposit growth. The growth of demand deposits accelerated during this phase, while that of time deposits tended to decelerate resulting in the overall slowdown in aggregate deposit expansion. The deceleration in time deposits growth was the outcome of a number of forces, *viz.*, slowdown in expansion of branch network and substitution of time deposits held in banks with other saving instruments such as units of mutual funds, shares and debentures, and deposits of non-banking financial intermediaries (NBFCs).

The share of bank deposits in household sector declined to 38.4 per cent by 1994-95 mainly due to disintermediation in the financial system on account of households' preference for capital market instruments (Table 13.2).

The substitution of funds, particularly in favour of units of mutual funds during the latter part of the 1980s and the early 1990s, to some extent, was facilitated by the availability of Tax benefits under Section M of the Income Tax Act. As a result, corporates and individuals invested large funds in the UTI and other mutual funds. In the face of increased competition from newly set up mutual funds, UTI also followed an aggressive policy of launching new schemes, especially during the latter half of the 1980's to meet investors' diverse income and liquidity needs. In view of buoyant capital market conditions in this phase, units of mutual funds and direct investment in shares provided higher returns than interest rates on bank deposits. This encouraged switching of household financial savings from bank deposits to shares and debentures and units of mutual funds. Deposits mobilized by NBFCs also increased during this phase. An empirical study conducted for India also found that time/term deposits of SCBs were substituted in favour of units of mutual funds, non-convertible debentures (NCDs), life insurance policies of LIC and small savings.[5]

◈ Phase III (1995-2005)

Bank deposit growth continued to decelerate further during this phase with the average aggregate deposit registering an increase by 15.7 per cent, although income levels sported further reflecting the impact of improvement in real GDP growth. This deceleration was caused by deceleration in demand deposits and to some extent time deposits. The sharp deceleration was caused by deceleration in demand deposit growth was owing to the successive reduction in the stipulated minimum maturities of domestic term deposits. This led to switch of funds from saving deposits (demand liability portion) to term deposits. In order to provide banks the flexibility in their operations and improve efficiency, not only the minimum maturity period of term deposits was brought down but also banks were gradually accorded freedom in fixing the interest rates in their domestic term deposits for specific maturities.

In this phase, bank deposits faced competition mainly from post office deposits and savings, the collection under which soared by more than four times.

This phase also witnessed sharp decline in interest rates on term deposits of all maturity spectrum from 12-13 per cent to 4.00-5.50 per cent between 1995-96 and 2003-04. Although, the decline in interest rate on other saving instruments also took place, this decline was much lower than on term deposits. As a result, growth rate of bank deposits tended to decrease.

Consequent upon increased competition from post offices, which was mainly from rural and semi-urban areas, the relative proportions of rural, semi-urban and urban deposits in total deposits decreased from their peaks in the 1980s and the early 1990. Concomitantly, the share of metropolitan deposits in total deposits of banks increased from the early 1990s, partly reflecting the growing significance of new private sector banks, which are operating largely in urban and metropolitan areas. Thus, the share of the rural sector in total bank deposits which had surged from 12.6 per cent in 1980 to 15.3 per cent by end-March 1990s, declined to 12.9 per cent by end-March 2004. Similar trends were also noticeable in respect of shares of deposits in semi-urban and urban areas. In contrast, the share of metropolitan areas in total bank deposits persistently moved up in this decade.

As regards ownership of bank deposits, it may be observed that the proportionate share of the household sector in banks' total deposits nosedived from 69.2 per cent in 1995 to 58.4 per cent in 2004. The share of the Government sector in total deposits of SCBs increased from 9.2 per cent in 1995 to 14.5 per cent by end-March 2004. This could be attributed mainly to improved public sector savings rate which, in turn, was due to improved performance of non-departmental government enterprises. The share of corporate sector in total bank deposits also increased.

As regards the trend in share of various types of bank deposits, it may be noted that the relative share of term deposits soared from 59.2 per cent at end-March 1995 to 64.4 per cent at end-March 2002 that of savings deposits declined from 24.2 per cent at end-March 1995 to 23.7 per cent at end-March 2000. However, the share of saving deposits increased to about 26.1 per cent by end-March 2007, while that of term deposits decreased to 61.5 per cent.

◈ Phase IV (2005-2010)

There was significant acceleration in growth of bank deposits in this phase, particularly between 2005 and 2009. Thus, average growth rate of bank deposits buoyed up from 15.7 per cent during the period 1995-96 to 2004-05 to 22.4 percent in 2008-09. This sharp rise was owing to remarkable improvement in term deposits which, in turn, was due to extension of the tax benefits under Section 80C for fixed deposits in scheduled banks with maturity of five years and above. Rise in interest rates on term deposits of different maturity above the small savings rates rendered the various deposit schemes of the banks more attractive and hence the increase in growth rate of bank deposits. The introduction of bank deposit schemes for senior citizens at higher interest rates also led to improved mobilization of time deposits. In 2009-10 bank deposits registered significant slowdown from 22.4 per cent in 2008-09 to 17.0 per cent in 2009-10. This was caused by sharp deceleration in term deposits due to prevalence of low interest rates for a major part of the year.

In the fourth phase, the growth of non-resident (NRI) deposits decelerated significantly. As a result, the share of NRI deposits in aggregate deposits of SCBs nosedived from 15.5 per cent at end-March 1993 to 6.4 per cent at March end 2007. The sharp decline could be attributed to the rationalization of various NRI deposit schemes and decline in the ceiling interest rates prescribed by the RBI for various deposit schemes as part of the strategy to manage capital flows as well as increased recourse to foreign currency borrowings by banks in view of lower interest rates abroad.

A notable shift was witnessed in the various components of household sector financial savings. Thus, proportion of bank deposits in household sector financial savings surged remarkably from 36.9 per cent during 1995-96 to 2004-05 to almost 56 per cent during 2006-07. However, there was significant decline in its share in 2010-11 (Table 13.2).

It is interesting to observe from Table 13.3 that bank deposits constitute the single largest source of domestic savings. Not only have bank deposits maintained their predominant position in domestic savings but also have played an important role in stepping the share of financial savings of the household sector in gross domestic savings from an average of 1.9 per cent in the 1950s to 10.8 per cent during 2000-07 (Table 13.3). It is also significant to note from the

TABLE 13.3: Gross Domestic Saving Rates

(Per cent of GDP)

Sector	1950s	1960s	1970s	1980s	1990s	2006-07	2009-10
1. Household Sector (A+B)	6.6 (68.2)	7.6 (61.7)	11.4 (66.5)	13.5 (71.0)	17.7 (77.0)	23.2 (80.9)	19.5 (69.5)
A. Financial Savings	1.9 (18.8)	2.7 (21.8)	4.5 (26.0)	6.7 (35.4)	9.9 (43.3)	10.8 (37.9)	9.8 (34.9)
B. Physical Savings	4.7 (49.4)	4.9 (39.9)	6.9 (40.5)	6.8 (35.6)	7.8 (23.7)	12.3 (43.0)	9.7 (34.6)
2. Private Corporate Sector	1.0 (10.4)	1.5 (12.0)	1.5 (9.1)	1.7 (9.2)	3.8 (16.3)	5.3 (17.8)	6.7 (24.1)
3. Public Sector	2.0 (21.4)	3.2 (26.3)	4.2 (20.3)	3.7 (19.9)	1.5 (6.7)	0.7 (1.3)	1.8 (6.4)
4. Gross Domestic Savings (1+2+3)	9.7 (100.0)	12.3 (100.0)	17.2 (100.0)	19.0 (100.0)	22.0 (100.0)	29.2 (100.0)	28.0 (100.0)

Source: Figures in brackets are percentages to gross domestic savings.

table that physical savings of the household sector have also moved in tandem with the increase in gross financial savings. Quite a significant part of the physical savings is reported to be locked up in unproductive assets.

Although the bank deposits to GDP ratio in India moved up gradually over the years, it was still lower than almost all advanced countries and several emerging countries in Asia (Table 13.4).

TABLE 13.4: Bank Deposits to GDP Ratio: Cross Country Evidence

Country/Year	*1960*	*1980*	*2006*
Developed Economies			
Australia	0.38	0.33	0.75
France	0.17	0.65	0.68
Germany	0.32	0.55	0.99
Japan	0.40	1.32	1.90
U.K.	0.32	0.26	1.32
U.S.A.	0.55	0.65	0.68
Emerging Market Economies			
India	0.12	0.26	0.53
Malaysia	0.14	0.62	1.16
Philippines	0.12	0.18	0.47
South Africa	—	0.46	0.57
Thailand	—	0.32	0.94

Source: World Bank's New Database on Financial Development and Structure, October, 2007.

One of the major factors for the low-deposit-GDP ratio in India was the high share of physical savings in total savings even as India's savings rate compared favourably with several advanced and emerging economies.

D. CHALLENGES BEFORE COMMERCIAL BANKS IN INDIA

Undoubtedly, there has been phenomenal growth in bank deposits during the post nationalization period, rising from ₹ 4,661 crore at the June end 1999 to over ₹ 47 lakh crore as at end March 2010. However, this unprecedented surge has been mainly because of the Government fiscal policy and the RBI monetary policy as well as its persuasive approach to prod banks to offer attractive interest rates and offer new products to attract potential customers. Banks in India never made strategic efforts to expand their deposit base.

What is most disturbing to note that despite massive branch expansion of PSBs and entry of private sector banks and continued rise in household savings rate, the share of financial savings in total household savings has declined considerably to 50 per cent at present and almost 50 per cent of the savings are still in real estate. Accordingly, a major challenge before the banks would be to raise financial saving rate. According to McKinsey, a 5 per cent conversion of the physical assets into financial assets can enable banks to garner an additional ₹ 60,000 crore deposits.

Another challenge would be to release resources of the household sector held in physical assets over and above the genuine requirement for savings in various financial assets. Nevertheless, there has been significant shift of small savings from Post office deposits to bank deposits in recent years owing to attractive interest rates, it is a moot issue if the current trend would be sustained. Therefore, to sustain the recent trend in deposits, banks need to tap hitherto untapped savings, particularly in rural areas. This is also necessary to meet growing resource requirements for sustaining the high growth momentum of the Indian economy.

Bankers must remember that as the financial sector develops, the share of non-deposit saving instruments tends to rise at the expense of bank-deposits. This trend is expected to accentuate in the coming years. The challenge, therefore, for the banks is to mobilize hitherto untapped savings and to improve their services to not only retain their existing depositors but also attract new depositors.

Another formidable challenge before banks is to mobilize resources from the rural sector which throws up opportunities for the banks to reap the benefits of low cost large deposit base, which may not be available to other financial intermediaries. The main problem faced by banks in rural areas is that deposit transactions often involved small amounts and display irregular patterns reflecting seasonality and erratic nature of small scale income generating activities. Another major challenge lies in identifying appropriate lies in identifying appropriate technologies to significantly reduce the costs of doing rural business that result from low population density and poor physical infrastructure. While technological and management information system (MIS) solutions are necessary to overcome this challenge, their impact on the efficiency, quality of services, bottomlines and outreach potential of the banks need to be carefully assessed.

With increasing development of financial markets and concomitant emergence of a number of specialized intermediaries/markets which are able to cater to the evolving investor requirements, equity market related instruments such as equity shares and units of mutual funds have been gaining importance in view of their higher returns, albeit with higher embedded risks. This has already led to shrinkage of traditional deposit base. There is, therefore, strong need for banks to extend their outreach to prospective depositors/investors.

Besides the above challenges, commercial banks in India are facing operational constraints compared to non-banks while diversifying their activities. First, non-banks are able to manage their resources more effectively by having a leaner cost structure and quickly adopting new technologies thereby offering higher returns. Further, non-banking intermediaries such as brokerages, asset-management firms and mutual funds are able to offer specialized services like cash management and wealth management for various investors including high net worth individual (HNI). Second, unlike non-banks, banks are often subjected to various regulatory requirements such as statutory stipulations of reserve requirements, directed lending, prudential regulations driven provisioning requirements and limits on capital market exposure. While these measures promote financial stability, they constrain the diversification opportunities and thus constrict the banks' ability to earn higher income on their deployed funds and thereby offer higher interest rates on the deposits.

D. STRATEGIC MARKETING APPROACH TO OVERCOME THE CHALLENGES

The above challenges, which commercial banks in India are facing in mobilisation of deposits, can be overcome by adopting strategic marketing approach which signifies identification of the most profitable markets now and in future, assessment of the present and future needs of customers, setting business development objectives and developing suitable plans to meet them, management of the various services and promotion of these services to execute plans.

Although Indian bankers hold the view that they have been doing marketing since long without calling it by name, marketing in Indian banking in its correct perspective is of recent origin. In fact, until very recently hardly any bank had adopted 'marketing' as the guiding principle of its operations or as its organisational culture. There has been a general absence of synergistic effort in this direction.

The Indian bankers claim to have practiced marketing approach in their operations even before the nationalisation of banks but the fact is that they have been doing only selling. They have been very conservative and inward looking concerned with increasing volume of deposits and profits. They were primarily concerned with subserving the interests of controlling business houses and had scant concern for public at large. Banks were essentially product oriented organisations, placing before the customers their limited range of services so that the latter would choose the one that suits them, presuming that they had the requisite knowledge, time, interest and skills.

In fact, the banking system in India, SBI chairman rightly pointed out, has grown up in an environment where it provides what it wants to provide, where it wants and when it wants.[6]

It should, however, be noted that the selling concept of marketing is more relevant where the environment is static and there is no competition.

But in a fast-paced competitive milieu characterised by path-breaking advancement in technology, expanding scale of business operations, ever increasing competition, growing internationalization of business, changing socio-economic and political environment, fast changing familial and personal values, the selling concept has lost its relevance. The banks are, therefore, supposed to change their selling approach so as to meet the exacting demands of the customers and provide what they want, when they want and where they want.

Recent developments in Indian economy provide enough cue that the bankers cannot expect the hitherto easy growth in their deposits in the ensuing years. Already, growth rate of deposits of the PSBs has slackened in recent few years. This is essentially because of emergence of new financial institutions and financial instruments offering better returns and services to their customers. The entry of new generation banks and mutual funds and emergence of equity market related instruments has already begun showing its impact on market share of PSBs.

In addition to the above, deterioration in consumer services has also been the bane for decline in deposit growth. In the context of the limited package of services available at banks and feudalistic mind set of the banks, functionaries, the accent was on the quantity and the pace of branch expansion. Banks were asked to go predominantly to unbanked and underbanked areas and were required to ensure opening of branches within a time frame. But ability to upgrade the quality of services effectively was not built up. Although during post nationalisation period there has been expansion in the spectrum of services of banks, efforts at bringing in more customers within the orbit of the branches and educating the customers as to the benefits that would accrue to them by making one or the other of the services available at the branch have not been done as aggressively and systematically as possible. What is, therefore, necessary is to build up orientation in favour of the customers. Primacy of the customer has to be brought under sharper focus.

In contrast to the above, vast deposit potentials existing in the country have yet not been fully tapped. According to the survey conducted by the Indian Bank's Association, the household sector contributes 75 per cent of the domestic savings. But of its total, only 45 per cent land in the banks. Banking, the survey reveals, has been a habit of literate Indian citizens (86 to 94 per cent of banks savers). However, a majority (30 to 40 per cent) of the non-bank savers are illiterate. Further, 58 to 70 per cent of literate non-bank savers are not tapped by the banks. The production workers or the blue jean community which constitute about 28 to 32 per cent of the non-bank savers, are potential bank depositors.

Furthermore, large untapped segments in vast rural areas exist for bank deposits. The inability of the banks to attract depositors to the extent they would have attributable to the absence of marketing orientation in their efforts.

Further, more aggressive and concerted marketing efforts will have to be made by commercial banks to mobilise burgeoning amount of deposits from the people so as to meet the growingly large credit demands of not only existing clients but of new ones also. Increased emphasis on the development of agriculture and cottage and small-scale industries will result in considerable pressure on banking institutions for funds. The banking system cannot meet this demand without a corresponding rise in the growth rate in deposits. It is true that a part of the surpluses generated out of additional income in the rural sector stemming out of increased agricultural production and development of cottage and small-scale industries will flow into banks. However, the growth in such deposits will be moderate, particularly because of the fact that the saving income ratio is smaller in the rural sector than in others. Accordingly, banks will have to make serious efforts to raise the rate of savings in the form of deposits; otherwise, there is a danger that savings would be diverted into unproductive investments or into financing non-priority sectors. Moreover, banks have to mop up the resources that will be released in the unorganised sectors because of increased reliance of the neglected sectors on bank loans.

Above all, the very survival of a banking organisation depends on how successfully it balances the needs of customers with its resources. Marketing approach provides ways and means of matching customer's needs with the resources in such a fashion as to meet its socio-economic objectives. In fact, the increase in deposit interest rates accompanied by a high decibel marketing campaign with hoardings on every main street advertising 9.5% to 10.5% return on bank deposits led to burgeoning surge in term deposits.

Unlike selling concept, where products are first made and then offered for sale followed by a strong sales drive and where focus is on the salesman, marketing approach involves ascertainment of wants or needs of people and production of goods and services on the basis of identified needs. Organisations try to earn their profits through need satisfaction of its customers. They follow proactive approach towards market demand. Marketing concept focuses on the customer.

The keystone of strategic marketing approach is the realisation that the reasonable satisfaction of the customer's want is the economic and social justification for the continued existence of the organisation satisfying the want; that it is the customer in the final analysis, who makes the economic system function and that in a volatile and competitive market, significant efforts in the bank must be mobilised to determine the customer needs and then satisfy them by an appropriate product or service of a package of products and services.

Thus, strategic marketing concept rests on four main pillars, *viz*., a market focus, customer orientation, co-ordinated marketing and profitability; the selling concept takes an inside-out perspective. It starts with the factory, focuses on the bank's existing products and calls for heavy selling and promoting to produce profitable sales. The strategic marketing concept takes an outside-in perspective. It starts with a well-defined market, focuses on customer needs, co-ordinates all the activities that will affect customers and produces profits through creating customer satisfaction.[7] It stresses that the organisation should achieve its objective by satisfying customer needs better than competitors can do. Organisations having adopted marketing approach are highly involved in identifying and analysing the profit potential of different marketing opportunities whereas selling concept focuses on means of achieving a certain volume of sales.

Although a perceptible change is now discernible on the horizon and the bankers have started thinking in terms of product development, market penetration and market development. The evidence of increasing customer orientation of commercial banks becomes available by witnessing a liberal mushrooming of myriad of new financial services offered by them in recent years.

However, considering the ferocity of competitive challenges to the banks, rapid developments in socio-economic conditions and changing profile of the customers' preferences and the life styles, bankers have still to do a lot to formulate and reformulate suitable marketing strategy and translate it into action to achieve the desired results.

E. FORMULATING MARKETING STRATEGY FOR A COMMERCIAL BANK

Marketing strategy of a bank focuses on a service/market and fleshing out the detailed plans and programmes for achieving the service objectives in that market. The marketing strategy serves as the central instrument for directing and co-ordinating the marketing effort. It is the marketing strategy that determines what the customers' needs are, how these needs are to be met, what actions on product innovations are to be brought out and what should be its pricing strategy for well sustained market growth.

Marketing strategy should be formulated within the overall framework of corporate objectives and strategy of a bank. In fact, marketing strategy making begins with strategic corporate planning. For instance, several market forces are analysed during the overall premising strategy and many basic questions about the marketing objectives are answered while establishing the ultimate corporate objective.

The process involved in formulation of marketing strategy for deposit mobilisation purpose involves the following steps:

- Undertaking marketing opportunity analysis;
- Selecting target market;
- Determining competitive positioning;
- Making marketing strategic decisions.

◈ Undertaking Marketing Opportunity Analysis

Strategic marketing planning begins with the effort to identify an attractive set of opportunities for the bank. This calls for an in-depth environmental analysis. For instance, economic survey of the country may reveal that owing to various developmental measures taken by the Government during the plan period, not only urban prosperity has increased but also rural folk prospered considerably resulting in the rise in per capita savings. There is also tendency for the economy to buoy up in future, resulting in rise in per capita savings. The new economic and industrial policy, the fast technological upgradation and changes and focused attention on infrastructure development are likely to result in steep increase in demand for bank funds. Public sector undertakings are also expected to lean more heavily on bank's assistance. As a result, credit creation capacity of banks will increase leading to rise in growth of deposits. All these developments provide sufficient indication of existence of whooping deposit potentials in the ensuing years.

In assessing market opportunity the banker must evaluate sales potential of each opportunity. For this purpose, it is necessary to investigate as to who would buy the service, what are their special features, how many would buy, where they are located, who will be the competitors, what distribution channels would be needed, etc.

A survey of the competitive environment will show that commercial banks as noted earlier, are facing a fierce competition from a variety of financial instruments and institutions. Bankers themselves often feel that these instruments of competitors are more attractive than banks' schemes in terms of rates of interest and tax concessions.

It should also be noted that deposit potentials exist both in urban and rural areas. While rural and semi-urban pockets of the economy have almost remained untapped, in the urban areas, banks have played a game of shuttle cock. Although banks are fanning out into rural and semi-urban areas, banks' branches in these areas have not been effective to identify potential savers and attract their savings.

Thus, despite rich deposit potentiality that exists for banks, their market share in total savings of the community is declining because not only newly emerging private bankers but also non-banking agencies have made good inroads into the market and are taking a good share in the market by not only offering attractive return for savers but also bringing out their attractive schemes to suit people belonging to various walks of life. This tendency is very likely to persist in future and competitive posture is going to be more fierce.

A banker to survive successfully in the long-run must be responsive to changing attitudes, values, desires, beliefs and customs of people in a society. It is because of the fact that profile of customers and their needs are fast changing due to various environmental factors. For instance, those who were first class customers two decades ago, like upper/middle service class, now do not find bank deposit schemes enough attractive. Their main concern is in reducing the incidence of income tax by investing their savings in such instruments as are eligible for tax rebate. For interest income, they find other avenues like company deposits, shares, debentures, etc., more lucrative and high yielding.

◈ Selecting Target Market

Bank marketing analyst should make detailed probe in each of the potential market areas so as to choose the target market — particular groups of customers to whom the bank wishes to appeal. Since the customers are too numerous, widely scattered, heterogeneous in their needs and buying behaviour, it will be more helpful to the banker to identify the composition of the market, *i.e.*, the command area in which he is going to operate and the customers to be dealt with. This calls for two steps. The first is market segmentation — the task of breaking the total market into segments that share common practices. The bases for segmentation can be income (economically affluent, middle class, poor sections), age (retired, employed, young people in universities, colleges as well as kids) and profession (lawyers, teachers, doctors, engineers, contractors, officers, workers).

In the case of corporate sector, the categorisation could be according to nature and size of industries (manufacturing industry, trading firm, retail business, giant, small, etc.). Geographically, market can be divided into metropolitan, urban, semi-urban and rural areas. These segments may be further stratified so that the bank can focus its activities sharply on target strata. The banker should try to find out the specific needs of different customer segments so that suitable package of services can be made available.

The tasks of identification of potential customers, segmentation of these customers and determination of specific needs of the customers can be entrusted by the central office to branch managers who after conducting informal interviews and focus groups with customers, prepare questionnaires which are administered to a sample of potential depositors. On the basis of the information collected through questionnaires branch managers prepare profile of the customers in terms of their distinguishing attitudes, behaviour, demographics, age, profession, etc. These information will be very useful for a bank in formulating suitable deposit schemes.

Another task involved in targeting market is to evaluate the various segments and decide the segments which the bank can serve most effectively. The bank must look at three major factors while evaluating different market segments, *viz.*, segment size and growth, segment structural attractiveness and bank's objectives and resources. A banker should choose the one that has growing tendency. However, he should ensure that the segment is attractive from the point of view of growth of deposits. For instance, urban people could be a good segment for a bank so far as their size and growth prospects are concerned. However, the same may not be very attractive because of existence of several strong and aggressive banking non-banking competitors and high-possibility of emergence of new competitors to attract urban savers. In contrast, rural segment of the country will be the obvious choice in view of its vastness of size and growing prosperity and limited competition.

Bank's resources should also be kept in view while choosing the target market. Even if a segment has positive size and growth characteristics and is structurally attractive, the banker needs to consider its own objectives and resources. Some attractive segments can be dismissed because they do not mix with the company's long-run objectives. Even if the segment fits the bank's objectives, it must consider whether it possesses the requisite skills and resources to succeed in that segment. Each segment has certain success requirements. The segment should be dismissed if the bank lacks one or more necessary competencies and is in no opposition to acquire the necessary competence. But even if the bank possesses the requisite competence, this is not enough. If it is really to win in that market segment, it needs to develop some superior advantages to the competition. It should not enter market segments where it cannot produce some form of superior value.

While choosing the target market, it is also essential for a bank to study the population group-wise data. If a particular bank has more of rural/semi-urban branches, identification of large group of customers in these areas and devising suitable schemes to suit their need would give positive results because the branch net work in these areas would help the bank in tapping the potential of the identified target group.

◈ Determining Competitive Positioning

In addition to the above, banker should also assess the strengths and weaknesses of the existing bank's schemes and services *vis-a-vis* those of the competitors with a view to determining competitive positioning of the bank. This will help in developing a general idea of what kind of offer to make to the target market in relation to the competitor's offer. This again calls for market research to learn what competitors are offering to customers in the target market and what customers really want.

An analysis of strengths and weaknesses of the bank's deposit schemes and services *vis-a-vis* those of competitors will reveal that savers with strong motive for high income prefer company deposits and corporate shares and debentures, those desiring to reduce their tax liability prefer NSCs and NSS and savers saving for future contingency opt for provident fund scheme of the Government. However, NSCs cannot be encashed prematurely before the expiry of full years. Loans against them from banks are granted less freely than against their own deposits at a higher rate of interest and upto a limited amount.

Despite lower interest rate and absence of tax concessions on bank deposit schemes, commercial banks have an edge over their non-banking agencies in respect of the services the former offer to the public. Thus, bank deposits are almost fully liquid. The depositors can get their money back immediately in case of demand. They always have the benefits of good yields and safety.

Another major strength of banks is their easy accessibility. A wide network of branches allows customers to choose a convenient nearby branch. Thus, the customers can without any problem contact branch functionaries personally. Provisions of facilities like repayment of deposits, transfer of accounts from one branch to the other, heavy withdraws at short notice, loans against security of bank deposits at convenient terms, remittances, lockers, etc., are other inherent advantages of bank schemes which no non-banking agency offers. Thus, capital market is highly speculative and even the more well versed and skilled persons have burnt their fingers in it. The long phase of depression after the boom of '85 has left many with loss of even their capital.

Company deposits provide upto 14% interest but as there is no exemption from income-tax on the interest to a tax payer, even in 25% bracket, the effective yield will be only 10.5%. There is no facility of loan or premature payment from the company. Similar is the case with company debentures with the only difference that they can be disposed off in stock exchanges if the holders so desire. Such disposal is generally made at below the face value. Again several companies default in payment of the principal and interest on the due date. Loss/delay in mail of interest warrants/letters/repayment can cause further inconvenience.

In the light of the above, the management has generally two basic alternatives. One is to take position next to one of the existing competitors and fight for the customers who want the present service. This option should be chosen where it is felt that the bank can render better service, the market buying this kind of service is large enough for the competitors and the company and it has more resources than the existing competitors. The other choice is to render a service which is not currently offered to the target market. In this case, the bank would gain instant leadership in this market. However, before making these decisions, careful consideration of certain critical factors such as technical and economic feasibility of the service and strong preference for the service by sufficiently large number of customers must be made.

◈ Making Marketing Strategic Decisions

Once the management has identified strengths and weaknesses and assessed the trends in the environment to isolate opportunities and threats, suitable strategy has to be formulated to achieve the bank's avowed objective of garnering deposits on an increasing scale from different corners of the country and maintain its market share in total deposits of the country. In the present circumstances, it will be more useful for a bank to adopt growth and competition strategies.

Growth strategy is intended to increase business from existing clients by selling new products/services to them and consolidating relations with them. Competition strategy involves getting new customers. A bank can expand its deposits and maintain its market share through market development or market penetration. In market development strategy, bank management should always look for new markets whose needs might be met by its current products. In product development strategy, the management looks for ways to increase the market share of its current deposits in the current markets. This can be done by encouraging the bank's current customers to deposit their savings more. Attempt could also be made to attract the competitors' customers by offering better services. Finally, the banker could try to convince current non-banking savers to put their surpluses with bank. This would be very useful particularly in rural areas where there are a lot of people who still are not familiar with banking facilities.

Whatever be the marketing strategy adopted by a bank, the management must concentrate on three vital aspects of marketing, *viz.*, product, price and place.

◈ Product

In product part of marketing, the bank management should be essentially concerned with developing new saving schemes and services keeping in view current needs and future preferences of target market, changing life styles, technological upgradation, schemes of competitors, etc. Such a product/service mix should be developed that will not only attract savings of the target market but also create surpluses by curbing the conspicuous consumption of the potential customers.

So as to offer most suitable product mix to the target market, the banker should keep in view current and future needs and preferences of target customers, services offered by the existing competitors and present and future state of environment.

In recent years, commercial banks have in their attempt to attract savings, evolved new schemes such as Monthly Interest Schemes, Annuity or Retirement Schemes, Farmer's Deposit Scheme, Insurance Linked Savings Bank Account, Housing Deposit Scheme, Insurance Linked Savings Bank Account, Housing Deposit Scheme, Automatic Extension Deposit. A brief review of these schemes is made below:

(i) **Monthly Interest Schemes:** These are fixed deposit accounts on which the depositors get interest which is paid monthly either in cash or is carried in the depositor's current or savings deposit account. A loan facility on appropriate terms is granted to the depositors against such deposit. Banks also provide the refund facility before maturity.

(ii) **Annuity or Retirement Schemes:** Under this scheme, monthly deposits are collected for a number of years. After a certain stipulated period, the amount, inclusive of interest, or double the amount in monthly instalments is repaid.

(iii) **Farmer's Deposit Scheme:** This scheme has been introduced by commercial banks to benefit farmers. Under the scheme, farmers have the freedom to deposit their savings once or twice a year. They may run down one-tenth of their deposits every month.

(iv) **Insurance Linked Savings Bank Account:** This scheme has been introduced to provide life insurance protection to the person depositing in a "Special Insurance Linked Savings Bank Account." Men not below the age 18 years and not above 49 years, and women in the same age group with an independent regular income, are entitled to operate the account, provided that they agree to keep the specified minimum balance. Joint accounts may be opened by two persons closely related to each other; but only one of the joint account holders will be insured. A minimum balance of ₹ 500 in rural areas and ₹ 1,000 in urban areas must be maintained in the account. The insurance cover is provided by the LIC under a special agreement with the bank. Premium at 1.25 per cent is paid by the bank. Interest at 4 per cent per annum is given by the bank to the account holder on the minimum balance.

An account holder has the benefit of repayment of the balance in the account. In the event of the premature death of the account holder before the age of 41 years, the successor will get twice the amount of the deposit maintained during the half-yearly account period immediately preceding the date of death, subject to a maximum of ₹ 10,000. In the event of the premature death of the account holder above the age of 41 years, the successor will be entitled to get an amount equal to the average monthly minimum amount of deposit maintained during the half-yearly accounting period immediately preceding the date of the death, subject to a maximum of ₹ 5,000.

However, a bank has to evolve further a wide variety of specific deposit schemes and render diversified services so as to garner surpluses of diverse target customers by satisfying their needs. Thus, a bank with a dense branch network of over 56% of the total branches in rural areas and majority of population having agriculture as the main occupation can attract savings of farmers by introducing a suitable scheme.

The deposit scheme would be a loan linked or otherwise. A recurring deposit scheme would not be suitable for agriculturists since they may not be able to save fixed amount every month. A scheme which facilitates them to save unequal amounts even at irregular intervals during a fixed total period would be suitable and the interest paid as regular monthly return to the farmers would prove very useful to the latter. Say, in this scheme a deposit or may be allowed to deposit for about a period of 25 years so that he gets back after 50 years of age or so principal and interest put together as equal monthly instalments just like pension. This would take care of the uncertainties in the later part of the life of the farmer when his energies do not permit him to work and earn.

In order to attract savings of urban non-bank savers who have strong preference for investments in physical assets compared to financial assets (according to IBA survey, 76% of household savings in urban areas are converted in consumer durables, business assets and house property), it is worthwhile exploring the possibility of developing some deposit linked credit schemes, so that at least the amount to be spent on such items could remain in the banks as deposits till such purchases are made.

In order to accelerate the pace of deposit mobilisation, banks need to tap hitherto untapped savings, especially in rural areas, by introducing appropriate deposit schemes suitable to savers with risk and return profiles. Further to tap small amounts of household savings which display irregular patterns, banks are advised to adopt 'piggy banking' concept (as in Philippines) whereby small locked boxes are provided to the savers to be maintained at their homes after opening of the savings account with a minimum deposit. The key are kept with the banks. This allows the clients to save small amounts on a daily basis in their boxes and bring them to the banks when they intend to deposit their savings. Banks may also employ technological and MIS solutions to expand their outreach in the rural sector and boost rural savings. The experience of other countries can be a guide to the banks in this regard.

With traditional deposit base of banks shrinking in recent years, there is a need for them to extend their outreach to prospective depositors/investors by expanding the ambit of specialised financial services offered by them by repackaging and redesigning of products to suit individual needs.

By offering investment services to depositors a bank may attract new deposits. A large number of savers, particularly in the middle-income group, are willing to invest their saving surpluses in profitable securities; but they abstain from doing so mainly because of complexity of investment affairs and their limited knowledge of them. If a bank promises to collect profitable and safe securities for the depositors, collect interest on these securities and manage their disposal, when required, a good number of savers would be tempted to put their idle funds in the bank.

Banks may also introduce such deposit schemes as would suit the people and as would provide for the collection of deposits and their repayment. Farmers, for example, have after the harvest, a substantial amount; if these savings are not mobilised, they will find their way into unproductive channels. A bank may devise a scheme by which farmers' savings are collected immediately after the harvest and by which they would have the freedom to withdraw their deposits during the year, as and when needed. This scheme would ensure to the depositors the triple benefits of certainty of regular interest income, the safety of funds, and the withdrawal facility. Farmers, if educated about the merits of this scheme, may be tempted to deposit their savings in the bank.

Another scheme, deposit — linked with bequeath may be introduced to fulfil one of the basic motives of the people in low and middle-income groups — to bequeath some property to their children. Under the scheme, an account will be operated in the name of the child. The bank will accept the deposits weekly, monthly or quarterly. The sum of deposits, plus the interest thereon, would be repaid to the child after attaining the age of majority. In this way, a person may give some wealth to his child, which would otherwise not have been possible because of his limited income.

Most persons in low and middle-income groups do not have a sufficient source of earnings to satisfy their bare needs in their old age. Such persons may be induced to save and deposit regularly in the form of a social security deposit after they attain 45 years of age, if the persons are assured of a regular monthly interest income after their retirement. Salaried persons may also be induced to keep the sum, which they get in a lumpsum at the time of retirement, in the form of a social security deposit if they are certain to get a steady monthly interest income on it.

Small entrepreneurs and farmers may be encouraged to save more and more if they are assured of credit facilities for investment purposes after depositing a certain sum over a period of years. For example, a small entrepreneur under the investment deposit scheme may be assured of a loan sufficient to buy a machine if he deposits a sum equal to 25% of the price of the machine. This could be a loan with 35% margin.

Bank should evolve schemes to attract young who constitute the best potential market. The young today are acquiring more and more spending power and this is more so in urban and metropolitan centres. To attract young, mostly students suitable scheme of education deposits could be introduced. Likewise, other deposit schemes such as marriage deposits and medical deposits may be started. The basic principle underlying these schemes is that a person who saves in these forms consistently over a long period of time should be assured of meeting his liabilities by providing a sum that is double his savings. Linking of deposits with loans for different purposes would prove to be an effective instrument for introducing a higher rate of saving.

A bank can also attract terminal benefits of a retired official who would appreciate counselling from the banker as to how he could apportion his investments in such a way as to get the permissible tax shelter, a specified monthly income to meet his ordinary needs and invest the balance in different maturities in various securities consistent with his need for funds.

By rendering assistance to needy persons, a banker can produce the latter to put their surpluses in the bank. Thus, a professional like a doctor, who is just setting up a practice would greatly appreciate the bank's help to acquire a few necessary equipments. One who has a growing practice would benefit by the bank's assistance for acquiring sophisticated equipment he may need for enlarging his clientele. The needs of other professionals may vary and would need to be studied, so that the customer would get a conviction that his bank is the most dependable friend.

The success of a bank depends on its establishing rapport with its customers and potential clients, gleaning their needs and offering such services as would be appropriate.

◈ Pricing

In respect of pricing, a bank has limited choice due to fixation of interest rates and services charges by RBI and IBA, respectively. However, a combination of several services in package, with judicious use of the limited discretion with banks, could be made sufficiently competitive and attractive for customers. Although the recent hike in cost of bank's services has invited a lot of public criticism, the fact is that customers are mostly concerned with the quality of services rather than costs. With improved quality of service and capacity to provide a wide range of services, price may not remain the deciding factor of customer preference.

◆ Place

Another vital element of bank marketing is the place from where the product is being offered. A bank should be so located that customers do not feel inconvenienced in making transactions with the bank. Location of bank branches assume considerable importance for effective distribution. In this respect, banks suffer from several limitations for reasons beyond their control. Many of the branches of commercial banks are quite inconveniently located. Such branches will have to strive harder in compensating the customers by offering better service to attract them. Besides, customers provide due consideration to conveniences in terms of amenities and comforts in choosing a particular bank branch. Therefore, an inviting outlook and physical comforts offered by a bank are no less important. It is intriguing to note that most of the bank branches in India are far short of these requirements. They not only lack in the conveniences, and comforts needed by the customer, but also lack an appropriate air of friendliness. Many of the branches are overgrown in size, resulting in congestion, chaos and confusion. Such branches with their unmanageable sizes are unable to service and control even their existing business efficiently and effectively, resulting in dissatisfaction of the customers. This is an organisational problem for the banks to which a solution will have to be found.

In the performance of a service, personal competence and efficiency constitute critical inputs. It is not only a matter of knowledge and skill alone, but more importantly of attitude — the disposition of the server towards the served that determines the quality of service. Direct personal contact with the customers helps the bank to attract more and more savings by familiarising them with benefit of new deposit schemes and explaining and counselling a customer for helping him to select the right product.

Of late, emergence of virtual banking providing ATM, Telebanking and Internet banking facilities has eased the problems of customers in transacting with banks.

◆ Promotion

Promotion is a vitally important ingredient of the marketing mix. Modern marketing calls for more than developing a good product, pricing it attractively and making it really accessible to target customers. It requires effective tools with which to inform, persuade or remind target customers about the bank's marketing mix and the bank itself for maintenance or improvement of market share or improvement of climate for future sales. A bank must, therefore, choose useful and effective methods for promoting the bank's products.

There are three major tools of promotion, *viz.*, mass selling, personal selling, and sales promotion.

Mass selling is intended to communicate with large number of customers at the same time. Advertising is a highly public mode of communication. Banks can play a crucial role in spreading the message among masses on need to save through scientific advertising campaign. Till now, banks have used posters display at own premises. It attracts the attention of those who visit its premises and are literate enough to read and understand and also have time and willingness to read these posters. Banks have also started putting up hoardings at the prominent places in towns and many banks put up welcome boards at the entrance of cities even at the small centres.

Press advertisements by individual banks are presently not allowed. IBA is doing this job collectively, obviously with a view to achieving uniformity and economy. It is really surprising to see that TV as a media of advertising remains neglected by IBA. It covers more than 70% area of the country and touches both at the literate and illiterate masses, urban, rural and semi-urban masses. It will be more useful if specially developed documentaries and serials could be sponsored by IBA on TV network. This will become an effective tool for inculcating savings habits among masses.

Advertisements by banks for developing saving habits should be based on effective theme messages touching upon economic, social, psychological, security and nationalist motives in a scientific and balanced manner. Their advertisements should not only convey to the public about benefits of the scheme but also its superiority to those of the competitors.

Here the IBA should commission marketing research projects to study the depositors' behaviour in various regions of our country. Such research studies will help in identifying dominating factors affecting deposit habit behaviour. While pursuing the goal of development of saving habits, bankers should not ignore the needs for socio-culture reforms. To cite, some theme messages based on "Dowry of a Daughter" are objectionable from this point of view. Positive contribution should be made by aggressive and persuasive marketing of concepts like 'small family,' 'hard work', 'honesty', 'savings and investment', 'simple living', etc.

Personal selling is the most direct form of promotion and a very powerful one at that. Personal selling device is very useful promotional device particularly for a banking intending to penetrate in rural areas where vast majority of the people are still unfamiliar with economic implications of various saving schemes. While LIC, UTI and National Small Savings Organisation, etc., are resorting to personal selling for promotion of savings and saving habits, banks in India have almost ignored this promotional technique. It is, therefore, necessary for banks to develop a specially trained and motivated cadre of 'Bare Foot' Bankers who can work hard to spread the message of 'simple living,' 'avoid wasteful social and conventional expenses', 'save more', 'deposit', 'invest more for better future of your family' and 'contribute in nation's development' to every nook and corner of the country. It should be treated as a mission and a process of education be adopted with patience and perseverance. This task is in the nature of concept selling which requires special skills and traits much different from those needed for product selling. Such persons must be ready and willing to do all paper work like filling of forms etc., for illiterate/semi/literate persons.

Service orientation in marketing efforts of bankers is necessary for winning over new clients. The best form of publicity of a bank is customers' satisfaction. All banks have some interest rates etc., to offer basically similar schemes but some of them can attract more customers than others because of superior quality of service. Some important elements of service are upkeep of the premises and utmost cleanliness, availability of physical facilities for services, trained and motivated staff, speed and efficiency, knowing the customers and welcoming them by name and with a smile, improvement in systems and procedures to cut delays, quick decision-making, punctuality and discipline etc.

Another strategic move which an Indian commercial bank should make in order to improve its market share in deposits is adoption of 'single window service' concept in marketing of banking services. This strategy has been suggested in view of the fact that the new generation private sector banks and foreign banks have embarked on full computerisation for quite sometime and have been able to achieve competitive edge over the PSBs. The new private sector banks have been able to respond quickly to the changes and introduced sophisticated technology such as ATMs, Networking of branches, Electronic Fund Transfer, Tele-banking, Internet banking, shared payment Net-work, E-Commerce. The significant difference between the computerised branch of a private sector bank and a public sector bank is that the former operates on the single window concept, while the latter, despite computerisation, continues to operate almost along the existing manual system. Nevertheless, PSBs have introduced single window service system partially by opening teller counter, its impact is limited. However, things are gradually improving in as much as many PSBs have, of late, decided to extend business hours especially in respect of their computerised branches.

It is suggested that PSBs should quickly act upon the plans of extension of business hours, Sunday banking, 24-hours banking by installation of more number of ATMs and above all quick net-working of branches. Further, technology driven banking should not be restricted to metro or urban areas only but should also be extended to other important centres as the same will provide over other competitors. Since most of the PSBs are losing grounds in metro and urban areas, at least they can avoid similar happenings in semi-urban and rural areas by taking proactive measures before competition intensifies in these areas as well.

It will, therefore, be in fitness of things to introduce the Single Window Service system once a branch is computerised. This move will not only improve customer service but will be economical. In case this is not done, banking services will not only be labour intensive but also capital intensive.

F. IMPLEMENTING MARKETING STRATEGY

For implementing marketing strategy for deposit mobilization purpose, considerable work will be involved at all levels. At the branch level, extensive market survey and analysis of data will have to be undertaken. The final market plan would emerge after a series of discussions and negotiations between the manager and his controller. This plan throws light on number of personal calls in a mouth publicity campaign schemes to be launched in target markets.

It is necessary for a bank to develop and train a band of devoted staff having zeal and zest to work hard to achieve the results. Skill of salesmanship has to be developed. A successful salesman is one who creates demand by drawing attention, creating interest, arousing desire and securing action. This requires communicative ability, emotional stability, tactfulness, judgement, courage, determination, self-confidence, imagination, technical knowledge, enthusiasm, dynamism coupled with prudent attitude, etc. The manager should develop a personal rapport with and concern for the customers and motivate the staff to do the same. Banks will have to empower the employees more and chalk out new schemes for motivating them. Newly set up private sector banks have performed exceedingly well in the area of market share development as the level of employee involvement, motivation, productivity and profitability has been found to be exceptionally of high order.

Thus, banks, especially PSBs need to invest significantly in skill enhancement at all levels, for developing innovative products and delivering new service modes in the face of increased competition.

G. CONCLUSIONS

Banks in India have played a significant role in supporting the growth process by mobilizing savings particularly after the nationalization. They have been instrumental in garnering savings from the household sector.

A host of forces have influenced the banks' deposit mobilization efforts which include external forces — environmental forces — and internal forces. External forces include state of national economy, characteristic of local economy, role of government, relative changes in policy, economic policy of government, policy central banks and household's decisions. Internal forces influencing a bank's capability to mobilize deposits comprise physical features of the bank, personnel of the bank and services rendered by it, fundamental policies and financial position of the bank and size of the bank.

Surge in deposits of the SCBs during the post nationalization period was the result of significant rise in net financial savings of the household sector and large expansion of banks. However, pace of deposit growth slackened during 1984-95 mainly due to slowdown in economy~ slowdown in expansion instruments. This tendency continued during the subsequent decade (1995-2005) due to successive reduction in the maturities of term deposits and concomitant decrease in interest rates on the one hand and fierce competition from post offices offering higher interest rates on their deposits.

It is gratifying to note surging trend in growth of bank deposits in recent few years. This has been mainly owing to rise in interest rates on term deposits and extension of tax deposits.

Although there has been unprecedented spike in bank deposits since nationalization of banks, this surge has been mainly due to fiscal policy of the Government and monetary policy of the RBI and banks in India have made very limited efforts to expand their deposit base.

The biggest challenge before the banks in India is to sustain the acceleration of deposit growth in view of emergence of new saving instruments and effective competing institutions. To overcome this challenge and to cater to the growing credit requirements, banks have to tap hitherto vast untapped savings from rural and unbanked regions of the country. For that the banks have to adopt strategic marketing approach. They have to formulate marketing strategy that involves undertaking marketing opportunity analysis, selecting target market, determining competitive positioning and making marketing strategic decisions. They have also to implement the strategy effectively for which they need to invest significantly in skill enhancement at all levels.

KEY TERMS

- Derivative deposit
- Financial savings
- High net worth individuals
- Physical savings
- Piggy banking
- Strategic marketing approach

DISCUSSION QUESTIONS

1. Discuss, in brief, various forces that bear upon a bank's ability to mobilize savings.
2. Critically assess the efforts made by commercial banks in India to mobilize savings of the household sector since nationalization.
3. What factors have influenced deposit mobilization efforts of the bank m India during post nationalization?
4. What are the major challenges commercial banks in India are going to face in near future?
5. What strategic measures should banks in India take to overcome the challenges?
6. What is strategic marketing approach to deposit mobilization by banks? How will this approach help a bank in garnering savings of the household sector?
7. What is 'piggy banking' approach of deposit mobilization? How will it enable a bank to tap small savings of the people?

REFERENCES

1. RBI Report on Currency and Finance, 2006-08, Volume I, p. 43.
2. JBS Davies, A Shorrocks Sandstrom and E.N. Wolf, "Estimating the Level and Distribution of Global Household Wealth," Research Paper No.2007/77, UNU — Wider, United Nations University, Nov. 2007.
3. J. Richard Resen, "Banking Market Conditions and Deposit Interest Rates," Journey of Banking and Finance, 31, 2007.
4. RBI Report, Op cit, pp. 146-148.
5. Janak Roy, "A study of operations of Non-Banking Financial Intermediaries in India with special reference to their implications for monetary policy", unpublished Ph.D. thesis, IIT, Mumbai, 1999.
6. Economic Times, July 4, 2007.
7. Weyer Deryk, Quoted in Marketing Financial Services, by McLever Colin Naylor Geoffrey, p. 5.

❁ ❁ ❁

Relationship Banking

Chapter 14

Learning Objectives:

The present chapter attempts to:

- Provide a conceptual exposition of relationship banking and its distinguishing features.
- Provide an incisive idea about utility and fundamentals of relationship banking and customer experience management in banks.
- Provide an insight into the process of developing relationship with customers.
- Provide a methodology for formulating relationship banking strategy.
- Provide a discussion on customer relationship management operations in commercial banks in India.

Chapter Outline:

- Introduction.
- Concept of relationship banking.
- Distinguishing features of relationship banking.
- Utility of relationship banking.
- Fundamentals of relationship banking.
- Process of developing relationship with customers.
- Formulating relationship banking strategy.
- Customer experience management in banks.
- Customers relationship management operations by commerical banks in India.
- RBI policy regarding customers services by commercial banks.
- Conclusions.

A. INTRODUCTION

With unleashing of forces of competition and large scale disintermediation in recent years following the policy of deregulation, liberalisation and privatisation and growing awareness of customers due to pathbreaking technological developments, Indian customers have become more finicky and sophisticated demanding better service and higher value and aspiring for personal care, continuous attention and involvement. Sensing the need for retaining the existing customers in highly competitive market in view of much higher costs involved in wresting new customers than those in servicing extant ones and also realising that losing a customer means more than losing a single sale,[1] Indian organisations including commercial banks have, of late, started focusing on customers' service. Thrust of quality customer service is on more involvement and choice and building on-going customer relationship. Although use of sophisticated technology has helped the new players in improving their operational efficiency and achieving an edge over their competitors, it is quite doubtful if it can totally substitute the human element from the process especially in the context of banking business. Maintaining relationship with the customers certainly requires people who can give a personal touch to the transactions and retain the customers in the bank's fold.

Realising, though belatedly, that it is customers on whom depends the ultimate survival of banks and it is they whose willingness to pay for a product or service converts economic resources into wealth and things into goods and it is they who determine what is its business and, what it produces and whether it will prosper, commercial banks have, of late, embarked upon long-term marketing plan with focus on customers. However, they are still finding it too difficult to woo new customers and retain the existing ones because of higher value offered by the new players in terms of cost, quality, product differentiation, delivery and service. The mind boggling question before Indian bankers today is how to attract customers and retain them.

A cursory look at the marketing strategies of various commercial banks in India reveals that they are more keen on attracting new customers rather than retaining existing ones. As a matter of fact, their approach to marketing is transaction-oriented, the aim of which is to help sales people to close a specific sale with a customer. The focus of transaction banking is on customer creation, and product-orientation with little emphasis on building long-term relationship with customers, limited customer care and commitment.

In an age of decreasing customer loyalty, bankers have to place greater emphasis on managing customer relationships so that they can sell more products to their existing customers. Beyond designing strategies to attract new customers and create transactions with them, they have to go all out to retain current customers and build lasting customer relationships. They must build strong economic and social ties by promising and consistently delivering high-quality products, good service and reasonable cost. Indian bankers need to shift from trying to maximize profit on each individual transaction to maximizing mutually beneficial relationships with customers. This is what is known as 'Relationship Banking' or 'Customer Relationship Management' in banks.

B. CONCEPT OF RELATIONSHIP BANKING

Relationship banking or Customer Relationship Management (CRM) in banks is a comprehensive management system which seeks to touch all areas and functions of banking business connected with value creation and delivery chain of the organization. CRM is neither a product nor a service; it is an overall business strategy that enables organizations to effectively manage relationships with their customers by providing an integrated view of the customers to everyone in the organization. It is a philosophy that places the customer at the heart of an organization's processes and culture to improve his satisfaction and, in turn, maximize profits for the organization.

Relationship banking involves creating, maintaining and enhancing strong relationships with customers. It is the process of attracting, maintaining, enhancing and commercializing a relationship between a buyer and a seller. Attracting customers is only the first step in relationship management, while it is the be-all and end-all in a transaction approach. In fact, the actual relationship starts when transaction ends. A sale merely consummates the courtship at which point the marriage depends on how the seller manages the relationship.

Thus, relationship banking emphasizes on building and maintaining profitable long-term relationships with customers by creating superior customer value and satisfaction. Relationship banking is oriented toward the long-term. The objective is to deliver long-term value to customers and the measure of success is long-terms customer satisfaction.

The relationship banking is based on the premise that customers do not merely buy banking products or services, but solutions to their problems. This is more so in the case of high value customers of critical importance, who mostly belong to the corporate sector.

In relationship banking, bank's people, processes and technology are integrated in such a way as to maximize the relations of the bank with all types of its customers. The true value of relationship banking is to transform strategy, operational processes and business functions so as to retain customers and increase customer loyalty and profitability.

What is most important to note that high level allegiance to customers can be sustained in the long run if it is based on emotions. Everyone in the organizations has to be emotionally attached to the targeted customers.

C. DISTINGUISHING FEATURES OF RELATIONSHIP BANKING

Thus, relationship banking has certain cardinal features making it distinct from transaction banking:

- Relationship banking is a proactive strategic system to deal with customers on an enduring basis, keeping in view, *inter alia*, needs, perceptions, social, cultural changes, lifestyles, spending and consumption habits of core customers, competitors' strategies and the firms' core competencies. It is not just important to understand who your customer is today, but to identify the drivers of his behaviour, how these are changing his future needs.
- Excellence and not the effectiveness is the rule of relationship banking. Excellence in all the spectrum of activities, right from identification of customer needs to the customers' satisfaction, signifies doing superb and superior things with accent on productivity, cost, quality, products innovativeness, delivery of world class services and understanding of customers' needs. A bank to be dandy and excellent will have to provide unparalleled guarantee of reliability of product and service. This demands passion and perseverance among the people at all levels of the organization. The 'Total Quality Management' is, thus, an adjunct to relationship banking.
- Relationship banking is a comprehensive approach. It does not belong just to sales and marketing. It is a way of doing business that touches all areas, it is way of thinking about and dealing with customer relationship.
- Relationship banking is based on customer centric approach which signifies configuration of strategic aspects of the bank to fulfill customers' needs. Since success of an institution depends on healthy concoction of strategic thinking and strategic action, the best chance of surviving and thriving in today's and tomorrow's competitive and turbulent terrain lies in customerization of these two major aspects of business so that the vision, mission, objectives, strategy, process, people, structure, information systems and culture are cohered to customers' delight. It is important to touch the customers' nerve and create empathy so as to capture customers and retain them.
- Everyone in the organization has to be emotionally attached to the targeted customers.

- Relationship banking focuses on customer retention and therefore places high premium on building and strengthening long-term relationships with customers. As against this, transaction banking is about customer catching.
- Unlike the transaction banking which is only converting a prospect to a customer, the relationship banking assiduously cultivates the customer to take him further up in the relationship ladder to a client, a supporter and finally to a partner.
- Relationship banking is based on basic premise that customers need focused and constant attention.
- Relationship banking thrusts on creating superior value and satisfaction to customers that result in strong customer loyalty.
- Relationship banking believes in maximizing mutually beneficial relationships with customers instead in maximizing profits on each individual transaction.
- Basic objective of relationship banking is to earn customer loyalty and as such it emphasises on sustained post-sale nurturing.
- There is high degree of customer commitment and care, and greater and consistent involvement of customers in operations of relationship building.
- Relationship banking rests on mutual trust and confidence whereas transaction banking is based on "Exchange." Hence, transparency is the crux of relationship banking.
- Relationship banking is more concerned with the repeat customers than with the market share. Accordingly, service encounters with a customer are not of episodic nature (as in the case of transaction banking) but of a continuous one of mutual dependency.
- Relationship banking is based on team system of working. It demands that all of the bank's operating units work together with marketing as a team to serve and satisfy the customer.

D. UTILITY OF RELATIONSHIP BANKING

Relationship banking based on philosophy of nurturing and building long-term relations with customers is significantly useful to banking institutions in as much as it enhances their competitive advantages through revenue growth and cost savings. Retention proves more profitable as current customers place frequent orders and buy more. It is much easier to discover client needs and concerns in an existing client setting. With growing confidence of clients, and so also increasing image, more of new business opportunities may emerge.

Costs shrink too. The need for prospecting new customers tends to decline with higher retention rate. Extant customers prove less sceptical and price sensitive — everything may offer a price premium. Since the need for comfort building measures is less, services can be delivered by the operating executive themselves without much demand on the time and effort of the top management.

Further, with growing competitive pressure, costs of attracting new customers are rising. In competitive markets it might cost five times as much as to attract a new customer as to keep a current customer happy.[2] By reducing customer dissatisfactions by only 5 per cent, organisations can improve profits anywhere from 25 to 85 per cent.[3]

As such, focus of a bank's first line of defence should lay on customer retention. The best approach to customer retention is to deliver high customer satisfaction and value that results in strong customer loyalty. Loyalty is an invaluable asset of an organisation. It does not exist on its own unless it is earned. Once earned it will appreciate in value, as satisfied customers become the bank's most vocal sales person. Thus, relationship begets loyalty which, in turn, multiplies cash flows.

E. FUNDAMENTALS OF RELATIONSHIP BANKING

A focus on customer is pivotal to relationship banking. It is, therefore, essential to have an understanding of what customers aspire. Customers normally aspire for higher value from a bank to be derived from the services of both tangible and intangible attributes, features and benefits.

There are four different levels that constitute a total product concept. These are core, expected, augmented and potential. For a banking service such as a deposit account, the core element might be safety and return on deposits.

The customer also expects that the transaction must be completed without undue delay and a neat and accurate statement of account should be sent to him, besides warm and friendly atmosphere in the bank. This is the expected element of bank product.

The banker on his own provides additional services such as a loan facility, a locker or credit card and also makes frequent customer calls which differentiate the product from that of competitors. This is augmented element of products.

Potential element of bank product consists of all potential additional features which a banker is capable of packing into the banking product, besides forging personal rapport with the target customer. At this stage the banker becomes a friend, philosopher and guide to customers.

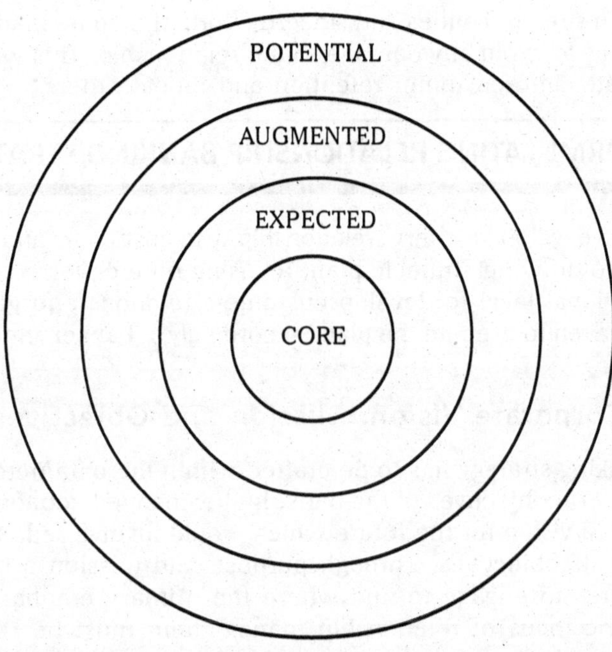

Fig. 14.1

While at the first (core) level, the customer's basic need is satisfied, he derives greater benefit through the second (expected) level and the third (augmented level). As the service extends to the fourth and final (potential) level, the building up of lasting customer relationship is complete. At each of these levels, more and more value addition takes place. It is at the fourth level that customer value addition attains its peak.

Thus, in relationship management quality of service constitutes the crucial element. Creating and retaining a customer are the driving forces of delivering high quality service. The bank has, therefore, to determine what the customers value most in terms of products and services.

Unfortunately, Indian bankers have been all along accustomed to creating a steady stream of customers through the front door and losing them through the back door. However, in recent few years it is being realised that product-oriented and transaction-oriented efforts to augment their business may not achieve desired results and hence the new approach of relationship banking is receiving focus. They have come to believe that relationship banking is the new paradigm for survival and success, embracing a 'care and customer' approach to growth by identifying, nursing and deepening customer relationships.

F. PROCESS OF DEVELOPING RELATIONSHIP WITH CUSTOMERS

Process of developing relationship with customers is a circular one. It begins with identification of customer needs which may be manifest in needs and arouse incipient needs through proactive marketing approach. Further, entire range of needs of the customer should be discerned.

Once the needs of the customer have been determined, the banker must try to find out an agreed price for the product for delivering the product with value. This value could be by way of product quality, optimum cost, timely delivery, post sales service package, etc. Besides, the value would be both actual (seller's point of view) and perceived (buyer's point of view). It is the creation of value that helps maintain and enhance relationship between the buyer and the seller.

Third step involved in the process of relationship banking is to get feedback from the clients about the product offerings and suggestions about improved product use of helpful new products. This will enable the banker to determine the gap, if any, between the upfront promises and the down stream realities and sincere efforts should be made as early as possible to remove the gap so as to avoid any damage to the relationship. This will generate customer loyalty which culminates into customer retention and repeat orders.

G. FORMULATING RELATIONSHIP BANKING STRATEGY

So as to nurse and develop long-term relationship with customers and to generate customer loyalty, a banker has to draw up strategic plan, focusing on long-term course of action to be taken at the organisational level to develop customers relations and gain customers loyalty and steps to be undertaken to execute the plan. Accordingly, a banker should take the following steps:

◆ Articulating Corporate Vision, Mission and Objectives of the Bank

Relationship banking strategy has to be crafted within the parameters of vision, purpose and mission and long-term objectives of the bank. In the changed economic milieu the banker will have to think with a vision for the future which would involve redefining its purpose and mission and resetting its objectives. Through purpose and mission a bank has to visualise what business it desires to engage in and where the primary emphasis has to be placed. Customer being centric focus of relationship management must be reflected in corporate vision of the bank. The primacy of the customer and his needs and a realization that a bank exists only because of the customers have to permeate the entire organisation so that its entire efforts are focused on creation of customers value and customers satisfaction.

While visualizing vision and mission it must be remembered that the banker projects a good corporate image before the customers and the general public. One of the crucial aspects influencing customer decision is the perceived risk associated with the service provider. If a bank is perceived to be risky or unsafe, whatever innovative and pioneering efforts that it makes are likely to be viewed with a tinge of suspicion. In the absence of good corporate image entire efforts to focus on customers would be futile.

The vision so articulated needs to be shared with employees, customers, collaborators and other enlightened people of the society to solicit their opinions so that path of the bank may be expressed as dedicated to provide hassles-free services to people they want any time, any where.' This simple statement of purpose and mission will catch attention of people in and outside the organization.

Statements of purpose and mission provide a long-term direction to the bank and bind all the elements together toward customer service.

Within the framework of vision and mission, the banker should spell out its long-term objectives which serve as guide post to strategic decisions and as standard to evaluate performance of the organization. These objectives focus on getting a customer and retaining him and creation of value to customers and provision of quality services. Keeping in view these objectives, quantified goals may be stated in terms of how many new customers, what percentage of repeat business, what amount of business from a single customer, etc.

◈ Evolving a Strategy

With a view to achieving purpose and objectives, suitable strategy of market segmentation has to be drawn up. Segmentation makes relationship strategy focussed, helps devise appropriate delivery system and tailor the relationship programmes to customer needs. Market segment is nucleus of relationship management because the latter is effort-oriented and cannot spread too thin on all and sundry. As such, only those segments, which are accessible, measurable and of minimum critical size should be the thrust of relationship building.

Within a segment, it is imperative to compute the life time value of the customers. The lifetime value is the net present value of the contribution of a customer over the anticipated retention period. This analysis will help decide the intensity of relationship effort necessary and the cost to be incurred thereon.

Once the target customer has been identified, the banker should build a relationship chain to keep him. The relationship attempt begins with the provision of a relationship manager to take care of all the needs of a customer. The relationship manager acts as a bridge between the customer and the bank. This bridge becomes a chain when the relationship manager is able to develop interdependence between the customer and the bank.

The task of a relationship manager is to satisfy the entire needs of the customer and to mobilise the resources of the bank for the purpose. He has to understand customer's value chain to find areas of contribution. He will have to reengineer the delivery process to maximize customer value. Thus, relationship becomes a bank-wide process and the entire organisation gets pivoted on the relationship management.

◈ Designing Appropriate Structure

With a view to executing customer focused strategy, the banker must strive for organisational structure which is market driven, responsive to customers' needs and performance based. Lean and flat structure with clearly defined authorities and responsibilities coupled with self-managed teams is the demand of the day.

The existing hierarchically and functionally oriented structure of a bank in which every product group contacts the client separately and thinks that it only owns the client and none is responsible for providing the quality of service is not suitable for achieving the objective because on the one hand the cost of multiple contacts is higher and the return is limited to the specific products and material time only and on the other hand, the client gets desperate contacts and fractured view of the organisation and he has to run to different outlets for various needs resulting in untapping of his incipient and his satisfaction left no chance. In brief, the existing organisational set up of Indian commercial banks can at best optimize individual functions at the cost of total business and customers.

The changed structure for relationship management purpose must have multi-disciplinary teams for customer satisfaction. In such a structure, the relationship manager is the sole person who interfaces with the customer and skilled product groups and lends support to him in product delivery. For example, the client may express his need for three different products to the relationship manager who delivers the same with the help of the respective product groups. In sum, the entire structure is organised around the customer and not the product.

◆ Designing a Service Delivery System

Since the market driven delivery system has to be process-based instead of function-based, logistics should be so designed as to ensure a cost effective, yet constant output. Besides, product quality is also guaranteed. In fact, product quality is critical particularly when repeat sale is the primary concern of an organisation.

So as to ensure quality, service delivery should be designed as a system rather than as uncoordinated series of activities. For this purpose, detailed flow chart should be prepared, outlining all the components, identifying the fail points, setting execution standards and showing delivery points. With the help of the flow chart, the bank can eliminate non-value added activities, redundancies and identify the areas of improvement.

Further, service quality should be embedded into the process. Accordingly, the existing process needs to be reset keeping in view critical service issues as identified by the customers and as practised by the best in the banking industry. It is worth noting that the service quality and standards are not determined by the bank itself but by the customers and the competitors.

In order to ensure effective service delivery system, the banker should emphasise on co-ordination of all the activities involved therein. There should be a clear accountability for co-ordination in delivery. For example, a high value customer of a bank may deposit cash, purchase a draft, ask for a auto loan, etc. In such a situation a single interface to co-ordinate these activities will be meaningful as multiple interfades are likely to lead to inconsistent output and loss of quality. In a single interface system, the co-ordinator is accountable to the client and all the delivery points, in turn, are accountable to him. It is, therefore, necessary that the co-ordinator has sufficient authority to drive cross-functional teams and is himself not bogged down by any of the product execution responsibilities.

◆ Cultivating Skill

For relationship management to be effective a banking organisation must have three skills, *i.e.*, marketing skill, product skill and listening skill. While relationship manager requires marketing skill, product executive needs product skills. Of course, every executive including top management needs listening skills.

Relationship manager is expected to identify customer's needs, sell products and manage post sale feedback. He has to be proactive in need identification and arousal of incipient needs. He should be adept in offering value to a need. Likewise, while selling products, relationship manager should be cross selling (another product), upselling (higher value products), renewal selling, revival selling, etc.

Since the customer needs higher value and satisfaction, product executives must have competencies to offer products which meet the customer and competition standards. Product delivery in time and at reasonable cost, performance criteria, tolerance limits, etc. bear testimony to product skill.

People working in a service-oriented organisation must possess listening skills. Getting constant feedback from the customers goes a long way in gaining customers loyalty. Relationship needs empathic listening even though it is a bitter complaint. Complaints act both ways: more of it may show a systematic future and none of it may show a decaying relationship. Even satisfied customers, feedback must be obtained so as to strengthen the existing relations and earn their lasting loyalty.

◆ Creating Invigorating Organisational Ambience

Successful relationship banking demands creation of an organisational climate where there is least resistance to any change in the organisation. Corporate bank managers have to foster trust, generate a sense of pride and ownership in the organisation and provide life satisfaction to the people and sustain it through culture, useful traditions, practices and systems.

A sense of belongingness and commitment to quality and service culture has got to be inculcated. Organisational people have to retain customers through best services. Two important factors that help in sustaining motivation of the people are empowerment and open communication..

Empowerment of the staff facing customers is a must. He should be equipped with adequate skill and authority to provide quick solutions. Empowered staff may deliver more than anticipated as they rise to progressive challenges.

Openness in communication is a prerequisite to effective relationship efforts. It helps employees in imbibing the culture of customer service that in the ultimate analysis differentiates the leaders from the laggards.

Healthy organisational climate demands developing suitable performance appraisal system and reinforcing it through top management interventions.

Performance appraisal system for relationship staff and product staff should be based on a twin track system, i.e., to reward repeat business and to reinforce skilled products. For appraisal of performance of relationship executives, customer loyalty is the cornerstone. Loyalty can be measured in terms of net cash inflow. However, there are other parameters which must be kept in view while determining magnitude of loyalty generated by the bank staff. For example, extensive ground work may have been undertaken to launch a new product or to win over a client from a competitor. This will certainly have its positive influence on the bank's future cash inflow which is no less than milching the extant cash. Likewise, performance of product staff may be evaluated in terms of the earnings and quality.

◈ Creating Transformational leadership

All the above strategic measures cannot achieve the desired results without profound change in perceptions and mindsets of corporate leaders and paradigm change in style of leading people from transactional to transformational so as to move from exercising gross power of authority, which not only produces compliance to the subtle power of influence which secures commitment and passes ownership down the line. Transformational leaders direct their employees through vision, inspiration, ideas and fire their desire to reach destination, generate a sense of pride and ownership on the organization and provide life satisfaction to them.

H. CUSTOMER EXPERIENCE MANAGEMENT IN BANKS

◈ Concept

With deepening competitive pressures, traditional demands of product function, reasonable price and quality have lost their relevance. Even concept of customer relationship management with focus on strengthening long-term relationship has not been found significantly helpful in retaining customers. Everyone is now realizing that no matter what the firm's product offering is, there will always be competitors willing to do it cheaper or better. One can always find a cheaper car, a better-looking designer shirt, a mobile service offering more freebies, an airline with better seats, a bank with more ATMs. As such, if one wants to retain one's premium positioning and higher margins, one is left with only one option: delver a really powerful and pleasant customer experience, and reinforce it in as many ways as possible, so that the customer no longer cares if the rival product is cheaper or has more frills.

Research shows that customer satisfaction is not enough to guarantee sustained superior performance in the market place; for that a company needs enthusiastic customers.[4]

Emerging competitive pressures centre around the customer's experience and the crucial issue is how to provide customers with compelling experiences that create enduring memories and lasting relationships. The only differentiator that bank can rely on for lasting advantage is the experience that a customer carries within her head. If a customer starts believing in a brand and starts taking some degree of ownership of it, the brand will have become a part of her. From then on, as long as the brand delivers overall customer value and keeps on innovating, it will be tougher for competitors to dislodge.

The question, thus, arises is what is customer experience and how it is created. Customer experience is an intangible quality which is different from one person to the other. Experiences are built around feelings, emotions, smells, colours, spaces, sounds, human contact, branding and a thousand other factors and time. A great experience is created because it does not happen by accident and it is not only the result of better product features and functions or better services but because of how it makes people feel.[5]

The objective of any market programme of a bank is to create a platform on which customers can experience something of value. New focal points of a bank should include such things such as feelings, emotions, ideas, actions and connections, able to fulfill people's demands from the heart, whilst also helping enterprises identify new niches in which to operate. The concept of 'experience' is closely related to the process of behaviour, which is not restricted to enabling to buy whatever they want. It involves all activities and events experienced as part of the purchasing process. Experience is created when the individual interacts with the enterprise and it is, therefore, important to ensure that these interactions are as perfect as possible as seen from the customer's perspective.[6]

Explaining the reasons of management of customer experiences becoming a key differential factor for many brands, Joseph Pine II and James Gilmore observed that technology, that powers so many experiences, and increases competitive intensity are the main reasons. But the most encompassing answer resides in the nature of economic value where there is a natural progression of a commodity to goods, product, service and experiences.[7]

◈ Components of Customer Experience Management

Service:

Service is a critical component of experience, and providing good service requires many characteristics, including empathy, sensitivity and caring. It also requires proper tools-the right information delivered at the right time, the right products and the authority to do the right thing.

Technology:

Emerging technologies are enhancing value of products and services and also facilitating greater experiences. For banks, technology becomes the centerpiece because it is the interface to the customers. However, the relevant software has to be designed, customer needs to be anticipated and right information to be provided to users.

Look Beyond the Product:

The key to managing customer experience lies in taking the story well beyond the product. A bank has to provide a comfortable space where human minds can relax and interact freely. Similarly, instead of merely looking at providing 'luxury', a bank can think of catering to the exploratory and entertainment needs of the customer.

The Critical Intangible-Trust:

Most of the factors in the customer experience management are intangible and the very first thing on this list is trust. If a banker has built trust in customers, they will not switch over to other institutions. In real world, the sad truth is that most organizations are not giving their employees any tools for building trust, and as a result there is a systematic breakdown in the ties that make a market strong.

Realign People Practices:

Every company has to realign its people practices because managing the internal customer is no different from managing the external customer.[8] Without employees' enchanting experiences, there is no customer experience. Employees are the creators of customer experiences. If they do not have great delightful experiences, they will not deliver one to the customer. Either through product and service innovations, or through exceptional customer service, employees are the people that cement the relationship with customers. Employees' experiences are the ways to make them want to do it.

In reality, employees are not machines. If they are not inspired, they function only at partial capacity. They will conduct the transaction they were trained to do but they will not care. Financial incentives cannot make the employees perform by hearts. It will never unlock their passion, risk taking, willingness to work in teams, ability to excel or lead change. The key to unlocking their hearts is their experiences.

Re-engineering employees' experiences requires the same amount of commitment and resources as is required to redesign the customers' experiences. Bankers have to ensure that they have provided their employees with necessary tools and access to relevant information so that they become more effective. They must be inspired by trust, and empowerment to perform their job.

The employees should be trained and developed in such a manner that they understand the business ground rules and then give them opportunity to use their common sense to delight customers. They need to understand that different customers are treated differently based on their total business with the bank. They should understand its margins and annual customer value so that they can select the right compensation for certain problems.

In sum, if a bank is building a case for a customer experience strategy and counting on the great financial rewards that it can deliver by a reduction of customer churn and an increase in business per existing customer, it must always remember that the employee's experience is the path to customer's experiences. One cannot happen without the other.

I. CUSTOMERS RELATIONSHIP MANAGEMENT OPERATIONS BY COMMERCIAL BANKS IN INDIA

During the past decade commercial banks in India have been working hard to improve customer relation management operations and spending enormous funds annually on CRM initiatives as the banks are facing challenge of catering to a more demanding customers-someone who is less tolerant of errors or omissions. With the cost to acquire new customers rising ever markedly against the cost to retain customers, they want to hang on for a long time. In addition to building new relationship, bankers are looking at deepening relationships. The bankers are gradually realizing that the cornerstone of the business rests on providing superior products and services designed to add value for customers. There is a huge demand for innovative, value added products and services that enhance the overall customer experience. The bankers' move to provide creative solutions for customers spending needs is in that direction.

Commercial banks in India have, of late, taken several steps to improve services to their customers.[9] The most important ones are outlined below:

Introducing Multiple Delivery Channels

In their endeavour to ease customer dealings with the banks, most of them have gradually introduced multiple delivery channels, like ATM, Phone Banking, Net Banking to shift the customers away from the traditional brick and mortar banking.

Extended Banking Hours Facility

Since in Indian situation branch banking cannot be totally relegated to the backseat because of continuing customer preference for such system, some of the banks like SBI, ICICI Bank, Punjab National Bank and Bank of Baroda have resorted to extended banking hours from 8 a.m. to 8 p.m. in select branches.

Management of Customer Complaints

Banks have begun taking serious note of customer complaints. Reply within 24 hours is ensured informing the status of complaint. Even the highest authority personally monitors the progress regarding customers' compliant in certain banks.

Customer Retention

Banks are now keeping regular track of number of accounts closed and the accounts wherefrom heavy withdrawal is taking place. Reasons for closure of accounts are ascertained to arrest customer attrition.

Designing Products and Services to suit Customers

Most of the banks concentrating on their retail portfolio are in the process of aligning their products to suit specific customer needs. Product innovation and modification of existing products are undertaken on an ongoing basis to match the changing needs of the customer.

Relationship Pricing

Sensing the fact that relationship pricing strategies encourage customers to have multiple facilities and services with the bank, many banks have introduced various schemes with freebies to attract new customers on the one hand and to establish a long standing relationship through a spectrum of products, on the other.

Customizing the Relationship

Most banks have redesigned their account opening forms with plethora of information primarily with a view to establishing an abiding relationship with the customer and also cross selling bank's various products.

Focus on Quality Customers

According to CRM, the level of customer should be aligned with the status of the customer. A high net worth customer deserves greater focus because 20% of such customers contribute to 90% of the bank's profit. According to a survey in a nationalized bank, 67% of the bank's savings deposits customer maintain an average balance of less than ₹ 1,000/- in their accounts, 25% maintain an average "balance between ₹ 1000/- and ₹ 10,000/- and the remaining 8% maintain balance over ₹ 10,000. The customers belonging to the last category are "profit" and "quality" customers. The bank should, therefore, concentrate on this category of customers while at the same time it should make efforts to convert most of the loss customers into profit customers.

Unfortunately, Indian banks have yet not been able to create enthusiastic customers because of the absence of pleasant ambience and human touch and warmth in dealings by the branch level staff. The customers do not feel being cared by the bank functionaries. It must be noted that no amount of product offerings and technological sophistication are going to attract new customers and retain the existing ones if the bank functionaries do not create pleasant and powerful customers experience and their emotions and feelings are not deeply respected everytime.

Nevertheless liberalization of financial services and competition have improved customer services, experience shows that customers' interests are not always accorded priority. More importantly, concerns have been raised with regard to banking practices that tend to exclude vast segments of the population. This is why, the RBI has announced its intention to implement policies to incentivise banks to provide extensive services responsive to the needs of the underprivileged.[10]

According to a survey conducted by "Consumer Voice", backed by the Consumer Affairs Ministry, Syndicate Banks, State Bank of Mysore, Central Bank and Karnataka Bank scored the highest in overall satisfaction. Citibank had the highest number of dissatisfied customers with nearly 45% reporting a problem with the bank.[11]

The study "Assessment of Quality of banking Services in India" analyzed the perception of consumers and their satisfaction levels within their banks covering over 3,000 customers in 8 cities. The surprise winner was United Western Bank with loyal customers rise in Western India, over 70% of its customers would recommend the Bank to their friends. Contrary to popular perception, private sector banks did not score as well as their nationalized peers, with the exception of Vysya Bank and Standard Chartered Bank.

UTI Bank, Bank of Baroda, Canara Bank and HSBC were some of the banks where nearly 60% customers would recommend the banks to friends.

Nearly half the customers of State Bank of Hyderabad, Citibank and HDFC Bank would not recommend them to friends.

Citibank was the worst offender with 45.5% of its customers saying that they had problems including unauthorized transactions, excess fee or hidden charges, delay in crediting of cheques and difficulties in closing an account. As many as 56% customers said that they would not recommend the bank to their friends.

Only 14% of the consumers in the survey reported knowledge about the fees charged by their banks.

While most banks swear by credit card operations, the survey reports that the good old cheque deposit and draft facilities still drive the banking sector, with 98% of the consumers endorsing the cheque facility.

Country's largest lender-SBI-witnessed largest customer migration followed by PNB. Most customers are moving to ICICI Bank or HDFC Bank.

Banks that delay collecting cheques from drop boxes and further charge late fees or interest, according to the survey, were ING, Vyasya Bank, Syndicate Bank, ABN Amro Bank, Bank of India and Canara Bank.

J. RBI POLICY REGARDING CUSTOMERS' SERVICES BY COMMERCIAL BANKS

In November 2003, while presenting the mid-term review of the annual monetary and credit policy for the year 2003-04, RBI Governor, Dr. Reddy, brought into sharp focus the inadequacy in banking services available to common person and the need to benchmark the current level of service, review the progress periodically, enhance the timeliness and quality, rationalize the processes taking into account technological developments and suggest suitable incentives to facilitate change on an ongoing basis. Accordingly, he set up a Standing Committee on Procedures and Performance Audit on Public Services under the chairmanship of Shri S.S. Tarapore. The Committee, after undertaking incognito visits to bank branches, including the RBI offices for a first hand experience of difficulties faced by the public at large, made a host of recommendations covering an individual customer's dealing with banks in the areas of foreign exchange, currency and government transactions including pension, besides the main relationship as an account holder. In the light of these recommendations, the RBI adopted the approach to customer service by empowering the common person in availing banking services and strengthening customer-service delivery in banks through a consultative process with banks. Specifically, the focus is on (*a*) sensitizing banks to customer service and encouraging the involvement of boards of banks, especially in matters relating to banks' own grievance redressal machinery, (*b*) insisting on transparency in all dealings with the customers and ensuring reasonableness in pricing; (*c*) promoting adherence to self-imposed codes by banks on commitments to bank customers and monitoring compliance by an independent agency, *viz*., Banking Codes and Standards Board of India (BCSBI); (*d*) strengthening and empowering institutional mechanisms for dispute resolution; (*e*) using regulation prescription only when essential, while encouraging IBA to take initiatives; and (*f*) rationalizing the RBI's own system and procedures.

Bearing in mind the above principles, the RBI issued the following directives to banks.[12]

- Banks are required to inform customers upfront about the requirement of minimum balances and the charges if such balances are not maintained. They are also required to inform customers one month in advance about any changes in such minimum balances and charges.
- Banks are required to provide a choice of a 'no frills account' where the minimum balance is nil or very small but having restrictions on number of withdrawals, etc., to facilitate common man's access to bank accounts. Banks have been asked to give wide publicity to this facility so as to ensure greater financial inclusion.
- In case of collection of cheques, banks are required to formulate and disclose their policy for affording immediate credit, time frame for collection and interest payment for delayed collection, taking care to ensure that the interests of the small depositors are fully protected. The policy should clearly lay down the liability of the banks by way of interest payments due to delays for non-compliance with the standards set by the banks themselves. Compensation by way of interest payment, where necessary, should be made without any claim from the customer.
- Banks are required to provide both the drop box facility and the facility for acknowledgement of cheques at the regular collection counters and no branch should refuse to give an acknowledgement if the customer tenders the cheques at the counters.
- Depositors cannot be forced to sign a declaration that despatch of cheque book by courier is at the depositor's risk as it constitutes an unfair practice. Banks should also ensure that cheque books are delivered over the counters on request to the depositors or to his authorized representative.
- Banks have been advised to ensure that brief and intelligible particulars are invariably entered in passbooks/statements of account and they adhere to the prescribed monthly periodicity while sending statement of accounts.
- It has been clarified to banks that payment to the survivor/nominee of a deceased depositor where there is a valid nomination or where the account has been opened with a survivorship clause is a valid discharge of liability provided inter alia it has been made clear to the survivor(s)/nominee that he would be receiving the payment from the bank as a trustee of the legal heirs of the deceased depositor, i.e., such payment to him shall not affect the right or claim which any person may have against the survivor (s)/nominee to whom the payment is made. In such cases, insistence on production of legal representation is unwarranted and would invite serious supervisory disapproval. In such case, therefore, while making payment to the survivor (s)/nominee of the deceased depositor, the banks have to desist from insisting on production of succession certificate, letter of administration or probate, etc., or obtain any bond of indemnity or surety from the survivor (s)/nominee, irrespective of the amount standing to the credit of the deceased account holder.
- In case where the deceased depositor has not made any nomination or for the accounts other than those styled as "either or survivor" (such as single or jointly operated accounts), banks have been told to adopt a simplified procedure for repayment to legal heir(s) of the depositor keeping in view the imperative need to avoid inconvenience and undue hardship to the common person.
- In the case of term deposits, banks are advised to incorporate a clause in the account opening form itself to the effect that in the event of death of the depositor, premature termination of term deposits would be allowed. The condition subject to which such

premature withdrawal would be permitted may also be specified in the account opening form. Such premature withdrawal would not attract any penal charge.

- In order to avoid hardship to the survivor (s)/nominee of a deposit account, banks are advised to obtain appropriate agreement/authorization from the survivor (s)/nominee with regard to the treatment of pipeline flows in the name of the deceased account holder.
- Banks are advised to settle the claims in respect of deceased depositors and release payment to survivor (s)/nominee(s) within a period not exceeding 15 days from the date of receipt of the claim subject to the production of proof of death of the depositor and suitable identification of the claim(s) to the bank's satisfaction.
- Information should not be gathered in the name of 'Know Your Customer',(KYC) with the intention of using it for cross-selling of services. The banks should obtain the information required for opening an account independent of any other information that they seek for cross-selling purposes with the consent of the customer. The forms containing this information must not be a part of the account opening form.

Considering the significant growth in credit cards in recent years and the experiences of banks and customers with this product, the Reserve Bank issued detailed guidelines on credit card operations of banks in November 2005. These guidelines, aimed at protecting customer's interest, include clear disclosures of terms and conditions including rate of interest on annualized basis, prohibit issue of unsolicited cards, ensure customer confidentiality, and also cover matters such as 'do not call' registry, fair practices in recovery and collection.

◈ Banking Ombudsman Scheme

Understanding the importance of customer service in banking, the RBI set up Banking Ombudsman (BO) offices in 15 major banking centres. Since its inception, BO has been an effective form for redressing complaints received from customers.

Keeping in view the large number of complaints continuously being received against banks, the Banking Ombudsman Scheme was revamped in 2006 to enlarge its extent and scope of the authority and functions to specifically cover redressal of grievances against deficiency in banking services, including a variety of banking products/services, such as, loans and advances, credit cards, non-payment/inordinate delay in the payment or collection of cheques, drafts, bills, non-issue of drafts to customers., non-adherence to prescribed working hours by branches, etc. Banking Ombudsman (BO) functions as an arbitrator in respect of any dispute with mutual consent of both the parties provided that the value of the claim in such dispute does not exceed rupees ten lakh. Under the new scheme, the complainants will be able to file their complaints in any form, including online. The complainant can appeal against the awards given by the Banking Ombudsman.

A quick review of the complaints received at the various offices of the Ombudsman since the revised scheme came into force reveals that the number of complaints received by the BO's offices has more than doubled to 13,483 during the quarter ended March 31, 2006. This increase could be attributed to the complainants tending to approach the BO's office or the RBI directly instead of first approaching the concerned bank's internal machinery for redressal. There was considerable increase in the number of complaints received by the BO offices across the country from 26062 in 2006 to 79,266 in 2009-10. However, year 2010-11 witnessed a decline from 79,266 to 71,274; the decline being particularly visible in metropolitan regions, viz., New Delhi, Mumbai and Chennai.

It is also interesting to note that there was an increase in complaints against PSBs in 2010-11 over the previous year whereas number of complaints against private sector banks and foreign banks registered a decline.

In 2010-11, almost one-fourth of the total complaints were received against credit/debit/ATM cards. The second largest number of complaints were received against pension followed by loans and advances.

◈ Ensuring Reasonableness of Bank Charges

As the Reserve Bank was receiving several representations from public about unreasonable service charges being levied by banks, it was felt that the existing institutional mechanism in this regard is not adequate. Accordingly, and in order to ensure fair practices in banking services, the RBI has recently issued instructions to banks making it obligatory for them to display and continue to keep updated, in their offices /branches as also on their website, the details of various service charges in a format prescribed by it. The Reserve Bank has also decided to place details relating to service charges of individual banks for the most common services on the website. Furthermore, the Reserve Bank has since constituted a working group headed by the Banking Ombudsman, Mumbai and including nominee of IBA representative of customers to formulate a scheme for ensuring reasonableness of bank charges and to incorporate this in the Fair Practices Code, the compliance of which will be monitored by the Banking Codes and Standard Board of India (BCSBI).

So as to ensure reasonableness of product pricing by banks, the RBI is highly concerned with the methodology of rate fixation by commercial banks that has hindered the transmission of monetary policy measures.

The base rate, introduced in July 2010, replaced the benchmark prime lending rate and was aimed at increasing the transparency on pricing of loans and to improve transparency of monetary policy. However, the RBI feels the banks' interest rates were reduced in tune with reduction of CRR and repo rates.

Another contentions issue is 'spreads'. Some of the banks such as the SBI have changed their spreads, which has led to a reduction in the interest rate. However, the lower interest rate is offered to only the bank's new customers while the RBI is of the view that if the spreads are changed, that should be applicable to both new and old customers.

The RBI is also concerned with a significant variation in deposit rates on similar tenure and has been asking banks to correct the anomaly.[13]

◈ Customer Service — Institutional Machinery

In the area of customer service, the institutional machinery in banks should comprise:

- At the Board level, every bank has been asked to constitute a Customer Services Committee of the Board including, as invitees, experts and representatives of customers to enable the bank to formulate policies and assess the compliance thereof internally.
- Every bank has been asked to convert the ad hoc committee of executives on customer service headed by the CMD/ED into a Standing Committee that periodically reviews the policies and procedures and working of the bank's own grievance redressal machinery. These committees have been found to be very useful as the CEO of the bank and his top management team is singularly focused on matter relating to customer services at the meetings of these committees and decisions for improving services, tend to get taken instantly, cutting across different departments.
- Each bank is expected to have a nodal department/official for customer service in the Head Office and each controlling office, whom customers with grievances can approach in the first instance and with whom the Banking Ombudsman and the RBI can liaise. More interaction between the RBI/BO and the nodal officers will enable banks to take necessary correctives at the local level.

In its efforts to further protect the interests of Banks' customers, the RBI released the Code of Bank's Committee to customers on July I, 2006.[14] The code, formulated by the Banking Codes and Standard Board of India (BCSBI), constituted by the RBI as an autonomous body-in February, 2006 and the IBA, provides protection to individual customers and explains how banks are expected to deal with customers in their day-to-day operations. It contains details of the information a bank would give before a person becomes its customer and the information a person would get after he becomes a customer. It is a document that lays down the rights of a bank customer which can be enforced against the bank. The code also provides form of compensation, the customer can get if the bank defaults.

Banks are expected to voluntarily adopt this as their code. The BCSBI would keep a watch on each bank's adherence to this code. If banks do not voluntarily adopt the code, then the RBI will publicize their names. This public censure is enough to ensure compliance of the code.

The RBI Working Group on "Reasonableness of Bank Charges" is of the opinion that banks should provide basic services such as issue of passbook, cheque facility, balance inquiry, stop payment, issue of DD, pay order, telephonic transfer, etc. at reasonable charges.[15]

In July, 2006 the RBI constituted a separate customer service department so as to bring all the activities relating to customer service in banks under a single umbrella. This department performs the functions of disseminating instructions/information relating to customer service and grievance redressal by banks; administering the Banking Ombudsman Scheme; acting as a nodal department for the Banking Codes and Standards Board of India (BCSBI), ensuring redressal if complaints received directly by the RBI on customers service in banks; and liaising between banks, IBA, BCSBI, BO offices and the regulatory departments within the Reserve Bank on matters relating to customer service and grievance redressal.[16]

The periodic feedback that the department receives from the complaints dealt at the Banking Ombudsman offices has become one of the most important inputs for policy initiatives in the RBI.

The RBI in its directive issued on May 24, 2007 permitted banks to deliver cash and drafts at the door step of the individual customer also, either against cheques received at the counter or requests received through phone/internet banking. The banks will bear all risks involved in reaching cash to the customer's door step. According to the guidelines, the service should be seen as mere extension of banking services offered at the branch and liability of the bank should be the same as if the transactions were conducted at the branch.[17]

So as to improve further services to banks' customers, the RBI issued detailed guidelines in 2007-08 regarding engagement of recovery agents, strengthening of grievance redressal mechanism in banks, branch level committee on customer service, furnishing a copy of loan agreement to borrowers, settlement of claims in the case of missing persons, etc.

During 2009-10, focused attention was paid to customer services in the banking sector by sensitising banks to render an efficient customer service. The RBI has also taken a number of steps to disseminate instructions/guidelines relating to customer service and grievance redressal by banks through the multilingual website by placing all customers related notifications and press releases in a specific page titled "For Common Person". Customers of commercial banks can also approach the RBI with their grievances and querries through "Contact Us" mode of the website.

A comprehensive Master circular on Customer Service was issued on July 1, 2010 incorporating various issues, such as customer service, operations of deposit accounts, levy of service charges, service at counters, disclosure of information, operation of accounts by old and incapacitated persons, facilities to visually impaired persons, guardianship in deposit accounts, remittances, drop box facility, collection of instruments, dishonour of cheques, dealing with complaints, safe deposit lockers, nomination facility settlement of claims of deceased depositors missing persons, etc.

In 2010, the RBI constituted a committee on customer service in banks under the chairmanship of Shri M. Damodaran to look into banking services rendered to retail and small customers including pensioners and also to look into the system of grievance redressal mechanism prevalent in banks, its structure and efficacy and suggest measures for expeditious resolution of complaints. The committee has submitted its report to the RBI and it has also posted on the RBI's Website to seek public feedback. The committee in its report has suggested a toll-free common call centre number for all banks, which a customer could call and then be diverted to the bank concerned. On the deposits side, the committee emphasised that bank customers be treated fairly, all banks should offer plain vanilla saving accounts, with certain privileges like cheque facility, ATM card, etc. without prescribing a minimum balance. It also suggested that all fixed deposits schemes offering different rates for different tenures should indicate the annualised yields so that the customer could take an informed decision.

It has also been suggested that banks should not auto-renew deposit accounts without written customer consent.

As regards charging discriminatory interest rates from new and old borrowers of home loan, the committee suggested that in a floating interest rate scenario, when an entire class of borrowers has the same characteristics and risk level, the point of entry in time (old customers and new customers) should not create discrimination in the interest rate offered.

The committee has also suggested that banks should not impose exorbitant penal rates for foreclosure of home loans and ensure that the customers are not denied the benefit of lower rates offered by other financial institutions.

Lately, the RBI took several initiatives to further improve quality of services to bank customers. It has also appointed a committee under Shri M. Damodaran to suggest to the customers and addressing complaints expeditiously.

K. CONCLUSION

In the wake of pathbreaking economic reforms leading to increased competitiveness and fast changing social, familial and personal values of people, bank's customers have, of late, become finicky demanding better service and higher value as also personal care, and the management's growing realization that retaining existing customers is as important as attracting new customers and for that matter developing long-term relationship with customers is imperative, concept of customer relationship management (CRM) in banks has become cliche for commercial banks the world over.

CRM, in fact, involves creating, maintaining and enhancing strong relationships with customers with a view to delivering long-term value to customers.

So as to nurse and develop long-term relationship with customers and to generate customer loyalty, a banker has to draw up strategic plan focusing on long-term course of action to be taken at the organizational level.

With deepening competitive pressures, concept of CRM has been found lacking in retaining customers. It is, therefore, being realised that if a bank intends to retain one's premium positioning and higher margins, one is left with only one option: deliver a really powerful and pleasant customer experience and reinforce it in as many ways as possible so that the customers no longer cares if the rival product is cheaper or has no frills. Thus, concept of customer experience management (CEM) is gaining prominence these days.

Focus of CEM is on customers, technology, look beyond the product, trust, realignment of people practices.

Regarding CRM operations by commercial banks in India, it has been noted that during the past decade the banks have been striving hard to improve customer relationship management operations and spending enormous funds yearly on CRM initiatives. They have, of late, taken several steps to improve services to their customers.

Realising the inadequacy in banking services, the RBI issued in recent times specific guidelines to the banks. Even the Banking Ombudsman Scheme has been revamped in 2006 in order to enlarge its extent and scope of,the authority and make the scheme more effective.

The RBI has also directed the banks to build adequate institutional machinery, for formulating policies and executing them to the benefit of customers.

The RBI permitted banks to deliver cash and drafts to the individual customers at their doorsteps on request.

KEY TERMS

- Banking Codes and Standard Board of India
- Banking Ombudsman
- Customer Centric approach
- Customer Experience Management
- Flow Chart
- High Networth Customers
- Life Time Value
- Relationship Banking
- Transformational leadership
- Transaction Banking
- Vision and mission

DISCUSSION QUESTIONS

1. What is customer relationship management? How is it different from customer experience management?
2. Bring out distinguishing features of customer relationship management.
3. Discuss the utility of customer relationship management for commercial banks.
4. How would you formulate customer relationship strategy for a bank?
5. What are the major components of customer experience management?
6. Discuss, in brief practices followed by commercial banks ion India with respect to customer relationship.
7. Discuss various initiatives taken by the RBI in relevant few years to improve quality of services to banks' customers.

REFERENCES

1 Philip Kotler and Gary Armstrong, *Principles of Marketing*, Prentice-Hall of India Pvt. Ltd., New Delhi, 1996, p. 14.
2. Kevin J. Clancy and Robert S. Shulman, *Breaking the Mode*, Sales and Marketing Management, pp. 82-84.
3. Fredrick F. Rerchheld and W. Eard Sasser Jr., *Zero Defections: Quality Comes to Services*, Harvard Business Review, September-October, pp. 301-307.
4. David Szymanski, *Indian Management*, March, 2004.
5. Alexandra Thusy and Lagdon Morris, —— *CRM to Experience Management*, Indian Management, January, 2005.
6. Liau Chih-te, Customer *Experience Management*, Productivity News, Nov-Dec, 2004.
7. Joseph Pine II and James Gilmore, *The Experience Economy*.
8. Lior Arussy, *Treating Employees Like Customers*, Indian Management, January, 2005.
9. Annual Report on Currently and Finance, RBI, 2004-05.
10. Rakesh Mohan, Reforms, *Productivity and Efficiency in Banking:* The Indian Experience, RBI Bulletin, March, 2006.
11. The Economic Times, July 31, 2006.
12. Usha Thorat, *Treating Bank Customers Fairly – Regulatory Initiatives*, RBI Bulletin, June, 2006.
13. Business Standard, July 25, 2012.
14. The HINDU – *Business Line*, July 2, 2006.
15. Business Line, September 16, 2006.
16. Report on Trend and *Progress of Banking in India*, 2005-06, pp. 45-46.
17. Times of India, May 25, 2007.

* * *

Chapter 15

Management of Loans in Commercial Banks

Learning Objectives:

The present chapter attempts to provide:

- An outline of redeeming features and fundamentals of bank lending.
- Discussion on process of formulating lending policy in a commercial bank.
- Insight into the forces influencing lending policy in a bank;
- Contents of bank loan policy.
- Detailed understanding of how credit applicant is evaluated.
- An idea of how bank lending activity is organized.

Chapter Outline:

- Characteristics of commercial bank loans.
- Cardinal principles of sound bank lending.
- Formulating loan policy for a commercial bank.
- Factors influencing loan policy in a commercial bank.
- Contents of bank loan policy.
- Evaluating credit applicant.
- Organisation of bank lending.
- Conclusions.

Lending is one of the two principal functions of commercial banks not only because of their social obligation to cater to the credit needs of different sections of the community but also because lending is the most profitable activity, for the interest rates realised on business loans have always been well above those realised on investments. Having sterilized a portion of deposits in cash reserve and highly liquid assets, which yield little or no earnings for the purpose of satisfying the liquidity requirements, a bank has to deploy the residual funds in profitable outlets so that it may be able to pay interest on deposits, salary to the staff, meet other establishment expenses, build up reserves and pay dividend to the shareholders. This is why bank loans account for a major portion of residual funds of a commercial bank. An examination of some of the important characteristics of bank loans would provide us an insight into the lending activities of a commercial bank.

A. CHARACTERISTICS OF COMMERCIAL BANK LOANS

Most important characteristics of bank loans in India are given below:

- The bulk of the bank loans in India is provided to trade and industries. Banks are lackadaisical in making advances to the agricultural sector because of the relatively greater credit risks inherent in them and because of the inability of agriculturists to furnish good security. However, since nationalisation, banks have evinced keen interest in this sector as also in infrastructure sector.
- Another striking feature of a bank loan in our country is that nearly three-fourths of it is given for a period of less than one year. This is essentially because of the high liquidity of such loans. The short-term loans are given to finance the seasonal needs of businessmen and also for working capital purposes to facilitate the process of production and distribution. Seasonal loans are primarily for the purpose of increasing the inventory of a business firm and are repaid as the inventory is liquidated. Short-term funds are borrowed for increasing the current assets and for expanding production. Such loans are repaid out of the net operating earnings of the firm. Working capital loans are always for a year or less, but may extend for a period in excess of one year. On the other hand, seasonal loans are sought for a few months.

Short-term loans may take the form of cash credit and overdraft, demand loans, and the purchase and discount of bills. Among these, cash credit and overdraft are the most prominent.

However, in recent few years banks have also begun providing term loans to the borrowers to meet their long term requirements leading to significant reduction in the proportionate share of short-term loans in the loan portfolio. Thus, as on 31st March, 2010 term loans accounted for over 55 per cent of the loans provided by the PSBs.

- Bank borrowers generally fall in the average profitability group. A highly profitable firm would rely less on bank loans to finance expansion or current needs because it has sufficient earnings to do so. Contrary to this, the less profitable concerns or the less self sustaining concerns need bank support to help them tide over the financial difficulties caused by the shortage of liquid funds. There may be many specific reasons for the current tight position of a firm; but meagre earnings or losses are the most frequent ones. This suggests that bankers should be very careful while granting loans to firms and should take all possible protective steps to minimise their risk.
- Another characteristics of bank borrowers is that most of them own relatively small, young and growing business. Smaller firms depend more on bank loans to finance their needs because of their limited access to other sources of finance. Young concerns which have sufficiently established themselves and which do not have enough accumulated earnings make frequent trips to the bank. Growing concerns rely more on bank credit than their older and more established counterparts because the former are not capable of generating sufficient income to take care of their growing financial needs. As a matter of fact, growth is one of the very best reasons for the extension

of bank credit. The banker is averse to making advances to firms which suffer losses even though they have the remnants of a reasonably satisfactory current position.

B. CARDINAL PRINCIPLES OF SOUND BANK LENDING

Lending is the most profitable business of a commercial bank; but at the same time, it is highly risky. Loans are always accompanied by the credit risk arising out of the borrower's default in repaying the money. A banker should, therefore, manage his loan business in a profitable and safe manner. He should take all the necessary precautions to minimise the risks associated with the grant of a loan. In considering a loan proposal, he should bear in mind certain general principles of lending. These principles help him to establish some credit standards by which to evaluate the loan applications of particular borrowers. Some of these principles are incompatible, e.g., liquidity and profitability; but an astute banker strikes a satisfactory compromise between these two. These principles are discussed below:

◆ Safety

The safety of funds is the most important guiding principle of a banker. While lending out funds, he should ensure that it would be safe to do so; otherwise the banker will not be in a position to repay the deposits. Consequently, he will lose public confidence which may subsequently spell the ruin of the bank itself. The safety of funds implies that the borrower would repay the principal sum and the interest thereon in the manner and on the conditions provided for in the loan agreement. Every care should be taken to ensure that a loan to a particular borrower does not involve any avoidable risk of non-payment. A bank follows an aggressive policy of lending in its bid to maximise earnings; but it has always to be defensive at the same time because it cannot afford to lose the people's money. A banker should always take a calculated risk. This is why he always insists upon collaterals, margins and guarantees in addition to the personal promise of the borrower.

◆ Liquidity

Since a major part of commercial bank liabilities is payable either on demand or after a short notice, the banker should ensure that the loan is liquid. Liquidity, as already defined, signifies the readiness with which the bank can convert its assets into cash with no or insignificant loss. A loan will be liquid if it has been given for a short period to finance some purchases of stock, raw materials, etc. A banker should, therefore, provide short-term advances which can be recalled in time to satisfy the demands of the depositors. He cannot afford to lend short-period funds for a long time because in that case the loans and advances will tend to be less liquid, and it would be a great problem for him to realise cash in case of an emergency. Furthermore, loans, to be liquid, should be provided against the security of highly shiftable assets so that in the event the borrower defaults in repaying the principal sum, these might be readily converted into cash.

There is another reason for paying adequate attention to the liquidity principle. The cost of borrowing from the Reserve Bank of India is related to the net liquidity ratio which is the ratio of the net liquid assets of the borrowing bank to its aggregate demand and time liabilities. The net liquidity ratio of a bank must be equal to the specified limit or above it so that it may obtain a loan from the Reserve Bank at the bank rate. With every one per cent drop in the net liquidity ratio of the borrowing bank, the cost of lending by the Reserve Bank goes up by one per cent.

◆ Diversification of Risks

A bank manager should adhere to the principle of diversification while lending out funds. Diversification implies dispersal of funds over a large number of borrowers and borrowing firms situated in different parts of the country. It is a means of minimising the risks inherent in the grant of loans. It is not merely a defensive policy to protect the bank against risk but also a device for increasing the average return on a fund that might otherwise, for the sake of safety, be confined to risk-free assets providing little or no yield. The manager should remember that he can face his loss with greater equanimity if he does not lay all his eggs in one basket. If all the eggs are put in one basket he will lose his entire capital in case the basket is upturned and all the eggs are broken. In view of this, he should avoid concentrating the bank's funds in a few customers. He should diffuse lending and offer advances to different firms belonging to different industries which are situated over different geographical areas, so that he may not be badly mauled by the failure of one industry or a few big borrowers.

The most important form of diversification is maturity diversification. Under maturity diversification the loan portfolio is staggered over different maturity periods so that a certain amount of loans mature at regular intervals and are utilised to meet the depositor's demand. If such funds are not needed, they may be lent out or invested in securities that best fit into the bank's loan and investment portfolio.

◈ Profitability

Equally important is the principle of profitability. Like other commercial institutions, banks must make sufficient income to pay interest to the depositors, meet establishment costs retain a portion of the income for the future and pay dividends to owners. The difference between the lending and borrowing rates constitutes the gross profit of the bank; and no banker will ordinarily think of an advance without a satisfactory margin between lending rates and borrowing rates.

The lending rates are affected by the bank rate, inter-bank competition and inter-bank agreements, where they have been agreed upon. Different rates are charged, depending on the credit risk involved in lending to borrowers, the nature of security, the mode of charge, the margin requirement and the form and type of advance. While charging interest, the banker must ensure the liquidity and safety of the loans. A particular customer may offer a higher rate of interest; but an advance made to him may be subject to imminent risk and default. A banker should avoid making profit at the expense of the liquidity and safety of his capital. Within the limits of liquidity and safety, and the national policies as laid down by the government and the Central Bank, a banker should strive for accomplishing the profitability objective.

◈ Purpose

Bankers should inquire into the purpose for which the loan is taken. As a matter of fact, safety and liquidity of loan depend on the purpose to which it will be put. If an advance is given for productive purposes, say, for financing the purchase of inventories; in all probability it will be repaid because the grant of the loan will generate additional income for the borrower to enable him to repay it. An advance made for non-productive and speculative purposes is subject to greater credit risk because the purpose for which the loan was sought would in no way improve the repaying capacity of the borrower. A banker should, therefore, avoid making loans for wasteful expenditure on social functions and speculative transactions. Admittedly, it is very difficult to ensure that the loan has been utilised for the purpose for which it was required. Funds borrowed for a productive use have often been used for speculative purposes. The banker should, therefore, take follow-up steps to see to it that the end-use of credit is not for a purpose other than the one for which it was given.

◈ Customers Satisfaction

While considering credit application of the borrower and disbursing loans, banker must ensure that the applicant is least inconvenienced. The applicant should be aided in filling the application form and complying with formalities. This will help the bank in the long run in attracting and retaining customers.

C. FORMULATING LOAN POLICY FOR A COMMERCIAL BANK

A bank has the social obligation of meeting the diverse credit needs of different sections of the community; but it cannot afford to lend the funds of its depositors and owners indiscriminately, and incur losses. It has to conduct its lending business in an orderly and safe manner so that its loan portfolio remains balanced from the standpoint of size, type, maturity and security, and promises reasonable and steady earnings. This calls for a clear-cut and definite credit policy, spelling out detailed guidelines for the size of the loan portfolio and its composition, the maturity periods of the loan for acceptable security and creditworthiness, for the liquidation of loans, for the compensating balance, the limits of lending authority, the loan territory, and similar other matters. Such a policy provides a direction to the use of funds, controls the size and make-up of the loan portfolio, and influences the credit decisions of the bank. With a systematic loan policy the banker will find it easy to reach the goals of the bank and serve the public concurrently. A loan policy is, therefore, a necessity for a bank.

This loan policy may be written or oral. However, it is advisable to have a written policy, for that would eliminate chances of misunderstanding between the credit department, which is seized with the job of granting credit, and the top management, which is concerned with formulating policies. It should also help maintain uniformity in, and standardisation of, lending practices. As against this, oral policies are easy to forget, and there is always a risk of misunderstanding and misinterpretation of what was said long before. But oral policies have the advantage of being flexible, an element which is lacking in written policies. One of the most important objections against a written loan policy is that it suffers from inflexibility and rigidity. At times, a bank with a written loan policy may find itself restricted in its loan activities and exposed to public criticism. Credit officers of the bank may become tight-fisted. If they provide credit facilities exceeding the maximum limit, as set out in the loan policy, they would be accused of having violated the loan policy; if they did not do so, and kept themselves within the loan limits, the bank and its credit officers would be the subject of seething public criticism — that they do not care for the customers. Too much inflexibility in written policy can be avoided if it is reviewed frequently and attuned to changed conditions. Formulating and implementing loan policies is amongst the most important responsibilities of bank directors and management. Since formulating a definite loan policy for the bank calls for expertise, knowledge and experience in various aspects of bank credit, the Board of Directors must call upon the services and co-operation of the bank's credit officers, who are well versed in the techniques of lending and are familiar with external and internal forces that have their bearing on the lending activities of the bank. The credit policy is, in fact, the outcome of the joint efforts of the Board of Directors and the credit officers of the bank.

In deciding the loan policies, the policy formulators must be very cautious, for the lending activity of the bank affects both the bank and the public at large. They should give serious consideration to all the factors that are likely to influence the loan policies, and work out their policies accordingly. A discussion in brief of all these factors is, therefore, necessary before dwelling upon how a bank formulates its loan policies.

D. FACTORS INFLUENCING LOAN POLICY IN A BANK

Important factors which go into the determination of the loan policies of a bank are:

◆ Capital Position

The capital position of a bank is probably the most important factor influencing its loan policy. As observed earlier, capital provides the cushion which absorbs the losses that may occur. It serves as a protective factor against losses for depositors and guarantees funds for the creditors. A bank with a strong capital position can assume more credit risks than one with a weak capital position. Accordingly, the former can follow a liberal lending policy and provide different types of loans, including long-term loans promising higher interest rates, which the latter cannot do because of the greater risk involved.

◆ Earnings Requirement

Profit making is one of the principal objectives of a commercial bank. Some banks may be in a position to emphasise the importance of income, while others may lay stress on liquidity. Banks which have set income as the principal goal of their lending policies would follow an aggressive policy and might make a larger amount of term loans or customer loans which normally are made at higher interest rates because of the relatively greater amount of risks involved in them. This does not mean that banks should take undue risks to accomplish the objective of profitability. Where earnings receive a greater emphasis in the loan policy of a bank, it may mean that it would include in its investment account securities which carry shorter maturity periods and possess relatively less risk.

◆ Deposit Variability

Banks that have experienced erratic movements in their deposits will have to follow a conservative lending policy. They cannot afford to incur undue risks by extending their term-lending facilities. A similar policy should also be followed where banks are faced with declining deposits. In a refreshing contrast to this, a liberal lending policy can be pursued by banks whose deposits show little or no fluctuations, and which can easily predict the fluctuations in deposits and loan demands, and make a provision for them in their secondary reserve. Banks, whose deposits have shown a rising tendency in the past, and which expect the rising trend to persist in future, can also be liberal in their loan policy.

◆ State of Local and National Economy

In formulating the lending policy, banker should keep in mind the economic conditions that prevail in the region served by the bank. A bank operating in an area which is subject to seasonal and cyclical fluctuations can ill afford to adopt a liberal policy because that would entail the hazards of illiquidity. But in a stable economy, where the possibility of fluctuations in the level of deposits and loan demands is limited, banker may follow a liberal loan policy. Consideration should also be given to national economy. If the economic conditions of the country are expected to improve, and the level of business activity is likely to increase, banks may liberalise their lending policies and accommodate those borrowers who were hitherto refused banking facilities because of a stiff credit policy. If the economy is likely to recede in the future, banker must revise the existing policy and design a new one with stiffer terms and conditions of lending, so that only borrowers of a very high credit character are eligible for bank accommodation.

◆ Monetary Policy

Monetary policy of the central banking authorities goes a long way in determining the lending policy of a commercial bank. By bringing about variation in the minimum reserve requirement and the net liquidity ratio, the Central Bank influences the lending policy of banks. For example, by reducing the proportion of the minimum cash reserve, which a commercial bank is required to carry with the Central Bank, and by reducing the net liquidity ratio, the bank would get additional funds which can be utilised in making further advances. If the cash reserve ratio and the net liquidity ratio are increased, lending ability of banks would be somewhat restricted.

◆ Ability and Experience of Loan Officers

Loan officers of a bank play a significant role in the execution of its loan policies. The Board should, therefore, consider the skill and competence of its loan officers while laying down a loan policy. When a bank is staffed by a large number of credit officers having expertise, knowledge and rich experience in diverse forms of loans, the banker can afford to provide different types of lending facilities, and formulate his policy accordingly. But this cannot be done by banks whose credit officers are competent to deal with only certain types of loans. This is why smaller banks have limited their lending business to short-term loans. Most of these banks have abstained from consumer lending and term lending to business enterprises because they are ill-equipped with skilled personnel.

◈ Competitive Position

In formulating a loan policy, the management should have consideration to the competitive position of the bank. Where a bank finds that strong competing institutions exist, say, in the field of term lending and, the management feels that it cannot afford to provide loans on the terms that are offered by other existing institutions, it might follow a policy of refraining from entering the sphere of term loans.

◈ Credit Needs of the Area Served

The credit needs of the area served by the bank would also influence its loan policy. A bank is supposed to meet the loan demands of all the local borrowers, who present logical and economically sound loan requests the grant of which is not contrary to prudent banking practices. If this cannot be done, there will be little justification for an institution to exist in that region. For example, in an economy predominantly dependent on agriculture, the bank must tailor its loan policy to meet the seasonal loan demands of the farmers.

E. CONTENTS OF BANK LOAN POLICY

Loan policy of a bank must be definite and broad-based to include all the important dimensions of its lending business so that credit officers may not face any problem in evaluating the creditworthiness of the loan applicants and in taking credit decisions. A commercial bank should set down specific guidelines in respect of the size of the loan portfolio, the compensation of the loan portfolio, acceptable security and creditworthiness, maturities, excess lines, liquidation of loans, interest rates, compensatory balances, lines of credit and limitations of the lending authority. In the following paragraphs, we shall discuss the characteristics of a loan policy with respect to each of the above aspects.

◈ Size of Loan Account

An intelligent loan policy spells out clearly the amount of the total advances that a bank would sanction. Determining the size of the loan account is not an easy job. There is no iron-clad formula for fixing the size of the loan. The rule that, as long as the bank has funds for lending, it should continue to lend, does not provide a logical rule for determining the size of a loan account. The primary social and business excuse for the commercial banking system is its ability to supply credit to the community. A commercial bank should lend as long as it is possible to do so prudently. In deciding the question of the size of the loan account, a banker is in dilemma: should he opt for profitability or liquidity. A satisfactory trade-off between these conflicting goals calls for a due consideration of various factors.

Within the framework of the banking legislation regulating the size of the loan portfolio of banks, a bank has to determine the optimum size of its loan portfolio keeping in mind the environment within which it is operating.

In India, Banking Companies Act does not put any limitation on the size of the loan account. However, an indirect control over the magnitude of the loan account is provided in the *Credit Authorisation Scheme* (CAS), which was introduced in November, 1965. Under this scheme, banks were required to seek the prior permission of the Reserve Bank before releasing fresh credit limits in excess of ₹ 4 crores or more to any single party or any limit that would take the total limits enjoyed by such party from the banking system as a whole to ₹ 1 crore or more on secured or unsecured basis. The amount of credit limits falling within the purview of the CAS underwent changes over the years. Until recently, banks were required to refer projects for sanction of credit limits aggregating over ₹ 6 crores to the RBI for prior approval under the CAS.

Of late, the RBI has decided to withdraw the credit authorisation scheme. Instead of the present system of prior authorisation by the RBI for sanction of working capital credit limits and term loans, banks will now have to send all proposals involving sanction of aggregate working capital limit beyond ₹ 5 crore for only post sanction security to ensure that the basic disciplines were being observed. This was the most welcome step which will help big borrowers of banks to overcome the delays in obtaining sanction for their proposals from the RBI.

This limit was raised to ₹ 50 crore by the RBI in April 1993 in its attempt to resuscitate the cash-starved Indian industry. Banks were allowed syndication if it suits both banks and borrowers.

Further, the size of the loan account would depend upon the central banking policy on the proportion of funds to be held in cash by bank with the central bank and with itself in the form of liquid assets.

Recently, the RBI has fixed limits on bank lending. Thus, a bank can lend upto 25% of the outstanding to a borrower and 50% of the outstanding exposure to a corporate group, and 20% to an industry. In case of infrastructure project, the group exposure norms can be stretched to 60%.

RBI has, of late, allowed commercial banks to sanction term loans upto ₹ 50 crores for an individual project. Simultaneously, it has also allowed them to relate the sanction of term finance to the quantum of the loan rather than on the cost of the project.

Earlier a bank could sanction term loans for project costing up to ₹ 10 crores only. The banking system as a whole can now sanction loan upto to ₹ 200 crores for an individual project as against the earlier ceiling of ₹ 150 crores or 25% of the total terms loan assistance, whichever was less.

However, for projects requiring term finance assistance in excess of ₹ 20 crores, banks should continue to participate jointly with all India financial institutions subject to the share of an individual bank not exceeding ₹ 50 crores and that of the banking system not exceeding ₹ 200 crores. The RBI further liberalised banks' term lending norms in October, 1994. Keeping in view importance of the infrastructure development and the need for banks to participate in the financing of such projects the earlier ceiling of ₹ 50 crores individually and ₹ 200 crores collectively for projects has been abolished with the limit now raised to ₹ 500 crores. With effect from 11-5-2001 the RBI has clamped 5% limit on bank's exposure to capital markets which will include loans/advances to individuals/corporates and stockholders, besides investment in shares and debentures.

In its endeavour to improve credit delivery system, the RBI — apart from freedom to assess working capital needs of corporates — has allowed banks to extend loans to corporates against shares held by them to enable such corporates to meet promoters' contribution to the equity of new companies. Loan component has been raised to 80 per cent and 75 per cent for borrowers with working capital limit of ₹ 20 crores and ₹ 10 crores and above, respectively.

The ceiling for banks to offer credit / non credit facilities to Indian joint ventures / wholly owned subsidiaries abroad, which was fixed at 5 per cent of the unimpaired Tier I capital, was raised to 10 per cent of banks' unimpaired capital fund (Tier I and Tier II capital).[1]

The exposure ceiling in respect of an individual borrower which was fixed earlier as 25 per cent was reduced to 20% of the banks capital fund effective April, 2000. The exposure ceiling is to be computed in relation to Tier capital in India as defined under capital adequacy standards (Tier I and Tier II) effective March 3, 2002.[2]

Recently, the RBI has permitted banks to assume single/group borrower credit exposure up to 15 per cent and 40 per cent of capital funds respectively with respective additional allowance of 5 per cent and 10 per cent of capital funds for exposure to the infrastructure sector.

In addition, it has been decided in June 2004, that banks may, in exceptional circumstances, with the approval of their boards, consider enhancement of the exposure to a borrower up to a further 5 per cent of capital funds (i.e., 20% for single borrower and 45% for group borrowers). In respect of exposure to infrastructure, banks could consider additional sanctions up to 5 per cent and 10 per cent as indicated above, over and above the limits of 20 per cent and 45 per cent, respectively. The exposure limits will be applicable even in the case of lending under consortium arrangement wherever formalized.[3]

However, the above limits do apply to: (*i*) Credit facilities granted to weak sick industrial units under rehabilitation packages (*ii*) Borrowers to whom limits are allocated directly by the Reserve Bank for food credit principal and interest that are fully granted by the Government of India and Loans and advances granted against the security of bank's own term deposits.[4]

The RBI has enhanced the existing limits on unsecured exposures by banks to public financial institutions to 100 per cent for credit risk and 2.5 per cent for market risk effective April 1, 2005.[5] The limit of loans under Differential Rate of Interest scheme has now been raised from ₹ 6,500 to ₹ 15,000 and that of the housing loans under the same scheme from ₹ 5,000 to ₹ 20,000 for beneficiary.

While deciding the size of the loan account of the bank, the management must foresee the economic situations that would obtain in the economy in general and in the region in particular. A bank expecting bullish conditions in the economy and an expanding level of business activity would increase the size of the loan account to satisfy the increased loan demands from the business community. The expected rise in the level of deposits, coupled with less deposit withdrawals, is conducive to a rise in the size of the loan account. The economic state of the region where the bank is situated would also affect the size of the bank loan. The loan demand in an agricultural region rises during the busy season and declines during the lean periods. The bank, operating in an agricultural area, will, therefore expand the size of its loan account to satisfy the increased credit needs of the community in the busy period, and contract it during the lean seasons. Similarly, the size of the loan account of a bank operating in an area predominantly dependent on one or few industries will be tailored to the changed loan demands of these industries which, in turn, are influenced by seasonal and cyclical factors.

An analysis of the resource position of the bank and the priorities of the use of funds should also be made before taking a policy decision regarding the size of the loan portfolio. Where the capital position of the bank in relation to its total deposit liabilities is very good, the size of the loan account may be fixed at a higher limit because, with a strong capital position, the bank can boldly withstand stresses and strains. The composition of the deposit of the bank would also affect the size of the loan portfolio. A bank having secured a substantially large portion of deposits in the current account may experience sharp fluctuations in its deposits. In such a situation, the size of the secondary reserve will have to be higher and that of the loan account lower so that the bank may protect itself against the dangers of illiquidity. Simultaneously, the ownership of deposit accounts should be studied because that, too, would affect the size of the loan account. Where a large portion of the current account of a bank is owned by businessmen and stock-brokers, the management must keep a larger portion of funds in highly liquid assets, and deploy a smaller portion of funds in loans. The reverse policy would be followed where the current account holders belong to the salaried class and/or the wage-earners whose withdrawals are predictable and infrequent. Finally, the size of the loan portfolio will be kept at a lower level when a larger proportion of funds is held in the form of primary and secondary reserves for liquidity purposes. A bank having held a smaller proportion of funds in highly liquid assets because of its relatively lower liquidity needs can have a bigger size of the loan portfolio.

◈ Composition of Loan Portfolio

Policy decisions on the type of loan to be made must also be taken. Different types of loans carry different degrees of risks; the extent of risks which a bank can assume would depend upon the adequacy of its capital fund, and the structure and stability of its deposits.

When a bank decides to provide short and long-term loans to business, agriculture and other sectors of society, the policy statement should clearly spell out the forms in which these loans will be made, and the proportion of each of these forms of loans to the total bank loan. If the bank, because of its weak capital position and deposits variability, decides to refrain from making long-term loans, this must be clearly stated in its policy statements. More often than not, when banks, in their attempt to minimise credit risks, decide to diversify their loan portfolio, the policy statement should clearly set forth the various broad categories of borrowers among which the bank's advances will be diffused, specifying the proportion of the loan for each such category. When the management strives to bring about a considerable diversification within these broad categories, the policy statement should mention the maximum amount of the loan that might be granted to a particular borrower.

The management should also take into account the technical acumen and experience of the loan officers of the bank while taking policy decisions on the composition of the loan portfolio. It would not be prudent to engage in a particular lending activity if the bank does not possess experienced personnel in that line. Where the credit department of a bank is equipped with personnel who have specialized in different types of loans, as is the case in the large commercial banks, it should make use of its staff and make different types of loans.

There are certain purposes for which banks generally refrain from lending not only because of the larger risks involved in granting such loans, but also because such loans are not justifiable, economical as well as socially. (A loan for speculative purposes is one such example). If the bank management holds this attitude, this should be clearly spelt out in the policy statement.

While formulating policy regarding composition of loan, the management must keep in mind the directives of the RBI. Recently, the RBI advised all commercial banks to implement the measures, announced by the Union Finance Minister, for doubling of credit to agriculture.

Further, banks have also been directed to provide lending assistance for development of waste land and follow land, improving staffing in the rural areas to promote retail lending to agriculture, relying on village functionaries for credit disbursal, using individual volunteers, farmers' clubs or NGOs/SHGs as direct selling agents, building synergy between good working primary agricultural credit societies and commercial banks, using information technology in rural branches, working out appropriate incentive structure for prompt repayment making the rates of interest on small loans reasonable and improving the efficiency of credit delivery to small borrowers and association with contract farming.[6]

As regards the flow of credit to SSI sector, in the light of the decision of the group of Ministers, the RBI advised banks that, while sanctioning/renewing credit limits to their large corporate borrowers (i.e., borrowers who enjoy working capital limits of ₹ 10 crore and above from the banking system), they should fix separate sub-limits, within the overall limits, specifically for meeting payment obligations in respect of purchases from SSIs either on cash basis or bill basis. Banks may ensure that sale proceeds/other receipts of the borrower are credited to this account on a pro-rata basis.[7]

In view of tight liquidity position and interest rate hikes following increase in bank and repo rates, public sector banks and other banks have decided to give loans only to select high quantity borrowers.[8]

Banks have recently been advised to ensure that no loans were sanctioned for acquisition of investment in small saving instruments. Further, the banks have been advised to take sufficient care to ensure that the minority communities also receive an equitable portion of the credit, within the priority sector lending.[9]

◈ Credit for Infrastructure

In view of the national importance attached to infrastructural development, operational guidelines on financing infrastructural projects were issued to commercial banks in April, 1999. Accordingly, banks would be free to sanction term loans for technically feasible, financially viable and bankable projects undertaken by both public and private sector undertakings subject to prescribed criteria. In this context, four modes of financing were identified and these included:

(*i*) financing through funds raised by way of subordinated debt, (*ii*) entering into take-out financing; (*iii*) direct financing through term loans, deferred payment guarantees, foreign currency loans etc. and (*iv*) investments in infrastructure bonds issued by project promoters/financial institutions. Banks have also been permitted to issue inter-institutional guarantees subject to certain norms. The banks can now grant term loans up to ₹ 500 crores or ₹ 1,000 crores for power projects in a single project subject to such loans being within prudential norms as applicable to each bank. To give a boost to the infrastructure lending, banks have been allowed to raise long-term bonds with minimum maturity of 5 years.[10]

◈ Acceptable Security

While determining the policy regarding the security aspect of a bank loan, the management should see to it that the security requirements do not violate statutory provisions. The Banking Regulation Act of 1949 made the following provisions in respect of security and margins:

(*i*) A banking company cannot provide a loan, secured or unsecured, to a director, interested concerns, or to any individual for whom a director stands as a guarantor or with whom a director is a co-partner in a firm.

(*ii*) It cannot grant any loans or advances on the security of its own shares.

(*iii*) Unsecured loans in any case cannot be exceeded by 15 per cent of the total outstanding advances of a bank.

(*iv*) A bank is required to maintain 50 per cent margin in respect of advances against equity shares.

Besides, the Reserve Bank of India was authorised by the provisions of the Banking Regulation Act of 1949 to give directions to banks in respect of margins to be maintained for secured loans. The policy on margin requirements must be made within the directives received from the Reserve Bank from time-time.

The RBI had prescribed a uniform margin of 40% for guarantees and advances (w.e.f. 11-5-2001) extended by Banks against shares including a minimum cash margin of 20%. This uniform margin requirement was against the existing stipulation regarding the minimum cash margin of 25 per cent for issue of guarantees and advances against demat shares and 50% for advances against physical shares. This margin requirement will also be applicable to guarantees issued by banks on behalf of commodity brokers in favour of the national level commodity exchanges, in lieu of margin requirements as per the commodity exchange regulations.

The margin requirement on all advances/financing of IPOs/issue of guarantees by banks has been raised from 4 per cent to 5 per cent. Further, banks were advised to maintain a minimum cash margin of 25 per cent (with in the overall margin of 50%) in respect of guarantees issued by banks.[11] However, with effect from May 18, 2004, when the equity market slipped sharply the margins have been restored statue quo and margin requirement on all advances against shares/financing of IPOs/issue of guarantees has been reduced to 40 per cent. In respect of guarantees issued by banks for capital market operations, banks were advised to maintain a minimum cash margin of 20 per cent (with in the overall margin of 40 per cent).[12]

The requirements of margin/security for agricultural loans up to ₹ 50,000 and in the case of agro-business and agri-clinics for loans up to ₹ 5 lakh has, of late,[13] been waived.

The existing limits on unsecured exposures by banks have been withdrawn, allowing banks to set their own limits for unsecured exposures. However, unsecured sub-standard assets would attract 20 per cent provisioning.[14]

In respect of free sale sugar, the hitherto prescribed margin was withdrawn in the year 2001 and the banks were permitted by the RBI to decide the margin based on their commercial judgement.[15]

Further, banks can increase the limits on dispensation of collateral requirements for loans to SSI units, each having an investment of ₹ 5 crore. Further, they may increase the limit of collateral requirements from ₹ 5 lakh to ₹ 15 lakh on the basis of good track record and financial health of the units. The requirements of margin/security for agricultural loans up to ₹ 50,000 and in the case of agri-business and agri-clinics for loans up to ₹ 5 lakh waived.[16]

◈ Lending Criteria

In order to minimise the risks in lending, a bank should make loans only to deserving parties whose credit character, capacity and integrity are beyond reproach. The criteria of evaluating credit character and capacity to generate income should be set forth in the policy statement. For example, if the borrower's liquidity position is to be judged, the loan policy statement should contain guidelines to the measurement of liquidity. It may state that a study of the trends in the current ratio and quick ratio for the past three years should be made. Besides, the nature and composition of current assets and current liabilities should also be looked into. Furthermore, to judge borrower's capacity to generate income and repay the loan, the policy statement may set forth the specific tools, such as profitability ratios, cash budget, etc., that may be used for the purpose. A mere statement of the ways and means of evaluating the creditworthiness of borrowers may not be enough, unless credit norms are spelt out very specifically. For example, to state that the borrowers whose financial and earning positions in the past have been satisfactory may be considered creditworthy may not facilitate the task of loan officers because they still have no guidelines to determine which state of financial and earning affairs would be considered satisfactory. An intelligent loan policy contains specific standards expressed in terms of the range of ratios and percentages. For example, it should be spelt out in the policy statement that the borrower's liquidity position will be considered satisfactory if their current ratio ranges between 2:1 and 1.5:1, and their quick ratio ranges between 1.5:1 and 1:1.

The standard liquidity ratios cannot be uniform for all the groups of industries and trading concerns; they will have to be different, depending on the nature of the borrower's business. Similarly, the range of profitability ratios, too, may be fixed by keeping in mind the market rates of return. The norms of judging the funds management capacity of the borrower's firm may also be included in the policy statement. This will, besides saving the time of the credit department and easing the job of the lending officers, bring about uniformity in the extension of credit and reduction in the risks of lending.

◈ Maturity

A loan policy should also address the issue of loan maturities. One of the most constructive characteristics of a good loan policy is to make a loan for a period after which it may be called back in times of need to satisfy the liquidity needs of the bank and ensure that it is not exposed to risk. Short-term loans, carrying a maturity period of 30 days, 60 days or 90 days, are relatively more liquid and less risky. With an increase in the maturities of loans, the money and credit risk associated with them would tend to increase. Some banks may be averse to the grant of loans (long-period) to business firms; some may decide to provide real estate loans but not for more than a period of five years. There may be some banks who wish to grant loans for the purchase of automobiles for a period of two to three years. Definite policies with regard to the maturities of the loans to be given for different purposes should, therefore, be stated. This will serve as a useful guide to the loan officers.

There are banks which have the general policy of making short-term loans which are subsequently renewed, depending on the progress of the borrower's firm and the liquidity needs of the bank. If the bank management wishes to pursue this policy, the policy statement should spell out its wishes to pursue this policy, the policy statement should spell out, in unequivocal terms, the types of loans which would be eligible for renewals, and the circumstances under which these renewals would be possible, the period of the renewals and also the number of times the renewal facilities will be extended. In a sharp contrast to this, there are some banks which straight-away grant a loan for a long period, say, five years and its repayment schedule is tailored to the yearly income flows of the borrower. Such banks believe that if a credit is drawn in terms of a specific plan of repayment, the borrower is much more likely to perform in a satisfactory manner than if he is subject to nothing more compelling than the vague threat of a loan maturity that probably will be renewed if everything goes all right. If the management of the bank in question holds this view, it should be clearly stated in the policy statement.

A commercial bank can also sanction term loans for projects costing up to ₹ 10 crores only. Now the RBI has allowed commercial banks to sanction term loans upto ₹ 50 crores for an individual project. The banking system as a whole can now sanction loan up to ₹ 200 crores for an individual project. However, for projects requiring term finance assistance in excess of ₹ 200 crores, banks should continue to participate jointly with all Indian financial institutions subject to the share of an individual bank not exceeding ₹ 50 crores.

In December, 2006, the RBI issued directives asking banks not to exceed their aggregate exposure to the capital markets to 40% of their net worth.[17]

Minimum period of loans and spread over various maturities subject to roll-over would now be decided by banks and they could invest short-term/temporary surplus of borrowers in money market instruments.

◈ Compensating Balance

Banks often require borrowers to maintain a deposit balance bearing some relationship to the aggregate amount of the loan made or the maximum line of credit. This is done with a view to increasing the effective rate of interest. Moreover, the compensating balance is a protective device to save the bank from the risk of default. If it appears that the default is imminent, the bank can apply the balance on deposit to the loan. This practice is also known as the *right of offset*, i.e., the right to use all the deposit balance a bank customer has with the bank to offset a portion of any loan to this customer. By virtue of this device, the bank tends to get a slightly better settlement if it is the general creditor of the bankrupt customer.

The compensating requirement may not be common for all the customers. It may not be applicable to certain customers, while some customers may be asked to observe the minimum rules without fail. In considering a new loan application, the banker may be influenced by the amount of deposit held by the applicant in the bank at the time of the loan request. Further, unsecured borrowers may be asked to carry a relatively larger amount of deposit balance with the bank in view of the greater credit risk involved in extending loans to them.

The way in which the compensating requirement is applied seems to vary from bank to bank. Generally, there are two methods of computing a compensating balance — one is to require the borrower to keep a certain percentage of the maximum loan; the other is to require a certain percentage of the average loan during the year. Some banks apply the rule in an even more rigid fashion, and expect the borrower to carry the balance at the minimum, or not to allow the borrower's balance to fall below the minimum as long as the borrower is indebted to the bank. This may prove to be burdensome to the borrower during a part of the year, for the time when he has to borrow is naturally the time when he would be most disposed to draw his balance down to the minimum.

The policy statement on the compensating balance should include, among other things, a statement on the manner of computing the compensatory balance, the type of borrowers to whom the compensating requirement would apply, and the specific percentages of the loans that different borrowers would be required to hold as deposits in the bank.

◈ Limitations on Lending Authority

A large-scale commercial bank, having a big credit organisation consisting of a number of loan officers, should specifically determine the loan authority of different officers; otherwise there may be overlapping and duplication of efforts, resulting in considerable wastage. The demarcation of the lending authority of different credit officers may take the form of prescribing the lending limits for each lending officer. Some may be given the authority to make loans involving moderate amounts, say, between ₹ 5,000 and ₹ 25,000, while others may be authorised to lend between ₹ 25,000 to ₹ 1 lakh, still others between ₹ 1 lakh to ₹ 10 lakhs. Lending limits of the different lending officers should be based on the lending ability of the officers, which itself is a product of his knowledge and experience. When such limits are fixed, loan request in excess of the lending limits of the officer must be submitted to the other officer who has the authority to make the decision.

The management must set forth in the policy statement lending limits of each lending officer which should be stated on the lines mentioned above.

As present, the sanctioning powers of the Chairman – Managing Directors of Indian Commercial banks stand as a maximum of ₹ 15 crore for banks having aggregate loan portfolio of ₹ 5,000 core, while for CMDs of banks having a credit portfolio of above ₹ 5,000 crore, the cap is set as ₹ 30 crore. There has been an urgent need for a hike in the powers keeping in view the multi-fold growth in business since March, 1997 when the last revision took place. The new proposal is to divide banks into these with loan portfolio up to ₹ 25,000 crore and there above that limit. In the former, it is proposed that CMDs would have powers to clear loan proposal upto ₹ 60 crore for a singe borrower and ₹ 120 crore for group exposure. CMDs of banks with credit portfolio of above ₹ 25,000 crore would have powers to sanction up to ₹ 100 crore for single borrowers and ₹ 200 crore for group exposure. The Executive Directors' powers stand as 75% of the CMD's power.[18]

◈ Loan Territory

Some banks may wish to limit their lending business to certain areas. Some others may extend their lending operations all over the country. The loan policy statement of a bank must, therefore, include the regions to be served by the bank. This will save the time and efforts of the credit department which will, in that case, know from whom to receive a loan application. Territorial limit to the lending business may be imposed because of the limited size of the resources of the bank and because of the inadequacy of the loan staff to supervise the work. A bank whose customers come from particular region may wish to limit its business to these regions. When the loan territory clause does not appear in the policy statement, as is the case in larger banks, the lending officers are free to consider the loan applications pouring in from within the country or outside of it.

◈ Consortium Lending

The RBI issued guidelines (September 1999), recommending that banks help each other to 'take out financing' to avoid asset-liability mismatches. For instance, an eight-year loan could be disbursed by one bank for five years and another bank could extend the tenure by four years of the same borrower. By so doing, banks would be able to avoid an asset-liability mismatch, identified as a major risk for the financial sector by the Second Narasimham Committee report.

This is for the first time that the RBI is suggesting that banks to a form of consortium financing, where one bank takes on the liability for a minimum number of years while the second steps in for the remaining tenure for the rest of the liability. The consortium could include more than two banks depending on the size of the project.

◈ Recovery of Loans

Banks have been advised by the RBI that they are free to design and implement their own policies for recovery and write off including compromise and negotiated settlements with the approval of their Banks, particularly for old and unresolved cases falling under NAP" category.[19]

However, banks which have large exposure to corporates were advised to monitor and review on a monthly basis, through a suitable reporting system, the unhedged portion of the foreign currency exposures of these corporates whose total foreign currency exposure is relatively large (say about us $ 25 million or equivalent).[20]

F. EVALUATING CREDIT APPLICANT

Mere information on the formulation of an appropriate loan policy will not help accomplish the overall objective of maximising earnings and shareholders value while keeping an adequate amount of liquidity, unless the creditworthiness of the applicants is evaluated to ensure that they conform to the standards prescribed by the bank. The credit evaluation process involves three steps, *viz*., gathering information about the credit of the applicants, determining the creditworthiness of the applicants, and finally taking a decision to grant lending facilities. In the following paragraphs, the details of each of these aspects of credit evaluation have been examined.

◈ Gathering Credit Information

Credit department of a bank gathers from different sources the requisite information on which customer evaluation must necessarily be based. Two important factors should be kept in mind while searching for credit information — cost and time. A bank cannot afford to spend a lot of money in the investigation of some loan applicants, particularly the smaller ones; in such cases, the credit officer should take a decision on the basis of the limited information available to them about the applicant. Further, how much time the credit department should spend on an analysis of the creditworthiness of an applicant must also be considered. Spending a lot of time on investigation may be justified in cases of new and large credit customers.

There are a number of sources of soliciting credit information that would enable the banks to determine the creditworthiness of the potential borrowers. Their use will depend upon the nature of the business of the applicant, the form of loan required and the amount of the loan requested.

Interview: An interview with the applicant enables the bank to secure the information about the history of the borrower's business — its record of growth, the types of product made, the services rendered, the competitive position of the firm and its market — and check it against other sources. In an interview, the lending officer discovers the purpose of the loan sought and the applicant's plan for repayment. An idea about the applicant's honesty and ability may also be gathered in the course of a talk with him. In the course of discussions with the credit applicant, the lending officers should endeavour to determine whether the former would fulfil the credit standards, as established in the loan policy. If the applicant does not satisfy the credit norms, the lending officer may stop making a further probe into his creditworthiness. Where the applicant is considered, on a preliminary investigation, to be up to the standards expected of him, he may be asked to submit the various financial reports and records that will help the bank to evaluate his creditworthiness.

Financial Statements: The financial statements, including the balance sheet and the profit and loss account of the prospective borrower, are invaluable sources of credit information. Such statements are most readily available from the applicant himself. The financial statements of the last few years, the proforma balance sheet and income statement and budgets should also be obtained. An analysis of these financial statements would provide an insight into the borrower's financial position, funds management capacity, liquidity, profitability and loan repaying capacity.

The balance sheet enables the banker to judge the creditworthiness of the borrower; it is a snapshot, a photograph of the financial worth of the borrower's firm at a point of time. It depicts the financial position of his business on a particular date. On the one side, it shows the properties and on the other the liabilities, including the capital. Lending officers with analytical brains can learn a lot from the balance sheet about the liquidity of the business of the applicant, its credit policy, paying habits, and the ability to manage funds. With the help of this statement, the lending officer can discover whether the applicant has sufficient assets in his business to generate an income that would be adequate enough for the repayment of the loan, and whether the assets available in the business can be used as a security for the loan.

Equally important is the profit and loss statement. It is a motion picture which presents the financial result of operations during a particular period. It depicts the financial position of his business on a particular date. On the one side, it shows the properties and on the other the abilities, including the capital. Lending officers with analytical brains can learn a lot from the balance sheet about the liquidity of the business of the applicant, its credit policy, paying habits, and the ability to manage funds.

The management's ability to control cost as well as the competitive strength of the firm within the industry can also be judged with the assistance of the income statement.

Thus, both the balance sheet and the profit and loss statement are very useful financial statements for a bank. Although they are listed separately in the annual report of a business, there is a close relation between the two. While the balance sheet is a statement of the wealth of an entity at a time, the income statement explains the changes in this wealth between two points of time.

It would also be useful for a bank to collect information on the budgets, particularly on cash and capital budgets of the firm. These budgets are the expressions in financial terms of the plan of operations designed to achieve the objectives of the firm. The cash budget summarises the estimated cash inflows and the estimated cash disbursements of a business over the budget period. It is from this report that the lending officer can gauge whether sufficient cash resources would be available to the firm for debt repayment, besides meeting other cash obligations. The capital budget is a projection of the expected expenditures for fixed assets for a period of one year. With this, the bank can know the future developmental programmes of the business which, in turn, will help it to assess the debt-repaying capacity of the borrower.

◆ Reports of Credit Rating Agencies

Commercial banks can gather information on the creditworthiness of the applicant by procuring financing reports from credit-rating agencies, wherever they exist. These agencies collect information on the financial, managerial and other aspects of a large number of business concerns, and keep it up-to-date. It is their full-time job to get information from all possible sources (market places, private agencies, newspapers, etc.), to analyse and arrange and incorporate the information in their periodical reports. The information provided in a typical credit report includes the name and address of the firm, the date of formation, the type of business, the financial structure, management, bankers and credit rating. In America and England, there are a large number of credit rating agencies which publish detailed reports on companies in their periodicals. Dun and Bradstreet is the most important credit rating agency which reports on more than 3 lakh business houses in a year. Syed and Company Limited, the most promising agency in England, collects reports on all business houses and keeps them up-to-date. In addition to its rating services, Dun and Brandstreet supplies credit reports on request to individual firms — on the history of the business, the biographies of owners or chief officers, a description of the method of operation, a simple balance sheet, and recent payment experience of the suppliers of the firm.

In India for the first time the Credit Rating Information Services of India Ltd., was established in 1987 to rate companies as well as fixed interest bearing securities coming to the capital market. This will provide individual as well as corporate investors a useful tool in making investment decisions.

Bank's Own Records: If the applicant happens to be the bank's customer, the lending officer studies his past records. Every bank maintains a central file of all depositors and borrowers. An examination of the customer's record provides an insight into his past dealings with the bank, *i.e.*, the customer's paying habits of previous loans, and the balances carried by him in current and savings accounts. If an examination of the applicant's account reveals that the bills discounted for him have always been duly honoured, this will count as a plus point in his favour.

Bazar Reports: Reports on the applicant can be obtained from the various markets, particularly from businessmen carrying on the same trade, and from suppliers — those from whom the borrower buys for his firm. The bank may ask these businessmen and suppliers about the payment habits of the applicant, the promptness of the borrower in repayment, his practices in availing of all cash discounts, etc. Some businessmen may happen to be the borrower's friends, others his rivals. Some may, therefore, give exaggerated reports about the applicant's means, while others may try to run him down. All such reports, sometimes contradictory to each other, have to be weighed independently, and a balanced opinion has to be formed about the creditworthiness of the applicant.

Reports from Other Banks: The credit department of the bank may check with other banks with which the applicant has had dealings. Such a check with the other banks reveals the character, ability and management of the applicant.

Other Sources: Other sources of credit information on business firms, especially the larger ones, may be trade journals, periodicals, newspapers, trade directories, public records, such as income-tax statements, wealth tax returns, sales tax returns, reports about actions and decrees in the Government Gazette, registration, revenue and municipal records.

With the retail credit rising rapidly, banks will soon be relying on credit scores to access customers. Credit and Information Bureau of India (CIBIL) is expected to roll out. Credit score is built on data bases provided by various banks. As per the RBI regulations, banks and financial institutions have been instructed to facilitate submission of details of all borrowal accounts to the bureau for compilation of credit information. This data will soon be accessible to member banks to help improve the quality of credit appraisal and decisions.

In view of the rapid increase in loans to the real estate sector and the systematic risks posed by such exposure, banks were advised in March, 2006 that while appraising loans proposals involving real estate, they should ensure that the borrowers have obtained prior permission from the Government/local Governments/other statutory authorities for the project, where ever required.[21]

◈ Credit Analysis

After assembling the credit information on the potential customer, the lending officer analyses it to evaluate the creditworthiness of the applicant and to determine whether he is up to the standard or not. Such an analysis is known as *credit analysis*. A credit analysis involves the credit investigation of a potential customer to determine the degree of risk associated with the loan. The capacity of the applicant to borrow and his ability and willingness to repay the debt in accordance with the terms of the loan agreement must be studied. An analysis for the creditworthiness of the applicant, therefore, calls for a detailed investigation of the five 'C's of credit — character, capacity, capital, collateral and conditions.

The term *credit character* refers to the reputation of the prospective borrower in meeting his obligations to the bank. This includes certain moral and mental qualities of integrity, fairness, responsibility, temperance, trustworthiness, industry, and the like. Credit character is a relative matter. It is not difficult for a person to be honest and be willing to repay the debt when his income is high, his business is good and his profits are substantial. But when he is willing to repay his debts even during hard times, when his business has been poor and his profits low, he may be said to be a person with a high credit character. It is very difficult to measure a person's credit character exactly. However, he can collect information about the person's reputation in so far as the payment of his obligations is concerned, which sheds light on his credit character. Generally, those who have an excellent record of quick payment may reasonably be expected to behave so in the future as well. However, prosperous conditions can amend bad traits. That is why a person's credit character should be judged on the basis of his performance in bad times.

Capacity refers to the ability of the potential borrower to repay the debt when it falls due, and is indicative of the borrower's competence to utilise the loan effectively and profitably. This is a very important variable of credit analysis, for the customer's ability to repay is primarily dependent upon his earning capacity. The repayment of loan may be made by the sale of assets, by borrowing funds from others, and by earnings. Banks are always interested in loan repayment out of earnings because the repayment of the debt by the sale of assets is an expensive and time-consuming process, and may strain the banks' relations with the borrower. Nor does the bank like the loan to be repaid by borrowing from other lending institutions because the ability of the borrower to borrow from others, to do so is conditioned by his financial strength. With a deterioration in the financial position of the borrower, the chance of his repaying the loan by borrowings diminishes. The earning capacity of a borrower, if he is a businessman, is dependent upon the purpose of his present loan, his present debt structure and his income from business. The income from business is a product of the sale of goods or services, which is determined by such factors as the location of the store or plant, advertising, the quality and variety of goods or services, the nearness to the market, the distribution methods, advertising competition, and public relations. The cost of operation, too, affects the net earnings of the business.

In assessing the earning capacity of an applicant, the bank is vitally interested in his net earnings. The high earnings of a firm do not always suggest that the prospects of repayment are bright because it is possible that the bulk of the earnings will be used to repay other lenders having a claim on his income, and very little may be left for the discharge of other obligations. Thus, the debt may be so large that it may impair the repaying capacity of the borrower. Alongside this, the dividend policy of the firm should also be evaluated.

It is necessary to evaluate thoroughly the calibre of the management, which is referred to as the management factor. Such an investigation is vital to any judgement of the earning capacity of the applicant. The calibre of the management can be judged with reference to its know-how, its ability to assemble agents of production and manage them in such a manner as to ensure the flow of income and profits. The ability of the management is also reflected in its skill in hiring productive labour, its excellent advertising and public relations' programmes, the quality of its products and the introduction of new products, and the organisation of research and development programmes.

Capital represents the general financial position of the potential borrower's firm, with special emphasis on tangible net worth and profitability (which indicates the ability to generate funds continuously over time). The net worth figure of the business enterprise is the key factor that would determine the amount of credit that would be made available to the borrower. Here, the lending officer has to determine the amount of immediate liabilities that are due for retirement and the relation these bear to the firm's available assets. A true estimate of capital can be made if the market value rather than the book value of the assets is taken into account.

Collateral is represented by the assets that may be offered as a pledge against the loan. Collateral, thus, serves as a cushion or shock absorber if one or several of the first three "C"s are insufficient to give a reasonable assurance of repayment of the loan on maturity. The collateral in the form of pledged assets serves to compensate for a deficiency in one or several of the first three 'C's.

The term *conditions* refers to the economic and business conditions which affect the borrower's ability to earn and repay the debt and which are, or may be, beyond the control of the borrower. Economic conditions include all those factors which have a bearing on the economic processes of production, distribution and consumption. Borrowers may have a high credit character and potential ability to produce income; but the existing or ensuing conditions may be such as to render the extension of credit imprudent. In periods of economic recession, the banker may be averse to the grant of a loan because of the greater chance for the dissipation of the capital and shortfall in income, which would undermine the character of the borrower. In contrast with this, men with limited ability to earn an income may secure a loan from the bank because it is expected that the borrower would fare well in an improved business environment of the country. For a proper evaluation of the creditworthiness of the borrower, the lending officer of a bank should, therefore, have his fingers on the economic pulse of the nation. Alongside this, an analysis of the conditions obtaining in the industry to which the firm belongs should be undertaken to ascertain whether the industry has good growth prospects *vis-a-vis* other industries in the country. A study of the growth rate of the firm over the past few years and its comparison with that of other firms engaged in the same line would provide an insight into prospects to the other firms of the same size and age, the bank may not favour the extention of credit to him.

◈ Techniques of Credit Analysis

There are a number of useful techniques with which a banker can evaluate the five 'C's of an applicant. Important among these are:

(*i*) Ratio Analysis;
(*ii*) Cash Flow Projections;
(*iii*) Funds-Flow Statement; and
(*iv*) Credit Scoring.

A brief discussion of these tools are as follows:

◈ Ratio Analysis

Ratio analysis is an important tool available to a lender to judge the liquidity, profitability and funds management capacity of the credit applicant. It is the process of determining and presenting in arithmetical terms the relationship between figures and groups of figures in financial statements. The ratio may be expressed in one of the three forms:

(*i*) As a pure ratio; *e.g.*, 2:1;
(*ii*) As a rate; *e.g.*, inventory turnover so many times a year;
(*iii*) As a percentage; *e.g.*, return on the shareholders' investment is 10 per cent.

The financial ratios become meaningful in an assessment of the financial strength and other related aspects of the firm only when there is a comparison. In fact, an analysis of the ratio involves two types of comparisons:

(*i*) A comparison of the present ratio with the past and expected future ratios for the same firm; and
(*ii*) A comparison of the ratios of the firm with those of similar firms or with the industry averages.

Ratios as a tool for the evaluation of creditworthiness should, however, be used with extreme care and considered judgement because they suffer from certain serious drawbacks. In the first place, ratios can sometimes be misleading if an analyst does not know the reliability and soundness of the figures from which they are computed and if he is unaware of the financial position of the business at other times of the year. Second, ratios are a quantitative measurement. They do not tell us anything about the qualitative aspects of the relationship. A business firm, for example, may have a high current ratio of 4:1, but a larger part of the current assets may be composed of uncollectable receivables. When these are deducted, the ratio may be 2 :1. Third, price changes make the ratio analysis somewhat difficult.

The ratio as a tool for measuring the liquidity, profitability, efficiency and financial position of a firm may be classified into four basic types: Liquidity, Leverage, Activity and Profitability.

◈ Liquidity Ratio

The bank loan officer is very keen in determining the immediate ability of the concern to honour its current obligations. A calculation of the liquidity ratios and their interpretation provide a considerable insight into the present cash solvency of the firm and its stability to continue to be solvent in times of adversity. The commonly used liquidity ratios are: current ratio and quick or acid test ratio.

Current Ratio: The current ratio expresses the relationship between current assets (cash, marketable securities, accounts receivables and inventory turnover) and current liabilities (accounts payable, short-term notes payable, current maturities of long-term debt, accrued income taxes and other secured expenses). It is computed by dividing current assets by current liabilities. A higher current ratio is a clue to the ability of the company to pay its debts on maturity. On the other hand, a low current ratio points to the possibility that a firm may not be able to pay its short-term debts. However, from the management's point of view, a higher current ratio is indicative of poor planning, for an excessive amount of funds lies idle. A low ratio would, however, pin-point the inadequacy of working capital which may hamper the smooth functioning of the enterprise.

A current ratio of 2 : 1 was long considered to be the minimum in a sound business. This rule-of-thumb has, however, since succumbed to the rule of reason. An excess of current assets over current liabilities does not necessarily mean that the debts can be paid promptly. If current assets contain a high proportion of uncollectable accounts receivable or unsaleable inventories, there will be slow down in the intake of cash. Therefore, while computing the current ratio, it would be pertinent to take note of the nature and proportion of the various types of current assets, the nature of current liabilities, the nature of cash flows and the future expectations.

Acid Test Ratio or Quick Ratio: It is a measure of judging the immediate ability of the firm to pay off its current obligations. It is obtained by dividing the quick current assets by current liabilities. Quick current assets include those assets which can be liquidated immediately and at minimum loss in order to meet the pressing financial obligations of a firm or bank. They consist of cash, marketable securities and accounts receivables. Inventories are excluded from the quick assets because they are slower to convert into cash and generally exhibit an uncertainty insofar as conversion prices are concerned.

A ratio of 1:1 is usually considered adequate. But again while using this ratio as a measure of immediate ability to pay off short-term obligations, the liquidity of receivables must be kept in mind, for the receivables which are not collectable are not adequate to support the liquidity of the concern. Therefore, such factors as the size, age and location of the accounts receivables must be analysed before reaching any final decision.

◈ Leverage Ratios

Bank lending for medium and long-term periods is determined by the ability of the borrower to pay his long-term loan in future. This is measured with the help of the leverage ratios. Under this group are included:

- The debt to total assets or debt asset ratio;
- The debt-equity ratio;
- Long-term debt to capitalisation; and
- Times interest earned.

Debt to Total Assets Ratio: This ratio indicates the proportion of the total assets created through a debt, including short-term and long-term liabilities. It is computed by dividing the total assets by the total debt. It is of considerable significance to creditors in as much as it highlights the long-run solvency of the firm. The lower the ratio, the greater the cushion against credit losses in the event of liquidation. A bank prefers the moderate ratio.

The Debt-equity Ratio: This ratio relates all the creditor claims on the assets to the owner's claims. It is computed by dividing the total debt, both current and long-term, of the business by its tangible net worth, consisting of common stock, reserves and surplus. If the ratio is greater, it would mean that the creditors have invested more in the business than the owners; that is, the creditors would lose more in times of distress than the owners. This is why creditors prefer a low debt-equity ratio. A low debt-equity ratio may, however, indicate that the firm is not taking advantage of a proper mix of debt and equity, and may be passing up an opportunity to engage in financial leverage with a view to increasing its earnings.

Long-term Debt to Total Capitalisation: This ratio reflects the relationship between the long-term borrowed capital and the owner's capital contribution. It is found by dividing the long-term debt by total capitalisation (all long-term + net worth). Although there is no hard and fast rule concerning the proper relationship that should obtain here, one rough rule-of-thumb method indicates that the maximum percentage of long-term debt should not exceed 33.3 per cent of capitalisation for manufacturing firms and 50 per cent for railroads and public utilities.

Times Interest Earned: This measure is used to indicate the times interest charges have been earned and how much safety margin is available to the shareholders. It is computed by dividing profits before interest and taxes (PBIT) by interest charges. A high ratio is a sign of low burden of borrowings on the business and a lower utilisation of the borrowing capacity.

◈ Activity Ratios

A banker is also interested in knowing how efficiently funds are managed by the firm. For this purpose, activity ratios are calculated. These ratios express the relationship between the level of sales and investment in various assets, *viz.*, inventories, receivables, fixed assets, etc. The important activity ratios are:

- Inventory turnover;
- Average collection period; and
- Total assets turnover.

Inventory Turnover: The inventory turnover is computed by dividing the cost of goods sold by the average inventory for the period. This ratio gives the number of times the inventory is replaced during a given period, usually a year. Presumably, the higher the turnover, the better is the performance of the company, for it has managed to operate with a relatively small average locking up of funds. A low sales to inventory ratio may indicate a slow moving inventory, suffering possibly from obsolescence; or it indicates a none too aggressive sales force.

Average Collection Period: The average collection period is a measure of receivable turnover. Its computation involves two steps. In the first place, annual sales are divided by 365 days to get the average daily sales. In the second stage, the daily sales are divided into accounts receivables to find the number of days the sales were tied up in receivables. This gives an average collection period because it represents the average period of time that the firm must wait after making a sale before receiving cash. The formula is:

$$\text{Average collection period} = \frac{\text{Receivables (Net sales)}}{\text{No. of days in year}}$$

$$\text{OR} \quad \frac{\text{Receivables} \times \text{No. of days in a year}}{\text{Net sales}}$$

This ratio reflects the credit and collection policies of the firm and the effectiveness of its collection machinery. A longer period of collection indicates the leniency of credit policy and/or none too strenuous collection efforts.

This ratio, to be of value, must be compared with the selling terms of the business firm. If the selling terms of the firm are 2/10 net 30, the collection period of 30 days would appear to be acceptable. If, however, the period is 90 days, it would indicate that there are three months' receivables still on hand.

Total Assets Turnover: This ratio expresses the relationship between the amount invested in the assets and the results accruing in terms of sales. This is calculated by dividing the net sales by the total assets.

The total assets turnover indicates the efficiency with which the assets of the firm have been utilised. A higher ratio would mean a better utilisation and *vice versa*. However, care should be exercised in drawing a conclusion. Sometimes, the purchase of assets may not result in higher sales, but may, on the contrary, cause a reduction in cost and thereby result in an increase in profits. In such cases, even if the ratio declines, the situation is considered favourable.

◈ Profitability Ratios

Profitability ratios, as a matter of fact, are the best indicators of the overall efficiency of a business concern because they compare the return of value over and above the values put into a business with the sales or services by the firm with the help of the assets employed. Profitability ratios are of two types: Profitability as related to sales and profitability as related to investment.

(a) Profitability as Related to Sales: Under this group of profitability ratios are included:

- Gross profit to sales;
- Operating profit to sales;
- Net profit to sales; and
- Final net profit to sales.

Gross Profit to Sales: This ratio establishes a relationship between gross profit with sales to measure the relative operating efficiency of the firm and to reflect its pricing policies. It is computed by dividing sales minus the cost of goods sold by sales.

Sometimes, it is calculated by taking the cost of goods sold instead of sales. That indicates the position of the trading result.

Operating Profit to Sales: This ratio expresses the relationship between operating profit and sales. It is worked out by dividing the operating profit by net sales. With the help of this ratio, one can judge managerial efficiency, which may not be reflected in the net profit ratio. For example, a firm may have a larger amount of non-operating income in the form of dividend and interest, which represents a major proportion of its net profit. The net profit ratio may, in such cases, show the high efficiency of the management. However, the operating profit ratio will make it crystal clear that the efficiency is extremely low, for non-operating income has no relation with the operating efficiency of the management.

Net Profit to Sales: The net profit to sales, also referred to as the net profit margin, is calculated by dividing the net income (after tax) by net sales. This ratio provides a considerable insight into the overall efficiency of the business. A higher ratio is an indication of the higher overall efficiency of the business, and better utilisation of total resources. A low ratio, on the other hand, would mean poor financial planning and low efficiency.

(b) Profitability as Related to Investment: Under this group of profitability following ratios are included:

Return on Capital Employed: This ratio is computed by dividing the net profit figure by the total capital employed in the business. The net profit in this case means profit before taxes, less interest on short-term borrowings. The figure of the capital employed is found out by subtracting current liabilities from the total investments. This ratio is the only dependable measure of the overall performance of a firm. A higher ratio is an index of better utilisation of funds.

Return on Net Worth: This ratio is obtained by dividing profits before tax by net worth. It measures the productivity of the shareholders' funds. A higher ratio indicates a better utilisation of owners' funds and a higher productivity.

◈ Cash Flow Projections

In considering the loan application of a firm, a banker wants to know whether the borrowing firm would have adequate cash earnings to repay the loan requested for. Where it is found that the firm's cash earnings may not be sufficient to repay the debt on the expiry of the loan period, the loan request may be turned down despite the high credit character and fairly good earning capacity of the borrower. This is why the borrowing firm is required to prepare a projected cash flow statement. In essence, this statement is simply a cash budget. The cash budget of a firm predicts for some future period the amount of cash receipts from different sources, cash disbursements for different purposes, and the resulting cash position, generally on a monthly basis. For a banker, such statements tend to shed a lurid light on the cash surplus or shortfalls, and enables him to determine the amount of the loan that should be granted and the duration for which it should be granted.

◈ Fund Flow Analysis

Another technique, which has come to be increasingly used by bankers to evaluate the creditworthiness of the borrowing firms, is the funds flow analysis. This analysis is undertaken to highlight changes in the financial condition of a business concern over a given period of time. A funds flow statement is a report which summarises the events taking place between two accounting periods; it spells out the sources from which funds were derived and the uses to which these funds were put. This statement is derived from an analysis of the changes that have occurred in the assets and liabilities items between the two balance sheet dates. With the help of this statement, an analyst can judge the liquidity position of the firm, and the spending and financing habits of the management. In several instances, a firm has a fairly good earning record; yet it may experience a shortage of liquid resources, which may often impel it towards liquidation. Contrary to this, despite low profits, a firm may be placed comfortably with respect to working capital. Furthermore, the funds flow statement provides an insight into the financing pattern of an enterprise. An analysis of the major sources of funds in the past reveals what portion of the growth was financed by internal resources and what portion by external resources. It shows whether the firm has been expanding its scale of business by building up additional plant and equipment or by increasing its sales, or whether it is involved in purely routine affairs of distributing dividends and redeeming long-term debts.

There are two aspects of the funds flow statement — the inflow of funds and the outflow of funds. The inflow of funds is shown on the left hand side and the outflow of funds on the right hand side. This statement can be prepared in a number of ways, depending on the sense in which term *funds* is used. There are three concepts of the term *funds* — the cash concept, the total resources concept, and the working capital concept. We shall now discuss in detail the mechanism of the preparation of the funds flow statement under each of the three concepts will be touched upon.

The funds statement prepared on the "cash concept basis" depicts sources side of the following items:

- A net decrease in any asset other than cash or fixed assets;
- A gross decrease in fixed assets;
- A net increase in any liabilities;
- Proceeds from the sale of stock of capital;
- Funds provided by operation.

Uses of funds in the statement show the following items:

- A net increase in any fixed assets;
- A gross increase in fixed assets;
- A net decrease in any liability;
- Retirement of debt or purchase of stock;
- Payment of cash dividends.

According to the "total resources concept," all the changes that result in an increase in the funds of the firm constitute sources of funds. Generally, funds flow in a business firm from the following sources:

- The earnings of the enterprise;
- Expansion in liabilities through increased use of borrowed funds or increased trade credit;
- Decrease in assets such as liquidation of current assets, sale of fixed, miscellaneous or tangible assets, and earned depreciation on such assets;
- Contribution of additional funds by the owners of the firm.

The use of funds side of the funds statement depicts all such changes as cause a decrease in the total funds of the business. The following items are shown on the "uses" column of the statements:

- Decrease in liabilities:
- Increase in assets;
- Decrease in capital funds;
- Net losses.

According to the *working capital concept*, the term *funds* refers to the net working capital (current assets – current liabilities). Since the prime objective of the funds flow statement, prepared on the basis of the net working capital, is to show the ebb and flow of funds through the working capital and to focus on factors contributing to these movements, two statements are prepared under this concept. In the first statement are recorded the changes in the net working capital. This statement records the changes in the net working capital, and is called the *schedule of working capital*. The second statement, called the *Funds Flow Statement*, is prepared to highlight the factors contributing to the variances in working capital, as displayed by the above schedule.

The schedule of working capital is designed to measure the flow of funds through the working capital. As a matter of fact, one has to ascertain the changes in current assets and current liabilities during the two balance sheet dates, and record the variations in the net working capital over the period in the schedule of the working capital. An increase in current assets would result in a rise in the net working capital; but a decrease in it causes a reduction in the level of the net working capital. On the other hand, the net working capital would decline with an increase in current liabilities and rise with a decrease in them. The funds statement under the working capital is prepared to reflect the causes of the variances in the net working capital of a firm. In the column of the sources of funds are shown only those credits in the fixed accounts (fixed assets or fixed liabilities) which were offset by debits to current accounts (any current asset or current liability). Likewise, under the heading *application of funds* only those debits in fixed accounts are shown in the funds statement which were offset by credits to current accounts.

In simpler words, only the following changes in the fixed part of the balance sheet are shown as sources of funds in the statement:

(*i*) Such increase in fixed liabilities as caused a decrease in current liabilities or an increase in current assets;

(*ii*) Such decrease in the value of fixed assets as caused an increase in current assets or a decrease in current liabilities.

Similarly, under the heading, *use of funds*, the following changes in the fixed assets and liabilities are shown:

(*i*) Such decrease in fixed liabilities as caused a rise in the current liabilities or a decrease in value of current assets;

(*ii*) Such increase in fixed assets as caused a reduction in current assets or expansion in current liabilities. The following format of the funds flow statement will make the above points very clear:

Sources of Funds	*Uses of Funds*
1. Net profit (before charging such expenses as do not affect the level of the working capital, such as depreciation, charges to write off goodwill, and other intangible assets (+)	1. Net Loss (before charging such expenses as do not affect the level of the working capital) (–)
2. Increase in long-term liabilities (+)	2. Decrease in long-term liabilities (–)
3. Decrease in the value of fixed assets (–)	3. Increase in value of fixed assets (+)
4. Acquisition of additional capital (+)	4. Refund of capital (–)

It should be remembered that the statement would not record such changes in fixed assets and liabilities, as it does not affect the level of the working capital.

◈ Credit Decision

After determining the creditworthiness of the applicant, the lending officer has to decide whether or not credit facilities should be provided to him. The creditworthiness of the applicant should be matched against the credit standards set out in loan policy. If the applicant is above or upto the standards, the loan should be made to him. The difficulty in taking a credit decision arises where the applicant is marginally creditworthy. In such cases, the decision should be taken only after matching the potential profitability against the cost of the debt loss. The applicant who does not satisfy the standard of acceptability may be told of the bank's helplessness in view of its loan policy. The applicant may be asked to approach other existing financial institutions for assistance. In many instances, the bank lending officer finds that the borrowing firm's earnings would not be sufficient to repay the loan within the period set out in the bank's policy statement, but that the liquidity and security position of the firm is very strong. The bank may advise such firms to approach term-financing institutions whose terms and conditions might be fulfilled by the firm.

◈ Supervision of Loans

In order to ensure the end-use of the loan, it is necessary for the bank to keep track of the loans outstanding. It keeps in touch with the borrowers during the life of the loan. The supervision of the loan is the responsibility of more than one department of the bank. The credit department regularly obtains the financial reports of customers indebted to the bank and analyses them to assess the progress made by the customers. The lending officer keeps track of his clients. When special problems arise in connection with outstanding loans, they are referred to the higher echelons of bank management, as in the case of new loans. Usually, the outstanding loans are supervised in the following ways:

Inspections: Team of financial and technical officers visits the borrower's firm to find out how the customer's affairs are developing. The borrower is required to maintain records showing the utilisation of the disbursed loan, and the operations and financial results of the firm. In addition to a close scrutiny of these records, they make a physical verification of stocks. The borrower may also take the opportunity of discussing any special problem with the visiting team, which may sometimes avert problems of workouts and liquidations. Frequent visits to the borrower enable the bank to discover such things as may not be reflected in their financial statements. For example, an inspection of the borrower's firm makes it possible for the bank to assess the general state of the repairs and maintenance of plant and equipment. Inadequate maintenance is very often an early sign of distress. Uncovering the discrepancy between the claims made in statement and the actual affairs is also possible by personal visits to the borrower. The visiting staff may also get the opportunity to discuss matters with the employees and junior officers of the firm and acquire a *feel* about the morale of the employees and the general state of affairs of the firm.

Keeping Track of the Deposit Balance: By inspecting the deposit balance required to be held by the borrower, the bank can learn a good deal about him. It observes the way the agreement regarding the amount of the deposit balance is observed because it gives clues to the borrower's affairs. If the borrower has all along kept a bare minimum balance, it may not be a healthy sign. On the other hand, some surplus over the minimum is considered a good sign.

Checking with Other Creditors: As in the case of the grant of loans, the bank continually checks with other creditors for the supervision of loans. Such checking is very useful, for it acquaints the bank with the borrower's paying habits, his ability to avail of all the discount facilities, and similar other matters. Frequent enquiries about the debtor should be avoided, for they cast doubts on the creditworthiness of a quite satisfactory debtor. When other creditors receive repeated requests for credit information, they may suppose to start wondering just what it is that prompts this frequent inquiry.

Obtaining Half-Yearly and Yearly Financial Reports: Where the bank has provided term loans, the assisted firms are required to send half-yearly and yearly financial reports and circulars and minutes of shareholders' meetings to the bank. The credit department carefully studies and analyses these to assess the progress of the assisted concerns, their profitability and other financial aspect.

While obtaining these reports, the credit department has to ensure that the liquidity position is maintained in accordance with the loan agreement, that property is kept in good condition, and that profits have been distributed according to the terms of agreement. Where deviations from the terms of the loan agreement are discovered, the borrower should be asked to correct the position.

Obtaining Budgetary Report: A budgetary report is an effective tool in the hands of a bank to supervise long-term loans. Budgets are valuable only if used. The bank should require the borrower to submit budgetary reports which show the actual results, budget amounts and the differences between the actual results and the budget amount. If the budgetary report discloses disappointing results, the bank should ask the borrower to explain the reasons. Where disappointing results are due to factors beyond the control of the borrower, the banker has every reason to be sympathetic, but he should not fail to take such protective action as may be required. Often, the intelligent banker can plan a sort of economic retreat which, in the long run, works to the advantage of the borrower as well as the bank. If the unsatisfactory performance was due to lapses on the part of the borrower, the banker should collect the loan if he is satisfied that the borrower would not reform his way of working in the future.

In view of the increase in growth of advances to the real estate sector in the recent years, banks have been advised by the RBI to contain the risk involved. Banks were also advised to put in place a system for ensuring proper checking and documentation of related papers before sanctioning/disbursing such loans. They were also directed to report their real estate exposure and disclosure their gross exposure to the real estate sector and the detailed break-up in their annual reports.[22]

The banks have, of late, been advised to monitor credit flow to minorities in 103 minority concentration districts, which have at least 25 per cent minority population.[23]

G. ORGANISATION OF BANK LENDING

The principal responsibility for formulating a loan policy for a bank and its implementation lies with the Board of Directors. Since the members of the Board are preoccupied with other important activities, they do not attend to the day-to-day lending functions of the bank. They constitute a separate lending body, known as the *credit department*, to carry into effect the loan policies which they formulate.

Broadly speaking, the credit department of a bank performs the following functions:

(*i*) It receives loan applications;

(*ii*) It collects credit information about the applicants from numerous sources and conducts interviews with the applicants to solicit additional information and to verify the accuracy of the information given by them in the application;

(*iii*) It investigates the creditworthiness of applicants by making use of numerous tools of credit analysis;

(*iv*) Once the loan has been granted, it supervises loans by visiting the borrowers, keeping a constant vigil on their deposit balances, obtaining financial and other reports and checking with other creditors and calling the attention of the borrowers to their unsatisfactory performances;

(*v*) It maintains records of credit information and revises them constantly so that bank officers may come to know the status of their accounts;

(*vi*) It furnishes credit information to other banks and creditors who seek it.

In an ideal situation, the credit policy statement is usually prepared by the Board of Directors, and its implementation is done by the loan committee and loan specialists because, in most banks, all the directors do not meet each week. All the loan applications are received by the credit department manager, which are then referred to the concerned individual loan officer possessing the sanctioning authority. Where the loan requests exceed the stipulated amounts of the individual officer's loan authority, they are referred to the loan committee. This loan committee consists of the chairman of the Board, two or three Directors and one or two senior loan officers. Besides approving or recommending action on specified credit applications, this committee makes a complete report on all the applications handled each week or month, as the case may be, and the decision communicated to the Directors under whose supervision it operates.

Next to the loan committee is the Chairman of the Board, who is a full-time officer and exercises the greatest amount of control over bank loans. All the important loans are referred to him by the credit manager or senior loan officers for approval or disapproval. Ordinarily, the Chairman does not go into the matter in great detail, and acts largely on the recommendation of his subordinate officers, who analyse the situation with great care. In respect of small loan requests, the loan committee delegates powers to senior loan officers, who interview the borrowers and review their financial conditions with a view to establishing lines of credit. In a big commercial bank, there may be a number of senior loan officers, each possessing expertise and knowledge in a specific credit line. For example, a loan officer who has specialised in bill discounting may be given charge of the discount section; another loan officer, with special knowledge and experience in consumption loans, may be assigned the responsibility of the consumption loan section; still another may be in charge of real estate lending; and the loan officer who has specialised in agricultural science would be empowered to handle agricultural loans.

The manager of the credit department exercises general supervision over all the operations of his department. Among his numerous duties, important one is to appraise the risk or to determine whether any investigation should be initiated. He interviews customers and prospects for the purpose of obtaining the information required by the loaning officers in making loan decisions. He acts as an intermediary between the loan committee and his department. Often serving as secretary of the loan committee, he knows not only the voted decisions but also the opinions of the individual members of the committee, and is well enough informed to carry out the policies and wishes of his executive officers.

Still another function is to communicate with other banks and commercial houses requesting for credit information, and to receive and classify information from credit applicants and others. Finally, he inspects all the new and revised folders prepared during the day by his staff.

To aid the management in reaching the credit decision, the credit department is broken up into several subdivisions, one of which receives the loan applications, the other is concerned with the collection of credit information from different sources, still another division may be concerned with the interpretation of financial statements and other information and the calculation of the ratios for the use of the lending officers, and another division may be looking after filing and records.

A clear understanding of the organisational pattern of the lending work of a commercial bank may be had from the chart below which depicts the organisational set-up of a hypothetical bank:

The organisational set-up of the loan function in a bank would depend upon a number of factors, including the size of the bank, the magnitude of the loan portfolio and its composition, and the attitude of the Board of Directors, the extent of the authority delegated. In a small bank, two or three officers perform all the necessary credit functions, and the routine functions of the credit department are performed by a clerk. There is little or no specialisation. Each officer is responsible for securing the credit information that is necessary and for maintaining his own credit files. At the other extreme, in the larger banks, the loan function is highly departmentalised, and there is a considerable amount of specialisation of the lending activities. There are usually separate lending offices, each for real estate, business or commercial, consumer, agriculture and many others. There may be further sub-specialisation in each of these credit lines. For example, the business loan function may be categorised industry-wise, with a lending officer in charge of each industry or of related industries. Some large banks having nation-wide operation may divide their lending activities on a territorial basis. In such banks, loan requests exceeding the lending limit of the loan officers are considered by the loan committee which would, besides other members, consist of the senior loan officer of the concerned area.

Chart 15.1: Organisation of Bank Lending Work

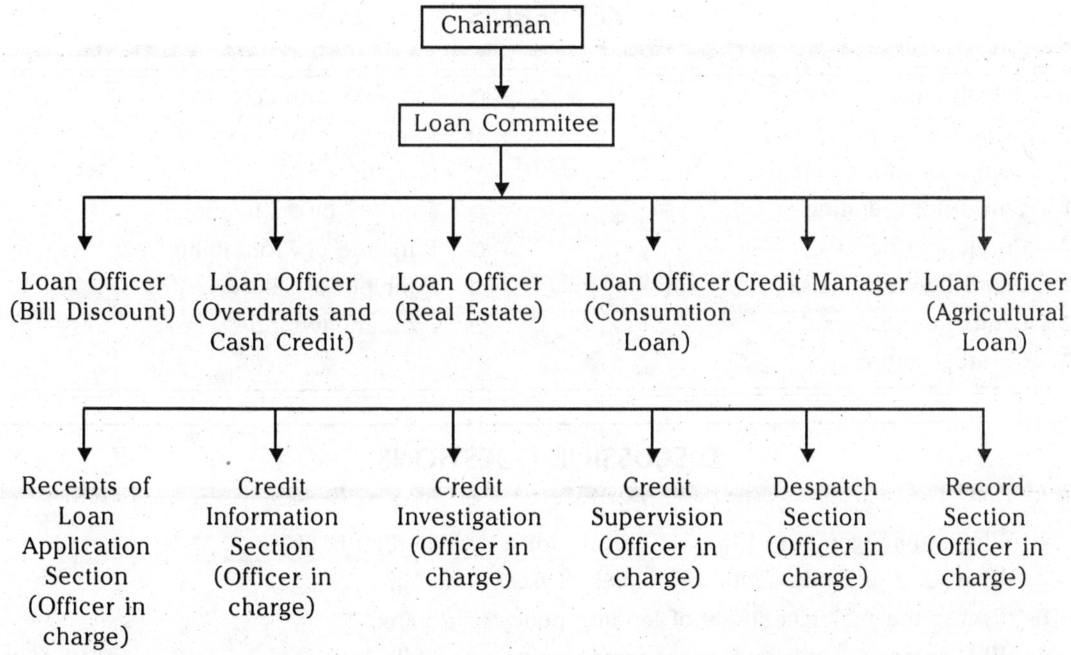

Chairman

Loan Commitee

Loan Officer (Bill Discount)

Loan Officer (Overdrafts and Cash Credit)

Loan Officer (Real Estate)

Loan Officer (Consumtion Loan)

Credit Manager

Loan Officer (Agricultural Loan)

Receipts of Loan Application Section (Officer in charge)

Credit Information Section (Officer in charge)

Credit Investigation (Officer in charge)

Credit Supervision (Officer in charge)

Despatch Section (Officer in charge)

Record Section (Officer in charge)

In medium sized banks, there is greater delegation of authority and specialization in respect of lending work than in small banks. Many banks of medium size have loan committee, which considers loan requests falling outside the sanctioning limits of the loan managers.

The bank with a large number of branches has a big lending organization with chairman of the bank as its head. Branch managers are given loan sanctioning authority up to a certain limit. A loan request beyond this limit is referred to the regional manager with in his limit or referred to the Head office. In large branches, there may be a good deal of specialization in lending work, as in the case of big bank. For expeditious disposal of credit requests, it is desirable to delegate more powers to branch/regional managers. Borrowers, particularly those requesting for a small amount of loans, cannot be expected to wait for a long-term for credit decisions. Moreover, the personal touch with the borrowers is maintained, which is necessary for the development of the banking business.

H. CONCLUSIONS

Lending being one of the principal business of a bank accounts for a major portion of its funds. Banks provide loans to different sectors of the economy for different purposes. Of courses, lending is main business of a bank but as the same time it is highly risky. As such, while lending money to borrowers, a banker must consider cardinal principles of safety, liquidity, diversification of risks, profitability and customer satisfaction.

Keeping in view these principles, bank has to formulate loan policy, specifying strategic guidelines with respect to size of loan and its compensation, acceptable security and margin requirements, lending criteria, maturity period, limitations of lending authority etc.

So as to ensure that lending facilities are granted to genuine persons, a banker is supposed to evaluate credit worthiness of the applicant keeping in view credit character, capacity, capital, collateral and economic and business conditions. This can be objectively assessed with the help of financial techniques.

With a view to ensuring the end use of the loan, it is necessary for the bank to keep a track of the loans outstanding. This task is performed by credit department with the help of lending officers.

KEY TERMS

- Activity ratio
- Cash flow analysis
- Compensating balance
- Consortium lending
- Credit scoring
- Diversification of risk
- Funds flow analysis
- Leverage ratio
- Liquidity principle
- Liquidity ratio
- Margin money
- Maturity diversification
- Principle of Profitability
- Principle of safety
- Profitability ratio

DISCUSSION QUESTIONS

1. Why is management of loan important for a commercial bank?
2. What are the fundamental principles of bank lending?
3. Discuss the major contents of lending policy of a bank.
4. What factor should bank management consider while formulating lending policy of the bank?
5. How should creditworthiness of a potential borrower be assessed?
6. How can profitability and liquidity of an applicant be measured?
7. A firm approach a bank manager for financing its working capital needs. What steps should a manager take to decide about the sanction of working capital loan to the firm?

REFERENCES

1. Report on Trend and Progress of Banking in India, RBI, 2003-04, p. 27.
2. Report on Trend and Progress of Banking in India, 2002-03, p. 159.
3. Annual Report 2000-01, Supplement to RBI Bulletin, September 2001, p. 162.
4. Report on Trend and Progress of Banking in India, 2002-03, p. 159.
5. Report on Trend Progress of Banking in India, 2004-05, p. 215.
6. Annual Report, 2000-01, Supplement to RBI Bulletin, September 2001, p. 236.
7. Annual Report, RBI, 2004-05, p. 213.
8. Economic Times, June 30, 2007.
9. Annual Report, RBI, 2006-07, pp. 259-262.
10. *Op. cit.*, p. 223.
11. Annual Report, RBI, 2004-05, p. 210.
12. Report on Trend and Progress of Banking in India, 2003-04, p. 27.
13. *Op. cit.*, p. 225.
14. Annual Report, RBI, 2004-05, p. 211.
15. Annual Report, RBI, 2001-02, p. 235.
16. Report on Trend and Progress of Banking in India, 2003-04, p. 225.
17. Business Today, December 17, 2006, p. 190.
18. Annual Report, RBI, 2001-02, p. 233.
19. Report on Trend and Progress of Banking in India, 2001-02, p. 142.
20. Economic Times, December 5, 2006.
21. Report on Trend and Progress of Banking in India, 2005-06, p. 28.
22. *Ibid.*
23. Annual Report, RBI, 2006-07, p. 263.

Chapter 16

New Norms of Working Capital Financing by Banks

Learning Objectives:

The present chapter aims at:

- Shedding lurid light on recommendations of Daheja Study Group and Tandon Committee on working capital financing.
- Pinpointing Reserve Bank of India's action on Tandon Committee recommendations.
- Providing a brief idea of Nayak Committee and Chore Committee Norms for working capital.
- Sensitizing to RBI guidelines regarding working capital financing.

Chapter Outline:

- Daheja Study Group: An appraisal.
- Tandon Committee recommendations — An appraisal.
- Reserve Bank of India action on Tandon Committee recommendations.
- Nayak Committee recommendations.
- Chore Committee norms for working capital.
- RBI guidelines regarding working capital financing.
- Conclusions.

A. DAHEJA STUDY GROUP — AN APPRAISAL

Until recently, commercial banks in India, following the British banking practices, confined themselves to short-term lending activity. Industry and trade had the privilege of receiving the bulk of the lending facilities provided by the banks. In fact, they were the major suppliers of working capital to trade and industry. Commercial banks met, on an average, 50 per cent of the inventory finance. The percentage was as high as 66 to 70 for sugar and iron and steel. Such assistance was provided through cash credit accounts. These advances were given usually against the security of the current assets of the borrowing company. The security-oriented system adopted by the banks tended to favour borrowers with strong financial resources, irrespective of their economic function. This, in effect, aided the concentration of economic power. What was more intriguing was that the increase in bank credit was not commensurate with the expansion in the levels of inventory and production. Bank funds were very frequently used by a few resourceful business units to pile up large inventories of scarce resources to create artificial shortages and make speculative gains out of it, while others experienced a shortage of inputs, lower capacity utilisation, higher cost of production and eventually the threat of breakdown.

The Daheja Study Group,[1] which was appointed in October 1968 to examine the extent to which credit needs of industry and trade had been inflated and how such trends could be checked, found that during the period from 1964-65 to 1966-67, bank credit expanded at a higher rate than the rise in industrial output valued at current prices, and that the ratio of short-term bank credit to inventories went up from 40 per cent in 1961-62 to 52 per cent in the 1966-67. The Study Group concluded that, in value terms, there was a tendency on the part of the industry generally to avail itself of short-term credit from banks in excess of the amount required for growth in production based on industries. The Group also found that there was a diversion of short-term bank credit for the acquisition of long-term assets. This, it felt, was due to the generally sluggish conditions in the capital market since 1962, limited appraisal of applications for short-term loans compared to medium-and long-term loans, and the stipulations of repayment schedule for medium-term loans.

Another potent cause for the diversion of bank funds, in the Study Group's view, was the existing lending system. Commercial banks granted working capital advances by way of cash credit limits. The system was adopted by the banks because of its convenience in the context of the emphasis placed by them on security. By and large, banks relate their credit limits to the security offered by their clients, and do not generally attempt to assess the overall financial position of the borrower through a cash flow analysis. Short-term advances, under the cash credit system, are not necessarily utilised for short-term purposes. The result was that cash credit advances did not remain short-term or self-liquidating, although the cash accruals arising from sales were periodically adjusted in a cash credit account. In a large number of accounts, no credit balance existed, nor was a debt balance fully wiped out over a period of years, because the withdrawals were in excess of receipts.

To control this tendency of over-financing and the diversion of the bank's funds, the Daheja Study Group recommended that the banking system should finance industry on the basis of a total study of the borrower's operations rather than on security considerations alone. Another recommendation was that the present as well as the future cash credit accounts should be distinguished as between "the hard core" and the short-term components. The hard core would represent the minimum level of raw materials, finished goods and stores which the industry is required to hold in order to maintain a given level of production. The short-term component of the account would represent the requirement of funds for temporary purposes, e.g., a short-term increase in inventories, tax, dividends and bonus payments, etc., the borrowing being adjusted in a short-term period out of sales. The Group suggested that the hard core part of the working capital of companies with a strong financial position should be segregated and put on a formal term-loan basis, subject to a repayment schedule. In other cases, the borrowers should be asked to arrange for long-term funds to replace bank borrowing.

Despite the Daheja Study Group's recommendations, the enigma of expansion in bank credit, in commensurate with the level of production and inventory, continued to persist. It was felt that unless the style of bank lending was changed and objective norms were fixed for financing working capital requirements, a few financially well-off industrial units would continue to thrive on bank credit, making nonsense of all the monetary and fiscal attempts at overcoming shortages and controlling pressures, and that a large number of new credit claimants will starve of funds. It is in this context that the Reserve Bank of India appointed the Study Group under the Chairmanship of Shri P.L. Tandon in August, 1975:

(*a*) To make recommendation for obtaining periodical data from borrowers regarding their business production plans and credit needs, which would enable banks to formulate their own credit plans more meaningfully;

(*b*) To suggest norms for inventory holding by industries in both private and public sectors with the help of bank credit;

(*c*) To lay down criteria for determining the satisfactory financial structure of borrowers *vis-a-vis* their borrowings;

(*d*) To make recommendations on the sources of finance for minimum working capital requirements;

(*e*) To make recommendations as to whether the existing pattern of financing working capital requirements by the cash credit/overdraft system, etc., requires to be modified; and if so, to suggest suitable modifications; and

(*f*) To make recommendations on another related matter as the Group may consider germane to the subject of the enquiry, or any other allied matter which may be specifically referred to it by the Reserve Bank of India.

B. TANDON COMMITTEE

◈ Tandon Committee Recommendations — An Appraisal

The Tandon Committee recommendations may be classified into six broad categories, *viz.*, norms for inventory and receivables, new approach to bank lending, style of lending credit, information system and follow-up, supervision and control, and norms of capital structure. We shall evaluate each of these recommendations in the following paragraphs.

◈ Norms for Inventory and Receivables

Starting with the rationale for holding inventory at the minimum proportionate to production requirements, the Committee envisaged that the entire system of credit planning had to be dovetailed into production planning. It rightly felt that it was unable to accept the fact that the uncertainties of the procurement of inventory could be regarded as a reason for not laying down norms. On the other hand, it emphasised that uncertainty itself was a good reason for justifying the need for its planning.

The Committee suggested norms for inventory and receivables in as many as 15 industries, excluding heavy engineering industry. The norms represented the maximum levels for holding inventory and receivables in each industry. Borrowers were not expected to hold inventories and receivables at higher levels than these and the norm was not an entitlement to hold inventories or receivables upto this level. The norms were fixed after taking into consideration the companies' studies published by the Reserve Bank of India, deliberations with bodies representing the interest of various industries, and discussions with experts in the concerned industries. The suggested norms are contained in Table 16.1.

The Committee rightly pointed out that the norms could be absolute or rigid and that allowances had to be made for some flexibility when circumstances justified a need for a variation from the norms.

However, the conditions of an operational nature, such as bunch receipts of raw materials, including imports, power cuts, strikes and other unavoidable interruptions in the industry, transport delays and bottlenecks arising out of infrastructure inadequacy, etc., would have to be accounted for while fixing the norms. These causes were of a perennial nature. The mere fact that they were identified as those which required exemption did not appear to fulfil the final objectives and the responsibility undertaken. The absence of weightage to be given to each of the factors was likely to become a plea for exemption under each situation. The norms, by and large, were to be considered seriously. It was also unlikely that both the borrowing individual at a point of time and the lending agency would beforehand be aware of the fact that such operational factors were beyond their control. In the event of the occurrence of such a factor, the borrower would claim and request for additional weightage to these factors. The lending agency might consider these with a discount. Finally, by following the ultimate discretion for deviation from the norms at the operating level, the Committee left a vacuum in the system. This would trigger off issues of a complicated nature in the application of norms between the smaller and larger units, which would in all likelihood, affect the smaller units with levels within the norms, not because they planned that way but because they could not afford to hold more. On the other hand, the larger units might be able to withstand the pressure till they come within the mark. The bitter fact remains that the absence of a rating scale of validity of the assurance for a uniform application of norms was ruled out.

The Tandon Committee saw the inventory and credit receivables problems through an American banker's looking glass. But, the US and the Indian economies are different. One is a free enterprise economy and the other a controlled economy. The banker's directive to entrepreneurs to reduce inventories and receivables can succeed only if the latter are free agents, that they are free to take decisions, and that inventories are available on tap. In large areas of the Indian industry, the inventory decisions of units are decided by government policies and controls. The sugar industry is a classic example of the fact that Indian entrepreneurs have very little maneuverability in reducing finished goods inventories. Similarly, in the fertiliser industry, the basic raw materials are imported and, to that extent, there is uncertainty about their availability. In the cement industry, almost three-quarters of the inventory consist of stores and spares (for which the Committee did not fix norms). The long delivery time of spare parts of indigenous make and import restrictions on the imported parts resulting in the uncertainty of regular supply encourage a large stocking of these items. These problems seem to have been vaguely understood by the Tandon Committee.

◆ New Approach to Bank Lending

As regards the new approach to bank lending, the Committee maintained that the bank's main role as a lender would be to supplement the resources carrying a reasonable level of current assets in relation to his production requirements. It, therefore, argued that the total current assets would be carried purely by a certain level of credit for purchases and current liabilities. The funds required to carry the remaining current assets were termed as the working capital gap, which had to be partly filled by the borrower's own funds and long-term borrowings and partly by bank borrowings. In the context of the above approach, the Committee developed three alternatives for working out the maximum permissible level of bank borrowings:

(*i*) Under the first method, the bank would finance a maximum of 75 per cent of the working capital gap, *i.e.*, the total current assets minus current liabilities other than bank borrowings, and the balance was to come out of long-term funds, i.e., owned funds and term-borrowings.

(*ii*) In the second alternative, the borrower would have to provide for a minimum of 25 per cent of the total current assets out of long-term funds and the bank would provide the balance. The total current liabilities, inclusive of bank borrowings, would not exceed 75 per cent of the current assets.

(*iii*) The third alternative was almost the same as the second one except that it excluded the core current assets (permanent portion of current assets) from the total current assets to be financed out of the long-term funds.

TABLE 16.1: Suggested Inventory Norms

Industry	Raw Materials	Finished Goods	Receivables and Inland Bills Discounts (Exclusive of Foreign Bills Discounted)
1. Cotton Textiles	1½ (Mumbai and Ahmedabad) 2½ (Bihar, Orissa, West Bengal & Assam) 2 (Other areas)		2
2. Synthetic Textiles	1-1½	½ to 1	¼
3. Jute Textile	2-2½	1 (for domestic sales) 1½ (for export)	1
4. Pharmaceuticals	2-2½	2	1
5. Rubber Products	2	½	½
6. Fertilisers			½–1
(i) For Nitrogenous Plants	½-¾ (near the refinery)	¾ (where stocks are on plant site)	- do -
	1-1½ (for inland units)	1½ (where stocks are also in uncountry centres)	-do-
(ii) For Phosphatic Plants	2 (for units in port areas)	-do-	- do -
	3 (for inland units)		½
7. Vanaspati	1		
8. Paper			
(i) Bamboo and Wood	4-8 (to be built up in stages from November to May and thereafter to be brought down)	(i) Controlled sales ¾ (ii) Free sales ¼	½ - do -
(ii) Chemicals	2½		2
9. Light Engineering	3		- do -
10. Medium Engineering	3		

Notes: 1. Raw materials are expressed as so many months' production.

2. Finished goods and Receivables are expressed as so many months' sales. These figures represent only the average levels. Individual items of finished goods and receivables may be for different periods, which may exceed the indicated norms, so long as the average overall level of finished goods and receivables does not exceed the amounts as determined in terms of the norm.

The three alternatives are illustrated below with the help of the following illustration:

Illustration 16.1:

The data on the working capital position of a company are furnished below. Calculate the maximum permissible level of bank borrowing, as recommended by the Tandon Committee under the three alternatives:

Current Assets:	(₹)
Raw Materials	400
Stocks in Process	40
Finished Goods	180
Receivables	100
Other Current Assets	20
	740

Current Liabilities:

Creditors for Purchases	200
Other Current Liabilities	100
	300
Bank Borrowings, including bills discounted with Brokers	400
	700

Solution:

Calculation of Maximum Permissible Level of Bank Borrowing

First Alternative:	(₹)
Total Current Assets	740
Less: Current Liabilities other than Bank Borrowings	300
Working Capital Gap	440
Less: 25% of Working Capital Gap from Long-term Sources	110
	330
Excess Borrowing	70
Second Alternative:	
Total Current Assets	740
Less: 25% of Current Assets from Long-term Sources	185
	555
Less: Current Liabilities other than Bank Borrowings	300
	255
Working Capital Gap	440
Maximum Bank Borrowings Permissible	255
Excess Borrowing	145
Third Alternative:	
Total Current Assets	740
Less: Core Current Assets Long-term Sources	190
	550
Real Current Assets	138
	412
Less: Real Current Liabilities other than Bank Borrowings	300
Maximum Bank Borrowing Permissible	112
Working Capital Gap	440
Excess Borrowing	288

The Committee was of the opinion that the banks should start with the first method and move on to the second and third in a time-bound programme in respect of the excess credit above ₹ 10 lakhs to be reviewed on an annual basis. The banks were also required to work out the position of the existing customers, and in the case of those who were having over-the-limits recommended under the present formula, they were to persuade them to reduce this excess progressively. This it intended to do by converting the excess amount into a term loan to be authorised over a suitable period, depending on the cash generating capacity, and/or by entry into capital market for additional equity.

It is a high ideal to eliminate the existing excessive borrowings through all the three methods, starting with the first and ending with the third, and that, too, on a gradual but definite basis in the shortest span of time possible. The objective of reducing the excess credit and channelling of the funds into a more productive purpose appears noble in theory, but its attainment in reality appears to be doubtful. Furthermore, the suggested alternative that the excess credit should be reduced by entry into the capital market would only tilt the balance in favour of the established units. The borrower will have to compete in the capital market with the established units which, with their records of proven success and high dividend, are also likely to enter the market following pressure from the bank to wipe out their excess credit.

As for raising the cost of equity to satisfy the company's needs, it has to declare a dividend at the rate prevailing in the market. If supposing, the dividend rate is 12 per cent, this means its has to earn a pre-tax profit of 15% (presuming a 30 per cent tax rate). This would be so provided that a gross margin of profit on the incremental investment is at least as high as 25 to 30 per cent after accounting for the escalation in price and operating expenses. Therefore, as to what would be the cost of capital to an industry in raising the money through debt or meeting its additional requirement through equity in order to wipe out the excess debt or meet the additional requirement is a matter to be very seriously considered. In the alternative, if the money is raised by debt, and if, at the same time, the objective is to maximise the earnings per share, assuming that the potential is that large to cover the additional cost of the debt without diluting the earnings per share, is another factor which one cannot discount. In the ultimate analysis, it boils down to the fact that if it is not through bank credit, it has to be through a wider capital base or at a higher cost of debt to ensure the continuity of operations. In either case, the objective of reducing the ultimate price line and thereby controlling the inflationary pressure can be least met by these processes.

◈ Style of Lending

The Committee also felt that the current style of extending bank credit should be changed. The cash credit system, in its present form, has been expensive to operate, and a hindrance to any systematic credit planning efforts. In order to introduce a degree of stability, the Tandon Committee suggested that, instead of making available the entire credit limit as a cash credit for a year, it should be bifurcated into a loan and demand cash credit, and that it should be reviewed annually.

Under the new approach, while the minimum requirements of current assets would be financed through a loan account, the fluctuating levels of current assets would be financed by a sub-limit for cash credit or by bill finance limits. The latter will essentially be for seasonal requirements, which will be automatically squared off at the end of the business cycle. The former is, however, a continuous requirement, constant for the year, and will increase as the level of operation increases.

The new style of bank credit on the above lines was suggested with a view to enabling the borrower plan his credit needs in line with the operational demands and including financial discipline in the utilisation of bank credit. To ensure the success of this disciplinary measure, the Committee applied the principles of behavioural science and attempted to take advantage of cost consciousness among the borrowers. It felt that as the loan would carry interest throughout the year, it would discipline the customer to plan his needs carefully to ensure that as little of it as possible lay idle, ideally none. To further strengthen the principle of bifurcating the credit limits, the Committee recommended that the demand portion of working capital finance might be subject to interest at a higher rate of one per cent above that of the loan account.

As a direct consequence of this change in the structure of the interest rates, the interest payable by the borrower will be on the higher side. Even the borrower operating within the acceptable level of financial discipline and able to rationalise the bifurcation between the loan and demand components will be affected, albeit to a small extent.

To argue that interest payment can be reduced by availing of more working capital finance through a loan account carrying a lower rate of interest seems to be illusory, for the loan account carries interest throughout the year, and hence any temporary flush of funds cannot be used to repay the credit liability to reduce the interest burden. Another factor that will inflate the cost of bank credit is the present drawing in excess of the norms laid down by the Committee. It was recommended that the excess drawings should be transferred to a term loan account and that a higher interest of one and a half per cent over the demand position be charged till the term loan account is amortized. The present market condition being what it is, the inventory held by the borrowings will obviously be over the specified norms, hence the drawings would be correspondingly over the eligible limits. The borrower will find it difficult to dispose of the inventory and liquidate the excess drawings resulting in higher interest costs for quite some time.

The second important change recommended in the approach to lending is to encourage, as far as possible, the grant of bill finance instead of cash credit against book debt. Though bill finance is amenable to easy control and imposes a greater financial discipline on the borrower, it is always costlier. This is mainly so because, in the case of cash credit, the interest is paid periodically, usually every quarter after using the funds, whereas in the case of bill finance, the interest is to be paid before availing of the credit. Further, the drawing of bills will attract stamp duty that will depend upon the amount of the bill, which is usually done by the borrower.

◆ Credit Information System

In order to follow up and supervise bank credit from the point of view of ensuring a proper end use of funds, and keep a watch on the safety of the advance, it is essential that some operational data must be forthcoming from the borrowers so that their total operations may be judged. The Tandon Committee recommended a quarterly budgeting reporting system for operational purposes on the basis of which the requirements of working capital finance would be calculated with reference to the borrower's future production needs. In the absence of such information system, the application of the new mechanism of credit appraisal was not possible. Under the proposed information system, as recommended by the Committee, borrowers enjoying credit limits aggregating ₹ 1 crore and above from the banking system were required to submit the following statements:

(*a*) Quarterly operating statement, including the actual and budgeted figures — Form I (Part A) — Table 16.2.

(*b*) Quarterly statement of current assets and current liabilities (both actuals and budget) — Form I (Part B) — Table 16.3.

(*c*) Quarterly Funds Flow Statement.

In addition to the above statements, the borrowers were required to submit monthly stock statements and a projected balance sheet and profit and loss account at the end of the financial year. Though the system was to be introduced, to start with, for borrowers with a working capital limit of a crore of rupees and above, it would be progressively extended to other similar borrowers.

The cash credit limits to be sanctioned to the borrowers will be determined once a year with reference to their annual business production plans, and the accounts will have to be reviewed every quarter on the basis of the quarterly operations statement and quarterly projected figures for current assets and liabilities. The permissible level of bank finance will be controlled through the funds flow statement. The actual drawings will be on the basis of the stock statement.

The sanctioned limit will be determined by the customer's inflow and outflow of funds. The deficit in cash during the quarter will be the level of additional demand of cash credit borrowings required in that quarter. The permissible level of drawing in any quarter within the sanctioned limit will thus be the level at the end of the previous quarter, plus or minus the deficit or surplus shown in the funds flow statement.

Within the overall permissible level of drawing, the day-to-day operations in the accounts will be regulated on the basis of the drawing power (subject to the margins stipulated by the banker against the different components of inventory and receivables) as per the monthly stock statements, which will continue to be submitted.

The proposed information system calls for the compilation and study of enormous data. The borrowing concern will have to maintain elaborate records or change the existing methods to get at the data required by the bank. This will require additional manpower and professional skill which will ultimately increase the cost of the borrower.

◈ Follow-up: Supervision and Control

With a view to verifying whether the assumptions of lending in regard to the borrower's operations continue to hold good and ensuring that the end-use is according to the purpose for which the credit was given, the bank should follow up and supervise the use of credit. This would be necessary if the banker has to shift from security-oriented lending to production-oriented credit.

Since the projected funds flow statement would form the basis of determining the line of credit, a banker would be justified in laying down the condition that any material change, say, about 10 per cent of the figure projected earlier, would require his prior approval. He may manipulate certain minimum terms and conditions relating to matters having a material impact on the funds flow of the borrower. From the quarterly forms, he will verify whether the operational results conform to earlier expectations, and whether there is any divergence. However, a variance of, say, around 10 per cent may be treated as normal. Besides, the larger borrower should be required to submit a half-yearly proforma balance sheet and profit and loss account within two months of the end of the half-year.

After the close of each year, a detailed credit analysis should be done, as of new advances, when the banks will re-examine the terms and conditions, and make the necessary changes.

In order to ensure that the managerial efficiency of the borrowing firms may be properly judged, the Committee made a recommendation for inter-firm and industry-wise comparisons. In making inter-firm comparisons, besides examining financial and operating ratios, certain productivity ratios might also be examined to determine labour efficiency, capital efficiency and fixed assets efficiency.

For the purpose of better control, the Committee recommended a system of turnover classification in each bank within the credit rating scale. To illustrate: There may be a five-point scale, on which the borrower may be classified as excellent, good, average, below average or unsatisfactory. Such a system of classification on the basis of credit risk would facilitate an easy identification of the borrower whose affairs require to be watched with more than ordinary care.

To ensure the end-use of funds, the Committee suggested that the banker should call for appropriate operational data and figures relating to the borrower's financial position at periodical intervals, that the borrower's current ratio and the respective shares of bank finance and the borrower's long-term funds in meeting his working capital gap did not change adversely. If the position in this regard did not change adversely, the conclusion would be that bank finance is headed towards the build-up of current assets.

◈ Norms for Capital Structure

The debt-equity relationship, the Committee felt, is a relative concept, which is dependent upon several factors and circumstances, such as the state of the capital market, the government's policy on created money, the need for maintaining current assets at a specific level, the marginal efficiency of capital or the opportunity cost, etc. In discussing norms of the capital structure, a banker should keep in mind the relationship of equity to long-term debt and of equity to the total outside liabilities of the borrowers. Where a company's long-term net debt to net worth and total outside liabilities to net worth ratios are worse than the medians, the banker should endeavour to persuade the borrower to strengthen his equity base as early as possible. According to the Committee, this would be a worse practical approach for the banker than attempting to legislate absolute standards of long-term debt-net worth and total outside liability-net worth ratios for all industries or even for an industry.

C. RESERVE BANK ACTION ON TANDON COMMITTEE RECOMMENDATIONS

Acting upon the recommendations of the Tandon Committee, the Reserve Bank introduced a reform on 21st August, 1975. The reform was designed to reduce the industry's resort to excessive borrowings from commercial banks. Though, in the short run, the penal interest on borrowings in excess of the inventory norm was visualized to curtail borrowings, the basic strategy of the reform was to convert excess borrowings into term loans, to be amortized out of the industry's earnings under a phased programme.

The RBI accepted the first two methods. It advised banks to assess credit needs of units above ₹ 10 lakhs and upto ₹ 50 lakhs and above ₹ 50 lakhs under I and II Methods, respectively.

The Reserve Bank advised all the scheduled banks to initiate immediate action with respect to all the borrowers belonging to any of the fifteen industry groups, having credit limits in excess of ₹ 10 lakhs from the banking system, to ensure that they finance not more than 75 per cent of the working capital gap. Beginning with borrowers having a relatively weak financial position, the process should be completed within a period of one year. In respect of borrowers seeking an enhanced credit limit, such action might be taken at the time of sanctioning the credit limit.

The Reserve Bank instructed banks that the excess over the finance for which borrowers would be eligible under the new formula will be identified and converted into a long-term loan, which may be amortized gradually over the period of amortization, depending upon the borrower's cash generating capacity, his ability to raise additional equity, and other relevant factors. Additional credit might be provided to borrowers with excess borrowings under certain conductions.

Banks were also advised that they should ensure that the borrowers who were already in Position Two (second alternative of financing Working Capital Gap as per the Tandon Committee Recommendation) should not slip back to Position One. As regards the third alternative as per the Tandon Committee's recommendation, the Reserve Bank did not take any view for the present. However, it advised that, in respect of borrowers, who were already in a better position where more than 25 per cent of the current assets were financed by owned funds and long-term borrowing, banks might take a case-by-case view if there was a possibility of increasing their reliance on bank finance.

As regards the style of bank credit, the Reserve Bank advised the banks that instead of making available the entire credit limit as a cash credit, the limit might be bifurcated into a loan comprising the minimum level of borrowing which the borrower expected to use throughout the year, and a demand cash credit to take care of the fluctuating requirements, both being reviewed annually. Within the overall availability, bill limits might also be allowed. Such bifurcation of credit limits should be done in all cases at the time they were required to conform to the criteria specified in Method One.

The Reserve Bank accepted the forms designed by the Tandon Committee for credit information purposes. These forms were circulated to all commercial banks with deposits of ₹ 50 crores and above. The proposed information system was to be introduced, in the first instance, in respect of borrowers with limits aggregating ₹ one crore and above from the entire banking system, and the process was to be completed within six months. The banks were asked to call for the quarterly data straight-away from such borrowing companies as have already the information system. The other borrowers should be asked to build up the system for requisite information as soon as possible, so that they also start submitting the requisite data within the aforesaid period of six months.

TABLE 16.2: Quarterly Operating Statement

	Actuals for Previous Accounting Year (Whole Year)	Projections for Current Accounting Year (Whole Year)	Previous Quarter Ended			Current Quarter Ending .. Actuals/ Estimates	Net Quarter Ending .. Budget	Subsequent Quarter Ending .. Budget
			Budget	Actual	Variance			
	(1)	(2)	(3)	(4)	(5)	(6)	(7)	(8)
1. Sales								
2. Less Excise Duty								
3. Net Sales (Item 1 – 2)								
4. Cost of Sales								
(*a*) Raw Materials Consumption								
(*b*) Power and Fuel								
(*c*) Salaries and Wages								
(*d*) Consumable Stores								
(*e*) Repairs and Maintenance								
(*f*) Other Manufacturing Expenses								
(*g*) Depreciation								
Sub-total								
Add: Opening Stock (in Process and Finished Goods)								
Sub-total								
Deduct: Closing Stock — (in Process) and Finished Goods								
Total Cost of Sales								
5. Gross Profit (Item 3–4)								
6. Other Overheads:								
(*a*) Interest								
(*b*) Selling, General and Administrative expenses								
7. Operating Profit (Item 5–6)								
8. Other Income/Expenses — Net (±)								
9. Profit Before tax (Item 7 to Item 8)								

TABLE 16.2 (Contd.)

	(1)	(2)	(3)	(4)	(5)	(6)	(7)	(8)
PART - B								
Current Assets:								
(*i*) Inventory								
(*a*) Raw Material								
Imported - Indigenous								
(*b*) Stocks in Process								
(*c*) Finished Goods								
(*d*) Consumable Stores								
(*ii*) Receivables (Including Bills Discounted with Bankers)								
(*iii*) Advances to Suppliers of Raw Materials and stores								
(*iv*) Other Current Assets								
Total Current Assets								
Current Liabilities:								
(*v*) Short-term Bank Borrowings (including Bills Discounted with Bankers)								
A.								
B.								
C.								
(*vi*) Creditors for Purchases of Raw Materials and Stores								
(*vii*) Advances from Customers								
(*viii*) Accrued Expenses								
(*ix*) Statutory Liabilities								
(*x*) Other Current Liabilities								
Total Current Liabilities								

Notes: When estimates have been given under the head actuals, the reasons may be given.

As the form has to be furnished during the current year, the actuals would not be available for the whole quarter. For the periods the actuals are not available, estimates may be taken into account for arriving at this figure to be furnished in Column 6 of Part A and Column 4 of Part B.

Outstandings with different banks should be given separately.

Where the audited Balance Sheet and Profit and Loss Account for the previous accounting year are not available, estimated/provisional figures for the previous year may be furnished in Column (1) and the figures for preceding year based on the audited balance sheet, should be given in an additional column before Column (1).

The amount of bills discounted with bankers included in item (ii) of Part B, should be indicated separately.

The amount of bills discounted with bankers in repect of purchases, including in item (v) of Part B, should be indicated separately.

TABLE 16.3: Quarterly of Current Assets and Current Liabilities Statement

	Actuals for Previous Accounting Year (Whole Year)	*Projections for Current Accounting Year (Whole Year)*	*Previous Quarter Ended*			*Current Quarter Ending ... Actuals/ Estimates*	*Net Quarter Ending... Budget*	*Subsequent Quarter Ending... Budget*
			Budget	*Actual*	*Variance*			
	(1)	(2)	(3)	(4)	(5)	(6)	(7)	(8)
SOURCES								
Long-term								
1. Profit before Tax (+) Loss (–)								
2. Depreciation								
3. Sub-total (Items 1 + 2)								
4. Sale of Fixed Assets								
5. Capital Issue								
6. Term Loans/Debentures/Deferred Credits								
7. Public Deposits								
8. Others								
9. Sub-total (Item 3 to 8)								
Short-term								
10. Decrease in current assets								
(*a*) Inventory								
(*b*) Receivables								
(*c*) Others								
11. Increase in Current Liabilities								
(*a*) Creditors for Purchase of Raw Materials and Stores								
(b) Short-term-Bank Borrowings, including Bills Discounted with Bankers								
(c) Other Short-term Payables								
(d) Others								
12. Sub-total : (Items 10 + 11)								
13. Grand Total								

TABLE 16.3 (Contd.)

	(1)	(2)	(3)	(4)	(5)	(6)	(7)	(8)
USES								
Long-term								
14. Additions to Fixed Assets								
15. Repayments of Term Loans								
16. Repayments of Public Deposits								
17. Investments in Subsidiaries and Affiliates								
18. Advances to Subsidiaries and Affiliates								
19. Payment of Taxes								
20. Dividends								
21. Others								
22. Sub-total (Items 14 to 21)								
Short-term								
23. Increase in Current Assets								
(*a*) Inventory								
(*b*) Receivables, (including Bills Discounted with Bankers)								
(*c*) Others								
24. Decrease in Current Liabilities								
(*a*) Creditors for Purchase or Raw Materials and Stores								
(*b*) Short-term Bank Borrowings (including Bills Discounted with Bankers)								
(*c*) Others								
25. Sub-totals (Items 23 + 24)								
26. Grand Totals (Items 23 + 25)								
27. Balance (Item 13 – Item 26) Surplus (+) Shortfall (–)								
28. Opening Cash and Bank Balance								
29. Closing Cash and Bank Balance (Items 27 + 28)								

Notes: Where estimates have been given under the head **actuals**, the reasons may be given.
As the form has to be finished during the current quarter, the actuals would not be available for the whole quarter. For the periods the actuals are not available, estimates may be taken into account for arriving at the figure to be furnished in Col. 6.
If any significant amount is included in this item, particulars thereof may be furnished separately.
The figure should tally with item (9) in Part A of Form I.

D. CHORE PANEL'S RECOMMENDATIONS AND CASH CREDIT SYSTEM

The Reserve Bank of India appointed a Study Group under the Chairmanship of Mr. K.B. Chore to review the working of the cash credit system in commercial banks in India.

The main proposal of the Chore Study Group was in line with the trend of thought that became increasingly forceful over time. Unfortunately, it became increasingly difficult for business enterprises to obtain loans to finance their working capital requirements. Within the framework of the situation created by its proposal for a reduction in bank financing of the working capital requirements of medium and large enterprises, the Study Group's recommendations aimed at curbing the use of cash credit and increasing the role of short-term loans and bill finance in the overall scheme of bank finance. This proposed shift in the pattern of bank finance stemed from the widely held view that the cash credit system, because it permits the borrower to draw funds whenever these are required by him within the sanctioned limits, does not encourage the borrower to manage the cash resources properly.

The Study Group advocated for better discipline and planning consciousness among borrowers by requiring them to submit quarterly projections of cash credit limits. Accordingly, it recommended that the banks, while assessing the credit requirements, should fix separate limits, wherever feasible, for the normal non-peak level as also for the peak level credit requirements, indicating the periods during which the separate limits would be utilised by the borrowers. If, however, there was no pronounced seasonal trend, peak level and normal requirements should be treated as identical, and the limits should be fixed on that basis.

The Study Group was of the view that the borrowers should be discouraged from approaching the banks frequently for *ad hoc* or temporary limits in excess of sanctioned limits to meet unforeseen contingencies. Requests for such limits should be considered very carefully and should be allowed only for pre-determined short durations and given as a separate demand loan on non-operable cash credit account. As any such additional accommodation would put the bank credit planning out of gear, and as such contingencies form part of business risks, banks should charge an additional interest of one per cent per annum above the normal rates on these limits.

About the enhancement of a borrower's contribution to at least 25 per cent of the total current assets, the Study Group suggested that in case where the borrowers might not be able to comply with this requirement immediately, the excess borrowings should be segregated and treated as a working capital term loan, which should be made repayable in half-yearly instalments within 5 years. The working capital term loan should carry a rate of interest which should, in no case, be less than the rate for the relative cash credit limit. But banks might, at their discretion, charge a higher rate to encourage an early liquidation of the working capital term loan. Further, suitable provision should be made for charging a penal rate of interest in the event of any defaults in the timely repayment of the working capital term loan.

Since the drawal of funds would be regulated through quarterly statement, it was recognised that there was a need for the timely submission of quarterly reports. The statements should form the basis for a quarterly review of the account, and the operative limit indicated by the borrower should virtually set the level of drawings in that quarter, subject to a tolerance of 10 per cent either way. If a borrower did not submit the returns within the prescribed time limit, the bank might charge penal interest of one per cent per annum on the total outstandings for the period of default in the submission of the quarterly returns. The borrower might also be warned that, in case the default persists, the account might be frozen without further notice.

The Chore Committee recommendations were accepted by the RBI. However, the concept of drawee bill could not take off.

E. NAYAK COMMITTEE RECOMMENDATIONS

The Reserve Bank of India constituted in December, 1991 a Committee under the Chairmanship of Shri P.R. Nayak, Dy. Governor Reserve Bank of India, to go into the difficulties experienced by Small Scale Industries (SSI), particularly in securing finance. It was in the light of a widespread belief among the industry that, though RBI guidelines issued were wholesome, the banks did not always follow them and that was at the root of the travails of the SSI, which was substantiated by a sample study conducted by the RBI during 1989 revealing that, even one year after the issue of the guidelines, the compliance at the field level was deficient in certain respects and that, in one-third of the branches surveyed, full working capital according to the instructions had not been sanctioned.

The major recommendations of the Committee were as under:

(*i*) Village Industries and the smaller Tiny Industries with credit limits upto ₹ 1 lakhs should have the first claim on the priority sector credit to the SSI.

(*ii*) Bank branches should give priority to those Village Industries and the Smaller Tiny Industries which can use working capital efficiently, having established facilities but unable to make further progress for lack of working capital.

(*iii*) The new priority sector credit dispensation, when adopted, should fully provide for the working capital requirements of all tiny units into credit limits of ₹ 10 lakhs, after first taking care of the working capital allocation made for Village Industries and the smaller Tiny Industries with credit limits upto ₹ 1 lakh. A specific allocation to the larger tiny units should be made by fixing their proportion of the credit to the total priority sector credit.

(*iv*) In regard to the larger SSI, there should be flexibility in the application of the inventory norms as per Tondon Committee recommendations and that in respect of units for which the norms are not presently applicable or have not been prescribed, 25% of the output values should be freely allowed as working capital, of which at least four-fifths should be provided by the banking sector. The working capital requirements of the larger SSI should be fully met by the commercial banks and the Chief Executive of each bank shall ensure that this was done.

(*v*) The reorientation of the banker will be facilitated by the following modifications in the existing instructions/guidelines issued to commercial banks by the RBI.

(*a*) The branch manager should be vested with adequate discretionary power which will enable them to grant 'ad-hoc' increases upto 10 per cent over the sanctioned limits to meet unforeseen contingencies, including escalation in raw material/input costs, even if the quantum of such 'ad hoc' limits is beyond the powers granted to him for sanctioning credit without reference to higher authorities.

(*b*) Where the borrower is unable to bring in the additional margin money immediately, banks should not insist on the additional margin to be brought in by the entrepreneur in one instalment at the time of granting 'ad-hoc' increases in enhancement of working capital limits to meet unforeseen contingencies. Such additional margin should be permitted to be built up within a reasonable period from future cash accruals.

(*c*) Applications for fresh limits/enhancement of existing limits which are considered favourably by the appropriate sanctioning authority, should be referred to the next higher authority with all relevant particulars, and the latter should scrutinise each case and come to his own judgement. The final decision should invariably be based on such review by the higher authority and should be taken within a reasonable time.

(*d*) A similar procedure should be evolved whereby the curtailment of limits applied for will also be reported to the next higher authority by the sanctioning officials and the decision conveyed in a time-bound manner.

(e) Four types of application forms might be evolved for use by SSIs on the basis of aggregate credit limits: *(a)* not exceeding ₹ 50,000, *(b)* between ₹ 50,000 and ₹ 15 lakhs, *(c)* between ₹ 15 lakhs, and ₹ 25 lakhs, and *(d)* above ₹ 25 lakhs. RBI and SIDBI might take early necessary steps for the simplification of these forms.

(f) Collateral security and/or third party guarantee should be dispensed with as a rule, irrespective of the amount of credit involved. Exceptions may be justified only in the case of larger advances of over ₹ 2 lakhs in the undernoted circumstances:

(i) The technology was new and untried and the bank/SFC considered the lending risk to be higher than normal.

(ii) The proposal was only marginally viable but the bank/SFC would like to support the same with due care being taken to cover the extra risk involved.

(iii) The entrepreneur/promoter had adequate own assets which could be charged to the bank/SFC, as there should normally be no objection to offering such assets as collateral security for the credit limits.

Where collateral security was taken, the bank should return it to the borrower, after a stipulated minimum period, if the unit has been functioning well and the operations in its various borrowal accounts have been satisfactory. No applications for advances should be rejected merely for collateral security.

(vi) Where the bank had a first charge over the fixed assets of the units either singly or jointly with the SFC on a pari-passu basis, it should not ask for cash margin from SSI borrowers for non-fund-based facilities provided, such fixed assets leave adequate surplus, after covering the existing facility, to provide for the non-fund-based facilities.

(vii) Insistence on compulsory deposit mobilisation by the banks for the sanction of credit limits would have to be prevented through the issue of unambiguous guidelines.

(viii) To facilitate timely decisions on credit proposals by successive tiers in the hierarchy, a committee approach would be helpful in which decisions were taken by the competent authority after a structured discussion with the branch manager and also the intervening levels.

(ix) An effective grievance redressal machinery within the bank which could be approached by the SSI in case of difficulties with banks/FIs, as well as other agencies connected with SSI. This was likely to reduce the real or perceived helplessness of the SSI. The arrangements made in this regard so far should be preserved. The creation of an 'ombudsman' type of authority, on a full time basis, at the regional/controlling offices within the bank would be an effective measure to assist this machinery. Customers' complaints should be heard and investigated by the ombudsman who will report directly to the Chairman. In order to make the aforesaid measures meaningful it is of the utmost importance to lay down time limits within which decisions on the complaints are communicated to the complainants.

(x) Under the multi-agency approach for financing SSI, term finance is usually provided by SFC and working capital by the commercial bank. The lack of co-ordination between the two has been a major cause of the difficulties faced by SSI entrepreneurs. In this regard, SFCS and banks should endeavour to cover the financial requirements of SSI and the Single Window Scheme (SWS) to the maximum extent. SIDBI as the apex finance institution will have to support, and if necessary, supplement the SFCs efforts in creating the necessary organisation to discharge the responsibility. Out of 85 districts, having concentration of SSI units, for about 40 districts SFCs and for the

remaining ones commercial banks should act as principal financing agency for SSIs.

(*xi*) To discharge their responsibility well under this scheme, the commercial banks should open specialised branches to cater to the SSI clientele.

◈ Adequacy of Term Credit Provided to the SSI Sector

The major share of the demand for investment credit for SSI would have to be met by SIDBI. The Committee recommended the following measures to augment the resources of SIDBI:

- If future allocations would not be available to SIDBI from the National Industrial Credit (Long-Term Operations) NIC (LTO) Fund of RBI, it would be necessary for RBI to relend to SIDBI, IDBI's repayment of past borrowings from the Fund.
- SIDBI should be permitted to float tax-free bonds with a GOI Subsidy towards interest differential between LTO Fund rate and the bond rate.
- SIDBI's share of SLR bonds should be increased.
- RBI should examine the feasibility of diverting the resources of foreign banks to the extent of their shortfall in achieving Priority sector targets.
- Government of India may permit SIDBI to mobilise deposits from SSI sector with suitable tax incentives to the depositors.
- SIDBI should be enabled to tap the resources of international finance agencies through foreign lines of credit/commercial borrowings.
- SIDBI should explore the feasibility of raising its refinance to SSI units from the present level of 61% of its total disbursements by suitably rearranging its priorities.
- LIC and GIC should be persuaded to lend a portion of their funds at reasonable rates to SIDBI for on-lending to SSI units.
- SIDBI, Banks and SFCs should take necessary steps to provide information inputs to small-sized companies in the SSI sector to enable them to tap the capital market through the OTCEI route wherever such a course is feasible.
- The Government's SSI policy of August 1991 envisages that non-SSI units could invest up to 24% of the equity of SSI. The non-SSI units should be encouraged to maximise the flow of capital resources to SSI through this mechanism.
- The enactment of Limited Partnership Act should be expedited to facilitate the flow of equity to the SSI.

◈ Evaluation of Nayak Committee Recommendations

Nayak Committee recommendations are essentially guided by those of other Committees and it has not made any innovative suggestions to improve working capital finance to SSI Sector.

The Committee's presumption based on misconceived notion of the World Bank that all priority sector lending was heavily subsidised and should, therefore, be drastically pruned down does not always hold true.

The recommendation of the Committee to accord priority to those tiny sector units having established production successfully will not help new entrepreneurs and militates against the Government's declared policy of encouraging first generation entrepreneurs.

The Committee fails to furnish specific guidelines regarding opening of specialised branches for financing SSI. It has also not fixed responsibility on lead banks for observance of the RBI guidelines.

F. RESERVE BANK GUIDELINES REGARDING WORKING CAPITAL FINANCING

On the basis of recommendations of the Nayak Committee and the Group headed by Ms. Vaz, Executive Director, RBI, the following guidelines were issued in 1993:

Norms for inventory and receivables: The Banks are required to make their own assessment of credit requirement of borrowers based on a total study of borrowers' business operations i.e., taking into account the production/processing cycle of the industry as well as the financial and other relevant parameters of the borrowers. The Banks can decide the levels by holding each item of inventory as also receivables, which in their view would represent a reasonable built up of current assets for being supported by bank finance. Reserve Bank of India will not prescribe detailed norms for each item of inventory as also of receivables, it would only advise the overall levels of inventory and receivables for different industries for the guidance of banks to serve as broad indicators. Banks may also consider evolving suitable internal guidelines for accepting the projections made by their borrowers relating to item, 'Sundry creditors' (Goods appearing as per item enables "other current liabilities" in the Balance sheet).

The above guidelines apply to all borrower enjoying aggregate final based working capital limit of ₹ 1 crore and above from the banking system. The guidelines set out for arriving at working capital facilities, for village and tiny industries and other SSI units enjoying fund based working capital limit upto ₹ 50 lakhs on the basis of a minimum 20% of their projects annual turnover are extended to all borrower enjoying aggregate fund based working capital limits of less than ₹ 1 crore from the banking system.

◈ Method of lending (Minimum Current Ratio) and Maintenance of Minimum Margin

For sanction of credit limits borrowers enjoying aggregate fund based credit limits for amounts less than ₹ 1 crore from the banking system, banks should ensure maintenance of minimum margin of 5% of the annual turnover of such borrowers as margin money. In other words 25% of the output value should be computed as working capital requirement, of which at least four-fifth should be provided by banks and the balance one-fifth should be by way of promoter's contribution towards margin money. Sanction of aggregate fund based working capital limits of ₹ 1 crore and above from the Banking system would be subject to the second method of lending so as to ensure maintenance of minimum current ratio of 1.33%. The following credit liabilities will be exempt from the application of second method of lending.

(*a*) Units engaged in export activities - borrowing units engaged in export activities need not bring in any contribution from their long-term sources towards financing that portion of current assets as is represented by export receivables.

(*b*) Additional credit needs of exporters arriving out of firm order/confirmed LC — additional credit needs of exporters arising out of firm orders/confirmed letter of credit (and which were not taken into account while fixing the regular credit limits of borrowers) should be met in full, even if sanction of such additional credit limits exceeds MPBF.

(*c*) Units marketing/trading exclusively products and merchandise manufactured by village tiny and SSI units. The borrowing units marketing/trading exclusively (100%) the products and merchandise manufactured by village tiny and SSI units will be subject to the first method of lending while assessing their MPBF provided dues of the said village, tiny and SSI units have been settled by such borrower within a maximum period of 30 days from the date of supply. This relaxation is also available to that portion of marketing business related to the products manufactured by village, tiny and SSI industries in respect of cases where borrowing units also market products manufactured by medium and large industries and or have manufacturing activity of their own.

(*d*) Sugar industries — credit limits of borrowing units in the sugar industry may be determined on the basis of a current ratio of 1:1 up to September 30, 1994.

(*e*) Sick/weak units under rehabilitation will be exempted from the approach of the second method of lending as hitherto.

G. CONCLUSIONS

Until recently commercial banks in India confined themselves essentially to meet working capital needs of trade and industries and ignored the priority sectors of the economy. To curb this practice, the Daheja study group was appointed in 1968. The group, after noting the excess financing of working capital needs and the diversion of such funds, recommended for change in style of bank lending and fixing objective norms for funding working capital needs.

Tandon Committee was, therefore, appointed in 1975 to suggest norms for inventory holding by industries, lay down criteria for determining the satisfactory financial structure of the borrowers, and suggest sources for of financing maximum working capital needs. The Committee after making comprehensive study of the working capital requirements of different categories of industries and the existing financing practices made comprehensive recommendations in respect of norms for inventory and receivables, approach to bank lending, style of lending, credit information system, supervision and control and norms of capital structure.

The RBI appointed another study group under the chairmanship of Mr. K. B. Chore to review the working of the cash credit system in commercial banks. The Group in its recommendations advocated for better discipline and planning consciousness among the borrowers by requiring them to submit quarterly projections of cash credit limits. It recommended that the banks while assessing the credit requirements should fix separate limits, wherever possible, for the normal non-peak level and for the peak level credit requirements. The Chore Committee recommendations were mostly accepted by the RBI.

Sensing the problems being experienced by the small scale industries (SSI) in obtaining bank credit, the RBI constituted Nayak Committee in 1991. The Committee gave recommendations regarding adequacy and flow of institutional credit for working capital and adequacy of term credit to the SSI sector.

In the light of the Nayak Committee recommendations and those of the study group headed by Ms. Vaz, the RBI issued norms to banks in 1993. These norms relate to inventory and receivables and method of lending.

KEY TERMS

- Chore Panel
- Daheja study group
- Hardcore working capital
- New approach to bank lending
- Short-term working capital
- Style of lending
- Tandon Committee
- Working Capital Gap

DISCUSSION QUESTIONS

1. Why was Daheja study group appointed? Evaluate the major recommendations of the Daheja study group.
2. What were the major recommendations of Tandon Committee?
3. Discuss the new approach to bank lending as suggested by the Tandon Committee.
4. Examine new style of lending recommended by the Tandon Committee.

5. What action did the Reserve Bank take to implement the Tandon Committee recommendation.
6. Discuss the norms of the RBI regarding working capital financing by commercial banks.

REFERENCES

1. The National Credit Council constituted in October 1968 under the Chairmanship of V.T. Daheja.
2. Report on Trend and Progress of Banking in India, 2000-01, p. 148.

Inclusive Growth and Commercial Banks

Chapter 17

Learning Objectives:

The present chapter aims to provide an incisive view of inclusive growth and financial inclusion and the role of commercial banks in promoting financial inclusion in India.

Chapter Outline:

- Inclusive growth.
- Financial inclusion.
- Financial inclusion and international experiences.
- Financial inclusion and Indian experiences.
- Financial inclusion and commercial banks in India.
- Progress under financial inclusion plans.
- Conclusions.

A. INCLUSIVE GROWTH

A country aiming at gaining prosperity and eliminating poverty across the country and achieving superiority on global marquee on sustainable basis must focus on inclusive growth. This is why for the first time the 11th Plan of India placed thrust on inclusive growth and the 12th five-year plan decided to continue and strengthen inclusive growth programme.

Inclusive growth means growth of a kind that the benefits flow to everyone and the participation in the benefits of growth is very high. Inclusive growth programme focuses on growth of, for and by the people. This signifies growth of all sections of the society including unprivileged and neglected ones, allowing people to contribute to and benefit from higher economic growth.

Inclusive growth concept has several implications, as outlined below:

- Pace and pattern of growth, which are interlinked, need to be addressed together. Rapid pace of growth is indubitably necessary for substantial poverty reduction. Besides, growth has to be broad-based across sectors, implying a direct link between macro and micro determinants of growth. Further, growth needs to be balanced sectorally and geographically. One of the major factors responsible for exclusive and unsustained growth of India has been neglect of agriculture and infrastructure sectors since independence. Good quality infrastructure is the most critical physical requirement for faster growth. Furthermore, economic growth across regions has not been balanced, with some of the most backward areas yet to experience any significant growth.
- Inclusive growth entails responsible and sustainable creation as well as just distribution of both wealth and welfare. Social cohesion and human dignity lay at its core.

  The vision of inclusiveness must go beyond the traditional objective of poverty alleviation to encompass equality of opportunity as well as economic and social mobility for all sections of society. There has to be equality of opportunity to all with freedom and dignity. Equality of opportunity implies equality in terms of access to markets, resources and unbiased regulatory environment for business and individuals. This must be accompanied by an improvement in the opportunities for economic and social advancement. This can be ensured only if there is a degree of empowerment that creates a true feeling of participation and the individuals are provided adequate opportunities to develop their skills and strengthen their capacity to contribute to growth programmes. It may not be out of point to observe that lack of quality education and skills development has been a major hurdle for India to achieve sustainable growth at a faster pace.
- Inclusive growth focuses on productive and fuller employment rather than on direct income redistribution, as a means of increasing income for excluded groups. Hence, the thrust is not only on employment growth but also on productivity growth. Employment growth generates new jobs and income for the individuals — from wages in all types of firms, or from self employment, usually in micro firms — while productivity growth has the potential to lift the wages of those employed and the returns to the self-employeds.

  It must be noted that the inclusive growth approach takes a longer term perspective because of the emphasis on improving the productive capacity of individuals and creating conducive environment for employment.
- Inclusive growth is typically fuelled by the market driven forces of growth with the government playing a facilitating role. Policies for inclusive growth have to be an important component of government strategies for sustainable growth. For instance, a country like India that has grown rapidly over a decade, hut has not seen substantial reduction in poverty rate will need to focus specifically on inclusiveness of its growth strategy.

- Inclusive growth demands a clear commitment to pursue a development process which is sustainable. Natural resources are limited and their per capita availability is actually diminishing because of growing population and also because of traditional exploitation of common pool resources. As such, it is necessary to ensure not only preservation and maintenance of natural resources but also provide equitable access to those who do not have access at present. The degradation of natural resources reduces the well-being of the people, and the poor and women suffer more as they depend much more on natural common resources for fuel and water and also have fewer resources to take defensive actions.
- Good governance — understood as a mechanism linking inclusion, decision making and accountability — is fundamental to advancing each of these pillars. Over the years, the governments at the centre and the states have launched a large number of initiatives at substantial public expense to achieve the objective of growth with poverty alleviation and inclusiveness. However, many of these initiatives have floundered because of poor design, insufficient accountability and also corruption at various levels. There is, therefore, strong need for major improvements in governance which would make government funded programme in critical areas more effective and efficient.
- For inclusive growth it is unquestionably necessary to ensure the delivery of financial and non-financial services by the formal financial system to all people in a fair, transparent and equitable manner at an affordable cost.

B. FINANCIAL INCLUSION

◈ Conceptual Framework

Access to safe, easy and affordable credit and other financial services by the poor and vulnerable sections, disadvantaged areas and lagging sectors has come to be recognised as a pre-condition for accelerating economic growth, reducing income disparities and squalor, and achieving the equity objective so as to sustain the growth momentum. Despite the broad international consensus regarding the importance of access to finance as a crucial alleviation measure, it is estimated that globally over two billion people are currently excluded from access to financial services.[1] In most developing countries, a large segment of society, particularly low income people, has very little access to financial services, both formal and semi-formal. As a consequence, many of them have to necessarily depend either on their own or informal sources of finance and generally at usuriously high cost. The situation is worse in most least developed countries where more than 90 per cent of the population is excluded from access to the formal financial system.[2] In India too, a very large number of the poorest of the poor continue to remain outside the reach of the formal banking. Half of India's population does not have bank account, 90 per cent has no access to credit or life insurance cover, 95 per cent has no general insurance, while 98 per cent has no participation in the capital market.[3]

It was, therefore, strongly felt in India that the existing banking policies, systems and procedures and deposits and loan products were not well suited to meet the credit needs of the vulnerable. This led to the search for alternative policies and mechanism for reaching out to the poor to satisfy their felt needs.[4] As such, financial inclusive became the policy imperative.

Financial inclusion is the process of ensuring access to appropriate financial products and services needed by vulnerable groups at an affordable cost in a fair and transparent manner from main-stream institutional players. According to Asian Development Bank, financial inclusion refers to the provision of a broad range of financial services such as deposits, loans, payment services, money transfers and insurance to poor and low income households and their enterprises.[5] While this concept of financial inclusion is very broad covering all sorts of financial services provided by various financial institutions, a very important elements of adequacy, timeliness and affordability factor are missing in this concept. The Committee on Financial

Inclusion (CFI) constituted by the Government of India in June, 2006 under the chairmanship of Dr. C. Rangarajan rightly defines financial inclusion as the process of ensuring access to financial services timely and adequate credit when needed by vulnerable groups at an affordable cost[6] inclusive finance does not require that everyone who is eligible uses each of the services, but they should be able to choose them, if desired. Contrary to this, financial exclusion signifies restricted access to banking, insurance and other financial facilities to a few privileged sections, depriving the vast sections of helpless and vulnerable segments of the society from low cost, few and safe financial products and services of organized financial institutions. Thus, timeliness, adequacy and transparency are the hallmarks of financial inclusion.

Financial inclusion is an immanent feature of a well developed financial system which broadens access to funds to people at large. Conversely, financial exclusion is characteristic feature of an undeveloped financial system in which access to funds is limited and people are constrained by the availability of reasonably fair cost of formal sources of finance. As banking services are in the nature of public good, it is essential that availability of banking and payment services to the entire population without discrimination should be prime objective of the public policy.

◈ Role of Financial Inclusion in Inclusive Growth

Addressing the recent Bancon 2006 Banker's Conference, Dr. Y.V. Reddy, Former RBI Governor, rightly observed that "financial inclusion is not a matter of philosophy but an approach that can lead to a win-win situation for the banks and the customers. Treat financial inclusion as an investment for business. It is the mass moves that make money."[7] In other words, financial inclusion can prove to be a boon to the consumer, banker and the economy alike.

Hassle free assistance to affordable financial services-especially credit and insurance enlarges livelihood opportunities and empowers the poor to take charge of their lives. Such empowerment aids social and political stability. It also imparts formal identity, provides access to the payments system and to savings safety not like deposit insurance.

Establishment of an account relationship can enable the customer to avail of the benefits of a menu of economical and safe financial products which are regulated and supervised by credible regulators. The banks accounts can also be used for multiple purposes, such as, making small value remittances at low cost and making purchases on credit. Financial inclusion also enables the poor households, and micro and small enterprises to make proper financial institutions. This will, in turn, be extremely useful to the people to generate savings, and making productive use of the savings. It, thus, saves them from resorting to non-formal lenders who extort the former by all means.

Financial inclusion approach can be gainfully utilized by the banks to enhance their credibility and social acceptance. By involving the masses in the banking business and helping them in generating savings and deploying these savings productively banks can scale up their business. They can further improve their business and gain societal acceptance by penetrating in rural hinterlands and engaging in developmental activities particularly rural infrastructure to improve availability of electricity, connectivity through provision of rural road and telecommunications and construction of warehouses. This will lead to better overall supply change management, enhance productivity of physical resources in rural areas and add value to agricultural activities. Thus, financial inclusion will not only enhance overall financing intensity of agriculture but also help increase rural non-farm activities and ultimately lead to development of rural economy and improve economic lot of downtrodden people. In fact, mass banking with "no-frills" can become a win-win situation for both the people at large and the banks.

Sustainable credit expansion and growth of banking business without adequate deposit growth is not possible in the case of financial exclusion. Financial inclusion has the immense advantage of ensuring sustained economic and banking growth without putting undue pressure on real interest rates and impacting the overall stability of the financial system.

Economy as a whole stands to gain from financial inclusion in as much as greater funds become transparently available for efficient intermediation and allocation, for uses promising highest returns. Thus, the single gateway of a banking account can be useful for manifold purposes and represents a beneficial situation for all the economic units in the country. As such, financial inclusion is considered to be critical for achieving inclusive growth; which itself is required for ensuring overall sustainable growth in the country.

Financial inclusion drives economic growth and poverty alleviation by mobilising savings and investing in the growth of the productive sectors. Delivery of timely, appropriate and affordable financial services to poor people is critical for securing sustained growth. Thus, financial inclusion is no longer a policy choice but a policy compulsion.

Banks and other financial services players are, therefore, expected to mitigate the supply side bottlenecks that hinder the poor and disadvantaged social groups from gaining access to the financial system. Empirical evidence suggests that access to financial products is constrained by several factors such as lack of awareness about the financial products, unaffordable products, high transaction costs and products which are inconvenient, inflexible, not customised and of low quality. Micro finance and financial literacy play pivotal roles in addressing these issues.

Empirical evidence shows that countries with large proportion of population excluded from the formal financial system also show higher poverty ratios and higher inequality. The empirical findings strengthen the argument that financial exclusion in indeed a reflection of social exclusion, as countries having low GDP per capita, relatively higher levels of inequality, low rates of literacy, low urbanization and poor connectivity appear to be less financially inclusive.. Financial inclusion, therefore, assumes importance as a policy objective.

D. FINANCIAL INCLUSION AND INTERNATIONAL EXPERIENCES

In view of its paramount significance in economic and banking growth, financial inclusion is being practiced in different developed countries of the world with greater thrust on empowerment of the common person and low income groups. The Financial Inclusion Task Force in the U.K. has identified three priority areas for the purpose of financial inclusion, *viz*., access to banking, access to affordable credit and access to free face-to-face money advice. The U.K. has established a Financial Inclusion Fund to promote financial inclusion and assigned responsibility to banks and credit unions in removing financial exclusion. An enhanced legislative environment for credit unions has been established, accompanied by tighter regulations to ensure greater protection for investors.

A Post Office Card Account (POCA) has been created for those who are unable or unwilling to access a basic bank account. The concept of a 'Savings Gateway' has been piloted. This offers these on low-income employment pound 1 from the state for every pound they invest, upto a maximum of pound 25 per month. In addition, the Community Finance Learning Initiatives (CFLIs) were also introduced with a view to promoting basic financial literacy among housing association tenants.

In the USA, a civil rights law, *viz*., Community Reinvestment Act (CRA) prohibits discrimination by banks against low and moderate income neighbourhoods. The CRA imposes an affirmative and continuing obligation on banks to serve the needs for credit and banking services of all the communities in which they are chartered. Further, the state of New York Banking Department, with the objective of making available the low cost banking institution, offers basic banking account and in case of credit unions the basic share draft account, which is the nature of low cost account with minimum facilities. Some key features of the basic banking account are:

- The initial deposit amount required to open the account shall not exceed US $ 25.
- The minimum balance required to maintain such account shall not exceed US $ 0.10.
- The charge for periodic cycle for the maintenance of such accounts to be declared up front.
- A withdrawal shall be deemed to be made when recorded on the books of the account holder's banking institution.

- An account holder shall not be restricted as to the number of deposits which may be made to the account without incurring any additional charge.
- Every periodic statement issued for the basic banking account should invariably cover on it or by way of separate communique maximum number of withdrawals permitted during each periodic cycle without additional charge.
- The banking institution has to furnish, prior to opening the account, a written disclosure to the account holder describing the main features of the scheme, *i.e.,* the initial deposit amount required to open the account, minimum balance to be maintained, charge per periodic cycle for use of such account, maximum number of withdrawal transactions without any additional charge and other charges imposed on transactions for availing electronic facility not operated by the account holder's banking institutions, etc.

In Sweden, banks cannot refuse to open a saving or deposit account under Section 2 of the Banking Business act, 1987. In France, Article 58 of the Banking Act, 1984 recognized the principle of the right to a bank account. In Germany, a volunteer code was introduced by the German Bankers Association in 1996, providing for an 'everyman' current account, offering basic banking transaction, without an overdraft facility. In Belgium, a banking bill was enacted which was implemented since October, 2003. In addition to setting out the minimum standards for basic bank account, it also specifies the ceiling on charges and a minimum number of free face-to-face transactions. In Canada, the relevant legislation enacted in June, 2001 requires all banks to provide accounts without minimum opening balances to all Canadians, regardless of employment or credit history, with minimum identification requirements. A Financial Consumer Agency of Canada has been established to monitor whether financial institutions adhere to their public commitments.

D. FINANCIAL INCLUSION AND INDIAN EXPERIENCES

Despite banking expansion, improvement in financial performance, greater competition and diversification of ownership of banks leading to both enhanced efficiency and systematic resilience in the banking sector, existing banking practices tend to exclude rather than attract vast sections of population. Declining share of deposits and credits in rural and semi-urban areas, lower share of credit than that of deposits in all regions except metropolitans areas, falling share of farming loans and credit to SSI units speak volumes of existence of financial exclusion in banking system in India.

Notwithstanding various efforts taken by the Government and the RBI to increase banking penetration in the country, such as creation of SBI in 1955, nationalization of commercial banks in 1969 and 1980, initiation of the Lead Bank Scheme in 1970, establishment of RRBs in 1975, introduction of Self-Help Group (SHG) – Bank Linkage Programme in 1992 and formulating the Kisan Credit Card Scheme in 2001, little headway was made by banks to attract vast sections of population, in particular, pensioners, self-employed and those employed in unorganized sector.

Based on the available data on the number of savings banks accounts and assuming that one person has only one account it is found that on an all India basis 60 per cent of adult population in the country has bank accounts. In other words, 40 per cent in population is unbanked. In rural areas the coverage is 40 per cent against 60 per cent in urban areas. This figure is far lower than even some of the developing countries. Kerala, where about 89 per cent of the population has bank accounts, has high coverage. On the other hand, the North East and backward Eastern states have a low coverage with just 21 per cent. It is interesting to observe that the state of Himachal Pradesh is the only state in the country to achieve full financial inclusion.[8]

The magnitude of exclusion from credit markets is much more, as number of loan accounts constituted only 14 per cent of adult population. In rural areas, the coverage is 9.5 per cent against 14 per cent in urban areas. Regional differences are significant with the credit coverage at 25 per cent for the Southern Region and as low as 7.8 and 9 per cent, respectively, in North Eastern, Eastern and Central regions.

The extent of exclusion from credit markets can be observed from a different viewpoint out of 203 million households in the country, 147 million are in rural areas- 89 million are former households. 51.4 per cent of farm households have no access to formal or informal sources of credit.

The financial excluded sections largely comprise marginal farmers, landless labourers, oral lessees, self employed and unorganized sector enterprise urban slum dwellers, migrants, ethnic minorities and socially excluded groups, senior citizens and women. While there are pockets of large excluded population in all parts of the country, the North East, Eastern and Central regions contain most of the financially excluded population.

There are a host of factors contributing to financial exclusion. In remote, hilly and sparsely populated areas with poor infrastructure, physical access itself acts as a deterrent. From the demand sides, lack of awareness, low incomes/assets, social exclusion and illiteracy act as barriers, branch timings, cumbersome documentation and procedures, unsuitable products, language and staff indifferent attitudes are common reasons for exclusion. The combined impact of these forces resulted in higher transaction cost apart from procedural hassles. The requirement of independent documentary proof of identity and address can be a very important barrier in having a bank account, especially for migrants and slum dwellers.

Expressing serious concern on prevailing banking practices of financial exclusion the RBI Governor, DR. Reddy, observed that while commercial considerations are no doubt important, banks in India are bestowed with several privileges, especially of seeking public deposits on a highly leveraged basis, and enabling regulation and supervision of the RBI, they should be obliged to provide banking services to all segments of the population, on equitable basis.[9]

The Indian policy approach towards financial inclusion since 2008 has been focussed on ensuring inclusion at the individual and household level. Accordingly, the scheme of no-frills accounts (no pre-condition, low minimum balance maintenance) was initiated by the RBI in 2005 to provide an easy financial savings facility to the population at large, which can act as a means of their entry into formal banking system.[10]

In November, 2005 the RBI advised all the banks to make available a basic banking 'no-frills' account with low or nil minimum balances as well as charges that would make such accounts accessible to vast sections of population. All banks were also advised to give wide publicity to the facility of such a 'no-frills' account including on their websites indicating the facilities and charges in a transparent manner.

Further, in August 2005, RBI advised the banks to ensure that customers belonging to poor sections of the society are not kept away from banking system on account of difficulties in meeting the 'know your customers' (KYC) requirements for opening bank account. The KYC procedure for opening bank account was further simplified for persons who intend to keep balances not exceeding ₹ 50,000/- in all their accounts taken together and the total credit in all the accounts taken together is not expected to exceed ₹ 2,00,000/- in a year. The customer is allowed to exceed the threshold limit only after the full compliance with the KYC norms. More recently, in January, 2006, banks were permitted to utilize the services of NGOs/SHGs, micro-finance institutions and other civil society organization as intermediaries in providing financial and banking services through the use of business facilitator and business correspondent models.[11]

To extend hassle-free credit to bank customers in rural areas, the guidelines on general credit card (GCC) schemes were simplified to enable customers' access to credit on simplified terms and conditions, without insistence on security, purpose or end use credit. With a view to providing hassle free credit to customers, banks were allowed to issue general credit cards akin to 'Kisan Credit Cards'. A simplified mechanism for one time settlement of loans with principal amount upto ₹ 25,000 which have become doubtful and loss assets as on September 30, 2005 was suggested for adoption.

In February 2007, banks were directed to prepare a scheme for offering 'door step banking' services to their customers, with the approval of their boards, thereby dispensing with the need for approval from the RBI. Under the scheme, banks can offer doorstep services, such as pick up of cash/instruments, delivery of cash against cheques received at the counter and delivery of demand drafts to Corporates/Government departments/PSUs and pick up of cash/instruments and delivery of demand drafts to individuals. In May 2007, banks were also permitted to offer delivery of cash/demand draft to individuals. Furthermore, the delivery of cash/draft to individuals/corporate/Government departments/PSUs was permitted against requests received through any secure convenient channels.[12]

In order to give further impetus of financial inclusion, the RBI advised banks in May 2008 to classify overdrafts upto ₹ 25,000 (per account) granted against 'no frills' account in rural and semi-urban areas as indirect finance to the agriculture sector under priority sector with immediate effect.

Thus, broad strategy adopted by the RBI for financial inclusion in India in recent years comprises the following elements.[13]

(*i*) Encouraging penetration into unbanked and backward areas and encouraging agents and intermediaries such as NGOs, MFUs, CSOs and business correspondents (BCS);

(*ii*) Focusing on a decentralised strategy by using existing arrangements such as SLBC and district consultative committees (DCCs) and strengthening local institutions such as cooperatives and RRBs;

(*iii*) Using technology for furthering financial inclusion;

(*iv*) Advising banks to open a basic banking 'no frills' account;

(*v*) Emphasizing on financial literacy and credit counselling; and

(*vi*) Creating synergies between the formal and informal segments.

Based on the recommendations of the Committee of financial inclusion set up by the Government of India, two funds, viz. the "Financial Inclusion Fund" for meeting the cost of developmental and promotional interventions for ensuring financial inclusion, and the "Financial Inclusion Technology Fund", to meet the cost of technology adoption were set up with NABARD, with an overall corpus of ₹ 500 crore each which was subsequently increased to ₹ 600 crore each.

The RBI continues to foster financial inclusion in a mission mode through strategies ranging from relaxation of regulatory guidelines, provision of innovative products, encouraging use of technology and other supportive measures for achieving sustainable and scalable financial inclusion.

(*i*) Mandating opening of Branches in Rural unbanked centres: To further step up penetration of banking services in the rural areas, the RBI directed banks to allocate at least 25 per cent of their total number of branches to be opened during a year to unbanked rural centres. Further, in October 2011, to provide enhanced banking services in Tier 2 centres (with a population of 50,000 to 99,999 as per Census 2001), it has been proposed to permit domestic SCBs (other than RRBs) to open branches in these centres without the need to take permission from the RBI in each case, subject to reporting. The opening of branches in Tier 1 centres (centres with population of 1,00,000 and above as per Census, 2001) will continue to require prior permission of the RBI.[14]

(*ii*) Relaxation of KYC norms: In 2010-11, KYC norms were relaxed vide circular date January 27, 2011 to include job cards issued by/under National Rural Employment Guarantee Act (NREGA) duly signed by an officer of the state government or the letters issued by the Unique Identification Authority of India containing details of name, address and Aadhaar number can also be taken as the basis for opening small bank accounts.[15]

(*iii*) Widening the definition of Business Correspondence: Discussed in Chapter 30.

(*iv*) Introduction of Innovative and Simple Products.

Banks have been advised to provide in-built overdraft of small amount in 'no-frills' accounts so that customers can avail of credit of small amount without any further documentation, for meeting emergency requirements.

The RBI directed on July 10, 2012 to drop the 'no-frills' tag from the basic saving accounts as the nomenclature has become a stigma. It has asked banks to provide the zero balance facility in the basic banking accounts alongwith ATM-cum debit cards without any extra charge. Banks have been directed to convert the existing 'no-frills' accounts into 'Basic savings bank deposit accounts.' This account shall not have the requirement of any minimum balance ...... Further, no charge will be levied for non-operation/activation of in-operative-basic savings bank deposit account.

E. FINANCIAL EDUCATION

Taking cognizance of the fact that financial literacy facilitates financial inclusion, which, in turn, results in inclusive growth and development, the RBI strongly felt the exigency of promoting the financial literacy and improving the level of education among consumers of banking services.

Financial education is the process by which financial consumers/investors improve their understanding of financial products and concepts, develop the skills and confidence to make informed choices to improve their financial well being.[16] Financial education thus, aims at familiarizing the bank customers at large with fundamental features of financial market products, especially the risk-return trade off and developing the ability to make informed choices, enabling the individuals to take prudent financial decisions in their personal life and to avoid any distress in their personal life. The rapid growth of retail banking business in India and concomitant large influx of a growing number of retail borrowers into the banking system as also increasing complexity of financial markets leading to emergency of a wide variety of products have increased the necessity of financial literacy, particularly if the markets are to expand and operated efficiency.

Adequate financial education to the bank customers equips them with the basic financial skills and discipline to manage their financial affairs by appropriately balancing their expenses, borrowing and savings. Such customers can afford a better quality of life and also help in improving the integrity and quality of the markets.

In India, the need for financial education is even greater in view of the low levels of literacy and a large section of the population being still out of the formal financial set up. Furthermore, economic and financial sector reforms have placed higher disposable incomes in the hands of the public. Availability of a variety of new financial products on both credit and investment sides which are provided by a host of financial intermediaries, has necessitated that the investing public understand the nuances of each product and product supplier and take an informed decision about investments. At the same time, those who are not part of the formal financial system need to be educated about what banking is and why they should have a relationship with banks so that they also participate in and benefit from the growth process.

The RBI has taken a number of measures for increasing financial literacy.

(*i*) The RBI has undertaken a project titled "Project Financial Literacy" with the objective of disseminating information regarding the central bank and general banking concepts to various target groups including school and college going children, women, rural and urban poor, defence personnel and senior citizens.

(*ii*) A multilingual website in 13 Indian languages on all matters concerning banking and the common person was launched by the RBI in June, 2007.

(*iii*) With a view to introducing banking to school children, illustrated books have been made available on the website. Similar books have been prepared for different target groups and are widely distributed in regional language through various regional offices of the RBI.

(*iv*) Financial literacy programmes are being launched in each state with active involvement of the state governments and SLBC. These programmes include skits, road shows, exhibitions, workshops, seminars and dissemination through radio and television.

(*v*) A model scheme on financial literacy and credit counselling centres (FLCCs) was formulated by the RBI and communicated to all SCBs and RRBs with the advice to set up centres as distinct entities, such that the FLCCs' services are available even to other banks' customers in the district.

(*vi*) Financial education focuses on the capacity building measures to enable small and marginal borrowers to avail of the entire suite of financial products and services, i.e., savings, remittance, insurance and pension from the banking sector, in addition to credit. In view of the utility of these centres as expressed by state governments and other stakeholders, banks have been advised to set up FLCCs in all districts. As on March 2011, 252 FLCCs were set up in various states of the country.

F. FINANCIAL INCLUSION AND COMMERCIAL BANKS IN INDIA

At the outset it may be noted that commercial banks in India have never been enthusiastic to provide assistance on their own to all those who need it. In fact, they have been averse to penetrate in rural and semi-urban areas and help the weaker and unprivileged sections mainly because of higher risk perception. This is why the Government of India and the RBI have been pushing the banks hard through their policy interventions to penetrate unbanked regions and render financial support to all the needy persons timely and adequately.

◈ Progress before Pre-liberalisation period

Before 1990, several initiatives were undertaken for enhancing the use of the banking system for sustainable and equitable growth. These included nationalisation of private sector banks, introduction of priority sector lending norms, branch licensing norms with focus on rural/semi-urban branches, interest rate ceilings for credit to the weaker sections and creation of specialised financial institutions to cater to the requirements of the agriculture and the rural sectors having bulk of the poor population. The immediate tasks set for the nationalised banks were mobilisation of deposits on a massive scale and lending of funds for all productive activities. A special emphasis was laid on providing credit facilities to the weaker sections of the economy.

Since the 1970s, the promotional aspects of banking policy have come into greater prominence. The major thrust of the branch licensing policy during the 1970s and the 1980s was on expansion of commercial bank branches in rural areas. This resulted in a significant expansion of bank branches and decline in population per branch.

The National Bank for Agriculture and Rural Development (NABARD) was set up in 1982 mainly to provide refinance to the banks extending credit to agriculture, Regional Rural Banks (RRBs) were set up in 1975 to cater, *inter alia,* to the credit requirements of the rural poor.

◈ Progress during Post-liberalisation period

Despite massive banking expansion, existing banking practices tended to exclude rather attract vast sections of population. Declining share of deposits and credits in rural and semi-urban areas, lower share of credit than that of deposits in all regions except metropolitan areas, falling share of farming loans and credit to SSI units speak volumes of existence of financial exclusion in banking system in India.

Taking cognizance of the sordid fact that one person had only one account it is found that on an all India basis 60 per cent of adult population in the country had bank accounts and 50 per cent of the population across the country was unbanked; in rural areas, the coverage was 40 per cent against 60 per cent in urban areas.

The RBI decided to create a strong, vibrant and competitive banking system in terms of micro finance to bring financially excluded people within the fold of formal financial sector. Accordingly, the Self-Help Group-bank Linkage (SHGBL) programme was launched by the NABARD in 1992, with policy support from the RBI.

SHG is a group of about 15 to 20 people from a homogeneous class who joins together to address common issues. They involve voluntary thrift activities on a regular basis, the end use of the pooled resources to make interest-bearing loans to the members of the group. Once the group is stabilised, and shows mature financial behaviour, which generally takes up to six months, it is considered eligible to be linked to a bank which opens a savings bank account for the SHG and offers loans upto 4 times the group's savings. The SHG can then on lend to its members, helping them to engage in some income generating activities and capacity building.

The SBLM for purveying micro finance was started in India in 1989 as an action research project. The findings of the project led to the launching of the pilot project by NABARD in 1992. The pilot project was designed as a partnership model among three agencies, *viz.*, SHGs, banks and NGOs. These SHGs were expected to facilitate collective decision making by the poor, leadership development and provide doorstep banking. The banks as wholesalers of credit were to provide the resources while the NGOs were to act as agencies to organize the poor, build their capacities and facilitate the process of improving them.

Three different models that have emerged under the SBLM are:

- Model I: This involves lending by banks directly to SHGs without intervention/facilitation by an NGO.
- Model II: This envisages lending by banks directly to SHGs with facilitation by NGOs and other agencies.
- Model III: This involves lending, with an NGO acting as a facilitator and financing agency.

The RBI has been encouraging banks to lend financial support to the poor and unprivileged persons through SHGs.

Commercial banks' lendings under SHG-bank linkage have made rapid strides since its inception in the early 1990s. It may be noted form Table 17.1 that the number of bank-linked SHGs registered meteoric rise from 33,000 during 1992-99, 74,60,000 as on March 2011. These SHGs have been funded by banks. Loans granted by banks to SHGs surged sharply from ₹ 57 crore during 1992-99 to over ₹ 31,221 crore as on March-end 2011. In 2009-10, 1590 lakh new SHGs were credit linked with banks and bank loans, of ₹ 14,453 crore were disbursed to these SHGs. Further, at end March, 2011, 7460 lakh SHGs maintained savings accounts with banks. In 2010-11, 1200 lakh new SHGs were credit linked with banks and bank loans of ₹ 14,547 crore were disbursed to these SHGs.

TABLE 17.1: Banks' lending under SHG-Bank Linkage Programme

Year	No. of SHGs Financed ('000)		Bank Loans (₹ in crore)	
	During the year	Cumulative	During the year	Cumulative
1992-99	33	33	57	57
1999-00	82	115	136	193
2000-01	149	264	288	481
2001-02	198	461	545	1026
2002-03	256	717	1022	2049
2003-04	362	1079	1856	3904
2004-05	539	1618	2994	6898
2005-06	620	2239	4499	11398
2006-07	1106	2985	6570	12366

2007-08	1228	3626	8849	17000
2008-09	1610	4224	12254	22680
2009-10	1590	4850	14454	28038
2010-11	1200	7460	14547	31,221
2011-12	1100	7960	16500	36300

Source: RBI's Reports on Trend and Progress of Banking in India.

Among the commercial Banks rendering assistance to the SHGs, the contribution of commercial banks, particularly the PSBs has been as high as two-thirds of the total.

Furthermore, of the three models under SBLP, the model II, *viz.*, SHGs promoted by NGOs/Government agencies and financed by banks as the most dominant model, accounting for over four-fifths of the total assistance under the programme.

Another striking feature of SBLP is greater concentration of the assistance in the southern region, claiming over half of the assistance. The share of north-eastern region has been as low as 2.8 per cent. Nevertheless, the spatial disparity has declined in the last few years with some increase in the share of other regions, particularly the eastern region.

It appears that SBLPs have flourished more in the states with the well-developed banking infrastructure. This indicates that micro finance under SBLPs seems to be a supplementary rather than a substitute for a developed banking infrastructure.

Consequent upon the RBI directive to banks to open no-frills accounts in 2005, commercial banks opened such accounts for the poor and marginal individuals. Thus, it may be noted from Table 17.2 that number of no-frills accounts stood at 4,89,497 as at the end of March, 2006. This surged significantly in the subsequent years to reach 75,00,000 accounts as on March-end, 2011. Thus, no-frills accounts have grown phenomenally. However, an important challenge before the banking system is to keep these accounts operational, as many such accounts are found to be dominant since the poor often find it difficult to save and deposit money into these accounts. In order to keep these operational, banks have been advised to provide small overdrafts in such accounts; upto March 2010, ₹ 27.54 crore were provided as overdrafts by banks in such accounts.[18]

TABLE 17.2: Number of No-frills Accounts with Commercial Banks in India

As on March end	Number
2006	4,89,497
2007	67,32,335
2008	158,37,862
2009	330,24,761
2010	506,00,000
2011	750,00,000
2012	1417,00,000

Source: RBI Reports on Trend and Progress of Banking in India.

Nevertheless banks have been trying to expand, there are limitations to increase their physical presence. Out of the 6,00,000 habitations in the country, only about 5 per cent have commercial bank branch. People with debit cards comprise 13 per cent and those with credit cards comprise only 2 per cent.[19]

So as to enhance penetration of banking system in rural hinterlands the RBI adopted BC model in 2006 wherein an individual or a group is assigned the role of providing financial services on behalf of banks and permitted banks to use the services of various entities. The RBI has directed banks to reach all villages with a population of 2,000 or more by 2012 and those with a population of less than 2,000 over the next 3 to 5 years. There are about 1,00,000 such habitations across the country, of which about 35,000 have bank branches. The BC model is expected to work there since brick-and-mortar branches may not be viable in all such locations. In order to ensure that the BC model is viable, the RBI recently permitted banks to collect reasonable service charges from customers in a transparent manner.

In compliance with the RBI directive, banks had submitted their financial inclusion plans to the regulator, according to which around 2,00,000 business correspondents and customer service points would start work over next two-and a-half years. Also, 4,000 branches in unbanked villages and 100 million no-frills accounts would be opened.[20]

It has been noted with concern that the financial inclusion process was slow in many regions and states and banks are facing enormous problems in this regard. Barriers to access financial services are on both the demand and the supply side. Limited financial literacy is a major hindrance in achieving financial inclusion. Many general financial products are unsuitable for the poor and there is not much effort to design products that are suitable to their needs. The high customer acquisition and transaction costs are found deterring financial intermediaries from serving the unbanked areas. Banks do not find it cost-effective to serve poor customers because of the low business volumes, at least in the initial stages. The lack of basic physical and social infrastructure increases the cost of servicing the unbanked areas.

Most of these problems can be overcome with adoption of technology and change in the mindset of the bankers. According to the RBI governor, "Commercial banks should see financial inclusion as an opportunity rather than an obligation."[21]

G. PROGRESS UNDER FINANCIAL INCLUSION PLANS

As a result of the RBI efforts to encourage the banking sector to expand the banking network, there has been improvement in the status of financial inclusion in 2010-11 over the previous year/ (Table 17.3). It may be observed from the table that the bank branches opened in the hitherto.

TABLE 17.3: Progress of Financial Inclusion

Sl. No.	Indicator	End-March 2010	End-March 2011	End-March 2012
1.	Total number of customer service points deployed	33,042	58,361	1,16,548
2.	Total number of villages covered	54,757	9984	1,81,753
3.	Villages covered with population > 2000	27,743	53,397	—
4.	Villages covered with population < 2000	27,014	46,447	—
5.	Villages covered through branches	21,499	22,686	37,471
6.	Villages covered through BCs	33,158	76,801	1,41,136
7.	Villages covered through Mobile and ATM	100	355	3,146
8.	Credit - GDP	53.4	54.6	—
9.	Credit - deposit	73.6	76.5	—
10.	Population per bank branch	14,000	13,466	—
11.	Population per ATM	19,700	16,243	—
12.	Percentage of population having deposit accounts	55.8	61.2	—
13.	Percentage of population having credit accounts	9.3	9.9	—
14.	Percentage of population having debit cards	15.2	18.8	—
15.	Percentage of population having credit cards	1.53	1.49	—
16.	Branches opened in Tier 3-6 centres as a per cent of total new bank branches	40.3	55.4	—
17.	Branches opened in hitherto umbanked centres as a per cent of total new bank branches	5.6	9.7	—
18.	Number of KCC's outstanding (in millions)	20	23	30
19.	Amount in KCCs outstanding (₹ crore)	1,07,519	1,43,862	2,06,800
20.	Number of GCCs outstanding (in millions)	6	1	
21.	Amount in GCCs outstanding (₹ crore)	814	1308	4200

Source: RBI Report on Trend and Progress of Banking in India, 2010-11.

Unbanked centres increased from 281 in 2009-10 to 470 in 2010-11. Of the total new bank branches opened in 2010-11, almost 10 per cent were opened in hitherto unbanked centres as compared with 6 per cent in the previous year. However in comparison with the latest policy prescription, the share of new bank branches opened in unbanked centres in 2010-11 was low. There has been significant improvement in total number of villages covered by the banks in 2011 over the previous year. It can be seen from the table that banks have been heavily relying on BCs to expand the banking network in the unbanked areas under FIPs. In 2011-11, almost 77 per cent of the total villages covered were through BCs. The number of Kisan Credit Cards (KCCs) and General Credit Cards (GCCs) witnessed growth of 15 per cent and 49 per cent respectively in 2010-11 over the previous year.

In order to foster progress of financial inclusion, the RBI advised all public and private sector banks to put in place Board approved three-year financial inclusion plans (FIPs) from April 2010 onwards. The FIP should broadly contain self-set targets with respect to: (i) Opening rural brick and mortar branches; (ii) Deployment of BCs; (iii) Coverage of villages with population of more than 2000 as also other un-banked villages with population below 2,000 through branches/BC/other modes; (iv) Opening no-frills accounts including through BC-ICT; (v) Issuing Kisan Credit Cards (KCCs) and general credit cards, and other specific products designed by them to cater to the financially excluded segments.

The progress, so far, by banks in achieving FIP during 2010-11 and 2011-12 has been impressive. A brief analysis of the progress shows that penetration of banking has increased multi-fold in rural areas. As at end-March, 2012, villages covered through BCs constituted more than 80 per cent of the total villages covered under FIP. This is indicative of move towards widespread acceptance of BC model of financial inclusion by banks as well as consumers in rural India.[22]

Despite all the attempts made by the RBI, the extent of financial exclusion continues to be significant in India, when compared with some of the advanced as well as developing countries (table 17.4). This underlies the need to strengthen financial inclusion drive through well thoughtout policies.

TABLE 17.4: Select Indicators of Financial Inclusion — Cross country comparison for 2011

Country	Number of Branches (per 0.1 million adults)	Number of ATMs (per 0.1 million adults)	Bank loans as % of GDP	Bank Deposits as % of GDP
India	10.64	8.90	51.75	68.43
Australia	29.61	166.92	128.75	107.10
Brazil	46.15	119.63	40.28	53.26
France	41.58	109.80	42.85	34.77
Mexico	14.86	45.77	18.81	22.65
U.S.	35.43	—	46.83	57.78
Korea	18.80	—	90.65	80.82
Philippines	8.07	17.70	21.39	41.93

Source: Financial Access Survey, IMF.

H. CONCLUSIONS

Inclusive growth is necessary for achieving higher economic growth with reduced poverty on sustainable basis. Inclusive growth signifies growth of, for and by the people. For inclusive growth to take place, pace and pattern of growth need to be addressed together. There should be productive employment rather than on direct income redistribution. It should be fuelled by the market driven forces of growth with the government playing a facilitating role. Inclusive growth demands a clear commitment to pursue a development process which is environmentally sustainable. Above all, good governance is fundamental to the accomplishment of inclusive growth programmes.

For inclusive growth it is unquestionably necessary to ensure the delivery of financial services by the formal financial system to all in a fair, transparent and equitable manner at an affordable cost. Thus, financial inclusion is an important instrument of inclusive growth. Financial inclusion is the process of ensuring access to appropriate financial products and services needed by vulnerable groups at an affordable cost in a fair and transparent manner from main stream institutional players. Delivery of timely, appropriate, and affordable financial services to poor and marginal income groups is critical for ensuring sustainable growth.

In view of the above, financial inclusion is being practiced in various developed and developing countries with greater thrust on empowerment of the common people and low income groups. In India, both the Government of India and the RBI have, of late, been making concerted efforts to improve lot of poor and unprivileged persons through penetration of banking system in unbanked areas of the country. The basic policy approach towards financial inclusion in India since 2005 has been focused at the individual and household level.

For carrying out the task of executing financial inclusion programme, commercial banks have been assigned the major responsibility. Taking cognizance of the sordid fact that the existing banking practices have not been effective in lending to vast sections of the population, the RBI decided to create a strong, vibrant and competitive banking system in terms of micro finance so as to bring financially excluded people within the fold of formal financial sector. Accordingly, the banks have been directed to help the poor through self-help groups. There has been rapid stride in SHG-bank linkage programme since its inception. As on March end 2012, more than ₹ 36,000 crore has been lent out to 25,60,000 self groups by the banks. However, such assistance has been highly concentrated in the southern region.

In consonance with the RBI directive, the banks have opened more than 5 crore no-frills accounts. However, substantially large number of such accounts have remained dormant since the poor often find it difficult to save and deposit money into these accounts.

So as to enhance penetration of the banking system in rural and remote areas, the RBI adopted BC model in 2006 and allowed banks to use the services of various entities. The BC model is expected to work in all such locations where brick and mortar branches may not be viable.

KEY TERMS

- Basic Savings Bank Deposit Account
- Business correspondent model
- Doorstep banking
- Financial exclusion
- Financial inclusion
- Inclusive finance
- Know your customers
- National Mission on Financial Inclusion
- National Rural Financial Inclusion Fund
- No-frills accounts
- Self-help group-bank linkage programme

DISCUSSION QUESTIONS

1. Define inclusive growth. Discuss the role of inclusive growth in accelerating pace of growth and reducing poverty.
2. What are the pre-conditions to inclusive growth?
3. What is financial inclusion? Discuss the redeeming features of financial inclusion.
4. "Financial inclusion acts as powerful instrument of inclusive growth." Comment.
5. What triggered the adoption of the concept of financial inclusion in India?

6. What part has the RBI played in promoting financial inclusiveness in Indian banking system?
7. Discuss the role played by commercial banks in India in delivering financial services to financially excluded persons.
8. What is "No-Frills Accounts"? What steps have been taken by the RBI in this regard and with what result?
9. Is increase in number of "No-Frills Account" a conclusive evidence of greater financial support to deprived sections of the society? If not, give reasons.
10. What is self-help group bank linkage programme? Discuss in brief, various model of such programme.
11. What is the role of financial education in fostering financial inclusion and poverty alleviation programmes?
12. Critically examine the progress made under financial inclusion plans.

REFERENCES

1. United Nations, Advisors Group on Inclusion Financial Sector, 2006.
2. Asian Development Bank, 'Finance for the Poor', Micro Finance Development Strategy, 2000.
3. K.C. Chakravarty, RBI Deputy Governor, Business Standard, January 24, 2011.
4. RBI, Report on Trend and Progress of Banking in India, 2006-07, p. 152
5. Business Line, November 8, 2006.
6. RBI, Annual report on Currency and Finance, 2006-08, p. 315.
7. Business Line, November 8, 2006.
8. *Ibid.*
9. RBI Bulletin, November, 2006.
10. RBI Report on Trend and Progress of Banking in India, 2009-10.
11. RBI Bulletin, *op cit.*
12. RBI Annual Report, 2006-07, pp. 165-166.
13. RBI Annual Report on Currency and Finance, 2006-08, *op cit.*, p. 194.
14. RBI Report on Trend and Progress of Banking in India, 2010-11.
15. *Ibid.*
16. RBI Annual Report, 2006-07, p. 139.
17. RBI Annual Report, 2010-11, p. 87.
18. RBI Report on Trend and Progress of Banking in India, 2009-10, p. 93.
19. Report on Trend and Progress of Banking in India, *op cit.*, p. 13.
20. Business Standard, December 7, 2010.
21. *Ibid.*

Asset-Liability Management in Commercial Banks

Chapter 18

Learning Objectives:

The present chapter attempts at:

- Tracing out evolution of concept of Asset-Liability Management Approach.
- Providing conceptual understanding of Asset-Liability Management, its objectives and functions.
- Dilating upon the process of Asset-Liability Management.
- Assessing the utility of Asset-Liability Management Approach.
- Laying down Preconditions to the Effectiveness of Asset-Liability Management.
- Assessing the Relevance of Asset-Liability Management Approach to Commercial Banks in India.

Chapter Outline:

- Evolution of Asset-Liability Management Approach.
- Concept of Asset-Liability Management in Banking System.
- Objectives of Asset-Liability Management.
- Functions of Asset-Liability Management.
- Focus of Asset-Liability Management Approach.
- Process of Asset-Liability Management.
- Utility of Asset-Liability Management Approach.
- Prerequisites to the Effectiveness of Asset-Liability Management.
- ALM policies and practices of banking system in India.
- Conclusions.

A. EVOLUTION OF ASSET-LIABILITY MANAGEMENT (ALM) APPROACH

The overall success of banks and financial institutions in a competitive and market driven environment hinges essentially on how effectively they discharge their intermediation operations to obtain maximum yield.

In a regimented and controlled environment, the interest spread is primarily a function of a central bank of the country because banks accept deposits at regulated rate and lend at the regulated rate and earn the stipulated spread. This, however, does not happen in a deregulated environment. Intense competition for business and increasing fluctuations in both domestic interest rates as well as foreign exchange rates put pressure on the management of banks to maintain spreads, profitability and long-term viability without increasing market risk.

There are two major types of risks that a commercial bank is exposed to in the course of its operations, *viz*., credit risk and market risk.

Banking business in regulated economy is looked upon as the business of taking on credit risk. Market risk arising out of fluctuations in interest rates, foreign exchange rates, equity price risk and commodity price risk is virtually not existent in such a regime where market rates and prices are stable for relatively long periods of time. Banks are exposed to market risk in market driven and liberalised environment where there is free play of forces of demand and supply. Unlike in the repressed financial market banks have to manage not only credit risk but also market risk. They require a managerial approach to control the viability of market risk and so also of net interest income and net economic value of the bank. Emergence and growing popularity of Asset-Liability Management (ALM) all over the world during the last three and half decades is a strategic response of banks to inflationary pressure, severe volatility in interest rates and severe recessionary trends which marked the global economy in the seventies and eighties.

ALM as a discipline is nearly three and half decades old in the developed and deregulated western world. The debacle of 'Savings and Loan (S & L) Associations' experience (Thrifts) in the USA during 80's drives home the importance of ALM as a strategic approach for survival in a deregulated environment. 3-6-3 banking was a standing joke in the USA on thrift managers during 60s and early 70s. It used to be said in a lighter vein in those days that a Thrift Manager takes deposits at regulated rate of 3%, lends at regulated rate of 6% and goes for golf at 3 p.m., secure himself in the spread of 3%. So in regulated environment, more the deposits, more the loans and more the spread. All that was expected of the manager who was selling and networking. This game went on merrily for decades. But deregulation of interest rates in 80's saw the demise of 3-6-3 banking, giving blow to S & L debacle which had cost the US tax payers a couple of hundred billion USD (nearly 70 times of an own security scan losses) due to the benign neglect of interest rate risk arising out of deregulation. Banks' managers obsession of increasing deposits and loans, failure to recognise interest rate risks and maturity mis-matches had nearly wiped out thrift industry. This disastrous experience brought ALM to the center stage of financial intermediation. Financial liberalisation, deregulation, interest rate volatility and capital adequacy requirements redefined intermediaries' role in the late 80's.

With the tectonic changes in Indian economic policy in early 90s leading to deregulation of interest rates and free play of market forces, entry of new players, emergence of new financial instruments and new products at competitive rates and enhancement of risks, and income recognition and provisioning commercial banks in our country began to face tremendous problem of asset-liability mis-match. The interest rate gyrations witnessed during Sept. 1995/ Feb. 1996 exposed the vulnerability of mis-matches. Banks and financial institutions, which ignored ALM, were caught in a severe asset-liability mis-match in 1997-98. The banks having funded term assets through short-term loans with low interest rate and inherent organisational deficiencies were caught napping when the call money skyrocketed to dizzy heights of 80 to 90% or even higher. This made bank managers realize that they would have to survive the onslaught on their bottom lines amid uncertainty caused by deregulation and fierce competition from other players in the financial services system. Recent Asian crisis and global financial crunch further buttressed the bankers beliefs. With growing tendency of greater integration of money market, foreign exchange market and capital market and greater volatility in the market condition with the emergence of an active debt-market, Indian commercial banks are more under pressure to adopt the new approach so as to emerge as active players in the market.

Banks felt strongly the necessity of pursuing an integrated approach to financial management, requiring simultaneous decisions about the types of amounts of financial assets and liabilities — both mix and volume — with the complexities of the financial markets in which the institution operates. ALM has, therefore, come to be recognised in recent few years in India as a strategic approach of making business decision in a more comprehensive and disciplined framework to control asset-liabilities mis-match with an eye on the risks that the bank is exposed to. Although the process is too complex to practice, it is perhaps the only solution for banks to survive in a dynamic environment which demands focus on total balance sheet management.

B. CONCEPT OF ASSET-LIABILITY MANAGEMENT IN BANKING SYSTEM

ALM is an integrated strategic managerial approach of managing total balance sheet dynamics having regard to its size and quality in such a way that the net earnings from interest in particular are maximised with the overall risk preference of the institution. This approach is concerned with management of net interest margin (net interest margin is ratio of net interest income or spread, to total earnings/assets) to ensure that its level and riskiness are compatible with the risk-return objectives of the bank. This is sought to be done by matching of the liabilities and assets in terms of maturity, cost and yield rates. In fact, the asset-liability management by banks is critically dependent on the maturity profile of their assets and liabilities. As banks generally raise resources through short-term liabilities to finance assets ranging from short to long-term, the liquidity and credit risks get multiplied particularly during the periods of crisis. The maturity mis-matches and disproportionate changes in the level of assets and liabilities can cause financial liquidity and interest rate risks. The degree of mis-match may be very high in most banks. This is because banks fund their long-term assets with short-term liabilities. The problem is compounded by volatile call money market which exists for most part of a year. Mis-match is also caused by a bank's lending substantial portion of liabilities by way of cash credit amounting to 70% of the total advances. The fluctuations in balances of cash credit accounts compound the liquidity problems of commercial banks as normally these accounts are utilised in full to take advantage of tight money condition, anticipating general price rise, inflation, speculative trend, etc. Further, a bank's investment in government securities - both central and state are for a period of 10 to 15 years whereas funds received are of shorter maturities. Selling the Government securities would be difficult whenever need for funds arises as there is no active and liquid secondary market for debt instruments.

ALM approach involves quantification of risk and conscious decision-making with regard to asset - liability structure in order to maximise interest earning within framework of perceived risk. ALM can, therefore, be defined as the process of managing the net interest margin within the overall risk bearing capacity of a bank. Thus, it calls for an integrated approach towards financial management conditioned to simultaneous decision-making with respect to types and size of financial assets and liabilities, their mix and volume so as to insulate the spread from moving in adverse direction. Thus, the secret of effective banking deregulated and competitive environment hinges essentially on matching of assets and liabilities in terms of rate and maturity with a view to deriving optional yield. ALM has to be closely integrated with business strategy of the bank as the latter has bearing upon the risk profile of the bank.

Thus, the focus of ALM is not on building up of deposits and loans/assets in isolation but on net interest income and recognising interest rate and liquidity risks. This is essentially a guide for survival in a deregulated environment.

Diagrammatic presentation of ALM and asset-liability mis-matches is brought out in the following charts:

CHART 18.1: Asset-Liability Management Structure

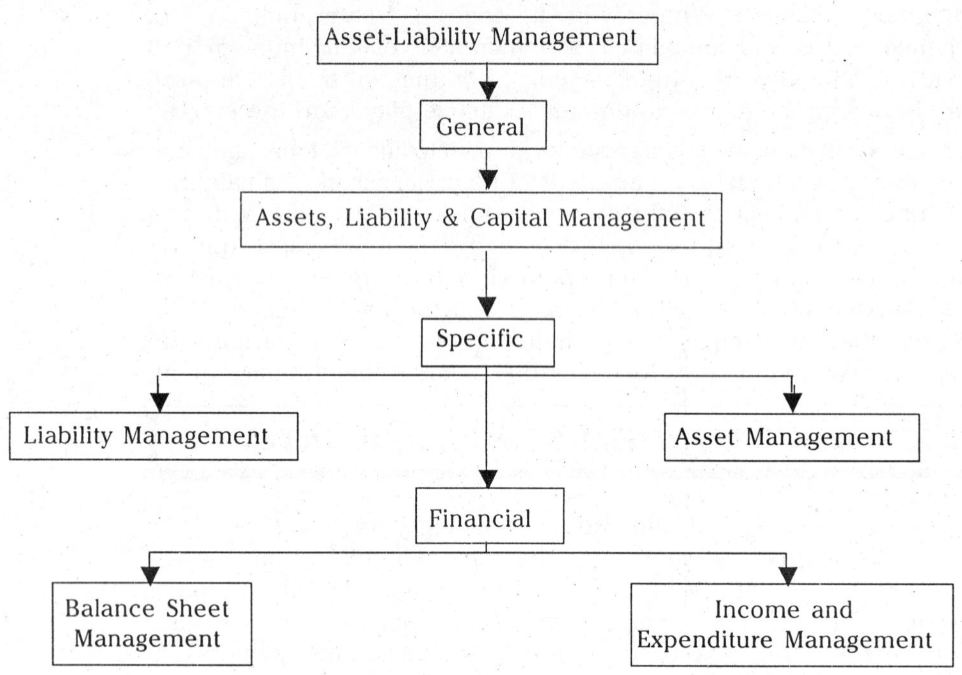

Chart 18.2

Asset-Liability Mismatches in a Bank

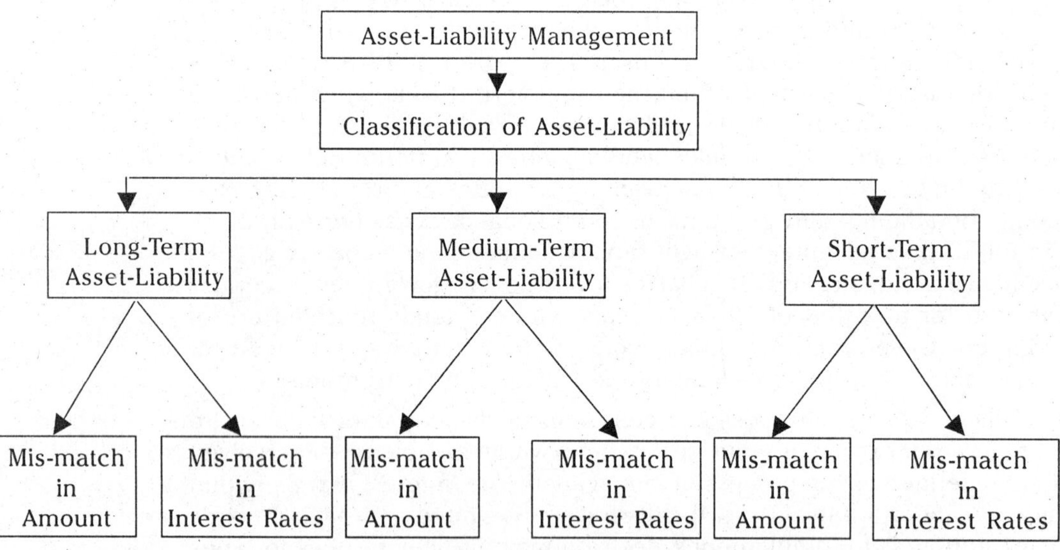

Precisely speaking, ALM is a co-ordinated approach to managing a bank's balance sheet to allow for alternative interest rates and liquidity scenarios. It is the process of planning, directing and controlling the flow, level, mix, costs, yield and duration of funds for the purpose of maximising yield with minimum financial risks.

C. OBJECTIVES OF ASSET-LIABILITY MANAGEMENT

Primary objective of ALM approach is to manage market risk in such a way as to minimise the impact of net interest income fluctuations in the short run and protect the net economic value of the bank in the long run. Precisely speaking, ALM has the following objectives:[1]

1. To control the volatility of net interest income and net economic value of a bank.
2. To control volatility in all target accounts.
3. To control liquidity risk, and
4. To ensure an acceptable balance between profitability and growth rate.

D. FUNCTIONS OF ASSET-LIABILITY MANAGEMENT

The basic function of ALM is to guide the management in establishing optimal match between the assets and liabilities of the bank in such a way as to maximise its net income and minimise the market risk. This it seeks to do by informing the management as to what the current market risk profile of the bank is and the impact that various alternative business decisions would have on the future risk profile.[2] The manager can then choose the best course of action depending on the Boards' risk perception.

Suppose for example, existing asset and liability structure of a bank is such that in aggregate the maturity of assets is longer than the maturity of liabilities. This would obviously expose the bank to greater interest rate risk because if interest rates tend to increase in future, it would adversely effect the bank's net interest income. So as to reduce the risk, the bank would have to either reduce the average maturity of its assets (possibly by reducing its holdings of Government securities) or by increasing the average maturity of its liabilities (perhaps by reducing its reliance on call/money market funds).

Thus, the bank manager equipped with the interest rates related information about existing risk profile of the bank can reduce its future risk by marketing its long-term deposit products more aggressively and wherever necessary even by increasing the rates offered on long-term deposits and/or decreasing rates on the short-term deposits.

In order to make prudent decisions with regard to procurement of funds and their allocation among assets, the bank manager may need other information such as competitive pressures, demand and supply factors, the impact of the decision on the bank's retail lending products, etc. ALM approach focuses on supplying these information to the management for better and more rational decision.

E. SCOPE OF ASSET-LIABILITY MANAGEMENT APPROACH

The main focus of asset-liability management, in a nut shell, is the matching of the liabilities and assets in terms of maturity, cost and yield rates. The maturity mismatches and disproportionate changes in the portfolio of assets and liabilities cause financial risks. Thus, ALM approach comprises the following aspects:

- Review of interest rate scenario.
- Fixation of interest/product pricing on both assets and liabilities.
- Assessment of existing loan portfolio.
- Assessment of existing investment portfolio.
- Measurement of financial risks.
- Managing financial risks.

- Review of actual performance *vis-à-vis* projections in respect of net profit, interest spread and other balance sheet ratios.
- Strategic planning and budgeting.
- Examining profitability of new products.

F. PROCESS OF ASSET-LIABILITY MANAGEMENT

Strategic approach to manage asset-liability and for that purpose to measure, manage and monitor the financial risks involves four stages:

- Identification of risks.
- Measurement and determination of risks.
- Enhancement of long-term profitability for a given level of risks.
- Management of risks.

◈ Identification of Risks

Risk is inherent in banking business. Given the complexities of bank balance sheets and rapidity of changes, chances of loss or risks are not only complex in nature but also varied in dimension. Inter-play of simultaneous risks makes the exercise to move beyond a workout for insulating profitability risk. Hence, the first step of ALM in a bank is identification of various types of financial risks a bank is exposed to. It is, therefore, imperative to comprehend each of these risks and find out how they arise.

There are six kinds of financial risks, *viz.*, Credit Risk, Interest Rate Risk, Liquidity Risk, Capital Risk, Market Risk, Foreign Exchange Risk and other risks. Credit risk arises when the counterparty fails to perform the repayment obligation on due date. Misjudgement of credit risks may lead to eventual fall of banks. The problems of many of the Japanese banks, failure of savings and loan association in the USA in the eighties and sub-prime mortgage lending in the USA in 2008 are cases in example. Even though the credit risk is managed by credit policy, there is a strong inter-relationship between market risk and credit risk. To the extent credit risk arises because of market risk variables, management of such risks becomes part of ALM. In a highly volatile interest rate environment loan defaults may increase, thereby deteriorating the credit quality.

Interest rate risk means risk resulting from changes in the interest income owing to interest rate fluctuations. Interest rate risk may be viewed from two different but complementary perspectives — earning sensitivity to interest rate fluctuations and price sensitivity of instruments/ products to changes in interest rate. Absence of appropriate management of interest rates is one of the primary factors for accentuating the spell of liquidity problems of banks in the recent past.

Liquidity risk is the potential inability to generate cash to cope with the decline in deposits or increase in assets. It stems out of mis-matches in the maturity patterns of asset and liability. Banks endeavour to protect their liquidity position generally by controlling mis-match between maturities of assets and liabilities, focusing on core deposits – the most permanent source of liquidity and other liquid assets. Since banks deal with assets and liabilities with varied maturity pattern and risk profile, they are expected to strike a reasonable trade-off between overtly liquid and relatively illiquid assets.

Capital risk arises from the inadequacy of capital of a bank to cope with statutory as well as business requirements. Each bank, as stated earlier, has to assess how much capital it would require to fulfill the regulatory norms. Further, banks require adequate capital to insulate themselves from the risks of business they undertake and hence, risks relating to credit, liquidity, interest rates and movement of market prices. Hence, management of capital risk is one of the important planks of the overall balance-sheet management.

Another kind of financial risk is market risk that results from adverse movement in market prices. Primarily the impact of market prices is observed in the movement of portfolio value. There exists strong relationship between interest rate risk and market risk variables. Inadvertently taken, market risk could prove to be dangerous for banks.

Another category of risk is foreign exchange risk that arises due to fluctuation in exchange rates. Such risk arises out of adverse movements of foreign exchange rate which may affect a bank's open position, either spot or forward, or a combination of the two, in any individual foreign currency.

Other risks comprise strategic risk and earnings risk. Strategic risk arises when business policy decisions, changes in economic and political environment, ineffective implementation of decisions or bank's future to cope with environmental changes negatively affect capital and earnings of a bank. Earnings risk results from inadequate diversification of a bank's earnings structure or its inability to attain a sufficient and lasting level of profitability.

◈ Measurement of Risk

The next step to ALM approach in a commercial bank is measurement of risk. For that purpose, it would be pertinent to decide what should be the risk measurement parameters that the management would need to focus on. The appropriateness of risk measurement parameters depends upon the degree of volatility in the operating environment, availability of supporting data and expertise within the bank and expected market and business developments.

The risk parameters chosen should be capable of capturing the risks to the immediate profitability as well as the risk to the long-term viability, i.e., future spreads between balance sheet value and economic capital adequacy, with changes in interest/exchange rates.

Generally, there are two major parameters which banks' across the globe employ to measure their balance sheet risks, *viz.*, risk to the Net Interest Income and Market Value of Portfolio Equity. While the former seeks to measure the risk to the immediate profits that emanate from cash flow mis-matches occurring in the accounting year, the latter measures the degree of risk arising out of the maturity mismatches in its assets and liabilities over the future years. These two parameters together attend to the short-term and long-term balance sheet risks.

There are several methods to measure interest rate risk, important being Gap method, Duration Method, Simulation and Value at Risk Method.

◈ Gap Method

Gap analysis is the most important technique used to analyse interest rate risk. It measures the difference between a bank's assets and liabilities and off-balance sheet positions which will be repriced or will mature within a pre-determined period. In other words, this technique measures the difference between the absolute value of rate sensitive assets and rate sensitive liabilities over a gapping period. However, the rate sensitivity gap can be mathematically expressed as:

RSG = RSA/RSL

Where RSG = Rate Sensitive Gap

RSA = Rate Sensitive Assets

RSL = Rate Sensitive Liabilities

Ratio of one indicates perfect match of rate sensitive assets to liabilities. If spread is positive at the beginning of the period, this perfect match protects the same even in the wake of subsequent changes in interest rates. If the ratio is greater than one, higher income is produced with increase in interest rates. Ratio of less than one produces higher losses with fall in interest rates.

Major drawback of Gap analysis is that it ignores the timing of repricing. In actual practice, repricing of assets and liabilities rarely takes place at the same time. If the gap horizon is one year, the timing difference can play havoc with measurement of interest rate risk.

◈ Duration Method

This method attempts to assess the effect of interest rate changes on the market value of assets and liabilities of the bank. The duration of an asset or liability is computed as the weighted average maturity of the resultant cash flows, the weights being the present value of the cash flows. Duration is less than the maturity for coupon bond. Greater the duration gap, higher is the interest rate risk exposure of the assets/liabilities.

This method is better than Gap method because it takes into account the timing and market value of cash flows.

◈ Simulation

Simulation model attempts to analyse the impact of changes in interest rates on the net income under different interest rate and market price scenarios. It requires forecasting the asset-liability picture under different scenarios, ascribing probabilities to them and choosing the most optimal model. This method is more dynamic and its utility depends upon the accuracy of forecasts.

◈ Value at Risk Method

In this method, attempt is made to workout depreciation/appreciation in the value of assets/liabilities because of change in interest rate with a view to indicating the trend in economic value of portfolio. Thus, for evaluating the opportunity cost/benefits carrying off-market items of balance sheet such as loan, deposits, etc., in a longer time frame, impact of interest rate changes on the value of such assets/liabilities under different interest rate scenarios will have to be calculated. This method is becoming popular because of its utility to compute the net worth of the organisation at a particular time which will be helpful in ascertaining long-term risk implications of the decisions which have already been taken or are to be taken.

◈ Enhancement of Long-term Profitability

The third stage of ALM process is identification of favourably priced assets/liabilities and off-balance sheet items so as to enhance long-term profitability for a given level of risk. In this sphere branch managers play crucial role. They should resist the temptation of accession to easily found high priced liabilities. Instead, every effort should be made to find low priced liabilities. While building up core business and creating assets and liabilities for the bank, thrust of the management has to be on client market and not on financial market. Mis-matches are usually built in client markets as assets and liabilities are created sequentially but not simultaneously and the same are managed in financial markets.

◈ Management of Risk

For effective management of financial risk of a bank, the Board of Directors should formulate overall investment policy, liquidity policy and policy regarding financing. It should also determine the acceptable level of risk in terms of the parameters chosen.

Within the framework of these policies the bank should undertake strategic planning exercise for its asset-liability. This exercise has to be done at the corporate level. It involves managing the CRR and SLR for the bank as a whole, formulating schemes having refinance facilities to have better leverage in managing the asset-liability and as a spin-off earning better profit. While formulating plan, the management should focus on products and services that are made available to branches which have special advantage like acquiring funds at low cost, providing services which do not entail funds outflow but results in additional income, schemes which provide for faster recycling of funds, instruments that provide hedge against exchange rate fluctuations, interest rate fluctuations and depreciation in value of assets.

The policies and strategies of the bank need to be reviewed from time to time keeping in view the bank's liquidity experience and developments in the business.

So as to ensure that policies and strategies are regularly reviewed and monitored, a comprehensive mechanism needs to be developed. The Board should also determine how frequently risks are to be monitored keeping in view the availability of data, fluctuations of interest and exchange rates and the pace of change of the risk profile of the bank's balance sheet.

With a view to ensuring effective management of risk, banks should set up an Asset-Liability Management Committee (ALCO) endowed with responsibility of deciding on business and risk management strategy. ALCO consisting of the bank's senior management with CEO as its head has to be responsible for drawing up strategic plans for the bank's asset-liability. It should periodically review the plans in terms of market trends, interest rate movements, deposit growth, financing needs of the bank, etc.

The ALCO has to address crucial issues like product pricing for both deposits and loans, the desired maturity profile of incremental assets and liabilities, the extent of exposure in long-dated government securities, the impact of a large business deal on the bank's risk profile, etc. In addition to monitoring the risk levels of the bank, the ALCO should review the results/progress in implementation of the decisions. It should also articulate the current interest rate view of the bank and base its decisions for the future business strategy in this regard.

For better planning and implementation, it will be advisable for banks to constitute sub-committees to handle certain important activities such as credit, investment, liability, etc. These sub-committees should comprise senior level managers of the bank. As a strategic planning exercise, committee on credit can evolve a system to evaluate, on an ongoing basis, rate sensitivity of loans, loan pricing, due date, problem, collateral, etc. The committee can draw forecasts of loan assets with respect to their quality and quantity after gathering information on fixed and variable rate loans having their approximate maturity schedules coupled with break-up on maturity rates and yields. The committee can also think of prognosticating the likely gaps and means of funding the gaps. It can also devise an internal control mechanism to evaluate quality rating of loans on a regular basis. Similarly, committee on investments can set goals on strategies, like desired mix of securities, desired mix of maturities and yield pattern and formulate broad operating functional guidelines on ceiling, limit stipulation, exceptional reporting, etc. As a strategy, instruments like ready forward REPOs, etc., can be thought of in the event of mismatch of SLR.

Strategic planning exercise should also be done at the branch level. At this level, assets and liabilities of the branch should be bifurcated into core and non-core. Reasonable estimates on assets and liabilities under core/non-core category can be made by scanning through the individual deposit accounts and advance accounts. Matching core deposits with core advances could be attempted by identifying some of their lending schemes like term loan, housing loan, consumer credit loan, vehicle loan, etc. The extent of non-core deposits could be matched with non-core discounting facilities, cheque purchase facilities, etc.

A robust mechanism needs to be built in so as to enable constant monitoring by the senior management of the risk parameters and to ensure adherence to policy limits. The frequency of monitoring the risks would be determined keeping in mind the availability of data, volatility of interest and exchange rates and the pace of change of the risk profile of the bank's balance sheet. In the current Indian scenario, banks should attempt to measure their risk once in every quarter initially. This needs to be eventually extended to monitoring risk on a monthly basis once the ALM process stabilises in the bank.

G. UTILITY OF ALM FOR COMMERCIAL BANKS

Utility of ALM for banks lies in its effectiveness to enable the management to achieve the bank's basic objective of maximising income while controlling its risk exposure and maintaining reasonable amount of liquidity in an environment of competitiveness and discontinuity. ALM allows a bank to plan for risks well ahead of the time they can prove damaging, to price its loans and deposits in a competitive manner and to structure its products in such a way as to attain optimum level of income with acceptable risk. It also facilitates the bank management to enhance the quality of its earnings by imparting stability to its interest margins. A higher quality of earnings would result into higher shareholder value which is the central focus of a risk management programme.

The ALM programme plays crucial role in ensuring adequate liquidity in the bank by assessing liquidity needs of the bank and managing simultaneously assets and liabilities of the bank.

Significance of ALM increases further when there is volatility of interest rates and forex market. Banks having freedom with respect to fixation of aggregate gap limit and cross currency position require the use of this approach so as to maintain respective net exposure in foreign currency within their risk taking capability.

It is argued that ALM programme is costly and involves direct costs in the form of cost of developing a software model, acquiring hardware and personnel cost of the ALM staff. It also involves indirect cost in terms of the time spent by ALM and the costs incurred in accessing date for ALM. However, the benefits of the ALM programme outweigh the costs involved therein. Further, costs ascribed to ALM programme can help the bank in providing better customer service and tighter monitoring of borrowed accounts.

H. PREREQUISITES TO THE EFFECTIVENESS OF ALM

ALM as an approach of managing asset-liability can help a bank in achieving the desired result if the following conditions are fulfilled:

- ALM requires dedication to acting on the basis of the contemplated future, a determination to plan and monitor regularly and systematically as an integral part of management. Importance of ALM in overcoming problems of asset-liability mis-match has to be recognised by the top management. Top management must not only have a passionate desire for planning but also back their wish by positive action. They must establish invigorating organisation culture which stimulates managers and employees at all levels of the organisation to practice the ALM approach. They should make others feel that they are interested in employing the new method for overcoming the problems of the bank arising out of the mismatch. A clear communication of the benefits of risk management would be the first step towards inculcating an organisation-wise risk culture.
- The ALM presupposes the team approach in decision-making and action. This implies involvement of all functionaries of the Bank in planning and implementation of the ALM programme for the success of the ALM programme. This is for the fact that ALM has organisation wide verification and involves in lending, borrowing, investing and trading activities in addition to financial planning and economic research activities. Thus, approach to ALM creates a congenial atmosphere for the discussion of problems and encourages the growth of creative ideas which serve as a diet needed for the successful survival of a bank. Besides, it helps the management in enlisting the support and commitment and building confidence and trust among the employees who will work harder to make it succeed.
- Visualization of the bank's vision and its articulation in terms of purpose and mission is the hallmark of ALM. Vision not only provides driving fuel, direction to the ALM strategy, but also helps the management in evaluating the practices and making prudent decisions. The bank management must also spell out the bank's objectives and strategies with respect to net interest income, loans, investments, overall risk framework and the trade-off between them. In the absence of clear objectives, it is not possible to assess a particular decision in the context of its contribution to the accomplishment of overall objectives.

- The top management should evolve a system to provide to all levels of management a thorough understanding and awareness of risk and all its parameters. The management must be equipped to undertake product planning and pricing and be familiar with the implications of their decision on the overall ALM.
- Technological and infrastructural support system in the bank would be an important prerequisite to implement effectively the ALM system. The database of the bank has to cover all operations of branches for a detailed analysis of assets and liabilities, gap between the two profitabilities and maturity of patterns of loans and deposits and for forecasting a comprehensive projection of liquidity conditions under various scenarios.

It is, therefore, essential to install an appropriate software. The software packages used must be tested and have extensive computing power to analyse the massive amount of asset/ liability data under different interest rate scenarios.

An appropriate software model would be able to correctly reflect the risk profile of the bank's products on both the asset and liability side, analyse the impact of non-standard, structured products on its risk profile.

- ALM system must continually be reviewed and its results appraised so as to conform that the standards set are being achieved. In course of the review, greater focus should be made on liquidity review because every financial transaction or commitment has implications for a bank's liquidity.

A schedule of liquidity reviews should be provided for so as to re-examine and refinance the bank's liquidity policies and practices keeping in view the bank's liquidity experience and developments in the business.

- The bank must develop human resource and craft a well thought out strategy for developing skills and competencies of its functionaries for risk definition, risk quantification and risk analysis. It should be equipped with the expertise of pricing of products on the basis of cost and risks involved and skill for forecasting and analysing the market trends.

I. ALM POLICIES AND PRACTICES OF BANKING SYSTEM IN INDIA

The maturity profile of assets and liabilities of Indian banks in general shows greater reliance on short-term deposits matched by short-term and medium term loans and long-term investments on the assets side. Indian banks began facing serious problem of mismatches in their asset-liability particularly after the economic liberalisation and globalisation leading to volatility in interest rates and foreign exchange rates. Problem of the banks deepened in 1999 when the RBI tightened their belt by bringing about income recognition, assets classification and provisioning norms straining the profitability of these banks. Emergence of new players, new instruments and new products offering competitive rates in the market following the reform process further increased banks' risks.

The above development forced commercial banks in India to take a re-look on the assets and liabilities management and put in place an appropriate system of asset-liability management.

Keeping in view the imperativeness of the adoption of the ALM system in the resolution of the problems facing the banks, the RBI vide its circular dated February 12, 1998 advised commercial banks to tighten their asset-liability system and put in place an appropriate system of asset-liability management. The following guidelines were issued by the RBI.[3]

- 20-25% of the demand deposits, including savings, should be considered as withdrawable on the demand and shown under the 1/14 day time bucket.
- Banks should study the behavioural pattern of deposits on the basis of historical trends and based on this banks should classify the deposits into volatile and core portions. While volatile portion is in the 1-14 day bucket, the core portion should be placed in the one-two year bucket. The term deposits will fit into the respective

maturity bucket, a saving bank deposit is sensitive to interest payment and repricing is possible only when RBI changes the rates while announcing the monetary policy. This time buckets should be co-terminus with the timing of the announcement of credit policy. For time deposits and certificate of deposits, the account should be distributed to different buckets on the basis of remaining maturity.

- NPA, net of provisions, should be shown under the two to five-year bucket and sub-standard assets in one to two-year bucket.
- Banks should study the behavioural and seasonal pattern of drawal in credit, based on outstanding, the core and volatile portion should be identified. While the volatile portion could be shown as an outflow of inflow, the core portion may be shown under the one or two years' bucket time. For cash credit, overdrafts and loan repayable on demand and term, repricing is needed when PLR is changed.
- Excess balance over the required CRR and SLR should be shown under 1-14 day bucket. The statutory CRR balances may be distributed under various time buckets corresponding to the DTL placed in their buckets with a time lag of 14 days.
- For borrowing on floating rate, the amount should be distributed to the appropriate bucket which refers to the repricing date while for the zero campus, it should be distributed to the maturity bucket relating to the matter of April and October, since the reprice is done only when RBI changes rates.

The Reserve Bank however, stated that due to the diversity and varying size of balance sheet items between banks, it may neither be possible nor may it be necessary to adopt a uniform risks management system. The design of risk management framework, as per the directive, should, therefore, be oriented towards the bank's own requirements dictated by the size and complexity of business, risk philosophy, market perception and the existing level of capital. In other words, banks can evolve their own systems compatible with the type and size of operations as well as risk perception. While doing so, banks may critically evaluate their existing risk management in the light of the guidelines issued by the Reserve Bank and put in place a proper system for covering the existing deficiencies and requisite upgradation. The Reserve Bank advised banks to identify the gaps in the existing risk management practices and the policies and strategies for complying with guidelines.

The RBI advised banks in February, 1999 to put in place an ALM system, effective April 1, 1999 and set up internal Asset-Liability Management Committee (ALCos) at the top management level to oversee its implementation. Banks were expected to cover at least 60 per cent of their liabilities and assets in the interim and 100 per cent of their business by April 1, 2000. The Reserve Bank also released ALM system guidelines in January, 2000 for all India term-lending and refinancing institutions, effective from April 1, 2000. As per the guidelines, banks and such institutions were directed to prepare statements on liquidity gaps and interest rate sensitivity at specified periodic intervals.[4]

During the period 2004-07, commercial banks in India were facing serious asset-liability mis-match, for the fact that while more and more bank credits have been going for infrastructure lending and commercial real estate financing, the liability structure of the banks is getting shorter and shorter due to heavy reliance on bulk deposits. Most of the bulk deposits have been from insurance companies, money market mutual funds, state governments and large corporates and these deposits were mopped up for tenures upto a year by offering rates upto 11.4 per cent. Between December 31, 2006 and March 2, 2007, aggregate deposits went up by ₹ 1.04 lakh crore. Time deposits during the same period rose by over ₹ 90,000 crore. The bulk deposits accounted for about 40-45 per cent of the deposits of the banks. The problem of mismatch was compounded by the fact that both on assets and liabilities sides there were rigidities in the absence of tradeable assets and liabilities instruments.

So as to rectify this malady, public sectors banks began capping their bulk deposit acceptances. The caps were in the range of 30-35 per cent of their net liabilities.[5] The cap imposed, it is believed, would take care of any impact on costs.

So as to ensure that banks put in place a sound system of asset-liability management and thereby instill more discipline among banks in managing their liquidity, the RBI issued the following new guidelines on September, 2007.[6]

- Banks were not permitted to have a negative gap in their funds outflows for the next day. Negative gap refers to a mismatch in which interest-sensitive liabilities exceed interest-sensitive assets.
- Banks must adopt a more granular approach to measurement of liquidity risk by splitting the first time bucket of 1-14 days in the statement of structural liability into three times buckets-next days, 2-7 days and 8-14 days. The net cumulative negative mismatches during the next day, 2-7 days, 8-14 days and 15-28 days should not exceed 5 per cent, 10 per cent, 15 per cent and 20 per cent of the cumulative cash outflow in the respective buckets in order to recognize the cumulative impact on liquidity.
- The basic idea was that in short duration, bank's outflow should not be more than inflow. This means, for instance, in the first bucket, next day- the outflow should not be more than 5 percent of the expected inflow.
- Banks were required to report this data to the RBI on fortnightly basis.
- Banks could finance the gap from call money market, bills rediscounting, repos and deployment of foreign currency resources after conversion into rupees.
- The new norms were implemented from 1st January, 2008.

The analysis of the maturity profile of long-term assets and liabilities indicates that at the aggregate level, the long-term assets are financed by short-term liabilities. The ALM calculated as long-term assets minus long-term liabilities never turned out to be negative during the recent years implying that the higher growth observed in the long-term loan segment is leading to asset-liability mismatches in the banking sector.

The maturity profile-wise composition of assets and liabilities indicates that almost half of the total deposits and borrowings of the banking sector were short-term as at end-March 2012 (Table 18.1). However, almost one-fourth of the total loans and advances and more than half of the total investments were long-term during the same period. There was no significant shift in the maturity profile-wise composition of assets and liabilities of the banking sector in 2010-11 over the previous year indicating the persistence of asset-liability mismatches (Table 18.1)

The persistent mismatch in the average maturity of assets with that of liabilities has been a concern for Indian banking sector in recent years. The proportion of short-term liabilities registered an increase from 2008 onwards. On the other hand, the proportion of short-term assets in total assets exhibited a declining trend from 2008 onwards.

Almost 20 per cent of the long-term assets of the Indian banking sector were financed by short-term liabilities in 2010-11.

The percentage of long-term assets financed by short-term liabilities witnessed a marginal decline over the previous year (Table 18.2).

On the financing side, almost 23 per cent of short-term liabilities were used to finance almost 20 per cent of long-term assets in the banking sector. The percentage share of short-term liabilities used to finance long-term assets also witnessed a marginal decline in 2010-11 over the previous year. (Table 18.2)

TABLE 18.1: Maturity Profile of Select Liabilities/Assets of Commercial Banks in India
(As at end-March)

(per cent to total and under each item)

Liabilities/Assets	2010	2011	2012
I. Deposits			
(*a*) upto 1 year	49.4	48.5	50.0
(*b*) over 1 year and upto 3 years	29.4	30.3	26.3
(*c*) over 3 years	21.2	21.1	23.7
II. Borrowings			
(*a*) upto 1 year	44.2	46.2	52.8
(*b*) over 1 year and upto 3 years	15.3	13.9	11.7
(*c*) over 3 years	40.5	40.0	35.7
III. Loans and Advances			
(*a*) upto 1 year	38.9	37.8	35.9
(*b*) over 1 year and upto 3 years	33.3	35.4	36.3
(*c*) over 3 years	27.8	26.8	27.8
IV. Investments			
(*a*) upto 1 year	28.1	27.6	30.4
(*b*) Over 1 year and upto 3 years	14.4	15.0	13.7
(*c*) over 3 years	57.5	57.3	55.9

Source: RBI report on Trend and Progress of Banking in India, 2010-11.

TABLE 18.2:Asset-Liabilities mismatches in the Indian Banking Sector

(Per cent)

Bank Group	Long-term Assets Financed by Short-term liabilities		Per cent of Short-term Liabilities used to finance long-term assets	
	2009-10	2010-11	2009-10	2010-11
1. Public Sector banks	22.6	22.0	28.5	27.9
2. Private Sector Banks	14.4	15.7	19.6	21.0
3. Foreign banks	–16.2	–25.2	–6.4	–9.0
All Scheduled banks	19.7	19.5	23.4	23.3

Source: RBI Report on Trend and Progress of Banking in India, 2010-11.

Asset-liability mismatch problem has been accentuated during the last two years (2009-2011). One of the major factors responsible for this crisis has been that banks have been lending more than what they get as deposits. The incremental credit-deposit ratio (ICDR) of the banking sector was at 1.2 per cent as at the end of December 2010, up from 58 per cent in the corresponding period of the previous year.[7] The high ICDR was mainly on account of lower deposit growth as compared to credit growth. While credit growth was a little over 24 per cent during 2009-10, deposit growth has been 16 per cent. The ICDR indicates that Indian banks have been lending more than their deposit. For instance, lending ₹ 102 against the maximum amount of deposit of ₹ 70 (after setting aside ₹ 30 in the form of CRR and SLR). According to Bank chiefs, banks have been using excess liquidity and alternative sources to fund their credit growth.[8] However, the RBI's main anxiety is whether banks were using daily borrowings to fund their credit growth, which can create a systematic problem in future. This is why the RBI has been pushing banks to increase the pace of deposit growth and find other long-term resources to fund their business.

Another reason for the existing asset-liability mismatch problem was a shift in deposit liabilities of the PSBs during 2009-10 towards the short-term end of the maturity spectrum alongside a shift in their loans and investments towards the long-term end. In 2009-10, there was a shift towards the short (upto 1 year) and medium-term (over one and upto three years) deposits mobilised by banks. As a result, there was a decline in the share of deposits with long-term maturity of over three years. While the maturity distribution of loans and advances remained largely unchanged in 2009-10, there was a shift in favour of long-term investments by banks.[9]

Interestingly, new private sector banks, which normally relied heavily on short-term deposits, exhibied a shift to favour of medium and long-term deposits in 2009-10, while their loans moved closer towards the short-term end of the spectrum.[10]

The problem of mismatches is going to bc deepened further in future. While deposit tenures are becoming shorter due to low interest rates, there is the huge pipeline of sanctions, on which banks are sitting so far, mostly for core sector projects, will now get disbursed. The RBI feels banks are heading for deep trouble if corrective steps are not taken immediately. The RBI has, therefore, asked banks to do a good job on asset and liability management, as also liquidity, and not go over board on duly providing funds.[11]

J. CONCLUSIONS

ALM is an integrated approach towards financial management conditioned to simultaneous decision-making with respect to types and size of financial assets and liabilities, their mix and volume so as to insulate the spread from moving in adverse direction. The secret of effective banking in deregulated and competitive environment hinges essentially on matching of assets and liabilities in terms of rate and maturity with a view to deriving optimal yield. ALM has to be closely integrated with business strategy of the bank as the latter has bearing upon the risk profile of the bank.

The basic function of the ALM is to guide the management in establishing optimal match between the assets and liabilities of the bank in such a way as to maximise its net income and minimise the market risks.

ALM as a strategic approach to measure, monitor and manage the financial risk of a bank involves the following steps:

(*i*) Identification of risk,

(*ii*) Measurement and determination of risk,

(*iii*) Enhancement of long-term profitability for a given level of risk,

(*iv*) Management of risk.

Consequent upon the new economic policy of the Government and concomitant competitiveness, banks in India, facing serious problem of mismatches in their asset-liability due to volatility in interest rates and foreign exchange rates, felt the necessity of adopting the ALM approach to withstand the risks associated with management of assets and liabilities. The RBI has also advised banks to tighten their asset - liability management and put in place an appropriate system of asset - liability management. The RBI has also issued guidelines in this respect. In recent years, problem of asset-liability mismatch in Indian banking system has deepened for various reasons.

KEY TERMS

- 3-6-3 Banking
- Capital risk
- Duration method
- Earnings risk
- Foreign exchange risk
- Gap method
- Incremental credit-deposit ratio
- Liquidity risk
- Market risk
- Savings & Loan Associations
- Strategic risk
- Value at risk method

DISCUSSION QUESTIONS

1. Discuss the concept of asset-liability management in banking system. Why is this concept gaining importance across the world?
2. Discuss the prime function of asset-liability management in a bank.
3. Outline the scope of asset-liability management of a bank.
4. What are the different kinds of risks, which commercial banks confront? Discuss various methods of measuring interest rate risk.
5. What are the major pre-requisites to the effective asset-liability management?
6. Bring out critical analysis of current asset-liability management policies and practices in banking system in India.
7. Why is commercial banks in India facing serious crisis of asset-liability mismtach in recent years?

REFERENCES

1. Report on Trend and Progress of Banking in India, 1999-2000.
2. The Journal of Indian Institute of Bankers, 1997.
3. S. Kannon, Relevance and Importance of Asset-Liability Management in Banks, The Journal of the Indian Institute of Bankers, 1999.
4. RBI Annual Report, 1999-2000.
5. Business Line, March 21, 2007.
6. Economic Times, September 6, 2007.
7. Business Standard, February 8, 2011.
8. Business Standard, January 25, 2011.
9. RBI Report on Trend and Progress of Banking in India, 2009-10, p. 67.
10. *Ibid*.
11. Business Standard, January 25, 2011.

Management of Non-performing Assets (NPAs) in Commercial Banks

Chapter 19

Learning Objectives:

The present chapter attempts to:

- Provide conceptual understanding of NPAs.
- Examine the present state of NPAs in Indian commercial banks.
- Assess the impact of priority sector advances on NPAs.
- Sensitize to the initiatives taken by the Government and the RBI.

Chapter Outline:

- Epilogue
- Conceptual exposition of NPAs.
- NPAs in Indian commercial banks.
- NPAs in priority sector advances
- Steps taken by the Government and the RBI.
- Impact of steps taken by the Government and the RBI on NPAs.
- Future challenges
- Conclusions.

A. EPILOGUE

Non-performing assets, also known as non-productive assets (NPAS), constitute integral part of banks' operations. A bank gives out money upfront and earns income over time on the promise of a borrower to repay. When loans are not repaid, the bank loses both its income stream, as well as its capital. The level of non-performing loans is recognised as a critical indicator for assessing banks' credit risk, asset quality and efficiency in allocation of resources to productive sectors.

The most calamitous problem facing commercial banks all over the world in recent times is spiralling non-performing assets which are affecting their viability and solvency and thus posing challenge to their ultimate survival. NPAs adversely affect lending activity of banks as non-recovery of loan instalments as also interest on the loan portfolio negates the effectiveness of credit-dispensation process. Non-recovery of loans also hurts the profitability of banks. Besides, banks with high level of NPAs have to carry more owned funds by way of capital and create reserves and provisions and to provide cushion for the loan losses.

The solvency crisis of financial systems, such as the American Savings and Loan crisis in the 1980s, the Nordic banking crisis at the beginning of 1990s and more recently, the banking sector problems in Japan and Turkey and of late sub prime crisis in the USA have, in large measure, been a consequence of accumulation of problem loans overtime.

NPAs, thus, make two-pronged attack on the bottom-lines of commercial banks; one, interest applied on such assets is not taken into account because such interest is to be taken into account only on its realisation unlike interest on performing assets which is taken into account on accrual basis; two, banks have to make provisions on NPAs from out of the income earned by them on performing assets.

Persistently high level of NPAs in loan portfolio of banks make them fragile, leading ultimately *to* their failure. This will shake confidence both of domestic and global investors in the banking system which will have multiplier effect, bringing disaster in the economy.

Thus, managing bad loans and keeping them at the lowest possible level has become a keyword for the banking industry in recent years which is critical for banks. It may be noted at this juncture that world class banks do not have NPAs of over 2% of the total portfolio.[1] An NPA level of over 5% is indicator of poor quality of loan portfolio. With growing competition and shrinking spreads, banks should strive to keep NPAs much below the level of 10% to make net earnings necessary for their survival and growth. Thus, the most critical condition for bringing about an improvement in the profitability of banks is reduction in the level of NPAs. In fact, it is a pre-condition for the stability of the financial system.

B. CONCEPTUAL EXPOSITION OF NON-PERFORMING ASSETS (ADVANCES)

The RBI introduced in 1985-86 the Health Code System for commercial banks advising them to recognise income only on realization basis, initially in respect of accounts under Health Code Nos. 6 and above, subsequently for those under Health Code No. 5 also. While the Health Code classification was serving as a useful monitoring and Management Information Mechanism, absence of a transparent, objective and uniform yardstick for measurement of problem (sticky) advances was the major drawback of this system.

In order to ensure greater transparency in the borrowal accounts and to reflect actual health of banks in their balance sheets, the RBI introduced prudential regulations pertaining to income recognition, asset classification and provisioning recommended by Narasimhan Committee with certain modifications in a phased manner over a three-year period beginning 1992-93. These regulations have put in place objective criteria for asset classification, provisioning and recognition of income which was lacking hitherto. This change has brought in necessary quantification and objectivity into the determination of NPAs. Thus, as per the asset classification, "an asset (advance) is considered as non-performing in case interest or instalments of principal or both remain unpaid for more than two quarters and if it has come past due, *i.e.*, 30 days after the due date."

An advance is to be classified as 'sub-standard' if it remains NPAs upto a period of two years and will be classified as 'Doubtful' if it remains NPA for more than two years (which was reduced to 18 months from the year ending 31st March, 2001). An account will be classified as 'loss' without any waiting period where the dues are considered uncollectible or only marginally collectible.

In order to move towards international best practices and impart greater transparency, it was decided by the RBI to introduce classification of loans as non-performing when interest and/or instalments of principal remain overdue for a period of more than 90 days from the year ending March 31, 2004.[2]

C. NPAs IN INDIAN COMMERCIAL BANKS

NPAs came into Indian financial systems consequent upon introduction of Prudential Accounting Norms. An era of treating Profits (even unrealized) was changed to providing for expected loss. Days of 'counting the chickens before the eggs hatch' came to an end.[3] However, non performing loans did exist even before the introduction of present prudential norms. According to the RBI study,[4] the proportion of problem loans (sticky loans) of PSBs to their gross advances stood at 17.91 per cent as on March 31, 1989. This soared to 23.5 per cent as on March 31, 1994. (Table 19.1). Reasons for the high level of NPAS are given below:

◈ Originating Factors

According to the RBI study, dues to the banking sector are generally related to the performance of the unit/industrial segment. In a few cases the cause of NPA has been due to internal factors of the banks such as weak appraisal or follow-up loans but more often than not, it is due to factors such as management inefficiency of borrowal units, obsolescence, lack of demand, non-availability of inputs, environmental factors, etc. Wherever the unit/segment is doing well the credit relationship is generally maintained except in cases of willful default/ misappropriation/diversion of funds. The problems to the unit/segment arising out of various internal/external factors were felt to be originating point for NPAs in banks.[5]

◈ Internal Factors

Among the internal factors responsible for high level of NPAs in Indian commercial banks, the most important ones have been project appraisal deficiencies regarding technical feasibility, economic viability and project management deficiencies in regard to implementation, production, labour, marketing, financial and administrative matters.

The culture of Indian banking system in respect of permitting excess or irregular drawings to some extent even during the processing stage has also contributed to poor quality of loans and NPAs. Further, PSBs have had the culture of consuming longer time even more than a year in appraising loan proposals.[6] As per the new norms if interest is not paid for two quarters, the advance is classified as NPA. If proposal for genuine enhancement remains pending for more than six months and the borrower has already gone ahead with implementing his projected plan, the account becomes irregular for more than six months even if higher credit assistance was deserving on merits.

There has been large number of cases of camouflaging irregularities by routinely rescheduling repayment or granting ad hoc facilities so as to avoid slippage of loans accounts into NPAs. Since this practice of ever greening cannot be continued indefinitely, loan accounts partook the character of NPAs.

Weak credit appraisal, non-compliance to lending norms and willful default as also ineffective credit monitoring and follow-up mechanism of the commercial banks have also contributed to slippage of standard loans into bad loans. In India greater focus is made on enhanced recovery of NPAs which may be effective to contain NPAs in the short run but very little efforts are made to follow-up once the loan is sanctioned. No serious efforts are made to study loan portfolio on multiple dimensions to monitor the aggregate exposure of the bank to industries, groups, regions, rating, classes, etc. As a result, the bank lacks any direction which can be pursued at an individual loan level. Further, collection machinery has been found lax in most of the banks in India.

Diversion of funds mostly for expansion/diversification/modernisation, and taking up new projects and for helping/promoting associated concerns have been reported to be the single most prominent reason for high level of NPAs.

The wide prevalent practice among commercial banks in India of providing working capital facility subject to annual renewal with or without enhancement has also been responsible for persistently high level of NPAs. If existing company, which was performing well in the past, turns sick due to its inability to face competition or due to the changing economic and policy environment or sometimes due to inefficient management, there is no scope for the bank to withdraw the facility unless the promoters decide to close down the company to merge it with some healthy unit. The bank finds it difficult to lay hands on the security against which working capital facility was given because of inadequate legal measures.

◈ External Factors

An important reason for the bulging of NPAs was the 'euphoria' generated with liberalisation, a dream of globalisation led to huge investments which unfortunately could not be utilised due to hesitant liberalisation policies.[7] Dominance of traditional industries in credit portfolios, industrial sickness, labour problems, the overall economic slow down-global as well as domestic-particularly in industrial sector have until recently adversely affected the bottom line of borrowal units and their capacity to service the debt leading to slippage of standard asset into NPA.

Among other external factors, the RBI study[8] noted that non-availability of raw materials, power shortage, transport bottlenecks, financial bottlenecks, change in Government policy, natural calamities, industrial sickness, increase in import costs, increase in overhead costs, market saturation, product obsolescence, fall in demand and others were responsible for weak performance in 48% of units assisted by the banks resulting into advances given to them turning bad.

Ineffective legal system is the most important factor contributing to enormously high level of NPAs in Indian commercial banks. Antiquated defaulter friendly legal system, extremely slow judicial system, and dismal record of enforcement machineries have also contributed significantly to high level of NPAs in India.

Commenting on the current legal system of the country, FITCHIBCA, an international rating agency, observed that "the Indian Legal System is sympathetic towards the borrowers and works against the banks' interest. Despite most of their loans being backed by security, banks are unable to enforce their claims on the collateral when the loans turn non-performing and therefore, loans recoveries have been insignificant"- Pannir Selvam Committee of IBA on NPAs clearly brought out that it takes decades for courts to decide cases and even after decrees are obtained, execution of decrees is virtually an impossible task. Languishing of thousands of cases in courts for decades is sad reflection of the speed of recoveries through the suit filing.

According to the RBI study, ineffectiveness of suit filing and recovery measures in the prescribed procedure for recovery of debts due to banks has resulted in blocking significant portion of their funds in unproductive assets, the value of which deteriorated with the passage of time. The multiple litigation opportunities available to the borrowal units delaying the verdicts/ enforcement, courts being burdened, as they are, with heavy work coupled with tardy decision-making process in the banks, have rendered legal process less useful.

Pending of significantly large number of suits speaks volumes about the recoveries made through the suit filing. In some cases, suits were pending for 15 to 20 years, but no progress was made in the suit. Out of all the suit filed cases of ₹ 1 crore and above, studied by RBI in 15 banks, there was only one case in which the suit filing was taken to the logical end.

As at June end, 1998, the PSBs had as much as 5.12 lakh suits involving an amount of about ₹ 12,000 crores pending before the courts.[9] As regards the time taken for disposal of suits filed by the banks, RBI study reveals that it took many years, in many cases more than a decade for the courts to settle the suits. Even after passing of court order, due to the multiple litigation opportunities, long-time is taken for settlement of the cases.

The legal process gets further elongated/complex in cases where legal actions are either delayed or the matter comes under the purview of the Board for Industrial and Financial Reconstruction (BIFR) and the Appellate Authority for Industrial and Financial Reconstruction (AAIFR). BIFR generally takes very long time to decide the case and approve rehabilitation package in case of sick units.

It is also interesting to note from the RBI study that Debt Recovery Tribunals (DRT) has not been effective. In fact, it has failed to achieve the declared objective of disposal of cases within six months in speedy recovery of advances. As at the end June, 1997, out of total number of 11,700 cases filed and transferred to DRTs involving ₹ 8,866.67 crores, only 1,045 cases had been decided and a meagre amount of ₹ 178.08 crores was realised as on June 30,1999.[10]

In the present Indian work culture, flouting rules, regulations and interpretation of rules to delay action or deny sanction have become very common. There are a number of cases of wrong claims of Government agencies or references to courts by filing legal action with the objective of getting direction of courts rather than making decision. This has led to growth of NPAs in the banks' loan portfolio.

The long drawn legal process not only encourages the incidence of NPAs but also prolongs their existence by placing a premium on default.

It is important to realize the havoc wrecked by the perennial and willful defaulters on the financial system. Their acts have raised the cost of credit, made bankers more risk averse and squeezed decent small and medium enterprise from accessing competitive credit. They have debased the banking system and, in the process, penalised the good borrowers. They need to be taken to task.

In view of its highly efficient legal system and regulatory framework, banks in Singapore have been rated as the lowest risk banks among banks of Asian countries.

◈ Recent Trends

However, in recent years, particularly after economic reforms, decline in proportion of gross NPAs to gross advances as also of net NPAs to net advances of all the Scheduled commercial banks was noticeable. Thus, it may be glanced from Table 19.1 that although both gross NPAs and net NPAs in absolute terms surged during 1997-2012, these increases have been at lower rate in correspondence with gross and net advances leading to fall in their respective share from 15.7% to 3.10% and from 8.1% to 1.40% respectively. Thus, there has been improvement in the asset quality of the banks. This seems to be the result of several policy measures taken by the Reserve Bank in conjunction with the Government to contain the NPAs of banks. In fact, the enactment of the Securitization and Reconstruction of Financial Assets and Enforcement of Security Interest (SARFAESI) Act and other steps taken by the Government and the RBI provided a significant impetus to banks to ensure sustained recovery and a menu of options to reduce level of NPAs.[11] An improved industrial climate also contributed to this state of affairs.

Interestingly, during the crisis year 2008-09, the gross NPA ratio remained unchanged for Indian banks. However, during 2009-10, both the gross NPA and net NPA of SCBs showed a rise (Table 19.1) clearly indicating greater defaults in repayment of banks' loans by the borrowers.

During 2011-12, both gross and net NPAs increased substantially. The spurt in NPAs could be attributed to the slowdown prevailing in the domestic economy as well as inadequate appraisal and monitoring of credit proposals.

It is noteworthy that the growth in NPAs of Indian banks has largely followed a lagged cyclical pattern with regard to credit growth. The empirical analysis taking growth rates of gross advances and gross NPAs since June 2000 indicated that NPA growth follows credit growth with a lag of two years. The co-efficients of credit growth were positive and statistically significant from the second lag onwards reflecting that credit growth fed into growth in NPAs in a lagged manner. This clearly indicates that asset quality can get compromised during periods of high credit growth which can result in the creation of non-performing assets for banks in the later years.[12]

Group-wise analysis of NPAs reveals that in case of Public sector banks, NPAs as percentage of gross advances declined significantly from 17.8 per cent in 1997 to 2.23 per cent in 2010. Likewise, net NPAs to net advances decreased from 9.2 per cent to 1.09 per cent during the corresponding years. This is due to persistent recovery set up coupled with close monitoring of the advances. Perceptible decline in the ratio of gross NPAs and net NPAs measured as percentage to advances was noticeable in case of the old private sector banks.

TABLE 19.1: Gross and Net NPAs of different Categories of Commercial Banks in India

(Amount in ₹ crore)

Bank Groups/ Years	Gross NPAs	Gross NPAs as % of gross advances	Net NPAs	Net NPAs as % of net advances
Scheduled Commercial Banks				
1997	473.00	15.7	22,340	8.1
2001	63,883	11.40	32,468	6.2
2005	58,300	5.20	21,441	2.0
2006	51,815	3.50	18,529	1.2
2007	50,486	2.50	20,101	1.0
2008	56,435	2.30	24,733	1.0
2009	68,328	2.25	31,564	1.05
2010	84,747	2.39	39,126	1.11
2011	97,922	2.25	41,813	0.97
2012	1,42,300	3.10	64,900	1.40
Public Sector Banks				
1997	43,577	17.8	20,285	9.2
2001	54,773	12.4	27,969	6.7
2005	47,325	6.0	16,642	2.7
2006	42,106	3.7	14,560	1.3
2007	38,968	2.4	15,145	1.1
2008	40,595	2.2	17,836	1.0
2009	44,957	2.0	21,155	0.94
2010	54,926	2.19	29,644	1.09
2011	74,614	2.23	36.071	1.09
2012	1,17,200	3.30	59,100	1.70
Private Sector Banks				
1997	2,325	10.7	1,385	6.6
2001	4,420	11.1	2,770	7.3

Bank Groups/ Years	Gross NPAs	Gross NPAs as % of gross advances	Net NPAs	Net NPAs as % of net advances
2005	4,206	6.0	1,859	2.7
2006	3,740	4.6	1,367	1.6
2007	2,969	3.1	891	1.0
2008	2,557	2.30	740	0.70
2009	3,072	2.36	1,159	0.90
2010	2,833	2.32	1,271	1.0
2011	18,420	2.25	4,430	0.56
2012	18,700	2.10	4,400	0.50
New Private Sector Banks				
1997	2.7	2.6	154	2.0
2001	1617	5.2	929	3.1
2005	1576	3.6	2,295	1.7
2006	4,336	1.8	1,793	0.8
2007	6,287	1.9	3,136	1.0
2008	10,426	2.5	4,906	1.2
2009	13,854	2.87	6,252	1.08
2010	14,541	2.83	5,068	0.56
2012	14,500	2.20	3,000	0.50
Old Private Sector Banks				
1997	2,325	10.7	1,385	6.6
2001	4,420	11.1	2,770	7.3
2005	4,206	6.0	1,859	2.7
2006	3,740	4.6	1,367	1.6
2007	2,969	3.1	891	1.0
2008	2,557	2.30	740	0.70
2009	3,072	2.36	1,159	0.90
2010	3,623	2.32	1,137	0.83
2011	3,699	1.97	982	0.53
2012	4,200	1.80	1,300	0.60
Foreign Banks				
1997	1,181	4.3	516	1.9
2001	2,616	7.0	844	2.4
2005	2,192	6.8	785	1.8
2006	1,928	1.9	807	0.8
2007	2,233	1.80	913	0.9
2008	2,664	1.80	1,250	1.20
2009	6,444	3.80	2,996	1.05
2010	9,205	4.29	2,975	1.82
2011	5,068	2.54	1,312	0.67
2012	6,200	2.60	1,400	0.60

Source: RBI reports on Trend and Progress of Banking in India.

As regards the new private sector banks, it may be noted from the Table that these banks had relatively lower NPAs during the initial years of operations. But as the banks expanded their operations, quality of their advances deteriorated. Thus, in 1997 gross NPAs of new private banks to their advance stood at 2.6 per cent, the lowest among all categories of banks. However, it tended to rise remarkably in the subsequent years to reach an all time high level of 8.9 per cent in 2002, reflecting increase in defaulters. Substantial progress was, however, witnessed during the last four years as is reflected in the steep fall in the ratio of NPAs to advances from 8.9 per cent in 2002 to 1.0 per cent during 2007, showing aggressive efforts made to monitor the advances and recover the same. However there was a rise in both gross and net NPAs during the last three years.

Foreign banks operating in India do not seem to be as serious in sanctioning and monitoring advances in the past as they are today. As a result, gross NPAs of these banks to their total advances initially shot up from 4.3 per cent in 1997 to 7.0 per cent in 2000. But the same tended to decline persistently to touch an all time low level of 1.8 per cent in 2008. There was increase on the gross and net NPAs of foreign banks during 2009-10.

Among bank groups, the new private sector banks have the lowest NPAs followed by foreign banks in India, old private banks and public sector banks.

Apart from the increase in NPA ratio, there was also deterioration in the distribution nof SCBs between 2009 and 2012 as was evident from an increase in the percentage of loss making and doubtful assets of SCBs, which represented the lower end of the NPA spectrum (Table 19.2). The shift in the distribution of NPAs in favour of doubtful and loss making assets was more prominent in the case of foreign and new private sector banks as compared to public sector banks.

The deterioration in asset quality was more pronounced in the case of the PSBs. During 2011-12, the gross NPAs of the PSBs increased at a higher rate as compared with the growth rate of NPAs at a system level. It is most disturbing to note that GNPAs of the PSBs, which account for about 80 per cent of the banking system, grew by over ₹ 43,000 crore during 2011-12 compared to only ₹ 320 crore in the case of private sector banks. This enormous difference is a reflection of better credit underwriting norms, recovery and upgradations.

TABLE 19.2: Classification of Loan Assets — Bank Groupwise

(Percentage to total advances)

Bank group	Year	Standard Assets	Sub-standard Assets	Doubtful Assets	Loss-making Assets
1. Public sector banks	2009	97.99	0.90	0.92	0.19
-	2010	97.81	1.05	0.93	0.21
	2011	97.77	1.04	0.99	019
	2012	97.0	1.60	1.20	0.20
1.1 Nationalised Banks	2009	98.25	0.72	0.87	0.16
	2010	98.05	0.99	0.81	0.15
	2011	98.11	0.93	0.83	0.14
	2012	98.10	0.90	0.80	0.10
1.2 SBI group	2009	97.44	1.27	1.03	0.25
	2010	97.30	1.18	1.19	0.33
	2011	97.00	1.31	1.37	0.32
	2012	95.9	1.90	1.90	0.30
2. Private Sector Banks	2009	97.10	1.81	0.86	0.23
	2010	97.27	1.37	1.02	0.34
	2011	97.76	0.56	1.33	0.35
	2012	98.10	0.50	1.10	0.30

Bank group	Year	Standard Assets	Sub-standard Assets	Doubtful Assets	Loss-making Assets
2.1 Old Private sector banks	2009	97.64	1.02	1.02	0.32
	2010	97.69	0.89	1.05	0.37
	2011	98.03	0.67	0.97	0.33
	2012	98.20	0.80	0.70	0.30
2.2 New Private sector banks	2009	96.94	2.04	0.82	0.21
	2010	97.13	1.53	1.02	0.33
	2011	97.68	0.52	1.44	0.36
	2012	97.7	0.50	1.40	0.40
3. Foreign banks	2009	95.70	3.46	0.59	0.25
	2010	95.74	2.94	0.86	0.45
	2011	97.46	0.94	1.06	0.55
	2012	97.30	0.90	0.90	0.80
Scheduled commercial banks	2009	97.69	1.22	0,89	0.20
	2010	97.61	1.20	0.94	0.24
	2011	97.75	0.95	1.06	0.24
	2012	97.20	1.30	1.20	0.20

Source: DSB Returns (BSA) submitted by respective banks.

D. NPAs IN PRIORITY SECTOR ADVANCES

There is a general perception that the prescription of 40 per cent of the net bank credit to the priority sector has led to higher level of NPAs because credit to these sectors is becoming sticky. However, the actual state of affairs existing till 2005 did not hold true (19.3). But the trend reversed thereafter when NPAs in priority sector were higher as compared to non-priority sector.

It is interesting to note that priority sector NPAs, which declined in 2008-09 due to implementation of the Agriculture Debt Waiver and Relief Scheme, 2008, witnessed an increasing trend thereafter. In 2010-11, the PSBs registered higher increase in agricultural NPA ratio as compared with the private sector banks.

Likewise, weaker sections NPAs and weaker sections advances also witnessed an increase in the PSBs and private sector banks.[13]

E. SUGGESTIONS TO CONTAIN NPAs OF COMMERCIAL BANK IN INDIA

It is generally argued that in view of lower percentage of advances to GDP and lower economic cost of bad loans as compared to those in Tiger economies, the impact of NPAs on the Indian economy is not that alarming as witnessed recently in the East African Region, Japan, USA and Euro Zone facing the crisis. This should, however, not lull the Indian bankers and RBI into sense of complacency because of growing competitiveness in the financial sector consequent upon globalisation of Indian economy, increasing inflatiionary pressures and rising interest rates.

Mere fact that even reduced level of NPAs of the Indian banks is still higher as compared to developed county standards of around 2 per cent warrants continued remedial actions. As

TABLE 19.3: Sector-wise NPAs in Indian Commercial Banks
(As on March 31)

(Percentages)

Bank Group	1996		1997		1998		1999		2000		2001		2002		2003	
	P	NP	P	NP	P	NP	P	NP	P	NP	P	NP	P	NP	P	NP
Public Sector Banks	51.8	48.2	50.7	49.3	49.4	50.6	46.7	53.3	46.5	53.5	48.5	51.5	44.5	55.5	47.2	52.78
Old Private Sector Banks	—	—	—	—	—	—	—	—	—	—	35.1	64.9	9.4	90.5	38. 0	62.0
New Private Sector Banks	—	—	—	—	—	—	—	—	—	—	15.2	84. 8	22.8	77. 2	9.5	90.5

Bank Group	2004		2005		2006		2007		2008		2009		2010		2011	
	P	NP	P	NP	P	NP	P	NP	P	NP	P	NP	P	NP	P	NP
Public Sector Banks	48.5	51.5	49.5	50.5	50.3	49.7	59.4	40.6	63.0	37.0	55.2	44.8	53.8	46.2	58.1	41.9
Old Private Sector Banks	41.9	58.1	42.1	57.9	43.9	56.1	47.7	52.3	52.5	47.5	40.2	59.8	44.7	55.3	43.3	56.7
New Private Sector Banks	11.4	86.6	9.5	90.5	15.1	84.9	23.4	76.6	20.0	80.0	17.4	82.6	23.1	76.9	22.6	77.4

Note: P = Priority Sector
NP= Non-Priority Sector

Source: *Reports on Trend and Progress of Banking in India for relevant years.*

such, strategic measures both at micro and macro levels — along the following lines have to be taken to effectively contain the magnitude of NPAs in the loan portfolio of the banks.

The approach to NPA management by the banks has to be multi-pronged, necessitating varied strategies suited to different stages of the passage of credit facility.

So as to reduce the level of NPAs in the loan portfolio, every commercial bank has to embark upon strategic plan to prevent the occurrence of the NPAs and stoppage of health accounts into bad loans. This calls for crystal clear policy guidelines in respect of credit appraisal and monitoring on the one hand, and streamlining credit assessment and supervision procedures and strengthening and the appraisal and monitoring cell, on the other.

Existing credit evaluation process is not adequate and focused and the staff handling the job is not endowed with required skills and expertise. It is, therefore, imperative to bring about radical change in credit evaluation process to ensure an in-depth appraisal focussed on risks inherent in the proposal and to lead to a credit rating of the potential borrower. Based on financial statements and their-in-depth appraisal and physical checking of stocks the bank should develop suitable model to assess health and repaying capacity of the credit applicants.

Serious attention needs to be paid to monitoring of the loans sanctioned by the bank. Since most bad loans have been due to poor credit monitoring than to poor credit approval, comprehensive preventive monitoring mechanism to maintain sound and health loan portfolio has to be developed. This mechanism has to lay emphasis on early detection of all signals relating to the health of the borrower, perspicacious analysis of those signals to take a view on the borrower's business and fast initiation of action upon warning signals to contain damage. Based on the information pertaining to financial performance of the borrowers, industry scenario, competitive position, and management charges, a bank can get invaluable information regarding the health of the borrowers, and early warning signals regarding a borrowing party. The loan review mechanism is to be adopted as a tool to bring about improvements in credit administration. Banks should also adopt their own risk-rating systems to assess the risk of lending. Sanctions above certain limits should be through a committee which can assume the status of an "Approval Grid". Exchange of credit information among banks would be of immense help to avoid possible NPAs.

While developing suitable policy guidelines, the focus has to be on measures to be taken at the branch level so as to identify danger signals, to diagnose the maladies and to take correct steps in potential NPA accounts in consultation with the controlling authority. Development of IT system at branch level to capture the danger signals followed by probe to ascertain the reasons behind its occurrence and taking quick action will go a long way in staying off the incipient sickness.

Whatever be the monitoring system developed by the bank, its thrust should be on prompt action. Introducing a credit rating of borrowers on the basis of all the available relevant information will be extremely useful. Rating index acts as a trigger for a hierarchy of predetermined actions. At the early stages of account irregularity, credit officers should check loan convenient maintenance but at the other end, when the company rating starts to slip, banks should be willing to call in loans.

In order to improve quality of the existing loan portfolio and maintain it on sustaining basis, the banks management should take a long-term view of each component in the portfolio and take decisions to exclude or include some components with specific features. Taking early decisions to reduce exposure to a sector or industry and making focussed marketing efforts to bring specific type of customers in the portfolio will help the banks in keeping the portfolio in healthy state.

The banking system ought to be so geared that a defaulter at one place is recognized as a defaulter by the system. The system will have to provide a mechanism to ensure that the unscrupulous borrowers are unable to play one bank against the other.

There is also a need to bring about change in the approach of banks towards legal action which is generally the last step. No sooner the account becomes bad, the bank should take immediate action to recover the loan.

With a view to ensuring effective and personalized appraisal, monitoring, speedy recovery of dues and maintenance of robust portfolio, the existing structure needs to be revamped to make lean, flat and responsive, equipped with employees possessing right kind of skills, experiences and aptitudes. These employees with clearly defined responsibilities should be empowered in its true sense to discharge their duties properly. Accountability of the employees with respect to credit appraisal, monitoring of loan accounts and recovery of dues should be fixed and communicated to them.

Banks should also conduct special audits on continuous basis to foil attempts of borrowers doctoring their accounts to show negative net worth and seek registration with BIFR so as to avoid/delay legal action initiated/to be initiated against them by the bank.

In view of ineffective and tortuous legal and judicial system and vitiated socio-political and ethical cultures, it would be in fitness of things to accord greater weightage to compromises as method of settlement of overdue accounts lying in the courts of law. In fact, compromises enable bankers to make better recoveries than those through court. The value of such amounts, if adjusted by the method of time-value of money, the losses incurred from the date of possible compromise can be worked out. Freedom to sue discretion for compromises and encouragement to it would go a long way in containing NPAs and nipping in the bud the potential court cases.

It is because of these reasons that the RBI recently came out with a one time measure — Settlement Advisory Committees (SACs) — to promote compromise settlement in small sector. However, unless there is an appreciation of the fact that compromise settlement is an effective and accepted non-legal remedy for recovery in chronic NPA accounts, the scheme is not likely to make much headway. The success of the schemes, as such, depends on banker's perception about compromise settlements. There is a need to impart necessary knowledge with a view to sharpening negotiating skills and reorienting attitudes of the employees.

The above internal arrangements will have to be supported externally by a proper legal framework where under quick action against a defaulting borrower could be taken. Though there are problems in affecting recoveries and write offs, it is of utmost importance that necessary changes are brought about in the related legislations for making recovery process more smooth and less time consuming.

DRATs, as stated earlier, have so far failed to achieve their stipulated objective of expeditious disposal of cases because of several factors. Apart from setting up more DRTs and Debt Recovery Appellate Tribunals (DRATs) and equipping them with proper and adequate infrastructure and manpower support, there is need to empower DRTs with a view to preventing the defaulters from stripping away the assets/securities during the pendency of cases. Suitable amendments in the Act/Rules should be made at the earliest.

For expeditious disposal of cases, DRTs should categorise borrowers on the basis of SWOT analysis into chronic willful defaulters with securities /assets, non-willful defaulters with securities/assets and defaulter without securities and prioritise them for action purpose.

In a landmark judgement pronounced on May 18, 2006, the Supreme Court of India observed that despite writing off, the debt is still recoverable by the bank. It is not true either in fact or in law that bad debts, which are written off cannot be recovered. The case relates to the Development and Credit Bank Ltd. (DCBL) deciding to write off from the financial records, debts that had turned into NPA over the years amounting to ₹ 120 crore. DCBL's Board of Directors and the principal shareholders of the bank in France approved this decision and the RBI approved this decision in March, 2003. However, the decision was challenged by one of the shareholders and hence the Supreme court verdict.[14]

F. STEPS TAKEN BY THE GOVERNMENT & RBI

From the regulator's perspective, there are four steps to the management of NPAs, *viz*; assessment, provisioning, recovery and prevention of fresh NPAs. The recent initiatives in the management of NPAs are related in greater measure to the third and fourth aspects, *viz*;

recovery and prevention aspects although norms relating to the first and second aspects have been progressively tightened to bring them at par with international best practices.[15] Major steps taken in recent years by the Government/RBI to contain NPAs are:

◈ One Time Settlement/Compromise Scheme

In May 1999, the RBI issued guidelines for the constitution of settlement advisory committees (SACs) for compromise settlements of chronic NPAs of the small sector. Modified guidelines were issued in July, 2000 to provide a simplified, non-discretionary and non-discriminatory mechanism for recovery of the stock of NPAs.

Under one-time settlement/compromise scheme of the RBI extended in May 2003 the time limit for processing of applications received under the revised guidelines for compromise and settlement of chronic NPAs of PSBs upto ₹ 10 crore upto December 31, 2003 which was further extended July 31, 2004. Amount of ₹ 608 crore was received through 21,311 compromise proposals upto March 2006.

◈ Lok Adalats

Lok Adalats have proved an effective institution for settlement of dues in respect of smaller loans. These Adalats have been conferred a judicial status. RBI issued guidelines to banks in 2001 indicating that:

(*i*) ceiling of amount for coverage under Lok Adalats would be ₹ 5 lakh;

(*ii*) the scheme may include both sent-filed and non-sent filed accounts in the doubtful and loss category; and

(*iii*) the settlement formula must be flexible.

Furthermore, DRTs have been empowered to organise Lok Adalats to decide on cases of NPAs of ₹ 10 lakh and above.

The monetary ceiling of cases to be referred to Lok Adalats organized by civil courts was enhanced to ₹ 20 lakh. Furthermore, banks were advised to participate in the Lok Adalats convened by various DRTs/DRATs for resolving cases involving ₹ 10 lakh and above to reduce the stock of NPAs.

◈ Debt Recovery Tribunals (DRTs)

The Recovery of Debts Due to Banks and Financial Institutions Act was enacted in 1993 to provide for the establishment of tribunals for expeditious adjudication and recovery of debts due to banks and financial institutions and for matters connected therewith and incidental thereto. The amendments made in 2000 to this Act and the Rules framed thereunder further strengthened the functioning of DRTs.

On the recommendation of the Reserve Bank, the Government of India set up a working group in July, 2004 to improve the functioning of DRTs. The working group is expected to examine issues and recommend appropriate measures regarding: (*a*) the need to extend the provisions of the Recovery of Debts Due to Banks and Financial Institutions Act to cases for less than ₹ 10 lakh; (*b*) redistribution of the jurisdiction of the various DRTs; (*c*) modification in the existing strength of the DRTs/Debt Recovery Appellate Tribunals (DRATs); and (*d*) Legal and Institutional provisions.

◈ Credit Information Bureau (India) Ltd. (CIBIL)

Taking cognizance of the utility of an effective institutional mechanism for sharing of information on borrowers/potential borrowers by banks, CIBIL was set up in 2001. Banks were advised to go for parallel reporting of data on suit filed accounts to both the RBI and CIBIL upto March 31, 2003 and switch over such reporting to the CIBIL effective from April 1, 2003.

Banks have been urged to make persistent efforts in obtaining consent from all their borrowers in order to establish an efficient credit information system which would help in enhancing the quality of credit decisions and improving the asset quality of banks, apart from facilitating faster credit deliver. Further, with a view to strengthening the legal mechanism and facilitating credit information on borrowers of bank/FIs, a draft credit information companies Regulation Bill, 2004 covering registration, responsibilities of the bureaus, rights and obligations of the credit institutions and safeguarding of privacy rights is under active consideration of the Government.[17]

◈ Securitization and Reconstruction of Financial Assets and Enforcement of Security In Interest (SARFAESI) Act, 2002

Until the enactment of Securitization Act, Banks/financial institutions had to enforce their security through court which was a very slow and time consuming process. There was also no provision in any of the present law in respect of hypothecation, though hypothecation is one of the major security interest taken by the Bank/financial institution. The Securitization Act was first enacted with effect from 21-06-2002 to overcome the hardships faced by the Banking industry.

The salient features of the Securitization Act are:[18]

(*i*) In case of any borrower having defaulted in repayment of secured debt or any instalment thereof and his account in respect of such debt is classified by the secured creditor as non-performing asset, then the secured creditor may require the borrower to discharge his liabilities within sixty days from the date of notice, failing which the secured creditor shall be entitled to take recourse to one or more of the following measures to recover his secured debt:

- Take possession of the secured assets of the borrower including the right to transfer by way of lease, assignment or sale for realising the secured assets;
- Take over the management of the secured assets of the borrower including the right to transfer by way of lease, assignment or sale and realise the secured asset;
- Appoint any person (hereafter referred to as the manager) to manage the secured assets the possession of which has been taken over by the secured creditor.

(*ii*) In the case of financing of a financial asset by more than one secured creditors or joint financing of a financial asset by secured creditors, no secured creditor shall be entitled to exercise any of the above powers unless exercise of such right is agreed upon by the secured creditors representing not less than three-fourth in value of the amount outstanding as on a record date and such action shall be binding on all the secured creditors.

(*iii*) No borrower shall, after receipt of the notice, transfer by way of sale, lease or otherwise any of his secured assets referred to in the notice.

(*iv*) Where the possession of any secured asset is required to be taken by the secured creditor or if any of the secured asset is required to be sold or transfer by the secured creditor under the provisions of this Act, the secured creditor may, for the purpose of taking possession or control of any such secured asset, request in writing the Chief Metropolitan Magistrate or the District Magistrate within whose jurisdiction any such secured assets or other documents relating thereto may be situated or found, to take possession thereof and the Chief Metropolitan Magistrate or as the case may be, the District Magistrate shall, on such request being made to him-

(*a*) take possession of such asset and documents relating thereto;
(*b*) forward such asset and documents to the secured creditor; and
(*c*) no act of the Chief Metropolitan Magistrate or the District Magistrate done in this respect shall be called in question in any court or before any authority.

(*v*) Any person (including borrower), aggrieved by any of the measures as referred to above taken by the secured creditor or his authorised officer, may prefer an appeal to the Debts Recovery Tribunal having jurisdiction in the matter within forty five days from the date on which such measures had been taken.

(*vi*) Where an appeal is preferred by a borrower, such appeal shall not be entertained by the Debts Recovery Tribunal, unless he deposits seventy five percent of the amount claimed in the notice as referred to above. However, the Debts Recovery Tribunal may, for reasons to be recorded in writing, waive or reduce the amount to be deposited.

So as to bolster the debt recovery efforts of lenders, the Lok Sabha passed on December 7, 2004 the Enforcement of Security Interest and Recovery of Debts Laws (Amendment) Bill. The Bill proposed to amend the Securitization Act by reducing the possibility of defaulters delaying the recovery process through frivolous appeals.

The Bill proposed to make it mandatory for borrowers who prefer an appeal to the Debts Recovery Appellate Tribunal (DRAT) to deposit upfront 50 per cent of the amount decreed by the Debts Recovery Tribunal. However, the Tribunal can reduce the upfront payment of 25 per cent.

Debts Recovery Tribunal shall have to dispose of cases within four months of any application being filed before it by borrowers whose assets are taken possession of by lenders. If the DRT fails to take a decision within the stipulated firms, a borrower can prefer an appeal to the DRAT for expeditious disposal.

The SARFAESI Act provides, *inter alia,* for enforcement of security interest for realization of dues without the intervention of Courts or Tribunals. The Security Interest (Enforcement) Rules 2002 was also notified to enable secured creditors to authorise their officials to enforce the securities and recover the clues from the borrowers.

In April 2004, a Supreme Court ruling on the SARFAESI Act 2003 struck down the provisions requiring the borrower pre-deposit 75 per cent of the liability in case the borrower wants to appeal against the order of attachment of the assets. The SARFAESI Act was amended in 2004, in order to dissuade the borrower from delaying the repayment of dues and to facilitate the speedy recovery of debt of secured creditors. By end March, 2008, public sector banks had issued 2,79,996 notices involving an outstanding amount of ₹ 56,000 crore. An amount of ₹ 15,415 crore was recovered in respect of 17,289 cases.[19]

Adequacy of the SARPAESI Act in recovering outstanding dues is doubtful, as evidenced from the recovery amount, for the fact that most of the big defaulters have taken consortia loans and before issuing the notice, the lead banker has to secure assent by secured creditors representing 75 per cent of the outstanding secured debt. Also, the core competence of bankers is to lend and receive money, not attach assets and fight cases. If there is even a small chance of borrower repaying, the banker is only too happy to oblige. As such, the NPA Act will be used only against hardcore defaulters.[20]

Already banks and financial institutions have started fighting pitched battles on sharing the spoils of the amounts recovered as a result of the new NPA Act. Some of the bankers feel that the cream of the spoils is going to the financial institutions and not to the banks as the former have the first charge on fixed assets.[21] Although banks lending working capital to companies normally have the first charge on receivables, inventories and cash flows, it is difficult for them to recover their dues as defaulting companies can always clean up the receivables and inventories before the banks can lay their hands on them as the lending agencies are required to give six weeks' notice before they can seize and sell assets.

It may also be noted that the minefield of complex Indian procedures may create stumbling blocks in putting the theory into practice. If we look at the broad scheme of the Act, a secured creditor has basically two choices in relation to an NPA:

- It can take possession of the secured assets; or
- It can take over the management of the borrower's company.

In the repossession option, if the borrower puts up substantial resistance, the lender may seek a magistrate's help. Theoretically, these proceedings should be short, but nothing prevents the borrower, or a third party for the matter, from raising the objections to repossession before the magistrate with the result that this proceeding could transform into a potentially endless inquiry into the nature of the secured asset, its proper status, the nature of the liability and so forth. More significantly, taking the magistrate's help, in effect, means dealing with the existential Indian reality of local loyalties and networking. And if the borrower is able to overcome the lethargy and the network, the magistrate is ultimately going to act through the local police. Getting the police help opens another can of worms.

There is also the alternative of taking over management control. This sounds simple in theory, but the reality is that to take over management is to accept the obligation to run the management. A currency glance at any ordinary compliance due diligence checklist will reveal that every company has to comply with 34 basic statutes, most carrying criminal liability if a default occurs. In effect, to take over management is to become responsible for compliance with these 34 statutes. The lender who picks up the courage to take over management will find that it will either assume comprehensive management or risk being dragged into a criminal court.

This brings up the whole issue on the indemnity being offered to lenders and their officials under this statute. Shorn of the legalese, the indemnity is limited to persons "exercising the rights of the secured creditor" in relation to "acts done or not done in good faith under the Act". Does this truly help the lender? In fact, the Act neither allows secured creditors to violate other laws, nor is such violation likely to be covered by good faith. Further, manager's takeover does not seem to be a plausible option, unless it is driven by the independent specialists.

Finally, the Act has not meaningfully addressed an overriding issue relating to repossession of the secured asset. Since time immemorial, every borrower intending to defeat the lenders' rights has created backdated arrangements and third party interest in secured assets, after the receipt of the notice preparatory to repossession. In fact, the extent to which the secured creditor may proceed against a third party acquirer of secured assets has also not been addressed, leading to another pandora's box of legal proceedings with a third party in the loop.

In a landmark judgement by the Bombay High Court in May, 2007 possession of secured assets has been made easier. The court has ruled that no notice or hearing needs to be given to a borrower or a third party when instance is taken from the Chief Judicial Magistrate to take possessions of the secured asset under the Securitization Act.[22]

With a view to ensuring healthy development of the securitization market, the RBI issued draft guidelines on securitization of standard assets on April 4, 2005, financial institutions and non-banking companies.

Under the proposed guidelines, for a transaction to be treated as securitization, it must follow a two-stage process. In the first stage, there should be pooling and transferring of assets to a bankruptcy remote special purpose vehicle (SPV). In the second stage, repackaging and selling the security interest, representing claims on incoming cash flows from the pool of assets to the third party investors should be effected. For enabling the transferred assets to be removed from the balance sheet of the seller in a securitization structure, the isolation of assets or 'true sale' from the seller or originator to the SPV would be an essential pre-requisite. Therefore, an arm's length relationship between the originator/seller and the SPV has to be maintained. The SPV would also be required to meet the criteria to enable originators to avail off-balance sheet treatments for the assets transferred by them to the SPV and also to enable the service providers and in the pass-through certificate (PTCs) to avail of the regulatory treatment for their respective exposures in a securitization structure.[23]

In its endeavour to protect interest of investors in securitized debt, the RBI has unveiled draft regulations on securitization on February 2, 2006. The regulations provide for a liquidity facility which helps borrowers to tide over temporary cash shortages and may result due to timing differences faced by SPVs, between the receipt of cash flows from the underlying assets and the payments to be made to investors. According to the guidelines, the liquidity facility should be capable of being drawn only when there is a sufficient level of non-default assets to cover drawings or the full amount of assets that may turn non-performing assets to be covered by a substantial credit enhancement. It has emphatically said that the liquidity facility to meet temporary mismatches in receivables should not be drawn for the purpose of providing credit enhancement, converting losses of SPV, serving as a permanent revolving funding and covering any losses incurred in the underlying pool of exposures. Further, liquidity facility will not be available for meeting recurring expenses of securitization, funding acquisition of additional assets by SPV, funding the final scheduled repayment of investors and funding breach of warranties. The RBI has further clarified that said securities issues by SPV would be in the nature of non-SLR securities. The counterpart for investors will not be SPV, but the underlying assets, of which the cash flows are expected from the borrowers. Such investments will, therefore, be included to reckon overall exposures to any individual or group borrowers, industry or geographic area wherever the obligators in the pool constitute 5% or more of the receivables or ₹ 5 crore whichever is lower.[24]

With a view to providing an additional option and developing a healthy secondary market for NPAs, the RBI issued guidelines in July 2005 on sale/purchase of non-performing assets where securitization companies and reconstruction companies are not involved. The guidelines include several specific provisions, *viz.*,

- A non-performing asset in the books of a bank shall be eligible for sale to other banks only if it has remained a non-performing asset for at least two years in the books of the selling bank and such selling should be only on a cash basis;
- A non-performing financial asset should be held by the purchasing bank in its books at least for a period of 15 months before it is sold to other banks;
- A bank may purchase/sell non-performing financial assets from/to other banks only on a 'without recourse' basis;
- Banks should ensure that subsequent to sale of the non-performing financial assets to other banks, they do not have any involvement with reference to assets sold and do not assure operational, legal or any other type of risks relating to the financial assets unsold;
- A non-performing asset may be classified as 'standard' in the books of the purchasing bank with reference to cash flows estimated while purchasing the asset. The asset shall attract provisioning requirement appropriate to its asset clarification status in the books of the purchasing bank;
- Any recovery in respect of a non-performing asset purchased from other banks should first be adjusted against its acquisition cost. Recoveries in excess of the excess of the acquisition cost can be recognised as profit;
- For the purchase of capital adequacy, banks should assign 100 per cent risk weights to the non-performing assets purchased from other banks;
- In case the non-performing asset is an investment, then it would attract capital charge for market risk also;
- The purchasing bank should ensure compliance with the prudential credit exposure ceilings (both single and group) after reckoning the exposures to the obligators arising on account of the purchase.

◈ Asset Reconstruction Companies (ARCs)

To solve the problem of bad loans, the SARFAESI Act provides for the establishment of ARCs. According to the Act, a securitization or reconstruction company with owned funds of not less than ₹ 2 crore or not exceeding 15 per cent of total financial assets acquired or to be acquired, as specified by the RBI, can commence or carry on business after obtaining a Certificate of Registration (COR). Existing securitization or reconstruction companies would have to apply for registration to the RBI within six months from the commencement of the Act.

For grant of COR to a company, the RBI has to ensure that the applicant company fulfills the following conditions:

- It has not incurred loss in any of the three preceding financial years;
- It has made adequate arrangements for realisation of financial assets for securitization or asset reconstruction;

- It submits periodical returns;
- It complies with the prudential norms of the RBI;
- Its Directors have adequate professional expertise and not have been convicted of any moral turpitude offence. Not more than half the Board members should be associated in any manner with the sponsor, and should not otherwise hold any controlling interest in such securitization or reconstruction company-

◈ Latest changes in SARFAESI & Debt Recovery Acts

On October 11, 2011 the Government approved amendments to the SARFAESI and Debt Recovery Acts to enable banks to effectively deal with the menace of bad loans and also encourage them to disburse credit freely to home and corporate loan seekers.

The Enforcement of Security interest and Recovery of Debts Laws (Amendment) Bill 2011 was passed in Parliament in December 2012. It seeks to convert any part of debt into shares of defaulting company by ARC. It also seeks to enable banks or any person to file a Caveat so that before granting any stay the bank or person is heard by the Debt Recovery Tribunal.[25]

◈ Provisioning Coverage Ratio (PCR) for Advances

As a macro-prudential measure, the RBI directed in October, 2009 to maintain PCR of 70 per cent of gross NPAs with reference to the position as on end-September, 2010. The surplus of the provision over and above the prescribed prudential norms should be segregated into a separate account styled as "counter-cyclical provisioning buffer" which will be allowed to be used during periods of system-wide downturn with the prior approval of the RBI.[26]

However, on April 24, 2011, the RBI specified that the earlier guideline requiring additional funds to be set aside for bad loans will not apply to loans that turn bad after September, 2010.[27] This move will certainly be beneficial to banks.

◈ Directing banks to recover NPAs from Promoters' money

Expressing his concern over a surge in banks' NPAs and cases of restructured accounts, finance minister asked banks on March 18, 2013 to take stern action for recovery of their dues. He observed that "we cannot have an affluent promoter and a sick company. Promoters have to bring in additional money and companies have the duty to pay back loans."[28]

G. IMPACT OF STEPS TAKEN BY THE GOVERNMENT & RBI ON NPAs

In view of several measures taken by the Government and the RBI, as outlined above, the banks have been able to recover a significant amount of NPAs leading to tremendous reduction in level of NPAs of the banks. (Table 19.4)

The setting up of the ARCIL provided a major boost to the banks' efforts to recover their NPAs. During 2004-05, several banks and financial institutions sold their NPAs to the ARCIL to the extent of ₹ 15,343 crore.

Among the various channels, the SARFAESI Act, 2002 has been the most important means of recovery of NPAs (Table 19.4). It comprised over half of the amount recovered during the period 2008-12. During 2011-12, of the total amount recovered through these channels, recoveries under the SARFAESI Act constituted almost 70 per cent.

DRTs have been another important channel which banks employed to recover bad loans. However, debt recovery is frustrating for any bank. In theory, DRTs are supposed to dispose of cases within six months. But the reality is that it can take years. Banks have been on a retail lending in recent years, so recovery is a bigger problem than before.

TABLE 19.4: NPAs Recovered by Scheduled Banks Through Various Channels

(Amount in ₹ crore)

Kind of Channels	2003-04			2004-05			2005-06			2006-07		
	No. of Cases Referred	Amt. Involved	Amt. Recovered	No. of Cases Referred	Amt. Involved	Amt. Recovered	No. of Cases Referred	Amt. Involved	Amt. Recovered	No. of Cases Referred	Amt. Involved	Amt. Recovered
1. One-Time Settlement/ Compromise Schemes	1,39,562	1510	617	132,781	1332	880	10.262	772	608	—	—	—
2. Lok Adalats	1,86,100	1063	149	1,85,395	801	113	2,68,090	2,144	265	1,60,368	758	106
3. DRTs	7544	12305	2117	4744	14317	2688	3,534	6,273	4,735	4,028	9,156	3,463
4. SARFAESI Act	2661	7847	1156	39288	13224	2391	41,180	8,517	3,363	60,178	9,058	3,749

Kind of Channels	2008-09			2009-10			2010-201			2011-12		
	No. of Cases Referred	Amt. Involved	Amt. Recovered	No. of Cases Referred	Amt. Involved	Amt. Recovered	No. of Cases Referred	Amt. Involved	Amt. Recovered	No. of Cases Referred	Amt. Involved	Amt. Recovered
1. One-Time Settlement/ Compromise Schemes												
2. Lok Adalats	5,48,308	4,023	96	7,78,833	7,235	112	6,16,018	5,254	151	4,76,075	1,700	200
3. DRTs	2,004	4,130	3,348	6,019	9,797	3,133	12,872	14,092	3,930	13,365	24,100	4,100
4. SARFAESI Act	61,760	12,067	3,982	78,366	14,249	4,269	1,18,642	30,604	11,561	1,40,991	35,300	10,100

Source: Report on Trend and Progress of Banking in India, 2004-05.

◈ Restructuring of Advances

It is important to note that restructuring of advances undertaken by the banking sector during the recent years also helped in reducing the GNPA ratio of the banking sector.

In the aftermath of the global financial turmoil in 2007, the RBI had proactively taken many steps to arrest the downward spiral, if any, in the economy and the banking sector. Amongst those steps, one important measure was allowing banks to restructure their advances, as a one-time measure. Accordingly, the RBI issued guidelines on restructuring of advances by banks in August 2008 by which banks were permitted to restructure accounts of viable entities classified as standard, sub-standard and doubtful. Though it was prescribed in August 2008 that accounts classified as standard assets should be immediately classified as sub-standard assets upon restructuring, in January 2009, an exceptional/special regulatory treatment was granted to all accounts, which were standard as on September 1, 2008. The exceptional/special regulatory treatment was granted to all accounts, which were standard as on September 1, 2008. The exceptional/special regulatory treatment permits treating standard accounts as standard after restructuring, provided certain conditions are met. The special regulatory treatment allowed to the standard accounts helped the banking sector to limit the growth of GNPA.[29]

Data on restructuring of advances by bank groups since September 2008 indicate that PSBs account for major portion of the restructuring of standard advances. At the system level, the restructured standard advances as a percentage of gross advances increased from 2.16 per cent as at end-March 2009 to 2..66 per cent as at end-March 2011.[30]

I. FUTURE CHALLENGES

The downgrading of financial health of the SBI — India's biggest commercial bank by one notch from C– to D+ by Moody's Investor Services — an internal rating agency — in October, 2011 has come as a shock to Indian banking system and so also the country's financial system. Low Tier-I capital ratio and deteriorating asset quality led to the lowering of rating of the SBI.

The SBI's Tier-I capital ratio at 7:6 per cent is currently below the eight per cent that the Indian government has committed to maintaining for public sector banks. Further, the growth in non-performing assets (NPAs) as a percentage of the Bank's loan portfolio was almost at a five-year high in the first quarter of the current fiscal year (2011-12). Concerns over the financial health of the SBI had already gained significant traction since its net profit plunged 99 per cent in the last quarter of 2010-11.

As a result of this downgrading, the SBI, despite the support of the full faith and credit of the Indian government, is now judged a weaker bank than private sector banks, such as Axis Bank, HDFC Bank and ICICI Bank.

While the SBI has decided to float rights issues of ₹ 5,000 crore in December, 2011 to raise its Tier-I capital ratio, Moody believes that the SBI will find itself capital constrained again in near future.

Moody's rating draws attention to two sordid and inconvenient truths about India's current banking system. The first is that the largest public sector bank lacks the capital required to support the credit expansion that the economy requires. Secondly, the government is poorly placed to provide the additional capital needed.

The situation is likely to aggravate in future for various reasons. One of the reasons is deteriorating quality of assets as banks may also have to restructure loans because of the borrowers' inability to service their debt due the slowdown in growth and rising interest costs. According to the Corporate Debt Restructuring Forum, a platform set up by banks and financial institutions, cases worth ₹ 34,562 crore went for debt restructuring in the first half of the current financial year (2011-12) compared to just ₹ 5,179 crore in the year-ago period. The number of companies referred rose from 21 to 35. According to RBI norms, banks have to make a provision at 2 per cent for the restructured account, which is treated as standard asset as against the normal standard loan provisioning at 0.4 per cent, putting additional pressure on the bottom line.

Maintaining capital adequacy in a rising NPA scenario is the biggest challenge for the PSBs. The government has estimated a capital infusion of ₹ 2 lakh crore into the PSBs by 2020. Given the state of Government's finances, capital infusion by the exchequer will put pressure on the already strained fiscal balances. Raising fresh capital from financial markets in a bearish scenario would entail its own cost for our banks.

In recent years, banks have resorted to using hyhrid capital (perpetual bonds) to shore up capital adequacy ratios. But Basel III norms no longer recognize perpetual debt as Tier II capital. The Basel Committee has also prescribed lower financial leverage of banks as global financial crisis was getting accentuated by higher leverage by some banks. According to the Basel Committee on Banking supervision (BCBs), no asset, including cash (which obviously has the least risk) should be excluded from leverage ratio.

Profitability of the banks will also tend to decline in future due to greater provisioning for restructured debts and other corporate loans, affecting Tier-I capital position of the banks.

In view of the above, commercial banks in India, especially the PSBs will require large additional capital to restore the minimum Tier-I capital position and for that purpose, the Government will have to infuse burgeoning capital into banks. Infusion of huge capital by the Government in the ensuring period will not be an easy task, given its fragile fiscal position. Under the circumstances, the monetary and fiscal authorities need to work in tandem in addressing the concerns of the banking sector. Capital infusion by the exchequer in systematically important banks and shift in focus of the central bank from inflation to growth could be part of such a strategy.

H. CONCLUSIONS

Managing bad loans and keeping them at the lowest level has become a key word for the banking industry in recent years because it adversely affects financial health of a bank.

NPAs in Indian banking system came into existence consequent to introduction of prudential accounting norms. However, non performing loans did exist even before the introduction of the present norms and its proportion to gross advances stood at 17.91 per cent as on March 31, 1989 and this soared to 23.5 per cent as on March 31, 1994. A slew of forces-both external and internal- contributed to high level of NPAs.

In recent years particularly after economic reforms, there has been substantial decline in level of gross NPAs in Indian banking system, touching an all time low level of 2.25 per cent in 2011. This is because of several policy measures taken by the RBI in conjunction with the Government. Net NPAs nosedived from 8.1 per cent to 0.97 per cent during the corresponding period.

However, level of NPAs in Indian banks is still higher as compared to those of other countries. As such, strategic measures both at macro and micro levels need to be taken. It is gratifying to note that in recent few years the Government and the RBI initiated several concrete measures which are now showing positive results.

KEY TERMS

- Approval Grid
- Bad Loan
- Credit Information Bureau
- Debt Recovery Tribunal
- Doubtful Asset
- Health Code System
- Lok Adalat
- Loss Making Asset
- SARFAESI
- Sticky Advances
- Substandard Asset
- Tiger Economics

DISCUSSION QUESTIONS

1. What do you understand by NPAs? Why should it be managed?
2. Bring out the main factors that are responsible for non-performing assets in commercial banks in India.
3. Discuss the recent trends in NPAs in Indian Commercial Banks.
4. How far NPAs affected financial health of Indian Commercial banks.
5. What have been the basic reasons for improved quality of banks' assets in recent years?
6. What means have, of late, been taken to contain NPAs in Commercial banks in India? What has been its impact on level of NPAs of the banks?
7. What have been main channels which Indian commercial banks have employed to recover bad advances. Discuss, in brief, the relative importance of these channels.

REFERENCES

1. Report on Trend and Progress of Banking in India, 2001-02, p. 25.
2. Report on Trend and Progress of Banking in India, 2000-01, p. 147.
3. Economic Times, July 11, 2000.
4. RBI Monthly Bulletin, July 1999, p. 918.
5. Report on Trend and Progress of Banking in India, 2002-03, p. 67.
6. Business Standard, December 27, 2000.
7. Economic Times, July 9, 2000.
8. Report on Trend and Progress of Banking in India, 1998-99.
9. SBI Monthly Bulletin, May 1999, p. 901.
10. Economic Times, May 5, 2001.
11. RBI's Annual Report, 2000-01, p. 160.
12. RBI Report on Trend and Progress of Banking in India, 2009-10. p. 174
13. RBI report on Trend and Progress of Banking in India, 2010-11, p. 78.
14. Times of India, May 18, 2006.
15. RBI Report on Trend and Progress of Banking in India, 2003-04, p. 36.
16. RBI's Annual Report, 2004-05, p. 136.
17. RBI Report on Trend and Progress of Banking in India, 2004-05, p. 35.
18. Government of India (2002), The Securitisation and Reconstruction of Financial Assets and Enforcement of Security Interest, New Delhi.
19. RBI Annual Report on Currency and Finance, 2007-08, p. 220.

20. Economic Times, December 5, 2002.
21. Trend and Progress of Banking in India, 2002-03, p. 36.
22. Times of India, May 3, 2007.
23. Economic Times, February 3, 2006.
24. Times of India, May 18, 2006.
25. Business Standard, December 11, 2011.
26. RBI on Trend and Progress of Banking in India, 2010-11.
27. Business Today, November 27, 2011.
28. Business Standard, March 19, 2013.
29. RBI report on Trend and Progress of Banking in India, 2010-11, p. 79.
30. *Ibid*.

Chapter 20

Operational Efficiency of Commercial Banks in India

Learning Objectives:

The present chapter attempts to:

- Provide a conceptual exposition of operational efficiency in a bank.
- Provide an overview of efficiency of Indian commercial banks.
- Outline parameters for measuring efficiency of commercial banks in India.
- Assess efficiency of commercial banks in India.

Chapter Outline:

- Backdrop.
- Efficiency of Indian commercial banks — An overview.
- Parameter of measuring efficiency of commercial banks in India.
- Assessing efficiency of commercial banks in India.
- International competitiveness of Indian banks.
- Conclusions.

A. BACKDROP

In a ferociously competitive environment, a firm, to achieve sustainable competitive prowess, must have competitive advantage over its rivals for all the time to come. This is possible if the firm has an edge over its competitors in attracting customers and defending against competitive forces.[1] When a firm possesses a unique strength that allows it to achieve superior efficiency, quality, innovation and customer responsiveness and thereby to create superior value- and the factors critical for success within its industry that permits the firm to outperform competitors, competitive advantage is said to exist

Banking industry is pre-eminently a service-oriented industry. For successful survival and sustained growth, a bank has to be efficient and effective in utilisation of resources and provide excellent services to the customers. Efficiency of a bank is reflected in its profitability. In fact, economic surplus is an index of efficient and effective deployment of resources. It is fundamental truth that operating revenue must exceed operating expenditure. A bank being essentially financial intermediary engaged in purchasing and selling funds is expected to earn a reasonable return to the savers, supply funds to investors and generate adequate margin for itself after covering cost of services. Profit provides cushion to the bank to support its credit risks and withstand any unforeseeable developments. A profitable banking organisation has sufficient resources in its command to finance its growth and diversification programmes in future. Since profitability is an index of efficiency of a banking enterprise, a profit making bank can infuse confidence in public at large which is necessary for its survival and growth. Profit constitutes the sinews of long-term survival and growth of a bank and contributes to its inner strength.

Productivity is one of the major factors affecting profitability of a bank. It is a function of an input-output relation. When for the same quantity of inputs, a greater quantity of output is generated or when same output is achieved with a lesser quantity of inputs, productivity is said to be high. It is usually argued that for a socio-economic institution like bank, earning profit should not be the prime consideration. It should primarily be concerned with fulfilling social obligations and promoting development of the economy and accordingly it should channelise its resources and efforts towards social ends. Pursuit of social obligations, it is contended, will interfere with the pursuit of economic goals to the extent that they prevent bank from making economically optimal decision. Acceptance of social responsibility increases the costs and risks of doing business which means dilution of profit. Social obligations, it is further argued, mean considerable diversion of managerial time and talent apart from scarce economic resources of bank. Thus, what is socially desirable may be economically suicidal.

The above line of argument emanates from all those who strongly believe that pursuit of economic goals as well as social goals is not possible as they oppose each other. There is no doubt that social obligations increase cost of operations and hence adversely affect profitability of the bank. However, in the long run economic goals and social responsibilities are compatible with each other; in fact, they reinforce each other.

Social actions of a bank enhance its image and creditability in the society and thus, ensure its existence. Rendering satisfactory services to customers at reasonable price and ensuring them adequate safety and liquidity coupled with reasonable return help the bank garner adequate resources comfortably. This is again necessary for the survival and growth of an institution.

Profit making goal of a bank has great social relevance. It contributes directly and indirectly to social welfare and development. As economic organs of society, commercial banks are socially responsible to pursue their goal of earning profit to the optimum extent by meeting the material needs of society. In fact, the major social responsibility of a bank is to operate profitably and efficiently utilise the resources at its disposal. Society does not stand to gain if banks' performance suffers.

A bank can serve society and help economy to develop only when it operates successfully. Generation of adequate operational surpluses by banks is necessary not only to provide adequate cushion to support their credit risks but also to satisfy their social obligations.

Thus, to fulfill its economic and social goals, a bank must lay focus on the efficient utilization of all resources or factors of production.

Sound financial health, as reflected in capital adequacy and asset quality, is *sine qua non* for sustained competitive superiority of a banking institution because it impacts its profitability.

The interest spread- the difference between interest income and interest expense- is an important indicator of efficiency of banks since it drives a wedge between interest received by depositors and the interest charged to borrowers on their loans. A high differential may adversely affect domestic savings and jeopardise economic growth. Financial system in developing countries typically exhibits significantly and persistently high spreads. These margins have persisted even though most countries have undertaken financial liberalisation. It has been observed that in many sub- Saharan African countries, the range of financial products remains extremely limited, interest rate spreads are wide, capital adequacy ratios insufficient and the share of non-performing loans quite high.[2]

B. EFFICIENCY OF INDIAN COMMERCIAL BANKS — AN OVERVIEW

The banking structure existing at present in India is the outcome of a process of expansion, reorganization and consolidation which has been going on for many years now. The banking system in India has undergone three phases. Pre-nationalisation period and post-nationalisation period are the two distinct phases of the development process. Of late, it has extended to a third phase, *viz.*, market development through innovation and diversification into new areas with exclusive focus on customers' services and through mergers.

Prior to nationalization, growth of banks was governed purely by economic considerations. However, post-nationalisation period witnessed greater emphasis having being accorded to social objectives resulting into widening of branch networks, the length and breadth of the country and greater mobilisation of savings through bank deposits and greater channelisation of resources into the neglected sectors. Till recently, managers' performance was being evaluated in terms of the business levels achieved by them, emphasising the quantitative aspect of productivity to the sad neglect of profitability. It is not that profitability has not been the concern of bank management but the priorities of policy directed lending to the neglected and socially desirable sections of society coupled with the desire to spread banking network to every nook and corner of the country forced productivity and profitability to take a back seat.

In fact, commercial banking in India has never been an area of high profitability and productivity. Proliferation of non-remunerative small loaning under Government sponsored schemes, excessive statutory pre-emptions, political interference and providing services at a price that had hardly purified the costs made matters worse for Indian commercial banks. Occasional sops of debt relief as populist political stance affected the behaviour of the borrowers towards repayment of bank loans and kept the level of bad and doubtful debts mounting with the banks. Subsequently, disintermediation took some of the very good and creditworthy borrowers away from the banks' fold to the capital market and the burgeoning Commercial Paper market, exposing the banks to the vagaries of market forces where efficiency and profitability are the watchwords.

While the social objectives of nationalization seem to have been achieved, there has been progressive erosion in the efficiency, profitability and viability of the system with consequential adverse impact on the economy.[3] This led to the Reserve Bank of India to appoint Productivity, Efficiency and Profitability Committee under the Chairmanship of J. E. Luther in 1977. The Committee emphasised on the necessity of using profitability and productivity as norms of assessing performance of commercial banks.

Financial strength and efficiency of banks operating in highly protected and regulated environment were not found measuring up to international standards so much so that they were unable to meet financial requirements of industry and other sectors of the economy. Unprecedented growth of banking industry during seventies and eighties accompanied inefficiency and loss of control. The persistent deterioration in the financial health and the looming danger of the very survival of the banking industry called for quick but comprehensive remedial measures. Accordingly, Narasimham Committee was appointed in 1991 to recommend measures to improve efficiency and effectiveness of Indian financial system after thoroughly examining all the relevant aspects.

Thus, to improve operating efficiency of commercial banks in India and so also the competitiveness in the process of financial intermediation, several banking sector reformatory measures were taken since the adoption of the Government policy of liberalisation, privatisation and globalisation in 1991. It was expected that banks would take advantage of the changing operational environment and improve their performance. Towards this end, the RBI initiated a host of measures for the creation of a competitive environment. Deregulation of interest rates on both the deposits and lending sides imparted freedom to banks to appropriately price their products and services. To compete effectively with non-banking entities, banks were permitted to undertake newer activities like investment banking, securities trading and insurance business. This was facilitated through amendments in the relevant Acts which permitted PSBs to raise equity from the market upto a threshold limit (49 per cent) and also enabling the entry of new private and foreign banks. This changing face of banking led to an erosion of margins on traditional banking business, promoting banks to search for newer activities to augment their fee incomes. At the same time, banks also needed to devote focused attention to operational efficiency in order to contain their transactions costs. Simultaneously with the deregulation measures; prudential norms were instituted to strengthen the safety and soundness of the banking system.

The ongoing banking sector reform with its thrust on transparency, efficiency and profitability has provided an opportunity for rebuilding the banking institutions into efficacious and vibrant engines by improving their productivity and viability and by toning up allocative efficiency of financial resources. This is all the more necessary when the Indian economy has embarked on the path of global competitiveness with concomitant thrust on competition, deregulation and technology.[4]

As such, Indian commercial banks are expected to improve their efficiency, enhance productivity and profitability on sustaining basis. These banks are aggressively engaged in gearing and bracing themselves up structurally, functionally and culturally to the needs of the hour. It is, therefore, pertinent to assess how far commercial banks in India improved their efficiency during the post reform period.

C. PARAMETERS OF MEASURING EFFICIENCY OF COMMERCIAL BANKS IN INDIA

Operational efficiency of a bank can be measured in terms of productivity, profitability, spread and financial soundness. However, measuring productivity in the case of banks bristles with several snags. Banking is a service industry whose output consists not of any physical product whose properties could be analysed in a laboratory and whose production could be quantified easily but of a bundle of services, not easy of measurement. Further, banks are not merely purveyors of credit and acceptors of deposits but also suppliers of financial assistance to economically and socially neglected sectors. The costs of the new services are higher, while the returns from them are lower. Therefore, a more comprehensive and multi-dimensional approach has to be adopted to judge the efficiency of banks.

Productivity of banks is generally measured in terms of business per employee, profit per employee, and business per branch. In India, average business handled per employee is taken as a measure of productivity for each branch. Average business here is the sum of average deposits and advances which is the output generated by the input of human efforts. This measure of productivity is, however, inadequate in as much as it ignores subsidiary services and relegates quality of the product to a secondary position. Quality of product/services is of paramount importance in a service industry where the product does not have a physical form. However, measuring quality aspect of banks' operations suffers from greater degree of subjectivity. This is why other sets of indicators such as quality of customers services, the percentage of bad debts written off in relation to total advances could be thought of for measuring productivity in bank. Even these measures lack objectivity. This led us to use quantifiable and objective techniques to measure productivity of a bank, *viz.*, profit per employee, business per branch, intermediation cost, interest spread, etc.

Another significant parameter of operational efficiency of a bank is profitability. Profitability of a bank provides useful insight into its effectiveness of the utilisation of funds and its managerial efficiency. We have employed three important profitability ratios, *viz.*, net profitability as percentage of gross operating income, net profit as percentage of working funds and return on total assets. Net profit as percentage of gross operating income indicates the capacity of a bank to generate residual income and the degree of cost control exercised by the management while net profit as percentage of working funds seeks to measure efficiency of funds management and productivity of capital employed in a bank. Return on total assets is an overall profitability rate which measures earning power and overall efficiency of a bank. It is a good measure of earning power inasmuch as it is an extension of the input-output analysis.

Improvements in efficiency of the banking system are expected to be reflected, *inter alia,* in a reduction in operating expenditure, interest spread and cost of intermediation.

Financial health of a bank- an important index of efficiency, solvency and soundness-can gainfully be judged on the basis of capital adequacy and asset quality. Capital adequacy of Indian banks will be judged on the basis of ratio of the Capital to Risk Weighted Assets (CRAR). Quality of assets of banks will be determined with the help of their gross NPAs to gross advances and net NPAs to net advances.

D. ASSESSING EFFICIENCY OF COMMERCIAL BANKS IN INDIA

◈ Efficiency of Banks in Terms of Productivity

Table 20.1 brings out data pertaining to business per employee, profit per employee and business per branch of Scheduled Commercial banks in India. It may be noted from the table that business per employee of Indian banks increased nearly seventeen fold in real terms from ₹ 54 crore in 1991-92 to ₹ 1137.60 crore in 2011-12, showing an annual compound growth rate of over 76 per cent. At the same time, the profit per employee soared more than five times from ₹ 20,000 to ₹ 6 lakh over the same period, signifying a compound growth of around 195 per cent. Branch productivity also registered concomitant improvement from ₹ 1099 crore in 1991-92 to ₹ 11,320 crore in 2009-10. Thus, there has been distinct improvement in the efficiency of banks during the post reform period. This can be attributed to constellation of forces such as technological advances, financial innovation and different strategies suited to their business philosophy and risk-return profile, changing composition of banks' input-output, and reduction in total cost. It is interesting to note that pick up in business per branch was not a sharp as in the case of business per employee, the rise in which, to an extent, was also due to voluntary retirement schedules introduced by public sector banks.

A comparative study of productivity of groups of banks in India (Table 20.2) shows that productivity of foreign banks has been higher as compared to their domestic counterparts. Thus, in 1997-98, business per employee in case of foreign banks was ₹ 529 lakh as compared to ₹ 82 lakh in case of PSBs and ₹ 292 lakh in case of private sector banks. Over the period of time, there has been spectacular improvement in the productivity of the PSBs which recorded a rise of over ten fold. As against this, the same surged by less than three fold in the case of private and foreign banks.

TABLE 20.1: Select Productivity Indicators of Scheduled Commercial Banks in India

(₹ in Lakh)

Year	Business Per Employee	Profits Per Employee	Business Per Branch
1991-92	54.0	0.2	1,099.0
2001-02	115.0	0.5	1,962.0
2005-06	419.80	2.80	6,410.0
2006-07	522.94	3.49	7451.0
2007-08	643.24	4.74	9,100.0
2008-09	753.44	5.63	10,354.0
2009-10	873.32	6.05	11,320.0
2010-11	1020.90	2.75	
2011-12	1137.60	3.40	

Source: A Profile of Banks, 2009-10, RBI.

As regards efficiency of banks in terms of profit per employee, Table 20.2 reveals that private sector banks had highest productivity in terms of profit per employee at ₹ 6.18 lakh in 1997-98 followed by foreign banks with ₹ 5.15 lakh.. Public sector banks with ₹ 0.74 lakh were least productive.

Over the period 1997-98 — 2011-12, there was significant surge in profit per employee across all the category of banks. However, it was highest in case of foreign banks followed by private and private sector banks.

An analysis of recent trends in profit per employee in respect of different categories of banks reveals that there was significant improvement in profit earned per employee across all bank groups.

TABLE 20.2: Productivity of Groups of Banks in India

(₹ in Lakh)

Year	Public Sector Banks		Private sector Banks		Foreign Banks	
	Business Per Employee	Profit Per Employee	Business Per Employee	Profit Per Employee	Business Per Employee	Profit Per Employee
1997-98	82.00	0.74	292.0	6.18	529.00	5.15
2003-04	230.00	1.84	371.0	3.09	858.00	14.27
2004-05	261.00	2.51	374.0	4.38	807.00	21.20
2005-06	471.18	2.76	704.0	4.71	974.77	16.13
2006-07	600.10	3.75	751.0	6.00	1037.10	19.47
2008-09	734.00	4.70	744.0	6.16	1282.74	25.39
2009-10	870.00	5.34	798.0	7.19	1445.87	17.09
2010-11	1016.70	5.90	958.1	9.40	1555.500	27.50
2011-12	1151.20	6.40	999.1	10.60	1831.00	34.00

Source: Statistical Tables relating to Banks, RBI.

In sum, productivity of foreign banks and private sector banks in terms of business per employee and profit per employee has been significantly higher than the PSBs.

◈ Efficiency of Banks in Terms of Operating Costs

As regards efficiency of Indian banks in terms of intermediation cost (ratio of operating expenses to total assets), it may be observed from Table 20.3 that intermediation cost of

Indian banks witnessed a gradual reduction in the post-reform period across various bank groups. Thus, operating costs to total assets in the case of PSBs tended to decline from 2.61 per cent in 1991 to 1.38 per cent in 2012 and in the case of private sector banks from 2.98 percent to 0.62 per cent during the corresponding period. This is reflective of various initiatives taken by the banks' management to streamline the operations and control operating expenses. However, this does not hold true in case of foreign banks. Thus, ratio of operating expenses to total assets surged from 2.26 per cent in 1991-92 to 4.2 per cent in 2008-09. This was because of rising burden of labour cost. Since 2009, the ratio of operating expenses to total assets in the case of foreign banks decreased steeply to 2.30 in 2012.

TABLE 20.3: Intermediation Costs in Different Group of Indian Banks

(Operating cost as Percentage To Total Assets)

Categories of Banks	1991-92	1999-2000	2001-02	2004-05	2005-06	2006-07	2007-08	2008-09	2009-10	2010-11	2011-12
Public Sector Banks	2.61	2.53	2.29	2.13	2.40	2.0	1.5	1.7	1.7	1.13	1.38
Private Sector Banks	2.98	1.79	1.00	2.02	2.40	2.4	2.6	2.5	2.3	0.86	0.62
Foreign Banks	2.26	3.22	3.03	2.85	3.30	3.2	3.1	4.2	2.9	2.50	2.30

Source: Reports on Trend and Progress of Banking in India, RBI for relevant years.

Further, there has been improvement in the efficiency of Indian banks during post reform period, as manifested from the declining trend in per unit cost of output, irrespective of the choice of outputs (Table 20.4). Thus, the operating cost per unit of earning assets (credit & investment) declined from 2.1 per cent in 1992 to 1.65 per cent in 2012. Likewise, operating cost per unit of total volume of business tended to slide from 3.4 per cent to 0.9 per cent during the corresponding period. Among the components of operating cost, employee cost per unit of output registered a remarkable decline during the post reform period. This trend is noticeable across all bank groups and especially for PSBs in post 2001 period due to the voluntary retirement scheme across several nationalised banks. On the other hand, the change in physical capital cost per unit of output has been marginal. This is indicative of the fact that Indian banks maintained a steady flow of investments towards physical capital formation, especially on automation and information technology.

TABLE 20.4: Operating Expenses and Its Components of Scheduled Banks

(Per cent)

Year	Operating Exp/Earning Assets	Labour Cost/Earning Assets	Non-Labour Cost/Earning Assets	Operating Exp/Total Business	Labour Cost/Total Business	Non-Labour Cost/Total Business
1992	2.08	1.40	0.68	3.42	2.30	1.12
1996	2.48	1.73	0.75	4.01	2.80	1.22
2001	2.16	1.47	0.74	3.55	2.35	1.20
2004	1.78	1.08	0.71	2.61	1.58	1.03
2005	2.10	1.30	0.80	—	—	—
2006	2.10	1.20	0.90	—	—	—
2007	1.90	1.0	0.90	—	—	—
2010	1.65	0.9	0.75	1.02	0.70	0.32
2012	1.55	0.9	0.70	1.90	1.70	0.70

Source: Statistical Tables relating to Banks in India for various years, RBI.

Another strand of improved performance of Indian scheduled banks is reflected in the cost-income ratio (ratio of operating expense to total income less interest cost) which recorded a declining trend from about 55 per cent of their total net income toward managing labour and physical capital in 1992 to 57.8 percent in 2012. The declining tendency was more pronounced in case of PSBs and private sector banks. (Table 20.5).

TABLE 20.5: Cost-Income Ratio of Scheduled Commercial Banks in India

(Per cent)

Year (end March)	Public Sector Banks	Private Sector Banks	Foreign Banks	Scheduled Banks
1992	58.4	58.9	30.9	55.3
1997	64.3	51.3	45.6	61.0
2001	67.0	51.8	50.0	63.4
2010-11	65.9	22.0	23.0	50.0
2011-12	34.4	21.5	43.1	57.8

Source: Statistical Tables relating to Banks in India for various years, RBI.

Inter-country comparison of intermediation costs shows that Indian banks have had lower ratio of operating costs to total assets (2.2%) as compared to the Canada (2.8%) and Spain (2.5%),[5] reflecting superiority of Indian banks to those of advanced countries on this score. Further, cost-income ratio of Indian banks is comparable internationally in as much as the same for the world's largest banks varied markedly from a low of 48 per cent to a high of 116 per cent, while in case of Indian banks, the range was between 45 and 72 per cent.[6] However, intermediation cost of banks in India tend to be higher as compared to major Asian countries (Table 20.6).

TABLE 20.6: Intermediation Cost of Banks of Major Asian Countries

(As Percentage To Total Assets)

Year	China	Indonesia	Korea	Malaysia	Philippines	Thailand	India
1997	1.24	4.50	2.55	1.49	3.28	1.50	2.60
2000	1.12	2.72	1.46	1.70	3.32	1.98	2.57
2003	1.01	2.94	1.38	1.61	3.00	1.71	2.19

Source: Bank Scope.

◆ Efficiency in Terms of Profitability

One of the important tools of measuring profitability of a bank is 'return on assets' (ROA) which gives an indication as to how much profits a bank is able to generate per unit of its assets. Higher value of the ratio is indicative of higher profitability.

It may be noted from Table 20.7 that despite increased competition in the banking system in India, the return on assets (ROA) improved significantly from 0.39 per cent in 1991-92 to 1.10 per cent in 2010-11. The significant improvement in the profitability ratio is all the more significant as the intermediation cost of the bank declined during the same period. However, there has been mismatch between assets and return of the banks. While total assets multiplied almost six-fold in a decade, returns have not been as good. However, there was decline in ROA of banks, particularly in case of the PSBs.

TABLE 20.7: Return on Assets of Commercial Banks in India

(per cent)

Year	Public Sector Banks	Private Sector Banks	Foreign Banks	All Commercial Banks
1991-92	0.28	0.57	1.56	0.39
2000-01	0.42	0.71	1.00	0.50
2005-06	0.82	0.87	1.54	0.88
2006-07	0.83	0.87	1.65	0.90
2009-10	0.97	1.28	1.26	1.05
2010-11	0.96	1.43	1.74	1.10
2011-12	0.88	1.53	1.76	1.08

Another measure of profitability is return on equity (ROE) which indicates the amount of profits a bank is generating for its equity investors. Table 20.8 exhibiting information about ROE of Indian commercial banks reveals that ROE of the bank fluctuated widely during 1991-92 to 2006-07 in consonance with the profitability and prevailing capital position in India. However, there has been continuous step up in ROE of the banks mainly in recent few years due to improvement in net operating income. Furthermore, the PSBs have shown relatively greater improvement in their ROE.

TABLE 20.8: Return on Equity of Commercial Banks in India

Year	Public Sector Banks	Private Sector Banks	Foreign Banks	All Commercial Banks
1991-92	11.02	26.77	42.76	14.77
2000-01	8.65	13.09	11.53	9.61
2005-06	8.13	13.55	12.62	13.43
2006-07	14.86	12.81	13.86	14.24
2009-10	17.47	71.94	7.34	14.31
2010-11	16.90	13.70	10.28	14.96
2011-12	15.33	15.25	10.79	14.60

Source: RBI Report on Trend & Progress of Banking in India.

However, the SBI group was an exception to the above general trend. The marginal decline in both ROA and ROE in the case of the SBI group was partly on account of the provisioning requirements for housing loans extended at teaser interest rates.

During 2011-12, ROA and ROE dipped marginally compared with the previous year, mainly reflecting the slow down in net profit caused by increased interest expenditure.

Inter-country comparison of ROA and ROE reveals that Indian commercial banks have performed much better than these in USA, France, Germany, Japan, Korea and China (Table 20.9). This clearly indicates that Indian banks have been managing their resources more prudently as compared to their counterparts in other countries.

TABLE 20.9: Profitability ratios of Select Countries

(Percentages)

Country	ROA		ROE	
	1999	2006	1999	2006
USA	0.84	0.99	8.81	12.00
UK	0.90	0.53	14.94	15.43
France	0.28	0.54	6.08	14.39
Germany	0.23	0.48	7.20	13.34
Japan	0.13	0.50	2.57	8.83
Brazil	1.62	1.85	15.87	18.00
Korea	–1.21	0.98	–24.75	14.86
China	0.17	0.62	2.58	11.83
India	0.83	0.85	14.18	14.76

Source: Bank Scope.

◆ Efficiency of Banks in Terms of Financial Soundness

(1) Capital Adequacy

Financial soundness of different groups of banks in India, as noted earlier, will be assessed on the basis of capital adequacy and asset quality. As such, from the perspective of regulatory and supervisory process, the capital to risk weighted asset ratio (CRAR) constitutes the most important indicator for assessing soundness and solvency of bank.[7]

As noted in Chapter 12, capital adequacy position of Indian banks has been satisfactory and CRAR has been well above the stipulated rate. Further, Indian banking system withstood the pressures of the global financial crisis. All the commercial banks have become Basel complaint as on March 31, 2009. They successfully managed to meet increased capital requirement under the changed framework. Thus, CRAR of Indian banks as at end March 2012 stood at 12.94 per cent and 14.24 per cent respectively under Basel I and Basel II framework, far above the stipulated minimum ratio by the RBI.

Core CRAR ratio — the prime measure of financial strength of any bank — of SCBs at end March 2012 stood at 9.4 and 10.4 per cent under Basel I and II framework, respectively against much above the RBI's stipulated 6 per cent.

Furthermore, CRAR across all the bank groups was well above the stipulated ratio. However, foreign and private sector banks are reported to have registered an increase in CRAR between 2009 and 2010. As against this, there was decline in the CRAR for the SBI group while nationalised banks maintain their position.

However, financial health of the banks in terms of capital adequacy deteriorated since 2010. The SBI, the largest bank of India, came under Moody's scanner which downgraded the Bank by one notch from C– to D+ in October, 2011. The downgrade indicates that India's banking sector is not in the best of health. The SBI's downgrading has been due to five-year high NPAs, decline in its net profit and impending capital challenges. Moody's rating draws attention to two sordid and sour truths about India's current banking system. The first, that the largest PSB lacks the capital required to support the credit expansion that the economy requires. Secondly, the government is poorly placed to provide the additional capital needed.

◆ Asset Quality

The level of non-performing assets (NPAs) is recognised as critical indicator for assessing bank's credit risk, asset quality and efficiency in allocation of resources to productive sectors.

As observed in the Chapter 18 on 'Management of Non-Performing Assets', there has been considerable improvement in the asset quality of banks despite tightening norms in recent years. Thus, gross NPAs to gross advances in case of the scheduled banks nosedived from 15.7 per cent in 1997 to as low as 2.25 per cent in 2011. Likewise, ratio of NPAs to net advances declined sharply from 8.1 per cent to 0.97 per cent during the corresponding period. Similar tendency was noticeable across all bank groups. The significant improvement in quality of assets of the banks since 1997 was the outcome of improvement in the credit appraisal process, upturn of the business cycle, new initiatives for resolution of NPAs (including enactment of the SARFAESI Act which provided several options to banks for dealing with NPAs), aggressive restructuring by banks in 2004-05 and greater provisioning and write offs of NPAs enabled by greater profitability.

However, tremendous improvement in quality of assets of the banks should not lull the bankers and the RBI into sense of complacency because of deepening competitiveness in financial sector. Mere fact that even reduced level of NPAs of the Indian banks is still high as compared to developed countries' standards of around 2 per cent warrants continued remedial actions.[10]

Already the PSBs witnessed deterioration in asset quality in 2010-11 because of deterioration in asset quality of the SBI group. With soaring inflation and high interest rates making it hard for families to repay debts, banks' bad assets are piling up fast, resulting in rise in gross NPAs of banks close to ₹ 1 trillion. There are also instances of stressed debt being converted into equity. Earlier 2011, over a dozen banks, including SBI, ICICI Bank, IDBI, Bank of India, UCO Bank and PNB agreed to convert their ₹ 750 crore debt in Vijay Mallya's Kiingfisher Airlines into equity.

The current economic downturn is proving to be a testing time for banks, with quality of assets further suffering. The gross non-performing assets (NGPAs) of banks was 2.9 per cent as at the end of March, 2012. Critically restructured assets and NPAs, which surged sharply in the past year and a half will rise further in 2012-13 and aggravate asset quality in the banking system.[11]

Most investors have serious concerns about asset quality of the PSBs and are convinced that NPA numbers are understated. As many former bankers point out, properly calculated, stressed assets for the banking system are already over 8 per cent of loans. This is based on the official NPA and restructured loan figures (adjusted for recoveries).[12]

Indeed, 85 per cent of the asset quality issues of the banks are due to infrastructure, real estate and priority sector obligations, and none of these areas seem to be getting any better.

◈ Efficiency of Banks in Terms of Spread

The spread or the net interest income, as noted earlier, constitutes an important indicator of efficiency of banks since it is the most important driver of profitability of banks. Behaviour of interest rate, in fact, has a direct bearing on banks' 'profitability'. The interest spread as percentage to total assets of groups of commercial banks in India is depicted in Table 20.10. It may be glanced from the Table that foreign banks had highest net interest income in relation to their assets at 5.08 in 2011-12. It was followed by private sector banks having spread at 4.00 per cent during the period.

TABLE 20.10: Net Interest Income (spread) as a Percentage of Total Assets of Banks in India

Group of Banks	1992-93	1995-96	1996-97	1997-98	1998-99	1999-2000	2000-01	2001-02
Public Sector	3.22	3.10	3.16	2.91	2.81	2.70	2.84	2.93
Private Sector	4.0	3.10	2.95	2.46	2.11	2.13	2.33	1.58
Foreign Banks	3.90	3.57	4.13	3.97	3.51	3.85	3.64	3.25
All Scheduled	3.30	3.15	3.22	2.95	2.79	2.72	2.84	2.57

Group of Banks	2002-03	2003-04	2004-05	2005-06	2006-07	2008-09	2009-10	2010-11	2011-12
Public Sector	2.51	2.58	2.97	2.85	2.70	3.07	3.02	3.52	3.46
Private Sector	1.91	2.24	2.34	2.30	2.60	3.67	3.77	4.00	3.85
Foreign Banks	3.36	3.47	3.33	3.52	3.72	6.10	5.49	5.00	5.08
All Scheduled	2.48	2.87	2.88	2.78	2.75	3.40	3.31	3.69	3.62

Source: Report on Trend and Progress of Banking in India.

Over the period, the interest spread of Scheduled banks tended to decline from 3.30 per cent in 1992-93 to 2.75 per cent in 2006-07 and similar trend was noticeable in case of all the public sector banks.

Persistently declining trend in interest spread of commercial banks in India during the last decade can be attributed to a number of factors. One such factor is competitive pressure arising from conditions of free entry and competitive pricing which tended to raise the functional efficiency of intermediation by decreasing the spread. Secondly, low non-financial costs have acted as a source of narrowing intermediation spreads. Thirdly, growing macro economic stability and healthy policy environment has also contributed to contraction in interest spread of the banks. Hardening of interest in recent years is an added fact.

In 2008-09, net interest margin of SCBs showed improvement because both deposit and lending rates of the banks, which influence the net interest margin of banks, had shown a generally upward movement during the first half of 2008-09. These rates, however, were on a decline during the second half of the year following the accommodative monetary policy stance pursued by the RBI. During a major part of 2009-10, the declining trend in the deposit rates of SCBs continued with the rates offered by the banks. The NIM of the Indian banking sector improved during 2010-11. During 2011-12, both cost as well as return on funds increased for the banks. However, the spreads narrowed due to the higher increase in cost of funds. At the bank group level, cost of funds was lower in the case of foreign banks, partly because low cost CASA deposits formed a higher proportion of total deposits for foreign banks. It is noteworthy, the NIM of the Indian banking sector continues to be higher than some of the emerging market economies of the world.[12] The decomposition of the NIM into NIM from core banking business (i.e., calculated as the difference between the interest income from loans and advances minus interest expenses on deposits as a per cent of average total assets) and NIM from others (i.e., mainly the difference between all other interest income and interest expenses) shows that NIM from others. (i.e., mainly the difference between all other interest income and interest expenses) shows that NIM from core banking business witnessed substantial increase during the last one decade (2000-01 to 2010-11). This indicates that the cost of financial intermediation increased in the economy during this period. There is therefore, a need to bring the overall NIM down by way of offering loans at lower rates of interest and offering attractive rates to deposition to boost investment through the efficient channelling of savings.[14]

TABLE 20.11: Spread As Percentage To Total Assets of Banks of Major Asian Countries

Year	China	Indonesia	Korea	Malaysia	Philippines	Thailand	India
1996	1.86	2.97	1.70	2.91	4.07	1.57	3.07
2000	1.76	2.21	2.06	3.02	2.54	1.43	2.74
2004	1.87	4.22	2.50	2.61	2.30	1.99	2.84

Source: Bank Scope.

However, the US banks had moderately higher net interest margin at 3.0 per cent.[13]

Thus, on score of interest spread, banks in India have faired better than others.

In fact, with operational flexibility, the PSBs are competing relatively with private sector and foreign banks.

E. INTERNATIONAL COMPETITIVENESS OF INDIAN BANKS

Indian banking sector faces much better than its Asian press in terms of key performance indicators. According to the Moody's Investor Services study (July 2007) based on the three years' average performance (i.e., from 2003 through 2006) Indian bankers have the highest 'Return on Equity' (ROE), in Asia as 20.38 per cent as against Indonesia as 20.19 per cent, New Zealand as 18.83 per cent and Japan as 6.42 per cent.[15]

Indian bankers have the lowest Average Gross Bad loans as percentage of total loans act 8.18 per cent. This ratio is as 15.05 per cent for Philippines 13.08 per cent for Thailand, 11.80 per cent for China and 9.73 per cent for Malaysia.

The 'cost to income' ratio for Indian banking sector is also relatively lower at 44.56 per cent. The banking sectors of only three countries have better cost to income ratios compared to India, notably, Singapore as 44.15 per cent, Taiwan as 42.61 per cent and Hong Kong as 40.05 per cent.

F. CONCLUSIONS

The foregoing analysis reveals that there has been discernible improvement in operational efficiency of commercial banks in India during the period of liberalisation. The increasing trend in efficiency has been fairly uniform, irrespective of the ownership pattern and PSBs and private sector banks in India did not differ significantly in terms of their efficiency measures. However, foreign banks recorded higher efficiency as compared to their Indian counterparts.

The pattern of efficiency improvement is broadly in consonance with what is expected from an industry undergoing deregulation and transformation. Ostensibly, all the bank groups registered efficiency gains even in the face of increasing competition in the financial market place. However, while sustaining the current trends in efficiency, there remains scope for banks to expand their asset base relative to their input usage by adopting innovations in product technology and to control operating expenditure. There is also a need to strengthen capital position and improve quality of assets of the banking industry.

KEY TERMS

- Asset quality
- Capital adequacy
- Fee-based activities
- Intermediation cost
- Interest spread
- Net interest margin
- Operating costs
- Productivity of banks
- Return on assets
- Return on equity

DISCUSSION QUESTIONS

1. What is the significance of efficiency and productivity on the financial health of Indian banking industry?
2. How can operational efficiency of a bank be measured?
4. Discuss operational efficiency of Indian banks.
4. What has been the impact of economic reforms on the efficiency of Indian banks?
5. How far has productivity of Indian banking industry improved during post liberalisation period? Identify the major contributory factors for this improvement.

6. "Despite improvement in operational efficiency of Indian banking sector, its financial health has deteriorated in recent years." Comment.
7. What steps would you suggest to improve further the efficiency and productivity of Indian banks to the global level?

REFERENCES

1. Michael E. Porter, Competitive Advantage, The Free Press, New York, 1985, p. 11.
2. A. Barajas (*et al*, 2000), R. Steiner and N. Salazar (1999), Interest Spread in Banking in Columbia, 1974-96, IMF Staff Paper 46, pp. 196-224.
3. Government of India, Discussion Paper, 1993, p. 2.
4. RBI Occasional Papers, Vol. 16, No. 4, December 1995, p. 313.
5. RBI Report on Trend and Progress of Banking in India, 2003-04, p. 78.
6. RBI Report on Trend and Progress of Banking in India, 2004-05, p. 85.
7. RBI Report on Trend and Progress of Banking in India, 2003-04, p. 85.
8. RBI Report on Trend and Progress of Banking in India, 2004-05, p. 93.
9. RBI Report on Trend and Progress of Banking in India, 2002-03, p. 65-66.
10. RBI Report on Trend and Progress of Banking in India, 2002-03, pp. 65-66.
11. Hindu, August, 2012.
12. Business Standard, July 31, 2012.
13. RBI Report on Trend and Progress of Banking in India, 2010-11, pp. 73.
14. *Ibid*.
15. The Indian Banks, December, 2007.

Chapter 21

Performance Budgeting in A Commercial Bank

Learning Objectives:

The present chapter aims at:

- Providing an overview of performance budgeting.
- Emphasising upon the need for performance budgeting in commercial banks in India.
- Highlighting mechanics for preparing performance budget for a commercial bank.

Chapter Outline:

- Performance Budgeting — An overview.
- Need for performance Budgeting in commercial banks in India.
- Mechanics for preparing performance budget for a commercial bank.
- Conclusions.

A. PERFORMANCE BUDGETING — AN OVERVIEW

Budgeting is an important managerial tool of planning, evaluation and control. Traditional budgeting emphasises the financial aspects, and does not establish any relationship between financial outlays and the physical targets of performance. It does not tell us what physical targets will be fulfilled from the budgeted expenditure on a particular head. It does not depict estimates in terms of the physical programmes of action or cost per unit or the cost-benefit ratio. The management, therefore, finds it difficult to evaluate the performance of work with the help of the conventional budgetary system. In order to overcome these deficiencies of the conventional budgetary system, the concept of performance budgeting was evolved for the first time in the USA during 1920s.

The performance budget may be defined as a managerial tool of estimating expenditure and earnings in terms of functions, programmes, activities and projects, and correlating the physical and financial aspects of the various programmes and activities forming part of a project. Indian Administrative Reforms Commission, which used the term performance budgeting for the first time, pointed out that performance budgeting focuses attention upon the general character and relative importance of the work to be done, or upon the service to be rendered, rather than upon the things to be acquired, such as personnel services, supplies, equipment, and so on. The important things in performance budgeting, therefore, are the work or services to be accomplished and what that work or services will cost. The main focus in performance budgeting is on activity analysis to achieve the lowest possible input-output ratio involving direct costs and benefits.

Performance budgeting seeks to accomplish many objectives, such as ensuring progress towards the long-term objectives envisaged and enunciated in the planning prospectus of the organisation, correlating the physical and functional aspects of programmes and activities, facilitating budget review and decision-making at all levels of management in the organisation, facilitating a more effective performance audit, and, finally, measuring the progress in time-bound objectives so that timely remedial action may be initiated.

The main parameters of performance budgeting system are:

(*i*) Formulation of objectives and goals;

(*ii*) Formulation of specific programmes, functional activities, and tasks for different levels of organisation within the realities of fiscal constraint;

(*iii*) Evolution of realistic and acceptable norms, yardsticks, standards and performance indicators, and expression thereof in quantifiable physical units;

(*iv*) Adoption of decentralised responsibility structure; and

(*v*) Development of a systematic accounting and reporting system to facilitate monitoring, analysis and review of actual performance in relation to the budget.

By providing a meaningful relationship between estimated inputs and expected outputs, performance budgeting serves as an effective instrument or tool in the hands of the management with which the latter can integrate the budgeting, costing, reporting and control a banking system of an enterprise. It facilitates the introduction of performance audit and a more purposeful and effective control through internal reports in the form of performance reports. By identifying the objectives and sub-objectives and the different levels in the organisation structure, it enhances the accountability of the management, and develops an awareness among the management cadres of the importance of their contribution to departmental programmes and the cost of their contribution. In view of these potentialities, performance budgeting is being growingly used in India in different private sector and public sector organisations, including commercial banks.

B. NEED FOR PERFORMANCE BUDGETING IN COMMERCIAL BANKS IN INDIA

The role and responsibilities of commercial banks in India have undergone phenomenal changes dimensionally, geographically and functionally. These institutions are no longer purveyors of short-term credit to the trade and industry located in urban areas. They now satisfy the varied credit needs of the farmers, businessmen, professionals and other weaker sections of society which have received importance in our economic planning. The banks have to penetrate into far flung areas of the country to garner the savings of the country folk and assist the poor and neglected people. In order to discharge its new responsibility, it is necessary for a commercial bank to spell-out its corporate purpose and mission and define its objectives in terms of deposit mobilisation and its channelisation, and communicate them to zonal or divisional offices and, through them, to branch offices, and then translate these goals into meaningful and feasible action programmes in consultation with zonal managers, who would, in turn, consult their respective branches.

Evidently, this process pre-supposes a grass-root budgeting system, under which the budgets of all the branches are sent to the regional offices, and the budgets of the regional offices are transmitted to the head office with a view to fixing the targets in different areas. After fixing the targets in terms of deposits and loans on the basis of the information supplied by branch level managers, the responsibilities of individual branch managers for the accomplishment of their respective targets are fixed, and their performance is evaluated against these targets. This is actually the process followed under the performance budgeting system.

Until recently, *ad hoc* targets for the growth of deposits and for lending to different sectors were fixed by the executives of the head office on the basis of the growth rate of bank business during the past couple of years, the current state of the economy in general and of industry in particular. Once this exercise was over, the head office issued a circular to all the regional offices, indicating a particular targeted growth rate of deposits for the next calendar year. The regional managers transmitted copies of these circulars to their divisional offices and branches. This practice of fixing the growth rate of deposits in advance by the head office and passing it on to all the divisions and branches was neither rational nor correct. The practice of fixing *ad hoc* targets for lending or formulating short-term plans for the busy season and the slack season was also unrealistic and unrelated to facts. Such a system was devoid of a complete sense of involvement on the part of the staff, who were expected to attain the targets. As a result, banks found it difficult to achieve the desired results.

In view of the above, as early as December 1972, public sector banks were advised by the Ministry of Finance to prepare annual plans for the year 1973 and to take steps to introduce performance budgeting, with special emphasis on priority sector lending. Following this, all public sector banks completed the preliminary work for the introduction of annual planning and performance budgeting. Some of these banks had already introduced the system in selected regions during the year 1974; the others adopted the system in the subsequent years.

C. MECHANICS FOR PREPARING PERFORMANCE BUDGET FOR A COMMERCIAL BANK

The preparation of performance budgeting in a commercial bank entails the following steps:

(*i*) Establishment of specific objectives and formulation of policies for the bank;

(*ii*) Formulation of action plans for different activities to achieve the objectives;

(*iii*) Fixing responsibilities at different levels of bank management in terms of the targets to be accomplished; and

(*iv*) Installation of the performance appraisal system for control.

◈ Establishment of Objectives and Formulation of Policies

The establishment of objectives is a pre-requisite to performance budgeting in a commercial bank. An objective is the end-point of any management programme and is needed in every area where performance and results directly and vitally affect the survival and growth of the enterprise. To be meaningful, objectives must be specific. A mere statement that the objective of the bank is to maximise profitability while fulfilling the socio-economic goals of the government without jeopardising its liquidity is not sufficient. The objectives must be verifiable, and the easiest way to get verifiability is to put them in quantitative terms. Instead of stating the objectives as above, we must say that the bank's objectives are to mobilise new deposits of the order of ₹ 100 crores next year and lend ₹ 150 crores to farmers, ₹ 50 crores to small-scale units, ₹ 10 crores to artisans, etc. Such verifiability of objectives is necessary because the branches and regional offices, which have to prepare their performance budgets for their incorporation in the overall performance budget of the bank, must know the top management's thinking on the future thrust and direction of the bank's activities. This also facilitates the formulation of the necessary policy guidelines.

In order to prepare the policy guidelines for the bank, the head office appoints a task force consisting of senior executives (including economists, financial and other experts on agriculture, small scale industries, large industry, trade, etc.) to prepare working papers relating to expected additions to deposits and advances to various sectors in each region during the ensuing year. This exercise should be undertaken by keeping in view the past trends of the business in each segment, as well as the likely economic regulatory and other current factors at the macro level which may affect the bank business in the following year.

These working papers are then consolidated and crystallised into draft policy guidelines for sectoral performance in various circles, regions and zones. These policy guidelines are prepared in the manner which is shown in Table 21.1. The draft guidelines are then presented before the top management; and, after discussions a consensus is arrived at about the broad direction and thrust of the bank and the expectations of the top management regarding the desired levels of sectoral achievements in various regions.

TABLE 21.1: Guidelines of a Bank

Region I		*Region II*		*Region III*		*Region IV*		*Region V*	
Existing	*Planned*	*Existing*	*Planned*	*Existing*	*Planned*	*Existing*	*Planned*	*Existing*	*Planned*
D = 100	120	D = 210	225	D = 140	150	D = 80	90	D = 270	280
A = 60	70	A = 240	210	A = 40	70	A = 60	75	A = 210	225
CD Ratio		CD Ratio		CD Ratio		CD Ratio	CD Ratio	CD Ratio	CD Ratio
60%	59%	101%	93%	20%	47%	75%	83%	79%	80%

Regional managers should be asked to collect information pertaining to their "*business*" and "*general*" environment of their own regions, and to identify the business potentiality in their areas.

Before finalising the policy guidelines for different regions, the head office invites the regional managers to a meeting with the Managing Director and other senior executives of the bank. Thus, regional managers are fully associated with the formulation of the central office policy guidelines.

The central office policy guidelines so finalised are then sent to each regional office. Within the framework of these guidelines, the regional manager prepares the guidelines for the regions. He sends these guidelines to various branch office managers, together with printed performance budget sheets, with the request that they prepare the budget in conformity with the guidelines.

◈ Formulation of Action Plan

Performance budgeting pre-supposes a grass-root planning. Every branch prepares feasible action programmes in terms of budgets for different activities, such as deposits, advances, income and expenditure, and send them to the regional office, which will, after assimilating the budgets of different branches, prepare the budget for the whole region. On receiving the budget of different regions, the head office prepares the performance budget for the bank as a whole.

The branch manager prepares the performance budget for his branch, keeping in view the corporate goals and the overall requirements of the bank, and the physical and human resources available with the branch. This involves the following exercises:

- **Determination of Command Area of the Branch:** The performance budget at the branch level begins with the determination of the command area of the branch for the budget year. The command area is the main area of operations which the branch can effectively serve during the budget year. In identifying the command area, the branch manager should keep in view a host of factors, such as the area from where the major chunk of branch business comes at the moment, and the pockets of business potentials that can possibly be converted into real business. The command area can thus be segregated on the basis of the geographical spread and services pockets. Geographically, it will cover the area around the branch premises, over which the various types of customers' clusters are spread. According to service pockets, it will cover even an area which is geographically far off, but functionally very close to the branch. For instance, a residential colony is situated far from the branch; but the branch manager has been able to attract a number of customers of this colony. Likewise, the branch manager has provided financial assistance to a number of industrial establishments of an industrial estate located at a great distance from the branch. Both areas form the command area on the basis of the deposits and advance services, even though they are distantly situated.
- **Collecting the Area Profile:** The command area is then divided into smaller possible sub-divisions, such as Road No. 1, 2, 3, 4... etc., or village A, B, C, etc. The branch manager's next task in the sequence is to collect the data on the occupational profile of the population and the productive units within each segment of the command

TABLE 21.2: Population — The Command Area (No. of Household Units)

Occupations	*Road A*	*Road B*	*Road C*	*Road D*	*Total*
1. Agriculturists					
2. Traders' families					
3. Professionals					
4. Salaried class					
5. Others					
6. Wholesalers					
7. Retailers					
8. Small-scale industrialists					
9. Large and medium industrial units					
10. Educational institutions					
11. Health institutions					
12. Religious and social units					
13. Functional units					
14. Government offices					

area. To facilitate this task, each bank branch is supplied a bunch of printed sheets by its head office. The proforma of one of these sheets is shown in Table 20.2. The branch manager fills this sheet on the basis of his personal knowledge and impressions, the knowledge of his staff and also on the basis of some government publications, such as the District Census Handbook.

- **Determination of Potential Customers:** After collecting the data pertaining to the occupations of the residents of the different segments of the command area, the branch manager should prepare a comprehensive table which will contain occupation-wise, details of the residents, as also of the existing customers. This will serve as a guide to business development for the budget year. This is illustrated in Table 21.3. This list will enlighten the branch manager on the total number of farmers in the area and the number of farmers having accounts with the branch; the total number of traders families and the number of such families having accounts with the branch, and such other details of the area. With this information, the branch manager must undertake an analysis to determine why others have no dealings with the branch. On investigation, a number of reasons may be discovered. These reasons may be:

(*a*) Some are banking upon the branches of other banks located in the areas;
(*b*) Some are too poor to save anything;
(*c*) Some have dealings with branches away from the command areas;
(*d*) Some have surpluses, but they do not keep them with any bank branch; and
(*e*) Any other.

TABLE 21.3: Guide for Business Development of the Command Area for 200...

Occupational Types	*Total No.*	*Existing No. of A/cs.*	*Potential No. of A/cs.*	*Individual Addresses*	*Services to be Adopted*	*Strategy to be Adopted*
Agriculturists						
Traders' families						
Professionals						
Salaried class						
Wholesalers						
Small-scale industrial units						
Retailers						
Schools and colleges						
Clubs/Societies/Offices						

With this information, the branch manager should identify the potential customers and devise suitable strategies for attracting them. For instance, he may, by promising better banking services, attract the traders of the command area having their accounts with a branch away from the command area. The personal approach for this purpose will be very useful. Similar exercises may also be undertaken for other classes of households, commercial or industrial units, services and religious organisations.

The branch manager should examine the possibilities of the new activities likely to come up in the command area, and assess whether he can seize upon one or more of these activities during the budget year. At the same time, the possibility of available expertise and entrepreneurship in the area, who can exploit local natural resources and formulate a viable project that can be financed by the branch on the basis of its feasibility, should be explored.

- **Planning for Deposits, Advances, Ancillary Business, Income and Expenditure:** One the basis of the information collected, the manager should prepare separate budgets for deposits, advances, ancillary business, income and expenditure, and estimate the total deposits, total advances, income and expenditure during the budget period.

Most banks use planning sheets for the purpose. For instance, the deposit planning sheet is used to estimate deposits precisely. A proforma of a simple deposit planning sheet is given in Table 21.4. In this sheet, information pertaining to present and future deposits from persons of different occupations are shown.

The planning exercise for advances for budget year is made on the sheet, the proforma of which is given in Table 21.5. In the advance sheet, the branch manager has to fill in different columns, showing the existing advances to agriculture (in terms of number and amount), industries and traders, the expected increase in such advances, and the total advances during the budget year.

On the basis of the planning sheet, the performance budgets for deposits and advances are constructed. These budgets are prepared for the whole year as well as for each quarter. The performance budget for deposits, the proforma of which is shown in Table 21.6, contains information on the actual deposits of the last year and the anticipated deposits in the next year and the quarterly deposit position of the branch.

The proforma budget for various advances contains the details of the actual amount of advances for the whole of last year, the anticipated amount of advances for the whole budget year as well as for each quarter. The proforma budget for advances is shown in Table 21.7.

Besides, the branch manager should prepare the budget for the revenue likely to be received from agency services, such as collections, safe deposit, locker services, remittances, guarantees, exchange, etc. Unlike the deposits and advances, the manager may find it difficult to estimate revenue from these services in precise terms. However, he should endeavour to assess the potentialities of these services in the light of the existing and ensuing changes in the environment, and so estimate the income from these ancillary services.

Once the budgets for deposits, advances, and ancillary services are ready, the branch manager should consider whether the existing staff and facilities are adequate enough to carry into effect the anticipated budget, or whether additional staff and facilities will be required. The input budget is prepared for this very purpose.

Finally, the income and expenditure budget is prepared to estimate the revenues from, and the expenditures on, the budgeted (existing as well as incremental) business of the branch. This budget is prepared on the basis of the deposits, advances, ancillary business and input budgets. A proforma of the income and expenditure budget is given in Table 21.8. The expected income and expenditure on deposits and advances should be calculated on a monthly accrual basis; otherwise the figures of the profit budget would be wrong. For instance, if the budgeted deposits for the full one year of a branch amount to ₹ 12 lakhs, and if they are evenly spread at ₹ 1 lakh every month, the interest burden of the branch should be calculated by decreasing the number of months, i.e., the interest on deposits of ₹ 2 lakhs garnered in the first month will have to be calculated for all the twelve months, but interest on the subsequent ₹ 2 lakhs for February should be computed only for eleven months; on the deposits of March, the interest burden will be calculated for only 10 months, and so on. Similarly, the interest on advances should be computed.

- **Finalising the Performance Budgets:** When the performance budgets are prepared by the branch manager, they are discussed with the regional manager and finalised. The regional manager should discuss these budgets objectively, and ensure that whatever figures are contained in the budgets are real and attainable.

After the finalisation of the budgets of different branches, the regional manager adopts them for the preparation of the performance budget for the region. This budget is then sent to the head office. The head office convenes a meeting of all the regional managers at which their respective budgets are discussed and finalised. Finally, the performance budget of the bank as a whole is constructed region-wise.

TABLE 21.4: Deposit Planning Sheet of ... Branch of 200....

Occupations	Potential Units			Present Deposits		Increase in the Deposits of Existing A/cs Planned	Deposits from New Accounts Planned		Total Increase in Deposits Planned
	Existing Nos.	Additions in Budget Year	Total	No. of A/cs	Amount Rs.		No. of A/cs	Amount	
A. Household Sector									
A - 1 Agriculturists									
A - 2 Salaried Class									
A - 3 Professionals									
A - 4 Traders' Families									
A - 5 Industrial Families									
A - 6 Remittances Received									
B. Traders									
B - 1 Wholesalers									
B - 2 Retailers									
B - 3 Others									
C. Industries									
C - 1 Large & Medium									
C - 2 Small-scale									
C - 3 Others									
D. Service Industries									
E - 1 Colleges/Universities									
E - 2 Schools									
E - 3 Hospitals									
E - 4 Others									
F. Financial Institutions									
F - 1 Bank Branches									
F - 2 Co-op. Banks									
F - 3 Others									

TABLE 21.5: Advance Planning Sheet

	Potential Units			*Financed During the Year*				*Additional Finance for Existing Units in Budget Year*		*Finance to New Units in the Budget Year*			
				Term Loan		*Working Cap.*				*Term Loan*		*Working Cap.*	
	Existing No.	*Additions in year*	*Total Amt.*	*No. of A/cs.*	*Amt.*	*No. of A/cs.*	*Amt.*	*Term*	*Working Cap. A/cs.*	*No. of A/cs.*	*Amt.*	*No. of A/cs.*	*Amt.*
A. Agricultural Sector													
A - 1 Cultivators													
A - 2 Dairy													
A - 3 Poultry													
A - 4 Others													
B. Industries													
B - 1 Large and Medium													
B - 2 Small-scale													
B - 3 Others													
C. Traders & Others													
C - 1 Wholesalers													
C - 2 Retailers													
C - 3 Others													
C - 4 Transport Operators													
C - 5 Professionals													

TABLE 21.6: Proforma Budget Sheet for Deposits

Branch Name
Year of Opening
Region
Budget for the Year 1983

(₹ in '000)

Types of Deposits	*1982 December (Actual)* ₹	*1983 December (Anticipated)* ₹	*Budget Year 1983*			
			I Qtr.	*II Qtr.*	*III Qtr.*	*IV Qtr.*
1. Current Account No. Amount ₹						
2. Savings Account No. Amount ₹						
3. Other Account No. Amount ₹						

TABLE 21.7: Proforma Budget Sheet for Advances

Branch Name
Year of Opening
Region
Budget for the Year 1983

(Rupees in '000)

Types of Deposits		*1982 December (Actual)* ₹	*1983 December (Anticipated)* ₹	*Budget Year 1983*			
				I Qtr.	*II Qtr.*	*III Qtr.*	*IV Qtr.*
A. Priority Sector							
A - 1	Agriculture						
A - 2	Small-scale						
A - 3	Exports						
A - 4	Professional						
A - 5	Retailers						
A - 6	Others						
Total							
B. Non-Priority Sector							
B - 1	Large & Med. Industries						
B - 2	Wholesalers						
B - 3	Others						
Total							
Grand Total							

TABLE 21.8: Income and Expenditure Budget Sheet

Name of Branch
Region
Budget Year

	Budget Year				(Amt. In 000' ₹) Total for the Budget Year
	I Qtr.	*II Qtr.*	*III Qtr.*	*IV Qtr.*	
EARNINGS					
1. Interest receivable on advances					
2. Interest receivable from EO					
3. Other Income					
Total					
EXPENSES					
1. Interest payable on deposits					
2. Interest payable at HO					
3. Salaries and allowances					
4. Other Expenditure					
Total					
Profit (+) Loss (–)					

◈ Fixing Responsibility

On the basis of the performance budgets of the bank's branches, the targets for different types of deposits, advances, inputs, etc., are fixed for the budget year for different regions, and the respective regional managers are required to achieve them. The regional managers allocate these targets among the different branches falling within their respective jurisdictions, and the branch managers are expected to achieve the target set for them. The branch manager then fixes the responsibility among his subordinates in terms of the target set for them. For instance, an employee may be charged with the responsibility of procuring new deposits from persons living in certain areas; the other employee may be entrusted with the responsibility of giving loans to farmers and small-scale units. The target amount may be fixed for each quarter. It should, however, be noted that the branch manager should discuss the targets with his staff and then allocate the responsibilities among them.

◈ Installation of Performance Appraisal System for Control

The performance budgeting system is a control device with which the bank management can measure the efficiency of different regional and branch offices. As a matter of fact, the budgetary system entails a comparison of the actual performance against pre-determined plans and objectives. A natural extension of the budgetary process is, therefore, the creation of periodic reports which will enable the management to check the estimated figures against the actual achievements. Therefore, a foolproof system of control should be installed with the creation of periodic reports. Such a system of control not only helps in evaluating performance, but also ensures a direct control of the various income and cost factors; probes into the reasons for the deviations from targets and takes corrective action, wherever necessary; promotes a feeling of cost consciousness and restricts expenditures to the minimum; encourages healthy competition between branches and helps in reviewing current policy and in determining future policy.

The budgetary report proforma of one branch is contained in Table 21.9, which shows actual results, the budget figures and the variance between the two, the causes of the variance, the corrective steps taken, and guidance for the future.

TABLE 21.9: Budgetary Report of ... Branch

Items	1st Quarter (January-March)				
	Actual	Budget	Variance	Course of Variance	Corrective Steps
Deposits Advance Profit Inputs					

For maintaining a continuing comparison of actual results with budgeted results, a monthly or quarterly report will be very useful. The observation of actual deposits and advances for every quarter will enable the management to determine whether the actuals are in conformity with the estimates; if not, what are the reasons for the variance. There may be two principal reasons for any variance. In the first place, environmental conditions may have changed since the determination of the budgets, rendering the entire estimates wrong. The actual deposit figures for a branch may have, therefore, been proper under the changed circumstances, even though they vary from the pre-determined standards. In such a situation, the only remedy left with the top management is to direct the concerned branch manager to revise the deposit budget in consultation with the regional manager, for this affects both the regional and the head office budgets. Another factor responsible for the deviation is the failure of the personnel to execute the policies and programmes of action. The branch manager should take the necessary action against those employees who are at fault in order to ensure that such deviations do not recur. All this indicates that the entire system of performance budgeting is rolling in nature and has to be taken as an on-going exercise.

D. CONCLUSIONS

Performance budgeting is an important managerial tool which exhibits estimated expenditure and earnings in terms of functions, programme as activities and projects and correlates the physical and financial aspects of various programmes and activities forming part of the projects.

Performance budgeting system comprises the following.

- Formulation of objectives and goals;
- Formulation of specific programmes, functional activities, and tasks for different levels of organizations;
- Evaluation of realistic and acceptable norms, yardsticks, standards and performance indicators, and quantify them into physical units;
- Adoption of decentralised responsibility structure; and
- Development of a systematic accounting and reporting system to facilitate monitoring, analysis and review of actual performance in relation to the budget.

KEY TERMS

- Action Plan
- Command Area
- Grass-root budgeting
- Objectives and goals
- Performance budgeting

DISCUSSION QUESTIONS

1. What is performance budgeting? Discuss parameters of performance budgeting.
2. Why should a commercial bank prepare performance budgeting?
3. Distinguish between traditional budgeting and performance budgeting.
4. Discuss how a banker should construct performance budget for his bank.
5. What is command area? What is its importance in preparing performance budget of a bank?
6. What is performance appraisal system? Discuss how a banker should design this system for his bank.

Zero-Base Budgeting in A Commercial Bank (ZBB)

Learning Objectives:

The present chapter aims at:

- Highlighting the relevance of ZBB to commercial banks in India.
- Providing conceptual understanding of ZBB.
- Dilating upon methodology of preparing ZBB.
- Examining utility of ZBB approach.
- Describing methodology for adoption of ZBB in a commercial bank.

Chapter Outline:

- Relevance of Zero-Base Budgeting (ZBB) to commercial banks in India.
- Concept of ZBB.
- Preparing ZBB.
- Utility of ZBB approach.
- Adoption of ZBB in a commercial bank.
- Conclusions.

A. RELEVANCE OF ZERO-BASE BUDGETING (ZBB) TO COMMERCIAL BANKS IN INDIA

Commercial banks in India have come to be recognized as vital catalytic agent engaged in the hurculean task of stoking the engine of economic development and uplifting the teeming hapless and neglected masses of the country. Post nationalisation period has witnessed unparalleled expansion of branch network, growth in deposits and dimensional, functional and geographical increase in lending operations of the commercial banks. Today, they constitute one of the pillars of the Indian economy and control the commanding heights of the economy. To ensure the uninterrupted growth at a rapid pace, it is necessary that these banks function efficiently.

However, it is intriguing to observe that until recently there has been a steady erosion of bank's profitability. While social orientation alone is not responsible for profit erosion as it is widely made out to be, the fact remains that bank's future march on the road to social banking will depend only on how effectively the resources are being carved. Among the various factors that contributed to the deplorable profitability performance of the banks, lack of proper utilisation of financial resources has been the major one. This is mainly due to ineffective planning and monitoring system. Although they have launched formal planning and performance budgeting system more than a decade back to plan and control their operations, these have not fructified for the fact that the existing planning and monitoring system do not provide any mechanism for constant evaluation of efficacy and effectiveness of the current operations. The existing systems review only a fraction of total activity because detailed analysis of only those expenditure items which are likely to increase (or decrease) is made. The reasonableness of the previous year's level performance is not critically reviewed; it is taken for granted. This leads to entire planning system to be based on incremental growth. Certain percentage growth is indicated as a corporate objective *vis-a-vis* the previous year's performance. As a result, if the past performance has been unsatisfactory, the incremental results achieved in the subsequent year are higher than the average of the banking industry and this is applauded as meritorious, while the fact remains that the bank may have provided more than necessary resources by way of manpower, equipment, etc., in the previous year and goes on providing more resources for the current year for achieving the incremental growth of outputs.

Further, the present budgeting system does not pay any attention to cost factor which is very important for a banking enterprise facing the problem of deteriorating profitability. The existing level of cost, which is generally based on a traditional "business as usual" position is hardly winnowed and the "unit cost" is presumed to be valid perpetually. It has become fancy for bank managers to place entire blame on the Government for the continued decline in their profitability rate because the social responsibility function imposed on banks is generally not as remunerative as their traditional commercial activities. Although there is some truth in it, but to what extent social obligations adversely affect profitability of the bank has not been precisely determined because the costs involved in undertaking both traditional and non-traditional activities are not examined at every managerial level. In the existing budgeting system, where expenses are budgeted, the basis is the permissible extent of incremental growth depending on the activities undertaken by a branch. This leaves the individual activities undertaken by the branch totally out of focus and a "branch position" (which is after all, only a composite entity) is relied upon.

So as to arrest the deteriorating profitability performance of Indian commercial banks, the top management has to install such a planning and control system as could force the executive to identify and analyse what they are going to do in total the 'cost' involved in performing the activities, set objectives and goals, make requisite operating decisions and evaluate changing responsibilities and work load as an integral part of the monitoring system. This is done only under "Zero-Base Budgeting" (ZBB).

The Government of India, decided to introduce ZBB in its various department from the financial year 1987-88 and directed all the State Government and Public Undertakings to install this control system.

With a view to ensuring optimal utilisation of resources and economising costs it is high time for the bank managers to launch this approach. However, success of ZBB approach lies in its proper implementation by the functionaries who require thorough understanding of the concept of ZBB as also the sequence of activities that have to be performed under this approach. The following paragraphs are, therefore, devoted to dilate upon these aspects.

B. CONCEPT OF ZBB

According to Peter A. Phyrr, who first introduced this system in a U.S. based firm, Texas Instrument in 1970, ZBB is an operating, planning and budgeting process which requires each manager to justify his entire budget request in detail from scratch and shifts the burden of proof to each manager to justify why he should spend any money at all. ZBB implies constructing a budget without any reference to what has gone before, based on a fundamental reappraisal of purposes, methods and resources. It attempts to re-evaluate all programmes and activities in terms of cost-benefit. ZBB is not based on last year's budget but rather on ground zero, thus avoiding the common tendency in budgeting to look at changes from the previous period. Under this approach the entire banking business programme is divided into goals and activities and cost of each activity is then calculated from the ground up. Each expenditure is reconsidered from the very beginning. It is like assuming that a zero expenditure has been defrayed on an activity at the time of its review, although the activity is being performed for a long period and may have already involved some expenditure.

In ZBB, a bank is required to justify not only the new programme and the funds therefor but also the on-going activities and the funds for them. Thus, provisions for existing programmes are also required to be justified in the budget rather than adding them in the budget as a matter of routine. As such, the existing programmes will not be treated as immutable but will be examined afresh as to their continued utility and effectiveness, thereby freeing resources for new programmes. The basic idea underlying this approach is not just to cut expenditure but to make the entire programmes more effective by a more purposive allocation of resources to various programmes.

ZBB thus differs markedly from the traditional budgeting as also from performance budgeting. In their traditional budgeting the current expenditure levels are used as an established base from which an analysis in detail of only those items that involve increases or decreases is made. In contrast, ZBB requires evaluation of the whole project so as to establish its need, and not just the additional requirements. In performance budgeting, evaluation of the entire programme expenditures takes place and at the same time the expenditures continue almost as in the routine budgeting practice. But in ZBB entire expenditures are reconsidered to justify their continuation.

C. PREPARING ZBB

Budget making exercise under ZBB involves the following:

(*a*) Identification of "Decision Units";

(*b*) Formulation and development of "Decision Packages";

(*c*) Review and rank of the "Decision Packages"; and

(*d*) Allocation of Resources.

◈ Identification of "Decision Units"

Preparation of ZBB begins with identification of decision units. A decision unit is a full description of each individual activity which a manager undertakes and the decisions made by him in respect thereof. These decisions pertain to the level of expenditure and the scope, direction or quality of work to be performed. The decision units are ultimately the modules which will be assessed for their achievements under ZBB. Identification of decision units calls for breaking down the conglomeration of operations at each managerial desk into the relevant-elementary activities (which are, of course, inter-related to other activities). This can be done effectively if organisation structure, management and objectives of the enterprise are known.

The benefit of this sort of analysis is that the relevance of each activity to the total role of that manager as well as to the corporate objective is focused sharply. It also helps the manager to realise why he is performing a particular activity and also what resources, by way of manpower and other facilities like transport etc. (which all involve expenditure) are necessary and whether there are alternative methods of performing the same activity at a lower cost. For instance, a branch manager has to undertake a number of activities, such as appraisal of agricultural loan applications the objective of which is to ensure that overdues are reduced, inspection of small-scale industrial units so as to detect the incidence of sickness or incipient sickness, and organising deposit mobilisation weeks/fortnights/months so as to attract more and more savings of the community. All these involve cost. ZBB insists that the manager conceives of the alternative strategies of carrying out the above activities at lower cost. Even activities like O & M, organisational planning, economic research etc., which are relatively more difficult to plan and control can be subjected to the system of ZBB and performed at a most economical cost. In sum, all those activities which are amendable to a cost-benefit analysis are within the orbit of ZBB.

◈ Formulation and Development of "Decision Packages"

Another vital exercise involved in ZBB is development of decision packages. A decision package is a budget request which lists the function or activity of the decision unit, goals and objectives of the activity, benefits to be derived from undertaking the activity/programme, financial consequences of not undertaking the activity, the estimated cost of the package and alternative ways of performing the same activity or achieving the same objectives. In addition, manager is expected to identify alternative levels of efforts and spending to perform a specific activity. A minimum level of effort package, which is actually the grass root's funding level necessary to keep an activity/programme alive (usually 70-75% of the current operating level) must be established and additional levels of efforts with its costs and benefits must be identified in separate decision packages have different performance output and separate funding requirements. This analysis forces every manager to consider and evaluate a level of spending lower than his current operating level, gives management the alternative of eliminating an activity or choosing from several levels of efforts and allows tremendous trade offs and shifts in expenditure levels among organisational units.

◈ Review and Rank of "Decision Packages"

Once the decision packages are developed, they are reviewed and ranked in order of decreasing benefit. This stage, thus, entails prioritisation of the various activities undertaken by each manager as well as by the managers. The ranking has to be done at various levels starting from the lowest level of the managers who identify decision units and prepare decision packages. The ranking of decision packages requires to be done in the light of the corporate priorities laid down for the ensuing budget period, and cut-off point on the total permissible cost to be incurred in the next year. Each concerned manager will rank his own decision packages. These are then sent upward through the management hierarchy where the decision packages are once again reviewed and ranked along with the other decision unit packages at selected levels and a single, consolidated ranking for all the packages is produced.

In the process of ranking, the "Volume Problem" will emerge particularly at the highest levels where thousands of packages are to be reviewed and ranked. In a large banking organisation the problem of ranking a large number of decision packages can be handled by a committee at each of the higher levels. Use of computer in this regard will be extremely useful in shuffling and reshuffling the numerous decision packages on the basis of the objectives and corporate priorities and cost considerations. In arriving at a progressive total of the costs involved and deciding upon the ultimate cut-off point the manager can make use of a computer. Thus, the decision packages falling below the cut-off point would have to be discontinued.

◈ Allocation of Resources

Once the decision packages have been finalised, resources are allocated as among various functions and sub-functions for the ensuing year.

D. UTILITY OF ZBB APPROACH

ZBB is a powerful managerial tool that will help the bank management in judicious allocation of resources, minimization of cost of operation and in deriving the optimum benefits out of the current deployment funds. By permitting constant review and appraisal of on-going programmes, it enables the management to spotlight redundant and relatively less deserving schemes and staves-off their perpetuation and thereby safeguards the organisation from suffering on account of them. Since ZBB requires justification of each budget request, it permits trade-offs within and across departments and relates costs and benefits of programmes and managers will be every careful in selection of projects in the very beginning. They will always be cost conscious and objective during the operation of the projects. Thus, the ZBB will foster a culture of efficiency and cost consciousness among the bank executives which is very much in demand in the present Indian banking scenario.

ZBB can also be employed as a very effective means of control system that establishes clear cut objectives and goals, measures progress towards these goals, indicates positive action required if the actual performance deviates from the plan and budget and displays potential for further improvement.

The management's efforts in directing and motivating employees are facilitated by ZBB because most managers have to work together in developing and finalising the decision packages and operating plans. It provides ample opportunity to the branch managers to identify problems that are likely to be faced by them in achieving the goals. It also commits the managers to a set of defined objectives and goals, performance standards and accomplishments that they will be held accountable for. This is because each branch manager is involved in decision-making.

However, the bank managers have to face several problems in formulation and execution of this technique. The most important problem experienced by the management is in the area of formulation of decision packages. Determining activities, functions or operations to develop decision packages for establishing the minimum level of effort and identifying work measures and evaluation of each activity involve lot of subjective judgement on the part of each activity manager and are, therefore, subject to question.

In ranking and reviewing the decision packages, the management faces problems of determining who will do the ranking, to what level within each organisation packages will be ranked and what method or procedure will be used to review and rank the packages.

There are certain fears and administrative problems which top management of a bank have to face particularly in the initial years of the implementation of ZBB. Branch Managers as well as regional managers may often be apprehensive of any process that forces decision-making and requires detailed scrutiny of their function for all to see. Administration and communication of ZBB process are likely to pose serious problems because more managers become involved in this process than in most budgeting and planning procedures.

E. ADOPTION OF ZBB IN A COMMERCIAL BANK

In view of the above, it is advisable to the bank management in India to select a pilot area where to implement it first and learn from it the difficulties experienced before extending it to all activities, areas, and branches. Thus, to start with, the top management may introduce ZBB in respect of certain vulnerable activities and regions where either the performance is not upto the desired level or the cost is suspected to be excessive. Even before the pilot implementation is taken in hand, the management will have to ensure that extensive leg-work has been undertaken so that there is intellectual and emotional acceptance of the system at all managerial levels.

In the light of the experience, this system should be extended to other areas and activities so that ultimately the entire banking organisation is covered in course of time.

It is further advisable that the entire work of implementation of ZBB system is monitored by a centralised staff department under the supervision of the chairman/managing director of the bank. Such a staff department will serve the purpose of keeping the top management informed of progress and also help to establish creditability lower down. In a large commercial bank having decentralised administrative set-up, each administrative office should have a staff department on the above pattern.

Another decision which top management of a bank will have to take in regard to implementation of ZBB system is as to what should be the appropriate level of managers who will be asked to identifying decision units and prepare decision packages. In a bank, it will be in fitness of things to restrict these tasks upto the level of branch managers and departmental heads at the administrative office. At branch level, each significant manager's desk will be subjected to prescribed scrutiny.

Time requirement is also an important factor to be considered while implementing ZBB approach. At present, annual performance budgeting exercise in a bank takes 14 and 16 weeks' time. It will be possible to adopt a similar time-frame for ZBB. Another moot question to be taken into account is how frequently ZBB exercise should be undertaken. Since ZBB exercise involves lot of cost, time and efforts and there my be radical changes in the decision units or the decision package from year to year, the management is advised to undertake this exercise once in three years. In the intervening two years, if necessary, the decision packages may be updated. The ranking exercise may be undertaken every year.

Whatever be the frequency of implementation of ZBB system that may be decided upon, it would be in the interest of a bank to make a critical analysis of the first year's ZBB process upon completion, and then identify the problem prone areas and the remedial measures. Appropriate changes should be incorporated when the exercise is repeated. Soon after this, the bank management will be in a position to draw up a ZBB manual for use by branch managers, regional managers and administrative heads at the corporate level of the organisation.

What is most important for effective implementation of ZBB approach in a bank is that the managers should be exposed to the basics of ZBB and imparted adequate training. It would be useful to repeat capsular training programmes on location so that even potential managers may be appropriately oriented.

F. CONCLUSION

ZBB is an operating, planning and budgeting process which requires each manager to justify his entire budget request in detail from scratch and shifts the burden of proof to each manager to justify the proposed spending. ZBB is not based on last year's budget but rather on ground zero.

In ZBB, budget making process involves the following steps:

- Identification of Decision units;
- Formulation and development of Decision packages;
- Review and rank of the Decision Packages; and
- Allocation of Resources.

ZBB is an invaluable managerial tool which helps the bank management in judicious allocation of resources, minimisation of cost of operations and in deriving the optimum benefits out of the current deployment of funds.

KEY TERMS

- Decision Package
- Decision unit

DISCUSSION QUESTIONS

1. What is zero-base budgeting? How is it different from traditional budgeting?
2. Discuss the utility of zero-base budgeting for a commercial bank.
3. What is the relevance of zero-base budgeting for Indian commercial banks? How can this approach help improve performance of Indian commercial banks?
4. Discuss how a banker should construct zero-base budget for his bank.
5. What is decision unit? How is this unit identified?
6. What is decision package? How can a banker develop decision package?

Management of Development Financial Institutions

Section Three

Section III: Learning Objectives

- Providing vivid account of evolution, growth and performance of Development Financial Institutions in India and abroad.
- Providing an understanding of mechanism of project evaluation by Development Financial Institutions.

Section Outline

- Development of Financial Institutions — An overview.
- Project Evaluation by Development Financial Institutions in India.
- Performance evaluation of All-India Financial Institutions.

Chapter 23

Development Financial Institutions in India — An Overview

Learning Objectives:

The present chapter aims at:

- **Providing a synoptic view of Development Financial institutions in India and abroad.**
- **Providing a brief profile of all India-term lending institutions.**
- **Familiarizing with the RBI policy guidelines for Financial Institutions.**

Chapter Outline:

- Development Financial Institutions across the globe — A synoptic view.
- Development Financial Institutions in India — A panoramic view.
- Profile of all India Financial Institutions.
- RBI Policy Guidelines for Financial Institutions in India.
- Conclusions and suggestions.

A. DEVELOPMENT FINANCIAL INSTITUTIONS ACROSS THE GLOBE — A SYNOPTIC VIEW

Development Financial Institutions (DFIs) emerged in different parts of the world to overcome the perennial problem of inadequacy of long-term resources for catering to the developmental requirements of the country. In view of the inadequate supply of long-term credit through banks and concomitant shortage of long-term investments and the perceived risk aversion of savers and creditors, many of these institutions had to be sponsored by national governments. Although the oldest such government sponsored institutions began with the establishment of the Societe Generale pour favoriser l'Industrie National in France in 1822, it was well over two decades later that development banking came into its own with the establishment of the Credit Mobiliser in France in 1848 for financing of Continental European railway expansion. In Asia too, such institutions were established as early as in the 20th century- an important example being the Industrial Bank of Japan (IBJ) founded in 1900. The IBJ assisted not only in the development of the domestic capital markets, but it also performed the role of obtaining portfolio capital for the industrial firms in Japan.

Historically, the DFIs played a key role in the speedy industrial development of Europe and Japan. DFIs have also been used for government support to the priority sector or to counter the effects of problems in any sector. For example, the Government of Japan took the support of the DFIs in resolving problems in banking sector in Japan; Malaysia used them for directing flow of funds to targeted sectors for its economic recovery. In Korea and Thailand, DFIs were set up to extend financial support to small and medium enterprises (SMEs). In these countries, the DFIs have been rendered support by Japanese and French governments by guaranteeing or underwriting their bonds.[1]

With drying of subsidized sources of funds and financial sector reforms in a number of countries, the DFIs have chartered into totally new areas, such as lending to the SME sector, infrastructure and basic industries, industrial restructuring, foreign trade, environment conservation programmes, preservation of natural resources, improvement of environmental quality, health environmental education, sustainable agriculture, energy venture financing and banking services. For example, Industrial Bank of Korea (IBK), a premier term-lending FI established in 1961 under the Industrial Bank of Korea Act, diversified overtime into other related activities, such as credit card services, electronic banking, venture capital, trust account management and treasury operations. The retail banking operations of IBK form an important source of steady and relatively low-cost funds for its SME lending activities. Brazil has also witnessed similar diversification. Some DFIs have transformed themselves into universal banks.[2]

In developing counties, however, DFIs which failed to transform themselves in consonance with the changing environment are facing problems of high and growing NPAs, poor cost-benefit evaluations of projects, and widespread mismatches in their asset-liabilities requiring large provision. Furthermore, their inability to mobilize long-term fixed resources led to erosion of profits and in some cases erosion of net worth.[3] Financial sector reforms to foster efficiency, transparency and stability in the financial system and calibrated globalisation have led to the debate on the role of DFIs and the support provided by the Government. Efficiency of government sponsorship can be enhanced with conditionalities as in the case of France. Besides, an appropriate legal framework for effective regulation and supervision needs to be customised to suit the macro-economic and socio-political conditions, the stage of financial development and the nature of industrial development to each country.[4]

Financial sector, with its concomitant processes of decontrol, deregulation and globalisation has led to increased competition for financial intermediaries across different segments. The competitive pressures came into the business domain of FIs on account of the entry of new players. Moreover, with the initiation of financial sector reforms in the early 1990s, access of FIs to assured sources of long duration/concessional funds from the Government has been gradually phased out. As a consequence, DFIs are required to raise funds from the capital market. With the removal of administrative controls on the interest rate structure, it has become increasingly difficult for DFIs to raise long-term funds. This, in turn, has affected their ability to offer competitive rate to their borrowers.

Apart from the competitive pressure for raising resources, the role of DFIs as an exclusive source of development finance has diminished since the intermediaries, especially banks have also entered into long-term and high risk project financing. As such, FIs are increasingly facing competition not only in terms of raising resources but also in the deployment of funds. In short, the change in the operating environment coupled with the legacy of high non-performing assets has led to serious financial stress in term-lending financial institutions.

It is against this background, the RBI appointed 'Working Group on Development Financial Institutions' in 2004 to review the experiences and prospects of DFIs for transformation into banks and to assess the financial position and recommend a regulatory framework for the existing financial institutions. The Group noted that:[5]

- The role of DFIs as exclusive providers of development finance has diminished during the 1990s with the emergence of a well-diversified banking system, operating efficiently and acquiring skills in extending long-term finance. The Group suggested that the banks should be permitted to raise long-term finance through development bonds to enable them to extend high-risk project finance.
- As a result of the exposure of DFIs to certain sectors with cyclical downturn, DFIs have accumulated large NPAs. To overcome this, Government should decide which sectors need development finance and which institutions can continue as DFIs. The rest of the DFIs should be converted either to a bank or a regular NBFC.
- The SFCs, according to the Group, have lost their relevance and there is hardly any scope for the revival of financially sick SFCs. It, therefore, recommended for their phasing out.
- DFIs seeking transformation should restructure themselves like a company with a large and diversified shareholding.
- The regulatory framework needs further strengthening and should be so designed as to ensure financial soundness of DFIs and overall systematic stability.

B. DEVELOPMENT OF FINANCIAL INSTITUTIONS IN INDIA — A PANORAMIC VIEW

The need for financial institutions in India was felt very strongly immediately after the attainment of independence to fill the gaps in the capital market. The Indian capital market at that time was ill-equipped to provide for the needs of long-term industrial finance. The existing financial arrangements were incapable of coping with the burgeoning financial requirements of up and coming enterprises. Although the country had a network of strong and developed commercial banks, these institutions, working on the British banking model, confined themselves to short-term financing activity, and abstained from supplying long-term financial assistance. The managing agency houses, which had served as important adjunct to the capital market, were not able to cope with the requirements of the planned industrial development owing to their apathy to investment in risky ventures and their keenness to finance only interested concerns. Furthermore, several malpractices, the most important among which were the misuse of funds, excess speculation and manipulations, the high cost of promotion, and financial and marginal managerial concentration that had emerged, were often detrimental to the interest of the investing public. Moreover, there were dearth of issue houses and underwriting firms which sponsored security issues. As against the limited arrangements for the supply of long-term financial facilities, there was an enormous increase in the demand for long-term capital. Not only did existing industries require substantially large amounts of capital to meet their reconstruction, modernisation, expansion and diversification programmes, the establishment of new industrial projects on a gigantic scale in the capital goods sector for the building of a strong and balanced structure of industrial development, called for enormous investment. But only a very small part of the total requirements could be met by the existing financial institutions; for the total requirements could be met by the existing financial institutions; for the other, it became necessary to devise new institutional machinery with ample financial resources and with relatively more comprehensive functions.

But this was not the first time that the urgency for the creation of special financial institutions was realised. The idea for such agencies was contemplated as far back as 1918, when the Industrial Commission recommended the establishment of an institution analogous to the Industrial Bank of Jápan. The Central Banking Inquiry Committee of 1929 also pinpointed the gaps in the Indian capital market, and strongly emphasised the need for the establishment of provincial industrial corporations which would increase the facilities for industrial investment. The Committee also contemplated the possible establishment of an All-India Industrial Financial Corporation. Towards the end of the Second World War, attention once again came to be focussed on the problem of industrial finance in India. This problem indeed assumed not only a peculiar importance but also an altogether new aspect. However, because of the lackadaisical attitude of the British Government, the proposal for the creation of special financial institutions did not see the light of the day. The question of establishing a special financial institution, however, received the serious attention of our government immediately after liberation of the country. Accordingly, Industrial Finance Corporation (IFC) was the first special institution established in 1948 by an Act of the Parliament with a view to making medium and long-term capital more readily available to industrial concerns, particularly in those circumstances in which normal banking accommodations were inappropriate or a recourse to capital issue channel was impracticable. This marked the beginning of the institutionalisation process in the country.

A landmark development in the history of Industrial Finance Corporation took place in 1993 when the Corporation was reconstituted as a company under the Companies Act with a view to imparting higher degree of operational flexibility in its operations and thus to enabling it to access the capital market and reducing its dependence as Government guaranteed funds.

At the time of setting up of the IFC, the necessity for the establishment of similar institutions, which would assist smaller industries in different States, had been recognised because it was not possible for a single institution to satisfy the capital needs of the smaller concerns sprawling all over the country. Accordingly, the State Financial Corporations Act was passed in 1951, which empowered State Governments to set-up financial institutions in their territories. The Punjab Government took the lead in organising a financial corporation under the above legislation when the Punjab Financial Corporation was set-up in 1953. Gradually, financial corporations were established in different States of India. These institutions are closely modelled on the lines of the IFC, but there is a difference in the scope of their activity. While the IFC limits financial help to larger industrial concerns, the SFCs are intended to extend financial help to smaller enterprises. Under no circumstances can a state financial corporation entertain a loan request for more than ₹ 90 lakhs from a single concern.

One of the features that was noted with great concern in the operations of the above institutions in the first few years was that they confined themselves to the lending activity and kept away from the underwriting and investing business, obviously because of the considerable risks involved in the latter, although they were authorised to help industrial concerns by way of lending and guaranteeing, underwriting and investing. The result was that large number of new entrepreneurs and smaller concerns continued to experience a tremendous problem in acquiring capital from the market because of their weaker financial position and poor creditworthiness. What was more intriguing was that they could not secure the desired amount of loan assistance from these institutions owing to thin equity base. For the encouragement of industrial development in the private sector, a substantial provision for underwriting facilities is always necessary. In order to fill the gap another institution, called Industrial Credit and Investment Corporation of India (ICICI) was set-up in January 1955. Unlike the above two financial corporations which were set-up as government-owned institutions, the ICICI was organised as a wholly privately owned institution. In fact, it was one of the development banks which the World Bank had actively sponsored in a number of underdeveloped countries in collaboration with their respective governments. The ownership of the Corporation was entirely in private hands; but certain safeguards were built against the acquisition of control by interested groups. The Corporation started its operation as an issuing-cum-lending institution.

Another milestone in the field of institutionalisation of the capital market was the formation of Life Insurance Corporation following the nationalisation of life insurance business in 1956. The Corporation came into existence with the avowed objective of helping in the task of national development. Though a small proportion of its total resources is channelled into the private sector, the size of the LIC's resources is such that even this small proportion constitutes the largest source of industrial finance in the country.

With a view to encouraging commercial banks to supply term finance facilities, the Refinance Corporation of India Limited was established in June 1958. This institution was meant to provide refinancing facilities to commercial banks and other financial institutions giving medium-term loans. The role of this Corporation was different from that of the other specialised institutions in that it was not designed to provide direct financial support to industrial enterprises but to refinance medium-term loans ranging between 3 and 7 years. The Corporation was merged with the IDBI in 1964 when the latter assumed, besides other roles, the role of a refinancier.

During the 1960s, different State Governments, in their desire to hasten the pace of industrial development in their regions, established industrial development corporations. The Andhra Pradesh and Bihar Governments took the lead. Except Maharashtra and Gujarat where industrial development corporations were organised as statutory bodies, they were incorporated under the Companies' Act of 1956. These institutions were intended to foster industrial growth in the States by undertaking developmental, promotional and financing functions.

One of the important points of discussion in every nook and corner of the country was the absence of an effective mobilising agency in the country. The role of the newly set-up institutions, excepting the LIC, was limited to the channelisation of funds. These institutions did not act as mobilising agencies. They, therefore, acted as intermediaries between the government and the corporate sector. Hence, the need was felt for an all-India institution which could, besides providing financial assistance, mobilise the savings of the people —particularly of persons of moderate means. The Unit Trust of India was, therefore, established in 1964 with a view to pooling the savings of the people by the sale of its units, the purchase of which ensures to their buyers the combined benefit of safety, liquidity and profitability, and directing the resources thus mobilised into newer as well as older industrial enterprises by subscribing directly to their shares and debentures, and by loaning to them. The UTI, thus, began to act as a link between savings and investment.

By this time, a plethora of financial corporations catering to the financial needs of a variety of industries had come into existence, each one functioning within the narrow framework set down by the statute or the memorandum that accredited it. The multiplicity of financial institutions operating in the same field with hardly any demarcation in their specific activities led to overlapping and duplication in their efforts with the result that financially well off concerns could manage to procure financial assistance from a number of institutions, while the weaker concerns were left high and dry. A co-ordination of functions and working of existing financial institutions was, therefore, considered necessary so that they might play a more useful role in the industrial development of the country.

Another important point that was noted with anxiety was that many gigantic projects of national importance were held up because of the absence of adequate financial arrangements. It was beyond the means of individual financial institutions to finance these projects because of their resource base. Furthermore, a large number of industrial projects were envisaged to be set-up during the fourth and succeeding plans to achieve self-sufficiency in the industrial sector; and this called for a substantially large amount of capital provision, which the existing institutions were not able to supply in view of their own limited resources. The establishment of a financial institution with a substantially larger amount of resources and capable of functioning undeterred by statutory rigidities, therefore, became inevitable.

The Industrial Development Bank of India (IDBI) was, therefore, set-up — as a wholly-owned subsidiary of the Reserve Bank of India and under its direct control and management to act as an apex institution, co-ordinating the functions of all the smaller financial institutions and supplementing their resources so that direct financial support might be extended to all the deserving projects of national importance. With the setting up of the IDBI, the control of the IFC was transferred from the government to the former; the IFC became a subsidiary of the IDBI so that it might play an enlarged role. In February 1976, the IDBI was restructured and separated from the control of the RBI. One of the principle objectives of the re-organisation was to enable the IDBI to play an enlarged role as the principal financial institution for financing industries in closer co-ordination with the all-India and State level institutions and public sector commercial banks.

Another addition to the institutional structure of the capital market was the Industrial Reconstruction Corporation of India, which was constituted in April 1971 as a public limited company under the Companies Act. This institution was set-up to reconstruct and rehabilitate the sick and closed industrial units with a view to accelerating the tempo of industrial activity in the country.

In March 1985, the Government of India constituted Industrial Reconstruction Bank of India (IRBI), to act as the principal credit and reconstruction agency for reconstruction and rehabilitation of rich industrial units. However, with the setting up of Board for Industrial and Financial Reconstruction (BIFR), the role of IRBI became irrelevant and as a sequel to that, Government of India decided to convert IRBI into full-fledged all purpose development finance institution. Accordingly Industrial Investment Bank of India Ltd. (IIBI) was incorporated under the Companies Act, 1956 in March 1997 to provide it with adequate operational flexibility and financial autonomy.

In 1973, the General Insurance Corporation of India (GIC) came into being on nationalisation of general insurance companies in the country. GIC had four subsidiaries, *viz.*, National Insurance Ltd., New India Assurance Company Ltd., Oriental Fire and General Insurance Company Ltd. and India Insurance Company Ltd.

In December 1986, SICICI Ltd., was promoted by ICICI together with other all-India financial institutions as a specialised financial institution for encouraging and assisting development and investing in shipping, fishing and related industries.

With a view to have a strong capital base and optimise operational efficiencies in the changing business environment, SCICI Ltd., was merged with ICICI with effect from April 1, 1996.

In view of growing significance of small sector in Indian economy, need for setting up a separate all-India institution to cater exclusively to the needs of small business enterprises all over the country was strongly felt. Accordingly, in 1990 Small Industrial Development Bank of India (SIDBI) was set up as a subsidiary of IDBI to take over the functions of small business financing of IDBI.

In addition, three more specialised institutions were organised to meet the needs of certain specialised sectors. In 1988 the Risk and Technology Finance Corporation Ltd. (RCTC) was set up by reconstituting the Risk Capital Foundation which was promoted by IFCI in 1975 to cater to the risk capital and venture capital assistance.

The Technology Development and Information Company of India Ltd. (TDICI) was established by the ICICI and UTI under the Companies' Act in July, 1988 as India's first venture finance company. It took over the venture capital operations of ICICI and commenced operations in August, 1988. TDICI, now designated as ICICI Venture Funds Management Company Ltd., provides assistance to small and medium industries conceived by technocrat entrepreneurs including first generation entrepreneurs in the form of project loans, direct subscription to equity and a quasi-equity instrument called conditional loan.

The third specialised financial corporation promoted by IFCI together with other all-India financial institutions and some nationalised banks was the Tourism Finance Corporation of

India Ltd. (TFCI). The TFCI is a specialised all-India development financing institution for the tourism industry.

Apart from specialised financial institutions in the industrial sector, a number of financial institutions were also set up in the export-import, agriculture and rural sector and the housing sector. National Bank for Agriculture and Rural Development (NABARD) was set up in 1982 as an apex development bank for promotion of agriculture, small-scale industries, cottage and village industries, handicrafts and other activities in rural areas. Export-Import Bank of India (EXIM Bank) established in 1982 acts as the principal agency for financing, facilitating and promoting India's foreign trade. National Housing Bank was set up in 1988 under the National Housing Bank Act as the principal agency to promote housing finance institutions and to render financial and other support to such institutions. In January 1997, Infrastructure Development Finance Company (IDFC) was incorporated under the Companies' Act, 1956 to provide impetus to the infrastructure sector.

Although setting up on the (DFIs) was an important feature in the overall development of the financial system, with the emergence of the capital market as an important source of finance in the late 1980s and early 1990s, and renewed role of banks in term financing, DFIs have been increasingly exposed to greater competition. Liberalisation of the financial sector, with its concomitant processes or decontrol, deregulation and globalisation has led to increased competition for financial intermediaries across different segments. The competitive pressures came into the business domain of FIs on account of the entry of new players. Moreover, with the initiation of financial sector reforms in the early 1990s, access of FIs to assured sources of long duration/concessional funds from the Government has been gradually phased out. As a consequence, DFIs are required to raise funds from the capital market. With the removal of administrative controls on the interest rate structure, it has become increasingly difficult for DFIs to raise long-term funds. This, in turn, has affected their ability to offer competitive rates to their borrowers.

Apart from the competitive pressure for raising resources, the role of DFIs as an exclusive source of development finance has diminished since the intermediaries, especially banks have also entered into long-term and high-risk project financing. As such, FIs are increasingly facing competition not only in terms of raising resource but also in the deployment of funds. In short, the change in the operating environment coupled with the legacy of high non-performing assets has led to serious financial stress in term-lending financial institutions.

It is against this background, the RBI appointed 'Working Group on Development Financial Institutions, in 2004 to review the experiences and prospects of DFIs for transformation into banks and to assess the financial position and recommend a regulatory framework for the existing financial institutions.

It is noteworthy that the last decade of 20th century witnessed innovation, sophistication and diversification in operations of DFIs, while restructuring and re-organisation of these institutions has been the phenomenon since the beginning of 21st century. In their relentless endeavour to improve productivity, profitability and make their operations cost effective and enhance their competitiveness in fiercely competitive environment, both ICICI and IDBI facing serious problem of bad debts decided to reposition themselves to become one of the largest universal banks in the country to meet global challenges, and opted for merger route. ICICI merged with its erstwhile subsidiary ICICI Bank with effect from October, 2002 and IDBI with IDBI Bank with effect from October, 2004. Both ICICI and IDBI were forced into banking business because their core business of providing long-term funding withered away. A move is on to merge IFCI with the new entity so as to create a mega bank with a development finance role. The Government is also considering to merge Infrastructure Development Financial Corporations (IDFCI) with SBI so as to enable the former to meet the burgeoning infrastructural needs of the economy more effectively.

Thus, Financial Institutions (FIs) in India can be broadly categorized as all India or State level institutions depending on the geographical coverage of their operations. Based on their major activity, All India financial institutions (AIFIs) can be categorised as (i) term-lending institutions (IFCI Ltd., IIBI Ltd., IDFCI Ltd., Export-Import Bank of India (EXIM Bank) and TFCI Ltd., which extend long-term finance to different industrial sectors; (ii) refinance institutions (National Bank for Agriculture and Rural Development (NABARD), Small Industries Development Bank of India (SIDBI) and National Housing Bank (NHB) which extend refinance to banking as well as non-banking financial intermediaries for on-lending to agriculture, small scale industries (SSIs) and housing sectors, respectively; and (iii) investment institutions (LIC and GIC) which deploy their assets largely in marketable securities. State/regional level institutions are a distinct group and comprise various State Financial Corporations (SFCs), State Industrial Development Corporations (SIDCs) and North Eastern Development Finance Corporation (NEDFI) Ltd.

With the conversion of two-term lending institutions, *viz*., ICICI and IDBI into banks, only eight institutions were regulated by the RBI. These institutions included IFCI, IIBI, IDFC, Exim Bank, TFCI, SIDBI, NABARD and NHB. However, as at end-March 2011, there were only five Financial Institutions (FIs) under the regulation of the RBI, viz, EXIM Bank, NABARD, NHB, SIDBI and IIBI. Of these, four FIs (EXIM Bank, NABARD, NHB and SIDBI) are under full-fledged regulation and supervision of the RBI. IIBI is under the process of voluntary winding up as on March 31, 2011.

C. PROFILE OF ALL INDIA INSTITUTIONS IN INDIA

In the present section we shall discuss, in brief, nature and scope of business of IFCI, IIBI, IDFC Ltd., EXIM Bank, NABARD, SIDBI, TFCI and NHB.

◈ Industrial Finance Corporation of India (IFCI)

The IFCI was set up to make medium and long-term funds readily available to organizations in corporate and co-operative sectors, particularly in those circumstances in which banking accommodation is inappropriate or recourse to capital market is impracticable. Such financial assistance is rendered for the purpose of setting up new industrial projects as also for expansion, diversification and modernisation of existing one.

Initially, the IFCI was authorised to assist only those public limited companies and co-operative societies organised in the private sector and incorporated by an Act of legislature or registered in India, which were engaged in the manufacture of processing of goods, or in shipping, or in mining, or in the hotel industry, or in the generation or distribution of electricity, or any other form of power. The IFCI Act was amended in 1960 to widen the scope of its activities by including in the definition of industrial concerns, those engaged or to be engaged in the preservation of goods. Public sector projects, private limited companies in private sector and proprietary and partnership concerns were, therefore, outside the ambit of the business of the Corporation.

In 1970 a far-reaching decision was taken by the Government of India, whereby the Corporation's business was broadened to assist such public sector undertakings as were organised as public limited companies under the Companies Act of 1956, or had declared at least a maiden dividend, built up sufficient internal resources to undertake expansion programmes, and had not approached, or did not approach, the government for budgetary support for their expansion programmes. Since most of the public sector projects are organised as private limited, they could not avail themselves of the assistance of the Corporation. Accordingly, the IFCI Act was further amended in 1973 to authorize the Corporation to finance private limited companies in the public sector.

The IFCI (Amendment) Act, 1986 made it possible for the Corporation to provide assistance *inter alia* for medical, health or other allied services.[5]

In the year 1992-93 the Central Government permitted the Corporation to do financing of industrial concerns engaged/to be engaged in the development, maintenance and construction of roads.[6]

Thus, at present any limited company in the public, joint or private sectors or a co-operative society incorporated and registered in India which is engaged itself in the manufacture, preservation or processing of goods or in the shipping, mining or hotel industry or in the generation or distribution of electricity or any other form of power, transport, setting up or development of industrial estates, fishing, maintenance, repair, testing or servicing of machinery, equipment, vehicles, etc., providing medical, health or allied services, providing services relating to information technology, telecommunications or electronics, leasing or sub-leasing, providing engineering, technical, financial, managerial, marketing and allied services, research and development activities is eligible for financial assistance from the services, research and development activities is eligible for financial assistance from the Corporation. It may be noted that the Corporation does not provide financial support to financial institutions. Further, it can extend assistance only for productive purpose such as purchase of new machinery, construction of factory building and purchase of land. Its finances are not available for purchase of raw materials or for the repayment of existing facilities, save in exceptional circumstances. Financial assistance is available for setting up of new industrial projects as also for the expansion, diversification, renovation or modernisation of existing ones. Further, companies engaged in the development, maintenance and construction of roads can also avail financial assistance from the Corporation.

Until the early 1990s, all was well for the IFCI. A munificent central government financed the Corporation with a never-ending supply of cheap, perpetually resolving treasury bills, the source of its long-term funds. The IFCI maximised its loans and advances without the slightest concern for the quality of borrowers. Unfortunately, the good old days ended in the 90s. A bankrupt central government cut off the financial tap, forcing the IFCI and other financial institutions to access the bond market. For funds at coup on rates ranging from 14% to as high as 17%. This resulted in rise in cost of funds and an asset-liability mis-match. To add to their woes, the RBI imposed increasingly stringent norms for asset recognition, classification of non-performing loans, provisioning and capital adequacy.

Owing to indiscriminate lendings, poor credit and cost control and tightening RBI policy, the IFCI suffered mounting losses, and deepening financial crises in terms of erosion of its assets and gross capital inadequacy. Consequently, the Corporation was directed to stop granting further assistance to the organisations. At present, the focus of the Corporation is on recovering its loans aggressively and pursuing settlements. In the Union Budget 2004-05, it was indicated that the IFCI will be restructured through transfer of its impaired assets to an asset reconstruction company and by affecting merger with a large public sector bank.[7]

The beleagured institution has made innumerable attempts over the year to climb bank into the reckoning. The IFCI has now decided for a 26 per cent sale of its assets and for that purpose, invited bids from potential investors. The management believes that there is no future of IFCI unless there is a breakthrough of the kind that can happen with a strategic sale.

Recently, the IFCI has been permitted to start lending in only a small way and is focusing on providing working capital to the top rated Indian Companies.[8]

After waiting for three years, the Government of India decided in February 2010 to appoint a consultant to look at various options for the IFCI. The consultant is mandated with the task of suggesting the best possible structure for the institution, including the induction of a strategic investor or merger with a public sector entity or continuing in its current status of a stand alone entity and also ways to safeguard its interest in case of a merger or induction of a strategic investor.

On October 17, 2012, the Government of India acquired strategic control of the IFCI. The Government used a option to convert debentures it had issued eleven years ago when the IFCI was in deep financial trouble to acquire control over the leader. The IFCI Ltd. issued 400 million shares worth ₹ 400 crore to the Government, making it the largest shareholder in the company.

◈ Industrial Investment Bank of India Ltd. (IIBI)

IIBI (erstwhile IRBI) was set up in 1985 under the IRBI Act, 1984 as the principal credit and reconstruction agency for aiding rehabilitation of sick and closed industrial units. With a view to converting IRBI into a full fledged all purpose development financial institution, it was incorporated as a government company in the name of Industrial/investment Bank of India Ltd., under the Companies' Act, 1956 in March 1997 thereby providing it with adequate operational flexibility and financial autonomy.

The primary objective of the IIBI was to provide customised financial assistance to industrial enterprises so as to cater to their financial needs. The thrust of the institution was on setting new standards in the industry as the most innovative financial institution. As a development bank, the IIBI rendered assistance in the form of term loans, underwriting, direct subscription, deferred payment guarantees and also under asset credit/equipment finance scheme and equipment leasing/hire purchase scheme. Besides, the IIBI was also assigned with the task of undertaking merchant banking activities.

Further, the IIBI provided short-term non-product asset-backed financing in the form of working capital and other short-term loans to companies to meet their fund requirements.

In sync with its objectives, the IIBI decided to provide financial support in various forms to both up and coming industrial projects. As a development bank, the IIBI performed developmental activities including provision of infrastructural facilities, raw materials, etc., renders consultancy, managerial and merchant banking services and provides equipment leasing and hire purchase facilities for development purposes.

In addition to provision of financial support, IIBI performed developmental activities including provision of infrastructural facilities, raw materials, etc., renders consultancy, managerial and merchant banking services and provides equipment leasing and hire purchase facilities for the purpose of reconstruction and development of industrial concerns.

The financial assistance granted by the Bank took the form of soft loans and guarantees. Reconstruction loans were provided to enable a unit to meet its essential capital expenditure and relieve it of pressing indebtedness to the extent necessary for the purpose of reconstruction and filling the liquidity gap. Besides, it extended assistance by way of underwriting of stock, shares, bonds and debentures. It provided finance for acquisition of equipment and makes available machinery and other equipment on lease or hire purchase basis. Working capital to the assisted units is arranged through banks, although the IRBI may provide a margin for it either through loans or guarantees.

The Bank's assistance was available to units organized on a corporate, co-operative, partnership or proprietary basis, which are closed or facing the risk of closure but which possess potential viability. It does not, however, consider the cases of companies where more than 50 per cent of the shares are held by State or Central Government.

In granting reconstruction assistance, the IIBI gave the first priority to the units that are passing through a crisis and are facing closures. The next in line were the cases of such units as are cutting down on cash losses because of their use of relatively modern machinery and techniques and the existence of a satisfactory order book position. These were followed by cases where there are possibilities of regaining viability through a process of reconstruction over a period of years. In the overall assessment, however, units which were comparatively labour-intensive, were given special importance.

As in the case of the IFCI, the IIBI suffered heavy operating losses and NPAs resulting in deep financial crisis in recent years due to indiscriminate lending and poor credit and cost control. As a result, the IIBI was directed by the Government to stop its normal operations and concentrate on collections and settlement of loans. IIBI is in the process of voluntary winding up.[9]

◈ Infrastructure Development Finance Company (IDFC) Ltd.

IDFC was established out of the need for a specialized financial intermediary to address the requirements of the infrastructure sector. The Corporation has been conceived as an institution to facilitate the flow of private finance to commercially viable infrastructure projects and help mitigate commercial and structural risks contained therein, by designing innovative products and processes.

IDFC, incorporated in January 1997 with an initial paid-up capital of ₹ 10,000 million by way of contributions from the Government of India, RBI, domestic financial institutions and foreign financial institutions, commenced its operations from June 1997.

The IDFCI began its business with a mission "to be the leading knowledge-driven financial services platform, creating enduring driven financial services platform, creating enduring value, promoting infrastructure and nation building in India and beyond." In 2005, the corporation defined its vision as "to be the one firm" that looks after the diverse needs of infrastructure development. Its focus is on supporting companies to get the best return on investments whether it is financial intermediation for infrastructure projects and services, adding value through innovative products to the infrastructure value chain or asset maintenance of existing infrastructure projects.

The IDFCI is India's leading financial institution at the forefront of developing infrastructure through its presence across financing, advisory, investment banking, development and asset management functions related to the sector with a balance sheet size of more than US$ 10 billion.[10]

A bird's eye view of the business of the IDFCI may be had from the following chart.

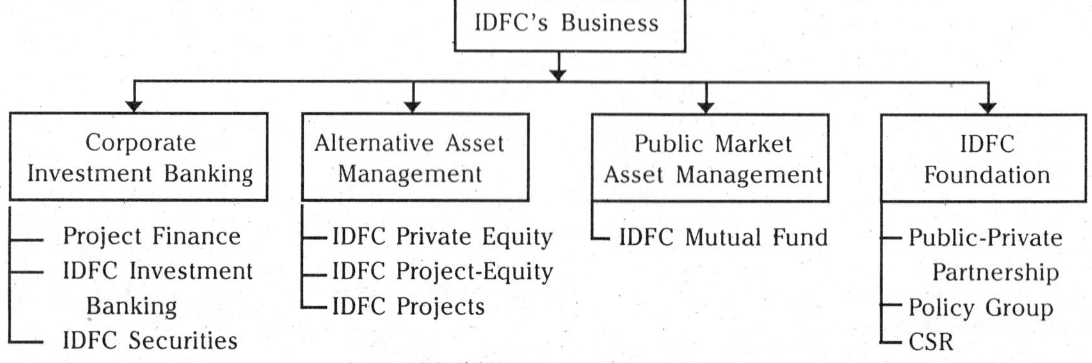

Chart 23.1: Showing IDFC's Business

◈ Corporate Investment Banking

(i) Project Finance

The IDFC Project Finance is a pioneer in lending for infrastructure projects. In fact, the corporation was founded with the sole objective of providing and promoting financing of Indian infrastructure. The IDFC has set up a wholly-owned subsidiary — 'IDFC projects' in December 2007, with the mandate to develop, finance, execute and manage infrastructure projects in the country. IDFC projects seeks to fulfill its mandate in active collaboration with the central and state governments as well as with the private sector from India and abroad.

(ii) Investment Banking

The IDFC provides a full suite of investment banking services to a diverse group of Indian and MNCs, banks and financial institutions across major industry sectors. The corporation has constituted IDFC capital as all-inclusive investment banking division.

(iii) Institutional Securities

IDFC Institutional securities has been one of India's leading equities broker for institutional investors catering to domestic as well as overseas financial institutions investing in Indian equities.

◈ Alternative Asset Management

(i) IDFC Private Equity

IDFC set up a wholly owned subsidiary 'IDFC Private Equity' in 2002 to manage three funds, viz, India Development Fund, IDFC Private Equity Fund II and IDFC Private Equity Fund III for the purpose of funding infrastructure including social infrastructure.

(ii) IDFC Project Equity

Another major initiative taken by the IDFC to catalyse India's infrastructure development was to establish wholly owned subsidiary, *viz.*, IDFC Project Equity, which focuses on creating sustainable, positive economic impact and long-term value for its investors, the infrastructure companies it invest in and the Indian economy. IDFC Project Equity was set up as part of the 'India Infrastructure Financing Initiative', a collaboration effort between the Government of India and leading Indian and global financial institutions to deploy US $ 5 billion in capital for infrastructure projects in India.

(ii) IDFC Projects

IDFC set up IDFC Projects Limited in December, 2007 as its development arm to develop, finance and manage infrastructure projects in India. In course of its activities IDFC Projects builds upon its parent's core strengths of government sponsorship, project financing and asset management to create a strong value proposition in the conceptualisation, development and implementation of infrastructure projects. It seeks to fulfill its mandate in active collaboration with the central and state governments as well as with the private sector from India and abroad.

◈ Public Market Asset Management

IDFC manages various mutual fund products for institutional and retail investors through IDFC Mutual Fund.

◈ IDFC Foundation

IDFC Foundation is actively involved in stimulating development of urban and rural infrastructure. Besides advising a number of government agencies and private bodies on suitable PPP models, it provides financial support to maintain and improve urban and rural roads. It has also committed ₹ 9,258 crore in telecom to connect villages and cities across India, bolstering rural entrepreneurship. IDFC Foundation is also involved in promoting education and healthcare.

IDFC Foundation advise on and manage infrastructure processes in commercialization and privatization of infrastructure assets.

◈ Exim Bank

Exim bank, wholly owned by Government of India, was set up in 1982 under the Export-Import Bank of India Act, 1981 with the objective of fostering India's international trade and functioning as the principal financial institution for co-ordinating the working of institutions engaged in financing exports and imports of goods and services.

Recognizing the dynamics of international trade and responding to the challenges of globalisation of production processes, accretion in private investment flows, diminishing role of financial intermediaries for large multinationals and emergence of world class commercial banks capable of infusing large capital and undertaking risks in project and trade financing,

Exim bank has over the years re-oriented its strategies to cater not only to the financing needs of exporters and importers and helping Indian companies create export capabilities but also in supporting them in the efforts to globalise their business.

Since its inception, the Exim Bank of India has been both a catalyst and a key player in the promotion of cross border trade and investment. Commencing operations as a purveyor of export credit, like other Export Credit agencies in the world, the Exim Bank of India, over the years, evolved into an institution that plays a major role in partnering Indian industries, particularly the small and medium enterprises, in their globalisation efforts through a wide range of products and services offered at all stages of the business cycle, starting from import of technology and export product development to export production, export marketing, pre-shipment and post-shipment and overseas investment.

Major business of the Exim Bank can be grouped into (*i*) Export financing (*ii*) Promotional (*iii*) catalytic and (*iv*) information and advisory.[11]

(i) Export Financing

As export financier the Exim Bank carries on the following activities.

- To grant in or outside India loans and advances by itself or in participation with any bank or financial institution whether in or outside India for purposes of export or import.
- To provide financial assistance by way of term loans in Indian rupees/foreign currencies for setting up new production facility, expansion/modernization/upgradation of existing facilities and for acquisition of production equipment/technology which go a long way in creation of export capabilities and enhancement of international competitiveness.
- To extend lines of credit to overseas financial institutions, foreign governments and their agencies, enabling them to finance imports of goods and services from India on deferred credit terms.
- To offer a variety of facilities for Indian investment and acquisitions overseas. The facilities include loan to Indian companies for equity participation in overseas ventures, direct equity participation by the Exim Bank in the overseas venture and non-funded facilities such as letters of credit and guarantee to facilitate local borrowing by the overseas venture.
- To support SMEs in their export marketing efforts including financing the soft expenditure relating to implementation of strategic and systematic export market development plans.

(ii) Promotional Activities

The Exim Bank of India has acted as a consultant for —

- Setting up an Exim Bank in Malaysia.
- Establishing an Export Credit Guarantee Company in Zimbabwe.
- Carrying out feasibility study for setting up the Afrexim Bank.
- Designing of Export Financing Programmes for Turkey and South Africa.
- Export development project for Ukraine, Vietnam and Armenia.
- Feasibility study for establishment of an export credit and guarantee facility for Gulf Cooperation Council countries.

(iii) Catalytic Role

The Exim Bank has also played the role of a catalyst. It introduced innovative products such as Export marketing finance, financing programme for software exports, etc. It was instrumental in creation of Asian Exim Banks Forum in 1996 to promote intra-regional trade and creation of Global Network of Exim Banks and Development Financial Institutions in 2006 to promote trade and development finance through cooperation and exchange of information.

(iv) Information and advisory services

The Exim Bank supplements its financing progammes with a wide range of value-added information, advisory and support services, which enable exporters to evaluate international risks, exploit export opportunities and improve competitiveness, thereby helping them in their gloablisation efforts.

The Bank also collects, compiles and disseminates market and credit information in respect of international trade.

Besides, it undertakes and finances research, surveys, techno-economic or any other study in connection with the promotion and development of international trade.

◈ Tourism Finance Corporation of India

Pursuant to the recommendations of the National Committee on Tourism set up under the aegis of Planning Commission, the Government of India decided in 1988 to promote a separate All India Financial Institution for providing financial assistance to tourism-related activities/projects. Accordingly, the IFCI Ltd. alongwith other All-India financial institutions and Nationalised Banks promoted a public limited company under the name of "Tourism Finance Corporation of India Ltd. (TFCI)" to function as a specialised All-India Development financial institution to cater to the financial needs of tourism industry. The TFCI incorporated as a public limited company under the Companies Act, 1956, commenced its operations from February 1, 1989.

Corporate mission of the TFCI is to catalyse and channelise investments into various segments of the tourism industry and across various locations in a need based manner and to take steps to promote the tourism industry within the overall framework of the Government of India policy.[12]

The principal objective of the TFCI is to render financial assistance to enterprises for setting up and/or development of tourism-related projects, facilities and services such as hotels, restaurants, holiday resorts, amusement parks, multiplexes and entertainment centres, education and sports, safari parks, ropeways, cultural centres, convention halls, transport, travel and tour operating agencies, air service, tourism emporia, sports facilities, etc.

The TFCI provides assistance by way of rupee loan, underwriting of public issues of shares/debentures and direct subscription to such securities, guarantee of deferred payments and credit raised abroad, equipment finance, equipment leasing, working-capital financing, take over financing, advances against credit card receivables and assistance under suppliers' credit.

The TFCI provides financial assistance to projects with capital cost of ₹ 3 crore and above. In respect of projects costing between ₹ 1 crore and ₹ 3 crore, the corporation will consider financial assistance to the extent of unavoidable gap, if any, remaining after taking into account assistance from state level institutions/banks. Unique projects, which are important from the tourism point of view and for which assistance from state level institutions/banks is not available, may be considered on exceptional basis even though their capital cost is below ₹ 1 crore. The TFCI considers assistance even if the total cost is less than ₹ 3 crore for existing concerns with satisfactory performance for renovation/upgradation, etc.

◈ Small Industries Development Bank of India (SIDBI)

Small Industries Development Bank of India (SIDBI), set up as a wholly-owned subsidiary of IDBI by an Act of Parliament in 1989, commenced its operations from April 2, 1990 by taking over the outstanding portfolio and activities of IDBI pertaining to the small sector. The basic idea underlying the formation of the SIDBI was to foster the growth of small-scale sector which occupies a pivotal position in Indian economy. Thus, the Bank has been assigned the role of the principal financial institution for promotion, financing and development of industry in the small, tiny and cottage sectors and to co-ordinate the functioning of institutions engaged in similar activities. It has to pay concentrated attention to the multi-dimensional growth and development of industries in the small scale sector with special emphasis on the village, cottage, and tiny sectors.

The vision of the SIDBI is to emerge as a profitable financial institution for providing competitive edge to the SSI sector with suitable credit and adequate promotional and developmental support.

Initially, the SIDBI's business comprised refinancing to term loans granted by SFCs, SIDCs, banks and other eligible financial institutions; direct discounting and rediscounting of bills arising out of sale of machinery/capital equipment by manufactures in the small scale sector on deferred credit and rediscounting of short-term trade bills arising out of sale of products of the small scale sector.

At present, the SIDBI renders equity type of assistance to special target groups like new promoters, women and ex-servicemen under National Equity Fund, and voluntary agencies working for development/to the upliftment of underprivileged women. It also provides resource support to NSIC and SSIDCs for their material supply and marketing of SSI products as well as their hire-purchase and leasing activities. For promotion, development and growth of small scale sector, SIDBI extends technical and related support services.

The year 2000 saw delinking of the SIDBI from the IDBI as subsidiary, in pursuance of the amendments approved by the Parliament, making it eventually not less than 51 per cent owned by IDBI/LIC/GIC/Public sector banks and other Government controlled institutions and the rest by public. The IDBI has decided to sell its 51 per cent stake in SIDBI to public sector banks and financial institutions. The restructuring of equity base is at advanced stage leading to a suitable re-organisation of the Bank in terms of its organisational set up and policy programmes.

Given the apex role, the approach of the SIDBI has been to supplement the efforts of existing institutions, strengthening their capacities through financial and support services and instituting suitable co-ordination mechanism while providing assistance for the small scale sector. While continuing with the schemes operated by the IDBI under Small Industries Development Fund (SIDF), the Bank took the initiative by identifying the gaps in existing credit delivery system and devised tailor-made schemes for direct lending to small scale sector so as to supplement the efforts of Primary Lending Institutions which include State Financial Corporation (SFCs), State Industrial Development Corporations (SIDCs), Scheduled Commercial Banks both in public and private sector, State Co-operative Banks, Scheduled Urban Co-operative Banks and Regional Rural Banks (RRBs).

Under indirect assistance, assistance to small scale sector is channelised through the large network of PLIs across the country by way of refinance, bills rediscounting and resource support in the form of lines of credit in lieu of refinance, etc.

The SIDBI, in tandem with the overall policy measures of the Government of India and keeping in view the expectations of the sector, has been refining its strategies and putting in place new policies and programmes for the development of small scale sector.

As an apex institution, the Bank has been expected to play a more proactive role in reaching out financial and support services to SSIs with the help of existing credit delivery structure and support service agencies. Besides co-promoting new intermediaries and strengthening the existing network of institutions engaged in development of small scale sector, the SIDBI has developed tailor-made schemes catering to specific requirements of SSIs, thus supplementing the efforts of PL's. A major challenge confronting the SIDBI is to devise strategies for development of all three distinct segments within small scale sector, viz., micro, tiny and modern SSI, the first two predominantly covering traditional industries.

In the given scenario, the SIDBI's policies, programmes and interventions have been aimed at promoting an orderly and healthy growth of these segments focusing on five prime factors, *viz.*, entrepreneurship credit, technology, market and infrastructure. While formulating the policies, emphasis has been laid on empowerment of women and generating self-employment opportunities for educated/skilled youth.

During 1998-99, the SIDBI launched 'SIDBI Foundation for Micro Credit' with a corpus of ₹ 100 crore as a measure to upscale its micro-finance activities. The new approach of the Bank not only envisages financial assistance but also building and strengthening the management capabilities of the micro finance capacity building inputs for achieving sustainability, economies of scale, desired outreach, etc.

The SIDBI has, of late, launched various schemes to help small scale sector. These schemes are in the fields of entrepreneurship, credit delivery, technology, market and infrastructure and small enterprises financial centre.

◈ Schemes on Entrepreneurship

So as to promote entrepreneurship and strengthen the existing enterprises to become competitive, the SIDBI has introduced a slew of programmes with special emphasis on employment generation and livelihood improvement of the rural poor by encouraging them to undertake income generating activities through self-employment schemes. The Rural Industries Programme of the Bank has endeavoured to develop viable and self sustaining enterprises in rural and semi-urban areas to address the problems of rural unemployment, urban migration and under utilisation of resources and skills in rural areas.

The Micro Credit Scheme was launched in 1994 to provide help to rural poor, especially women to set up micro enterprises. Besides, the Bank has sponsored establishment of Training-Cum-Production Centres for bringing about economic empowerment of Women under 'Mahila Vikas Nidhi Scheme.'

The SIDBI has taken several measures to encourage potential entrepreneurs by providing them with project ideas through mass media, training and escort services. The recently launched National Programmes on 'Innovation and Incubation for Small Industries' is yet another step in this direction with special focus on knowledge-based industries. To strengthen the existing enterprises, the Bank provides assistance, both financial and non-financial, for technological upgradation, marketing, quality certification and human resources development for the SSI sector.

◈ Schemes Relating to Credit Delivery

From a predominantly refinancing institution, the SIDBI has emerged as a major purveyor of a wide variety of financial services to the small scale sector. At present, the Bank renders financial assistance in the form of soft loan or quasi-equity assistance, term loan — both in rupee and foreign currencies, working capital term loan, bills discounting for equipment and components, factoring services, venture capital support and different forms of resources support to intermediaries engaged in assisting the small scale sector. The SIDBI operationalised Micro Credit Scheme (MCS) to extend small loans to poor people through NGOs for self-employment projects that generate income to enable them to rise above the poverty line. Encouraged by the success of the MCS programme, the Bank launched SIDBI Foundation for Micro credit during 1998 with the objective of upscaling its micro finance activities.

◈ Schemes on Technology

In view of pivotal role that technology plays in improving competitiveness of SSIs, the SIDBI, since its inception, has been according emphasis on technology upgradation of the SSIs and for this purpose, various measures have been taken by the Bank with a view to identifying their needs in terms of process technology, environment management, quality management, common facilities centre, etc., and taking suitable steps to address them.

Thus apart from meeting the credit needs of SSIs, the Bank has developed support mechanism and facilitated institutional and infrastructural framework for development and technology on an increasing scale. In 1995, the Bank set up Technology Bureau for Small Enterprises (TBSE) in collaboration with Asian and Pacific Centre for Transfer of Technology (APCTT), an outfit of United Nations. The TBSE is gradually emerging as a technology bank for SSIs providing information on range of technologies, sources and facilitating Technology Collaborations together with financial tie up, when feasible.

In April 1995, the SIDBI has set up out of its own funds, 'Technology Development and Modernisation Fund' (TDMF) with an earmarked amount of ₹ 200 crore for encouraging existing industrial units in the small scale sector to modernise their production facilities and adopt improved and updated technology. The Bank provides assistance at its Prime Lending Rate to beneficiary units. Though the assistance under TDMF since inception crossed the originally earmarked amount the Bank has decided to extend its operations for another 3 years by earmarking another ₹ 100 crore from out of its own resources.

The other major initiatives in this direction include cluster based intervention programmes for technology upgradation, organising Skill-cum-Technology upgradation programmes and expanding information base on status of technologies in specific sub-sectors within SSIs.

The SIDBI also acts as nodal agency in respect of specialised schemes of Government of India for technological upgradation of cotton textile industry and tanneries in the small scale sector.

◈ Schemes relating to Marketing

Sensing the need for giving serious attention to marketing problems of the sector, the SIDBI has undertaken suitable measures for creating and strengthening marketing infrastructure in villages, small towns, semi-urban and metropolitan cities by providing assistance for setting up of show emporia, trade exhibition centres, marketing complexes, etc. Under marketing finance, the Bank renders assistance for intangibles such as marketing research, research and development, product upgradation and standardisation, advertising, branding, participation in trade fairs/exhibition, sales promotion tours, etc.

◈ Schemes on Infrastructure

Recognising the infrastructural bottlenecks affecting adversely the growth of small scale sector, the SIDBI has made it a policy in 1990 itself to provide assistance for setting up industrial areas. In 1997, the Bank gave a renewed thrust to development of infrastructure in 1977 when it decided to cover all forms of organisations in public and private sector for setting up of industrial estates, development of existing industrial areas, setting up warehousing facilities, common facilities centres or any other infrastructural facility that would predominantly benefit SSIs. Besides, the SIDBI also operates scheme drawn up by the Government of India for Integrated Infrastructural Development (IID) envisaging assistance for setting up IID centres with facilities like water supply, power, telecommunications, common services centre including technological back-up services for SSIs in rural and backward areas.

In addition to the above, the SIDBI has operationalised many other programmes to help small scale sector to improve its competitiveness. Some of these schemes are outlined below.

◈ Schemes relating to Tiny and Micro Sector

So as to help develop tiny and micro sector the SIDBI has designed and developed tailor made schemes besides channelising assistance in respect of Government sponsored schemes and covering them under SIDBI's development activities. These schemes are National Equity Fund, Composite Loan Scheme and Mahila Udyan Nidhi. Under promotional and development activities, development of tiny and micro sector has been a thrust area of the SIDBI and various programmes devised for the purpose focus on areas such as enterprise promotion, technological upgradation, human resources development, market promotion, quality and environment management and information dissemination.

◈ Venture Capital Scheme

During 1998-99, the SIDBI launched Venture Capital Funds to provide financial support to small scale units in IT/software related sectors with participation from Central/State Governments. At national level, 'National Venture Fund for Software and IT Industry' (NFSIT) was set up with a corpus of ₹ 100 crore by the Bank in association with Ministry of Information and Technology. The NFSIT would meet the requirements of software and IT companies in the small scale sector to enable them to achieve rapid growth and competitive edge in domestic and foreign markets. The fund has become operational during 1999-2000.

Besides, the Bank took initiatives in launching state level dedicated venture capital funds in as many as 10 states. Five venture capital funds have become operational till March 2000.

◈ Refinance Scheme

The SIDBI modified its refinance scheme during the last two years (1998-2000) keeping in view the changes in the financial sector so as to make it more cost efficient and market friendly. The major features of the scheme are abolition of upfront fee, raising of loan ceilings for PLIs, raising of automatic refinance limit for banks, extension of line of credit facility to SFCs/SIDCs and increase in the extent of refinance to 100 per cent. Besides, a major exercise for simplification of refinance scheme is conducted and many sub-schemes are merged into the general scheme' so as to provide flexibility to PLIs in extending assistance to the target groups.

Under Refinance Scheme for Technology Development and Modernisation (RTDM), refinance facility is provided to PLIs at 2 percentage points below the Long-Term Prime Lending Rate (LTPLR) of SIDBI in respect of term loans of over ₹ 2 lakhs, with a condition that the PLIs extend assistance to SSI borrowers at SIDBI's LTPLR. Refinance against term loans upto ₹ 2 lakh is extended at 2.5 percentage points below LTPLR of SIDBI.

With a view to broadbasing the assistance for technology upgradation and modernisation, the limit of project cost under RTDM scheme of SIDBI was enhanced in 1998-99 from ₹ 50 lakh to ₹ 1 crore. Separate Lines of Credit were also provided to various state level institutions for assistance under RTDM, over and above the refinance limits available to them.

The SIDBI has also launched Refinance scheme for Small Road Transport operators. Under the scheme, the Bank has stipulated a minimum promoters' contribution of 15 per cent of the project cost. There is no debt-equity ratio norm for assistance under the scheme.

◈ Single Window Scheme

Single Window Scheme (SWS) of the SIDBI has emerged as a popular channel for SSI units to avail both term loan and working capital assistance from a single PLI.

◈ Composite Loan Scheme

With a view to widening the coverage of the composite loan scheme, the SIDBI modified the scheme in 1998-99 by enhancing the loan limit from ₹ 2 lakh to ₹ 5 lakh for village and cottage industries as also small scale industries in the tiny sector. This scheme has been extended to units located anywhere in the country in April 1999 for a period of 5 years.

The important feature of this scheme is interest reimbursement of 5 per cent on the interest actually charged by identified financial institutions in respect of rupee loans. Coverage for exchange rate fluctuation not exceeding 5 per cent per annum would also be provided in respect of foreign currency loans.

◈ Factoring Scheme

The SIDBI launched the factoring schemes in 1997-98 as a comprehensive package of receivables management services including advance against invoices and other allied services such as collection of proceeds from the purchaser, administration of sales ledger, etc. The Bank liberalised various norms of the scheme so as to impart renewed thrust to the scheme. Accordingly, partnership firms have also been made eligible. Relaxations were also made with respect to norms relating to customer base, debt concentration, profitability and fixation of the limit with regard to sales as against the earlier stipulation of net worth of SSI unit.

◈ Invoice Discounting Scheme

The SIDBI launched in March 2000 a scheme for Invoice Discounting in respect of goods supplied/services provided by SSI units to large purchaser companies in the public/private sector with sound financial position and payment period. Besides the transactions pertaining to supply of components, parts, sub-assemblies, etc., the scheme would also cover transactions arising out of other services rendered by SSI units to large companies such as, transportation, repairs, maintenance, computerisation, advertising, publicity, etc.

The assistance under the scheme is very likely to improve the liquidity position of small scale units by providing them with immediate cash against the goods sold and/or services provided to large companies.

◈ Scheme for Small Enterprises Financial Centre

Under this scheme, the SIDBI has entered into MOUs with 13 banks for joint/co-financing of projects relating to SME sector in the identified clusters. Select branches of the Bank have been designated as 'Small Enterprises Financial Centres'.

The SIDBI has formulated a scheme to broaden the financing option for infrastructure developments in clusters through public - private partnership.

◈ National Bank For Agriculture and Rural Development (NABARD)

NABARD, established in July, 1982 by a special act by the Parliament, is an apex development bank with mandate to uplift rural India by facilitating credit flow for promotion and development of agriculture, small-scale industries, cottage and village industries, handicrafts and other rural crafts. It has also the mandate to support all other allied economic activities in rural areas, promote integrated and sustainable rural development and secure prosperity of rural areas.

In discharging its role as a facilitator for rural prosperity NABARD is entrusted with —

(*i*) Serving as an apex financing agency for institutions providing investment and credit for promoting various developmental activities in rural areas.[13]

(*ii*) Providing refinance to lending institutions in rural areas.

(*iii*) Bringing about or promoting institutional development.

(*iv*) Coordinating the rural financing activities of all institutions engaged in developmental work at the field level and maintaining liaison with Government of India, State Governments, RBI and other national level institutions concerned with policy formulation,

(*v*) Undertaking monitoring and evaluation of projects refinanced by it.

(*vi*) Developing the institutions which help the rural economy.

Besides the above pivotal role, the NABARD also —

(*i*) Offers training and research facilities for banks, cooperatives and organisations working in the field of rural development.

(*ii*) Helps the state governments in reaching their targets of providing assistance to eligible institutions in agricultural and rural development.

(*iii*) Acts as regulator for cooperative banks and RRBs.

(*iv*) Keeps a check on its client banks.

(*v*) Prepares on annual basis, rural credit plans for all the districts in the country. These plans form the basis for annual credit plans of all rural financial institutions.

The NABARD operates throughout the country through its 28 regional offices and one sub-office, located in the capitals of all the states/union territories. It has 336 district offices across the country, one sub-office at Port Blair and one special cell at Srinagar. It also has 6 training establishments.

The NABARD is also known for its 'SHG Bank Linkage Programme.' It also has a portfolio of Natural Resource Management Programmes involving diverse fields like Watershed Development, Tribal Development and Farm Innovation through dedicated funds set up for the purpose.

The NABARD primarily functions through other agencies, the needs of the client institutions largely determine the knowledge and skill requirements of the bank's executives.

D. NATIONAL HOUSING BANK (NHB)

As a strategic institutional measure to boost housing sector, the National Housing Bank Act was passed in 1987 to establish a bank known, as the National Housing Bank with a view to promoting housing finance institutions both at local and regional levels and providing financial and other support to such institutions and for matters connected therewith or incidental thereto.

◈ Tasks of NHB

The NHB has been empowered to carry out the following tasks.

(*a*) To promote, establish, support or aid in the promotion, establishment and support of housing financial institutions;

(*b*) To make loans and advances or render any other form of financial assistance – whatsoever for housing activities to housing finance institutions, schedule banks, state co-operative agricultural and rural development banks or any other institution or class of institutions as may be notified by the Central Government;

(*c*) To make loans and advances for housing or residential township-cum-housing development or slum clearance projects;

(*d*) To subscribe to or purchase stocks, shares, bonds, debentures and securities of every other description;

(*e*) To guarantee the financial obligations of housing finance institutions and to underwrite the issue of stocks, shares, bonds, debentures and securities of every other description of housing finance institutions;

(*f*) To draw, accept, discount or rediscount, buy or sell and deal in bills of exchange, promissory notes, bonds, debentures, hundis, coupons and other instruments by whatever name called;

(*g*) To buy, sell or otherwise deal in any loans or advances secured by mortgage or charge of the immovable property relating to scheduled banks or housing finance institutions;

(*h*) To create one or more trusts and transfer loans or advances together with or without securities therefor to such trusts for considerations;

(*i*) To set aside loans or advances held by the NHB and issue and sell securities based upon such loans or advances so set aside in the form of debt obligations, trust certificates of beneficial interest or other instruments;

(*j*) To set up one or more mutual funds for undertaking housing finance activities;

(*k*) To undertake or participate in housing mortgage insurance;

(*l*) To formulate one of more schemes for the purpose of mobilization of resources and extension of credit for housing;

(*m*) To formulate one or more schemes for the economically weaker sections of society which may be subsidized by the Central Government or any State Government of any other sources;

◆ Obligations of the NHB

The NHB has the following obligations to comply with:

(*a*) The NHB shall establish a fund to be called the General Fund and all payment by the Bank shall be made out of this fund.

(*b*) The NHB shall prepare its balance sheet and accounts to be balanced and closed in such form and manner as may be prescribed.

(*c*) After making provision for bad and doubtful debts, depreciation of assets and all other matters for which provision is necessary or expedient or which is usually provided for by banker, the NHB shall transfer —

  (*i*) for a period of 15 years, following the accounting year during which the NHB is established, the amount remaining such of the funds as the RBI may specify; and

  (*ii*) after the expiry of the said period of 15 years, the NHB shall after making provision for the funds, transfer the balance of surplus to the RBI.

(*d*) The accounts of the NHB shall be audited by auditors appointed by the RBI

(*e*) The NHB shall furnish, from time to time, such information and returns as the RBI may require.

(*f*) The NHB shall make an annual report to the Central Government and the RBI on the trend and progress of housing in the country and in that report may make such suggestions as it may think necessary or expedient for the development of housing and the Central Government, as soon as the report is received by it, cause the same to be laid before each House of Parliament.

(*g*) The NHB shall not, except as otherwise required by this Act or any other Law, divulge any information relating to or to the affairs of its constituents except in circumstances in which it is in accordance with the law or practice and usage customary among bankers necessary or appropriate for the NHB to divulge such information.

(*h*) To provide guidelines to the housing finance;

(*i*) To co-ordinate with LIC, the UTI, the GIC, other financial institutions in the discharge of its overall functions;

(*j*) To act as agent of the Central Government institutions, the State Government or the RBI or of any authority.

The NHB may, for the purpose of carrying out its functions —

(*a*) Issue and sell bonds and debentures with or without the guarantee of the Central Government in such manner and on such terms as may be prescribed;

(*b*) Borrow money from the Central Government, scheduled banks, financial institutions, mutual funds and from any other authority organization or institution approved by the Government on such terms and conditions as may be agreed upon;

(*c*) Accept deposits repayable after the expiry of such period and on such terms as may generally or specially be approved by the RBI;

(*d*) Borrow from the RBI.

◆ Powers of the NHB

The NHB has been vested with following powers:

(*a*) No housing finance institution, which is a company in existence on the commencement of the NHB (Amendment) Act 2000, shall commence or carry on the business of a housing finance institution without obtaining a Certificate of Registration from NHB and having the net owned fund of ₹ 25 lakh or such other higher amount as the NHB may, by notification, specify.

(*b*) The NHB, after being satisfied that the applicant satisfies stipulated conditions, may grant a Certificate of Registration subject to such conditions which it may consider fit to impose.

(*c*) The NHB may cancel a Certificate of Registration granted to a housing finance institution if it:

(*i*) ceases to carry on the business of a housing finance institution in India; or

(*ii*) has failed to comply with any condition subject to which the Certificate of Registration has been issued to it; or

(*iii*) at any time fails to fulfill any of the conditions;

(*iv*) fails to comply with any direction issued by the NHB;

(*v*) fails to maintain accounts in accordance with the requirement of any law or any direction or order issued by the NHB;

(*vi*) fails to submit or offer for inspection of its books of account and other relevant documents when so demanded by an inspecting authority of the NHB.

(*vii*) has been prohibited from accepting deposits by an order made by the NHB

(*d*) The NHB may at any time direct any housing finance institution accepting deposits to furnish statements, information or particulars relating to or connected with deposits received by the housing finance institution.

(*e*) The NHB may, if it considers necessary in the public interest, give directions to housing finance institutions accepting deposits regarding the rates of interest payable on such deposits, and the periods for which deposits may be received.

◆ RBI Policy Guidelines for Financial Institutions

The RBI initiated several prudential and other regulatory measures during 2004-05 to bring the regulatory framework for FIs in line with that of banks.

◆ Asset Classification, Provisioning and Capital Adequacy

With a view to moving closer to international best practices and ensuring convergence of the norms applicable to FIs with those of banks, the RBI issued a directive that w.e.f. March 31, 2005, an asset will have to be classified as doubtful, if it remains in the sub-standard category for 12 months. However, FIs can phase out the consequential additional provisioning over a four-year period, commencing from the year ended March 31, 2005, with a minimum of 20 per cent each year.

The RBI introduced a graded highest provisioning according to the age of NPAs in 'doubtful for more than three years' category for FIs with effect from March 31, 2005. Consequently, the increase in provisioning requirement on the secured portion is required to be applied in a phased manner over three years as on March 31, 2004. On the unsecured portion, which is not covered by the realisable value of tangible security to which the FI has a valid recourse and the realisable value is estimated on a realistic basis, provision will continue to be to the extent 100 per cent.

◆ Prudential Credit Exposure Limits

The RBI directed FIs to strictly adhere the single/group borrower prudential exposure ceilings, i.e., 15 per cent (additional 5 per cent for infrastructure projects) and 40 per cent (additional 10 per cent for infrastructure projects), respectively. In exceptional circumstances, FIs with the approval of their respective Boards, can enhance their exposure to a borrower upto a further 5 per cent of capital funds (*i.e.* 20 per cent of capital funds for a single borrower and 45 per cent of capital funds for a group of borrowers), subject to the borrower consenting that FIs may make appropriate disclosures in their Annual Reports.

In respect of exposure to infrastructure, FIs could consider additional sanctions upto 5 per cent and 10 per cent over and above the limits of 20 per cent and 45 per cent, respectively.

FIs were advised to phase out exposures in excess of single/group borrower limits not in conformity with above by March 31, 2005, either by increasing capital funds or reducing exposures.

The RBI directed the financial institutions in 2009 to borrow not more than 10 times of net operating fund (NOF) with effect from March 31, 2010.[14]

◈ Holding of Instruments in Dematerialized Form

FIs were advised to hold their fresh investments in equity instruments effective August 30, 2004 in dematerialised form. All the outstanding equity investments in physical form were required to be converted into dematerialised form by end-December, 2004.

◈ Disclosures on Risk Exposures in Derivatives

With a view to making meaningful and appropriate disclosures of FIs' exposures to risk and their strategy to manage the risk, a minimum framework for disclosures on their risk exposures in derivatives was put in place in April, 2005. The framework, apart from the quantitative aspects, also includes qualitative aspects relating to derivatives with a particular reference to the extent to which derivatives are used, the associated risk and business purposes served.

◈ Guidelines on Investment by the FIs in Debt Securities

So as to provide greater transparency to investment by FIs in the debt securities issued by companies on private placement basis from time to time, and to provide protection of the interest of investors in such securities, the RBI directed FIs to adhere to the SEBI guidelines regarding disclosures (initial and continuing), listing agreements with the exchanges, credit rating of less than investment grade, appointment of a debenture trustee, issuance and trading of the debt securities in demat form, trading in stock exchanges and between Qualified Institutional Investors (QIIs) and High Networth individuals, and standard denomination of ₹ 10 lakh. If the FIs registered with SEBI associate themselves with the issuance of private placement of unlisted debt securities, they will be held accountable for such issues. They will also furnish periodical reports to SEBI in such format as may be decided by SEBI.

The RBI prohibited FIs from investing in unrated debt securities of original maturity of less than one year other than CPs and CDs.

◈ Other Guidelines

The RBI policy guidelines regarding lending under consortium arrangements/multiple banking arrangements, provisioning coverage for advances, prudential norms on creation and utilisation of floating provisions, additional disclosures in 'notes to accounts' and prudential norms on income recognition, asset classification and provision pertaining to advances — computation of NPA levels and projects under implementation issued to banks were *mutatis mutandis* applied to the select financial institutions with effect from July 1, 2010. Further, the guidelines regarding know your customer (KYC) norms/anti-money laundering (ALM) standards and sale of investments held under Held to Maturity category issued to banks were also made applicable to select financial institutions.[15]

E. CONCLUSIONS AND SUGGESTIONS

Financial institutions in India and abroad emerged to mitigate the chronic problem of inadequacy of long-term funds for catering to developmental needs of different sectors of the economy.

Since the independence of the country, a battery of financial institutions both at the country level and state level came into existence to provide long-term financial support to business enterprises. However, during the last two decades financial institutions faced perilous challenges in the wake of economic liberalisation and globalisation of financial markets. Concomitantly, these institutions encountered problems in raising resources and deployment of the funds to squeeze emerging opportunities, affecting their ability to offer competitive rates to their borrowers.

Thus, the predominance of these institutions as supplier of development finance diminished over a period of time in view of emergence of banks as powerful source of long-term funds.

Thus, in view of cataclysmic change in operating environment of the country and to overcome the serious financial stress of existing DFIs, the Government and the RBI decided to transform them into banks. Accordingly, ICICI was merged in ICICI Bank in 2002 and IDBI in IDBI Bank in 2004 and they were permitted to assume the role of a universal bank.

Although the efforts to convert DFIs into banks and enlarge their role in the context of fast changing domestic and global scenario, are laudable, it must also be remembered that the next decade in India is going to be the decade of infrastructure development. The financial institutions' dynamism and inclination towards financial innovation and technological change and their project appraising, financing and monitoring expertise will be greatly needed particularly for guiding such investments along commercially sound lines.

The Government and the Reserve Bank must remember that Indian financial system has to ensure supply of adequate funds to support infrastructure development on which depends the future economic development and sustained prosperity of the country. Despite the tremendous efforts made by DFIs and commercial banks in India during the last five decades or so, there still exists wide gap between the demand for funds by infrastructure sector and supply of funds for the same. It has been estimated that the country will require over ₹ 18 lakh crores during the next 5 years to meet its infrastructural requirements. Supply of funds to this sector has so far not been more than ₹ 15,000 crores. Software industry, despite its laudable performance, has yet to receive desired support from the existing financial institutions engaged in wide array of services. Mega projects in the field of oil, gas, petro-chemical sectors will require sufficient support from the existing institutions, particularly from Infrastructural Development Finance Corporation (IDFC) and Infrastructure Leasing and Financial Services (IL & FS) which were set up only to finance infrastructure and facilitate private capital flows into infrastructure projects. Unfortunately, these institutions which started their operations with funding infrastructure projects, agriculture, telecom, urban and transport sectors, subsequently diversified their operations and embraced investment banking, equity and derivatives, project finance and public-private partnerships (including education tourism, health and hospitals). Driven by commercial considerations, it was natural for these institutions to diversify into e-learning, mutual funds and car leasing. As such, the description of IL & FS as a project developer and IDFC as a project financier is at best artifice. There is thus no focus of these institutions on infrastructural financing.

What is, therefore, required is that these two institutions should be directed to concentrate themselves to funding of infrastructural projects and commercial banks. Both public and private sectors- including newly constituted ICICI and IDBI Banks — be asked to render support to the two institutions by way of equity share capital and long-term loans. Both the Government and the RBI should evolve suitable mechanism for the purpose.

KEY TERMS

- Central Banking Inquiry Commission
- Export-Import Bank
- Industrial Bank of Japan
- Industrial Credit and Investment Corporation of India Ltd.
- Industrial Finance Corporation of India Ltd.
- Industrial Investment Bank of India
- Infrastructure Development Finance Corporation of India
- Credit Mobiliser to Finance
- General Insurance Corporation
- Industrial Development Bank of India
- Life Insurance corporation of India
- National Agricultural Bank for Reconstruction and Development.
- National Housing Bank
- Small Industries Development Bank of India.

DISCUSSION QUESTIONS

1. Give a detailed account of evolution of development financial institutions the world over.
2. Why were development financial corporations set up in India? In what respects did they differ from the existing institutions?
3. Discuss in brief, profile of development financial institutions in India.
4. Describe the nature and scope of business of the IDFCI.
5. Why was Exim Bank established? Discuss nature and scope of activities of the Bank.
6. Describe objectives, functions, powers and obligations of the NHB.
7. Why was the IDBI formed? Under what circumstances was the IDBI converted into IDBI Bank?
8. Discuss the objectives and scope of business of the TFCI.
9. Why was the SIDBI constituted? Outline the major schemes launched by the SIDBI for fostering growth of small and medium segments of the industry.
10. Discuss, in brief, the role assigned to the NABARD as an apex development bank.
11. Bring out the RBI policy guidelines with respect to prudential and other regulatory aspects of the financial institutions.

REFERENCES

1. Beatriz Annendariz de Aghion, *Development Banking*, Journal of Development Economics, 1999 Vol. 58.
2. V. Murinde, *Development Banking and Finance*, Avebury, Ashgate Publishing, Aldershot, UK, 1999.
3. Y.C. Richard Wong and M.I,. and Sonia Wong, *Competition in China's Domestic Banking Industry*, Cato Journal, 2001, Vol. 21, No. 1 (Spring/Summer).
4. Report on Trend and Progress of Banking in India, 2002-03.
5. Annual Report of IFCI, 1987-88, p. 7.
6. Annual Report of IFCI, 1992-93, p. 4.
7. Report on Trend and Progress of Banking in India, 2003-04, p. 141.
8. Times of India, August 6, 2007.
9. Business Today, December 30, 2007.
10. www.idfc.com
11. eximbankindia.com
12. www.fciltd.com
13. www.nabard.org
14. RBI Report on Trend and Progress of Banking in India, 2009-10. p. 45.
15. *Ibid*. pp. 45-46.

Project Evaluation by Development Financial Institutions in India

Chapter 24

Learning Objectives:

The present chapter aims at:

presenting vivid account on how projects are evaluated and monitored by Development Financial Institutions in India.

Chapter Outline:

- General observations.
- Project evaluation by Development Financial Institutions in India.
- Follow-up by the Development Financial Institutions.
- Conclusions.

A. GENERAL OBSERVATIONS

Development Financial Institutions (DFIs) are supposed to play the role of catalytic agent to hasten the establishment of industrial projects of socio-economic importance, besides the conventional role of supplying term capital. As development agencies, these DFIs have to perform such functions of avowed social and economic significance as the dispersal of industries away from metropolitan areas and the total development of certain selected backward areas with a view to achieving a wide diffusion of entrepreneurship. As a financial agency, DFIs provide term loans and participate in the risk capital of those industrial concerns which are financially viable. The management of such institutions is confronted with the problem of carrying out both the tasks simultaneously. But it is primarily concerned with the profitability and safety aspects of the investment even while it is performing the role of a financier. However, these considerations become secondary when it acts as a development agency because in that capacity ,the order of the priorities of projects is laid down in terms of their economic significance to the nation. There may be certain projects which are highly bankable in terms of profitability and safety, but which do not fulfill the criterion of development. In a sharp contrast to this, projects of high national significance, which have received top priorities in development programmes may fail to satisfy the attribute of being bankable. As has been said aptly by Boskey: "All bankable projects are not necessarily economically important, nor is every economically important project necessarily bankable. A development bank will not achieve its development objectives if it devotes its limited capital exclusively to bankable projects, irrespective of their purpose; at the same time, as a bank it cannot afford to ignore the financial aspect of proposals and thereby run the risk of failing to preserve its capital intact."[1]

In view of the above, a judicious blending of banking and development criteria should be adopted for lending and investment policies of a development bank. The task of project appraisal in a DFI is often very difficult. It calls for a keen and an intuitive mind capable of going behind the facade of figures and charts to form a judgement.

Project appraisal is a techno-economic affair. It calls for an evaluation of the worthwhileness of a project from various angles. Among these, the technical basis of the project needs to be examined thoroughly, and it has to be seen whether the technical choices, including the choice of location, scale of operations, the processes, the arrangement for technical collaboration, the availability of power and transport facilities, are made correctly. Second, the demand for the product mix in India as well as abroad needs to be studied, and appropriate marketing arrangements worked out. Third, there has to be an appraisal of its management and the organisational set-up for project implementation. Fourth, the financial viability of the project in terms of its profitability has to be studied together with the financial arrangements made by the promoter for financing the project.

If a project is found suitable from all the four angles, its economic viability from the standpoint of the country's interest has to be examined. In this connection, the DFI, must have a clear understanding of the indices of significance from the national point of view. Two principal indicators of the project's economic significance are:

(*a*) The internal rate of return on a project; and

(*b*) The implicit exchange rate of the project.

On the basis of these two criteria, it is possible to select projects. All the projects are ranked in terms of these criteria, and such projects are chosen as offer the highest internal rate of return and the lowest exchange rate. This selection process should be such as to exhaust the total available investible funds during a given period of time. The projects which are left out would then have had a lower internal rate of return and a higher exchange rate than the marginal project which was selected.

However, in actual practice, this procedure is not workable for the simple reason that no such comprehensive list of well-worked out projects is available to an institution during a given time period. Hence, the project selection process begins to operate as and when a project seeks institutional assistance. In such a situation, a norm for the internal rate of return should be fixed in the light of the development objectives relating to the growth rate of industrial output. This would mean that all the projects which yield a rate of return per annum equal to, or more than, the norm tentatively fixed, deserve assistance by the institution. But this criterion by itself is not sufficient for a real economic choice. A project may yield an internal rate of return which is higher than the norm but which may still be such that it would be more advantageous for the country to import the products rather than produce them at home. In such a case, the project obviously is not economically viable and would certainly be inefficient from the country's point of view. The efficiency criteria, thus, should be related to the implicit foreign exchange rate of the project. The implicit exchange rate — domestic cost of earning/ saving, say, one U.S. dollar — should not be higher than the prevailing Reserve Bank exchange rate.

In applying the above criteria, it is necessary to take into account two basic considerations, *viz.*, that the export prices of certain products in developed countries are sometimes much lower than their domestic prices and that, in a new field, learning by experience is necessary. The criterion thus is that a project should not be selected unless its implicit exchange rate is equal to, or less than, the norm tentatively fixed (in terms of the rupees per US dollar). All transfer items like import duties, excise and sales tax need to be eliminated for the purpose of this calculation.

After a project has satisfied all the criteria referred to above, the DFI, before sanctioning assistance for it, must ensure that the cost estimates have been properly drawn up because both under-estimation and over-estimation are undesirable. While under-estimation is risky for the success of the project, a DFI, with its limited resources, cannot afford to go along with over-estimation. Ignorance and inexperience may be responsible for faulty estimates of cost. But, in many instances, deliberate misrepresentation leads to faulty estimates. A common source of under-estimation is the working capital.

After assistance has been sanctioned for a project, the DFI must keep a close watch on its progress with a view to ensuring that the assistance is utilised for the purpose for which it was sanctioned, to assess whether construction is progressing according to schedule, and to assess whether the project will be completed within the original estimates of capital cost; if not, to what extent there is likely to be an over-run; and to evaluate production performance and working results against the original expectations, and to find out, as early as possible, whether the realisation of targets and expectations is being impeded, and if so, to take the necessary remedial measures. Among the various ways in which the supervision of the project and the sanctioned loan may be effected are the receipt of periodical returns, visits to the site of the units, particularly in the early stages, periodic conferences with the promoters and reports from other quarters, including bankers and stockbrokers.

An effective control over the affairs of the assisted company may be exercised by the bank by nominating its own representative in the Board of Directors of that company. This may be necessary where the assistance is substantial or where the project is a complex one and is likely to face many serious problems initially, or where the management needs constant guidance. However, the DFI will have to ensure that its representative does not unnecessarily intervene in the day-to-day affairs of the company.

Finally, in order to ensure satisfactory progress of the project and proper utilisation of the sanctioned money, the DFI should see to it that qualified and experienced technical and managerial personnel are engaged by the assisted units. Where necessary, particularly in cases of over-run in costs and unsatisfactory working, it must exert pressure to bring about a suitable change in the personnel and help the units to hire suitable people. The DFI, however, is not expected to maintain a service for the purpose.

B. PROJECT EVALUATION BY DEVELOPMENT FINANCIAL INSTITUTIONS IN INDIA

While the DFIs established in India are required to act on business principles, they are, at the same time, expected to pay due regard to the interests of industry, commerce and the general public. As the industrial projects seeking assistance are in the nature of business risks, the DFIs examine them in the light of several factors, viz., the relative industrial and national priority of the project in the economy of the country, the technical, financial and economic viability of the project, the background of the promoters and their own financial contribution to project cost, and the quality of technical, financial and executive management for the construction and operation of the project.

(*i*) In considering loan application for financing a project, DFIs in India are guided by the national priorities indicated in the Five-Year Plans and the policies of the government, such as those which assist in the task of industrial development, the regional development of industries, and encourage technologists and new entrepreneurs to set-up projects.

(*ii*) Only those industrial concerns can apply for loans from the development banks which have received licences under the Industries Development and Regulation Act, 1951, and have got a Certificate of Incorporation.

(*iii*) While evaluating a project, the IDBI and IFCI pay due consideration to its relevant economic and social aspects, such as its employment potentiality, stimulation or growth of the ancillary industries, the benefits which are likely to flow from the project-towards rural and less developed areas, etc. The factors that govern the priority criteria of the DFIs are:

- Employment-oriented and labour-intensive nature of the project;
- Export-oriented projects, normally with an export obligation of 60 per cent of the production or above;
- Projects proposed to be located in the notified and less developed districts/ areas;
- Projects promoted by new entrepreneurs or technician-entrepreneurs; and
- Projects which contemplate harnessing the indigenously available technology or process, know-how and raw materials.

(*iv*) In respect of export-oriented projects, the DFIs endeavour to ensure that each project is viable as far as possible without any incentive or subsidies. Likewise, while appraising a project, the possibility of substituting the automatic and capital intensive process by a labour-intensive one is also examined in accordance with the directions received from the government. In this context, the scope for off-loading the existing low technology items from large units to small ancillary units is also considered.

(*v*) In terms of government guidelines, the DFIs have advised entrepreneurs to set-up their projects, as far as possible, either in the notified less developed areas or in areas which do not fall within the limits of large metropolitan cities. The setting up of projects in notified/selected less developed areas will also make them eligible for State and Central subsidies as applicable, as also for finance on concessional term from financial institutions, including the IFCI.

(*vi*) The DFIs follow project-oriented approach to evaluate the desirability of a project. Accordingly, they appraise its worthwhileness from the technical, financial, economic, commercial, managerial and social angles. We shall now examine each of these at a greater length.

◆ Technical Appraisal

A project, wherein all the relevant technical aspects have been taken into account by the promoters, and when the planned implementation of the project conforms to accepted engineering standards and practices, is regarded as technically sound.

The technical appraisal involves a critical examination of:

(*i*) Suitability of the selected technical process under prevailing conditions in the country, and the arrangements made or proposed to be made therefor.

(*ii*) The locational aspect, i.e., the project's nearness to sources of raw materials; the availability of utilities — water, power, transport facilities; the availability of fuel, skilled and unskilled labour, and market for the product; whether the location poses flood and earthquake hazards.

(*iii*) Adequacy of a plant and equipment and their specifications, plant layout, particularly with reference to production flow, the reputation of machinery suppliers, the balancing of the different sections of the plant, the proposed arrangements for the procurement of plant and equipment, etc.

(*iv*) The sale of operations, and whether the size of the unit would be adequate of the economic viability of the project.

(*v*) The availability of technical know-how during the implementation period and for the operation of the project.

(*vi*) Arrangements for the disposal of factory effluents and the utilisation of the by-products, if any.

(*vii*) The construction and installation schedules, and an examination of PERT and CPM charts with a view to judging whether the time estimate would be considered realistic.

(*viii*) Technical collaboration arrangements, if any.

◆ Financial Appraisal

A project promising earnings which are sufficient to cover fixed charges, operational and maintenance costs, and amortisation of loans, and which, in addition, gives an adequate return on the total investment, is considered to be financially sound. A scrutiny of the financial aspects involves an analysis of the working results, the balance sheet and cash flow for the past few years in the case of any existing concern, as also an examination of the following aspects in the existing as well as new projects:

(*i*) The basis and reasonableness of the cost of the project;

(*ii*) Financing plan, with particular reference to the capital structure, the promoter's contribution to the total project cost, the debt-equity ratio, and the availability of other resources or means of finance; in the case of an existing concern, an examination of the investment made outside the business and the justification made thereof;

(*iii*) An analysis of working results; an analysis of the profit and loss account and balance sheets, and estimates of profitability and cash flow, both during the construction and operation periods;

(*iv*) The internal rate of return, the debt services coverage, the expected return on share capital, the domestic resources, cost of import substitution, and export promotion aspects;

(*v*) In the case of an expanding concern, a critical appraisal of the statement of sources and the application of funds for at least five preceding years, so that the quality of its financial management may be properly evaluated.

These aspects will now be dealt with in detail in the following paragraphs:

◆ Appraisal of Cost Estimates

All the possible items of capital expenditure, particularly those mentioned below, together with the various contingencies, must be properly provided for. These items include:

(*a*) Cost of land, conveyance, laying roads, landscaping, factory and non-factory, buildings, boundary walls, ponds, etc.

(*b*) Plant and machinery, sales tax, octroi, other taxes, price escalation, freight insurance.

(*c*) Technical know-how and engineering fees.

(*d*) Miscellaneous fixed assets — furniture, office equipment, tools, vehicles, water facility, etc.

(*e*) Pre-operation expenses — promotional, organisational, training costs, rents, postage, stationery, printing, etc. In assessing the total cash requirements of the project, the instalments of interest and principal on deferred payments to be met during the construction period or before the project goes into commercial production and starts generating cash — these facts have to be taken into account and due provision should be made thereof in the means of financing of projects.

(*f*) Primary capital issues — mortgage expenses, stamp duty, legal charges.

(*g*) Initial or nucleus working capital (margin money).

(*h*) Start up expenses, including the cost of raw materials, direct wages, salaries, etc.

(*i*) A satisfactory provision for escalation in the costs of buildings, plant and machinery and overall contingency and firm costs.

(*j*) A separate assessment of the rupee costs of a project and the foreign exchange cost, both by way of capital expenditure and operating cost estimates.

(*k*) Inflationary conditions, fluctuations in the rates of foreign currencies, the impact of devaluation, which may affect the cost estimates.

In present-day conditions, the DFIs consider the provision for contingency at not less than 20 per cent (over and above the provision for escalation in accordance with quotations) on the items of cost for which the prices are not firm. This is not considered unreasonable. Its experience has been that pre-operation expenses frequently exceed the original estimates, generally as a result of delays in the implementation of projects. It expects that the assessment of the initial cash losses which often deplete a company's working funds or affect its liquidity has to be made on a liberal basis, if the possibility of over-runs is to be avoided.

It may observed here that an inter-firm comparison of projects cost serves as a useful starting point for cost estimates, making due allowance for such aspects as locational or geographical factors, the time factor, variations in capacity and product mix, special characteristics of the equipment or technical processes employed, the time taken for the implementation of the project, and attaining a comparable level of production. It is often useful to look for reasons for marked deviations under the various heads.

◆ Financing Pattern

Cost estimates have to be examined with reference to the sources from which the project is proposed to be financed. The DFIs ensure that an item of expenditure is financed from a right or most suitable source; public deposits are no substitutes for adequate equity or long-term loans for capital expenditure. They are good only as supplementary finance for well established concerns. There are various examples where concerns have come to grief by using such deposits for long-term expenditure.

The sources of finance should be:

(*i*) Share capital;

(*ii*) Long-term loans from financial institutions;

(*iii*) Foreign currency loans for financing the cost imported plant and machinery and other foreign exchange costs;

(*iv*) Deferred payments for plant and machinery, indigenous or imported;

(*v*) Unsecured loans from promoters and directors;

(*vi*) Public deposits;

(*vii*) Internal accruals in the case of existing concerns proposing to take up expansion or modernisation; and

(*viii*) Central government subsidy for projects set-up in selected backward districts.

The DFIs insist on a sound financial plan with a debt-equity ratio which is consistent with the nature of the industry, the capital outlay involved, the size of the project, the gestation period, and its expected profitability.

The DFIs adopt flexible approach in respect of debt-equity mix. Normally, debt-equity ratio of 1:1.5 is acceptable.

For the computation of the debt-equity ratio, the term *debt* includes all the borrowings repayable not earlier than five years from the date of borrowing, whether debenture loans or deferred payments, including interest thereon for the purchase of capital equipment, and preference shares redeemable not later than twelve years from the date of issue.

The term *equity* includes paid-up share capital, share premium, free reserves, preference shares and preference shares redeemable not earlier than twelve years from the date of issue.

The following refinements were suggested at the Inter-Institutional Meeting (IIM) of the IDBI, the IFCI and the ICICI, held on 21st June, 1977, in the computation of D-E ratio with regard to the appraisal:

(*a*) Term loans from financial institutions and debentures (including convertible debentures until they are actually converted into equity) would continue to be classified as debt.

(*b*) The minimum period of five years for treating all other borrowings as debt would be reduced to one year, and all the borrowings of more than one year's maturity (other than borrowings from banks or through short-term deposits for meeting the requirements of working capital) would be treated as debt. All debts with less than one year's maturity would be taken as current liabilities and will not be taken into account for calculating the debt-equity ratio.

(*c*) Unsecured loans from promoters for capital expenditure or long-term purposes, where these are not subordinated in all aspects to the loans from financial institutions, would be treated as debt. Subordinate unsecured loans from promoters/directors would otherwise be treated as *quasi-equity*.

(*d*) Redeemable preference shares, irrespective of the redemption period attached to them, would be treated as equity save under the following circumstances:

  (*i*) When the period between the due date of redemption of preference shares and the date, on which the debt-equity ratio is computed, is less than 3 years (in other words, when the redemption of preference shares is due within a period of 3 years), the preference shares would be treated as debt and not as equity. This procedure has been designed to enable the financial institutions to ascertain the measures proposed to be adopted by the assisted units to redeem the preference shares in time.

  (*ii*) When a period of only 12 months or less remains in the redemption of preference shares, they should neither be treated as debt nor equity but as a current liability.

(*e*) Equity would continue to include paid-up equity share capital, share premium, free reserves, including surplus or balance in the profit and loss account, irredeemable preference shares and redeemable preference shares, irrespective of the redemption period attached to them, provided that they do not fall in the two categories mentioned under (d) above. However, for the purpose of arriving at the equity in the case of an existing concern, the following items should be deducted from the figure of equity:

(*i*) All the items of assets which are of an intangible nature or which are expenditure that has not been written off;

(*ii*) Investments in other undertakings, where these, according to information available in the balance sheet, are considered *prima facie* as unrealisable;

(*iii*) Unabsorbed depreciation; and

(*iv*) Accumulated book losses.

(*f*) The Central Government's subsidy for projects in selected backward districts (presently raised to 30 per cent of the cost of project comprising land, building and machinery, subject to maximum limit of ₹ 15 lakhs) is not treated as the promoter's contribution. It is taken into account in the means of financing as a cushion for possible over-runs, and the D-E ratio is relaxed to that extent. But the Central Government's investment subsidy and unsecured sales-tax loans repayable in one or more instalments after a period of 12 years would continue to be treated as equity.

(*g*) Interest-free and/or unsecured development loans from State Government/State level developmental agencies are brought in by the promoters, and where these loans have been subordinated in all respects to the loans from the financial institutions, they would be treated as *quasi-equity.*

(*h*) Where there are certain items which are to be treated as quasi-equity, the D-E ratio would be worked out, both with and without the quasi-equity items. The first ratio, *i.e.,* with the *quasi-equity* items included in equity, is called the Adjusted Debt-Equity Ratio, and the other, i.e., without the inclusion of the *quasi-equity* items in equity, is called the normal debt-equity ratio.

Before financing a new project, the DFIs ensure that there are satisfactory arrangements for the underwriting/subscription of share capital for a new issue. It also examines the items of deferred payments, if any, particularly the grace period and maturities, with a view to determining if these are realistic and appropriate. The IFCI's experience is that, for a new project, with a long or even moderate gestation period, short-dated deferred payments and short-term obligations in the form of unsecured loans/public deposits are understandably not a satisfactory source of finance and should be discontinued. In view of the very poor public response to preference capital, the corporate planner should plan preference capital to the extent to which certain investment institutions at the all-India and State levels — such as LIC, UTI, or the SIICs - show interest in underwriting/subscribing it. The assisted concerns must bear in mind that the servicing of the preference share capital is costlier than the debt, for the dividends are paid out of taxed profits.

◈ Promoter's Contribution

The DFIs expect from the promoters a reasonable contribution to the financing of the project to ensure their continued interest in its successful implementation and operation. The normal requirement of the promoter's contribution is 25-30 per cent of the total project cost.

However, in the case of capital intensive projects costing above ₹ 200 crores, a lower contribution may be agreed upon, if desired by the promoter and is justified by the circumstances.

◈ Analysis of Working Results

Besides examination of D-E ratio on the lines mentioned above, the DFIs satisfy themselves on other important ratios which enable them to evaluate the financial and operational soundness of the concern. These ratios are:

(*i*) $\dfrac{\text{Net Worth} + \text{Term Liabilities}}{\text{Net Block}}$

(*ii*) Current Ratio

(*iii*) $\frac{\text{Cost of Production}}{\text{Capital Employed}}$

(*iv*) $\frac{\text{Net Project Cost}}{\text{Capital Employed}}$

(*v*) Return on Equity Capital

(*vi*) Net Profit before Tax/Net Sales

(*vii*) Gross Profit/Net Sales

(*viii*) Investment/Output

(*ix*) Receivables/Sales

(*x*) Stocks/Sales

The profit and loss account is also analysed to determine the added value.

The DFIs carry out an examination of the statement of the projected sources and the application of funds, and use it as a tool of financial appraisal. For existing concerns, this appraisal extends to the statement of sources and the application of funds for the past years as well. The prospective cash flow of the project is regarded as a real security for term loans which, in turn, depends on the viability of the project. It has been the experience of the DFIs that the physical security of land, buildings, plant and machinery is not the real security, for it is very difficult to find any buyer once the factory closes down. Moreover, on account of the existing political and social conditions in the country, foreclosure of mortgage of block assets has, in most cases, to be ruled out as a practical proposition.

In the evaluation of project, different viewpoints may have to be served. In the management view, the crucial test is the return on investment. From the shareholder's point of view, the earning per share is the focal concept. From the lender's view point, the real test is *debt services* coverage, which depends on the projected cash flow of the project. In the end, all the parties are interested in the commercial success of the project, each in his own interest.

The DFIs evaluate projected profitability and cash flow in terms of the three important indicators, namely:

(*i*) Debt service coverage ratio (DSCR);

(*ii*) Interest services coverage ratio (ISCR);

(*iii*) Internal rate of return (IRR).

These are calculated with a view to comprehending the implications of these indicators. The debt-service (*i.e.*, the number of times the total debt service, which includes the instalment of loans, the deferred payments, the interest on term loans, and deferred payments falling due in any year covered by the net distributable profit, with development rebate reserve, depreciation and interest added back) of at least two times is regarded as satisfactory.

The DSCR is to be worked out in the following manner:

$$\frac{\text{Net profit afer tax + Depreciation + Interest on term borrowings}}{\text{Repayment of term borrowings + Interest on term borrowings}}$$

A DSCR of 2:1 is adopted to estimate the cost available for meeting the term commitments; the period of the loans should be determined on this basis.

The interest service coverage ratio (ISCR) is calculated by relating the amount of interest on existing term loans/deferred payments, both existing, if any, as well as on proposed term loans/ deferred payments of a particular period to the amount of the net profit after tax but before interest. The ISCR between three and four times is considered to be satisfactory.

The internal rate of return (IRR) may be defined as the discount rate which equates the present value of investment of the project (known as cash outflows) to the present value of future cash benefits. In the case of expansion/diversification schemes, the IRR should be worked out on the incremental benefits accruing to the profit as a result of additional investment.

The internal rate of return of 15 per cent before depreciation but after interest on term loans and tax is considered to be good; between 10 to 15 per cent is considered to be satisfactory. The discounted equity return is also worked out; the equity divided is discounted to arrive at the present value. This is done while considering the proposal for underwriting equity shares.

◈ Economic Appraisal

The following aspects are considered while evaluating the economic justification of the project:

(*a*) The national and industrial priority of the project and its contribution to the economy;

(*b*) Savings in foreign exchange or prospects of exports;

(*c*) The extent to which the profit can bring about development in the areas;

(*d*) Employment potential;

(*e*) A critical study of the market for the product or products proposed to be manufactured, the existing and future demand, the licensed and installed capacity, the likely competition, a study of the pricing policy in relation to demand, the cost-volume-profit analysis (break-even point, level of operation and safety margin available on the break-even level of production);

(*f*) Scrutiny of the project in the context of

- (*i*) The Government's import and export policy;
- (*ii*) The Government's backward area development strategy;
- (*iii*) The Government's priority sector development strategy;
- (*iv*) Various other regulatory controls on production, prices, raw materials, collaboration agreements, foreign investment; and
- (*v*) Comprehension of the scope for growth and the establishment of new ancillary industries.

Projects of high national priority, as also export-oriented projects are given special consideration.

A novel technique, which evaluates the economic justification of the project by appraising the efficiency of saving or earning of foreign exchange, and known as Implicit Foreign Exchange Rate or Internal Exchange Rate, is described below. This rate is also known as the Domestic Resources Cost (DRC).

◈ Internal Exchange Rate

◈ Technique for Economic Appraisal of a Project

The efficiency of saving or earning foreign exchange cannot be measured with the technique of internal rate of return (IRR), which measures the productivity of the capital employed in a project. In the case of projects promising export growth or saving in foreign exchange or both, the appraisal has to be done to ascertain whether the benefit to the economy in terms of foreign exchange is really commensurate with the market exchange rate. For example, if the project is going to save foreign currency, say, of $ 1 by putting in an input of ₹ 25 when the market rate of $ 1 is only ₹ 46, there is no special advantage in encouraging the project despite the fact that the internal rate of return (IRR) on the project is very attractive. Hence, one must bear in mind that if the IRR on a project falls within the acceptable limit, the internal exchange rate (IER) may be disadvantageous. This is so because the cash flow computed for the IRR on the project may be inflated. For it may contain the various fiscal duties, taxes and subsidies which are not really the revenue for the country buying the projects. Similarly, there is no point in spending heavily on capital equipment and/or on raw materials in foreign exchange if the economy is going to have a benefit of ₹ 5 for every dollar spent, when the market rate of exchange is as above (*i.e.*, ₹ 46 per dollar), for there is no advantage in encouraging the project unless there are considerations other than economic and commercial, or there is some long-term interest. On the other hand, if the domestic resources' cost of a particular item meant for export and which earns foreign exchange of dollar 1 and which comes to ₹ 46, it is obvious that the export of such a product from the country would have a comparative advantage and should be supported and built up. This assessment of the economic justification of the export-oriented import substitution project is done by means of the internal exchange rate technique. This technique helps identify industries wherein the country has a comparative advantage for export promotion or import substitution. This technique helps identify industries wherein the country has a comparative advantage for export promotion or import substitution, and thereby helps in a rational allocation of scare resources, whether these relate to domestic capital or foreign exchange.

While calculating the IER, such costs as customs and excise duties, sales tax, subsidies and similar other payments should be excluded from the capital cost as well as from the current operating cost of a project. These fiscal levies are in the nature of transfer payments to the government and do not represent any genuine cost (or loss) to the economy. They come back to government as revenue. The IER calculation, therefore, involves the working out of the cost involved, less taxes, etc., in local currency to earn/save foreign exchange. The rate finally arrived at is the net cost in local currency to earn/save each unit of foreign exchange. This is known as internal exchange rate. In other words, this rate indicates at what domestic net cost each unit of foreign exchange will be earned.

This rate is compared with the market rate of exchange (the market rate of the dollar in terms of Indian Rupee) to judge the worthwhileness of the project. A project whose exchange rate is equal, or less than the market rate, may be considered worthwhile, for it denotes that manufacturing the product within the country costs as much as, or less than, the equivalent foreign exchange.

The current costs for the year, in which the optimum level of production is expected to be reached, need to be broken down into the following three broad categories:

(*i*) Charge on capital, *i.e.*, interest on capital employed;

(*ii*) Charge on account of depreciation;

(*iii*) Ongoing charges, *i.e.*, other current costs of production.

Charges on capital, both on the domestic and foreign exchange components thereof, may be taken at the respective net lending rates of interest in force at the time of the appraisal. The charge on inventories and block debts may be computed at 15 per cent, *i.e.*, at the commercial bank current average lending rate for working capital advances. The charge on depreciation may be calculated on a uniform annual rate $6^1/_4$ per cent on the gross value of depreciable assets, assuming a normal project life of 15 years, with a small residual value. The other current costs, consisting of variable and non-variable expenses, may also be examined to identify any direct or indirect foreign exchange component therein and other transfer payments. These are to be segregated item by item, and a complete picture of domestic and foreign exchange costs, exclusive of transfer payments, should be calculated in the form of an overall composite rate for the entire range of products.

This technique is applied by the DFIs mainly in the following cases:

(*i*) When the cost in terms of foreign exchange is 10 per cent or more of the total project cost, excluding the margin money for working capital; or

(*ii*) When the revenue expenditure in foreign exchange every year is more than 5 per cent of the total cost of production; or

(*iii*) When the export obligation is 10 per cent or more; or

(*iv*) When the estimated capital cost of a project is more than ₹ 1 crore.

For figuring out the internal exchange rate, the following information are required:

(*i*) The foreign exchange component in the capital cost of the project;

(*ii*) Import duties, excise duties, sales/purchase tax, octroi and other levies included in the capital cost;

(*iii*) Value in foreign exchange of imported components, raw materials, stores and spares, royalties and other services included in the revenue items;

(*iv*) The extent of import saving in the project or export potential or export obligation of the project;

(*v*) The current CIF prices for the finished products, if imported, and the FOB prices of the products, if exported;

(*vi*) The rates of export duties, duty drawbacks, cash and other incentives, etc., currently prescribed for the export of the products proposed to be manufactured.

◈ Mechanism of Computation Of Internal Exchange Rate

A. DATA

1.1 The estimated capital cost of project under broad heads is given below:

	₹ *in lakhs*
Land and Development, Buildings	54.00
Plant and Machinery, including Installation	190.00
Miscellaneous Fixed Assets	5.00
Preliminary and Pre-operation Expenses	22.00
Provision for Contingencies	6.00
Margin Money for Working Capital	13.00
Total	290.00

1.2 The estimated cost of plant and machinery includes the foreign exchange cost of imported machinery equivalent to ₹ 19 lakhs, the import duty thereon being ₹ 4.00 lakhs.

1.3 Excise duty, sales tax and octroi included in this project cost amount to ₹ 5.00 lakhs.

1.4 Pre-operation expenses include interest and commitment charges during the construction period. These are ₹ 11.00 lakhs.

1.5 No other transfer costs are included in the estimated capital cost.

2.1 The estimated cost of production and profitability for the optimum level (year of maximum achievable production):

Year of Operation	*Tonnes*
Installed Capacity	39,000
Production	36,900
Sales (Gross) (₹ in lakhs:)	461.80
Less: Excise Duty	32.29
Net Sales	429.51
Cost of Production/Sales	(₹ *in lakhs*)
Raw Materials	192.38
Consumable Stores	40.74
Utilities	33.62
Repairs and Maintenance	6.66
Direct Labour	11.44
Factory Supervision	9.25
Other Miscellaneous Expenses	15.31
Administrative Overheads	8.78
Selling Expenses	4.43
Total	322.61

Gross Profit Before Interest and Depreciation	106.90
Interest:	
On Working Capital Borrowing	1.10
On Term Loans	14.10
Depreciation	15.66
Net Profit Before Tax	75.44

2.2 The landed cost imported items comprises 15 per cent of the cost of raw materials and 50 per cent of the cost of consumable stores, the import duty on these items being 25 per cent. Excise duty, sales tax, octroi, etc., work out on an average of 5 per cent of the cost of indigenous items on both the cases.

2.3 **Inventories comprise**

	(₹ in lakhs)
Raw Materials	34.00
Consumable Stores	10.00
Finished Goods	14.00
Book Debts are Estimated at	15.00

2.4 While the project is mainly import saving, there is also an export obligation to the extent of 10 per cent of the output to meeting which the company has entered into arrangements for the export of its products to, say, some Middle East countries.

2.5 Current C.I.F. import price of the product is ₹ 1,202 per tonne and the F.O.B. export price is ₹ 900 per tonne.

B. Computation

3.1 Other than the charge on capital and depreciation, which are dealt with separately, the current costs projected for the optimum year of operations are as follows:

(₹ in lakhs)

	Imported	*Indigenous*	*Totals*
Raw Materials (25:75)	48.09	244.29	192.38
Consumable Stores (50:50)	20.37	20.37	40.74
Other Current Costs (0:100)	—	89.49	89.49
Total:	68:46	254.15	322.61

Transfer costs consisting of import and excise duties, sales tax, octroi, etc., included in the above figures, are required to be excluded. Assuming the import duty at a uniform rate of 25 per cent and local taxes at 5 per cent on the indigenous items, the foreign exchange and domestic cost elements in the current costs would be as under:

Current Foreign Exchange Cost *(₹ in lakhs)*

Raw Materials $\frac{100}{125} \times 48.09$	38.49
Consumable Stores $\frac{100}{125} \times 20.37$	16.30
Total:	54.79

Current Domestic Cost

$\frac{100}{105} \times 144.29$	137.42
Consumable Stores $\frac{100}{105} \times 20.37$	89.49
Other Current Costs (100%)	246.31

Summary	(₹ *in lakhs)*
Current Foreign Exchange Cost	54.78
Current Domestic Cost	246.31
Total Current Operating Costs (after excluding transportation payments)	301.09

3.2 Depreciation

Total Project Cost (excluding margin money)	277.00
Less: Value of Non-depreciable assets-say, on account of land	14.00
	263.00
Less: Transfer payments, *viz.*, import duty (₹ 4 lakhs); and excise duty and local taxes (₹ 5.00 lakhs); Preliminary expenses (₹ 11.00 lakhs).	20.00
	243.00
Of which imported machinery accounts for	19.00
Balance being indigenous assets	224.00
Depreciation on imported equipment (₹ 19 lakhs at $6^1/_4$%)	14.00
Total depreciation charge	15.20

3.3 Charge on Capital, *i.e.,* Interest on Capital Employed

The charge on capital has to be calculated not only on the investment by way of capital expenditure but also on the investment in inventories and book debts. Further, the foreign exchange component has to be identified in each case.

(a) On Capital Investment		(₹ *in lakhs)*
Total Estimated Project Cost		290.00
Less: Margin Money for Working Capital	13.00	
Transfer Payments, comprising import duty	4.00	
Excise, Sales Tax and Octroi	5.00	22.00
Balance on which charge on capital is to be calculated		268.00
Of which foreign exchange component is		19.00
Balance being domestic component of capital investment		249.00
Charge on capital at 11% (Present net effective rare applicable to rupee and foreign currency loans)		
On foreign exchange component		2.10
On domestic component		27.40
Total Charge on Capital Investment		29.50

(b) On Current Assets (Inventories and Book Debts)

The investment in inventories and book debts, when the optimum level of operations is reached in the third year of operation, is as follows:

		(₹ *in lakhs)*
(*i*)	Raw Materials	34.00
(*ii*)	Consumable Stores	10.00
(*iii*)	Finished Goods	14.00
(*iv*)	Book Debts	15.00
	Total:	73.00

The elements of foreign exchange and transfer payments in each of the assets have to be identified and segregated to arrive at the capital base for the purpose of calculating the charge thereon.

◈ Raw Materials

It is assumed that the stocks of raw materials are composed of 50 per cent imported and 50 per cent indigenous stocks. The foreign exchange and domestic cost components of the capital at charge under the head Raw Materials, after excluding the transfer payments relating to each, would work out as under:

Foreign exchange component

$$34.00 \times \frac{50}{100} \times \frac{100}{125} \qquad 13.60$$

Domestic cost component

$$34.00 \times \frac{50}{100} \times \frac{100}{125} \qquad 16.20$$

29.80

◈ Consumable Stores

It is assumed that the stocks of consumable stores are composed of 50 per cent imported and 50 per cent indigenous stocks.

The foreign exchange and domestic components of the capital at charge under the head Consumble Stores, after excluding the transfer payments relating to each, would work out as under:

(₹ *in lakhs*)

Foreign exchange component

$$10.00 \times \frac{50}{100} \times \frac{100}{125} \qquad 4.00$$

Domestic cost component

$$10.00 \times \frac{50}{100} \times \frac{100}{125} \qquad 4.80$$

◈ Finished Goods

It is assumed that the finished goods are valued at direct cost of production, in which case the raw materials component in the value of the stock of finished goods works out to approximately 70 per cent while the consumable stores component works out to 15 per cent.

The foreign exchange and domestic cost components in the value of the stock of finished goods of ₹ 14.00 lakhs may then be worked out as under:

Foreign exchange component in the value of raw materials used for producing finishing goods

$$14.00 \times \frac{70}{100} \times \frac{13.60}{125} \qquad 4.00$$

In consumable stores

$$14.00 \times \frac{50}{100} \times \frac{4.00}{10.0} \qquad 0.80$$

4.80

Domestic cost component in the value of raw materials used for producing finished goods

$$14.00 \times \frac{50}{100} \times \frac{100}{125} \qquad 4.79$$

In consumable stores

$14.00 \times \frac{50}{100} \times \frac{100}{125}$ 1.00

Other direct costs $= 14 \times \frac{15}{100}$ 1.00

Total Domestic Cost Component 7.80

◈ Book Debts

The book debts are assumed to represent only the domestic cost without any element of transfer payments included therein.

Summary of Break-up of Inventories, Exclusive of Transfer Payments

The investment in inventories and book debts, split up into foreign exchange and domestic cost components, would be as under:

(₹ in lakhs)

	Foreign Exchange	*Domestic Cost*	*Total*
Raw Materials	13.60	16.20	29.80
Consumable Stores	4.00	4.80	8.80
Finished Goods	4.80	7.50	12.60
Book Debts	—	15.00	15.00
	22.40	43.80	66.20

The charge (interest) on inventories and book debt at 15 per cent would work out as under:

On foreign exchange component	3.40
On domestic cost component	6.60
Total charge on inventories and book debt	10.00

Summary of charge on capital investment and inventories and book debts:

(₹ in lakhs)

	Foreign Exchange	*Domestic Cost*	*Total*
On Capital Investment	2.10	27.40	29.50
On Investment and Book Debts	3.40	6.60	10.00
	5.50	34.00	39.50

3.4 Summary of the cost indigenous production, both in terms of foreign exchange and domestic resources

(₹ in lakhs)

	Foreign Exchange	*Domestic Cost*	*Total*
Current Operating Costs	54.78	246.31	301.09
Depreciation	1.20	14.00	15.20
Charge on Capital	5.50	34.00	39.50
Total Current Costs (36,900 tonnes of production)	61.48	294.31	355.79
Cost: ₹ per tonne	167.00	798.00	965.00

Calculation of internal exchange rate (IER) of the project.

4.1 Foreign Exchange Saving Rate

	Reference percentage	₹/ *tonne*
(*a*) C.I.F. cost to import the finished product	2.5	1202.00
(*b*) P. E. cost incurred on domestic production	3.5	167.00
(*c*) Net saving of foreign exchange (F.E. on domestic production (*a*) – (*b*)		1035.00
(*d*) At US \$ = 17.00, net saving per unit of finished product in US \$ (*c*) + ₹ 9/-		\$ 60.90
(*e*) Domestic cost incurred to effect saving	3.4	798.00
(*f*) Domestic resource cost per US \$ (e) + (d)		6.94

4.2 Foreign Exchange Earning Rate

(*a*) F.O.B. realisation if exported	2.5	900.00
(*b*) Foreign exchange cost incurred on domestic production	3.4	167.00
(*c*) Net earnings of foreign exchange on export (a) – (b)		733.00
(*d*) At US \$ = ₹ 17/- Net earning per unit of finished production exported in US \$ (c) + ₹ 9/-		\$ 43.00
(*e*) Domestic cost incurred to effect this earning	3.4	798.00
(*f*) Domestic resources cost per US \$ (e) + (d)		9.73

4.3 Foreign Exchange Composite Rate

(*a*) 90% of the output is export savings and 10% export earning	2.4	
(*b*) Composite price per tonne is $\frac{(1202 \times 90) + (900 \times 10)}{100}$	2.4	1172.00
(*c*) Foreign exchange cost incurred on domestic production	2.4	167.00
(*d*) Foreign exchange saving/earning (*b*) – (*c*)		1005.00
(*e*) At US \$ = ₹ 17.00 foreign exchange saving/earning (d) + ₹ 9/-		\$ 59.00
(*f*) Domestic cost incurred to effect this saving/earning	3.4	798.00
(*g*) Composite exchange rate per US \$ (*f*) + (*e*)	7.12	

The above illustration shows that, from all viewpoints, *i.e.*, whether taken as an import substitution project or as an export promotion project, the rate is advantageous compared to the market rate of exchange.

It should, however, be emphasised that this indicator is not to be considered in isolation in deciding the financial and economic viability of a project. It need not necessarily be constructed that a project with a higher exchange rate is undesirable, for there are various other important factors, such as employment potential, utilisation of domestically available raw materials and other facilities, the strategic importance of the project, the products for other sectors of the economy, the desirability of securing a position in the international market for the products, etc., which should be taken into account before arriving at any decision on the project. Hence, as a thumb-rule, a rate upto 40 per cent above parity may be considered reasonable provided that other considerations, as indicated above, are favourable for the project. An exchange rate upto ₹ 18.70 per dollar may be considered reasonable at the present parity rate of \$ = ₹ 17.00.

Besides, Social Cost Benefit Analysis is also made, while appraising a project for which purpose Economic Rate of Return (ERR) based on accepted principles, is determined. Inter-firm comparison of the project with similar projects financed earlier is also made with a view to assessing the project cost and its profitability in as realistic a manner as possible.

◈ Commercial Appraisal

One of the crucial factors that determines the commercial viability of an industrial project is the market for the product(s) proposed to be manufactured by the new or existing unit. In the present economy such factors as recession, sickness in the industry, gradual switchover from the seller's to the buyer's market, etc., make it all the more imperative that a detailed market survey and a thorough appraisal thereof are carried out before launching a project. For this purpose, a study of the product(s) and product mix, an analysis of the demand and supply position of the product(s), their cost and price structure, demand patterns, trends in capacity utilisation and prices, demand growth rate, etc., and forecasts made therefor, marketing and sales strategies, sales organisation and selling arrangements and other relevant factories — all these are to be taken into account.

◈ Managerial Appraisal

As the promoters from the core of the management, the DFIs make an in-depth study of their background, the traits of the entrepreneurs and the quality of the management of their existing business. The overall background of the promoters, their academic qualifications, business and industrial experience, their past performance, are considered in great detail to assess their capabilities for implementing the project for which financial assistance has been sought. Further, the DFIs endeavour to ensure that the company has a competent Board of Directors and a qualified and competent technical, financial and executive management team, both for the implementation and operation of the project. In this connection, it may be observed that not only should the competence of the present management be studied but, at the same time, a study of the successor management is equally important, particularly when long-term loans are involved. It is possible that, before the final maturity of the loan which may be for terms of 10 to 15 years or more, the company may be deprived of the services of the present executives.

◈ Social Appraisal

The social benefits associated with the projects are examined under Social Appraisal. The projects which offer the following benefits, as also those which fall under priority area, are given special weightage. These projects are:

(*i*) Those which offer large employment potential;

(*ii*) Promoted by new entrepreneurs and/or technologists;

(*iii*) Those which provide inputs for increasing agricultural production as, for example, fertilisers, pesticides, agricultural machinery;

(*iv*) Those, which utilise agricultural output, thus promoting better income distribution in rural areas;

(*v*) Those which channelise the savings of the agricultural sector for productive purposes, e.g., sugar and textile co-operatives, thus encouraging the co-operative sector;

(*vi*) Those which are located in relatively less developed areas;

(*vii*) Those which stimulate the growth of ancillary industries;

(*viii*) Those which are based on indigenous technology and/or which aim at exploring new areas of technology;

(*ix*) Those which have prospects of earning foreign exchange or which would result in substitution of imports;

(*x*) Those which fulfil the increased demand for essential consumer goods, such as textiles and sugar, and which meet the basic needs of the people.

The DFIs are very much interested in ensuring that social goals of the enterprise are integrated into the financial and the organisational goals. The ingenuity lies in harmonising them. The above-mentioned social goals may not run counter to the financial soundness of the project, if properly managed. However, financial viability is emphasised because their own viability is heavily dependent on the viability of the project. These institutions are themselves large borrowers from the Government, the market and from foreign lending institutions. Hence, there is nothing incongruous if they regard the financial viability of the project in itself an important social goal.

◈ Appraisal of Energy Management and Ecological aspects

The DFIs also give due weightage to sociological and economical considerations. It is ensured that the applicant concern has made adequate provision for treatment of effluents so that environment remains pollution free.

In view of high priority and significant importance being given to the energy conservation and that of alternate sources of energy, the DFIs in India have been attaching considerable importance to the energy management while training industrial projects. For this purpose, the steps proposed to be taken for the conservation of energy or use of alternative sources of energy are then examined in greater depth while appraising a project.

However, the DFIs should not be very strict about imposing financial discipline on the companies seeking financial assistance. Since these institutions have been conceived as tools of planning, a careful blending of generosity and financial prudence will go a long way in accomplishing the avowed objective of a rapid industrialisation of the country.

C. FOLLOW-UP BY DFIs IN INDIA

In pursuit of the follow-up and supervision policy, the DFIs in India have devised some elaborate and rigorous procedures, as outlined below:

◈ Procuring Progress Reports

Loanee companies are required to submit half-yearly progress reports on the prescribed forms during the construction and operation periods. The progress reports help the institution to disburse funds for the project, keeping in view the progress achieved. The reports give it an idea of the problems encountered, the reasons for delays in implementation, over-runs in costs beyond the initial estimates, and deficiencies in management. The responsibility for obtaining the reports and taking the necessary follow-up action rests upon the various regional offices of the DFIs. The reports are examined by the regional offices, which are equipped with the necessary technical and financial staff, and only the adverse features or irregularities are brought to the notice of the assisted concerns directly by the office concerned, under intimation to the head office.

◈ Obtaining Annual Financial and Other Reports

Assisted concerns are required to send the annual audited balance sheet, circulars and minutes of the shareholders' meetings to the lending institution. These statements are carefully studied and analysed to assess the progress of the assisted companies, their profitability and other financial aspects, and are compared against the performance of at least three previous years. In such an examination, apart from drawing conclusions in respect of the overall performance of the assisted companies, the unusual features or breach of covenants with the institution, if any, are also examined.

◈ Inspections

From the date of the loan agreement, and so long as any part of the loan remains outstanding, the institution carries out site inspections, both during the construction and operation periods of the project, and inspects the books of accounts of the assisted concerns. Such inspections are usually carried out by teams of financial and technical officers of the DFIs. A prior notice of about 10 to 15 days is generally given to an assisted concern of the proposed inspection. To facilitate a proper inspection, the assisted concerns are required to maintain records, showing the expenditure incurred on the project, the utilisation of the disbursement by the banks, the progress of the projects, and the operations and financial working of the company. In carrying out technical and financial inspections, the officers of the institution visit the borrower's factory, examine the relevant records, accounts and schedules, cost estimates, plans and specifications of the plant, etc. In these inspections, the emphasis is on discussing the matters personally with the concerned officials of the company and seeking the necessary clarifications from them.

◈ Nomination of Directors

Where the commitments of the institution are comparatively large, or where defaults have been made in the payment of principal and/or interest, or where there are special circumstances calling for special vigilance in the operations of the concern, it nominates directors on the Boards of the assisted concerns. The persons nominated as directors are either the institution's own officers or non-officials, the latter generally being experts.

The persons nominated as directors hold office at the pleasure of the institutions and are not liable to hold any qualification shares or to retire by rotation. The nominated directors are expected to participate in the discussion of all the matters coming up at the Board's meetings, especially those which have a relevance to the assistance given by the institution and what affect its interests, or are otherwise important as matters of public policy. They shall not, however, interfere in the day-to-day management of the concerns.

To enable the nominated directors to keep themselves in touch with the operations of the company in matters like production in relation to installed capacity, sales, the reasonableness of inventories and receivables, the liquidity of the concern, the meeting of statutory obligations, changes in key personnel, etc., the IFCI devised a proforma on industry-wise basis to facilitate the reporting of certain information and operational data by the company for consideration at every meeting of its Board of Directors.

The follow-up and inspection of the loans and their utilisation should be done very carefully. This is inevitable, particularly in the context of Indian conditions because, unfortunately, in spite of careful planning in the initial stages, unforeseen problems and difficulties arise in the execution of many projects, which result in delays leading to increased costs.[2]

D. CONCLUSIONS

Project evaluation is a techno-economic affair which calls for an assessment of worthwhileness of a project from various angles. The DFIs in India are guided essentially by the national priorities and the policies of the Government. They follow project-oriented approach to evaluate the desirability of the project from the technical, financial, economic, commercial, managerial and social points of view.

The DFIs have also laid down elaborate and rigorous mechanism so as to ensure utilization of funds sanctioned for the project. This involves procurement of progress reports, Annual financial and other reports, periodic site inspections and nomination of their Directors of the Board of the Borrowing Company.

KEY TERMS

- Appraisal of energy management & ecological aspects
- Commercial appraisal
- Development bank
- Financial appraisal
- Financing pattern
- Internal exchange rate
- Managerial appraisal
- Project appraisal
- Social appraisal

DISCUSSION QUESTIONS

1. How is a capital expenditure project appraised by DFIs in India?
2. In what way is technical viability of a project evaluated?
3. What are the various considerations that DFIs in India factor in while appraising financial viability of a project?
4. What is internal exchange rate? How is it determined?
5. What critical factors do DFIs in India take into account while assessing commercial, social and managerial aspects of the project?
6. Discuss the procedures laid down by the DFIs for the follow-up of the assistance provided by the DFIs.

REFERENCES

1. Shirley Boskey, *Problems and Practices of Development Banks,* Baltimore, The Johns Hopkins Press, 1959, pp. 49-50.
2. IDBI Report of the Board of Directors, 1966-67, pp. 19-20.

Chapter 25

Performance Evaluation of All India Financial Institutions (AIFIs)

Learning Objectives:

The present chapter aims at:

- Providing vivid view of corporate purpose, mission, objectives, tasks and policies of AIFIs
- Evaluating performance of AIFIs

Chapter Outline:

- Backdrop.
- Corporate purpose, mission and objectives of AIFIs.
- Tasks of AIFIs.
- Corporate policies of AIFIs.
- Performance of AIFIs.
- Challenges before AIFIs.
- Conclusions and suggestions.

A. BACKDROP

In a ferociously competitive and combative milieu, as it exists across the globe, financial institutions to survive and thrive on the sustained basis must possess unique competencies that allow them to achieve superior efficiency in mobilising and utilising their resources, supplying innovative products and delivering world class quality services to the customers at large. Accordingly, performance of these institutions has to be evaluated against the parameters of intermediation function, profitability and financial soundness. Further, effectiveness of operations of these institutions can be judged with reference to their corporate objectives and tasks.

As such, performance of financial institutions in India will be examined along the above lines.

B. CORPORATE PURPOSE, MISSION AND OBJECTIVES OF AIFIs

In a developing economy, financial institutions are supposed to go far beyond the conventional function of providing term finance to qualifying entrepreneurs and mobilising resources for their lending operations. In fact, they have to ease the tasks of entrepreneurs by dispensing finance in time and even before by providing information on market and other related services.

It is to fulfill the above expectations that the financial institutions, as noted above, came into existence. Thus, the corporate purpose of these financial institutions is to help accelerate the level of economic growth of the country and to mitigate the gaps of capital and enterprise in the economy and provide total solutions to business organisations at competitive cost by developing long-term relationships with creditworthy corporate and institutional clients, by introducing product innovation, entering other businesses to capitalise on emerging opportunities and by increasing operational flexibility.

Within the framework of the above purpose and mission, financial institutions in India have set the following long-term objectives:

- To provide term-lending facilities;
- To subscribe to shares and debentures;
- To underwrite security issues of business enterprises;
- To provide indirect financial support to business enterprises through guarantees, discounting and other facilities;
- To provide lease financing and venture capital;
- To provide banking and non-banking financial facilities;
- To render managerial, technical and administrative services to the Indian Industry, and
- To garner resources directly from the public by floating shares and debentures in the stock markets.

While endeavouring to achieve the above objectives, the thrust of the financial institutions has been to supplement rather than supplant those agencies engaged in providing long-term financial support and entrepreneurial and managerial assistance to all the deserving projects whose access to the existing facilities is limited and which, because of this fact, would be likely to be held up.

C. TASKS OF AIFIs

So as to foster industrial and economic growth of a country, financial institutions should not only perform as an engine of growth but also act as the growth-inducing factor in desirable directives. These institutions just cannot be merely a lending agency. They have to take into account the strength of finance in the sense that it could command all resources and exploit this strength to the maximum benefit of the nation. As a matter of fact, the main instrument of working of these institutions is finance: to raise and disburse scarce resources in such a manner as to subserve the socio-economic objectives of the nation.

Accordingly, the primary tasks assigned to the financial institutions are to dispense financial assistance and services to the industrial and infrastructural projects of national importance and for this purpose they have to raise resources from national and international markets.

D. CORPORATE POLICIES OF AIFIs

The overall policy of the Indian Financial Institutions has been to dispense financial and other support for bolstering the growth of new industrial projects and for the modernisation, expansion, renovation and diversification of existing projects of national importance.

In tandem with the emerging needs of industries in the liberalised environment, the financial institutions have reoriented their operational policies and assistance structure with much sharper customer focus by developing and introducing a variety of products and services. During the post-reform period, these institutions set up several subsidiaries/associate concerns for offering a wide range of such newly developed products and services as also for capital market infrastructural development, covering areas such as commercial banking, investment banking, non-banking finance, custodial services, electronic trading in stock exchanges, capital market regulation, register and transfer services and credit rating.

E. PERFORMANCE OF ALL INDIA FINANCIAL INSTITUTIONS (AIFIs)

◆ Performance in terms of Intermediation Function

The competence of a financial institution in mopping up resources from savers and their attitude to do so influence considerably the success of resource mobilisation efforts of these institutions. The financial mechanism employed by the institution and its networking also play a significant role in garnering funds from the savers. Further, attitude and willingness of the institution to approach the savers and attract their surpluses by offering fascinating products bear upon the success of its funds mobilisation activity. Institutions restructuring themselves to investing or lending activity may prefer to approach government or governmental agencies for the financial support. At times, the government may constrict the resource mobilisation efforts of the financial institutions through policy interventions, prohibiting the public subscription to the security issues of these institutions.

In view of their avowed objectives, functions and expertise of financial institutions and their high credit standing in financial markets and closer linkages with the players of the markets, it is expected that these institutions might have made stupendous efforts to raise funds from outside.

The principal forms by which financial institutions may raise long-term funds from the market are issue of shares and debentures, acceptance of long-term deposits and recourse to long-term borrowings. They may also borrow funds on short-term basis to meet working capital needs of entrepreneurs.

◆ Procurement of Funds by AIFIs

An Aggregate View

Table 25.1 exhibits an overall resource position of AIFIs during the period 2000-2012. A peep into the Table shows that these institutions mobilised funds to the tune of ₹ 2,32,000 crore as on March 31, 2000 through private and public placement of debentures and bonds, borrowings from institutional agencies both from India and abroad and public deposits. This surged to ₹ 3,30,000 crores as on March 31, 2012.

TABLE 25.1: Overall Resource Position of AIFIs

(₹ in crore)

Sources of Funds	As on March 31 -----										
	2000	2001	2002	2003	2004	2005	2006	2009	2010	2011	2012
1. Paid up Capital	8,731 (3.8)	7,866 (3.2)	6,784 (3.7)	6,784 (3.7)	6,131 (4.7)	6,331 (4.4)	5,431 (3.7)	4,300 (2.0)	4,600 (1.3)	4,900 (1.7)	6,200 (1.8)
2. Reserves & Surplus	36,619 (15.8)	39,146 (15.9)	31,137 (17.7)	18,259 (9.9)	13,499 (10.4)	14,963 (10.5)	15,211 (10.5)	19,069 (8.8)	39,556 (15.9)	42,612 (14.7)	46,501 (13.8)
Total Owned Funds (1+2)	45,350 (19.6)	47,012 (19.1)	37,948 (21.6)	25,043 (13.6)	19,630 (15.1)	21,294 (14.9)	20,642 (14.2)	23,369 (10.8)	44,156 (17.7)	47,512 (16.4)	52,701 (15.6)
3. Borrowings	41,413 (17.8)	37,715 (15.3)	27,145 (15.5)	21,862 (11.9)	18,360 (14.1)	23,028 (16.1)	18,950 (13.0)	40,443 (18.6)	35307 (14.2)	42,681 (14.7)	49,521 (14.7)
4. Bonds and Debentures	1,14,017 (49.1)	1,25,597 (50.9)	81,717 (46.6)	89,639 (48.8)	50,545 (38.8)	60,801 (42.6)	67,145 (46.2)	52,390 (24.1)	71,011 (28.5)	90,097 (31.0)	1,07,290 (31.9)
5. Deposits	13,350 (5.8)	17,821 (7.2)	14,240 (8.1)	20,144 (11.0)	17,946 (13.8)	13,643 (9.5)	14,520 (10.0)	65,591 (30.2)	79,472 (31.9)	92,782 (31.9)	1,07,078 (32.4)
6. Other Liabilities	17,194 (7.7)	18,376 (7.5)	14,469 (8.2)	27,063 (14.7)	23,661 (18.2)	24,104 (16.9)	24,217 (16.6)	35,579 (16.4)	19,037 (7.6)	17,544 (6.0)	17,729 (5.3)
Total Debt (3+4+5+6)	1,26,695 (80.4)	1,99,511 (80.9)	1,37,572 (78.4)		1,10,572 (84.9)	1,21,576 (85.1)	1,24,832 (85.8)	1,94,003 (89.2)	2,04,827 (82.3)	2,43,104 (83.6)	1,83,618 (84.4)
Total Liabilities	2,32,045 (100.0)	2,46,523 (100.0)	1,75,520 (100.0)		1,30,142 (100.0)	1,42,870 (100.0)	1,45,474 (100.0)	2,17,372 (100.0)	2,48,983 (100.0)	2,90,616 (100.0)	3,36,319 (100.0)

It is revealing to note that the financial institutions appear to have made sincere efforts to mobilise resources in recent years. It may also be interesting to observe from the above table that they have placed heavier reliance on external sources of funds inasmuch as it contributed more than four-fifths to the total funds. Among the external sources, bonds and debentures and borrowings from the Government, RBI and other financial agencies contributed predominantly to total resources. Share capital, on the contrary, contributed about 4 per cent to the total resources and reserves and surplus proportioned 10–15 per cent. Predominance of bonds/debentures in the resource pattern of the financial institutions is due to their in-built flexibility and tradability.

In recent years, financial institutions relied greatly on borrowings, especially short-term borrowings to cater to working capital needs of entrepreneurs. Thus, other liabilities comprising short-term loans represented almost 6.0 per cent of the total funds as on March end, 2012 as against 7.7 per cent as on March end, 2000.

However, relative significance of borrowing from the Government, RBI and other Government owned agencies declined gradually. This trend in the pattern of resource mobilization is not without reasons. One such reason is the truncated flow of concessional financing by the Union Government and the RBI to the financial institutions following resource crunch. Rising cost of long-term borrowings due to paucity of funds as well as uncertainty about yields for long tenors are also responsible for declining significance of bonds and debentures in the resource pattern of the institutions in recent years. Another reason responsible for the above trend is growing preference of the DFIs for certificate of deposits (CDs) in view of their relatively low cost and assured availability. Recourse to short-term borrowing has also been facilitated by the RBI credit policy of 1993 permitting select financial institutions to borrow in the short-term money market from scheduled commercial banks and co-operative banks for periods in the maturity range of 3 to 6 months. Although raising deposits is found to be the easiest option, the financial institutions do not want to rely heavily on this because most of the deposits are short-term in nature unlike their assets, and hence to be rolled over or have to be replaced with similar maturity deposits. Moreover unlike debentures, deposits cannot be traded. Despite this, financial institutions are widely using CDs in recent years to meet their growing requirements.

The existing practice of advancing loans by the RBI to industrial and agricultural finance institutions from the long-term funds was discontinued subsequent to the announcement to this effect made in the Union Budget for 1992-93. Accordingly, the RBI has been making only token contribution to these funds from 1992-93.

It would also be in fitness of things to examine the overall debt-equity position of the financial institutions. The position is brought out in Table 25.2. It is evident from the Table 29.2 that the financial health of the Indian financial institutions has been sound when compared with the international norms of 12:1 prescribed by the World Bank.[1]

TABLE 25.2: Debt-Equity Position of the AIFIs on March, end ....

	1991	2000	2005	2006	2009	2010	2011	2012
Debt-Equity Ratio	9.1:1	5.1:1	6.9:1	6.1:1	8.2:1	4.5:1	5.1:1	3.7:1

◆ Institution-wise Procurement of Funds

Institution-wise funds mobilised by AIFIs (Table 25.3) reveals that NHB mobilised the largest amount of resources followed by SIDBI, NABARD and Exim Bank. IFCI and IIBI were barred from mobilising fresh resources on account of their poor financials.[2]

TABLE 25.3: Resources Mobilised by AIFIs

(₹ in crores)

	Resources Raised during the year								
Institutions	2001-02	2002-03	2003-04	2004-05	2005-06	2009	2010	2011	2012
IFCI	651	267	—	—	—	—	—	—	—
IIBI	551	150	176	—	—	—	—	—	—
TFCI	48	93	172	23	71	—	—	—	—
Exim Bank	625	2,505	6,881	5,430	7,198	15,902	18,395	23,752	54,700
IDFC	250	400	4,253	3,975	—	—	—	—	—
SIDBI	1,224	961	2,972	2,364	3,489	15,797	30,186	34,090	44,000
NABARD	2,549	2,988	5,334	8,843	8,194	7,746	12,346	28,273	42,300
NHB	238	1,877	3,290	5,172	2,830	20,005	17,824	36,996	60,700
	6,136	9,250	22,401	26,085	21,782	59,450	78,751	1,23,111	2,01,700

The FIs also raise resources from the money market through various instruments such as commercial paper (CP), Certificates of Deposit (CDs), and term deposits.[3] It may be noted from Table 25.4 that CP is most popular source of funds of the FIs, contributing over 70 per cent of the resources. FIs are mandated to raise resources from the money market within the sanctioned umbrella limit. Though gross resources raised by the SIDBI from money market during 2011-12 were ₹ 9,035 crore, at no point of time during the year amount outstanding under the above instruments exceeded the umbrella limit. As CP is a short-term money market instrument, FIs kept resorting frequently to this instrument during the year taking the cumulative amount raised through CP to a higher level.

TABLE 25.4: Resources mobilised by AIFIs from Money Market as on March-end, 2012

(Amount in ₹ crore)

Instruments	NABARD	SIDBI	NHB	EXIM	Total
A. Total	4,935	9,035	2,895	5,091	21,956
(*i*) Term deposits	819	7	218	842	1,886
(*ii*) Term money		438			438
(*iii*) Certificate of Deposits	53	1,281	—	—	1,334
(*iv*) Commercial paper	4,063	7,309	488	4,250	16,110
(*v*) Short-term loans from banks	—	—	2,188	—	2,188
B. Umbrella Limit	7,546	20,794	4,155	8,967	41,462
C. Utilisation of umbrella limit (A as percentage of B)	65.4	43.5	69.7	56.8	53.0

◆ Deployment of Resources by AIFIs

AIFIs have utilised major portion of their funds in fresh deployment in the form of project loans, venture capital, direct subscription, underwriting, guarantees, refinancing bills, rediscounting, direct discounting, loans to housing finance companies, etc. Thus, it may be observed from Table 25.5 that fresh deployment claimed over half of the resources of these institutions in 2000-01 which tended to rise to over 70 per cent of the total funds in 2006. This is because of resurgence of industrial development in the country. Taking advantage of the falling interest rate environment, the AIFIs retired their high cost old debts and replaced them with cheaper debts. Other deployments tended to decline steeply from 30.9 per cent in 2001 to 15.5% in 2009 mainly on account of a decline in interest payments. However, there was steep decline in fresh deployments during the recent years, mainly owing to economic and industrial slump.

TABLE 25.5: Deployment of Funds By AIFIs as on March end

(₹ in crores)

Deployment Funds	2001	2002	2003	2004	2005	2006	2009	2010	2011	2012
(*i*) Fresh Deployments	41,564 (51.0)	48,289 (49.5)	52,028 (54.4)	56,555 (65.0)	61,635 (65.0)	72,273 (71.9)	1,94,911 (65.5)	1,71,922 (56.8)	1,74,674 (58.7)	2,73,900 (64.4)
(*ii*) Repayment of past Borrowings	14,694 (18.0)	20,815 (24.2)	17,478 (18.3)	17,590 (20.2)	21,069 (22.2)	14,402 (14.3)	56,592 (19.0)	1,15,015 (38.0)	83,971 (28.2)	1,29,000 (30.4)
(*iii*) Other Deployments	25,200 (30.9)	28,509 (29.2)	26,056 (27.3)	12,845 (14.8)	12,106 (12.8)	13,781 (13.7)	45,993 (15.57)	15,673 (5.2)	39,139 (13.1)	22,200 (5.2)
Total	81,458 (100.0)	97,613 (100.0)	95,562 (100.0)	86,990 (100.0)	94,810 (100.0)	1,00,456 (100.0)	2,97,496 (100.0)	3,02,610 (100.0)	2,97,784 (100.0)	4,25,200 (100.0)

Note: Figures in brackets denote percentage to total.

◆ Provision of Assistance by AIFIs

A synoptic view of funds dispensed by AIFIs in recent years may be had from Table 25.6. It is interesting to find that total funds provided by AIFIs nose-dived from ₹ 97,337 crore during 2000-01 to ₹ 11,942 crore in 2005-06. This is reflective of declining role of these institutions in project financing – being the core activity. With financial liberalization, banks have also started financing projects and thus have been competing with FIs. The withdrawal of concessional sources of funds and restrictions on raising short-term funds of maturities of less than one year forced the FIs to raise high cost funds directly from a relatively under – developed long-term debt market.[4] The blue chip companies could raise financial resources for industrial projects more cost effectively. As a result, demand for funds from AIFIs declined. Transformation of ICICI into a bank in October 2002 and IDBI in October 2004 and hence their exclusion in the computation of sanctions also contributed to the above sharp change. There has been significant increase in amount of assistance sanctioned by FIs during the recent few years due to increase in assistance dispersed by the SIDBI to small scale industries.

Regarding trends in utilisation of sanctioned assistance, it may be observed from the above table that there was remarkable improvement during the period 2000-2003, when over 70 per cent of the assistance was utilised. However, the position has not been satisfactory during the subsequent (2003-05) two years when level of disbursed assistance declined to 53.1 per cent in 2005. The major contributory factors for this trend were:

(*i*) Applicants concerned did not avail of loan facilities sanctioned because they had fully or partly cancelled or deferred their projects. Some applicants refused to accept the terms prescribed by financial institutions for the disbursement of assistance.

TABLE 25.6: Assistance Sanctioned and Disbursed by AIFIs

(Amount in crore of ₹)

Year (1)	Sanctions (2)	Disbursements (3)	Percentage of 3 to 2 (4)
2000-01	97,337	59,449	61.2
2001-02	63,222	44,905	71.1
2002-03	19,335	14,501	73.7
2003-04	21,708	14,634	67.0
2004-05	9,091	6,279	53.0
2005-06	11,942	9,237	79.0

2006-07	11,102	10,225	92.0
2007-08	16,181	15,098	93.0
2009-10	39,589	37,581	97.5
2010-11	52,901	52,603	99.5
2011-12	47,800	47,800	100.0

(*ii*) In many instances, financial institutions stopped disbursing further installments of loans because of the unsatisfactory progress on the construction of projects.

(*iii*) A portion of loans sanctioned was left unutilised by some applicant companies which preferred to utilise them according to their convenience.

However, the position improved significantly since 2005-06 when assistance utilized accounted for cent-per cent of the sanctioned assistance.

◈ Mode of Assistance

AIFIs have endeavoured to cater to the diverse needs of business entrepreneurs through variegated schemes. Thus, for asset creation purpose, these institutions render assistance directly as well as in indirect forms, in addition to underwriting and guarantees. Direct assistance is dispensed by way of rupee loans, foreign currency loans, direct subscriptions, direct discounting of bills, suppliers/buyers/deferred credit, special deposits with industrial concerns, seed capital and equipment leasing. Indirect assistance takes the forms of refinancing, bills rediscounting, assistance to leasing companies, loans and subscription to securities of financial institutions.

Table 25.7 showing forms of assistance provided by AIFIs reveals that bulk of the assistance was rendered in the form of loans comprising loans, foreign currency loans and guarantees underwriting and direct subscription accounted for less than one-tenth of the total assistance. 'Others' comprising short-term/bridge loans formed a small portion.

Over the period 2000-2006, loans as component of assistance portfolio of AIFIs gained in significance, while other forms of assistance lost their importance.

Predominance of loans in the assistance portfolio of the all-India financial institutions is a clear testimony to their continued strong preference for safer investment. In fact, financial institutions seem to have pursued the policy of sleeping well-to eating well, while deploying their resources and are loath to take risk for higher return.

Another important factor responsible for the predominance of the loan as form of assistance is the growing demand from industrial enterprises for loan from the institutions. Corporate borrowers generally prefer loans to equity for a variety of reasons. First, debt is generally the cheapest form of financing and coupled with the fact that interest in it is tax deductible, it offers great attraction to business enterprises. Secondly, debt introduces financial leverage which may, under favourable circumstances, boost up earning per share and raise the value of the firm. Uncertainty in getting equity share capital from this market due to its subdued condition in recent few years has further increased the pressure for loans from the industrial enterprises on the financial institutions.

In recent years, financial institutions rendered assistance to corporate enterprises by way of underwriting and direct subscriptions. (Table 25.7).

TABLE 25.7: Forms of Assistance by AIFIs

(Amount in ₹ crores)

Year	Loans	Underwriting & Direct Subscription	Others	Total
2000-01	74,444 (76.3)	13,796 (4.3)	9,098 (9.4)	97,338 (100.0)
2001-02	41,993 (66.7)	9,065 (4.9)	12,163 (18.4)	63,222 (100.0)
2002-03	17,013 (86.3)	2,208 (13.1)	114 (06)	19,335 (100.0)
2003-04	18,708 (89.0)	458 (9.0)	2,542 (12.0)	21,708 (100.0)
2004-05	9,091 (100.0)	—	—	9,091 (100.0)
2005-06	11,942 (100.0)	—	—	11,942 (100.0)
2010-11	59,800 (59.7)	40,100 (40.3)	—	99,900
2011-12	49,300 (56.0)	38,300 (44.0)	—	87,600

Note: Figures within brackets denote percentage to the total.

◈ Performance in terms of income, cost and profitability of AIFIs

Income, cost and profitability are important indices of financial performance of an institution. Table 25.8 exhibits information pertaining to income, expenditure and profitability of AIFIs. It may be discerned from the Table 25.8 that interest income constituted major source of total income of AIFIs. Over a period, interest income tended to rise from 91.3% in 2000-01 to 95.7% in 2011-12 while non-interest income declined from 8.86% to 4.3% during the corresponding period. This is reflective of decreasing level of fee-based business of AIFIs.

Likewise, interest expenditure represented over 90 per cent of total expenditure of AIFIs. Over a period of time, interest expenditure recorded rise from 82% in 2000-01 to 91.4% in 2011-12 whereas other operating expenses shot up from 7.58% to 8.6% during the period.

Net profit as percentage of assets after showing decline from 1.35% in 2000-01 to 0.9% in 2002.03 improved significantly to reach 1.9% in 2004-05. This is on account of sharp decline in expenditure from 9.6% to 4.7% during the corresponding period. What is most important to note is that profitability of AIFIs showed improvement despite IFCI and IIBI continued to incur net losses. Thus, barring these two institutions, all other institutions registered positive operating and net profits. There was shortfall in the profitability rate in 2005-06 mainly because of rise in expenditure.

Profitability performance of the AIFIs has improved significantly in recent years due to remarkable rise in operating income of these institutions, particularly during 2010-11.

A comparative study of profitability of AIFIs and PSBs reveals that the former has fared better than the latter. However, net interest income as percentage of total assets was higher in the case of PSBs in relation to the AIFIs.

◈ Financial Soundness

Financial soundness of a financial institution, as noted earlier, can be judged in context of capital adequately and NPAs.

TABLE 25.9: Income, Expenditure and Profitability of AIFIs

(Amount in crore of ₹)

Particulars	2000-01	2001-02	2002-03	2003-04	2004-05	2005-06	2007-08	2008-09	2009-10	2010-11	2011-12
A. Income (*a*+*b*)	27,064	17,196	15,822	9,346	9,451	9,599	11,541	14,274	15,624	17,965	22,664
(*a*) Interest Income	24,721	15,516	13,194	7,694	8,122	8,246	99.34	12,169	15,147	17,485	21,887
	(91.3)	(90.2)	(89.3)	(82.3)	(85.9)	(85.9)	(86.1)	(85.3)	(96.9)	(97.3)	(95.7)
(*b*) Non-Interest Income	2,343	1,679	2,628	1,652	1,329	1,353	1607	2,106	478.0	480.0	976.0
	(8.7)	(9.8)	(10.7)	(17.7)	(14.1)	(14.1)	(13.9)	(14.8)	(3.1)	(2.7)	(4.3)
B. Expenditure (*a*+*b*)	23,745	15,708	13,182	7,135	6,689	7,606	8707	10,492	10,492	13,337	16,290
(*a*) Interest Expenditure	19,572	13,287	11,825	6,203	5,660	5,691	7,292	8,977	9,611	11,862	14,885
	(82.42)	(84.59)	(90.2)	(86.9)	(84.6)	(74.8)	(83.8)	(25.6)	(91.6)	(88.9)	(91.4)
(*b*) Other Expenditure	2,598	1,296	1,358	932	1,029	1,915	1,414	1,516	880	1,475	1,406
	(7.58)	(5.41)	(9.8)	(13.1)	(15.4)	(25.2)	(16.2)	(14.4)	(8.4)	(11.1)	(8.6)
C. Profit:											
Operating Profit (PBT)	4,895	2,784	2,640	2,212	2,762	1,993	2,834	—	4,332	3802	4,885
Net Profit (PAT)	3,319	1,487	1,693	1,545	2,036	1,402	1,898	2,592	2,773	2,554	3,240
Financial Ratios											
Operating Profits as % of Total Assets	1.99	1.59	1.40	1.70	1.90	1.40	1.60	1.70	1.90	1.40	2.81
Net Profit as % of Total Assets	1.35	0.85	0.9	1.2	1.4	1.0	1.0	1.20	1.20	0.90	1.03
Income as % of Total Assets	10.98	9.80	8.6	7.2	6.6	6.6	6.50	6.60	6.70	6.70	7.23
Interest Income as % of Total Assets	10.03	8.84	7.2	5.9	5.7	5.7	5.60	5.60	6.50	6.50	6.92
Other Income as % of Total Assets	0.95	0.96	1.4	1.3	0.9	0.9	0.90	1.0	0.20	0.20	0.31
Expenditure as % of Total Assets	9.63	8.95	7.2	5.5	4.7	5.2	4.80	4.80	4.50	4.90	5.20
Interest Expenditure as % of Total Assets	7.94	7.57	6.4	4.8	4.0	3.9	4.10	4.10	4.10	4.40	4.75
Other Operating Expenses as % of Total Assets	1.05	0.64	0.7	0.7	0.7	1.3	0.8	0.70	0.40	0.50	0.45
Spread (Net Interest Income)	2.09	1.27	0.7	1.1	1.7	1.8	1.50	1.40	2.40	2.10	2.17

The performance of the select FIs in respect of the maintenance of a minimum capital to risk-weighted assets ratio (CRAR) is presented in Table 25.9. It may be noted from the table that except IFCI and IIBI, all FIs had a CRAR much above the norm of 9.0 per cent throughout the period. Trend analysis of CRAR during the period 1999-2009 reveals that except TFCI, CRAR of all FIs declined. Notwithstanding the decline, CRAR of AIFIs remained substantially higher than the stipulated rate.

On the score of capital adequacy, position of AIFIs barring the IFCI and IIBI has been more stronger than as compared to commercial banks.

TABLE 25.9: Capital Adequacy Ratio of AIFIs

(Per cent)

Institution	1999	2000	2001	2002	2003	2004	2005	2006	2007	2008	2009	2011	2012
IFCI	8.4	8.8	6.2	3.1	0.95	-17.0	-23.0	-27.9	14.0	—	—		
IIBI	11.7	9.7	13.9	9.2	-11.0	-20.1	-41.1	-64.2	—	—	—		
TFCI	15.4	16.2	18.6	18.5	19.8	22.8	27.4	34.9	40.9	—	—		
IDFC	235-5	119.7	85.5	56.7	51.3	36.9	28.6	—	—	—	—		
Exim Bank	23.6	24.4	23.8	33.1	26.9	23.5	21.6	18.4	16.4	15.1	16.8	17.0	16.4
NABARD	53.3	44.4	38.5	36.9	39.1	39.4	38.8	34.4	27.0	26.6	25.9	21.8	20.6
NHB	17.3	16.5	16.8	22.1	27.9	30.5	22.5	22.3	24.0	24.7	17.7	20.7	19.7
SIDBI	26.9	27.8	28.1	45.0	44.0	51.6	50.7	43.2	37.5	41.8	34.2	31.6	29.2

As regards quality of assets of the AIFIs, it may be observed from Table 25.10 that the net NPAs of AIFIs except TFCI and Exim Bank -tended to increase during the period 2000-2004. This was on account of time and cost over-runs in projects, slippages in the standard assets, increase in legal expenses relating to NPAs, impairment of major assets of the assisted units, contraction of credit portfolios etc. During 2004-05, the asset quality of all FIs, except SIDBI, improved significantly, reflecting the combined impact of recovery of dues and increased provisioning. Sub-standard assets across all the AIFIs declined at the end – March, 2005 in comparison with the previous year. While doubtful assets of the IFCI and IIBI declined those of SIDBI and Exim Bank increased.[5]

In the case of the IFCI, high NPAs arising out of large scale slippage from standard assets to the NPAs category, thereby negating the effect of additional provisioning led to the squeezing of cash flow. This, in turn, resulted in restructuring of liabilities. Further, their continued losses, *inter alia*, led to mismatches in assets and liabilities, resulting in erosion of the IFCI's capital. Similarly, in the case of the IIBI, rising NPAs and consequent provisioning coupled with the problem of declining profitability were some of the factors behind the negative CRAR.

TABLE 25.10: Net Non-performing Assets/Net Loans at end-March

(Per cent)

	2000	2001	2002	2003	2004	2005	2006	2009	2010	2011	2012
IFCI	20.7	20.8	22.5	34.8	32.3	28.0	9.1	—	—	—	—
IIBI	16.7	22.9	24.1	40.3	38.0	27.3	13.1	—	—	—	—
TFCI	14.7	20.5	20.2	20.5	21.0	11.0	3.0	—	—	—	—
IDFC	—	—	00	0.1	—	—	—	—	—	—	
Exim Bank	8.1	8.2	7.4	2.2	1.3	0.9	0.6	0.23	0.20	0.20	0.3
NABARD	3.5	—	—	—	—	—	—	0.03	0.03	0.02	0.02
NHB	—	—	—	—	—	—	—	—	—	—	—
SIDBI	1.3	1.2	3.0	3.8	2.4	3.9	1.9	0.08	0.20	0.30	0.4

The year 2005-06 witnessed remarkable improvement in the asset quality of AIFIs. Thus, net NPAs of the IFCI, IIBI and TFCI declined sharply during the year, reflecting the combined impact of recovery of dues and increased provisioning.[6] As at end March, 2006, while NABARD and NHB did not have any NPAs, NPAs of Exim Bank and SIDBI were at less than one and two per cent, respectively. During the recent years, net NPAs of Exim Bank, NABARD and SIDBI were almost negligible.

A comparative study of NPAs of the AIFIs with those of scheduled banks adumbrates that the position of the latter has been far better than that of the former. This is attributable mainly to focused efforts of the banks' management to reduce NPAs, and facilitated by the Government and the RBI.

F. CHALLENGES BEFORE AIFIs

In recent few years the AIFIs are saddled with serious problems arising out of reduced access to cheap funds, increasing reliance on market borrowing, rapid disintermediation, growing complexities of the financial sector and the brunt of a 'developmental' tag and mismatch of asset and liability resulting in substantial increase in cost of funds hovering between 14-15 per cent and rise in lending rates in the region of 16-17 per cent which in many cases are higher than the prime lending rates of commercial banks. This has obviously resulted in drop in net spreads and decline in profitability.

Further, due to cost factor these institutions are finding it difficult to keep highly rated companies with themselves particularly when the money market is flush with liquidity and interest rates are falling. Only high risk companies are reported to have approached these institutions for funds which, in turn, is affecting quality of their loan portfolio.

Further, role of these institutions as supplier of development finance has diminished during the last two decades in view of emergence of banks and mutual funds as powerful source of long-term funds.

Despite the landmark efforts of the AIFIs over the last five decades, there is verisimilitude of existence of whopping chasm in Indian capital market in the next millennium which would require considerable drive, dynamism, expertise and financial support from them. There is going to be burgeoning demand for funds from infrastructural sector on account of its deterministic influence on overall economic growth. It has been estimated that the country will require about ₹ 18 lakh during the next 5 years to meet its infrastructural requirements. Supply of funds to this sector has so far been not more than ₹ 15,000 crores. Fast developing software industry despite their laudable performance has yet to receive desired support from the financial institutions. Mega projects in the field of oil, gas, petrochemicals, pharmaceutical sectors and projects in textiles, sugar and food projects will continue to bank upon the DFIs because of prolonged sluggishness of new issue market, absence of debt market and strong network of underwriting system and limited supply of term financing by commercial banks.

As such, the AIFIs will continue to remain harbinger in project financing in the current millennium and it will not be in the national interest to relegate them to the status of a bank or non-banking financial intermediary.

Crucial role played by these institutions in rendering term financial and promotional support to Indian corporates and catalyse industrial-growth and unique competencies and acumen that they possess with respect to project appraisal, risk management and expertise in convoluted investment business have earned them encomiums for being resilient, vibrant and pragmatic and customer-friendly segment of Indian financial system. They enjoy high creditability among the investing public, as evidenced by the all India survey of household investors conducted by the society for Capital Market Research and Development in late 1997. As such, these institutions can become household names. It takes a long time and much effort to build a brand image which needs to be preserved and enhanced.

G. CONCLUSIONS AND SUGGESTIONS

India witnessed institutionalisation of capital market in post independence period when battery of financial institutions came into existence to mitigate gaps of capital and enterprise through supplementing rather than supplanting the existing agencies engaged in providing term financial support, entrepreneurial and managerial assistance to all those deserving industrial projects whose access to the existing channels was limited. These financial institutions have put in gargantuan efforts to pump in burgeoning amount of funds of over ₹ 5 lakh crore to render support to several thousand strategic industrial projects of national priority for their growth, expansion, diversification and rationalisation and played seminal role in deepening all-round industrial development and widening entrepreneurial base through identification of growth potential areas in the country, and the project ideas to exploit the potentials and assisting the state levels to undertake feasibility studies of the ideas and implement the viable ones, formation of Technical Consultancy organisations all over the country to provide consultancy services to various state developmental and financial institutions engaged in the task of industrial development and sponsoring entrepreneurship development programmes. Besides, they have promoted new financial agencies all over the country to give fillip to development of small industries.

Besides, they have offered innovative financial products to suit the needs of upcoming enterprises. They have also commenced rendering financial services to the deserving entrepreneurs and are thus on the way out to assume the role of an universal bank.

In order to meet the recent challenges of the emerging competitive environment and impending risks arising from one-product dominant portfolio they formulated market oriented strategy and reengineered their business to offer variety of innovative products and services to the customers. Although project finance remains the sheet anchor of their business, the behemoths forayed into activities of syndication, securitisation, retail banking, working capital, insurance, lease financing, factoring, venture capital, asset management, custodial services, credit rating, stock broking, investors related services and merchant banking and set up as many as 12 subsidiaries with 100 present shareholding and 6 with majority holding equipped with skilled an dextrous manpower so as to provide high quality customised services to their clients. As a part of strategy, the DFIs have laid strong emphasis on the development and marketing of corporate finance products. Within the project finance segment, these institutions have achieved substantial diversification through increased focus on infrastructure and oil, gas and petro chemical projects.

Thus, the financial institutions in India have emerged as most dynamic, and matured species of Indian financial system and possess tremendous resilience and potentiality to face any challenge to them.

However, to be highly competitive and more useful, existing role of the financial institutions needs to be rationalised. They will have to focus on core business with market orientation, have risk-identification and project management skills and strengthen their infrastructural network.

So as to meet fast expanding financial requirements, the DFIs will have to make vigorous efforts to access retail investors and attract their surpluses. In view of growing investment habits, especially of middle class people and their awareness about the operations of financial markets, it will be in fitness of things for the institutions to offer their shares in the open market. Shares of low denomination with buy back facility may certainly entice moderate savers who predominate the community. High credit standing and sound financial health of the national level institutions certainly provide them the cutting edge over others in garnering savings of the people. Besides, they should offer stock options with buy back facility to their employees. This will, besides raising resources for the institutions, qualify the employees to have a say in policy decisions which will give them a sense of ownership and belongingness which will, in turn, help in improving efficiency and productivity of the employees leading to improvement in the overall performance of the institution.

However, they have to ensure provision of adequate working capital to the approved projects so that they are not hamstrung in want of the same. Besides, they have to pep up their efforts in rendering underwriting facility especially to new and nascent projects. Unfortunately, we do not have strong underwriting institutional set up in the country. As a result, new enterprises are still confronted with problem in raising share capital from the market on account of which they are finding it too difficult to borrow funds from the financial institutions.

A strong underwriting institutional structure should be organised under the aegis of LIC and leading stock brokers of the country should join the UTI to bolster the primary market. So as to enable the UTI to play its role effectively in project financing, the RBI should take its supervisory role and transfer refinancing of SFCs to SIDBI.

In their bid to improve earnings the DFIs have, of late, diversified into several fee-based activities. Some of them are planning to embrace into commodities trading, courier business and events management. There is no point in being in any line of business where one is not capable of achieving number one or two positions.

In fact, decision to enter into a line of business must be made on the 'concept of fit' which demands matching of market opportunities with organisational strengths. The concept of fit will have to be supplemented by 'concept of leverage' which signifies that an organisation with limited resources should focus on convergence, accumulating, complementing, conserving and recovering of resources and diversify only in those business where one has core competencies and tremendous scope of synergies. This will lead to useful value addition and optimal resource utilisation which are essential prerequisites to face emerging challenges. Further, every institution will have to set up business units for each of its critical activities and evolve suitable strategy in respect thereof specifying how the unit intends to compete in that specific business and what would be its contribution to the institution as a whole.

With a view to achieving competitive excellence both in the fields of resource mobilisation and channelisation, the present infrastructural set up of the institution needs to be strengthened. Every institution should have wide marketing network of branches all over the country, each equipped with competent manpower and electronic gadgets. It may also go for financial tie up with commercial banks and other agencies so as to avail of their existing branch networking facilities both in respect of mobilisation and channelisation of resources. This will certainly reduce cost of operations and improve quality of services and thereby expand delivery platforms for covering wide range of customers.

The AIFIs in their strategy oriented rationalised role are poised to make seminal contribution to Indian corporates in their endeavour to achieve objectives of successful survival and growth on sustainable basis in the current millennium.

Regarding profitability performance of AIFIs, it may be observed that profitability of these institutions has improved modestly in recent years despite continued losses suffered by the IFCI and IIBI. This is on account of sharp decline in their operating cost. On this count, AIFIs have fared better than the public sector banks.

It is most interesting to note that AIFIs, barring the IFCI and IIBI, have had sound capital adequacy position, as evidenced by higher CRAR. As compared to scheduled banks, capital adequacy position of the AIFIs has been highly satisfactory.

However, quality of assets of the AIFIs has not been as satisfactory as that of the banks.

Thus, in order to improve financial performance of the AIFIs so that they can contribute significantly to the development of the country, these institutions have to focus on augmenting their earnings through fee-based business. Although these institutions have, of late, entered into fee-based business, the same is too limited considering their enormous skill and expertise. What is expected of the top management is to develop performing culture in the organisation where the people feel enthused and enthralled to use their expertise in this field.

KEY TERMS

- Capital Adequacy
- Corporate Policy
- Corporate Purpose & Mission
- Deployment of Funds
- Financial Soundness
- Intermediation Function
- Non-performing Assets
- Procurement of Funds
- Profitability

DISCUSSION QUESTIONS

1. Discuss in brief, corporate purpose, mission of the AIFIs.
2. Describe the tasks assigned to the AIFIs.
3. Outline the overall policy formulated by the AIFIs to achieve their objectives.
4. How far have the AIFIs been effective in achieving their objectives?
5. Assess profitability performance of the AIFIs.
6. Examine financial health of the AIFIs.
7. What are the challenges before the AIFIs in the changed economic milieu of the country?

REFERENCES

1. IDBI Annual Report, 1993-94, p. 82.
2. Report on Trend and Progress of Banking in India, 2004-05, p. 144.
3. RBI, Report on Trend and Progress of Banking in India, 2010-11.
4. Report on Trend and Progress of Banking in India, 2002-03, p. 116.
5. Report on Trend and Progress of Banking in India, 2004-05, p. 148.
6. Report on Trend and Progress of Banking in India, 2005-06, p. 156.

Management of Investing Institutions

Section Four

Section IV: Learning Objectives

The present section seeks to provide deep insights into strategic and operational aspects of institutions engaged in the investing business.

Section Outline

— Insurance industry in India.

— Operational polices and practices of LIC.

— Operational policies and practices of mutual funds.

Chapter 26

Insurance Industry in India

Learning Objectives:

The present chapter aims at:

- Providing insight into the emergence of insurance industry in India and abroad and drivers of their growth.
- Furnishing an incisive account of Performance of Indian Insurance Companies during the post reform period.
- Familiarizing with the emerging challenges to Indian insurance industry.

Chapter Outline:

A. EPILOGUE

Insurance industry is a direct descendant of the economic order and its preservation and progression has a direct and proportionate relationship with the levels of growth and sustainability of the economy. Significance of insurance business covering wide variety of risks increases with degree of changes in the environment. In fact, everything has a life cycle- the universe, the planet, the civilization, the economies, the companies and the products. The journey of progress is being traversed by the world on the vehicles of various economic orders, but the life of every new economy is becoming shorter and shorter. The hunting and gathering nomadic economy drove the life on the planet Earth for hundreds and thousands of years. The agricultural economy's dominance sustained for about ten thousand years. The industrial economy was dwarfed by the information economy within a span of only 200 years.

Today it is the information economy that rules the various facets of the environment-social, political and economic. The overwhelming influence of the information economy can be perceived in every aspect of life. Yet, the conclusion of the information economy's life span is within viewing distance and a new economy-christened the Bio-economy appears to be emerging and is likely to overshadow the information economy during the lifetime of the new generation.

The global economy is undergoing unremitting transformation. The thumb rule of 5-5-5 from concept to consumer; 5 years from concept to prototype, 5 years from prototype to product and 5 years from product to Billion Dollar Business had undergone substantial contraction and even the most progressive and optimistic persons are not able to predict the velocity of change. There is befogging of businesses and emergence of new economic models. The Law of Diminishing Returns is getting replaced by the Law of Increasing Returns. The markets and not the strategies tend to price, sell and manage offers.

B. INSURANCE INDUSTRY—A GLOBAL PERSPECTIVE

Insurance industry is crowded in North America, Western Europe, Japan and Oceania. These countries account for 90.7% of global premiums with a planetary average penetration of 7.8% of the GDP. With a per capital premium of US $3165, the Japanese are the greatest savers through the vehicle of life insurance and the Swiss with US $1571 per capita are the biggest spenders in non-life insurance premium. Insurance companies wrote US $2443.7 billion in premium worldwide in the year 2000, reflecting a growth of 9.1% and 2.7% in life and non-life, respectively.

The drivers of growth of life insurance business were private pension in the U.S. and Western Europe along with index-linked policies buoyed by the stock market rallies upto mid-2000. The upswing is also attributable to a dramatic rise in the single premium business since the year 1995. The volatility of single premium business is likely to introduce capriciousness in the otherwise steadily growing life insurance industry.

Non-life insurers reported higher growth rates as compared to the 90s. Growth motors were a robust global economy and recovery from financial crisis. The China, Hong Kong, S.A.R and Taiwan regions registered growth rates in excess of 10%. The premium upsurge in Asian and Russian markets outpaced their respective GDP growth rates. However, the earning of the insurance industry remained lackluster despite good growth and reporting fewer major losses.

C. EVOLUTION AND GROWTH OF INSURANCE INDUSTRY IN INDIA

The insurance sector in India has made a full circle from being an open competitive market to nationalisation and back to a liberalized market again. Tracing the developments in the Indian insurance sector reveals the 360 degree turn witnessed over a period of almost two centuries. The business of organised life insurance in India started with the opening of Oriental Life Assurance Company in 1818 in Calcutta followed by Bombay Life in 1823 and Madras Equitable in 1829. The Bombay Mutual Life Insurance Society started its business in 1870. It was the first company to charge same premium for both Indian and non-Indian lives. The Oriental Assurance Company was established in 1880. The General Insurance business in India, on the other hand, can trace its roots to the Tritors (Tital) Insurance Company Ltd., which established in the year 1850 in Calcutta by the British. Till the end of 19th century, insurance business was almost entirely in the hands of overseas companies. In 1907, the Indian Mercantile Insurance Ltd. was set up- the first company to transact all classes of general insurance business.

Insurance regulation formally began in India with the passing of the Life Insurance Companies' Act of 1912 and Provident Fund Act of 1912. Several frauds during 20's and 30's allied insurance business in India. By 1938, there were 176 insurance companies operating in the country. The first comprehensive legislation was introduced with the Insurance Act of 1938 that provided strict state control over insurance business. As the industry traversed the path of development and diversification, innumerable operators joined the bandwagon, more to harness riches from the business of spreading risks than to generally protect and indemnify individuals, organizations and the society against an array of hazards causing to life and property and economic distress.

The industry received sharper focus after independence and then managers of the Indian economy for a variety of considerations believed that in particular the business of long-term security-Life insurance- deserved to be organised and orchestrated in a better fashion. Although there were 245 insurance companies and provident societies operating in 97 centres, these institutions were found serving urban customers having vested interests of a few big business houses at the expense of national economic growth. It was, therefore, felt that if these institutions were merged and operated to encourage nation building activities, they would prove to be a valuable asset for the nation. The integrated strength of these insurance companies would mobilise in an organised manner the enormous savings of the people in different parts of the country and make them available for the industrial development programmes envisaged in the country's Second five-year plan. The need to cater to the burgeoning financial requirements of five-year plans and to shun the vagaries of private enterprises led to the nationalization of the insurance industry in India and emergence of Life Insurance Corporation in October 1956, following the enactment of the LIC Act, 1956. This was in conformity with the Government's chosen path of state led planning and development.

The (non-life) insurance business continued to thrive with the private sector till 1972. Their operations, however, were restricted to organised trade and industry in large ones. In 1972, the General Insurance Business (Nationalisation) Act, 1972 nationalised 68 Indian Insurance and 45 non-Indian insurance companies conducting general insurance business. 113 insurers amalgamated and grouped into four companies, *viz.*, the National Insurance Company Ltd., the New India Assurance Company Ltd., the Oriental Insurance Company Ltd., and the United Indian Insurance Company Ltd. The GIC was incorporated as a company.

◆ Insurance Sector Reforms

In 1993, Malhotra Committee headed by Former Finance Secretary and RBI Governor, R.N. Malhotra, was formed to evaluate the Indian insurance industry and recommend its future directions. The reforms were aimed at "creating a more efficient and competitive financial system suitable for the requirements of the economy keeping in view the structural changes currently underway and recognising that insurance is an important part of the overall financial where it was necessary to address the need for similar reforms".

In 1994, the Committee submitted the report and some of the key recommendations included:

(i) Structure

Government stake in the Insurance companies to be brought down to 50%. Government should take over the holding of GIC and its subsidiaries so that these subsidiaries can act as independent corporations. All the insurance companies should be given greater freedom to operate.

(ii) Competition

Private companies with a minimum paid-up capital of ₹ 100 crore should be allowed to enter the industry. No company should deal in both life and general insurance through a single entity. Foreign companies may be allowed to enter the industry in collaboration with the domestic companies. Postal Life Insurance should be allowed to operate in the rural market. Only one state level Life Insurance Company should be allowed to operate in each state.

(iii) Regulatory Body

The Insurance Act should be changed. An Insurance Regulatory body should be set up. Controller of Insurance (currently a part from the Finance Ministry) should be made independent.

(iv) Investments

Mandatory investments of LIC Life Fund in government securities to be reduced from 75% to 50%. GIC and its subsidiaries are not to hold more than 5% in any company.

(v) Customer Service

LIC should pay interest on delays in payments beyond 30 days. Insurance companies must be encouraged to set up unit-linked pension plans. Computerisation of operations and updating of technology to be carried out in the insurance industry.

The Committee emphasised that in order to improve the customer services and increase accessibility of the various insurance products in India, the insurance industry should be opened up to competition. But at the same time, the Committee felt the need to exercise caution as any failure on the part of new players could ruin the public confidence in the industry. Hence, it was decided to allow competition in a limited way by stipulating the minimum capital requirement of ₹ 100 crore. The Committee felt the need to provide greater autonomy to insurance companies in order to improve their performance with economic motives. For this purpose, it had proposed setting up an independent regulatory body *viz.*, the Insurance Regulatory and Development Authority (IRDA).

Reforms in the insurance sector were initiated with the passage of the IRDA Bill in Parliament in December 1999. As per the Provisions of IRDA Act, 1999, the Insurance Regulatory and Development Authority (IRDA) was established on 19th April, 2000 to protect the interests of holders of insurance policy and to regulate, promote and ensure orderly growth of the insurance industry. The IRDA, since its incorporation as a statutory body in April 2000, has fastidiously stuck to its schedule of framing regulations and registering the private sector insurance companies. Having being set up as an independent statutory body the IRDA has put in a framework of globally compatible regulations. The other decision taken simultaneously to provide the supporting systems to the insurance sector and in particular, the life insurance companies was the launch of the IRDA online service for issue and renewal of licenses to agents.

◆ Present Scenario

Enactment of the IRDA Act, 1999 paved the way for entry of private players into the insurance market which was hitherto the exclusive privilege of public sector insurance companies/ corporations. Under the new dispensation, Indian insurance companies in private sector were permitted to operate in India with the following conditions:

(*i*) Company is formed and registered under the Companies Act, 1956;

(*ii*) The aggregate holding of equity shares by a foreign company, either by itself or through its subsidiary' companies or its nominees, does not exceed 26%, paid up equity capital of such Indian Insurance Company;

(*iii*) The company's sole purpose is to carry on life insurance business or general insurance business or reinsurance business;

(*iv*) The minimum paid up equity capital for life or general insurance business is ₹ 100 crore;

(*v*) The minimum paid up equity capital for carrying on reinsurance business is ₹ 200 crore;

(*vi*) Insurance companies are required to invest not less than 15 per cent of their funds in infrastructure and social sectors.

◆ Micro Insurance

IRDA has issued the Micro Insurance Regulations which provide for a tie up between a life and a non-life insurance company for distribution of insurance products to improve the penetration of insurance in the rural areas. This regulation allows cross selling of insurance products which is not being allowed in general. As per these regulations, the Self Help Groups (SHGs), Micro Finance Institutions and Government organisations can act as micro insurance agents. This would certainly improve the distribution channels in rural India for marketing low value products.

◆ Insurance Companies Registered by IRDA

IRDA has so far granted registration to 48 insurance companies which include 24 life insurance companies & 24 non-life insurance companies. General Insurance Corporation has been approved as the "Indian reinsurer" for underwriting only re-insurance business. (Table 26.1)

◆ Deployment of Funds

According to the IRDA directive, life insurance companies can invest 50 per cent of their investible assets in government securities, 15 per cent in infrastructure bonds and similar instruments while holding a discretionary control, subject to conditions, on 35 per cent of the assets. Similarly, general insurance companies' discretionary quota stands at 45 per cent of the investible assets. At least 75 per cent infrastructure investment should be in AAA rated bonds.

The IRDA has, of late, changed the rules of the game for insurance companies by amending investment regulations. Accordingly, it has enlarged the investment universe by including debt securities, venture capital and follow-on offers as approved investment avenues. Further, no insurer can hold more than 10 per cent equity in any company. Investment in debt has also been capped at a sum of 10 per cent of the paid-up capital, free reserves and debentures and bonds.

In February 2008, the IRDA notified amendments to obligations of Insurers to Rural or Social sectors Regulations, prescribing the percentage of rural business in the range of 5 to 20 per cent for life and general insurers and 25,000 to 50,000 lives in the social sector, depending on the operations of a particular company.

On February 8, 2013, the IRDA permitted raising of the investment limit of insurance companies. Accordingly, insurance companies can now increase their exposure in equity in a given company from the present level of 10 per cent to a higher level of 12 per cent and 15 per cent depending upon the size of the controlled fund of any given insurer.

On March 8, 2013 the IRBI mandated that a life insurance company should invest not less than 25 per cent of its total corpus in central government securities. The total investment of such a company in central and state government securities and other approved securities — all put together — should not be less than 50 per cent.

The IRDA also prescribed the investment limit for life insurance firms in housing and infrastructure bonds. While permitting them to invest in these bonds, the regulator made it clear that a life insurance company's total exposure to these bonds should not be less than 15 per cent of its corpus. However, the IRDA prescribed that a double 'A' rating of bonds a must for insurance firms to consider investment.

For companies carrying on pension funds, annuity and group business, the IRDA prescribed that not less than 40 per cent of their total funds should be invested in government bonds and approved securities.

In the case of unit-linked insurance business, the IRDA prescribed that the investment in approved securities shall not be less than 75 per cent of such fund(s) in each such segregated funds.

◈ Procurement of Funds

In a historic move to improve resource position of insurance companies, the insurance laws were amended in 2009 to amend Sections 10A of the Insurance Act, 1938, allowing insurance companies to raise capital on the lines of the banking sector in the form of subordinated debt or through preference shares or through perpetual bonds. Lately, the government decided to lift the FDI cap in private sector insurance firms to 49 per cent from 26 per cent and permit overseas reinsurers to enter the market through branches. This was intended to ease the resource constraint of the private insurers.

◈ Protection of the Interest of Policyholders

IRDA has the responsibility of protecting the interest of insurance policy-holders. Towards achieving this objective, the Authority has taken the following steps:

(*i*) IRDA has notified protection of policy holders Interest Regulations 2001 to provide for policy proposal documents in easily understandable language; claims procedure in both life and non-life; setting up of grievance redressal machinery; speedly settlements of claims; and policyholders' servicing. The Regulation also provides for payment of interest by insurers for the delay in settlement of claim.

(*ii*) The insurers are required to maintain solvency margins so that they are in a position to meet their obligations towards policyholders with regard to payment of claims.

(*iii*) It is obligatory on the part of the insurance companies to disclose clearly the benefits, terms and conditions under the policy. The advertisements issued by the insurers should not mislead the insuring public.

(*iv*) All insurers are required to set up proper grievance redress machinery in their head office and at their other offices.

(*v*) The Authority can take up with the insurers any complaint received from the policy holders in connection with services provided by them under the insurance contract.

◈ IRDA's New Tariff Guidelines – A critique

IRDA's new tariff guidelines came into effect from 1st January, 2008. The new guidelines have removed price controls and shared in a free pricing regime for fire and engineering risks. It is only in the case of the motor third party risk that the regulator would apply pricing controls. The rate scheme approvals would be done only if the operating ratio did not exceed 100%.

Although IRDA appears to have axed controls, in reality, all rates being offered to customers would have to be approved by the regulator under the file and use guidelines. In fact, in September, 2007, when public sector insurers were planning to push down the tariffs by offering discount in excess of 60 per cent, in the wake of intense competition, the regulator had interviewed to impose a ceiling on the maximum discounts that insurers could offer.

However, the approval is required if the operating ratio does not exceed 100 per cent. PSU insurers have positive underwriting margin anywhere between 7 and 10 per cent implying high level of profitability. But the underwriting margins in the case of private sector were higher due to absence of legacy losses and high reliance on reinsurance.

For the first time since the non-life insurance market was opened, public sector insurance were in a position to flex their muscle. Tariffs in the low claims segments – fire and engineering — have dropped by about 50 per cent. In fact, during the year 2007, public sector insurers were planning to push down the tariffs even by offering still higher discount. They were in a position to do so in view of their large capitalization. To check this practice and to ensure level playing field that IRDA had to detariff fire and engineering risks.

◈ Re-insurance Business

In December 2000, the GIC subsidiaries were restructured as independent insurance companies. Accordingly, the GIC which was the holding company of the four public sector general insurance companies has since been delinked from the latter and has been approved as the 'Indian Reinsurer" since 3rd November, 2000. The share capital of the GIC and that of the four companies are held by the Government of India. All the five entities are Government Companies registered under the Companies Act. Thus, while GIC's subsidiaries look after general insurance, the GIC itself has been the major reinsurer. Currently, all insurance companies have to give 20 per cent of their reinsurance business to the GIC. The aim is to ensure that the GIC's role as the national reinsurer remains unhindered.

D. RECENT REFORMATORY MOVES IN INSURANCE SECTOR

The year 2010 was a landmark year when IRDA and SEBI found themselves in a turfwar which led to repositioning unit-linked insurance plans (ULIPs) more as insurance products, by providing higher protection and focus on long-term savings for pension plans.

The lock-in period for all ULIPs has been increased from three years to five years. All limited premium ULIPs, other than single premium products, will have premium paying term of a least 5 years. Further, all ULIP pension or annuity products will offer a minimum guaranteed return of 4.5 per cent per annum or as specified by the IRDA from time to time. The new guidelines became effective from September 1, 2010.

The IRDA is contemplating on norms whereby life insurance policies must come will a minimum of five years of regular premiums. It is not in favour of single premium policies or two-pay or three-pay policies as it feels that life insurance industry cannot sustain on a single premium policies and insurance, by nature, has to be long-term.[2]

The IRDA introduced new rules in May, 2010 stipulating that pension and annuity products should have a minimum sum assured, just like in single premium policies and all partial withdrawal be allowed only after 5 years of the existence of the policy.[3]

The IRDA directed insurance companies in May 2010 to give benefit illustration of net and gross yields at 7 and 10 per cent for schemes upto 10 years. Earlier, they used to give this illustration at 6 and 10 per cent. The IRDA also limited fund management charge at 1.35 per cent for a 10-year and 1.25 per cent for policies of more than 10 years.

The IRDA mandated insurers to give details of the commissions being paid from July, 2010. Further, insurance companies cannot introduce pension plans without life cover. Earlier, there were a number of ULIP pension plans without any sum assured, leaving the policyholder completely at the mercy of market dynamics.[4]

The IRDA has of late, recommended that the overall exposure in the promoter's group companies should be brought down to five per cent from 25 per cent. According to the current guidelines, an insurance company can invest up to 10 per cent in equity and 2.5 per cent in debt in the promoter's group companies. Additionally, in infrastructure firms of the parent company, another 12.5 per cent exposure is allowed, which means the total exposure can go up to 25 per cent.

The above initiatives were intended to bring transparency in operations of insurance companies and render their products customers' friendly.

In a move to take insurance products to the doorsteps of customers the IRDA is giving final touches to guidelines for "monoline" insurance agents — agents who will be authorised to sell only one simple insurance product.[5]

The IRDA has directed life insurance companies not to dilute more than 10 per cent stake through initial public offers (IPOs). The IRDA has capped the stake dilution by life insurers in the first three years of listing.[6] This directive is intended to put a check on the hugh valuations of life insurance firms which will be difficult for the market to absorb.

Insurance companies that have completed 10 years of operations and have strong financial position will be allowed to access capital markets through public offer.[7] Insurance company planning public offer has to seek formal approval from IRDA and then approach the SEBI for final approval. As part of eligibility criteria, the insurance company should have maintained the prescribed regulatory solvency margin as at the end of the preceding six quarters.

In a recent communication to all life insurers, the IRDA has said "The marketing of products labelled as highest NAV product shall not be allowed."[8] Thus, the life insurers have been asked to stop selling highest net asset value guaranteed products which contribute almost 20 per cent to the total premium collection of life insurers. Highest NAV-guaranteed products are those that promise to pay the highest value the fund achieves during a certain period, say, five or seven years. The regulator's argument is that such products led to systemic risks associated with the way funds were managed and posed the risk of heavy sell-off in equities when stock markets fell.

In another move, the IRDA has mandated a minimum death benefit of at least 10 times of the annualised products, as there were some products offering a limited dealt benefit. The regulator has also discouraged the use of single premium or limited premium payment term policies as these could impact the cash flow management companies.[9]

Another reformatory move made in May 2012 by the IRDA pertains to the retention limit. In a communication to the CEOs of insurance companies, IRDA said companies operating for more than 10 years would not be able to cede more than 30 per cent of their risks to reinsurance companies. Those operating for less than 10 years would have to retain half the risk in their books.[10]

The idea underlying this move is to discourage the current practice of insurance companies from passing on most of their risk to reinsurers against a ceding commission. According to the IRDA, if an insurer has low retention limit, then such insurers only net as an insurance service provider than as a risk bearing insurer. This amounting to fronting. Fronting insurers only rely on ceding commission without developing national retention capacity and underwriting expertise necessary for development of a viable domestic insurance industry.

As such, the IRDA has directed insurance companies to formulate its retention policy for each type of product, based on emerging claims experience, financial standing, underwriting capacity and on the annual reinsurance programme it gives to the authority.

E. PERFORMANCE OF INDIAN INSURANCE COMPANIES DURING THE POST REFORM PERIOD — A PANORAMIC VIEW

The insurance industry in India has come a long way in terms of bouquet of innovative insurance products offered, quality of services rendered and concomitant increase in penetration in untapped market since the year 2000, when the government opened up the market to private players. From just LIC offering the standard cover plan, today there are 24 players in the private sector offering a plethora of products. Thus, the entry of private players into the insurance industry has seen a veritable explosion of products that offer customers a much richer menu of options. For a choice- starved customer, their entry has been a god send. It has infused a new flavour into what was perceived as a sober industry and has resulted in the market leader, the LIC, adopting a more market-friendly approach in its bid to retain its premier position. (Table 26.1)

It is notable that the perception of the people about the life insurance and its changing dynamics in recent few year has been transformed by the fledgling private insurers who have been able to sign up Indian customers faster than anyone ever expected with their triple whammy combination and aggressive distribution. Earlier, life insurance was seen more as a savings instrument and tax saving device and not so much as risk cover, people are now suddenly turning to the private sector players and snapping the new innovative products on offer. These insurers are coining money in new niches that they have introduced.

It is also interesting to observe that life insurance industry has, of late, become highly competitive. The market share of the LIC, for example, has declined from 91 per cent in 2009 to almost 71 per cent in 2005 mainly due to aggressive marketing strategies and smart distribution networks of the private insurers. However, the LIC with its massive distribution network across the country and concerted efforts improved its market share to 73 per cent in 2011. In fact, the deregulated tariff environment unleased since January 2007 prompted the public sector insurer to pursue an aggressive strategy for top line growth.

The private insurers seem to be scoring big in other ways. They are persuading people to take out bigger policies. For instance, the average size of the life insurance policy before privatisation was around ₹ 50,000 which has now risen to ₹ 80,000. But the private insurers are ahead in this game and the average size of their policies is around ₹ 1.10 lakh to ₹ 1.20 lakh — way bigger than the industry average.

Among the private players in life insurance market, the ICICI Prudential with market share of 25 per cent topped the list followed by Birla Sun Life with a market share of 15 per cent.

Currently, over 80 per cent of life insurance sold is either endowment or money back schemes and the state-owned companies still dominate these segments. But the annuity or pension products have already wrested over 33 per cent of the market. The current flavour in the insurance market is the unit-linked insurance plan (ULIPs), which provides cover as well as an opportunity to invest through the same product. In the unit-linked insurance schemes, insurance companies have a virtual monopoly, with over 90 per cent of the customers.

Today, an individual has a banquet of products to choose from to address his various his financial needs. Within this portfolio, ULIPs as a product category has found tremendous popularity and acceptance among consumers due to its twin benefits of protection and long-term wealth creation. Added to this is the flexibility it offers customers to structure it as per financial goals and appetite for risk. With the introduction of the new regulatory guidelines, ULIPs now offer a better and improved value proposition to consumers. This will reinforce the trust of customers in life insurance.

Consequent upon the above changes, there has been tremendous growth in the insurance industry in India. From a size of ₹ 50,000 crore in 2005, the insurance business in terms of premium collection surged to over 1,28,700 crore in 2011-12 recording growth rate of over 10 per cent over 2010-11 (Table 26.2) Of this, life insurance business accounted for over 60 per cent of the total business. The exponential growth of the insurance business can be explained by the entry of high profile new private insurers. The insurance industry grew (premium as percentage of GDP) from 2.3 per cent in 2001 to 5.2 per cent in 2011.[11]

Insurance penetration (percentage of total insurance premium to GDP) surged from 1 per cent in 2001 to 5.1 per cent in 2010. It slipped for two years to 4.1 per cent in 2011. This has been attributed to a slower rate of growth in life insurance premiums, compared with the rate of growth of the Indian economy. Likewise, Insurance density (per capita insurance premium) recorded rise every year from 2001 but saw the first-ever fall in life insurance density to $ 49 (about ₹ 2,695) in 2011 from $ 55.7 (about ₹ 3063).[12]

TABLE 26.2: Insurance Business in terms of Premium Collection *(April-Jan)*

(₹ crore)

	2011-12	2010-11
Life insurance		
Private insurers	22,351.32	27,864.73
LIC	59,145.36	67,135.31
Total	81,496.68	85,000.04
General Insurance		
Private	19,839.39	15,778.63
Public	27,375.90	22,257.63
Total	47,215.29	38,036.26
Total insurance business	1,28,711.97	1,23,036.30

Source: IRDA report, 2011-12.

A granular look at Table 26.2 shows that while life insurance business during 2011-12 declined by 14.21 per cent from ₹ 95,000 in 2010-11 to ₹ 81,500 crore, the general insurance business grew by 24.13 per cent from ₹ 38,000 crore to over ₹ 47,000 crore during the corresponding period. The major force for the decline in life insurance business in recent years has been the lacklustre performance of pension and ULIPs. Since the new guidelines on ULIPs were introduced in September, 2010, sales have taken a beating. Life insurance business has also suffered due to volatile market conditions. Even the country's largest insurer, LIC, saw a six per cent drop in new business premiums for April-January, 2012-13. Private insurers collected ₹ 21,220.45 crore — a dip of 5 per cent over 2011-12.

It may further be noted from Table 26.2 that since the new regulations pertaining to unit-linked pension plans and plans were introduced in September 2010, sales of life insurance products have been going down. It was expected initially that the industry would require six months to recover, but things did not turn out that way. This is for the fact, insurers believe, that "it is not easy to realign the business model overnight. The changes for betterment are always welcome, but the regulator should understood that the industry should be given adequate time to adjust." When the pension plans guidelines come into force in September 2010, it was the largest selling product accounting for almost a third of the sales of the life insurance industry. As a result, premium collected from pension plans dwindled to ₹ 597 crore in the first six months of 2011, compared to ₹ 17,675 crore during 2010-11. Also, in terms of the number of policies issued, the share of pension plans dropped to a mere 0.36 per cent in the first six months of 2011, compared to 16 per cent in the corresponding period a year ago.

It is noteworthy that the share of single premium business in total insurance business in 2011-12 was 46.20 per cent. The share of single premium business in case of LIC was 52 per cent while it was 31 per cent in case of the private insurers.[12] This suggests that the life insurance industry cannot sustain on single premium policies and insurance, by nature, has to be long-term. Ideally, premium's tenure should be a minimum of five years. In view of this, the current move of the IRDA assumes importance.

The life insurance industry is currently going through a period of adjustment, as companies are busy in aligning their business models with the new environment. While insurers call this a defining change that will go a long way in making life insurance a preferred financial tool for long-term savings and protection needs, the immediate situation is not rosy.

Along with cutting down on sales of new policies, insurers are trying to bring down cost through rationalisation of infrastructure, better vendor management and squeezing discretionary expenses. Insurers are now emphasizing need-based selling. As a result, most companies have brought down the proportion of ULIPs in total sales to 50 per cent from 85-90 per cent earlier. During the last one year (2011-12), companies have adopted the new mantra of improving persistency, reducing costs and rolling out new distribution channels. Most insurance companies have set up a separate desk to look into their persistency ratio. Insurers are cajoling distributors to sell products on the basis of customer needs encouraging transparency and understanding of the features and ensuring timely renewal payments to retain customers. Also, training and incentives are being provided to distributors to focus on longer term sales and higher persistency in their portfolio.

In the new regime, insurance companies are focusing more sharply on managing expenses. They are launching new distribution models to bring down costs. Online sellers are becoming popular with insurers.

In this connection, it may be noted that the country's top private life insurers have significantly reduced branches and employees over the last couple of years to cut costs and improve efficiency. ICICI Prudential, the second largest private life insurer in the country, has reduced its branches by nearly a half from 1,923 to 1,000 in the last two years. The top six private insurers, barring SBI Life, reduced nearly 30 per cent of branches, while the head count was scaled down 27 per cent in the same period.[13]

Contrary to life insurance industry, the general insurance industry registered spike by 24.13 per cent during 2011-12, compared to the year-ago period. Thus, the general insurance industry collected premiums worth ₹ 47,215 crore by writing new policies during the April-January 2011-12 period compared with ₹ 38,036 crore in the corresponding period of the previous year.

The public sector general insurance companies accounted for around 60 per cent of the premium collected during the period. Among these, New India Assurance with a market share of about 17 per cent claimed the largest amount during 2011-12 followed by United India (15%) and National Insurance (14.36%).

Among the private sector non-life insurance companies which collected about 40 per cent of the total premiums collected during 2011-12, the ICICI Lombard with a market share of almost 10 per cent topped the list followed by Bajaj Allianz (6.8%).

In view of entry of 18 non-life insurance companies in the private sector, the market share of public sector non-life insurers recorded fall from 73 per cent in 2001 to 60 per cent in 2011-12. The largest state-owned company, New India Assurance, saw its market share fall from over 20 per cent to 17 per cent during the corresponding period.

However, during the recent few years, private sector insurers are facing problems of low retentions resulting in solvency pressures, large chunk of the liabilities were added to the national re-insurers and global re-insurers through treaties, or through the facultative re-insurance route. The public sector, on the other hand, had high retentions on account of motor insurance, impacting their solvency for picking up high value big ticket business and resorting to undercutting of tariffs.

Insurance companies in India have made significant contribution to India's economic growth. LIC has provided ₹ 7,04,151 crore in the 11th Five-year Plan (2007-12) while the four general insurance companies and GIC of India have contributed about ₹ one lakh crore.

According to the World Economic Forum Financial Development Report, 2012, insurance penetration in India is much greater than in countries with a per capita income that is 10 times higher. It is remarkable that with a per capita GDP of $ 1,388.80, India has achieved a life insurance penetration of 3.61 per cent as against 3.56 per cent of the USA with a per capita GDP of $ 48,386.77. It is also a matter of pride that the report places India at the top of global rankings in terms of Life Insurance Density (measured as a ratio of direct premium to per capital GDP of 2011).[14]

As regards profitability performance of the insurance industry, the life insurance industry in the private sector in the county has suffered losses to the tune of ₹ 6,421 crore during the period 2006-2008. Only four private insurers were able to report profits during 2007-08. The public sector giant, LIC managed to post a modest growth in profits at ₹ 845 crore in 2007-08 compared with ₹ 774 crore in 2006-07. Among private sector general insurers, Reliance General Insurance suffered the biggest loss of ₹ 165 crore in 2007-08. The four public sector insurance companies saw their conbined profits come down by about 24 per cent to ₹ 2,205 crore.Hamstrung by income pressurers due to steep fall in premium income and mounting capital requirements, private sector insurance companies are shifting focus to retail products. For instance, ICICI Lombard has made significant progress with a retail focus to become the largest insurer in general insurance sector in 2011-12. This has given impetus to other players to focus their attention on the retail space. Retail insurance, however, is a small ticket and low-loss business. As a result, capital requirements are low. In fact, retail focus is essentially a derisking mechanism. Further, the retail sector is an untapped market with large growth potential. Currently, non-life insurance cover is less than one per cent of the country's GDP.

TABLE 26.1: List of Insurance Companies Registered by IRDA

LIFE INSURERS	
Public Sector	
1.	Life Insurance Corporation of India
Private Sector	
2.	Bajaj Allianz Life Insurance Co. Ltd.
3.	Reliance Life
4.	Birla Sun-Life Insurance Company Ltd.
5.	HDFC Standard Life Insurance Co. Ltd.
6.	ICICI Prudential Life Insurance Co. Ltd.
7.	ING Vysya Life Insurance Company Ltd.
8.	Max New York Life Company Ltd.
9.	MetLife Insurance Company Ltd.
10.	Kotak Mahindra Life Insurance Co. Ltd.
11.	SBI Life Insurance Company Limited
12.	TATA AIG Life Insurance Company Ltd.
13.	Aviva Life Insurance Co. Pvt. Ltd.
14.	Sahara India Life Insurance Co. Ltd.
15.	Shriram Life Insurance Co. Ltd.
16.	Bharti AXA Life Insurance Co. Ltd.
17.	Future Generali Life Insurance Co. Ltd.
18.	IDBI Federal Life Insurance Co. Ltd.
19.	Canara HSBC OBC Life Insurance Co. Ltd.
20.	AEGON Religare Life Insurance Co. Ltd.
21.	DLF Pramerica Life Insurance Co. Ltd.
22.	Star Union Dai-ichi Life Insurance Co. Ltd.
23.	India First Life Insurance Co. Ltd.
24.	Edelweiss Tokio Life Insurance Co. Ltd.
GENERAL INSURERS	
Public Sector	
1.	National Insurance Company Limited
2.	New India Insurance Company Limited
3.	Oriental Insurance Company Limited
4.	United India Insurance Company Limited
5.	Export Credit Guarantee Corporation
6.	Agriculture Insurance Corporation

Private Sector

7. Bajaj Allianz General Insurance Co. Ltd.
8. ICICI Lombard General Insurance Co. Ltd.
9. IFFCO-Tokio General Insurance Co. Ltd.
10. Reliance General Insurance Co. Ltd.
11. Royal Sundaram Alliance Insurance Co. Ltd.
12. TATA AIG General Insurance Co. Ltd.
13. Cholamandalam General Insurance Co. Ltd.
14. HDFC Ergo General Insurance Co. Ltd.
15. Future Generali India Insurance Co. Ltd.
16. Universal Sompo General Insurance co. Ltd.
17. Shriram General Insurance co. Ltd.
18. Bharti AXA General Insurance Co. Ltd.
19. Raheja QBE General Insurance Co. Ltd.
20. SBI General Insurance Co. Ltd.
21. L&T General Insurance Co. Ltd.
22. Star Health & Allied Insurance Co. Ltd.
23. Aollo Munich Health Insuranc Co. Ltd.
24. Max Bupa

F. CHALLENGES BEFORE INSURANCE INDUSTRY IN INDIA AND SUGGESTIONS TO COMBAT THE CHALLENGES

Indian insurance industry despite remarkable performance, as noted above, are going to face many challenges in its operations because of deepening liberalization and globalization, increasing disasters, declining interest rate, convergence and heightened customer expectations. Most important challenges are brought out below:

◈ Under Market Penetration

A critical issue facing the insurance industry in India is to increase the insurance penetration, which, though comparable to most emerging market economies, is much lower than that of OECD countries. (Table 26.3) Life insurance penetration in India is only 4.1 per cent of GDP, despite the fact that insurance companies have come up with specialised plans, with premium as low as Re. 1 a day for the rural market and introduced bancassurance to widen their reach. Still only 20-25 per cent of the over 200 million potentially insurable population is covered. Further, 99 per cent of the households are uninsured, and so are 80 per cent of two wheelers in India and only 2 per cent of the total health spends in the country via insurance.[15]

There has been 50 per cent increase in insurance penetration during the last 7 years and about a three-fold increase in insurance density in the same period. Still India ranks 19th in the global insurance market, with an income premium of $ 17 billion, as compared to China whose premium income is $ 47 billion, or the US, who ranks number one with an income premium of $ 1,055 billion.

Low penetration and density of Indian insurance companies may be discovered from Table 26.3. It may be noted from the table that on the parameters of insurance penetration and density as compared to even other BRIC nations, leave alone the developed countries, India ranks low.

TABLE 26.3: Penetration and Density of Insurance

Country	Insurance Penetration			Insurance Density		
	2003	2004	2005	2003	2004	2005
USA	9.61	9.36	9.15	3637.70	3755.10	3875.20
Brazil	2.96	2.98	3.01	82.60	101.10	128.90
U.K	13.37	12.60	12.45	4058.50	4508.40	4599.00
Russia	3.25	2.83	2.27	98.20	114.40	122.80
South Korea	9.63	9.52	10.25	1243.00	1419.30	1706.10
India	2.88	3.17	3.14	16.40	19.70	22.70
China	3.33	3.26	2.70	36.30	40.20	46.30

Source : IRDA Annual Report, 2005-06.

Under penetration of insurance market in India to the extent of almost 80 per cent of human beings and major natural resources remaining uninsured offers lot more opportunities to insurers. The major factor was the lack of awareness of life insurance across both rural and urban parts of the country. Exploiting these opportunities through innovative product offerings suited to the needs of the people, driving down premium rates/charges in respect of certain products and through improving the utility of services is the major challenge facing Indian insurance companies.

Under the circumstance, the IRDA directed the insurers to gradually increase their coverage of the rural sector to 15.0 per cent of total policies within direct by the fifth year in respect of a life insurer and 5 per cent of total gross premium income written direct by the third year in respect of a general insurer besides covering 20,000 lives in the economically vulnerable social sector by the fifth year in the case of all insurers. Further, life insurers have to adopt innovative marketing strategies to target lower income groups.

So as to sell policies, insurers are looking at other chanels, in addition to agents and banks. These channels are post offices, Kirana Stores and even malls. For instance, ICICI Lombard has tied up with 22 post office circles in the country for distribution of insurance products. Max New York has embarked on an initiative wherein the company would be tapping kirana stores to sell Max Vijay, which caters to the insurance needs of the low income groups. Future Generali has already bagged over 50,000 customers through the 'mallassurance' route with average premium for life insurance being about ₹ 20,000 and general insurance business being ₹ 3,000.[16]

◆ Deepening Competitive Pressure

Ferocity of competitiveness in insurance industry following dismantling of the tariff regime since January 2007 and entry of public sector banks in the insurance business will tend to accentuate competitive pressure both on public sector and private sector insurance companies in the country. Developments like removal of floor rates, freedom to structure new products and half a dozen new entrants are expected to dramatically change the general insurance landscape in future. Indian companies are now barred from issuing motor policies which provide for a replacement vehicle when the insured car is in the garage following an accident. From next year (2007-08) they will be able to provide such covers as is the practice in many foreign companies and there will be competition in the true sense.

The real disruption will, however, come from the new entrants, and renewed aggression by incumbents, including Reliance General Insurance. Three banks Allahabad Bank, Indian Overseas Bank and Karnataka Bank are partnering Japanese insurer 'SOMPO' for a joint venture in non-life insurance, where Dabur will also be a partner. HDFC, which recently broke up with Chubb, is looking for a new partner and is keen on being among the top three. The SBI has decided to get into general insurance and is looking out for a partner. The future Group

(Pantaloons), which has tied up with Italian insurer 'GENERALI', is also expected to enter the business during the current year. The increased competitive pressure led to decline in premium rates and decline in margins and increase in exposure to much higher risk at lower prices. Intense competition is driving the general insurance business to lower premium by about 50 per cent.

◈ Risk Management

In view of cataclysmic changes in macro policies of the Government and concomitant changes in every economic activity leading to metamorphic changes in the risk complexion, the major challenge before the management of the insurance industry will be balancing the business and risk management. The risks before the industry could be segmented into insurance risk, credit risk, business market risk and operational risk. The totality of the industry has been influenced in the recent past by the Gulf War, 11th September incident, 1987 Market Crash, 1991 Black Wednesday, Asian crisis, Dot.com boom and bust, volatile fluctuations in share price during 2005-06, recent terrorist attacks across the country, in addition to substantial impact of factors like AIDS/HIV, CJD, Heart/Lung transplant, Cloning, mortality improvements, disability discrimination limitation and use of genetic information on longevity and the quality of life of the people.

The management has to manage the risks through their identification, assessment, monitoring and control process. The process involved includes reporting of risk, risk adjusted performance evaluation, liability and reserve administration, asset-liability matching and credit risk management. Both the Board of Directors and the executive management will have to be actively engaged in meeting the challenge of risk management; while the former will have to get involved with the policy architecture, the latter will be charged with the responsibility of building an operational framework. Any laxity in this exercise may be ruinous.

◈ Multi-channel Distribution Network Management

In insurance market, competitive edge provided by product innovation can sustain only for a couple of months, since products can be cloned. Tomorrow's business will be dictated by distribution networks of far reach. This is why insurers are pumping in big money in scaling up their agency force and opening new branches.

Segmentation of market, selling segment-oriented products, focusing on fuller satiation of customers aspirations commandeers multiple channel distribution networks. Presently, product-market relationship is dominated by personalised selling rendered by tied agents. However, developments in the market are likely to be different in view of the information explosion, technology-led delivery system, emergence of financial conglomerates and universal banking revolutionising the geometry of financial products.

The market is expected to witness the onslaught of multiple distribution channels, which will be product-specific, segment-centric or market wide. The insurance companies will have to balance between comfort and the motivation levels of the existing tied agency channel and promotion and push to new channels. There may be conflicts in market access, product allocation, compensation structure, service supports and even publicity orientation. Developing suitable approaches not only for sapient and pragmatic propositions in products formulation, compensation structure, market segmentation and technology architecture in a market hitherto served by single distribution network will be an awesome challenge for the insurance companies.

◈ Talent Crunch

Sharp acceleration in growth in insurance business in recent years is putting great pressure on the industry, especially in terms of getting suitable sales and marketing people. Across the industry, trained man power, consumer education and awareness and good quality data and use of technology at the customer interaction level are already getting in the way of growth. There is a demand for two lakh agents every year to add to the 15 lakh already available. Further, there is acute shortage of specialised skills such as actuarial, underwriting, and investment.

Quite a large number of agents are not properly trained. They do not mind how they sell and what they sell to the customers.

To overcome the talent shortage, insurance industry is currently poaching from other aligned industries such as telecom and retail, but then it is equally at risk of attrition due to people leaving for other industries.

◈ Capital Inadequacy

The biggest hurdle in the way of the insurance industry's growth is a lack of capital. Although it is believed that there should be no dearth of capital to fund the scorching growth of insurance companies, the task of garnering funds from the market is not so easy. It is not possible for insurance companies to raise funds through IPO before 10 years. There is a 10-year cooling period and it will definitely be after 10 years, although the law does not prohibit any early IPO. But it takes 10 years for an insurance company to stabilise its operations. The fast growth of the insurance industry is pushing back profitability of these companies much further than the usual 7-8 years. And in any case, the retail investor is not likely to understand the dynamics of the insurance business, especially since it loses money hand-over-first in the early years. Insurance companies are more interested in chasing growth and market share on the expense of profitability. In such a scenario, listing in itself would bring in a lot of discipline.

The nature of the business is such that needs regular capital infusions for growth. This is why the insurance regulator requires to maintain a 150 per cent solvency margin. Thus, they must maintain capital 1.5 times their liabilities. This means the need for capital rises in proportion to growth. Private insurers (including general insurers) have invested more than ₹ 10,000 crore as equity capital into the industry since liberalisation in 2000. Some promoters (especially Indian promoters who own 74 per cent of the business) are getting fatigued with this constant ploughing in of capital. There is, therefore, clamour for relaxation of the FDI cap in insurance from 26 per cent to 49 per cent.

◈ Customer Relationship Management

Providing satisfaction to finicky customers in terms of risk, return and respect and dispensing the value proposition accordingly would be a tremendous challenge before the insurance companies. According to the recent consumer voice study on the insurance sector, private companies have scored better ranks as compared to the government owned companies in terms of quality of services offered. The private sector players, the study noted, have instilled deeper roots into the insurance segments, wherein PSU for the same a way behind. The responses of the customers associated with these PSUs draw facts that PSU's need to improve on a lot of parameters in order to gain a better position amongst their customers. The findings show that the customers of private companies are more satisfied than customers of PSUs. This could lead to serious issues for the PSUs as it is doubly hard to retain an unsatisfied customer than it is to obtain a new customer. Essentially, PSUs' need to take advantage of their huge customer base of providing them better service quality would result in retention of their huge customer base as well as help to create a positive association amongst their customers. The study further shows that on some parameters or the other, both the sectors lag and hence one could clearly say that there exists need for improvement amongst the players in the insurance sector. Thus, the message is clear; understanding the customers is crucial to business. The entire customer aspiration syndrome will get built on the platform of power of information and the right of choice. The current emphasis on providing quality service or customised products will pave way to developing appropriate marketing campaigns, lowering cost and providing profound and pleasant experience to customers to build their loyalty. In fact, the value proposition of each of the companies will be scrutinised through microscopic lenses. The CRM challenge will have the pyramid of four sub-challenges-product development, pricing mechanism, technology management and customer experience management.

◈ Fund Management

The task of fund management is going to be complex and convoluted because of competing economies, competing institutions, competing financial instruments and geographically disperse initiatives, sharp decline in the interest rates and the emergence of a new generation of demanding investors with greater focus on return satisfaction have rendered the job more complicated.

Fund management is a futuristic function and its success depends on a high level of analytical power, forecasting capability, technical skill to perceive and monitor micro and macro financial factors and the impact thereof. The ability of the management to make use of new instruments like derivatives, insurance-based capital market bonds, solvency bonds, catastrophe bonds, C-swaps, exchange traded C-options, contingent capital and live securitisation can keep a company ahead of others. Intriguingly, these instruments have yet not seen light of the day in Indian capital market. Transparency in operation and corporate governance in investment decision- making will be yet another challenging task.

◈ Knowledge Management

Indian insurance market because of its immense potentiality is going to be fiercely competitive in which bigwigs and transnationally competitive insurance companies will aggressively participate and some kind of guerrilla warfare may ensure in the battle for supremacy. Key to the survival and success in the terrains of competition war will be human resource adroitness and core competence. Hence, insurance companies will have to equip themselves with capability to assimilate information for building, conserving, utilising and updating of knowledge and have human resources acumen. This demands focused efforts on the structural requirements and long-term policy of procurement, retention, organisational culture building and an ambience of creativity, connectivity and continuity along with co-ordinated and continuous relationship with academic world.

◈ Convergence Management

Convergence and consolidation have come to be recognised as powerful means to cope with business challenges emerging out of rapid structural transformation, triggered by an emerging class of highly informed, demanding and value conscious customers and tectonic changes in the socio-economic milieu and growing inter-economy transaction and deregulation.

However, convergence should be well articulated in terms of objectives and it should be need based and should not promote an oligopolistic market to defeat the objective of competition.

Convergence in the financial services is creating ever-growing demands on skill sets to meet the organizational desideratum. New knowledge in the technology-led market place has made yesterday's expertise obsolete, leaving little room for precedent-oriented decision making or perception-based management. The management will have to make quantitative and qualitative decision based on hard facts, research findings and human ingenuity.

◈ Stakeholders' Conflicts Management

Efficient management of demanding stakeholders' conflicts is key to organisational success. It would be a daunting task for any insurance company to balance the interest and country interest of various stakeholders. It would, therefore, be in fitness of things to put in place a sound and fool-proof mechanism to resolve stakeholders' conflicts while protecting embedded customers values.

◈ Corporate Governance

Future of corporate organisations including insurance companies will be contingent not only upon value creation but also upon the quality of governance. Insurance companies will, therefore, have to indicate how they conduct themselves as an ideal corporate citizen. For this, high degree of integrity, transparency, disclosure and structured internal processes will have to be maintained. The rampant mis-selling in the insurance industry is the greatest problem with which the IRDA is seriously concerned. According to a survey conducted by NCAER, more than 60 per cent insured households were not able to clearly understand the extent of the coverage and the benefits being offered under an insurance plan, resulting in lower insurance penetration.

◈ Regulatory Challenge

In a market-driven economy, regulation plays a crucial role in promoting entrepreneurship, creating space for a healthy growth of the industry and sharpening focus on customer concerns. The IRDA has been playing significant role by promulgating a sagacious, internationally benchmarked regulatory architecture and in the development of the market However, the regulatory challenges will emerge as much from regulating insurance companies and their products in the Indian market as also from cross border operations, inter-regulatory space for supervision, inter-institutional conflict and convergence in the financial services.

Ostensibly, this will call for greater co-ordination among various regulators. Over the medium term, a regulatory shift from micro-managing the insurance market and companies focusing on risk management, asset protection and asset-liability management, cost controls and solvency-based supervision is expected. This will be driven by more informed and demanding customers, proliferation of products, blurring of boundaries and the need for foreign capital. Eventually, self- regulation will assume a pivotal role and insurance companies will have to get together to meet the challenge of co-ordination and collaboration in a fiercely competitive market place.

There is a need to provide greater flexibility to insurers, especially in combining or bundling products without changing the standard terms and conditions. This will allow more innovation in products. Globally, while insurance products are by and large standard, innovations are usually based on packaging. What distinguishes policies from each other is the combination of various products that are offered to the consumer. Currently, the market has a few examples of bundled products like the householder's insurance policy which combines a host of covers like fire and burglary among others.

G. FUTURE OF INSURANCE INDUSTRY IN INDIA

Despite enormous challenges, future prospects of insurance industry in India are very bright and growth is by no means exhausted not only because of under penetration but also due to growing prosperity of the people, demographic dynamics and their changing behaviour and perception. According to Mckinsey's recent study, Indian household incomes will almost triple over the next two decades if the economy moves at an annual growth rate of 7.3 per cent from 2005 to 2025. There is a raft of opportunities for insurance companies as nearly half a billion of 25-30-year-olds take the economy forward in the next few years. Over the next 25 years, they will have investment needs, protection needs and education needs for their children. In 5-10 years, they seriously start thinking about what they will do when they retire. This will certainly increase demand of insurance products.

Affluent households, the growing middle class and an emerging bankable population are distinct segments that need to be served in fundamentally different ways. Affluent consumers largely look for wealth management services with life insurance services forming an integral part of their portfolio. The middle class is an attractive segment due to its sheer numbers and buying power. It is constantly looking for solutions in tax savings, retirement, and health and wealth categories. The bottom of the pyramid and rural markets are emerging segments that look for composite products and health insurance. Bottom-of-the pyramid products such as micro-insurance will have to be the order of the day.

Players need to offer a balanced mix of ULIPs and traditional products. Single-premium, structured products, health and pension products to suit various life and savings needs of customers will be crucial. One of the key products which can drive future growth is pensions and pension annuities. This is one of the largest products globally. Even with regard to health, currently only 14 per cent of the population in the country is covered under any health insurance of any form. There is a large untapped opportunity in the pensions and health segments for life insurance companies.

Further, in view of fast changing consumption patterns and consumers aspiring to move up the value chain in terms of goods and services consumed, spurring of higher entrapreneurial abilities and opportunities, everyone is seriously thinking to create a financial safety net to secure and protect their family as they strive for growth and development. Insurance is the only instrument that will be able to create this safety net for people to fallback on in times of exigency.

Further, perception of the people about insurance is changing fast. Earlier, insurance was seen more as a saving instrument and not so much as risk cover, but now with events like the earthquakes and tsunamis, there is greater awareness.

With opening of the insurance business to private sector and growing opportunities attracting new players, insurance market has become ferociously competitive. Aiding this process is aggressive marketing strategies and multiplicity of delivery channels. In such a landscape, insurance players need to grab a share of the new policies that are sold. Much will depend on their product configuration, their reach and the sales force team they have.

Cost is increasingly becoming a critical issue in general or non-life insurance. We have not been able to cost-effectively service a huge market. However, in the wake of increased competition, detariffing and deregulation of overall portfolio of non-life companies, there has, of late, been price war. Rates for fire and engineering covers have dropped by 25 to 30 per cent. In fact, price competition has been so immense that IRDA has had to step in to set a floor level for the drop in prices. On a month-to-month basis, discounting has doubled since February, 2007. While customers may relish the price war, it is not in their interest in the long-term, especially, if the profitability of insurer gets affected. If the insurer is not healthy, then the very reason for taking an insurance cover gets defeated. A financially precarious insurer may be in no position to pay claims. Cost effectiveness will drive the growth of alternate channels such as internet channels, direct marketing and variants in agency channels. Further, players will have to rationalise costs by incorporating e-issuance of policies, straight through processing and increased process optimisation to provide cost effective customer service. Leveraging the internet and other technology options to provide single window service so as to cross-sell and retain customers will become the norm.

Further to survive and thrive in stiffer competition, insurance companies will have to consider entering into new lines of business. Since the squeeze on margins is particularly severe in corporate and commercial lines of business, insurance companies are looking to tap retail customers to cushion against the pricing pressures. Another move is towards the hinterland or non-urban India, promising huge opportunities for non-life companies.

Besides product innovation, distribution looks to be key ingredient for driving growth in the insurance sector. Insurance is still a push product in India. Agents have to create the need for insurance, especially in our country where research shows that life insurance is the last thing in the list of future purchases for the middle class. So while the industry's fate may depend on the evolution of the need-based insurance products, the growth of individual companies would hinge on their distribution reach. In a market that is quite homogenous, as far as insurance products are concerned, relationships with clients may be the only differentiating factor. This is for the fact that while popular insurance products that manage to stir interest are easily imitable and can be offered by other players almost immediately, distribution capabilities and network cannot be easily replicated by competition. It is heartening to note that in the recent few years insurance companies are focusing on training of agents, operational efficiency and cutting costs and new channels of distribution including online sales.

The Indian insurance market has matured over the last 10 years. The regulators want the insurance companies to be more focused on customers. The insurers to survive and succeed need to move quickly towards becoming customer-centric. They have to customerise their strategies and operations if they have to stay ahead of their competitors.

The life insurance landscape continues to remain heavily untapped. The need is to leverage its strengths, fasten growth drivers to emerge stronger and build an exemplary model on the basis of consumer trust and valuable distributor relationships. These strategies will the industry to sustain its growth momentum over the years to come.

H. CONCLUSIONS

Insurance industry plays a significant role in prompting economic growth of a country. Insurance companies not only provide risk cover to infrastructure projects, but also contribute long-term funds.

Insurance industry is crowded in North America, Western Europe, Japan and Oceania, accounting for about 91% of global premiums with a planetary average penetration of around 8% of the GDP. The drivers of growth of life insurance business in these countries were private pension provisions along with index-linked policies.

Insurance industry in India started without any regulations in the 19th century. The business of organized life insurance in the country began with the opening of the Oriental Life Assurance Company in 1818. Till the end of 19th century, insurance business was entirely in the hands of overseas companies.

By 1938 there were 176 insurance companies operating in India. In 1938, the Insurance Act was passed which provided for strict state control over insurance business. The industry received greater focus after independence. In 1956 erstwhile private life insurance companies were nationalised to establish LIC. The non-life insurance business continued to thrive with the private sector till 1972 when General Insurance Business Act was passed to nationalize 113 insurance companies and the GIC was formed.

The Indian Insurance industry has, of late, come a long way in terms of bouquet of innovative insurance products offered, quality of services rendered and concomitant increase in penetration in untapped market. The entry of private insurers has infused a new flavour into what is perceived as a sober industry and has forced the LIC to adopt a more market-friendly approach in its bid to retain its premier position.

Nevertheless, the LIC continued to play predominant role in the life insurance market, its market share has tended to shrink from 90% to 73% because of private insurance companies eating into the share of the LIC.

At present, over 80% of life insurance sold is either endowment or money back schemes and the Governments owned companies still dominate these segments. However, in the annuity or pension products business, the private insurers have already wrested over 33% of the market The private insurers also seem to be scoring big in many other ways.

Despite remarkable growth, Indian insurance industry is going to face many challenges such as under market penetration, risk management, multi-channel distribution network management, customer relationship management, fund management, knowledge management, convergence management, stakeholders' conflicts management, corporate governance and regulatory challenges. Both the Government and insurers have to formulate suitable strategies to meet these challenges so that the insurance industry is able to achieve its mission of insuring people in every nook and corner of the country. In fact, there is going to be tremendous increase in demand of insurance products in future.

KEY TERMS

- Corporate Governance
- Customer Relations Management
- Fronting
- General Insurance Industry
- Highest NAV guaranteed products
- Insurance Regulation and Development Authority
- IRDA Act
- Life Insurance Industry
- Malhotra Committee
- Micro Insurance
- Monoline Insurance
- New Tariff Guidelines
- Regulatory challenges
- Re-insurance business
- Single premium business
- Unit linked Insurance Plans

DISCUSSION QUESTIONS

1. How did insurance industry evolve across the world?
2. Discuss the evolution and growth of insurance industry in India.
3. What were the important recommendations of the Malhotra Committee on insurance sector?
4. Outline the salient features of the IRDA Act.
5. How has the IRDA Act liberated the insurance sector in India?
6. Assess the recent performance of the insurance industry in India.
7. Comment upon the recent reformatory steps taken by the Government in the insurance sector.
8. What are the major challenges facing the insurance industry during the post liberalisation period? Suggest measures to combat these challenges.
9. Present your own view on future of insurance industry in India.

REFERENCES

1. Economic Times, July 23, 2007.
2. Business Standard, Jan. 31, 2012.
3. Business Standard, May 5, 2010.
4. Business Standard, May 6, 2010.
5. Business Standard, September 9, 2011.
6. Business Standard, Feb. 22, 2011.
7. Business Standard, Dec. 20, 2011.
8. Business Standard, May 14, 2012.
9. *Ibid.*
10. Business Standard, May 18, 2012.
11. www.greenworldinvestor.com
12. Insurance Gazette, Business Standard, March, 2013.
13. Business Standard, May 21, 2012.
14. HINDU, February 26, 2013.
15. Business Standard, December 14, 2009
16. Business Standard, Feb. 2, 2012.

* * *

Strategic Policies and Practices of Life Insurance Corporation of India (LIC)

Chapter 27

Learning Objectives:

The present chapter aims at:

- Providing insights into objectives and strategic policies of LIC.
- Describing the pattern of deployment of Fund by LIC.
- Highlighting the role of LIC in corporate financing.

Chapter Outline:

- Introduction.
- Objectives of LIC.
- Strategic policy of LIC.
- Growth of LIC.
- Deployment of fund by LIC.
- Diversified activities of LIC
- Liberalisation and LIC
- Conclusions and suggestions.

A. INTRODUCTION

Life Insurance Corporation (LIC), formed by an Act of Parliament, *viz*, LIC Act 1956, with a capital contribution of only ₹ 5 crore from the Government of India, a vast net work of 2048 branches, 101 divisions and 7 zonal offices and 24 satellite offices across the country, enjoyed monopoly position till March, 2000, when the Government of India opened the insurance sector, lifting all entry restrictions for private players and allowing foreign players to enter the market with a limit of 26 per cent equity capital for foreign partners in an insurance company. The opening up of the sector has infused competitiveness in the industry leading to greater spread and deepening of insurance in the country and restructuring and revitalising of the public sector companies. Thus, the monopoly of the LIC came to an end in 2000 and since then 24 private sector players have taken the plunge.

B. OBJECTIVES

The emergence of LIC as the largest single channel of individual savings and the biggest investing institution is a significant event in the socio-economic development of the country.

Explaining the benefits of the LIC, the late C.D. Deshmukh, the then Finance Minister observed: "With Second Plan involving an accelerated rate of investment and development, the widening and deepening of all possible channels of public savings has become more than ever necessary," and of these, the nationalisation of the life insurance business was a vital part. He added: "The nationalisation of life insurance will be another milestone on the road the country has chosen in order to reach its goal of a socialistic pattern of society. In the implementation of the Second Five-Year Plan, it is bound to give material assistance. In the lives of millions in the rural areas, it will introduce a new sense of awareness of building for the future in the spirit of calm confidence, which insurance alone can give. It is a measure conceived in a genuine spirit of services to the people to respond, confound the doubters and make it a resounding success."

Main objectives of the LIC are as follows:

- To protect the interest of the policy holders against embezzlement of funds by the insurers.
- To spread life insurance much more widely and in particular in the rural areas and in the socially and economically backward class with a view to reaching all insurable persons in the country and providing them adequate financial cover against death at a reasonable cost.
- To maximise mobilisation of people's savings by making insurance linked savings adequately attractive.
- To deploy funds in the best advantage of the investors as well as the community as a whole keeping in view national priorities and obligations of attractive return.
- To conduct business with utmost economy and with the full realisation that the money belongs to the policy holders.
- To act as trustees of the insured public in their individual and collective capacities.
- To cater to the various life insurance needs of the community that would arise from the changing social and economic environment.
- To involve all people working in the Corporation to the best of their capabilities in furthering the interests of the insured by providing efficient service with courtesy.
- To promote amongst all agents and employees of the Corporation a sense of participation, pride and job satisfaction through discharge of their duties with dedication towards achievement of corporate objectives.

C. STRATEGIC POLICIES OF LIC

The LIC is essentially an investment institution. Its investment policy has been designed after providing a thoughtful consideration to cardinal principles of safety of principal, diversification of investments in terms of types of securities, number and types of enterprise, maturities and regions. The Corporation is supposed to act on business principles and its investment policy is governed by consideration of interest of its policy holders unless it be in the larger interest of the country.

The investment policy of the LIC is subject to regulation by the provision as contained in Section 6(i) of the LIC Act, 1956, enjoining on the Corporation the duty of carrying on its business to the best advantage of the community and the primary obligation of holding the policy holders' money in trust with the help of dynamic and vigorous management imbued with a spirit of trusteeship.

The pattern of investment of the LIC was until recently governed by Section 27A of Insurance Act, 1938. As per this Act, the Corporation was required to invest at least 50 per cent of the controlled funds in central and state government securities and other approved securities, 35 per cent in other approved investments and the remaining 15 per cent in unapproved investments as decided by the Corporation's investment committee.

The Section 27A of the Insurance Act, 1938, was amended in April 1975. The amended section stipulates that accretion to the controlled fund (all funds of the Corporation pertaining to its life insurance business and capital redemption insurance business) of the LIC shall be invested as under:

(*i*) In Central Government marketable securities: Not less than 25 per cent

(*ii*) In Central Government, State Government securities, including government guaranteed marketable securities including (*i*) above: Not less than 50 per cent.

(*iii*) In socially-oriented sector including Public sector, co-operative, houses built by policy holders, OYH schemes including (*ii*) above: Not less than 75 per cent.

In respect of the balance 25 per cent of the accretion to the controlled fund, the government has indicated that: *(a)* about 18 per cent would be required for loans against policies within the surrender values; *(b)* about 2 per cent may be invested in immovable properties; and *(c)* about 10 per cent may be invested in private corporate sector. This would leave about 5 per cent of the controlled fund which may not be available for investment as it would constitute funds in the pipeline. It may be noted here that Section 27-A, as initially made applicable to the LIC, stipulated that balance of the funds after investment in government and other approved securities would have to be invested in scheduled investments. Of late, IRDA changed the pattern of deployment of funds by life insurance companies. Accordingly, LIC can now invest upto 50 per cent of its investible resources in government securities, 15 per cent in infrastructure bonds and similar instruments while holding a discretionary control, subject to conditions, on 35 per cent of the assets. This balance of 35 per cent can be put into equities, corporate bonds and mutual funds.

Main features of investment policy of LIC are as under:

- The crux of the Corporation's investment policy should be that the funds shall be invested in such a manner as to safeguard and promote to the maximum extent possible the interest of the policy holders. The larger interest of the country should not, however, be ignored.[1]
- Investments are be dispersed over different classes of securities, industries and regions. The Corporation's policy has been not to acquire more than 30 per cent of the outstanding equity shares of company.
- It is the policy of the Corporation to act purely as an investor and not assume the role of an operator or speculator and try to take advantage of temporary fluctuations in the market prices.

- The Corporation would underwrite security issues after careful investigation of the project from financial, economic, technical, managerial and social angles. Another notable feature of underwriting of the LIC is that the Corporation's participation in underwriting is in the form of 'firm' underwriting in the sense that it underwrites issue of capital invariably by way of firm commitment. Through underwriting, it purchases a large block of sound securities for its investment portfolio. The approach of the LIC in this regard is that of an investor and one of a catalytic agent to generate public subscriptions.

It is the policy of the Corporation to lay relatively more emphasis on senior securities because fixed return, and preferential claims on income and assets fit into the cannons of sound investments for an insurance organisation like LIC.

In sum, the approach of the LIC to underwriting is that of an investor and not one of a catalytic agent to generate public subscriptions.

The IRDA Act 1999 has permitted the LIC and other newly formed insurance companies to invest more in corporate equity and debt instruments. The Act has also allowed insurance companies to invest in venture capital funds with a proven track record under its category of approved investments.

The Act has specified 2:1 debt-equity ratio for convertible debentures. However, in the case of capital investment project, higher ratio upto 4:1 would be considered. For debentures, the interest cover should at least be 2.5 times, including interest on proposed loans and the debt-equity ratio would not exceed 2:1.

- As regards investments in time deposits, the regulatory body has specified that the insurer has to place the deposits with a view to cater to working capital needs of the corporate sector. The placement of the deposit would have to be decided after evaluating financial and non-financial aspects of the performance parameters of the companies. The maximum amount of short-term deposits that can be placed with any company should not exceed ₹ 2 crore or 10 per cent of networth including the proposed loan subject to the networth of the borrowing company being not less than ₹ 15 crore.
- It is the policy of the corporation to review its investment portfolio from time to time and make changes in its composition as may be warranted under the circumstances.
- The Corporation's investment policy is not to acquire control or participate in management of any concern in which it has interest as an investor unless exceptional circumstances warrant such participation. Over the years, the LIC has become more aggressive and consumer-centric in its approach.[2]
- As regards assistance policy of the LIC, the Corporation assists public sector undertakings and public limited companies and abstains from assisting private limited companies. The Corporation assists industrial enterprises directly by underwriting of capital issues, subscription of shares and bonds and long-term loans to enterprises. Besides, the Corporation finances the private industry indirectly through subscriptions to the shares and bonds of the special industrial financial institutions such as the IDBI, SFCs, IFCI and so on. In sanctioning loans, the Corporation accords priority to production and generation of electricity, housing schemes, supply of water and drainage, road transport development and financing of industrial development.

During the year 1997-98 the LIC was given greater autonomy in utilising its investible funds. The restriction of investing 25% of investible funds in specified proportion has been removed to enable it to invest the entire amount available under the ceiling of 25% on the basis of commercial judgement but subject to prudential norms. The investment pattern of the Group schemes fund has also been liberalised. The revised pattern provides for investments at not less than 40% in Government securities (Centre and States) and Government guarantee securities, thereby leaving 50% with LIC for market investment.

In 2008, the IRDA, as noted earlier changed the rules of the game for insurance companies by amending investment regulations, prohibiting an insurer to hold more than 10 per cent equity in any company. Investment in debt has also been capped at 10 per cent of the paid-up capital, free reserves and debentures and bonds.[3] However, the LIC has of late, received regulatory forbearance from the government allowing it to breach the investment limit. The relaxation has been allowed largely to enable the Corporation to hike stake in public sector banks.[4] Further, the IRDA is willing to allow the LIC to invest up to 20 per cent in debt in a particular company. However, this additional exposure will be allowed only for the exchange-traded debt issues.[5]

On November 21, 2012, the Government allowed the LIC to invest in a company upto 30 per cent of the latter's paid-up capital; up from the current limit of 10 per cent, nevertheless the IRDA has not been willing to concede this long standing demand of the LIC.

The rule was being eased to allow the Government to dip into the LIC's large coffers while off-loading PSU shares through disinvestment.

In order to make available contractual savings for infrastructure projects, the scope of the socially oriented investment has been widened to include ports, roads including highways and railways. LIC has also been permitted to make such investment in the private sector, subject to prudential norms fixed by the LIC Investment Committee/LIC Board from time to time.

- In consonance with the Government thrust on rural development, the LIC has made it a policy to make sustained and conscious efforts to carry the message of life insurance to the rural areas, especially the backward and remote areas. This has resulted in steady growth of new business from these areas. Further, it has been the constant endeavour of the Corporation to provide security to as many people as possible and to channelise the savings mobilised for the welfare of the people at large.

While granting loans, which constitute one of the major avenues of investment for the corporation's funds, it lays emphasis on the following.[6]

- Projects/Schemes for generation and transmission of electricity for agricultural and industrial use,
- Housing Schemes,
- Piped water supply and sewerage projects/schemes in rural and urban areas and townships,
- Development of road transport, and
- Industrial development.

D. GROWTH OF LIC

The LIC commenced its tryst with trust on 1st September, 1956 with formidable challenges of restoring the confidence of the insuring public and efficacious channelisation of people's savings for economic rejuvenation. The Corporation in its career of 50 years has passed through several phases of trials and tribulations. The success of the organisation benchmarked with the growth of other segments of the financial services industry and with reference to the environmental ethos attracts the envy of all. In particular it has been the run up of the last 16 years just before liberalisation – 1984-2000 with compounding annual growth rate of 20.6% and not many industries can boast of such an enviable track record. LIC is the front runner in the insurance sector with market share of 73 per cent in terms of policies.

The LIC business is conducted through individual insurance plans, group insurance plans and social security plans.[7] Individual insurance plans comprise four basic life insurance such as whole life Assurance, Endowment Assurance, Jeevan Anand and LIC's Jeevan Tarang, six term assurance plans, viz., Temporary Assurance, Mortgage Redemption Assurance, Convertible Term Assurance, LIC's Anmol Jeevan and LIC's Amulya Jeevan, Specific plans for children, pension plans, unit linked plan, micro insurance plans, health insurance plan, plan for handicapped dependents and other plans such as Money Back Plans, Jeevan Mitra, Jeevan Saathi, Jeevan

Surabhi, etc. Group Insurance schemes include Group Term Insurance Schemes, Group Gratuity Scheme, Group Leave Encashment Scheme, Group Superannuation Scheme, Group Annuity Scheme, Group Flexible Income Plan, Group Saving Linked Insurance Scheme, Group critical Illness Rider Benefit and Group Mortgage Redemption Assurance Scheme. Besides, the LIC has offered social security schemes, such as Janashree Bima Yojana, Shiksha Sahayog Yojana and Aam Admi Bima Yojana.

An analysis of total new business of the LIC according to schemes shows the predominance of individual schemes over the group schemes. (Table 27.1). Amongst the individual schemes, individual assurance occupies the most prominent position. Amongst group schemes, group assurance including linked business represented the bulk of the total business.

Further, an analysis of trends in new business of the Corporation shows phenomenal spurt. Thus, the new business under individual assurance rose from ₹ 1,78,343 crore in 2007-08 to over 4,44,000 crore during 2010-11. The similar tendency was noticeable in respect of group schemes. However, new business under ULIP suffered decline during 2010-11. This was mainly because of new ULIP norms. Taking cognizance of this trend the LIC took a conscious decision to make a paradigm shift from ULIPs to conventional products, which offer a regular flow of premium. As a result, 60 per cent of the products of the LIC are now traditional nature (as against 20 per cent three years ago).[8]

TABLE 27.1: New Business of LIC according to Schemes for the year

	No. of Policies (in lakhs)			Sum Assured (₹ in crores)		
	2007-08	2009-10	2010-11	2007-08	2009-10	2010-11
Individual Schemes						
(*a*) Individual Assurance	1,925.27	3,059.10	3,145.90	1,78,342.60	3,97,157.64	4,44,301.90
(*b*) Annuities	18.85	19.00	23.00	222.97	645.18	509.58
(*c*) Linked	356.84	821.80	550.90	20,070.08	36,951.06	29,403.47
Group Schemes	No. of Schemes					
Group Insurance (including linked business)		18,305	18,073	40600.90	84576.95	91861.17
Annuities per annum					520.38	1,332.03
Social security Group Schemes		5,190	5,446			
Group Superannuation	15	268	1,990			

Source: Annual Report of LIC for relevant years.

TABLE 27.2: Life Fund of LIC as at the end of March:

Year	₹ in crore
1957	410.40
1967	1,123.90
1977	3,952.89
1987	14,502.20
1997	87,759.96
2005	3,85,639.07
2006	4,63,147.00
2007	6,13,266.58
2008	6,86,616.45
2011	7,63,285.83

E. DEPLOYMENT OF FUND BY LIC

As regards utilisation of fund by the LIC, it may be noted from Table 27.3 that there has been astounding increase in quantum of investments by the LIC during the period 1956 to 2011, recording a rise from ₹ 348 crore to over ₹ 1265000 crore during the corresponding period.

TABLE 27.3: Pattern of Deployment of Fund by LIC

(*₹ in crore*)

Particulars	1956		2002		2008		2011	
	Amt.	%	Amt.	%	Amt.	%	Amt.	%
1. Loan	33.8	9.7	34,913.00	15.9	76,166.21	10.8	85,464.75	6.9
2. Securities	294.8	84.5	1,81,825.48	82.1	6,75,537.76	88.3	11,46,610.04	90.5
3. Other Investments	19.8	5.8	4,378.95	2.0	4,110.68	0.9	33,045.41	2.6
Total	348.4	100.0	2,21,117.43	100.0	7,55,814.65	100.0	12,65,120	100.0

Regarding pattern of investment of the LIC, over four-fifths of the fund was invested in government and corporate securities. The remaining one-fifth of the fund was used for lending for housing development and infrastructure facilities as also in other forms of investments comprising social security fund investment, contribution to the UTI's initial capital, LIC Mutual Fund, etc.

In recent years, the LIC also invested its resources abroad in the form of loan, stock exchange securities and house property. Table 27.4, showing investment by the Corporation out of India, reveals that the LIC invested about 1.2 per cent of its funds outside the country. Bulk of foreign investment was in the form of stock exchange securities.

TABLE 27.4: LIC Investment out of India as on March end

(*₹ in crore*)

Items	2002	2006	2008	2011
Loan	70.87	117.77	113.29	110.88
Stock Exchange Securities (out of India)	478.91	793.77	909.48	1248.52
House Property	30.29	35.58	53.08	59.44
Other Investments	3.30			
Total	580.07	951.53	1075.86	1266539.04

Thus, pattern of LIC's investment and the changes therein during the period since inception have, by and large, been in accordance with investment policy of the Corporation.

As regards the pattern of the LIC's investment, it may be seen from the Table that as on March end, 1956 more than two-thirds of the funds was deployed in Government and other approved securities. Less than one-tenth of the funds was utilised in the form of lending for housing development and infrastructural facilities. Corporate and co-operative sector claimed 16 per cent of investible funds of the Corporation. Other investments representing contribution to initial capital of UTI, ICMF, LIC HFL and LIC International Kisan Vikas Patras, house property etc., accounted for about one-fifth of the investible funds.

Over the period of time, there has been significant change in the pattern of deployment of funds. Thus, for example, investment in government and other approved securities which stood as 84.5 per cent on March end 1956 accelerated to over 90 per cent as on March end,

2011. As against this, loans for social oriented schemes declined during the period. This was because of greater investment in securities of public sector undertakings.

◆ Sectoral Distribution of Investment by LIC

Sector-wise distribution of the LIC's investment is shown in Table 27.5. It may be seen from the table that public sector has been the largest beneficiary, having received about ₹ 76,000 crore by the end of March, 2011 accounting for over 77 per cent of the total investment. It was distantly followed by private sector with an investment of the order of ₹ 2,65,800 crore, representing over one-fifth of the total.

TABLE 27.5: Sector-wise investment by LIC

(₹ in crore)

Year	Public		Private		Joint		Co-operative		
end-March	Amt.	%	Amt.	%	Amt	%	Amt.	%	Total
1980	3915.5	71.7	770.1	14.5	0.0	00	602.1	13.8	5287.7
1990	16404.3	80.2	2640.7	13.2	125.5	0.6	1332.2	6.0	20503.7
2000	117059.0	80.4	19268.4	13.6	575.5	0.4	2129.3	5.6	139032.2
2010	678374.5	73.9	236134.7	25.7	70.9	0.0	3336.5	0.4	717916.5
2011 39.4	775992.5	77.2	265798.3	22.7	82.1	—	3666.6	0.3	1045539.4

Source: Handbook of Statistics on the Indian Economy, RBI, 2010-11.

It is notable that the LIC's investment in PSUs and PSBs has been higher than the stipulated 10 per cent ceiling (table 27.6). The IRDA is worried about this trend as it may lead to a risk of concentration. Nearly 26 per cent of the LIC's equity investment is in banks, while nearly 39 per cent of its equity exposure is in stocks of PSUs.[9] The IRDA is also concerned that returns from these stocks were not great, particularly in the year 2011-12.[10] In the current financial year (2011-12), though the Corporation raised its stakes in most of these firms, the market value of the stocks have declined owing to the volatile equity market conditions.

TABLE 27.6: LIC's Top 10 Investments in PSUs (December, 2011)

	Value (₹ crore)	Stake
Corporation Bank	1,722.34	24.81
MTNL	390.47	18.81
PTC India	270.72	15.92
Orissa Minerals	352.71	15.42
Shipping Corporation of India	457.10	14.13
State Bank of India	18,236.93	12.76
Oriental Bank	1,022.41	12.09
HPCL	1,233.81	11.58
GNFC	149.18	10.92
Syndicate Bank	640.58	10.27
Others	54,349.51	

Source: Business Standard, March 6, 2012.

Although the LIC has, of late, been allowed to increase its exposure by more than 10 per cent in corporate entities, the caveat is that the insurance behemoth would have to prune its book in illiquid stocks and unlisted investments, which constituted around ₹ 5,000 crore or 2 per cent of its total equity investment corpus. LIC's total investment corpus stood at nearly ₹ 11 lakh crore as on March 31. 2011, of which 20 per cent or ₹ 2.2 lakh crore was in equity shares. During 2010-11, the LIC invested ₹ 1.96 lakh crore, of which ₹ 43,000 crore was invested in equities. The equity investment portfolio of the insurer includes investments in more than 400 unlisted firms. The finance ministry is of the opinion that the LIC's exposure in these companies (unlisted and illiquid stocks) is more than desirable and will have to be brought down to comfortable levels.[11]

E. DIVERSIFIED ACTIVITIES OF LIC

In recent years, the LIC has diversified its activities in housing finance and mutual fund and set up wholly owned subsidiaries to handle these activities.

(a) LIC Housing Finance Limited (LICHFL)

The LICHFL — wholly owned subsidiary of the LIC sanctioned loan of ₹ 51,090 crore up to March 31, 2011 to state governments for housing schemes, Apex cooperative Housing Boards and National Housing Bank. The sanctioned loan was more than two and half fold of what was sanctioned up to March-end 2008 (₹ 21,936 crores)

◆ LICHFL Care Houses Ltd.

LICHFL Care Houses Ltd. — a wholly owned subsidiary of LIC Housing Ltd. — was established in 2006 to fulfil a great corporate social responsibility in securing the retired life of senior citizens in a homely way of setting up senior citizens retirement villages.

With the pilot project at Bangalore completed, construction of the second at Bhubaneshwar in full swing, and half a dozen on the anvil, this organisation is catering to the needs of the seniors with a competitive edge.

(b) LIC Mutual Fund

The LIC entered into mutual fund business in June 1989 with a view to attracting savings particularly of middle class people in rural and semi-urban areas by providing easy accessibility of the investment media. The Corporation set up LIC Mutual Fund AMC Ltd. to manage, mutual fund business. The LIC Mutual Fund entered into joint venture with Nomure Asset Management Strategic Investments Private Ltd. on January 18, 2011 and thus becoming LIC Nomure Mutual Fund with its investment manager, renamed as LIC Nomura Mutual fund Asset Management and Trustee as LIC Nomure Fund Trustee Company Pvt. Ltd. wherein Nomura acquired 35 per cent stake.

Since inception, 100 schemes have been launched and continuous sale and repurchase is available under 26 ongoing schemes. During the year 2010-11, the AMC has mobilised a substantial sum of ₹ 4,67,187.72 crore from all live schemes.

LIC Nomura Mutual Fund stood at number 14 among 41 mutual funds industry as on March 31, 2011 on AAUM basis.

(c) LIC Pension Fund Ltd.

LIC Pension Fund Ltd. has been sponsored by the LIC with a specific purpose of managing pension funds under new pension system regulated by Pension Fund Regulatory and Development Authority (PERDA) for the employees of Central Government who have joined services w.e.f. January 1, 2004. for state government employees, this scheme is applicable as per above as and when it is adopted by the respective state governments.

LIC Pension Fund Ltd. is a fund management company which manages 3 schemes of new pension system. *i.e.*, Central Government scheme w.e.f 02-04-2008, state government scheme w.e.f. 25-06-2009 and NPS Life (Government Pattern). Since 4-10-2010, the authorised capital of the company in ₹ 25 crore and paid-up capital ₹ 15 crore. LIC Pension Fund Ltd. is the first company of its kind in India to manage pension funds under New Pension system.

This company started its operations with allocation of 5% Central Government New Pension system fund in 2008-09 which increased to 29% in 2009-10. During 2010-11, the company emerged as number one fund manager by receiving 35% of New Pension system fund of Central Government employees. State governments also followed the same pattern of allocation.

During the financial year 2010-11, LIC Pension Fund Ltd. received an amount of ₹ 1,044.60 crore under 3 schemes. The total assets under management was ₹ 1,878.93 crore as on March 31, 2011.

(d) LIC Cards Services Ltd.

LIC Cards Services Ltd. — a wholly owned company of the LIC was incorporated on November 11, 2008 with the objective of providing access to LIC Card Customers, the payment products through strategic alliance/s. During 2010-11, the company distributed gold and silver cards in tie up with Corporation Bank and distributed 11,813 credit cards.

With a view to extending the product line and further improving the quality of card issuance, the company entered into another tie-up with Axis Bank. It has planned to distribute more than one lakh cards in the current financial year (2011-12)

F. LIBERALIZATION AND LIC

Until recently, the life insurance market in India remained underdeveloped with the LIC having monopolised the market. Its penetration was 19 per cent of the insurable population. The LIC sold insurance as a tax instrument, not as a product giving protection. Most customers were underinsured with no flexibility or transparency in the products. With the entry of the private insurers, the LIC lost its monopoly position.

Nevertheless, LIC continues to occupy predominant position the life insurance market. However, its market share has fallen from 91% to almost 73% because of emergence of private insurance players who have forayed into the market aggressively. The entry of private insurers into the insurance industry has seen a veritable explosion of products that offer customers a much richer menu of options. They have infused a new flavour into what was perceived as a sober industry and has resulted in the market leader LIC adopting a more market-friendly approach in its bid to retain its premier position. The action is mainly on the products front.

Private insurance players have established their image as those known for innovative products, smart marketing and aggressive distribution. Investing public are increasingly turning to these insurers and snapping up the new innovative products on offer. They are coining money in new niches launched by them. Although LIC still dominates endowments and money back policies, private insurers have already wrested over 33 per cent of the market in annuity or pension products. In the popular unit-linked insurance schemes they have a virtual monopoly with over 90% of the customers.

Nevertheless, the LIC is no stranger to ULIPs, it was only in 2003-04 that it began focussing sharply on such plans. By March 31, 2008, these policies accounted for 85 per cent of its total premium income, as against 42 per cent two years earlier. The LIC continues to ride on ULIPs.[12]

Buoyed by their quicker than expected success, nearly all private insurers are fast forwarding the second phase of their expansion plans. The impact of liberalization and conquest aggressive foray of private sector life insurers with their new and innovative products and customer friendly approach has had telling effect upon the LIC whose proportion in financial year decreased to 13.5 per cent in 2005-06 from 15.1 per cent in 2004-05.

The aggressive stance of private insurers has forced the public sector behemoth LIC to rejuvenate itself to fight back to woo new customers and even it has recently run a catchy advertising campaign featuring a customer saying he had bought an LIC when he actually meant that he had bought an insurance policy. The Corporation was trying to convey, in a not too subtle fashion, that 'LIC' was a byword for insurance in the 'Customers' mind.

Because of aggressive marketing strategies and launching of slew of innovative products the LIC has transformed itself from annual growth rates of 16-17 per cent in 2004-05 to 34 per cent the following year and it has closed 2006-07 with a 9 per cent growth and thus managed to arrest the steady decline in its market share.

In its endeavour to improve its market share, the LIC has, of late, decided to change its focus from geographies to modern distribution channels and banks work of a pan-India basis and give channel-specific relationship. Given that insurance is not as transaction-heavy as a bank, the Corporation would rely more on web-based solutions down the line, so that people are encouraged to these channels.[13]

Furthermore, the LIC, as noted earlier, decided to change the product mix in favour of conventional products, which offer or regular flow of premium. Thus at present, 60 per cent of the products are traditional in nature. This conscious decision has been taken in view of the recent volatile market conditions affecting sale of ULIP.

It is important to not that the LIC's investment policy has, of late, been directly influenced by the Government to reach its disinvestment target and for that matter, rescue issues of public sector undertakings in case the public response was lukewarm. For instance, LIC and a couple of banks had to rescue the Hindustan Copper disinvestment which attracted poor bids till the last 15 minutes before the sale closed. In March, 2012, when the ONGC's disinvestment floundered, LIC came out to bail it out by contributing ₹ 11,500 crore of the total of ₹ 12,767 crore raised from the ONGC share sale.

On the same day when the Government announced a relaxation in single company investment norms, LIC was involved in yet another bailout, that of Air India. The company was investing ₹ 3,000 crore alongwith the Employees Provident Fund Organization (EPFO) in Air India's bond issue. How can LIC or for that matter the EPFO justify investing such a large sum in a troubled airline with a doubtful future?

G. CONCLUSIONS AND SUGGESTIONS

The LIC has made remarkable progress in the field of mobilisation of resources and their channelization. It has built up a big reservoir being used for financing socio-economic schemes of national importance and needs of public and private sector undertakings.

Although the LIC has played an important role in garnering burgeoning amount of savings from the people, even then there is ample scope for tapping savings from vast untapped section of the society. Life insurance penetration in India is only 6 per cent of GDP and only 20-25 per cent of the over 200 million potentially insurable population is covered.

The LIC has, therefore, a long way ahead to penetrate the untapped market. It has to focus more on pension and annuity schemes – the preferred products of the customers and bring in innovative features in these schemes from time to time so as to attract new customers and retain the existing ones. The Corporation should also provide flexibility to its customers to switch between the various investment options to maximize returns round the years.

So as to combat competitive challenges from private players, the LIC should take mileage of its huge customer base and country wide distribution network by providing customers better service qualities. The Corporation needs to take initiatives aggressively to generate awareness amongst its customers about its new product offering or assistance. Greater focus on training and development of different levels of its staff is required so as to develop their skills to cope with the new developments.

As regards deployment of investible funds, major portion of the Corporation's fund is invested in public sector. There has also been greater concentration of the Corporation's equity investment in PSUs and PSBs, causing great concern to IRDA and the Government. The equity investment portfolio of the LIC comprises of unlisted and illiquid stocks of firms which is much higher than the desirable level. As such, the Corporation's investment policy needs to be revised to minimise its investment in unlisted and illiquid stocks and to include equities of robust companies.

In recent years, the LIC has diversified its business to embrace mutual fund and housing finance activities and set up wholly owned subsidiaries to handle these activities.

Recent moves of the Government in using the LIC to reach its disinvestment target is causing great strains to the Corporation's profitability particularly when the LIC is asked to buy shares of PSUs at private higher than the market price. The LIC is supposed to take an independent call on investing at the disinvestment programme.

KEY TERMS

- Consumer-centric
- Conventional Products
- IRDA
- LIC Card Services Ltd.
- LIC HFL
- Life Fund
- LICHFL Care Homes Ltd.
- LIC Pension Fund
- Pension Fund regulatory and Development Authority.

DISCUSSION QUESTIONS

1. What triggered the formation of the LIC?
2. Discuss broad features of strategies of the LIC. How far has new economic policy impacted the strategies of the LIC?
3. Discuss salient features of investment policy of the LIC.
4. Critically assess the pattern of deployment of funds by the LIC.
5. In what respects has the sectoral distribution of investment by the LIC increased its exposure in recent years?
6. How far has entry of private life insurers affected the market position of the LIC?
7. What strategic initiatives have the LIC taken in recent years to improve its competitive position?

REFERENCES

1. Annual Report, LIC, 2004-05.
2. Annual Report, LIC, 2001-02.
3. Business Today, September 28, 2008.
4. Times Business, March 5, 2012.
5. Business Standard, September 21, 2011.
6. Annual Report, LIC, 2001-02.
7. Annual Report, LIC, 2011-12.
8. Business Standard, October 14, 2011.
9. Business Standard, March 6, 2012.
10. *Ibid*.
11. Business Standard, September 28, 2011.
12. Business Standard, March 8, 2011.
13. Business Standard, March 9, 2010.

* * *

Operational Policies and Practices of Mutual Funds

Chapter 28

Learning Objectives:

The present chapter aims at:

- Familiarising with concept, types and significance of mutual funds.
- Providing a succinct view of mutual funds in India and abroad.
- Evaluating policy guidelines for mutual funds in India.
- Assessing performance of mutual funds in India and suggesting for making them effective institutional agencies in the country.

Chapter Outline:

- Concept of mutual funds.
- Types of mutual funds.
- Significance of mutual funds.
- Evolution and growth of mutual funds abroad.
- Evolution and growth of mutual funds in India.
- Organizational structure of mutual funds in India.
- Policy guidelines for mutual funds in India — A critique.
- Policies and strategies of mutual funds in India.
- Operations of mutual funds in India — A synoptic view.
- Suggestions to make Indian mutual funds more effective.
- Conclusions.

A. CONCEPT OF MUTUAL FUNDS

Mutual fund concept, which has been in vogue in the Western world since long, is gaining popularity in developing countries including India as an institutional device to bridge the gap between supply and demand of capital in the market. An understanding of the concept of the mutual fund and its significance in economic development and state of mutual fund in India is, therefore, inescapable.

Mutual fund is an American concept and the terms, 'Investment Trust', 'Investment company', 'Mutual fund', 'Money Fund' etc., are used interchangeably in American literature. Mutual funds are corporations which accept dollars to buy stocks, long-term bonds, short-term debt instruments issued by business or government units. These corporations pool funds and thus, reduce risk by diversification.[1] The term 'mutual' signifies that all gains or losses resulting from the investment accrue to all the investors in proportion to their subscription. Mutual fund is, thus, a concept of mutual help of the subscribers for portfolio investment and management of these investments by experts in the field.

According to Hirch, a mutual fund is a professionally managed investment company that combines the money of many people whose goals are similar and invest this money in a wide variety of securities.[2]

As per the UK Investment Trust and Companies, a mutual fund is a vehicle that enables a number of investors to pool their money and have it jointly managed by a professional money managers.[3]

Investment company institute, USA defines the term mutual fund as a type of investment company that gathers assets from investors and collectively invests those assets in stock, bonds or money market instruments.[4]

Securities and Exchange Board of India (Mutual Fund) Regulations, 1996 defines mutual fund as a fund established in the form of a trust to raise monies through the sale of units to the public or a section of the public under one or more schemes for investing in securities including money market instruments.

Mutual fund generally refers to open-end investment trusts whose distinctive feature is regular sale and purchase of securities. Further, mutual funds must redeem their shares at the funds current net asset value at the time the shareholders request redemption.

In sum, mutual fund is a form of collective investment brought in by a large group of investors for the mutual benefit of savers as well as investors. Each fund is divided into equal portions or units. Anyone investing in the fund is allocated units in proportion to the size of one's investment. The price of these units is governed principally by value of the underlying investment held by the fund. The flow chart, as brought out in Chart 28.1, presents the working of mutual funds.

The above chart throws lurid light on rationale of mutual funds. They receive money from many investors, pool them and then purchase securities. The individual investors receive the benefits of professional management and diversified portfolio at relatively low cost with much convenience and flexibility.

B. TYPES OF MUTUAL FUNDS

So as to cater to the varying needs and preferences of large number of savers across the country and abroad, many types of mutual funds have come into existence. Choice of a fund by a saver would depend on what he desires his money to earn for him and how much risk he is willing to assume. Thus, mutual funds can be classified into the following three major groups:

Chart 28.1

Mutual Fund operation Flow Chart

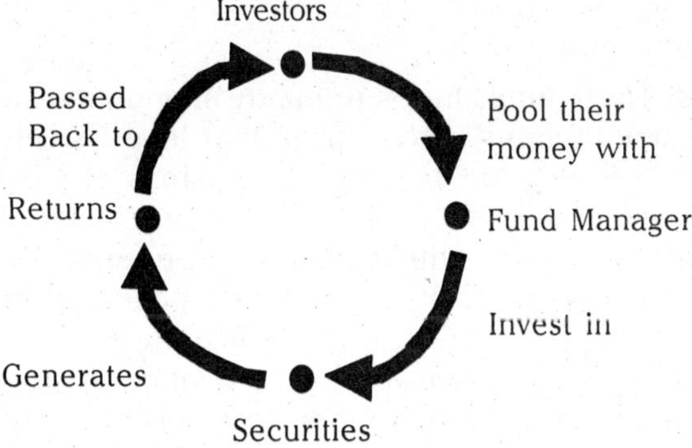

(*i*) Functional classification

(*ii*) Portfolio classification

(*iii*) Geographical classification.

(i) Functional Classification

Functional classification, based on basic characteristics of the mutual fund schemes opened for public subscription, can be grouped into:

- Open-ended funds
- Close-ended funds
- Interval funds.
- **Open-ended** funds continuously offer new shares for sale and always stand ready to buy securities at any time. The capitalization of the funds is constantly changing as investors buy and sell their shares directly with the fund. US-64, CanClgr and Franklin Blue Chip are examples of such funds.
- **Open-ended Dynamic bond funds:** In view of uncertainty of interest rates, a number of fund houses (IDBI Mutual Fund, Pramerica MF Union KBC, Daiwa MF and Principal MF) have, of late, launched open-ended dynamic bond funds. Dynamic bond funds are able to take advantage of rate cuts or rises by altering their portfolio. But here lies the danger as well. Sometimes, fund managers can get their churning right or it can go haywire as well. So returns can widely fluctuate. The trick in these funds lies in being made to predict the rate fluctuations correctly and change the portfolio. When the interest rate is rising, bond prices fall and the fund manager should be able to decrease the duration of the bond; short-term bonds face a lower impact. In contrast, when the interest rate is falling, they should be able to increase the duration of the bond.
- **Closed-ended** mutual funds are open for subscription only once and can be redeemed only after a fixed investment period. These funds have a fixed number of shares that can be owned by the investing public. Morgan Stanley Growth fund, Canpep 95, UTI Master Equity 98, Pru ICICI premier, UTI/UGS 2,000 and UTI/UGS 5,000 are some examples of such funds.
- **Interval funds** are the variations of the above stated two concepts. Thus, some funds are close-ended for the first couple of years and become open-ended after some time- some funds allow fresh subscriptions and redemptions as fixed intervals every year in order to reduce the hassles of daily entry and exist, yet providing reasonable liquidity.

(ii) Portfolio Classification

Mutual funds can be categorized according to the type of instruments in which the funds have been invested. As such, different funds are designed to meet the diverse notions of savers and generally designated as Stock funds, Bond funds, Balanced funds, Money market /liquid funds and other funds.

- **Stock Funds:** These funds invest primarily in common stocks. There is a broad range of common stock funds — from those that invest solely in the new, unestablished companies. There may be several sub-divisions of stock funds. Thus, *Growth and Income funds* place relatively equal weight on capital growth and dividend income and accordingly invest in equity stock and preference shares. *Growth funds* invest their funds in common stocks primarily for capital growth purpose. They meet the investors' need for appreciation, high risk-bearing capacity and ability to defer liquidity. As such, the investments by growth-oriented funds are predominantly made in equities. *Income funds* aim at ensuring to their investors high current income; growth in the value of the portfolio is of small importance. Such funds employ their funds in high yielding common stock. There are two basic groups within the income funds: those that focus on constant income possible even with the use of leverage. Naturally, the greater the anticipated return of any investment, the higher the potential risk of the investment.
- **Bond Funds:** Bond funds obviously employ their funds in bonds so as to ensure regular and fixed income to their investors. In the U.S.A., it is common to have two types of bond funds, one emphasising high-yielding but risky bonds and the other low-yielding but high grade bonds.
- **Balanced Funds:** Balanced funds combine bonds and/or preferred stocks with the ownership of common stock, usually at some pre-determined percentage relationship. Several balanced funds keep one-half of the portfolio in common stocks and one-half in bonds and preferred stocks. Balanced portfolios are more conservative than common stock funds and they generally do not have significant price movement either up or down. The main purpose of balanced funds is to earn an adequate return in the form of interest and dividends from the fixed portion of the portfolio, while at the same time gaining a modest growth in the common stock portion. Balanced fund are most suited for the investors who have an appetite for some risk, but are wary of taking to 100 per cent equity route through an equity fund.
- **Money Market/Liquid Funds:** These funds invest in highly liquid money market instruments such as Treasury Bills (issued by the Government), certificates of deposits (issued by banks) and commercial papers (issued by companies). Hall marks of such funds are safety and high liquidity. Pru ICICI liquid funds, Birla Cash plus and Templeton India Liquid fund are some examples of liquid funds.
- **Other Schemes**

With in each of the above categories, there can be further variants of the funds. For instance, debt funds may be diversified debt funds, focused debit funds and high yield debt funds. Likewise, equity funds may be diversified funds, sector funds, index funds and equity linked savings schemes.

Diversified Funds have investment portfolios spread across industries and companies. Choice of stock is the discretion of the fund managers. Can equity diversified fund of Canara Bank is the example of such funds. HDFC Top 200 fund is another diversified equity funds.

Sector Funds deploy funds in stocks of a particular business sector or industry, like information technology (IT), fast moving consumer goods (FMCG) or pharma. The degree of diversification of risk is very limited in this type of fund, making it extremely risky. Of course, the potential earnings can be high if the sector does very well. Franklin pharma, Franklin FMCG, Franklin Infotech, Kotak Tech, Tata Life Science and Tech, UTI Petro and UTI Pharma and Health-care are some examples of this type of fund.

Index Funds: Index funds are equity funds that replicate a particular equity index by investing in stocks that the index tracks. As each stock has different weightage in an index, the portfolio of an index fund is allocated in a way to mirror that of the index. For example, if Reliance industries has a weightage of 10 per cent in an index, a fund based on the index would also allocate 10 per cent of its portfolio to the stock. Investing in index funds has the advantages of no risk for fund management, lesser portfolio churning, low expense ratio and greater marketability.

(iii) Geographical Classification

Mutual funds can also be grouped according to geographical boundaries of their operations, as domestic mutual funds, off - shore funds and overseas funds.

Domestic Funds are open for mobilizing savings of the nationals within the country. These funds may be of various kinds, as outlined above under the portfolio and functional groups.

Off-shore Funds represent mutual funds with investments source abroad. Thus, subscription to these funds is mobilized from international financial markets for its investment in the economies and capital market instruments of specific country (ies). These funds are cross border investments facilitating capital movement of investible surpluses from cash rich countries to high growth or potentially high growth economies of the world. Kotak Global India Fund, SBI's Magnum Global and Global opportunity fund are few examples of overseas funds.

Indian mutual funds have been permitted to invest in foreign debt securities in countries with fully convertible currencies. In the recent past, mutual funds have also been permitted to invest in equity shares of listed overseas companies having shareholding of as least 10 per cent in an Indian company listed on a recognized stock exchange in India.[5]

Thus, a host of mutual funds have come into existence to garner savings from the savers for investment outside the country. Such kind of mutual funds are called **'Overseas' funds.** There are three types of overseas funds, *viz.*, global funds, international funds and country funds. While global funds invest in the domestic funds as well as foreign stocks and bonds, international funds invest strictly in foreign countries. Country funds invest in the stocks and bonds of a particular country or region.

The basic idea underlying formation of overseas mutual funds is to exploit the bright investment opportunities abroad and thereby augment the fund's overall rate of return.

C. SIGNIFICANCE OF MUTUAL FUNDS

Mutual funds are financial intermediaries concerned with mobilising savings of those who have surplus income and channelisation of these savings in those avenues where there is demand of funds. These institutions employ their resources in such a manner as to afford for their investors the combined benefits of low risk, steady return, high liquidity and capital appreciation through diversification and expert management.

Savers of moderate means in the underdeveloped regions are generally reluctant to invest in corporate securities because of their lack of adequate knowledge about complicated investment affairs. Moreover, their resources being small, they can at best hold securities of one or two or just a few industrial concerns only and as such, the fate of their savings and prospects of earnings therefrom are tied to the fate of such unit or units. Investment in securities of mutual funds takes care of both these problems, for such investment, in effect, represents a part of the funds' entire portfolio diversified in terms of securities, units, industries and geographical regions. These institutions employ expert investment analysts and thus professional knowledge and expertise go into the selection and supervision of their investment portfolio. Diversification and expert investment knowledge ensure steady and regular earnings to the fund and a share in the general prosperity. Accordingly, investors in the shares of mutual funds are assured of low risk, steady return, liquidity and capital appreciation. By taking upon themselves the problems which confront the small savers in investing their savings and dealing with them effectively, mutual funds help mobilise savings of the people and promote thrift.

Mutual funds also provide benefits of flexibility in as much as investors can systematically invest or withdraw funds, or switch to other schemes according to their needs, through features provided under their different schemes, such as regular investment, withdrawal plans and dividend reinvestment options.

Tax benefits to investors in certain schemes constitute an added attraction for mutual funds. Dividends paid by mutual funds to unit holders are taxed only at the time of distribution of dividends. These dividends after this deduction are tax-free in the hands of investors. On the contrary, investment in bonds or other deposits that earn interest (over and above ₹ 12,000 that is eligible for exemption under Section 80L) is taxed at 30 per cent.

Savings pooled by mutual funds are invested largely in industrial securities. They usually finance long-term business requirements largely by way of direct subscription to share capital of industrial enterprise. Mutual funds, while themselves raising resources from a large number of small savers, make funds available to industrial concerns in relatively bigger lots and thus reduce their burden and botheration involved in raising finance directly from individual savers.

Thus, by playing the role of financial intermediation mutual funds provide a convenient and effective link between savings and investment. Well managed mutual funds would be mutually beneficial arrangement. While, on the one hand, they help the investing community by offering share of corporate growth, on the other they have a salutary impact on the stock markets. By blending caution with aggression and analysis with intuition, the funds can successfully convert market opportunities into lucrative returns for the investors.

Role of the mutual funds is not limited to domestic sphere only. In addition to attracting domestic savings, these funds can offer their units abroad and attract foreign capital just as UTI has recently done by offering India Fund, India Growth Fund schemes. Similarly, they may serve as useful institutions for securing profitable investment avenues abroad for domestic savings. Investment in foreign industrial securities requires fairly detailed knowledge of the state of the foreign economy in general and of industries in particular as also of fiscal position of industrial enterprises and their future prospects. As a result, despite attractive investment prospects abroad for surplus domestic savings, individual investors would find it an extremely difficult task to make foreign investment on their own. Mutual funds have, as in the case of domestic investment, stepped in to solve these problems for the savers.

D. EVOLUTION AND GROWTH OF MUTUAL FUNDS ABROAD

The USA is a pace setter in the development of mutual funds in terms of growth of number of household investors, funds and types of schemes.

The origin of mutual funds dates back to 1822 when - societe General De Belgique was established in Belgium, employing the concept of risk sharing. The birth of modern fund industry, however, can be traced back to 1968 when the foreign and colonial investment trust (F & CIT) was formed in London. It introduced the concept of close-ended funds for the first time. It is still one of the most successful investment trusts in the U.K. Most of the early British investment companies or trusts resembled today's close-ended funds by issuing a fixed number of shares to groups of investors whose pooled assets were invested in various companies. The Scottish American Investment Trust, constituted in February, 1873 by Fund Pioneer, Robert Fleming was significant in as much as it invested in the economic potential of the US, chiefly through American railroad bonds. Many other trusts that followed this Trust not only targeted investment in America but also led to the introduction of the investment fund concept on the US shares in the late 1900s and early 1990s.

The formation of the Massachusetts Investor's Trust in the USA in 1924 paved the way for modern day open-ended funds. These funds introduced important innovations to the investment company concept by establishing a simplified capital structure, continuous offering of shares, the ability to redeem them and a set of clear investment restriction and policies.

By 1929, a handful of mutual funds were formed, managing funds to the tune of $ 140 million. The stock market crash of 1929 followed by the Great Depression gave a big jolt to the growth of mutual fund industry until a succession of landmark securities laws, beginning with the Securities Act of 1933 and concluding with the Investment Company Act of 1940, re-engendered investor's confidence in funds, resulting into relatively steady growth in industry asset from $ 448 million in 1940 to $ 7.4 trillion by year-end 2003.[6]

It is interesting to note that worldwide individual investors have over the years shown rising interest in the securities market. There has been marked change in their investment behaviour, as reflected by shift in their preference from bank deposits to acquire financial instruments, to obtain higher returns and capital gains. This phenomenon gave fillip to the growth of mutual fund industry.

Although a beginning was made in 1960, when the concept of mutual fund was familiarized in most of the developed nations, it made tremendous growth only in 1980s. During 1980s mutual funds had recorded big surge in many developed countries. For instance, mutual funds in Italy grew at 200 per cent, Japan 600 per cent, the UK 350 and Germany 330 per cent.

There has been tremendous growth of mutual fund industry in the USA, with number of various kinds of mutual funds having soared from 1,243 in 1984 to 8034 in February 2005. Net assets of mutual funds in the USA stand at, $124.5 billion as on February, 2005.[7] One of the basic reasons for attraction of the US citizens to mutual funds is stringent regulatory framework administered by Securities and Exchange Commission (SEC) which safeguards investors' interests through strict regulation of the mutual fund industry to conform to the desirable norms offering stability and liquidity of the investment, creditability of mutual fund companies, assuring fair play in disbursement of income to the investors in the form of return and growth.

A peep into number of mutual funds in the world reveals that there were 55,528 mutual funds in operation at the end of 2004. USA with 14,067 mutual funds topped the list of the countries followed distantly by France (7,908), Luxemburg (6,855), Republic of Korea (6,636), Spain (2,599), Japan (2,552), Ireland (2,088), U.K. (1,710), Belgium (1,281), Italy (1,142) and Germany (1,041).[8]

Globally, the total net assets of mutual funds as at the end of 2004 amounted to $ 16,152,429 millions. The US with $ 16,152,429 millions has been at the top of the world in terms of assets generated followed distantly by Luxemburg ($13,96,131 million), France ($1,370,954 millions), Italy ($5,11,733 millions), U.K. ($492,726 millions) and Japan ($3,99,462 millions).[9]

Thus, US mutual fund industry is the largest in the world, accounting for half of the $16.2 trillion total net assets.

E. EVOLUTION AND GROWTH OF MUTUAL FUNDS IN INDIA

Historical evolution and growth of mutual funds in India can be divided into four distinct phases, viz.,

Phase I: 1964-1987
Phase II: 1987-1993
Phase III: 1993-2003
Phase IV: 2003 onwards

Phase I: 1964-1987

The Shroff Committee, in its report submitted in 1954, recommended for the establishment of unit trusts both in public and private sectors as they were most suited to India, where in order to increase capital available for industries, small savings could be drawn into the investment market. However, the Government did not take cognizance of this recommendation.

In 1963 when the whole stock market was in a state of despondency, and uncertainty engulfed the entire economy, joint stock companies found it difficult to raise capital from the market owing to the diffidence of investors, with the result that industrial development of the country came to grinding halt. The Government, therefore undertook aggressive programmes to mobilise the long-term savings of the people and direct them into productive channels with a view to fostering industrial growth in the country. The emergence of the Unit Trust of India in 1964 was part of these efforts. The Trust was established in 1964 under the creation of the Unit Trust Act, 1963 to afford the small savers as a means of acquiring a share in the widening prosperity based on a steady industrial growth of the country through facilities for investment combining the benefits of wide diversification, a reasonable return and expertise of management.

The Trust commenced its operations from July 1, 1964. The first decade of UTI operations (1964-74) was the formative stage. It introduced unit-linked insurance plan (ULIP) in 1971. The period 1974-84 witnessed a state of consolidation and expansion of the UTI. During the period 1984-87 the Trust launched several new schemes such as Children's Gift Growth Fund (1986) and Master Share (1987). The first Indian offshore was brought out. The total investible funds of the UTI which amounted to ₹ 24.67 crore as the end of June 1965, surged to ₹ 4,563-68 crore by the end of June 1987.[10]

Phase II: 1987-1998

The UTI enjoyed monopoly position till 1987 when Banking Regulation Act was amended to permit commercial banks to launch mutual funds in the country. Financial corporations were also permitted to engage in mutual fund business. This infused some degree of competition in the industry.

The SBI was the first bank to launch a mutual fund called SBI Mutual Fund in July 1987. This was followed by Canbank Mutual fund (December, 1987), Punjab National Bank Mutual Fund (August, 1989), Indian Bank Mutual Fund (November, 1989), Bank of India (June, 1990), Bank of Baroda Mutual Fund (October, 1992).

LIC set up its mutual fund in June 1989 with a view to providing easy accessibility of the investment media including the stock market in the country to one and all especially the small investors in rural and semi-urban areas. The GIC entered in the field of mutual fund business when it brought out two schemes *viz.*, GIC safe 1991 and GIC Rise 1995.

The IDBI floated an offshore mutual fund in 1991. The Fund is being managed by a subsidiary set up in the joint sector, *viz.*, 'Fidelity International' - The World's largest privately managed investment company.

Thus, the mutual fund industry came to be ruled by 7 PSBs in addition to LIC, GIC and UTI. From 1987-1993, the mutual fund industry registered almost seven times expansion in terms of assets, rising from ₹ 6,700 crore (in 1987-88) to ₹ 47,000 crore (in 1992-93).[11]

Phase III: 1993-2003

Until 1992, the mutual funds were in public sector. So as to enhance degree of competitiveness and provide the investors with wider outlets for investment, Dave committee recommended that private sector should also be permitted to sponsor mutual funds through asset management companies. Accordingly, the Government permitted entry of private sector in mutual fund business. Mutual Fund Regulations came into being in 1993 and SEBI was empowered to regulate and control all mutual funds except UTI. For the first time in February 1993 SEBI allowed six private sector mutual funds, *viz.*, 20th Century Finance Corporation, Tata sons, Credit Capital Finance Corporation, ICICI, Cat financial services and Apple industries. Kothari group was also granted premium of floating mutual fund scheme in October, 1993. Morgan Stanley, Taurus Mutual Fund, JM, Shivram, CRB, Alliance and Birth Mutual Fund were also allowed to operate in mutual fund business. The total funds mobilized by all mutual funds reached ₹ 75,050 crore by March end, 1995. Interestingly, foreign fund management companies were also permitted to operate in India in association with Indian partners. The private sectors mutual funds brought sufficient dynamism in their operations through product innovations, investment management techniques and investor servicing technology.

An important development took place in 1996 when a comprehensive set of regulations *viz.*, SEBI (Mutual Fund) Regulations was introduced for unified governance of all mutual funds operating in India. Further, Union Government Budget 1999 provided a big fillip to the growth of the industry by exempting all mutual fund dividends from income tax in the hands of investors. This resulted in tremendous growth in assets of the mutual funds in just one year from over ₹ 68,000 crore in 1998-99 to ₹ 1,13,005 crore in 1999-2000.[12]

The number of mutual funds also increased during this period. There were several mergers and acquisitions. As at the end of January 2003, there had existed 33 mutual funds with total assets of ₹ 1,21,705 crore.[13]

Phase IV: 2003 onwards

A significant development took place in February 2003, when UTI was bifurcated into UTI-I and UTI-II. UTI-I is the specified undertaking of the UTI (SUVTI) with asset under management of ₹ 44,541 crore as at the end of January, 2003. It manages the assets of US-64 scheme and 25 assumed return schemes as also development reserve fund of the UTI. This specified undertaking is managed by an administrator and governed by the rules framed by the Government of India. It does not come under the purview of SEBI. UTI-II, known as UTI Mutual Fund Ltd., is sponsored by SBI, PNB, Bank of Baroda and LIC, each holding 25 per cent stake. The UTI-II comprises 36 net asset value schemes of UTI. The UTI mutual fund is managed by the Asset Management Company (AMC). The AMC is registered with SEBI and subject to Mutual Fund Regulations 1996. It had total assets of ₹ 19,847 crore as at the end of April, 2004. The basic objective of restructuring UTI was to protect interests of small investors.

There were in all 34 registered mutual funds in India with a corpus of ₹ 1,98,662 crore by the end of March, 2004. The number of registered mutual funds increased to 49 at the end of March, 2011 with a corpus of ₹ 5,92,250 crore. The AUM of the mutual fund industry has doubled over the last five years to around ₹ 6 lakh crore as of December, 2011.[14] With re-entry of Bank of India in mutual fund industry on May 28, 2012 by forging a joint venture with AXA Investment Managers, the number of mutual funds increased to 49 on May 28, 2012.

F. ORGANIZATIONAL STRUCTURE OF MUTUAL FUNDS IN INDIA

The SEBI, regulatory body of the mutual funds in India, has laid down a unique organizational structure for the mutual funds with inbuilt checks and balances, as brought out in Chart 28.2. It may be observed from the chart that the constituents of the Indian mutual funds are Sponsor, Trustees, Asset management company, Custodian and Registrars/Transfer agents.

Chart 28.2: Organization of a Mutual Fund

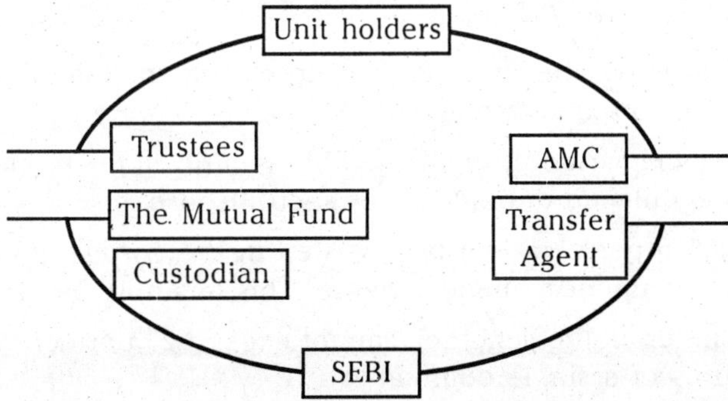

Mutual fund in India is constituted in the form of a public trust created under the Indian Trusts Act, 1882 as a trustee of any other mutual fund. Besides acting as the fund manager, AMC can engage in certain specified activities such as advisory services and financial consulting, subject to the conditions laid down by SEBI.

A custodian is an entity independent of the sponsors and is required to be registered with SEBI. The custodian is appointed by the Board of Trustees for safe keeping of physical securities or participating in any clearing system through approved depository companies on behalf of the mutual fund in case of dematerialized securities. Thus, deliveries of a fund's securities are given or received by a custodian or a depository participant at the instruction of the AMC.

Registrars/transfer agents handle sales and redemption-related activities of the fund. They also maintain records of the shareholders and remit the payment cheques to the investors. The AMC may choose to carry out this activity in - house and charge the scheme for the service at a competitive market rate or it can appoint a SEBI approved registrar and transfer agent.

The fund sponsor is one who establishes the trust, contributing to its initial capital and appoints a trustee to hold the assets of the trust for the benefit of the unit holders, who are the beneficiaries of the trust. The trust or fund, under the Indian Trusts Act, has no independent legal capacity itself, rather it is the trustee(s) who has (have) the legal capacity and therefore, all acts in relation to the trusts are taken on its behalf by the trustees. The trustees hold the unit-holders' money in a fiduciary capacity, *i.e.*, the money belongs to the unit-holders and is entrusted to the fund for the purpose of investment. Being public trusts, mutual funds can invite any number of investors as beneficial owners in their investment schemes.

The trustees do not directly manage the portfolio of the securities. For this purpose, the sponsors or trustees, if so authorized, appoint the AMC. The AMC so appointed is required to be approved by SEBI. Once approved, the AMC functions under the supervision of its own Board of Directors as also under the direction of the trustees and SEBI. The AMC of a mutual fund is required to have as least ₹ 10 crore at all times.

G. POLICY GUIDELINES FOR MUTUAL FUNDS IN INDIA — A CRITIQUE

Guidelines by the Government

The Government of India has, of late, come out with comprehensive guidelines governing the formation and operations of all mutual funds and the SEBI has been vested with wide ranging statutory powers to oversee the constitutions and working of mutual funds. These guidelines are:

1. All mutual funds shall be authorised for business by the SEBI and operated only by separate asset management companies.
2. Mutual funds can invest only in transferable securities either in the money market or in the capital market.
3. No mutual funds will be promoted to do option trading, short selling or carrying forward transaction in securities.
4. Mutual funds can invest only in transferable security in the money and capital markets or any privately placed debentures or securitised debts.
5. Not more than 5 per cent can be invested in the corpus of any company's shares and investments under a single scheme. This has now been raised to 10 per cent.
6. Investment under all the schemes cannot exceed 25 per cent of funds in the shares and debentures of a single company.
7. Investments in rated debt instruments of a single issuer has been limited to 15 per cent of the NAV of the schemes (upto 20% with prior approval of Board of Trustees and AMC). SEBI will grant registration to only those mutual funds which can conduct their business smoothly and efficiently. Parameters for deciding this will include a track record of sponsors, a minimum experience of 5 years in the relevant field of financial services, integrity in business transactions and financial business.

8. The minimum net worth of such an Asset Management Company (AMC) is stipulated to be ₹ 5 crores; of which the minimum contribution of the sponsor should be 40%.
9. The mutual funds should have a custodian, not associated in any way with the asset management company and registered with the Board.
10. The minimum amount to be raised with each close ended scheme should be ₹ 20 crores and for the open scheme ₹ 50 crores.
11. In case of low subscription, the entire amount has to be refunded within 6 weeks from the date of closure of the scheme, otherwise an interest @ 15% p.a. from the date of expiry of 6 weeks has to be paid.
12. Mutual funds will have to maintain books of accounts, expenses, and make appropriation of expenses among the individual schemes, fix limit of the expenses of the AMC that can be charged to the mutual funds, provide for depreciation and bad debts.
13. Mutual funds have to publish schemewise annual reports, furnish annual statements of accounts, furnish six monthly unaudited accounts, quarterly statements of movements and net asset value and quarterly portfolio statements to SEBI.
14. Mutual funds should ensure adequate disclosures to the investors. The SEBI also restricted mutual funds from making assurance or claims that could mislead the public.
15. In case of violations of the provisions of the SEBI Act, 1992 or the regulation, SEBI can withdraw authorisation to any AMC.
16. Mutual funds can make private placement to foreign institutional investors to the extent of 24% of their equity.
17. The SEBI issued a code of conduct restricting MFs from making assurance or claims that could mislead the public.
18. A mutual fund should not invest in any unlisted security issued by way of private placement of any associate/group companies of the sponsor or listed security of group companies of the sponsor in excess of 30 per cent of the net assets.
19. A mutual fund can borrow except to meet temporary liquidity needs for the purpose of repurchase, redemption of units or payment of interest or dividend to the unit holders. In any case, it cannot borrow more than 20 per cent of the net assets of the scheme for a period exceeding six months. It is profited from advancing any loans for any purpose. However, it can lend securities in accordance with the stock lending scheme of SEBI.
20. The funds of a scheme cannot in any manner be used for trading or in short selling or carry forward transactions. However, they are permitted to enter into derivative transactions in a recognized stock exchange for purposes of hedging and portfolio balancing in accordance with SEBI guidelines.
21. Mutual funds may enter into an underwriting agreement after obtaining a Certificate of Registration in terms of the SEBI (underwriters) Rules and Regulations, 1993, authorizing it to carry on activities as underwriters.
22. Every mutual fund must compute the NAV of a scheme as determined by dividing the net assets of the scheme by the number of outstanding units on the valuation date, carrying out valuation of its investment portfolio and publish the same in accordance with the valuation norms.

RBI's Major Policy Guidelines

1. Every mutual fund shall be constituted as a Trust under the Indian Trust Act and the sponsoring bank should appoint a Board of Trustees. The Board of Trustees should have at least two outside trustees. The overall superintendence, direction, control

and management of the affairs and business of the funds should vest in the Board of Trustees.

2. Mutual funds should have a full time Executive Trustee.
3. There must be a "Terms length" relationship between the sponsor bank and the Board of Trustees.
4. The sponsor bank's contribution to the corpus of the fund should be a minimum of ₹ 25 lakh or such higher amount as may be specified by the RBI.
5. In addition to the contribution to the corpus, the sponsor bank should contribute and maintain in each of the fund's schemes by way of its stake an amount equivalent to 1 per cent of the total amount outstanding. This stipulation will, however, not apply to special schemes wherein the sponsor bank cannot participate.
6. Mutual funds cannot undertake direct or indirect lending, underwriting, bills discounting and money market operations.
7. Bank sponsored mutual funds cannot invest in finance companies.
8. The investment objectives and policies of the mutual fund should be laid down in the trust deed and every scheme to be launched by the fund must be in accordance with such broad objectives and policies.
9. The subscription amounts collected by mutual funds are primarily intended to be channelised into the capital market instruments like government and other trustee securities, shares/debentures of public limited companies, bonds of public sector undertakings, etc.
10. The mutual funds should invariably take delivery of scripts purchased and, in case of scripts sold, give delivery thereof to the purchaser.
11. The mutual funds cannot make investments in any other unit trust, mutual fund of similar collective investment scheme. They should also not invest in the shares, etc., of investment companies/corporations.
12. Mutual funds shall not hold, under any one scheme, more than 5 per cent of issued share capital or debenture stock of any company. In case more than one scheme is operated by a fund, such holdings in respect of all its schemes put together should not exceed 15 per cent of the paid-up capital or debenture stock of a company.
13. The total amount invested by a fund from any of its schemes in the shares, debentures, etc., of any specific industry should not exceed 15 per cent of a scheme's fund.
14. The maximum spread between the purchase and selling prices of units/shares of any scheme should not be more than 5 per cent.
15. The total cost of managing any scheme under a fund including management fees and other administrative costs should be kept within 5 per cent of the total income of the scheme.
16. Mutual funds can invest in ADRs and GDPs of Indian companies, rated debt instruments and equity of overseas companies listed on a recognized stock exchange overseas. However, these companies should have a shareholding of at least 10 % in a listed Indian company. However, to enable funds to invest in a large number of stocks overseas, the requirement of a 10% reciprocal share holding in listed Indian companies by overseas companies has been done away with.

The RBI has, of late, raised the ceiling on mutual fund investments in the overseas market. The aggregate ceiling on overseas investments by funds has been increased to $2 billion from $1 billion in overseas exchange traded funds. However, this is subject to SEBI's permission.[15] This has been further raised to US $ 4 billion, and subsequently as a reformatory move to US $5 billion.[16]

SEBI's Major Regulatory Provisions

1. Mutual funds shall be authorized for business by the SEBI.
2. Mutual funds shall be sponsored by the registered companies with sound track, general reputation and fairness in all their business transactions.
3. Mutual funds shall be established in the form of trusts under Indians Trusts Act. The sponsoring institution will be free to work out the details regarding the Constitutions of the Trust.
4. The Trust shall be authorized to float one or several different schemes under which units shall be issued to the investors.
5. Mutual funds shall be operated by separately established Asset Management Companies (AMC) to be approved by the SEBI.
6. AMC cannot act as the Trustee of Unit Trusts.
7. AMC cannot undertake any other business activity than management of mutual funds and such other activities as financial services constantly, exchange of research and analysis on commercial basis as long as these are not in conflict with the management activity itself.
8. The mutual funds shall use the services of a custodian registered with the SEBI.
9. The custodian shall be totally delinked from the AMC.
10. Each authorized mutual funds shall be allowed to float different schemes as long as the AMC concerned meets the required capital adequacy criteria.
11. Each scheme floated by a mutual fund shall have prior registration with SEBI.
12. Mutual funds can start and operate both closed-end and open-end schemes.
13. For each closed-end scheme, the mutual fund shall be required to raise at least ₹ 20 crore and for each open-end scheme at least ₹ 50 crore.
14. Mutual funds cannot keep closed-end schemes open for subscription for more than 45 days. For open-end schemes, the first 45 days of the subscription period should be considered for determining the target figure or minimum size.
15. Mutual funds shall provide continuous liquidity. Closed-end scheme shall have to be listed on exchanges. For open-end schemes, mutual funds shall sell and repurchase, units at pre- determined prices based on net asset value.
16. Mutual funds are allowed to invest only in transferable securities either in the money market or in the capital market, including any privately-placed debentures or securitized debt. Privately placed debentures, securitized debt and other unquoted debt instruments holdings shall not exceed 10% in case of growth funds, and 40% in case of income funds.
17. Mutual funds shall not be allowed to provide term loans for any purpose.
18. No individual scheme of the mutual fund shall invest more than 5 per cent of its corpus in any-one company's shares.
19. No mutual fund under all its schemes shall own more than 5 per cent of any company's paid-up capital carrying voting rights.
20. No mutual fund under all its schemes taken together shall invest more than 10 per cent of its funds in the shares or debentures or other securities of a single company.
21. No mutual fund under all its schemes taken together shall invest more than 15 per cent of its funds in the shares or debentures of any specific industry.
22. No scheme shall invest in or lend to another scheme under the same AMC.
23. The AMC may charge the mutual fund with investment management and advisory services which should have been disclosed fully in the prospectus subject to the following ceiling:

(a) 1.25% of the weekly average net assets outstanding in the current year for the scheme concerned as long as the net assets do not exceed ₹ 100 crore, and

(b) 1% of the excess amount over ₹ 100 crore, where net assets so calculated exceed ₹ 100 crore, and

(c) All mutual funds must distribute a minimum of 90 per cent of their profits in any given year.

The SEBI has recently allowed the Mutual funds to invest 100% of funds raised in Money Market upto 6 months and thereafter 30% of funds for 6 months to one year and only 25% in Money Market and again 100% of funds in Money market, 6 months prior to repayment to investors.

24. Every scheme should have at least 20 investors and no single investor should hold more than 25 per cent of the fund's assets.

25. Every mutual fund will have to furnish to SEBI at least the following periodic reports, in addition to any other SEBI may ask for:

    (a) Copies of the duly audited annual statement of account including the balance sheet and the profit and loss account for the funds and for each scheme, once a year.

    (b) Six-monthly unaudited accounts as above.

    (c) A statement of movements in net assets for each of the schemes of the funds, every quarter.

    (d) A portfolio statement, including changes from the previous periods, for each scheme, every quarter.

26. All mutual funds are required to adopt a written code of ethics designed to deal with the potential conflicts of interest that may arise from transitions by the affiliated persons or companies.

27. Every mutual fund shall have to copy with a common advertising code laid down by the SEBI. The fund is expected to submit to the SEBI the texts of the marketing literature and advertisements issued to the investors.

    Mutual funds shall have to disclose in their marketing and publicity brochures for each scheme, the investment objectives, the method and periodicity of valuation of investment, the exact method and periodicity of sales and purchases and other details considered by to SEBI to be essential for investors.

28. SEBI can, after due investigation, impose penalties on mutual funds for violating the guidelines as may be necessary. However, for cases of penalties of suspension or deauthorisation of mutual fund entities, prior concurrence of the RBI and the government is necessary.

29. The SEBI scrapped entry load on investments in mutual funds w.e.f. August 1, 2009.

30. The SEBI issued in September, 2009, a code of conduct for intermediaries including distribution of mutual funds, emphasizing that clients' interests are to be protected and the intermediaries should highlight the risk factors of each scheme and avoid misinterpretation and exaggeration.

31. On August 10, 2011, the SEBI allowed Qualified Foreign Investors (QFI) to invest upto \$ 10 billion in equity and debt schemes of mutual funds in India. A QFI is a person resident in a country compliant with Financial action Task Force (FATF) standards and that is signatory to the international organisation of securities commission's Multilateral Memorandum of Understanding. QFIs should not be resident in India or registered with SEBI as a FII or sub-account. The ceiling of \$10 billion was subsequently raised to \$20 billiion.

    In order to shore up the inflow of foreign funds and thereby, stem the steady depreciation of the rupee against the dollar, the Government allowed on May 29, 2012 QFIs from six-member-countries of the Gulf Co-operation Council (GCC) to invest in the Indian capital market. Thus, a $1-billion window over and above the current $ 20-billion limit has been created for AFI investment in corporate bonds and mutual fund debt schemes.

32. In July, 2011, the SEBI allowed mutual funds to charge transaction cost upto ₹ 150 for a minimum investment of ₹ 10,000 to be paid to the distributors.
33. On January 28, 2012, the SEBI decided to exempt mutual funds (and insurance companies), which are broad-based investment vehicles representing the public at large, from regulations related to sale and lock-in of their pre-preferential shareholding in pre-preferential shareholding in issuer companies.

This relaxation has already proved boon to Indian corporates as they have been able to garner huge funds from the market so far.

The regulatory framework for mutual funds smacks of ineffective panning, clarity of thought and suffers from several shortcomings. There does not seem to be any justification for separate regulatory framework to govern the operations of the mutual funds the UTI Act with comprehensive guidelines already in existence. It would have been more logical to broaden the scope of the UTI Act to make it applicable to all the mutual funds. Some of the guidelines issued by the RBI and SEBI are contradictory. For instance, while the RBI prohibits bank sponsored mutual funds from investing in finance companies, SEBI has actually made reservations for mutual funds in public issues of finance companies. The existing rules and regulations are quite comprehensive to ensure greater transparency about the operations of mutual funds. However, there is some scope of effectively curbing the malpractices, particularly in the field of distribution of mutual fund products by regulating the activities of intermediaries. Further, some of the rules and regulations, *viz.*, restrictions on investment, requirements of underlying securities in the derivative market, individual investor's communication and recording of all secondary transactions have been identified as very stringent. These have had an adverse impact, to some extent, on the performance of mutual funds.

SEBI rules regarding late trading and rapid trading are either ineffective or nonexistent. Although SEBI has introduced a specific regulation against late trading since March, 2004, it has failed to check late trading. As a result, there is rampant late trading by mutual funds to the detriment of common investors. What is most disturbing to note is that there are still no regulations to deter rapid trading in mutual funds, even though the regulator is aware of how it can harm long-term investors. While late trading is nothing short of cooking the books, rapid trading is not a crime but need to be discouraged.

H. POLICIES AND STRATEGIES OF MUTUAL FUNDS IN INDIA

Mutual funds in India seem to have pursued policy of garnering their resources from corporate sector. This is more so in the case of private sector and joint sector funds that confine their operations in metropolitan and other big cities. To attract resources from corporate sector customized schemes are brought out frequently. In recent years, they are drifting towards retail investors so as to widen their customer base.

For mobilization of resources the industry's strategy is to employ agents and distributors, train and develop their skills so that they can educate the investors properly and offer them suitable products to meet their requirements. Rationalization of product distribution arrangements, continuous R & D for improving product handling and phased shift from scheme-oriented investor services to single window personalized client-oriented services are the hallmarks of Indian mutual funds' strategies.

The crux of investment policy of mutual funds is management of its portfolio assets, consisting primarily of industrial securities. Management, therefore, requires constant vigilance over the trends emerging in the financial markets. The broad aim of the investment strategy should, therefore, be to maximize income on the portfolios as a whole, given the conditions in the capital and stock markets.

In formulating investment strategy the management is guided mainly by considerations of the safety of funds, reasonable return and capital appreciation on the security instruments. Most of the funds have decided to build and maintain a balanced portfolio, comprising both variable dividend and fixed income-yielding securities so as to strike a proper balance between the two fundamental principles of the safety of the principal and return on capital. Marketability of the securities is an important consideration for the mutual funds in India so that investors may avail the benefits of capital appreciation and a reasonably high return on their investments.

Accordingly, strategy of majority of the mutual funds has been to invest major chunk of the funds of growth schemes in equities while bulk of investible funds of income schemes is deployed in fixed-yielding securities so as to be able to honour their commitment of paying the assured return to their investors.

In view of the carnage in the stock markets following the snowballing of global financial crisis during 2008-09, mutual funds decided to trim their exposure to equity and increase holding on to cash looking for the best opportunity (over 12 per cent of their corpus).[17]

In their endeavour to ensure security of capital and a reasonable return, mutual funds in India have adopted the principle of diversification as the basic tenet of its investment policy. Accordingly, they have decided to diffuse their investible resources over different type of securities of about 25 companies belonging to 10-11 industry groups. A ceiling in terms of proportion of the resources to be deployed in an individual company and industry is fixed, keeping in view the SEBI framework.

Within the overall guidelines laid down by the Trustees, managers have high level of freedom and flexibility to bring about change in the portfolio in consonance with the changing economic and business conditions.

In view of immense potentiality of infrastructural sector in the economic development of India and the concomitant government policy directives to financial institutions, public sector mutual funds have recently decided to invest in equity issues of infrastructural projects. It could subscribe to the 'start up' capital for core projects in power, telecom, ports and roads.

Of late, mutual funds have decided to tap investors' appetite for global markets with schemes aimed at investing in other countries which would also act as a hedge against fall in the domestic stock market.

I. PERFORMANCE OF MUTUAL FUNDS IN INDIA — A SYNOPTIC VIEW

Performance in Terms of Assets

Mutual fund industry in India witnessed continued growth after 2001.

TABLE 28.1: Assets under Management of Mutual Funds

(₹ in crore)

Year (end-March)	Amount
1998	97,228
1999	68,193
2000	1,07,946
2001	90,587
2002	1,00,594
2003	1,09,299
2004	1,39,616
2005	1,49,616
2006	2,31,862
2007	3,26,292

2008	5,05,152
2009	4,17,300
2010	6,13,979
2011	5,92,250
2012	6,64,792
2013	7,94,297

Source: SEBI.

During the period 2001-2013, the industry surged by over eight fold, touching an all time peak level of ₹ 7,94,297 crore as on March end, 2013. According to a survey by ASSOCHAM, the mutual fund sector would grow at compound annual rate of 13 per cent in next three years to become ₹ 9,50,000 crore industry.[18]

Major driving forces that have contributed to the surge in the industry's growth are:

- A buoyant domestic growth coupled with a booming stock market.
- A conductive regulatory regime as manifested in the increased efforts by the SEBI to improve the market surveillance and protect investors' interest.
- Increased focus on product and distribution innovation by the fund players.
- Launching of slew of customized fund schemes.
- Lesser outflow of cash.
- Large inflows into liquid funds due to record low call rates below 10% for all of the month of July, 2007.
- Mega size public offers leading to spurt in size of liquid funds flowing to MFs.

The increase in the size of Indian mutual fund industry as a percentage of GDP has been substantial. However, a global comparison using AUM figures from the Investment Company Institute (and from the SEBI for domestic data) and World Bank figures for GDP shows that India has plenty of scope for growth. India's mutual fund industry is 8 per cent of GDP as against Australia's 105 per cent, the US 77 per cent, France 50 per cent and Brazil 40 per cent of GDP.[19]

A notable feature of this growth has been the predominance of the private sector funds from less than one-half of the assets to over three-fourths during this period.

Reliance Mutual Fund maintains its top position as the country's largest fund house with AUM of ₹ 66,420 crore as on July end, 2007. ICICI Prudential remained at the second slot with total wealth of ₹ 48,688.55 crore. PSU major UTI MF holds the third rank with assets worth ₹ 42,547.60 crore as at July end, 2007.

Recent rise of the foreign investment cap for MFs by the RBI has given fillip to mutual funds to go global on a larger scale with schemes aimed at investing in other countries. While DSP Merrill Lynch and Kotak MF have launched their global funds in July, 2007, one of the country's biggest fund houses UTI MF and HSBC Asset Management Company are also planning to launch new schemes that would invest overseas. Besides, there are various schemes from Sundaram BNP Paribas, Principal MF, Fidelity International and Franklin Templeton that provide an opportunity to Indian investors to get an exposure to global markets. A diversified portfolio spread across the boundaries is likely to protect the investors against the bouts of volatility in domestic stock market.

An Interesting development that took place during 2007 was MF houses' rush to launch infrastructure funds and at least three of them relatively opened schemes primarily dedicated to this sector. While strange performance of existing infrastructure funds have given enough reasons for fund houses to launch schemes dedicated to this sector, the government's keenness to develop India's infrastructure is another reason managers are bullish on these schemes. Enthused by its 150% return during the last two years, the fund house launched Indo Global Infrastructure Fund, which in addition to investing in Indian infrastructure relates firms, will also look for global players. Lotus India MF is the other player to launch its scheme for the sector while DBS Cholamandalam MF closed its scheme. Apart from scheme's growth potential, other driver is diversification of portfolio.

During 2010-11, assets of the mutual fund industry registered decline. This was mainly due to economic slowdown both in domestic and overseas economies, uncertainty in equity markets, high rate of inflation and reluctance of investors to invest in mutual funds schemes.

As amongst 48 mutual funds as on December-end 2011, the top ten managed assets to the tune of ₹ 5,22,308.27 crore which accounted for over 80 per cent of the total assets under management.[20] HDFC Mutual Fund with average assets under management of ₹ 88,628 crore topped the list followed closely by Reliance Mutual Fund with assets of ₹ 82,305 crore. (Table 28.2)

It is interesting to note that HDFC Mutual Fund with average assets under management of over ₹ 1 lakh crore continued to top the list of mutual funds followed by Reliance Mutual Fund. ICICI Prudential Mutual Fund with AUM of about ₹ 88,000 crore ranked third. (Table 28.2)

Table 28.2: Top ten Mutual Funds in terms of Average Assets under Management

(Amt. in ₹ Crore)

Name	As on December 31, 2011	As on March 31, 2013
1. HDFC Mutual Fund	88,628.03	1,01,720.27
2. Reliance Mutual Fund	82,305.81	94,580.19
3. ICICI Prudential Mutual Fund	69,367.79	87,835.07
4. Birla Sun Life Mutual Funds	60,217.27	77,046.43
5. UTI Mutual Fund	57,817.34	69,450.39
6. SBI Mutual Fund	41,551.51	54,905.44
7. Franklin Templeton Mutual Fund	35,641.63	41,564.26
8. DSP Black rock Mutual Fund	30,564.90	32,342.26
9. Kotak Mahindra Mutual Fund	29,738.06	35,361.35
10. IDFC Mutual Fund	26,475.43	32,885.99

Scheme-wise analysis of net assets held by mutual funds industry in India reveals that (Table 28.3) open-end schemes have been more popular than close-end schemes, like any other developed market. Thus, the open-end schemes pocketed assets to the tune of ₹ 5,44,815 crore, which represented over 80 per cent of the total assets under management. Among the open-end schemes, income-oriented schemes dominated the market, accounting for the largest share of the assets followed closely by equity and money market schemes.

Two striking developments have taken place during the last three years (2009-12), one such development is big investors' shift to debt mutual fund schemes from equity fund schemes because of uncertainty in the security market and the falling rate of return on equities. According to the Association of mutual funds in India, gross equity sales in November 2011 were ₹ 3,183 crore, the lowest since April 2009. Interestingly, among the ten top performing fund categories, seven are debt funds, with ultra short-term schemes being the best performing of income funds. This momentum will tend to increase.

Another major development has been the edge of close-ended mutual fund schemes over the open-ended schemes. According to the Association of Mutual Funds in India, the number of close-ended schemes reached 368 in 2011 as against 202 last year, a jump of over 82 per cent only. In contrast, the number of open-ended schemes grew by 13 per cent only. The majority of the rise happened in the income category with number of schemes more than doubled, registering growth of 134 per cent. It is mainly on the back of the industry's emerging preference for fixed maturity plans.

AUM distribution in India shows a heavy skew (approximately 68 per cent) in favour of income- and debt-oriented schemes which are short-term investments. Growth and equity schemes account for 28 per cent of the total AUM and balanced and exchange traded funds, two per cent.

Distribution is skewed and shrinking. In March 2012, there were 84,793 mutual fund distributors certified by the Association of Mutual Funds in India. Of these, 78,282 were individuals and 6,511 were corporate distributors. The number was 1,14,000 on June 30, 2010.[21]

TABLE 28.3: Scheme-wise Assets under Management
(As on Feb. 29, 2012)

(₹ *in crore*)

Scheme	Open-end	Close-end	Total
Balanced	16,741	11	16,752
ELSS	21,486	2,512	23,998
Equity	1,61,695	29	1,61,724
Gilt	3,675	—	3,675
Gold ETF	9,795	—	9,795
Income	1,69,669	1,20,974	2,90,643
Liquid/Money Market	1,57,455	—	1,57,455
FOF Investing overseas	2,639	—	2,639
Other ETF	1,660	—	1,660
Total	5,44,815	1,23,526	6,18,341

Performance in Terms of Financial Intermediation

Mutual funds in India have come into existence to mobilize savings of the people and channel them into productive outlets so as to ensure triple benefits of certainty of income, safety of funds and liquidity to the investors.

Regarding mobilization of resources, it may be noticed from Table 28.4 that since the beginning of the decade of 70s till 1986-87, UTI, the solitary institution in the industry, garnered resources through its diverse schemes to the tune of ₹ 4016 crore. There was phenomenal surge in the amount of resources raised by the mutual funds during the period 1987-88 — 1991-92 in as much as funds mopped up during this period amounted to ₹ 32,000 crore, almost eight fold increase over what was raised during 1970-71 — 1986-87.

TABLE 28.4: Net Resources Mobilized by Mutual Funds

(₹ *in crore*)

Year	UTI	Public Sector Mutual Funds	Private Sector Mutual Funds	Total
1970-71 - 1986-87	4,016.1	—	—	4,016.1
1987-88-1991-92	24,735.8	7,296.3	—	32,032.1
1992-93-1996-97	19,608.0	4,183.4	3,877.9	27,669.3
1997-98-2001-02	26,631.0	4,497.0	45,179.1	76307.1
2002-03-2004-05	-11,106.2	1,979.2	62,594.8	53,467.8
2006-2007	7,326	7,621	79,038	93,985
2007-2008	10,677	9,820	1,33,304	1,53,801
2008-2009	-3,659	9.38	-34,018	-28,297
2009-2010	15,653	14,726	48,166	78,545
2010-2011	-16636	-15684	-15594	-47914

Sources: Handbook of Statistics on the Indian Economy, RBI, 2010-11.

This was partly because of entry of public sector banks in the industry but mainly due to expansion of the operations of the UTI and incredible efforts made by the Trust to mobilize funds through several innovative schemes and planned publicity and aggressive promotional efforts.

However, performance of the mutual funds industry suffered heavily during the period 1992-93 — 1996-97 when total resources procured from the market declined substantially to an all time low level of ₹ 27,669 crore, even though mutual funds in the private sector also started raising resources since 1994 and could mop up about ₹ 3,900 crore during the period. The primary factor responsible for the declining trend was failure of UTI and public sector mutual funds to sustain their tempo. Further, there was greater amount of outflow of funds than the inflow in the case of the UTI during the period 1995-96 and 1996-97.

The subsequent period- 1997-98 — 2001-02 witnessed spectacular spurt in amount of resources garnered by the mutual funds. Major portion of the resources mopped during this period was by the private sector mutual funds.

A peculiar trend was noticeable during the three years of 2002-03 — 2004-05 when private sector mutual funds mobilized net resources to the tune of ₹ 62,594.8 crore as against negative trend in the case of UTI mainly because of the steep increase in redemptions and repurchases of the order of ₹ 11,000 crore. This led to sharp decline in the amount of funds garnered during the period.

It, thus, emanates from the above analysis that private sector funds have played crucial role in mobilizing savings of the public, accounting for about 70 per cent of the resources garnered since 1993. This is attributable to introduction of host of innovative saving schemes carrying features suiting the needs of diverse sections of the society, vigorous and planned publicity, promotional drive, relatively attractive rates of return and better service standard. Further, private sector funds were found more investor friendly and efficiently managed, compared to their public sector counterparts.

During the last two years 2005-07, a whopping sum of ₹ 3,20,000 crore was mobilised by the mutual funds industry. This is primarily due to launching of a large number of innovative saving schemes and smart and customer friendly marketing and distribution strategies. The contribution of private sector funds has been astoundingly very high. The emerging trend is indicative of growing investor's confidence.

A new concept of investing in gold through a mutual fund is now evolving. A handful of mutual funds have, of late, decided to offer this investment option. The first gold mutual fund product was launched by Benchmark Mutual Fund in 2006 and DSP Merrill Lynch World Gold Fund in July 2007. Others like UTI Mutual Fund and Prudential ICICI too are getting ready with their schemes. Under this scheme, the money is deployed to purchase gold in physical form. As such, the performance of the fund would depend on the price movement in gold.

During 2008-09, net resource mobilisation by mutual funds turned negative; there was a net outflow of ₹ 28,297 crore during the year as compared to a net inflow of ₹ 1,53,801 crore during 2007-08. Both the number of schemes and net resource mobilisation declined steeply, reflecting uncertainty in the stock markets and redemption pressures from banks and corporates on account of tight liquidity conditions prevailing at that time.

The year 2009-10 witnessed significant improvement in the resource mobilisation efforts of the mutual fund industry when net resources of the order of ₹ 78, 545 crore were garnered. This was because of improved economic conditions and boom in equity markets. Major portion of the resources was mobilised by the private sector funds.

Economic slump, global crisis, high inflation rate and sluggish security market during 2010-11, hurt the sentiments of the investors resulting in a net outflow of ₹ 47,917 crore during the period.

Among 48 mutual funds operating in India, ten top funds including ICICI Prudential Mutual Fund, Birla Mutual Fund, HDFC Mutual Fund have displayed sterling performance in so far as net resources garnered by them. (Table 28.5). They together mobilised resources to the tune of ₹ 59,604.71 crore during 2009-10 accounting for over 100 per cent of the total net resources mobilised by all the 48 funds.

TABLE 28.5: Top Ten Performers in Mobilisation of Net Resources

(*₹ in crores*)

Name of the Mutual Fund	Year 2009-10
1. Birla Mutual Fund	12,492.3
2. HDFC Mutual Fund	11,358.3
3. ICICI Prudential Mutual Fund	10,371.5
4. IDFC Mutual Fund	6,603.0
5. Franklin Templeton Mutual Fund	5,775.7
6. Kotak Mahindra MF	4,601.7
7. CRB Mutual Fund	3,129.9
8. Axis Mutual Fund	2,448.6
9. Reliance Capital Mutual Fund	1,429.0
10. J.M. Mutual Fund	1,394.7

Source: Handbook of Statistics on the Indian Economy, RBI, 2010-11.

Scheme-wise analysis of resources garnered by the mutual funds industry (Table 28.6) reveals that the bulk of the resources mobilized during the past five years were under liquid/ money market schemes and growth/equity-oriented schemes.

TABLE 28.6: Net Mobilization of Resources by Mutual Funds according to Types of Schemes

(*₹ in crore*)

Type of Schemes	2000-01	2001-02	2002-03	2003-04	2004-05	2005-06	2007-08
Money Market Schemes	2,564	3,291	5,005	24,576	10,348	4,205	14,976
Govt. Securities	—	1,563	—	2,232	-1,345	-1,560	434
Debt Instruments	4,839	8,210	1,467	12,795	-14,247	13,977	88,457
Equity Oriented Schemes	—	—	43	7,219	-194	3,592	46,933
Others	2,782	—	—	—	7,698	32,325	5,768
Total	**10,185**	**13,064**	**6,515**	**46,822**	**2,260**	**52,539**	**1,56,568**

Source: Trend and Progress of Banking in India, RBI an Report on Currency and Finance for relevant years.

Mobilization under debt schemes, which have traditionally been garnering the largest amount of resources, declined sharply during the year 2004-05 due to a hardening of yields. Equity oriented schemes attracted higher funds mainly due to attractive returns in buoyant secondary market.

Net resources mobilized under the equity oriented schemes increased by about five times during 2005-06 to ₹ 35,231 crore from ₹ 7,100 crore in the previous year, driven by attractive returns from these schemes in view of buoyant secondary market conditions.

In line with the recent trend, bulk of the net resources mobilised by mutual fund during 2007-08 was accounted for by income/debt-oriented schemes and equity oriented schemes. While higher interest rates seemed to have made the debt schemes more attractive to the investors, resource mobilisation through growth/equity oriented schemes during the year was supported by the robust performance of the domestic stock markets.[20]

During 2008-09, income/debt oriented schemes witnessed a net outflow of ₹ 32,161 crore, while growth/equity schemes registered a net inflow of ₹ 4,024 crore.

In the wake of the tight liquidity condition since June 2008, mutual funds have faced redemption pressure. For instance, while sale of new schemes amounted to ₹ 11,476 crore for the month ended Feb. 29, 2012, amount of redemption during the period amounted to over ₹ 5,00,000 crore. This is why most fund managers have adopted a cautious approval and preferred to invest only in non-convertible debentures.

Performance in terms of Return

Until recently, majority of investors were not satisfied with performance of the mutual funds because of poor returns, *i.e.*, less than expected income and even loss of capital in several cases. Shockingly, most of the investors in growth funds and US-64 scheme expressed loss of faith in mutual funds.

However, the scenario has remarkably changed in recent few years. Indian mutual funds are rewarding their investors better than any other funds in the world. According to a report by Lipper, a leading market research agency, Indian funds have grabbed eight of the top ranks over a 10-year period. If one takes the last five years, they account for 7 out of the top 10 and over a 3-year period, six of the 10 best performing mutual funds are from India.

A bird's eyeview of top performers may be had from Table 28.7.

Table 28.7: Best Performing Mutua Fund in 2011

Schemes	Plan	Types	% Returns
Reliance Pharma Fund - Dividend	Dividend	Open	91.52
Franklin Pharma Fund - Dividend	Dividend	Open	89.67
DSP Black Rock Micro Cap Fund - regular growth	Growth	Open	67.90
SBI MSFU - FMCG Fund	Growth	Open	64.91
UTI - Pharma & Healthcare Fund - Income	Dividend	Open	61.76
ICICI Prudential Discovery Fund - Institution Option-I Growth	Growth	Open	61.37
Religare MID N SMALL CAP Fund - Dividend	Dividend	Close	58.28
UTI - Transportation and Logistics Fund - Income	Dividend	Open	55.18
Birla Sun Life MNC Fund - Dividend	Dividend	Open	54.98
SBI MSFU - IT Fund	Growth	Open	54.03
SBI MSFU Pharma - Dividend	Dividend	Open	53.71
Franklin Infotech Fund - Dividend	Dividend	Open	53.26
UTI - Master Value Fund - Income	Dividend	Open	51.72
Religare Mid Cap Fund - Dividend	Dividend	Close	51.36
ING Dividend Yield Fund - Dividend	Dividend	Open	51.21
DSP Black Rock Small and Mid Cap Fund - Institutional - Dividend	Dividend	Open	50.81
HDFC Mid - Cap Opportunities Fund - Dividend	Dividend	Open	50.65
Franklin FMCG Fund - Dividend	Dividend	Open	50.39
DSP Black Rock Technology.com Fund - Institutional - Dividend	Dividend	Open-ended	40.93
Reliance Equity Opportunities Fund - Institutional - dividend	Dividend	Open	49.63
ICICI Prudential FMCG Plan - Dividend	Dividend	Open	48.78
ICICI Prudential Emerging Star Fund - Institutional - I - Growth	Growth	Open	46.93

Source: http://money.sulekha.com

A peep into table 28.7 shows that rate of return on different schemes of the mutual funds has surged significantly in the year 2011. For instance, Reliance Pharma Fund — dividend offered as high as 91.52 per cent and Franklin Pharma Fund — Dividend 89.67 during the year. Rates of return in the case of other outstanding players ranged between 46.93 per cent and 67.90 per cent.

Profitability performance of mutual fund industry has not improved during the year 2010-11. Twenty-three of the 44 fund houses for which data are available have been carrying forward losses and among the profitable AMCs, 12 saw their profits decline in 2010-11. Many have blamed big-shift regulations, including the ban on entry loads since August, 2009 for the industry's woes.[22]

It is generally believed that the profitability of the mutual fund industry may not improve significantly in future due to increasing cost incurred to develop distribution channels and falling margins due to greater competition among fund houses.[23]

However, top players in the industry have continued to remain profitable. Thus, Reliance Mutual Fund continued to remain the most profitable asset manager in the industry during 2011-12 with ₹ 276 crore as net profit. HDFC MF, the country's largest fund house, grew faster to ₹ 269 crore as compared with ₹ 242 crore in 2010-11. ICICI AMC, the third largest fund house, grew fastest in terms of profitability at 22.5 per cent to ₹ 88 crore against ₹ 72 crore earlier.[24]

A Critical Appraisal

Mutual funds in India are ostensibly vehicles of democratic capitalism. They allow millions of ordinary investors to own equity, and this is one reason why the industry is lavished with tax breaks. But in real world, mutual funds have become vehicles of power and privilege instead, doing all they can to help a few favoured investors. Contrary to the philosophy of mutual funds of focusing on individual investors, in India the industry particularly in the private and joint sectors is highly focused on corporates, deriving 60-80 per cent of their corpus from them, giving scant attention to the retail investors.

There exists structural flaws in the business models of the mutual fund industry. First, there is sharp variance in the investor mix. Corporate investors account for less than one per cent of the mutual fund population. But their share of AUM stood at 46.7 per cent in September 2011. Again, high net-worth individuals account for less than two per cent of the investor population, yet their share of AUM was 23.7 per cent. But retail investors, who make up 97.4% of the investor population, accounted for a mere 23.6 per cent of the industry's AUM. This is in sharp contrast to the United States, where retail investors owned 87 per cent of the $ 11.8 trillion invested in mutual funds as of December, 2010.[25] Thus, in India, the mutual fund industry, which osensibly exists to multiply the small investors hard-earned money, has been hijacked by corporate India.[26]

Entry ban load, imposed by the SEBI in 2009 to attract retail investors, failed to be a game changer even after three years. The investor base in equities has shrunk since by four million; monthly sales are down from ₹ 9,000 crore to less than ₹ 3,000 crore, new fund offers are down and most fund houses are struggling to make money.[25]

No doubt, the entry load was positive step which made MFs one of the cheapest products. But new investors did not come, as it created a disconnect between the industry and investors. The problem remains disinterest among distributors for selling MF plans, as they get low commissions.

Another disconcerting trend in respect of mutual fund industry in India is its low penetration. As a percentage of household savings the share of the fund is a meagre 4 per cent in India as compared to 16 per cent in the West. Close to three-fourth of the fund industry's assets come only from the country's top five cities, viz., Mumbai, Delhi, Bangalore, Chennai and Kolkata.[27]

Low financial literacy has made its difficult to attract customers. According to a recent study — Visa's 2012 Financial Literacy Barometer, India ranked 23rd amongst 28 markets assessed by it. Brazil fared the best, followed by Mexico, Australia, the U.S. and Canada. The survey found that Indian families hold money management discussions infrequently, and that even educated people lack knowledge of investment plans.

In connivance with mutual funds, fund managers and corporate investors have been found indulging in numerous irregular practices and the SEBI has remained a mute spectator. One such unethical practice being adopted by fund managers is 'front-running'. In this, fund manager buys the shares of a company through his secret account merely hours before his fund buys them. Prices normally rise when a lager fund picks up thousands of shares of a particular company. Once the prices rise, the fund manager would quietly sell his holdings and make a neat profit. This has become common practice among funds managers but SEBI has failed to curb this practice.

Late trading and rapid trading are another kind of unethical practices pursued by big investors with the help of asset management companies. Inappropriate NAVs have been given to large investors for a long time. The biggest culprits have been public sector financial institutions and banks that have been arm twisting MFs, especially debt and liquid funds. Late trading deflates NAVs of the funds they manage and NAV performance is what fund managers are judged by. SEBI does not have any mechanism to check past late trades.

Rapid trading practices are being indulged by most of the private sector mutual funds in India to help the institutional investors to pull out money in uncertain or volatile times. For this purpose, the funds go to the extent of selling its liquid holdings first just to repay the larger investors with the result that the long-term investors, who typically react later to the market developments, are left with the relatively illiquid ones. This problem is compounded because the funds also offer lower or zero exit loads to larger investors. So while a retail investor may need to pay a 0.5 per cent exit load for leaving a fund within six months, big investors pay nothing or a much lower load. This encourages frequent trading by large investors. Unfortunately, SEBI has so far not been able to take effective steps to curb this nefarious practice.

Still another irregular practice indulged in by mutual funds in India is dominance of a fund by single or few large investors. As of March end, 2004, a whopping 110 or nearly one-third, out of the total 350 schemes in the industry were single-investor schemes. Although SEBI has advised mutual funds that no single investor should hold more than 25 per cent of the funds assets, this does not serve the purpose much, for the fact that a big investor or a fund can easily rope in 19 small investors into the scheme to meet the legal requirements. Even a maximum holding of 25 per cent for a single investor is too large to marginalize other investors with their moves.

Several fund houses have reportedly been offering assured returns to Provident Funds (PFs) and indulging in unethical practices. In their bid to increase the size of assets under their management, funds are paying scant attention to the means adopted to show results. In the case of PFs, for instance, money meant for investing in gilts was diverted to equities in order to earn a higher rate of return. This despite the fact that PFs are prohibited by law from investing in equities. Such instances do nothing for investor trust in MFs. As it is, many common investors view MFs suspiciously. This is why funds have failed to become as popular in India as they are in other markets.

Mutual funds in India have been found splurging on marketing expenses. When 75 per cent of assets under a fund's managements are in commoditised debt and cash funds, differentiating one scheme from another depends on what the fund houses can do for distributors —from giving extra commission in particular periods or on meeting some targets, to furnishing their offices, gifting them cell phones, laptops and sending them abroad on pleasure trips. Although SEBI is aware of the mad short-term incentivisation going around in the industry, it has yet to take concrete steps to control cozy distribution deals and marketing incentives.[28]

It has also been noted with concern that some Indian mutual funds turn over their portfolios so many times in a year that moderate hedge funds would be put to shame. The industry claims this is because the Indian investors only invest for the short-term and there is no equity cult to speak of in the country. However, distributors have huge role to play here. In fact, retail investors rarely shift funds. It is distributors who keep encouraging high-net worth individuals to churn their investors so that they upfront commissions ranging between 1.5-1.75 per cent. SEBI is either unaware of the games of mutual funds play, or it prefers to ignore.

Another disturbing trend is that investors profiles have not changed over the years because of geographical reasons. The top five cities still account for a whopping 73 per cent of the industry AUM, with Mumbai alone accounting for 44.59 per cent, according to data from Association of Mutual Funds of India. Another weakness of Indian mutual fund industry is that it suffers from the copycat syndrome. Within days of an AMC launching a fund, the others follow suit and try to lure the same investor.[29]

In recent years, the MF industry has been asking for a higher expense ratio. Already expense ratios are very high in India, roughly ten times the norm in developed equity markets. Since India is a high-volume, well-developed equity market with very low brokerage, the demand for higher expense ratios is unreasonable. There are 48 AMCs each offering multiple schemes. This should lead to lower expense ratios. It is, therefore, necessary for the MF industry to introspect its operations. It needs to find ways to restructure, market and sell its products to face competition from insurance.

In view of the above, the bulk of the estimated 20 million investors across the length and breadth of the country, appear to be reposing more faith in investment alternatives other than MF schemes; these include plain vanilla bank deposits, or insurance products or buying stocks, etc.[30]

J. SUGGESTIONS TO MAKE INDIAN MUTUAL FUNDS MORE EFFECTIVE

Nevertheless the transparency level in terms of disclosure of portfolios of the schemes is higher in the mutual fund industry compared to other establishments such as banking, post offices and provident-funds, there is still scope for mutual funds to further enhance it through more disclosures. Specifically, they need to explain the risk factors in detail, disclosure portfolio turnover and associated transaction costs, exhibit their financial performance, profile of the managers, distribution expense, percentage of fees charged by SEBI and total expense ratio.

For long-term success and survival, mutual funds should focus on retail investors so as to widen their investor base. The SEBI is considering offering incentives to AMCs that increase their reach beyond the top cities.

So far mutual funds in India have confined themselves to urban areas; leaving vast saving potentials in rural hinterlands untapped. By penetrating in rural areas and introducing saving schemes tailored to the diverse preferences in rural community and by educating them about the benefits of the schemes, mutual funds can raise burgeoning resources which can be gainfully employed for the national development.

For wooing the retail investors, the MF industry has got to focus sharply on two fronts: Performance and products areas where most fund managers will agree, Indian MFs have yet to deliver.

While it is fine to advertise good performance of a particular scheme by a fund in order to attract more investment, the times are fast approaching when an honest view based approach would compel a mutual fund to advise investors on "sell" or "switch" between schemes, as emphatically as it would advise on the purchase. So as to attract investors, it is, therefore, advisable to mutual funds to offer this sort of counselling which will certainly make a mutual fund different from other institutions.

In order to improve penetration of mutual fund industry, it is necessary to expand the reach beyond established markets and top cities and for that purpose focus has to be on the distribution network and smaller branches need to be set up in rural areas to bring in new investors. There is also strong need to develop awareness programme to educate the masses about investment nuances.

The industry also needs to sharpen distribution and adopt new models. AMCs need to go beyond traditional channels such as independent financial advisors and large bank branches and tap into intermediaries with low-cost access to remote locations. Tying up with India Post, public sector and RRBs, self help groups, micro finance institutions and the like will also help expand the investor base.

Broadening the market will encourage the launch of more innovative products. Of late, the industry has many innovative products, such as the Reliance ATM Card. This card, issued by a partner bank, is linked to mutual fund schemes and allows investors to withdraw cash at ATMs or make payments at merchant establishments. The investor has the opportunity to earn market-linked returns every day and he also gets liquidity through the ATM Card.

In order to ensure that mutual funds are operating in the vital interests of retail investors, SEBI must take the following steps without further delay:

(*i*) SEBI should ensure that monthly portfolios of mutual funds are published in at least one national newspaper in English, in addition to, a regional newspaper in local language.

(*ii*) For effective implementation of the code of conduct for the mutual fund intermediaries, it is desirable to have more specific guidelines instead of laying them down in general terms.

(*iii*) So as to prevent late trading practices, SEBI should ask mutual funds to vouch to their boards and endorse it in their prospectus that their fund house has never done late trading.

(*iv*) With a view to checking rapid trading practices of mutual funds, SEBI should adopt the rules existing in other nations and apply its mind a bit.

(*v*) In its endeavour to discourage the existing practice of dominance of single investor in investors portfolio of funds schemes, SEBI should make it mandatory to mutual funds to disclose on a regular basis as to how many investors hold more than 10 per cent, 20 per cent or 25 per cent of the NAV. Fund managers should also disclose what the possible impact of these investors would be and how they would deal with such situations.

(*vi*) SEBI should also make it mandatory to the intermediaries to disclose that they are tied agents of specified mutual funds and the rate of commission earned by them. This information should be placed in their offices so that it is clearly visible to the investors.

(*vii*) So as to curb unethical practices of the mutual funds, SEBI, apart from improving its market intelligence, setting up a system that allows investors and even mutual funds participants blow the whistle on unethical practices, strict follow up action and stiff punishment, whenever such a practice comes to light, will go a long way in disciplinary industry participants.

(*viii*) The Government should give powers to SEBI to punish the wrong doers. Stringent punishment needs to be given to those involved in misleading advertisements of the scheme. SEBI should also expose such defaulters in public through the print and electronic media.

(*ix*) There is a need to incentivise long-term savings in mutual funds. Liberalising third-party investment management, particularly for insurance and pension industry would benefit from investment expertise, too. In the U.S., mutual funds account for 26 per cent of the $ 17.9 trillion retirement market.

(x) Tax rates do not encourage retail investors. For mutual funds, dividend distribution tax on equity schemes is zero. It is 12.5 per cent on other schemes, and 25 per cent on money market and liquid schemes. Long-term capital gains tax is 10 per cent with indexation and 20 per cent without indexation for non-equity oriented schemes short-term capital gains tax is 15 per cent for equity schemes and 30 per cent for non-equity schemes. It is, therefore, advisable to simplify taxation and give retail investors incentive to put their money in mutual funds.

In view of surging economy and its various segments, growing awareness of investors and tremendous potential of mutual funds, the industry has bright future, provided the Government, the RBI and SEBI take concrete steps along the lines suggested above.

K. CONCLUSIONS

Mutual fund is a financial intermediary concerned with garnering savings of the people to invest in a diverified portfolio of securities with a view to ensuring the savers triple benefits of minimum risk, steady return and capital appreciation to tighten governance and disclosure rules and develop effective monitoring system to curb the existing unethical practices.

Mutual funds are of various types evolved to cater to the varying needs and preferences of large number of savers across the country and abroad. Thus, there may be different categories of mutual funds based on functional, portfolio and geographical types.

The USA is the pace setter in the development of mutual funds in terms of growth of number of household investors, funds and types of schemes. One of the basic reasons for the popularity of mutual funds in the USA is the stringent regulatory framework. The US mutual fund industry is the largest in the world, accounting for half of the $16-2 trillion total net assets.

In India, Unit Trust of India was the solitary mutual fund until 1987 when Government permitted public sector banks and insurance companies to engage in mutual fund business. For the first time in February 1993, SEBI permitted private sector to enter into mutual fund business. Thus, there are at present 34 registered mutual funds in India with a corpus of ₹ 4,86,513 crore by the end of July, 2007.

So as to ensure smooth functioning of mutual funds, the Government, RBI and SEBI have laid down policy guidelines. However, these guidelines have not been enforced effectively leading to a number of unethical practices by the mutual funds to the detriment of the retail investors.

As regards performance of mutual funds, private sector and joint sector funds have played crucial role in mopping up savings of public, accounting for about 70 per cent of the total resources garnered so far by the mutual funds. Among the various saving schemes, liquid/money market schemes and growth/equity-oriented schemes have been very popular. Further, open-end schemes have had edge over close-end schemes in attracting savings.

It is intriguing to find that mutual funds in India have become vehicles of power and privileges, doing all sorts of favour to a few institutional/High Net Income (HNI) investors at the expense of retail investors. In connivance with mutual funds managers and distributors, corporate and HNI investors have engaged in numerous unethical practices such as late trading, rapid trading, dominance of fund by a single or few large investors, diversion of funds, etc. mutual funds have also been found splurging on marketing expenses.

Although mutual funds in India have bright future because of surging economy and robust industrial growth, the Government, RBI and SEBI need to tighten governance and disclosure rules and develop effective monitoring system to curb the existing unethical practices.

KEY TERMS

- Asset Management Company
- Balanced Funds
- Bond Funds
- Close-ended Funds
- Copycat Syndrome
- Diversified Funds
- Domestic Funds
- Front running
- High Networth Individuals
- Index Funds
- Infrastructure Funds
- Late Trading
- Money Market Funds
- Off-Shore Funds
- Open-ended Funds
- Rapid Trading
- Stock Funds
- Taxation Funds

DISCUSSION QUESTIONS

1. What do you understand by the term mutual funds?
2. Discuss the significance of mutual funds in industrial development of a country.
3. What are the distinguishing features of different types of mutual funds?
4. Discuss, in brief, growth of mutual fund industry in India.
5. Evaluate the present policy guidelines for mutual funds in India.
6. Critically assess the performance of mutual funds in India.
7. Discuss the unethical practices of mutual funds in India.
8. "Mutual funds industry in India has been hijacked by corporate India." Comment.

REFERENCES

1. Western J. Fred and Eugene F. Brighan, *Essentials of Managerial Finance*, Dryden Press, Hinsdale, Illinois, 1985, p. 36.
2. Michael D. Hirch, *Multifund Investing: How to Build a High Performance Portfolio of Mutual Funds*, Dow Jones-Irwin, Homewood, Illinois, 1987, p. 57.
3. UK Investment Trusts and Companies, Freshfields Bruckhans Derringer, Jan. 2005, (Source: www.rinpipe.com/wharmf.htm).
4. Investment Company Institute, Mutual Fund Fact Book, Washington DC, USA, 2004, p. 12.
5. S. Sankaran, *Indian Mutual Fund Handbook*, A Guide for Industry Professionals and Intelligent Investors, Vision Books Pvt. Ltd., 2003, p. 24.
6. Investment Company Institute, Mutual Fund Fact Book, Washington DC, USA 2004, pp. 11-13.
7. Investment Company Institute, Investment Company Fact Book, 45th Ed., p. 205.
8. Investment Company Fact Book, *op. cit.*, p. 103.
9. Investment Company Fact Book, *op. cit.*, p. 102.
10. SEBI, Mutual Funds 2002 Report, p. 3.
11. Association of Mutual Funds in India, Mutual Fund Testing Programme for Distributors and Employees of Mutual Funds in India, Workbook, 2nd Ed, December 2001, p. 8.
12. Association of Mutual Funds in India, *op. cit.*, p. 9.
13. www.mutualfundsindia.com
14. Business Today, April 1, 2012.

15. Times of India, July 29, 2006.
16. Business Line, September 27, 2007.
17. Business Line, February 23, 2009.
18. Business Times, September 27, 2007.
19. Business Today, August 5, 2012.
20. www.mutualfundsindia.com
21. Business Today, *op. cit.*
22. Business Today, April 1, 2012.
23. Business Standard, August 14, 2009.
24. Business Today, April 1, 2012.
25. Business times, December 8, 2007.
26. Business Standard, May 22, 2012.
27. Business Standard, August 1, 2012
28. Business Today, August 12, 2007.
29. Business Standard, July 23, 2012.
30. Business World, July, 2004.

Non-Banking Finance Sector

Section Five

Section V: Learning Objectives

The present section aims at providing insights into the profile and operations of NBFCs and Micro Finance Companies in India.

Section Outline

— Non-Banking Finance Companies in India.

— Micro Finance Companies in India.

Chapter 29

Non-banking Finance Companies

Learning Objectives:

The present chapter aims at:

- Acquainting with nature and Significance of Non-banking Finance Companies (NBFCs).
- Presenting an overview of NBFCs in India.
- Focusing on regulatory framework of NBFCs in India.

Chapter Outline:

A. NATURE AND SIGNIFICANCE OF NON-BANKING FINANCE COMPANIES

Non-banking Finance Companies (NBFCs) representing companies engaged in transferring the funds from lender to borrowers have come to be recognized all over the globe as an integral part of financial system to supplement the efforts of commercial banks and development financial institutions.

According to the Reserve Bank (Amendment Act) 1997,[1] 'a non-banking Finance Company' means:

(*i*) a financial institution which is a company;

(*ii*) a non-banking institution which is a company and which has as its principal business the receiving of deposits under any scheme or arrangement or in any other manner or lending in any manner;

(*iii*) such other non-banking institution or class of such institutions as the RBI may with the previous approval of the Central Government specify.

Thus, NBFCs encompass an extremely heterogeneous group of intermediaries. They differ in various attributes, such as, size, nature of incorporation and regulation, as well as the basic functionality of financial intermediation. Notwithstanding their diversity, NBFCs are characterised by their ability to provide niche financial services in the Indian economy.[2]

Because of their relative organizational flexibility leading to a better response mechanism, they are often able to employ innovative marketing strategies and devise tailor made services relatively faster than banks and financial institutions. This enables them to build up a clientele that ranges from small borrowers to established corporates.

B. TYPES OF NBFCs

NBFCs can be classified on the basis of the kind of liabilities they access, the type of activities, they pursue, and of their perceived systematic importance.[3] On the basis of liabilities, there are two categories, (i) Category 'A' Companies (NBFCs holding and accepting public deposits or NBFCs-D), and Category 'B' Companies (NBFCs not having public deposits or NBFCs -ND). NBFCs-D are subject to requirements of capital adequacy, liquid assets maintenance, exposure norms (including restrictions on exposure to investments in land, building and unquoted shares), ALM discipline and reporting requirements. NBFCs-ND are subject to minimal regulation as they were non-deposit taking bodies and considered as posing little threat to financial stability. However, recognizing the growing importance of the segment and its inter-linkages with banks and other financial institutions, capital adequacy, exposure norms, ALM discipline and reporting requirements have been made applicable for NBFCs - ND that are large and systematically important since April 1, 2007, such entities are referred to as NBFCs - ND — systematically important.

On the activity-based classification, NBFCs can be grouped into five categories: (*i*) Loan Companies (LCs), (*ii*) Investment Companies (LCs), (*iii*) Asset Finance Companies (AFCs), (*iv*) Infrastructure Finance Companies (IFCs) and (v) Systematically important Core Investment Companies (CICs – ND – SI). A new category of CIC-ND-SI was created in August, 2010 for those companies with an asset size of ₹ 100 crore and above that was only in the business of investment for the sole purpose of holding stakes in group concerns, but not trading in these securities and accepting public deposits. Principal business of four major categories of NBFCs is listed in the following table:

TABLE 29.1: Types of Non-Banking Financial Entity and Their Business

Non-Banking Financial Entity	Principle Business
I. Non-Banking Financial Company	In terms of the Section 45-I(f) read with Section 45-I(e) of the RBI Act, 1934, as amended in 1997, their principal business is that of receiving deposits or that of a financial institution, such as lending, investment in securities, hire purchase finance or equipment leasing.
(*a*) Equipment leasing company (EL)	Equipment leasing or financing of such activity.
(*b*) Hire purchase finance company (HP)	Hire purchase transactions or financing of such transactions.
(*c*) Investment Company (IC)	Acquisition of securities. These include Primary Dealers (PDs) who deal in underwriting and market making for government securities.
(*d*) Loan Company (LC)	Providing finance by making loans or advances, or otherwise for any activity other than its own; excludes EL/HP/Housing Finance Companies (HFCs).
(*e*) Residuary Non-Banking Company (RNBC)	Company which receives deposits under any scheme or arrangement, by whatever name called, in one lumpsum or in instalments by way of contributions or subscriptions or by sale of units or certificates or other instruments, or in any manner. These companies do not belong to any of the categories as stated above.
II. Mutual Benefit Financial Company (MBFC) *i.e.*, Nidhi Company	Any company which is notified by the Central Government as a Nidhi company under Section 620A of the Companies Act, 1956 (1 of 1956).
III. Mutual Benefit Company (MBC), *i.e.*, Potential Nidhi Company	A Company which is working on the lines of a Nidhi company but has not yet been so declared by the Central Government, has minimum net owned fund [NOF] of ₹ 10 lakh, has applied to the RBI for COR and also to Department of Company Affairs (DCA) for being notified as Nidhi company and has not contravened directions/regulations of RBI/DCA.
IV. Miscellaneous Non-Banking Company (MNBC), *i.e.*, Chit Fund Company	Managing, conducting or supervising as a promoter, foreman or agent of any transaction or arrangement by which the company enters into an agreement with a specified number of subscribers that every one of them shall subscribe a certain sum in instalments over a definite period and that every one of such subscribers shall in turn, as determined by lot or by auction or by tender or in such manner as may be provided for in the arrangement, be entitled to the prize amount.

C. NON-BANKING FINANCE COMPANIES IN INDIA — EVOLUTION AND GROWTH

Non-banking finance companies in India emerged in a small way in the late 60s and early 70s as support companies for big industrial houses to act as fixed deposits collection centres and to work out leasing deals for clients on behalf of these houses as also to cater to the needs of those primarily not satisfied by the services offered by the general banking system. Most of the NBFCs located in Southern part of India commenced their operations as Nidhis or Chitfunds. There were in all 2941 such companies in 1971 which could not make any perceptible impact on the financial system of the country because of their limited scope of activities.

However, number of NBFCs surged phenomenally from 2041 in 1971 to 25,085 towards the end of 80s. Growing demand of financial services and substantial tax benefits contributed to this remarkable growth. Tax benefits were so tempting that one out of every two NBFCs came into existence to avail these benefits. With the introduction of comprehensive regulatory framework for NBFCs during 1997 and 1998, as many as 37,400 companies which were carrying on the financial business were eligible for registration with the Reserve Bank for continuation of business. As on June 2000, the RBI approved 9,130 companies for registration. Applications of 13,150 companies are at various stages of consideration.

The most important factor that contributed to this phenomenal increase in number of NBFCs during 80s was tax benefit. When NBFCs acquired assets in addition to those hypothecated to banks, the same was leased from NBFCs rather than being purchased. The lease rentals on these assets were shown as an outflow on the profit and loss account, resulting into reduction of profit to that extent. Another tax benefit was that the NBFCs could also charge depreciation on the assets owned by them and thus reduce their tax liability.

Another important reason for the surging growth of NBFCs during 1980s was the emergence of first generation entrepreneurs in large numbers. Since many people who were low to moderate on capital but high on entrepreneurial ambitions could not meet all the formalities of financial institutions for funds borrowings, this provided the right kind of environment for the emergence of entities equipped with capital and willingness to take risks.

There was also a relaxation on the amount of funds that a lessor could raise from the market in the form of fixed deposits. This led to the formation of new species known as leasing companies to deal primarily with equipment leasing and hence the flood of NBFCs during 1980s.

The growth of NBFCs was also fuelled by Policy changes in auto and consumer durable sectors. As the banking system was reluctant to lend for consumption, pent up demand for consumer durables was met by liberal lendings by NBFCs. The primary market took off mobilising equity impacting operations of NBFCs. Once the SEBI came into existence and it was empowered to regulate activities, a large number of NBFCs got into merchant banking.

NBFCs proliferated by the early 1990s. This rapid expansion was driven by the scope created by the process of liberalization in fresh avenues of operations in areas such as hire purchase, housing, equipment leasing and investment. The business of asset reconstruction has recently emerged as a greenfield within this sector following the passage of securitization (SARFAESI) Act, 2002. Not only existing companies expanded their operations but a large number of these finance companies were set up to squeeze these opportunities in 1990s leading to rise in their number to 13,014 by June end, 2006 with total assets ₹ 57,453 crore. Total number of NBFC-D declined to 12,385 at end-June, 2012. (Table 29.2) A similar trend was also observed in case of deposit taking NBFCs (NBFCs-D) during 2010-11. The declining trend was mainly due to cancellation of certificates of Registration and their exit of NBFCs from deposit taking activities resulting in conversion of NBFCs from deposit taking into non-deposit taking companies.[4]

TABLE 29.2: Number of NBFCs Registered with RBI

End June	NBFCs	NBFCs-D
2000	8451	679
2001	13,815	776
2002	14,077	784
2003	13,849	710
2004	13,764	604
2005	13,261	507
2006	13,014	428
2007	12,968	401
2008	12,809	364
2009	12,740	336
2010	12,630	308
2011	12,409	297
2012	12,385	271

Source: RBI report on Trend and Progress of Banking in India for relevant years.

NBFCs have, thus, become an integral part of Indian financial system. Over the years NBFCs have moved from traditional areas of operations like fixed deposits and hire-purchase to newer avenues like merchant financing, bill discounting, asset management, etc. While most NBFCs operate in a variety of areas so as to even the spread, each has its own particular field of strength which remains its major bread earner. NBFCs are finding it difficult to handle all areas successfully under one roof because each field of operation has its own dynamics, set of rules, set of investors and separate market. As a result, most of the big NBFCs are hiving off few of their business segments into separate joint ventures with other specialized concerns.

Another emerging development is that large NBFCs are extending dedicated lines of credit to their smaller counterparts. While large NBFCs see this as an alternative to finding corporate sectors which are prone to large-scale defaults, smaller NBFCs view this as a solution to their problem of resource crunch. Under this scheme, larger NBFCs can restrict their exposure to one or two smaller NBFCs instead of lending to a large number of customers directly.

Further, NBFCs in India are planning to shift their focus from fund-based activities to fee-based activities so as to cope with the problem of paucity of funds and to earn adequate income to sustain their growth. Until now, the major thrust of the NBFC's business was on leasing and hire-purchase. But with credit from banks and financial institutions becoming increasingly difficult to come by, they have decided to move towards non-fund based activities.

Fierce competition is also forcing NBFCs to shift from auto and consumer goods financing to newer areas like office equipment financing which is growing at a rate of over 30 per cent.

Another remarkable trend witnessed in recent years is growing preference of NBFCs for retail financing where the risks are lower and margins better.

D. REGULATORY NORMS AND DIRECTIONS FOR NBFCs

Since the NBFCs are engaged in financial intermediation affecting interests of the investors and so also the economy as a whole, it is imperative to regulate the operations of these finance companies. In the absence of effective regulatory measure, industrial houses may escape from the provisions of credit and monetary policies of the Central Banking authority by taking recourse to the system of financing through public deposits. Besides, any one could approach NBFC at any time and obtain a loan and the Central Bank had no say over it. Further, there was no transparency and disclosure of operations of these companies. Several residuary

NBFCs were reported to be operating with meagre capital and some of them even with negative capital. Quite a large number of these companies were found issuing misleading advertisements to tempt the savers. Under the circumstances, Central banking authority could not bring about financial discipline among the constituents of financial markets of the country.

In view of the above, the regulation of the deposit acceptance activities of the NBFCs was initiated by the Reserve Bank in the sixties with a view to safeguarding depositors' interests and to ensuring that the NBFCs function on healthy lines. Accordingly, in 1963, a new Chapter III-B was inserted in the RBI Act, 1934 to effectively supervise, control and regulate the deposit acceptance activities of these institutions.

However, the powers vested with the Reserve Bank were very limited in that it could regulate only the limits upto which, manner in which and conditions, subject to which the deposits could be accepted by NBFCs, depending upon the classification based on their principal business. The RBI had no control over the asset-side of balance sheets of NBFCs. In 1985 the Chakravarty Committee recommended for the introduction of a system of licensing (based on the level of business) for NBFCs in order to protect the interests of depositors.

The Narasimham Committee (1991) outlined framework for streamlining the functioning of the NBFCs. The Committee recommended for evolving specific regulatory framework to govern the operations of these institutions. Such framework should include, in addition to the existing requirements of gearing and liquidity ratios, norms relating to capital adequacy, debt-equity ratio, credit-concentration ratio, adherence to sound accounting practices, uniform disclosure requirements and assets valuation.

In the light of the above, the RBI constituted a Working Group on Financial Companies under Dr. A.C. Shah in 1992[5] to make detailed study of working of NBFCs and to suggest regulatory and control measures to ensure healthy growth of these companies. Following the wide-ranging recommendations of the Committee, the RBI initiated a series of measures, including: (*i*) the widening of the definition of regulated deposits to include intercorporate deposits, deposits from shareholders and directors and the borrowers by issue of debentures secured by immovable property, (*ii*) the introduction of a scheme of registration of NBFCs having net owned fund of ₹ 50 lakh and above, (*iii*) the issuance of guidelines on prudential norms so as to regulate the asset side of the balance sheet of NBFCs. However, these measures could not be given statutory backing at that time since the provisions of the RBI Act, 1934 did not confer it with adequate powers to make them mandatory.

In January 1997, an Ordinance was issued by the Government effecting comprehensive changes in the provisions of the RBI Act 1934. This was subsequently replaced by the RBI (Amendment) Act in March, 1997. The RBI announced in January, 1998 a new set of regulatory measures, as brought out below: (Table 29.3)

TABLE 29.3: Regulatory Norms As per Chapter III B of the RBI Act

1. Certificate of Registration	No company, other than those exempted by the RBI, can commence or carry on the business of non-banking financial institution without obtaining a COR from RBI. The pre-requisite for eligibility for such a COR is that the NBFC should have a minimum net owned funds of ₹ 25 lakh (Now raised to ₹ 2 crore.)
2. Maintenance of Liquid	NBFCs have to invest in unencumbered approved securities, valued at a price not exceeding current market price, an amount which, at the close of business on any day, shall not be less than 5.0 per cent but not exceeding 25.0 per cent, specified by RBI, of the deposits outstanding at the close of business on the last working day of the second preceding quarter.

(Contd...)

3. Creation of Reserve Fund*	Every non-banking financial company shall create a reserve fund and transfer thereto a sum not less than 20.0 per cent of its net profit every year as disclosed in the profit and loss account and before any dividend is declared. Such fund is to be created by every NBFC irrespective of the fact whether it accepts public deposits or not. Further, no appropriation can be made from the fund for any purpose without prior written approval of RBI.

* *Nidhis* and *Chit Fund* companies exempted.

B. Directions applicable to NBFCs

The RBI has issued comprehensive deposit acceptance and asset side regulations as under for the NBFCs. While all the prudential norms are applicable to public deposit accepting/holding NBFCs only, some of the regulations are applicable to non-deposit accepting companies.

(I) Deposit Acceptance Related Regulations

1. Ceiling on quantum of public deposits	• Loan and investment companies - 1.5 times of NOF if the company has NOF of ₹ 25 lakh minimum investment grade (MIG) credit rating, complies with all the prudential norms and has CRAR of 15 per cent. • Equipment leasing and hire purchase finance companies — if company has NOF of ₹ 25 lakh and complies with all the prudential norms. (*i*) with MIG credit rating and 12 per cent CRAR - 4 times of NOF (*ii*) without MIG credit rating but CRAR 15 per cent or above — 1.5 times of NOF or ₹ 10 crore, whichever is less.
2. Investments in liquid assets	• NBFCs — 15 per cent of outstanding public deposit liabilities as at the close of business on the last working day of the second preceding quarter, of which (*i*) not less than 10 per cent in approved securities and (*ii*) not more than 5 per cent in term deposits with scheduled commercial banks. • RNBCs - 10 per cent of outstanding deposit liabilities as at close of business on last working day of second preceding quarter. • These liquid asset securities are required to be lodged with one of the scheduled commercial banks or Stock Holding Corporation of India Ltd., or a depository or its participant (registered with SEBI). • Effective October 1, 2002, government securities are to be necessarily held by NBFCs either in Constituent's Subsidiary General Ledger Account with a scheduled commercial bank or in a demat account with a depository participant registered with SEBI.

(Contd...)

	• These securities cannot be withdrawn or otherwise dealt with for any purpose other than repayment of public deposits.
3. Period of deposits	• No demand deposits • NBFCs — 12 to 60 months • RNBCs — 12 to 84 months • MNBCs (Chit Funds) — 6 to 36 months
4. Ceiling on deposit rate	• NBFCs, MNBCs and Nidhis — 12.5 per cent per annum (effective November 1, 2001) • RNBCs — Minimum interest of 4.0 per cent on daily deposits and 6.0 per cent on other than daily deposits. • Interest may be paid or compounded at periods not shorter than monthly rests.
5. Advertisement and	Every company, which accepts deposits by advertisement, has to comply with the advertisement rules prescribed in this regard, the deposit acceptance form should contain certain prescribed information, issue receipt for deposits, maintain a deposit register, etc.
6. Submission of Returns	All NBFCs holding or accepting public deposits have to submit periodical returns to RBI at quarterly, half yearly and annual intervals.
(2) Prudential Norms applicable to only those NBFCs which are accepting/holding public deposits	
1. Capital to Risk Assets Ratio (CRAR)	• The NBFCs holding/accepting public deposits are required to maintain CRAR as under: (*i*) Equipment leasing companies/hire purchase finance companies (with MIG credit rating) 12 per cent (*ii*) Equipment leasing companies/hire purchase finance companies (without minimum investment grade credit rating) 15 per cent (*iii*) Loan/investment companies 15 per cent (*iv*) RNBCs 12 per cent • CRAR comprises — tier I and tier II capital. • To be maintained on a daily basis and not merely on the reporting dates. • Tier I capital — core capital or NOF but includes compulsory convertible preference shares (CCPS) as a special case for CRAR purposes. • Tier II capital — all quasi-capital like preferences shares (other than CCPS) subordinated debt, convertible debentures, etc. • Tier II capital not to exceed tier I capital. • General provisions and loss reserves not to exceed 1.25 per cent of the risk-weighted assets.

(Contd...)

		• Subordinated debt issued with original tenor of 60 months or more.
2.	Restrictive norms	• Acceptance of public deposits not allowed if the prudential norms are not complied with fully. • Any NBFC defaulting in repayment of the matured deposits prohibited from crating any further assets until the defaults are rectified. • Investments in real estate, except for own use, restricted to 10 per cent of the owned fund. • Investments in unquoted shares restricted as under: EL/HP Companies 10 per cent of owned fund Loan/investment companies 20 per cent of owned fund • No further investments in real estate or unquoted shares in case of excess position held till its regularization. • Sufficient adjustment period allowed - further extension on merits of each case.
3.	Credit/investment concentration norms	• Single borrower exposure limits Credit: 15 per cent of owned fund Investments: 15 per cent of owned fund • Single group of borrowers exposure limits credit: 25 per cent of owned fund investments: 25 per cent of owned fund • Composite (credit and investments) exposure limits Single borrower: 25 per cent of owned fund Single group of borrowers: 40 per cent of owned fund • Exposure norms also applicable to own group companies and subsidiaries. • Includes all forms of credit and credit related and certain other receivables as also off balance sheet exposures. • Debentures/bonds to be treated as credit for the purpose of prudential norms but as investments for the purpose of balance sheet and compliance with investment obligations.
4.	Reporting System: Half-yearly return	• Half-yearly returns to be submitted as at the end of March and September every year. • Time allowed for submission — 3 months from the due date. • The return to be certified by the statutory auditors of the company. However, it need not wait for audit and the figures furnished therein could be the unaudited figures but must be certified by auditors.

(Contd...)

(3) Prudential Norms applicable to all NBFCs irrespective of whether they accept/ hold deposits or not	
1. Income Recognition Norms	• The recognition of income on the NPA is allowed on cash basis only. The unrealized income recognised earlier is required to be reversed.
2. NPA Norms	• Recognition of income on accrual basis before the asset becomes NPA as under: Loans and Advances: Upto 6 months and 30 days past due period (past due period done away with effect from March 31, 2003) Lease and Hire Purchase Finance: 12 months
3. Restrictive Norms	• Loans against own shares not allowed.
4. Policy on Demand/ Call Loans	• Companies to frame a policy for demand and call loans relating to cut-off date for recalling the loans, the rate of interest, periodically of such interest, periodical reviews of such performance, etc.
5. Accounting Standards	• All the Accounting Standards and Guidance Notes issued by Institute of Chartered Accounts of India (ICAI) are applicable to all NBFCs in so far as they are not inconsistent with the guidelines of RBI.
6. Accounting for Investments	• All NBFCs to have a well defined investment policy. • Investments classified into two categories: (*i*) long-term and (*ii*) current investments. • Long-term investments to be valued as per Accounting Standard, AS-13 of ICAI. • Current investments to be classified into: (*a*) quoted and (*b*) unquoted. • Current quoted investments to be valued at lower of cost or market value. • Block valuation permitted — Notional gains or losses within the block permitted to be netted — but not inter-block, net notional gains to be ignored but notional losses to be provided for. • Valuation norms for current unquoted investments are as under — (*i*) Equity shares (at lower of cost or break up value or fair value) (*ii*) Re. 1/- for the entire block of holding if the balance sheet of the investee company is not available for the last two years (*iii*) Preference shares at lower of cost or face value (*iv*) Government securities at carrying cost (*v*) Mutual Fund units at net asset value (NAV) for each scheme and (*vi*) Commercial Paper (CP) at its carrying cost.

(Contd...)

7.	Asset Classification	All forms of credit (including receivables) to be classified into four categories - • Standard asset • Sub-standard asset • Doubtful asset • Loss asset.
8.	Provisioning for Non-performing Assets Loans and Advamces	• Standard assets — No provision • Sub-standard assets — 10 per cent of outstanding balance • Doubtful assets — on unsecured portion 100 per cent and no secured portion 20, 30 and 50 per cent depending on the age of the doubtful assets • Loss asset — 100 per cent of the outstanding.
9.	Provisioning for Non-performing Assets Equipment Lease and Hire Purchases Accounts	• Unsecured portion to be fully provided for • Further provisions on net book value (NBV) of EL/HP assets • Accelerated additional provisions against NPAs NPA for 12 months or more but less than 24 months — 10 per cent of NBV NPA for 24 months or more but less than 36 months — 40 per cent of NBV NPA for 36 months or more but less than 48 months — 70 per cent of NBV NPA for 48 months or more — 100 per cent of NBV • Value of any other security considered only against additional provisions. • Rescheduling in any manner will not upgrade the asset upto 12 months of satisfactory performance under the new terms. • Repossessed assets to be treated in the same category of NPA or own assets — option lies with the company.
10.	Risk-Weights and Credit Conversion factors	• Risk-weights to be applied to all assets except intangible assets. • Risk-weights to be applied after netting off the provisions held against relative assets. • Risk-weights are 0, 20 and 100. • Assets deducted from owned fund like exposure to subsidiaries or companies in the same group or intangibles to be assigned 0 per cent risk-weight. • Exposures to all-India financial institutions (AIFIs) at 20 per cent risk-weight and all other assets to attract 100 per cent risk-weights. • Off-balance sheet items to be factored at 50 or 100 and then converted for risk-weight.

(Contd...)

11. Disclosure Requirements	(1) Every NBFCs is required to separately disclose in its balance sheet the provisions made as outlined above without netting them from the income or against the value of assets. (2) The provisions shall be distinctly indicated under separate heads of accounts as under; (*i*) provisions for bad and doubtful assets; and (*ii*) provisions for depreciation in investments. (3) Such provisions shall not be appropriated from the general provisions and loss reserved held, if any, by the NBFC. (4) Such provisions for each year shall be debited to the profit and loss account. The excess of provisions, if any held under the heads general provisions and loss reserves may be written back without making adjustment against them.

In recent years, focus of regulatory initiatives in respect of NBFCs has been on deposit acceptance norms and improved disclosures. Thus, in order to protect depositors interests, all NBFCs accepting/holding public deposits have, of late, been directed to ensure that there is full cover available at all times for public deposits accepted by them. While calculating this cover, the value of all debentures (secured and unsecured) and outside liabilities other than the aggregate liabilities to depositors may be deducted from total assets. For this purpose, the assets will have to be evaluated at their book value of realisable/market value, whichever is lower. In case, the assets cover so calculated falls short of the liability on account of public deposits, the same has to be reported to the RBI. They have also been asked to create a floating charge on the statutory liquid assets invested as required under section 45-1B of the RBI Act, 1937 is favour of their depositors and that the charge should be duly registered in accordance with the requirements of the companies Act.[6]

◈ Latest RBI's Policy Directives to NBFCs

The RBI has been strengthening the regulatory and supervisory framework for NBFCs since 1997 with the objective of making the NBFC sector vibrant and healthy. These efforts were pursued further during 2006-07. During the year, a major thrust was on strengthening the regulatory framework with regard to systematically important non-banking financial companies so as to reduce the regulatory gaps. Some of the major regulatory and supervisory policy directives, issued by the RBI during 2006-07 are stated below:[7]

◈ Reclassification of NBFCs

Until December 6, 2006, NBFCs were classified as equipment leasing, hire purchase, investment companies and loan companies. However, on December 6, 2006 all NBFCs were asked to regroup themselves into new categories, as asset finance companies (AFC), investment companies and loan companies.

AFC is defined as any company which is a financial institution carrying on as its principal business of financing the physical assets supporting productive/economic activity such as automobiles, tractors, generator sets, earth moving and material handling equipments, moving on own power and general purpose industrial machines. Aggregate financing of the above assets and income from the principal business must not be less than 60% of the total assets and total income, respectively. The companies satisfying these conditions should approach the Regional office of the RBI along with the original Certificate of Registration (COR) to reorganize their classification as asset finance companies. The change in classification would be incorporated in the COR issued by the RBI as NBFC — Asset Finance Company (NBFC-D-AFC), if accepting deposits and NBFC-ND-AFC, if not accepting deposits.

◈ Policy Directives regarding Systematically Important NBFCs

All NBFCs-ND with an asset size of ₹ 100 crore and more all now be called as systematically important NBFCs-ND (NBFC-ND-SI). These NBFCs are required to maintain a minimum CRAR of 10 per cent. They are not allowed *(i)* to lend to any single borrower/group of borrowers exceeding 15%/25% of their owned funds; *(ii)* invest in the shares of another company/single group of companies exceeding 15%/25% of their owned funds; and *(iii)* lend and invest exceeding 25% of their owned funds to a single party and 40% of their owned fund to a single group of parties.

In case of the additional exposure on account of infrastructure loan and/or investment, the NBFCs are allowed to exceed the prescribed limit of credit/investment for a single party or a single group of parties, i.e., 5% for a single party and 10% for a single group of parties.

AFCs are permitted to exceed the exposure to a single party and a single group of parties upto a further 5% points of their owned fund in exceptional circumstances with the approval of their boards.

The Government owned NBFCs are exempted from certain provisions of Non-Banking Financial Companies Prudential Norms (Reserve Bank) Directions, 1998, at present. However, there is a proposal to bring all deposit-taking and systematically important Government owned companies under the provisions of the Directions, 1998.

With a view to ensuring adherence to compliance with the regulatory framework for systematically important non-deposit taking/holding NBFCs (NBFC-ND-SI) as on December 12, 2006, such companies were advised on April 27, 2007 to put in place a system for submission of an annual statement of capital funds and risk asset ratio, among others, as at end of March every year.

◈ Exposure Norms & Risk Weights

The RBI amended the NBFCs Prudential Norms (Reserve Bank) Directions, 1998. Under the amended directions, NBFCs were advised on September 20, 2006 that while calculating the aggregate of funded exposure of a borrower for the purpose of assignment of risk weight, they may 'net-off' against the total outstanding exposure to the borrower advances collateralized by cash margins/security deposits/caution money against which the right to set off is available.

◈ Guidelines on Fair Practices Code

The RBI asked NBFCs on September 28, 2006 to prescribe the broad guidelines on fair practices that are to be framed and approved by the boards of directors of all NBFCs. The fair practices code so framed and approved by the board of directors is to be publicized and disseminated on the website of the company, if any, for the information of public.

The salient features of the guidelines are:

(*i*) Loan application form to include necessary information affecting the interest of the borrower.

(*ii*) To devise a system of giving acknowledgement for receipt of all loan applications and preferably the time frame, within which loan applications are to be disposed off.

(*iii*) To communicate in writing to the borrower by means of sanction letter or otherwise, the amount of loan sanctioned, alongwith the terms and conditions.

(*iv*) To give notice to the borrower of any change in the terms and conditions including disbursement schedule, interest rates, service charges and prepayment charges, among others.

(*v*) To release all securities on repayment of all dues.

(*vi*) To refrain from interference in the affairs of the borrower except for the purposes provided in the terms and conditions of the loan agreement.

(*vii*) Not to resort to undue harassment in the matter of recovery of loans.

(*viii*) The board to put in place the appropriate grievance redressal mechanism within the organization to resolve disputes in this regard.

◆ Prior Public Notice about change in Control/Management

NBFCs were advised on October 27, 2006 to give public notice 30 days prior to the transfer of the ownership by sale of shares, or transfer of control or by way of amalgamation/ merger of an NBFC with another NBFC or a non-financial company.

◆ Distribution of Mutual fund products by NBFCs/issue of co-branded credit cards

With a view to strengthening the NBFCs through diversification, the RBI permitted vide its annual policy statement for the year 2006-07 on October 31, 2006 to market and distribute mutual fund products as agents of mutual funds, with prior approval of the RBI, for an initial period of two years, to be reviewed thereafter.

It was also decided on December 4, 2006 to allow NBFCs, selectively, registered with the RBI to issue co-branded credit cards with scheduled commercial banks, without risk sharing, with prior approval of the Bank for an initial period of two years. NBFCs fulfilling the following minimum requirements are eligible to apply:

(*i*) Minimum net owned funds of ₹ 100 crore.

(*ii*) The company should have made net profit as per the last two years audited balance sheets.

(*iii*) The percentage of net NPAs to net advances of the NBFC as per the last audited balance sheet should not be more than 3 per cent and

(*iv*) NBFCs-ND should have CRAR of 10 per cent and NBFCs-D should have CRAR of 12 per cent or 15 per cent, as applicable to the company.

In addition, for distribution of mutual funds products the NBFC (*i*) should comply with the SEBI guidelines/regulation; (*ii*) should not adopt any restrictive practice of forcing its customers to go in for a particular mutual fund product sponsored by it; and (*iii*) the customers should be allowed to exercise their own choice.

In the case of co-brand credit card business, the role of the NBFCs under the tie up arrangement should be limited only to marketing and distribution of co-branded credit cards and the co-branded credit card issuing bank would be subject to all the instructions/guidelines issued by its concerned regulatory authority.

◆ Creation of Floating Charge

NBFCs accepting/holding public deposits have been directed to create floating charge on the statutory liquid assets invested in terms of Section 45-1B of the RBI Act, 1934.

◆ Submission of Returns and Certificates

(*i*) NBFCs and RNBCs with total assets of ₹ 100 crore and above the required to submit the monthly return on capital market exposure from April, 2007. Earlier only deposit taking NBFCs with deposits of ₹ 50 crore and above were submitting the return on capital market exposure.

(*ii*) NBFCs are required to submit a certificate from their statutory auditors every year to the effect that they continue to undertake the business of NBFI requiring holding of COR.

◆ Ceiling on Interest Rate

NBFCs/miscellaneous non-banking companies (Chit fund companies) can pay a maximum interest rate of 12.5 per cent per annum on their public deposits. The new rate of interest would be applicable to fresh public deposits and renewals of matured public deposits.

According to the RBI directives issued in January, 2009, the Board of each, NBFC should adopt an interest rate model taking into account the relevant factors, such as cost of funds, margin and risk premium and determine the interest rate accordingly.

◈ Acceptance of Deposits by Chit Fund Companies

MNBCs were prohibited w.e.f. August 18, 2009 from accepting deposits from public except from the shareholders, which was subject to the conditions specified in the MNBC Directives, 1977.

◈ Regulatory Framework for Core Investment Companies

Under the current regulatory framework, Core Investment Companies (CICs) with an asset size of less than ₹ 100 crore are exempt from the requirements of registration with the RBI. However, CICs with an asset size of ₹ 100 crore or more and accessing public funds would be considered as systematically important Core Investment Companies (CICs – ND – SI) and would be required to obtain Certificate of Registration from the RBI.

◈ Introduction of Provision of 0.25 per cent for Standard Assets of NBFCs

In the interest of counter-cyclicality and also to ensure that NBFCs create a financial buffer to protect themselves from the adverse effects of economic downturns, the RBI introduced in 2010 provisioning of 0.25 per cent of the outstanding standard assets.[8]

◈ Enhancing CRAR to 15 per cent

The RBI raised the minimum capital ratio of all deposit-taking NBFCs from 12 per cent to 15 per cent, effective from March 31, 2012. Accordingly, all deposit taking NBFCs shall maintain a minimum capital ratio consisting of Tier-I and Tier-II capital, which shall not be less than 15 per cent of the aggregate risk. Weighted assets in balance sheet and risk adjusted value of off-balance sheet items effective from March 31, 2012.[9]

◈ Entry of NBFCs into Insurance Business

The RBI permitted in 2010 NBFCs registered with it to set up a joint venture (JV) company for undertaking insurance business with risk participation, subject to certain safeguards: (i) the maximum equity contribution such an NBFC can hold in a JV company is 50 per cent of the paid-up capital of the insurance company; (ii) subsidiary or company in the same group of an NBFC or of another NBFC engaged in the business of a non-banking financial institution or banking business shall not be allowed to join the insurance company on risk participation basis. In case more than one company in the same group of the NBFC wishes to take a stake in the insurance company, the contribution by all companies in the same group shall be counted for the limit of 50 per cent prescribed for the NBFC in such an insurance JV.[10]

◈ Tightening norms for jewel loans

In a significant move to tighten the rules for lending by NBFCs, the RBI issued directive on March 21, 2012, making it mandatory for NBFC to maintain a loan-to-value (LTV) ratio of not exceeding 60 per cent for loans granted against the collateral of gold jewellery. Also, NBFCs will have to disclose in their balance sheet the percentage of such loans to their total assets.

Furthermore, NBFCs engaged in lending against gold jewellery (such loans comprising 50 per cent or more of their financial assets) must maintain a minimum Tier-I capital of 12 per cent by April 1, 2014.

NBFCs should not grant any advance against bullion/primary gold and gold coins.[11]

◈ Return to be submitted

All NBFCs (excluding RNBCs) are required to file various returns related to deposit acceptance prudential norms, capital market exposure, among others.

◈ RBI Panel Recommendations on Governing norms of NBFCs.[12]

A committee set up by the RBI headed by former RBI deputy governor Usha Thorat made the following recommendations:

(*i*) The provisioning and asset classification norms of NBFCs should be brought in line with these for commercial banks.

(*ii*) The liquidity ratio may be introduced for all registered NBFCs.

(*iii*) Tier-I capital of systematically important NBFCs should be at 12 per cent within three years of registration.

(*iv*) Risk weights for NBFC not sponsored by banks may be raised to 150 per cent for capital market exposure and 125 per cent for real estate exposure.

(*v*) NBFCs not accessing public funds may be exempted from registration, provided their assets were below ₹ 1,000 crore.

(*vi*) Minimum asset size of ₹ 50 crore should be insisted for registering any new NBFC. Existing NBFCs below this limit may deregister or be asked to seek a fresh certificate of registration a the end of two years.

◈ Revamping of the Fair Practices Code by RBI

On March 26, 2012, the RBI revamped the fair practice code (FPC) to the adopted by NBFCs while doing lending business and directed the NBFCs to modify FPC with the approval of their boards within one month of the issue of the circular.

The RBI issued the following guidelines to be incorporated in the NBFC's FPC:

- NBFCs should mention the penal interest charged for late repayment in bold in the loan agreement.
- NBFCs must furnish a copy of the loan agreement and enclosures quoted in the loan agreement to the borrower so as to avoid any dispute between with regard to the terms and conditions on which the loan was granted.
- Boards of NBFCs should lay appropriate internal principles and procedures in determining interest rates and processing and other charges.
- NBFCs should lay down the auction procedure that would be followed in case of auction of jewellery due to non-repayment. There should be no conflict of interest and the auction process must ensure that there is arm's length relationship in all transactions during the auction.
- NBFC themselves should not participate in the auctions held. Gold pledged will be auctioned only through auctioneers approved by the board.
- Micro Finance Institutions (Development and Regulation) Act, 2012.

The Government enacted Micro Finance Bill in December 2012 to empower the RBI to regulate the NBFCs in the customers' interest. A bird's eye view of the Micro Finance Bill can be had from Chapter 30.

E. ENFORCEMENT OF REGULATORY MEASURES

So as to ensure that the NBFCs adhere to the regulatory guidelines, the RBI laid down supervisory oversight a four-pronged strategy including (*a*) on-site inspection based on capital adequacy, assets quality, management, earnings and systems (CAMELS) methodology, (*b*) off-site monitoring supported by state – of the art technology, (*c*) market intelligence, and (*d*) exception reports of statutory auditors. The degree of supervisory oversight is based on the three criteria, *viz*, size of the NBFC, the type of activity performed and acceptance (or otherwise) of public deposits.

For close monitoring of linkages of NBFCs with capital market, a system of quarterly reporting which was subsequently changed to monthly reporting for companies having public deposits of ₹ 50 crore and above, was put in place. In case of large exposure to the capital market, companies have also been required to submit funds flow statement.

With a view to addressing issues relating to systematic risk and monitoring the affairs of financial conglomerates, the RBI put in place a reporting framework for such entities. Entities having significant presence in more than one financial segments under the jurisdiction of specified regulators (RBI, SEBI, IRDA, etc.) have been covered under this framework. NBFCs subject to this reporting discipline are required to submit returns at periodic intervals on their intra-group relationships.

Recently, a quarterly reporting arrangement has been introduced for NBFCs not accepting/ holding public deposits and having assets size or ₹ 500 crore and above as on March 31, 2004.

However, the periodicity for the submission of the return, which was found to be too long to take informed and timely decisions, was changed from quarterly to monthly from September 2005. Similarly, with a view to increasing the coverage of NBFCs, the threshold level was raised by making the reporting system applicable to NBFCs with assets size of ₹ 100 crore and above, beginning September, 2005, instead of ₹ 500 crore and above earlier.

A closer view of the above reveals that the RBI regulation and supervision system is comprehensive for companies accepting or holding public deposits to ensure protection of interests of depositors. Thus, companies holding or accepting deposits are required to comply with all the directions on acceptance of public deposits, prudential norms and liquid assets and should submit periodic returns to the RBI. They are supervised, using all the supervising tools. On the contrary, other NBFCs are regulated and supervised in a limited manner. They are required to comply only with prudential norms relating to income recognition, accounting standards asset classification and provisioning against bad and doubtful debts. Such companies are less frequently inspected. Recent measures and proposed moves of the RBI are intended to align the prudential norms for both deposit taking and non-deposit taking NBFCs and thereby reduce the regulatory arbitrate between banks and NBFCs. However, the RBI regulatory measures are considered far more stringent for deposit taking NBFCs. Life is going to be tougher for NBFCs catering to the securities market and real estate sector as their margin funding business will get affected, since the higher risk weight will increase the impact on the cost of funds and margins. Due to the higher provisioning norms, a substantial amount of money would be unproductive and it will impact the cash flow reserves, thereby impacting the margins.

TABLE 29.4: Ownership Pattern of NBFCs
(As on March 31, 2012)

(Number of Companies)

Ownership	NBFCs ND-SI	Deposit-taking NBFCs
A. Government companies	9 (2.4)	7 (12.6)
B. Non-government companies	366 (97.6)	266 (97.4)
1. Public Limited Companies	198 (52.8)	263 (96.3)
2. Private Limited Companies	168 (44.8)	3 (1.1)
Total No. of Companies (A+B)	375 (100.0)	273 (100.0)

Note: Figures in parentheses are percentage share in total number of NBFCs.

F. BUSINESS PROFILE OF NBFCs IN INDIA

◈ Ownership pattern of NBFCs

NBFCs in India have been predominantly non-government companies.[13] Table 29.4 exhibiting the ownership pattern of NBFCs-ND-SI as well as deposit taking NBFCs, show that the percentages of non-government companies (Public limited companies in nature) were 97.6 per cent and 97.4 per cent, respectively in NBFCs-ND-SI and deposit taking NBFCs as against government companies having a share of 2.4 per cent and 2.6 per cent, respectively at end-March, 2012.

◈ Resource Profile— An Overview

NBFCs in India procure resources for meeting their financial requirements through owned funds (comprising share capital and surplus), Public deposits and borrowings. Table 29.5 exhibiting information pertaining to resources structure of NBFCs shows that bulk of the fund requirements of these companies is met through outside sources (Public deposits and borrowings) while owned funds comprise not more than one-fourth of the total funds.

TABLE 29.5: Resources Profile of NBFCs
(As on March end)

(₹ crore)

Year	Owned Funds	Public Deposits	Borrowings & Other Liabilities	Total
1999	8026.6 (26.4)	9,784.7 (32.2)	22,620.6 (41.4)	40,431.9 (100)
2000	6,665.7 (17.8)	8,338.0 (22.3)	22,448.4 (59.9)	37,452.1 (100.0)
2001	4,089.5 (16.0)	5,350.9 (15.1)	16,163.0 (68.9)	25,603.4 (100.0)
2003	7,605.0 (20.1)	5,035.0 (13.4)	25,069.0 (66.5)	37,709.0 (100.0)
2004	6,741.0 (20.6)	4,317.0 (13.2)	21,556.0 (66.3)	32,614.0 (100.0)
2005	6,750.0 (18.7)	3,926.0 (10.9)	23,044.0 (70.3)	33,720.0 (100.0)
2006	6,787.0 (19.1)	2,667.0 (7.5)	23,641.0 (73.4)	37,095.0.0 (100.0)
2007	8,258.0 (17.2)	2,042.0 (4.3)	37,699.0 (78.5)	48,000.0 (100.0)
2008	11.870.0 (16.9)	2,038.0 (2.9)	56,385.0 (80.2)	70,293.0 (100.0)
2009	12,845.0 (17.0)	1941.0 (2.6)	60,730.0 (80.4)	75,516.0 (100.0)
2011	18,000 (15.4)	12,000.0 (10.2)	86,900 (65.6)	1,16,900.0 (100.0)
2012	22,500 (18.1)	10,000 (8.6)	91,800 (73.3)	1,24,400.0 (100.0)

Note: Figures in parentheses are percentage share in total.

Over the period 1999-2012, reliance on outside sources has increased at the expense of the owned funds. Thus, it may be seen from Table 29.6 that while relative share of owned funds in total funds nose-dived from 26.4% in 1999 to 18.1% in 2012, that of outside funds recorded sharp increase from 73.6% to 81.9% during the corresponding period. So as to increase bank's lending to NBFCs, the erstwhile guideline regarding bank's ceiling of 5 per cent of its networth and upto 40 per cent to a group of NBFCs has been increased to 10% for a single NBFC borrower with effect from April 1, 2007. The base has been changed to the bank's capital funds from its networks.[14]

◆ Deposit Profile of NBFCs

Deposits of NBFCs in India have recorded tremendous progress, indicating growing popularity of these companies among public at large. Thus, it may be seen from Table 29.6 that the deposits of the reporting NBFCs surged from ₹ 119 crore as on March end 1970 to over ₹ 24,500 crore as at March end, 2007, recording almost 200 times increase during the period. This can be attributed to simplified sanction procedures, orientation towards customers, attractive rates of return on deposits and flexibility and timeliness in meeting the credit needs of specified sectors like equipments leasing and hire purchase. However, amount of deposits garnered by NBFCs declined steeply and continuously to reach a low level of ₹ 10,100 crore as on March end, 2012. This was due to economic slump, high inflation, liquidity crunch and uncertainty in the economy. Among NBFCs, Residuary Non-Banking Companies (RNBCs) claimed over 80 per cent of the total deposits.

TABLE 29.6 :Aggregate of Deposits of NBFCs (As on March end)

Year	₹ in crore
1970-71	119
1975-76	444
1981-82	1,477
1987-88	5,942
2001-02	18,084
2002-03	18,822
2003-04	20,100
2004-05	19,644
2005-06	20,576
2006-07	24,697
2007-08	24,400
2008-09	21,567
2009-10	17,247
2010-11	11,964
2011-12	10,100

◆ Activity-wise Profile of Deposits

Predominance of RNBCs in total deposits held by all NBFCs has been the characteristic feature of the NBFCs operating in India. It may be observed from Table 29.7 that in 1999 RNBCs accounted for more than half of the public deposits garnered by NBFCs. This was followed remotely by EL and HP companies.

Over the period, 1999-2003 there has been significant surge in the relative share of NBFCs from 52.2 per cent in 1999 to 75.0 per cent in 2003. However, during the last two years, HP emerged as the largest NBFC group, constituting as high as 74.6 per cent at end-March, 2006.

TABLE 29.7: Activity-wise Profile of Deposits of NBFCs

Nature of business	1999	2001	2003	2005	2006
1. Equipment Leasing (EL)	1,172.91 (5.7)	1,450.21 (8.0)	511.0 (2.5)	4,727.0 (12.2)	3,489.0 (9.8)
2. Hire Purchase (HP)	3,339.78 (16.3)	3,659.19 (20.2)	3,539 (17.6)	20,500.0 (51.8)	28,682.0 (74.6)
3. Investment and Loan (IL)	4,455.80 (21.8)	785.82 (4.3)	329.0 (1.6)	2,894.0 (22.9)	2,987.0 (7.8)
4. RNBCs	10,644.27 (52.2)	11,625.24 (64.3)	15065 (75.0)	3,926.0 (10.9)	2,667.0 (7.0)
5. Other NBFCs	816.17 (4.0)	564.18 (3.1)	656.0 (3.3)	816.0 (2.2)	317.0 (0.8)
Total	20,428.93 (100.0)	18,084.64 (400.0)	20100 (100.0)	38,908.0	38,228.0

* includes Miscellaneous Non-banking companies, unregistered and unnoticed Nidhis, etc:
Note: Figures in brackets indicate Percentage to Total.

This broadly is the reflection of the impact of the efforts made in the field of deposits and borrowings.

◈ Size-wise Profile of Deposits of NBFCs-D

Majority of NBFCs in India have accepted public deposits of smaller amount. Thus, it may be noted from Table 29.8 that over four-fifths of the NBFCs accept deposits in the range of less than ₹ 2 crore. On the contrary, NBFCs holding deposits more than ₹ 20 crore represent only 5 per cent of total number of companies. However, these companies have accounted for over four-fifths of total public deposits held by all the NBFCs during the period 2002-2011.

A sharp increase was discernible in the share of the NBFCs-D with a deposit size of 5 crore and above, accounting for about 92.3 per cent of total deposits at end-March 2012. However, only 7 NBFCs-D belonged to this category, constituting about 3-6 per cent of the total number of NBFCs-D. It indicates that only relatively larger NBFCs-D were able to raise resources through deposits.

◈ Region-wise Profile of Deposits of NBFCs-D

One of the distinguishing features of the NBFCs in India is their localized operations. It may be discerned from Table 29.9 that Southern region predominated the total number of NBFCs, while Eastern region dominated the public deposits of all the NBFCs, essentially because a leading RNBC being based in Kolkata.

Over the period 1999-2003, relative share of deposits held by NBFCs in Eastern and Southern regions declined sharply from 61.4% in 1999 to 55.4% in 2003. In contrast, the share of Central region spurted sharply from 22.2% to 38.6% during the corresponding period. During the last seven years, southern region emerged as the largest region in so far as mobilization of deposits by the NBFCs is concerned. The presence of NBFC in the North-Eastern region reduced to nil since 2006.

◈ Maturity Pattern of Deposits of NBFCs-D

Table 29.10 displays information pertaining to maturity pattern of deposits held by NBFCs during the period 1999-2012. A close scrutiny of the table shows that deposits in the maturity range of more than one year and up to 3 years accounted for over two-thirds of the total deposits of the NBFCs as on March end, 2012.

TABLE 29.8: Size-wise Profile of Deposits Held by NBFCs-D
(As at end-March)

(₹ in crore)

Deposit Range	No. of NBFCs										Amount of Deposit										
	2002	2003	2004	2005	2006	2007	2008	2009	2010	2011	2002	2003	2004	2005	2006	2007	2008	2009	2010	2011	2012
Less than 0.5	518	491	428	368	264	218	213	177	184	134	83 (1.4)	65 (1.3)	53 (1.2)	43 (1.1)	37 (1.4)	30 (1.5)	28 (1.4)	22 (1.1)	21 (8.00	19 (0.5)	13 (0.2)
0.5-2.0	237	233	210	197	120	29	85	53	60	38	234 (3.9)	225 (4.5)	206 (4.8)	195 (5.0)	116 (4.3)	83 (4.1)	82 (4.0)	51 (2.6)	64 (2.3)	44 (1.1)	38 (0.6)
2.0-10.0	97	90	82	84	48	34	38	30	27	28	416 (7.0)	360 (7.1)	352 (8.2)	375 (9.6)	201 (7.5)	152 (7.4)	186 (9.0)	133 (1.9)	128 (4.4)	129 (3.2)	113 (2.0)
10.0-20.0	11	21	18	18	14	7	4	6	5	7	160 (2.7)	284 (5.6)	242 (5.6)	265 (6.7)	196 (7.3)	93 (4.6)	61 (3.0)	76 (3.9)	69 (2.5)	108 (2.7)	109 (1.9)
20.0-50.0	14	12	17	18	6	4	2	3	4	2	396 (6.7)	364 (7.2)	569 (13.2)	601 (15.3)	199 (7.5)	151 (7.4)	56 (2.7)	115 (5.9)	133 (4.8)	81 (2.8)	120 (2.1)
50.0 and above	28	23	19	15	11	7	8	6	10	8	4,644 (78.3)	3,737 (74.3)	2,895 (67.0)	2,447 (62.3)	197 (71.9)	1533 (75.1)	1629 (79.8)	1544 (79.5)	2416 (78.0)	3681 (91.5)	5447 (92.2)
Total	**905**	**870**	**774**	**700**	**463**	**359**	**350**	**275**	**290**	**217**	**5,933 (100.0)**	**5,035 (100.0)**	**4,317 (100.0)**	**3,926 (100.0)**	**2,682 (100.0)**	**2042 (100.0)**	**2042 (100.0)**	**1941 (100.0)**	**2831 (100.0)**	**4062 (100.0)**	**5,840 (100.0)**

Note: Figures in parenthesis denote Percentage to Total.

TABLE 29.9: Region-wise Break-up of Deposits held by NBFCs-D
(As at end-March)

(₹ in crore)

Region	1999		2001		2003		2005	
	No.	Amt.	No.	Amt.	No.	Amt.	No.	Amt.
Northern	204	484.07	253 (2.4)	575.0 (3.0)	271	543.0 (2.7)	200	351.0 (8.9)
North Eastern	30	0.89 (–)	—	—	1	484.07 (2.4)	0	0
Eastern	64	7,711.91 (37.7)	24	7932.0 (44.0)	21	7634.0 (38.0)	15	178.0 (4.5)
Central	244	4,533.94 (22.2)	126	4105.07 (23.0)	83	7752 (38.6)	72	920 (2.4)
Western	180	2,851.08 (14.0)	81	2041.0 (11.0)	63	687.0 (3.4)	32	280.0 (7.1)
Southern	825	4847.04 (23.7)	497	3432.0 (19)	436	3482.0 (17.3)	381	3,204.0 (77.0)
Total	**1,547**	**20,428.93 (100.0)**	**981**	**18084.0 (100.0)**	**875**	**20,100.0 (100.0)**	**700**	**3926.0 (100.0)**

Region	2006		2007		2010		2011		2012	
	No.	Amt.	No.	Amt.	No.	Amt.	No.	Amt.	No.	Amt.
Northern	215	333.0 (13.6)	191	288	189	335.0	144	188.0	125	328.5
North Eastern	1	0	0	0	—	—	—	—	—	—
Eastern	12	59.0 (5.4)	8	21 (1.0)	9	9.0	8	4.0	5	3.9
Central	63	34.0 (1.4)	59	27 (1.3)	—	—	—	—	—	—
Western	27	104.0 (3.9)	23	86 (4.2)	27	612.0	20	929.0	17	1.488.0
Southern	114	1917 (78.3)	78	1620 (79.3)	65	1,876	45	2,942	49	4,020
Total	**432**	**2,447 (100.0)**	**359**	**2042 (100.0)**	**290**	**2.831.0**	**217**	**4,062**	**196**	

Note: Figures in parenthesis denote Percentage to Total.

TABLE 29.10: Maturity Pattern of Deposits held by NBFCs-D
(As at end-March)

(₹ in crore)

Maturity Period	Amount of Deposits									
	1999	2001	2003	2005	2006	2007	2009	2010	2011	2012
Less than 1 year	1,694.6 (17.3)	1,721.0 (26.7)	1,203.0 (23.9)	1,208.0 (30.8)	878 (35.9)	695 (34.1)	698 (36.0)	1034 (36.5)	982 (24.2)	1172 (20.1)
1-2 years	2,904.3 (29.7)	1,741.0 (27.0)	1,241.0 (24.6)	940.0 (24.0)	648 (26.5)	473 (23.2)	506 (26.1)	595 (21.0)	794 (19.6)	1,553 (26.6)
2-3 years	2,895.8 (29.6)	2,038.0 (31.5)	1,927.0 (38.3)	1,357.0 (34.6)	559 (22.8)	560 (27.4)	593 (30.6)	1031 (36.4)	1988 (48.9)	2,498 (42.8)
3-5 years	2,122.2 (21.7)	842.0 (13.0)	619.0 (12.3)	402.0 (10.2)	360 (14.7)	234 (11.4)	84 (4.3)	81 (2.9)	222 (5.5)	617 (10.6)
5 years and above	167.8 (1.7)	118.0 (1.8)	45 (0.9)	19.0 (0.5)	3 (0.1)	80 (3.9)	60 (3.0)	90 (3.2)	77 (1.9)	1 (0.0)
Total	**9,784.7 (100.0)**	**6,460 (100.0)**	**5,035.0 (100.0)**	**3,926.0 (100.0)**	**2,447 (100.0)**	**2,042 (100.0)**	**1941 (100.0)**	**2,831 (100.0)**	**4,062 (100.0)**	**5841 (100.0)**

Note: Figures in parentheses denote Percentage to Total.

In 2010-11, there was sharp increase in the proportionate share of deposits belonging to more than 2 years and upto 3 years, while the shares of deposits belonging to almost all maturity categories showed a decline. In 2011-12, the relative share of deposits having maturity period of more than one year but less than 2 years surged sharply.

◈ Borrowings By NBFCs-D

NBFCs in India borrow funds from various sources, *viz.*, Governments, banks and financial institutions, debentures, foreign and other sources. It may be discerned from Table 29.11 that banks and financial institutions and debentures are major source of borrowings by NBFCs. Other sources comprising inter-corporate borrowings, commercial paper, borrowings from mutual funds, Directors, etc., constitute another important source of borrowing.

TABLE 29.11: Sources of Borrowings of NBFCs-D
(As on March end)

(₹ in crore)

Sources	1999	2001	2003	2005	2006	2007	2008	2009	2010	2011	2012
1. Government	2,739.6 (12.11)	3,041.0 (13.5)	1,570.0 (6.4)	972.0 (4.2)	533.0 (2.3)	25.0 0	2,319 (4.6)	1,824 (3.3)	4710 (7.4)	5908 (8.4)	5,400 (6.7)
2. Banks and Financial Institutions	7,582.9 (33.5)	8,959.0 (36.5)	6,954.0 (36.6)	8,796.0 (30.2)	9197.0 (38.9)	14,923.0 (42.8)	18,995 (38.0)	24,565 (44.5)	31,853 (49.8)	35,320 (50.0)	40,100 (50.0)
3. Debentures	4,001.8 (17.7)	3,758.0 (16.7)	5,352.0 (21.9)	6,976 (30.3)	8,171 (34.6)	8,777.0 (26.9)	13,054 (25.8)	13,066 (23.6)	14,973 (23.4)	14,330 (20.0)	23,800 (29.4)
4. Foreign Sources	624.2 (2.8)	670.0 (3.0)	694.0 (2.8)	510.0 (2.2)	621.0 (2.6)	1201.0 (3.6)	1,455 (2.1)	1463 (2.6)	757 (1.1)	3 (0)	—
5. Others	7,672.1 (33.9)	6,851.0 (33.3)	7,905.0 (32.3)	7,632.0 (33.1)	5,519.0 (21.4)	7,637.0 (26.7)	14,753 (29.5)	14,371 (26.0)	11,785 (18.3)	14,256 (21.6)	14,300 (13.9)
Total	**22,620.6 (100.0)**	**22,559.0 (100.0)**	**24,480.0 (100.0)**	**23,044 (100.0)**	**23,641 (100.0)**	**32,563 (100.0)**	**50,577 (100.0)**	**55,289 (100.0)**	**64,078 (100.0)**	**69,816 (100.0)**	**80,900 (100.0)**

Note: Figures in parentheses denote Percentage to Total.

During the period 1999-2006, debentures emerged as the most important source of funds for NBFCs. Its share to total borrowings shot up from 17.7% in 1999 to 34.6% in 2006. On the contrary, borrowings from banks and financial institutions declined in significance; from 33.5%

in 1999, it fell to 30.2% in 2005. However, in 2006-07, NBFC's borrowings from banks and financial institutions shot up to 38.9%. Borrowing from external sources and from banks and financial institutions increased sharply by 95.9 per cent and 52.6 per cent, respectively during 2006-07, leading to surge in their proportionate share to the total borrowings. However, borrowings from the Government declined sharply during 2006-07. There is one state owned NBFC operating in the Southern region. During 2008-2012 borrowing from banks and financial institutions surged remarkably while borrowing through debenture and from government declined.

◈ Asset Profile of NBFCs-D

◈ Pattern of Assets — An Overview

Table 29.12 displays pattern of deployment of funds of NBFCs-D sector in India. It can be seen from this Table that funds of the NBFCs are utilized in the form of loans and investment and other financial assets. Security investments comprise government securities, corporate securities and others. Other financial assets of the NBFCs include hire purchase, equipment leasing and bills discounting.

TABLE 29.12: Asset Composition of NBFCs-D
(As on March end)

(Amount in crore of ₹)

Components	2001	2002	2003	2004	2005	2006	2009	2010	2011	2012
Loans and Advances	8,090.9 (31.2)	8,592.0 (28.7)	13,398.0 (35.5)	12,363.0 (37.7)	12,749.0 (35.4)	9,199.0 (25.9)	57305 (38.6)	71,119 (37.9)	77,901 (38.2)	87,400 (39.0)
Investments	2,882.4 (11.3)	3,302.0 (11.0)	4,338.0 (11.6)	3,817.0 (11.6)	3,957.0 (11.0)	3,589.0 (10.1)	14,813 (10.0)	18,498 (10.9)	21,102 (10.3)	19,100 (8.5)
Other Financial Assets	14,630.7 (17.7)	18,001.0 (60.3)	19,973.0 (52.9)	16,574.0 (50.7)	19,297.0 (53.3)	22,773.0 (54.0)	75,516 (51.4)	94,212 (51.2)	1,05,431 (51.5)	1,16,900 (52.5)
Total	25,604.0 **(100.0)**	29,895.0 **(100.0)**	37,709.0 **(100.0)**	32,754.0 **(100.0)**	36,003.0 **(100.0)**	35,561.0 **(100.0)**	1,47,634 **(100.0)**	1,83,829 **(100.0)**	2,04,434 **(100.0)**	2,23,400 **(100.0)**

Note: Figures in parentheses denote Percentage to Total.

It is interesting to note from the above table that more than half of the funds of these companies are invested in other financial assets, especially in hire purchase form. Other important component of the assets is loans and advances which constitute one-third of the total assets. Among security investment, NBFCs appear to have shown greater interest in corporate securities, obviously for enhancing their earnings.

◈ Activity Profile of Assets of NBFCs-D

Table 29.13 showing activity-wise distribution of assets of NBFCs reveals that the major portion of the assets of NBFCs are in the form of hire purchase assets. Over the period 1999-2006 while hire purchase assets gained in significance, other forms of assets lost their sheen. Thus, it may be seen from the Table that loans and inter-corporate deposits had claimed almost one-third of the assets of the NBFCs in 2001 which, however, tended to decline to 3.9% in 2005. Likewise, declining tendency was noticeable in respect of security investment. In contrast, percentage share of hire purchase assets soared from 33.4% to 80.7% during the corresponding period. In 2009, phenomenal surge in loans and investments was witnessed. Surge in these two categories of assets of NBFCs continued during 2010 and 2011. These two categories of activities constituted 93.9 per cent share in total assets of the NBFCs-D sector.[15]

TABLE 29.13: Activity-wise Deployment of Assets of NBFCs-D (As at March end)

(Amount in crore of ₹)

Components	2001	2002	2003	2004	2005	2006	2009
Loans and Inter-Corporate deposits	8,090.0 (31.2)	13,710.0 (34.4)	4,109.0 (10.9)	5,485.0 (16.7)	6,964 (9.3)	1,377 (3.9)	21,073.0 (27.9)
Investments	2,882.4 (11.3)	4,334.0 (10.9)	2,208.0 (5.9)	2,422.0 (7.4)	1,890 (5.2)	1,160 (4.5)	14,813.0 (19.6)
Hire Purchase	8,341.0 (33.4)	13,202.0 (33.1)	22,163.0 (58.8)	19,929.0 (60.8)	20,500 (56.9)	28,682 (80.7)	35,647.0 (47.2)
Equipment Leasing	3,187.2 (12.8)	3,112.0 (7.8)	7,996.0 (21.2)	3,744.0 (11.4)	4,727 (13.1)	3,489 (9.8)	585.0 (0.8)
Other Assets	3,102.5 (11.3)	5,475.0 (13.8)	1,233.0 (3.3)	1,173.0 (3.6)	1,922 (5.3)	404 (1.1)	3398.0 (4.5)
Total	**25,604.0 (100.0)**	**39,833.0 (100.0)**	**37,709.0 (100.0)**	**32,754.0 (100.0)**	**36,003 (100.0)**	**35,561 (100.0)**	**75,516.0 (100.0)**

◈ Size-wise Distribution of Assets of NBFCs-D

Deployment of resources by different size groups of NBFCs is exhibited in Table 29.14. It may be noticed from this table that asset size of NBFCs varies significantly from less than ₹ 50 lakh to above ₹ 500 crore. Most of the companies were those having assets of less than ₹ 10 crore. However, bulk of the assets were held by NBFCs in the large assets size. Thus, 15 NBFC companies with assets size of above ₹ 500 crores held more than 95 per cent of the total assets of all the NBFCs-D as at March end, 2011.

A peep into the table reveals that over the period, assets size of the NBFCs particularly those having less than ₹ 2 crore declined sharply. This is reflective of utilization of assets to liquidate high cost deposit liabilities.[16] Another reason for the reduction in the asset size of many of the companies may be attributed to conversion of a few large sized deposit taking companies to non-deposit taking companies.[17]

It is interesting to observe that while small NBFCs often specialize in addressing local credit needs, their large number continues to pose a regulatory challenge for the RBI.[18]

G. NBFCs AND INSURANCE AND CREDIT CARD BUSINESS

Recently, the RBI has decided to permit NBFCs to enter into insurance business subject to the following conditions:

(*a*) NBFCs should possess owned funds of not less than ₹ 500 crore;

(*b*) CRAR of not less than 12.0 per cent (15.0 per cent in case of NBFCs engaged in loan and investment activities holding public deposits);

(*c*) Level of Net NPA not more than 5.0 per cent of the total outstanding leased/hire purchase assets and advances taken together;

(*d*) Net profit for the last three continuous years;

(*e*) A satisfactory track record of the performance of the subsidiaries; and

(*f*) Regulatory compliance and servicing of public deposits held.

A NBFC will normally hold 50 per cent of the paid-up capital of the insurance company. The RBI may permit a higher equity contribution by the NBFC initially, pending divestment of equity within the prescribed period.

TABLE 29.14: Size-wise Distribution of Assets of NBFCs *(As at March end)*

(₹ in Crore)

Range of Assets (₹ crore)	1999		2001		2003		2005		2006		2007		2010		2011	
	No. of Comps.	Assets	No. of Comps.	Assets	No. of Comps.	Assets	No. of Comps.	Assets	No. of Comps.	Assets	No. of Comps.	Assets	No. of Comps.	Assets	No. of Comps.	Assets
Less than 0.50	1,055	79.30 (0.2)	153	42.0 (0.1)	139	34.0 (0.1)	129	31.0 (0.1)	45	14.0	56	12.0	23	8	11	3
0.50-2	332	307.41 (0.9)	389	421.0 (1.1)	354	388.0 (1.0)	258	284.0 (0.8)	187	215.0	155	176.0	105	125	70	80
2.00-10	55	961.49 (2.8)	280	1,193.0 (3.2)	245	1,131.0 (3.0)	185	816.0 (2.3)	119	551.0	97	418.0	91	416	73	347
10.00-50	64	1,701.31 (4.7)	89	1,981.0 (5.3)	68	1,394.0 (3.7)	77	1,865.0 (5.2)	48	1,127.0	43	1,024.0	37	831	34	822
50.00-100	11	1,709.95 (4.7)	15	1,019.0 (2.7)	19	1,315.0 (3.5)	18	1,216.0 (3.4)	7	473.0	5	339.0	10	702	8	508
100.0-500	18	5,122.76 (22.6)	28	7,130.0 (18.9)	28	6,492.0 (17.2)	16	3,119.0 (8.7)	12	2,362.0	8	1,598.0	7	1,377	6	831
Above 500	1	23,085.78 (64.1)	20	25,848.0 (68.7)	17	26,950.0 (71.5)	17	20,672 (79.6)	14	33,085.0	15	44,433.0	17	90,753	15	1,02,839
Total	**1,536**	**35,968.00 (100.0)**	**974**	**37,634.0 (100.0)**	**870**	**37,709.0 (100.0)**	**700**	**36,003.0 (100.0)**	**432**	**37,828.0 (100.0)**	**359**	**47,999.0 (100.0)**	**290**	**94,212 (100.0)**	**217**	**1,05,431 (100.0)**

Note: Figures in brackets denote Percentage to Total

Earlier NBFCs entering into insurance business were required to seek prior approval of the RBI. NBFCs can now enforce insurance business without approval of the RBI on fee basis and without risk participation subject to certain conditions. However, NBFCs intending to set up insurance joint ventures with equity contribution on risk participation basis on making investments in the insurance companies would have to obtain the prior approval of the RBI.

NBFCs have also been permitted to enter into credit card business on their own in association with another NBFC or a scheduled commercial bank. This permission is granted on a selective basis keeping in view the financial position of the company and its record compliance. However, they are not allowed to issue any debit card. For entering in credit card business, NBFCs will have to obtain a certificate of registration apart from specific permission to enter into this business from the RBI. The NBFC would have to satisfy the requirement of a minimum owned fund of ₹ 100 crore and such other terms and conditions as the RBI may specify to this effect from time to time.

Towards the end of 2006, as stated earlier, the RBI permitted NBFCs having a minimum net owned fund of ₹ 100 crore, a net profits for two years and NPAs of less than 3 per cent to distribute mutual funds and issue co-branded credit cards (with commercial banks) with its prior approval. The non-deposit taking NBFCs should have a capital adequacy ratio of 10 per cent and deposit taking NBFCs should have 12 per cent or 15 per cent as applicable to the company.

H. FINANCIAL PERFORMANCE OF NBFCs-D

Financial performance of NBFCs-D can be objectively assessed in terms of profitability and financial soundness. While profitability of these companies can be judged by relating net profit to total assets and financial soundness, as is reflected in asset quality and capital adequacy.

Table 29.15 showing financial ratios of NBFCs-D during the period 1998-99 to 2010-12 reveals that profitability of NBFCs has improved significantly in recent years. Thus, net profit as percentage of total assets, which stood at 0.3% in 1998-99, surged over five-fold to reach an all time high level of 1.6% in 2004-05. This is primarily because of the persistently declining trend in total expenditure of the companies, which recorded a fall from 17.8% to 10.3% during the corresponding period. Profitability performance of NBFCs suffered a set-back during the next two years primarily because of increase in expenditure. However, profitability performance of NBFCs-D witnessed improvement, as reflected in the increase in their operating profits during 2010-12. This increase in profit was mainly on account of growth in income while expenditure declined marginally.

TABLE 29.15: Financial Ratios of NBFCs-D

	1998-99	2000-01	2002-03	2004-05	2005-06	2006-07	2008-09	2009-10	2010-11	2011-12
1. Net Profit as % of Total Assets	0.3	0.3	0.9	1.6	1.5	1.2	2.7	1.6	2.7	2.8
2. Income as % of Total Assets	18.9	16.9	13.5	12.7	12.2	12.0	15.6	14.5	14.4	15.5
3. Fee Income as % of Total Assets	0.7	1.0	1.0	1.0	0.4	0.3	6.4	0	0	0.1
4. Total Expenditure as % of Total Assets	17.8	15.9	11.9	10.2	9.0	10.0	11.6	11.7	10.4	11.4

It is gratifying to note that profitability rate of the NBFCs has been higher as compared to commercial banks. This can further be boosted if NBFCs lay more focus on fee-based activity. At present, fee-based income is infinitesimally small, as evidenced from the above table.

Regarding financial soundness of NBFCs, it may be observed from Table 29.16 that net NPAs in relation to total advances tended to decline from 6.7% in 1998 to as low as 0.4% in

2007. Net NPAs remained negative with provisions exceeding NPAs for the last four consecutive years upto end-March 2011. This is indicative of significant improvement in the asset quality of the NBFCs. On this score also, NBFCs' position is better as compared to commercial banks.

TABLE 29.16: Net Non-Performing Assets of NBFCs-D
(As on March end)

Year	(Per cent of credit exposure)
1998	6.7
1999	7.0
2000	9.5
2001	5.6
2002	3.9
2003	2.7
2004	2.4
2005	2.5
2006	0.4
2007	0.4
2008	9
2009	0
2010	—
2011	—
2012	0.5

From the perspective of regulatory and supervisory process, the capital to risk weighted assets ratio (CRAR) constitutes the most important indicator for evaluating soundness and solvency of NBFCs.

CRAR norms were made applicable to NBFCs in 1998 in terms of which every deposit-taking NBFCs is required to maintain a minimum capital consisting of Tier-I and Tier-II capital of not less than 12 per cent (15 per cent in the case of unrated deposit-taking loan/investments companies) of its aggregate risk-weighted assets and of risk adjusted value of off-balance sheet items.

TABLE 29.17: CRAR of NBFCs-D (As at March end)

CRAR (Range Per cent)	1999	2001	2003	2005	2006	2007	2009	2010	2011	2012
Less than 12	88	61	42	64	19	13	17	5	4	2
12-15	18	8	10	1	3	4	3	1	3	1
15-20	50	38	45	21	10	11	6	8	8	11
20-30	118	82	74	32	38	29	21	28	22	18
Above 30	403	525	487	206	252	275	150	235	169	158
Total	**677**	**714**	**658**	**324**	**322**	**332**	**207**	**275**	**204**	**190**

It may be seen from Table 29.17 that more than two-thirds of the NBFCs possessed a CRAR of above 30 per cent, far in excess of minimum statutory stipulations. Further, NBFCs having CRAR above 12 per cent but less than 30 per cent represented 25 per cent of the total number of companies. Thus, only a smaller number of NBFCs had CRAR less than the stipulated requirements.

At the end-March 2012, 187 out of 190 NBFCs had CRAR of more than 15 per cent or more (Table 29.17). This indicates that the NBFC sector is witnessing a consolidation process in the last few years, wherein the weaker NBFCs are gradually exiting and paving the way for stronger ones.[19]

On this score too, position of NBFCs has been more satisfactory as compared to commercial banks in India.

G. INTER-CONNECTENESS OF NBFCs AND COMMERCIAL BANKS IN INDIA

Recent global financial crisis has focused attention on inter-connectedness of the banking system with the NBFCs as excessive inter-institutional exposure tends to render the financial system vulnerable.

In recent few years, NBFCs in India are switching over from public deposits to borrowings in view of tightening of the prudential regulatory norms in respect of deposit taking companies. Thus, their total borrowigs as at the end of March, 2011 comprised as much as 66.2 per cent of their total liabilities (as against 31.8 per cent as at the end of March 2001), while the proportion of public deposits outstanding to their total liabilities declined sharply to 3.5 per cent at the end-March 2011 from 20.9 per cent as on March end 2001. Furthermore, nearly half of the total borrowings are from banks and financial institutions. This ostensibly indicates closer financial relationship between the backing system and NBFCs.

Further, greater reliance on borrowing for funding their operations and that too from banks raises concerns about the liquidity position of NBFCs and the banks' own liquidity position is likely to become tight in the event of crisis.

The larger NBFCs with ₹ 100 crore and above assets size, classified as symmetrically important (NBFC-ND-SI), are also found depending on banking system for their resources. As these NBFCs are not deposits taking, they are subject to somewhat less rigorous rules compared with NBFCs-D. In the post global financial turmoil, the regulators' attention across the world focused on the systematically important financial institutions (SIFIs). In India, the RBI has recently made it mandatory for such institutions to get themselves registered with the former.

Thus, high reliance of NBFCs on the banking system will not only strain banks in times of crisis but also land NBFCs themselves into vulnerable situation as banks may in the event of liquidity crunch, deny lending to NBFCs which in that case would further aggravate the precarious condition. The recent global financial meltdown is a pointer in this direction.

In view of differential regulatory and cost-incentive structures of banks and NBFCs and the latter borrowing from the former for on-lending, it would be in fitness of things to laydown adequate checks and balances on operations of NBFCs so as to ensure that the banks' depositors are not indirectly exposed to the risks arising due to above differential. It is gratifying to note that the RBI has already moved in this direction to bring the regulatory norms pertaining to NBFCs on par with the banking system.

I. CONCLUSIONS AND SUGGESTIONS

NBFCs represent an extremely heterogeneous group of intermediaries concerned with mobilization of resources and their profitable deployment. NBFCs came late in India in late 60s and early 70s to extend financial support to industrial houses. These institutions witnessed remarkable growth in 90's because of the impetus given by the Government policy of economic liberalization. Not only existing companies expanded their operations but a large number of new NBFCs were set up to squeeze the opportunities.

With a view to ensuring that NBFCs operate in the best interests of the investors, the Government, the RBI and SEBI formulated policy guidelines with respect to their registration and operations. The RBI laid down supervisory system to ensure the effective implementation of the policies.

Within the overall framework of the policies, NBFCs have raised resources from different sources to meet their credit and investment requirements. A distinguishing feature of resource profile of the NBFCs in India is that they place greater reliance on external sources like deposits and borrowings than on their own.

Among the resources, public deposits constitute an important component. There has been tremendous growth in public deposits of the NBFCs, indicating growing popularity of these institutions among public at large because of their attractive rate of return, timely sanction of funds and high degree of flexibility.

Predominance of RNBCs in total deposits held by all NBFCs has been another redeeming feature of these companies.

Majority of the NBFCs in India accept public deposits of small amount.

Further, operations of the NBFCs are localized in character. For instance, Southern region predominates the total number of NBFCs in India, while Eastern region dominate the public deposits of these institutions.

Another striking feature of the NBFCs is that they accept deposits of shorter duration. This is reflective partly of the reluctance of depositors to enter into long-term commitments when interest rates are at historic lows.

Another significant source of funding of NBFCs is borrowing from financial institutions and debentures. Over the years, debentures have emerged as the most important source for the NBFCs.

Regarding utilization of their resources, the NBFCs have been found deploying their funds in granting loans, investing in securities and holding other assets. However, hire purchase assets occupy prominent position in the assets portfolio of the NBFCs.

Size-wise distribution of assets reveals that most of the NBFCs have assets of less than ₹ 10 crore. However, bulk of the total assets were held by a few leading NBFCs.

In recent years, NBFCs have been permitted to engage in non-fund business like insurance and credit card business. However, their operations in this sphere have remained limited so far.

As for financial performance of the NBFCs, it is interesting to find that over the years profitability and financial health of these institutions have remarkably improved. But there is still great scope for the NBFCs to improve their earning through expanding their fee-based business.

So as to ensure successful survival of NBFCs in the wake of highly competitive environment, they will have to enter into mergers and joint ventures so as to prune down their field of activities and hive off problematic areas. This will help them consolidating their position which in turn reduce cost of raising funds and other operations. It is heartening to note that the major finance companies such as, Alpic Finance, Apple Finance, Apple Credit Corporation and Sree International Finance have recently decided to explore the possibilities of merging their business.

NBFCs should also explore the possibilities of expanding their business into non-traditional fund based and fee based areas where they have core expertise. They should undertake in-dept market study to identify the niches keeping in view macro-economic variables, such as money supply, inflation, interest and rate movements. With the opening of the financial sector to overseas investors, there will be spate of tie-ups for requisite expertise and technology transfers. NBFCs having professional expertise and strong infrastructural base can take advantage of this opportunity. The need of the hour is to innovate, change and upgrade technology involved in raising funds and their deployment and to improve customers' services.

Growing inter-connectedness of the NBFCs and banking system in India, as reflected in switching over from public deposits to bank borrowings by the NBFCs, is causing deep concern among financial regulators about the vulnerability of the NBFCs and so also of the banking system in times of financial meltdown. To stave off the impending crisis, it is imperative to bring regulatory norms of the NBFCs on par with commercial banks. The RBI has, of late, moved in this direction.

KEY TERMS

- Chit Fund company
- Equipment Leasing Company
- Hire-purchase Finance Company
- Infrastructure Finance company
- Investment Company
- Loan Company
- Miscellaneous Non-banking Company
- Mutual Benefit Finance Company
- Nidhi company
- Residuary Non-banking Company (RNBC)
- Systematically Important Core Investment Companies.

DISCUSSION QUESTIONS

1. How has the RBI define a NBFC?
2. Discuss in brief, nature of business of different types of NBFCs operating in India.
3. Give an account of evolution and growth of NBFCs in India.
4. Describe regulatory framework of NBFCs.
5. Outline recent policy directives of the RBI to govern the operations of the NBFCs.
6. Assess resource profile of NBFCs in India.
7. Critically examine asset profile of NBFCs in India.
8. Evaluate financial performance of NBFCs operating in India.
9. Comment upon the growing interconnectedness of NBFCs and banking system in India.
10. What measures would you suggest the RBI to take to improve functioning of the NBFCs in India?

REFERENCES

1. RBI Report of the Committee on Financial Companies, 1992.
2. RBI Report on Trend and Progress of Banking in India, 2002-03.
3. RBI Report on Trend and Progress of Banking in India, 2010-11.
4. RBI report on Trend and Progress of Banking in India, 2011-12.
5. Report of the Working Group on Finance Companies, RBI, 1992.
6. Report on Trend and Progress of Banking in India, 2004-05.
7. Annual Report, RBI, 2006-07.
8. RBI Report on Trend and Progress of Banking in India, 2010-11.
9. Business Standard, February 18, 2011.
10. RBI Report on Trend and Progress of Banking in India, 2010-11.
11. Hindu, March 22, 2012.
12. Business Standard, August 30, 2011.
13. RBI report on Trend and Progress of Banking in India, 2011-12.
14. Business Line, December 1, 2006.
15. RBI Report on Trend and Progress of Banking in India, 2010-11.
16. RBI Report on Trend and Progress of Banking in India, 2010-11.
17. *Ibid.*
18. *Ibid.*
19. RBI Report on Trend and Progress of Banking in India, 2010-11.

❋ ❋ ❋

Micro Finance Institutions (MFIs)

Learning Objectives:

The present chapter attempts at:

- Providing an understanding of nature and significance of Micro Finance Institutions.
- Describing business models and forms of organizing Micro Finance Institutions.
- Tracing out evolution and growth of Micro Finance Institutions in India and abroad.
- Discussing MFI model in India.
- Focussing initiatives taken by the RBI, NABARD and SIDBI to foster microfinance.
- Assessing performance of MFIs in India.
- Identifying challenges before Micro Finance agencies
- Offering suggestions to improve MFIs in India.

Chapter Outline:

- Prologue
- Nature of MFIs.
- Significance of MFIs.
- Business models of MFIs.
- Forms of organization of MFIs.
- Evolution and growth of MFIs —A global scenario.
- MFIs in India — History and evolution.
- Legal structure of MFIs in India.
- MFI model in India.
- Policy initiatives by the RBI.
- Recent initiatives by the NABARD.
- Micro finance initiatives by the SIDBI.
- Performance of MFIs in India —An evaluation
- Challenges before Micro Finance Agencies
- Suggestions to improve MFIs in India
- Regulation of MFIs in India
- Conclusions

A. PROLOGUE

Despite the broad international consensus regarding the Importance of access to finance as a crucial alleviation measure, it is estimated that globally over two billion people are currently excluded from access to main stream financial services.[1] In most developing countries, a large segment of society, particularly low income people, has a very little access to formal financial services. As a result, many of them have to necessarily depend either on their own or informal sources of finance and pay usuriously high interest rate. The situation is worse in most least developed countries where more than 90 per cent of the population is excluded from access to formal financial system.[2] In India too, a very large number of the poorest of the poor continue to remain outside the reach of the formal banking system. Even today, half of India's population does not have bank account, 90 per cent has no access to credit or life insurance cover, 95 per cent has no general insurance, while 98 per cent has no participation in the capital market.[3] This is despite tremendous banking expansion, improvement in financial performance, greater competition and diversification of ownership of banks leading to enhanced efficiency and systematic resilience in the banking system during the post reform period.

The reasons behind the formal financial sector's failure to reach the vast segment of the poor population are manifold and operate in a self-reinforcing manner. The principal prohibiting factor is that banks face extremely high fixed and variable costs in servicing low income households, resulting in high delivery costs for relatively small transactions. Moreover, low income households are interested in the same products that are usually utilised by the rest of the population because they have different immediate needs, lower financial capacities and variable income streams. The unsuitability of existing credit products for low income households is exacerbated by a general unavailability of collateralizable assets. Additionally, the low income population is often illiterate and lacks financial knowledge, making it nearly impossible for it to even contemplate availing existing financial services, which provide no ancillary support to mitigate these challenges. In the absence to access to formal financial services, the low income segment has traditionally relied on local moneylenders to fulfill their financial needs. While this money is readily available, it is often exorbitantly priced at 60%-100% annual yields and forces the borrowers into a classific debt trap, entrenching them in poverty.

Thus to help the poor and deprived segment of the population to overcome their problems of poverty, meet their financial needs and improve their standards of living, an alternative system to main stream financial institutions was strongly felt. Microfinance Institutions have, in recent years, come to be recognised as an effective agent of financial inclusion to improve the economic and social lot of the deprived and helpless sections of the society across the globe by providing them small scale financial services, both credit and savings, at affordable price.

B. NATURE OF MFIs

A microfinance institution is an organization that provides microfinance services to an individual or an eligible client, either directly or through a group mechanism. This very broad definition includes a wide range of providers that vary in their legal structure, mission and methodology. However, all share the common characteristics of providing financial and other services to clients who are poorer and more vulnerable than traditional bank clients. MFIs are usually established to fulfill a mission — of reaching credit and financial services to the poor who are otherwise unreached by mainstream financial institutions. They try to simultaneously achieve the twin goals of access (by the poor) and sustainability (of the institution or its micro-credit portfolio).

Imminent features of MFIs that distinguish them from other institutions operating in financial market of a country are:

- Thrust of MFIs is not only on financial inclusion but also on poverty alleviation of the poor and deprived sections of the community.
- The mission of MFIs is to serve the poor and deprived sectors of the society and not to use poverty as business opportunity to mint money.
- MFIs are concerned with provision of financial as well as non-financial services to the unprivileged and deprived sections of the society. Most microfinance companies provide multiple financial services like lending, savings, insurance, crop insurance, etc. Non-financial services include capacity building, training, marketing of products, micro insurance, etc.
- Typically MFIs dispense small amount of loans to help the poor to pullout of priority. They generally provide first loan of not more than ₹ 5,000 a year. Those who repay qualify for a higher second loan, may be, of ₹ 7,000 and the third loan can still be higher. In the U.S., the term micro loans typically, refer to loans under $35,000. In Canada, a microfinance loan is restricted to a maximum of $25,000.
- Philosophy of MFIs is to play the role of responsible financiers. As a responsible financier, an MFI is supposed to provide support at reasonable and affordable price which the poor can afford. MFIs have to keep the overall cost to the borrowers at a level consistent with the repaying capability of the borrower. There should be transparency in determining lending interest rate. In the U.S., MFIs cannot charge more than 3.5 per cent over the prime rate, based on each individual's business and credit history.
- MFIs lend support essentially creating self-employment income generating activities. Focus of these institutions is always on helping the poor, especially women in unleashing their entrepreneurial talent and developing their leadership skill so as to enable them to improve their earnings and quality of life.
- MFIs extend financial support without any collateral. The whole mechanism of microfinance is based on mutual trust, accountability, participation and creativity and not on legal procedures, as is in existence in the Grameen Bank System of Bangladesh which has been replicated by micro finance organizations in several countries.
- MFIs follow informal and flexible approach to suit the credit needs of the poor. As such, each model is tailored according to the circumstances and the local needs.

  In terms of lending model, MFIs may be classified as lenders to groups or as lenders to individuals. In India, MFIs usually adopt group-based lending models, which are of two types — the self-help group model and the joint-liability group (JLG) model. The model of lending to individuals is similar to the retail loan financing model of banks. Detailed discussion on the business model follows.
- MFIs can also be differentiated on the basis of their loan repayment structures. Most MFIs adopt the weekly and fortnightly repayment structure; those under the SHG model have a monthly repayment structure. MFIs lending to traders in market places also offer daily repayment, while MFIs extending agricultural loans have bullet — and cash flow-based repayment structures depending on the crop patterns.
- Another distinguishing feature of MFIs is that they provide services at the doorstep of the poor based on the principle that the poor should not go to the suppliers of finance.
- MFIs also emphasize on mobilization of surpluses from poor sections of the society through introduction of need-based schemes. They offer savings services in two ways, viz., the savings are either collected by the MFI or the SHG. In the latter method, the MFI or NGO encourages the SHG to collect savings/thrift from each member of the group on a weekly monthly basis and rotate the savings/thrift among members. An MFI collecting savings from borrowers may either make it compulsory for borrowers/ members to have savings with it, or offer voluntary savings services to both members/ non-members.

C. SIGNIFICANCE OF MFIS

MFIs are emerging across the world as the most powerful agents of financial inclusion to ameliorate the economic and social lot of the poor and vulnerable people and ensure all found economic development with equity. This is because of the several reasons, viz., ability to reach out to the poor, promise of financial sustainability, the potential to build on traditional systems, provision of informal and flexible financial services to the poor for meeting their modest consumption and livelihood needs, availability of better financial products as a result of experimentation and innovation and provision of collateral-free micro credit to the poor.

The basic premise of micro financing is that access to credit allows poor people to take advantage of economic opportunities. MFIs act as a catalyst in the lives of the poor. They help them achieve a reasonable rise in their income level, build up assets, and improve their standards of living. They also create the habit of thrift among the members and thus provide cushion against external stocks.

By reducing vulnerability and increasing earnings and savings, MFIs allow poor households to make the transformation from "everyday survival" to "planning for the future". Empirical evident shows that, among the poor, those participating in microfinance programmes, who had access to financial services, were able to improve their well-being — both the individual and household level — much more than those who did not have access to financial services.

In view of the above, MFIs are emerging as important institutions to facilitate and foster inclusive growth in a number of countries. They provide powerful means for integrating the financial needs of poor people into a country's mainstream financial system.

D. BUSINESS MODELS OF MFIS

Broadly speaking, MFIs use two credit delivery models, *viz.*, (*i*) Group Model (*ii*) Individual Model.

◈ Group Model

This is one of the most common methodologies employed by MFIs for providing microfinance. Group model primarily involves a group of individuals, which becomes the basic unit of operation for the MFIs. As noted above, MFIs provide collateral free loans, group model helps in creating social collateral (peer pressure) that can effectively substitute physical collateral. Group becomes a basic unit with which MFIs deal.

Groups are trained to own joint responsibility for loans that are taken by individuals in the group. Groups ensure repayments from all individuals in that group. Group may have to jointly own the responsibility of defaults and pay on behalf of defaulting client. Group also helps in credit appraisal and provides opinion on creditworthiness of each individual in the group. Group methodology also helps in controlling cost. As such, group method ensures mat even without taking any physical collateral, the MFI is able to manage its credit risk.

Group model becomes more important in case of larger loan defaults, when a financial institution can take recourse to legal action. In small loans, legal course is not an economically sound option.

In view of the above, group model is widely accepted and used in microfinance across the world.

Group model may take the form of Self-Help Group and Joint Liability Group.

Self-Help Groups (SHGs) concept has its origin in India. SHGs have come to be recognized as very important bodies in rural development and are, therefore, found in almost all parts of the country. SHGs are formed by NGOs as well as government agencies and are used as channels for various development programmes.

A SHG is an association of generally upto 20 members, preferably from the same socio-economic background. A SHG can be all-women-group, all men group, or even a mixed group.

Joint Liability Group (JLG) model is based on the concept of joint liability. It is the brainchild of Prof. Muhammad Yunus, founder of Grameen Bank in Bangladesh. Grameen model is the most accepted and prevalent microfinance delivery model in the world today. Many MFIs have accepted this model as it has high focus on standardization and discipline. Grameen model is a joint liability group model. Here five-member groups are formed and eight such groups form a center. Hence, in a full-capacity center there are 40 members. However, over the years people have experimented with centers of different sizes and now these are variations of 5-8 groups within a center. Center is the operational unit for the MFI, which means that MFI deals with a center as a whole. Weekly meetings take place at the central level and individual groups do not meet. A Grameen model is focused on financial transactions. The Group and center are joint liability Groups, which signify that all members are jointly responsible for repayment. MFI recovers full money from center. If any member defaults, the group members pool in money to repay to the MFI. In case group members are unable to do it, center as whole has to contribute and share the responsibility.

Thus, the SHG and Grameen model have originated with two different approaches. SHG model has been developed with holistic view of development and empowerment of society where financial transactions are only one part of it, while Grameen model is specifically focused on providing financial services to the low-income clients.

◈ Individual Model

In individual lending model, MFIs provide loans to an individual based on his/her own personal creditworthiness. Individual lending is more prevalent with clients who generally need bigger size loans and have the capacity to produce guarantee and generate enough comfort to the MFIs. MFIs generally base their decision on personal knowledge of the client, his/her reputation among peers and society, client's income sources and business position. MFIs also ask for individual guarantors or take post-dated cheques from clients. Individual guarantors come from friends or relatives well known to the borrower and who are ready to take liability of repaying the loan, should the borrower fail to do so.

E. FORMS OF ORGANIZATION OF MFIs

In course of evolution and growth of micro finance movement around the world, MFIs have taken wide variety of forms, which may for convenience of discussion be categorized into four major groups, as listed below:

◈ Informal Finance Service Providers

These include moneylenders, pawn brokers, savings collectors, money guards, input supply shops, etc. They understand each other's financial circumstances and can offer very flexible, convenient and fast services, because they know each other well and live in the same community. These services are generally costly and the choice of financial products limited and of very short-term. Informal services, that involve savings, are also risky.

◈ Member-owned Organizations

These comprise self-help groups (SHGs), credit unions and a variety of hybrid organizations like 'financial service association'. Like their informal cousins, they are generally small and local, signifying their access to good knowledge about each others' financial circumstances and thus can offer convenience and flexibility. Grameen Bank is a member owned organization. Since they are managed by poor people, their costs of operation are low. However, these providers may have little financial skill and can run into trouble when the economy slumps or their operations become too complex.

◈ NGOs

The MSC counted 3,316 of these MFIs and NGOs lending to about 133 million clients by the end of 2006. Led by Grameen Bank and BRAC in Bangladesh, Prodem in Bolivia and FINCA International, headquartered in Washington DC, these NGOs have spread around the developing world in the past three decades; others like the Grameen Council address larger regions. They have proven very innovative, and pioneering banking techniques like solidarity lending, village banking and mobile banking that have overcome barriers to serving poor populations. However, with boards that do not necessarily represent either their capital or their customers, their governance structures can be fragile and they can become overly dependent on external donors.

◈ Formal Financial Institutions

This category comprises commercial banks and non-banking financial institutions. They are regulated and supervised, offer a wider range of financial services and control a branch network that can extend across the country and internationally. However, they have been found reluctant to adopt social missions, and due to their high costs of operations, often cannot deliver services to poor or remote population. The increasing use of alternative data in credit scoring, such as trade credit is increasing commercial banks interest in microfinance. With appropriate regulation and supervision, each of these institutional types can bring leverage to solving the microfinance problem. For example, efforts are being made to link SHGs to commercial banks to network member-owned organizations together to achieve economies of scale and scope and to support efforts by commercial banks to 'down-scale' by integrating mobile banking and e-payment technologies into their extensive branch network.

F. EVOLUTION AND GROWTH OF MFIs — A GLOBAL SCENARIO

The history of micro financing can be traced back as long to the middle of the 1800s when the theorist Lysander Spooner was writing over the benefits from small credit to entrepreneurs and farmers as a way of getting the people out of poverty. Independently to Spooner, Friedrich Wilhelm Raiffeisen founded the first cooperative lending banks to support farmers in rural Germany credit unions and lending cooperatives have been around hundreds of years. However, the pioneering of modern microfinance is often credited to Dr. Mohammad Yunus, who began experimenting with lending to poor women in the village of Jobra, Bangladesh during his tenure as a professor of economics at Chittagong University in the 1970s. He founded Grameen Bank in 1983 and won the Nobel Peace Prize in 2006. Since then, innovation in micro finance has continued and providers of financial services to the poor continue to evolve.

Historical context can help explain how specialized MFIs developed across the world over the last few decades. Between the 1950s & 1970s, governments and donors focused on providing subsidized agricultural credit to small and marginal farmers, in hopes of raising productivity and incomes. During the 1980, micro-enterprise credit concentrated on providing loans to poor women to invest in tiny businesses, enabling them to accumulate assets and raise household income and welfare. These experiments resulted in the emergence of NGOs that provided financial services for the poor. In the 1990s, many of these institutions transformed themselves into formal financial institutions in order to access and on-lend client savings, thus enhancing their outreach.

MFIs have come into existence around the world to help the poor. US Microfinance is most often thought of as "banking for the poor". In the late 1980s, MFIs developed in the US to serve low income and marginalized minority communities. By 2007, there were 500 MFIs operating in the US. According to Aspen Institute estimates, only 2 per cent of potential US microfinance customers are being served. Furthermore, a growing percentage of Americans are unbanked — 30 per cent of Americans have no banking relationship whatsoever.[4]

In Canada, microfinance history took shape through the development of credit unions. These credit unions provided financial services to the Canadians who could not get access to traditional financial means. Two separate branches of credit unions were developed in Canada to serve the financially marginalized segment of the population. Alphonse Desjardins introduced the establishment of savings and credit services in late 1900 to the Quebecois who did not have financial access. About 30 years later, Father Moses Condy introduced credit unions to Nova Scotia. Those models of modem institutions are still present in Canada today. Rise Asset Development, Alterna Savings, Access Community Capital Fund, Montreal Community loan fund, Momentum and Vancity are the leading MFIs operating in Canada.

Asia is the home of the largest number of MFIs and MFI outreach. Even then there is enormous demand for microfinance in the four most populous countries in Asia (China, India, Indonesia and Pakistan). For instance, China has a poor population of about 110 million people and the total number poor clients so far reached by NGO — MFIs, RCCs, the government and the city Commercial Bank for urban entrepreneurs is only slightly over 7 million.

About 26 per cent of 1.2 billion people in India are still under the poverty line. Only an estimated 10 to 12 per cent of the poor in India are reached by MFIs.

Indonesia, the fourth most populous nation (over 245 million) in the world has over 40 million people who are living below poverty line. Although there are several formal, semi-formal and informal microfinance providers working in the country and serving a few million, there is still need for increasing microfinance outreach to millions of both rural and urban poor who are still excluded.

In Pakistan, 32 per cent of its 164 million people are under poverty line. Although a number of microfinance providers including NGOs and banks are working in the country, their outreach is still less than one million. The country, therefore, needs a great breakthrough to increase the microfinance outreach at a faster rate.

Microfinance development in most of the Asian countries except Bangladesh has remained skewed and slow. Although the countries in the Pacific region have relatively small population, a large proportion of them live under the poverty line. They have microfinance programmes with little capacity, outreach and exposure to best practices.

The microfinance sector around the globe has grown over time with more and different types of players becoming involved, with increasing number of geographic regions being serviced, with new types of products and services being developed and with new ideas and technologies to support it.[5]

The global picture regarding microfinance outreach has been quite impressive. From a mere 7.6 million families in 1993, the Microcredit Summit Campaign (MSC) reported an outreach of more than 92 million clients by December 3, 2004. This number includes 66.6 million families who were among the poorest when they started with a programme. Of these 66.6 million poorest clients, about 84 per cent was served by the 52 largest individual institutions, all with 1,00,000 or more clients. Among these largest MFIs, 79 per cent were in Asia, 17 per cent in Africa and only 4% in Latin America. Of the 3,164 institutions that had reported to the MSC by December 31, 2004, 1628 were in Asia, 994 in Africa, 388 in Latin America and Caribbean, 48 in North America, 34 in the Middle East, 72 in Europe and the newly Independent States. Of the over 92 million people reached by the end of 2004, 81.5 million were in Asia, 7 million in Africa and 3.8 million in Latin America and the Caribbean. Only 5.2 million of 61.5 million poorest families in Africa and the Middle East were covered by microfinance programmes by the end of 2004. Asia, which is home to some 67 per cent of the world's people living on less than US $ 1 a day could, therefore, rightfully boast of a vibrant microfinance sector. In Asia, Bangladesh distinguishes itself by reaching more than 75 per cent of poor families with microfinance. MFIs in Bangladesh reached over 18 million poorest clients by the end of 2004. The intensity and density of microfinance is greater in Bangladesh than in any other country of the world. The pioneering role of Grameen bank, the bold initiative of NGO-MFIs, the participation of banks, the implementation of Government programmes and the strong commitment and competitive spirit of the major players in the field significantly contributed to such a development of microfinance in Bangladesh.

As of December end 2009, there were 1395 MFIs globally with an estimated borrower base of 86 million with a total outstanding portfolio of over 44 billion as reported by the MFIs to the Microfinance Information Exchange or Mix Market, excluding MFIs that do not report to Mix Market, if they did report, the total size of the global finance industry is estimated to be roughly 200 million borrowers. From 2003 to 2008, the global microfinance industry experienced a growth in borrowers at a CAGR of 12 per cent and a portfolio outstanding CAGR of 34 per cent. Inter-regionally, South Asia, East Asia and Pacific region had the highest growth rates in terms of borrowers. Sub-Sahara Africa, Middle East and North Africa experienced the slowest growth. Latin America continues to lead in terms of portfolio outstanding with $16 billion or 36 per cent of the total global portfolio. However, South Asia has the lead in terms of borrowers with over 50 per cent of the global borrower base. The disparity between these two trends is explained by the variance of average loan sizes in the two regions, which is a product of their economic well-being and the business models followed by their respective microfinance sectors.[6]

G. MFIS IN INDIA — HISTORY AND EVOLUTION

The evolution of Indian MFIs can be broadly divided into four distinct phases:

Phase 1: The Cooperative movement (1900-1960)

During this phase, credit cooperatives were vehicles to extend subsidized credit to villages under government sponsorship.

Phase 2: Subsidized Social banking (1960s-1990)

With failure of cooperatives, Government focused on measures such as nationalization of Banks, expansion of rural branch networks, establishment of RRBs and the setting up of apex institutions such as NABARD and SIDBI, including initiation of a government sponsored Integrated Rural Development Programme. While these steps led to reaching a large population, the period was characterized by large-scale misuse of credit, creating a negative perception about the creditability of micro borrowers among bankers, thus further hindering access to banking services to the low-income people.

Phase 3: SHG-Bank Linkage Programme and Growth of NGO-MFIs (1990-2000)

The failure of subsidized social banking to cater to 135 million or 72 per cent of the household having an annual household income below $1800 triggered a paradigm shift in delivery of rural credit with NABARD initiating the SHG-Bank Linkage Programme (SBLP), aiming to link informal women's groups to formal banks. The programme helped increase banking system outreach to otherwise unreached people and initiate a change in the bank's outlook towards low-income families from 'beneficiaries' to 'customers'. This period was, thus, marked by the extension of credit at market rates. The model generated a lot of interest among newly emerging MFIs, largely of non-profit origin, to collaborate with NABARD under this programme. The macro economic crisis in the early 1990s, that led to introduction of economic reforms in 1991, resulted in greater economy to the financial sector. This led to the emergence of private sector banks that became important players in the microfinance sector in the subsequent years.

Phase 4: Commercialization of Microfinance (2001 onwards)

Post reforms, rural markets emerged as the new growth drivers for MFIs and banks, the latter taking in the sector not only as part of their corporate social responsibility but also a new business line.

In view of burgeoning mismatch between micro credit demand (51.4 billion) and supply ($4.3 billion), there was mushrooming of MFIs during this period. However, few top MFIs accounted for over 80 per cent of the microfinance business.

What is interesting to observe is that the majority of the MFIs including the larger players operated mainly in South India till 2005-06. Since 2007, however, the large MFIs have extended their presence in states such as Maharashtra, Chhattisgarh, Orissa, Jharkhand and West Bengal. Over the past two years, the larger MFIs have established pan-India coverage. The growth of the microfinance sector in Eastern Indian was driven primarily by capacity enhancement initiatives by the apex MFIs and tapping of growth of opportunities in the eastern market by South India based MFIs and banks. Many of the large MFIs, nevertheless continue to have a significant exposure to South India.

In their desire to rake in quick money, large number of NGO-MFIs began transforming themselves into NBFCs, using poverty as business opportunity. These MFIs adopted commercial approach to attract private equity and best practices from the business world to scale and technology to overcome cost constraints. MFIs set up after 2000 saw themselves less in the developmental mould. The MFIs' move from public service to private purpose and super profiteering after 2000 became the potent causes for their debacle in 2010 onward which attracted the attention of the people around the world.

H. LEGAL STRUCTURE OF MFIs IN INDIA

With respect to legal structure, MFIs may be classified as:

◈ Not-for-Profit MFIs

(*i*) Societies (such as Bandhan, Rashtriya Seva Samithi, and Gram Utthan)

(*ii*) Public trusts (such as Shri Kshatra Dharmsthala Rural Development Project and Community Development Centre)

(*iii*) Non Profit Companies (such as Indian Association for savings and credit and cash for micro credit)

◈ Mutual Benefit MFIs

(*i*) Cooperatives registered under State of National Acts (such as Sakh Sahkari Samiti Ltd.)

(*ii*) Mutually-aided cooperative Societies (such as Sewa-Mutually Aided Cooperative Thrift Societies Federation Ltd.)

◈ For-Profit MFIs

(*i*) Non-banking Financial Companies (such as SKS Microfinance Ltd., Share Microfin Ltd., Spandan Sphoorthy Financials Ltd.)

(*ii*) Producer Companies (such as Sri Vijaya Visakha Milk Producers Co. Ltd.)

(*iii*) Local area banks (the only such MFI is Krishna Bhima Sannidhi Local Area Bank)

I. MFI MODEL IN INDIA

Micro-finance initiatives in India have been centred around two broad models, viz. Self-Help Group Bank Linkage Model (SBLM) and Micro-Finance Institutions (MFIs)-NBFC Model.

◈ SHG-Bank Linkage Model (SBLM)

SHGs form the basic constituent unit of the micro-finance movement in India. An SHG is typically an informal association of 15-20 poor people, mostly women, who contribute small amounts into a savings pool. After saving regularly for six months, lending small amounts and maintaining accounts, as SHG becomes eligible to be linked to a bank which opens a savings banks account for the SHG and offers loans upto four times the groups' savings. The SHG can then on-lend to its members, helping them to engage in some income generating activities and capacity building.

The SBLM for purveying micro-finance was started in India in 1989 as an action research project. The findings of the project led to the launching of the pilot project by NABARD in 1992 with the policy support from the RBI. The pilot project was designed as a partnership model among three agencies, viz., the SHGs, banks and NGOs. These SHGs were expected to facilitate collective decision making, by the poor, leadership development and provide 'doorstep' banking. The banks as wholesalers of credit were to provide the resources while the NGOs were to act as agencies to organize the poor, build their capacities and facilitate the process of improving them.

Micro-Finance Institutions (MFIs) Model

A growing component of inclusive banking in India is the lending by the MFIs. The MFI model in India is characterized by a diversity of institutional and legal forms. These MFIs are working in different forms and shapes, as noted earlier, such as societies, trusts, cooperatives or 'non-for profit companies' or non-banking financial companies (NBFCs) registered with the RBI.

Microfinance model takes the form of bank-partnership model (BPM) and banking correspondent model (BCM). In the BPM, the bank uses an MFI as its agents for handling credit, monitoring, supervision, recovery and for taking care of all relationships with the client, from first contact through final repayment. ICICI bank pioneered a 'partnership model' where the loans remain on the banks books and the MFI does for a fee, everything on behalf of the bank from loan origination to monitoring and collection. However, the MFI has to guarantee the bank against default (subject to a limit).

In January 2006, the RBI permitted banks to utilize the services of NGOs, MFIs (other than NBFCs) and other civil society organizations as intermediaries in providing financial and banking services through the use of business facilitator and business correspondent models. The BC model allows banks to do 'cash in-cash out' transactions at a location much closer to the rural population, thus addressing the last mile problem. The BC model uses the MFI's ability to get close to poor clients — a necessity for savings mobilization from the poor — while relying on financial strength of the bank to safeguard the deposits.

In SHG-bank linkage model the NABARD plays leadership role while in MFIs model NGOs play catalytic as well as enabling role at grass root level.

J. POLICY INITIATIVES BY THE RBI

The RBI took the following policy initiatives to give fillip to the micro finance movement in India:

(*i*) In January 1993, the RBI permitted the SHGs to open savings bank account with banks.

(*ii*) Financing of SHGs by banks will be treated as part of their lending to the weaker sections.

(*iii*) In 1999-2000, banks were advised that interest rates applicable to loans given by banks to micro credit organizations or by the micro credit organizations to SHGs/member beneficiaries, would be left to their discretion.

(*iv*) The RBI set up a micro finance and financial inclusion division in the RBI for mainstreaming micro credit and accelerating flow of credit to MFIs.

(*v*) In order to encourage NBFCs to engage in micro finance business, the RBI exempted in January 2000, such NBFCs as were engaged in micro financing activities, licensed under Section 25 of the Companies Act, 1956, and were not accepting public deposits, from the purview of Sections 45- 1A. (registration), 45-1B (maintenance of liquid assets) and 45-1C (transfer of a portion of a profits to Reserve Fund) of the RBI Act, 1934.

(*vi*) In February 2000, the RBI issued comprehensive guidelines to banks which, *inter alia*, stipulated that micro credit extended by banks to individual borrowers directly, or through any intermediary, would from than onwards be reckoned as part of their priority sector lending. Banks were permitted to formulate their own model/s or choose any conduit/intermediary for extending micro credit. Banks were also given freedom to prescribe their own lending norms so as to provide maximum flexibility with respect to micro lending. Banks were further directed to delegate adequate sanctioning powers to branch managers and to keep the loan procedures and documents simple for providing prompt and hassle-free micro credit.

(*vii*) Banks were advised to provide adequate incentives to their branches for financing the SHGs and that the group dynamics of working of the SHGs should be left to them.

(*viii*) In order to protect the interest of depositors MFIs would not be permitted to accept public deposits unless they complied with the extant regulatory framework of the RBI. However, as an additional channel for resource mobilisation, the RBI in April 2005 enabled NGOs engaged in microfinance activities to access External Commercial Borrowings (ECBs) upto US $ 5 million during a financial year for permitted end use, under the automatic route.

(*ix*) The RBI permitted banks in January, 2006 to use the services of NGOs/SHGs, MFIs (other than NBFCs) and other civil society organizations as intermediaries in providing financial and banking services through business facilitator and business correspondent models.

(*x*) On December 19, 2011, the RBI allowed MFIs to raise funds via external commercial borrowings upto $10 million or equivalent during a financial year for permitted end-uses under the automatic route.

K. RECENT INITIATIVES BY THE NABARD

NABARD, which has been playing a crucial developmental role for the microfinance sector in India, has taken the following steps to boost the micro finance programmes in the country:

(*i*) In March, 2006 NABARD launched the 'Micro Enterprise Development Programmes' (MEDP) for skill development with a view to enhancing the capacities of matured SHGs to take up micro enterprises through appropriate skill upgradation. The programme envisaged development of enterprise management skills in existing or new livelihood activities, both in form and non-form sectors. The duration of training can vary between 3 and 13 days depending upon the objective and the nature of training.

(*ii*) In 2005-06, a pilot project for 'promotion of micro enterprises' was launched among members of matured SHGs.

(*iii*) NABARD provides marketing support to the SHGs for exhibiting their products.

(*iv*) NABARD launched a pilot project in December 2003 to link post-offices with the objective of examining the feasibility of utilizing the vast network of post offices in rural areas for disbursement of credit to rural poor on an agency basis.

(*v*) In 2007, the NABARD decided to support SHG Federation, which are emerging as important players in nurturing SHGs, by way of granting assistance for training, capacity building and exposure visits of SHG members.

(*vi*) Recognizing the role played by the MFIs in extending micro finance services in the unbanked areas, NABARD extends support to these institutions through grant and loan-based assistance.

(*vii*) The NABARD manages Micro Finance Development and Equity Fund (MFDEF), created in 2000-01 for facilitating and supporting the orderly growth of the micro finance sector, scaling-up of the SHG-bank linkage programme, extending financial support to MFIs and undertaking various promotional initiatives.

So as to make the approach and design of SHG-BLP more flexible, guidelines were issued by NABARD on March 27, 2012 suggesting some client friendly product level changes in tune with the changing needs of customers under SHGs, such as allowing voluntary savings by members with surplus funds, which could be maintained separately or used for intra-group lending; providing need-based access to funds, and longer tenure of credit from banks through the introduction of a cash credit system to obviate the need for frequent documentation and also delays in the renewal of loans; extending JGG or other non-collateral lending models of higher credit needs to smaller livelihood groups, a self-rating mechanism to improve the quality of the group; and developing federations to continuously guide, nurture and cater to the needs of the groups.

L. MICROFINANCE INITIATIVES BY THE SIDBI

SIDBI was one of the first institutions that identified and recognized NGO/MFI route as an effective delivery channel for reaching financial services to those segments of population not reached by the formal banking network. As a result of bulk lending funds provided, coupled with intensive capacity building support to the entire microfinance sector, it has come to occupy a significant position in the Indian micro finance sector. Today, the SIDBI is one of the largest suppliers of micro finance through the MFIs. The SIDBI has taken the following measures to give fillip to the microfinance sector in India:

(*i*) The SIDBI launched its micro finance programme in February, 1994 on a pilot basis to provide small doses of credit to the NGOs across the country. NGOs acted as financial intermediaries and on-lend funds to their clients. Limited amount of capacity building grant was also provided to the NGOs.

(*ii*) The SIDBI took the initiative to do away with collateral-based lending in MF and pioneered the concept of capacity assessment rating (CAR) for the MFIs. As a part of its development agenda, the SIDBI encouraged a private sector development consulting firm to develop a rating tool for the MFIs which were rolled out in 1999. The SIDBI has also succeeded in developing a market for rating services. Two mainstream rating agencies, viz. CRISIL and CARE have also started undertaking micro finance ratings, besides M-CRIL.

(*iii*) The SIDBI introduced a product called 'transformation loan' in 2003 to enable the MFIs to transform themselves from an informal set up to more formal entities. This loan is a quasi-equity product with longer repayment period and features for conversion into equity at a later date, when the MFI decides to convert itself into a corporate entity.

(*iv*) The SIDBI also supports incubation of potential local community based organizations through two-tier/umbrella NGOs/MFIs. The approach not only helps the SIDBI to increase its outreach through double intermediation but also enables it to channelise finance to smaller NGOs. It also supports a few new intermediaries set up by experienced professionals. Another approach in this direction involves incubation of new start-up MFIs promoted by first-generation development/micro finance professionals. The incubation support is either given through well-reputed management institutes or through institutions specializing in capacity building and technical support services.

(*v*) The SIDBI has also taken initiatives to develop human resources of the MFIs. These initiatives are in the form of encouraging the MFIs to hire young management/accounting graduates from reputed institutes through campus placement, providing grant funds for hiring trained and experienced professionals and second line managers, providing support to some of the management training institutes in the form of training and exposure/visits of their faculty members to reputed national and international training programmes and inviting international experts to lend support to these institutes for developing a course on micro finance.

M. PERFORMANCE OF MFIs IN INDIA — AN EVALUATION

The post reform period witnessed paradigm shift in extending micro credit to the poor through microfinance initiatives, which were mooted as supplementary credit delivery networks, centred around two models — the SHG Bank Linkage Programme and the Micro Finance Institutions. These initiatives aimed at alleviating poverty and promoting thrift and credit has made immense contribution towards empowerment of rural folk, especially women.

Microfinance sector in India has grown phenomenally in recent few years. Some of the leading MFIs, such as SKS, Share, Spandan, Ujjivan and Basix are setting the pace for the sector with innovations in products, processes, funding structure and linkages with financial institutions.

◈ Performance in terms of amount of assistance

SHG-Bank Linkage Programme (SBLP) has completed two decades of existence since the early days of the pilot in 1992. The approach has received wide acceptance amongst a multiplicity of stakeholders, like the financially excluded poor households, civil society organizations, bankers and also the international community.

Number of bank-linked SHGs registered meteoric rise from 33,00 during 1992-99 to 79,60,000 as on March, 2012. These SHGs have been funded by banks which surged sharply from ₹ 57 crore during 1992-99 to over ₹ 36,300 crore as on March-end, 2012. In 2010-11, 12 lakh new SHGs of ₹ 14,547 crore was disbursed to these SHGs. Further, at end-March 2011, 80.00 lakh SHGs maintained savings accounts with banks. On an average, the amount of savings per SHG was ₹ 9,405 as compared to the amount of credit of ₹ 82,500 in 2011-12.[7]

It is interesting to note that over 75 per cent of the total number of SHGs Swings linked with banks belonged to those of exclusive women SHGs. Likewise, 80 per cent of total number of SHGs credit linked programme with banks belonged exclusively to women SHGs. As on March 2011, exclusive women SHGs represented over 50 per cent of the outstanding loans under SLBP. Furthermore, as on March end, 2010, total savings of SHGs with banks amounted to ₹ 6,198.71 crore, of which ₹ 4498.66 crore (72%) pertained to exclusive women SHGs. Further, total loans outstanding against SHGs as on March end 2010, figured out ₹ 28,038.28 crore, out of which ₹ 23,030.36 crore related to women SHGs.[8] Thus, under SBLP, major focus was on empowerment of women.

There is a strong belief that the SHG movement has the potential to satisfy the financial service needs of India's unbanked people in a sustainable way. However, the approach has faced a few concerns of being fundamentally focused on credit without adequate room for intensifying the space for thrift and savings. Similarly, the approach has also shown the need and scope for allowing greater flexibility to accommodate multiplicity of credit borrowings at the SHG level.[9]

Inspired by the Grameen Model of micro lending in Bangladesh, Indian MFIs have been growing by leaps and bounds over the last decade. The microfinance sector in India is fragmented. There are more than 3000 MFIs, NGOs and NGO-MFIs, of which about 400 have active lending programmes. The top 10 MFIs are estimated to account for around 74 per cent of the total loans outstanding for MFIs.[10]

According to data from www.mixmarket.org, Indian MFIs witnessed an extraordinarily high growth rate from 2004-2009, with an average annual increase of 91 per cent in number of clients and 107 per cent in outstanding portfolio size. Even during the global financial crisis from 2008-09, the MFI gross loan portfolio grew by 66.20 per cent and the number of borrowers increased by 76.50 per cent.[11] This is reflective of the increased acceptance of MFIs as commercially viable and their resultant ability to attract capital and resources during recent years. One of the factors that fuelled the stratospheric rise of MFIs loans was the fortuitous priority sector lending clause issued by the RBI which enabled banks to lend 40 per cent of their total loan portfolio and of which 45 per cent to be lent to agriculture. Private sector banks finding it difficult to meet the target preferred to lend MFIs who deliver 12 to 13 per cent interest rate.

Recognising the important role of micro-finance institution in channelling credit to the rural parts of the country, banks have funded these institutions on an increasing scale in recent years, as is evident from Table 30.2.

TABLE 30.2: Micro-Finance Institutions funded by banks

Items	Number (in million)			Amount (in billion)		
	2009-10	2010-11	2011-12	2009-10	2010-11	2011-12
Loans disbursed by banks	691	469	465	81	76	52
Loans outstanding with banks	1,531	2,176	1,960	101	107	115

Source: RBI Reports on Trend and Progress of Banking in India

TABLE 30.1: MFIs' Outstanding loans

Year	₹ crore
2004-05	1,500
2005-06	2,700
2006-07	4,400
2007-08	9,500
2008-09	18,500
2009-10	20,000
2010-11	30,000
As on December 5, 2011	20,000

Then began the sad strong story of debacle of MFI industry. In 2010, the Society for Elimination of Rural Poverty (Serp), set up by the Andhra Pradesh Government, listed 54 suicide cases alleged to have been committed by borrowers due to coercive recovery practices of MFIs. Taking cognizance of the suicides, allegedly due to strong-arm tactics of the MFIs for recovery of loans and their raking in hyper profits at the cost of rural poor, pushing multiple lending without conducting due diligence and thus forcing the poor into debt trap, the State Government promulgated an Ordinance on October 15, 2010 to regulate the MFIs. The ordinance was replaced by Andhra Pradesh Micro Finance Bill passed on December 14, 2010. The Act applies to all entities engaged in the state in the business of microfinance including NBFCs regulated by the RBI. Among others, the Act mandates that (*i*) every MFI has to register before the Registering Authority of the district, (*ii*) no member of an SHG can be a member of more than one SHG, (*iii*) no MFI can give a further loan to any SHG/its members without the approval of the registering authority where there is an outstanding bank loan, (*iv*) all repayments have to be made at the office of the Gram Panchayat or at a designated public place, (*v*) MFIs cannot use agents for recovery or use coercive methods of recovery, and (*vi*) loan recoveries have to be made only by monthly installments.

The Andhra MFI Act gave massive blow to the MFI industry, affecting severely, lending business and loan collections. Amount of MFIs' outstanding loan plummeted to ₹ 20,000 as on December 5, 2011; loan collections in Andhra plunged to 10 per cent from nearly 99 per cent prior to the ordinance. In 2010-11, the amount of loans in Andhra Pradesh alone was reduced from ₹ 5,000 crore to ₹ 8.5 crore, indicating massive flight of capital out of India. The impact translated into bad loans worth as much as ₹ 6,000 crore — toxic assets which may wipe out the net worth of several big Andhra Pradesh-based MFIs.

A sector that was booming — bringing to succor to the poor and profits to entrepreneurs — was rendered sick.

According to report of Business Standard, money lenders are back in rural Andhra Pradesh, "grabbing the space vacated by microfinance institutions following the state government's decision to curb the money-lending business of private players." It went on to say "money lenders, pawn brokers and middlemen are charging as high as 225 per cent interest rate per annum."[12]

◈ Performance in terms of Product offering

Thus far, MFIs in India have largely limited their product and service offering within the confines of financial inclusion. In fact, their product has been limited to credit which is intended to serve a variety of needs as shown by Table 30.2.

TABLE 30.2: Product Offering by MFIs in India

Product	Purpose
Existing Products:	
Micro-enterprise/small business loan	Working capital/business start-up
Agricultural Loan	Crop/Farm-related
Livestock Loan	Dairy /Poultry
General	Consumption
Education Loan	Academic/vocational
New/Niche Products:	
Housing Loan	Home improvement/new home

Despite following single-product model, the MF sector has experienced remarkable growth. This growth can be expected to continue as product innovation and diversified service offerings are necessary to attract and retain greater number of customers with a variety of needs. Recognizing the pent up demand of its products, mature MFIs have, of late, taken concrete steps toward expanding their product basket, at least within the context of financial services. They are heavily exploring the possibility of providing savings/deposit services, micro insurance and remittance services.

◈ Savings

Due to RBI regulations, non-banking Macro Finance Institutions cannot access public savings, unless they provide the service through a Section 25 Business Correspondent Conduit. This structure prohibits the conduit from charging any fees to execute this function and limits its reach within a limited radius of the bank branch. MFIs are lobbying the RBI to relax these regulations to allow NBFCs to operate as business correspondents, charge an extra fee for the deposit taking service and delimit the geographical reach of their operations. Such charges would not only make deposits a viable commercial product, but also allow the MFIs to offer it to a broader set of limits.

◈ Micro Insurance

MFIs have, of late, started offering insurance to their clients. Micro insurance schemes are mostly implemented as a compulsory element along with the micro credit provided. One of the best examples of micro insurance scheme is the one which is linked to the Grameen Bank scheme in Bangladesh. Grameen established a separate organization called 'Grameen Kalyan' which uses the women groups for the collection of annual premium for micro insurance.

Although several MFIs are entering the domain of micro insurance, the sector is still in its early days and evolving rapidly. More than half of the 83 MFIs that responded to a Sa-Dhan study in 2005 were offering insurance, with life insurance being more widespread than non-life insurance.

Generally, micro insurance schemes cover health care, life, accident expenses, maternity protection and disability. Both the public sector and private sector insurance companies have tied up with various MFIs in the country for the purpose. One of the problems in the implementation of micro insurance scheme is that the poor have a lesser understanding of risk pooling and are often loath to join schemes where payments have to be made with no immediate returns. This is why, companies such as Satin and BASIX usually tie the insurance products to their credit products, which make the availability of credit contingent on the client availing insurance. Similarly, Basix also links livestock loans to livestock insurance which cushions the financial risk and increases use likelihood of a successful loan recovery.

◈ Remittance

Sensing the growing need of domestic labour migrants for a fast, low-cost, convenient, safe and widely accessible money transfer service, some MFIs are providing remittance services by establishing their presence in a migrant destination to channel remittances back to the community in the migrant's area of origin or by establishing a tie up with another MFI, bank or money transfer company in the area of origin. Going forward, the role of technology will become more important in facilitating the development of alternative channels and payment mechanisms.

In an attempt to meet their clients' needs of healthcare and education as well as livelihood requirements which can enhance their income, employment potential or quality of life, MFIs in India have, of late, started delivering variety of non-financial services. For example, Basix provides low income customers with livelihood services, including agricultural and business development consulting services, to help them use their loans more productively. In addition to livelihood services, several MFIs are examining the feasibility of providing critical basic services to deliver low cost healthcare, education and vocational training. For example, Spandana is currently developing a comprehensive low cost healthcare delivery model based on the healthcare needs of women and children. BASIX has launched a vocational training academy to impart education in rural development and management to potential job seekers from low income communities. These participants are deployed in the rural/semi-urban areas with BASIX or other organizations offering financial services to the poor.

These types of services have a strong potential to reinforce long-term client relationships that will go a long way in addressing the last mile inclusion challenge.

Microfinance sector comprising the SHG-Bank linkage programme and MFIs made incredible efforts to reach around 94 million poor and deprived segments of the population across the country and lent out funds to the tune of over ₹ 60,000 crore by the March end 2011 at terms and conditions convenient to the borrowers. The efforts of the Microfinance sector to outreach even these helpless people, who remain deprived of the banking sector, have been laudable.

Missionary activities of various agencies engaged in micro finance business have indubitably transformed the rural landscape as they have provided organized credit access to some 2.6 per cent people which include most of the isolated communities. MFIs did cross the last mile, did bring about innovative practices and did contribute a credit deal to financial inclusion.

According to a study sponsored by NABARD, there has been a marked shift toward higher income slabs between pre and post SHG situation. The proportion of households having an annual income level of ₹ 22,500 declined from 74 per cent during pre-SHG situation to 57 per cent in the post-SHG situation, indicating increased income levels. Further, involvement in the group significantly contributed to developing self-confidence of the members. The members were relatively more assertive in confronting with social evils and problematic situations.[13]

In other assessment, it was observed that availing loans from money lenders and other informal sources with higher interest rate was remarkably reduced due to SHG intervention. Furthermore, consumption oriented loans were replaced by production oriented loans during the post-SHG situation.[14]

MFIs' many economic enterprises are generating significant direct and indirect employment mostly in rural areas.[15]

According to the study conducted by EDA Rural Systems and APAS (2006), 30 per cent of SHGs in the sample were involved in community services including water supply, education, health care, veterinary care and village road. These community actions, the study pointed out, inculcated a new boldness and confidence amongst women, often putting pressure on the authorities to do their job.

Some of the states like Andhra Pradesh are trying to implement various developmental and poverty alleviation schemes through SHGs.

In recent few years, a number of micro finance firms (in NBFC sector) have come into existence to provide door-step credit to the poor people and in that process, make tidy profits. In fact, poverty for them has now become a big business in India so much so that a slew of storied ventured capital outfits and wealth techies such as Sequoria and Michael Dell have now decided to park some of their capital with some of India's poorest people, using MFIs as intermediaries. These investors and their MFI outfits hope that handing out small loans that average ₹ 5,000 at a 28 per cent interest rate to India's impoverished will not only help their for — profit micro finance portfolio companies to make a tidy profits, but will also help reduce poverty in the country.[16]

A study conducted by EDA Rural System For SIDBI on 44 MFIs suggested that microfinance not only enhanced the choices available to the poor bur also helped develop strategies for coping the economic vagaries. The study also confirmed that there was definite impact of microfinance on alleviating the poverty and reducing the dependence of poor on money-lenders.

The impact of microfinance, studies reveal, has gone beyond business loans and enterprise investments. Microfinance initiatives have offered more than just material benefits. They are also addressing issue associated with "non-material" poverty, which includes social and psychological effects that prevent people from realizing their potential. Reports indicate that micro finance has brought changes in to the life style of the poor in terms of their opportunity to acquire assets, reduce dependency on money lenders and in some cases to accumulate personal savings. The poor also learn to invest in health and education and to meet the wide variety of other cash needs that they encounter.

However, everything is not hunky-dory in the microfinance sector. Studies on operational practices of micro finance institutions conducted from time to time by various agencies reveal several irregularities in their operations, raising serious doubts about their sensitivity to the needs of the poor clients.

MFIs (not bank-linked SHGs) were found charging interest rates as high as 32-42 per cent to provide finance to the poorer sections of the society when they themselves borrow funds from banks at 9-14 per cent. In addition, they employed strong-arm tactics to recover the loans, triggering the crisis in Andhra Pradesh.

According to Report of Malegam Committee on 'Microfinance' expansion led to multiple lending (the same borrower taking loans from more than one MFI). It was noted that number of micro finance clients was 10 times the number of poor households in Andhra Pradesh. So, the loan had transformed into consumer finance from microfinance. In Tamil Nadu, the ratio of MFI clients to poor households was 4.0 and in Karnataka and West Bengal, it was 2.8.

In their desperate race to grab as many clients as possible and increase their market share to make hefty profits, most of the microfinance firms are currently engaged in playing number game with the result that the most vulnerables are not clients of choice. It is horrifying to find from the report of the state of the Sector Report on microfinance for 2008, that in five MFIs out of eight, the proportion of non-poor clients was more than the poor. In other words, with a focus on the bottom line, the MFIs have abandoned those below the poverty line and gone after wealthiest segments of the poor, who can afford to take out bigger loans, which in turn, can generate heftier profits for the firm. This strategy is more about financial inclusion and less about poverty reduction.[17] In fact, professional management and private equity targets have set agenda for both lending and recovery. This led to a rampant multiple lending.

Another questionable practice of the micro finance firms is their irresponsible lending behaviour. Almost every MFI in India routinely tries to understate its interest rates to its clients and markets its loans as costing just 15 per cent which is actually 15 per cent "flat", a loan where the principal amount never declines, and therefore, is closer to an annualized 28 per cent rate. Many simply emphasize the weekly payments instead of highlighting the interest rate being charged.[18] Doubts are also expressed in different quarters about the effectiveness of the small loans in alleviating poverty. It makes sense that reasonably priced credit can be a life saver for the desperately poor, especially women. With the purchase of an inexpensive buffalo, a poor mother can generate a little more cash income and send her children to schools. However, the question of everyone is borrowing for entrepreneurial purposes. Even if loans are given to set up grocery shops the most common of microfinance activities — the borrower may not eke out enough of a living to get out of poverty because so many grocery shops lead to fierce competition.

Another questionable practice of large MFIs is that they operate mainly through middlemen. They pay a high commission (3-4%) to middlemen to ensure quick recovery. These middlemen use unacceptable means to recover dues from borrowers. Middlemen are also said to take a 3-4 per cent cut from borrowers to get them loans from MFIs. In many cases, this is shared with MFI loan sanctioning officials. Thus, these issues make the whole business of micro financing a money game, giving high returns in the name of financial inclusion. It is estimated that only one out of 7 MFIs follows proper governance practices and ethics.[19] These MFIs have deviated from their path of serving the poor. They are just pushing the poor into debt trap by multiple lending and lending beyond the capacity of borrowers.

All these unethical practices continued unabated under the very nose of the RBI, Government of India and lending banks in the absence of central regulation for coping interest rates, banning multiple lending, bringing greater transparency and monitoring the end-use of the loans, until October 2010 when Andhra Government clamped ordinance banning lending and recovery operations of all the MFIs operating in the state. This one measure has brought the MFIs particularly those in Andhra on the brink of collapse.

N. CHALLENGES BEFORE MICRO FINANCE AGENCIES

Indubitably, the MFIs have developed an important delivery mechanism for outreaching the deprived and underprivileged people of India. However, these firms are facing enormous challenges in achieving their solemn objective of alleviating poverty in the rural areas. Some of the major challenges before them are briefly enumerated as under:

◈ Cost of Operations

One of the most challenging issues facing the MFIs is high cost of operations affecting adversely their operational viability and sustainability of the process of providing financial services to the poor. Though financial inclusion provides an immense opportunity to the MFIs in terms of large customer base, the operating cost of expanding the coverage of financial services is so high to inhibit the MFIs to penetrate in rural and remote areas. Indian MFIs have the highest financial expense ratio (12.0 per cent) in the world.[20]

◈ Availability of Funds

Another serious problem being faced particularly by micro finance firms is availability of funds at reasonable rate. These firms are presently prohibited from accepting public deposits leaving them with limited option of arranging funds through private equity and venture capital funds.

◈ Availability of Financial Products

Owing to limited availability of funds, micro finance firms are finding it difficult to provide wide range of services/products for all purposes leaving the rural poor with little option than to transact with the informal sector which ultimately leads them to a situation of debt trap. The NBFCs' craze around outreach with very little depth and very little diversity of offering is actually creating serious risk and certainty represents a deep opportunity loss in terms of what the poor want. It is gratifying to note that some large MFIs are planning to extend loans between ₹ 50,000 and ₹ 1.5 lakh to its members and is in the process of teaming up with a partner. It is also financing the retail outlet by providing working capital to its customers who are running Kirana stores.

◈ Human Resource

Managing micro finance business demands, among other things, leadership, communicational and emotional skills. Acquiring the persons endowed with these skills and retaining them in highly competitive environment are posing enormous challenge to the MFIs. This is a gargantuan task, requiring an assembly line approach to recruitment, training and placement of personnel, like the highly standardized distribution process of Coke or MC Donald's. For a microfinance firm to be able to be operationally efficient, it needs to manage its retention rates and ensure that quality of staff does not take a dip in its frantic efforts to scale up.

O. SUGGESTIONS TO IMPROVE MFIs IN INDIA

The above discussions lead us to an unmistakable conclusion that MFIs in India have rendered yeomen services to improve economic and social lot of the poor. However, quite a few but big blac swans have brought bad name to the microfinance sector because of their nefarious practices to rake in money, forcing the Andhra Government to ban the operations of all the MFIs working in the State. Instead of killing the MFIs because of the misdeeds of few loan sharks, serious measures need to be taken to prevent the unfair practices of these so called MFIs and to ensure that the genuine MFIs become effective agent of growth of the poor and pauper of the country.

(*i*) MFIs need to charge interest rate which is affordable to the poor. The interest rate should not be out of alignment with the cost of funds, transaction costs, risk costs and a certain margin. In any case, there is a need for transparency in its determination and fairness in application.

(*ii*) MFIs should shun 'overlending' and 'multilending.' The joint liability system has to be ended because this aided by commission agents was the main source of unbearable pressure.

(*iii*) So as to avoid cases of multiple financing, there is a need to put in place a system of credit registries, (through which lenders share credit information about their clients' repayment records) through credit information bureau similar to that for the large corporates. Credit registries can increase access by establishing credit record of burrowers. This could, to start with, be done by one of the credit rating agencies which have been allowed to be sued by the banks rating the MFIs.

(*iv*) MFIs should design and develop tailor-made thrift, credit, insurance and remittance products for the poor and weaker sections taking into consideration their requirements and repayment capacity.

(*v*) Apart from the business of micro finance, the role of SHGs should be extended to address social problems faced by rural household and the community related to health care, sanitation, family planning, literacy, energy conservation, local ecology, management of common resources, etc. The developmental agencies will have to pay more attention to these issues and provide greater support, guidance and training to utilize the SHG movement as a catalyst of bringing transformation in the socio-economic development of rural areas.

(*vi*) The MFIs need to improve their compliance with disclosure and reporting norms and bring transparency.

(*vii*) Training and capacity building of the MFIs in core banking and finance, including risk management and cash flow analysis for projects and securitization is an area of high priority, which coupled with wide spread use of technology could reduce transaction costs and improve overall effectiveness while imparting robustness to the movement.

P. REGULATION OF MFIs IN INDIA

In India there is hardly any provision of micro savings, micro investments, micro insurance or micro pensions. This is mostly because of regulatory reasons, *i.e.*, accepting money is heavily regulated, whereas giving money is not. Hence, there has been unregulated and undue focus on loan pushing. It is not as if the poor have no need for savings and investment products.

Indifferent attitude of the RBI and the Central Government has been squarely responsible for the present day crisis in micro finance sector. The RBI failed to enforce effective regulation for profit MFIs that are registered as NBFCs and come under its supervision. Even an internal Committee of the RBI had warned of possible problems in the micro finance sector and recommended two months before the sector was mired in crisis that RBI withdraw priority sector status to MFIs for bank loans if they failed to bring down interest rates. But the RBI failed to step in timely.[21]

It was only after Andhra Pradesh Government introduced the historic ordinance in October 2010 that both the RBI and the Central Government woke up. The RBI appointed the Malegam Committee immediately thereafter to look into the issues concerning the MFI industry. The main recommendations of the Malegam Committee are:

◈ Malegam Committee Recommendations

(*i*) There should be a 24% of interest cap on microfinance loans to individuals.

(*ii*) There should be average margin cap of 10% for MFIs with a loan portfolio of ₹ 100 crore or more and 12% for smaller MFIs.

(*iii*) A new category of non-banking finance companies, *viz.*, NBFC-MFI be created.

(*iv*) An BFC-MFI to provide financial services predominantly to low-income borrowers.

(*v*) Lending to this sector be treated as priority sector lending.

(*vi*) To qualify as NBFC-MFI, a lender must hold no less than 90% of its total assets in the form of qualifying assets (excluding cash and bank balances and money market instalments). Also, an annual family income should not exceed ₹ 50,000.

(*vii*) An individual ceiling of ₹ 25,000 on loans to a single borrower.

(*viii*) At most, two MFIs can lend to a single borrower.

(*ix*) The pattern of repayment can depend on the nature of the loan. The schedule can be weekly, fortnightly or monthly as per the convenience of the borrower.

(*x*) NBFC-MFIs be exempted from State Money lending Acts.

(*xi*) Fast track courts be set up in every district for MFI-related issues.

(*xii*) All loans should be without collateral.

(*xiii*) MFIs be allowed to levy only three charges including processing fee, interest and insurance charge.

(*xiv*) In order to bring down defaults, the Committee recommended setting up one or more credit information bureaus.

(*xv*) The idea of joint liability be given up.

(*xvi*) MFIs should not employ coercive methods for recovery of loans. In case such methods are used, the management of the MFI should be punished.

(*xvii*) All MFIs would have to observe a specific code of corporate governance.

◈ RBI Action on Malegam Committee Recommendations

While accepting most of the recommendations of the Malegam Committee, the RBI created a separate category of NBFC-MFIs and issued following directives to all the SCBs on May 3, 2011.

1. Bank credit to MFIs extended on or after April 1, 2011 for on-lending of individuals and also to members of the SHGs will be eligible for categorisation as priority sector advances provided that:

(*a*) Not less than 75 per cent of the aggregate loans given by MFIs are extended for income generating activities;

(*b*) Not less than 85 per cent of the total assets of MFI (other than cash balances with Banks and financial institutions and money market instruments) are in the nature of "qualifying assets."

(*c*) Banks have to ensure that MFIs comply with the following caps on margin and interest rate as also other pricing guidelines:

(*i*) Margin cap at 12 per cent for all MFIs;

(*ii*) The interest cost is to be calculated on average fortnightly balances of outstanding borrowings and interest income is to be calculated on average fortnightly balances of outstanding loan portfolio of qualifying assets;

(*iii*) Interest rate on individual loans at 26 per cent p.a. to be calculated on a reducing balance basis;

(*iv*) Only three components are to be included in pricing of loans, viz., a processing fee not exceeding 1 per cent of the gross loan amount, interest charge and insurance premium.

(*v*) The processing fee is not to be included in the margin cap or the interest rate cap of 26 per cent;

(*vi*) Only the actual cost of insurance i.e., actual cost of group insurance for life, health and livestock for borrower and spouse can be recovered and administrative charges must be recovered as per IRDA guidelines.

(*vii*) There should not be any penalty for delayed payment.

(*viii*) No Security Deposit/Margin to be collected from borrowers.

2. Bank loans to MFIs, which do not comply with above conditions and bank loans to other NBFCs, will not be reckoned as priority sector loans with effect from April, 2011.

◈ Government of India's Microfinance Bill, 2012

On May 22, 2012, the Government of India introduced in Lok Sabha Microfinance Institutions (Development and Regulation) Bill 2012. The main objectives of the Bill are to provide a common regulatory framework for the microfinance industry in India and to provide greater protection to borrowers. Major features of the Bill are:[22]

(*i*) The Bill proposes to make the RBI the sole regulator of Microfinance sector. All entities involved in micro finance activity will have to be registered with the RBI.

(*ii*) The RBI will specify net worth and other norms such as those for creation of reserves, in addition to these related to fund-raising tools.

(*iii*) The draft bill also proposes to define systematically important MFIs that would be required to convert into Section 25 companies.

(*iv*) Apart from registration, the RBI is proposed to be empowered with prescribing rules, develop the market, inspect books and also issue cease and desist orders.

(*v*) The RBI is also proposed to be vested with power to mandate ceiling on amount of assistance that can be given to individual clients. In addition, it can prescribe the tenure for which the assistance is provided.

(*vi*) In addition to annual percentage rate and margin, the RBI would also have the power to prescribe the processing fees, interest rate and the life insurance premium that a MFI charges.

(*vii*) The RBI can prescribe governance norms, recovery methods, methods of operation and would facilitate credit rating.

(*viii*) The RBI would also prescribe that MFIs become members of credit information bureaus just like banks and credit card companies.

(*ix*) The draft bill has also suggested that self regulatory organizations be set up and banks be asked to follow a code of conduct formulated by it.

(*x*) MFIs would have to provide client Protection Codes and set up grievance redressal mechanism to address some of the concerns around their functioning.

(*xi*) Every MFI would have to set up a reserve fund and transfer a part of its annual profit, for staff training, capacity building and implementation of new technologies.

The Bill seeks to bring under the RBI's purview all institutions offering microfinance service. It also legitimizes other services offered by MFIs as insurance, remittances, collection of thrift and pension schemes. It allows MFIs to collect thrift and small savings by micro-clients that can be used to meet emergency credit needs. At present, NBFCs are not permitted to collect savings on behalf of their clients.

Another encouraging feature of the Bill is that it empowers self-regulatory outfits such as Microfinance Institutions Network and Sa-Dhan to take strict actions against erring MFIs. This provides multiple layers of consumer protection and avoids recurrence of incidents like those that happened in Andhra Pradesh.

The Bill which has been approved by the Parliament regulating the MFI sector in the customers' interest and avoiding a multitude of microfinance legislation in different states. Compulsory registration of the MFs would bring the erstwhile money-lenders into the fold of organised financial services in the hinterland who had been acting as MFIs hitherto.

Q. CONCLUSIONS

MFIs have in recent years emerged as a powerful agent of financial inclusion to improve the economic and social lot of the poor and pauper sections of the society. Thrust of MFIs is outreaching the most vulnerable and providing them financial as well as non-financial products at affordable terms and conditions.

MFIs around the world employ two credit delivery models, *viz.*, Group model and individual model. In group model, a group of individuals is involved. Group becomes a basic unit with which MFIs deal. Group model may take the form of Self-Help group and joint liability group. In individual lending model, MFIs provide loans to an individual based on his/her own creditworthiness.

MFIs have taken four major forms of organizations, viz., informal finance service providers, member-owned organizations, NGOs and formal financial institutions.

Modern concept of MFIs was evolved in Bangladesh by Dr. Mohammad Yunus in 1983 when he founded Grameen Bank in 1983. In the initial years, MFIs organized as NGOs concentrated on providing loans to poor women to invest in tiny business and increase their income. Subsequently, in the 1990s, many of these institutions transformed themselves into formal financial institutions in order to access and on-line client savings, thus enhancing their outreach.

MFIs came into existence in different parts of the world to help the poor. MFIs developed in the USA in the late 1980s to serve low income and marginalised minority community. In Canada, microfinance history took shape through the development of credit unions. Asia is the home of the largest number of MFIs. It is important to note that the microfinance sector around the globe has grown over time with more and different types of players becoming involved, with new types of products and services being developed and with new ideas and technology to support it.

The evolution of MFIs in India passed through four distinct phases, viz., the cooperative movement, subsidized social banking, SHG-Bank linkage programme and growth of NGO-MFIs and commercialisation of microfinance. In view of tremendous opportunities to serve the poor due to burgeoning mismatch between micro-credit demand and supply, the first decade of the current century witnessed mushrooming of MFIs and more so in South India. However, few top MFIs dominated the space. These MFIs adopted commercial approach to exploit the opportunity and used poverty as a means to mint quick money. They went to the extent of employing all sorts of unfair practices to quench their greed. This led Andhra Pradesh Government to enact microfinance legislation in 2010 to curb the unethical operations of MFIs. This legislation landed the MFIs particularly those in Andhra in grave crisis.

MFIs (both under SHG-Bank Linkage Programme and NBFC-MFI) have made laudable efforts in providing financial and non-financial support to the poor and brought about perceptible change in life style of the poor.

However, everything is not hunky-dory in the microfinance sector. Several studies on operational practices of MFIs conducted from time to time bring to the forth various nefarious practices to the detriment of the poor. All this happened under the very nose of the RBI and the Government of India. There was no central legislation, until the Andhra Government Micro Finance Act, 2010, to regulate the operations of the MFIs. It was only after the enactment of the Andhra Micro finance legislation that the RBI and the Government of India woke up. Malegam Committee was appointed to look into operations of the MFIs. The Committee recommended several measures most of which have been accepted by the RBI. The Government of India was also smart enough to draft Bill on Micro finance in 2011. It is hoped that these measures when implemented will bring the micro finance industry on right track.

KEY TERMS

- Business Correspondent
- Credit Unions
- Financial Products
- Formal Financial Institutions
- For-Profit MFIs
- Grameen Model
- Group Model
- Individual Model
- Joint Liability System
- Malegaon Committee Report
- Micro Insurance
- Mix Market
- Multiple Lending
- Mutual benefit MFIs
- Non-Financial Products
- Not-for-profit MFIs
- Responsible financing
- Self-Help Group (SHG)
- SHG-Bank Linkage Programme
- Social banking
- Social Collateral

DISCUSSION QUESTIONS

1. Bring out the redeeming features of Micro Finance Institutions.
2. Why are MFIs emerging an important sector of financial system around the world?
3. Discuss important business models of MFIs.
4. Outline the main forms of organisation of MFIs across the globe.
6. Briefly outline the developments of MFIs in India.
7. Discuss MFI model that exists in India.
8. Briefly discuss policy initiatives of the RBI, NABARD and SIDBI in respect of MFIs.
9. Critically evaluate performance of MFIs in India.
10. Why is MFI industry in India currently in deep crisis?

11. What measures have the RBI and Government of India taken in recent times to salvage the crisis and put the MFIs on strong footing?
12. What suggestions would you proffer to improve and strengthen functioning of MFIs in India?

REFERENCES

1. United Nations, Advisors Group as Inclusive Financial Sector, 2006.
2. Asian Development Bank, Finance For the Poor, Micro Finance Development Strategy, 2000.
3. K.C. Chakravarti, Business Standard, January 24, 2011.
4. www.opportunityfund.org
5. www.microcreditsummit.org
6. Microfinance industry in India, Lok Capital, March 2010.
7. RBI Report on Trend and Progress of Banking in India, 2011-12.
8. www.samn.eu/index.php?q=microfinance-india
9. RBI Report, *op cit.*
10. www.sksindia.com
11. Business Standard, December 6, 2011.
12. Business Standard, November 30, 2012.
13. V. Puhazendi & KJS. Satyasal, Microfinance For Rural People: An Impact Evaluation, NABARD, 2000.
14. V. Puhazendi & K.C. Badatya, SHG-Bank-Linkage Programme for Rural Poor — An Impact Assessment, 2002.
15. Business Today, March 8, 2009.
16. Business Today, November 10, 2009.
17. Business Today, November, 2008.
18. *Ibid.*
19. Business Standard, May 15, 2010.
20. Business Today, December 31, 2006.
21. Business Standard, December 3, 2010.
22. Business Today, August 21, 2011.

Management of Financial Services in India

Section Six

Section VI: Learning Objectives

- The present section aims at providing vivid account of how various institutions rendering financial services in India are managed.

Section Outline

- Financial services in India
- New issue market in India
- Secondary market in India
- Merchant banking in India
- Venture capital
- Custodial services in India
- Credit rating services in India

Chapter 31

Financial Services in India

Learning Objectives:

The present Chapter aims at:

- Providing conceptual understanding of financial services.
- Focusing on nature and significance of financial services.
- Presenting a synoptic view of recent trends in financial services in India.

Chapter Outline:

- Nature of financial services.
- Scope of financial services.
- Significance of financial services to economic growth.
- Financial services and virtualization.
- Financial services in India — Recent developments at a glance.
- Road ahead.
- Conclusions.

A. NATURE OF FINANCIAL SERVICES

Success of financial system in a country depends, *inter alia*, upon range and quality of financial services rendered by various agencies. In general, all types of activities, which are of a financial nature, could be brought under the term 'financial services'. The term financial service, in a broad sense, means "mobilizing and allocating savings". Thus, it includes all activities involved in the transformation of savings into investment. This is why financial services are also called financial mediation which is concerned with garnering funds from a large number of savers and making them available to all those who are in need of it.

Thus, financial services comprise products and services offered by finance industry which encompass a broad range of organizations that deal with the management of money.

The term 'financial services industry' includes all kinds of organizations which intermediate and facilitate transactions of both individuals and corporate customers. Among the financial services organizations are financial institutions of various kinds for the facilitation of various financial transactions and other related activities in the world of finance like loans, insurance, credit cards, security investment, money management as well as providing information on the stock market and other issues like market trends.

Thus, financial services are commonly associated with the supply of financial instruments such as debt securities, equity securities and insurance policies. As such, financial services form an integral part of financial system of a country in as much as it seeks to serve the needs of individuals, institutions and business enterprises, through the network of financial institutions, financial markets and financial instruments.

Financial services are intangible in nature. To be successful these services need to be innovative and customer centric. Based on customers' requirements, suppliers of financial services are expected to offer need-based products and services timely and at affordable cost. Communication between customers and the suppliers of financial services need to be crystal dear, the latter has to adopt compliance culture to enhance the trust. Besides, the products introduced should serve social purposes and needs rather than just being innovative so that retail participation is facilitated. Market players, therefore, need to innovate products with a social purpose taking into account the customers' preferences.

Effective financial services demands developing trust between companies, market participants and intermediaries by enhancing levels of integrity, transparency and governance.

Another redeeming feature of financial services is that functions of production and delivery of financial services need to be performed simultaneously. This calls for synchronization of understanding between financial services suppliers and their clients.

Efficacious financial services have to be dynamic. These services need to be constantly revisited and redefined in the light of fast changing environmental forces. As such, providers of financial services must be proactive and resilient so as to evolve new services on continuous basis by prognosticating the changes in preferences of the customers.

B. SCOPE OF FINANCIAL SERVICES

Financial services cover a wide range of activities. They can be broadly classified into fund-based activities and non-fund based activities.

Fund-based activities comprise all commercial banking activities (like acceptance of deposits, allowing withdrawals, issuance of debit and credit cards, allowing financial transactions at branches or by using Automatic Teller Machines, providing wire transfer of funds and electronic fund transfers between banks, facilitation of standing orders and direct debits, providing overdraft agreements for the temporary advancement of the Bank's own money to meet monthly spending commitments of a customer in their current account, providing a cheque guaranteed by the

Bank itself and prepaid by the customer), underwriting and investment in shares, debentures, bonds, etc. of new issues, dealing in secondary market activities, participating in money market instruments like commercial papers, certificate of deposits, treasury bills, discounting of bills, etc., involving in equipment leasing, hire purchase, venture capital, seed capital, and dealing in foreign exchange market activities.

Non-fund based activities also known as 'fee-based' activities include management of pre-issue and post-issue activities to the capital issue in accordance with the SEBI guidelines and thus enabling the promoters to market their issue, making arrangements for the placement of capital and debt instruments with investment institutions, arrangement of funds from financial institutions for the clients' project cost or his working capital requirements, assisting in the process of getting all government and other clearances, providing information relating to domestic and foreign market trends, providing counseling on business restructuring, etc.

C. SIGNIFICANCE OF FINANCIAL SERVICES IN ECONOMIC GROWTH

Financial services are fundamental to economic growth and development of a country. Financial services industry played the role of a financial intermediary provides the means and mechanism of transferring command over resources from myriad of savers to those who can make profitable use of the same with a view to adding to the volume of productive capital. Banking, savings and investment, insurance, and debt and equity financing help private citizens save money, guard against uncertainty, and build credit, while enabling businesses to start up, expand, increase efficiency and compete in local and international markets. For the poor, these services reduce vulnerability and enable people to manage the assets available to them in ways that generate income and options — ultimately creating paths out of poverty.

By acting as an entrepreneur, financial services industry prompts the pace of growth of underdeveloped countries. As an entrepreneur, as noted in Chapter 1, it undertakes the task of assessing growth potentialities of various regions of the country, identifying specific project ideas, evaluating these ideas so as to determine their feasibility in financial and non-financial terms. Based on the survey, it discerns need-based resource-based and foot-loose or merchant type of industrial projects. In order to ensure that these projects are executed successfully, it takes the responsibility of identifying individuals with entrepreneurial traits and motivates them to an entrepreneurial career by providing training facilities and dispensing financial, technical and managerial support so that they set up industrial enterprises.

Further, institutions associated with financial services facilitate business entrepreneurs in managing their business. Such facilitation may take the form of management of pre-issue and post issued activities relating to capital issues, making arrangements for the placement of capital and debt instruments, providing credit syndication services and assistance in getting all government and other clearances. They also provide consultancy services to business restructuring, procurement of foreign capital and overseas investment.

The financial services sector is the largest in the world in terms of earnings, comprising a wide range of businesses including merchant banks, credit card companies, among others, having the expertise, reputation and geographic reach to have significant direct impact and, through engagement and, to change the way entire markets operate. They are using increasingly deliberate strategies to expand economic opportunity through business models that serve the poor individuals and SMEs as clients. They are also developing initiatives to build human and institutional capacity and using their experience and influence to shape policy frameworks in the regions in which they work.[1]

Despite their immense potentialities to date the impact of financial services industry on expanding economic opportunity has remained limited in the developing world, where a vicious cycle of insufficient information, inappropriate products, inadequate infrastructure and inflexible regulatory environments have kept costs and therefore prices high, limiting companies' markets to clients within the top tiers of the economic pyramid.[2]

D. FINANCIAL SERVICES AND VIRTUALIZATION

Effectiveness of financial services sector in ferally competitive and fast changing global environment depends essentially on its agility, flexibility and responsiveness. It is no secret that customers, regulators and shareholders are all pressing, financial services organizations to adopt more advanced business models to achieve higher performance, offer better services and reduce industry — systematic risk. Financial services organizations are now réalizing the role of technology in their business to fulfill the expectations of wide sections of the society. Those financial organizations that do not commit to virtual transformation risk becoming costly, cumbersome and uncompetitive. Banking takeovers and consequent technology transformations bear testimony to this fact. Even if an actual merger or acquisition is not the instigator, in the wake of such activity, financial organizations are motivated to accelerate plans to use business technology to improve efficiency. However, this is not the only impetus to delivery more business-led, customer-focused technology solutions. Many more organizations are now testing the water with IT transformations and optimization programmes. These changes are driven through a combination of industrialization of the business, the introduction of dynamic IT, significant improvements in connectivity and selected use of business process outsourcing. Together, these forces are driving the evolution of financial services industry towards virtualization.

Virtualization — key to technology-based solutions — allows customers, employees and partners to access the organization's resources wherever they are, via whatever device. Virtualization can dramatically change the way corporate business is done and affect a company's ability to achieve improved performance, scalability, reliability and availability. Virtualization puts on accent on the existing components of market structure, business organization and IT systems as also on the opportunities financial institutions have to better exploit every single building block to add value to the overall organization.[3] By thinking the business environment as a set of independent components, financial organizations can go ahead with breaking up the value chain. This enables them to define new business models that add value, simply by rethinking the way the different blocks composing the financial services sector are organized. For instance, financial institutions can leverage more on selective sourcing to access best-of-breed services in the areas of payments, back-office processing, human resource management, or even distribution, with new technologies ensuring that no backlog will impact the overall service. At the same time, the finance company itself can reengineer its internal processes and break its many walls and silos. Typically, banks and insurance companies are established organizations that have worked for a long time in a highly regulated and protected environment that has grown dramatically in the last two decades. Many processes and organizational models are a legacy of this history and now need restructuring in order to achieve higher optimization, greater integration and enhanced flexibility. In fact, concept of virtualization focuses on optimization, collaboration and flexibility.

It should, however, be noted that adopting a virtualization strategy alone is no guarantee of success. The opposite is actually closer to reality as the concept of a virtual business becomes more accessible, so the entry of new competition becomes easier. It is difficult to tie a bank or an insurance company to a specific location because they have multiple premises or channels to market, some of which — for example, websites — are already virtual channels. Customers do not even need to use their own bank or insurer to access many of the services on offer.

The major challenge for businesses selling financial services (both existing providers and new players) is to virtualize the value chain while also virtualizing the organization and IT systems. It they are unable to do this, the implications are manifold. Poorly performing internal IT systems will not only negatively impact the benefits of virtualization, but also leave businesses in an even less competitive position than when they embarked on the modernization process. Banks, therefore, need to start by breaking away from the silos and the heritage of the past. One way to see how dynamic IT yields new, more resilient operations is to understand how financial institution has evolved into the unyielding complexity in which we work today.

It is noteworthy that the process of simplification and consolidation needs to be carried out with the objective of creating a more flexible system, and not just a cheaper one. The rapidly changing business environment renders even the most stringent single solutions definitively out of date. Therefore, the answer does not lie in banks defining stringent processes but in taking a more dynamic approach to exploit underutilized skills that already exist. Financial organizations must move to the next generation of application architecture to remain standing in future. To stay in the game, they must be both low-cost operators and growth-generating innovators.

E. FINANCIAL SERVICES IN INDIA — RECENT DEVELOPMENTS AT A GLANCE

Post reform period has witnessed remarkable improvement in financial services both quantitatively as well as qualitatively. The financial system of India has significantly impacted the pace and pattern of growth with financial services organizations responsible for the robust economic growth. The financial services sector contributed 15 per cent to India's GDP in financial year 2009 and is the second-largest component after trade, hotels, transport and communication all combined together. It is expected to enhance by 9.7 per cent for the year 2009-10 to 17.2 per cent of GDP (at a factor cost).[4]

Indian finance industry engaged in financial services business provides a wide spectrum of services which can be classified mainly into fund-based and fee-based services. Fund-based services being provided by financial organizations in India include banking, insurance, security investment, money management, car financing, housing financing, mutual funds, micro finance, equipment leasing and hire purchase.

Non-fund based (fee-based) services being provided by finance companies in India — both in public and private sectors comprise broking services, investment services, financial consulting, credit syndication, taxation services, project consultancy, factoring and similar other services for which the institutions charge fees.

Fund-based services in India have taken a giant leap during the post liberalization period. The policy of financial liberalization, privatization and globalization pursued by the Government since 1991 and frenetic to execute the various policy guidelines have substantially improved every segment of financial market of India (For details, see Chapter 4).

During post reform period every segment of financial market of the country significantly improved. Consequent upon the various initiatives of the RBI since the early 1990s, the Indian money market has undergone transformation in terms of instruments, participants and technological infrastructure, leading to emergence of deep, liquid and vibrant money market (for details, see chapter 4). Likewise, capital market in India has recorded landmark developments during the last two decades of reforms in terms of institutionalization and sophistication of secondary market, strengthening of equity market, demutualization of stock exchanges, and growing financial depth of capital market. (For details, see Chapter 4)

Development financial institutions in India transcended their traditional role to assume the role of a development bank to render various financial services to the needy entrepreneurs in addition to project finance. (For details, see Chapter 4)

Another category of institutions associated with rendering fund-based services in India is NBFCs. The NBFCs are mostly private sector institutions which provide a variety of services including equipment leasing, hire purchase, loans and investment. These NBFCs perform a diversified range of function and offer financial services to individual, corporate and institutional clients. With the growing importance assigned to financial inclusion, NBFCs have come to be regarded as important financial intermediaries particularly for the small-scale and retail sectors. (For details, see Chapter 4)

Amongst the institutions engaged in fund-based business banks have emerged most pivotal institutions providing wide variety of financial services including merchant banking. Banking industry in India has undergone tectonic transformation during the post liberalisation period from class banking to mass banking, from one engaged in short-term lending and offering pure deposit type products to universal banking, offering a bouquet of customized products through multiple channels to wide spectrum of customers. (For details, see Chapter 4)

Indian insurance industry has, of late, come a long way in terms of a bouquet of innovative insurance products offered, quality of services rendered and concomitant increase in penetration in untapped market. The entry of private insurers has infused a new flavour into what is perceived as a sober industry and has forced the public sector behemoth — LIC — to adopt a more market-friendly approach in its bid to attract the client. Indian insurance sector in recent times is in top-gear growth wherein the number of life policies in force has increase nearly 12-fold over 2000-2010 and those pertaining to health insurance have increased nearly 25-fold (For details, see Chapters)

Mutual funds in India have also been actively providing financial services by way of garnering savings of the people to invest a diversified portfolio of securities with a view to ensuring the savers triple benefits of minimum risk, strong return and capital appreciation. The ₹ 6.42 trillion Indian mutual fund industry has 44 asset management companies. The industry is poised to grow by leaps and bounds in the coming years due to lower penetration coupled with soaring assets under management. (For details, see Chapters)

Non-fund based financial services in India will be dilated upon in the subsequent chapters with reference to new issue market, secondary market, merchant banking, factoring, custodial services and credit rating agencies.

F. ROAD AHEAD

Indian financial services industry is a promising one and holds great potential for massive growth in future. Be it in banking, insurance, mutual fund or foreign investments, the country is making its mark in every sub-segment, nationally as well as internationally. According to a report by Boston Consultancy Group (BCG), and Indian Banks Associations (IBA), the Indian banking industry would stand as the third largest in the world by 2025 wherein its assets size is poised to mark US $ 28,500 billion by 2025 from the asset size of US $ 1,350 billion in 2010. Another report by an individual body and BCG suggests that India's insurance industry would reach US$350-400 billion in terms of premium income by 2020, making it among the top three life insurance markets. Also, India is expected to be one of the top 15 non-life insurance markets by 2020.[5]

G. CONCLUSIONS

Financial services concerning all activities involved in the transformation of savings into investment form an integral constituent of financial system of a country.

These services comprise fund-based and non-fund based activities, the former covers all commercial banking activities, insurance, underwriting and security investment, participation in money market instruments, equipment leasing, hire purchase, venture capital, seed capital and dealing in foreign exchange market activities, while the latter comprise activities that include merchant banking business, factoring, counseling, etc.

Financial services sector is fundamental to economic growth and development of a country. Financial agencies play significant role in fostering capital formation, project development, development of entrepreneurs and also facilitate in management of new issues, as well as in credit syndicate. They provide consultancy services particularly in respect of business restructuring, and overseas investment.

To provide quality financial services at an affordable cost, financial services institutions are increasingly embracing concept of virtualization — a concept-based solution. Virtualization allows customers, employees and partners to access the organization's resources wherever they are, via. whatever device. It can bring about dramatic change in the way the finance industry conducts its business and affect a company's ability to improve performance.

Financial services sector has recorded spectacular performance during the post-reform period, contributing almost 15 percent to India's GDP in 2009.

In recent years, Indian finance services industry has provided a wide range of financial services including fund-based and non-fund based activities to individuals and business enterprises. Development finance institutions, commercial banks, insurance companies, mutual funds and NBFCs have made tremendous progress to provide various fund-based services to individual institutions and corporate enterprises. Even they have changed their basic character in consonance with fast changing requirements of different sections of the society and exhibited resilience and vibrance in their operations.

As such Indian finance services industry holds out very bright future.

KEY TERMS

- Financial services industry
- Fund-based services
- Non-fund based services
- Value chain
- Virtualization.

DISCUSSION QUESTIONS

1. Discuss nature and significance of financial services.
2. What are the major types of financial services provided by finance industry?
3. Bring out redeeming features of financial services.
4. What is virtualization? In what respect can finance services industry be benefitted by virtualization approach?
5. Discuss, in brief, recent financial services scenario in India.
6. What is the future of financial services industry in India?

REFERENCES

1. Christopher, Suffon and Beth Jenkins, "The Role of Financial Services Sector in Expanding Economic Opportunity", Corporate Social Responsibility Initiative Report No. 19, Cambridge MA, Kenney School of Government, Harward University, 2007.
2. Ibid.
3. www.nortel.com/solutions/industry/collateral/financeidc.pdf
4. www.ie=bef.og/industry/financialservices.aspx
5. www.ibef.org/artdispvie.aspx?in

The New Issue Market in India

Learning Objectives:

The present Chapter aims at:

- Providing vivid account of functions, services and organization of new issue market in India.
- Dilating upon various ways of selling new securities in market.
- Describing the duties and responsibilities of various intermediaries of new issue market in India.

Chapter Outline:

- Introduction.
- Functions of new issue market in India.
- Services of new issue market in India.
- Organization of new issue market in India.
- Methods of distribution of securities.
- New issue market intermediaries in India.
- Role of the SEBI in new issue Market.
- Conclusions.

A. INTRODUCTION

Securities market of our country, where securities of corporate enterprises are traded, comprise two main markets, viz., New issue market (Primary market) and secondary market. In the new issue market, new securities are floated and exchanged for cash, credit or other securities. New security issues are floated both by the newly set up organizations and by the existing ventures. Contrary to this, in the secondary market buying and selling 'second hand' or existing securities are transacted. Stock market is the nickname of the secondary market.

B. FUNCTIONS OF NEW ISSUE MARKET IN INDIA

The major function being performed by primary market in India is to facilitate transmission of funds of those who have surplus income and are willing to invest to entrepreneurs seeking to set up new undertakings or expand, modernize and diversify the operations of the existing enterprises. Since activity of the primary market connects savings and investment, primary market is indispensable for economic and industrial development of the country. Besides, primary market has directed the flow of investment into long-term channels. The capacity of the market machinery to reach down all potential savers irrespective of size of their savings and investing institutions existing in the market have a direct bearing on volume of savings that may be channelled into industry.

C. SERVICES OF NEW ISSUE MARKET IN INDIA

To perform its functions, the new issue market renders the following services:

◈ Investigating services

The first important service rendered by new issue market agencies is to undertake comprehensive investigation of the proposed business. This investigation comprises activities like economic, financial and technical analysis as well as analysis of legal and environmental dimensions of the project. Investors are furnished information about the above so that they can make dispassionate decisions with respect to the type, quality and quantity of the issue.

◈ Advisory services

New issue market agencies aid and advise the investors in regard to choice of the issue, its price, the timing, its size, selling strategies, methods of floatation, and the terms of securities. Such specialized services help the investors in improving the quality of capital issue.

◈ Underwriting services

New issue market makes an institutional arrangement whereby the issuing companies are given the guarantee of buying all such new security issues as remain unsubscribed by the public. This arrangement is akin to insurance that provides protection to the issuer against the failure of an issue.

◈ Distribution services

New issue market also helps the issuer in selling the security issues to the ultimate investors. This, it does through stock brokers and dealers who are in constant touch with the issuers and the ultimate investors, on the one hand and other agencies of the capital market, on the other.

D. ORGANIZATION OF NEW ISSUE MARKET IN INDIA

The agencies associated with functions of originating underwriting and distributions constitute the organization of the new issue market in India. Subscribers also form part of the market. Issuers of new securities include agencies connected with the floatation of initial issues and those concerned with the floatation of existing issues. These agencies are known as promoters who conduct detailed investigations about the venture to be set up, formulates financial plan, prepares prospectus for capital issues, approaches underwriting and brokerage firms for underwriting the issues and makes arrangements for advertising and circulating the prospectus to procure subscriptions. Thus, a promoter is the issuer or supplier of new companies in the market. In the case of existing enterprise, they themselves are the suppliers of new issues when they float further issues. However, when the existing companies offer new security issues only to their existing stockholders, they will not constitute the suppliers of new issues in the new issue market. On the contrary, if they offer issues to public through prospectus, they are regarded as the suppliers of new issues in the market. In the case of existing enterprises, it is the Board of Directors who take decisions as to why, how and when new issues will be floated. They also enter into agreement with underwriters and brokers before floating public issues.

Underwriting is another important activity of primary market. In our country, all financial institutions and brokers undertake this business. Commercial banks have also entered into this market recently in a big way through their subsidiaries. Insurance and investment companies are also important underwriters. Underwriters in India have been found to have subscribed more for preference shares and debentures than for equity shares as the latter are more suited to the investing public and thus devolve less on the underwriters. Brokers help in the floatation of new issues not only through underwriting or as managing brokers but also as financial consultants, advising on the proper capital structure, methods of raising capital and requirements of the Companies Act and the Securities Contracts (Regulation) Act, and listing requirements.

In India, underwriting for public issues was compulsory till October, 1994 in the sense that an issue had to be underwritten if the issuer opted for it while applying for permission to make an issue, or if the SEBI felt that it has to be underwritten. The underwriting business was quite lucrative and devolvement on underwriters lost their money as many issues turned out to be dual; devolvement became enormous and underwriters backed out of their commitments. Since October 1994, the SEBI has made underwriting optional.

The distribution function of primary facilitates the sale of securities to ultimate investors. This function is performed by specialised agencies like brokers and dealers in securities. They maintain constant and close link with the issuers and the ultimate investors on the one hand, and issuers and other agencies of capital market, on the other.

E. METHODS OF DISTRIBUTION OF SECURITIES

Distribution of securities to prospective investors to mop up their surpluses is a highly specialised activity that requires a lot of expertise and experience. As such, companies seeking to garner funds from a large number of investors — both individuals and institutions — have to hire the services of the specialised agencies such as underwriters, brokers, merchant bankers, etc. Besides, there are other ways which can be employed for selling securities to the investing public. Distribution activity has become more important since June, 2010 when the Government of India mandated listed companies to make 25 per cent public holding. In India, following methods are usually employed to garner funds from the public through floatation of securities.

- Public issue through prospectus
- Offer for sale

- Private placement
- Rights issue
- Over-the-counter placement
- Stock-option
- Book-building

◈ Public issue through prospectus

In this method, a public limited company invites the public at large through prospectus to subscribe to the issue of securities. According to the SEBI norms, a minimum of 49% of the total issue at a time is to be offered to public prospectus is a document that provides information about the company and its proposed issue. The company and directors signing this document are personally liable for any false statement or misrepresentation of material facts in the prospectus.

Public issue through prospectus may take the form of direct selling, sale through investment intermediaries and underwriting of issues. Direct selling of securities method can be used when a company intends to approach a small number of large individual or institutional investors. However, there is no certainty of procuring the desired funds from investors through direct selling. This is why companies may take the help of intermediaries and specialized agencies such as brokers, merchant bankers, for selling such securities. These agencies charge commission for their service. However, they do not provide any guarantee to the issue regarding the sale of securities. To remove this deficiency and to ensure certainty of procurement of the desired funds, companies approach underwriting firms who, in lieu of commission, undertake the guarantee of buying the unsubscribed portion of the offer. Thus, an underwritten placement method is relatively more safe method of acquiring funds from the public at large.

The pure prospectus method of selling securities is very popular method because it is useful to both to the issuers as well as to the investors. The issuers have the benefit of wider diffusion of ownership of securities, thus avoiding the possibility of concentration of controlling power in the hands of few. Investors have the advantage of getting detailed information about the company and its issue through prospectus as per the SEBI requirements. This method also promotes confidence of investors through transparency and non-discriminatory basis of allotment. There is hardly any scope of artificial jacking up of prices if the issue is made public.

However, this method can be gainfully employed by large companies offering big issues because of high costs involved in raising capital. Further, it is a time consuming method as a lot of legal formalities need to be compiled with before floating an issue.

◈ Offer for sale

This method involves outright sale of shares enbloc by the company to issue houses or a group of brokers at an agreed price who in turn resell them to the public at large. In such cases, the issuing houses may act as agents of the company. The difference between the resale price and purchase price is termed as spread and represents the profit of the issue houses. In the USA, issuing companies cannot approach the public directly. They are under obligation to sell their shares in the first instance to underwriters, who then issue these shares to the investing public. In India, this method has been employed on an experimental basis under the name 'bought out deals' wherein the shares are first sold to the sponsor under an agreement that the sponsor shall sell them to public within a specified period of time.

This method of distribution of securities has the advantage of ensuring success of the issue and economizing on cost of new issues and thus the issuing company is relieved of the botherations involved in selling securities to the public. The issue houses also stand to gain by charging higher prices.

◈ Private placement

In this method, the issuing company offers issue privately to a select group of investors without the prospectus. In this process, the issuer may call upon the services of brokers or issue houses. This method works in a manner similar to the 'offer for sale method' whereby securities are first sold to issue houses etc. who then sell them at higher prices to individuals and institutions.

The SEBI has laid down certain restrictions on the reservation of securities in any public issues. For example, the maximum permissible allotment through reservation is restricted to 10% for permanent employees, 10% for shareholders of promoting companies, 20% for Indian mutual funds, 24% for FIIS and 20% for Indian and multi-lateral development financial institutions.

This method of selling securities is very economical and less troublesome. As such, it suits the requirements of small companies. To others, this method is useful especially when the stock market is in bearish state and the public response is poor. However, the disadvantage of this method is that the investor cannot resell the security for a specific period of time. This method may also lead to concentration of securities in few hands. There is also scope for creating artificial scarcity for the securities, thus jacking up the prices temporarily and misleading the general public.

◈ Rights issue

Rights issue method is an important method of distributing securities in which the existing company offers shares to its existing shareholders in proportion to their existing ownership. As per Section 81 of the Companies Act, 1956, existing shareholders get a right of 'pre-emption' and they have the option to exercise the right to renounce it or throwaway. For that purpose, a company intending to increase its subscribed capital by the issue of new shares either after two years of its formation or after one year of the first issue of shares whichever is earlier will have to offer the shares to the existing shareholders with the right to resolve them in favour of a nominee.

Rights issue is the cheapest and convenient method of raising funds and protects the interest of the existing shareholders against the dilution of their ownership.

◈ Over-the-counter placement

This method has come to be employed in recent years, especially after the commencement of the operations of Over-the-Counter Exchange (OTCE) in 1992. The OTC permits small companies to raise funds through its exchange. Under this method, the company intending to raise funds through OTCE appoints a member of the OTCE as sponsor. The sponsor appraises the project and values the shares of the company. The shares are placed by the sponsor with itself and other members and dealers of the OTCE. The sponsor ensures the success of the issue even if it is required to subscribe to all the shares by itself. The OTCE members and dealers operate counters to facilitate trading with investing public. The distribution of shares through OTCE has to be made as per the SEBI guidelines. This method of selling securities is most suited to small enterprises.

◈ Stock option

Stock option, also known as Employees Stock Option Plan, (ESOP) is a method of selling securities of a company to its employees. It is a voluntary scheme on the part of the issuing company to participate in the management of the company by offering shares at a discount to the market prices. This method of selling securities has in recent years been growingly used as an incentive tool to retain the talented employees in the organization.

According to the Government policy guidelines, shares allotted to the employees under the ESOP cannot exceed 5% of paid up capital in anyone year and any capital gains arising out of the sale shall be taxed accordingly. MNCs have also been permitted to offer shares under ESOP to their Indian employees at their discretion and not at the concessional rate.

Stock option under ESOP is subject to certain guidelines of SEBI. Accordingly, the approval of the shareholders through a special resolution is mandatory for the issue of stock option. There is no restriction on the maximum number of shares to be issued to a single employee. However, in case of employees being offered more than 1 per cent shares, a specific disclosure and approval would be mandatory at the AGM. A minimum period of one year between grant of options and its vesting has been prescribed. After one year, the company would determine the period during which the option can be exercised. The ESOP scheme is open to all permanent employees and to the directors but not to the promoters. It will also be applicable to the employees of the subsidiary or holding company with the express approval of the shareholders.

In India, this method is quite popular with most of the IT companies. Even some banks have also offered shares under ESOP to their employees.

◈ Book-building

This method of distribution of securities is distinct from other aforestated methods in the sense the quantum and the price of the securities to be issued is determined on the basis of the bids received from the prospective investors by the lead merchant bankers. Thus, the price of the share is not decided in advance by the company or underwriters. Share prices are decided on the basis of real demand for the shares at various price levels in the market and for that purpose, bids are invited from prospective investors from which the demand at various price levels is recorded. The merchant bankers undertake the sole responsibility for the issue.

Book-building method involves the following process:

(i) Appointment of Book runner

The first step involved in the book-building method is appointment of a book-runner from amongst merchant bankers by the issuing company. The book-runner so appointed will have to form a syndicate for the book-building. Bids invited from prospective investors are to be received by the syndicate members who must be member of National Stock Exchange (NSE) or Over-the-Counter Exchange of India (OTECI). These bids are recorded and stored in computer and are accessible to the company management or to the book-runner.

(ii) Filing Draft Prospectus

The prospectus containing all the information about the company and the issue except price of the share is filed with SEBI. The offer of securities through this method has to be separately disclosed in the prospectus under the heading, 'Placement Portion Category'. Likewise, the quantum of shares to be offered to the public will have to be shown under the heading 'Net Offer to the Public'.

(iii) Circulating Draft Prospectus

The book runner circulates a copy of the draft prospectus to the prospective institutional investors who are eligible for firm allotment and to the intermediaries who are eligible to act as underwriters for the purpose inviting bids. The draft prospectus to be circulated must state the price-band within which the securities are being offered for subscription.

(iv) Maintaining record of Bids

The book-runner keeps record of bids received from the investors. Bid once given by the investor cannot be withdrawn, although the same can be revised. The minimum period for which the book has to remain opened in 5 days and the closing date cannot be earlier than the period mentioned. The SEBI can anytime inspect the records.

(v) Analysis of Bids

Immediately after the expiry of the closure of the bid offer dates, the bids received are thoroughly analyzed by the book-runner to determine the price of the issue. The final price is generally fixed reasonably lower than the possible offer price so as to ensure the success of the issue.

(vi) Underwriting of the Issue

In case the issuing company has decided to make offer of shares to the public under the category of 'Net offer to the public', company is bound to get the entire portion to be offered to the public fully underwritten. An agreement with the underwriter specifying the number of securities as well as the price at which the underwriter would subscribe to the securities has to be entered into by the issuer.

(vii) Filing with ROC

The issuing company is required to submit a copy of the prospectus as certified by the SEBI within two days of the receipt of the acknowledgement card from the SEBI.

(viii) Collecting completed Application Forms

The book-runner collects on day before the opening of the issue to the public, application forms along with the application money from the institutional buyers and the underwriters to the extent of the securities proposed to be allotted to them or subscribed by them.

(ix) Allotment of securities

The allotment of securities under book-building method can be made on the second day from the closure of the issue. The issuing company has the option to choose one date for both the placement portion and the public portion.

(x) Placement schedule and listing

The underwriters to the 'net offer to the public' may be asked by the book-runner to pay in advance the amount involved in underwriting commitment by the eleventh day of the closure of the issue. In such a situation, the shares allotted as per the private placement category will become eligible for being listed.

(xi) Undersubscription

Where there is undersubscription in the 'net offer to the public' category, any spillover to the extent of under-subscription is to be permitted from the 'placement portion' group and the preference is accorded to the individual investors. In the case of undersubscription in the placement portion, spillover is to be permitted from the net offer to the public to the placement portion.

Following the recommendations of Malegaum Committee, the SEBI introduced the option of book-building in October, 1995. Accordingly, the issuing company has now the option for either reserving the securities for firm allotment or issuing the securities through book building. The cent per cent book building is permissible since 1998-99 in respect of issues of ₹ 25 crore and above. As per the recent SEBI guidelines, a company intending to issue shares to the public exceeding 5 times its existing net worth can do so only through the book building way and 60% of such issues must be picked up by institutions, 25% by small investors and the remaining 15% by those having applied for less than 1,000 shares.

Book-building route is becoming increasingly popular in securities market of India because of several advantages, such as determination of demand-based price of the share, minimization of the scope of unofficial premium market operations, reduction of the allotment and listing time from about 60 days to just 7-10 days, transparency in the process of issue of shares, reliable allotment procedure, and minimization of floatation costs. Besides, this method can be employed in case of public issue as well as private placement of both. In case any one of the two gets undersubscribed, it can be split· over.

F. NEW ISSUE MARKET INTERMEDIARIES IN INDIA

A number of intermediaries are associated with activities of the primary market in India. They are Merchant Bankers, Underwriters, Bankers to the Issue, Brokers to the Issue, Registrars and Share Transfer Agents and Debenture Trustees. A brief discussion of tasks and obligations of each of these participants, as per the SEBI guidance,[1] is brought out below:

◈ Merchant Bankers

Merchant bankers in India, akin to 'accepting and issue houses' of the U.K. and Investment banks of the USA, offer a package of financial services relating to the issue. A detailed discussion in this respect has been made in chapter on 'Merchant Banking'.

◈ Underwriters

A company intending to garner funds from the market is not certain about the availability of the desired quantum of funds through subscription of securities. To ensure the certainty, some sort of institutional arrangement needs to be made whereby the issuing company is given the guarantee of purchase of all unsubscribed securities. This arrangement is akin to insurance that provides protection against the failure of an issue of capital to the public. Such an insurance arrangement to ensure success of the issue is termed as 'underwriting'. Underwriters, therefore, undertake the guarantee offering the shares placed before the public in the event of non-subscription of the securities. Thus, an issuing company has to enter into an agreement with an underwriter who may be individual or institution for underwriting the issue. The obligation of the underwriter as per the requirement arises when the event of non-subscription of issues by the public takes place.

Underwriting may take different forms depending on nature of the agreement entered into between the issuer and the underwriter. Thus, there may be standby underwriting, outright purchase, joint underwriting, syndicate underwriting and sub-underwriting.

Under *standby underwriting*, underwriters enter into an agreement with an issuing company to take all such securities as are not subscribed in the market or to buy certain portion of the security issues. This type of underwriting is very popular in India.

In *outright purchase*, underwriters buy the entire issue outright and make the payment thereof. Thereafter, they arrange to sell them to investors through their own organization. This type of underwriting is very popular in the USA.

Joint underwriting takes place while capital issue is large and risk is too high and in such cases the issuing company approaches more than one underwriter. Each underwriter undertakes to guarantee for the issue of a certain portion of the whole issue offered to the public and thereby shares the risk proportionately.

In *syndicate underwriting*, a number of underwriters enter into an agreement among themselves to underwrite an issue particularly the one which is quite large and/or potentially risky. Syndicate underwriting seems to be akin to joint underwriting. But actually this is not so. In the case of joint underwriting, underwriters are approached by the issuer for underwriting an issue and no agreement takes place among the underwriters themselves. In contrast, in the case of syndicate underwriting, underwriters enter into a formal agreement among themselves to undertake the guarantee of buying shares or debentures of a public issue.

Sub-underwriting of an issue takes place when an underwriter enters into agreement with some other underwriters to underwrite the whole or part of the issue underwritten by him. In this case, sub-underwriters do not enter into agreement with the 'issuing company'.

◈ Tasks and Responsibilities of underwriters

The SEBI has laid down the following guidelines regarding tasks and responsibilities of underwriters:

(*i*) An underwriter is required to get itself registered with the SEBI and procure a certificate of registration for undertaking the business. The SEBI issues the certificate on being satisfied with the following conditions:

- Availability of necessary infrastructure like, sufficient office space, equipments, and manpower to carry out the duties effectively.
- Experience in underwriting or having a minimum of two persons equipped with the underwriting experience.
- Capital adequacy norm of a minimum net worth of ₹ 20 lakh.
- No conviction of the applicant (director, principal officer or partner) in any offence.
- Underwriting to fulfill obligations under the SEBI Act, rules and regulations.
- Underwriting to abide by the prescribed code of conduct.
- Payment of the prescribed fee of ₹ 2 lakh for the first and second years for grant on registration certificate and ₹ 20,000 p.a. for its renewal.

(*ii*) An underwriter is under obligation to comply with all the formalities with regard to registration with the SEBI, agreement with the issuing company and all other responsibilities as spelt out by the SEBI. These include disclosures in the prospectus and its filing with the Registrar of companies (ROC) before signing the underwriting agreement with the issuer, ensuring that the prospectus is delivered to the ROC within 30 days of the underwriting agreement or within such an extended time as approved by the underwriter in writing, subject to the limits within the law, complying with any additional disclosures that may be made in the interests of investors or stipulated by SEBI/lead managers.

(*iii*) An underwriter cannot take up total underwriting obligations, at any point of time, under all underwriting agreements, exceeding 20 times its net worth.

(*iv*) An underwriter will have to subscribe to securities under the agreement within 45 days of the receipt of intimation from the issuing company.

(*v*) An underwriter is required to observe codes of conduct which the SEBI has prescribed in respect of the conduct of the business. The codes include observing high standards of integrity and fairness in the conduct of the business, undertaking all efforts to protect the interest or its clients, rendering high standards of service, exercising due diligence and ensuring proper care and exercise of independent professional judgement, not making untrue statement or suppressing any material fact in any documents, reports, papers or information furnished to the SEBI, and not deriving any other direct or indirect benefit from underwriting the issue except receiving the underwriting commission at the agreed rate, the ceiling for which is 5% in case of underwriting of shares and 2.5% in case of debentures.

◈ Bankers to an Issue

Bankers represent an important segment of Indian new issue market. They carry out the function of accepting applications and application moneys from investors in respect of securities and refunding of application money to the applicants to whom securities could not be allotted. They also participate in the payment of dividends by companies.

◈ Tasks and Responsibilities of Bankers to an Issue

The following guidelines with respect to duties and responsibilities of bankers to an issue have been laid down by the SEBI:

(*i*) A banker intending to act as banker to an issue can do so by getting itself registered with the SEBI and obtaining a certificate of registration to that effect. The SEBI issues the certificate on being satisfied about the availability of the necessary infrastructure, communication and data processing facilities with the applicant and the adequacy of manpower to effectively perform activities relating to the issue.

(ii) An annual registration fee of ₹ 2.5 lakh for the first two years from the date of initial registration and ₹ 1 lakh for the third year has to be paid by the banker to an issue to the SEBI. The renewal fees are ₹ 1 lakh annually for the first two years and ₹ 20,000 for the third year.

(iii) A banker is required to enter into an agreement with the issuing company, specifying number of centres at which applications from investors will be collected and the time within which statements regarding applications and money received will be sent to the registrars to the issue by the designated branches or the banker to the issue.

(iv) A banker to the issue has to maintain books of accounts, records and documents for a minimum period of atleast 3 years regarding number of applications, names of investors, time with which applications received were forwarded to the issuing company/ registrar to the issue and dates and amount of refund to investors,

(v) A banker to the issue is required to furnish to the SEBI detailed information pertaining to number of applications received, number of issues for which he acted as banker to the issue, the dates on which applications from investors were forwarded to the issuing company/registrar to the issue and amount of refund to investors.

(vi) A banker to the issue has to observe all the codes of conduct ordained by the SEBI for the merchant bankers and underwriters. Besides, it has to adhere to the following norms laid down by the SEBI:

- Make all efforts to protect the interests of investors;
- Observe high standards of integrity and fairness in the conduct of the business;
- Exercise due diligence, ensure proper care and exercise independent professional judgement;
- Not to keep blank application forms bearing broker's stamp at the bank premises or at the entrance of the bank;
- Not to accept applications after office hours, on bank holidays or after the date of the closure of the issue;
- Not to act any time in collusion with other agents in a manner detrimental to the interest or small investors; and
- Abide by all acts, rules, relations,· notifications, directions, circulars, instructions and guidelines issued by the Government, the RBI, Indian Banks Association and SEBI that are relevant to his operation as banker to an issue.

◈ Brokers to An Issue

Brokers to an issue represent intermediaries who are concerned with procuring the subscription to the issue from prospective investors across the country. In this way, they serve as a vital link between the issuer and the prospective investors and assist in speedy subscription of the issue by the public.

An issuing company can appoint as many number of brokers as it wants provided the stock exchange of which the issuer is a member permits and the listing requirements are fulfilled. A copy of the consent letter should be filed with the Registrar of Companies alongwith a copy of the prospectus stating the names and addresses of the brokers to the issue.

The brokers to the issue must be endowed with the expertise, professional competence and must be honest so as to be able to carry out the various functions of an issue.

The issuing company has to pay brokerage according to the provisions of the Companies Act and rules and regulations the agreement between the brokers and the company and guidelines prescribed by the SEBI. Maximum brokerage rate, applicable to all types of industrial securities, whether underwritten or not, is 1.5 per cent. The brokers will have to meet all mailing costs, canvassing expenses and all other out of pocket expenses relating to the subscription of the issue out of their brokerage. On private placement, the listed company can pay brokerage at the maximum rate of 0.5%.

◈ Registrar to an Issue and Transfer Agent

Registrar and Transfer agent are the two categories of intermediaries who actively participate in the new issue activity of a company. The Registrar performs the functions of collecting applications from prospective investors, keeping a record of the applications and moneys received from the investors, assisting the issuing company in the determination of the basis of allotment of securities, processing and dispatching of allotment letters and refund orders, share and debenture certificates and other documents related to the issue and acting as Depository Participants (DPs).

Transfer Agent, on the other hand, carries out the activities, such as maintaining the record of holders of securities of the company for and on behalf of the company, handling all matters relating to transfer and redemption of securities of the company and acting as Depository Participants (DPs).

◈ Tasks and Responsibilities of Registrar and Transfer Agent

The SEBI has prescribed the following rules regarding duties and responsibilities of registrar and transfer agent:

(*i*) Both registrar and transfer agent have to obtain certificate of registration from the SEBI. The SEBI issues the certificate on being satisfied, about their ability to perform their functions efficiently and honestly, adequacy of their infrastructure and capital. Capital adequacy norm for Category I registrar (one who acts as registrar to an issue and transfer agent) is ₹ 6,00,000 and for Category II registrar (one who acts as registrar or as a transfer agent) ₹ 3,00,000. An annual fee of ₹ 50,000 and ₹ 30,000 has to be paid for initial registration by Category I and Category II registrars, respectively. Renewal fee for every 3 years for Category I registrar is ₹ 40,000 and for Category II registrar ₹ 25,000.

(*ii*) The registrar and transfer agent are required to maintain for a minimum period of 3 years records, books and documents containing details about the issue, rejected applications together with the reasons for rejection, basis of allotment, terms and conditions of purchase of securities, allotment of securities, list of allottees and non-allottees, names of transferors and transferees and the dates of transfer of securities. They have to provide for periodic reporting to and inspection by the SEBI.

(*iii*) Registrar and transfer agent are under obligation to observe various codes of conduct prescribed by the SEBI for merchant bankers and underwriters. Alongside this, they have to ensure that enquiries from investors are promptly dealt with and adequate steps are taken for proper allotment of securities and quickly refund of excess application money as per law.

◈ Debenture Trustees

A company contemplating to issue debentures to raise long-term funds from the market has to appoint a trustee to safeguard the interests of the debenture holders. The following may be appointed as debenture trustee:

(*i*) A scheduled bank, or

(*ii*) A public financial institution, as defined in Section 4-A of the Companies Act, 1956, or

(*iii*) An insurance company, or

(*iv*) A body corporate.

◈ Tasks and Responsibilities of Debenture Trustees

The SEBI has laid down the following guidelines with respect to tasks and responsibilities of debenture trustees:

(*i*) A debenture trustee must get certificate of registration from the SEBI for acting as trustee. The SEBI issues the certificate on being satisfied about the adequacy of the infrastructure of the applicant, its expertise and experience and professional qualification for a debenture trustee from an institution recognized by the government in finance, accountancy, law or business management.

(*ii*) A debenture trustee must accord consent in writing to the body corporate to act as debenture trustee before the debenture trustee.

(*iii*) A debenture trustee shall take possession of the trust property as per provisions of the Deed.

(*iv*) A debenture trustee shall carry out inspection of books of accounts/records/documents and registers and trust property.

(*v*) A debenture trustee shall enforce security in the interest of debentureholders.

(*vi*) A debenture trustee shall have to abide by various codes of conduct issues by the SEBI on 1-10-2003. Important among these codes are:

- Make all efforts to protect the interests of debenture holders;
- Maintain high standards of integrity, dignity and fairness in the conduct of the business;
- Fulfill its obligations in a prompt, ethical and professional manner;
- Exercise due diligence, care and independent professional judgement;
- Avoid conflict of interest and make adequate disclosure of its interest;
- Put in place a mechanism to resolve any conflict of interest;
- Not indulge in any unfair competition, which is likely to harm the interest of other trustees or debentureholders.
- Ensure full and adequate disclosures to ,the debentureholders so as to enable them to make a balanced and informed decision.
- Not to make untrue statement or suppress any material fact in any documents, reports, or information furnished to the SEBI.
- Ensure that good corporate policies and corporate governance is in place.

G. ROLE OF THE SEBI IN PRIMARY MARKET

The SEBI plays crucial role in the effective functioning of the primary market in the country. This it seeks to do in following ways:

(*i*) Prescribing detailed guidelines with respect to various methods that can be adopted by a company to sell its securities;

(*ii*) Laying down comprehensive rules with respect to duties and responsibilities of various players of the primary market;

(*iii*) Prescribing exhaustive codes of conduct for different players of the primary market for protecting interests of the investors;

(*iv*) Conducting the inspection of the working of different intermediaries of the primary market so as to ensure that the relevant books of accounts, other records and documents are maintained properly as per the rules;

(*v*) Suspending the certificate of registration granted to the intermediary in case of violation of the provisions of the SEBI Act, and rules, not observing the prescribed codes of conduct, failure to furnish information relating to his business as required by the Board, non-submission of reports as required by the Board, indulging the manipulating or price rigging or cornering activities, guilty of misconduct or improper or unbusiness like or unprofessional conduct, failure to pay the fees and violation of the conditions subject to which the certificate of registration granted to the intermediary;

(*vi*) Cancelling the certificate of registration in case of the repeated defaults with respect to the above, guilty of fraud, conviction of a criminal offence, violation of any provision of insider trading regulations, and violation of the provisions of the Companies Act.

H. CONCLUSIONS

New issue market of a country renders three major services: investigating and processing of proposals for new issues, underwriting of new security issues and distribution of new securities to ultimate investors. These functions are carried out by specialised agencies like financial institutions, brokers and dealers of securities.

There are various methods of selling securities, viz., public issue through prospectus, offer for sale, private placement, right issue, over-the-counter-placement, stock option and book building.

A host of players participate in the activities of the new issue market in India. They are merchant brokers, underwriters, bankers to the issue, brokers to the issue, registrars and share transfer agencies and debenture trustees. These players can carry on their business after getting Certificate of Registration from the SEBI. The SEBI has laid down comprehensive rules defining duties and responsibilities of each of these players and codes for conduct in their business. Violation of rules and failure to observe codes may lead to suspension of their business.

The SEBI plays vital role in the effective functioning of the new issue market in India by formulating comprehensive rules regarding issue of new securities, defining duties and responsibilities of various players of the market, and conducting the inspection of the working of these players.

KEY TERMS

- Bankers to an issue
- Book building
- Debenture Trustee
- Offer for sale
- Outright purchase
- Over-the-counter placement
- Private placement
- Public issue through prospectus
- Rights issues
- SEBI
- Share Transfer agents
- Stock option
- Syndicate Underwriting
- Underwriting

DISCUSSION QUESTIONS

1. Outline major functions of new issue market in India.
2. Discuss, in brief, about the agencies associated with activities of new issue market in India.
3. What are the various methods used in India for selling securities?
4. What is book-building? How is price determined under this method?
5. Discuss, briefly, the functions performed by various agencies associated with new issue market in India.
6. What do you know about underwriters? What are the duties and obligations which the SEBI ordained for the underwriters?
7. Who are the bankers to an issue? What are the duties and responsibilities of a banker to issue, as laid down by the SEBI?
8. Who are the brokers to an issue? How are they appointed? What are their duties towards the issuing company and the SEBI?

9. What duties and responsibilities have been laid down by the SEBI for registrars and share transfer agents?
10. Who is eligible to act as a debenture trustee? Outline duties and responsibilities which the SEBI has laid down for a debenture trustee?
11. What role the SEBI plays in the smooth functioning of the new issue market in India?

REFERENCES

1. Business Today, July 25, 2010.
2. www.sebi.gov.in
(This is the website of SEBI which contains information about the guidelines regarding primary market in India.)

Secondary Market in India

Chapter 33

Learning Objectives:

The present chapter aims at:

- Presenting discussion on nature and significance of secondary market.
- Providing discussion on procedure for listing of securities in Indian stock market and settlement of trade.
- Providing a vivid view of major stock exchanges in India.

Chapter Outline:

- Nature of secondary market.
- Objectives and services of secondary market.
- Importance of secondary market.
- Listing of securities.
- Procedure for securities trading in stock market in India.
- Mechanics of trade settlement in India.
- Secondary market intermediaries in India.
- Major stock exchanges in India —A brief view.
- Conclusions.

A. NATURE OF SECONDARY MARKET

Secondary market, also known as stock market, is a market where the trade of previously issued securities of governments, semi-governments and firms is made under a code of rules and regulations. It is a two-way market in which the investors and stakeholders are just as likely to be sellers as buyers. As per Section 2(3) of the Securities Contract (Regulation) Act 1956, the following securities can be traded at a stock market:

(*i*) Shares, scrips, stocks, bonds, debentures, debenture stocks or other marketable securities of a like nature in or of any incorporated company or other body corporate;

(*ii*) Government securities; and

(*iii*) Rights or interests in securities.

Redeeming features of secondary market are:

(*i*) A secondary market is a market for already existing long-term securities of governments, semi-governments and corporate enterprise. This market exists only if someone creates it. There are two types of market creators — dealers and brokers. Dealers stand ready to buy and sell at quoted prices. They hold on to the securities until someone else comes along wishing to buy them. In contrast, brokers do not themselves buy or sell the securities. They, instead of buying the securities, would find someone willing to buy them.

(*ii*) The secondary market can be wholesale and retail. The **wholesale market** is the market in which professionals, including institutional investors trade with one another. Transactions in this market are usually large. The **retail market** is the market in which the individual investors buy and sell securities.

(*iii*) Exchanges in the wholesale secondary market for capital securities may take place in either of the two markets, viz., **over-the counter market (OTC)** and **organized exchange market** Where the organization is more structured and communication is often face to face, the market is known as an organized exchange. Generally, the secondary market for government securities is an OTC market, and that the secondary market for corporate equities consists of both the OTC markets and exchanges. The wholesale market for bonds in the USA is principally an OTC market; fewer than 10% of all issues are traded in the stock exchanges.[1]

Thus, an organized exchange is characterized as auction market that uses floor traders who specialize in particular stocks. Exchange rules govern trading to ensure the efficient and legal operation of the exchange and the exchange board constantly reviews these rules to ensure that they result in competitive trading. In about 90% of trades, the specialist matches buyers with sellers. In the other 10%, the specialist may intervene by taking ownership of the stock themselves or by selling stock from inventory.

Unlike organized exchanges, OTC markets have market makers. Rather than trading stocks in an auction format, they trade on an electronic network where bid and ask prices are set by market makers.

(*iv*) In the secondary market, only those securities, which are listed in the stock exchanges, are traded. Unlisted securities are not permitted to be dealt in the market.

(*v*) Transactions in the secondary market must accord to the rules and by laws framed by the stock exchange to regulate its day-to-day operations.

B. OBJECTIVES AND SERVICES OF SECONDARY MARKET

Primary objectives of a secondary market are to provide marketability to existing securities and to facilitate the acquisition of capital by corporate enterprises. In order to accomplish these objectives, the secondary market performs the following functions:

(i) To provide for a regular market

The secondary market provides for a ready and continuous market where those desiring to deal in securities assemble to buy and sell securities during the business hour. This enables investors to liquidate their investments quickly and with the least possible loss. High marketability of securities enhances their value and facilitates the use of these securities as collateral for loan.

(ii) To provide stability in prices of securities

Through the mechanism of regular purchase and sale of securities, the secondary market ensures continuity and stability in share price which is an essential requirement of liquidity. Bulls, bears and stock brokers operating in the market deal in securities with the expected changes in security prices and buy or sell securities accordingly to take price advantage. For instance, speculators expecting rise in share prices in future buys shares at lower prices in the present and disposes them off in future. This results in gradual rise in prices and avoids violent fluctuations in share prices. Thus, regular transactions in securities prevent sharp movement in prices unless warranted by economic and political developments in the country and abroad. Stockbrokers render useful services in equalizing prices of securities of different markets. They make heavy buying in the market where share prices are ruling low and thereby increase pressure of demand of securities which would in consequence raise share prices. Where share prices are high, the stockbrokers tend to depress the rise by sale of securities substantially.

A mandatory 25 per cent public float since June 2010 would ensure better price discovery. This is for the fact that more shares available for trading in the secondary market would mean greater liquidity, in turn paving volatility and making the markets more stable. Diverse shareholding also makes price manipulation difficult.

(iii) Regular valuation of securities

Another redeeming function of the secondary market is to provide mechanism to evaluate securities properly. For proper valuation of securities, the market provides such an economic machinery which could produce prices of securities as close as possible to investment value based on present and future income yielding prospects of various enterprises capitalized at notional rate of interest, *i.e.*, the rate which will prevail if and when all the liquid savings are employed into productive avenues. This can be achieved by intelligent anticipation of future income yielding prospects of various enterprises and notional rate of interest. A well developed secondary market disseminates full information about listed companies to attract a large number of informed buyers and sellers from all walks of life and to arouse keen competition among them resulting in the establishment of fairest possible price.

(iv) To provide safety in dealings

A well organized and regulated secondary market ensures a greater measure of safety and fair dealings to the average investors because transactions are made publicly under well-defined rules, regulation and by-laws of the exchange. For any malpractice or for not observing the exchange rules, the member broker is severely dealt with by the stock exchange. A listed company is required to make a continuous disclosure of all material information for the benefits of the investors.

(v) To ensure wide provide ownership of securities

A secondary market ensures wider distribution of securities. If a company's securities are listed in different stock of markets of the country, its securities will be bought and sold by persons spread across the country and ownership of securities is widely diffused. Broad ownership also safeguards the corporate sector from government interference and protects genuine security markets from dominance by large institutions and government bodies.

C. IMPORTANCE OF SECONDARY MARKET

In view of the above conditions, secondary market plays crucial role in economic and industrial development of a country through promoting capital formation and efficient allocation of capital. Secondary market promotes capital formation by assisting in the effective mobilization of savings and their channelisation into appropriate avenue of investment. This it does by providing an organized market in diverse type of securities to suit the varying notions and whims of mass of savers about liquidity, profitability and risk element in their investments. The opportunity of constant evaluation of returns on one's investment compared to others, the liquidity that is important to investment in fixed capital and price continuity that it ensures, instill confidence in the minds of savers. On the other hand, by creating conditions which reasonably ensure availability of financial resources for creating real capital, whether in private or public sector, they give impetus to development.

A secondary market increases economic efficiency. An organized exchange helps allocate capital more efficiently by establishing fair prices for securities and by minimizing the costs of buying and selling them. A secondary market also helps in directing flow of savings into promising industries and checks the flow of capital in uneconomic and less profitable ventures. This, the secondary market seeks to achieve through keeping an eye on the exchanges. A permanent to surge in share price of a particular industry suggest that more capital can be absorbed by the industry with the advantage. On the contrary, if share price in an industry registers continued fall, it suggest that the industry cannot absorb the capital profitably. Through price mechanism the secondary market prevents gluts and scarcities of capital as between different industries and avoids misalignments between supply of capital and the demands of industry and effects economies in the use of capital.

In underdeveloped economies not only is the volume of savings low but a large part of it is dissipated in conspicuous consumption and in hoards because of lack of knowledge investment opportunities, high liquidity preference and other non-economic forces. The secondary market promotes conditions which take care of some of these inhibiting factors. It offers a ready market for conversion of securities into cash and thereby encourages investment and discourages hoarding. Again, its widely published operations and price quotations bring home to the savers various productive and desirable opportunities of investment.

The secondary market also facilitates an investor to shift from one type of investment to another according to his investment priorities without any significant depreciation in its real value. Accordingly, an investor does not get tied for the better or for the worse, to the particular enterprise whose shares he buys. It is this assurance that he does not have to sink or swim with it that makes him willing to venture into investment.[3] Further, by widening the opportunities for investment, a secondary market enables investors to spread their risk by acquiring securities of different industries, and in varying proportions, which is an essential concomitant to modern investment.

A secondary market helps to promote 'democratic capitalism'. By distributing the ownership of securities more widely among the public, a securities market ensures that the ownership of business is not confined to a small number of wealthy families or to big industrial financial conglomerates.

An efficient secondary market makes access to international capital easier. Foreign investors — both direct and portfolio investors — will be encouraged to invest because of their strong preference for investment in countries where their funds are complementing, rather than replacing domestic savings.

Thus, secondary markets serve the nation in several ways through their multifarious services. However, to many people the secondary market is inseparately associated with speculation with a word that carries with it a cluster of anti-social in applications and monstrously pervert its functions and advantages.[3] There is no denying fact that unscrupulous and unbridled speculations breed all sorts of misfortunes. But genuine speculations, which enable the stock exchange to render the services, stated above, need not be discouraged. As such, while the significance of the secondary market need not belittled, it must always be subject to the maintenance of normally conducive conditions and effective check over unscrupulous speculation.

It is important to note that both the segments of the capital market are equally important while not being mutually exclusive. Only when a country's primary market is alive, it is possible to ensure a good deal of activity in the secondary market, more so in developing economies. Looking from the other angle, if country's secondary market is only active but not transparent and disciplined, the cult of equity and related investment in the primary market will be difficult to be continuously developed and sustained because the liquidity which the secondary market imparts to such investment in the hands of the investors will be adversely effected.

D. LISTING OF SECURITIES

Only such securities can be traded in a stock market in India as are listed in the stock market. The stock market lays down certain standards which a firm must fulfill before getting the securities listed.

As per Securities Contracts (Regulation) Act, 1956, a company intending to get its securities listed in an exchange has to furnish the following documents and information to the concerned stock market:

(*i*) Memorandum and Articles of Association.

(*ii*) Copies of all prospectuses or statements in lieu of prospectuses.

(*iii*) Copies of audited financial accounts.

(*iv*) Agreements with promoters, underwriters, brokers, etc.

(*v*) Letters of consent from SEBI.

(*vi*) Details of shares and debentures issued and shares forfeited.

(*vii*) History of the company in brief.

(*viii*) An underwriting regarding compliance with the provisions of the Companies Act, 1956 and Securities Contracts (Regulation) Act, 1956.

(*ix*) A list of the highest ten holders of each class of kind of securities of the company.

On being satisfied with the above details, the firm is granted admission for trading. The stock exchange is empowered to withdraw or suspend the listing in case of breach of conditions.

In April, 2010, the SEBI vide its circular dated April 6, 2010, has made it mandatory for all listed entities to disclose their asset-liability and solvency positions every six months within 45 days from the end of the half-year, as a note to their half-yearly financial results.

On March 8, 2013, the SEBI announced a new set of regulations to govern issuance and listing of non-convertible preference shares with a view to safeguarding the interest of small investors from such high-risk securities. These guidelines are:

- The listing of privately placed non-convertible redeemable preference shares, would require a minimum application size of ₹ 10 lakh for each investor.
- The public issuance of such shares would require a minimum rating of 'AA' or equivalent investment grade.

The main objectives of listing of securities are to ensure proper supervision and control of dealings in securities and thereby protect the interests of the investors.

Listing of securities facilitates wider publicity in print and media and thus helps the firms in wider distribution of securities. Since the securities are traded as per certain rules and the rates of securities are regularly quoted, the investors are benefitted as they can make well informed decisions about the investment in companies and their securities. The listed securities have a ready market at stock market and the prices offered for securities are also competitive since a large number of buyers and sellers are always present at the market to trade in securities. Thus, listed securities ensure adequate liquidity.

E. PROCEDURE FOR SECURITIES TRADING IN STOCK MARKET IN INDIA

Trading in securities in a stock market is permitted through members of the stock market. Anyone intending to deal in securities has to approach brokers who are members of the stock market. National Stock Exchange of India (NSE) has laid down the following procedure for trading in securities in the exchange:

◈ Registration of client

A firm intending to buy securities has to approach the broker and execute a client registration form wherein all details about the buyer are furnished. Likewise, the seller has also to execute the registration form. This forms the basis for trading in the exchange through the broker.

◈ Agreement

An agreement between the buyer and the broker as specified by the exchange concerned is entered into. This agreement is known as the client member agreements.

◈ Placing an order

Buyer places the order in writing with the broker for the purchase of certain number of scrips at a certain specified price. In this respect, the broker guides the client about the type of securities to be purchased and the proper time for it. If a client is to sell the securities, then the broker tells him about the most appropriate time for sale. While placing an order, sometimes a definite price is given on which the purchase is to be made, sometimes the tentative price is given and sometimes the maximum price is given. The broker tries to make purchases as far as possible to the nearest price offered by the client. The broker is given some choice for bargaining. The same type of choice is given to the broker for selling the securities.

◈ Order confirmation

After collecting the order from the client, the broker places the order in his computer system, which is, in turn, transmitted to the computer system of the NSE at Mumbai. The order confirmation slip is obtained by the broker from the exchange.

◈ Trade confirmation

A trade confirmation slip is generated as soon as the order is matched by the computer against the price generated by the matching algorithm (price-time priority). The trade confirmation slip contains details of the trade executed. The buyer then makes payment of requisite margin money to the broker.

◈ Contract note

The broker issues a contract note to the buyer in respect of all the orders that are executed during the day. Such a note specifies the obligation of the parties concerned, for the buyer to make payment and the broker to make delivery of scrips. Accordingly, the buyer makes the payment and the broker delivers the scrips to the former. And thus, the contract is concluded.

F. MECHANICS OF TRADE SETTLEMENT IN INDIA

The spot dealings are settled in the market itself in full. The selling broker hands over the transfer form and share certificates to the buying broker after receiving the price. In the NSE, settlement of trade in stock takes a certain cycle.

There are two kinds of trade settlement in vogue in the NSE, viz., Rolling Settlement and Account Period Settlement.

(i) Rolling Settlement System

In this system, the trade executed on a certain day has to be settled after a certain number of days depending on the nature of settlement cycle practiced by the exchange. Thus, if a settlement cycle is specified as T + 4, it signifies the trade executed on the first day (say Monday) has to be settled on the fifth day (on Friday), *i.e.*, after a gap of 4 days.

(ii) Account Period System

Under this method, trading is allowed to continue for a certain period mutually agreed upon by the parties and it is possible for the client to buy or sell for a certain number of days, and thereby accumulate a certain position during the period. At the end of the period, his obligation in terms of shares purchased or sold and the amount to be paid by him is figured out and communicated to him. The obligations of a broker are calculated after netting the trades. The following example illustrates how the system is practiced in the NSE for its equity segment.

Settlement Cycle At NSE

Day 1	Monday	Commencement of trade cycle.
Day 2	Tuesday	End of trade cycle.
Day 3	Thursday	Work out of obligations and its communications to brokers.
Day 4	Friday	Delivery of shares by selling broker to the clearing house.
Day 5	Monday	Payment by buying broker for purchases made.
Day 6	Tuesday	Receipt of amount by the selling broker and receipt of shares by the buying broker.

Thus, it is evident from the illustration that the investor has liberty to trade in any pattern of his choice during a period between Monday and Tuesday. Once the period expires, the obligation of each broker in terms of the shares sold/purchased and the money to be received/ paid is figured out and duly communicated to the broker. The broker is expected to deliver the shares that he has sold on next Thursday and pay the amount due on Tuesday next.

◈ Mechanism for Guaranteed Settlement

At times, either or both the parties of the trading transaction commit default in honouring their respective commitments at the end of the settlement period. Such a situation, known as 'counterparty default' is likely to destabilize the functioning of the stock exchange and threaten the sanctity and integrity of the stock market. So as to avert the occurrence of such a situation, the NSE introduced a system called 'Settlement guaranteed mechanism'. According to this system, settlement of trade is undertaken by a separate statutory agency known as 'Clearing Corporation'. The NSE has set up a separate fully owned subsidiary to undertake this task.

The modus operandi of settlement guarantee mechanism is that the Clearing Corporation acts as a counterparty in respect of every transaction. In that capacity it ensures and verifies that the deliveries of proceeds and shares are made and passes them on to the respective brokers. In case a broker defaults, the clearing corporation ensures that the trade is carried out unhindered by making payment or making delivery of scrips on behalf of the defaulting brokers, who is thereafter dealt with by the corporation. Thus, this mechanism helps both the brokers and thereby their investors who are assured of prompt settlement irrespective of the fulfillment of obligations by the other party. Besides, minimizing market risk, the mechanism saves the sanctity and integrity of the stock market.

However, success of the settlement guarantee mechanism calls for

(*i*) Automated trading and settlement processes

(*ii*) Robust risk management processes

(*iii*) Well articulated settlement schedule

(*iv*) Clearance of all securities through clearing house

(*v*) Multilateral netting (netting across locations)

(*vi*) Funds settlement through clearing house

(*vii*) Well-defined procedures for post-settlement issues

◈ Settlement of Dematerialized Securities

In the traditional method of securities trading involving physical movement of scrips, investors experience several problems such as time-consuming process, involvement of heavy paper work, risks due to transiting through postal system and high percentage of bad deliveries due to the vulnerability of physical certificates to forgery, theft, mutilation, etc. The unprecedented growth in the number of investors and volume of transactions here sent the entire settlement system haywire.

To overcome the above problems, the Government of India enacted the Depositories Act in 1996 to institute **Depository system**. In depository system, the transfer and settlement of scrips take place through the system of effecting transfer of ownership of securities by means of book entry on the ledgers of the depository without the physical movement of scrips. The depository system, thus, eliminates paper work, facilitates automatic and transparent trading in scrips, shortens the settlement period and ultimately contributes to the liquidity of investment in securities. This system is also known as 'Scripless trading system'. Securities traded through depository system are called 'dematerialized securities'.

A depository is a firm wherein the securities of an investor are held in electronic form in the same way a bank holds money. It carries out the transactions of securities by means of book entry without physical movement of securities. The depository based settlement system is called 'book entry transfer settlement'. The depository acts as a defacto owner of the securities lodged with it for the limited purpose of transfer of ownership. It operates as a custodian of securities of its clients. At present, there are two depositories in India, viz.,

(*a*) National Securities Depository Ltd. (NSDL)

(*b*) Central Depository Services India Ltd. (CDSIL)

An investor intending to avail of the depository has to open an account with a depository participant (DP) also known as an agent of the depository.

The procedure for selling dematerialized securities in a stock exchange except one followed in physical securities is outlined below:

(*i*) Investor sells securities in any of the stock exchanges linked to depository through a broker.

(*ii*) Investor instructs his DP to debit his demat account with the number of securities sold and credit the broker's clearing account.

(*iii*) The broker transfers the securities to clearing corporation before the pay-in day.

(*iv*) The broker receives payment from the stock exchange.

(*v*) The investor receives payment from the broker for the sale of securities.

The procedure followed for purchasing dematerialized securities is given below:

(*i*) Investor instructs DP to receive credits into his account in the prescribed form.

(*ii*) The investor purchases securities in any of the stock exchanges linked to depository through a broker.

(*iii*) The broker receives payment from the investor and arranges payment to clearing corporation.

(*iv*) The broker receives credit of securities in clearing account on the pay-out day.

(*v*) The investor receives shares into his account by way of book entry.

G. SECONDARY MARKET INTERMEDIARIES IN INDIA

There are various intermediaries who operate at a stock exchange and are the registered numbers of the exchange. A brief discussion of functions and duties of these intermediaries is set out below:

(i) Jobbers

Jobbers are independent security merchants who buy and sell securities on their own account. They cannot deal on behalf of public and are barred from taking commission. They deal directly with brokers who, in turn, make transactions on behalf of public. Jobber generally quotes two prices, one at which he is prepared to sell a particular security. The difference between the two prices is the Jobber's profit which is known as **Jobber's turn**.

(ii) Brokers

Brokers represent those intermediaries of a stock exchange who bring together buyers and sellers and help them in making a deal. They charge commission from both the parties for their services. Brokers are the experts who forecast trends in prices and advise their clients in making fruitful transactions. They get orders from investors and execute the orders through jobbers.

A broker has to apply to the SEBI for registration as a member of stock exchange. The SEBI on being satisfied with the necessary infrastructure of the applicant will issue the certificate of registration. Once registered, the broker has to follow a specified code of conduct.

A stock broker is supposed to maintain high standards of integrity, promptitude and fairness in the conduct of his business. He has to act with due skill, care and diligence in the conduct of all his business. He shall not involve himself in excessive speculative in the market beyond reasonable level not commensurate with his financial health. He is obliged to abide by all the provisions of the Securities Contract (Regulation) Act and the rules and regulations issued by the Government, the SEBI and the stock exchange from time to time as may be applicable to him.

A stock broker shall faithfully execute the orders received from the clients for buying and selling securities at the best available market price. He shall issue a contract note to his client for the transaction without delay. He should refrain from furnishing false or misleading advice or information to the clients with a view to inducing him do business in particular securities and enabling himself to earn brokerage. While dealing with a client, he shall clearly disclose whether he is acting as a principal or as an agent and shall ensure at the same time that no conflict of interest arises between him and the client.

The SEBI has the power to suspend or cancel registration of and impose penalties on the broker, if he is found to be indulging in manipulation and rigging of prices and violates any of the provisions of the Securities Contracts (Regulation) Act and the regulations.

(iii) Sub-broker

A sub-broker is an agent of a stock-broker who helps the investors in dealing with the stock broker. He is required to apply to the SEBI for registration and submit along with the application a letter of recommendation from a stock broker of a recognized stock exchange, and two references one of which should be from his banker. On being satisfied that the applicant fulfills certain conditions such as that he is not less than 21 years of age, he is not convicted of any offense involving fraud or dishonesty, he has passed 12th standard from a recognized institute, he is a fit and proper person, the SEBI issues a certificate of registration.

A sub-broker is expected to maintain high standard of integrity, promptitude and fairness in the conduct of all his investment business. He shall act with due skill, care and diligence in the conduct of his business.

In his dealings with the clients and the general investing public, a sub-broker shall faithfully execute the orders for buying and selling of securities at the best available market price. He shall issue promptly to his clients purchase or sale notes for all the transactions entered into by him with his clients. He should not disclose or discuss with any other person or make improper use of the details of personal investments and other confidential information pertaining to his client.

A sub-broker is expected to cooperate with his broker in protecting the interests of their clients. He should not fail in carrying out his stock broking transactions with his broker nor shall he fail to meet his business liabilities or show negligence in completing the settlement of transactions with them. He should desist from resorting to unfair means of inducing clients from other stock brokers.

A sub-broker shall comply with the rules, bye-laws and regulations of the stock exchange and shall not indulge in disgraceful or improper conduct on the stock exchange nor shall he willfully obstruct the business of the exchange. He shall not indulge in manipulative, fraudulent or deceptive practices with a view to distorting market equilibrium or making personal gains.

(iv) Tarawaniwalas

Tarawaniwalas represents those members of stock exchange who make transactions on their own behalf like a jobber but they may also act as a broker on behalf of the public. They have been found indulging in malpractices to make earnings. For instance, they may sell their own securities to their clients when prices are higher and vice-versa.

The members of Banking Stock exchange have unofficially divided themselves into two categories, viz., brokers and Tarawaniwalas. The distinction between jobbers of Indian Stock Exchange and London Stock Exchange is that the former cannot act as brokers whereas the latter may act both as brokers and jobbers. Section 15 of the Securities Contract (Regulation) Act prohibits trade practices of tarawaniwalas.

(v) Portfolio Consultants

Portfolio consultants are the persons equipped with skill and high degree of expertise. They advise their clients in portfolio construction, formulation of investment strategy, evaluation and monitoring of portfolio. A person is allowed to act as portfolio consultant only if he possesses a certificate issued by the SEBI. A portfolio consultant is required to deposit a fee of ₹ 5 lakh as registration fee at the time of issue of certificate by the SEBI. After three years, he has to pay a renewal fee of ₹ 2.5 lakhs. Failure to pay fee in time will lead to suspension of certificate.

H. MAJOR STOCK EXCHANGES IN INDIA — A BRIEF REVIEW

BOMBAY STOCK EXCHANGE

◆ Evolution and Objectives

Of the 23 stock exchange in India, Bombay Stock Exchange is the oldest exchange established in 1875. The BSE is also the oldest in Asia. It was the first to be recognized and it is the only one that had the privilege of getting permanent recognition ab-initio. The exchange has built up mechanism to redress grievances of investors as well as members and provides information inputs to the investing public. Until 2002, the BSE was named as the "The Stock Exchange, Mumbai". On August 19, 2005 the Exchange changed into a corporate entity from an Association of persons and was renamed as Bombay Stock Exchange Limited. Business of the BSE is spread over 100 cities of the country. The BSE was established with the primary objective of safeguarding interests of the investors while providing an efficient market mechanism. It also seeks to ensure redressal of the investors' grievances. It strives to educate and enlighten the investors by making available necessary information inputs. It is the first exchange in India and the second in the world to obtain an ISO 9001:2000 certification. It has at present 1,383 broker members.

◈ Management

Until 2001, the BSE was administered by a governing body consisting of 9 elected directors (one-third to retire every year by rotation) an executive director, three government nominees, a RBI nominee and five public nominees. However, as per the SEBI directives in March 2001, the elected directors have been restrained from acting. Accordingly, the governing board now comprises of only 10 directors. The executive director acts as the chief executive officer and is responsible for the day-to-day administration of the exchange.

◈ Trading and Settlement System

As regards trading system, the BSE has adopted a fully automated computerized mode of tracing known as BOLT (BSE — On-Line Trading) system with effect from March 14, 1995. Through the BOLT System, the members can enter orders from Trader Work Stations (TWS) installed in their offices instead of assembling trading ring. The system is at present only order driven. It facilitates more efficient processing, automatic order matching and faster execution of orders in a transparent manner.

All trade done by members in all the securities in Compulsory Rolling System (CRS) are settled by payment of money and delivery of securities on T +2 basis which means that the final settlement of transactions made on a trade day by exchange of money and securities on the fifth business day after the trade day. Under a rolling settlement environment, the trades done on a particular day are settled after given number of business days instead of settling all trades made during a period at the end of according period. All deliveries of securities are required to be routed through the clearing house, except for certain off-market transactions.

◈ Functional Specialisation

The BSE has a well-established functional specialisation as among its members under the following categories:

- *Commission broker:* Almost all members act as commission brokers. They execute on the floor of exchange selling order placed by their constituents to whom they render service on a commission basis.
- *Floor broker:* Floor brokers, officially attached to other members, execute orders for any member and receive as their compensation a share of the brokerage charged by the commission broker to their constituent.
- *Tarawaniwala:* The tarawaniwala may be a jobber or specialist who specializes in stocks located at the same trading post. He trades in and out of the market for a small difference in price and as such is an important factor in 'making a market' (maintaining a continuous and liquid market) in stocks in which he specializes.
- *Dealer in non-cleared securities:* The dealer in non-cleared securities specializes in buying and selling on his own account shares which are not on the active list. He is generally prepared to buy what is on the offer at which he deals varies with the movement of the particular stock.
- *Odd-lot dealer:* The odd-lot dealer specializes in buying and selling in amounts less than the prescribed trading units. He buys odd lots and makes them up into marketable trading units. Likewise, he sells odd lots obtained to buying or by splitting up round lots. He earns his profit on the difference between the prices at which he buys and sells.
- *Arbitraguer:* The arbitraguer specializes in making purchases and sales in different markets at the same time and makes profits by the difference in prices between the two centres.

- *Security dealer:* Security dealer is specialised in buying and selling gilt-edged securities. He acts mainly as a jobber and is prepared to take risks inherent in the ready sale of securities to meet current requirements.

◈ BSE Sensex

The Sensex, short form of the BSE-Sensitive index, is a "Market Capitalization — weighted" index of 30 stocks representing a sample of large, well-established and financially sound companies. It is the oldest index in India and has acquired a unique place in the collective consciousness of investors. The index is widely used to measure the performance of the Indian stock markets.

Sensex was first compiled in 1896. It was calculated on a market capitalization weighted methodology of 30 component stocks, the base year of the sensex was taken at 1978-79.

There are some listing parameters. First, the scrip should have a listing history of atleast three months at the BSE and should have been traded on each and every trading day in the last three months at the BSE. Secondly, the scrip should figure in the top 100 companies listed by final rank. The weightage of each scrip in the sensex based on three month average daily average free-float market capitalization should be atleast 0.5 per cent of the index. The scrip should be a balanced representation of the listed companies in the universe of the BSE and must have a good track record in the opinion of the BSE Index Committee.

◈ Expansion of the BSE

During post liberalization period, the BSE grew exponentially in various dimensions. Thus, number of listed companies has grown from 197 in 1946 to 5000 today. The BSE accounts for over two-thirds of the total trading volume in the country. Average monthly turnover in the BSE surged from ₹ 1,65,567 crore in 2007-08 to ₹ 2,28,348 crore in June 2011.[4] Market capitalization of the companies listed in the BSE shot up from ₹ 5,72,198 crore in 2002-03 to ₹ 67,28,515 crore in June 2011.[5] The BSE has 721 registered stock brokers.

In view of rapidly growing economy and consequent increase in investing community, the BSE needs to really spruce up its operations.

In its strive to expand its business, increase reach and improve services to investors, the BSE tied up with the Deutsche Boarse Group, a strategic investor, to explore cross-listing of indices and other products. The BSE has also roped in the US-based International Securities Exchange to develop and launch derivates.[6] So as to improve its volume of business the BSE has, of late, forged an alliance with regional stock exchanges, viz., Madhya Pradesh Stock Exchange, the Vadodara Stock Exchange and Jaipur Stock Exchange.[7] The BSE has already a tie up with the Kolkata Stock Exchange, in which it has a 5 per cent stake.

NATIONAL STOCK EXCHANGE

◈ Evolution and Objectives

India's premier stock exchange today, National Stock Exchange (NSE), was born only as recently as November 1992. The NSE was sponsored by the IDBI, and co-sponsored by other term lending institutions, LIC, GIC, other insurance companies, commercial banks and other financial institutions. It was created to encourage stock exchange reform through system modernization and competition. Unlike the BSE, the NSE is professionally managed national market for shares, PSU bonds, debentures and government securities endowed with all the requisite infrastructure and trading facilities. It is an electronic screen based system where members have equal opportunity of trade irrespective of their locations in different parts of the country because of their connectivity through a satellite network. NSE was set up with specific objectives of:

(*i*) providing a nation-wide trading facilities for equities, debt instruments, etc.;

(*ii*) ensuring equal access to investors all over me country through an appropriate communication network;

(*iii*) providing fair, efficient and transparent securities market to investors using electronic trading systems;

(*iv*) enabling shorter settlement cycles and book entry settlement systems; and

(*v*) attaining current international standards of securities market.

The NSE has at present 1500 broker-members.

The NSE's strengths are technology, people and its processes. It always keeps the customer at its centre. In 5 years, since inception it changed the market from being entirely paper-based to entirely paperless. On any given day, the NSE completes 10 million trades and processes over 400 million messages.

◈ Management

In the NSE, being demutualized stock exchange, the ownership and management of the exchange is completely divorced from the right to trade on it. The NSE is managed by a Board comprising senior executives from promoter institutions, current professionals in the fields of law, economics, accountancy, finance, taxation, etc., public representative, three nominees of SEBI including a senior official of SEBI and one full time executive of the Exchange.

While the Board is concerned with broad policy issues, decisions pertaining to market operations are taken by an Executive Committee formed under the Articles of Association and Rules. The Executive Committee comprises representatives from trading members, the public and the management. The day-to-day management of the Exchange is delegated to the Managing Director who is supported by a team of professional staff.

◈ Trading and Settlement Mechanism

With a view to encouraging an institutional market where large volume of trades come up for settlement in Jumbo lots, two exclusive additional market segments — the institutional lot segment and trade — for trade segment — have been set up. The NSE has an order driven system, which permits members to undertake jobbing in securities of their choice. Several members undertake jobbing on account of the cease of entry and exit, and narrow margins which results in improved liquidity and reduced transaction costs.

The settlement cycle is completed within eight days from the last day of the trading cycle. The trading period is a week (Wednesday to Tuesday) and the settlement of trades takes place in the ensuing week.

◈ Segments of NSE

The NSE has two separate segments — Capital Market segment and the wholesale Debt Market segment. The former deals in equities, convertible debentures, derivatives, etc., the latter caters to banks, financial institutions and other institutions participants which deal in PSU bonds, Treasury bills, government securities, call money, CPs, CDs, etc.

◈ NSE Group

NSE group is composed of the following:

(*i*) India Index Services and Products Ltd. (IISL)

(*ii*) National Securities Clearing Corporation Ltd. (NSCCL)

(*iii*) NSEIT Ltd.

(*iv*) National Securities Depository Ltd. (NSDL)

(*v*) DOTEX International Limited

◈ NSE Indices

- S & P CNX Nifty
- CNX Nifty Junior

- S & P CNX500
- S & P CNX Nefty
- CNX Midcap 200
- Other IISL Indices
- CNXIT FMCG Index
- CNX Millennium Index
- CNX Segment Indices
- S&P CNX Industry Indices
- Customized Indices

◈ Derivatives

The NSE deals with the following derivatives:

- S & P CNX Nifty Futures
- S & P CNX Nifty Options
- Futures on Individual Securities
- Options on Individual Securities

◈ Expansion of the NSE

During short-period of time, the NSE expanded its business and became the largest exchange in India in terms of volume of stocks transacted. In 2007-08 its monthly turnover was ₹ 1,68,567 crore which shot up to ₹ 2,22,457 crore in June, 2011. What is most unique about the NSE is that derivative trading represents about four-fifths of the total trading. In terms of market capitalization, the NSE grew from ₹ 36,50,368 crore in April 2008 to ₹ 65,74,743 crore in July 2011.[8] It has 900 registered brokers, higher than the BSE. The NSE records an average daily turnover of about ₹ 1.5 trillion in equities, equity Euros and currency trading.

The NSE has recently embarked on consolidation and expansion so as to increase its volume of business and improve services. It has a license to list Dow Jones Industrial Average and S&P 500 through its alliance with the Chicago Mercantile Exchange. The NSE has also forged deal with the London Stock Exchange for working out a joint business strategy. This will lead the NSE's equity benchmark index, S&P CNX Nifty to become a globally traded contract. Also, the NSE will be able to offer a basket of top traded global indices once the NSE 100 Index is listed on its flow floor in India.

The NSE is now on the verge of establishing an exchange for the small and medium enterprises (SMEs) of India, to create broad asset classes and to deepen the financial markets so that households have access to a variety of savings and investment opportunities.

The main contribution of the NSE to Indian financial markets has been to incorporate forward-looking technology in the trading process and enabling equal and fair access to all investors through its electronic on-line trading platform. It played a pivotal role in implementing critical market reforms and establishing industry benchmarks in the adoption of best practices.

OVER-THE-COUNTER EXCHANGE OF INDIA (OTCEI)

◈ Genesis and Objectives

The idea underlying establishment of OTCEI was to overcome the problems beings faced by new and small companies in accessing funds from the market. Small investors all over the country were finding it difficult to get themselves listed in the existing exchanges because of their listing requirements and thus faced with the problems of access, liquidity, delays in payment and delivery, and uncertainty with respect to prices at which their shares were bought and sold. Thus, the country was bereft of a stock market option for small and medium companies who could raise capital through a public issue at reasonable cost and with least delays in realization of proceeds. The OTCEI was established to address the problems of relatively smaller companies. It was promoted by the UTI, ICICI, IDBI, IFCI, LIC, GIC, SBI Caps and Canbank as company under Section 25 of the Companies Act, 1956 in 1992.

The primary objectives of the OTCEI are:

- To enable small companies to raise capital from the market at cheapest costs and on optimal terms.
- To provide a convenient and an efficient avenue capital market investments for small investors.
- To inspire investor's confidence in the financial market by offering them the two-way best prices to the investors.
- To ensure transparency, redress investors' complaints and unify the country's securities market to cover even those places which do not have a stock exchange.
- To provide liquidity advantage to the securities trades.
- To promote organized trading in unlisting securities.
- To broad base the existing informal market in order to make it more liquid.
- To provide a source of valuation for securities traded.
- To act as a launch pad to an IPO.

◈ Immanent Features

The OTCEI is distinct from other stock exchanges because:

(*i*) It is a ringless and electronic national exchange without a specified trading floor.

(*ii*) It caters to the needs of the small business which have so far not met the requirements for listing on the stock exchange.

(*iii*) It has a nationwide reach. The market is spread across the country through numerous countries of the operators exchange.

(*iv*) Small and medium sized companies having a paid up capital between ₹ 30 lakhs and ₹ 25 crore can be enlisted.

(*v*) OTCEI deals in equity shares, preferences shares, bonds, debentures and warrants.

(*vi*) Trading is by way of negotiated bidding.

(*vii*) The trading in OTCEI is screen based. Transactions take place through satellite communication telephone lines.

(*viii*) A company, which is listed on any other recognized stock exchange in India, will not be eligible for listing on the OTCEI.

(*ix*) At the OTCEI, listing is granted only if the issue is fully subscribed to by the public and sponsor.

◈ Trading in OTCEI

Following the recommendations of the Dave Committee, the OTCEI has been permitted to trade in equity shares of all unlisted companies. Such trading provides an opportunity to make the stocks liquid and tradable. It also provides a source of valuation of mutual funds, facilitates inter-institutional trades and enables placement of these shares with FIIs. Derivative instruments like futures and options, forward contracts on stocks, other forms of forward transactions and stock lending can also be traded on the OTCEI.

◈ Trading Services

An investor can buy and sell any listed scrip at any of the OTC exchange counter. He can also make an application for services like transfer of shares, splitting and consolidation of shares, nomination and revocation of nomination, registering power of attorney, transmission of shares and change of holder's name, etc.

Trading Mechanism

Unlike other stock exchanges, the OTCEI is a ringless security exchange equipped with computers and electronic equipments instead of a trading hall of conventional stock exchanges. The dealings are carried on through counters scattered all over the country and linked with communication network. For the purpose of trading, the investors can choose the price quoted by the market-makers scattered all over the country. Every counter at OTCEI displays these quoted prices continuously on every working day. Once the decision is taken about the price and the market-maker, the investor may proceed ahead for the purchasing sale of scrips.

The mechanism of trading followed at OTCEI is different for listed securities and permitted securities (securities listed on other stock exchanges and permitted for trading on OTCEI).

Trading in listed securities begins three days after listing and after due notice to the public and OTCEI counters, *i.e.*, members and dealers. Trading commences with compulsory market-maker, offering quotes for the minimum depth depending on the issue price of the security. In case the issue price is ₹ 50, the market-makers have to give quotes for atleast 10 market lots. In other case, the minimum depth is five market lots.

Settlement Mechanism

A separate system of settlement is adopted for the listed securities and permitted securities. The OTCEI does not permit short selling or forward buying in listed securities. All deals get completed after the CRs, SCs and AASs are confirmed, matched and issued.

In case of the permitted securities, settlement mechanism has a five-day trading cycle. Short-selling and squaring up by the counters is to be completed within the trading cycle. Delivery and payment is on net basis, not on trade basis. A transaction of any value generates a single conformation slip. Certificates must be delivered to the investors within a fortnight from the date of purchase of the security.

Significance of the OTCEI

The OTCEI has been very useful particularly to small companies. It helps companies in raising funds from the capital market in a cost-effective manner and provides a convenient and effective avenue of capital market investment for investors at large. While the other recognized stock exchanges require that in order to have its securities listed the company should have an issued capital of not less than ₹ 3 crore out of which normally 25% is to be offered to the public, the minimum issued equity share capital of a company for eligibility for listed on the OTCEI is ₹ 30 lakh. Further, listing on the OTCEI is advantageous to companies because of the high liquidity of these securities, which is the result of compulsory market making, improved access and speed of transactions resulting from the extensive network of electronically interlinked counters arial. Companies can obtain a fair price of their securities by negotiating the same with the sponsors (who are members of the OTCEI) and save unnecessary issue expenses by placing their securities to the public. This mechanism is now popularly known as a bought out deal. Above all, OTCEI's wide computerized network is spread all over India and will make investment easier. All deals are entered into through remote terminals which are concerned to the main frame computer of the OTCEI. The exchange enables transactions to be completed quickly and investors can settle the deals across the counter within a few days. The exchange also provides liquidity to investments as every scrip listed on the OTCEI will have atleast two makers who will continuously give two day quotes. With the national network of operations, the presence of the OTCEI was expected to add dynamism to the functioning of the capital market in India.

Despite being pioneer in technology based trading system and advantageous to small companies, the OTCEI has been languishing since its inception. Even the reforms of the OTCEI in terms of Dave Committee recommendations failed to nudge it. This seems to be due to lack of speculative element and capital appreciation. Besides, the method of listing and trading involving market marking did not attract many brokers and sub-brokers into this market. Lack of commitment on the part of the sponsors and poor settlement system also hindered the growth of the market.

INTERCONNECTED STOCK EXCHANGE OF INDIA LTD. (ISEI)

Interconnected Stock Exchange of India Ltd. was promoted in 2000 by 14 Regional Stock Exchanges to provide cost-effective trading linkage to all the members of the participating exchanges with the objective of widening the market for the securities listed on these exchanges. The ISEI is a national level stock of exchange and provides trading, clearing, settlement:, risk management and surveillance support to its traders and dealers. It seeks to address the needs of small companies and retail investors with the guiding principle of optimizing the existing infrastructure and harnessing the potential of regional markets so as to transform these into a liquid and vibrant through the use of the state-of-the-art technology and networking.

The participating exchanges of the ISEI have in all about 4500 stockbrokers, out of which more than 200 have been currently registered as traders on the ISEI. In order to leverage its infrastructure and to expand its nation-wide reach, the ISEI has also appointed over 4500 dealers across 70 cities in addition to the participating exchange centres. The dealers are administratively supported through the regional offices of the ISEI at Delhi (North), Kolkata (East), Coimbatore (South) and Nagpur (Central), besides Mumbai (West).

The ISEI has also floated a wholly-owned subsidiary, *viz.*, ISEI Securities and Services Limited (ISS), which has taken up corporate membership of the NSE in both the Capital Market and Futures & Options segments and the BSE in the Equities segments so that the traders and dealers of the ISEI can access other markets in addition to the ISEI market and their local market. Thus, the ISEI provides the investors in smaller cities on-stop solution for cost-effective and efficient trading and settlement in securities.

The ISEI has, of late, started offering the full suite of the DP facilities to its traders, dealers and their clients with a view to broad basing the range of its services.

CALCUTTA STOCK EXCHANGE

◈ Evolution and Objectives

Calcutta Stock Exchange was formed in May 1908 as an association which was subsequently registered on June 7, 1923 as a limited liability company with an authorized capital of ₹ 3 lakh. In April 1980, the CSE was granted permanent recognition by the Government. In the year 1997, the CSE ushered in a new era by replacing the old manual trading system with completely computerized on-line trading and reporting system with 101 'B' Group scrips. Subsequently with effect from 07-03-1997, remaining 'B' Group and all 'Permitted Group Scrips' were transferred on to the C-Star Systems. The CSE finally shifted the entire 'A' group scrips to the computerized with effect from April 4, 1997.

The CSE was established to protect the interests of investors through provisions of meaningful services including timely supply of necessary information inputs to them and redressal of grievances against the brokers.

◈ Management

The CSE is managed by a governing body comprising a President, and Vice-President who are elected from me members of the CSE. From among the 8 elected members, 3 are Government nominees (appointed by SEBI) and 6 are public representatives. The Executive Director appointed by the Exchange with SEBI's approval, is charged with the responsibility of carrying out day-to-day executive functions. The governing body is responsible for policy formulation and for ensuring smooth functioning of the exchange.

◈ Trading and Settlement Mechanism

The CSE has an auction type of trading with bids and offers being made by open outcry. There is no compulsory market-making at the CSE. However, it has an informal system of jobbers. Communication in me trading ring is either verbal or through and signals. The traders with the ring can communicate with their offices on intercoms provided by the CSE within the trading ring. The jobbers standing at specific locations in the trading ring regularly announce the two-way quotes for me scrips traded at me post. The members are free to do jobbing on any day since there is no prohibition on a jobber acting as a broker and the vice-versa. However, an identifiable group emerges which confines its activities to jobbing alone.

On stroking a deal, traders enter abbreviated details in small "Soudo books". At the end of the trading all deal details are transferred to a Soudo sheet and is handed over to the CSE computer division.

◈ Expansion of CSE

At the time of establishment, the CSE had 150 members which tended to increase to 959 at present, consisting of several corporate and institutional members. In terms of membership the CSE has outpaced the NSE (900), OTCEI (895) and BSE (721) to distant second, third and fourth positions. In terms of active brokers, the NSE ranks number one, while the BSE and CSE score second and third positions. The CSE had 1962 companies listed having market capitalization of ₹ 77, 131 crore in 2002-03.

◈ MCX Stock Exchange Limited (MCX-SX)

MCX-SX, India's New Stock Exchange, commenced operations in the Currency Futures Segment on October 2008 and currently provides trading facility in currency futures and options. The Exchange currently has 750 members participating from 714 towns and cities across India.[9]

MCX-SX received permission from the SEBI on July 10, 2012 to trade in equity, futures and options on equity, interest rate derivatives and debt segment.

Taking cognizance of existing weaknesses in Indian equity markets: lack of products and shallow market depth, MCX-SX focuses on innovation around products. The Exchange introduced first differentiated product in currency option contracts on August 21, 2012 in order to induce efficiencies in currency risk management.

MCX-SX is committed to introduce better services in every sphere of its operations.

The Exchange has offered membership on September 4, 2012. A person can apply for any membership category and be a Trading Member (TM)/Self Clearing Member (SCM)/Trading-cum-Clearing Member (TCM)/Professional Clearing Member (PCM). MCX-SX has embarked on aggressive membership drive by offering lower membership fee of ₹ 25 lakh, which is nearly 80 per cent less than what the NSE charges (₹ 1.5 crore), to become a trading member of the exchange. It has also announced a lower deposit structure and net worth requirement for its members than the NSE and also doled out discount schemes for those from the rural areas and professionals.[10]

The MCX Stock Exchange intends to take on the country's two most popularly traded equity indices, the sensex-30 and the Nifty-50, with its benchmark SX-40. It seeks to select top stocks from the BSE and the NSE to create the SX-40. The stock will be traded on MCX-SX.

The MCX-SX's strategy is to position itself as a premium bourse, by keeping its pricing structure lower than the NSE and higher than the BSE. It has followed the same strategy with its index, by having 40 shares in it.

The new exchange has collaborated with Indian Statistical Institute for its indices. It also has an international partnership with FTSE and its other Indian partner, Financial Technologies Knowledge Management Company, for developing benchmark domestic and global indices.

MCX-SX follows delivery-based settlement system in equities. Under the system a seller of stock futures or options will have to deliver shares to the counter-party when the contract expires. This pattern is followed by all leading derivative exchanges around the world and also the BSE, but the latter has not been able to capitalise on it due to lack of marketing strategy.[11]

The setting up of the MCX-SX has infused competitiveness in Indian stock market leading to the price war between stock exchanges. To counter the aggressive membership drive of MCX-SX, the NSE has cut its deposit and networth criteria by upto 50 per cent under the new 'Alpha Category.'

I. CONCLUSIONS

Secondary market is a market for trading of previously issued securities. It provides for a regular market of securities, stability in prices of securities and provides safety and liquidity in dealings. Besides, secondary market helps in wider distribution of the securities. As such, it plays significant role in fostering capital formation and economic development of a country.

In the secondary market, only such activities can be traded in a stock exchange as are listed in the exchange.

In any stock market trading in securities can be done only through stock brokers. An investor intending to buy or sell securities has to enter into agreement with a broker and places the order for the purchase or sale of securities which is subsequently confirmed by the broker.

In a stock market, spot dealings are settled in the market itself in the NSE, settlement of trade takes a certain cycle. There are two kinds of settlement in vogue, viz., Rolling Settlement and Account Period settle. So as to ensure that both the parties of me trading transaction honour the commitment and functioning of me stock market is not destabilized, the NSE has introduced a system what is known as 'Settlement guarantee mechanism'.

In view of several problems experienced by investors, the Government of India enacted the Depository Act in 1996 to introduce Depository system wherein settlement of scrips takes place through the system of affecting transfer of ownership of securities by means of book entry on the ledgers of the depository without the physical movement of scrips.

There are various intermediaries who operate at a stock market, they are the registered members of the exchange. Main functionaries in Indian stock markets are Jobbers, brokers, sub-brokers, tarawaniwalas and portfolio consultants.

Among 23 Indian stock exchanges in India, the BSE is the oldest exchange in the country as also in Asia. The BSE has a well established functional specialisation as among its members, the NSE in India is premier stock exchange. It has two segments, *viz.*, capital market segment and the wholesale debt market segment. Besides, we have a ringless and electronic national exchange in OTCEI having no specified trading floor. Another stock exchange, viz., ISEI was promoted in 2000 by 14 Regional Stock Exchanges to provide cost-effective trading linkage to the members of the participating exchanges. Both the BSE and NSE are forging alliances with overseas stock exchanges in their strive to expand their business and improve quality of services.

The CSE — the largest stock exchange in India in terms of membership — was formed in 1908 to protect the interests of investors through timely supply of necessary information inputs and redressal of grievances against the brokers. The CSE has an auction type of trading with bids and offers being made by open outcry.

KEY TERMS

- Account Period Settlement
- Bolt
- Broker
- Counterparty default
- Contract note
- Delivery-based Settlement System
- Dematerialized securities
- Depository
- Depository system
- Jobber
- Jobber's turn
- Organized exchange market
- Over-the counter market
- Portfolio consultants
- Scripless trading
- Settlement guaranteed mechanism
- Tarawaniwalas

DISCUSSION QUESTIONS

1. Discuss, in brief, redeeming features of secondary market.
2. Enumerate the various services rendered by the secondary market.
3. Bring out the role of the secondary market in a country's economic development.
4. Describe briefly the procedure for securities trading in an Indian stock market.
5. Discuss the mechanism of trade settlement of dematerialized securities.
6. What is depository system? Discuss the procedure for selling dematerialized securities in a stock exchange.
7. Outline the functions and duties of Jobbers, brokers and sub-brokers.
8. Briefly outline functional specialisation of the Bombay Stock Exchange.
9. Discuss trading and settlement mechanism of the NSE.
10. Briefly outline objectives and trading and settlement mechanism of the Calcutta Stock Exchange.
11. Write a brief note on newly set up stock exchange in India.

REFERENCES

1. Meir Kolm, Financial Institutions and Markets, Tata McGraw-Hill, New Delhi, 2004, p. 589.
2. H.D. Herman, The Stock Exchange, Sir Isacc Pitman & Sons Ltd., London, IV ed., p. 2.
3. *Ibid.*
4. RBI Annual Report for relevant years.
5. *Ibid.*
6. RBI Annual Report, *op. cit.*
7. Business Standard, April 6, 2010.
8. *Ibid.*
9. Business Today, August 5, 2012.
10. Business Standard, September 6, 2012.
11. Business Standard, October 19, 2012.

Merchant Banking in India

Learning Objectives:

The present chapter aims at:

- Presenting a conceptual view of merchant banking.
- Providing an inclusive view of services rendered by merchant bankers and their role in Indian economy.
- Providing vivid view of history and growth of merchant banking.
- Describing, in brief, regulatory framework of merchant banking in India.

Chapter Outline:

- Conceptual exposition.
- Services of merchant bankers.
- History and growth of merchant banking.
- Role of merchant banking in Indian economy.
- Conclusions.

A. CONCEPTUAL EXPOSITION

The term 'merchant banking' eludes any precise definition because it is widely and loosely used, being sometimes applied to banks which are not merchants and sometimes to merchants who are not banks, and sometimes to houses that are neither merchants nor banks. Furthermore, the term merchant banking has been used differently in different parts of the world. While in the UK, a merchant banking refers to the 'accepting and issuing houses' which provide a variety of services such as issue management, portfolio management, underwriting of issues, rendering advice on project development, on mergers and amalgamation, Eurocredits, etc. In the USA, it is known as 'Investment banking' which is concerned with garnering savings and channelling them into profitable outlets. Investment bankers act as the intermediaries to provide specialised service in securities for long-term. They simply buy the securities in bulk with a view to selling them to investors at large. They also provide other services involved in marketing of securities.

However, a merchant bank may be regarded as an institution which embraces a wide range of activities such as project counselling, pre-investment activities, feasibility studies, project reports, foreign currency finance, portfolio management, credit syndication, acceptance credit and other services.

According to the Securities and Exchange Board of India (Merchant Bankers) Rules, 1992, "A merchant banker is any person who is engaged in the business of issue management either by making arrangements regarding selling, buying or subscribing to securities or acting as manager, consultant, adviser or rendering corporate advisory services in relation to such issue management".

Merchant banking is a skill based activity and involves serving financial needs of every client. Merchant bankers can turn to any of the activities depending upon resources, such as capital, foreign tie-ups for overseas activities and skills.

A merchant bank differs from a commercial bank. While a commercial bank is primarily concerned with accepting public deposits for lending purpose, providing working capital finance, allowing its customers to withdraw of money by cheques, providing cash credit, overdraft, bill discounting facilities, issuing credit cards and providing facilities relating to transfer of funds, a merchant bank renders a number of services incidental to the promotion and development of projects such as corporate counselling, project consultancy, corporate restructuring, issue management, loan syndication, portfolio management, leasing services, providing assistance for technical and financial collaborations, etc.

B. SERVICES OF MERCHANT BANKERS

Traditionally, merchant banks have been concerned with the acceptance of credit for the financing of international trade and raising of loans for overseas borrowers by new capital issues. However, in recent years they have extended their business to cover a wide variety of services. At present, merchant banks across the globe are engaged in providing the following services.

◈ Project Counselling

As a project counsellor, a merchant banker carries out project feasibility study, prepares project report in consultation with technical, financial and marketing experts, decides upon the financing pattern to fund the cost of the project, appraise the project report with banks and financial institutions, fills up of application forms for obtaining funds from financial institutions and securing government approval.

◈ Issue Management

Another major service that is provided by a merchant banker is the issue management. This service comprises preparation of prospectus, registration of prospectus, obtaining approval for the issue from the SEBI, arranging underwriting for the proposed issue, preparing other documents for the stock exchange, selection of the registrar to the issue, printing press, advertising agencies, brokers and bankers to the issue, organizes a meeting with company representatives and advertising agencies to finalize arrangement relating to date of opening and closing of issue, launching publicity campaign and fixing date of board meeting to approve and sign prospectus and pass the necessary resolutions. Pricing of issues is done by the companies in consultation with the merchant bankers.

In the case of management of debentures, apart from the above, the merchant banker has to finalize the terms of the issue that will make the debenture issue attractive and assist in the finalization of the relative security or mortgage documents and obtaining approval thereof from the company's solicitors and trustees.

◈ Credit Syndication

Merchant banks undertake the preparation of the project profile, loan applications for financial assistance on behalf of promoters from various financial institutions for term loans, working capital finance for new projects, etc. They also arrange finance for projects from foreign countries.

◈ Servicing of issues

Many merchant bankers act as paying agents for servicing the long-term loans taken in the past, for keeping a register of shareholders and debenture-holders for companies, acting as paying agents for their dividends and debenture issues, arranging investment of funds and for the safe custody of securities on account of clients in the country and abroad.

◈ Investment Management

Merchant bank render expert advice on matters pertaining to investment decisions; for example, they assess the effects of taxation and inflation on gilt-edged and other securities. They also tender advice on investment in government securities, trusts, charitable institutions and companies. They buy and sell securities on behalf of their client companies.

◈ Placement and distribution

Merchant bankers help their client companies in distributing different securities like equity shares, debt instalments, mutual fund products, insurance products, commercial paper, etc. The distribution network of a merchant banker can be classified as institutional and retail in character. The institutional network comprises mutual funds, FIIs, private equity funds, pension funds, financial institutions, etc. The size of such a network signifies the wholesale reach of the merchant banker. The retail network is exclusively dependent on networking with investors.

◈ Services to non-resident investors

Merchant bankers do provide services to non-resident investors in terms of identification of investment opportunities, choice of securities, investment management and operational services like purchase and sale of securities.

◈ Off-shore financing

The merchant bankers help their clients in the following areas involving foreign currency:

(*i*) Long-term foreign currency loans.

(*ii*) Joint ventures abroad.

(*iii*) Financing exports and imports.

(*iv*) Foreign collaboration arrangements.

◈ Arranging fixed deposits

Merchant banks act as brokers for their clients to help them in raising finance by way of fixed deposits. For this purpose they render the following services:

- Guiding the client company in determining the amount that could be raised by it in the form of deposits from the public.
- Drafting advertisement for inviting deposits.
- Filing a copy of advertisement with the Registrar of Companies for registration.
- Arranging for the issue of advertisement in newspapers, as required by the Companies Act.
- Drafting and printing of application forms.
- Making arrangement for the collection of deposits at the banks' branches.
- Submission of periodical statements to companies concerned.
- Tendering advice to the company on the terms and conditions of fixed deposits, and deciding on the appropriate rate of interest, keeping in view the prevailing capital and money market conditions.
- Helping the company to observe all the rules and regulations in this regard.
- Assisting in maintenance of records and registers for the purpose, as per Section 58(A) of the Companies Act, 1956 and the rules thereunder.

◈ Other specialized services

Besides the above basic activities, a large number of merchant banks also render highly specialized services including corporate counselling. Some of them also assist their clients in cost audit and recruitment of executives.

As a corporate counsellor, merchant banks tender advice to corporate enterprise in almost all the matters pertaining to their business, *viz.*, choice of business and form of organization, product line, diversification of business, incorporation of firm, issue management, credit syndication, capital structuring, corporate restructuring, overseas operations, foreign collaborations, leasing, venture capital etc.

Thus, merchant bankers provide variegated services to the benefit of business enterprises. Effectiveness of a merchant banker in rendering these services depends essentially on his expertise and experience. A successful merchant banker should have wide network with potential investors. He should have high degree of probity to command confidence of the public at large.

C. HISTORY AND GROWTH OF MERCHANT BANKING

The history of merchant bank can be dated back to the late 17th and early 18th centuries when it first started in Italy and France. This was started by the Italian grain merchants. It comprised of merchant bankers who intermediated or assisted in financing the transactions of other traders and their own trade too. With the passage of time, the merchant banking in the modern era started from London where the merchants started to finance the foreign trade through acceptance of bills. Later they extended their services to the governments of underdeveloped countries to raise the long-term funds through the floatation of bonds in the London money market. Over the period, they extended their services to loan syndication, underwriting the issues, portfolio management, etc. The post war period witnessed huge increase in the merchant banking activities.

Merchant banking activity was officially commenced in the Indian capital market when the RBI granted license to Grindlays Bank in 1967 to do merchant banking activity. Grindlays started its operations with management of capital issues, recognized the requirements of upcoming class of entrepreneurs for diverse financial services ranging from production planning and system design to market research. Apart from this, it also provides management consultancy services to meet the requirements of small and medium sector.

It was followed by Citibank in 1970 and the SBI in 1970. Later, the ICICI set up its merchant banking division followed by a few other banks like the Syndicate Bank, Canara Bank, Bank of India, Bank of Baroda, Punjab National Bank, Central Bank of India, and UCO Bank.

The merchant banking business got more importance in the year 1983 when there was a tremendous boom in the primary market where companies were floating huge amount of new issues. To squeeze this opportunity, merchant banking activities were organized and undertaken in several forms. Commercial banks and foreign development finance institutions organized their merchant banking business through formation of divisions. Nationalized banks formed subsidiaries. Sharebrokers and consultants constituted themselves into public limited companies. Some merchant banking companies entered into collaboration with merchant bankers of foreign countries abroad with several branches.

As of now there are 135 merchant bankers who are registered with the SEBI. It includes public sector, private sector and foreign players. Prominent among them are:

◈ Public Sector Merchant Bankers

- SBI Capital Markets Ltd.
- Punjab National Bank
- Bank of Maharashtra
- IFCI Financial Services Ltd.
- State Bank of Bikaner & Jaipur

◈ Private sector Merchant Bankers

- ICICI Securities Ltd.
- Axis Bank Ltd.
- Bajaj Capital Ltd.
- Tata Capital Markets Ltd.
- ICICI Bank Ltd.
- Reliance Securities Ltd.
- Kotak Mahindra Capital Company Ltd.
- Yes Bank Ltd.

◈ Foreign Players in Merchant Banking

- Goldman Sach (India) Securities Ltd.
- Morgan Stanley India Company Pvt. Ltd.
- Barclays Securities (India) Pvt. Ltd.
- Bank of America, N.A.
- Deutsche Bank
- Deutsche Equities India Pvt. Ltd.
- Barclays Bank Plc
- Citigroup Global Markets India Pvt. Ltd.
- DSP Merrill Lynch Ltd.
- FEDEX Securities Ltd.

D. ROLE OF MERCHANT BANKING IN INDIAN ECONOMY

The above discussion reveals that merchant bankers play crucial role in fostering growth in an economy. As a promoter, they translate the project ideas into productive and profitable ventures. Once the enterprise starts functioning, they provide myriad of services to the entrepreneur in its successful functioning. They guide entrepreneurs not only in choosing suitable pattern of financing the project but also help them in procuring the required funds at reasonable cost both from domestic and foreign markets. They also help the entrepreneurs in entering overseas markets, forging alliances with domestic and foreign plays for expanding and diversifying the business. At times, entrepreneurs intending to recapitalize and restructure their firms resort to expert guidance of merchant bankers.

In view of the above, merchant bankers have gained prominent place in financial markets across the world. The role of merchant bankers is becoming more pronounced in emerging economies like India. Despite rapid progress made in almost all sectors of the economy during the post reform period and India — emerging as the second fastest growing economy in the world, the growth has not been balanced in as much as it is influenced by services and manufacturing sectors that have mainly contributed to growth. Agriculture is still lagging behind. Even the growth rate has not been sustainable as is evidenced from the declining performance of the manufacturing sector in recent years.

Further, the growth has not been equitable and size of population below poverty line has not declined significantly during the post liberalization period. Geographically too, the country has lacked balanced growth. This is why the Government of India pursued inclusive growth approach in eleventh plan to ensure rapid and balanced development on sustainable basis and reduce the degree of inequality and poverty and decided to continue the same during the twelfth five year plan. This requires huge investment especially in agriculture, manufacturing and infrastructure sectors. Infrastructure sector alone is expected to require $1000 billion during the next five years. The 12th Five-year Plan (2012-17) envisages investments worth $1000 billion 50 per cent of which would come from the private sector. So, about $100 billion would be required in the private sector in both equity and debt, every year from April 2012 onwards.[1] Arranging such a burgeoning amount of funds for infrastructure and other sectors needs services of merchant bankers. The growing emphasis on development of fertilizers, petrochemicals and electronic industries, which are highly specialized and complex in character, requires specialized services which merchant banker can afford to provide. With changing emphasis in the lending policies of banks and other financial institutions from security orientation to project orientation, corporate enterprises would require the expert services of merchant bankers for project appraisal, financial management etc.

Growing role of agro-based and small scale industries in Indian economy portends great demand of merchant bankers for project counselling, issue management, loan syndication, etc.

In the wake of globalization of financial markets of India and consequent inflow of FIIs in Indian stock markets, increased complexity in investment activities and volatility of the markets, corporate demand of expertise of merchant bankers has increased tremendously. These merchant bankers' services are required to help the entrepreneurs in project and issue management and managing resources from overseas markets. Further, companies aspiring to enter off-shore markets to expand their operations need expert advice of merchant bankers in locating the market, choosing product line, selecting suitable partner and taking all statutory and other steps to set up the enterprise in the foreign country.

Thus, the role of merchant bankers in India is very likely to surge significantly in years to come in view of robust economic growth, increasing globalization of the economy and greater internationalization of domestic business as well as increasing FIIs.

E. REGULATION OF MERCHANT BANKING

Merchant banking business in India is regulated by SEBI (Merchant Bankers') Regulation Act, 1992. According to the Act, any person or body proposing to engage in the business of merchant banking would need authorization by the SEBI in the prescribed format. Thus, no organization can act as a merchant banker without obtaining a certificate of registration from the SEBI.

(a) Categories of Registration

The categories for which registration is required are:

Category I : To carry on the activity of issue management and to act as adviser, consultant, manager, underwriter, portfolio manager.

Category II : To act as adviser, consultant, co-manager, underwriter, portfolio manager.

Category III : To act as underwriter, adviser or consultant to an issue.

Category IV : To act only as adviser or consultant to an issue.

(b) Capital Adequacy Requirements

The SEBI has prescribed the following capital adequacy requirements for different categories of merchant bankers:

Category I : ₹ 5 crore

Category II : ₹ 50 lakh

Category III : ₹ 20 lakh

Category IV : Nil

(c) Procedure for Getting Registration

An application should be moved to the SEBI in Form A of the SEBI (Merchant Bankers) Regulations, 1992. The SEBI shall consider the application and on being satisfied issue a certificate of registration in Form B of the Act. Within 15 days of the receipt of the intimation from the Board, the merchant banker shall pay a sum of ₹ 5 lakh as registration fees. Further, to keep registration in force he shall pay renewal fee of ₹ 2.5 lakh every three years from the fourth year from the date of initial registration.

(d) Code of Conduct

While issuing certificate of registration, the SEBI issues code of conduct which has to be observed by the merchant banker. Important contents of the code are listed below:

- A merchant banker shall make all efforts to protect the interests of investors.
- A merchant banker shall maintain high standards of integrity, dignity and fairness in the conduct of his/her business.
- A merchant banker shall fulfill its obligations in a prompt, ethical and professional manner.
- A merchant banker shall at all times exercise due diligence, ensure proper care and exercise professional judgement.
- A merchant banker shall endeavour to ensure that inquiries from investors are adequately dealt with, and grievances of investors are redressed in a timely and appropriate manner.
- A merchant banker shall ensure that adequate disclosures are made to the investors in time in accordance with the applicable regulations and guidelines so as to enable them to make informed decisions.

- A merchant banker shall refrain from making any statement or becoming privy to any act, practice or unfair competition, which is likely to be harmful to the interests of other merchant bankers.
- A merchant banker shall not indulge in making any exaggerated statement to the client, either about the qualification or the capability to render certain services or achievements in regard to services rendered to other clients.
- A merchant banker shall not divulge to other clients, press or any other party, any confidential information about the client and deal in the securities of any client without disclosing to the SEBI.
- A merchant banker shall endeavour to ensure that copies of the prospectus, offer document, letter of offer or any other related literature are made available to the investors at the time of issue of the offer.
- A merchant banker shall always endeavour to render the possible advice to the clients having regard to their needs.
- A merchant banker shall put in place a mechanism to resolve any conflict of interest situation that may arise in the conduct of his business or where any conflict of interest situation takes place, shall take reasonable measures to resolve the same in an equitable way.
- A merchant banker shall abide by the provisions of the Act, rules and regulations which may be applicable and relevant to the activities carried out by the merchant bankers.
- A merchant banker shall have internal control procedures and financial and operational capabilities which can reasonably be expected to protect its operations, its clients and other registered entities from financial loss.
- A merchant banker shall ensure that good corporate policies and corporate governance are in place.

It is noteworthy that while the SEBI's code of conduct requires a merchant banker to conduct due diligence of a company while bringing it to the capital market, the regulatory framework does not specifically define what constitutes due diligence. The SEBI, therefore, wants to put in place standard guidelines for due diligence process carried out by merchant bankers for public issues. This is intended to protect interests of investors and enhance the quality of companies coming to the capital markets. Accordingly, the SEBI has asked the Association of Merchant Banker of India (AMBI), the umbrella body of merchant bankers, to frame the due diligence guidelines for its members.[2]

So as to prevent misuse or diversion of IPO proceeds, the SEBI is planning to make merchant bankers managing an issue responsible for the end use of the issue proceeds. Accordingly, the merchant bankers may have to submit a quarterly report to the SEBI on the status of the proceeds for a period of upto one year after raising the money.[3]

F. CONCLUSIONS

A merchant bank is any person who is engaged in the business of project counselling, issue management, portfolio management, credit syndication, acceptance credit and corporate consultancy. A merchant banker renders wide variety of services right from conception of business ideas to floatation of the enterprise and its management. This, he acts as project counsellor, manager of issue, credit syndicator, and manager of portfolio. Besides, he helps the client companies in distributing their securities and arranges fixed deposits and foreign currency financing for them.

The history of merchant banking can be dated back to the late 17th and early 18th centuries when it first started in Italy and by the Italian grain merchants. With the passage of time, merchant banking in modem era started from London where the merchants began to finance the foreign trade through acceptance of bills. Subsequently, they extended their services to issue management, credit syndication and *portfolio* management. The post war period witnessed tremendous expansion of merchant banking business.

In India, merchant banking started in 1967 when the RBI allowed the Grindlays Bank to do merchant banking activity. Later on, Citibank and the SBI embraced merchant banking activity in 1970 followed by other banks and institutions. At present there are 135 merchant bankers registered with the SEBI.

In view of variety of services provided by merchant bankers, they have come to be recognised as an important institution to foster growth of a country. This is why they have gained prominence in financial markets across the world. The role of merchant bankers is becoming more pronounced in emerging economies like India in view of surging industrial growth, growing new issue activity, globalisation of financial markets and increasing inflow of FIIs.

Merchant banking business in India is regulated by SEBI (Merchant Bankers') Regulation Act, 1992. As such, no person can undertake merchant banking activity without being registered with the SEBI.

KEY TERMS

- Corporate counselling
- Credit syndication
- Investment bankers
- Investment management
- Project counselling

DISCUSSION QUESTIONS

1. Give a conceptual understanding of merchant banking.
2. Discuss, in brief, nature and functions of merchant banking.
3. Discuss various categories of merchant bankers as per SEBI.
4. Discuss the role of merchant banking in India.
5. Discuss various relevant provisions regarding registration of merchant bankers under the SEBI (Merchant Bankers) Regulation Act, 1992.
6. What are the various services rendered by merchant bankers in India?
7. Discuss, in brief, code of conduct prescribed by the SEBI for merchant bankers in India.
8. How do merchant bankers help their corporate clients in accepting fixed deposits?
9. What are the issue management and investment management services provided by merchant bankers in India? Explain.

REFERENCES

1. Business Standard, December 19, 2011.
2. Business Standard, July 08, 2011.
3. Business Standard, January 17, 2012.

Chapter 35

Venture Capital

Learning Objectives:

The present chapter aims at:

- Providing conceptual exposition of venture capital.
- Familiarizing with characteristics, dimensions and functions of venture capital.
- Focusing on state of venture capital in India.
- Describing regulatory framework of venture capital in India.
- Prognosticating about future of venture capital in India.

Chapter Outline:

- Concept of venture capital.
- Immanent attributes of venture capital.
- Dimensions of venture capital.
- Functions of venture capital.
- Process of venture capital financing.
- Venture capital in international arena.
- Venture capital in India.
- Regulatory Framework for venture capital in India.
- Future of venture capital in India.
- Conclusions.

A. CONCEPT OF VENTURE CAPITAL

An emerging source of long-term finance, which is playing a strategic role in recent years in corporate development in different parts of the world, is 'Venture Capital'. Venture Capital (VC) concept as source of long-term financing for new industrial enterprises is essentially of American origin. Over a period of time, ideas behind venture capital developed into the present form in the U.S.A. where it has been a significant source of equity finance for over the last 30 years. The concept of VC is gradually coming into vogue in developing countries like India but it is understood in somewhat different sense.

Narrowly speaking, VC refers to the risk capital supplied to growing companies and it takes the form of share capital in the business firms. Both money provided as start up capital and as development capital for small but growing firms are included in this definition. In developing countries like India, VC concept has been understood in this sense. In India, VC comprises only seed capital finance for high technology and funds to turn research and development into commercial production.

In broader sense, VC refers to the commitment of capital and knowledge for the formation and setting up of companies particularly to those specializing in new ideas or new technologies. Thus, it is not merely an injection of funds into a new firm but also a simultaneous input skills needed to set the firm up, design its marketing strategy, organize and manage it. In western countries like the USA and UK, VC perspective scans a much wider horizon along the above sense. In these countries, venture capital not only consists of supply of funds for financing technology but also supply of capital and skills for fostering the growth and development of enterprises. Much of this capital is put behind established technology or is used to help the evolution of new management teams. It is this broad role which has enabled VC industry in the West to become a vibrant force in the industrial development. It will, therefore, be more meaningful to accept broader sense of VC.

VC can be divided into many different types according to the characteristics of the shareholders and sources of investment such as private equity firms, banks, financial institutions, private corporate firms, government or insurance companies.

B. Immanent Attributes of Venture Capital

VC as a source of financing is distinct from other sources of financing because of its unique attributes, as set out below:

- VC is essentially financing of innovation and ideas, which have a potential for high growth but with inherent uncertainties.
- VC makes long-term investment in highly potential ventures of technical savvy entrepreneurs whose returns may be available after a long period, say 5-10 years.
- VC does not confine to supply of equity capital but also supply of skills for fostering the growth and development of enterprises. Venture capitalists ensure active participation in the management which is the entrepreneur's business and provide their marketing, technology, planning and management expertise to the firm. In broader sense, venture capital connotes financial as well as human capital. The big focus is on technology.
- VC financing involves high risk return spectrum. Some of the ventures may yield very high returns to more than compensate for heavy loss on others which may also have earning prospects. In fact, the fundamental principle underlying VC fund is 'no return without risk and greater the risk, greater the return'.
- VC funding may be by way of investment in the equity of the new enterprise or by way of debt or a combination of both, though equity is the most preferred route.

C. DIMENSIONS OF VENTURE CAPITAL

VC is associated with successive stages of the firm's development with distinctive types of financing, appropriate to each stage of development Thus, there are fours stages of firm's development, viz., development of an idea, start up, fledgling and establishment.

The first stage of development of a firm is development of an idea for delineating precise specialisation for the new product or service and to establish a business-plan. The entrepreneur needs seedling finance for this purpose. Venture capitalist finds this stage as the most hazardous and difficult in view of the fact the majority of the business projects are abandoned at the end of the seedling phase.

Start-up stage is the second stage of the firm's development. At this stage, entrepreneur sets up the enterprise to carry into effect the business plan to manufacture a product or to render a service. In this process of development, venture capitalist supplies start-up finance.

In the third phase, the firm has made some headway, entered the stage of manufacturing a product or service, but is facing enormous teething problems. It may not be able to generate adequate internal funds. It may also find its access to external sources of finance very difficult. To get over the problem, the entrepreneur will need a large amount of fledgling finance from the venture capitalist.

In the last stage of the firm's development when it stabilizes itself and may need, in some cases, establishment finance to exploit opportunities of scale. This is the final injection of funds from venture capitalists.

It has been estimated that in the U.S.A., the entire cycle takes a period of 5 to 10 years.

D. FUNCTIONS OF VENTURE CAPITAL

VC is growingly becoming popular in different parts of the world because of the crucial role it plays in fostering industrial development by exploiting vast and untapped potentialities and overcoming threats. VC plays this role with the help of the following major functions:

- VC provides finance as well as skills to new enterprises and new ventures of existing ones based on high technology innovations. It provides seed capital to finance even in the pre-start stage. In the development stage that follows the conceptual stage, venture capitalist develops a business plan (in partnership with the entrepreneur) which will detail the market opportunity, the product, the development and financial needs. In this crucial stage, the venture capitalist has to assess the intrinsic merits of the technological innovation, ensure that the innovation is directed at a clearly defined market opportunity and satisfies himself that the management team at the helm of affairs is competent enough to achieve the targets of the business plan. Therefore, venture capitalist will seek to establish a time frame for achieving the predetermined development marketing, sales and profits targets. In each investment, as the venture capitalist assumes absolute risk, his role is not restricted to that of a mere supplier of funds but that of an active partner with total investment in the assisted project. Thus, the venture capitalist is expected to perform not only the role of a financier but also a skilled faceted intermediary supplying a broad spectrum of specialist services — technological, commercial, managerial, financial and entrepreneurial.
- Venture capitalist fills the gap in the owner's funds in relation to the quantum of equity required to support the successful launching of a new business or the optimum scale of operations of an existing business. It acts as a trigger in launching new business and as a catalyst in stimulating existing firms to achieve optimum performance.
- Venture capitalist's role extends even as far as to see that the firm has proper and adequate commercial banking and receivable financing.

- Venture capitalist assists the entrepreneurs in locating, interviewing and employing outstanding corporate achievers to professionalise the firm.

E. PROCESS OF VENTURE CAPITAL FINANCING

The VC activity involves six steps, viz., deal origination, screening, evaluation, deal negotiation, post investment activity and exit plan.[2] Normally, these processes last for 10 years.

◈ Deal origination

VC financing begins with origination of a deal. For venture capital business, stream of deals is necessary. There may be various sources of origination of deals. One such source is referral system in which deals are referred to venture capitalists by their parent organization, trade partners, industry association, friends, etc. Another source of deal flow is the active search thought, networks, trade fairs, conferences, seminars, foreign visits, etc. Certain intermediaries, who act as link between venture capitalists and the potential entrepreneurs, also become source of deal origination.

◈ Screening

Venture capitalist in this endeavour to choose the best ventures first of all undertakes preliminary scrutiny of all projects on the basis of certain broad criteria, such as technology or product, market scope, size of investment, geographical location and stage of financing. Venture capitalists in India ask the applicant to provide a brief profile of the proposed venture to establish prime facie eligibility. Entrepreneurs are also invited for face-to-face discussion for seeking certain clarifications.

◈ Evaluation

After a proposal has passed the preliminary screening, a detailed evaluation of the proposal takes place. A detailed study of project profile, track record of the entrepreneur, market potential, technological feasibility future turnover, profitability, etc. is undertaken.

Venture capitalists in Indian factor in the entrepreneur's background, especially in terms of integrity, long-term vision, urge to grow managerial skills and business orientation. They also consider the entrepreneur's entrepreneurial skills, technical competence, manufacturing and marketing abilities and experience. Further, the project's viability in terms of product, market and technology is examined.

Besides, venture capitalists in India undertake thorough risk analysis of the proposal to ascertain product risk, market risk, technological and entrepreneurial risk.

After considering in detail various aspects of the proposal, venture capitalist takes a final decision in terms of risk return spectrum, as brought out in Chart 35.1.

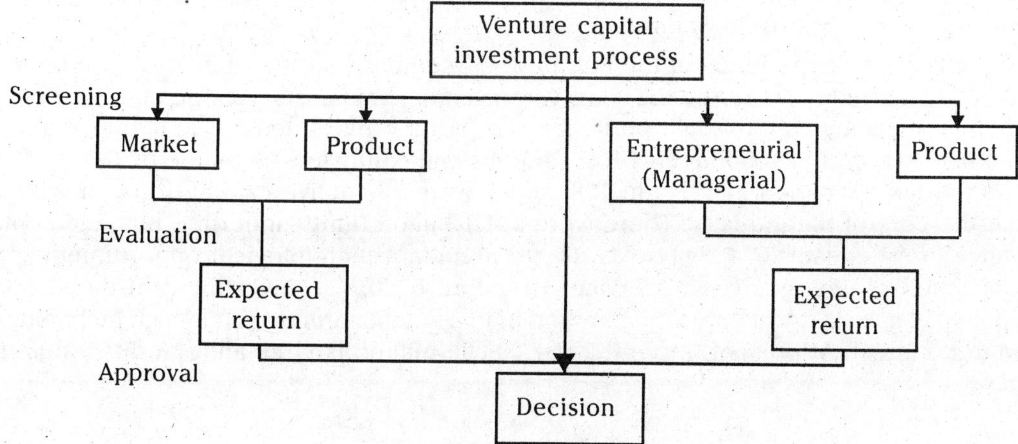

Chart 35.1: Venture Capital Investment Process

◈ Deal negotiation

Once the venture in found viable, the venture capitalist negotiates the terms of the deal with the entrepreneur. This it does so as to protect its interest. Terms of the deal include amount, form and price of the investment. It also contains protective covenants such as venture capitalist's right to control the venture company and to change its management, if necessary, buy back arrangement, acquisition, making IPOs.

Terms of the deal should be mutually beneficial to both venture capitalist and the entrepreneur. It should be flexible and its structure should safeguard interest of both the parties.

◈ Post investment Activity

Once the deal is financed and the venture begins working, the venture capitalist associates himself with the enterprise as a partner and collaborator in order to ensure that the enterprise is operating as per the plan. The venture capitalist's participation in the enterprise is generally through a representation in the Board of Directors or informal influence in improving the quality of marketing, finance and other managerial functions. Generally, the venture capitalist does not meddle in the day-to-day working of the enterprise, it intervenes when a financial or managerial crisis takes place.

◈ Exit Plan

The last stage of VC financing is the exit to realize the investment so as to make a profit/ minimise losses. The venture capitalist should make exit plan, determining precise timing of exit that would depend on a myriad of factors, such as nature of the venture, the extent and type of financial stake, the state of actual and potential competition, market conditions, etc.

At exit stage of venture capital financing, venture capitalist decides about disinvestments/ realization alternatives which are related to the type of investment, equity/quasi-equity and debt instruments. Thus, venture capitalist may exit through IPOs, acquisition by another company, purchase of the venture capitalist's share by the promoter and purchase of the venture capitalist's share by an outsider.

F. VENTURE CAPITAL IN INTERNATIONAL ARENA

The natural birth place of VC is the U.S. The development of the venture capital industry has taken place over quite a long period. VC industry in its present form started in 1946 — the year of the formation in Boston of the American Research and Development Corporation. The legislation used to spur VC was 'Small Business Investment Companies Act' with tax advantage and government loan money. By 1962, there were 585 such companies with total capital of 205 million. However, these companies ran into difficulties due to lack of understanding of VC principles on the part of the management and their inexperience. Inappropriate government legislation also contributed to the failures.

Learning from the experience of the 60s, new VC companies formed in 70s were better structured and organized. These were the years when venture capitalists became more involved in development financing both for their portfolios and for new investments. The pool of capital employed which stood at $2.5 billion in 1975, surged significantly to $7.6 billion by the end of 1982 due to the tax deduction in 1978. In 1988 there were 587 active capital firms, of which 200 formed the core of the industry. There were $24.1 billion funds under the management. The buoyancy in American VC activity was due to abundant technological opportunities for commercialization of new goods and services, freedom of foreign investment in the U.S.A. and large potential gains associated with equity and management participation in high technology ventures and tax relief. At present, more than $7,00,000 million is circulating in this industry in the U.S.A.

The most important feature of American venture capitalists is that they are totally involved with the firms based on high technological innovation right from the stage of conception of business ideas to the final stage of their establishment. They provide, in addition to risk capital, managerial, commercial, technical, financial and entrepreneurial services so as to enable the firms to achieve optimum performance. They are almost a full-fledged partner in the business along with the entrepreneur, sharing the risk and added value created in the process.

In the U.K., VC activity flourished in the years since 1980. There were only 10 companies in the market supplying VC at that time. In 1987 Britain had 140 such companies with total investment of 800 million. The major factors contributing to this phenomenal growth in venture capital activity in Britain were strengthening of the enterprise culture, i.e., public acceptability of being in business of taking risks for oneself, of starting a business, of trying to make a profit now exist, and development of the unlisted securities market.

Both these factors were the outcome of strong government support. The government launched guarantee scheme and business expansion scheme to render fiscal and financial incentives to venture capitalists.

The British venture capital funds have certain characteristics. They have come into existence to fill a potential gap in the market unfilled by the banks of the various government schemes. That potential is for close involvement in the management of the company being backed and in the planning and ownership of the company over a period of perhaps 5 to 7 years. Some venture capitalists provide funds even right from the research stage.

VC as such has not been a popular of financing in developing countries. Only a few Asian countries made serious efforts to establish VC organization. These VC organizations were usually set up by development banks as subsidiaries or separately managed funds. Besides, in some developing countries such as Philippines and Argentina, commercial banks constituted VC organizations.

However, it is interesting to observe that private sector organizations did not take much interest in setting up VC firms until recently. In some countries, VC firms came into existence with the support of International Finance Corporation (IFC) since 1978. IFC played crucial role in setting up SOFINNOVA in Spain, VIBES in Philippines, Brasilpai in Brazil, IPS in Kenya, KDIC in Korea and SEAVI in South East Africa.

In recent years, few VC firms have come up in countries such as Korea, Taiwan and Malaysia on the initiative of some private sector institutions. In Korea, for example, a number of VC firms have been established with the help of Korea Technology Advancement Corporation (KTAC). KTAC is a venture capital group set up in 1974 with the sole objective of investing in high tech business, especially by commercializing the R&D results from the Korean Advanced institutes for Services and Technology.

Foreign VC firms have not been in existence in developing countries excepting Taiwan which has been able to attract foreign VC firms since the initiation of venture capital in 1983.

VC organizations in these countries have not made much headway because of several factors. One such factor is dearth of funds available for funding high risk technology ventures. Another factor contributing to slow growth of VC firms is absence of entrepreneurial approach among development banks and commercial banks. These institutions have also been found lacking flexibility, drive and managerial skills needed for venture financing. Further, inefficient performance of the government, and sponsored VC firms have retarded the growth of venture capital companies. Absence of tax incentives is another crucial factor responsible for slow growth of the companies. In a number of developing countries including India, tax laws favour debt against equity. Finally, disinvestment factor has hindered the progress of VC firms in developing counties. Investors are attracted towards equity investment only when they are assured of making capital gains by disposing off equity shares. Unfortunately, financial markets in most of the developing countries are not properly developed to provide scope for sale of shares as and when desired by their holders.

G. VENTURE CAPITAL IN INDIA

VC in India is of recent origin, dating about two decades back. Before its evolution in 1987, development finance institutions (DFIs) were playing informally the role of venture capitalists by providing equity financing to ventures in the pre-public issue stage and supplying technological support to promising entrepreneurs. Although the DFIs came with VC schemes as early as 1986 to provide finance to technology-based entrepreneurs to support their research and development projects, the concept was operationalized in fiscal budget for 1987-88 when a cess of upto 5 per cent was introduced on all technology import payments to create a pool of funds, venture fund, to be operated by the Industrial, Development Bank of India. Industrial Credit Investment Corporation of India (ICICI) launched a venture capital scheme in 1986 to encourage new technocrats in the private sector in new fields of high technology with inherent risk. The real thrust was imparted by the finance minister in the budget speech of 1988-89 announcing the formulation of a scheme under which VC funds companies would be enabled to invest in fledgling enterprises and be eligible for concessional treatment of capital gains to non-corporate entities. This was followed by the announcement of comprehensive guidelines in November, 1988 by the Controller of Capital Issues (CCIs) for setting up of VCFs/Cs of investing in unlisted companies and for availing concessional facility of capital gains tax.

These guidelines construed VC narrowly as a vehicle for equity-oriented finance for technological upgradation and commercialization of technology promoted by relatively new entrepreneurs. However, they institutionalised the VC concept which received official recognition through them.

To undertake the task on a continuous and systematic basis, the ICICI setup jointly with the UTI in 1988 venture capital fund with ₹ 20 crore. The fund was used for providing assistance mainly in the form of equity, conditional loans and convertible debentures to set up technological ventures having potential for fast growth. In 1989, the ICICI established with the UTI another fund, the Technology Development and Information Company of India Ltd. (TDICI). This fund started providing venture capital, R/D, and technical and managerial services including technology and information. During the same period, two venture capital companies, *viz.*, Gujarat Venture Finance Ltd., and Andhra Pradesh Industrial Development Corporation Venture Capital Ltd. promoted by the state development financial institutions came into existence. In January 1990, ICICI and UTI jointly launched another venture fund for ₹ 100 crore.

In July 1990, the Gujarat Industrial Corporation Ltd. launched a venture capital finance scheme through a newly registered subsidiary with the help of the capital trust fund worth ₹ 24 crore to cater to projects that will enhance the growth of the national economy. The new subsidiary – Gujarat Venture Finance Ltd. — financially supports the entrepreneurs having both indigenous and imported technologies through equity participation.

Among commercial banks, State Bank of India and Canara Bank, Grindlays Bank launched venture fund schemes to support projects which need venture financing.

In the private sector, first VC company 'Credit Capital Venture Fund' was set up in April 1989. The other private venture capital firms set up in India were '20th Century Venture Capital Corporation', Indus Venture Capital Fund, Credit Capital Venture Fund and Infrastructural Leasing and Financial Services Ltd.

Small Industries Development Bank (SIDBI) launched its first ₹ 100 crore venture capital fund in 2001 which focused on the 17 sector. Its second a ₹ 500 crore fund, was SME-focused fund. The SIDBI has decided to launch its third venture capital fund during 2012, to be viewed as India Opportunity Fund.

Thus, the VC funds/schemes in India are essentially in the nature of equity assistance funds/schemes. There are no full-fledged individual corporate or institutional venture capitalists in India offering a broad spectrum of multifaceted specialist services like the venture capital finance in India, the size of the funds appears to be very small.

Following the repeal of Control of Capital Issues in 1985, the VC funds came to be regulated by the SEBI.

With a view to promoting VC financing India, income of the approved VCFs/Ca by way of dividends and long-term capital gains from equity investment in unlisted companies in the manufacturing sector was exempted from tax in July 1995. So as to augment availability of venture capital, the Government of India issued guidelines in September 1995 for overseas VC investment India. SEBI Venture Capital Fund Regulations were issued in 1996.

Taking cognizance of the necessity for rapid development of venture capital activities in India, SEBI appointed the Chandra Shekhar Committee to identify the impediments in the growth of venture capital industry in the country and to suggest suitable measures for its rapid growth. The Committee submitted its recommendations in January 2000. These recommendations pertained to harmonization of multiplicity of regulations, venture capital fund structures, resource raising, investments exit, SEBI regulation, Company Law related issues and other related matters.

In recent years, there has been a steady increase in the number of VC funds and the investment made by them indicating keen interest evinced by the venture capital funds in supporting high tech, small and medium sized enterprises. Number of VC funds registered with the SEBI surged from 8 during 1996-98 to 150 at present. There has also been sharp increase in investment in VC. Thus, it may be noted from Table 1 that total investment made by venture capitalists in India's IT., software and services sector surged from ₹ 7,000 lakh in 1996 to ₹ 9,00,000 lakh in 2008.

TABLE 35.1: Venture Capital Investment in India

Year	₹ lakh
1996	7,000
1997	32,000
1998	61,000
1999	1,40,000
2000	3,20,000
2001	5,00,000
2008	9,00,000
2009	5,83,000
2010	5,77,500

The main factor contributing to this accelerating trend is a major liberalization of the tax treatment for venture capital funds in the year 2000 to promote the flowering of knowledge-based enterprise and job creations. Besides, the SEBI was made the single point nodal agency for registration and regulation for both domestic and overseas VC funds. However, there has been steep decline in VC investments since 2008 to touch a low figure of ₹ 5,77,500 lakh in 2010. This was mainly because several segments in IT start-up space did not show good returns.

A peep into the operations of leading venture capitalists in India reveals the following:

- Early stage financing is to the tune of 73% viz, seed 27%, start-up 39%, other early stages 7% and later stages 26% ad turnaround 1%.
- Venture capitalists have funded the enterprises mainly by way of equities which comprise 62% of the total investment. Convertible instruments from 14% and debt 24%.
- Private venture capitalists have put 99% of their funds in equities and only 1% in debt finance.
- The assistance has gone mainly to new entrepreneurs (62%) who were first generation entrepreneurs.

- Average investment by venture capitalists in India is reported to be around ₹ 75 lakh which is relatively lower than in the USA and UK.
- Investment portfolio of venture capitalists has in recent years tended to be more diversified and broad-based. It may be noted from Table 2 that VC investments in IT and ITES accounted for over 72 per cent of their total investments in 2006. However, this share nosedived to 40 per cent in 2010. Reasons for steep decline in investments in IT and ITES sector, as noted earlier, have been the diminishing opportunity in this sector. According to several, venture capitalists, the opportunity in the start-up ecosystem lay beyond just IT and ITES.[5] There is growing shift of the VC's investments in consumer services sectors (Table 3). The decline in share of IT investments, according to CEO of venture intelligence, is probably due to shift in VC's interest from export orientation sectors like IT service and BPO towards more domestic consumption sectors.[6] Another reason for the fewer investments in the IT segment is that many verticals in IT services industry are no more at a nascent stage to attract early stage venture funding.

TABLE 35.2: Venture Capital Investments during 2006-10

Year	Total Investments (Amount in Lakh of ₹)	% of share of IT & ITES
2006	5,10,000	72
2007	5,38,000	66
2008	9,00,000	55
2009	5,83,000	41
2010	5,77,500	40

Source: Times Business, December 20, 2010

TABLE 35.3: Investment Portfolio of Venture Capitalists

(*Percentages*)

Industry	2009	2010
IT& ITES	41	40
Education	1	10
Health care	8	9
BFSI	13	8

Source: Times Business, December 20, 2010.

- An important trend lurking in recent years in the domain of VC in India is that some venture capital firms, viz., Cannon Partners, Helion Ventures, IDG Ventures India, and Everstone Capital, are incubating their own business idea which is in contrast with the traditional VC model of investing in and mentoring the business ideas of other entrepreneurs.[7] This new concept is very popular in the US, where VCs develop an in-house business idea and look out for external management teams to run the business. The people who form the management team are typically those who have several years of experience in the areas that the VC is looking to set up the business in. This includes top business executives, technology professionals and evangelists who have previously incubated start-ups.

VC firms — Cannon Partners, Helion Ventures, and IDG Ventures India have been forerunner in forming companies using this model. IDG formed Aujas, a company in the digital security products space in 2007. Before setting up Aujas, IDG screened over 60 companies in the digital space but did not find a single one worthy of being funded. So it appointed Manjula Sridhar as an entrepreneur in-residence (EIR). Sridhar was the founder of a company called Virefree Technologies with several years of experience in the telecom and datacom industry.

After going through resumes, they roped in Srinivas Rao, Senior VP in Cisco India and Sameer Shelke, an expert in information security to form the core management team. Today Aujas has over 100 clients and has executed 200 projects in 15 countries. Aujas was also selected to be the security partner for the government's Adhaar Unique Identification Programme (UIDAI).[8]

The success rate of ventures in India is reported to be about 50-60% which is quite high in comparison with the score in the west where it is reported to be only 20-30%. This is believed to be on account of careful selection of projects by Indian VCs and their active involvement with the assisted units at different stages.

H. REGULATORY FRAMEWORK FOR VENTURE CAPITAL IN INDIA

Venture capital in India is subject to regulations by the SEBI. The main elements of the SEBI Regulation 1996 are outlined below:

◈ Registration

All VCs must be registered with the SEBI. Only such funds are eligible for registration as are either a (*i*) company under the Companies Act or a (*ii*) trust under the Indian Trust Act, 1982 or under an Act of Parliament or state legislature or a (*iii*) body corporate set up under the law of the central or a state legislature.

◈ Investment Size

Each scheme launched/funds set up by a VCF should have a firm commitment from the investors for contribution of atleast ₹ 5 crore before the start of its operations.

◈ Restrictions on Investment

A VCF cannot invest more than 25 per cent of the fund in one venture. It cannot invest in associated companies.

Atleast 75 per cent of the investible funds of the VCF should be invested in unlisted equity shares/equity linked instruments (convertible securities/share warrants/preference shares, debentures compulsorily convertible into equity). Not more than 25 per cent may be invested by way of (*a*) subscription to initial public offer of a VCU whose shares are proposed to be listed subject to a lock-in of one years and (*b*) debt/debt instruments of a VCU in which the VCF has already made an investment by way of equity.

◈ Prohibition on Listing

No VCF would be entitled to get its units listed on any recognized stock exchange till the expiry of three years from the date of issuance of units by it.

◈ General Obligations

A VCF is not permitted to issue any document/advertisement inviting offers from public for subscription/purchase of any of its units. It may receive money from investment in the VCF through only private placement of its limits. It must maintain books of accounts/records/documents for a period of 8 years.

◈ Winding-up

A VCF established as a company can be wound up in accordance with the provisions of the Companies Act. A scheme of the VCF set up as a trust would be wound-up:

- When the period of the scheme mentioned in the placement memorandum is over;
- If in the opinion of trustees/trustee company the scheme should be wound up in the interest of the investors in the scheme;

- When 75 per cent of the investors in the scheme resolve in a meeting of the unitholders;
- When SEA directs in the interest of the investors.

A VCF set up as a body corporate would be wound up in accordance with the provisions of the statutes under which it is constituted.

SEBI Foreign Venture Capital Investors (FVCIs) Regulations 2000

A foreign venture capital investor (FVCI) established outside India and proposes to invest in venture capital funds/venture capital undertakings (VCUs) in India is governed by SEBI Foreign Venture Capital Investors (FVCIs) Regulations, 2000. The main highlights of the regulation are:

Registration

A FCVCI should be registered with SEBI to carry on business in India. The eligibility criteria for registration of an applicant are:

- Track record, professional competence, financial soundness, experience, general reputation of fairness and integrity;
- The RBI's approval for investing in India;
- It is an investment company/trust/partnership, pension/ mutual/endowment fund, charitable institution or any other entity incorporated outside India;
- It is authorized to invest in VCFs/carry on activity as a VCF;
- It is regulated by an appropriate foreign regulatory authority or is an income tax payer or submits a certificate from its banker of its promoters track record where it is neither a regulated entity nor an income tax payer;
- It has not been refused a certificate by SEBI; and
- It is a fit and proper person.

Investment Criteria

FVCTs should satisfy the following norms prescribed by SEBI regarding investment:

- They should disclose their investment strategy to SEBI.
- They cannot invest more than 25 per cent of the funds committed for investment in India in one VCU.
- At least 75 per cent of their investible funds should be invested in unlisted equity shares/equity linked instruments.
- Not more than 25 per cent of such funds may be invested by way of (a) subscription to initial public offer of a VCU whose shares are proposed to be listed, (b) debt or debt instruments of a VCU in which the VCFs have already made in investment by way of equity.

General Obligations

The FVCIs have to maintain, for a period of 8 years, books of accounts/records/documents which would give a true and fair picture of their affairs and intimate to SEBI the place where they are being maintained, They have also to ensure that the domestic custodian takes steps for monitoring their investments in India, furnishing periodic reports to SEBI.

Inspection and Investigation

The SEBI has the right to, *suo moto* or upon receipts of information/complaints, order an inspection/investigation in respect of conduct and affairs of any FVCI by an officer to (i) ensure that the books/accounts/documents are being maintained in the specified manner, (ii) inspect/investigate into complaints from investors/clients/any other person on any matter having a bearing on its activities, (iii) ascertain whether the provisions of the SEBI Act and FVC's regulations are being complied with and inspect/investigate, suo moto, into affairs in the interest of the securities market/investors.

◈ Suspension/Cancellation of Registration

The registration of an FVCI can be suspended by SEBI if it (i) contravenes any of the provisions of the SEBI Act or SEBI FVCI Regulations, (ii) fails to furnish any information relating to its activities as required by SEBI, (iii) furnish to it, information which is false/misleading in any particular material (iv) does not submit periodic returns/reports as required by it, and (v) does not cooperate in any enquiry /inspection conducted by it.

I. FUTURE OF VENTURE CAPITAL IN INDIA

Rapidly changing economic environment accelerated by the high technological explosion, emerging needs of new generation of entrepreneurs in the process and inadequacy of the existing venture capital funds/schemes are indicative of the tremendous scope for VC in India and a pointer to the need for the creation of a sound and broad-based venture capital movement in India. Knowledge based industries, which are growing fast and mostly global and less affected by domestic issues, offer tremendous opportunity for VC in India.

There are many entrepreneurs in India with good project ideas but no previous entrepreneurial track record to leverage their firms, handle customers and bankers, hire key personnel and borrow money. VC can open a new window for such entrepreneurs and help them to launch their projects successfully.

With rapid international march of technology, demand of newer technology and products in India has gone up tremendously. The pace of development of new and indigenous technology in the country has been slack in view of the fact the several processes developed in laboratories are not commercialized because of unwillingness of people to take entrepreneurial risk, i.e., risk their funds as also undergo the ordeal of marketing the product and process. In such a situation, venture financing assumes more significance. It can act not only as a financial catalyst but also provide a strong impetus for entrepreneurs to develop products involving newer technologies and commercialise them. This will give a fillip to the development of new technology and would go a long way in broadening the industrial base, creation of jobs, provide a thrust to exports and help in the overall enrichment of the economy.

Increasing ability of entrepreneurs to move beyond supplier of low-cost services to higher value products is pointer to bright future of VC in the country.

In addition, VC will be needed urgently to solve the serious problems of sickness which has plagued many Indian industries. There are large numbers of sick companies which offer opportunities for turnaround, either through a change in the product line or use of existing facilities in a different way but do not have required funds. The supply of equity to persons who have fertile ideas and necessary expertise can save the sick units from liquidation.

Another type of situation commonly found in our country is where the local group and a multinational company may be ready to enter into a joint venture but the former does not have sufficient funds to put up its share of the equity and the latter is restricted to a certain percentage. For personal reasons or because of competition, the local group may not be keen to invite anyone in its industry or any major private investors to contribute equity and may prefer a VC company as a less intimately involved and temporary shareholder. Venture capitalists can also lend their expertise and standing to the entrepreneurs.

A large number of smaller units serving as ancillaries to major industrial groups need capital, expertise and contacts, of venture capitalist of upgradation of their technology in tune with the demands from the major industrial units. It is generally found that small suppliers are faced with a choice of going out of business, losing their major client, being acquired by the client or obtaining capital at an exorbitant rate, from a source outside the industry. Venture capitalists can help these units and save them from the crisis.

In service sector, which has immense growth prospects in India, venture capitalists can play significant role in tapping its potentiality to the full. For instance, venture capitalists can provide capital and expertise to organizations selling antique remodeled jewellery, builders of resort hotels, baby and health care market, retirement homes and small houses.

In view of the above, it will be desirable to establish a separate national VC fund to which the financial institutions and banks can contribute. In scope and content such a venture capital fund should cover (i) all the aspects of venture capital, financing all the three stages of conceptual, developmental and exploitation phases in the process of commercialization of technological innovation and (ii) as many of the risk stages — development, manufacturing, marketing, management and growth as possible under Indian conditions. The fund should offer a comprehensive package of technical, commercial, managerial and financial assistance and services to budding entrepreneurs and be in a position to offer innovative solutions to the various problems faced by them in business promotion, technology transfer and innovation. To this end, the proposed national venture capital fund should have at its disposal massive financial resources at its command and multidisciplinary technical expertise. The major thrust of this fund should be on the promotion of viable new business in India to take advantage of the upcoming high growth industries so as to take the Indian economy to commanding heights.

J. CONCLUSIONS

VC is emerging as a potent source of risk financing to new ventures. Venture capitalist also provides managerial as well as technical expertise to the potential entrepreneurs.

VC financing involves six stages, viz., deal origination, screening, evaluation, deal negotiation, post investment activity and exit plan.

VC funds are highly developed in the USA and UK. They provide, in addition to risk capital, managerial, commercial, technical, financial and entrepreneurial services to the potential ventures so as to enable them to achieve optimum performance. Main factors contributing to the advanced growth of venture capital funds in these countries are enterprising culture and provision of tax incentives.

VC in India developed recently is in its nascent stage. Venture capitalists in India have confirmed themselves to early stage financing. They provide funds to the enterprises by way of equities. These entrepreneurs are finally first generation entrepreneurs. Success rate of ventures in India is reported to be between 50-60% which is quite high.

One of the factors responsible for the stunted growth of venture capital in India is the restrictive legal and financial framework.

Future of the VC in India is very bright in view of the liberalized environment, emergence of new generation of entrepreneurs and inadequacy of the existing schemes to cater to the bargaining demands.

KEY TERMS

- Establishment Finance
- Fledgling Finance
- Fledgling Enterprises
- In-house business idea
- Private Equity Firms
- Seedling Finance
- Start-up Finance
- Venture Fund

DISCUSSION QUESTIONS

1. What do you understand by Venture Capital? Discus functions of Venture Capital.
2. What are the distinguishing features of Venture Capital fund in India?
3. Discuss dimensions of Venture Capital.
4. Trace out the development Venture Capital in international arena.
5. Examine the present state of Venture Capital in India.
6. In what respects is Venture Capital in India different from the USA and the UK?
7. Outline briefly the operation of Venture Capital firms in India.
8. What is the future of Venture Capital in India?
9. What are the requisites to the success of Venture capital in India?

REFERENCES

1. G. Auson, Venture Capital in Europe, Europe Venture Capital Association Year Book, London 1992, p. 49.
2. T.T. Tyebjee and A.A. Bruno, A Model for Venture Capital Investment Activity, Management Science, 30, 1981, pp. 10151-66.
3. Economic Times, December 13, 2003, p. 3.
4. Times, Business, December 20, 2010.
5. Times Business, *op. cit.*
6. *Ibid.*
7. Times Business, April 18, 2004.
8. *Ibid.*

Internet Resources:

- www.venturecapital.org/india/india_research.htm

  This is the website of Indian Venture Capital Association that contains findings of survey of venture capital in India.
- economictimcs.indiatimes.com/ articleshow8844710 cms

  This is the website of economic times that provides information about current state of venture capital in India and its future prospects.
- www.indiainfoline.com/lega/vefu/ch01.html

  This is the website of Indian information about introduction funding in India, SEBI regulation and other laws.
- www.karvy.com/articles/vcindia.htm

  This is the website of karvy that contains details about current venture capital in India and its future aspects.
- www.hydonline.com/business/finance/venture_capital

  Thls is the website of the hydonline which provides conceptual understanding of venture capital and its state of affairs across the globe.

Chapter 36

Custodial Services in India

Learning Objectives:

The present chapter aims at:

- Provide a conceptual exposition of custodial services.
- Provide an insight into various players in custodial business and services offered by them.

Chapter Outline:

A. CONCEPTUAL EXPOSITION OF CUSTODIAL SERVICES

As the name suggests, custodial services are all about safe custody services. In context of financial market transactions, custodial services refer to the safe custody of share certificates and securities or keeping deposits of them for physical handling of receipts and deliveries or for keeping accounts and delivering after sales services, such as collection of dividend, rights, bonus, etc.

The custody business provides a range of security services, including safekeeping and settlement, reporting, corporate actions, dividends collection and distribution, proxy voting, tax reclaim, fund administration and providing market news and information. Thus, a custodian providing core domestic custody services typically settles trades, invests cash balances as directed, collects income, processes corporate actions, prices securities positions, provides record keeping and reporting services and keeps the client informed of the actions taken or to be taken by the issuer of securities, having or bearing on the benefits or rights accruing to the client. Such services are provided to individual as well as institutions.

A typical process flow is portrayed through Figure 36.1.

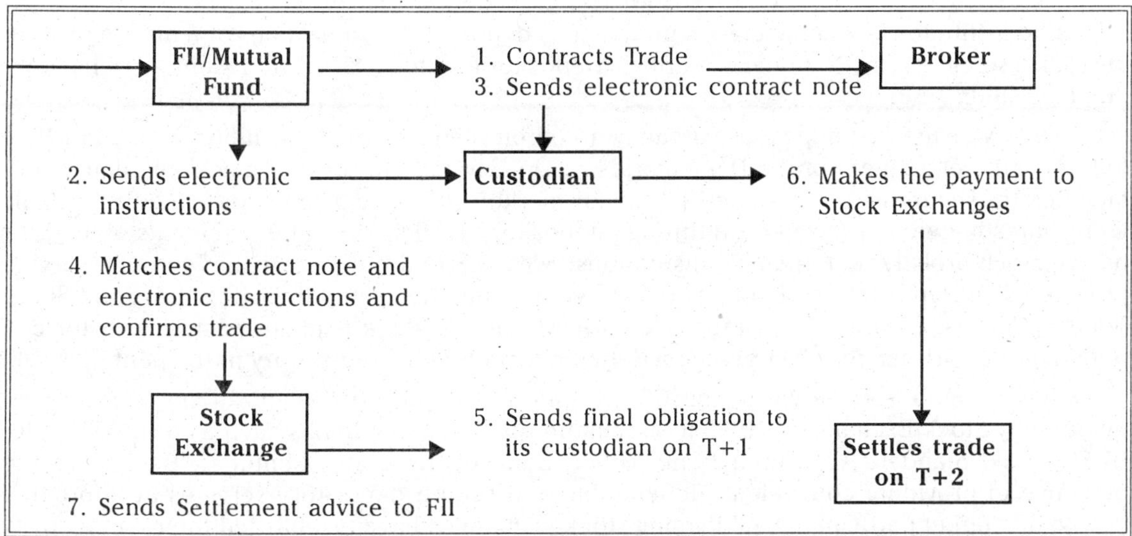

Figure 36.1: Typical Process Flow

There are two types of custodial service structures which are prevailing in financial markets across the globe — Direct custody and Global custodian relationship. Direct custody is an arrangement wherein the client directly enters into a contractual agreement with the custodian in the local market. Global custodian is an entity who safe keeps and settles the trades on the stock exchange for their end clients. Thus, custodians operating in India primarily play the role of sub-custodians and enter into a contractual agreement.

B. CUSTODIAL SERVICE PLAYERS IN INDIA — A SYNOPTIC VIEW

There are 16 SEBI-registered custodians operating in India. These may broadly speaking, be classified into banking institutions and specially constituted custodial and depository corporations. While the former offer custodial services in addition to their core banking business, the latter have been established for rendering custodial services to their sponsors and others.

There are 5 foreign banks, *viz.,* CitiBank, HSBC, Deutsche Bank, JP Morgan and Standard Chartered Bank, which dominate the Indian market today.

Among domestic banks, SBI, ICICI Bank, HDFC, and Kotak Mahindra are playing crucial role in providing custodial services. SBI Fund Management formed joint venture in 2004 with Societe Generale Securities to offer custody and related services to both foreign and domestic investors and clients.

As regards specially constituted and depository corporations, Stock Holding Corporation of India Ltd. (SHCIL) was the first institutional agency setup in 1988 jointly by IDBI, IFCI, ICICI, UTI, LIC, GIC and IIBI as a company under the Companies Act. Initially, the SHCIL provided custodial services to its sponsors. But it extended them for a fee to others like some private mutual funds, banks and other institutions who are active in the capital market. The SHCIL has membership of the stock exchanges in Mumbai, New Delhi, Kolkata and Chennai so that it can participate in clearing and settlement on behalf of its sponsors and clients. SHCIL will be merged with government owned IDBI Bank. Broking services of SHCIL, which is a subsidiary known as SHCIL Services Ltd. would be merged with IDBI Capital Market Services. With this merger, IDBI will emerge as a major player in financial services segment of the country.[1]

The OTCEI, set up in 1990, formed OTC Exchange Custodian to provide for custodial services to its members. OTC Exchange Custodian is an important constituent of the Exchange, as the shares traded on OTCEI need not be physically handled and simple counter receipts can be used as transferable property in lieu of share certificates.

Two institutions, which were set up to act as depository organizations and also to provide custodial services, are National Securities Depositories Ltd. (NSDL) and Central Depository Services (India) Ltd.

NSDL was the first depository organization promoted by IDBI, UTI and NSE set up in 1996 following the enactment of the Depositories Act in July 1996 to provide electronic depository facilities for securities being traded in capital market. NSDL, registered with the SEBI, deals with shares in dematerialized form through depository participants who are agents of investor banks, stock brokers and financial institutions. NSDL carried out its activities through service providers like Depository Participants (DPs), issuing companies and their Registrars and Share Transfer Agents, Clearing Corporations/Clearing House of stock exchanges. The investor can obtain depository services by opening a demat account with a depository participant of NSDL.

Central Depository Services Ltd. (CDSL) is another depository organization was promoted by Bombay Stock Exchange in 1999 in association with leading banks such as SBI, BOI, BOB, HDFC Bank, Standard Chartered Bank, Union Bank of India and Centurian Bank with the objective of providing convenient, dependable and secure depository services at affordable cost to all market participants. All leading stock exchanges have established their connectivity with CDSL.

C. SERVICES PROVIDED BY CUSTODIAL SERVICES INSTITUTIONS IN INDIA

◈ Services by Banking Institutions

As a part of their banking business, banking players in India are providing complete range of custodial services through their custodial service division. These can be grouped into the following categories:

(i) Custody and Settlement Services

Banks are providing a bouquet of tailor made solutions for overseas and domestic investors who would be investing in the Indian capital market across debt and equity instruments, derivatives, depository receipts and mutual fund units. They assist their clients for the custody account opening documentation requirements and facilitate clients during the SEBI registration process. As a clearing member with the clearing houses of leading Indian stock exchanges, banks perform clearing and settlement of cash and securities on behalf of clients. They provide safekeeping services for securities held — both in electronic as well as physical forms.

(ii) Depository Services

SBI, ICICI and Kotak Mahindra banks offer depository services including dematerialization and rematerialization (conversion of physical certificates into the electronic book entry format). They are also custodians for ADR/GDR issues. Kotak Mahindra Bank and ICICI coordinate with local custodians to ensure prompt receipt underlying securities against cancelled depository receipts and report the same to clients on priority basis.

(iii) Fund Accounting Services

Banks, particularly ICICI and Kotak Mahindra banks, offer accounting services as a value addition to their custody clients. They offer investment accounting for all purchases and sales alongwith the profit and loss, valuation for all securities, unit capital accounting for recording capital inflows and outflows from the fund/portfolio, income and expense accounting of daily accruels, reconciliation with third parties like registrar, bank or custodian.

(iv) Corporate Actions

SBI, ICICI and Kotak Mahindra are also engaged in tracking and collecting of corporate benefit entitlements which also include primary market auctions, open market operations/ value free transfer, calculation of interest and redemption.

(v) Standardized and Customized Information Services

Investors need meaningful information that offers insight to their investment portfolios. Apart from the very comprehensive standard suite of reports, both ICICI and Kotak Mahindra banks provide customized reports to clients at various frequencies to enable clients to efficiently manage their securities portfolios, cash balances and take more informed investment decisions.

(vi) Compliance Monitoring and Regulatory Reporting

Banks monitor compliance to existing guidelines by investors and facilitate reporting to regulators and local authorities on behalf of the client.

(vii) Other Services

Both the ICICI and Kotak Mahindra banks have web based reporting system to report on position limit utilization, margin movement, activity summary, and scripwise margin. They also provide proxy services and for that matter, act on client instructions and participate and vote on their behalf in shareholders' meeting of companies.

For rendering the above custodial and other services, banks have set up separate custodial division which is endowed with state of art clearing, settlement and risk management systems. They have dedicated client relationship personnel.

◈ Services by SHCIL

The SHCIL is offering the following services to its sponsors and others:

(i) Custodial services

The SHCIL having a state of art custody vault offers custodial services and stores millions of scrips. The corporation has a system of inspection and audit of all certificates received from members sent for transfers received from the company and deposited in safe custody in its vaults. It also provides services related to collection of dividend warrants, and interest cheques. It attends to the necessary consolidation or splitting of shares, redemption and collection of bonus and rights and other privileges attached to securities.

(ii) Clearing services

Being member of major stock exchanges, the SHCIL provides the post-trading agency for the institutions. It receives and/or delivers the securities on behalf of the institutions after each settlement of the stock exchange. The SHCIL monitors the execution of the purchase/sale orders of the institutions by the brokers. It ensures that the securities are duly and timely transferred to the names of the institutions.

(iii) Support services

The SHCIL renders support services by way of arranging to monitor interest/dividend payments due to the institutions and ensuring that the warrants received from the companies are deposited in the banks to the credit of the institutions without delay.

(iv) Corporate actions

The SHCIL renders personalized services of collection of warrants, dividends, rights and bonus, etc. It has tie up with an all-India financial services company for courier network for this personalized service from the company. It has also a system of computerized accounting after deposit of its warrants, dividends, interest, etc. and sending reconciliation statements to all its members and clients.

(v) Information services

The SHCIL has an on-line system of sharing various information relating to corporate activity, book closures, record dates, dividend dates, etc. It has a shift communication system for informing offshore clients as also those from across long distances to share information and eliminate unnecessary movement of paper.

◈ Services by NSDL

(i) Depository services

The NSDL provides depository and clearing services through depository participants, issuing companies and their registrars and share transfer agents, Clearing Corporation/Clearing House of stock exchange. The investor can obtain depository services by opening a demat account with a depository participant of the NSDL. The issuer company can make dematerialization services available to its shareholders by entering into an agreement with the NSDL and by establishing an electronic link with the NSDL.

A clearing member has to open a clearing account in the depository system for receiving the securities from its clients for delivery to the Clearing House/Clearing Corporations as pay-in and to distribute the pay-out to its clients received from the Clearing Corporation/House. The Clearing Corporations/Houses of stock exchanges are linked between electronically receive securities delivered by clearing members towards pay-in and to give out securities to clearing members towards pay-out.

The NSDL is electronically linked to each of service providers, through Very Small Aperture Terminals (VSATs) or through Leased Landlines. It has launched 'Certificate Programme' on depository to enable the participants to understand and adopt the procedures to be followed in conducting various transactions in the NSDL depository system.

(ii) Other services

Besides the major services of electronic custody and trade settlement services, the SDL provides other services like pledge, hypothecation of securities, automatic delivery of securities to clearing corporations, distribution of securities to allottees in case of public issues, internet based services for clearing members, 'speed'. Speed is a common infrastructure of the NSDL and any depository participant of the NSDL can subscribe to it. Speed-e enables demat account-holders (including clearing members) to submit delivery instructions directly on the internet through speed-e website.

◈ Services by Central Depository Services (India) Ltd.

The CDSL provides depository services at affordable cost to all market participants. Depository participants (DP) can provide on-line depository services since the CDSL's system is based on centralised database architecture. It stores records describing the ownership of securities. This service makes it possible for securities settlement in India to be conducted electronically.

The CDSL provides other facilities including dematerialization, rematerialization, pledging or hypothecation of dematerialized securities, freezing of demat accounts, and custody of securities.

D. FUTURE OF CUSTODIAL SERVICES IN INDIA

As noted earlier, capital market in India has 16 SEBI-registered custodians carrying out custodial business. The size of the business is estimated to be around ₹ 2,000 crore. Opportunities from local mutual funds wanting to outsource their non-core administrative functions such as fund accounting and growth in the domestic organized pension sector are expected to take the industry to more than double its current size.

Sensing the growth of inflows in the Indian equity market, overseas and domestic players in the stock broking business are lining up to offer custodial services. Lining up to enter the fray are French banking major BNP Paribas, SBI-Societe, Hong Kong based JP Morgan & domestic players like Religare, Prabhudas, Liladhar & Ananda Rathi Securities.

Till recently, only FIIs, insurance companies and mutual funds were being serviced by custodians. Now, newer client segments including high-net worth individuals, increasingly understand the need and value of engaging a custodian. The SEBI guideline making it mandatory for portfolio managers with over ₹ 500 crore assets to appoint a custodian has also given a fillip to growth in the industry. With markets on an upswing, it is expected more business flow to custodians.

E. CONCLUSIONS

Custodial services signify the sale custody of share certificates and securities. The custody business provides a range of security services.

There are 16 SEBI registered custodians operating in Indian financial market including foreign and domestic banks, SHCIL, OTCEI, NSDL and CDSL. These institutions are providing a bouquet of custodial and depository services as also fund accounting services, corporate actions, customised information services, compliance monitoring and regulatory reporting. For rendering these services, these institutions have set up a separate custodial division equipped with competent and skilled personnel.

Custodial service businesses hold bright future in view of the growth of inflows in the Indian equity market, and likely, increase in demand of the service by local mutual funds wanting to outsource their non-core administrative function to the custodians.

KEY TERMS

- CDSIL
- Corporate actions
- Custodian
- Customized information services
- Depository services
- Direct custody
- Global custodian relationship
- NSDL
- OTCEI
- SHCIL
- Speed-e

DISCUSSION QUESTIONS

1. What do custodial services signify?
2. Outline various players operating custodial business in India.
3. What are the various services rendered by commercial banks as custodians?
4. Discuss the objectives and functions of Stock Holding Corporation of India Ltd.
5. Describe various services being rendered by National Securities Depositories (India) Ltd.
6. Bring out, in brief, range of services being provided by Central Depository Services Ltd.
7. Give your own perception about future of custodial service business in India.

REFERENCE

1. Hindu, November 1, 2012.

Internet Resources:

- www.ehow.com
- www.wikinvest.com/wiki/custodialservices
- e.business.icicibank.com
- www.hdfc.com
- www.financialexpress.com

Credit Rating Services in India

Learning Objectives:

The present chapter aims at:

- Providing an understanding of credit rating and credit rating agencies.
- Familiarising with credit rating process.
- Focussing on role of credit rating agencies.
- Providing vivid view of credit rating agencies in India and services rendered by them.

Chapter Outline:

- Prologue.
- Contours of credit rating.
- Nature of credit rating agencies.
- Credit rating process.
- Business models of credit rating agencies.
- Role of credit rating agencies in financial markets.
- Credit rating agencies in India — An overview.
- Services of credit rating agencies in India.
- Regulation of credit rating agencies in India.
- Conclusions.

A. PROLOGUE

In market driven economy efficacy and effectiveness of financial markets in allocation of resources among competing uses depends, *inter alia*, on availability of systematic and reliable information on a regular basis about dynamics of macro and micro environment including dynamics of interest rates, fiscal and monetary policies containing opportunities and risks across the different countries of the globe. Enlightened investors — both individual and institutional — need detailed and dependable information, in addition to general economic and business conditions of the country and abroad, about the current financial health of the enterprises seeking funds from the market, their credit character, ability to meet the obligations, likely future income, before making rational investment decision. These investors draw upon the desired information from varied sources such as offer documents of the enterprises, research reports of various market intermediaries and governmental agencies, media reports, websites of the enterprises, etc. Besides, they can make use of independent, research-based information provided by reputed and specialised agencies containing their credible opinions on the creditworthiness of different organizations, governments and countries. Such opinions are popularly known as credit rating and suppliers of these opinions, as credit rating agencies.

B. CONTOURS OF CREDIT RATING

Credit rating, also known as debt rating, signifies an assessment of the creditworthiness of individuals and companies and countries. It is forward-looking opinion about credit character in terms of the ability and willingness of an issuer of debt investment, such as a company or state or city government, to meet its financial obligations in full and on time. Credit ratings can also speak about the credit quality of an individual debt issue, such as a corporate note, a municipal bond or a mortgage-backed security, and the relative likelihood that the issue may default.

Credit rating, based upon the history of borrowing and repayment as well as the availability of assets and extent of liabilities, provides a relative ranking of the credit quality of debt/ financial instrument. Such rating is specific to a debt instrument. It is intended as a grade and an analysis of the credit risk associated with that particular instrument. Rating is neither a general purpose evaluation of the issuing enterprise nor an overall evaluation of credit risk likely to be involved in all the debts/financial instruments contracted or to be contracted by such issues.

Although credit rating reflects the opinion expressed by an independent professional organization, it does not amount to buy, sell or hold recommendations or a measure of asset value. It is also not intended to signal the suitability of an investment. Credit rating speaks about one aspect of an investment decision — credit quality — which in some cases may include the evaluator's view of what investors can expect to recover in the event of default.

However, the assignment of credit ratings is not an exact science, for the fact that there are future events and developments that cannot be foreseen. As such, ratings opinions should not be treated as guarantees of credit quality or as exact measures of the probability that a particular debt issue will default. Instead, ratings express relative opinions about the creditworthiness of an issuer or credit quality of an individual debt issue, from strongest to weakness, within a universe of credit risk.

Credit ratings may be sovereign and corporate. A **sovereign** credit rating is the credit rating of a sovereign entity, *i.e.*, a national government. The sovereign credit rating takes into account three main elements, viz., public debt as a percentage of gross domestic product, the budget deficit and debt affordability. It indicates the risk level of the investing environment of a country and is used by investors looking to invest abroad.

As a part of its sovereign rating, Standard and Poor's (S&P) warned a number of highly rated Group of 20 countries in January 2012 that it may downgrade them from 2015 if their governments fail to enact reforms to curb rising healthcare spending and other costs related to ageing populations.[1] Likewise, S&P cautioned India in February, 2012 that its sovereign credit rating could slightly tilt towards 'negative', if effective action was not taken to counter the "balance of risk factors" emanating from economic uncertainties at home and abroad.[2]

On April 25, 2012, S&P revised long-term outlook of Indian economy to negative from stable and warmed further deterioration of economic fundamentals posed the grim possibility of a rating downgrade. According to the rating major, diminishing growth prospects, worsening external situation and a lack of fiscal discipline are the prime reasons for the outlook revision.[3]

Corporate credit rating is rating of a company or a financial institution's ability to meet its debt obligation. Corporate credit rating is usually of a financial instrument such as bond, rather than the whole corporation. In October 2011, when Moody had downgraded SBI's stand-alone rating, citing inadequate capital and declining asset quality, it was a corporate credit rating.

Credit rating may be a short-term and long-term. A short-term rating is a probability factor for an individual going into default within a year. This is in contrast to the long-term rating which is evaluated over a long time frame. In the past, institutional investors preferred to consider long-term ratings. Nowadays, short-term ratings are commonly used.

C. NATURE OF CREDIT RATING AGENCIES

Credit ratings are provided by independent professional organizations who are specialized in evaluating credit risks of individuals, and institutions. These agencies are organized as companies that assign credit ratings for issuers of certain .types of debt obligations as well as debt instruments. In some cases, services of the underlying-debt are also given ratings. These agencies express their opinions on creditworthiness of the issuer in terms of alphabetical or alphanumeric symbols. These symbols are assigned with reference to the debt instruments being rated. They are simple and easily understood, enabling the investor to distinguish between debt instruments on the basis of their underlying credit quality. Each agency applies its own methodology in measuring creditworthiness and uses a specific rating scale to publish its ratings opinions. Typically, ratings are expressed as letter grades that range, for example, from 'AAA to D' to communicate the agency's opinion of relative level of credit risk.

Agencies that assign credit ratings for institutions include:

- A.M. Best (U.S.)
- BayCorp Advantage (Australia)
- Bulgarian Credit Rating Agency (Bulgaria)
- Capital Intelligence (Cyprus)
- Capital Standards Rating (Kuwait)
- Dagong Global (People's Republic of China)
- Dominion Bond Rating Service (Canada)
- Egan-Jones Rating Company (U.S.)
- Fitch Ratings (Dual-headquarters U.S./U.K.)
- CRISIL (India)
- ONICRA (India)
- Japan Credit Rating Agency Ltd. (Japan)
- Moody's Investors Service (U.S.)
- Standard & Poor's (U.S.)
- Weiss Ratings (U.S.)

Amongst the above, the big three credit rating agencies of the world are Standard & Poor's, Moody's Investor Services and Fitch Ratings. Moody's and S&P each control about 40 per cent of the market. Third-ranked Fitch Ratings has about a 14 per cent market share. Sometimes, it is used as an alternative to one of the other majors.[4]

Standard & Poor's and Moody conduct extensive research on the bond issuer before assigning a credit rating to them. Each of the credit rating agencies rate debt securities with a slightly different ratings scale. Table 36.1 shows what each of these credit rating agencies considers investment grade and non-investment grade securities.

TABLE 37.1: Rating Grades of Moody's and Standard & Poor's

	Moody's	Standard & Poor's	
Highest quality	Aaa	AAA	
High quality	Aa	AA	Investment Grade
Upper medium	A-l, A	A	
Medium	Baa-l, Baa	BBB	
Speculative	Ba	BB	Non-investment Grade
Highly speculative	B, Caa	B, CCC,CC	
Default	Ca, C	D	

Thus, it may be noted from the table that global rating scale at Moody's contains nine grades and goes from the highest grade to the lowest grade (in increasing order of risking: Aaa, Aa, A, Baa, Ba, B, Caa, Ca, C. Likewise, the long- term globating rate scale at S&P contains nine grades and goes from the highest grade to the lowest grade (in increasing order of riskiness): AAA, AA, A, BBB, BB, B, CCC, CC, C. In both the cases, debt instruments of me companies having grade between Aaa (Moody's) AAA (S&P) and A-1, A (Moody's) and A (S&P) are considered investment grade and others are rates as non investment grade. The likelihood of default (Ca, C in Moody's and D in S&P) is the single most important factor in the two agencies' assessment of creditworthiness.[5]

D. CREDIT RATING PROCESS

Credit rating procedures adopted by rating agencies are, by and large, the same. The process begins when an issuer approaches the agency and requests for rating of me instrument. An agreement is then entered into between the two and rating committee is constituted to rate the instrument and assess a major transaction or event having bearing on current rating or consider putting a rating on review of change.

Rating committee comprises a lead credit analysis, area supervisors and junior analytical staff. Ratings are based on a variety of public and non-public information. Public information typically includes filings with the Commission (SEBI in case of India), news reports, industry reports, bond and stock price trends, data from central banks, etc. Non-public information can include me issuer's credit agreements, acquisition agreements, private placement memoranda, and general business projections and forecasts, on-public information is often provided pursuant to the confidentiality agreement between the rating agency and the issuer. Rating committee also gathers information from the issuer through questionnaires and the detailed document. However, rating agency does not conduct audits or due diligence review of the issuer-provided information.

Before providing an opinion on the relative credit risk associated with the financial instrument the rating committee tries to estimate the cash generation capacity of the issuer, on the basis of primary cash flows operations, vis-i-vis, its requirements for servicing obligations during the tenure of the instrument. While doing so, an assessment is also made of the secondary cash flow available through the sale of marketable securities. There can be liquidated, if need be, to supplement the primary cash flow. This is for the fact that secondary cash flows have a greater bearing on the short-term ratings. The long-term ratings are generally based on adequacy of primary cash flows.

While assigning rating to a particular instrument the committee factors into a host of relevant factors such as basic characteristic of the industry to which the issuing firm belongs, product positioning, perceived quality of products or brand equity, proximity to the markets, distribution network, efficiency of operations, project risk, quality of management, etc. Besides, a myriad of financial forces including financing policies, flexibility of financial structure, past financial performance and quality of accounting policy, are also looked into.

Once the desired information has been analyzed and relevant factors are considered, the committee decides about the rating of the instrument. Before finalizing the rating decision, the rating agency generally informs in advance of the imminent rating action and allows the issuer to appeal the decision. However, the right of appeal is limited both in time and to the submission of new and vital information. On receiving the new information the rating committee reviews its rating decision. Rating agencies generally survey ratings over time by reviewing corporate findings, monitoring industry trends, and maintaining a dialogue with corporate management.

E. BUSINESS MODELS OF CREDITING RATING AGENCIES

There are two business models, *viz.*, "submission-based" and "issuer-pays". Originally, all CRAs relied on a "submission-based" business model where the CRA would not distribute the ratings for free but would instead only provide the ratings to subscribers to the CRA's publications. Submission fees would provide the bulk of the CRA's income. Today, most smaller CRAs still rely on this business model which, proponents believe, allows the CRA to publish ratings that are less likely to be tinged by certain types of conflicts of interest.[6]

By contrast, most large and medium-sized CRAs (including Moody's, S&P, Fitch, Japan Credit Ratings, R&I, AM. Best and others) today rely on an "issuer-pays" business model in which most of the CRA's revenue comes from fees paid by the issuers themselves. Under this business model, while subscribers to the CRA's services are still provided with more detailed reports analyzing an issuer, then services are a minor source of income and most ratings are provided to the public for free. Proponents of this model argue that if the CRA relied only subscription for income, the last majority of bonds would go unrated since subscriber interest is low for all but the largest issuances. Further, while rating agency faces a clear conflict of interest vis-i-vis, the issuer, it rates, tile subscriber-based model, the subscriber-based model also presents conflicts of interest, since a single subscriber may provide a large portion of the CRA's revenue and the CRA may feel obligated to publish ratings that support that subscriber's investment decisions.

In October, 2011, a new collaboration based business model called "wikirating" was developed by Austrian mathematician Dorian Crede. This is an on-line community credit rating platform which aims at providing a transparent source of credit rating information, received by a worldwide community.

F. ROLE OF CREDIT RATING AGENCIES IN FINANCIAL MARKETS

CRAs equipped with professional acumen and dexterous expertise play crucial role in financial markets by providing to investors, issuers, investment banks, broker-dealers, and government regulators insightful and independent opinions of credit risks of individuals, institutions and countries based on research-based information. For e ample, CRAs increase the range of investment alternatives and provide objective, dispassionate, easy-to-use measurements of relative credit risk; this generally increase the efficiency of the market, lowering costs for both borrowers and lenders. This, in turn, increases the total supply of risk capital in the economy, leading to stronger growth. They also open the capital markets to categories of borrowers who might otherwise be shut out altogether: small governments, start-up companies, hospitals and universities.

CRAs aid investors in making prudent investment decisions and building an optimal investment portfolio promising high return with low risk by providing them with an independent and professional judgement of the credit quality of the instrument which an individual investor would not otherwise be able to evaluate. In fact, rating provides low cost supplement to the in-house appraisal system of organized institutional investors. CRAs also supply information through the industry reports. Company reports, investor information and protection seminars and other on-line assistance rendered by the rating agencies.

Issuers of financial instruments can gainfully use the service of credit rating agencies as the latter help the former in accessing the market in raising funds. Credit rating, by a reputed agency instills confidence in the investing public about creditworthiness of the issuer and thus widens the investor base. This is why, in most cases, a significant security issuance must have at least one rating from a respected CRA for the issuance to be successful. Studies by the US Bond Market Association note that many institutional investors now prefer that debt issuance has at least three ratings.

Credit rating agencies may also play a key role in structured financial transactions. Unlike a "typical loan or bond issuance, where a borrower offers to pay a certain return on a loan structured financial transactions may be viewed as either a series of loans with a different characteristics, or else a number of small loans of a similar type packaged together into a series of "buckets" (different loans called "tranches"). CRAs often determine the interest rate or price ascribed to a particular tranche, based on the quality of loans or quality of assets contained within that grouping.

Companies involved in structured financing arrangements often consult CRAs to help them determine how to structure the individual tranches so that each receives a desired rating. For example, a firm may wish to borrow a large sum of money by issuing debt securities. However, the amount is so large that the investors may demand prohibitively high rate of return on a single issuance. Hence, the firm may decide to issue three separate bonds, with three separate credit ratings — A (medium low risk), BBB (medium risk), and BB (speculative), using S&P's rating system. The firm expects that the effective interest rate it pays on the A-rated bonds will be much less than the rate it a must pay on the BB-rated bonds, but overall, the amount it must pay for the total capital it raises, will be less than it would pay if the entire amount were raised from a single bond offering. As this transaction is devised, the firm may consult a CRA to see how it must structure each tranche — in other words, what type of assets must be used to secure the debt in each tranche — in order for that tranche to receive the desired rating when it is issued.

Services of CRAs may also be useful to intermediaries of financial markets, particularly merchant bankers and underwriters in as much as their ratings can serve as an effective tool for them in planning, pricing, underwriting and placement of issues. Stock brokers and dealers can make use of ratings as an input for monitoring their risk exposure. Merchant banks have been found employing credit rating for pre-packaging issues through asset securitization/structured obligations.

Regulators too parlay credit ratings or permit ratings to be used for regulatory purposes. For example, under the Basel II agreement of the BCBS, banking regulators can allow banks to employ credit ratings from certain approved CRAs (called External Credit Assessment Institutions) while calculating their net capital reserve requirements. CRAs have facilitated regulatory authorities across the world to issue policy directives based on their credit ratings. For example, specific rules restrict the entry of new issues that are rated below a particular grade. Institutional investors are advised not to hold instruments that are rated below a particular level. Even regulatory authorities stipulate different margin requirements for the mortgage of rated and unrated instruments.

However, operations of CRAs across the world have been subject to criticism on scores of their inability to prognosticate the future, error of judgement, arbitrariness in rating and conflicts of interest.

The CRAs have often been accused of not being able to predict future problems associated with the issuer and resultant defaults. This is partly due to the rating process which relies heavily on past numerical data and standard ratios with lower usage of judgement and understanding of the underlying business. It also fails to capture all aspects of the situation, especially in today's complex financial world. These agencies miserably failed to predict the defaults of Lehman Brothers and other investment bankers and estimate the potential impact of adverse events for structured credit products. The CRAs in India have lost creditability in recent years because their failure to predict defaults in many companies.

The CRAs have been found making errors of judgement in rating structured products, particularly in assigning AAA ratings to structured debt, which in a large number of cases was subsequently downgraded or defaulted. They are also blamed for not downgrading companies promptly. For example, Enron's rating remained at investment grade four days before the company went bankrupt, despite the fact that the CRAs had been aware of the company's problems for months. Likewise, Moody's gave Freddie Mac preferred stock the top rating until Warren Buffet talked about Freddie on CNBC and on the next day Moody's downgraded Freddie to one tick above junk bonds.

CRAs are criticized very often for being arbitrary in rating certain companies for having too familiar relationship with the management. These agencies, it is alleged, meet frequently in person with the management and advise on actions the company should take to maintain a certain rating. Further, larger CRAs, (Moody's and Standard & Poor's) are often found as promoting a narrow minded focus on credit ratings, possibly at the expense of employees, the environment or long-term research and development. They are also accused of being too cozy with the companies they rate, and on the other they are accused of being too focused on a company's "bottom line" and unwilling to listen to a company's explanations for its actions.

Besides being accused of too close to company management of their existing clients, the CRAs have also been criticized for engaging in heavy-handed "blackmail" tactics in order to solicit business from new clients, and lowering ratings for those firms. For instance, Moody's published an "unsolicited" rating of Hannover Re, with a subsequent letter to the insurance firm indicating that "it looked forward to the day Hannover would be willing to pay". When Hannover management refused, Moody's continued to give Hannover Re ratings, which were downgraded over successive years, all while making payment requests that the insurer rebuffed. In 2004, Moody's cut Hannover's debt to junk status, while the insurer's other rating agencies gave it stray marks. The shareholders were shocked by the Moody's downgrade and Hannover lost $175 million US$ in market capitalization.

It has also been suggested that CRAs are conflicted in assigning sovereign credit ratings since they have a political incentive to show they do not need stricter regulation being overly critical in their assessment of governments they regulate.

In view of the above pitfalls, it has been suggested that financial regulators, instead of relying on CRA ratings, should ask banks, broker-dealers and insurance firms (among others) to use credit spreads when calculating the risk in their portfolio. Furthermore, the issuing firm should, as far as possible, set its instrument rated by atleast three prominent agencies to instil public confidence.

G. CREDIT RATING AGENCIES IN INDIA — AN OVERVIEW

Evolution of CRAs took place in the USA following the financial crisis in 1837. The first mercantile credit agency was set up in New York in 1841 which assessed the ability of the merchants in paying their obligations. John Bradstreet established rating agency in 1849 which published its ratings book in 1857. In 1900, John Moody founded Moody's investors service which published "Manual of Railroad Securities" in 1909. It was followed by the rating of utility and industrial bonds in 1914 and rating of bonds of U.S. cities and other municipalities in the early 1920s.

CRAs in India came into existence very late in 1987 when the first rating agency, viz., Credit Rating and Information Services in India Ltd. (CRISIL) was set up. CRISIL, jointly promoted by the ICICI nationalized and foreign banks, initiated and popularized the concept of credit rating in India. In 1996, Standard & Poor's picked up 9.66 per cent stake, and became the majority equity holder in 2005 with a 52.4 per cent shareholding. CRISIL is an independent organization. It has no trading interest or association. It is equipped with experienced and dedicated analysts supported by multidisciplinary database who provide incisive and proactive analysis for their clients. CRISIL has an in-depth understanding of the Indian business and financial markets.

Although CRISIL remains the leader among the rating agencies in the country, it derives 60 per cent of its revenues from non-rating business. The bulk of the revenues from non-rating business comes from research (global research that includes equity and derivatives research and risk and analytics and Indian research that includes economy, industry and capital markets).

In 1991 another leading rating agency, viz, Investment Information and Credit Rating Agency of India Ltd. (ICRA Ltd.) was sponsored by the IFCI and nationalized and foreign banks and insurance companies. Moody's — the global rating agency — has taken a small 11% stake in ICRA. ICRA endowed with over 100 analysts is a prominent player focused on developing innovative concepts and products in a dynamic market environment, generating wider investor education, and enhancing efficiency and transparency of the financial markets.

CARE Ltd. is the third credit rating and information services institution promoted by the IDBI in 1993 jointly with financial institutions, public and private sector banks and private finance companies. CARE undertakes credit rating of all types of debt instruments.

The latest entrant in the credit rating business in India is 'Duff and Phelps'. It is a joint venture between the international credit rating agencies Duff and Phelps and JM Financial and Alliance Group. This agency commenced its business in 1996.

Thus, there are at present four major credit rating agencies in India. CRISIL is the largest rating agency having over two-fifth market share followed by ICRA with about two-thirds, and CARE with less than one-fifth. Duff and Phelps is the fourth agency with a nominal market share of less than 4 per cent.

H. SERVICES OF CREDIT RATING AGENCIES IN INDIA

CRAs in India have been providing wide range of services which, for convenience of discussion, can be categorized into four major groups, *viz.,* credit rating, infrastructure advisory and other services.

(i) Credit rating service

CRAs in India are providing rating and evaluation services across the cross-section of companies in the Indian economy. Rating services of CRISIL cover the rating of long, medium and short-term debt instruments, securitized assets and other structured obligations, debt issues of large infrastructure projects, mutual funds and municipal bonds. ICRA rates rupee dominated debt instruments such as bonds and debentures, (long-term) fixed deposits (medium-term), commercial paper and certificates of deposit (short-term) and structured obligations and sector specific debt obligations of infrastructure companies. ICRA offers rating services to a wide range of issuers including manufacturing and service companies, power companies, financial institutions, non-bankers finance companies, municipal and other local bodies, telecom companies and companies involved in infrastructure.

CARE evaluates credit risks of debt instruments and sector specific industry reports. Besides, it provides credit analysis rating service which is issuer specific and not instrument specific.

Duff and Phelps rates debt instruments and also evaluates companies and countries on request.

(ii) Infrastructure Services

CRAs in India provide infrastructure with a view to making available information on any company, industry or sector required by a business enterprise. CRISIL has set up the Global Data Services of India Ltd. as its 100 per cent subsidiary to provide high quality, reliable and timely financial analysis of Indian corporates, covering more than 1500 of the largest companies listed on the Indian stock exchanges. CRISIL has also established 100 per cent subsidiary to render information services. Likewise, ICRA set up a separate division to service the unique information needs of investors and capital markets community. The division, while leveraging on ICRA's core competencies and its wide research base, focuses on providing up-to-date credible and value-added information in user-friendly format to supplement investment & decision-making ICRA's information services endeavours to constantly upgrade its products and introduce new ones in cognizance of the dynamic and evolving nature of Indian business environment. ICRA information services division has built to the increasing market requirements for value-added information and analysis.

The information services of ICRA also include related services, viz., Equity Grading and Equity Assessment. The ICRA's equity grading service is designed to comment upon the relative inherent quality of equity reflected by the earning prospects, risk and financial strength associated with the specific company. It grades the fundamentals of a company, which ultimately acts as an important input in the price behaviour of the stock of such a company over the medium-term and long-term. Equity assessment process commences at the instance of an investor and at the consent of the company being assessed. ICRA mayor may not disclose the investor's identity to the company depending upon the investor's performance.

(iii) Advisory Services

In view of the growing need in the country for an unbiased and professional view on adopting the best business practices in the context of economic deregulation and increasing competition, both CRISIL and IRCA have engaged in advisory services, taking mileage of their cumulative expertise in different industries and sectors.

CRISIL has set up a separate division, CRISIL Advisory Services (CAS), to render an array of advisory services covering the areas of energy, urban infrastructure, corporates, capital markets, e-consulting, and banking and finance. CAS has been involved in both policy issues and transactions in these sectors. It has been actively involved in the adaptation of new principles and paradigms to cope with emerging business challenges.

With its extensive knowledge of business and management practices spanning the major sectors of the Indian economy, as a repository of high quality analytical talent, the ICRA is rendering advisory services to different Indian organizations, regulatory authorities and other organizations having business interests in India. The ICRA's advisory services are in the areas of strategy-making, risk management and strategy execution.

(iv) Other Services

CRISIL provides a wide spectrum of training programmes including the tailor-made programme, to meet the specific needs of various agencies and individuals concerned with credit and investments. These programmes are especially useful for credit analysts, lending and investment officers of banks and financial institutions, portfolio managers, corporate treasurers and finance managers.

Besides providing credit rating and information services, CARE Ltd. undertakes extensive research study of the shares listed/to be listed in the major stock exchanges in order to identify the potential winners and losers among them on the basis of the fundamentals affecting the industry, market shares, management capabilities, international competitiveness and other relevant factors. CARE provides the equity research service with specific objectives to be accomplished by them.

Recently, ICRA has launched the corporate governance rating services with a view to offering its current opinions on the relative level of adoption of corporate governance practices.

The focus of this service is on corporate's business practices, and quality of disclosure standards with respect to the regulatory norms and interests of the stakeholders.

I. REGULATION OF CREDIT RATING AGENCIES IN INDIA

CRAs in India are regulated by the SEBI. Major regulatory provisions are outlined below:

◈ Promotion

A CRA can be promoted by a (*i*) public financial institution, (*ii*) scheduled bank, (*iii*) foreign bank operating in India, (*iv*) foreign credit rating agency, having at least 5 years with a minimum net worth of ₹ 100 crore at the time of filing of the application.

◈ Registration

A CRA to carry on rating business must be registered with the SEBI. For this purpose, the application should be moved to the SEBI in Form A along with a non-refundable fee of ₹ 25,000.

◈ Eligibility

A CRA to be registered must satisfy the following eligibility conditions:

(*i*) It should specify in its Memorandum of Association rating activity as one of its main objects;

(*ii*) It has a minimum net worth of ₹ 5 crore;

(*iii*) It has adequate infrastructure;

(*iv*) It has professional competence, financial soundness and general reputation of fairness and integrity in business transactions to the satisfaction of SEBI;

(*v*) It is not involved in any legal proceedings connected with the securities market which may have an adverse impact on the interests of the investors and has not been convicted of any offence involving moral turpitude or any economic offence.

◈ Grant of Registration Certificate

On being satisfied with the eligibility of the applicant, the SEBI will grant a certificate of registration on payment of a fee of ₹ 5,00,000, subject to certain specified conditions set out below:

(*i*) The CRA would comply with the provisions of the SEBI regulations, guidelines, circulars of the SEBI.

(*ii*) Where any information/particulars furnished to the SEBI are found to be false/misleading any material particular or has undergone change subsequent to its furnishing at the time of application, it would immediately inform SEBI in writing, and

(*iii*) The certificate of registration is valid for three years, renewable on payment of a renewable fee of ₹ 3,00,000 for another three years.

◈ Code of Conduct

The SEBI has prescribed the following code of conduct for CRAs:

- It should observe high standards of integrity and fairness in all its dealing with its clients;
- It should fulfill its obligations in an ethical manner;
- It should render, at all times, high standard of service, exercise due diligence, ensure proper care and exercise independent professional judgement. It should also, wherever necessary, disclose to the clients, possible source of conflict of duties and interest, while providing unbiased services;

- It should not indulge in unfair competition nor wean away client(s) of any other rating agency on assurance of higher rating;
- It should not make any exaggerated statement, oral or written to the client either about its qualification or its capability to render certain services or its achievements in regard to services rendered to other clients;
- It should ensure that all dealings with the clients are handled promptly and efficiently;
- It should not divulge to other clients, press or any other party any confidential information about its client(s), which has come to its knowledge, without disclosing it first to the person concerned of the rate company/client;
- It should not make untrue statement(s) or suppress any material fact in any documents, reports papers on information furnished to SEBI or to public of stock exchange(s);
- It should maintain an arm's length relationship between its credit rating and any other activity; and
- It should abide by the provisions of the SEBI Act, regulations and circulars which may be applicable and relevant to the activities carried on by it.

◈ Agreement with the Client

The CRA should enter into a written agreement with each client, spelling out rights and liabilities of each party, and client's agreement to cooperate so as to enable the CRA to arrive at, and maintain a true and accurate rating of the client's securities and provide the former accurate and adequate information timely.

◈ Monitoring of Ratings

The CRA is duty bound to monitor the rating of securities rated by its during its lifetime and disseminate information regarding newly assigned ratings from releases and websites and to all the stock exchanges where the securities are listed.

◈ Disclosure of Rating Definitions and Rationale

The CRA should make public the definitions of the concerned rating, along with the symbol, and also state that the ratings do not tantamount to recommendations to buy, hold or sell any securities. It should make available to the general public the details for its ratings.

J. CONCLUSIONS

Credit rating, which signifies an assessment of creditworthiness of individual, corporates and countries, has come to be recognised as an important process in making rational investment decisions in today's market driven competitive world. Credit ratings may be sovereign as well as corporate. It may also be short-term and long-term.

Credit rating is done by independent professional organizations, known as credit rating agencies. These agencies express their opinions on creditworthiness of the issuer in terms of alphabetical symbols. Each agency applies its own methodology in measuring creditworthiness and uses specific rating scale to publish its ratings opinions. Three major credit rating agencies of the world are S&P, Moody's and Fitch.

Rating process adopted by CRAs is, by and large, the same. Rating process begins when the issuer approaches the agency. The task is done by a rating committee constituted for the purpose. Ratings are based on a variety of information including estimated cash flows during the tenure of the instrument. While assigning rating to a particular instrument the committee factors into a host of other relevant factors. Before according final rating action, CRAs generally review ratings over a period of time.

Three business models used by the CRAs across the world are subscriber-based, issuer-pays and wikirating.

The CRAs play significant role in financial markets of a country by furnishing to investors, issuers, financial intermediaries and government regulators independent opinions of credit risks of individuals and countries based on research-based information. However, operations of these agencies are subject to several criticisms. This is why it is suggested that the issuer should get its instrument rated by atleast three reputed agencies.

The CRAs in India came into existence in 1989 with the formation of CRISIL. It was followed by ICRA Ltd. in 1991 and Care Ltd. in 1993. The fourth CRA, viz., Duff and Phelps, was set up in 1996. Amongst these, CRISIL with over two-third market share is the biggest agency.

The CRAs in India render a range of useful services such as credit rating, information providing, advisory and other services.

The CRAs in India are regulated by the SEBI. A CRA to operate its business has to comply with various provisions of the SEBI stipulated therefor.

KEY TERMS

- Advisory services
- CARE Ltd.
- Credit Rating Services
- Corporate credit rating
- CRISIL
- Duff & Phelps
- ICRA Ltd.
- Issuer-pays model
- Information services
- Long-term rating
- Short-term rating
- Sovereign credit rating
- Structured financial transactions
- Subscriber-based model
- Wiki rating model

DISCUSSION QUESTIONS

1. Discuss, in brief, contours of credit rating.
2. Distinguish between sovereign credit rating and corporate credit rating.
3. Discuss the credit rating procedure generally followed by the CRAs.
4. What role does a CRA play in financial markets of a country?
5. Bring out, in brief, major drawbacks noticed in the operations of the CRAs across the world.
6. What are the business models that the CRAs generally employ?
7. Why should issuer not rely exclusively on rating by one agency?
8. Discuss, briefly, various services rendered by the CRAs in India.
9. Describe major provisions prescribed by the SEBI for regulating operations of the CRAs in India.

REFERENCES

1. Business Standard, February 1, 2012.
2. THE HINDU, Feb. 7, 2012.
3. THE HINDU, April 26, 2012.
4. www.mysmp.com
5. www.crisil.com
6. www.investopedia.com